T0408147

# Understanding Salafism

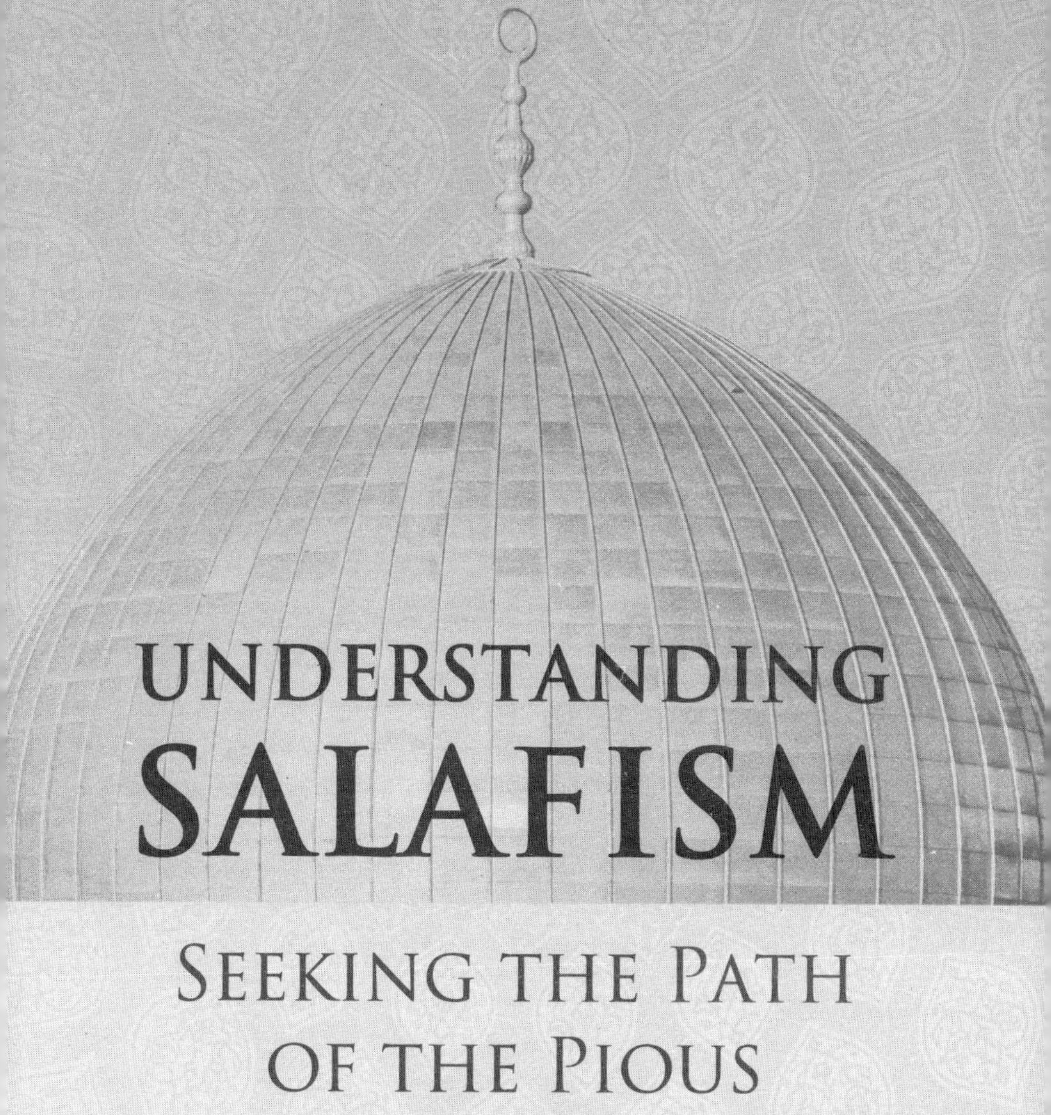

# UNDERSTANDING SALAFISM

## SEEKING THE PATH OF THE PIOUS PREDECESSORS

YASIR QADHI

ONEWORLD ACADEMIC

A Oneworld Academic Book

First published by Oneworld Publications Ltd in 2025

Copyright © Yasir Qadhi, 2025

The moral right of Yasir Qadhi to be identified as the
Author of this work has been asserted by him in accordance with the
Copyright, Designs and Patents Act 1988

All rights reserved
Copyright under Berne Convention
A CIP record for this title is available from the British Library

ISBN 978-1-78607-848-3
eISBN 978-1-78607-849-0

Typeset by Geethik Technologies
Printed and bound in Great Britain by Clays Ltd, Elcograf S.p.A.

No part of this publication may be reproduced, stored in a retrieval system, or
transmitted, in any form or by any means, electronic, mechanical, photocopying,
recording or otherwise, without the prior permission of the publishers.

The authorised representative in the EEA is eucomply OÜ,
Pärnu mnt 139b–14, 11317 Tallinn, Estonia
(email: hello@eucompliancepartner.com / phone: +33757690241)

Oneworld Publications Ltd
10 Bloomsbury Street
London WC1B 3SR
England

Stay up to date with the latest books,
special offers, and exclusive content from
Oneworld with our newsletter

Sign up on our website
**oneworld-publications.com**

MIX
Paper | Supporting
responsible forestry
FSC® C018072

*For all those brave enough to venture on the real path of the salaf...*

# CONTENTS


*List of Figures* xiii
*Preface* xiv
*Conventions* xvii

**1 Introduction: A Bird's Eye View of Salafism** **1**
1.1 The Problem of Belonging: What is Salafism? 1
1.2 Theology 7
1.2.1 Monotheism (Tawḥīd) 8
1.2.2 The Conception of Faith (Īmān) 11
1.2.3 Association and Dissociation (al-Walāʾ wa-l-Barāʾ) 11
1.2.4 The Saved Sect (al-Firqa al-Nājiyya) 12
1.3 Law 15
1.3.1 Shariʿa and Fiqh 15
1.3.2 Sunna and Bidʿa 21
1.4 Spirituality 22
1.5 Political Activism and Jihad 26
1.6 Typology and Categorization of Modern Salafi Strands 29
1.6.1 Analysis and Critique of Previous Salafi Typologies: Wiktorowicz, Pall, and Wagemakers 29
1.6.2 Towards a Multivariable Open-Ended Typology 36
1.7 Conclusion 41

**2 A Comprehensive History of Salafi Thought: From its Origins to Modernity** 43
2.1 The Formative Years (650–850 CE) 44
2.1.1 The Sunni Origins of Salafi Thought 44
2.1.2 The Traditions of the Divine Attributes and the Emergence of Proto-Salafism 46
2.2 The Consolidation and Flourishing (850–1000 CE) 51
2.2.1 Aḥmad b. Ḥanbal (d. 241/855) 51
2.2.2 ʿUthmān b. Saʿīd al-Dārimī (d. 280/894) 53
2.2.3 Abū Bakr b. Khuzayma (d. 311/923) 54
2.2.4 Al-Ḥasan b. ʿAlī al-Barbahārī (d. 329/941) and the Rise of the Ḥanbalīs in Baghdad 56
2.2.5 Ibn Baṭṭa (d. 387/997) and Other Seminal Figures 58
2.2.6 The Caliph al-Qādir bi-llāh (d. 422/1031) and his Creed 59

2.3 The Decline (1000–1275 CE) 60
2.3.1 Karrāmī and Ḥanbalī Dominance under the Ghaznavids and the Early Seljuks 60
2.3.2 The Rise of Niẓām al-Mulk (d. 485/1092) and the Path to Ashʿarī Dominance 61
2.3.3 The Diverse Ḥanbalī Responses to Ashʿarī Dominance 65
2.4 The Taymiyyan Revival (1275–1400 CE) 67
2.5 The Interlude (1400–1700 CE) 76
2.5.1 The Qāḍīzādelī Movement in the Ottoman Heartlands 76
2.5.2 Ibrāhīm al-Kūrānī (d. 1101/1690) and his Revival in the Arab Lands 79
2.6 The Wahhabi Movement (1700–1800 CE) 83
2.7 Yemen and its Zaydī Converts (15th–18th Centuries) 85
2.8 The Ahl-e Ḥadīth Movement of the Indian Subcontinent (1800–1900 CE) 87
2.8.1 Sayyid Aḥmad Shahīd (d. 1831) and Shah Muḥammad Ismaʿīl (d. 1831) 88
2.8.2 Sayyid Nadhīr Ḥusayn (d. 1902) and Ṣiddīq Ḥasan Khān (d. 1890) 90
2.9 Salafism in the Arab Lands (1900 CE) 95
2.9.1 Salafism in Egypt 96
The ʿAbduh 'Enlightenment' project 96
Rashīd Riḍā (d. 1935) 98
Muḥammad Ḥāmid al-Fiqī (d. 1959) 102
2.9.2 Salafism in Ottoman Damascus 103
ʿAbd al-Razzāq al-Bīṭār (d. 1917) 103
Jamāl al-Dīn al-Qāsimī (d. 1914) 104
Muḥibb al-Dīn al-Khaṭīb (d. 1969) 106
2.9.3 Salafism in Ottoman Baghdad 107
Maḥmūd al-Ālūsī (d. 1854) 107
Nuʿmān al-Ālūsī (d. 1899) 108
Maḥmūd Shukrī al-Ālūsī (d. 1924) 108
2.9.4 Muhammad Nasir al-Din al-Albānī (d. 1999) 109
2.10 Conclusion 117

**3 Wahhabism and Salafism** **120**
3.1 Muḥammad b. ʿAbd al-Wahhāb: His Life, Beliefs, and Works 122
3.1.1 Ibn ʿAbd al-Wahhāb: His Life from Two Paradigms 122
Muḥammad b. ʿAbd al-Wahhāb: The reviver of the prophetic message 122
Muḥammad b. ʿAbd al-Wahhāb: The fanatical deviant 127
Conclusion 131
3.1.2 The Theology of Muḥammad b. ʿAbd al-Wahhāb 131

God's sole right to be venerated: Tawḥīd al-Ulūhiyya 132
Takfīr (excommunication) 134
Politicizing theological dissent: al-Walāʾ wa-l-barāʾ 136
The central role of jihad in Wahhabism 138
3.1.3 Ibn ʿAbd al-Wahhāb's Excommunication of Other Muslims 139
3.1.4 The Writings of Muḥammad b. ʿAbd al-Wahhāb 145
3.1.5 Was Ibn ʿAbd al-Wahhāb's Thought Original or Based on Scholarly Precedent? 147
3.1.6 The Reactions to the Wahhabi Movement 149
3.2 The Influence of the Saudi States on the Development of Wahhabism 152
3.2.1 First-Wave Wahhabism 153
The First Saudi State 154
The Second Saudi State 157
The Third Saudi State 159
The Ikhwān and the Battle of Sibilla (1929) 160
3.2.2 Second-Wave Wahhabism 163
Muḥammad b. Ibrāhīm and the winds of change in Second-Wave Wahhabism 167
The Siege of Mecca in 1979 170
3.2.3 Third-Wave Wahhabism 175
ʿAbd al-ʿAzīz b. ʿAbd Allāh b. Bāz (d. 1999) 176
Muḥammad b. Salih al-Uthaymīn (d. 2001) 180
Salih b. Fawzan al-Fawzan (b. 1933) 183
Conclusion 183
3.2.4 The Ṣaḥwa Movement 185
3.2.5 Madkhalism 189
3.2.6 Jihadi-Salafism and the Wahhabi-Jihadi-Salafi Strand 193
3.2.7 Fourth-Wave Wahhabism? 195
3.3 The Islamic University of Medina (IUM) 199
3.3.1 The Founding of the IUM 199
3.3.2 Departments, Pedagogy, and Student Life 201
3.3.3 Brief Survey of the Impact of the Alumni of IUM 204
3.4 Conclusion 206

**4 Salafism and Islamism: A Case Study of the Muslim Brotherhood 208**
4.1 Al-Bannā, Qutb, and Salafism 209
4.2 The Salafi–Brotherhood Relationship in the Kingdom and Egypt 213
4.2.1 The Initial Mutual Attraction (Mid-1930s to 1949) 213
4.2.2 The Engagement: Brotherhood Migration and Exile to Saudi Arabia (1950s to 1961) 216

4.2.3 The Marriage (of Convenience?): Support for the Muslim Brotherhood (1962 to 1978) 219
4.2.4 The Child: Political Salafism (1979 to 2000) 223
4.2.5 The Bitter Divorce (2001 to 2010) 229
4.2.6 The Post-Divorce Hostility (2011 to the Present) 232
4.3 Salafism and the Muslim Brotherhood in Other Middle Eastern Countries 244
4.3.1 Syria 244
4.3.2 Jordan 247
4.3.3 Kuwait 248
4.4 Conclusion 250

**5 The Phenomenon of Jihadi-Salafism** 252
5.1 Defining Jihadi-Salafism 253
5.1.1 The Concept of Jihad in Islam 253
5.1.2 Categorizing Jihadi Movements 255
5.1.3 Key Doctrines of Jihadi-Salafis 258
A Salafi conceptualization of Tawḥīd 259
Al-ḥākimiyyah as the fourth category of Tawḥīd 259
Takfīr 260
Violence as the central method for social change 261
Al-Walāʾ wa'l-Barāʾ 263
5.2 Important Events and Personalities That Influenced Jihadi-Salafism 263
5.2.1 Wahhabism 263
5.2.2 The Muslim Brotherhood and Sayyid Qutb 264
5.2.3 Afghanistan: The Breeding Ground of Jihadi-Salafism 266
5.2.4 Abdullah Azzam (d. 1989) 269
5.3 The History of Jihadi-Salafism 276
5.3.1 Egypt 276
The origins of Jihadi-Salafism 276
The murder of Sadat as the public announcement of JS in Egypt 280
The repentance of major Jihadi-Salafis in Egypt 282
5.3.2 Saudi Arabia 286
5.3.3 Morocco 290
Harakat al-Shabibah al-Islamiyyah: The first public proto-SJ movement 290
SJ in Morocco from the Afghan–Soviet war to the present 292
5.3.4 Algeria 293
The fight for independence and the norm of war 294
The Armed Islamic Movement (MIA) and the birth of jihadism 294

The failed path to the Islamization of Algeria 295
Opening the road to JS: From the GIA after 1992 until the AQIM 296
5.3.5 Afghanistan, the North-West Frontier, Al-Qaeda and the Launch of Global Jihadi-Salafism 301
An overview of the path toward global Jihadi-Salafism 301
The history of Al-Qaeda in Afghanistan, leading to Islamic State 302
5.3.6 The Malay Archipelago 309
The Darul Islam movement: From jihadism towards Jihadi-Salafism 310
Jemaah Islamiyah and the birth of Jihadi-Salafism 311
5.4 The Main Ideologues of Jihadi-Salafism 313
5.4.1 Osama bin Laden (d. 2011) 313
5.4.2 Ayman al-Zawahiri (d. 2022) 315
5.4.3 Abu Muhammad al-Maqdisi (b. 1959) 318
5.4.4 Abu Mus‘ab al-Zarqawi (d. 2006) 320
5.5 The Main Jihadi-Salafi Movements After Al-Qaeda 323
5.5.1 ISIS in the Middle East 323
5.5.2 Boko Haram in West Africa 328
5.5.3 Al-Shabaab in East Africa 331
5.6 Leading Jihadi-Salafi Preachers in the English-Speaking West 335
5.6.1 Anwar al-Awlaki (d. 2011) 336
5.6.2 Abu Hamza al-Misri 342
5.6.3 Abdullah al-Faisal 343
5.7 Conclusion 345

**6 Global Salafism in the Contemporary World** 350
6.1 Africa 352
6.1.1 Morocco 352
6.1.2 Algeria 358
6.1.3 Libya 361
6.1.4 Nigeria 367
6.1.5 Sudan 369
6.1.6 Mauritania 371
6.2 The Middle East 373
6.2.1 Syria 373
6.2.2 Jordan 375
6.2.3 Lebanon 379
6.2.4 Kuwait 381
6.2.5 Yemen 384

6.3 Asia and the Far East 388
6.3.1 India and Pakistan 388
6.3.2 Malaysia 390
6.3.3 Indonesia 391
6.4 Europe 394
6.4.1 The United Kingdom 394
First phase: The activism of the Ahl-e-Hadith 394
Second phase: The rise of JIMAS 396
Third phase: JIMAS and UK Salafism splinters 398
A note on Salafi literature in the UK 399
UK Salafism and the war on terror 400
Looking to the future 401
6.4.2 Türkiye 402
6.4.3 Bosnia and Herzegovina 403
6.4.4 France 405
6.5 North America 406
6.6 The Phenomenon of Post-Salafism 414
6.6.1 Definitions and Trajectory 414
6.6.2 History and Origins 416
6.6.3 Key Figures 417
Salman al-Oudah 417
al-Sharif Hatim al-Awni 419
Adil al-Kalbani 420
Post-Salafism as maqāsid al-sharīʿa discourse 420
Post-Salafis in the English-speaking West 420
6.6.4 Post-Salafi Jihadism? 421
6.7 Conclusion 422

*Epilogue* 425
*Notes* 431
*Bibliography* 512
*Index* 560

# LIST OF FIGURES

| | | |
|---|---|---|
| 1.0 | Wicktorowicz's Salafi Typology | 30 |
| 1.1 | Pall's Salafi Typology | 32 |
| 1.2 | Wagemaker's Salafi Typology (*Wiktorowicz with a Twist*) | 34 |
| 1.3 | Typology of al-Albānī Salafism | 38 |
| 1.4 | Typology of Saudi-Establishment Salafism | 39 |
| 1.5 | Typology of the *Ṣaḥwa* Movement | 40 |
| 1.6 | Typology of the Jihadi-Salafism (ISIS) | 40 |

# PREFACE

*Alḥamdulillāh.*

One balmy summer evening in August 1995, having just weeks before left my engineering offer at Dow Chemical and taken on studies at the Islamic University of Medina (IUM), I found myself sitting in the Holy City of Medina, in the Prophet's Mosque, knee to knee, in front of one of the iconic figures I had heard so much about, Shaykh Muḥammad b. Salih al-Uthaymin. I could not believe what was happening. A few weeks earlier, I had been busy taking my final exams in engineering at the University of Houston, and now here I was thousands of miles away in the holiest of cities, as a student at one of the prestigious centers of Islamic scholarship, literally touching the great sage I had already grown to admire. The overwhelming feeling of awe that enveloped my being is difficult to describe. This would be the first of many experiences I had with Shaykh Ibn al-Uthaymin, and during the next ten years, I would have the opportunity to interact with some of the greatest icons of Islamic scholarship in that region, including the Grand Mufti of the Kingdom, Shaykh ʿAbd al-ʿAzīz b. ʿAbdullah b. Bāz.

I had chosen to apply to IUM because at the time I felt it was one of the only Islamic seminaries teaching the 'correct' version of Islam, a strand that describes itself as 'Salafi.' I had already embraced the principles of this movement during my first year in university, and even before traveling to Medina, had studied enough about the movement to be intellectually convinced of its strengths and spiritually convinced of its orthodoxy. I completed a BA (in the Sciences of Hadith), and an MA (in Islamic Theology) at the University, before the horrific events of 9/11 prompted me to return to the country of my birth.

After returning to America and while pursuing my PhD at Yale, I began to read the secondary literature on the movement that I had subscribed to and even taught to fellow believers (I wear multiple hats: I am a cleric and an academic). I was appalled by the crass generalizations and superficial stereotypes that characterized most of these works. But what most frustrated me about the monographs and articles was that none of them seemed to give an insider's holistic perspective of the movement.

The idea of this book was first suggested to me by Professor Omid Safi while we were having lunch at a soul food diner in Memphis, Tennessee (catfish and fries) when I was an assistant professor at Rhodes College. I complained about how Salafis were always misrepresented and misunderstood, even by academics who were supposed to know better. He stopped eating and waved a fry at me, 'You know, *you* should write a book on Salafism! You're the ideal person for it. Let me put you in touch with my dear friend at Oneworld.' That meal, almost a decade ago, was the genesis of this work that is now in your hands.

This book consists, alongside this Preface, of six chapters and an Epilogue. Chapter 1 is meant as both an introduction and stand-alone chapter. If a reader only has limited time, this chapter should be sufficient to gain a working understanding of the movement. Chapter 2 is a detailed historical survey of the trends and figures that generated modern Salafism. We begin with the *ahl al-ḥadīth* movement of the classical period, and work through its various iterations over the last fourteen centuries, ending at the middle of the twentieth century, with the seminal figure of al-Albānī. In Chapter 3, we discuss the most common manifestation of this movement in our times, the version known as Wahhabism. Chapter 4 demarcates the complicated relationship between the political Islamist movement known as the Muslim Brotherhood and mainstream Salafism. Next, in Chapter 5, we summarize the history and pertinent aspects of perhaps the most studied reality of modern Salafism, the Jihadi-Salafi movements and their thought. And in the last chapter, Chapter 6, a selection of geographic regions is chosen to provoke a discussion of some contemporary aspects of the movement around the globe, ending with the modern phenomenon of post-Salafism. In the Epilogue, I share some personal reflections regarding my own association with the movement, along with a plea for greater understanding, both for those within and those without.

I make no claims to being comprehensive or wholly impartial. A level of personal analysis is necessary, and no doubt readers who are familiar with this topic, or who subscribe to the movement, might find my treatment of some areas unsatisfactory. I make no excuses for this: my aim has been to provide a holistic overview and critical analysis of a deeply contested – and contentious – movement and tradition. It would be impossible to please everyone, nor is perfection humanly possible. And while it is inevitable that some readers, especially those associated with the movement, will not agree with some of the analysis they read, I can only state that it is not my desire to unfairly criticize, and that to this day I have nothing but genuine respect for all my teachers and my alma mater. I can only hope that the work is of overall benefit, and its strengths ultimately outweigh its unavoidable weaknesses. For all its limitations, I hope my care and concern comes through in every page, and the reader finds it useful. I am optimistic that my attention to the movement's nuances and the development of its theology and history will provide a perspective that is rarely found in other books.

This book has taken over eight years to write, in between my constant travels and lectures and career changes and family commitments. So much has changed during that time, not just within the movement, but concerning my association with it. I have 'moved on' from the movement, after being one of its main faces in the English-speaking world for more than a decade. Some of the reasons for this are mentioned in the Epilogue. Moreover, the movement itself has fractured into so many other sub-strands, and the events of the Arab Spring and the current geopolitical realties of the Middle East are impacting it in real-time, thus making an up-to-date summary impossible. Given the speed of change taking place, in a few years, perhaps another monograph will be needed to supplement this one!

Many have helped me along the way. I would like to thank (in alphabetical order): Hira Amin, Christopher Anzalone, Andrew Booso, Jonathan Brown, Cole Bunzel, Shaakirah Edwards, Suleiman Hani, Ismail Ibrahim, Ismail Kamdar, Huzaifah Islam-Khan, Azhar Majothi, Salman Nasir, and Kashif Zakiuddin for their feedback, input, and ideas that helped shape this work. Of course, Oneworld and its editors deserve special thanks for their patience and help with the manuscript. Obviously, all faults and errors are my own.

On a personal note, while this is by no means the first book I have written, it is the first monograph to be published by an academic press. Hence, it does mark a different milestone in my life (one that I admit is long overdue), and I am, as always, humbled by and eternally grateful for all of these milestones. I remain indebted to my teachers for all they have taught me; to my parents for having raised me to always love knowledge and excel in my studies; to my children Ammaar, Yusuf, Sarah, and Zaynab, who are no longer children but young adults and who make life worth living; and of course, to my life partner and loyal supporter for the last three decades, my wife Rumana, who truly has been a Divine blessing to me in helping me be who I am.

*Wa mā tawfīqī illā billāh...*

Yasir Qadhi<br>Plano, TX<br>10 April 2024 (Eid al-Fiṭr, 1445)

# CONVENTIONS

Initially, I planned to use as little Arabic in this book as possible. However, as this book covers the history and theology of several Muslim groups spanning over a millennium, it is not possible to do justice to this topic without using Arabic terms. Many of these terms would, in fact, be lost in translation if we had to use English alternatives. For transliteration of these terms, classical Arabic names, and various other Arabic terms utilized throughout the book, I have generally followed the conventions of the *International Journal of Middle East Studies* (*IJMES*).

In keeping with the rule of *IJMES*, I have dropped the ending 'h' for *tā marbūṭa*; thus, 'Sunnah' appears as 'Sunna.' Similarly, I have also retained the Arabic definite article 'al-' found in many proper names such as ʿAbd al-ʿAzīz. However, for the sake of simplicity, I have generally dropped the special characters from Arabic names that are commonly known in the English language and have instead opted to spell them as per their common English spellings (thus, it is Gamal Abdel Nasser and not Jamāl ʿAbd al-Nāṣir). Similarly, for commonly known Arabic words, I omit italicization and special characters, hence: Qurʾan (not *Qurʾān*), hadith (not *ḥadīth*), and Salafi (not *Salafī*). It should also be noted that in Arabic names, people are often referred to by their fathers with the title 'ibn/bin' (son of) or 'bint' (daughter of). For ease of reading, I have abbreviated these words as 'b' whenever they form part of a longer name. The exception is when a name starts with Ibn or Bint; then I have written it in full.

Dates before 1800 CE appear in the dual format of AH/CE (*Hijrī* dates followed by the Common Era). Names of locations appear in their common English spelling as found in widely used maps unless the places no longer exist. In the latter case, places are referred to by their historical name in Arabic transliteration.

This book follows the reference system of the *Chicago Manual of Style* (17th Edition). However, on occasion, when different volumes (or parts) are referenced, the volume (or part) reference is divided from the page reference by a colon. For example, the reference '3:210' means that the relevant text can be found on page 210 in the third volume (or part) of the cited work. The only unusual citation conventions in this book are those for citing Sunni hadith collections. In those cases, I have followed the standard Wensinck system of citing the chapter (*kītab*) and subchapter (*bāb*) of every book (e.g., *Ṣaḥīh al-Bukhārī: kitāb al-shahādāt, bāb lā yushhad 'alā shahādat jawr idhā ushida*). All translations are my own unless otherwise noted in the footnotes.

# 1

# INTRODUCTION: A BIRD'S EYE VIEW OF SALAFISM

*'The Salafi methodology is Islam as understood correctly.'*
*~ Muḥammad Nasir al-Din al-Albānī*[1]

The aim of this chapter is to provide an introductory overview of the Salafi movement. While certain concepts presented here will be investigated in greater depth in subsequent chapters (and hence, there will be overlap), this chapter itself will make allowances when discussing these concepts in a simplified manner for introductory purposes. This chapter will also concentrate on the modern manifestation of the Salafi movement. It should, however, be noted that in many circumstances, the *modern* practitioners within this tendency – contrary to what they may believe – are not actually emulating the earlier icons to which they subscribe.

In the first section of this chapter, we will attempt to define Salafism, after which four key topics will be covered in each subsequent section. We will begin with theology, which is the *sine qua non* of Salafism, and then move on to law, spirituality, and political activism. For each of these topics, the goal will be to illustrate how Salafism – as a whole – is distinct in its understanding of these topics from other movements and, where relevant, to mark internal divisions between Salafi sub-strands. In the concluding section, the primary typologies of the Salafi movement will be summarized, and a new, more comprehensive one will be proposed.

## *1.1 The Problem of Belonging: What is Salafism?*

One of the most defining aspects of Sunni Islam is the respect that is given to the Companions of the Prophet, and of the early Muslims, in light of a famous tradition of the Prophet Muhammad: 'The best of all generations is my generation, and then the generation that follows them, and then the generation that follows them.'[2] Yet such reverence among Sunni scholars for the Predecessors (*salaf*) or, more accurately put, the Pious Predecessors (*al-salaf al-ṣāliḥ*) does not, in general, translate into viewing the early generations as constituting a unified and monolithic scholarly tradition.[3] Although certain doctrines have been described in classical Islamic scholarship with the adjective *salafī*, the use of Salafism (*al-salafiyya*) as an abstract noun – claiming to represent some comprehensive system – is a recent phenomenon.[4]

The popularity of the use of the term Salafism began in the 1920s as an Orientalist method to describe specific reformist currents in the Muslim world from the end of the nineteenth century. The most distinctive of these trends was the one associated with Muḥammad ʿAbduh (d. 1905) and his students, which took an 'enlightenment' (*tanwīr*) view of the *salaf* and sought to throw off the shackles of popular Islamic scholarship by means of the type of freedom and dynamism that they saw in the *salaf* (this modernist movement will be discussed in detail in Chapter 2). Although it is debatable whether these scholars saw themselves as 'Salafis' in a technical sense, or proponents of something called Salafism, this group was and has remained a popular academic designation for the term 'Salafism.' Nonetheless, despite the undeniable impact of some of these modernist scholars on the later articulation which emerged in the 1960s, this book is about this other latter form of Salafism that came to exemplify the term itself in the last quarter of the twentieth century, namely 'puritan' (as opposed to 'enlightenment') Salafism. When one uses the term 'Salafi' in any context today, it is undeniably understood as a reference to the puritan Salafi movement, and not the revivalist efforts of a group of thinkers in the early part of the twentieth century.

The fullest and most well-known version of puritan Salafism today is also modern – being itself the product of the twentieth century. Salafis themselves would, of course, dispute this claim. According to them, they belong to the group that follows the teachings of the original Muslims, being linked to this early community by a pristine and unbroken intellectual chain of succession starting with the Prophet Muhammad himself, which is then, in turn, passed through each successive generation until the present Salafi sect (a claim that is explored in detail in Chapter 2).[5] However, as this book will demonstrate, this modern phenomenon of trying to define Salafism as a specific group has been contentious and has led – quite predictably and understandably – to numerous rival claimants to the title of true representatives of Salafism. An outsider might well ask: Is it even possible for anyone to give a correct and absolute representation of the movement? Hence, one finds the necessary attempts at outlining a typology of Salafism that elaborates a core basis of broad concepts that enjoy consensus and other ideas that are contested and have led to sub-division within the broader movement.

All of this is to underscore the fact that defining a particular strand of any religion is not an easy task, and Salafism is no exception. Firstly, the term 'Salafism' itself is highly contested. Its understanding among adherents of the movement typically differs from that of Muslims belonging to other strands (some of whom employ it with a pejorative undertone), or academics who study this trend from outside the faith. Even then, not all those who fall within the purview of the movement are eager to embrace the term and be labeled as 'Salafi.' Secondly, Salafism is a term that can be applied to describe a myriad of groups, each competing with the other for the exclusive claim to this label. Thus, Salafism is a broad strand of Islam that encompasses multiple sub-strands, each situating itself along a particular point on a theological, legal, political, and methodological spectrum. In fact, some sub-strands even hereticate other groups that might vie for this same label. As a result, any proposed definition will be hotly contested by those who actually adopt it and seek to reserve it exclusively for themselves. Thirdly, the movement, like all other movements, is very much a social construct that adapts to and is affected by the prevailing political and social climate in which it finds itself. Hence, there are geographical variations in the way the Salafi movement manifests across the world. And so, the Salafism of Pakistan, for instance, differs significantly – both socially and culturally – from, say, that of Nigeria. Fourthly, Salafism can be viewed as being part of a historical continuum, with various figures and trends that later Salafis associate with the movement, spanning the entirety of the fourteen centuries of Islam. However, most of these earlier figures and trends did not explicitly use the term 'Salafi' for themselves. As such, their 'Salafi' identity is highly debatable – especially in light of a modern definition. Hence, there is the question of whether definitions of Salafism should seek to accommodate such historical figures or instead solely concentrate on its modern manifestations as it exists today. And, lastly, since Salafism is a trend of Sunni Islam that occupies a specific range on a larger spectrum, it is almost impossible to demarcate where 'Salafism' ends and, say, 'Islamism'[6] or some other strand begins.

These issues are raised merely to point out that any definition is bound to be contested, and rightfully so. Whatever approach one follows in addressing the above questions (and even more besides these) will inevitably dictate one's methodology in defining the movement. Nonetheless, and with all of these caveats in mind, it would be useful to begin our discussion regarding some key factors that all Salafi groups agree on in order that these may serve as a starting point for a working typology.

If Salafism had a motto, it would be, following 'The Qurʾan and Sunna[7] upon the understanding of the Pious Predecessors' (*al-Qurʾān wa-l-sunna*

*ʿalā fahm al-salaf al-ṣāliḥ*). Salafis, like all Muslims, believe in the Qurʾan (the speech of God) as the primary authority in all matters. And Salafis, like all Sunni Muslims, believe in the Sunna. It could be said that all Sunni strands of Islam value, to some degree, the Sunna – after all, the term itself (viz., '*sunnī*') literally means 'those who follow the Sunna.' However, the beliefs of the Salafis about the Sunna are not equally exemplified in other Sunni groups. Salafis view the Sunna as being of equal legal importance – but not of equal spiritual blessings – as the Qurʾan. This love for the Sunna is demonstrated in many aspects, ranging from the emulation of the most mundane acts reported about the Prophet to the utmost care given to editing and publishing works of hadith.[8] It is also manifested in their attitude towards the canonical schools of Islamic law (*madhāhib*, sing. *madhhab*), as they tend to be more dismissive of unrestricted obedience to later jurists and feel that approaching the Sunna directly is more authentic.

*Historically*, the Salafi movement considers itself to be a direct continuation of the prototypal manifestation of Sunnism, which they view as *the* orthodox and original form of Islam itself as propagated by the Prophet. The *ahl al-ḥadīth* (The Partisans of Hadith) movement of the second/eighth century is the earliest Islamic movement that best corresponds with modern Salafism. In fact, a chronological chart of a continuous line of thinkers and writings can be traced from the classical *ahl al-ḥadīth* school to the modern Salafi movement itself (this will be done in the next chapter). Of course, no Salafi would ever consider any individual on that genealogical chart as a 'founder,' including notable figures such as Aḥmad b. Ḥanbal (d. 241/855), the eponymous founder of the Ḥanbalī school of law, Ibn Taymiyya (d. 728/1328), the Damascene Ḥanbalī theologian, or Muḥammad b. ʿAbd al-Wahhāb (d. 1792), the founder of the Wahhabi movement. Instead, all of them are viewed as being part of a historical continuum, with the real founder of the movement – at least as argued by the Salafis themselves – being none other than the Prophet himself.

*Theologically*, Salafis uphold certain doctrines about God's divine attributes (*al-asmāʾ wa-l-ṣifāt*), predestination (*qadar*), orthodoxy, orthopraxy, and particular understandings of worship (*ʿibāda*) that distinguish them from all other Islamic sects and trends. They consider these theological beliefs to be the primary core of what defines orthodoxy. Hence, any deviation from these beliefs, even in the slightest, is considered an evil innovation (*bidʿa*) and heresy or – depending on the severity of difference – even unbelief (*kufr*). The tenets and specifics of this theology will be discussed later in this work.

*Methodologically*, Salafis hold both the Qurʾan and the hadith as two co-equal sources of the religion. They believe that the earliest generation of Muslims – specifically the first three generations after the Prophet – achieved religious perfection. Therefore, they hold that subsequent generations should strive to emulate the beliefs and practices of those righteous individuals by drawing on their understanding of the two primary sources. In this vein, any form of progression or deviation from these beliefs is viewed as regression and corruption, especially given that those early predecessors perfected Islam. Any beliefs or rituals that have no basis in early Islam are viewed as reprehensible innovations (*bidʿa*) and are considered destructive to the purity of the faith.

In fact, the very term 'Salafi' itself is a manifestation of this doctrine, as it is derived from the noun '*salaf*,' literally meaning 'those who have preceded.' In Islamic theology, the '*salaf*' or '*al-salaf al-ṣāliḥ*' (the Pious Predecessors) refers to the first three generations after the Prophet, as outlined in the famous hadith quoted at the beginning of this section. The aforementioned tradition is one of the most often-quoted hadith in Salafi circles, as it serves to legitimize the movement while also allowing the adherents to view themselves as the only group truly following it. Hence, a *salafī* is someone who strives to follow the *salaf*. To achieve this, Salafis believe they are to engage in a twofold process of studying the teachings of the rightly guided scholars of that era while simultaneously purifying the faith of any syncretic practices or deviations that might have crept in since then.

Hence, based on the discussion so far, a definition of Salafism may be proposed:

> Salafism is a strand of Sunni Islam whose origins lie in the *ahl al-ḥadīth* school of the classical period of early Islam. It considers the Qurʾan and authentic hadith as the only authoritative and divine sources. The movement strives to emulate what it views as the perfect understanding of these sources via the theology and practices of the earliest generations of Islam (the *salaf*). Salafism prioritizes the importance of creed and abhors any syncretic ritual practices not found in the earliest generations. Typically, and especially in matters of theology, Salafism wishes to interpret the Qurʾan and hadith in the most literal way possible. It has a unique understanding of specific theological doctrines, in particular, the understanding of God's divine attributes (*al-asmāʾ wa-l-ṣifāt*) and God's exclusive right to be worshiped (*tawḥīd al-ulūhiyya*). Since it views the first three generations as being the ideal role models, any new developments in the interpretation or practice of the faith are seen in a negative light.

As noted earlier, modern Salafism is characterized by a diversity of interpretations when it comes to matters of theology, Islamic law, politics, and jihad. Consequently, it is neither appropriate nor feasible to pigeonhole all Salafis into one monolithic category. Therefore, in this introductory chapter, I have avoided adding qualifiers to this definition of Salafism in order to encompass the full spectrum of these diverse groups. The remainder of this chapter will focus on the contours of contemporary Salafism.

Before we proceed regarding the internal issues that define Salafism, it is pertinent to make a brief comment on the extent of the following the Salafi movement has today. Unfortunately, a definitive response is not possible for the simple reason that, like almost all Islamic movements, nobody keeps membership records. There is no form to fill in to become a Salafi; you simply choose to live your life differently. It is impossible to guess numbers. What further complicates a quantitative analysis is the reality that Salafism's reach, without a doubt, extends far beyond those who subscribe to it. Many Muslims all over the world who would not see themselves as Salafi, or are even in disagreement with the movement, have nonetheless absorbed ideas about Islam that are clearly derived from the Salafi movement.

Additionally, the impact of this movement is geocentric. Muslims in the Gulf countries (particularly Saudi Arabia, the United Arab Emirates, Kuwait, and Qatar) predominantly subscribe to Salafi beliefs – at least at on some level – as the clerical training of those countries is Salafi in nature. The movement, on the other hand, has a much smaller following among the Muslims of, say, Türkiye or Indonesia. The situation gets more complicated in the Levant and North Africa. For example, in Egypt, in the first free elections held after the Arab Spring, almost a quarter of the seats in the new parliament were won by candidates who came from Salafi parties.[9] In almost all Western countries, Salafism has had a discernible impact at almost every level. Even lay-Muslims are aware of the ideas and figures of the movement. Hence, all that can be said for the purposes of this work is that Salafism is clearly a seminal strand of Sunni Islam, with tens of millions of committed followers, and no serious study of the Muslim world can ignore its teachings and impact. Yet, it is definitely *not* the main strand of Sunnism, and large swaths of the Muslim world remain unaffected by – or even opposed to – Salafism.

The contentiousness of the Salafi label must be viewed in conjunction with related terms like 'Ḥanbalī' and 'Atharī,' as they are all viewed as either synonyms or alternative labels. In terms of the group being discussed in this book, these labels are synonyms for the same methodology: *Salafi* in the commitment to the Pious Predecessors; *Ḥanbalī* in that Aḥmad b. Ḥanbal and his approach in theology and general ethics were likewise an adherence to the Pious Predecessors; and *Atharī* in that they have fealty to the 'reports' (*athār*) of the Pious Predecessors. In contrast, other Sunni opponents of the Salafis, such as Sufis, Ashʿarīs, and even others who claim to be *true* Ḥanbalīs or Atharīs, take the Salafis to be an aberration and not a faithful representation of the Ḥanbalī school or the *athār* of the Pious Predecessors.

## 1.2 Theology

In the modern Western world, it is safe to say that theology is a forsaken discipline. Perhaps this is not surprising: it was only a few centuries ago that Western civilization went to war over theological rifts and ecclesiastical differences. These internecine battles and religious civil conflicts resulted in political and social changes whose effects can still be seen, and perhaps even gave rise to the modern notion of 'secularism.' Hence, it was only natural that the bitter after-effects of Europe's obsession with abstract theology resulted in the relegation of that discipline to small departments in specialized academic programs at institutions of higher learning. Even the largest churches of modernity tend to shy away from conceptual notions of belief, feeling that emphasizing abstract doctrines over positive messages will turn away potential attendees. Moreover, the Anglophone West is slowly losing its religion: in 2021, for the first time since the census began, fewer than half of people in England and Wales identified themselves as Christian.

Given this tendency – and the fact that most modern readers are not too concerned with theology – it is understandable that the majority of writings on Salafism pay scant attention to the theology that underpins it. In attempting to portray Salafis as 'the other,' most journalists (and even academics) end up mentioning matters that Salafis themselves would not primarily associate with, but which Western readers will immediately find eccentric. As Edward Said points out in his *Orientalism*, in choosing how to describe 'the other,' more is typically revealed about the one who describes than the one who is described.[10] Consequently, most descriptions of Salafism in academia and the media tend to concentrate on legal or cultural issues, such as their views on gender interactions, the impermissibility of music, the details of dress codes, and other mundane societal matters. Yet, these issues – all of them – are tertiary manifestations of *any* given strand of traditionalist Islam, and no strand views them as being the primary subject that identifies their faith. Ironically, any social practice that is typically pointed out as being 'Salafi' (for example, women veiling in *niqāb*) is hardly ever unique to Salafi Islam and can be found in many opposing groups as well. Many Shiʿis, for instance, cover their face, yet Salafism and Shiʿism are mutually exclusive strands and view each other with great animosity.

In order to appreciate the worldview from within, it will be essential for an outsider to discard his or her own biases and see what matters most to Salafis themselves. And this leads us back to theology first and methodology second. The primary importance of theology for Salafis is understood by appreciating the centrality of faith (*īmān*) in the Islamic tradition. This is highlighted in the famous hadith of Gabriel (*ḥadīth Jibrīl*), whereby the Prophet outlined the facets of the religion, with faith (*īmān*) constituting the second of three components – the other two being bodily actions (*islām*) and spiritual excellence (*iḥsān*).[11] This demarcation engenders the differentiation between a simple Muslim (i.e., one who conforms to outward manifestations of the faith), a believer (*mu'min*, who actually possesses faith), and a person of spiritual excellence (*muḥsin*, who believes and acts in accordance with the law of Islam in a heightened spiritual state). Thus, there is a hierarchy in Islam, as Ibn Taymiyya notes: 'Every person of excellence (*muḥsin*) is a believer (*mu'min*), and every believer (*mu'min*) is a Muslim. Yet not every believer is a person of excellence, nor is every Muslim a believer.'[12] For Salafis, theology is the real core of one's Islamic identity, hence the Salafi conception of Islamic theology is what makes them unique.

### *1.2.1 Monotheism (Tawḥīd)*

Of utmost importance is the Salafi understanding of monotheism (*tawḥīd*). For most Muslim groups, monotheism entails belief in the Oneness of God: He has no partners, nor is there any entity similar to Him. For Salafis, it is more precise than that. In order to be truly monotheistic, they claim that a believer must perfect his understanding not only of the uniqueness of God's existence (*al-rubūbiyya*) but also the affirmation of His divine names and attributes (*al-asmā' wa-l-ṣifāt*) and the implementation of that in venerating God and God alone through acts of worship (*ulūhiyya*). This tripartite division of *tawḥīd* is a fundamental principle unique to Salafi Islam, which we will analyze in more detail.[13]

Of course, an essential aspect is the belief that there is only one ultimate Creator and Lord, and no other entity exists with unlimited divine power except the one God, Allah Himself. This aspect of monotheism – which no Muslim would disagree with – is called 'Oneness of Lordship' (*tawḥīd al-rubūbiyya*). But according to Salafis, every single religion in the world, even paganism, ultimately affirms this notion – at some level – of one All-Powerful Creator. Therefore, it is not enough to say that God is One: in order to be truly monotheistic, one must also affirm 'God's unique right to be venerated and worshiped' (*tawḥīd al-ulūhiyya*). According to this doctrine, no other entity must be shown ultimate respect, asked anything supernatural, or shown the reverence of a religious devotee, other than God Himself.

While conceptually, all Muslims would agree to such a premise, Salafis define 'worship' and 'reverence' in a manner that excludes many practices that other non-Salafi Muslims would justify as a part of religious rituals. Examples of these practices include veneration of saints, invoking the Prophet for one's needs as a form of 'intercession' (*shafā'a*), or the belief – as some Sufis and Shi'a hold – that a category of people are given supernatural powers. Consequently, Salafis are at ease with using phrases like 'saint worship' and 'grave worship' to characterize practices that are common among other strands of Islam[14] without accounting for alternative interpretations that negate idolatrous connotations. For example, many trends (a third view) consider them to be unlawful practices but not inherently polytheistic in nature.[15]

Salafism's preoccupation with monotheism (*tawḥīd*) seems wholly natural, bearing in mind that monotheism is, in fact, a cardinal position of the Islamic faith. However, to an uninformed observer, even a devout Muslim, their excesses in this regard may not be easily apparent. The modern Salafi movement, heavily influenced by the works of Ibn ʿAbd al-Wahhāb (whose Wahhabi movement will be recounted in detail in Chapter 3), displays an almost single-minded obsession with the antithesis of monotheism: idolatry (*shirk*). Ibn ʿAbd al-Wahhāb did not simply condemn prevalent practices in the Muslim world as blameworthy religious innovation (*bidʿa*), he regularly labeled masses of Muslims as idol-worshippers (*mushrikūn*) due to what he perceived as practices that he considered idolatrous, such as the Sufi veneration of saints and the Shiʿi belief in Imams. In fact, he not only deemed these Muslims to be idol-worshippers, but also went so far as to consider the pre-Islamic idolatry of the Prophet's time to be 'less severe' (*akhaff*) than the modern 'idolatry' of his fellow Muslims.[16] This obsession with idolatry, in such terms, has led modern Salafis to view *shirk* as a widespread phenomenon within the Muslim world. Consequently, like the movement of Ibn ʿAbd al-Wahhāb, some Salafis can be prone to casual excommunication (*takfīr*) of other Muslims[17] – with its worst manifestation being among militant Salafis (also known as Jihadi-Salafis), and which often results in legitimizing violence (as detailed in Chapter 5). In less extreme instances, it fosters harsh accusations against other Muslims that often lead to Salafis splitting off from Muslim communities and forming their own mosques and associations.

The last of the tripartite division is the affirmation in God's divine names and attributes (*tawḥīd al-asmāʾ wa-l-ṣifāt*). While this is being discussed last, historically, this was the first and most important cornerstone of the earliest prototypes of Salafism – and where the first divisions in Sunni Islam occurred (as explored in more detail in Chapter 2). This point entails the belief that God is not only unique in His absolute sovereignty and exclusive right to be worshipped but also unique in the reality of His divine names and attributes. Since the intellect cannot fully comprehend God, Salafis believe that the only way to know Him is via revelation (that is, the Qurʾan and hadiths). The language that God Himself uses in the Qurʾan, or the Prophet used in the hadith, must be held in the highest of regard, and hence, all nouns, adjectives, and descriptions given of God should be taken at face value. Affirming a divine attribute 'literally' (*ḥaqīqī*) means that one understands the apparent meaning of the attribute according to the Arabic language, but not its reality or modality (*kayfiyya*). Furthermore, since God is obviously not like any other being, the divine attribute will be understood in a unique manner, negating any perceived anthropomorphic connotations from it.

Of particular importance is the Salafi focus on God's attributes of transcendence (*al-ʿuluww*), speech (*kalām*), ascent over the throne (*al-istiwāʾ*), and descent (*nuzūl*). All divine attributes that might possibly be perceived as overtly anthropomorphic – such as God's face (*wajh*), hands (*yad*), and shin (*sāq*) – are also all affirmed as being divine, but with the caveat that their precise modality is not known and cannot resemble anything of the creation. It is of note that these divine attributes mentioned do not occupy a different theological status to other divine attributes since, for Salafis, all of God's divine names and attributes are equally important. Rather, these particular attributes have historically been the ones that were the most contentious and generated the most controversy, specifically with their rival claimants to Sunnism, the Ashʿarī and Māturīdī schools of theology.[18]

The essence of the differences between the Salafis and Ashʿarī/Māturīdī schools can be reduced to each school's attitude on speculative or rationalist theology (*ʿilm al-kalām*).[19] Speculative theology has a clear set of guidelines on how God's attributes should be interpreted and a complex categorization of the divine attributes. Salafis feel that such a categorization and classification is itself a blameworthy heresy (*bidʿa*) and that *all* attributes should be understood in the same manner. For an outsider, this topic quickly becomes confusing because both trends seek to affirm all of God's attributes and deny His resemblance to His creation (*tashbīh*) while affirming His complete divine transcendence (*tanzīh*). However, Salafis insist that *all* of the divine attributes must be literally (*ḥaqīqī*) understood, whereas other trends would insist that some attributes should be understood in a figurative (*majazī*) manner. Hence, a Salafi would claim that God has a face and hands, becomes angry, laughs, is merciful, and hears and knows (because all these attributes are mentioned in the scripture), but would then add, 'in a manner that befits His majesty, and not in a way that resembles the creation.' The Ashʿarī/Māturīdī schools, however, would claim that while God is indeed hearing and knowing, attributes such as 'mercy' and 'anger' should be interpreted to imply God's intending to reward or punish. As for the reference to the divine face and hands, the Ashʿarī/Māturīdī schools would claim that these are clearly figurative (*majāzī*) and not meant to be understood literally. Ultimately, the Salafis completely reject the use of speculative theology (*kalām*) or the use of figurative interpretation, while the Ashʿarī/Māturīdī approach is either (1) to prefer an affirmation while simultaneously leaving the true meaning to God (*tafwīd*), or (2) to resort to figurative interpretations (*ta'wīl*) if they are deemed acceptable.[20]

Thus, it is unsurprising that the Salafi insistence on the literalness of such phrases used in the sacred texts has led them to be accused of anthropomorphism. In fact, the most iconic figure of Salafism, Ibn Taymiyya, was put on trial and jailed for this very charge.[21] The Salafi antagonism of those Sunnis who are highly sensitive about literal interpretation – because of the fear of falling into corporealism (*tajsīm*) – is clearly exemplified in a short work composed for lay Muslims by Ibn al-Uthaymin. This work, *ʿAqīdat ahl al-Sunna wa-l-jamāʿa* (*The Creed of the People of the Sunna and the Community*) – often printed with a preface of endorsement from the previous Grand Mufti of Saudi Arabia ʿAbd al-ʿAzīz b. Bāz (d. 1999) – has a section titled, 'The Face, the Two Hands, and the Two Eyes,' referring to the attributes of God.[22] While references to such divine attributes are scattered through the sacred texts, it was uncommon for classical theologians to gather them together and make them a cardinal point of creed. Since this unique understanding of God's attributes is an important aspect of Salafism, we shall return to it in our next chapter.

### *1.2.2 The Conception of Faith (Īmān)*

Another cornerstone of Salafi theology involves its conception of faith (*īmān*). The Qurʾan refers to *īmān* as the most important aspect in the life of a believer. Hence, it frequently addresses the believers as 'O people of *īmān*.' But what exactly does it mean to have faith or to believe? Does mere acknowledgment of God's existence count as legitimate *īmān*? Or must one also believe and act in a specific manner? What if one professes to believe but then willfully ignores each and every commandment of God and abandons the most basic rituals? Mainstream Salafism defines *īmān* as consisting of (1) faith in the heart, (2) acknowledgment of the tongue, and (3) actions of the limbs. In other words, not only must a person believe in God and the fundamentals of faith, but one must also acknowledge verbally – via the testimony of faith (*shahāda*) – that one is a Muslim, and one must then have a bare minimum quantity of actions that demonstrate such faith. For most scholars of the movement, at a bare minimum, a person must be observant of the five daily prayers (*ṣalāt*) to be considered a believer – abandonment of the prayer is tantamount to abandonment of the faith. For the vast majority of non-Salafi Muslims, anyone who does not pray remains a Muslim, albeit a sinful one.

### *1.2.3 Association and Dissociation (al-Walāʾ wa-l-Barāʾ)*

Another important and unique aspect of Salafi theology is the doctrine of 'association and dissociation' (*al-walāʾ wa-l-barāʾ*).[23] While each strand of Salafism interprets this doctrine differently, at its core, it deals with the level of permissibility of associating with individuals or entities outside one's own strand and subsequently identifying when such association becomes theologically problematic. Hence, as a general rule, Salafis believe one should ally with like-minded and pious believers while refraining from supporting Muslims guilty of deviant beliefs (*mubtadiʿa*). And while this notion might seem more of an ethical issue, with a distinctly social and political manifestation – rather than a theological tenet of faith – Salafis themselves deem the matter to be theological. Interestingly, this doctrine is not explicitly found to be a prominent topic in the writings of Ibn Taymiyya. In fact, the modern fixation on the doctrine is largely drawn from Ibn ʿAbd al-Wahhāb's reading of the Qurʾan, who considered it to be a fundamental principle of monotheism (*tawḥīd*), without which one's faith in God was in question.[24] Consequently, Salafism – due to this tendency – has received a reputation as being somewhat 'cultish.' Of course, Salafis would reject this characterization vehemently since, from their perspective, it is the other groups that have strayed or broken from the true teachings of Islam while they have remained steadfast and correct themselves.

At its most extreme manifestation, understandings of *al-walāʾ wa-l-barāʾ* would even allow Salafis to consider a fellow Muslim as an apostate (*kāfir* or *murtadd*) if the said individual crosses a certain threshold in their association with individuals or groups they deem to be deviants or apostates. An example of this would be if a Muslim were to ally with a non-Muslim in order to fight against a fellow Muslim. Far more common, however, is the claim that one's own piety and probity are affected if one is deemed too lax in associating with those who are deviant. In particular, the dogmatic-loyalist branch of Salafis, the Madhkhalīs (who shall be discussed later in this chapter and in Chapter 3), became notorious for their constant usage of this concept in declaring others as being misguided. Jihadi-Salafis also use this doctrine in considering some Muslims as legitimate military targets because they view them as having offered aid to their enemies.

### *1.2.4 The Saved Sect (al-Firqa al-Nājiyya)*

One of the seminal features of Salafism is the certainty with which they identify as *the* correct understanding of Islam and *the* only saved group of Muslims. To understand this point, one must first understand a series of traditions in the hadith corpus that reference schisms and splinter movements, praising only one group and criticizing all others. These traditions form a staple motif in Salafi discourse, and these concepts permeate throughout much of their rhetoric and form a foundational block in understanding Salafism.

Among them are the following three hadiths:

(1) The Messenger of God, may God's blessings and peace be upon him, stood among us and said: 'Those who came before you of

the People of the Book [meaning the Jews and Christians] split into seventy-two sects, and this nation (*umma*) will split into seventy-three: seventy-two shall be destined for Hell, and one for Paradise, and that is the *jamāʿa* [the rightly guided group].'[25]

(2) The Prophet, may God's blessings and peace be upon him, said, 'My nation (*umma*) shall divide into seventy-three sects, all of them will be in the Fire except for one, and that is the *jamāʿa* [the rightly guided group].' It was asked of him, 'And who are they, O Messenger of God?' He responded, '[Those who remain on] what I and my Companions are upon today.'[26]

(3) The Messenger, may God's blessings and peace be upon him, said, 'There shall always be a group of my nation (*umma*) clearly upon the truth, subjugating their enemies. Those who oppose them will not vanquish them. And they shall remain upon this until the command of God [i.e., the Day of Judgment] comes.'[27]

While some of these narrations (in particular the first two) are considered problematic by several Sunni theologians, the general scholarly consensus of Sunnism is that the hadiths that mention schisms (*ḥadīth al-iftirāq*) are considered as authentic statements uttered by the Prophet.[28] However, it is not the authenticity of these hadiths that is hotly debated by Muslim scholars, but the understanding and application of them.

Salafis view that their specific understanding of Islam, *and only their understanding*, is what is intended as the 'saved faction' in such narrations. Hence, from these hadith, they derive other descriptions for themselves, such as 'the Saved Sect' (*al-firqa al-nājiyya*) – since they are the only one destined for Paradise – and 'the Aided Group' (*tāʾifa al-manṣūra*) – since God shall always protect them in spreading the truth against their enemies. When understood in this light, Salafis then view 'the other' as every single understanding and schism besides their own. Hence, not only do non-Sunni groups like the Shiʿa become 'the other,' even mainstream Sunni movements that are not Salafi (such as the Ashʿarīs, Māturīdīs, and Sufis) are categorized as one of the seventy-two misguided sects.

The appellation '*ahl al-Sunna wa-l-jamāʿa*' (The People of the Sunna and the Community)[29] – which is the term Sunnism is abbreviated for – is considered by Salafis as exclusively applying to them in its proper and fullest sense. Hence, for Salafis, they and they alone are the true 'Sunnis,' that is, the Saved Sect and the Aided Group. Authorities within Salafism, whether proto-Salafis like Ibn Taymiyya or modern Salafis like Muḥammad b. Salih al-Uthaymin (d. 2001) – one of the leading icons of the movement in the twentieth century – have, however, acknowledged 'a general, technical usage' (*istilāḥ al-ʿamma*) of the term '*ahl al-sunna*' as encompassing other non-Salafi groups which are opposed to the Shiʿa.[30] Thus, 'Sunnis,' in this generic sense, encompasses the Ashʿarīs, Māturīdīs, and even many Sufis. However – as explicitly noted by Ibn al-Uthaymin himself – Salafis argue that *ahl al-sunna* is, in reality (*ḥaqiqa*), 'the Pious Predecessors' (*al-salaf al-ṣāliḥ*), which excludes Ashʿarīs, Māturīdīs, Sufis, and the Muʿtazila.[31] In this manner, Salafis claim to be the only adherents to the path of the Pious Predecessors.

Of course, the concept of the Saved Sect is a wholly theological construct. However, many Salafis conceive of the notion in a comprehensive sense that entails praxis – both personal worship and sociopolitical interaction – and spirituality, especially in its opposition to the practices and beliefs of Sufism. Thus, Salafis will articulate a theological basis for the Saved Sect mentality but also manifest this belief in a distinct set of actions and attitudes, which are not simply theological. They would, however, argue that such external and non-theological matters are subsumed under the 'Salafi methodology' (*al-manhaj al-salafī*). According to Egyptian scholar ʿAmr ʿAbd al-Munʿim Salīm, in his *al-Manhaj al-Salafī ʿinda al-Shaykh Nāṣir al-Dīn al-Albānī* (*The Salafi Methodology According to Shaykh Nāṣir al-Dīn al-Albānī*), Salafism is 'the methodology which takes the Predecessors as a basis and acts according to their beliefs (*iʿtiqādihim*), public dealings (*muʿāmalatihim*), legal rulings (*aḥkāmihim*), pedagogy (*tarbiyātihim*) and the purification of their souls (*tazkiyat nufūsihim*).'[32]

Critics argue that adherents to Salafism display strong sectarian tendencies and demonstrate groupthink, ready to demarcate lines between 'authentic' Islam and heresies (*bidʿa*). From the Salafi perspective, they see that they are defending the purity of the faith against syncretism and corruption in line with the above-mentioned narrations. However, it has been acknowledged, in part, by Salafi leaders like Ibn al-Uthaymin, that the Salafis have been beset with extremes that should be dismissed as being 'Salafi-like.' These people, he argues, have adopted what is termed a 'partisan methodology' (*manhaj ḥizbī*) within a narrowly defined and uniform Salafi group, which divides from others on the basis of superficial differences or legitimate legal and creedal differences (for even the Predecessors differed on some matters of belief).[33] Nonetheless, such interventions have not been frequent or adamant enough to temper a general trend of argumentation and disruption on the part of those who define themselves as Salafis. Hence, modern Salafism is beset with constant internal factionalization on various issues, at times theological, at times legal and methodological, with each group claiming that *they* are representing *true* Salafi thought in that field. Since the presumption is that only one opinion or way will be correct, it then becomes natural for there to be a competition between strands for authority and leadership, as will be demonstrated in a later part of this chapter – and indeed throughout the work.

## *1.3 Law*

### *1.3.1 Shariʿa and Fiqh*

The term ‘shariʿa,’ meaning ‘path,’ captures the importance Muslims place on Islamic law. This is because they believe that only by traversing this *‘path’* does one attain righteousness and piety. Muslims view the Shariʿa as a comprehensive legal system and code of ethics that embodies God’s infallible and immutable law, revealed to guide and govern their lives. It is primarily derived from the Qurʾan, and the precedent of the Prophet as recorded in the hadith literature; secondary sources include the consensus (*ijmāʿ*) of the Islamic scholarly community, scholarly interpretations (*ijtihād*), among others. Besides matters of ritual conduct (*ʿibāda*), Islamic law encompasses a wide range of legal areas, including criminal law, family law, commercial law, and even international law. Moreover, it regulates all aspects of individual and communal life, from personal behavior to political governance.[34]

It is important to note here that while the Shariʿa itself is God’s infallible and immutable law, *fiqh* denotes the human interpretation and approximation of God’s law. As such, it is fallible and susceptible to modification. This distinction not only highlights the difference between the law and its sources – as perceived by Muslim jurists – but also underscores the implicit assumption that the Shariʿa is not entirely self-evident. In fact, Muslims believe that God did not reveal the law itself but only the scripture containing indications (or indicants: *adilla*, sing. *dalīl*) of God’s *intended* law. After all, if scripture were self-evident, it would *not* be the source of law but the law itself, and as a consequence, there would be no need for interpretation since there would be nothing to interpret.[35] So unless a *dalīl* is conclusive (*qaṭʿī*), it only serves as a guide for the jurist to *infer* what he thinks is a correct ruling for a particular case at hand. Therefore, *fiqh* – and the individual ruling it produces – is traditionally understood as the result of the juristic interpretation (*ijtihād*) of what the Shariʿa entails.

So the primary role of any qualified Muslim jurist (*mujtahid*), explains Wael Hallaq in *The Origins and Evolution of Islamic Law*, is to identify the relevant *adilla* within the authentic sources of law and subsequently derive a normative rule that would fall into one of five distinct legal categories: (1) obligatory (*wājib*), (2) recommended (*mandūb*), (3) permissible (*mubāh*), (4) repugnant (*makrūh*), and (5) prohibited (*harām*).[36] While the sources must be known with certainty, the legal conclusions drawn from them do not necessarily have to be more than probable. This is because Islamic jurisprudence – except in cases where the *adilla* are conclusive (*qaṭʿī*) – was dominated by probability. In fact, certainty and probability became the fundamental categories with which Muslim jurists approached every legal question, leading to the norm of juristic disagreement (*ikhtilāf*) in

Islamic jurisprudence. Consequently, it was understood that not only could incorrect rulings occur but also that a plurality of different opinions would emerge for any given case. After all, one jurist's inference is as good as that of another, as the two cardinal maxims state: 'All qualified jurists (*mujtahid*) are correct,' and 'The *mujtahid* whose opinion is correct is rewarded twice [i.e., both for exercising his effort and for getting it right], while the *mujtahid* whose opinion is incorrect is rewarded only once [for his effort].' Therefore, every ruling resulting from an individual *ijtihād* of a jurist is classified as being conjectural (*ẓann*) and not conclusive (*qaṭʿī*).[37]

Of course, most concede, in theory, that there can be only one correct ruling for a given case, regardless of whether the community of jurists knows which one it is. So, except for cases where there is juristic consensus (*ijmāʿ*) on a ruling, one opinion is considered superior to the others and is, therefore, chosen by a jurist (or his school) to be the authoritative ruling to be applied for a given case. This selection does not claim absolute certainty regarding the ruling but rather emphasizes its *highest probability*. This notion is particularly evident through their use of operative legal terms to describe their rulings, such as the relied-upon opinion (*al-muʿtamad*), the stronger opinion (*al-aqwā*), and the more correct opinion (*al-aṣaḥḥ*).

Aron Zysow, at the beginning of *The Economy of Certainty*, observes that Muslims from a very early period 'came to treat the question of [legal] legitimacy along explicitly epistemological lines.'[38] This is because, as with most legal systems, the Shariʿa does not offer resolutions to every legal question and leaves room for Muslim jurists (*fuqahāʾ*, sing. *faqīh*) to exercise their intellectual efforts (*ijtihād*) in order to make judgments. Consequently, this has resulted in numerous rulings (*fatāwā*, sing. *fatwa*) on a range of issues, culminating in the development of the science of Islamic jurisprudence (*fiqh*) and, with it, the schools of law (*madhāhib*, sing. *madhhab*), most notably the Ḥanafī, Mālikī, Shāfiʿī, and Ḥanbalī schools. These four schools of law have been understood by mainstream Sunni Muslims, from at least the tenth century, as all being equally valid attempts at interpreting the Shariʿa. Hence the default is that a Muslim should subscribe to one of these four schools (typically, the school that is predominant in his area or that his family follows).[39]

Salafis, like all other mainstream Muslim groups, consider Islamic law to be a necessary and crucial component of the religion. However, Salafis exhibit a spectrum of opinions regarding the proper methodology for interpreting Islamic law and the validity of certain principles of Islamic legal theory (*uṣūl al-fiqh*). This spectrum ranges from those who advocate adherence to one of the traditional legal schools to those who advocate breaking away from them.[40] This division is rooted in a broader debate on the clarity of scripture and the permissibility of uncritical adherence (*taqlīd*) to a legal school (or scholar). These conflicting views have resulted in internal divisions among Salafis and set them apart, at least to some degree, from non-Salafi Sunnis.

As mentioned previously, a historical normative emerged in which the four schools of law (the *madhhabs*) were deemed to be the exclusive mechanism that a lay-Muslim had to resort to in order to follow the Shariʿa. The notion that these schools should be rigorously adhered to (*taqlīd*) became widespread, since it gave the perception of consistency and reliance on a large body of scholarship that spanned many regions and centuries. Salafism, on the other hand, conceives of this tradition, and of the schools of law, in a radically different manner. For those whose primary goal was to purify the religion and return to the original understanding of Islam as revealed to the Prophet and understood by the earliest generation, the school of law became a barrier, or even a deviation, to their pursuit. After all, there were no *madhhabs* in the time of the Prophet and the earliest generations, so what need is there for scholars to act as mediators when God has made clear what He intends in the Qurʾan and the Sunna? They assert that the words of a human scholar, regardless of their eminence or antiquity, should not – and do not – hold any weight in the absence of explicit evidence (*dalīl*) from the Qurʾan and Sunna. It is the Prophet of God alone who should be followed, not some fallible jurist with their subjective interpretation of the law.

Within this paradigm, the books of jurisprudence (*fiqh*), along with the more intricate, hermeneutically developed legal frameworks (*uṣūl*) that form the bedrock of traditional Islamic law, might be dismissed and bypassed in favor of going straight to the literal proof texts of the Qurʾan and hadith. Consequently, it is a norm among lay Salafis to challenge scholars who deliver a verdict on any opinion with the question, 'What is the evidence (*dalīl*)?' This question is at once empowering and debilitating: empowering because it seeks to provide lay individuals with direct access to the sacred sources themselves and debilitating due to the inherent challenge posed by the absence of the necessary methodological and hermeneutical training required to effectively analyze those sources and extract legal principles.

Salafis, at least in rhetoric if not in practice, tend to oppose *taqlīd* and, at times, the *madhhabs* as a whole. This critical stance toward *taqlīd* and *madhhabs* is, in fact, a typical stereotype associated with Salafis among non-Salafis. However, the level of opposition varies among Salafis themselves and has led to internal divisions among their ranks. Consequently, Salafis can broadly be divided into three factions: (1) soft-madhhabists, (2) critical-madhhabists, and (3) anti-madhhabists. The three greatest figureheads of Salafi scholarship of the past century best exemplify each of these factions: Ibn Bāz, Ibn al-Uthaymin, and – the famous Albanian hadith scholar from Jordan – Nasir al-Din al-Albānī, respectively.

The first faction, the soft-madhhabists, are those who follow a particular *madhhab* but are rhetorically anti-*taqlīd*. They would, in theory, be opposed to following a *madhhab* if it contradicts the proof text from scripture. Nonetheless, they concede that a lay Muslim should follow a *madhhab* as long as the individual is aware of the evidence (*dalīl*) for the position the *madhhab* advocates. This faction, along with their fellow critical-madhhabists, commonly displays a stronger affinity toward the Ḥanbalī – and, to a lesser extent, Shāfiʿī – school of law. Both of these schools rely more on a hadith-based approach in legal derivation, and the Ḥanbalī school in particular has always had a close association with the movement, as the next chapter will demonstrate. In contrast, the Ḥanafī school's heavy reliance on transmitted opinions and juristic precedent does not resonate well with them. Ibn Bāz exemplifies this faction since, despite being a Ḥanbalī, he demonstrated his anti-*taqlīd* edge by issuing independent verdicts that deviated from the accepted Ḥanbalī *madhhab* (such as his following Ibn Taymiyya's opinion on the triple-divorce opinion).[41] He claimed that it was best to follow a *madhhab* but that if stronger evidence was found outside the school, it would be permissible for a qualified jurist to leave that school.

The second faction, the critical-madhhabists, are those who, despite adhering to a *madhhab*, retain their anti-*taqlīd* stance not just in rhetoric – unlike their fellow soft-madhhabists – but also oftentimes in practice. They live up to their claim that the strong *dalīl* supersedes the teachings of a *madhhab* by, at times, adopting opinions outside their respective *madhhab* that they feel are better substantiated by the textual evidence from scripture. Ibn al-Uthaymin serves as an emblematic figure within this faction – his overall teaching was through the Ḥanbalī school, but he frequently departed from that school if he felt that evidence from the hadith was sounder. He authored a renowned commentary of the classical Ḥanbalī legal text, *Zād al-Mustaqniʿ* (*The Provision of the Seeker*) by Mūsā al-Ḥajjāwī (d. 968/1561),[42] but in the commentary would regularly champion positions that the text did not, claiming that the 'evidence' indicated that the Ḥanbalī school was incorrect in its position.[43]

The third faction, the anti-madhhabists, vehemently opposes adherence to the *madhhabs* and advocates for the abandonment of *taqlīd* in favor of direct engagement (*ijtihād*) with the textual evidence found in the Qurʾan and hadith. This faction, primarily identified with al-Albānī and his brand of Salafism, contends that *taqlīd* obstructs the intellectual development and genuine understanding of Muslims regarding the foundations of Islamic law. They argue that blind adherence to the *madhhabs* has led Muslims astray from the authentic teachings of the Prophet, resulting in confusion, religious innovations (*bidʿa*), and disunity within the Muslim community. The anti-madhhabists even claim that the founders of the *madhhabs* would themselves have altered their opinions had they been aware of the evidence and proofs (*dalīls*) presented by this faction. Consequently, they believe that Islamic law is in need of purification from the *madhhab*s – a traditionalist barrier that impedes and obscures the true teachings of Islam. They maintain that this purification can be achieved by directly examining the primary sources – the Qurʾan and hadith literature – and by independently verifying the scriptural authenticity of legal rulings. Some among them argued, and many tacitly fell into, the notion that individuals can arrive at correct rulings without the need for extensive scholarly interpretation, which they view as fallible, subjective, and a source of uncertainty and deviation. Hence, for them, the application of the simple and apparent literal meaning of scripture took precedence over the study of hermeneutics and the science of *usūl al-fiqh*.

Although it has been said that the anti-madhhabist stance of al-Albānī may have been influenced by figures such as Ibn Taymiyya, Ibn Qayyim al-Jawziyya (d. 751/1350), Ibn ʿAbd al-Wahhāb, and the literalist approach of the Ẓāhirī school of law[44] – famously championed by the Andalusian scholar ʿAlī b. Ḥazm (d. 456/1064) – it represents a relatively recent development within the broader Islamic intellectual history. This is because although all these figures displayed anti-*taqlīd* tendencies to varying degrees, they did not reject the *madhhabs* entirely and held sentiments more aligned with the madhhabists and critical-madhhabists. Ibn Taymiyya, for instance, was a Ḥanbalī who frequently referenced the four *madhhabs* in his legal discussions and did not prohibit *taqlīd* for the layperson. Even a regular scholar was permitted to perform *taqlīd* with an exception for matters where the evidence is demonstrably clear that the *madhhab's* position contradicts scripture.[45] Similarly, Ibn ʿAbd al-Wahhāb was a faithful adherent to the Ḥanbalī *madhhab*. There have, of course, also been scholars who adopted a semi-independent approach to *fiqh*, seeking to derive Islamic rulings directly from the textual evidence of scripture – primarily from the hadith literature – without considering the transmitted rulings of the *madhhabs*. Prominent Yemeni scholars such as Muḥammad b. Ismāʿīl al-Sanʿānī (d. 1182/1768) and Muḥammad b. ʿAlī al-Shawkānī (d. 1834), who based their *fiqh* on hadith, exemplify this approach, and they are to some degree precursors of al-Albānī's anti-madhhabist stance. They did not, however, entirely undo Islamic law from *madhhabs*; their works demonstrate an affinity to comparative *fiqh* by weighing the positions of one school over another in relation to scriptural evidence.

However, unlike any of these figures – who displayed varying degrees of anti-*taqlīd* tendencies – al-Albānī vehemently rejected *taqlīd* of the *madhhabs* with an unprecedented harshness and confidence in his methodology. He refused to follow any scholar or *madhhab* besides the Prophet. He stated:

> Those who are called Wahhabis, they are Ḥanbalīs… as for me, I refused to be Ḥanafī, therefore I will also refuse to be called a Ḥanbalī. Because when I affiliated [myself] with the Messenger of God, blessings and peace be upon him, it has sufficed me from all other affiliations. I worship God alone, and I follow Muhammad alone. God has no partner in worship, and Muhammad has no partner in following.[46]

This refusal to be labeled as Ḥanafī or Ḥanbalī stemmed from his belief there is a dichotomy between the true teachings of Islam as embodied within the Qurʾan and Sunna – as recorded in the authentic hadith collections – and the deviant beliefs found within the fallible opinions of the *madhhabs*. By stating that he worships God alone and follows Muhammad alone, he implies that adhering to a *madhhab* and engaging in *taqlīd* constitutes a type of potential rejection of the Prophet's Sunna – a charge rarely levied by any other scholar, Salafi or otherwise.[47] Al-Albānī's stance towards *taqlīd* and his position of being anti-*madhhab* became extremely popular globally with the spread of his sermons on audio cassettes, so much so that modern Salafism in most parts of the world is largely associated with al-Albānī's stance on the *madhabs*.

Consequently, of the three Salafi legal strands, the one advocated by al-Albānī and his followers is the one that has brought about the most vehement opposition, especially as the wordings used by him and his followers in their critique of *taqlīd* has led to accusations that they have advocated legal anarchy. Throughout history, Muslims have relied upon scholars and the scholarly class (*ʿulamāʾ*) in matters of religious understanding, due to their expertise. Within the traditionalist paradigm, it is inconceivable for a lay Muslim, without requisite legal training, to challenge a scholar and demand the textual evidence (*dalīl*) for an issued ruling, choosing instead to independently engage with the scriptural proof text themselves. Hence, those wishing to bypass the tradition and the *madhhabs* in favor of going directly to the Qurʾan and Sunna would be seen as committing a 'Protestant error'[48] and are likened to a non-qualified patient questioning a professional physician's treatment and diagnosis based on their own internet research about the appropriate course of action. Salafis of the al-Albānī persuasion are, nevertheless, dependent on the interpretive control of scholars who they insist must be followed.[49]

The Salafi insistence on not 'blindly following' one of the schools of law but rather the evidence results in the rather ironic reality – as detractors of the movement note – of Salafis invariably following a scholar or scholars whom they view as having followed the evidence: i.e., doing exactly what followers of the existing legal schools do.

### *1.3.2 Sunna and Bid*ʿ*a*

One aspect that is salient in all three trends mentioned above is a strict adherence to the Prophetic Sunna and an aversion to adding – or tampering with – the rituals of the faith. Salafism is associated (critics would use the term 'obsessed') with its attempt at eradicating blameworthy religious innovation (*bidʿa*). Of course, at some level, all mainstream Muslims seek to condemn actions that are properly deemed to be such innovations. This is based on various warnings attributed to the Prophet, such as the narration in *Ṣaḥīḥ Muslim* which is routinely recited in most Friday sermons around the globe: 'the worst of matters are introduced novelties (*muḥdathāt*), and every innovation (*bidʿa*) is an error (*ḍalāla*).'[50] Hence, it is not in the rejection of 'innovation' per se that Muslims differ as much as in the definition of what constitutes a reprehensible innovation.

For most non-Salafi schools, some types of innovation are acceptable – those known as 'praiseworthy innovations' (*bidʿa ḥasana*) – whereas others are reprehensible. Taking a well-established practice, and fine-tuning it, or specifying a time or place for a ritual, would not typically be considered a reprehensible innovation. Examples of this would include singing praises of the Prophet on his birthday (*mawlid*), or devotees gathering at a mosque or house and chanting invocations in a particular manner (group *dhikr*). The fact that the earliest generations did not celebrate the birthday of the Prophet is not relevant: since showing love to the Prophet is a matter of faith, and singing devotional poetry is an established practice, it makes sense for later generations to organically adopt and fine-tune mainstream concepts and participate in such celebratory gatherings. An innovation would only be reprehensible, according to most non-Salafi schools, if a completely alien concept or ritual were to be introduced into the faith (for example, the claim that the daily prayers should be done with music).

For Salafis, on the other hand, *all* ritualistic innovations are, by default, reprehensible and must be rejected. If a religious practice is not sanctioned in the Qurʾan or the Sunna and was not done by the earliest generations, it should be rejected as an evil innovation: there is no such thing as a 'praiseworthy innovation' (*bidʿa ḥasana*). Hence, the very act of celebrating the Prophet's birthday is a reprehensible innovation since it was not done by the first generations.[51] Likewise, group *dhikrs*, which are a staple part of almost all non-Salafi religious gatherings, become problematic as well.

Such a cautious attitude applies only to acts that are religious in nature; hence, technological 'innovations' such as computers and cell phones would not be issues of contention.[52] Salafis have absolutely no problems with technology. In fact, in the last few decades, they have, by all accounts, excelled and surpassed other groups in the usage of modern technology in propagating their opinions (a simple search on Google of almost any

Islamic topic will bring up Salafi responses far more than other trends). However, some activities that might be treated as non-religious in common understanding are classified as religious by Salafis and hence subject to the same prohibitions. An example of this is celebrations: the majority of Salafis view *all* celebrations as being religious in nature and hence consider personal celebrations like birthdays, anniversaries, and commemorative days like Mother's Day to be an innovation.[53]

## *1.4 Spirituality*

It is a common trope that Salafism is contrasted as the 'other' vis-à-vis the Islamic mystical tradition of Sufism (*taṣawwuf* in Arabic).[54] From scholarly treatises to online debates, the constant back and forth between these two strands is a hallmark of intra-Muslim polemics – so much so that even lay Muslims are acutely aware of the bitter rivalry between them.

This has led some to assume that Salafis are opposed to spirituality as a whole. However, this is not strictly accurate and is not how Salafis themselves view it. Salafis are generally opposed to the *methods* and *philosophy* underpinning Sufi spirituality and mysticism, but not the actual notion of spirituality itself.[55] Just like all other Muslims, they affirm spirituality as being a part of the Qur'anic notion of purification (*tazkiya*) and the Prophetic concept of spiritual excellence (*iḥsān*). In fact, they often write and teach on the topic of 'purification of the heart.' Perhaps it might be more accurate to state that Salafis are not opposed to spirituality but to mysticism – which for the Sufis are one and the same. Hence, in order to understand the nuanced nature of the Salafi conception of spirituality and how it fundamentally differs from Sufi mysticism, we will briefly summarize Sufism and its key tenets before examining Salafism's response to it.

Sufism refers to the broad tradition of Islamic mysticism and has a controversial history, even among those who claim to adhere to its ideal. It can even be argued that the term itself is as contentious as 'Salafism,' with rival claimants to both its title and its principles. It emphasizes the inward search for God and the attainment of spiritual closeness or union (*jamʿ*)[56] with the divine. The Sufi mystical tradition is characterized by a particular worldview – influenced by Gnostic[57] and Neoplatonic thoughts[58] – in which the soul is viewed as having a divine origin and, hence, of higher importance than the body. The soul, being directly created by God Himself, is what will eventually return to Him, but only after its sojourn in the temporal world, imprisoned, as it were, in the physical body. The goal of Sufism is to protect the purity of the soul from the corruption of the body and the material world. In doing so, it aims to expedite the eventual reunification (*jamʿ*)

of the soul with the Divine as perfectly and swiftly as possible, realized through the annihilation of the soul in God (*fanāʿ fī Allāh*). This notion is encapsulated in the doctrine of the 'unity of being' (*waḥdat al-wujūd*), wherein God is seen as the only 'ontologically real' existent. The meaning of this doctrine is highly debated both within and without the Sufi tradition, with some maintaining the union to be merely *experiential* (trying to maintain a monotheist dichotomy between the Creator and His creation), while others believe it to be *existential* and ontological (subscribing to a monistic cosmology, wherein God alone really exists).[59]

Regardless of the exact nature of this reunion, Sufis generally believe that the way that it is achieved is by means of receiving spiritual guidance from a master (*murshid*) – or more colloquially, a Sufi shaykh – who has already achieved such a status, in a supposedly unbroken chain of spiritual authorization leading back to the Prophet himself.[60] Under the guidance of the master, the initiate (*murīd*) undergoes a continual series of spiritual exercises and rituals that allow the soul to journey from one spiritual station (*maqām*) to another until it reaches the ultimate goal of reunification and annihilation in God. Consequently, joining a specific Sufi order (*ṭarīqa*), in which this mystical path is clearly delineated, becomes a common Sufi practice. This often entails pledging allegiance (*bayʿa*) to the spiritual leader (*shaykh*) of the order, adhering to a strict regimen of worship and spiritual purification as taught by the shaykh, and desiring to experience mystical states (*aḥwāl*, sing. *ḥāl*) that facilitate the soul's journey. And since Sufism is concerned with mystical experiences that can only be bestowed by the Sufi master, there is an emphasis on the role and miracles (*karāmāt*) of saints (*awliyāʾ*) and on the persona of the Prophet himself. This also translates into a heavy emphasis on being in the presence of a Sufi master, who is presumed to possess some inherent blessings or powers bestowed on them by God, and which perpetuate even after their death, making their tombs exude a holiness that is conducive to one's spiritual betterment. Sufism is also associated with various rituals and practices that are unique to them, such as their distinctive methods of remembering God (*dhikr*).

Salafis find all of the aforementioned mystical notions and practices problematic. They believe that true spirituality is manifested in a state of God-consciousness (*taqwā*), which is achieved by a strict adherence to the sacred law (Shariʿa). Such adherence, contrary to Sufi beliefs, does not require a spiritual guide. In fact, believing that certain people are inherently holy and pious opens the door to extreme veneration of people – a notion that Salafism is completely averse to. According to the Salafis, the first steps to idolatry (*shirk*) are couched in saint-veneration. Hence, even the Prophet of God himself should only be respected insofar as he is the ultimate human guide to understanding who God is and how to worship Him. Unlike Christians, whose equation of Jesus with God is considered polytheism in most Islamic thought, Muslims should take care in not exaggerating the status of the Prophet himself or blurring the boundaries between creation and the Creator. Salafis, as a whole, eschew the mystical terminology associated with the soul's alleged journey on to God and completely reject the concept of annihilation (*fanāʾ*) within the divine. Monism (*ittiḥād*), in particular, as understood in the reality of the doctrine of the unity of being, is viewed as an ultimate form of heresy (*kufr*), because it erases all distinction – which for Salafis is an absolute and necessary condition for true monotheism (*tawḥīd*) – between God and His creation. For the Salafis, the real spiritual goal is thus the proper *worship* of God and not the (*re*)*unification* (*jamʿ*) of the soul with divine essence.[61] Hence, spirituality is automatically achieved via adherence to the Prophetic practice – and not via innovated practices and beliefs.

Salafis do not deny the existence of pious people or saints (*awliyāʾ*). However, for them, only God knows who these saints are and, as such, they do not and cannot dispense any blessings nor do they have any intercessory powers. Consequently, the graves of saints are not to be venerated or visited with any rituals special to them.[62] Even the grave of the Prophet is not intended as a place of visitation. Ibn Taymiyya (in)famously issued a verdict (*fatwā*) claiming that traveling to visit the grave of the Prophet was a religious innovation (*bidʿa*) and that the journey to the city of the Prophet should be done with the express purpose of praying in the blessed mosque of the Prophet and not with the purpose of venerating his grave.[63] Salafism thus stresses that the Prophet is a divinely appointed role model to emulate, *not* a manifestation of the divine on earth.

This distinction leads to one of the most recognizable points of contention between Salafis and Sufis: the question of the celebration of the Prophet's birthday (*mawlid*). For Sufis, the answer is obvious: anything that shows love for the Prophet is inherently praiseworthy, for how can God not be pleased with those who express genuine love for His most favored creation? However, for Salafis, such a celebration is an evil heretical innovation (*bidʿa*), imported from Christianity and lacking any real basis in the practice of the earliest of generations of Pious Predecessors (*salaf*) themselves.

It is not only the practice of celebrating the birthday that Salafis find reproachable, but also activities associated with it. Among those practices deemed problematic is the recitation of the *Qasīdat al-Burda* (*Ode of the Mantle*), a renowned poem authored by the Egyptian Sufi master Muḥammad b. Saʿīd al-Būṣīrī (d. c. 694/1294). This poem is arguably the most famous Arabic poem ever composed as an expression of love for the Prophet and is regularly recited in many Sufi gatherings throughout the year. Yet Salafis consider this poem a textbook example of excessive veneration leading to *kufr* and *shirk*. According to them, the poem is guilty of attributing to the Prophet divine-like attributes and qualities exclusive to God alone.

However, the harshest criticism that the Salafis reserve for the Sufis (and for Shiʿa) is regarding the highly contentious practice of invoking God through the rank of the Prophet (*tawassul*) and of seeking assistance and invoking the Prophet or saints directly (*istighātha*).[64] *Tawassul* is an extremely common Sufi practice that involves asking God by the status and rights of the Prophet (typically by saying, 'O God, grant me such-and-such by the rank of the Prophet'). Ibn Taymiyya famously wrote an entire treatise claiming that not only was this an evil innovation (*bidʿa*), it was also a potential stepping-stone to extreme veneration of a created being and hence a pathway to idolatry (*shirk*).[65] Since *tawassul* entails ultimately asking God – albeit through the status of a created being – Salafis do not consider it to be idolatry in and of itself. The same cannot be said, however, of the practice of 'praying to' the saints (*istigātha*).

For Salafis, supplicating to other than God for one's needs is essentially the same as idolatry (*shirk*). Hence, the common practice of standing in front of the grave of the Prophet (or any saint) and asking him directly for one's needs is viewed not merely as an innovation, but as tantamount to idolatry – the only unforgivable sin in Islam. Many Salafis accuse those Sufis who practice *istighātha* of being actual pagans (*mushrikūn*, sing. *mushrik*) or of being one step shy of paganism (*shirk*). Salafis draw a parallel between the Sufi practice of invoking the Prophet and the Christian invocation of Jesus, asserting that both actions contradict the fundamental essence of monotheism (*tawḥīd*). Historically, some Salafis (like the Wahhabi movement, further discussed in section 3.1.2 below) have gone as far as excommunicating (*takfīr*) Sufis and engaging in military conflict with them due to this practice. In response, Sufis view Salafis as being devoid of any genuine love for the Prophet and as being dogmatic in the application of the letter of the law while forgetting its spirit. For the Sufis, invoking the Prophet is *not* the same as the Christian invocation of Jesus for the simple fact that the Sufi recognizes that the Prophet is a mortal, and invoking him is merely done because God loves him, and not because the Prophet is presumed to be divine or the son of God. Sufis argue in this regard, as Muḥammad b. ʿAlawī al-Mālikī al-Ḥasanī (d. 2005) wrote: 'The people only request them [the saints] to be a means unto their Lord in fulfilling what they seek from Allah; it is He, the Exalted, who fulfills the need as a result of their intercession, supplication, and entreaties.'[66] Sufis would argue that asking the dead (*istighatha*) is, in such an instance, a type of *tawassul* in its essence and hence cannot be considered idolatry.

It is important to point out that the tension between Salafism and Sufism is not as simplistic as portrayed here. This section merely summarizes the modern reality and tension between these two strands. Historically, the relationship has been more nuanced, and figures like Ibn Taymiyya and in particular his luminary student Ibn Qayyim, were more open to aspects of Sufism than later figures like Ibn ʿAbd al-Wahhab. In particular, Ibn Qayyim's seminal work *Madārij al-Sālikīn* (*The Ranks of the Divine Seekers*) can be viewed as a proto-Salafi attempt to reclaim Sufism and recast it in a Taymiyyan form[67] – something that the later Ibn ʿAbd al-Wahhāb did not attempt to do.

Furthermore, it has been argued from within Salafism in the West that, despite the importance placed in the religion on spiritual rectitude,[68] their group has suffered from being, in the words of one of the preachers of Salafism in America, Jamaal al-Din Zarabozo, 'divided, fighting, bickering, following their desires and so forth…[hence they] themselves are solely in need of a reminder concerning the purification of the soul and the true way to achieve that purification.' He further adds, 'Some of the *Ahl al-Sunna* [namely the Salafis] have a tendency to concentrate on other essential matters (such as academic matters of belief, fiqh [jurisprudence], the grading of hadith and so forth) while failing to also concentrate on the question of purification of the soul.'[69] This type of internal concern is one that can be taken seriously, as it seems to be aimed at raising the standards of the group. It also speaks to something of a crisis that Salafi activists have perhaps yet to fully address in their works and speeches.

## *1.5 Political Activism and Jihad*

One of the most contested notions between various strands of modern Salafis is the ideal relationship Salafis should have with their Muslim rulers and government and the mechanism of political engagement with the state. As with all matters, Salafis believe that religion must inform their methodology in politics and that they need to look to the texts of the Qurʾan, the hadith, and the actions of the Pious Predecessors in order to obtain the political methodology that is most pleasing to God. Of course, which texts are chosen, how they are interpreted, and which early role models are invoked, is where and how differences occur. The question of political engagement has proved to be the most controversial in the modern Salafi movement, not least because of the vast spectrum of Muslim governments.

It is possible to divide the current Salafi movement's attitude toward politics into five broad categories: (1) apolitical, (2) soft-loyalist, (3) dogmatic-loyalist, (4) activist, and (5) militant. The Salafis of the Kingdom of Saudi Arabia provide a fascinating example of this division and the impact it has had on Salafi unity. Of course, these categories are fluid and part of a continuum – there are overlapping areas and contested notions within each part of this spectrum. Nonetheless, these five divisions serve as useful milestones for understanding this phenomenon.

In the mid-1990s these five divisions clearly manifested in competing factions within the Kingdom, with independent ideologues leading each one of them. Every splinter claimed to be upon the correct understanding of Islam and accused the others of deviation. The split was extremely polemical and – due to the central nature of the Kingdom – affected all Salafi movements around the globe. The catalyst that caused these fault lines to appear was the Kingdom's alliance with the United States during the Gulf Wars of the early 1990s and the subsequent American invasions of Iraq. Since this topic will be discussed in detail in Chapter 3, only a brief overview will be provided here.

On one side of the spectrum, a primary strand of Salafis felt that the ideal Muslim should eschew political involvement to the greatest extent possible since politics corrupted the soul and tainted one's purity in the eyes of God. For them, Salafism is manifested in its theological beliefs and strict adherence to the Sunna: it is these factors that God loves and through which He grants salvation. It makes no sense, therefore, to taint that salvation by getting involved in the mundane matters of this world. This stance was popularized by the Jordanian strand of Salafism associated with al-Albānī, arguably the most influential Salafi cleric of his time. Al-Albānī's stance of not meeting politicians and remaining aloof from global politics in general shaped his followers' political participation, or lack thereof, around the world. Many Salafi organizations throughout the Muslim and Western world today are influenced by this strand and could be classified as apolitical. This strand minimized political engagement, but this did not mean that they never commented on global affairs or refrained from showing support to a particular Muslim country or leader. More precisely, the focus for this strand was never politics: the teachings of Islam were to be spread via propagation (*daʿwa*), purification (*taṣfiya*), and education (*tarbiya*). Al-Albānī famously remarked, 'Establish an Islamic State in your heart, and it shall be established for you in your lands.'[70]

Moving one degree along our spectrum, another strand felt that it was religiously praiseworthy to express loyalty to the rulers as long as those rulers allowed clerics to preach the faith. Hence, public criticism of the rulers was religiously prohibited because such criticism resulted in potential chaos and even civil war.[71] This strand was most famously manifested in the senior Saudi clergy and the office of the Grand Mufti of Saudi Arabia, Ibn Bāz. When the decision was made to allow American troops access to the Kingdom during the first Gulf War, the Mufti supported this decision and warned against voices that were critical of the king. While this group disdained public criticism of the rulers, they too did not emphasize political attitudes as part of propagating Islam.

This support for the rulers proved to be a catalyst for the breaking away of another strand: the *Ṣaḥwa* movement (Awakening), led by a younger generation of clerics such as Safar al-Ḥawalī and Salman al-ʿOudah. This strand, while not rebelling against the king, was openly critical of the ruler's unchecked authority. They interpreted Islamic teachings as sanctioning a level of accountability for the rulers and providing the people with the freedom to criticize and participate in shaping government policy. The *Ṣaḥwa* movement proved to be especially popular among the youth, eventually leading to a confrontation and clampdown by the authorities. Almost all the icons of this movement were jailed or forced into exile, but their ideology continues to live on.

In response, an even more radical pro-government movement emerged, in which fierce loyalty to the ruler became a mark of piety, and any hint of criticism was deemed a deviation. The most iconic figure of this strand was a professor at the Islamic University of Madinah, Rabīʿ b. Hādī al-Madkhalī, and this strand became notorious for enacting McCarthyite witch-hunts against opponents merely for having been seen with people from other strands. An entire phenomenon was created and named after him; a '*Madkhalī*' is someone whose fidelity to the faith is marked by one's associations with only pro-government Muslims (who were described as being 'of sound methodology,' or with the catchphrase: 'on the *manhaj*'). Any hint of being 'soft' with people from other strands betrayed an internal religious corruption that must be warned against.

The final strand on our list viewed all the previous strands as being too quietist and pacifist. Believing that the Islamic doctrine of jihad applied in the current context, this strand resorted to militancy and outright war in order to achieve its goals (hence, the term Jihadi-Salafi commonly used to describe this trend). Militant groups like Al-Qaeda and Islamic State of Iraq and Syria (ISIS) may be viewed as examples of this strand, and due to the high profiles of these organizations, a very public and visible linkage was created between Salafism and the notion of jihad.[72] But the topic of jihad is not a notion exclusive to Salafism, and as a Qurʾanic term, it is a recognized part of Islamic law according to mainstream Islam. The split between Jihadi-Salafis and other Salafis is with respect to the permissibility of engaging in jihad in the current context. Most Muslims and mainstream Salafis view jihad as a legitimate part of the religion. However, they restrict it as something that can only be declared by a legitimate Muslim government and against a legitimate threat or enemy. In the absence of either or both conditions, jihad remains a theoretical concept rather than a practical reality for the vast majority of Muslims. The Jihadi-Salafi movement fundamentally disagrees with mainstream Islam on this issue. We shall have much more to say on this strand – the entirety of Chapter 5 is dedicated to their ideas and history.

This is an intentionally simplified summary. Many factors must be considered when accounting for each group and their ideas comprehensively, such as the influences of the Muslim Brotherhood and jihadist thought. We'll explore these factors and others in more depth in subsequent chapters.

## *1.6 Typology and Categorization of Modern Salafi Strands*

Salafis exhibit substantial internal diversity with regards to a number of key issues, adopting different and often contradictory interpretations on matters of law, politics, and jihad, among other things. Consequently, this has led to the emergence of multiple competing factions within Salafism, each group claiming to be the legitimate, pure, and 'true' Salafism while denouncing all others as adherents to unorthodox and heretical beliefs (*bid'a*). It has become a hallmark of Salafism to factionalize to the extent that what separates these factions is treated as more significant than what unites them. Even categorizing different types of Salafism is highly subjective, often revealing more about the classifier's presumptions about Salafism than the features of the tendencies they are trying to define. While scholars have made numerous attempts over the last twenty-five years to identify and explain the fundamental characteristics of Salafism,[73] we'll explore three of the most influential typologies in the next section.

### *1.6.1 Analysis and Critique of Previous Salafi Typologies: Wiktorowicz, Pall, and Wagemakers*

In his 2006 paper, 'Anatomy of the Salafi Movement,'[74] the American political scientist Quintan Wiktorowicz introduces one of the earliest systematic classifications that served as a template for all other subsequent Salafi typologies. Wiktorowicz argues that Salafis should be divided primarily based on their attitude toward politics and political engagement. According to him, to be a Salafi is to essentially adhere to three primary beliefs: (1) a strict understanding of the Oneness of God (*tawḥīd*), (2) the belief that the Qur'an and Sunna are the exclusive sources for human guidance, and (3) a general aversion to the application of human reason or desire in religious matters. Beyond this, and especially in their attitude toward politics and political engagement, Salafis can diverge sharply. This division, Wiktorowicz argues, is due to the 'inherent subjective nature of applying religion to new issues and problems,'[75] especially in regard to contemporary politics.

As such, Wiktorowciz divides Salafis into three major factions: (1) purists, (2) politicos, and (3) jihadis. The *purists*, Wiktorowicz argues, are those who emphasize nonviolent methods for implementing the Salafi creed

| Salafism | | |
|---|---|---|
| **Purists** | **Politicos** | **Jihadis** |
| al-Albānī<br>Ibn Bāz<br>Ibn al-Uthaymin<br>Rabīʿ al-Madkhalī | Ṣaḥwa movement<br>Safar al-Ḥawalī<br>Salmān al-ʿOuda | Al-Qaeda<br>Abū Musʿab al-Zarqawi<br>Osama bin Laden |

***Figure 1.0*** *Wicktorowicz's Salafi Typology*

through propagation (*da'wa*), purification (*tazkiya*), and education (*tarbiya*). They see politics as a diversion that leads to deviancy and 'discourages activism of any kind, even under conditions of repression.'[76] Wiktorowciz includes in this category figures like al-Albānī, Ibn Bāz, Ibn al-Uthaymin, and Rabīʿ al-Madkhalī, all of whom are known to have rejected peaceful political resistance of governments through parties or organizations. In contrast, the *politicos* are distinguished by Wicktorowciz as those who engage in politics through activism and discourse. They are characterized by the rise of a new and younger generation of politically astute scholars critical of the (elder) purists' perceived negligence and ignorance of national and, especially, international politics. They instead seek to apply 'the Salafi creed to the political arena, which they view as particularly important because it dramatically impacts social justice and the right of God alone to legislate.'[77] This faction, also identified with the *Ṣaḥwa* movement, is represented by clerics like Safar al-Ḥawalī and Salman al-ʿOudah. The members of the third and final category, the *jihadis*, explains Wiktorowicz, do not stop at merely being critical of political regimes like the politicos but believe in taking 'a more militant position and argue that the current context calls for violence and revolution.'[78] The most infamous examples included in this category are the Jordanian jihadist Abū Musʿab al-Zarqawi (d. 2006), Osama bin Laden (d. 2011), and the Al-Qaeda movement he founded.

Although Wicktorowicz's categorization is quite influential and has broadly been accepted by many academics writing on Salafism, it has several key problems. Zoltan Pall, a Hungarian scholar of Salafism, leveled one critique while positing his own alternative typology. Firstly, Pall points out that Wicktorowicz's categories are tied to a specific 'sociopolitical context at a certain point in time,'[79] namely modern-day Saudi Arabia, and thus fail to adequately capture the dynamic and evolving nature of the global and transnational Salafi movement. Secondly, Wiktorowicz's categories are too rigid and clear-cut to accurately reflect the complexity of Salafis in actual practice. Pall provides an example of ʿAbd al-Rahmān al-Nuʿaymī, a Qatari political Salafi, who claimed to have the same ideological views as Bin Laden while at the same time defining himself as part of the *Ṣaḥwa* movement with plans to participate in the elections in Qatar.[80] Al-Nuʿaymī, as per Wiktorowicz's typology, could be classified as belonging to both the politicos (the *Ṣaḥwa* movement) and the jihadis (Bin Laden) – and not exclusively to one or the other as Wiktorowicz's rigid classification would propose. Thirdly, and most importantly, Pall believes that Wiktorowicz's classification is incomplete because it neglects the theological debate on the obedience towards the ruler (*ḥakim*) that underlies and motivates the activity, political and otherwise, of all Salafis. The theological beliefs and interpretations of Salafis regarding the authority of rulers are crucial in shaping their attitudes toward politics and political engagement and thus cannot be ignored. For instance, the reasons why al-Albānī refused political participation are markedly different from those of Ibn Bāz and the establishment of Saudi Salafism.

Pall offers a refined version of Wiktorowicz's typology to account for these nuances within Salafism. He proposes primarily dividing Salafis into two factions based on their stance on the theological debate of obedience to the ruler. The two main factions are the *purists*, who obey the rulers unconditionally, and the *harakis* (activists), who refuse to do so. Each faction is then further subdivided into two groups based on how they apply this creed, what Pall calls 'preference.'[81] The members of the first faction, the purists, are split into purists-rejectionists and politico-purists. *Purist-rejectionists* (Wiktorowicz's purists) reject political participation altogether, do not permit public criticism of the ruler, and only allow for giving secret advice (*nasīḥa sirriya*). Examples included in this subgroup are figures like al-Albānī and Rabīʿ al-Madkhalī. On the other hand, *politico-purists* (or *purist-politically oriented*, as Pall calls it) are those *purists* who see political participation, with the permission of the ruler, as another platform for *da'wa* and propagation of 'pure' Islam.[82] Ibn Bāz is an example of this subgroup.

The second faction, the *harakis*, is divided by Pall into politicos and jihadis. *Politicos* (Wiktorowicz's politicos) are those who not only permit public criticism of the ruler but also seek to achieve change in the realm of politics via peaceful reform and various forms of political participation. Figures such as Salman al-ʿOudah, together with the *Ṣaḥwa* movement and the Haraka al-Salafiyya (a Kuwaiti Salafi movement), are examples of this sub-orientation. The second sub-faction of *harakis*, the *jihadis* (Wiktorowicz's jihadis), are those who 'believe that removing secular regimes and imposing Islamic legislation could happen only through armed jihad.'[83] Figures such as Bin Laden would be included in this camp. It should be noted here that although Pall *initially* categorized jihadis as a second subset of the *harakis* along with the politicos, he later amended them – and rightfully so – as a separate (third) faction in their own right.[84] This amendment is justified as it accurately reflects the fact that jihadis are not always closer to politicos than they are to purists. In practice, jihadis may come from a political background as much as a purist one since the political

<table>
<tr><th colspan="4">Salafism</th></tr>
<tr><td colspan="2">Unconditionally obedient towards the ruler</td><td colspan="2">Critical towards the ruler</td></tr>
<tr><td colspan="2">Purists</td><td>Harakis (Activists)</td><td>Jihadis</td></tr>
<tr><td>Purist-rejectionists</td><td>Purist-politicos</td><td rowspan="2">Haraka al-Salafiyya<br>Ṣaḥwa movement<br>Safar al-Ḥawalī<br>Salmān al-ʿOuda</td><td rowspan="2">Osama bin Laden</td></tr>
<tr><td>Al-Albānī<br>Rabīʿ al-Madkhalī</td><td>Ibn Bāz</td></tr>
</table>

***Figure 1.1*** *Pall's Salafi Typology*

isolationism of purists can sometimes lead to radicalization. Hence, Pall's amendment of jihadis as a separate third faction provides a more accurate typology of Salafis in practice.

Joas Wagemakers, in an article published in 2016 entitled 'Revisiting Wiktorowicz,' expands upon Pall's typology.[85] While he agrees with Pall's basic framework and definition (adopted from Wicktorowicz) of using politics as a yardstick to divide Salafis, he argues that Pall's categories (and subcategories) were still too broad to account for the diversity and differences within each Salafi faction sufficiently. And since there are only three positions on which one can be divided on the basis of politics, namely: apolitical, political, and anti-political (as implicit within Wicktorowicz's own template), Wagemakers too divides Salafis into three primary branches (what he later calls 'Wiktorowicz with a Twist').[86] These are (1) quietists (apolitical), (2) politicos (political), and (3) jihadis (anti-political). Each branch is then further subdivided into smaller groups to reflect internal differences and diversity.

First, Wagemakers prefers the term *quietist* (as in 'politically quietist') to purist, stating that being 'purist' does not say anything about Salafis' attitudes toward politics, especially since all Salafis see themselves as bearers of the pure and pristine Islam as it was originally revealed. Hence, 'quietists' would be a more accurate term for Wiktorowicz and Pall's purists – those characterized by political quietism in favor of preaching and propagating Salafism. Wagemakers here notes that being a quietist does not mean that they do not have political opinions or never comment on political issues.[87] Rather, it means that they believe these views should be expressed privately in religious terms or as discreet advice to the rulers. But if this is the case, quietists can hardly be called apolitical, for the private advice that some of them offer to the rulers is itself a political act. Not only that, by virtue of being quietists, they are supporting a political status quo, essentially making them political. And although Wagemakers himself contends with these points – he argues that accepting them would make it virtually impossible to apply the term *political* to Salafis – to illustrate the varying attitudes of quietists themselves, he subdivides them into three sub-factions: aloofists, loyalists, and propagandists. The first sub-faction, the *aloofists*, are those Salafis who stay entirely aloof from politics altogether and maintain a certain independence to and from the ruler. They believe that society is not yet ready for genuine Islamic political action and that politics inherently involves compromises that could corrupt the purity of their faith. The most prominent figure from this trend is al-Albānī. The second sub-faction, the *loyalists*, are those quietists who share the aloofists' rejection of political engagement but believe that they can (or should) show loyalty and support to the ruler and the regime's policies by justifying them whenever asked. Such support for the ruler stems from a genuine sense of loyalty or, to the contrary, fear of the regime itself. This sub-faction includes figures such as Ibn Bāz and Ibn al-Uthaymin. The third sub-faction of quietists consists of the *propagandists*, those whose support for the ruler almost becomes a tenet of faith. And due to this extreme loyalty and reverence, they not only actively propagate support and obedience towards the ruler but also fiercely denounce the more politicized Salafi critics of the regime. The propagandists are often called 'Jāmīs' or 'Madhkhalīs' because of their ties to figures such as Muḥammad b. Amān al-Jāmī (d. 1996) and Rabīʿ al-Madkhalī, respectively.

The second branch of Salafis Wagemakers distinguishes is the *politicos* (Wiktorowiciz's politicos and Pall's *harakis*). They distinguish themselves from the quietists not only by their belief in the correctness of political involvement but also by having more sophisticated views regarding (international) politics. Politicos, too, are not homogenous and are thus subdivided into two sub-groups: politicians and activists. *Politicians* are those who actively engage in elections, political debates, and parliamentary politics. Examples included in this subgroup are various Salafi political parties across Kuwait, Lebanon, and Egypt. Wagemakers, however, notes that some of those involved in this subgroup engage in politics only so far as they wish to use parliament to propagate their version of Islam. This would essentially make them Pall's purist-politicos. On the other hand, the second sub-faction of politicos, the *activists*, do not engage in parliamentary politics but are instead active in demonstrations, political discourse, or societal activism. Examples included in this group are Salman al-ʿOudah, Safar al-Ḥawalī, and the *Ṣaḥwa* movement in Saudi Arabia, and *Jamʿiyyat al-Kitāb wa-l-Sunna* (*The Book and Sunna Association*) in Jordan.

Following Wiktorowciz and Pall, *jihadis* constitute the third and final branch of Wagemaker's classification. He defines them 'as those Salafis who believe in solving intra-Muslim problems of supposed apostasy of rulers and allegedly un-Islamic legislation through revolutionary (and often global) jihad.'[88] He is, however, sure to point out that all Salafis see jihad (at least on a theological and conceptual level) as an integral part of Islam. So, what differentiates jihadis from other Salafis is not *if* they support jihad but rather what *type* of jihad they support. Whereas all 'Salafis support classical jihad, with its strong roots in Islamic law, they are vehemently against the overthrow[ing] of regimes for religious reasons, which they often believe to be based on an extremist interpretation of *takfīr* [excommunication].'[89] Hence, on this basis, Wagemakers splits jihadis into three sub-factions: revolutionaries, global jihadis, and caliphate jihadis. The first sub-faction, the *revolutionaries*, advocates jihad as a means to overthrow the ruler for their alleged refusal to apply Islamic law. They believe the ruler has committed apostasy by this very refusal and is therefore no longer fit to rule – hence the basis for their jihad. A prominent example given of this subgroup is a Palestinian-Jordanian scholar Abū Muḥammad al-Maqdisi. The second sub-faction, whom Wagemakers calls *global jihadis*, consists of those who seek to attack Western powers, primarily to make them 'withdraw their support for dictatorial and supposedly apostate rulers in the Muslim world.' This sub-faction is exemplified by groups such as Al-Qaeda. The third sub-faction of jihadis, proposed by Wagemakers later in his 2020 paper entitled 'Salafism: Generalisation, Conceptualisation and Categorisation,' is that of the *caliphate jihadis*.[90] They are defined as those Salafis 'who actively and concretely work to re-establish a caliphate instead of the states in the Muslim world'[91] and are best embodied by ISIS.

| | | | |
|---|---|---|---|
| **Salafism** | **Quietists** | *Aloofists* | al-Albānī |
| | | *Loyalists* | Ibn Bāz<br>Ibn al-Uthaymin |
| | | *Propagandists* | Muḥammad b. Amān al- Jāmī<br>Rabīʿ al-Madkhalī |
| | | | (*for more groups*) |
| | **Politicos** | *Politicians* | Salafi political parties in:<br>Egypt<br>Kuwait<br>Lebanon |
| | | *Activists* | Jamʿiyyat al-Kitāb wa-l-Sunna<br>*Ṣaḥwa* movement<br>Safar al-Ḥawalī<br>Salmān al-ʿOuda |
| | | | (*for more groups*) |
| | **Jihadis** | *Revolutionaries* | Abū Muḥammad al-Maqdisi |
| | | *Global Jihadis* | Al-Qaeda |
| | | *Caliphate Jihadis* | ISIS |
| | | (*for more groups*) | |

***Figure 1.2*** *Wagemaker's Salafi Typology (Wiktorowicz with a Twist)*

Each of the typologies assessed above – Wiktorowicz, Pall, and Wagemakers – share the same premise of using politics as the yardstick for categorizing Salafis. Insofar as this has its advantages in political science, the premise remains not only simplistic and arbitrary but fundamentally flawed for several reasons. Firstly, by reducing Salafis solely to their relationship to politics, it mischaracterizes the movement as essentially a political one. Secondly, these divisions, based on political attitudes (apolitical, political, and anti-political), exist across all strands of Islam and hence are in no way peculiar to Salafism alone. For example, quietists, politicos, and jihadis exist among Shiʿa and non-Salafi Sunnis (such as Sufi movements) as much as they exist within Salafis. Thirdly, classifying Salafis based on these differing political attitudes without proper consideration of the underlying motive(s) for their differences – such as the varying theological and legal interpretive methodologies – has resulted in typologies that obscure the substantial differences that exist within each category. Although there was a general awareness in Pall and even more so in Wagemakers about the role theological and legislative differences play within the internal divisions of Salafism, none of them have attempted to categorize Salafis primarily on these factors. Yet the political divisions among Salafis are a manifestation of their diverse interpretations of theology and jurisprudence. Fourthly, categorizing Salafis from an outsider's perspective, particularly on a single issue deemed relevant by the classifier, fails to give a clear picture of what Salafi tendencies themselves see as significant.

The question that should be asked is not what *outsiders* find definitive but rather how *insiders* view their movement. For example, the *Ahl-e Ḥadīth* movement in India is primarily concerned with questions related to the (right) juristic tendencies rather than proper methods of political engagement. Their main point of contention revolves around whether (and how) one should adhere to an established *madhhab* (school of law). Therefore, not only would it be inaccurate to classify them based on the aforementioned typologies, but even if that were possible, it would say very little about the group itself. Hence, to develop a comprehensive and meaningful Salafi typology, it is crucial to consider how Salafis perceive themselves *internally* and what issues they consider *most significant* as their points of difference. Lastly, as we've seen, Salafism is a global and dynamic movement that defies classification based on a single issue. This tendency to prioritize politics as the sole basis for classification often leaves scholars unable to account for or explain new and emerging divisions. Even when classified based on one issue alone, the need to expand and refine the posited categories becomes evident as new Salafi groups emerge over time.

Subsequent scholars, such as Pall and Wagemakers, made more nuanced revisions of Wiktorowicz's typology, but even then, their expanded classifications proved to be still too limited and needed further revisions of their own. This is because all these classifications stem from an erroneous attempt to construct a fixed and unchanging typology for a multifaceted and evolving movement. Wagemakers himself notices this limitation – his own typology notwithstanding – and attempts to address it by proposing an open-ended typology. He suggests that although the three broad categories of dividing Salafis into quietists, politicos, and jihadis will remain fixed, there is room within each of these categories for 'micro analyses of local forms of Salafism (that) can easily be integrated.'[92] He provides an example of the newly risen ISIS Jihadi-Salafis, who could not be accommodated within his original typology. Wagemakers instead posits a third subgroup of jihadis (the caliphate jihadis) alongside his original two subgroups of revolutionaries and global jihadis, thereby integrating the ISIS Jihadi-Salafis into his typology. While Wagemakers deserves credit for his effort to capture the nuances of different positions among Salafis, his exclusive focus on political attitudes neglects other arguably more significant factors that influence and shape different Salafi groups. As a result, his classification still falls short of being a comprehensive typology that accounts for the diverse array of Salafi groups across the spectrum.

### *1.6.2 Towards a Multivariable Open-Ended Typology*

From the analysis above, it is evident that merely expanding upon Wiktorowciz's typology while accepting his basic premise of using politics as a yardstick for the Salafi divisions is both insufficient and ineffective. To propose a more comprehensive and holistic typology that accurately captures the nuances of each Salafi group, factors beyond politics, including theological, legal, methodological, and social aspects, along with many other relevant factors, should all be equally considered. The system needs to take into account not only how *outsiders* view the movement but also, more importantly, what *insiders* view as being the most significant to their interpretation of the faith. Therefore, I propose *a multivariable open-ended typology* capable of not only accommodating existing groups and their differences but also accounting for future trends and their potential differences.

Firstly, this proposed typology would classify Salafis based on multiple varying factors, beginning with their respective locations and eras, before encompassing a wide array of issues that are considered important and divisive within each faction. These variables would serve as the defining parameters and criteria for classifying a particular faction and may include, but not be limited to, issues such as political stance towards the ruler; political engagement; theological importance of heresy (*bidʿa*) and excommunication (*takfīr*); interpretation and applicability of jihad; and juristic tendencies; as well as many other context-specific variables that are (and will be) unique to various Salafi groups across the spectrum. Furthermore, as this typology is open-ended and not fixed, it allows for the addition of new variables, if needed, as is the case with all dynamic and global movements.

Secondly, once the variables involved in classifying a particular faction are identified, the variables would be *structured* in an orderly list based on the level of significance attributed *internally* to each of them by the faction. This ordering will thus reflect what each faction sees as the crucial issue of self-definition and, consequently, a matter of division in relation to others. For instance, in a typology aimed at classifying the *Ṣaḥwa* movement, the political stance towards rulers would be the first variable ordered, followed closely by involvement in the political process as the second variable, and so on. However, the same typology would look quite different when applied to another group, such as the *Ahl-e Ḥadīth* movement, where the first variable listed would not be the political stance towards the ruler but rather the variable of juristic tendencies (which is their defining characteristic).

Thirdly, after establishing the parameters, each variable should be considered a mini-typology with its own subcategories that are distributed along a continuum of opposing views. For instance, when examining the variable of political stance towards the ruler, there are two extreme positions: total obedience to the ruler (as represented by Wagemakers' quietist-propagandists) and excommunication (*takfīr*) and overthrowing of the ruler (Wagemakers' jihadis) on the opposite end. However, between these two extreme stances, there are multiple positions that vary, ranging from quietists to caliphate jihadis, and possibly even newer and unique positions that may emerge within the Salafi ideology as the need arises. So, for example, when classifying the *Ṣaḥwa* movement within this particular variable (of which this is the first variable to be considered), it would be positioned somewhere towards the middle of the spectrum, reflecting its critical stance towards the ruler and so falling into the category of Wagemaker's activists. Similarly, when it is classified against the variable of *involvement in the political process*, there are three primary markers: shunning politics in the left end, involvement out of necessity for propagation (*da'wa*) in the intermediate position, and full-out being politically active on the right end. Therefore, the *Ṣaḥwa* movement would be placed somewhere between, if not within, the intermediate position of involvement out of necessity for propagation and the right end due to being politically active position. And when they are finally categorized in terms of their juristic tendencies (which is an irrelevant and tertiary matter of contention among them – and hence will appear lower on our *structured* list), they will fall under the semi-critical madhhabist branch, which represents the intermediate position of the spectrum, with the uncritical adherence to *madhhab* on the left and absolute rejection of *madhhab* on the right.

Hence, the proposed *multivariable open-ended structured typology* offers a more accurate and pragmatic approach to categorizing Salafi groups. In addition to providing a holistic classification of all existing Salafi groups, this typology also facilitates an internal understanding of each Salafi faction from the perspective of its members. Such nuanced comprehension has the potential to aid in predicting future trends and contribute to a more comprehensive conceptualization and comprehension of Salafism as a dynamic and globally active movement. As can be seen in the following examples, the purpose of my typology is not to box Salafi sub-trends into neat and rigid categories, which would only then be problematized by the reality on the ground. Instead, it seeks to inform practitioners as to how any given sub-strand of Salafism can be unpacked into various factors and positions assumed, which contributes to its own articulation during a specific context and locality. The result of this exercise may not always lead practitioners to simplistic labels like those proffered by Wiktorowicz, Pall, or Wagemakers – which obviously appeal to researchers; yet this can be seen as a necessary sacrifice if one is to accurately depict the nuances of a specific movement within the movement, in *real-time.*

In the first example (Figure 1.3), Al-Albānī Salafism in Jordan is typified according to four central factors: (1) juristic tendency; (2) attitude towards non-Salafis; (3) involvement in the political process (specifically in Jordan); and (4) attitude towards jihad. As highlighted in the following chapter, al-Albānī's particular brand of Salafism has spread far and wide in the Muslim world as well as the Anglosphere. In the latter, however, it would not be accurate to describe all Salafis in the United States or Britain,

<table>
<tr><td rowspan="11">AL-ALBĀNĪ SALAFISM</td><td colspan="12">(1) Juristical Tendency</td></tr>
<tr><td colspan="4">soft-madhhabist</td><td colspan="4">critical-madhhabist</td><td colspan="4">anti-madhhabist</td></tr>
<tr><td colspan="12">(2) Deviancy (Bid'a) and Excommunication (Takfīr)</td></tr>
<tr><td colspan="4">neutral</td><td colspan="4">hereticize</td><td colspan="4">excommunicate</td></tr>
<tr><td colspan="12">(3) Involvement in the Political Process</td></tr>
<tr><td colspan="4">quietist-aloofist</td><td colspan="4">purist-politico</td><td colspan="4">politico-activist</td></tr>
<tr><td colspan="12">(4) Political Stance Towards the Ruler</td></tr>
<tr><td colspan="2">apolitical</td><td colspan="2">dogmatic-loyalist</td><td colspan="3">soft-loyalist</td><td colspan="3">activist</td><td colspan="2">militant</td></tr>
<tr><td colspan="12">(5) Interpretation and Applicability of Jihad</td></tr>
<tr><td colspan="3">inapplicable</td><td colspan="3">applicable theoretically</td><td colspan="4">applicable contextually</td><td colspan="2">applicable</td></tr>
<tr><td colspan="12">for more variables…</td></tr>
</table>

***Figure 1.3*** *Typology of al-Albānī Salafism*

<table>
<tr><td rowspan="11">SAUDI-ESTABLISHMENT SALAFISM</td><td colspan="5">(1) Deviancy (*Bid'a*) and Excommunication (*Takfīr*)</td></tr>
<tr><td>neutral</td><td colspan="3">**hereticize**</td><td>excommunicate</td></tr>
<tr><td colspan="5">(2) Juristical Tendency</td></tr>
<tr><td>**soft-madhhabist**</td><td colspan="3">**critical-madhhabist**</td><td>anti-madhhabist</td></tr>
<tr><td colspan="5">(3) Involvement in the Political Process</td></tr>
<tr><td>quietist-aloofist</td><td colspan="3">**purist-politico**</td><td>politico-activist</td></tr>
<tr><td colspan="5">(4) Political Stance Toward the Ruler</td></tr>
<tr><td>apolitical</td><td>dogmatic-loyalist</td><td>**soft-loyalist**</td><td>activist</td><td>militant</td></tr>
<tr><td colspan="5">(5) Interpretation and Applicability of Jihad</td></tr>
<tr><td>inapplicable</td><td colspan="2">**applicable *theoretically***</td><td>applicable *contextually*</td><td>applicable</td></tr>
<tr><td colspan="5">*for more variables…*</td></tr>
</table>

***Figure 1.4*** *Typology of Saudi-Establishment Salafism*

for example, as al-Albānī-like because while they are generally anti-madhhabist, their learned preachers tend to be trained in Saudi Arabia, where the *fiqh* curriculum is comparative or critical-madhhabist in the Ḥanbalī tradition. Moreover, several of the senior students/associates of al-Albānī have since passed away, and the remaining few have fractured.[93] Delineating these changes would require a typology for each faction in the 2000s.

In the second example (Figure 1.4), Saudi-establishment Salafism includes the same factors as above but with the addition of their political stance towards the king. Here, we are specifically typifying Saudi-establishment Salafism in Saudi Arabia during the 1990s and 2000s. This captures two brief decades in the aftermath of the Gulf War, which gave rise to the political crackdown on the *Ṣaḥwa* movement and, following 9/11, a clampdown on local terrorist networks. In 2015, Saudi's role in the civil war in Yemen led establishment-Salafis to theoretically and practically support the Kingdom's military campaign. This shift is best represented in a fluid and open-ended typology.

In the third example (Figure 1.5), there are three key factors that define the *Ṣaḥwa* movement in Saudi Arabia during the 1990s: (1) their attitude towards the king, (2) their involvement in the political process, and (3) their interpretation of jihad. The movement was entirely suppressed following the arrest of several *Ṣaḥwa* leaders, several of whom, upon being released, publicly recanted their earlier views. The movement outside Saudi Arabia, albeit remnants in the Middle East and Europe, would require their own typologies to encapsulate shifting discourses and changing political contexts.

| THE ṢAḤWA MOVEMENT | | | | |
|---|---|---|---|---|
| (1) Political Stance Towards the Ruler | | | | |
| apolitical | dogmatic-loyalist | soft-loyalist | **activist** | militant |
| (2) Involvement in the Political Process | | | | |
| quietist-aloofist | purist-politico | **politico-activist** | | |
| (3) Interpretation and Applicability of Jihad | | | | |
| inapplicable | applicable *theoretically* | ***applicable contextually*** | applicable | |
| *for more variables…* | | | | |

***Figure 1.5*** *Typology of the Ṣaḥwa Movement*

| JIHADI-SALAFISM (ISIS) | | | | |
|---|---|---|---|---|
| (1) Deviancy (*Bid'a*) and Excommunication (*Takfīr*) | | | | |
| neutral | **hereticize** | **excommunicate** | | |
| (2) Interpretation and Applicability of Jihad | | | | |
| inapplicable | applicable *theoretically* | applicable *contextually* | **applicable** | |
| (3) Political Stance Towards the Ruler | | | | |
| apolitical | dogmatic-loyalist | soft-loyalist | activist | **militant** |
| (4) Involvement in the Political Process | | | | |
| quietist-aloofist | purist-politico | **politico-activist** | | |
| *for more variables…* | | | | |

***Figure 1.6*** *Typology of the Jihadi-Salafism (ISIS)*

In the final example (Figure 1.6), ISIS-Salafism highlights the same factors as above in addition to their attitudes toward non-ISIS members (including Salafis). Here, a typology is offered for the faction's brief establishment of the infamous Islamic State (IS). It differs from the general classification of Jihadi-Salafism in former years because its function as a 'Caliphate' pitted itself against all outsiders, Al-Qaeda members notwithstanding. A typology of ISIS-Salafism following the fall of the state in 2019 would need to reflect how its branches in countries like Afghanistan and Nigeria continue to wage militant-extremism without significant control of territories. Further variables would need to be added to IS Africa, for example, to reflect internal fissures between competing groups.

The abovementioned nuances demonstrate the limitations of earlier typologies in encapsulating the shifting contours of Salafi-led movements outside the timeframes in which they were first introduced. Nevertheless, the four typologies suggested here are by no means final; instead, it is left to the practitioner to reflect on what other factors and variables are required to fully capture any given Salafi faction during a particular time period and within a specific location.

## *1.7 Conclusion*

In this introductory chapter, key concepts within Salafism were identified pertaining to theology, law, spirituality, and politics. The core ideas and figures of this movement can be traced back through a line of thinkers to the dawn of Islam. However, each of its thinkers, and hence each iteration of the movement, has brought forth unique nuances that complicate any attempts at making definitive claims about the movement as a whole. The difficulties of providing basic typologies of Salafism have thus been highlighted, and a more open-ended and fluid typology has been proposed. Despite being far from monolithic, it does continue to possess certain features that remain central to all strands. It is, therefore, still possible, at least on a surface level, to describe Salafism as a movement.

In terms of theology, all Salafis believe that there has always been only one correct interpretation of the faith, from the dawn of Islam until modernity. This correct understanding entails an uncritical and literal acceptance of the Qur'an and the authentic hadith literature, specifically when it comes to aspects of theology. The belief that the sacred texts are not in need of external hermeneutics to understand them is a cornerstone of the movement. It is for this reason, for instance, the entire discipline of 'speculative theology' (*ʿilm al-kalām*) is viewed with great suspicion. The best of generations is (1) the Companions of the Prophet, (2) and then their students, and (3) then their students after them – all of whom constitute the actual *salaf*. Salafis claim that all of the *salaf* were united in their creed and understanding of Islam. The figure of Ibn Ḥanbal and all of the early traditionalists and scholars of hadith of the third and fourth Islamic centuries are especially admired. Throughout the last millennia, two figures spearheaded revivalist attempts and, in the process, helped shape and nurture the movement in different ways. These two figures were Ibn Taymiyya and Ibn ʿAbd al-Wahhāb. While the former had no political backing and was actually persecuted by the state, the latter helped found a regional empire, and the rise of that empire in recent times, along with the effects of oil wealth, has helped launch a global revival of unprecedented proportions. Ibn Taymiyya, in particular, is viewed as one of the most gifted defenders and elucidators of the correct teachings of Islam. But from an internal perspective, the Salafi movement has no founders, nor does any one person after the Prophet have the right to elucidate and derive new doctrines. The belief that the earliest three generations are the best role models automatically necessitates that conformity and precedent are the default, and any changes, modifications, or adaptations of theology and rituals should be eschewed and classified as reprehensible innovations (*bidʿa*). There is also a strong spirit of proselytization among all adherents: other Muslims, and even non-Muslims, should be invited to this understanding of Islam.

In terms of law, throughout its history, various icons have emphasized different aspects: whether it was rejecting analogical reason (*qiyas*) in deriving Islamic law, a preference for weak hadith over other sources of law, or a particular interpretation with understanding what constitutes 'worship' and innovation (*bid'a*). All of these aspects have remained a historical legacy that modern Salafis must take into account. Yet the movement is not united within itself: there are a variety of opinions regarding some aspects of the Shari'a and how it should be approached, even though overall there is a dislike of the blind-following (*taqlīḍ*) of the established legal schools (*madhhabs*). Modern geographic manifestations of the movement differ in what aspects of the faith to prioritize and how one should go about preaching to fellow Muslims. However, the most contentious issue that divides modern Salafism is political in nature: what is the ideal relationship between the laity and rulers, and what is the best approach to bringing about societal change?

As with all movements, Salafism responds to external forces. With radical developments taking place around the world, in particular, the rise of Islamophobia and the Far-Right in the West and the failure of the Arab Spring in the East, coupled with a new generation of leaders in the Muslim world, Salafism is again fracturing in real-time, and the changes of today are yet to be analyzed. To better understand these changes, the following chapter analyzes the historical context behind the modern phenomenon of Salafism in all its forms.

# 2

# A COMPREHENSIVE HISTORY OF SALAFI THOUGHT: FROM ITS ORIGINS TO MODERNITY

*'Therefore, whoever turns away from the divinely legislated Salafi way shall undoubtedly go astray, and fall into contradiction, and remain in either complete or partial ignorance.'*
*~ Shaykh al-Islām Ibn Taymiyya*[1]

This chapter provides an overview of the development of Salafi thought from early Islam to now. I am not arguing, much less presuming, that there's a single, teleological trajectory from early Islam that arrives at modern Salafism. However, it is possible to identify common features in earlier Islamic movements that can be read as a continuity of thought establishing a distinctly Salafi tradition.

Furthermore, I have employed the term 'Salafi(sm)' or 'proto-Salafi(sm)' to describe figures in all of these eras not because the term was known or used by them in the contemporary sense, but because the contemporary Salafi movement views these figures as being faithful to their paradigm. Of course, the term 'proto-Salafi,' depending on the era and context (especially in classical and medieval periods), can be synonymous – or at least overlap – with the *ahl al-ḥadīth* movement of early Islam, (proto-)Ḥanbalism, and (proto-)Sunnism. One should, however, bear in mind that this identification of proto-Salafism with these three movements only holds insofar as we are able to acknowledge that these tendencies are distinct from Salafism today, and there are many elements within them that the modern Salafi movement rejects.

## 2.1 The Formative Years (650–850 CE)

### 2.1.1 The Sunni Origins of Salafi Thought

One of the key hallmarks of Salafism today is its claim to be a continuation of a pure, pristine, and uncorrupted theology that dates back to the earliest generations of Islam. It is as if contemporary Salafis feel that Islamic theology – or at least their version of it – has remained a pure, unblemished diamond that has been handed down from the Companions of the Prophet to their students and then onward to later generations until it has been entrusted to the care of current-day adherents, carefully preserved and maintained – impervious to all changes. Hence, the concept of organic evolution or development of ideas threatens the foundation of the modern movement.

While Salafis today do not object to the idea that later scholars, like Ibn Taymiyya, defended the movement using techniques that earlier ones did not, it is extremely rare to find a scholar who would admit that most of later Salafi theology would have been unknown and unrecognizable to the earliest Muslim community. Conversely, non-Salafis dispute the assertion that modern Salafism is an accurate representation of the early generations' religious thoughts and practices. In the case of adherents to the late Sunni tradition – comprising of adherents to the prevalent four schools of law, the accepted schools of *kalām* theology,[2] and Sufism[3] – they too claim that it is *their* inherited tradition that goes back, pure and uninterrupted, to the early Muslims.

In addition to upholding the Qurʾan and Sunna, with normative or acceptable interpretations according to principles largely upheld by Sunni authorities, the Salafi movement idealizes the first three generations of Islam, 'the Pious Predecessors' (*al-salaf al-ṣāliḥ*). In fact, they receive their name from their claim of loyal adherence to them. These three generations are known by special designation: beginning with (1) the actual 'Companions of the Prophet' (*ṣaḥāba*) who saw and interacted with him, then (2) their 'Successors' (*tābiʿūn*), those who interacted with the Companions, and finally (3) the 'Successors of the Successors' (*tābaʿū al-tābiʿīn*), meaning those who studied and interacted with the Successors. There are also sub-categories within each of these three groups. For example, those who interacted with the Prophet for a longer period (i.e., the earliest batch of converts) are held in higher esteem than those who might have converted later and narrated only a hadith or two from him. Similarly, those Successors who managed to study with some of the more senior Companions take precedence over those who only interacted with one or two of the younger Companions.[4]

Of these three generations, the Companions occupy a class of their own. Respect for the Companions is not just a common courtesy extended to those who interacted with the Prophet. Rather, it is a major tenet of Sunni theology. This is due to the numerous verses in the Qurʾan and the authentic hadith traditions that elaborate on the virtues of those who accompanied the Prophet. '*God is pleased with them, and they are pleased with God,'* is a common Qur'anic phrase in describing the Companions.[5] Even from a logical perspective, Salafis argue, who better to interpret the Qur'an than those who witnessed its revelation? Who is more qualified to opine on the words of the Prophet than those who directly interacted with him? This type of argument underpins the appeal of Salafism to large numbers of Muslims seeking out orthodoxy.

Although the Companions are not considered to be all at the same level, all of them, *without exception*, are considered pious and noble. No criticism of their integrity and motives may be tolerated according to Sunni theology. Nonetheless, one may disagree with an individual Companion's legal verdict or even find fault with a political decision or course of action. After all, the orthodox Sunni position is that it is only the Prophet who is deemed to be divinely protected from major error. But the prevailing theological principle is that one is never allowed to impugn the character of a Companion or call into question their integrity. In this regard, one can see the maxim found in early hadith textbooks: 'The Companions, all of them, are trustworthy' (*al-ṣahaba kulluhum ʿudūl*). This is because the Companions are seen as having been faithful to the teachings of the Prophet and the message of Islam. So, even the civil wars that took place among the Companions are considered to be simply political differences that do not impinge on their piety and character. The sentiment is that all sides of the conflicts were theologically in unison and that evil third parties – such as the proto-Khārijīs[6] or cryptic figures like the Yemeni Jewish convert to Islam ʿAbd Allāh b. Sabāʾ (d. 50/670)[7] – were the primary cause of the bloodshed and division. Unconditional respect for the Companions is a hallmark of all strands of Sunnism. But for the Salafis in particular, it takes on an even more heightened significance. In contrast to this, other strands of Islam during the first three centuries – such as proto-Shiʿism,[8] Khārijism, Muʿtazilīsm, or Jahmism[9] – are viewed as having strayed away from orthodoxy and are deemed misguided because *inter alia*, they do not view the Companions as being role models.[10]

Since no theological texts have survived from the first century of Islam, Salafis rely on the works, often credos, written in the following centuries and trust the *isnād* system (chains of narrators) that traditionalist hadith narrators used to authenticate reports from earlier times.[11] This is often summarized into a single slogan: 'We follow the Qur'an and Sunna according to the understanding (*fahm*) of the Pious Predecessors (*al-salaf al-ṣāliḥ*).' Using this hermeneutic, Salafis are able to construct an image of the *salaf* as being largely pietistic in their rituals, fideistic to the Qur'an and hadith, ascetic in their lifestyles, and uniformly orthodox in their theology. Salafis recognize and accept the diversity of legal opinions within Islamic law and jurisprudence. However, they would not afford the same generosity to the realm of theology.

Therefore, at the foundational level, there are many primary theological issues that are important to Salafis that also overlap with all basic Sunni tenets: (1) the view that both the Qur'an and hadith are the two primary sources of Islam, (2) belief in the political authority of the Rightly Guided Caliphs (*al-khulafā' al-rāshidūn*), (3) respect for the Companions (*'adāla al-ṣaḥāba*), (4) belief in divine predestination (*qadar*), and (5) other general factors, like adherence to Islamic law, common to all strands of Sunnism.

### *2.1.2 The Traditions of the Divine Attributes and the Emergence of Proto-Salafism*

One key distinguishing factor that contributed to the emergence of proto-Salafism is the informal contest between two schools of legal thought during the second/eighth century: the *ahl al-ḥadīth* (Partisans of Hadith, usually translated as 'traditionalists') and *ahl al-ra'y* (Partisans of Legal Reasoning);[12] the former asserting the authority of the Qur'an and hadith over the latter's occasional preference for reason and logical interpretations. Debates between the two schools largely remained limited to matters of law. Another key factor that can be seen as a distinguishing marker of proto-Salafism vis-à-vis other Sunni movements was its understanding of God's attributes (*ṣifāt*), as found in the Qur'an and in the hadith literature (*aḥādīth al-ṣifāt*). Proto-Salafism demarcated itself primarily from both other Sunnis (like the Ash'arīs and Māturīdīs) and non-Sunnis (like the Mu'tazila and the Shi'a)[13] through its interpretation of this genre.

As the first hint of Neoplatonic thought[14] made its way to Arab lands via Christian-Muslim interactions in the newly conquered territories of Syria, talk began of the meaning and nature of these divine attributes. The Mu'tazilī school – along with the rather obscure Jahmī school, founded by Jahm b. Ṣafwān (d. 128/745–6) – separated itself from proto-Sunnism by its refusal to take the hadith corpus as a primary source of theology. Rather – as one of the founders of the school, Wāṣil b. 'Aṭā' (d. 131/748–9),[15] put it – they would rely on 'Qur'anic statements, unanimously agreed upon reports, intellectual proof, and consensus.'[16] This is because, as Wāṣil claimed, he distrusted hadith reports due to the presence of perceived biases arising after the assassination of the third Caliph 'Uthmān (d. 35/656).

In not taking the hadith corpus into their theological considerations, coupled with a nascent version of early *kalām* theology, the Mu'tazila were able to affirm man's ultimate free will and rejected the Sunni doctrine of predestination (*qadar*). Additionally, and more importantly for our purposes here, they rejected much of the divine attributes reported in the hadith literature (*aḥādīth al-ṣifāt*). They argued that the divine attributes found in revelation, even those found in the Qur'an alone, could not imply *ontologically real* attributes. This is because, according to them, if the attributes were *real* entities that existed eternally alongside God's essence, then it would mean that there is a plurality of eternal existents. This, in turn, would violate the principle of God's perfect unicity (*tawḥīd*), which for them meant that God alone is the only eternal existent and that He is not composed of parts – since an ontologically real multiplicity in God's essence would imply such a composition.[17] In fact, this principle of God's perfect unicity is so central to Muʿtazilī theology that it comprises the first of five fundamental theological principles (*uṣūl al-khamsa*) of Muʿtazilism.[18] This does not mean that they 'rejected' the divine attributes and, *ipso facto*, the entirety of revelation – contrary to how they were characterized in Sunni heresiography – but they rejected the *literal* interpretation of being ontologically *real* attributes. So, in trying to steer a middle path between the transcendentalist conception of God (influenced by Neoplatonism) that He is beyond human descriptions and the positive (and anthropomorphic) descriptions of God found in revelation, the Muʿtazila maintained – at least some of them – that God's essence and His attributes were identical. Hence, any and all language in the Qurʾan that described God was merely figurative. So, for them, God did not *actually* rise over the throne, descend to the lower heavens, laugh, or speak – as these were all human attributes. And this, they opined, is the meaning of the Qurʾanic verse: '*There is nothing like unto Him*' (Qurʾan 43:11).[19]

In response to this trend, a number of prominent *ahl al-ḥadīth* scholars began preaching that God's attributes, as mentioned in the hadith traditions, needed to be affirmed *literally* because they were taught by the Prophet himself. Some modern authors have characterized the *ahl al-ḥadīth* trend as 'proto-Ḥanbalism' because this explicit affirmation of the attributes would become a hallmark of the later Ḥanbalī school. However, it should be noted that one finds an unconditional affirmation of the attributes across all spectrums of – what would later be called – Sunnism.[20]

In fact, later Salafis consider *all* proto-Sunnis during this early phase as sharing the same theology – in contradistinction to other groups like the Muʿtazila and the Shiʿa. Of course, the historical reality is more nuanced, and – as with all movements – there were competing narratives within Sunnism itself. Nevertheless, it is accurate to assert that, during this time frame, the dominant narrative of proto-Sunnism would have been simply to narrate these Prophetic traditions and assume that people understood that God is characterized by the nouns and adjectives mentioned in the sacred texts. For instance, a famous hadith scholar from Baghdad, Abū ʿUbayd al-Qāsim b. Sallām (d. 224/838) recited to his students a series of hadith regarding various divine attributes – such as God's throne and God's laughter – and then remarked:

> These traditions are authentic and valid. The scholars of hadith and the jurists transmitted them from generation to generation. For us,

> they reflect undeniable truth. But when we are asked, 'How does He laugh? How does He place His feet?' We should answer, 'We do not interpret them [i.e., the attributes]. We have never heard anyone interpreting them.'[21]

This latter quotation indicates that questions had already begun regarding the modality (*kayfiyya*) of the attributes and that the doctrine of 'without (knowing) how' (*bi-lā kayfa*, referred to here as *balkafa*) was now in vogue in proto-Sunni circles. It is important to stress that at this early stage, the *balkafa* doctrines were not just popular among proto-Salafis. Rather, it was a broad trend that permeated many different schools of law and could be found in all proto-Sunni movements. Ibn Sallām, it must be pointed out, predates Aḥmad b. Ḥanbal and hence cannot be considered a 'Ḥanbalī' in any sense of the term. However, modern Salafis claim Ibn Sallām as an icon of early Salafism.

As almost all famous traditionalists of this era espoused a version of the *balkafa* doctrine, later Salafi authorities co-opted these scholars – regardless of their affiliation to any particular legal school – into the category of the actual *salaf*. Furthermore, they would go on to claim that later Salafi theology was, in fact, a direct extension of earlier proto-Sunni inclinations. For example, there are many references to figures as diverse as the Syrian al-Awzāʿī (d. 157/773–4), the two 'Kufan Sufyāns,' – al-Thawrī (d. 161/778) and Ibn ʿUyayna (d. 198/814) – the Egyptian al-Layth b. Saʿd (d. 175/791), and the famous jurist of Medina and eponymous founder of the Mālikī school of law, Mālik b. Anas (d. 179/796), along with a whole cadre of scholars of that generation, all of whom affirmed various notions of *balkafa* regarding God's attributes.[22]

Perhaps the most famous quotation in this regard – and one that is repeated in almost all treatises on the topic – is the response of Mālik b. Anas when he was asked about the verse: '*The Ever-Merciful has risen over* (*istawā*) *the throne*' (Qurʾan 20:5). A man, after reciting the verse, queried, 'But *how* did He rise over the throne?' The reaction that those who reported the incident recorded also embodies the early community's view on the sanctity and sensitivity of this topic. According to eyewitness reports, Mālik's face scowled, and in silence and anger, he lowered his face. Eventually, beads of perspiration were seen on him – a manifestation of the boiling anger within him – and when he finally managed to compose himself, he raised his head, anger still etched in every line of his brow and every wrinkle on his face, and boomed, 'God's *rising* (*istawā*) is known. *How* [He has risen] is unknown. Belief in this [rising] is obligatory, and asking questions about it is a heresy (*bidʿa*). I see that you are an evil man…' and he commanded that the questioner be expelled from his gathering.[23] This statement from Mālik is viewed by modern Salafis as a general rule that needs to be applied to *all* the divine attributes: (1) the linguistic meaning of the *attribute* is known, (2) *how* it (ontologically) exists in God is unknown, (3) believing in this *attribute* is obligatory, and (4) delving too deeply into the reality or modality of it leads to heresy (*bidʿa*). Similar answers abound in early proto-Salafi literature. For example, the renowned jurist of Khurasan, Isḥāq b. Rāhawayh (d. 238/852–3) was asked by a nephew of the ruler of the region, 'Is it true that God descends to the lowest skies every night?' He sharply responded, 'This is our belief! If you truly believed in a God in the heavens, you wouldn't have needed to ask me about this!'[24]

However, it is not just God's descent and His rising over the throne that are affirmed in such an explicit manner by proto-Salafis. For example, Muḥammad b. Ismāʿīl al-Bukhārī (d. 256/870) – universally considered to be the epitome of hadith scholars during the Golden Age of Compilation – writes:

> And it is mentioned by the Prophet that God shall speak with a voice – those who are near will hear it as clearly as those who are far away shall. And this is the case only for God Himself. Thus, in this, is clear evidence that the voice of God (*ṣawt Allah*) is not similar to the voice of the creation… Hence, when it comes to the divine attributes, there is no similarity or replication or any semblance to the attributes of the creation.[25]

In another now widely printed credo, the 'two Rāzīs' – Abū Zurʿa (d. 264/878) and Ibn Abī Ḥātim (d. 277/890) – declared a consensus of all scholars throughout the major Muslim lands, affirming God's rising over the throne (*istiwāʾ*), and being separate from His creation (*bāʾin min khalqihi*).[26] Examples of such a trend among the scholars of this era are too numerous to mention. Hence, it was easy for later Salafis to claim that proto-Sunnism was essentially Salafism. In other words, from the perspective of Salafis, the Salafi creed was *the* creed of early Sunnism, and all famous scholars of this era – regardless of legal school – followed the same creed. This would change when proto-Ash'arism, sometime in the third Islamic century, began to differentiate between types of divine attributes, understanding such statements to indicate a concept known as '*tafwīḍ*,' in which the actual word is affirmed but the meaning is left unknown. During this time, leaders of proto-Salafism were taken to task for their articulations on certain creedal points, and some were even boycotted or harassed, including al-Bukhārī and the famous exegete and historian Muḥammad b. Jarīr al-Ṭabarī (d. 310/923).[27] Other icons of this era would assert ideas at odds with the majority of proto-Salafis, including Abū Jaʿfar al-Ṭaḥāwī (d. 321/933);[28] such anomalies are often reinterpreted by later Salafis in an effort to project an alleged homogeneity in creed.[29]

During this time, a group of the *ahl al-ḥadīth* began compiling and narrating hadith about the divine attributes in order to refute these more philosophically inclined trends. This phenomenon led to another moniker that was used for the *ahl al-ḥadīth* faction: 'the gatherers of fluff' (*ḥashwiyya*), a pejorative term implying that they picked up anything they could.[30] The explicit intent of their detractors was to assert that the *ahl al-ḥadīth* lacked the intellectual sophistication to think matters through, instead taking ambiguous or dubious reports at face value and 'hurling' them at their detractors as if the mere act of narrating these traditions was itself sufficient to silence the philosophical points made against them. This tension and the accusation of being literalist-fundamentalists and anti-rationalists would plague the Salafi movement from its inception until modernity.

The growing tension within the Muslim community at that time in relation to the divine attributes – and within the *ahl al-ḥadīth* movement itself – can be exemplified through one figure who was typical of this period: the intellectual polymath and long-serving judge under the Abbasids, ʿAbd Allāh b. Muslim, commonly known as Ibn Qutayba (d. 276/889). What is especially fascinating about Ibn Qutayba is that he does not, in any manner, conform to the stereotype of a literalist-traditionalist (or proto-Ḥanbalī). Yet, in his exposition on creed, one finds clear elements of the same defense of the divine attributes that later became a hallmark of Salafism. Ibn Qutayba wrote half a century before the rise of the Ashʿarī school, and his works are reflective of his broad, encyclopedic knowledge of philology, Arabic poetry, and the works of Greek, Hindu, and Persian *belles lettres*. While he wrote many books, the two that are of most interest regarding this topic are his *Taʾwīl mukhtalif al-ḥadīth* (*Concerning the Interpretation of Conflicting Hadith Narrations*)[31] and his *al-Ikhtilāf fī al-lafẓ wa-l-radd ʿalā al-Jahmiyya* (*Concerning the Word [of God] and Refuting the Jahmiyya*).[32]

In both these works, we find a clear tendency to affirm a literal understanding of God's attributes, with a healthy criticism of two groups: (1) those whom he viewed as rationalists, and (2) those whom he dismissively called *ḥashwiyya*. The first group is clearly identifiable as the Muʿtazila. The second group seems to be a section of the hadith scholars – although he does not name them – who appear to extract excessive meanings from their reading of such traditions and assume a precise knowledge of the exact connotations of the divine attributes. In a chapter entitled, 'A Refutation of Those who Claim the Divine Hands Imply "Grace,"' after quoting a selection of Qurʾanic verses and hadith that mention God's two hands (*yadayn*), he writes:

> So, we speak exactly as God Himself and His Prophet, and we do not fall into folly (*natajāhal*), nor do we allow our desire to deny anthropomorphism to negate what God Himself described Himself with.

> As well, we do not say how these hands are, and if asked regarding them, we restrict ourselves to speaking exactly as the texts speak and do not say what the texts do not say.[33]

Ibn Qutayba appears to confidently speak on behalf of mainstream Sunnism, and his intellectual standing and subsequent fame permit him this status.[34]

## *2.2 The Consolidation and Flourishing (850–1000 CE)*

The period of consolidation and flourishing of proto-Salafi theology is defined by the works of a number of key figures, discussed below, and one event, namely the composition of the Qādirī Creed, which underscored a continuation of proto-Salafi ideas surrounding God and His attributes. Together, these provide the foundations that the modern Salafi movement continues to try to emulate. Their main rival at the time, and indeed to this very day, were the Ashʿarīs, a theological school that emerged during the ninth century. Despite its Muʿtazilī roots (although they do not view the Muʿtazila as having influenced them), it became a serious contender in theology from the tenth century, having absorbed key tenets of earlier proto-Salafis, and the growing influence of Neoplatonic philosophy. Eventually, Ashʿarism would supplant proto-Salafism as the dominant trend of Sunnism.

### *2.2.1 Aḥmad b. Ḥanbal (d. 241/855)*

The single greatest primogenitor of proto-Salafi theology is the icon of the movement, Aḥmad b. Ḥanbal, the eponymous founder of the Ḥanbalī school of law. Much has already been written about this important figure; hence, all that is required here is a summary.[35]

Born in Baghdad, Aḥmad b. Ḥanbal rose to become not only a hadith scholar of the highest caliber – he compiled the largest extant collection of hadith in his famous *Musnad*,[36] which totals around thirty thousand traditions – but also the founder of the school of law that emphasized the primacy of hadith more than any other school. More importantly, he propagated Sunni theology in many treatises and is seen as a hero for the brave stance he took during the 'Great Inquisition' (*Miḥna*) when – due to the corruption of the rulers – 'the deviant and corrupt' beliefs of the Muʿtazila regarding God and the nature of the Qurʾan became politically dominant. It was during this precarious time – when people were forced to proclaim the *createdness* of the Qurʾan – Ibn Ḥanbal stood almost entirely alone against the tidal wave of heresy, facing imprisonment and torture but steadfastly refusing to recant the orthodox view of the eternal nature of the Qurʾan. Popular support for 'the truth' eventually won the day and forced the political establishment to acquiesce in the face of public pressure.[37]

Ibn Ḥanbal left an indelible mark not just on Salafism but on Sunnism as a whole. Perhaps his most critical legacy is the establishment of Sunni theology regarding the Qurʾan, which remains an untouchable shibboleth to this day: 'The Qurʾan is the uncreated and eternal speech of God; whoever claims otherwise is a heretic.' Ibn Ḥanbal would remark, 'God recited the Qurʾan to Jibrīl [the Archangel Gabriel]; Jibrīl to the Prophet; and the Prophet to us. Whoever says otherwise is a disbeliever.'[38] No group that wanted to claim the title of Sunnism could contradict this mantra. Hence, the Ashʿarīs, who developed a doctrine of 'the internal divine speech' (*al-kalām al-nafsī*), held that although the enunciated words of the Qurʾan (*al-kalām al-lafẓī*) were created, the Qurʾan *itself* is *still* the uncreated speech of God (*kalām Allāh ghayr makhlūq*).[39]

Another key contribution of Ibn Ḥanbal was to solidify the notion that *all* hadiths that pertain to the divine attributes (*aḥādīth al-ṣifāt*), without any exceptions, needed to be affirmed as they were – literally – based on the principle of *balkafa* (however one understood that). He wrote:

> Faith is to believe in all that has been narrated [regarding the divine attributes] … without asking 'How?' or 'Why?' Rather, faith requires one to affirm and believe. Yet, if someone does not understand the interpretation of the hadith or his mind cannot comprehend it, then let him just believe and submit.[40]

It is for this reason that he affirmed the divine attributes that were contentious, even among other traditionalists, such as the 'form' (*ṣura*) of God, and man having been created in God's image.[41]

A final feature worthy of mention is Ibn Ḥanbal's strict admonitions to avoid association with deviant groups, and to socialize only with pious believers who shared his understanding of truth. Such was his forthrightness in this regard, he even dissociated himself from the famous scholar al-Ḥārith al-Muḥāsibī (d. 243/857), and entreated others to do likewise.[42] An entire sub-genre of harsh criticisms and calls for boycotting of infamous narrators and figureheads was subsequently subsumed into biographical works of hadith narrators. Later movements would appropriate this notion of *jarḥ* (condemnation) in different ways. Perhaps the most radical development of this attitude would be the manifestation of the doctrine of *al-walāʾ wa-l-barāʾ* (association and dissociation) that was employed by Ibn ʿAbd al-Wahhāb and his movement to justify their excommunication (*takfīr*) of the Ottomans.[43]

### *2.2.2 ʿUthmān b. Saʿīd al-Dārimī (d. 280/894)*

While Ibn Ḥanbal is undoubtedly the most iconic figure of this era, he is not the only one. Another key figure was ʿUthmān b. Saʿīd al-Dārimī,[44] who came to be highly praised by later scholars like Ibn Taymiyya for seeking to adhere to the way of the *salaf.* Al-Dārimī was from the city of Herat in the province of Khurasan. Here, he achieved great fame in hadith circles due to his association with some of the traditionalist luminaries of the previous generations, such as Ibn Ḥanbal himself, ʿAlī b. al-Madīnī (d. 234/849), and Isḥāq b. Rāhawayh. This made him a highly sought-after scholar. He was also of the Shāfiʿī school of law, underscoring the previously mentioned fact that *ahl al-ḥadīth* theology (and oftentimes approach to law) permeated all of the Sunni legal schools. Al-Dārimī led the charge against a sect known as the Karrāmīs – the purported archetypal anthropomorphists in early Islam – and was instrumental in expelling their founder, Muḥammad b. Karrām (d. 255/868)[45] from Herat.

Yet al-Dārimī's impact was not in hadith or law but in theology. Part of his legacy lies in authoring two books, both of which are among the cornerstones of Salafi theology and are still extant and in print. Ibn Qayyim, the luminary pupil of Ibn Taymiyya, wrote:

> And his [al-Dārimī] two works are the most beneficial ever written with regard to the Prophetic tradition, and it should be required reading for every student of that discipline. By reading these works, a student will be able to see what [creed] the Companions and Successors and the early scholars were upon. In fact, Shaykh al-Islām [Ibn Taymiyya] would always encourage the reading of these works with the highest of encouragement, and he would hold them in high regard. In these two works, one will find an explanation of monotheism (*tawḥīd*) and God's names and attributes from both scriptural and logical perspectives that are not found elsewhere.[46]

A summary of these two works demonstrates some of the key aspects of proto-Salafi theology – aspects that would remain crucial for the next millennia. Both works are set up as refutations of 'heretics' – those who figuratively reinterpret Qurʾanic passages about God's attributes and outright reject hadith on the topic.

The first work, in particular, is directed against the 'Jahmiyya' – a generic term that early traditionalists used to describe all those who rejected the reality of God's attributes. Hence, this work is aptly entitled *al-Radd ʿalā al-Jahmiyya* (*Refutation of the Jahmiyya*).[47] In it, Al-Dārimī engages in key theological debates, presenting the views of the opposing group while affirming his own beliefs. Here, he claims that his views are in line with the earliest of generations, the Companions, and the great scholars of hadith of the past – all of whom, in turn, transmitted this message exactly from the Prophet himself.[48] Within this context, al-Dārimī discusses Qurʾanic verses and hadiths about God's throne (*ʿarsh*); the fact that God has risen over (*istawāʾ*) this throne – which proves that He is transcendent and above the creation while negating that He is in 'no place' or 'every place'; God's descent (*nuzūl*); the Beatific Vision (*ruʾya*) that God will bless the believers in the afterlife; and the belief that the Qurʾan is God's uncreated speech. In the final chapter of this work, al-Dārimī argues that those who believe contrary to this should be asked to repent or otherwise be executed for blasphemy.

Al-Dārimī's second work, entitled *Radd ʿalā al-Marīsī al-ʿanīd* (*Refutation of al-Marīsī, the Arrogant*),[49] was written as a response to an unnamed opponent, who was a follower of Bishr b. Ghiyāth al-Marīsī (d. 218/833), about whom little is known. Bishr is classified as a Jahmī in traditional heresiographical works, and is attributed with the composition of theological treatises – the contents of which are only preserved in the form of refutations against him.[50] According to al-Dārimī, his opponent held that God could not be perceived through any of the five senses.[51] In response to this, al-Dārimī discusses – in addition to almost all of the issues mentioned in the aforementioned work – that God has two hands, one right and one left; that those hands have fingers;[52] that God moves with a motion (*ḥaraka*);[53] and that God has a form (*ṣūra*).[54] He affirms all of the phrases found in the texts literally, as divine attributes, but always with the caveat of God's uniqueness and a version of the *balkafa* doctrine. Such extreme literalism in the face of the figurative interpretations of the Muʿtazila and later the Ashʿarīs and their closest equivalent, the Māturīdīs, would become a source of embarrassment to later Ḥanbalī theologians, with even Ibn Taymiyya having to clarify that some of these excesses are not theologically tenable.[55]

### *2.2.3 Abū Bakr b. Khuzayma (d. 311/923)*

Another seminal work in early proto-Salafi theology is *Kitāb al-tawḥīd wa-l-ithbāt ṣifāt al-rabb* (*The Book of Monotheism and Affirmation of the Attributes of the Lord*)[56] by Abū Bakr Muḥammad b. Isḥāq, better known as Ibn Khuzayma. This work is significant for three reasons: the fame and reputation of its author; the encyclopedic nature of its content; and that its author was a pillar of the Shāfiʿī school who propagated Salafi-cum-Ḥanbalī theology. Ibn Khuzayma is regarded as one of the icons of hadith scholarship of his era. He attempted, like al-Bukhārī before him, to compile a book of authentic (*ṣaḥiḥ*) hadith, of which only a portion remains and has been published, not surprisingly, as *Ṣaḥīḥ Ibn Khuzayma*.[57] The caliber of both his teachers and students is sufficient to indicate the esteemed stature that he enjoyed.[58] In addition to his fame as a hadith scholar, he was also the most senior Shāfiʿī judge in the city of Nishapur and was consulted by the rulers on affairs of a religious nature.[59]

*Kitāb al-Tawḥīd* is perhaps the most thorough explication of proto-Salafi/Ḥanbalī theology of the fourth/ninth century. It consists of around eighty chapters, with an aggregate of six hundred Prophetic narrations, interspersed with Qurʾanic verses and his occasional commentary. In its introduction, Ibn Khuzayma claims that what prompted him to write the work was that some of his students were being unduly influenced by 'the *Muʿaṭṭila* (negators of the divine attributes), the *Qadariyya* (proponents of free-will) and the Muʿtazila.'[60] Fearing for his students' salvific safety, he felt compelled to defend two fundamental pillars of theology:

> [1] to affirm that God's decree is pre-eternal and that foreordination (*al-maqādīr*) will be executed before man himself acquires the deed, and [2] to believe [and affirm] in all of the attributes of the divine – may He be exalted – mentioned in His book… or authentically narrated and confirmed with accurate chains from our Prophet.[61]

Hence, all eighty chapters deal with two fundamentals: (1) proving predestination (*qadar*), and (2) detailing God's attributes (*ṣifāt*) as found in scripture. What makes this work unique is the extremely detailed list of divine attributes that Ibn Khuzayma claims cannot be understood except in a literal manner: God's face, his two hands, fingers, eyes, feet, speech, knowledge, laughter, His throne and His rising over it, His transcendence above His creation, and other such attributes.

Nonetheless, Ibn Khuzayma is explicit in his claim that such attributes should not be understood in anthropomorphic terms. After quoting Qurʾanic verses and Prophetic hadith that mention God's face (*wajh*), he writes:

> So, God affirmed for Himself a face (*wajh*), and He described that face as a face of majesty and generosity, and He affirmed that it shall be eternal and never perish. The methodology that we follow, as well as all of our scholars from the people of Hijaz, Tihama, Yemen, Iraq, Syria, and Egypt, is that we affirm for God what He has affirmed for Himself. We verbally testify with our tongues and believe with our hearts [what He has affirmed] without comparing God's face with the face of any creation – may God be exalted from resembling any created being! And may He also be exalted from the methodology of the negators of the attributes (*muʿaṭṭilīn*), for He is too exalted to be non-existent as the negators assert, since a being that has no attributes is, in fact, non-existent. And we exalt Him above what the Jahmiyya claim, for they deny the attributes of our Creator – the very attributes

that He has revealed in His book and upon the tongue of His Prophet Muhammad – may God's blessing and peace be upon him.[62]

### *2.2.4 Al-Ḥasan b. ʿAlī al-Barbahārī (d. 329/941) and the Rise of the Ḥanbalīs in Baghdad*

The Islamic capital city of Baghdad witnessed the ascent of the Ḥanbalīs after the death of their founder, Ibn Ḥanbal, up until the fourth/tenth century. The most famous representative of the Ḥanbalīs in Baghdad at this time, and hence of this era, was al-Ḥasan b. ʿAlī al-Barbahārī. Al-Barbahārī studied with some of the most famous students of Ibn Ḥanbal, and his reputation as a hardline, uncompromising preacher of truth greatly increased his following. It is said that he once sneezed during a teaching session on the side of the river Tigris and, as is Islamic custom, he praised God for it. The murmuring generated by the students' customary response of invoking God's blessings – a Christian and Muslim tradition of saying 'Bless you!' – was so loud, due to the sheer number of students, that the Caliph himself, in his palace at the city center, was alarmed and had to inquire as to the source of the commotion. When informed, he expressed his concern that such a large crowd had gathered around the preacher.[63]

Al-Barbahārī achieved notoriety during his lifetime – with some even calling him a 'troublemaker'[64] – for enforcing morality on the streets of Baghdad, and not allowing any preacher of non-Ḥanbalī background to gain a platform in the capital. Due to his popularity, even the Caliph was apprehensive and gave him much leeway – although Ḥanbalī sources portray the Caliph as a genuine admirer. However, in due course, the Caliph was forced to order the arrest of al-Barbahārī due to the public outcry over the vigilante antics he instigated. Nonetheless, the latter retained widespread popularity among a significant number of supporters from the people of Baghdad, and lived the remainder of his life in hiding, worshipping in the houses of admirers and followers until his death.[65]

Two key aspects are of particular interest in our examination of al-Barbahārī's life. Firstly, his purported authorship of a significant work entitled *Sharḥ al-Sunna* (*The Explanation of the Sunna*)[66] and secondly, his engagement with the founder of a scholarly tradition that would emerge as a contender – ultimately surpassing Ḥanbalī Islam in the contest for the mantle of Sunni orthodoxy – the Ashʿarī school.

*Sharḥ al-Sunna* is the sole extant work attributed to al-Barbahārī, and is one of the few early Ḥanbalī texts to have been translated in its entirety into English.[67] Current scholarship has demonstrated that the work was *not* in fact authored by al-Barbahārī, but rather attributed to him by later authorities in order to authorize emerging proto-Salafi trends.[68] However, in Salafi circles, the book is assumed to be al-Barbahārī's, and it is with this assumption in mind that we shall proceed, as it has influenced the practice of a number of contemporary Salafis.

The work is representative of Ḥanbalī thought: it emphasizes the importance of hadith and the Sunna; warns against deviation and heresy; affirms the divine attributes in detail while negating knowledge of their modality; and lists many other points of theology, and even law, deemed essential to Islam.[69] Of interest, is the exclusivist claim – representative of some strands of Ḥanbalism and modern Salafism – that the book is the decisive factor in affirming the orthodoxy of a person: 'So whoever believes in what has been mentioned in this book and affirms it and takes this book as a guide without doubting a single letter in it or denying a single word, that person is upon the Sunna and with the orthodox community (*jamāʿa*), standing [with them] in perfection. Whoever doubts any word in this book, or denies it, is a person of deviation.'[70] Such is the author's enmity towards 'the people of blameworthy religious innovation' (*ahl al-bidʿa*) that he commands people not to even listen to the recitation of the Qurʾan by those deemed to be miscreants, let alone speak to them.[71]

The encounter between al-Barbahārī and the eponymous founder of Ashʿarism, Abū al-Ḥasan al-Ashʿarī (d. 324/935–6), is a common feature in the folklore found in later writings which, for Salafis, proves the higher status of al-Barbahārī. According to the earliest telling of this incident, al-Ashʿarī came to Baghdad and visited al-Barbahārī, seeking to ingratiate himself with the leading scholar of the city. In order to impress him, al-Ashʿarī began chronicling the long list of famous authorities that he had refuted, including prominent Muʿtazilī figures and theologians of other faiths. But all of this seemed to fall on deaf ears, and the stern figure of al-Barbahārī contemptuously dismissed the stranger by saying, 'I understand neither heads nor tails of what you speak! I only understand that which Aḥmad b. Ḥanbal has said.'[72] Frustrated, al-Ashʿarī left the gathering and composed his work *al-Ibāna ʿan uṣul al-diyāna* (*An Elucidation of the Foundations of the Religion*),[73] which is an atypical work that has garnered much controversy and discussion in academic circles, because it is the clearest of al-Ashʿarī's writings that seems, at some level, to be sympathetic to Ḥanbalī doctrines. He then returned to present this book as a gift, but al-Barbahārī rejected it, and this, in turn, caused al-Ashʿarī to remain a pariah in Baghdad until the latter's departure from the capital.[74]

The story is apocryphal at best, with most later authorities – including Ibn Taymiyya himself[75] – dismissing it as an outright forgery, despite the fact that it appears in Ibn Abī Yaʿlā b. al-Farrāʾ's (d. 526/1133) *Ṭabaqāt al-Ḥanābila* (*The History of the Ḥanbalīs*).[76] However, in Ḥanbalī circles, it serves a necessary function: to demonstrate the clear edge that Ḥanbalism had in Baghdad during the time of al-Ashʿarī himself. Ironically, later

Ḥanbalīs did not need to resort to this suspicious vignette to prove their point. A number of well-documented incidents clearly show that Baghdad was a pro-Ḥanbalī city at this time and that the introduction of Ashʿarism caused a literal battle, as will be discussed in the next section.

### *2.2.5 Ibn Baṭṭa (d. 387/997) and Other Seminal Figures*

Another significant theologian of this era was ʿUbayd Allāh b. Muḥammad al-ʿUkbarī (of Ukbara, Iraq), commonly known as Ibn Baṭṭa. He wrote a number of theological treatises, two of which are still extant and have been printed recently: *al-Ibāna al-kubrā* (*The Large Elucidations*)[77] and *al-Ibāna al-ṣughrā* (*The Small Elucidations*).[78] In both of these works, Ibn Baṭṭa stresses the need to remain firmly upon the Sunna, to adhere to the community of believers, to believe in the fundamentals of faith, and in particular, to affirm the Qurʾan as being the eternal, uncreated speech of God: 'not one letter of which is created and whoever claims otherwise is an unbeliever worthy of execution.'[79] Both works emphasize the divine attributes and the unconditional belief in their descriptions as found in the Qurʾan and hadith literature.[80] His presence in Ukbara extended the influence of Ḥanbalism outside Baghdad, as did his theological tracts, which conformed with similar works by non-Ḥanbalīs during the same era.

One prime example is that of Hibat Allāh al-Lālakāʾī (d. 418/1027).[81] Although he was born in Tabaristan, he spent his professional life in Baghdad, excelling in Shāfiʿī law. There, he authored an encyclopedic commentary entitled *Sharḥ uṣūl iʿtiqād ahl al-Sunna wa-l-jamāʿa min al-kitāb wa-l-sunna wa ijmāʿ al-ṣaḥāba* (*The Explanation of the Creed of the Partisans of the Sunna and the Community Based on the Book, the Sunna, and the Consensus of the Companions*).[82] This work is one of, if not *the*, most encyclopedic work that can be viewed as a *summa theologica* of early pre-Ibn Taymiyyan proto-Salafi theology. It has extensive chapters dealing with all salient issues of theology, including predestination, the status of the Companions and the *salaf*, controversies over the definition of faith (*īmān*), and, of course, the divine attributes, which, not surprisingly, takes up the bulk of the work. As far away as Khurasan, Ismāʿīl al-Sābūnī (d. 449/1057), a leading Shāfiʿī scholar, authored a similar but much shorter work, notably entitled *ʿAqīdat al-salaf wa aṣḥāb al-ḥadīth* (*The Creed of the Predecessors and the Partisans of Hadith*).[83]

The works of scholars like Ibn Baṭṭa, al-Lālakāʾī, and al-Ṣābūnī (among others not mentioned here) preserved credos and collections of theological statements from earlier *ahl al-ḥadīth* leaders and cemented a counter theology to the growing influence of the Ashʿarī and Māturīdī schools, along with Shiʿi and Muʿtazilī thought. Their influence helps us to understand why scholars such as al-Khaṭīb al-Baghdādī (d. 463/1071), Abū Bakr al-Bayhaqī

(d. 458/1066), and Abū al-Faraj b. al-Jawzī (d. 597/1201) – claimed by modern Ashʿarīs as being of their school (or, in Ibn al-Jawzī's case, of being sympathetic to their school) – not only recounted the aforementioned works but oftentimes agreed with them on seminal points. These works give the impression of *continuity* of the creed: that proto-Salafi theology has been the same from the dawn of Islam as upheld by the Companions, the Successors, and the icons of scholarship of every generation after them until the era of the authors. Also, the fact that these figures come from different legal schools underscores the observable phenomenon of proto-Salafi theology transcending any one legal school.

### *2.2.6 The Caliph al-Qādir bi-llāh (d. 422/1031) and his Creed*

In approximately 409/1018, the long-reigning Abbasid Caliph al-Qādir bi-llāh (d. 422/1031)[84] commissioned and disseminated a confession of faith that was popularly known as *al-Iʿtiqād al-Qādirī* (The Qādirī Creed),[85] also entitled *al-Risāla al-Qādiriyya* (The Qādirī Epistle).[86] This brief creed presented salient features of Sunni theology and was clearly intended to challenge the growing influence of the Muʿtazila and Shiʿa and demonstrate the triumph of Ḥanbalī theology over all other strands of this era. Politically, the issuance of the creed, along with the command that it be recited after the Friday sermon and at specific ceremonies, served the purpose of consolidating the religious authority of the Caliph himself and of ascertaining his rightful role as both political *and* religious heir of the Prophet.

The Qādirī Creed was thus meant not only to be a final arbiter of what constituted 'orthodoxy' but also sought to both pacify the concerns and gain the unrestricted support of the Ḥanbalī masses. In no uncertain terms, it declared the Muʿtazila to be outside the fold, not just of orthodoxy, but of Islam itself: 'Whoever says that the Qurʾan is created in any of the above-mentioned forms, is a heretic whose blood may be lawfully shed if he refuses to publicly repent when requested to do so.'[87] Tellingly, it also employed language that demonstrated its siding *with* the Ḥanbalīs and *against* the Ashʿarīs. However, in a sign of political pragmatism, it neither hereticized nor even indirectly criticized the Ashʿarī school, being content with merely employing language that would appease the Ḥanbalīs: 'He [God] should be described only by his attributes that He used to describe Himself, or the attributes that His Prophet used to describe Him.'[88] Nonetheless, it is clearly unsympathetic to emerging Ashʿarī thought, as is shown in a number of key phrases, such as its proclamation that the Qurʾan is the speech of God, uncreated in all of its aspects and however it exists[89] (the Ashʿarīs claim that the wording of the Qurʾan is created while the speech of God is not). Further, in defining faith (*īmān*), the creed clearly affirms the Ḥanbalī definition that it consists of internal intentions, words, and actions.[90]

George Makdisi opines that the two main targets of the creed were contemporary scholars in Baghdad who were gaining popularity and threatening the stability of Ḥanbalism: the Muʿtazilī al-Qāḍī ʿAbd al-Jabbār (d. 415/1025) and the Ashʿarī ʿAbd al-Qāhir al-Baghdādī (d. 429/1037).[91] The creed, which was first read in the Caliph's palace in an elaborate ceremony attended by all of the senior judges and scholars of the city, served to officially verify the dominance of Ḥanbalism in the public sphere and effectively marginalized – for the time being at least – the possibility that any other dogma could be officially sanctioned or endorsed in the capital. It has also been proposed that the interplay between the Shiʿi Buyid and the nascent Ashʿarī Seljuk dynasties aided the Abbasid Caliphate's decision to side with a local theology and power base to maintain a semblance of neutrality.[92] Indeed, the creed has been interpreted as being a direct response to Shiʿi power and popular support, enabling Sunnism to be no longer defined simply in opposition to Shiʿism but on its own terms, thereby placing a clear dividing line between Sunnis and Shiʿis.[93] But in trying to settle the terms of Sunnism, the creed, in fact, opened the door to disputation about the nature of Sunnism itself.

Early Sunni trends clearly seemed to favor a literalist reading of the divine attributes and a reliance on transmitting the hadiths of the Prophet as evidence that the attributes should not be reinterpreted figuratively. This school, due to Ibn Ḥanbal's popularity, became mainstream in the Muslim capital of Baghdad and sustained dominance for a period of time, co-opting even the Caliph.

## *2.3 The Decline (1000–1275 CE)*

If, for a period of time, Ḥanbalism was so popular in the capital that it was supported by the Caliph himself, how then did the rival strand of Ashʿarism become the dominant trend in most cities including Baghdad, Damascus, and Cairo, within the span of two short centuries? In this section, we will attempt to answer this question. It was in this era that specific events took place that would have a domino effect on later Sunnism, allowing Ashʿarī theology to take center stage in Mamluk times. The consequence was to effectively marginalize the Ḥanbalī trend and create a dominant interpretation of 'traditionalist' Sunnism that would last until modernity.

### *2.3.1 Karrāmī and Ḥanbalī Dominance under the Ghaznavids and the Early Seljuks*

Our story begins not in the capital of Baghdad but in the outlying city of Nishapur, the intellectual and political capital of the province of Khurasan during Abbasid rule. Nishapur was host to many different trends of Islam, including the Ismāʿīlīs, Ashʿarīs, Ḥanbalīs, and Karrāmīs. As mentioned previously, the Karrāmīs are a now-extinct sect who maintained a close connection with the Ḥanbalīs due to their founder's status as a student of Ibn Ḥanbal.[94] Theologically, they shared similar beliefs with the Ḥanbalīs about the divine attributes, although they differed on some other finer points of theology and law. It is also highly likely that at this stage, they were not a separate sect per se and saw themselves as a part of the greater *ahl al-ḥadīth* movement.[95]

When the Ghaznavids came to power, both the dynasty's founder, Sabuktigin (d. 387/997), and his son, Maḥmūd (d. 421/1031), were ardent supporters of the Karrāmīs, giving them free rein to take charge of religious affairs, and as a result, their teachings became the dominant trend in the city of Nishapur. When the Ghaznavids were ousted by the Seljuks in 431/1040, the Seljuk ruler, Tughril Beg (d. 455/1063), being completely uninformed about religious trends, allowed a local vizier he had appointed to run the city, ʿImād al-Dīn al-Kundurī (d. 456/1064), to launch an inquisition against all other sects. Al-Kundurī, regarded as a fanatic by all accounts, issued a public decree in 445/1053 that resulted in all non-Karrāmī clerics and judges being removed from office. As his power increased unchecked, with the backing of popular religious sentiment, al-Kundurī ordered that Ashʿarīs and Shiʿa be cursed publicly from the pulpits of the mosques every Friday. Eventually, he issued a decree calling for the arrest of specific prominent clerics, including some of the most famous Ashʿarī scholars of the era: Abū al-Qāsim al-Qushayrī (d. 465/1072) and Abū al-Maʿālī al-Juwaynī (d. 478/1085). The former was imprisoned for a period of time, while the latter, with the help of friends and supporters, fled the city and sought refuge in the Hijaz – becoming known as '*Imām al-Ḥaramayn*' (Imam of the Two Holy Sanctuaries) after he led prayers in the Two Holy Mosques of Mecca and Medina. This incident became known as 'The Inquisition (*Miḥna*) of the Ashʿarīs' in later works.

During the five-year period of the Inquisition, there was an awkward friendship between the Ḥanbalīs and the Karrāmīs of the city of Nishapur. The dominant Karrāmīs viewed themselves as being the true Ḥanbalīs and thus tolerated the non-Karrāmī Ḥanbalīs. So, while the Ḥanbalīs were removed from office, they were neither persecuted nor harmed in any way. This was later interpreted by those persecuted as being evidence of tacit Ḥanbalī support of the Inquisition.[96]

### 2.3.2 The Rise of Niẓām al-Mulk (d. 485/1092) and the Path to Ashʿarī Dominance

After five years of the Inquisition, Alp Arsalan (d. 465/1072) succeeded his father as Seljuk ruler and proceeded to imprison and then execute al-Kundurī. Thereafter, he appointed as vizier one of the most successful diplomats the Muslim world has ever seen, al-Ḥasan b. ʿAlī b. Ishāq, otherwise known as Niẓām al-Mulk (d. 485/1092). The placement of Niẓām al-Mulk as the vizier and the educational reforms that he instituted in order to counteract the effects of the Inquisition were to be the single most crucial factor in the spread of Ashʿarī theology in the medieval era.

As fate would have it, as a young man, Niẓām al-Mulk had traveled to Nishapur and studied with a famous Ashʿarī theologian – one whose son was a colleague to Niẓām and who was also imprisoned and harassed during the Inquisition. Not only did Niẓām al-Mulk identify with the Ashʿarī school, but he was also personally affected by the harsh crackdown. Hence, when he was appointed as the vizier to Alp Arsalan and given carte blanche authority in the running of the administration, he carefully planned an effective strategy to push the Ashʿarī school into the mainstream of the Islamic world. Yet even he could not have imagined that this drive would be so successful, essentially allowing a hitherto small and marginalized strand of Sunnism to become *the* definitive interpretation of Sunni orthodoxy for centuries to come.

Within a year of becoming vizier under Alp Arslan, Niẓām al-Mulk had established the first of a series of prestigious madrasas, all of which he named after himself, the Niẓāmiyyas. The vizier personally oversaw and (with state funds) financed these colleges. Through these schools, the first of which opened up in his own hometown of Nishapur, Niẓām al-Mulk was able to revolutionize the entire madrasa educational system: firstly, by the sheer scale of the colleges; secondly, by financing the students to study there (a first in the Muslim world); thirdly, by introducing the concept of bringing multiple teachers together in one location to teach different subjects (another first); and, lastly, by standardizing the curriculum and building a similar network of institutions in several key cities of the Muslim lands.

The prototype model, established in Nishapur, witnessed the assumption of leadership by none other than al-Juwaynī himself. Following his return from a disconcerting period of exile, he undertook the role of effective headship at this establishment, where he engaged in uninterrupted teaching for the subsequent three decades. He was also given the position of chief sermonizer (*khaṭīb*) of the large mosque of Nishapur – a position that Ḥanbalīs had previously held. The Niẓāmiyya in Nishapur did not face much opposition, as the popularity of the Karrāmīs (and, along with them, the Ḥanbalīs) appears to have dwindled in the aftermath of the Inquisition.

Yet the opening of the Niẓāmiyya in the capital of Baghdad would cause a major scandal and even result in all-out brawls and the accidental death of an innocent bystander. This sordid episode is called the 'Trial (*fitna*) of al-Qushayrī,' and its story marks the beginning of the ascent of Ashʿarism and the displacement of Ḥanbalism from the capital. The Niẓāmiyya of

Baghdad was inaugurated in 455/1067, and Niẓām al-Mulk chose the young and somewhat brash ʿAbd al-Raḥman b. ʿAbd al-Karīm al-Qushayrī (d. 514/1120) to be president of the college. This al-Qushayrī was the son of the one jailed in the Inquisition. The younger al-Qushayrī was sent from Nishapur to Baghdad, and in the year 469/1077, for the very first time in Baghdad, a mosque-chair dedicated to teaching Ashʿarī theology was publicly permitted. As part of his teachings, the fiery al-Qushayrī had no qualms labeling the Ḥanbalīs – who were still the dominant majority in Baghdad – deviants for having affirmed all of the divine attributes in an anthropomorphic manner. This, of course, deeply upset the Ḥanbalī clerics, and in the next few days, both sides fomented sectarian strife and incitement between their followers.

With tensions running high, all that was required was a spark to set alight the growing anger. That spark came in the form of a market brawl when one of the students of al-Qushayrī started proclaiming loudly in the bazaar that the Ḥanbalīs had blasphemed against God in their affirmation of the divine attributes. Immediately, he was hit on the head with a brick thrown by an unknown assailant. After months of religious propaganda from both sides, an all-out melee ensued, with weapons being brought from houses. Over a dozen of those directly involved were killed, along with at least one innocent bystander. The people had to rush to the local army officials to get them to intervene, and it was only then that public order was grudgingly restored. Sadly, while this was the worst outbreak, it was not the only physical altercation between the Ḥanbalīs and the Ashʿarīs, and at least two other incidents of violence were reported the following year.

These violent encounters led to a forced intervention from both the Caliph in Baghdad at the time, al-Muqtadī (r. 467/1075–487/1094), and from Niẓām al-Mulk, remotely from Nishapur. The Caliph needed to balance his own pro-Ḥanbalī power base in Baghdad with this new intervention from the powerful Seljuks under the vizier Niẓām al-Mulk. After all, he himself, along with his predecessors, had been helpless barely a decade ago under the Shiʿi Buyid dynasty (r. 334/945–447/1055).[97] It was under his own orders (or perhaps 'pleadings' would be more accurate) that the Seljuks entered Baghdad and displaced the Buyids in 447/1055. It must be recalled that, for much of its existence, the Abbasid Caliph was more a titular sovereign than a powerful monarch. So, during this crucial phase, it was the Seljuks who controlled the armies and financed the treasuries. Hence, it would have been imprudent for the Caliph to risk the ire of the vizier in Nishapur, who effectively acted as the primary envoy of the Sultan and wielded more power. Although Niẓām al-Mulk might have technically been more powerful, he too had to pursue a delicate balancing act to ensure that he did not do anything to invoke the ire of the Caliph. As the titular head of Sunni Islam, people were bound to him by the dictates of Islamic theology and law.

The Caliph was powerless to intervene in the Niẓāmiyya itself, as that was under the control of Niẓām al-Mulk directly. Instead, in light of the preceding events, and at the behest of Niẓām al-Mulk, the Caliph requested his chief vizier (accused by the Seljuks of agitating the Ḥanbalīs), Fakhr al-Dawla (d. 482/1090), to reside as his permanent 'guest' in the palace, effectively placing him under house arrest. The net result was that he was unable to foment any further agitation – or so it was alleged.[98] Niẓām al-Mulk sent a harsh letter to the provost of the school, accusing him of provoking the Ḥanbalīs unwisely: 'for it is not in our power to tackle Baghdad and its surrounding areas or to convert them from what they have been accustomed to from before since what is the norm in that region is the theology of Imam Ibn Ḥanbal.'[99] Eventually, Niẓām al-Mulk called the brash al-Qushayrī back to Nishapur and, after an interim president, selected the brilliant luminary Abū Ḥāmid al-Ghazālī (d. 505/1111) to take over the most prestigious of the Niẓāmiyyas in the capital itself, where he remained almost until his death.

The significance of Niẓām al-Mulk's letter and his selection of al-Qushayrī and later al-Ghazālī cannot be overstressed. It indicates unequivocally the vizier's primary goal: the propagation of Ashʿarī Sunnism. This intent was reinforced by the presence of a plaque at the college's entrance that bore the inscription 'The Ashʿarī Niẓāmiyya College.' Ignaz Goldziher sums up this era succinctly. He writes concerning the rise of Ashʿarī thought:

> For it was not possible for them to teach theology in public. It was not until the middle of the eleventh century, when the vizier of the Seljuks, Niẓām al-Mulk, created public chairs in the great schools founded by him in Nishapur and Baghdad for the new theological doctrine that Ashʿarī dogmatic theology could be taught officially, and was admitted into the system of orthodox theology; its most illustrious representatives could have chairs in the Niẓāmiyya institutions. It is, then here, that the victory of the Ashʿarī school was decided in its struggle against Muʿtazilism on the one hand, and the intransigent orthodoxy [viz., Ḥanbalī traditionalism] on the other.[100]

In the following century, the Niẓāmiyya, backed by the official endorsement from the Seljuk state, played a pivotal role in supplanting Ḥanbalī influence. This led to the proliferation of multiple educational institutions throughout the Muslim world, often with teachers drawn from the main Niẓāmiyya. It served as the initial catalyst, igniting an intellectual transformation that spread globally. This transformative trend extended as far as India in the East and Andalusia in the West. It involved the institutionalization of madrasas by rulers to consolidate their popularity, gradually emerging as a conventional practice. And the Niẓāmiyya, being the 'Ivy League' of this movement, was able to export professors and graduates who carried its Ghazālian notions of Sunnism across the Muslim world. The most important of these madrasas was al-Azhar University. Although initially established by the Shiʿi Ismāʿīli Fatimids, its ownership transitioned to the Ayyubids following the Fatimid dynasty's decline. Subsequently, it evolved into an enduring emblem and stronghold of Ashʿarī ideology, persistently representing a benchmark for 'traditionalist' Sunnism.

Thus, the Seljuks and Niẓām al-Mulk set in motion a 'Sunni Revival' against the dominance that the Shiʿa had achieved under the Fatimids. While the Sunni Revival spread west through the Almoravids by the end of the eleventh century – conquering parts of what are now Morocco, Algeria, and Spain – the crowning glory of this Sunni Revival would be seen in the great warrior-ruler Ṣalāḥ ad-Dīn Ayyūbī (d. 589/1193), known famously in the West as 'Saladin.' The latter not only ended Fatimid rule in Egypt in 1171, but he also recaptured Jerusalem from the Crusaders in 1187. Furthermore, he adhered to the intellectual path of Niẓām al-Mulk and hence, he not only supported the patronage of Islamic seminaries but also made them adhere to Ashʿarī theology.[101]

### *2.3.3 The Diverse Ḥanbalī Responses to Ashʿarī Dominance*

Concomitant with the loss of political power was the diversification of Ḥanbalī thought at this time. This era marked the onset of exploration, growth, and departure from the theological tenets of earlier generations among Ḥanbalī scholars. While each individual undoubtedly possessed distinct attributes, it is possible to broadly categorize three principal ideological threads.

One strand became increasingly strident in affirming the literal meanings of God's attributes. This strand embraced accounts that were often deemed apocryphal by other groups. For instance, they would accept the notion that Muḥammad would occupy God's throne at face value – an idea present in exegetical commentaries but not in established hadith traditions. Most famous among this group were al-Ḥasan b. Ḥāmid (d. 403/1012), al-Qāḍī Abū Yaʿlā (d. 458/1065), and Abu al-Ḥasan b. al-Zāghūnī (d. 527/1132). All three of these scholars represent a continuous strand within the Ḥanbalī tradition: Abū Yaʿlā had studied under Ibn Ḥāmid, and Ibn al-Zāghūnī under one of the primary protégés of Abū Yaʿlā. While most theological writings of Ibn Ḥāmid and Ibn al-Zāghūnī are no longer extant,[102] al-Qāḍī Abū Yaʿlā has left us one of the main theological works that represent this tradition of medieval Ḥanbalī Islam: *Ibṭāl al-taʾwīlāt li-akhbār al-ṣifāt* (*The Annulment of False Interpretations Regarding the Divine Attributes*).[103] This trend was characterized, even by other Ḥanbalīs, as being a case of crass literalism, as they claimed, *inter alia*, that God exists in the form of a young man with curly hair (based on narrations that are highly disputed in all other tendencies); that God sits back and rests one foot over the other on the throne; and that God will place the Prophet on the throne next to Him on Judgment Day.[104] Ironically, despite the literalism, Abū Yaʿlā, Ibn al-Zāghūnī, and the like were known to embrace *kalām*-methods in their works.[105]

In response to this, we can discern a countermovement within Ḥanbalism in Baghdad. This second strand was even more sympathetic to *kalām*-based theology, and they were not as strident as others in their literalism. Foremost among this group was Abū al-Wafāʾ b. ʿAqīl (d. 513/1119), who caused so much consternation among his fellow Ḥanablīs that they felt compelled to take it upon themselves to hold an internal inquisition of sorts and force him to publicly recant some of his views – which were deemed too sympathetic to Muʿtazilism.[106] Another famous Ḥanbalī on this side of the spectrum was Ibn al-Jawzī, who admired the writings of Ibn ʿAqīl and also felt that his legal and theological school had taken an anthropomorphic turn in betrayal of the school's eponymous founder. Ibn al-Jawzī argued that Ibn Ḥanbal had said about the traditions of the divine attributes, 'We transmit these reports as we find them.'[107] Therefore, he took it upon himself to author two critiques against members of his own school: *Dafʿ shubah al-tashbīh* (*Refuting the Erroneous Belief of Anthropomorphism*)[108] and *Kitāb akhbār al-ṣifāt* (*The Book on the Traditions of the [Divine] Attributes*)[109] – the latter being larger than the former.[110] These are the only extant internal critiques of trends in Ḥanbalī theology and are, therefore, quite remarkable scholarly contributions. Despite having received education from esteemed Ashʿarī or Ashʿarī-leaning scholars like Abū Bakr al-Bayhaqī,[111] Ibn al-Jawzī maintained an anti-Ashʿarī position in alignment with the Abbasid caliphs' policy during his era. He also critically studied al-Lālakāʾī's work *Sharḥ uṣūl iʿtiqād ahl al-Sunna.*[112] Nevertheless, as the Abbasids adopted a more lenient stance toward the Ashʿarīs, Ibn al-Jawzī also adjusted his approach. This shift ultimately enabled the still-influential Ḥanbalī faction to effectively persuade the authorities in Baghdad to exile Ibn al-Jawzī to Wāsit between 590/1194 and 594/1199. Yet the intercession of the Caliph's mother led to Ibn al-Jawzī's return to Baghdad in 594/1199, which indicated that fanatical Ḥanbalī power had weakened since the time of Ibn ʿAqīl.[113]

Finally, there was a third trend in Ḥanbalī thought during this time that is best represented by the famous Maqdisī family of Palestine (also known as Banū Qudāma).[114] They were the primary bastions of Ḥanbalī thought in that region and produced several scholars, notably ʿAbd al-Ghanī al-Maqdisi (d. 600/1203)[115] and Muwaffaq al-Dīn b. Qudāma (d. 620/1223)[116] – the latter being the leading Ḥanbalī of his time. These scholars staunchly resisted both the Ashʿarīs and the practice of *kalām*-theology. ʿAbd al-Ghanī was essentially expelled from Damascus due to opposition from Ashʿarī authorities, which culminated in his temporary imprisonment and subsequent exile to Egypt. This situation arose after the Ḥanbalī preaching pulpit within the Umayyad Mosque in Damascus was demolished, and the Ḥanbalīs were prevented from praying there.[117] His cousin, Ibn Qudāma, authored the standard encyclopedic reference of Ḥanbalī law, *al-Mughnī* (*The Enricher*).[118] Both these figures authored several seminal theological works which generally did not align with either the crass literalism of Abū Yaʿlā or Ibn al-Jawzī's critiques and engagement in metaphorical interpretations. The Maqdisī strand claimed that jurisprudence and law were of greater importance and more practical significance than abstract theology and that it was sufficient to merely believe in the divine attributes without asking too many questions. Furthermore, their writings demonstrate a far more tolerant approach to the veneration of saints and the visitation of graves. Hence, later Ḥanbalīs would accuse them of being too vague in their affirmation of the divine attributes and too soft on the 'heretics,' – meaning the Ashʿarīs.[119] Their practicality is indicated by their cooperation with non- Ḥanbalīs in pursuit of the public welfare. Both Ibn Qudāma and ʿAbd al-Ghanī joined the army of the Ashʿarī-patron Salaḥ al-Dīn Ayyūbī during the Battle of Ḥaṭṭīn against the Crusaders in 1187. Of course, even in such company, they openly maintained their Ḥanbalism in creed: as the army marched, ʿAbd al-Ghanī conducted a reading for the public of a Ḥanbalī theological text by Ibn Baṭṭa – an instance which highlighted the complexities of the tense relationship during those times between such theological parties.[120]

In summary, this era saw both the political waning of Ḥanbalī thought and the splintering of its teachings. Various theological strands emerged, each competing for the banner of 'orthodox' Ḥanbalism. Ironically, none of these strands would eventually be given the ultimate status as legitimate heirs to Ibn Ḥanbal. That honor would go to the greatest reviver of Ḥanbalī thought and the undisputed leader of later Salafism, the 'Shaykh of Islam' Ibn Taymiyya al-Ḥarrānī.

## *2.4 The Taymiyyan Revival (1275–1400 CE)*

It is impossible to overstate the significance of Ibn Taymiyya to the modern Salafi movement. Without Ibn Taymiyya, it is likely that Salafism – if it even existed today – would be almost unrecognizable to us. This towering Mamluk-era figure not only shaped Salafi beliefs and codified them but, more importantly, *legitimized* this strand as being worthy of respect and *validated* the classical *ahl al-ḥadīth* movement as one that was viable, robust, and completely capable of taking on the criticisms of its detractors. The momentous impact of Ibn Taymiyya is all the more remarkable when one considers how opposition to *kalām*-theology had all but disappeared as an influential movement by his time, with Ashʿarism and Sufism long held to be part of the orthodoxy – supported by the generous patronage of the Mamluk rulers in the two lands in which Ibn Taymiyya would reside: Syria and Egypt.[121] Nonetheless, while his modern reputation is largely framed in terms of his rational and creedal expositions – and our discussion will focus on these matters as his legacy is defined in this manner – it is often forgotten that he was also committed to calling the Muslim community to the highest spiritual and ethical standards, such as love of the God and His Prophet.[122]

Indeed, Ibn Taymiyya was one of the most brilliant and prolific defenders of proto-Salafi theology in Islamic history, arguing for the purity of its methodology and creed against – from his perspective – the charges of the philosophers (*falāsifa*), the hecklings of the speculative theologians (*mutakallimūn*), the aspersions of the Shiʿa, and the innuendos of the Sufis. He challenged almost every group he perceived to be standing in opposition to his reading of the early Muslims' religious thought. But more significantly than merely defending the creed of the *salaf*, Ibn Taymiyya was compelled to take a simplistic, literalist creed that he cherished and imbue it with intellectual life and academic vigor hitherto completely absent from it. He was thus seminal in single-handedly developing a new fourth (taking into account the three identified above) current of Ḥanbalī theology that was so powerful and imposing that it completely and totally eclipsed all previous iterations. After Ibn Taymiyya, all strands of Salafism linked back to him and claimed to be his true heirs, and that remains the status quo until this day. Since his specific thought is similar, but not identical, to the Maqdisī current, it is perhaps unsurprising that modern Salafis consider it a mere continuation of an unbroken chain of *ahl al-ḥadīth*, passing the torch from one century to another.

So much has been written[123] about Ibn Taymiyya that a brief synopsis will suffice for our purposes.[124] Ibn Taymiyya was born in 661/1263 into a scholarly family of Ḥanbalīs who were based in the Mesopotamian city of Harran. His father was a local cleric, and his grandfather, Majd al-Dīn b. Taymiyya (d. 652/1254) had achieved some repute as an author and jurisconsult. In 667/1269, his parents fled the Mongol invasion with the young child and found refuge in the bustling, cosmopolitan city of Damascus. Here, Ibn Taymiyya was exposed to a wealth of knowledge and was also able to demonstrate his capabilities to a larger and more well-connected audience. He took to religious learning with a single-minded pursuit and spent his entire life immersed in reading, writing, and lecturing. He authored his first book when he was seventeen, and shortly after he was given a lectureship, or 'chair,' in the local school. He never married, nor did he take a position as a sermonizer at any mosque – by all accounts, he lived a simple and ascetic life. Throughout his life, he had a tenuous relationship with the authorities and with some of his fellow Ḥanbalīs who opposed some of his positions.[125] Accused of various crimes ranging from 'riling up the masses' to 'delivering verdicts that conflict with official decrees,' he was sent to jail seven times, eventually passing away while confined in a citadel with his brother.[126]

He stood apart from other proto-Salafi theologians for several reasons. The first and foremost reason among them was his intellectual acumen and erudite grasp of the views of his critics. He was no simple *ḥashwī*, flinging snippets of the sacred texts to refute his critics. On the contrary, he was extremely well-read, and even his critics could not help but be impressed with his knowledge of his opponents' views. He is credited with an almost photographic memory, being able to quote not just the Qur'an and hadith by heart (not a rarity in scholarly circles), but also writings from many disciplines and schools of thought. In his works, he skillfully attempts to demonstrate *why* the views of his opponents are incorrect, basing his criticism not only on the literal meanings of the sacred texts but also from a rational perspective. Typically, he would attempt to demonstrate why the views of his opponents were logically inconsistent from within their own paradigms as well.

A second reason for Ibn Taymiyya's profound legacy was that he had a powerful and authoritative demeanor that enabled him to cultivate a following of students and admirers. This devoted group of followers not only defended him in life but continued his legacy after death. Most prominent among his students are Ibn Qayyim, Sham al-Dīn al-Dhahabī (d. 748/1348), and Abū al-Fidāʾ Ismāʿīl b. Kathīr (d. 774/1373), and in the next generation, there was Ibn Rajab al-Ḥanbalī (d. 795/1393) and a host of others.

Thirdly, the sheer quantity of his writings helped solidify and spread his ideas. He is regularly listed among the most prolific authors Islam has ever produced. In fact, his student al-Dhahabī, a respected historian and biographer in his own right, remarks, 'and it is possible that his verdicts and writings reach 300 volumes; actually, no, they are even more!'[127]

One of Ibn Taymiyya's lasting contributions to proto-Salafi theology was his adoption and popularization of the tripartite division of *tawḥīd* which was rooted in earlier credos: that God must be unified in His lordship (*tawḥīd al-rubūbiyya*), His divine names and attributes (*tawḥīd al-asmāʾ wa-l-ṣifāt*), and His exclusive right to be worshipped (*tawḥīd al-ulūhiyya*).[128] Ibn Taymiyya stressed that all three aspects are equally important and must be accepted in order for one to be considered a pure monotheist. Therefore, a rightly guided Muslim must have correct beliefs about the divine attributes and not simply affirm that God is one. Ibn Taymiyya thus effectively allowed the discourse about the reality of God's attributes to take a far more pronounced importance in Islamic theology.

His theorizing provided a clear exposition of Islam's main doctrine of monotheism. In the process, his schema enabled factions loyal to his thought to easily declare groups who disagreed as having deviated from *true* Islam – for a misunderstanding in *tawḥīd* could not possibly be a trivial matter. Ibn Taymiyya's tripartite division of monotheism focused on the divine attributes – although he did write about the concept of worship (*tawḥīd al-ulūhiyya*), the focus was not as pronounced. This theological argumentation was initially preserved in the generation of Ibn Taymiyya's students, most prominent among them being Ibn Qayyim, and among the next generation of famous Ḥanbalī scholars, Ibn Rajab. Ibn Qayyim, in particular, championed the paradigm of his teacher quite faithfully. His writing style, which was more accessible than Ibn Taymiyya's notorious technical language, rendered his works appealing and accessible to the masses – often surpassing the appeal of his teacher's writings in various aspects.[129] Al-Dhahabī, too, authored a number of works reiterating his teacher's confidence in the positions of proto-Salafi theologians.

Among Ibn Taymiyya's most widely read books is a series of treatises that were written as responses to questions posed to him from three separate cities: *al-Risāla al-Tadmuriyya* (*Epistle to Palmyra*),[130] *al-Fatwā al-Ḥamawiyya al-kubrā* (*The Large Verdict from Hama*),[131] and *al-ʿAqīda al-Wāsiṭiyya* (*The Wāṣit Creed*).[132] These are still taught to all serious adherents to Salafism, offering a straightforward yet effective presentation – interlaced with Qurʾanic verses, hadith narrations, and rational argumentations – of Ibn Taymiyya's conception of the divine attributes. In these works, he asserts that since God obviously knows His attributes, speaks the truth, does not deceive, has the ultimate command over language, and desires to guide His creation, God would not – *could not* – employ language that is problematic or figurative. Rather, Ibn Taymiyya's famous principle that he stated over and over again was that all attributes that occur in the Qurʾan and authentic Sunna must be taken at face value, without reinterpretation (*taʾwīl*), distortion (*taḥrīf*), anthropomorphism (*tashbīh*), or ascribing modality (*tamthīl*). In yet another principle, he stated that anyone who affirms any attribute with *balkafa* must by necessity be able to affirm *all* attributes: this was an explicit attack on the Ashʿarīs.

Ibn Taymiyya's contention against the Ashʿarīs on this point can be framed in the following terms: How could they affirm, for example, that God has the 'seven attributes' of life, knowledge, power, hearing, seeing, will, and speech, and understand that these attributes were unique to Him, and yet problematize and reinterpret all other attributes, like mercy, ascent over the throne (*al-istiwā*), and transcendency (*ʿuluww*)? He further argued, for those like the Muʿtazilīs who wished to claim all attributes are figurative, how could they affirm the existence of God and deny His attributes? Surely, just as they understood that His existence was beyond the understanding of men, even as they affirmed that He 'existed' (*wujūd*), they should also understand that His attributes can use the same words as those of men, even as the reality of those attributes was beyond the understanding of men.

Ibn Taymiyya did not subscribe to the literal (*ḥaqīqa*) and figurative (*majāz*) dichotomy theory as conventionally argued. Thus, for him, the word 'lion' could be a 'predator' or a 'brave person,' without the latter being a figurative expression of speech, but rather as one of the proper, or *ḥaqiqī*, uses of the term. Hence, his theory was not a simplistic denial of figurative speech and metaphors in the Arabic language, but it accommodated what is often deemed to be figurative as being the *literal* usage. The real purpose of this linguistic theory, for Ibn Taymiyya, was to avoid giving people a way of denying a divine attribute – through recourse to linguistic explanations which were unknown, in his estimation, to the earliest community.[133]

His critique of Hellenistic thought is a masterpiece of its time. It shows a thorough understanding of the views of Plato and Aristotle and their influence on Neoplatonism and *kalām*-theology. This topic was of great interest to him since he viewed Ashʿarī *kalām*, in particular, as having emerged from Hellenistic principles and being a watered-down version of Neoplatonism.[134]

In writing extensively against *kalām*, Ibn Taymiyya took the famous post-*kalām* Ashʿarī theologian Fakhr al-Dīn al-Rāzī (d. 806/1209)[135] as his main interlocutor. Of particular importance is his ten-volume *Bayān talbīs al-jahmiyya* (*The Elucidation of the Deception of the Jahmiyya*),[136] which refutes one of al-Rāzī's main Ashʿarī treatises. This work is one of the most elaborate expositions of Ibn Taymiyya's views on divine attributes, including a thorough treatment of the notion of God's transcendency (*ʿuluww*). Another seminal work, and perhaps his magnum opus, is the brilliant *Dar' taʿāruḍ al-ʿaql wa-l-naql* (*Averting the Conflict Between Reason and Revelation*),[137] which consists of ten volumes.[138] While this work is ostensibly a refutation of al-Rāzī, Ibn Taymiyya presents a novel model for the harmonization of logic and rationality with God's revelation. Al-Rāzī had argued through his famous 'Universal Rule' (*al-qānūn al-kullī*) that when reason and revelation conflicted, reason should take precedence over revelation. Ibn Taymiyya took this principle to task in over forty-four points and a thousand pages of arguments, claiming that the positing of such a clash was simply an impossibility: there could never be an actual conflict between reason and revelation. After all, reason was God's gift to man, and revelation was God's speech. Far from being anti-rational, Ibn Taymiyya is seen here as a rational defender of submitting to God's scripture.[139]

His influential refutation of Shiʿi thought, an eight-volume work entitled *Minhāj al-sunna al-nabawiyya* (*The Prophetic Way of the Sunna*),[140] took on a contemporary, the famous Shiʿi cleric, al-ʿAllāma Ibn Muṭahhar al-Ḥillī (d. 726/1325), who had written a defense of the doctrine of Imamate in a treatise entitled *Minhāj al-karāma* (*The Way of Miracles*).[141] Ibn Taymiyya's title was a direct assault on the notion of the miracle of the Imams. In this treatise, he argues that Shiʿi notions of theology are incorrect, historically and textually. Almost all Sunnis consider this treatise – even those who disagreed with Ibn Taymiyya – to be one of the most thorough medieval defenses of Sunnism against the competing claims of Shiʿism.[142] He also issued a seminal fatwa against the Nuṣayrīs (used many centuries later by ISIS), in which he declared this breakaway sect of Shiʿism to be outside the fold of Islam.[143]

His writings did not restrict themselves to intra-Muslim polemics. In yet another work that is considered seminal to medieval Muslim thought, Ibn Taymiyya wrote a seven-volume refutation of Christianity entitled *al-Jawāb al-ṣaḥīḥ li-man baddala dīn al-Masīḥ* (*The Correct Response to Those who Altered the Message of Christ*).[144] Many of the arguments that Ibn Taymiyya championed in this work, such as the Islamic view of the corruption of Jesus' original doctrines, eventually became mainstream in Muslim circles.[145] He also wrote a two-volume work on preserving Muslim identity in a multicultural milieu, entitled *Iqtiḍāʾ al-ṣirāṭ al-mustaqīm li-mukhālafat aṣḥāb al-jaḥīm* (*Following the Straight Path by Opposing the People of Hellfire*).[146] In it, he argues that Muslims should be visibly different from Christians and Jews and that they are totally forbidden to celebrate festivals or holidays that are not Islamic in origin. He also claimed that celebrating the Prophet's birthday (*mawlid*) was an innovation (*bidʿa*) based on concepts imported from Christianity and, hence, should be avoided. These notions would become hallmarks in Salafism later and take on a new vigor with the rise of Wahhabism.

In addition to all of this, he wrote copiously on Islamic law, theology, hadith commentary, and Qurʾanic exegesis and authored hundreds of miscellaneous fatwas.[147] Perhaps his most controversial rulings, for which he was jailed, were the following: Firstly, his prohibition of traveling with the intention to visit the Prophet's grave; he viewed this as a stepping-stone to extreme veneration, arguing that one should travel to the Prophet's city to pray in his mosque and then, incidentally, visit the grave. Secondly, his fatwa that a triple-divorce did not constitute a final irrevocable divorce but rather was a revocable one – which was viewed as contravening unanimous consensus (*ijmāʿ*), although Ibn Taymiyya denied such unanimity.[148] However, there is a lesser-known position attributed to him that many modern Salafis find problematic: his supposed denial of the eternality of hell for disbelievers. This position was allegedly one of his last scholarly articulations and not very well publicized. Indeed, its relative secrecy is understandable in light of its rejection by what are considered to be the authoritative Sunni and Shiʿi positions on the matter – for it was normatively argued within Sunni Islam that the denial of the eternality of hell for disbelievers is itself disbelief (*kufr*) because of contravening the consensus (*ijmāʿ*) on the matter.[149]

In many ways, one can see Ibn Taymiyya's views on Sufism as bringing together his theological, legal, and societal vision. In essence, his stance was balanced, which is why it still attracts supporters to this day – among Salafis, Sufis, and others. He wrote,

> Some people accept everything of Sufism, what is right as well as what is wrong; others reject it totally, both what is wrong and what is right, as some scholars of *kalām* and fiqh do. The right attitude towards Sufism, or any other thing, is to accept what is in agreement with the Qurʾan and the Sunna and reject what is not.[150]

Furthermore, he divided Sufis into three camps. The first group consists of those Sufis who are rightly-guided. They are leaders to be exemplified and are not overcome with mystical intoxication (*sukr*). Examples of figures in this group include Sufi masters like Ibrāhim b. Adham (d. 160/777), al-Fuḍayl b. ʿIyāḍ (d. 187/802), Maʿrūf al-Karkhī (d. 220/835), Sarī al-Saqaṭī (d. 253/867), Sahl al-Tustarī (d. 283/896), al-Junāyd b. Muḥammad al-Baghdadī (d. 289/910), and then later ʿAbd al-Qadir al-Jilanī (d. 561/1166). The second group consists of those he identified as Sufis who fell into mystical intoxication (*sukr*) and utter ecstatic and extravagant statements (*shaṭaḥāt*) – those he deems religiously problematic – while in that state. However, these Sufis recognize the error of those words upon regaining sobriety. In this group are Sufis like Abū Yazīd al-Bisṭāmī (d. 261/875), Abū al-Ḥusayn al-Nūrī (d. 295/907), and Abū Bakr al-Shiblī (d. 334/946). The third and final group of Sufis, for Ibn Taymiyya, are those who had fallen into practices that were condemned in the sacred law – such as magic and sorcery; they espouse doctrines that are wholly heterodox, such as, in his opinion, the monistic doctrine of Muḥyī al-Dīn b. ʿArabī (d. 638/1240)[151] or the theory of indwelling with the Creator (*ḥulūl*) of Manṣūr al-Ḥallāj (d. 309/922).[152]

While modern Salafis have not adopted Ibn Taymiyya's nuanced view on Sufism *in toto*, they have embraced his harsher criticisms of certain prevalent Sufi practices – such as calling upon the dead (*istighātha*).[153] In what seems to be the clearest denouncement of calling upon the dead, Ibn Taymiyya said, 'Those who call upon prophets and righteous men after their death, at their graves and elsewhere, are among the polytheists who call upon other than God.'[154] However, Ibn Taymiyya's views are not as simplistic as those of Ibn ʿAbd al-Wahhāb, and many would argue that there is a marked difference between the two. This is because there is no evidence that Ibn Taymiyya actually anathematized individuals and cast them out of the faith for engaging in such practices. In one of the most telling manifestations of this, a contemporary of his, by the name of Nūr al-Dīn al-Bakrī (d. 724/1324), wrote a treatise in which he justified invoking the saints. Ibn Taymiyya wrote a detailed response entitled *al-Istighātha fi al-radd ʿalā al-Bakrī* (*Seeking Aid in the Refutation of al-Bakrī*),[155] and while he did employ extremely harsh language – even going so far as to describe this constituting disbelief (*kufr*) – Ibn Taymiyya never actually accused al-Bakrī himself of being outside the fold of Islam. This is despite the fact that al-Bakrī had no qualms in regularly considering Ibn Taymiyya to be a disbeliever (*kāfir*). In an interesting turn of events, the authorities later had a political dispute with al-Bakrī, and when they seemingly wanted to have him arrested or possibly killed, Ibn Taymiyya actually gave him shelter and protected him against the state.[156] This complicates how we are to view Ibn Taymiyya's position and might undermine the absolutist stance that Ibn ʿAbd al-Wahhāb and other modern Salafis have adopted from Ibn Taymiyya's words, even going so far as to use them as a pretext to justify acts of murder or to boycott those they deem to be innovators.

Yet, Ibn Taymiyya's contemporary importance for Salafis and non-Salafis is not merely intellectual and concerned with personal praxis only but extends to the socio-political arena as well.[157] In this regard, he has received both fame and notoriety. Perhaps the most defining moment for the latter case was the citation of him in *The 9/11 Commission Report*, in decidedly negative terms, which is indicative of how certain quarters view him as a leading figurehead for what is defined – in contrasting terms – as modern terrorism and fundamentalism (sometimes cynical alternatives for variations on Salafism).[158] Nonetheless, his fame in Islamic circles rests on his numerous political pronouncements and activism. He had a concerned social ethic – based upon the Qur'anic concept of 'enjoining the good and forbidding evil.' As argued by Ovamir Anjum, the construction of political justice as the 'qur'anic arch-obligation' was his main insight into political leadership in Islam.[159] Thus, the state's legitimacy was only derived from being the 'representative of the Community,' and 'if political authority is based on the practice of commanding and forbidding, the entire Community now becomes the site of political authority.'[160] Hence, for Anjum, Ibn Taymiyya's theory of an Islamic state 'politicizes the Community,' who are, in turn, to engage the rulership, through 'mutual advice and cooperation'; and so, we here have a 'Taymiyyan moment' in Islamic political theory, so often overlooked by those who treat his theory as identical to 'fundamentalism' today.[161]

Ibn Taymiyya also urged public officials to work in a utilitarian manner in pursuit of the 'public good' (*al-qaʿida al-ʿāmma*), and he participated in its societal implementation. For example, he engaged in overturning chessboards and eradicating taverns that served wine – although he in no way advocated mob anarchy in general. Moreover, he himself participated as a soldier in military expeditions, which he considered to be part of the lofty ideal of jihad, combatting the Mongol invasion of Syria that commenced in 1299. Nonetheless, he was something of a political pragmatist. While he acknowledged the existence of corrupt kings, he did not advocate revolution without an upright caliph. He recognized that civil war could cause more harm than the good it aimed to achieve. In addition, he dissuaded his followers from imposing the Islamic prohibition against wine consumption among the Mongol and Georgian armies that occupied Damascus in 1300 on the basis that they committed fewer atrocities when they were drunk.[162] Likewise, he wrote of how the Prophet Joseph's employment as overseer of the storehouses for the disbelieving Pharaoh was evidence that legitimated working under an unjust, disbelieving regime if one could implement some good.[163] However, as a demonstration of the centrality placed on justice (*ʿadl*) by him, he approved of the saying, 'God gives victory to a just state, even if it is unbelieving, and He does not give victory to the unjust state, even if it is Muslim.'[164]

The fourteenth century witnessed the continuing presence of Taymiyyan thought. He and his students lived through the century, with Ibn Rajab being perhaps the last significant scholar of the group, passing away in 795/1393. The end of the century saw a few outbreaks of activity from scholars who were not direct students of Ibn Taymiyya but exhibited Taymiyyan tendencies, which got them into trouble with authorities. For instance, there was the trial in 1382 or 1383 of Ṣadr al-Dīn b. Abī al-ʿIzz (d. 791/1389), a student of Ibn Kathīr – whose commentary on the *Ṭaḥāwiyya* creed is laden with Taymiyyan argumentation and lauded by contemporary Salafis – after he condemned a poet for using intercession (*tawassul*) through the Prophet. When news of the case reached Cairo, the sultan ordered that the scholar be questioned in Damascus, and the royal decree included the wording, 'We have been informed that a group of Shāfiʿīs, Mālikīs, and Ḥanbalīs manifest innovations and the doctrine of the Taymiyyans (*madhhab al-taymiyyin*).'[165] However, Ibn Abī al-ʿIzz – who was not a direct student of Ibn Taymiyya – was imprisoned and dismissed from his post after the interrogation. Moreover, one can see the case of the Ḥanbalī Muḥammad b. Khalīl al-Harīrī (d. 803/1400–1401), Imam at the al-Jawziyya seminary, who was tried and punished in 1383 for espousing Ibn Taymiyya's triple-divorce fatwa and believing that God is 'in the sky' (*fī al-samāʾ*),[166] and then in 1397 for again supporting the contentious divorce fatwa.[167]

Ultimately, the intellectual movement sparked by Ibn Taymiyya had no state support in his lifetime. This lack of political backing, together with relatively little scholarly and social popularity, caused his influence to vacillate radically in the succeeding centuries. It would be another three centuries before the views and teachings of this Mamluk theologian gained new prominence – through the adoption and radical adaptation of his thought at the hands of the Najdī Wahhabi revival of the eighteenth century. This does not imply, however, that his legacy was neglected during this interlude. There are a few interesting movements and personalities that carried forth some aspects of Taymiyyan thought and which passed the torch of this luminary even as they modified and adapted it to their own circumstances. It is to these movements and personalities that we shall next turn our attention.

## *2.5 The Interlude (1400–1700 CE)*

The interlude period for Salafism is really a tale of the impact of Ibn Taymiyya, as proto-Salafism was mainly preserved and conveyed through his works and those of his circle during this time. There has been a perception among some academics that Ibn Taymiyya's thought disappeared or had minimal impact after his death until recent times.[168] While it is true that figures like Ibn Qayyim, championing almost all of Ibn Taymiyya's views and remaining faithful to the broad strokes of Taymiyyan thought, were not broadly read, this does not mean that Ibn Taymiyya's influence waned completely. On the contrary, it is as if Ibn Taymiyya's intellectual ashes, still latently burning with his ferocity, were scattered by his students and carefully kindled across the Muslim world. Thus, they were the spark that significantly fueled certain movements that, if not faithful in all aspects, most definitely were a direct result of some of Ibn Taymiyya's thought.

This section will discuss two primary geographic regions of this time frame: the Ottoman heartlands and the Arab Middle East. This is, of course, with the caveat that this time frame still remains somewhat understudied, and much work needs to be done.

### *2.5.1 The Qāḍīzādelī Movement in the Ottoman Heartlands*

In identifying the continuing influence of Taymiyyan thought in the Ottoman lands during the Interlude period – albeit somewhat peripheral to the mainstream religious culture and consciousness – three distinct traditions can be identified: (1) Muḥammad b. ʿAlī al-Birgawī, also known as Birgili Meḥmed Efendi (d. 981/1573) and his 'Birgawīs,' (2) Aḥmad al-Rūmī al-Āqḥiṣārī (d. 1042/1632), and (3) Qāḍīzāde Mehmed (d. 1045/1635) and his Qāḍīzādelī movement. The fact that these Ottoman trends seem to adopt Taymiyyan trends later than their Arab counterparts is hardly surprising when one considers that the Ottomans gained control of Syria in 1516 and Egypt in 1517.

The Qāḍīzādelī movement was a short-lived attempt among Turkish scholars in the Ottoman heartlands to revive a puritanical understanding of Islam based on certain key teachings of Ibn Taymiyya. The movement emerged during the late 1500s and eventually faded away in the early 1700s, just a few decades before the rise of Wahhabism.[169]

This fascinating movement, named after Qāḍīzāde Meḥmed, reached its peak in the middle of the seventeenth century (more precisely, from 1621 to 1685) and was clearly influenced by select writings of Ibn Taymiyya and Ibn Qayyim, albeit with a very Ottoman character.[170] In contrast to the Ḥanbalī teachings regarding the divine attributes, most, if not all, of the members of this movement remained faithful to the tenets of the official Māturīdī school of the Ottoman lands and hence did not take the same theological stances of Ibn Taymiyya vis-à-vis the divine attributes. Rather, this movement took its cue from Ibn Taymiyya's critiques of aspects of Sufism and added to it a harsh criticism of popular social practices of the time, such as smoking, which had just become in vogue in Sufi circles.

Initially, the Qāḍīzādelīs were called 'Birgawī followers' (Tur. *Birgivī ḫulefāsı*) or simply 'Birgawīs' (Tur. *Birgivīler*), since all of them were religiously and intellectually inspired by the influential conservative religious scholar Muḥammad b. ʿAlī al-Birgawī (Birgili Meḥmed Efendi). Al-Birgawī was a Sunni scholar and moralist who lived during the height of the Ottoman Empire. He wrote extensively on a variety of topics ranging from jurisprudence to Qurʾanic recitation, and his books are still popular and widely read today.[171] Al-Birgawī was clearly influenced by the writings of Ibn Taymiyya[172] and made it his mission to rectify Sufi practice in the Ottoman Empire.[173] His book *al-Ṭarīqa al-Muḥammadiyya* (*The Muhammadan Path*),[174] which highlighted problematic practices of Sufism, became a primary textbook of the Qāḍīzādelī movement.[175] Another strong influence on this movement was the Ottoman scholar Abū al-Saʿud al-Afandī (*Tur.* Ebusuûd Efendi; d. 982/1574), who was very vocal in condemning the practices of the Shiʿa and various Sufi orders. Al-Birgawī also explicitly referenced Ibn Qayyim – and quoted extensively from his *Ighāthat al-lahfān* (*Aid for the Afflicted*) in a treatise in which he deals with the 'visitation of graves' (*ziyārat al-qubūr*), something that Ibn Taymiyya himself wrote extensively about.

Aḥmad al-Rūmī al-Āqḥiṣārī was born to a Christian family in Cyprus but was snatched as a child by the Ottomans upon Cyprus falling to the Turks. He later became an Islamic scholar and a Sufi.[176] He lived in Akhisar (western Anatolia) and did not spend a substantial amount of time in Istanbul. His most popular work is the *Majālis al-Abrār* (*The Councils of the Pious*),[177] in which he quotes freely from Ibn Qayyim in condemning prevalent practices around graves. He never refers to Ibn Taymiyya by name, but he reworks passages from the latter's work, namely *Iqtiḍā al-ṣiraṭ al-mustaqīm*, in denouncing the imitation of disbelievers and blameworthy religious innovation. However, it must be acknowledged that this adoption of Taymiyyan thought was rather restrictive, as al-Āqḥiṣārī remained a Ḥanafī, a Māturīdī, and a Sufi (like al-Birgawī) – all targets for contemporary Salafis. Yet, we are then left with a query: who was responsible – al-Birgawī or al-Āqḥiṣārī – for Taymiyyan thought arriving at the next semi-'Taymiyyan moment' in the Ottoman heartlands: the Qāḍīzādelīs?[178]

Qāḍīzāde Meḥmed Efendi studied Islam under the students of al-Birgawī and then started his career as a preacher at a mosque in Istanbul. But soon, he developed an antagonistic approach towards Sufis and gained a following. This increased when he was promoted to Friday imam at the Yavuz Selim Mosque. He translated some of Ibn Taymiyya's books into Ottoman Turkish and promoted them to his followers.[179] As his popularity grew, Qāḍīzāde gained the favor of Sultan Murād IV (d. 1049/1640). The Qāḍīzādelī movement's emergence as a fundamentalist challenge and discordant revivalist movement can be traced from its origins as a fervently devout and notably anti-mystical assembly of Muslim mosque preachers – positioned at the outskirts of the Ottoman religious establishment. This movement eventually ascended through the ranks, attaining recognition within the Ottoman ulama hierarchy, referred to as the '*ʿilmiye*' in Ottoman Turkish. Although they acquired the reputation of being strict, rigorous, and pious Muslim preachers among their supporters, they were designated by some Ottoman sources, and by their Sufi adversaries, as 'people of bigotry' (*ehl-i taʿaṣṣub*). The Qāḍīzādelīs prevailed over their rivals in seventeenth-century Istanbul under the successive leaderships of Qāḍīzāde Meḥmed Efendi, Usṭuvānī (d. 1071/1661), and Vānī Meḥmed Efendi (d. 1095/1684). They came to public prominence during the reign of Sultan Murād IV but began to be identified as 'Qāḍīzādelīs' during the height of their activities around the middle of the seventeenth century – a time coinciding with the reign of Sultan Meḥmed IV.

The strict verdicts of Qāḍīzāde and his followers helped Sultan Murād establish a stricter form of Islamic law. During his reign, coffeehouses and tobacco were banned on pain of death under Qāḍīzādelī pressure.[180] Smoking infractions resulted in a huge number of executions by dismemberment, impaling, or hanging. The eminent Ottoman historian Ḥajjī Khalīfah, known as Kātib Çelebi (d. 1067/1657), relates the execution of 'fifteen or twenty leading men of the army'[181] on a charge of smoking during a military expedition against Baghdad undertaken by Murād IV.

The rise of the Qāḍīzādelī movement was short-lived. By the late 1600s, they were already losing power and fading into obscurity. Sultan Mehmed IV fell out of favor with his people due to his harshness and for losing a major battle at the gates of Vienna. Eventually, he was dethroned through a military coup. His successor, Suleiman II (d. 1102/1691), was more inclined toward Sufism and did not give the Qāḍīzādelīs the same authority that Meḥmed did. Under Suleiman's rule, the Qāḍīzādelī movement slowly faded away.[182] After losing authority in Istanbul, the Qāḍīzādelī movement moved to Damascus, where it lingered on for a few more decades but never rose to the same level of authority again.

In Damascus, we know about the existence of the Qāḍīzādelī movement primarily from the writings of their main opponent, ʿAbd al-Ghanī al-Nābulsī (d. 1144/1731). The latter was a famous Ḥanafī-Sufi scholar who penned a number of writings to refute the beliefs of the Qāḍīzādelī movement, where he justified certain maligned Sufi practices and beliefs. He spent seven years in seclusion writing a commentary on al-Birgawī's *al-Ṭarīqa al-Muḥammadiyya*, in which he tried to neutralize the criticism of Sufism in the book.[183] The fact that ʿAbd al-Ghanī al-Nābulsī focused so much time writing against the Qāḍīzādelī movement, which included writing a book proving the permissibility of music in Islam[184] – an issue the Qāḍīzādelī movement strongly opposed – shows that they were still seen as a movement that needed engagement and refutation in the early 1700s. The debates between the Qāḍīzādelī movement and al-Nābulsī seem to go all the way up into the 1730s, which is just a decade before the rise of Wahhabism. This has led some scholars to theorize that Ibn ʿAbd al-Wahhāb was influenced by this movement, drawing a link between him and them through his chain of teachers.[185]

Yet, the fact remains that the Qāḍīzādelī movement remains largely unknown outside Ottoman lands. There remains work to be done to sift out the precise relationship between the Qāḍīzādelī movement in Türkiye and the revivalist movement spearheaded by Ibn ʿAbd al-Wahhāb in Najd. Whether this movement directly or indirectly influenced Ibn ʿAbd al-Wahhāb is still unclear. Either way, the end of the Qāḍīzādelī movement coincided with the rise of Wahhabism, which we will turn our attention to in the next chapter. Even if the Qāḍīzādelī movement's impact on Ibn ʿAbd al-Wahhāb remains ambiguous, there is another movement sparked by Ibn Taymiyya that clearly did have an impact on Ibn ʿAbd al-Wahhāb, and that is the intellectual movement of al-Kurānī and his legacy.

### *2.5.2 Ibrāhīm al-Kūrānī (d. 1101/1690) and his Revival in the Arab Lands*

The influence of Ibn Taymiyya persisted in the Arab lands during the Interlude. His works were read, and they influenced scholarly circles during this period – even if they were not a standard reference point. This was despite the fact that he remained a controversial figure with prominent detractors. Nonetheless, he continued to have supporters. Hence, his thought remained relevant in scholarly debates in Damascus and Cairo until around the 1450s. A dispute arose in Damascus around 1431 or 1432, when a Ḥanafī scholar called ʿAlā al-Dīn al-Bukhārī (d. 842/1438) declared that anyone who honored Ibn Taymiyya by giving him the rank of *Shaykh al-Islam*, was in turn a disbeliever – as was Ibn Taymiyya himself! This outraged a fellow Damascene scholar called Ibn Nāsir al-Dīn al-Dimashqī (d. 842/1438), who then penned a lengthy endorsement of Ibn Taymiyya entitled *al-Radd al-wāfir* (*The Ample Response*).[186] Notably, it included critical endorsements from illustrious scholars, including Ibn Ḥajar al-ʿAsqalānī (d. 852/1449) and the judges of the four schools of law in Cairo after the work was sent to them from Damascus for approval. Furthermore, there was the embrace of aspects of Taymiyyan thought in Yemen in the early fifteenth century until the nineteenth century[187] and in Egypt by Badr al-Dīn al-ʿAynī (d. 855/1453) and Jalāl al-Dīn al-Suyūṭī (d. 911/1505) – both of whom embraced aspects of Ibn Taymiyya's thought, such as his criticism of logic, and praised him as a great scholar capable of independent legal reasoning (*mujtahid*).[188]

Nonetheless, the major revivalist spark of Taymiyyan thought occurred in the learning circles of the Kurdish scholar Ibrāhīm b. Ḥasan al-Kūrānī.[189] Al-Kūrānī rehabilitated many of Ibn Taymiyya's ideas – in particular, his theology of divine attributes, causation, and predestination. Moreover, he started an intellectual revival that lasted at least two centuries and sparked many great reformist movements around the globe.

Al-Kūrānī was born in Iranian Kurdistan but studied for periods of time in Baghdad, Damascus, and Cairo before settling in Medina. It was in Damascus that he first encountered the intellectual descendants of Ibn Taymiyya – by this time, a small, marginal group in the city. Al-Kūrānī adopted many of the views of Ibn Taymiyya and obtained several of his works. Once settled in Medina, al-Kurānī appears to have attempted a critical engagement within his Ashʿarī theological school and Naqshbandī Sufi order. He called for reforms from within, advocating what he viewed as a purer form of Islam, which he derived, in part, from the writings of Ibn Taymiyya.[190] At times, he used selected texts from Ibn Taymiyya as textbooks for his public courses and defended the latter openly from charges of anthropomorphism.[191] Yet, despite this defense, he was neither Ḥanbalī in *fiqh* nor fully Taymiyyan in theology. His actual views are eclectic, combining aspects of Ashʿarism with Ibn Taymiyya's views and propagating a seemingly orthodox interpretation of the aforementioned doctrine of the 'unity of being' (*waḥdat al-wujūd*)[192] – itself derived from the thought of Ibn ʿArabī[193] – something that Ibn Taymiyya most likely would have found highly objectionable! Nonetheless, his main legacy was to keep the name and writings of Ibn Taymiyya alive and introduce them to a very tight-knit and highly influential circuit of intellectual revivalists.

While al-Kūrānī's impact deserves further study, it is clear that his thought directly impacted movements in, *inter alia*, India, Yemen, Arabia, and even Indonesia. For example, his son Muḥammad b. Ibrahīm, known as Abū Ṭāhir al-Kūrānī (d. 1146/1733), was one of the main influences on the famous polymath and reviver of the hadith sciences in India, Shāh Walī Allāh al-Dihlawī (d. 1176/1762). Almost all of Shāh Walī Allāh's hadith chains go through the father al-Kūrānī from his son. The originality of Shāh Walī Allāh's revival in the Indian landscape and his moving away from the Ḥanafī school to a more hadith-based *fiqh*, along with his unique views on Sufism, hint at the impact that Ibn Taymiyya's writings had on him via the Kūrānī father-son duo. This sentiment is further enshrined in a short treatise in which Shāh Walī Allāh defends Ibn Taymiyya from common objections, including the latter's proto-Salafi position that God is above His throne, on the basis that 'not one of these things [was brought against him] except that he had his evidence from the Book, the Sunna and the narrations of the *salaf*.'[194]

Shāh Walī Allāh al-Dihlawī is considered to be perhaps the most influential Islamic scholar to emerge from India around the onset of modernity.[195] All of the current major Islamic factions in the Indian subcontinent – *viz.*, Deobandīs, Barelwīs, *Jamaat-e-Islami*, and the *Ahl-e Ḥadīth* – today consider Shāh Walī Allāh to be a key figure in their history, especially the latter movement which alone identifies as a Salafi strand of Islam in the region.[196] Nevertheless, Shāh Walī Allāh remains a complex individual who does not wholly fit in with any one specific group or movement. His ideas contain elements of (proto-)Salafism, Sufism, Ashʿarism, and his own independent thought. Perhaps the ambiguity of Shāh Walī Allāh's legacy is partially due to his pragmatism. For instance, SherAli Tareen has argued that Shāh Walī Allāh held that 'the maintenance of social order took precedence over judging the niceties of everyday ritual life.' This is illustrated in an incident where he protected a scholar – who was his guest – and raised his hands in the ritual prayer (*rafʿ al-yadayn*). The locals, who largely followed the Ḥanafī school, in which the raising of hands was not practiced, were enraged. After Shāh Walī Allāh appeased the group on the basis that he also engaged in the practice, he admitted to the guest that he did not: 'I actually don't [practice the raising of the hands], but had I not said so, you would have been killed today!'[197] This pragmatism was continued by his children on the issue of *rafʿ al-yadayn* until his grandson Shāh Muḥammad Ismāʿīl (d. 1831), the later army commander, broke with any social conformity on the matter.[198] Furthermore, Shāh Walī Allāh argued that one must adhere to the Ḥanafī school if one lived in India or Central Asia and there were no scholarly experts from other schools.[199]

However, what is of particular interest to us here is another strand of al-Kūrānī's thought that led to the greatest revival of Salafism in our times. One of al-Kūrānī's main students was Abū al-Ḥasan Muḥammad b. ʿAbd al-Hādī al-Sindī (d. 1138/1726), an Indian émigré to Medina who achieved renown as a specialist in hadith, eventually becoming the most prominent teacher of hadith studies in the Prophet's Mosque. Another Indian émigré, also from the province of Sindh, was drawn into this circle of knowledge as a young man, mesmerized by this trend's intellectualism until he became its primary proponent. This was the famous Muḥammad Ḥayāt al-Sindī (d. 1163/1750).[200] Muḥammad Hayāt al-Sindī is considered by many to be the most prominent scholar of the Hijaz in this era. He wrote dozens of treatises, although only a few have been published. The reformist streak in his writings is very clear. While he was nominally affiliated with the Ḥanafī school and the Sufi Naqshbandī order, his writings clearly condemned the uncritical conformity (*taqlīd*) of legal schools in which authentic hadith were rejected, as well as Sufi practices like building mausoleums over graves.[201]

Al-Sindī eventually took over his teacher's chair of hadith after the latter's death and held the post until his own passing. Over the course of these decades, he left his mark on many theologians and thinkers. The most prominent among them was the prolific Ḥanbalī jurist based in Palestine, Muḥammad b. Aḥmad b. Sālim al-Saffārīnī (d. 1188/1774), renowned for his comprehensive poem on theology entitled *al-Ḍurra al-muḍiyya fī ʿaqd al-firqa al-marḍiyya* (*The Radiant Pearl on the Doctrine of the Delighted Party*).[202] Al-Saffārīnī followed this work with an encyclopedic commentary entitled *Lawāmiʿ al-anwār al-bahiyya* (*The Shining of the Magnificent Lights*),[203] the most detailed exposition of Taymiyyan Ḥanbalī theology of the late sixteenth century. In fact, this work remains a standard reference among Salafi theologians to this day and saw publication in the twentieth century by al-Maktab al-Islāmī, a Salafi publishing house in Beirut. Later Salafis, however, would criticize specific aspects of his thought, including his ecumenical claim that the Ashʿarī and Māturīdī schools were legitimate representations of Sunni Islam, along with the Atharī/Salafi school.[204] Of course, Salafi defenders of al-Saffārīnī would argue that such presentations are in relation to the generic Sunnism, which excludes the Shiʿa, rather than a reference to the specific 'pure' Sunnism of Atharī creed.

Another important student of al-Sindī was the highly influential former-Zaydī cleric from Yemen, Muḥammad b. Ismaʿīl, more commonly known as Ibn al-Amīr al-Ṣanʿānī (d. 1182/1768). Following his conversion to Sunnism, he sparked a Taymiyyan-based intellectual revival when he returned to his native land.[205] Al-Sindī's influence, like that of his teacher al-Kūrānī, continued after his death, and several of al-Ṣanʿānī's students went on to teach many prominent reformers and thinkers. Noteworthy among them are Muḥammad Murtaḍā al-Zabīdī (d. 1204/1790) and, albeit via another student, Muḥammad b. ʿAlī al-Shawkānī (d. 1834). The latter was another Zaydī convert to Taymiyyan Sunnism and was a polymath and prolific author. In fact, as shall be discussed later in this chapter, one of al-Shawkānī's students would play a formative role in the emergence of the *Ahl-e-Ḥadīth* movement of India.[206]

As we look at each of these major figures and attempt to simplify the complex webs of learning, it is clear through their writings that the thought of Ibn Taymiyya influenced all of these figures to varying degrees. Each of these figures was an independent thinker in his own right, and none simply parroted the ideas of their teachers before them in a simplistic and blind manner. On the contrary – as every reader of their works knows – these figures selectively took ideas from Ibn Taymiyya and infused aspects of Taymiyyan thought with a new life. In doing so, they introduced their own unique perspectives and interpretations, giving rise to distinctive theological outlooks. A common thread among all these figures, without exception, is a shared inclination toward revivalism based on a return to the texts, particularly the Qurʾan and Sunna. Their endeavors were characterized by a commitment to 'purify' what they deemed to be unwholesome additions to Islam in their respective times and cultures. In doing so, they all sought to rediscover the original Prophetic truth in every aspect of the faith. In this, the spirit of Ibn Taymiyya was clearly manifested. Another common thread was the critical attitude they took toward blind conformism (*taqlīd*) and the willingness to break away from the established schools if it appeared that the Prophetic evidence favored another opinion.

But there is one important figure left. For in the famous circles of Muḥammad Ḥayat al-Sindī, there was yet another spark of Taymiyyan thought who was to pass on his ideas and emerge as the most prominent influence for the modern age. It was in this circle in Medina, the holy city of the Prophet, that a young Arab man in his early twenties first encountered notions of the tripartite divisions of *tawḥīd* and was exposed to ideas about the dangers of extreme veneration of graves and the excesses of Sufi thought. This man had traveled to Medina from his hometown of ʿUyayna, in the province of Najd. And after studying with al-Sindī, he decided to write a book that would, in a short span of time, spark a movement that eventually became the basis of a Kingdom. He entitled his book *Kitāb al-tawḥīd* (*The Book of Monotheism*),[207] and his name was Muḥammad b. ʿAbd al-Wahhāb. The comprehensive account of his life and the unfolding of his movement will be the central focus of the forthcoming chapter. Still, a brief introduction is warranted here.

## *2.6 The Wahhabi Movement (1700–1800 CE)*

Of all the figures and movements that Ibn Taymiyya inspired, none are as prominent as that of Muḥammad b. ʿAbd al-Wahhāb.[208] There are a number of reasons for this.

Firstly, during the interval extending from the era of Ibn Taymiyya's immediate disciples until the eighteenth century, there existed no individual who more explicitly embraced an identification with Ibn Taymiyya and his doctrines than the persona of Ibn ʿAbd al-Wahhāb. How faithful he was to the actual teaching of his intellectual mentor is a matter of dispute, but what is undeniably true is that his followers view both Ibn Taymiyya and Ibn ʿAbd al-Wahhāb as the primary originators of their thought and on an equal footing in terms of authority. Ibn ʿAbd al-Wahhāb's writings are infused with the teachings of this great scholar who so inspired him, and his followers revived the books and carried the legacy of Ibn Taymiyya and his students.

Secondly, no other Taymiyyan-inspired movement was able to acquire as much political support as Wahhabism. The Saudi emirates and kingdoms, in all three of their historical iterations, enabled the teachings of Ibn Taymiyya to spread widely. Indeed, a modified version of 'Taymiyyan Islam,' derived from Wahhabism and its interpretation of Ibn Taymiyya, remains the official and dominant interpretation of Islam in Saudi Arabia, Kuwait, Qatar, and parts of the UAE, with support among clerics all over the Gulf, and indeed the Middle East.

Thirdly, in part because of its wealth, the modern Kingdom of Saudi Arabia has been able to establish various institutes and centers of learning, most prominently the Islamic University of Medina (IUM), which has successfully exported this Taymiyyan-cum-Wahhabi ideology and helped spark a global movement.

Finally, in the last century in particular, the movement has been instrumental in collecting, translating, publishing, distributing, and teaching not only the works of Ibn Taymiyya but also a vast array of Ḥanbalī and proto-Salafi theological texts. There has been an intellectual revival globally and an increased awareness of the *ahl al-ḥadīth* school, owing to the sheer quantity of publications and research they have produced.

While the followers of the movement view the teachings and thought of their founder as being identical to Ibn Taymiyya, critics believe that the Ibn ʿAbd al-Wahhāb reinterpreted – and perhaps radicalized – the Taymiyyan division of *tawḥīd* in an unprecedented manner. Ibn Taymiyya's emphasis in his *oeuvre* was primarily on the divine attributes, while Ibn ʿAbd al-Wahhāb wrote almost exclusively on the Taymiyyan notion of *ulūhiyya* (God's exclusive right to be worshiped), and developed doctrines that seem to be out of sync with Ibn Taymiyya's thought. Most significantly, Ibn Taymiyya never fought against fellow Muslims and did not declare any of his opponents outside the fold of Islam, regardless of how harshly he criticized them. The same cannot be said of Ibn ʿAbd al-Wahhāb. The Wahhabis' understanding of *tawḥīd* and the development of a doctrine they call *al-walāʾ wa-l-barāʾ* (association and dissociation) allowed them to excommunicate (*takfīr*) fellow Muslims for specific practices associated with saints and graves, and to wage war and kill their opponents while establishing a political base for their ideas.

With the rise of influence of the Kingdom, prominent clerics were able to yield global influence, and an entire cadre of scholars became household names, not just among Salafis, but all religious movements. Most prominent among them were the Grand Mufti, ʿAbd al-ʿAzīz b. ʿAbd Allāh b. Bāz, Muḥammad b. Salih al-Uthaymin, ʿAbd Allāh b. Jibrīn (d. 2009), and Salih al-Fawzan (b. 1933). These figures represented a slightly different version of Salafism, infusing Ibn Taymiyya's thoughts with the ideas and interpretations of Ibn ʿAbd al-Wahhāb. Due to the significance of this movement, the entirety of the next chapter will be dedicated to it.

## *2.7 Yemen and its Zaydī Converts (15th–18th Centuries)*

Yemen plays an important role in the development of modern Salafism. Considering Yemen's historic association as the bastion of Zaydī Shiʿism, a status it has maintained since the third/tenth century, such a link is somewhat surprising. It may be that the Zaydī emphasis on *ijtihād* (independent scholarly reasoning) made it easier for its scholars to explore other ideas and adopt opinions outside the mainstream Zaydī school. More work remains to be done regarding this era and region, and our goal here is only to provide a basic overview.[209]

Three iconic figures of Yemeni Salafism will be discussed here. Perhaps the first Yemeni scholar to have gravitated towards proto-Salafism was the enigmatic Muḥammad b. Ibrāhīm b. al-Wazīr (d. 840/1436). Although he is earlier than the two most important icons of Yemeni Salafism, his writings influenced both of them: Ibn al-Amīr al-Ṣanʿānī and Muḥammad b. ʿAlī al-Shawkānī. All three of these figures started their careers as Zaydī scholars, but their personal research led them towards a more Taymiyyan understanding of Sunni Islam.

Information regarding Ibn al-Wazīr is scarce, with most of the extant sources being recorded by al-Shawkānī, who himself was an admirer of the former's ideas.[210] It is not certain why he abandoned the Zaydī tradition for Sunni Islam. His writings, though, clearly indicate that he was influenced by Ibn Taymiyya and Ibn Qayyim and had access to their works. Perhaps his most famous work is a nine-volume defense of his theological and legal views, which he entitled *al-ʿAwāṣim wa-l-qawāṣim fi al-dhabb ʿan Sunna Abī al-Qāsim* (*The Protectors and Destroyers of the Sunna of Abu al-Qasim*).[211] This work is one of a kind. It acts as an encyclopedia of views and opinions on dozens of issues, providing the opinions of various sects and authorities, along with Ibn al-Wazīr's own opinions and his defense of them. Of particular note is his detailed discussion of *taqlīd* and his rejection of blindly following any authority, which takes up the entirety of the first two volumes. He also makes a passionate defense for following the Prophetic Sunna. Ibn Taymiyya is quoted fairly frequently, typically to mark the author's agreement with his views. One of the most striking examples of Ibn Taymiyya's impact on this Yemeni theologian is with regards to the issue of the eternality of Hell. While the general Sunni consensus is that Hellfire is eternal, Ibn Taymiyya and Ibn Qayyim allegedly entertained the possibility of Hell being temporal – that God's infinite mercy would eventually cause Hell to cease to exist. Ibn al-Wazīr wrote an entire treatise in which he defended the basis for the Taymiyyan idea on this topic while maintaining a neutral position between the two opinions, entrusting the final destination of the disbelievers to God.[212]

The next figure in this series is Ibn al-Amīr al-Ṣanʿānī. His status became particularly significant in the history of Salafism and Wahhabism because he was a contemporary of Muḥammad b. ʿAbd al-Wahhāb and was aware of the rise of Wahhabism. Al-Ṣanʿānī clearly shared some of Ibn ʿAbd al-Wahhāb's theological ideas and even supported his early career. However, as the Wahhabi call became more militant and extreme, al-Ṣanʿānī distanced himself from the movement and warned against it.[213] His main legacy for modern Salafism lies in his explanations of hadith, in particular, his commentary on the Ibn Ḥajar al-ʿAsqalānī's (d. 852/1449) *Bulūgh al-Marām* (*Attainment of the Objectives*)[214] entitled *Subul al-Salām* (*The Pathways of Peace*).[215] This work remains one of the iconic legal works written from outside the domain of the four schools of law and is studied in Salafi institutes across the Muslim world.

However, the most important thinker to emerge from Yemen, and whose impact is still felt among modern Salafis, is without a doubt, Muḥammad b. ʿAlī al-Shawkānī. He was a prolific writer, authoring works on legal theory, law, hadith, and Qurʾanic exegesis. One of his most influential works is a treatise against blind following (*taqlīd*), *al-Qawl al-mufīd fī adillat al-ijtihād wa-l-taqlīd* (*The Useful Speech Regarding The Evidences For Juristic Reasoning and Blind Following*),[216] in which he argued that it was impermissible for a person of knowledge to blindly follow any of the legal schools. He was also skeptical of the widely accepted jurisprudential notion of scholarly consensus (*ijmāʿ*) and often adopted minority opinions outside the known opinions of the four legal schools. No earlier authority took a more hardline stance against the *madhhabs* than al-Shawkānī. His ideas would go on to strongly influence the Indian *Ahl-e Ḥadīth* movement and also arguably the most iconic Salafi figure of our generation, al-Albānī.[217] Some of his works were actually incorrectly printed in Saudi Arabia in the twentieth century under the name of Muḥammad b. ʿAbd al-Wahhāb, due to the perceived similarity between them (notwithstanding the differences that al-Shawkānī had with ʿAbd al-Wahhāb).[218] Nonetheless, for all of his seemingly Taymiyyan trajectory, al-Shawkānī was a conciliatory figure who served willingly under three Zaydī-Shiʿi imams and did not call for a Sunni or Salafi revolt. Hence, he is often seen in contemporary Yemeni society as somebody who brought together the Zaydīs and the Shāfiʿīs (i.e., the Sunnis) in Yemen.[219]

## *2.8 The Ahl-e Ḥadīth Movement of the Indian Subcontinent (1800–1900 CE)*

Shāh Walī Allāh al-Dihlawī sparked a revivalist movement that eventually split, during British colonial rule, into three competing and highly diverse groups: (1) the Barelwī, (2) the Deobandī, and (3) the *Ahl-e Ḥadīth* factions. These three groups continue to dominate Sunni Islam in the Indian subcontinent.[220] Each retains a deep animosity for the others, despite the fact that all three – and especially the latter two – claim Shāh Walī Allāh as a 'progenitor' of sorts.[221]

The Barelwī and Deobandī movements, which comprise the two largest groups in the region, promote a staunch following (*taqlīd*) of the Ḥanafī legal school for both scholars and the laity alike – with rare exceptions.[222] Our concern is with the smallest of these three, the *Ahl-e Ḥadīth* movement. The *Ahl-e Ḥadīth* movement is a continuation of the Kūrānī-Dihlawī tradition mixed with the thought of al-Shawkānī, but only insomuch as Shāh Walī Allāh called for scholars – not laypeople – to seriously engage with the hadith corpus in their legal understanding. The movement eventually eschewed Shāh Walī Allāh's deeply mystical Sufism and his overall endorsement of adhering to the four accepted legal schools. They emphasized a complete rejection of the dominant Ḥanafī school, instead claiming that law should be derived directly from the hadith corpus. Their slogan is 'Qurʾan and rigorously authenticated (*ṣaḥīḥ*) hadith.' The method of their ritual prayer became a hallmark of the movement and a clear and visible sign of them breaking away from the Ḥanafī school; in particular: (1) the raising of the hands while going into bowing and then rising from the posture in the ritual prayer (*rafʿ al-yadayn fī al-ṣalāt*), a practice not done by the Ḥanafīs, (2) the placing of the hands on the chest rather than the Ḥanafī practice of below the navel, and (3) saying the *āmīn* (amen) loudly after the recitation of *Sūra al-Fātiḥa* in every unit (*rakʿa*) of the ritual prayer.[223] Other specific legal practices became, and remain, distinctive to the movement[224] and their theology is sympathetic to many aspects of Wahhabi theology – with indications of potential crossovers.

While its roots can be traced back to the 1820s, making it contemporaneous to the rise of Wahhabism itself, its coherent identity as a group solidified only in the 1860s.[225] Notably, a large portion of the movement's early adherents hailed from the urban upper echelons of northern India, resulting in heightened literacy levels among its followers compared to lower literary norms among other religious groups.[226] The leadership within the United Provinces and Delhi similarly held distinguished social status, often including individuals from the Prophet's family (known as '*sayyid*' in the Indian subcontinent).[227] It made a global impact on the revival of a strand of Salafism and continues to play an important role in that region today.

Research remains to be done regarding the complex set of influences that shaped the current iteration of the movement. However, it is clear that multiple thinkers were involved, all of whom were inspired in part by Ibn Taymiyya via reformist trends in the interlude identified above. There are two important epochs associated with this movement: the original founders of the early-nineteenth century (who first used the term '*Muḥammadī*' to describe their movement) and the next generation who crystalized the modern movement and named it by the appellation *Ahl-e Ḥadīth* before the turn of the twentieth century.

### *2.8.1 Sayyid Aḥmad Shahīd (d. 1831) and Shāh Muḥammad Isma'īl (d. 1831)*

The historical roots of the *Ahl-e Ḥadīth* movement can be traced back to a grandson of Shāh Walī Allāh, Shāh Muḥammad Ismā'īl, and his mentor Sayyid Aḥmad Shahīd (d. 1831) – both of whom died in the Battle of Balakot.[228] Sayyid Aḥmad was born in the town of Raebareli in 1786 and eventually traveled to Lucknow to study with Shāh 'Abd al-'Azīz (d. 1824), the son and spiritual heir of Shāh Walī Allāh, and uncle to Shāh Muhammad Ismā'īl.

Shāh 'Abd al-'Azīz spoke of Sayyid Aḥmad's spiritual brilliance and his ability to ascend the highest spiritual states of the Sufi path,[229] with reports mentioning his numerous visions of the Prophet, 'Alī, and Fāṭima.[230] Around 1811, Sayyid Aḥmad joined the military general Amir Khan (d. 1834) in the region he controlled in central India, who was, it has been argued, 'then the only Muslim independent chief in India who possessed the courage and power to cross arms with the foreigners (namely the British) threatening to become the supreme power in the country.'[231] Eventually, Sayyid Aḥmad left the service of Amir Khan in disappointment and disgust when the latter signed a peace treaty with the British in 1817 – but not after Sayyid Aḥmad tried earnestly to convince him not to become a tributary chief to the British.

Upon returning to Delhi, Shāh 'Abd al-'Azīz directed spiritual aspirants to pledge their allegiance to Sayyid Aḥmad. Many took the spiritual oath at his hands, including his own nephew, Shāh Muḥammad Ismā'īl, and Sayyid

Aḥmad's fame grew substantially. The critical disposition which would be a later hallmark of the *Ahl-e Ḥadīth* is clearly discernible in the character of Sayyid Aḥmad: after pledging his spiritual allegiance to Shāh ʿAbd al-ʿAzīz and progressing along the spiritual path, he questioned Shāh ʿAbd al-ʿAzīz to prove, from the Qurʾan, hadith, or consensus of the scholars (*ijmāʿ*), how it was not idolatry for him to meditate on the image of the spiritual guide (*tasawwur-e-shaykh* or *rabitat-e-shaykh*), in the tradition of the Naqshbandī order. When he later became a spiritual guide in his own right, he reformed the method of instruction and based the invocations on the Qurʾan and Prophetic wordings.

Unsurprisingly, Sayyid Aḥmad came to give the name *Tariqa-e-Muḥammadiya* (*The Muhammadan Spiritual Order*) to his movement in light of its perceived inspiration being solely from the Prophet. Mohiuddin Ahmad thus described this reformed Sufism of Sayyid Aḥmad in the following terms:

> The new mystical order puts moderation and sobriety above spiritual intoxication, social service above solitude and jihad above musical recitations [*samaʿ*] resorted to by the mystics belonging to other schools of mysticism for attaining spiritual trance and ecstasy. The Saiy[y]id's method of spiritual ascent demands abhorrence of every innovation in religion and punctilious devotion to the Law of Islam.[232]

Sayyid Aḥmad then began to undertake missionary tours throughout the region, which entailed – in part – tackling what he held to be un-Islamic beliefs and practices that had crept into Muslim behavior. The goal of the movement was to purify Islam of superstition and innovation. In the same way that he was open to reforming Sufism, he was inclined to be flexible in his application of the law, breaking away from Ḥanafī rulings in a number of key matters – including the issue of the permissibility of combining the prayers for the traveler.

By 1818, Sayyid Aḥmad had come to the conclusion that India was now, in the terms of classical Islamic law, an 'abode of war' (*dar al-ḥarb*). This was an opinion championed also by his teacher Shāh ʿAbd al-ʿAzīz, since the British controlled the majority of India.[233] In 1821, he undertook the arduous journey to Mecca to perform the pilgrimage, and it was here that he was introduced to the descendants of the Kurānī school. His keenness to identify forged hadith manifested in an interest in al-Shawkānī's work on the topic of fabricated hadith (*mawḍūʿāt*). During his visit to Medina in 1822, he refused to participate in a celebration of the Prophet's birthday (*mawlid*) unless he could be presented with valid religious evidence for its permissibility.[234]

In light of the precarious political situation faced by Muslim rulers in India, coupled with Sayyid Aḥmad's love for military activity, it was not surprising that in 1822, at the historic site of al-Hudaybiyya in the Hijaz, Sayyid Aḥmad made his spiritual aspirants take a pledge to perform jihad against the British upon their return to India. It was around this time as well that Shāh Muḥammad Ismāʿīl wrote a theological treatise in Arabic called *Radd al-ishrāk* (*The Refutation of Idolatry*),[235] which became the basis of a primary text of the movement and shares remarkable similarities to the Wahhabi theological primer *Kitāb at-tawḥīd* by Ibn ʿAbd al-Wahhāb.

In 1829, Sayyid Aḥmad planned to establish his own Islamic polity, basing himself at the Afghan frontier and leading an attack against the Sikh state of Ranjit Singh (d. 1839), who was reported to be committing atrocities against the Muslim population of the Punjab. But the movement was defeated by Singh's powerful army at the base of the Himalayan mountains,[236] with both Sayyid Aḥmad and Shāh Muḥammad Ismāʿīl being killed by the Sikh army in the Battle of Balakot.[237]

Sayyid Aḥmad's achievements would be lauded by twentieth century Islamic revivalists. Among them, Sayyid Abu al-A'la Mawdudi (d. 1979) said, 'History bears evidence that the soil of the sub-continent had neither witnessed the real Islamic jihad before them nor has ever seen such a phenomenon after them.'[238]

After the defeat of the Battle of Balakot, the remnants of this movement found themselves constantly in trouble with the British administration in India, who identified them as subversives and rebels. They labeled them 'Indian Wahhabis' due to their similarities to Wahhabi pirates threatening British interests in the Persian Gulf.[239] The British subjected the followers of *Tariqa-e-Muḥammadiya* to 'Wahhabi' trials between 1868 and 1871 in a crackdown on suspected rebels following the 1857 Mutiny.[240] Eventually, in 1883, the movement was militarily suppressed by British forces. Seeing this vicious crackdown, another movement with a similar shared heritage took lessons, and this new movement, which called itself the *Ahl-e Ḥadīth*, decided from its inception to be apolitical and declared loyalty to the British rulers, which resulted in the British softening their approach and dropping the harassment of them.[241] This new movement was sparked primarily by two intellectuals, to whom we shall now turn our attention.

### *2.8.2 Sayyid Nadhīr Ḥusayn (d. 1902) and Ṣiddīq Ḥasan Khān (d. 1890)*

While the origins of the *Ahl-e Ḥadīth* movement go back to Sayyid Aḥmad Shahīd, the actual birth of the modern intellectual movement and the creation of the appellation *Ahl-e Ḥadīth* goes back to Sayyid Nadhīr Ḥusayn (d. 1902).[242]

He was born in 1805 into a wealthy Shiʿi family descended from the Prophet in the city of Monghyr, whose near ancestors had been *qadī*s (judges) under the Mughals but had since fallen into penury.[243] He abandoned

Shiʿism in his youth and devoted his life to studying and teaching Sunni Islam. Sayyid Nadhīr studied under Shāh ʿAbd al-ʿAzīz's grandson Shāh Muḥammad Isḥāq (d. 1846).[244] He considered himself an heir to the Dihlawī tradition and began his career as a notable Ḥanafī scholar. Soon after his teacher migrated to the Hijaz, Sayyid Nadhīr abandoned his former *madhhab* and dedicated the rest of his life to preaching the Qurʾan, Sunna, and *ijtihād*.[245] Indeed, one learns of his gradualism in this regard if one believes the claim of the modernist Sayyid Aḥmad Khān (d. 1898) that it was he who convinced Sayyid Nadhīr to publicly perform the raising of the hands in the ritual prayer (*rafʿ al-yadayn*), after Nadhīr had believed in the practice but had not acted upon it.[246]

Although Sayyid Nadhīr was imprisoned by the British during the period when they were prosecuting the remnants of Sayyid Aḥmad's *Tariqa-e-Muḥammadiya* movement between 1864 and 1871, he was later acquitted of any ties with the militants. He further promoted the idea that India, under British rule, was still an Islamic land and argued that jihad against the British was religiously forbidden. Not only that, he claimed that Muslims were obligated to obey and accept them as their political leaders.[247] Due to his role in founding the movement and shifting its focus away from militancy toward reform, he is considered by some as arguably the most important propagator of the *Ahl-e Ḥadīth* movement, having personally instructed a host of next generation scholars.[248] It was this vision of his that ensured the *Ahl-e Ḥadīth* movement would never be a militant anti-British one but rather an apolitical, loyalist one.

Sayyid Nadhīr spent most of his life – over six decades – as a teacher of hadith studies in Delhi, and it was here that scores of scholars from across the country, and even other parts of the world, including Yemen and Central Arabia, obtained *ijāza* (license to teach) in the works of hadith.[249] He was also the primary teacher of many Deobandī and modernist icons as well. Hence, he was given the title '*Shaykh al-kull fī al-kull*' (The Shaykh of everyone in everything). To this day, a significant amount of *ijāzas* in books of hadith throughout the Muslim world go through him.

If Sayyid Nadhīr lived a somewhat professorial life, away from the limelight of politics and public office, the same cannot be said of the second individual who is associated with the emergence of the *Ahl-e Ḥadīth*, Ṣiddīq Ḥasan Khān (d. 1890). Also claiming descent from the Prophet, he grew up in an impoverished yet scholarly family. They were from a Shiʿi background and had been in the service of the nawabs of Oudh.[250] However, his father, Sayyid Awlād Ḥasan (d. 1837), had converted to Sunni Islam before his birth. The poverty that the family faced was on account of his father refusing to take his inheritance from the lands of Hyderabad owned by his Shiʿi family.[251]

Ṣiddīq Ḥasan's father was a disciple of Shāh ʿAbd al-ʿAzīz and studied under a student of the sons of Shāh Walī Allah.[252] Sayyid Awlād Ḥasan followed Sayyid Ahmad to the northwest frontier for his jihad campaign,[253] and was sent by Sayyid Aḥmad as his missionary representative to Oudh.[254] While in his later life, Sayyid Aḥmad countered accusations of religious deviation for not following the Ḥanafī legal school in the same way as his forebears,[255] it became evident that the movement would embrace the current of legal studies centered around hadith. For instance, Ṣiddīq Ḥasan grew up in the ambit of Sayyid Aḥmad's movement, with familial links to the leaders. Under the guidance of Wilayat ʿAlī (d. 1852),[256] one of Sayyid Aḥmad's successors, he embarked on a study of Ibn Ḥajar's *Bulūgh al-Maram*.[257] Within his father's revivalist circles, Siddiq Ḥasan received a thorough Islamic education, studying in Farrukhabad, Kanpur, and Delhi.[258]

Ṣiddīq Ḥasan, like Sayyid Aḥmad, was born in Raebareli, but he would find his fortune after moving to Bhopal. At first, he worked as a bodyguard for the prime minister of the state. After taking up employment for eight months with the Nawab of Tonk and living with the family of Sayyid Aḥmad, he returned to work for the prime minister of Bhopal. He soon became a scholar of the Nawab's court. However, the transformation of his social status in Bhopal was not due to his scholarly pursuits but rather through his marriages. His first wife was the daughter of the prime minister, who was eleven years his senior. He then married the monarch Shāh Jahān Begum (d. 1901), the Sultana (Queen) of the princely state of Bhopal, in 1871.[259]

This marriage was highly controversial and aroused the suspicions of the British. They suspected Ṣiddīq Ḥasan of being a Wahhabi and, hence, a rebel at heart, while the monarch was a British loyalist. In his defense, he wrote a book entitled *Tarjumān-e-Wahhābīyya* (*A History of Wahhabism*),[260] in which he attempted to prove that he was not a Wahhabi[261] and that the *Ahl-e Ḥadīth* movement were loyal subjects of British rule in India. He explained how the movement views the British as the established political power of the land and that Bhopal had supported Britain's war in Egypt.[262] Yet, the Queen's adoption of veiling, and corresponding primarily through her husband, caused heightened tension between her family and Ṣiddīq Ḥasan's family, due to their clash of cultures and different socio-economic backgrounds. In 1881, the British intervened and launched an investigation into Ṣiddīq Ḥasan and the risk he posed due to his religious conservatism. In 1885, the British formally stripped him of his official titles and reduced Shāh Jahān Begum to the role of a titular sovereign under the control of one of their ministers.[263]

Early in Ṣiddīq Ḥasan's career, he was influenced by the Yemeni reformer al-Shawkānī.[264] During a trip to Mecca for the pilgrimage, he also came across additional works of Ibn Taymiyya, which further influenced his way of thinking.[265] He is credited with producing, with the help of scholars employed in his royal court, a large number of works throughout his life. These works were composed in Arabic, Urdu, and Persian languages, with estimates indicating no less than eighty-four works in Urdu, fifty-four in Arabic, and forty-three in Persian.[266] In these works, he drew upon reformist arguments and summaries from the vast collection of manuscripts he possessed. At times, he reproduced al-Shawkānī's works, adding little to no additions while claiming them as his own. It should be noted that he refrained from publishing complete versions of classical works, leaving this task to be undertaken by succeeding generations of scholars who played a pivotal role in advancing Salafism in the modern era. The most prominent among them was Maḥmūd Shukrī al-Ālūsī (d. 1924), who worked closely with Jamāl al-Dīn al-Qāsimī (d. 1914) in this regard – both of whom will be discussed later in this chapter.[267]

Through his literary efforts, extensive network, access to wealth, free press, and prestigious status in Bhopal, Ṣiddīq Ḥasan was able to exert his influence over the Arab scholarly world. He achieved this by disseminating his works not only within India but also in prominent urban centers such as Istanbul and Cairo. Moreover, he came to establish powerful links for the distribution of his books in the Hijaz, through the Ottoman provinces and North Africa.[268] His endeavors, however, were not without contention, as they provoked sharp criticism from Ḥanafī scholars such as ʿAbd al-Ḥayy al-Laknawī (d. 1886), and he and his associates responded to such accusations with vigor and equal harshness.[269]

Ṣiddīq Ḥasan's marriage to the monarch of Bhopal resulted in the migration of several *Ahl-e Ḥadīth* scholars to the city who, having faced oppression in other locales, sought refuge and gained government positions in their newly adopted residence. A notable example was Salamatullah Jairajpuri (d. 1955), a leading student of Sayyid Nadhīr, who moved to Bhopal from north India and obtained employment as the director of the large city mosque and the Islamic seminaries in the city.[270] Ṣiddīq Ḥasan's international travels and links also led to non-Indian scholars coming to Bhopal, most notably from Yemen, including Ḥusayn b. Miḥsan al-Anṣārī (d. 1909), who was made the *qāḍī* of Bhopal when he came to the city.[271]

Another interesting facet of the history of this movement is the direct ties it had with Saudi Wahhabi clerics. One of the great-grandsons of Ibn ʿAbd al-Wahhāb himself, Iṣḥāq b. ʿAbd al-Rahmān Āl al-Shaykh (d. 1901), studied under Sayyid Nadīr and Ṣiddīq Ḥasan. Another prominent Wahhabi cleric of the time, Hamad b. ʿAtīq (d. 1884) wrote a laudatory letter to Ṣiddīq Ḥasan, praising some of the latter's works that he had read and offering constructive criticism. He even asked him to write a commentary on Ibn Qayyim's famous theological poem *Qasīda al-Nūniyya* (*An Ode Ending with the Letter Nūn*),[272] and eventually sent his own son, Saʿd b. Ḥamad (d. 1930), to study under both Sayyid Nadhīr Ḥusayn and Ṣiddīq Ḥasan in India.[273] Saʿd would become one of the senior Wahhabi clerics of the early twentieth century. More than twenty famous Wahhabi clerics studied with and, in turn, influenced *Ahl-e Ḥadīth* scholars and students of Sayyid Nadhīr.[274]

Ṣiddīq Ḥasan died in 1890 from hepatitis. Publicly, he played a pivotal role in distancing the *Ahl-e Ḥadīth* from their Arabian counterparts, as did Muḥammad Ḥusayn Batalwī (d. 1920), the editor of a popular *Ahl-e Ḥadīth* magazine. Both published treatises on India as an Islamic state under British rule and advocated for peaceful reform.[275] Privately, *Ahl-e Ḥadīth* leaders like Ṣiddīq Ḥasan, Batalwī (d. 1920), and Thanāʾ Allāh Amritsarī (d. 1948) entertained Wahhabi clerics and celebrated Āl Saud's victories in Arabia. A student of Sayyid Nadhīr translated Ibn ʿAbd al-Wahhāb's *Kitāb al-tawḥīd* as early as 1872, while the sons of another student started to print the works of Ibn ʿAbd al-Wahhāb alongside those of Ibn Taymiyya. Yet another student, Bashīr Aḥmad Sahsawānī (d. 1908), published a Wahhabi defense in 1908 while stationed in Bhopal – one of eleven written by *Ahl-e Ḥadīth* scholars at the time. Evidently, by this juncture, Arabian Wahhabis were also coming to India to pursue studies with the *Ahl-e Ḥadīth* community, marking a noteworthy exchange and collaboration between these two strands.[276]

Nonetheless, as British anti-Ottomanism became more strident, the loyalty of the *Ahl-e Ḥadīth* toward the British was tested. This was particularly evident in the activities of the Amritsārī, who had been a loyal pro-British subject before World War I. Thereafter, Amritsārī changed direction, in the face of open British hostility toward the Ottomans. He joined the *Khilafat* movement[277] with fellow *Ahl-e Ḥadīth*, Deobandīs, and other factions in campaigning to protect the Ottoman Caliphate.

Furthermore, the influence of late-traditionalist Sunni elements from the movement's origins persisted during its early years. Sayyid Nadhīr still took an oath of spiritual allegiance from his followers, affirmed the sainthood of Ibn ʿArabī, and did not endorse the literal acceptance of the scriptural references to God's attributes. Ṣiddīq Ḥasan considered himself a Naqshbandī Sufi despite his criticism of extreme Sufi culture – which included his scrutiny of the relationship between spiritual guides and their followers. According to Ṣiddīq Ḥasan, Sufism was an individual's vocation.[278]

Amritsārī also encountered opposition from his own followers within the *Ahl-e Ḥadīth* movement due to his approach to interpreting the Qurʾan. The contention arose from his application of figurative interpretations to verses referencing anthropomorphic divine attributes. Here, Amritsārī drew heavily from the works of Ashʿarī scholars like al-Ghazālī and al-Rāzī instead of submitting to Ibn Taymiyya and his supposed proto-Salafi literalism. When Amritsārī requested the guidance of the renowned reformer, Rashīd Riḍā (d. 1935) on the matter, the latter endorsed his use of figurative interpretations and pointed out prominent figures favored by Salafis, such as al-Shawkānī and Shāh Walī Allāh, had likewise employed figurative understandings in these contexts. In 1926, Amritsārī proceeded to attend the Islamic World Conference in Mecca as a representative of the *Ahl-e Ḥadīth*, accompanied by fellow members of his strand. This led to a rival faction of the *Ahl-e Ḥadīth* sending a delegation to the conference in order to alert the Āl Saud and their scholars to his interpretations. In response, the Saudi king refrained from taking sides and instead urged both factions to seek reconciliation. Amritsārī recanted his previous views at odds with the *Ahl-e Ḥadīth* and Wahhabis; such was the relationship between the two movements by that time that its scholars were expected to toe a single line on matters related to theology (in *fiqh*, however, the Wahhabis remained Ḥanbalīs).[279]

It is possible that the process of being theologically and spiritually '*taymiyyanized*' took some time for the movement. In this respect, it is not far-fetched to contend that Ṣiddīq Ḥasan's propagation and patronage of Ibn Taymiyya's works eased the wholesale acceptance of recognizably Salafi literalism in the realm of theology and spirituality. This influence might have further extended to the eventual disavowal of maintaining the Sufi orders, even under a reformed framework; following the deaths of both Sayyid Nadhīr Ḥusayn and Ṣiddīq Ḥasan, the *Ahl-e Ḥadīth* evidently distanced themselves from past iterations which favored Sufi saints and practices.[280] Consequently, members of the movement have increasingly adopted the term 'Salafi' to describe their movement.

Although the *Ahl-e Ḥadīth* strived to be puritanical Sunnis, their iconoclastic approach to the prevalent Sunni intellectual tradition had some unforeseen and unintended consequences, with critics of the movement claiming that their spirit of reform and desire to instigate a counterculture to the normative tradition paved the way for heterodoxy.[281]

The *Ahl-e Ḥadīth* movement is still active in India, Pakistan, and parts of Bangladesh today, and though the movement has grown steadily across the Indian subcontinent, it remains a minority among the Muslims in that region. Nonetheless, their international importance to the global Salafi movement is often neglected in much of the modern literature. Members of the movement have played a pivotal role in the formation of several Islamic universities in Saudi Arabia, and a number of its leaders graduated from Medina and Mecca, respectively. Moreover, diasporic communities, particularly in post-war Britain, have been instrumental in propagating Salafism in the English language.[282]

## *2.9 Salafism in the Arab Lands (1900 CE)*

In the late nineteenth and early twentieth century, during the final stages of the Ottoman era, various thinkers emerged across the Arab world who were influenced, in varying degrees, by the intellectual legacy of Ibn Taymiyya. Some of these figures were primarily interested in reviving what they viewed as a stagnated Ottoman Islam that was impeding progress in the Muslim world. Others felt that the ideas of this movement could play a role as part of a broader attempt of the Arabs to break away from Ottoman rule. The most significant among these figures – so much so that he typically eclipses all of the other names mentioned – is Rashīd Riḍā. It, therefore, becomes imperative to delve more deeply into his intellectual contributions and commence with an in-depth exploration of Salafism in Egypt. This focus, however, should not lead to the oversight of the significant contributions made by numerous other pivotal thinkers within this context.

### *2.9.1 Salafism in Egypt*

Several organizations and figures played an important role in the development of Salafi ideas throughout Egypt during the nineteenth and twentieth centuries. These included Muḥammad ʿAbduh (d. 1905), Rashīd Riḍā, and Muḥammad Ḥāmid al-Fiqī (d. 1959).

#### *The ʿAbduh ʿEnlightenment' project*

The 'Enlightenment' project is the name given to the movement associated with the famous triumvirate scholars who flourished at the end of the nineteenth century, culminating with Rashīd Riḍā. To understand the phenomenon of Riḍā, we need to first summarize his teacher and mentor, Muḥammad ʿAbduh, and ʿAbduh's own teacher and mentor, Jamāl al-Dīn al-Afghānī (d. 1897).

Jamāl al-Dīn al-Afghānī was an influential Muslim scholar of the eighteenth century, credited as one of the founders of Islamic modernism. His birthplace is disputed;[283] although he claimed to have been born in Afghanistan – hence his title al-Afghānī – later evidence seems to indicate that he was from Iran, having been born into a Shiʿi family and trained in Shiʿi seminaries.[284]

Al-Afghānī lived during a time of political turmoil. Colonialism was in full swing, and various Muslim lands were slowly falling to European powers. He is credited for his vision of a pan-Islamic unity to act as a bulwark against the colonizers, and to this end, he traveled across the Muslim world and involved himself in political intrigues in almost every land he visited. Despite gaining some level of popularity during his lifetime, al-Afghānī was unable to change the minds of the majority of Muslims. He cannot be considered a 'Salafi' in any sense of the term, nor did he ever refer to himself that way. He was not interested in theology in the slightest and rarely spoke of legal rulings or any of the standard classical aspects of Islamic thought. Rather, he created an Islamic discourse related to political engagement and anti-colonialist thought that would spark many thinkers and movements after him. He lived the last few years of his life in Istanbul, possibly under house arrest for promoting ideas that clashed with those of the Ottoman government.[285] He passed away from throat cancer in 1897,[286] leaving behind a contested legacy and one particularly active student who would develop his ideas in a different manner. That student was Muḥammad ʿAbduh.

Born in Egypt to a Turkish father and an Egyptian mother, ʿAbduh emerged as a pivotal figure in the landscape of Islamic thought. A protégé of al-Afghānī, his mentor wielded significant influence in shaping ʿAbduh's intellectual orientation. Nonetheless, it is ʿAbduh who is often credited as being the true founder of Islamic modernism. He graduated from the prestigious al-Azhar University in 1877 and began working as a teacher there. ʿAbduh was heavily involved in political and educational reform during his lifetime. His involvement extended to anti-British propaganda as he, alongside al-Afghānī, co-founded the newspaper *al-ʿUrwa al-wuthqā* (*The Firm Bond*) in Paris. Yet, the most important position he gained was that of Grand Mufti of Egypt in 1899. He held this position until his death six years later, and it was from here that he was able to produce many fatwas that clashed with the views of the traditional *ʿulamāʾ* of Egypt. Unlike al-Afghānī, ʿAbduh *was* interested in the details of Islamic theology and law and was eager to propose new interpretations and ideas regarding Islamic doctrine and *fiqh* that he felt were more in line with modernity.

ʿAbduh wrote an exegesis (*tafsīr*) of the Qurʾan which focused on reinterpreting it in light of modern science and rationale. His approach was very controversial, leading many traditional scholars to derogatorily label him a neo-Muʿtazilī. ʿAbduh was critical of the Muslim world, particularly of the scholars, and is quoted as saying, 'I went to the West and saw Islam, but no Muslims; I got back to the East and saw Muslims, but not Islam.'[287] This statement encapsulates ʿAbduh's view on his relationship with the Muslim community. He saw them as not reflecting Islam properly in their practice and understanding. To counter this, he disassociated himself from all labels besides Islam. ʿAbduh claimed to be calling people back to the way of the *salaf*, i.e., to abandon *taqlīd* and reopen the doors of *ijtihad* – so that *fiqh* could be reinterpreted for the modern world. He could be extremely critical of the Islamic intellectual tradition, as seen in his dismissal of Islamic theological studies after al-Ghazālī until the modern period as being banal and poor.[288] Yet his criticism also led to some positive outcomes. For instance, his bemoaning the loss of so many classical works led to him initiating the discovery of manuscripts of such neglected classics as the Qurʾanic exegesis of al-Ṭabarī[289] and having them edited and published. This zeal on his part significantly bolstered the modern print culture which has given new impetus to the study of classical Islamic literature. While he was the Grand Mufti, he sought to obtain manuscripts and books from other lands, often through his personal efforts of convincing collectors to donate from their collections, and in the process, enlarged the library of Al-Azhar University. His revival of book culture coincided with his efforts to revive the Arabic language in Al-Azhar and the general society.[290] Nonetheless, ʿAbduh's ideas on the religious sciences were rejected by the majority of observant Muslims, for they were often too *modernist* and seemingly at odds with mainstream intellectual traditionalism. However, he continued to preach to them in his books, lectures, and writings until his death in Alexandria on 11 July 1905.

There are conflicting reports on whether ʿAbduh coined the term 'Salafi' or whether this was done by his student Riḍā. Evidence suggests that while ʿAbduh did call for returning to a revival (*tajdīd*) as existed in earlier times, it was Riḍā who first popularized the term 'Salafi' as an identity.[291] Although ʿAbduh did promote the idea of following the *way of the salaf*, this phrase did not mean to him what it means to the Salafi movement of today. For him, this simply meant abandoning the blind following (*taqlīd*) of legal schools, reopening the doors of *ijtihād*, and reinterpreting the religion for modern times. Hence, in contrast to the Salafi movement, for ʿAbduh, the *way of the salaf* was neither a call to focus on theology nor an emphasis on the ritualistic practices and lifestyle of the early Muslims. In fact, ʿAbduh praised Ibn Taymiyya and described him as:

> *Shaykh al-Islam*, the great reviver…who's like has not been seen in the mastery of both tradition and rational sciences and in the power of argument! Egypt and India have revived his books and the books of his student Ibn Qayyim after a time when they were only available in the Najd. Now, they have spread to both the East and the West and will become the main support of the Muslims of the world.[292]

Still, Ibn Taymiyya is rarely quoted in his writings, and there is little to indicate that ʿAbduh was inspired by him directly. ʿAbduh's ideas are in such direct conflict with modern Salafism that Salafi groups today have no relationship with his writings and consider him a 'misguided modernist.' The same, however, cannot be said of his protégé, to whom we shall now turn our attention.

*Rashīd Riḍā (d. 1935)*

Muḥammad Rashīd Riḍā's profound impact has engendered extensive academic focus on his life, thought, contributions, and development.[293] Born in Ottoman Syria, he lived through the end of the Ottoman caliphate and was a leading thinker whose ideas shaped various movements of the twentieth century. He was, at one point in his youth, a member of the Naqshbandī Sufi order and seemed to maintain a favorable opinion of 'true' Sufism, but he would warn against excesses in attributing miracles (*karāmāt*) to Sufi saints.[294] Although his initial training was in traditional Islamic studies, he later adopted more political and reformist ideas. It began when he was exposed to *al-ʿUrwa al-wuthqā* – the publication by al-Afghānī and ʿAbduh – that inspired him to leave his home in Tripoli for Egypt in 1897 and collaborate with ʿAbduh. In Cairo, Riḍā teamed up with ʿAbduh to launch another weekly journal called *al-Manār* (*The Lighthouse*).[295] This journal was the first of its kind and influenced many hundreds of thinkers around the globe on a variety of modern topics and Qurʾanic commentary. Riḍā continued as the editor of the journal until his death in 1935.[296]

Although ʿAbduh heavily influenced his initial writings, Riḍā drifted away from ʿAbduh's ideas after the downfall of the caliphate. This change was reflected in Riḍā's adoption of a more politicized understanding of Islam and a focus on the revival of an Islamic state – although there is dispute about the specifics of his suggestions in this regard.[297] This may be because Riḍā lived in a different time from his teacher. While ʿAbduh witnessed the colonization of Egypt and other lands, the caliphate still existed during his lifetime. Riḍā, on the other hand, witnessed the collapse of the Ottoman Empire, the abolishment of the caliphate, and the post-World War I division of the Arab lands. So, it is not surprising that a scholar like Riḍā, whose life was dedicated to reviving Islam, would shift his interests.

Yet his presence in Egypt exerted a more direct influence than merely the impact of his *al-Manār* in the emergence of what we now see as puritan Salafism. In the last twenty years of his life, he became increasingly conservative, which coincided with his desire to see a developed Islamic polity. He searched among the present options, and from the mid-1920s, he became increasingly supportive of the Wahhabis (a period before Saudi Arabia exploited oil from the 1930s) by editing and publishing works, both modern and pre-modern, in support of them. Riḍā saw genuine virtue in the reign of ʿAbd al-ʿAzīz b. ʿAbd al-Raḥman al-Saʿūd, commonly known as Ibn Saud (d. 1953) – the founder of the third Saudi state. But he also sought to reform the Wahhabi scholars. Hence, he supported some of his students – such as ʿAbd al-Ẓāhir Abū al-Samḥ (d. 1951) and Muḥammad ʿAbd al-Razzāq Ḥamza (d. 1972) – to go to Mecca and Medina as scholars and advisors. This was done to exert an influence, with the patronage of the king, and not merely to imitate the Wahhabis.[298]

Indeed, Riḍā viewed the Saudi Wahhabis as being closer to the truth than normative-traditional understandings of Islam. He was sympathetic toward their cause, influencing his conceptualization of Salafism. Riḍā had celebrated Ibn Saud's victory over their rivals the Rashidīs, who were allied with the Ottomans, in 1904. Post-World War I, he began to actively promote the Wahhabi understanding of Islam. He claimed that Ibn ʿAbd al-Wahhāb was a reviver of Islam, and that the latter had renewed Islam in the Najd region. Riḍā was pleased when the Saudis conquered Mecca and considered it the beginning of the renewal of Islam in the region.[299]

The most important aspect of Riḍā's teachings is his active use of the term 'Salafi' to self-identify his movement and thought – making him perhaps the first prominent modern Muslim to do so.[300] Between his rejection of the traditional legal schools, his praise for the Saudi-Wahhabi regime, and his call for *ijtihād*, it is easy to understand why some people assume he was Salafi in the sense of the modern movement of the same name. However, in many ways, Riḍā's understanding of Salafism was different from that of the current movement. In fact, the modern Salafi movement today has an ambiguous relationship with him. While some embrace him as a positive reformer with perhaps some mistaken ideas, others view him as being too influenced by modernist thought and hence, not a positive role model. To understand this, we need to look deeper at his ideas and what the term 'Salafi' meant to him.

When Riḍā referred to himself as a Salafi, he applied this concept primarily to legal and methodological matters. Riḍā did not seem to concern himself as much with theological issues and did not subscribe entirely to the modern Salafi understanding of theology. In fact, several of Riḍā's early viewpoints directly contradict modern Salafi doctrines, like his reinterpretation of *jinn* as a reference to microbes and his support for Darwin's theory of evolution. He also denied aspects that he considered not affirmed explicitly in the sacred text – such as the existence of a messianic '*al-Mahdī*' reviver that is mentioned in the hadith corpus, the return of Jesus toward the end of times, and the miraculous occurrence of the splitting of the moon.[301] All these beliefs of his would not only receive rebuke in Salafi circles today but would be considered outright heretical.

Riḍā's focus was primarily on reforming Islamic law in order to make it more suitable to the modern world. In doing so, he called for the abandonment of *taqlīd* in favor of direct engagement with the texts of the Qurʾan and hadith. In this sense, there is an element that overlaps with contemporary Salafism. A significant number of Salafis today agree with the rejection of *taqlīd*, and they, too, call for following the Qurʾan and hadith. However, the major difference is that they call for following the Qurʾan and hadith as understood by the early generations, while Riḍā wanted to directly (re-)interpret the sacred text the way the earlier generations did, but for modern times. A clear example of this is the case of usury (*ribā*). Salafis, like other traditionalist authorities of Islamic law, consider usury to be prohibited and a major sin – as clearly stated in the Qurʾan and hadith. Nonetheless, Riḍā argued that usury could be permitted in modern times due to necessity (*ḍarūra*). Riḍā also encouraged women's education and was considered an iconic figure in his time for rethinking traditional attitudes about the role of women – a stance that the modern Salafi movement continues to find problematic.[302]

Whatever the nature of his project, Riḍā was clearly breaking away from his two predecessors: al-Afghānī and ʿAbduh. These two mentors of his were concerned with modernizing Islam to reconcile it with the *zeitgeist*. ʿAbduh, in particular, wished to do away with the rigidity of the schools of law. He believed that doing so would give him and fellow thinkers the freedom needed to become compatible with modernity. In all this, one can clearly see strong European influences on his approach to the religious texts and earlier religious sentiments.

Riḍā, on the other hand, was clearly more conservative than ʿAbduh. He was a vocal fan of Ibn Taymiyya and saw the rise of the Wahhabi-Saudi state as a positive sign. He used his journal, *al-Manār*, to extol the virtues of Ibn ʿAbd al-Wahhāb and the new King of Arabia – considering Wahhabism to be a revivalist movement that should be supported. During the course of his tenure, his journal printed more than two dozen Wahhabi treatises. Yet, while he appreciated aspects of Wahhabi theology, he most certainly did not take their approach in *takfir* (excommunication), *al-walāʾ wa-l-barāʾ* (association and disassociation), or in most areas of Islamic law. In one instance, he removed – without referencing this fact – a statement in a Wahhabi treatise that excommunicated the rest of the Muslim world.[303] This made Riḍā a target of criticism by the senior Wahhabi clerics of his time, who referred to him as 'a person of innovation and misguidance.'[304]

Ultimately, Riḍā was a complex persona whose ideas evolved over time, just like his teachers and students. Early in his career, he was clearly more liberal in his thinking, but his later works seem to indicate a growing sympathy towards Wahhabism and Taymiyyan theology. He may not have foreseen how Wahhabism and his own movement would merge into a new form of Salafism. Nonetheless, he and many of his students played a vital role in this process. Yet, Riḍā's role and status in the history of Salafism remains complicated and is, in many ways, ambiguous. Salafis are themselves divided in their assessment of whether to classify Riḍā within their ranks or not. Some contend that he was a modernist, while others assert he was a 'true' Salafi follower of Ibn Taymiyya.[305]

Despite this controversy over his status, he plays a crucial role in the history of Salafism for four reasons. Firstly, he is the one who popularized the term 'Salafism' and its usage, especially through the wide reach of *al-Manār*, influencing many revivalist thinkers (perhaps the most famous for our purposes would be al-Albānī, whom we will discuss later in this chapter). Secondly, his writings contributed toward a growing global acceptance of Wahhabi doctrine and ideas – especially since Riḍā did much to print their works and praise the efforts of the Kingdom. Thirdly, he contributed toward reopening the doors of *ijtihād*, a central concept in Salafism today, and helped spark many non-traditionalist thinkers. Fourthly, his political activism was the direct precursor to the Muslim Brotherhood, and he directly inspired its founder, Ḥasan al-Bannā (d. 1949). This organization would intersect with, influence, and be influenced by Salafism in many ways over the next century.[306]

*Muḥammad Ḥāmid al-Fiqī (d. 1959)*

Muḥammad Ḥāmid al-Fiqī was a graduate of Al-Azhar University and stands out as one of Egypt's foremost scholars who adhered to the teachings of Ibn Taymiyya. His significant role in the resurgence of Salafism in Egypt positions him as a pivotal figure in this revival. His father was a colleague of ʿAbduh at al-Azhar, and having been blessed with four sons, he decided to train each of them in one of the four Islamic schools of law. This was how al-Fiqī was assigned the Ḥanbalī tradition, and it appears this is how he was introduced to the thought of Ibn Taymiyya and his student Ibn Qayyim.[307]

Al-Fiqī was also a student of Riḍā's and associated with the circles of Syrian Salafi Muḥibb al-Dīn al-Khaṭīb (d. 1969).[308] Despite this, it seems that he was not satisfied with their seemingly tame adoption of Taymiyyan views. Out of all the Egyptian figures of this era, there is no question that al-Fiqī was a through-and-through Taymiyyan, adopting and defending strict Ḥanbalī theology and becoming the most vocal critic of Ashʿarism in his era.

In 1926, he founded the first, and what would eventually become the largest, Salafi organization in Egypt, the Jamāʿat Anṣār al-Sunna al-Muḥammadiyya (The Group of Helpers of the Prophetic Sunna).[309] While the ethos of the movement was essentially quietist and focused on propagating Salafi dogma, there were reports that some of their preachers would teach from the books of the Islamist Sayyid Qutb (d. 1966), at least as late as the 1970s.[310] In addition to concentrating on establishing mosques throughout Egypt, which often came to focus on social services,[311] the Ansār al-Sunna edited and published books that were foundational for constructing or re-enforcing the Salafi worldview. Through this activity, it became the leading Salafi organization in Egypt, to such an extent that it received quasi-official status from the Saudi ruling family, especially after al-Fiqī – often with the help of Muḥammad ʿAbd al-Razzāq Ḥamza – edited and published works on behalf of the Saudis. When the Saudi Prince Nayef (d. 2012) visited the organization in Cairo in 1954, he said, 'If [the Saudi diplomat] ʿAbdallah Al Ibrahim al-Fadl is our political ambassador in Cairo, [then] you are our religious ambassadors everywhere.'[312]

This organization influenced an entire generation of Salafi Egyptian scholars, many of whom eventually moved to Saudi Arabia as teachers or imams. It was his group that cooperated with *al-Maṭbaʿa al-Salafiyya* (*The Salafi Press*), the first Salafi publishing house of its kind in Egypt, and printed its own writings and editions of classical works of theology from the Ḥanbalī school such as Muḥammad b. al-Mawṣilī's (d. 774/ 1372)

*Mukhtaṣar al- ṣawāʿiq al-mursala ʿalā al-Jahmiyya wa-l-muʿaṭṭila* (*A Summary of the Blazing Meteorites Sent Against the Jahmī Negators*)[313] in 1929 and ʿUthmān b. Saʿīd al-Dārimī's refutation of Bishr al-Marīsī in 1939. Yet al-Fiqī's contempt for following the popular schools of law even made him critical of the Wahhabis – which was a foreshadowing of al-Albānī's demeaning analysis of Ibn ʿAbd al-Wahhāb's standing in relation to adhering to a legal school[314] – speaking of them as 'fanatically loyal' (*mutʿaṣṣibūn*) to the Ḥanbalī legal school.[315]

A further work that al-Fiqī arranged to be published, in a highly antagonistic Salafi move, was the single volume containing al-Khaṭīb al-Baghdādī's critical biography of Abū Ḥanīfa, extracted from the latter's vast *Tārīkh Baghdād* (*History of Baghdad*).[316] Not only did al-Fiqī arrange this Arabic printing, but he also sent a copy to the Indian subcontinent, a Ḥanafī heartland, where it was swiftly translated into Urdu and published. This early effort presaged a common Salafi trait of the twentieth century – attacking Abū Ḥanīfa – which has brought the ire of Ḥanafīs since the time of Muhammad Zahit Kevseri (Ar. Muhammad Zahid al-Kawthari, d. 1952).[317]

Al-Fiqī moved to Saudi Arabia for a few years and established a very cordial relationship with its first king, Ibn Saud. In Saudi, he founded a magazine, took charge of a seminary in the holy city of Mecca, and – at the request of the king – brought in key Egyptian Salafi scholars. These scholars played a vital role in educating a new generation of Saudi scholars.[318] Notably, al-Fiqī played a seminal role in broadening the horizons of the Wahhabi clerics of Saudi Arabia, a group traditionally wary of any and all technological innovations.[319] He passed away in the first days of 1959 after a botched operation in Egypt.

### *2.9.2 Salafism in Ottoman Damascus*

In Damascus, a number of key figures played an important role in reviving the teachings of Ibn Taymiyya. For our purposes, we shall mention three seminal personalities: (1) ʿAbd al-Razzāq al-Bīṭār (d. 1917), (2) Jamāl al-Dīn al-Qāsimī,[320] and (3) Muḥibb al-Dīn al-Khaṭīb.

#### *ʿAbd al-Razzāq al-Bīṭār (d. 1917)*

ʿAbd al-Razzāq al-Bīṭār, who was a late Ottoman reformist Sunni scholar, is generally regarded as one of the main icons of the Taymiyyan revival in Damascus. In fact, no less a figure than Riḍā referred to him as 'the reviver of the Salafi school in Damascus.'[321] Al-Bīṭār was born into a scholarly family and began studying Islam at a young age. Due to his early studies, he began preaching and teaching in his youth.

Although he spent most of his life as a traditional scholar, al-Bīṭār embraced Salafism in his fifties after meeting ʿAbduh.[322] Compared to his contemporaries, al-Bīṭār played more of a background role in the revival of Salafism. He organized gatherings where scholars, thinkers, and academics could meet and discuss contemporary issues. A large amount of early Salafi ideas in Damascus developed during these meetings, and many influential Salafi thinkers of that time list al-Bīṭār as one of their influences. One of these thinkers was a scholar named Jamāl al-Dīn al-Qāsimī.

*Jamāl al-Dīn al-Qāsimī (d. 1914)*

Jamāl al-Dīn al-Qāsimī was born in Damascus to a scholarly family and received a traditional education. In 1888, he composed a work celebrating the birth (*mawlid*) of the Prophet Muhammad, in which he declared his belonging to the Ashʿarī school of theology, the Shāfiʿī school of Islamic law, and the Naqshband Sufi order. However, by 1895, he had become a reformist, distancing himself from the Sufi order and criticizing some of the Sufi practices popular in Syria at the time.

During his twenties, he met a few Salafi scholars and was influenced by them, with al-Bīṭār being particularly prominent; they became life-long friends.[323] Together, they organized gatherings of scholars and thinkers to discuss issues, but these became controversial over time.[324] It might be said that the Salafism of al-Qāsimī and al-Bīṭār was more legalistic in nature – as their focus was on not adhering to one of the dominant Sunni legal schools – although they were concerned with reforming Sufism.[325] In calling for independent legal reasoning (*ijtihād*), al-Qāsimī embraced the thought of Ibn Taymiyya via al-Shawkānī, especially in so much as he did not adhere to a specific school of Islamic law.[326] This call for *ijtihād* placed the group in opposition to the prohibition laid down by the Ottoman administration, and they were accused of forming a new legal school (*madhhab*), whose supposed adherents were named the 'Jamālīs.'[327] The fact that they were referred to as 'Jamālīs,' a reference to al-Qāsimī, indicates that he may have been the most influential member of this movement.

Al-Qāsimī wrote several books which clearly show his Salafi leanings, most notably, his exegesis of the Qurʾan, as well as his most popular book, *Irshād al-khalq* (*Guiding the Creation*),[328] which promoted Ibn Taymiyya's theology. However, al-Qāsimī's changing perspectives were not straightforward, and they complicated the notion that he was simply a reformist Salafi in the tradition of ʿAbduh and Riḍā or merely a traditionalist Salafi in the mode of Ibn Taymiyya. Even though he seemed to no longer belong to the Naqhshbandī order under Muḥammad al-Khānī (d. 1898) – with whom he studied between 1885 and 1891 – he maintained a close relationship with him. Furthermore, while he called for *ijtihād* and opposed blindly following (*taqlīd*), the Sunni schools of law, he utilized Ibn ʿArabī for this purpose – even defending the latter's doctrine of *waḥdat al-wujūd* (unity of being) in the face of criticism from Ibn Taymiyya. He asserted that Ibn Taymiyya had mistakenly understood the concept in monistic terms.[329] His apparently sympathetic treatment of the Jahmiyya in his *Tārīkh al-Jahmiyya wa-l-Muʿtazila* (*History of the Jahmiyya and Muʿtazila*)[330] brought anger from Salafis as well. Hence, al-Qāsimī must be seen as a reformist with his own tradition, and he does not fall neatly within reformist versus traditionalist Salafi dichotomous paradigms.[331] In addition, his relationship with Sufism – a favorite target of Salafism – is particularly complex, albeit largely favorable, notwithstanding a perceptible reformist attitude.[332]

As one would expect, al-Qāsimī faced the rebuke of the dominant clerical class for his opposition to Syrian scholarly tradition. This was because the Salafism of Wahhabism would meet with firm Syrian condemnation, specifically in Damascus,[333] but also in other cities such as Hama.[334] The unanimous Damascene opposition to Wahhabism from the time of the latter movement's beginning is hardly surprising, especially in light of the loyalty shown by the Syrians to their Ottoman rulers, who had fought the Wahhabis to regain the holy cities of Mecca and Medina after the Wahhabis had taken control of them from the Ottomans – the latter destroyed the first Saudi capital in 1818. Moreover, Ibn ʿAbd al-Wahhāb's doctrines on divinity, intercession through the righteous (*tawassul*), and matters of excommunication (*takfīr*), radically differed from the approach of centuries of Syrian scholarship, as with the rest of the Muslim world. However, this type of unanimity only continued until the late nineteenth century in Damascus, as well as Baghdad. In the early 1900s, al-Qāsimī was in correspondence with Maḥmūd Shukrī al-Ālūsī[335] in Baghdad, and these interactions reveal the scholarly and merchant links that extended from these lands to Najd and Jeddah. However, the level of antipathy against Wahhabis meant that when Riḍā came to the Umayyad Mosque in Damascus, a riot broke out, and he was accused of being a Wahhabi.

Then, in 1909, indicating something of a changing attitude in Syria towards Arab Bedouins and Wahhabis, al-Qāsimī's younger brother, Ṣalāḥ al-Dīn (d. 1916), wrote of how 'Wahhabi' had become a pejorative term to divide the community from reformist scholars. He further described the Wahhabis as adherents of the Ḥanbalī school, as well as being devoted to God, righteousness and knowledge, and detesting idolatry (*shirk*), stating that Ibn ʿAbd al-Wahhāb had merely followed scholarly tradition. Furthermore, Muḥammad Bahjat al-Bīṭār (d. 1976), a student of Riḍā who was later recruited by Ibn Saud, wrote an attempted conciliation in 1922, which was a soft defense of the Wahhabis, under the pseudonym Abū al-Yasār al-Dimashqī al-Maydānī. This work, in part, extolled the Wahhabis' virtue in spreading the valuable works of Ibn Taymiyya, Ibn Qayyim, and Ibn Qudāma and explained away Ibn ʿAbd al-Wahhāb's views on divinity and idolatry as a mere stratagem to dissuade people from incorrect practice. Likewise, in 1922, an administrative official by the name of Aḥmad

Fawzī al-Sā'ātī (d. 1924) composed a treatise that sought to bring the two opposing parties together. He even said that Ibn 'Abd al-Wahhāb's works had been endorsed by Syrian scholars but that some of his followers had adopted an extreme course.[336] In addition, there was the case of 'Abd al-Qādir b. Badrān (d. 1927). He edited a local paper and became a Ḥanbalī after claiming to compare the four schools. His attacks on popular practices as unsanctioned innovations (*bid'a*) led to him being called a 'heretic' (*zindīq*) and a 'Wahhabi.'[337]

Al-Qāsimī and his movement were accused of plotting against the Ottomans and, as a result, were investigated several times. Due to such political unrest, al-Qāsimī withdrew from public activities and spent the remainder of his life focused on writing books and articles in which he explored his ideas. These books influenced a new generation of scholars. Al-Qāsimī, along with others, such as Maḥmud Shukrī al-Ālūsī, worked to produce classical works that influenced the growth of Salafism. These works introduced scholarly arguments from figures like Ibn Taymiyya, effectively challenging the established scholarly framework. Moreover, these works provided an impetus to a growing appreciation of what was seen as Salafi thought.[338]

Even if al-Qāsimī was not strictly speaking a Salafi in the contemporary technical sense, his work was vitally important – both directly and indirectly – in providing a context, both intellectually and institutionally, for the puritan Salafism of al-Albānī[339] that emerged at the end of the twentieth century in Syria and then spread throughout the world. The link between al-Qāsimī and al-Albānī, notwithstanding their obvious differences, was made by the latter's associate 'Ali al-Halabi (d. 2020), who mentioned how in 1914 – the date of al-Qāsimī's death and the year of al-Albānī's birth – 'the setting of one star announced the rise of another star…in the skies of Syria.'[340]

*Muḥibb al-Dīn al-Khaṭīb (d. 1969)*

Al-Khaṭīb was a Syrian Salafi scholar and writer who played a crucial role in popularizing the term 'Salafi' during the early twentieth century. Born in Syria, al-Khāṭib was influenced by the Salafi teachings of al-Qāsimī and al-Bīṭār. Following World War I, al-Khāṭib migrated to Egypt, where he collaborated with fellow Syrian 'Abd al-Fattāh Qatlān (d. 1931) to establish a publishing house called *al-Maṭba'a al-Salafiyya* (*The Salafi Press*).[341] Al-Khaṭīb dedicated much of his time to contributing to journals and publishing classical manuscripts. While his publishing venture encompassed a diverse range of books, it assumed a pivotal role in promoting the term 'Salafi,' particularly through al-Khāṭib's journal entitled *al-Majalla al-Salafiyya* (*The Salafi Review*). Subsequently, these works were translated into English and disseminated across various countries.[342] With this, many people began to associate this bookstore and its publications with authentic knowledge.

Over the next few decades, many important Salafi and Wahhabi books were published by *al-Maṭbaʿa al-Salafiyya*, with the Kingdom of Saudi Arabia financing a large number of these publications. This helped revive and spread Salafi literature in the Middle East. Nonetheless, not much is known about al-Khāṭib, as he lived a quiet life dedicated to writing and publishing. But his role in popularizing the term 'Salafi' in the twentieth century cannot be overlooked.

### *2.9.3 Salafism in Ottoman Baghdad*

Around the same time as the Damascus Salafi revival was taking place, a similar resurrection of Salafi ideas was emerging in Baghdad. In this city, though, the Salafi revival took place primarily through a single family: the al-Ālūsīs.

*Maḥmūd al-Ālūsī (d. 1854)*

Abū al-Thanā Maḥmūd al-Ālūsī (d. 1854) was a prominent nineteenth-century Salafi scholar who is famous for his exegesis (*tafsīr*) of the Qurʾan, *Rūh al-maʿānī fī tafsīr al-Qurʾān al-ʿaẓīm wa sabʿ al-mathānī* (*The Soul of Meaning in the Exegesis of the Great Qurʾan and the Repeated Seven Verses*).[343] Despite his Salafi leanings, he served as a mufti in the Ottoman Empire for a large portion of his life.[344] It seems that al-Ālūsī was a traditional Ḥanafī scholar early in his life and developed Salafi ideas later on. Initially, he did not openly preach Salafism, probably due to his government position. However, after losing his job, he became more vocal about his thoughts. The contentions featured in *Rūh al-maʿānī* were so polemical in nature, presenting seemingly Salafi arguments against the prevailing scholarly traditions, that the leading traditionalist of that era, the aforementioned al-Kawtharī, contended that the published edition had been adulterated by the author's son, Nuʿmān al-Ālūsī (d. 1899). This assertion contradicted the original manuscript version preserved in Istanbul, a copy of which the author had presented to the Ottoman ruler in 1850. However, a recent publication in 2010 based on the Istanbul manuscript proved that al-Kawtharī was wrong and had employed 'a pious lie as textual criticism' in order to defend the tradition against reformist efforts.[345]

While it is unclear where al-Ālūsī first learned about Ibn Taymiyya's ideas, two of his teachers link him to the broader Salafi tradition. The first is Shaykh ʿAlī al-Suwaydī (d. 1821), who was an Iraqi scholar sympathetic to the Wahhabi movement and shared some of their ideas.[346] The other was Maulānā Khālid Naqshbandī (d. 1826), a Kurdish scholar who migrated to India and took from the tradition of Shāh Walī Allāh, preaching the latter's blend of Sufism and Salafism.[347] Both these teachers had a strong impact on the intellectual development of Maḥmūd al-Ālūsī.

The development of al-Ālūsī's thoughts can be seen in the evolution of ideas in his work of *Rūh al-Maʿānī*. This thirty-volume book was written over a fifteen-year period, and the sections written in the early part seem more Sufi and Ashʿarī in nature, while the latter parts promote a Salafi understanding of Islam. Al-Ālūsī seems to have developed his Salafi ideas later in life and as a result did not write much other work about them.[348] His son and grandson, however, played an important role in reviving Salafism in Baghdad.

*Nuʿmān al-Ālūsī (d. 1899)*

Nuʿmān Khayr al-Dīn al-Ālūsī was the son of Maḥmūd al-Ālūsī. While his brother ʿAbd Allāh (d. 1874) became a traditional Sufi scholar, Nuʿmān became one of the most influential Salafi scholars in Ottoman Baghdad.[349]

Nuʿmān al-Ālūsī is famous for his book *Jalāʾ al-ʿaynayn fī muḥākamat al-Aḥmadayn* (*Revealing to the Eyes the Trial of the Two Aḥmads*),[350] which was written in defense of Ibn Taymiyya from the criticisms of Ibn Ḥajar al-Haytamī (d. 974/1566) – both called Aḥmad.[351] This book was highly controversial for its time, as it was written when tension was at an all-time high between the Ottomans and the Wahhabis. The book not only defended the figure that Wahhabis were said to take many of their ideas from, but also criticized the traditional theological school that the Ottomans followed.[352] Furthermore, the work was crucial in readdressing Ibn Taymiyya's reputation in the Ottoman lands as a heretic and providing a defense of his orthodoxy.[353]

Despite this tension, Nuʿmān al-Ālūsī developed a strong reputation among the scholarly community. His primary legacy resides in his written works, which impacted a new wave of scholarship and played a pivotal role in shaping the foundations of the modern Salafi movement. This influence extended not only to his own nephew, Maḥmūd Shukrī al-Ālūsī, but also to Riḍā. In fact, *Jalāʾ al-ʿaynayn* caused Riḍā to view Ibn Taymiyya in a positive light, given the rarity of writings that defended Ibn Taymiyya during that period.[354]

*Maḥmūd Shukrī al-Ālūsī (d. 1924)*

Following on from the work of his grandfather and uncle, Maḥmūd Shukrī al-Ālūsī would play a pivotal role in printing classical works from manuscripts – often diligently searching and obtaining manuscripts of hitherto unpublished works. In this pursuit, he was aided most notably by al-Qāsimī and utilized a widespread network of contacts. This network encompassed an eclectic array of individuals, ranging from the Ahl-e Ḥadīth scholar Ṣiddīq Ḥasan Khān to a Shiʿi associate in Najaf, the Orientalist Louis Massignon (d. 1962) and a Carmelite priest in Iraq. His efforts in uncovering and introducing a diverse range of works characterized by reformist or Salafi tendencies significantly contributed to the rise of Salafism. In addition, he engaged in reformist activities along Salafi lines with leading traditional scholars of the time, as seen in his criticisms of the leading Sufi scholar Yūsuf al-Nabhānī (d. 1932), albeit under the guise of a pseudonym. This stemmed from his fear of backlash in tackling a scholar greatly favored by the Ottomans.[355]

### *2.9.4 Muhammad Nasir al-Din al-Albānī (d. 1999)*

If there were to be one primary figure associated with the modern Salafi movement, without a doubt it would be Muḥammad Nāṣir al-Dīn, commonly known as al-Albānī (meaning 'the one from Albania'). Al-Albānī single-handedly shaped the modern Salafi narrative and influenced a global movement that is still reckoning with his legacy.[356] He accomplished this without any government support or institutional help, and his rise to fame and influence, regardless of one's personal stance on his views, is worthy of admiration.[357] One of the reasons for his success was his unshakable determination, which his followers esteemed, but which meant he could be seen as 'stubborn and ill-mannered, which al-Albānī himself admitted to being, as did his students.'[358]

Al-Albānī was born in 1914 in Shkodër, the capital of Albania at the time, to a father who was an Islamic scholar trained in the Ḥanafī school. At the age of nine, al-Albānī moved to Damascus with his family as the monarch Zog I tended towards secularization, which deeply frustrated his family. As a child, al-Albānī did not even know the Arabic alphabet; however, according to his own testimony, he quickly progressed in Arabic while at primary school, which would be the last formal stage of his education. As a student, he was known as 'al-Arnā'ūṭ,' the Ottoman Turkish term used for all Balkan people. His father, Nuḥ, was a highly respected teacher in the Damascene immigrant community and was seen as one of their experts in the Ḥanafī legal school. Nuh was skeptical of public schooling; Al-Albānī therefore completed his formal education at primary school and began to learn the Ḥanafī school with his father, who taught him the commentary of *Nūr al-'iḍaḥ* (*Light of Clarification*) called *Marāqī al-falāḥ* (*Steps to Success*), and *Mukhtaṣar al-Qudūrī* – (*Handbook [of Ḥanafī fiqh compiled by] al-Qudūrī*), both standard works of an intermediate level in the legal school. He also studied the rules of Qur'anic recitation (*tajwīd*) with his father and the Arabic language with the Sufi Sa'īd al-Burhānī (d. 1967). After a short spell learning carpentry, al-Albānī's father taught him how to mend watches, and he soon became proficient enough to open his own shop after first working with his father.

Al-Albānī was religious from a young age, and while working at his father's shop, he would – when lack of work permitted – take opportunities to read, in particular modern Arab novels, and attend classes on Islamic law in the Umayyad Mosque. He and his family were poor, so he would have to rent the books he wanted to read from a nearby bookseller. It was in such conditions that he first came across Riḍā and his journal *al-Manār*. Later, he would recount, 'Certainly, the *Manār* journal paved the way for me to work in the science of hadith.'[359] In particular, one article by Riḍā grabbed his attention; it discussed al-Ghazālī's *Iḥyā' 'ulūm al-dīn* (*The Revival of the Religious Sciences*) and its benefits, but also questioned some of the Sufi notions and criticized its use of weak hadith. In relation to the latter point, Riḍā had referenced Zayn al-Dīn al-'Irāqī's (d. 806/1403) notes on the authenticity and weakness of hadith in the *Iḥyā'*. This set off a frenzy in the young al-Albānī, who went searching for the book in the markets until he finally found it. Being too poor to buy the four-volume work, he was allowed to rent it from the seller. Al-Albānī then proceeded to write out the work and make notes on it, particularly in relation to obscure words in the hadith. This was the beginning of a critical interest in hadith, the passion of which led him to fall out with his father and leave the family home upon his father's ultimatum to change – he would remain largely estranged from his father until the latter's final years.

Very soon after engaging in his largely autodidactic study of Islamic literature, he came to dispute a number of positions taken by the Ḥanafī school on the basis of his reading of hadith, which he gave preference to, with what appears to be the most rudimentary of jurisprudential methods, perhaps resulting from his lack of a sophisticated education. However, it seems that the advanced Ḥanbalī legal text *al-Mughnī* – composed by the aforementioned Ibn Qudāma – and dealing with comparative legal matters, was important to al-Albānī in his self-study of law, as he used it for his notes on al-'Iraqī. A significant part of al-Albānī's self-study was his dedication to reading the holdings of the Ẓāhiriyya Library in Damascus, which was the second most significant Arab repository of manuscripts (along with the National Egyptian Library),[360] and al-Albānī secured a key to the building so that he could follow his passion for reading outside opening hours.

Not only did he argue against the positions of the Ḥanafīs and the Sufi community around him, but he also came to the conclusion – after his reading of Ibn 'Asākir's (d. 571/1176) *Tārikh Dimashq* (*History of Damascus*) – that it was impermissible to pray in the Umayyad Mosque, as it was reported that Prophet John (or Yaḥyā in the Islamic tradition) is buried somewhere in its grounds. This type of idiosyncratic legal reasoning would, at that time and later, not only upset devout adherents of the legal schools but also trouble many Salafis – in particular, the Wahhabi clerics who still followed the Ḥanbalī school.

In his early twenties, al-Albānī was part of a study circle with 'Salafi brothers,'[361] which focused on the study of hadith and their legal understanding. Hadith revival, especially with regards to authentication, would be his hallmark and legacy. These sessions started in the back of his shop and in the homes of people around Damascus from 1945. Soon, the gatherings became so popular that they had to rent a hall for the sessions. His association with intellectual rebels continued until he came to attend the sessions of the Syrian Muslim Brotherhood (SMB) in Damascus, who were open to his reformist methods, and some of whom he considered to be Salafi, such as leaders like ʿIṣām ʿAṭṭār (d. 2024)[362] and Zuhayr al-Shawish (d. 2013).[363] In the late 1960s, when the Aleppo branch of the Muslim Brotherhood fell out with the Damascus leadership, al-Albānī and al-Shawīsh engaged in debates with the leading scholar of the Aleppo faction, ʿAbd al-Fattāḥ Abū Ghudda (d. 1997), who was a staunch Ḥanafī and anti-Salafi (although later he would be reconciled with al-Shawish, as Yusuf al-Qaradawi (d. 2022) records).[364]

By the 1940s, his fame regarding hadith sciences had already attracted international attention, and al-Albānī was approached by a number of leading figures – including the leader of the SMB, Mustafa al-Sibaʿi (d. 1964), the Qatari Director of Religious Education, and the Najdi-Ḥanbalī scholar Muḥammad b. ʿAbd al-ʻAzīz b. Māniʿ (d. 1965) – to annotate the hadith found in the Ḥanbalī legal text *Manār al-sabīl* (*The Path of Light*), which he did in his seminal work *Irwā al-ghalīl* (*Quenching the Thirsty*), published in nine volumes.[365] In 1952, he began to publish articles in the journal of *Majallat al-Tamaddun al-Islāmī* (*Journal of Islamic Civilization*), which had an eclectic reformist agenda, and he continued to contribute until 1977 (the publication ceased in 1981). The publication was the official organ of the Jamʿiyyat al-Tamaddun al-Islāmī (Islamic Civilization Society), which had been established in 1932, with a number of al-Qāsimī's students as members and contributors, although they had good relations with the conservative clerics of Syria.[366] In this early period, al-Albānī also contributed articles to the Muslim Brotherhood's official journal, *al-Muslimūn*.[367]

In 1954, al-Shawish arranged for Damascus University to have al-Albānī trace the origins of the hadith on sales that were included in their *Mawsūʿat al-fiqh al-Islāmī* (*Encyclopedia of Islamic Law*), together with having al-Albānī lecture occasionally at the university. The very next year, he was conducting lessons at Damascus University on Wahhabi-Salafi theology by teaching *Fatḥ al-majīd* (*The Victory of the Exalted*) by ʿAbd al-Raḥmān b. Ḥasan b. Muḥammad b. ʿAbd al-Wahhāb (d. 1868). By the end of the 1950s, he had been appointed by the UAE to be a member of a delegation sent to Egypt on a task related to the science of hadith.[368] Between 1954 and 1968, al-Albānī composed the bulk of his *Silsilat al-aḥādīth al-ḍaʿīfah wa-l-mawḍūʿa wa-atharuhā al-sayyʾ fī al-umma* (*The Series of Weak and Forged Hadith Reports and Their Bad Influence on the Community*), and then from 1959 until 1966 he wrote *Silsilat al-aḥādīth al-ṣaḥīḥah* (*The Series of Sound Hadith Reports*). These two series would gain him much fame when they were published and led to his appointment at the Islamic University of Medina in 1961. Put together, these two works are an exhaustive collection of over 9,500 traditions, printed in twenty-four volumes, that display al-Albānī's mastery of classical hadith sciences. The goal was to sift through much of the hadith corpus and separate the 'authentic' from the 'inauthentic' through a detailed analysis of all of the collections of a particular tradition found in numerous source works, many of which al-Albānī culled from unprinted manuscripts. This work would do much to solidify his fame as a master of hadith sciences (although his critics would, of course, disagree).

Trouble grew, and as early as 1955, al-Albānī was called in front of a scholars' court before the Grand Mufti of Syria and warned not to cause unrest with the practices of his 'sect.' Furthermore, al-Albānī's speaking tours were often disrupted by the police, at the apparent instigation of the traditionalist scholars, and in 1967 (or 1969), he earned an eight-month prison sentence on account of the 'defamation of the shaykhs of the Sufi brotherhoods,' and was imprisoned a second time, as well as being placed under house arrest. Al-Albānī and his various supporters claimed that this government prosecution was inspired by the Sufi shaykhs of Damascus, or more specifically due to Muḥammad Saʿīd Ramaḍān al-Būṭī (d. 2013), a life-long arch-nemesis of al-Albānī, informing the government that he was an 'agent of colonialism.'[369]

Damascus was fertile ground for Salafi polemics in the late 1950s as the city was seen to be impoverished in the hadith sciences after the death of Badr al-Dīn al-Ḥasānī in 1935; the city only saw a revival in hadith studies at the end of the twentieth century, as a response to the Salafi movement.[370] Surprisingly, al-Albānī's efforts did also impact certain governmental policies. For instance, in 1956, certain songs in praise of the Prophet, which earned the ire of Salafis, were removed from public radio broadcasts; a celebration of Ibn Taymiyya was organized by the Higher Council for the Protection of Arts in 1960; furthermore, some public schools were named after Jamāl al-Dīn al-Qāsimī and Ibn Taymiyya, whom the Salafis revered.[371]

Al-Albānī's fame continued to grow abroad during this period. In this regard, al-Shawish would be crucial for the career of al-Albānī, as he had founded a publishing house named *al-Maktab al-Islāmī* (*The Islamic Bookshop*) in 1957 in Damascus. It was originally funded by the Qatari royal family (and later, with the help of the Saudi royal family), then relocated to Lebanon in 1963, when al-Shawish was forced to leave Syria for Lebanon.[372] This venture earned widespread renown for the quality of its publications, which were often editions of classical works with meticulous indexing, elaborate tables of contents, few errors and notes on the authenticity of the hadith. Al-Shawīsh employed al-Albānī as a hadith editor, and this work expanded al-Albānī's renown throughout the Arab world. Although he did occasionally publish with others, *al-Maktab al-Islāmī* would publish the bulk of al-Albānī's works until the 1990s, even after the two had a falling out in the 1980s.[373] Such was the central importance of this relationship, the famous Syrian scholar ʿAli al-Tantawi (d. 1999) said, 'Were it not for Zuhayr [al-Shawish], the views of Nāṣir (al-Din al-Albānī) would not have circulated.'[374]

This eventually brought him to the attention of the Saudi scholar Ibn Bāz (who would eventually become its Grand Mufti), who was at the time in charge of the administration of the Islamic University of Medina (IUM). It was Ibn Bāz who personally invited al-Albānī to come to teach hadith sciences at IUM during the first year of its inception in 1963. His stint at IUM helped boost his profile and his teachings globally, where many hundreds of students eagerly absorbed his fiery brand of anti-*madhhab* rhetoric and his emphasis on returning to the Qurʾan and Sunna directly.

However, his eccentric views and the brusque manner in which he dismissed mainstream-normative Ḥanbalī law began to raise the ire of some of his hosts. Another Wahhabi scholar, Ismāʿīl al-Anṣārī (d. 1997), an assistant to the Grand Mufti of Saudi Arabia – and the then-president of IUM, Muḥammad b. Ibrāhīm Āl al-Shaykh (d. 1969) – wrote refutations of al-Albānī on the instructions of the Grand Mufti, who deemed it below his rank to respond to a junior on such matters. Not only was al-Albānī's staunch anti-*madhhab* stance considered troublesome, he also held a number of radical opinions which were considered to be counter-productive or offensive: prohibiting women from wearing circular gold jewelry, his view on the number of units for the *tarawīh* night-prayer in Ramadan, and his criticism of the founder of Wahhabism, Ibn ʿAbd al-Wahhāb, as being weak in hadith and not a Salafi in law. For Saudi scholars, the last straw was al-Albānī's view that women could uncover their faces in public. This led to the Grand Mufti refusing to renew al-Albānī's contract at IUM in 1963.[375] Although Ibn Bāz tried to bring al-Albānī back to IUM, the Saudi authorities blocked the move. However, al-Albānī remained a member of IUM's Higher Council until 1975.[376]

He was forced to return to Syria, where he remained for the next fifteen years, at times courting trouble with the authorities but never directly confronting the Baʿathist regime. An important milestone in al-Albānī's career was his first visit to Jordan around 1967. Such was the popularity of his visits he started to go each month until the late 1970s, moving there in 1979.[377] This was an attractive proposition, as the Syrian regime was starting to pressure Syrian Salafis as a result of the intensifying animosity between the regime and Islamists. Yet, as al-Albānī's appeal grew in Jordan, he came under suspicion from the Jordanian authorities, who worried that this could develop into a political issue for them. Hence, al-Albānī was forced to leave the country in the early 1980s and travel, at various times, between Syria, Lebanon, and UAE.[378]

However, the Iran–Iraq war during the 1980s would provide an opportunity for his return. A Jordanian cleric with strong ties to the Hashemite King, Muhammad Ibrahim Shaqra (d. 2017), convinced the king that al-Albānī should be allowed to return to Jordan as an important tool to counteract the threat posed by the Shiʿa. The King was apparently convinced and agreed to the suggestion, allowing al-Albānī to return in 1983, where he remained on a permanent basis until his death.[379]

It has been argued that al-Albānī's thoughts on a *manhaj* (methodology) of Salafism reached maturity during his time in Jordan, and it is reported that it was in Jordan that he first used his famous slogan of Salafi reform that would define his work for the next twenty years: *al-taṣfiya wa-l-tarbiya* (purification and education), which focused on doctrinal and ritual 'purity.'[380] This refinement of Salafi methodology was constructed in the face of new challenges, such as the rise of Islamic activism and Jihadi-Salafism, which had an important base in Zarqa near where he lived. The refinement of the Salafi methodology, therefore, had to go further than a mere refinement of the hadith corpus.[381]

For al-Albānī, this phrase of *al-taṣfiya wa-l-tarbiya* was his methodological response to all other groups and movements. It earmarked his emphasis on *preaching* as the primary way of revival, and not *militancy* or *political activism*. That preaching was meant to, firstly, *purify* (*taṣfiya*) the religion from idiosyncratic practices and heretical beliefs (i.e., *bidʿas* in theology and rituals) and, secondly, *nurture* (*tarbiya*) people upon the correct understanding of *tawḥīd* and Sunna. Furthermore, it meant to *purify* texts of inauthentic hadiths in order to *nurture* Muslims according to 'authentic' Islam. It was also at this stage that al-Albānī began declaring that it was *obligatory* upon his followers to identify as 'Salafi' in order that truth be manifest from falsehood.[382]

In Jordan, he was able to influence a good number of associates despite not being permitted to publicly teach.[383] It is perhaps more appropriate to speak of his Jordanian *associates* rather than *students*, as al-Albānī's ability to formally teach was heavily restricted by the strict conditions put on him by the regime – in order to permit him to remain in the country. Most of his followers came from the lower economic classes, often without university qualifications (like al-Albānī himself) and were converts to Salafism – a point explained in Chapter 6 in relation to Jordan.[384]

His popularity continued to increase throughout the 1980s and especially in the 1990s via the propagation of his lectures and questions and answers on cassette tapes. One of his students, who went by the moniker of 'Abū Layla al-Atharī,' began recording his lessons and responses to the questions of locals and foreign delegates, spreading these recordings under the title *Silsilat al-hudā wa-l-nūr* (*The Series of Guidance and Light*).[385] These series were all meticulously documented, dated and numbered, and since they were not copyrighted, students were encouraged to replicate and distribute the tapes for free. It is difficult to overstate the impact that these cassettes had globally. The unique, eloquent speaking style of al-Albānī, coupled with his blunt, evidence-based responses that became representative of Salafi discourse, earned him a global following that no one else in his era could compete with. His lectures – via these cassettes – were religiously followed and memorized, and his fatwas became extremely popular, even though many of them were extremely eccentric.[386] In addition to these cassettes, al-Albānī and his students founded a magazine called *al-Aṣāla* (*The Foundations*) in 1993, which lasted until 2007, printing fifty-four journals. All of the articles were approved, directly or indirectly, by al-Albānī himself, and all of them reflected his points of view. It was in these magazines that many of his students and associates, like ʿAlī al-Halabi, Salim al-Hilali (b. 1957), Mashhur Hasan Salman (b. 1960), Muhammad Musa Nasr (d. 2017), and others, rose to prominence.[387]

Alongside his widely distributed cassette tapes, al-Albānī gained further fame through his many books, some of which were edited manuscripts of previously unpublished works, while others were dedicated to specific topics. What distinguished al-Albānī as an author was his usage of copious footnotes detailing the various sources for hadiths, their *isnāds* (chains of transmission) and, importantly, their grading in terms of authenticity. For example, he made the unprecedented move of critically examining the hadiths found in the four widely studied *Sunans* of Abū Dāwūd (d. 275/889), al-Tirmidhī (d. 279/829), al-Nasāʾī (d. 303/915), and Ibn Mājah (d. 273/887). It is perhaps impossible for those outside this subculture to fully comprehend how big an impact this *purification* process had on the direction of Salafi print culture specifically and in the wider Islamic book market more generally. It not only weaponized Salafis with 'authentic proofs' with which they could counter contesting trends (hence their oft-repeated mantra, *'What is your evidence?'*), but also encouraged a new genre of Islamic books that promised readers an authenticated treatment on any given topic (Al-Albānī himself authored an 'authentic,' albeit incomplete, biography of Prophet Muhammad). In particular, by acting as an adjudicator (*muḥaqqiq*) to the four canons out of the six of Sunni Islam,[388] and deciding which traditions should be accepted (his *Ṣaḥīh* editions of those canons), and which rejected (his *Ḍaʿīf* editions of those canons), the underlying presumption, rarely stated but very clearly believed by millions of his followers, was that al-Albānī was the final authority in hadith matters, and that this authority also then gave weight in deriving legal opinions and laws.

It was al-Albānī's treatment on the prayer, *Ṣifat ṣalāt al-Nabī* (*The Prophet's Prayer Described*), which roused a revolution of sorts in towns and cities across the Muslim world, including countries like Britain, where Salafis first translated it into English.[389] The book, one of three versions differing in size and complexity, as the full title would suggest, promised to provide readers with a description of the Prophet's prayer *as though you are seeing it.* It bypassed the voluminous debates between *madhabs* preserved in classic *fiqh* manuals and, instead, drew directly from a vast repository of hadith works and unpublished manuscripts. The impact of this work, as experienced in places as far and wide as Syria and the United States, was a perceptible drive for Muslims to alter their prayer method to fall in line with the hadith. Moreover, it contributed to the appeal of the Salafi dialectic, seemingly untangled from the opinions of men and solely based on textual evidence.[390] Naturally, several authors conforming to one of the four *madhabs* attempted to confute the work but, in doing so, only added to the turn towards scripturalism.

Even in Jordan, al-Albānī continued to court controversy with the mainstream Saudi Wahhabi establishment over a myriad of issues. Some of them were continuations of the issues of his sojourn in IUM back in the 1960s, perhaps most famously, over the Ramadan prayer of *tarawīh*, where the Saudi establishment, following the Ḥanbalī school, considered it as consisting of twenty units, whereas al-Albānī gave the unprecedented verdict that only eight units were allowed – anything in addition was not only invalid, it also actually constituted a religious innovation (*bidʿa*). The issue of the face veil (niqab) continued to be a source of constant back-and-forth, as al-Albānī argued, in contrast to Saudi Wahhabis, that a loose head-covering (hijab) was sufficient, and a face veil was not mandatory. However, the issue that generated the harshest response was theological. In a series of questions put to him regarding the verdict on the one who abandons the ritual prayer, al-Albānī answered that such a person, while committing a grave error, was still to be considered a Muslim, albeit a sinful one. This generated a series of responses from Saudi clerics, and in 1991, al-Albānī felt pressured to write a treatise defending his view, entitled *Ḥukm tārik al-ṣalāt* (*The Ruling on the One Who Abandons the Prayer*). Interestingly, his student ʿAlī al-Halabi wrote the foreword to this work.[391]

In response, Saudi scholars gave a flurry of fatwas, culminating in an extremely harsh reprisal by the Senior Committee of Scholars of the Kingdom, which, while not mentioning al-Albānī directly, did mention his students – including al-Halabi – and gave the verdict that anyone who claimed that faith was achieved without action had fallen into heresy and theological deviation (*bidʿa*), mirroring the heretical beliefs of the non-Sunni sect known as the *Murjiʾa*.[392] For a period of time, throughout the early and mid-1990s, the Salafi movement was thus divided between the Jordanian and the Saudi camps, and many fierce debates took place between advocates on both sides. However, in what appears to be an attempt at reconciliation by higher authorities in the Kingdom, in 1999, the year al-Albānī passed away, he was awarded the King Faisal International Award for Islamic Studies, the highest prize conferred not only by the Kingdom but by any Muslim land, in honor of his contributions to hadith studies. While al-Albānī did not attend in person – citing health reasons – he sent his colleague and student, the aforementioned Muḥammad Shaqra, to accept it on his behalf. He died a natural death, in Amman, Jordan, in October 1999. As a gesture of how sentimental he felt toward his time at IUM, he willed that his entire library be donated to the University.

The legacy al-Albānī left behind is still being carried on by his students and critiqued by his detractors. He left over a hundred works, many of them small pamphlets or treatises on specific topics, others being just a commentary of hadiths on various works. Most importantly, he left an indelible mark on Salafism, and single-handedly carved out an entire trajectory of modern Salafi thought that continues to inspire many hundreds of thousands of admirers around the globe. His version of 'Salafism' was the primary version that went global, and it has a complex relationship with other strands: at times tag-teaming off Wahhabism and mainstreaming their clerics (especially in non-Arab lands); at others, clashing with other variants (especially Wahhabism and the Ahl-e Ḥadīth movement on various issues). Still, the average Muslim around the globe came to know of the 'Salafi *manhaj*' and hence understand its contours through his lens, in particular his emphasis on bypassing the schools of law and of simplistically assuming the 'Qurʾan and Sunna' has a final, immediate, authoritative answer to any single question posed by a believer.

Countless Islamic works now refer back to al-Albānī's hadith gradings. The vast majority of these have been produced in the digital age, making it easier for some small-time publishers, particularly in Egypt, to market their books as 'authentic' for having no more than al-Albānī verdicts inserted into footnotes. Despite his death in 1999, al-Albānī's many cassettes, now entirely digitized and organized on various websites and YouTube, as well as his works, reprinted and reworked, ensure his continued influence on Salafism and the wider Islamic discourse.

## *2.10 Conclusion*

No history of Salafi thought can fully capture everything that contributed to its contemporary articulation. I have only attempted to outline a genealogy of ideas from which modern Salafism takes its inspiration.

It has been argued here that Salafi thought emerged during the formative centuries of Islam – during the era of the *salaf* itself. It was the classical *ahl al-ḥadīth* school which initially encapsulated the notion of proto-Salafi thought against rival trends, particularly in matters pertaining to God's divine attributes, but also finer points of creed related to predestination (*qadar*), the nature of the Qurʾan, leadership and, even occasionally, in formulating law. In the culmination of the early period, the school was firmly rooted in and around Abbasid Baghdad, after Aḥmad b. Ḥanbal almost singlehandedly assured its survival against the rise of non-scriptural and speculative theologies affecting Islamic discourse.

Ashʿarism only came to dominate over proto-Salafi thought when power shifted to the Seljuks. In response, remnants of the *ahl al-ḥadīth* evolved under changing circumstances and took varying directions leading up to the end of the thirteenth century. In Mamluk Syria and Egypt, the following century saw a renewed effort to enshrine the authority of revelation over *kalām*, and the *salaf* as an absolute reference point in matters of creed, led by Ibn Taymiyya and his circle of like-minded scholars. Despite their collective efforts failing to supplant the dominance of Ashʿarism in the Muslim world, their works did, in varying degrees, inspire Salafi (or, if one wishes to think in such terms, Salafi-esque) movements in succeeding years.

The eighteenth century witnessed the rise of the Wahhabi movement in Central Arabia, the Shawkānī school in Yemen, and the Ahl-e Ḥadīth in India – all of which saw themselves as reinstituting the original *ahl al-ḥadīth's* hermeneutic. All of these movements relied, to varying degrees, on the thought and writings of Ibn Taymiyya. They contributed to the idea of Salafism in the twentieth century in Egypt, Damascus, and Baghdad – a Salafism which evolved into a fully developed global movement, with a particular *manhaj* (methodology), albeit quickly contested, with al-Albānī as its foremost champion.

On a surface level, this history of Salafi thought suggests that at least up until the fifteenth century, there was a continuous chain of scholars who drew their conception of Islam, its creed, and practice, entirely from the *ahl al-ḥadīth* among the *salaf*. Modern Salafis, of course, would argue that these figures were Salafis, despite the fact that none claimed this title. This anachronism aside, there certainly is strong evidence to suggest that the *ahl al-ḥadīth* provided the basis for numerous works on an internally consistent creed, and affirming a particular approach towards the authority of scripture and the divine attributes of God. Their influence, if we are to count Ibn Taymiyya and his generation as the culmination of this trend, appears to have waned in the following two centuries, but found revivers in eighteenth century Central Arabia, Yemen, and India. Thereafter, the evolution of Salafi thought leads us to the present day, whereby Salafism is now largely a movement of self-identifying Salafis with a particular reading of history, one which lends itself to a modern projection of being connected directly to the past, in an uninterrupted chain of an orthodox theology and methodology.

However, a closer examination of the events leading up to the fifteenth century as outlined above, suggests that Salafi thought has undergone shifts and changes of direction from as early as the tenth century. These contours of change not only affected Salafi thought in later eras, but also informed the precise definition of a Salafi *manhaj* today. The following chapter explores how the Wahhabi movement, in particular, has played a significant role in how Salafi thought has been reworked from the Taymiyyan epoch in this regard.

# 3

# WAHHABISM AND SALAFISM

*'So if you can understand that the most ignorant of the pagans [of Mecca] understood from the testimony of faith [that God must be worshiped alone], then how strange is it that the one who claims to be a Muslim does not know from this testimony what a pagan knew... There is surely no good in a person who is more ignorant than the ignorant pagans [of Mecca]!'*
*~ Muḥammad b. ʿAbd al-Wahhāb*[1]

*'Before God blessed me with this knowledge, none of my teachers knew the meaning of "There is no god but Allah," or knew the meaning of Islam; whoever claims otherwise has lied, fabricated, led people astray, and falsely praised himself.'*
*~ Muḥammad b. ʿAbd al-Wahhāb*[2]

Of all the strands of Salafism, it is Wahhabism that has garnered the most scholarly attention. The rise of the Saudi state, coupled with the geopolitical importance of the oil-rich Kingdom, the horrific events of 9/11, followed by the meteoric rise and fall of Al-Qaeda and ISIS and their alleged association with this strand of Salafism, collectively serve as an obvious incentive for the abundance of literature here. Hence, a fundamental question arises: What exactly *is* Wahhabism, and how does it fit into the broader trend of Salafism?

We will explore the history of Wahhabism from several angles. We shall begin by looking at the life of the founder of Wahhabism, Muḥammad b. ʿAbd al-Wahhāb, through both a sympathetic and a hostile lens. This will then lead us to summarize his theology and works and the reception they received. In the second section, we will segue into a brief history of Saudi Arabia with its three political states and the evolution of Wahhabism in its three theological waves. The initial wave of Wahhabism encompasses the First (1744–1818) and the Second Saudi State (1824–91), while the onset of the second wave of Wahhabism is marked by the inception of the Third Saudi State in the 1930s, followed by the emergence of the third wave of Wahhabism (in the 1960s) within the same State. In the third section of this chapter, we will underscore the Kingdom's role in disseminating Wahhabism on a global scale, with specific emphasis on the instrumental role played by the Islamic University of Medina in proselytizing a distinctly Wahhabi-oriented Salafism. This chapter will conclude by introducing the jihadi trend of Wahhabism, which shall be discussed separately in Chapter 5.

Before proceeding any further, a necessary disclaimer regarding the nomenclature of the term 'Wahhabism' is needed. For outsiders, this moniker seems quite obvious: if Lutherans or Mormons (or even Christianity itself) can be named after its founders, why not name a movement begun by Ibn ʿAbd al-Wahhāb 'Wahhabism'? Consequently, this has become the standard term employed in almost all historical and academic works written on the movement. Indeed, the term was used during the lifetime of the founder by the Ottomans and other opponents, and it can be found in English sources within a decade of Ibn ʿAbd al-Wahhāb's death.[3] Moreover, as is common with such terms, the 'Wahhabi' label was eventually claimed by some followers of the movement, who referred to themselves with this term as an ascription to the name of God 'al-Wahhāb' (The Bestower), meaning that they were ascribing themselves to God as faithful Muslims. Furthermore, certain defenses of the movement used the term in a neutral and self-describing manner, as seen in certain works by Rashīd Riḍā and Muḥammad Ḥāmid al-Fiqī. Yet, this formalizing of the positive usage was halted in 1929 by then-King ʿAbd al ʿAzīz b. Saud, who saw the political benefits of prohibiting the usage of 'Wahhabi' and replacing it with 'Salafism' (*al-salafiyya*). By the middle of the twentieth century, Wahhabis had largely come to adopt the 'Salafi' label as a popular self-designation.[4]

Nonetheless, the term 'Wahhabi' is more often used with a pejorative undertone and is widely held by followers of the movement to be an offensive label. The pejorative nature of this term is itself worthy of deeper study, as it is regularly used within intra-Muslim polemics against groups whose association with the movement was tenuous. When used in this context, the term denotes crude literalism, fanaticism, denigration of the saints – and even the Prophet himself! For example, in colonial India, the term was even used by some Muslims against fellow believers for merely abstaining from Sufi festivals.[5] These connotations, combined with the movement's own perspective that does not perceive Ibn ʿAbd al-Wahhāb as a founder in the traditional sense, but rather as a 'reviver' of Islam's original and 'pure' theology, raise valid concerns regarding the usage of the term 'Wahhabi.' The initial followers of the movement referred to themselves as *Muwaḥḥidūn* (Monotheists), while a later iteration called themselves *Ikhwān* (Brothers). However, both terms have fallen out of use by contemporary followers of the movement. Instead, they prefer to call themselves 'Salafis' or simply 'Muslims.'

My usage of the terms 'Wahhabi' and 'Wahhabism' carries no intention of conveying a negative connotation or derogatory implication. Nevertheless, in almost all academic articles and books, this phenomenon is labeled as such, in a neutral and objective manner. For the sake of clarity, I employ it in this sense. The terms *Muwaḥḥidūn*, *Ikhwān*, and Salafi are either too obscure or indicate a wider intellectual trend beyond those who can be considered strictly as followers of the movement of Ibn ʿAbd al-Wahhāb.[6]

## *3.1 Muḥammad b. ʿAbd al-Wahhāb: His Life, Beliefs, and Works*

### *3.1.1 Ibn ʿAbd al-Wahhāb: His Life from Two Paradigms*

To fully understand the phenomenon of Wahhabism, it helps to have two competing narratives at hand: the sympathetic view and the adversarial view. These two interpretations are at such odds that it might be assumed we are reading two different histories. Yet, as every researcher quickly discovers, history is a very subjective and contentious exercise. The classification of figures as either heroes or villains can fluidly interchange based on the paradigm from which they are being observed. Furthermore, we are hindered in our quest to detail the life of Ibn ʿAbd al-Wahhāb because the paucity of sources prevents us from accurately establishing the accounts of his journeying to various locations from Najd and the length of time he spent in each place.[7]

We begin with the sympathetic view of an insider and then move on to a hostile analysis from an outsider.

*Muḥammad b. ʿAbd al-Wahhāb: The reviver of the prophetic message*

Muḥammad b. ʿAbd al-Wahhāb was born in the year 1704 within the province of Najd, located in the Arabian Peninsula.[8] Historically, this province was home to several prominent Companions of the Prophet and later Muslim scholars – a point that later Wahhabi authors highlight.

At the time of his birth, eighteenth-century Arabia was not a unified land. The most important province, the Hijaz – which contains the holy cities of Mecca and Medina – was under Ottoman control. However, the central province of Najd, although nominally under Ottoman rule, was politically independent for all practical purposes. It was very much a tribal land, where various Bedouin tribes fought one another over territory and limited resources, occasionally venturing outwards in more daring raids on trading and pilgrimage caravans.

Ibn ʿAbd al-Wahhāb was born into a scholarly family, and his father was the judge of the village of ʿUyayna. His grandfather, uncles, and older brothers were all scholars of Islamic law. Growing up in this environment steeped in Islamic scholarship, Ibn ʿAbd al-Wahhāb was nurtured within a milieu of devout Islamic practice and displayed a fervent commitment to religious pursuits from an early age. By the age of ten, he had successfully committed the entire Qurʾan to memory. His father recognized his intellectual acumen and appointed him as the imam for some of the five daily congregational prayers when he was just twelve. He also married at that age, which was quite common for that time and culture.[9] Ibn ʿAbd al-Wahhāb took a keen interest in Islamic studies and studied the Ḥanbalī legal school under his father.

In his early twenties, emulating Muslim scholars of the past, he began his quest for knowledge away from home. This led him to embark on travels to connect with scholars in Mecca, Medina, and Basra in Iraq. It was in Medina that he met the scholar that would arguably have the strongest impact on his understanding of Islam: the aforementioned great Indian scholar, Muḥammad Ḥayāt al-Sindī.[10] He soon took a particular interest in the writings of Ibn Taymiyya and Ibn Qayyim, and these writings profoundly impacted his understanding of monotheism, influencing his approach to law and theology.

In Medina, he also studied under ʿAlī al-Dāghistānī (d. 1199/1785) and Ismāʿīl al-ʿAjlūnī (d. 1162/1749). Another Medinan scholar who had a strong influence on him was ʿAbd Allāh b. Ibrāhīm (d. 1140/1728). It was while studying under these scholars that he developed a strong understanding of monotheism (*tawhīd*) and a concurrent dislike for innovation (*bidʿa*) and blind following (*taqlīd*).

Upon concluding his studies in Medina, he returned to his home city of ʿUyayna but then departed to continue his studies. While the exact reasons behind this decision remain ambiguous, his age was probably a determining factor. He was likely deemed too young to undertake significant communal responsibilities. This led him to opt for continued travel in his pursuit of Islamic scholarship. His second journey took him to Basra, where he was first exposed to Shiʿism and its rituals and practices. The unfamiliarity of these practices, in comparison to his more orthodox understanding of Islam, generated a lasting negative impression. Consequently, this experience laid the foundation for his enduring role as a harsh critic of Shiʿism throughout the rest of his life.

In Basra, he studied Islamic law, the Arabic language, and the books of hadith. His most famous teacher there was Muḥammad al-Majmūʿī (d. 1184/1770). It is claimed that he wrote his famous and most important book, *Kitāb al-Tawḥīd*, during this period. It was also here in Basra that he faced his first real test: many locals were unhappy at his attempts to command the good and forbid the evil. Eventually, he was forced to leave and return to Najd via the region of al-Ahsa. There he spent some time studying under the local scholars before moving to Huraymila, where his father had settled. It was in Huraymila that he began openly calling people towards 'the true Islam.'

According to his biographers, Ibn ʿAbd al-Wahhāb had by now surpassed his father in knowledge and people began to recognize this. Thus, we are told that large gatherings of people attended his lectures. It was here where he began to openly speak against the innovated practices of the people of his own land, accusing them of having strayed into polytheism. In an attempt to mimic the prophets, he began calling the people – many of whom he regarded as polytheists – towards 'true monotheism.'[11] At some point in this phase, a dispute occurred between Ibn ʿAbd al-Wahhāb and his father, most likely over a legal matter. Due to this, as an obedient son, he avoided lecturing in public and focused on his studies – or writing, according to some accounts, his most famous book, *Kitāb al-Tawḥīd*.

After his father passed away when Ibn ʿAbd al-Wahhāb was around thirty-eight years old, a scholarly vacuum was created, and he rose to greater prominence, becoming the leading scholar in his area. He became emboldened to be more open in his preaching against – and criticisms of – those he deemed to be innovators. His call attracted many followers, most importantly the chieftain of ʿUyayna, Uthmān b. Muʿammar (d. 1163/1750). However, in his own town of Huraymila, he faced opposition. Hence, he eventually moved back to ʿUyayna, where he could teach under Ibn Muʿammar's protection.

With the political backing of Ibn Muʿammar, Ibn ʿAbd al-Wahhāb's proselytization took on a political element. He now had the ability to physically remove the causes of polytheism and innovation, which he began to do in earnest. He felt that there were too many superstitious sites, where the veneration of saints and graves took place, dispersed throughout his land. This veneration was deemed to violate Islamic law and was, therefore, sacrilegious to the purity of the Muslim creed. He began uprooting all icons – graves, shrines, and trees – where such rituals and prayers were performed. He even leveled the most famous grave in Najd: the tomb of Zayd b. al-Khaṭṭāb (d. 11/632), the brother of the second Caliph of Islam, ʿUmar b. al-Khaṭṭāb (d. 23/644). By doing so, he felt that he had cleansed the land of the sources of polytheism.

Ibn ʿAbd al-Wahhāb's initiatives encountered resistance, prompting local inhabitants to voice their grievances to their respective community leaders. Ultimately, these complaints were brought to the attention of Ibn Muʿammar. The tribal leaders of al-Ahsa exerted pressure on him to curtail his support for Ibn ʿAbd al-Wahhāb. Succumbing to this pressure, Ibn Muʿammar acquiesced and requested that Ibn ʿAbd al-Wahhāb depart from ʿUyayna. This proved to be a blessing in disguise for Ibn ʿAbd al-Wahhāb, as he moved to the city of Diriyah, which was under the leadership of a chieftain belonging to the large Banu Tamīm tribe named Muḥammad b. Saʿūd (d. 1179/1765). It was here that a strategic and historic partnership was formed, and it would continue between their families for centuries.

Ibn ʿAbd al-Wahhāb explained to the chieftain that he was there to call people towards pure monotheism and that the locals were involved in polytheism and heresy. Ibn Saʿūd was completely convinced of Ibn ʿAbd al-Wahhāb's message and offered him his full support. He agreed to work with him in spreading this message on two conditions. The first was that Ibn ʿAbd al-Wahhāb would not leave Diriyah after they had fought together for the sake of God. Ibn ʿAbd al-Wahhāb agreed to this condition. The second was that Ibn ʿAbd al-Wahhāb must not stop Muḥammad b. Saʿūd from collecting the taxes on harvests. To this, Ibn ʿAbd al-Wahhāb simply stated that God would bless them with such war booty that they would no longer require taxes. Upon the agreement of both sides, they entered into an alliance to spread the message of 'pure Islam,' establishing the First Saudi State in around 1744.

Some historians claim that a third condition was added: that the political leadership would remain with the descendants of Ibn Saʿūd, and the religious guidance would be entrusted to the descendants of Ibn ʿAbd al-Wahhāb. Whether that was an actual condition made at that time is doubtful, but it nonetheless became a reality. The alliance between the two families remains to this day, in which the responsibilities are delegated in this manner.[12]

The spread of Wahhabism entered a critical stage in Diriyah. With the backing of the Ibn Saʿūd family, Ibn ʿAbd al-Wahhāb began to wage what he considered to be jihad against his enemies. From his perspective, he was inviting people to the pure message of monotheism, the genuine Prophetic message, yet those who called themselves Muslims were rejecting it. Therefore, he concluded that he had no choice but to eradicate their polytheism through war, which he believed was legitimate and sanctioned by God. Despite the militarily offensive nature of later expeditions conducted by the Wahhabis, Ibn ʿAbd al-Wahhāb claimed that the early violence, on the part of himself, his followers, and his allies, was only in self-defense after he and his community were excommunicated from the faith and attacked.[13]

Regardless of the truthfulness of these claims of self-defense, the armies of Ibn Saʿūd began to attack neighboring tribes, in what became 'an imperial effort.'[14] If defensive jihad was the nature of the early battles, it was clearly an offensive jihad by 1752, when they attacked Huraymila, after Ibn ʿAbd al-Wahhāb's own brother, Sulaymān (d. 1209/1794), called the town to rebel.[15] If this was indeed an authentic jihad, then according to Islamic law the lives and properties of those attacked would be forfeited. Ibn ʿAbd al-Wahhāb clearly believed that he was attacking actual apostates, not fellow Muslims, therefore there was nothing ethically unlawful about the attacks and the resulting wealth that his armies accrued.

Raids and skirmishes were a normal part of life in Najd, but they were usually conducted for worldly gain. The wars of Ibn ʿAbd al-Wahhāb took on a spiritual dimension that motivated his soldiers to excel in their battles. When some seemed uncomfortable that those being attacked were claiming to be fellow Muslims, Ibn ʿAbd al-Wahhāb convinced his followers that the locals had rejected the message of monotheism, and that their Sufi practices and veneration of saints was tantamount to open polytheism. Also significant was their loyalty to the Ottoman state, which was clearly a pagan empire in his assessment. This meant that their religious affiliations were not towards Islam for, as he preached, 'anyone who doubted the polytheism of a polytheist himself becomes a polytheist.'[16] As they had clearly become apostates, in this rationale, their blood was permissible to spill. Ibn ʿAbd al-Wahhāb taught that the polytheism of these nominal Muslims was worse than the polytheism of the pagans of Mecca at the time of the Prophet Muhammad, because at least those earlier pagans worshiped God directly at times of distress, whereas these contemporary 'Muslims' called out to saints. Hence, if the Prophet of God could wage war against the pagans of Mecca, then surely, he and his armies had even more right to wage war against those who were worse?

The first major battle was against the chief of Riyadh, Dahhām b. Dawwās (d. 1187/1773). Ibn Dawwās was an avowed enemy of Ibn ʿAbd al-Wahhāb, having launched an assault on a town allied with him. This gave the army of Ibn ʿAbd al-Wahhāb an excuse to fight back and declare jihad. Ibn Dawwās became a major opponent of the new Saudi state, and the war between the two states lasted almost twenty-eight years.

Further, there is great significance in the battle referred to earlier, which took place in Ibn ʿAbd al-Wahhāb's hometown of Huraymila, instigated by his own brother. Sulaymān b. ʿAbd al-Wahhāb had written a book refuting his brother's beliefs and sent it to the people of al-ʿUyayna. Ibn ʿAbd al-Wahhāb wrote a book of his own in response, and the Ibn Saʿūd clan sent an army to quash the rebellion. They were successful, and Sulaymān fled to the city of Sudair.[17]

The fledgling Saudi state was a threat to neighboring chiefdoms, in particular, the chief of al-Ahsa, and the Sharif clan of Mecca – which claimed descent from the Prophet and had governed the holy city for more than half a millennium. A war raged between the followers of Ibn ʿAbd al-Wahhāb and the people of al-Ahsa for twenty years before he emerged victorious. The battle with the Sharifs would take longer to resolve in favor of the Saudi-Wahhabi alliance. On another front, the Shiʿa of Najran attacked Ibn ʿAbd al-Wahhāb's armies, killing over 500 soldiers and taking 200 as prisoners of war. Consequently, Ibn ʿAbd al-Wahhāb signed a peace treaty with the people of Najran to focus on dealing with enemies closer to home.

In 1765, Ibn Saʿūd died, having served as the leader of his people for over thirty years. His son ʿAbd al-Azīz took over as leader of the fledging emirate and continued the jihad in support of Ibn ʿAbd al-Wahhāb. In 1773, Ibn Dawwās was finally defeated after a war that had commenced around 1746, and an important victory was declared as Riyadh was captured. With the conquest of Riyadh, the largest local opposition to the new state was eliminated. Multiple smaller cities immediately pledged allegiance to the new state, recognizing them as the new authorities of Najd. The state then continued to expand southward until the majority of Najd was under the control of the Ibn Saʿūd family by the 1780s, and from there, they began to view Hijaz and al-Ahsa as targets.[18]

Throughout this period, there was great tension between the Sharif of Mecca and the Saudi State. The people of Mecca did not understand this new Wahhabi call and were skeptical of the rising political power in Najd. During this time, the two states sent letters, delegations, and scholars back and forth to debate each other. There were even years in which the followers of Ibn ʿAbd al-Wahhāb were not allowed to perform Hajj. In a decisive battle in the year 1791, the followers of Ibn ʿAbd al-Wahhāb won a resounding victory over the forces of the Sharif.

Ibn ʿAbd al-Wahhāb passed away the following year, in 1792, at around ninety years of age. He left behind a legacy of great knowledge, particularly among his sons and grandsons, who would carry his mantle spiritually and academically as scholars and spokespersons for his thought. In the estimation of his followers, no one since the time of Ibn Taymiyya did more to revive the legacy of Ibn Ḥanbal and the earliest generations of Islam than the figure of Muḥammad b. ʿAbd al-Wahhāb.

Of course, this view is not shared by those who do not subscribe to his theology, and it is to their paradigm that we shall now turn.[19]

### *Muḥammad b. ʿAbd al-Wahhāb: The fanatical deviant*

The province of Najd, where Ibn ʿAbd al-Wahhāb was born, was underdeveloped and barren, and had historically been ignored by most Muslim rulers. Moreover, it was explicitly mentioned in Islamic sources as being a primary source of evil. The Prophet Muhammad warned about the trouble that would arise in this land:

> He said, 'O God, bless us in our Syria! O God, bless us in our Yemen!' They [the people] said, 'O Messenger of God, and [what about] our Najd?' The Prophet said, 'O God, bless us in our Syria! O God, bless us in our Yemen!' They said, 'O Messenger of God, and [what about] our Najd?' The Prophet said, 'Earthquakes and tribulations lie there [in anticipation], and the horn of Satan rises from there.'[20]

To many Muslims, the rise of Wahhabism from the province of Najd is a clear and explicit manifestation of the evils predicted by the Prophet.[21]

In light of the later Wahhabi rebellion, it is important to highlight that eighteenth-century Arabia, in general, formed an integral part of the Ottoman Empire and had done since the sixteenth century.[22] Although parts of it, including Najd, were often neglected and left to local rulers to run, it was without a doubt under the legitimate sovereignty of the Ottoman Caliphate. Many of the local chieftains would praise the Ottoman Sultans in their sermons, indicating they recognized and accepted Ottoman governance.

The scholarly family that Ibn ʿAbd al-Wahhāb was born into was the first to recognize his extremism. It is remarkable to note that his own family members became his strongest critics. For example, his father prevented him from preaching; and later, his brother Sulaymān went so far as to write a public treatise refuting the main points of Ibn ʿAbd al-Wahhāb's theology. Sulaymān argued that his brother was not qualified to dabble in matters of Islamic law and that he was contradicting the opinions of his role models, namely Ibn Taymiyya and Ibn Qayyim. He also argued that the issues Ibn ʿAbd al-Wahhāb raised were matters of valid dispute and that the practices of the people could, at most, be labeled as 'minor polytheism,' which does not take people out of the fold of Islam.[23]

Because Ibn ʿAbd al-Wahhāb spent the bulk of his twenties traveling and studying, there is a large gap in his life that is unknown. There is speculation regarding where he traveled and under whom he studied; some even say that he was influenced by British intelligence agencies during these travels.[24] Nonetheless, he did spend some time in Medina, where he was influenced by Muḥammad Ḥayāt al-Sindī, who would further introduce him to extremist ideas and embolden him to speak out against what they perceived to be polytheism and heresy.

After studying in Medina, he returned to ʿUyayna. Here, he tried to force his new views upon the community. But as he was very young, he failed to gain traction. Frustrated by the situation, he left and went to Basra, where he was exposed to Shiʿism. The practices and beliefs of the Shiʿa enraged him, and he soon found himself in serious trouble with local scholars. Unable to hold his tongue, Ibn ʿAbd al-Wahhāb was eventually forced to leave Basra.

Upon moving to Huraymila, where his father was now settled, Ibn ʿAbd al-Wahhāb began preaching his new message with vigor. This did not sit well with the scholars of the town, who all opposed him, including his own father. The clash with his father caused Ibn ʿAbd al-Wahhāb to step back for a while. His father, recognizing the errant ways of his son, was able to keep him in check while he was alive However, with his passing, Ibn ʿAbd al-Wahhāb was able to preach openly again. Slowly, he gathered a following among the less learned townspeople who were attracted to his ideas. Despite many scholars opposing him, the number of his followers swelled every day.

During this period – or before, while in Basra – he wrote his most famous book, *Kitāb al-Tawḥīd*. The book is a collection of the hadith without any substantive commentary, leaving it open to misinterpretation by the casual reader in that milieu. Such open-endedness is a common feature in the books of Ibn ʿAbd al-Wahhāb. The simplicity of his books caused many of his enemies to doubt his scholarly credentials, with some even referring to them as being akin to students' notes: bulleted generic points lacking any scholarly explanation or demonstrable acumen.

With the support of the chieftain Uthmān b. Muʿammar, Ibn ʿAbd al-Wahhāb grew bolder and began to physically impose his message upon people. He and his students began to uproot and destroy many important Islamic relics. They uprooted trees, leveled graves, and even destroyed sacred shrines. The worst offense he committed during this time was the destruction of the tomb of Zayd b. al-Khaṭṭāb, the brother of the second Caliph of Islam, ʿUmar b. al-Khaṭṭāb. His tomb had stood there for hundreds of years without any opposition, with people seeking blessings from it because it was the tomb of a respected companion of the Prophet. Ibn ʿAbd al-Wahhāb's command to destroy it – on the basis that it was a source of polytheism – started a tradition among his followers of destroying the tombs of pious people, a practice that continues to this day.

Due to his provocative actions, Ibn Muʿammar recognized his deviancy, and Ibn ʿAbd al-Wahhāb was forced to depart, seeking support in the city of Diriyah. In this new city, an unholy alliance was forged that would soon cast a dark shadow over Arabia. This alliance, which would prove devastating for the Muslims, saw Ibn ʿAbd al-Wahhāb joining forces with the local leader, Muḥammad b. Saʿūd. In this partnership, Ibn Saʿūd committed to safeguarding Ibn ʿAbd al-Wahhāb and spreading his teachings under the condition that he retained rule over the people. Empowered by this pact, Ibn ʿAbd al-Wahhāb's strategies took a more violent turn. With the ability to impose his beliefs on the people, he sought a religious pretext to justify his actions.

The pretext was simple. All he had to do was convince his followers that the neighboring tribes were not Muslims but, in fact, apostates, and hence, jihad against them was compulsory. To do this, he taught his followers that whoever shows respect to the pious saints, or seeks blessings from any sacred object, was engaging in polytheism (*shirk*), and was therefore no longer Muslim. Furthermore, he argued that someone who tacitly supported his townsfolk in such activities, even if he himself did not participate, essentially legalized polytheistic activities and, therefore, could be treated as a polytheist himself. Convinced by his argument, or perhaps persuaded by the lure of booty and power, the armies of Ibn Saʿūd declared jihad against their enemies, and anyone who opposed them became, by virtue of their opposition, pagans. Hence, they began conquering neighboring cities and massacring fellow Muslims in the name of Islam.

In the fifteen years following the declaration of war, the Saudi army conquered large areas of Arabia, inevitably destroying many holy sites and historic shrines. They began by conquering most of Najd, followed by some of the tribes of Central Arabia and parts of Yemen. When ʿAbd al-ʿAzīz succeeded his father Muḥammad b. Saʿūd, the bloodshed continued. He conquered Riyadh and set his sights on the Hijaz. This led to a series of clashes between the Sharif of Mecca and the Saudi army.

Even the death of Ibn ʿAbd al-Wahhāb could not stop the rise of the new Saudi-Wahhabi state. His followers had developed a taste for power and continued to fight the Ottoman Empire, taking over various Muslim lands long after his death. After the death of Ibn ʿAbd al-Wahhāb, the Saudi army raided Karbala in 1802, the site of the martyrdom of Ḥusayn (d. 61/680), the grandson of the Prophet Muhammad. This was a completely unprovoked raid: the sole desire was to impose their strand of Islam on a group they deemed heretical and to gain financial strength by looting the city. They entered the city by force, massacred over 2,000 pilgrims who were visiting the shrine,[25] destroyed the dome over Ḥusayn's grave, and pillaged the city of every valuable resource they could find. Soon afterward, they conquered the Arabian city of Taif, killing 200 citizens and pillaging the city, taking whatever they could amass as war booty. This became their pattern as they stormed through Arabia.[26]

Eventually, the Ibn Saʿūd family, alongside Ibn ʿAbd al-Wahhāb's descendants – now known as the Āl al-Shaykh family – succeeded in destabilizing the Ottoman representatives in the Hijaz, which allowed them to conquer Mecca and Medina. These two great cities passed back and forth between the Saudis and Ottomans multiple times before the collapse of the Ottoman Empire in World War I. With the Ottomans no longer a threat, the Saudi-Wahhabi state took on its current form.

By breaking away from normative Sunnism, his critics argue, Ibn ʿAbd al-Wahhāb resurrected extremist tendencies of the earlier fanatical Khārijīs, whom all mainstream Muslims condemn. They contend that he applied verses and rulings intended for idolaters to his fellow Muslims in a misguided manner. Moreover, he unjustifiably declared believers as apostates and used this as a basis to engage in war, resorting to violence and killing fellow Muslims for power and money. Thus, they argue, his ideas and teachings wreak havoc wherever they spread and disrupt peaceful communities by splintering them with internal disputes. He created a literalist do-it-yourself Islam in which every person feels qualified to challenge the scholars and demand simplistic proofs for complex problems. In the eyes of critics, Ibn ʿAbd al-Wahhāb is exactly what the Prophet warned against when he said that *fitan* (trials and tribulations) would come from the province of Najd.

*Conclusion*

The divergent perspectives on the narrative of Ibn ʿAbd al-Wahhāb, evident in the two accounts, underscore the significant contrast in how he is perceived. These viewpoints vary not only in terms of their interpretation but also extend to encompass specific aspects, including phrases, expressions, and descriptions, which remain subjects of contention. The supporters of Ibn ʿAbd al-Wahhāb view his story as the rise of a hero and the revival and purification of Islam, while his opponents view him as a heretical troublemaker who waged war against Muslims and caused chaos in Arabia. However, the story of the rise of Wahhabism does not end with Ibn ʿAbd al-Wahhāb. It continues with the rise of the Kingdom of Saudi Arabia – a story that will be continued in the next section. For now, it is important to take a deeper look at the message of Ibn ʿAbd al-Wahhāb and its unique theological beliefs.

### *3.1.2 The Theology of Muḥammad b. ʿAbd al-Wahhāb*

Ibn ʿAbd al-Wahhāb preached a theology that was based on his direct reading of the Qurʾan and hadith, as well as key concepts introduced by Ibn Taymiyya, but interpreted in novel ways (as will be demonstrated below). While certain concepts propagated by Ibn ʿAbd al-Wahhāb were not entirely unprecedented, his critics argue that they did not conform to the established norms of mainstream Islamic tradition. Additionally, he promoted unprecedented views, such as his politicization of the notion of *al-walāʾ wa-l-barāʾ* (association and disassociation).

The main concepts that we shall discuss here are: (1) his reception and subsequent reinterpretation of the Taymiyyan understanding of monotheism (*tawḥīd*) – in particular the notion of God's exclusive prerogative to be worshiped (*ulūhiyya*), (2) the implications of this understanding of monotheism on excommunication (*takfīr*), (3) his development of the doctrine of association with the believers and disassociation from the disbelievers (*al-walāʾ wa-l-barāʾ*), and (4) his application of jihad.[27]

### *God's sole right to be venerated: Tawḥīd al-Ulūhiyya*

Ibn ʿAbd al-Wahhāb promoted Ibn Taymiyya's tripartite division of monotheism (*tawḥīd*) into three categories: worship (*ulūhiyya*), lordship (*rubūbiyya*), and the names and attributes (*asmā wa-l-ṣifāt*). However, Ibn Taymiyya's writings focused primarily on the correct understanding of God's names and attributes and proving that the divine attributes – all of them – should be understood literally in a manner that befits God. While Ibn Taymiyya did speak out against certain issues regarding the veneration of saints and wrote some treatises on this topic, this was not the focus of his preaching.

In contrast, Ibn ʿAbd al-Wahhāb's preaching was almost exclusively preoccupied with his understanding of God's sole right to be worshiped (*ulūhiyya*). Throughout his writings, he continuously appeals to readers to direct all worship and veneration to God alone. Not even the prophets or angels were worthy of any special veneration, they were respected only because they perfected their servitude to God. True love for the prophets implied that one should worship God directly, emulating their humility and mannerisms.[28]

Of course, no Muslim theologian of any sect claims that any other than God should be worshiped. The Qurʾan clearly states[29] that the one unforgivable sin in the eyes of God is the opposite of monotheism, which is *shirk*. Hence, *all* Muslims abjure this heinous sin. It is in how he *defined* monotheism and worship, and consequently *shirk*, that Ibn ʿAbd al-Wahhāb departed from mainstream Muslim belief.

For most Muslims, monotheism (*tawḥīd*) implies believing in only One God, i.e., there is only One Supreme, All-Powerful Creator, Sustainer, and Nourisher, and that is Allah. The one unforgivable sin, that of *shirk*, would therefore only exist if a Muslim believed in another god besides the One True God, Allah. However, since Ibn ʿAbd al-Wahhāb adopted the Taymiyyan tripartite division of *tawḥīd*, he could then argue that it was possible for a person to believe that there is only One Supreme God (which would be *tawḥīd* in Lordship, or *rubūbiyya*), yet still fall into paganism by *worshiping* an entity that he did not believe was god (which would be an infringement in *tawḥīd* of *ulūhiyya*). Hence, even if a Muslim *claimed* to believe in One God, for Ibn ʿAbd al-Wahhāb, the *act* of diverting something he considered worship would nullify that Muslim's claim, and it would be permitted to accuse them of falling into *shirk*. For non-Wahhabi interpretations of Islam, no act of devotion directed to another entity could be considered *shirk* if one did not first believe that entity was a type of deity.

Of central concern to Ibn ʿAbd al-Wahhāb was the popular manifestation of saint veneration. One key aspect of his thought was that the primary path to polytheism was elevating exemplary pious people into saints. For Ibn ʿAbd al-Wahhāb, pre-Islamic idolatry was nothing but the veneration of saints. He pointed out that many of the famous Arabian idols were originally holy people whom their own nations had elevated and raised to the level of deities after their deaths.[30] Christianity was another example: Jesus was a noble prophet, and yet his people venerated him excessively to the point of committing idolatry by worshiping him. Hence, he warned that Muslims *must never* go down this path by excessively venerating their prophet or their saints.[31]

It was this preoccupation with what he perceived to be 'saint worship' on which Ibn ʿAbd al-Wahhāb focused his preaching. Prophets, angels, and saints, he taught, were all created beings who wielded no power. In fact, they were themselves worshipers of God, wanting His blessings and asking Him for forgiveness. If these beings were worshiping God, he argued, how could any Muslim then turn to them as objects of worship?[32]

Hence, any veneration that seemed to suggest the saint was somehow able to help the devotee was akin to idolatry. For Ibn ʿAbd al-Wahhāb, such practice then became polytheism (*shirk*), the one unforgivable sin in Islam. There were a number of key ideas and practices that he focused on which he deemed as manifestations of *shirk*, both major and minor. These included: (1) wearing talismans or amulets to ward off evil or procure good (a common practice among Sufis and lay-Muslims),[33] (2) praying in the vicinity of or traveling to the grave of a saint, believing that the saint's grave makes such a prayer more blessed,[34] (3) seeking blessings (*baraka*) from any item, such as a tree, or a mausoleum,[35] (4) making a religious oath (or *nadhr*) in the name of a saint or Prophet (for example by saying, 'If I am cured of such a disease, I vow to feed a poor person in the name of the Prophet'),[36] (5) sacrificing an animal to distribute its meat to the poor around a shrine, or in the name of a saint of a shrine,[37] (6) believing in omens,[38] (7) seeking spiritual refuge (*al-istiʿādha*) in a saint or prophet,[39] (8) possessing, much less venerating, any icon or statue or image,[40] and (9) practicing or believing in witchcraft and magic.[41]

However, the act that was the most reprehensible in his eyes was that of (10) *istighātha*, or calling out to the Prophet or the saints for one's needs. For Ibn ʿAbd al-Wahhāb, the invoking of *any* entity besides God for what he considered supernatural help was the essence of idolatry, on the basis of the fact that the Prophet was reported to have said, 'Supplication (*duʿa*) is the essence of worship.'[42] The response of his opponents, that they were not praying *to* the dead but *through* them in order to get to God, was soundly dismissed on the basis of his reading of Qurʾanic criticism leveled against the pagans of the Quraysh. He interpreted a number of Qurʾanic verses[43] as indicating that pagans worshiped idols with the excuse that they were using them as intermediaries to get to God. Hence, he argued, a Muslim who turned to any entity other than God with the same excuse automatically fell into paganism, *even if he did not consider that intermediary to be a god or intend an act of worship*. For him, it was irrelevant if a devotee claimed that saints were merely their intermediaries to God and that they were not viewing them the way pagans viewed idols: their invocation of the saints *made them gods*, even if they did not believe them to be such.[44] While it is true, he claimed, that God might allow prophets or saints intercession, as the Qur᾿an affirms, it is God that grants that right, not the prophet or saint. Hence, he argued, one should ask God directly for the Prophet's intercession and not go to the grave of the Prophet and ask *him* for it. Asking the Prophet directly after his death, he argued, was a type of *shirk*.

In fact, he went further than this and argued that Muslims in his time guilty of such practices were *worse* than the Meccan idolaters to whom the Qur᾿an was revealed because the pagans would invoke God directly at times of distress, whereas these 'Muslims' invoked their saints, or the Prophet himself, during such times.[45] Hence, the paganism of his opponents (which included Arab and Ottoman scholars) was clearer and more abominable than the paganism of the pre-Islamic Arabs to whom the Qur᾿an was revealed.

He agreed with Ibn Taymiyya's verdict that visiting the grave of the Prophet was not in itself a legislated act of worship, unless one happened to be in the holy city of Medina, in which case, just like any local grave, one may go and offer prayers for the deceased (the point being that one should not travel to another city for the sake of obtaining blessings from a grave, even the grave of the Prophet himself). He also taught that graves should be simple and level with the ground: just a mound of earth with a marker sufficed. Anything beyond this, especially a structure, should be demolished in case it leads to veneration and worship. A core practice of his movement was the demolition of all mausoleums and even headstones, as these were regarded as reprehensible innovations and stepping stones to polytheism.[46] His followers would become known for their iconoclastic practices of demolishing any structure on the graves of those deemed to be saints by non-Wahhabis.

*Takfīr (excommunication)*

Mainstream Sunnism is extremely hesitant to excommunicate fellow believers, believing that it is better to err on the side of caution rather than potentially incur the wrath of God.[47] Sunnis look to the excesses of the earliest splinter groups in Islam, the Khārijīs, who were the first to open the floodgates in the liberal application of *takfīr* (excommunication) upon all who disagreed with them – hence justifying fighting them – and realized that the door to *takfīr* leads to many dangers.

The writings of Ibn ʿAbd al-Wahhāb, however, are rife with accusations of *takfīr*. In one of his early letters, he stated, 'The belief in righteous persons (i.e., believing in saints) and others that most people profess today is polytheism.'[48] Similarly, regarding the Muslims of his region, he wrote, 'Know – may God guide you – that polytheism is what has filled the earth, and people call it "belief in righteous persons."'[49] As stated earlier, not only did Ibn ʿAbd al-Wahhāb effectively excommunicate the Muslim masses during his lifetime, he also claimed that their disbelief was worse than the disbelief of the polytheists of the past: 'If you know this, and you know what most people are doing, you will know that they are greater in disbelief and polytheism than the polytheists whom the Prophet fought.'[50]

The concept of *takfir* is clearly linked to how one defines monotheism and worship. For non-Wahhabi theologians, a Muslim could only be considered a non-Muslim if he believed or did something that clearly contradicted the testimony of faith; and even then, most Sunni movements would have a long list of conditions and impediments before specifying a person as having left the fold of Islam. In other words, to describe an *act* as polytheistic (*shirk*) or blasphemous (*kufr*) does not entail that the one who does it *becomes* an apostate, for one might have been coerced or unintentionally done something or perhaps was not aware that the belief or act was deemed blasphemous.

It appears, though, that Ibn ʿAbd al-Wahhāb generally did not consider such excuses as valid (we shall return to this point in the next section), and he gave immediate and overarching verdicts on large groups of Muslims who did not follow his teachings. In fact, he defined *shirk* as 'supplicating to others besides God.'

He did not stop at excommunicating those Muslims who venerated saints, but went further and excommunicated anybody who did not also excommunicate such Muslims, as well as anyone who merely doubted their disbelief. In his small treatise *Nawāqiḍ al-Islām* (*Nullifiers of Islam*), he listed as the third nullifier, 'Whosoever does not excommunicate the polytheists, or *is doubtful of their disbelief*, or affirms the validity of their doctrine, is a disbeliever by consensus.'[51] In a vacuum, this statement seems to fit within traditional Islamic theology. After all, anyone who considers the beliefs of another faith as valid along with Islam has clearly betrayed the normative claim of the exclusive truth the religion brings and hence fallen into serious error. However, the context in which it is stated here by Ibn ʿAbd al-Wahhāb gives it a somewhat ominous meaning. The 'polytheists' that he mentioned in his letters were the self-identifying Muslim peoples of Arabia, and those in the neighboring Ottoman lands, not people of other faiths. Hence, anyone who did not consider those tribes, or the Ottomans, as being outside the fold of Islam, or even doubted this fact and entertained the possibility that they were believers, was, according to Ibn ʿAbd al-Wahhāb, a disbeliever himself. In practice, this allowed Ibn ʿAbd al-Wahhāb and his early followers carte blanche to excommunicate all those who dared challenge their own verdict of disbelief. The claim that the majority of Muslims of Arabia and the Ottoman Empire at that time had abandoned Islam is what allowed the early Saudi-Wahhabi state to wage what it considered a holy war against them.

Despite the actions of Ibn ʿAbd al-Wahhāb being crystal clear in this regard, almost all modern followers of the movement have a very different understanding and claim that he did *not* excommunicate fellow Muslims. We shall, therefore, dedicate the next section to addressing this seeming contradiction (and later, explain how this shift occurred from what will be termed 'First-Wave Wahhabism' to 'Third-Wave Wahhabism').

*Politicizing theological dissent: al-Walāʾ wa-l-barāʾ*

The term *al-walāʾ wa-l-barāʾ* is often translated into English as 'allegiance and disavowal.' *Walāʾ* translates as 'loyalty and protection,' and *barāʾ* its opposite, 'dissociation and disavowal.' Mainstream Sunnism discusses such concepts as ethical manifestations of helping one's brethren in faith and of avoiding helping wrongdoers, in particular enemies of the faith wanting to attack Muslims and prevent them from worshiping God. There is a further ethical concept of 'loving what God loves, and being displeased at what God is displeased by,' and this is derived from a number of Qurʾanic verses and traditions of the Prophet. This concept does have some precedence in earlier writings of Ibn Taymiyya and others,[52] and there is clearly a fierce notion of 'refuting the people of deviation' among many early Salafi authors (perhaps most notoriously among the Ḥanbalīs, for example the pseudo-Barbahārī treatise *Sharḥ al-Sunna* mentioned in the previous chapter), but no interpretation of Sunni Islam ever named this doctrine as a fundamental pillar of the faith, nor did any Sunni group use it the way that Ibn ʿAbd al-Wahhāb did.[53] This notion remains, to this day, a core part of the teachings of all who are influenced by Wahhabism, particularly the jihadi groups.

Ibn ʿAbd al-Wahhāb used specific Qurʾanic verses and hadiths to derive a unique doctrine: in order to be a true believer, one must show outward *exclusive* loyalty to true believers, helping, aiding, and living among true believers. Faith, he argued, *required* 'dissociating' from unbelievers theologically, socially, culturally, and politically. Frequently, he would use the term *bugdh* (hating) for God's sake. As an integral aspect of genuine faith, Ibn ʿAbd al-Wahhāb contended that a believer must display 'loyalty' to the faith and its people and sever any affiliations that signify allegiance to those who oppose it. Not doing so jeopardized one's standing as a believer.[54]

The following quotations from Ibn ʿAbd al-Wahhāb demonstrate the importance of this belief in early Wahhabism:

> The foundation of Islam and its principle are two commands. The first is the command to worship God alone without a partner, to agitate for

> this, to demonstrate one's affinity to it, and to excommunicate those who do not practice it. The second is to warn against associating other beings in the worship of God, to be stern in this, to demonstrate enmity to it, and to excommunicate those who perpetrate it.[55]

He also said,

> Do not think that if you say, 'This is the truth. I follow it and eschew all else, but I will not confront them [i.e., those who oppose the truth] and will say nothing concerning them,' that this will profit you. Rather, it is necessary to hate them, to hate those whom they love, to revile them, and to show them enmity.[56]

There are many similar statements found in the letters of Ibn ʿAbd al-Wahhāb and the books of his descendants, which all prove the central importance of 'loyalty and enmity' to early Wahhabism. Ibn ʿAbd al-Wahhāb treated this doctrine as a necessary part of monotheism and excommunicated those who did not agree with him on this.[57]

This concept was then liberally applied by Ibn ʿAbd al-Wahhāb, both theologically and politically. By claiming that his followers were the *only* legitimate manifestation of Islam and true believers, he could then argue that '*walā*'' had to be shown to him and his political state; and that any group who showed loyalty to those that opposed him could, therefore, be seen as 'nullifying' their faith in Islam, and thus be deemed apostates.

Ibn ʿAbd al-Wahhāb's grandsons Sulaymān (d. 1818) and Abd al-Raḥmān (d. 1869), as well as the famous scholar of the Second Saudi State, Hamad b. ʿAtīq (d. 1884),[58] took this concept to its logical conclusion: this strict Manichean dichotomy was then easily applied against the invading forces of the Ottoman Empire and, hence, casually extended to include settlements and individuals who aligned themselves with the Ottoman cause from among the Arab tribes of the region. Moreover, it was even applied to those who assumed a neutral stance and refrained from taking any political positions within this conflict since they had not clearly 'dissociated' from the unbelievers (i.e., the Ottomans). These individuals, by virtue of them not showing loyalty to the true manifestation of Islam, according to the Wahhabi clerics, were showing loyalty to disbelief, and hence, *ipso facto*, were not Muslims.[59] Migration (*hijra*), a noble concept in Islam in its own right, was made an obligation on all non-Wahhabis to lands controlled by the Saudis. In fact, those who were unable to openly express hostility and enmity towards the non-Wahhabis in their own lands, they argued, were *obliged* to migrate to 'lands of Islam,' meaning Wahhabi territory. What this meant politically was that anyone who, for whatever reason, did not migrate to the lands ruled by Ibn Saʿūd was, once again, de facto a rejector of the faith.[60]

This understanding of *al-walāʾ wa-l-barāʾ* was the standard, mainstream position of early Wahhabism and was only tempered during the Third Saudi State as political alliances with foreign countries, especially the United Kingdom and the United States, became important, and tolerance towards Sufis and Shiʿis became necessary, as shall be discussed below.

However, the original understanding of *al-walāʾ wa-l-barāʾ* was recently revived by the Jihadi-Salafi movement, with copious quotations from early Wahhabi thinkers, including, of course, Ibn ʿAbd al-Wahhāb. Most infamously, Abū Muḥammad al-Maqdisi, in his book *Millat Ibrāhīm* (*The Creed of Abraham*), quotes liberally from early Wahhabi sources to justify the idea of allegiance towards the jihadi movement and enmity towards anybody who opposed them.[61] It was al-Maqdisi who reintroduced the original Wahhabi doctrine of *al-walaʾ wa-l-baraʾ*[62] that is now a fundamental belief of all Jihadi-Salafi movements. This notion will be elaborated on in more detail in Chapter 5 on Jihadi-Salafism.

*The central role of jihad in Wahhabism*

Combining all of the aforementioned concepts – the Wahhabi definition of *tawḥid* and its necessary corollary of *takfir*, coupled with their unique understanding of 'association and disassociation' – led to the inevitable result of believing in the legitimacy of waging jihad against all people outside the movement.

In the view of the early Wahhabis, those who opposed them were outside the fold of Islam – worse than pagans – hence, they reasoned that Islamic law allowed them to wage jihad as a means to bring them back into the fold. While Ibn ʿAbd al-Wahhāb implied that he drew inspiration from the writings of Ibn Taymiyya on the subject of jihad, the former, nonetheless, forged his own path in a decidedly more violent and extreme manner than anything Ibn Taymiyya had ever preached.[63]

It is important to note that while tribal warfare and Bedouin raids were a regular part of life in the Najd, Ibn ʿAbd al-Wahhāb and his followers brought in a uniquely religious element and utilized jihad as a tool to fight other Muslims and, subsequently, the Ottoman Empire. They justified this on the basis of excommunication (*takfīr*). Ibn ʿAbd al-Wahhāb imagined himself and his followers reliving the legacy of the Prophet Muhammad sent to fight the pagans of Arabia and turn them away from polytheism towards monotheism. Within this perspective, they construed their adversaries as pagans and apostates, thereby legitimizing theologically sanctioned warfare against them. In fact, early histories of the movement written by adherents, like the *Tārīkh* of Ibn Ghannām,[64] literally mention the raids of the Ibn ʿAbd al-Wahhāb in the same manner that the biographies of the Prophet and the *sīra* anthologies described the Prophet's battles: calling them by the specific term typically used for Prophetic battles, the *ghazawāt*.

A distinction can be made here between the early and later parts of Ibn ʿAbd al-Wahhāb's life. Before allying with the Ibn Saʿūd tribe, Ibn ʿAbd al-Wahhāb focused primarily on preaching and teaching his message. However, once he had the alliance of a political leader and command of his troops, the message turned violent. The second half of Ibn ʿAbd al-Wahhāb's life – as even the biographies sympathetic to him indicate – is full of stories of expeditions and battles against other Muslims. The evidence for this can be seen in both his writings and the criticisms raised against him by the scholars of his time.

Muḥammad b. ʿAfāliq (d. 1163/1750), for example, in his letters to Ibn Muʿammar, asked how he could justify the murder of Muslims in the name of jihad.[65] This letter may have been what caused Ibn Muʿammar to doubt his support for Ibn ʿAbd al-Wahhāb and turn against him, leading to his eventual assassination at the hands of Wahhabis. Others who criticized Ibn ʿAbd al-Wahhāb for waging war against Muslims included Salih b. ʿAbd Allāh al-Najdī (d. circa 1760),[66] ʿAbd Allāh al-Muways (d. 1761),[67] and his own brother, Sulaymān b. ʿAbd al-Wahhāb.[68]

To Ibn ʿAbd al-Wahhāb, however, his jihad was totally justified. Additionally, he invoked the historical precedent set by the first Caliph of Islam, Abū Bakr (d. 13/634), who engaged in warfare against those who resisted payment of the obligatory alms (*zakāt*). Ibn ʿAbd al-Wahhāb contended that if Abū Bakr was authorized to undertake a religious war against those who disregarded the third pillar of Islam, then it logically followed that he should be similarly sanctioned to wage a religious war against those who contravened the very first pillar of Islam – monotheism.[69]

These sentiments would, of course, eventually be watered down and reinterpreted by later Wahhabi scholars in the modern Kingdom until they would be resurrected in Jihadi-Salafi thought.

### *3.1.3 Ibn ʿAbd al-Wahhāb's Excommunication of Other Muslims*

Although excommunication (*takfīr*) of other Muslims was mentioned briefly above as being a central part of Ibn ʿAbd al-Wahhāb's theology, it is so contentious that it requires a fuller discussion here, with an elaboration on its meaning and the scope of its application. As shall be discussed in later sections, Wahhabism went through a number of critical, government-prompted reforms over the centuries, and modern Wahhabism is markedly different from its original manifestation. One of the most significant changes is the toning down of the concept of *takfīr*. In order to do this, modern clerics needed to reclaim the image of Ibn ʿAbd al-Wahhāb and exonerate him from his own actions.

The charge that Ibn ʿAbd al-Wahhāb excommunicated the bulk of the Muslim world is not new. It was something his own opponents accused him of early in his career, and he responded to those challenges with a vehement defense. Those defenses are used, especially by modern followers, to recast him in a different light. The newly refined image of Ibn ʿAbd al-Wahhāb presented to today's initiates claims he was not guilty of this heinous sin at all. Rather, this is a slander that results from the evil accusations of his opponents who wished to smear his reputation and besmirch his character.[70] Hence, the question must be asked: Did Ibn ʿAbd al-Wahhāb *actually* excommunicate the majority of the Muslim world?

Defenders of Ibn ʿAbd al-Wahhāb bring up specific statements from his letters to prove his innocence, such as the following quotes:

> We do not excommunicate anyone except the one who came to know the truth and rejected it after the proof had been established upon him, who is invited to it but does not accept it and shows stubborn resistance and obstinacy. What has been mentioned about us, that we excommunicate the one whose condition is other than this, is a fabrication against us.[71]
>
> As for what the enemies have mentioned about me, that I excommunicate on the basis of presumption and on the basis of loyalty [meaning: whether that person is loyal to the movement or not], or that I excommunicate the ignorant person upon whom the proof has not been established, then this is a mighty slander. They desire to make the people flee from the religion of God and His Messenger by way of it.[72]
>
> Regarding *takfīr*: I excommunicated the one who knew the religion of the Messenger, and then after he came to know of it, he reviled it, prevented the people from it, and showed enmity to the one who implemented it. This is the one I declare a disbeliever, and most of the Nation [of Muslims] – all praise is due to God – is not like that. As for fighting, then we did not fight anyone till this day except to protect our lives and honor. They are the ones who came to our lands and left [us] no [alternative] possibility. However, we may sometimes fight some of them from the angle of reprisal, and the reward for evil is its like.[73]

There are many more statements similar to these that are scattered throughout his letters and writings. These are used by his followers to demonstrate that he was, in fact, a mainstream Sunni. Pro-Wahhabi books and websites have large sections dedicated to reproducing and analyzing these quotations, taking them at face value.[74]

The dilemma here is that one faces a clear contradiction between what Ibn ʿAbd al-Wahhāb said in these letters and what he himself wrote elsewhere and clearly practiced in his life. (In a later section, we shall discuss the irony of the fact that Ibn ʿAbd al-Wahhāb *explicitly* clarifies his own message in these quotes and claims that any Muslim who is guilty of what he has classified as *shirk* automatically is excommunicated even if he did it unknowingly).[75] In response to scholars who accused him of *takfīr en masse*, Ibn ʿAbd al-Wahhāb wrote these letters claiming that this was a lie against him. Yet, the history of early Wahhabism, along with explicit quotations from other works of his, clearly shows that Ibn ʿAbd al-Wahhāb and his followers regarded the Muslims around them as pagans and waged religious wars against them. What underscores this point is the reality that *every single refutation* written against Wahhabism in its early history focuses on this reality: the charge that this movement accuses the rest of the Muslim world of being outside the fold of Islam. There seems to be a clear disconnect between these few statements from the founder on the one hand and how it was perceived by everyone else on the other. It is also undeniable that the early Wahhabis considered the Ottoman Empire to be a pagan empire – the Second Saudi State, during which time the sons and grandsons of the founder were in religious authority, went to war directly with it under the rubric of jihad and was quelled brutally, as the next section will detail.

Perhaps the most telling example of the application of this principle was in the case of Ibn Muʿammar. This story is mentioned quite factually in the earliest histories written by the supporters of the movement. When Ibn Muʿammar – who, it should be recalled, was the first political leader who supported Ibn ʿAbd al-Wahhāb – began to waver in his support and became sympathetic towards Ibn ʿAfāliq – the Ḥanbali scholar who was the main critic of Ibn ʿAbd al-Wahhāb – this wavering was deemed to be apostasy. News reached Ibn ʿAbd al-Wahhāb that his one-time supporter was now in direct correspondence with an arch-enemy: a rival cleric who, ironically, was not as much pro-Ottoman and pro-Sufi as he was anti-Wahhabi. Some disgruntled followers of Ibn Muʿammar visited Ibn ʿAbd al-Wahhāb, and they were told in no uncertain terms that Ibn Muʿammar was an apostate and hence, was permitted to be executed. Therefore, upon explicit orders from Ibn ʿAbd al-Wahhāb, Ibn Muʿammar was assassinated in a surprise attack in his own mosque after praying the Friday prayers.[76] It is important to stress that Ibn Muʿammar was executed as an apostate and not merely for political expediency and that this assassination is celebrated in early histories of the movement as a victory. So strict was Ibn ʿAbd al-Wahhāb's implementation of *takfīr* that there was no room for doubt in his message, or in the disbelief of his enemies, for that matter.

Nonetheless, the question remains: How do we reconcile the stark contrast between his letters, in which he claims not to practice *takfīr*, and the actions of his movement itself? There are several different ways that this can be done; four are mentioned here.

The first is taken by the modern followers of Ibn ʿAbd al-Wahhāb, who wish to reclaim his legacy and exonerate him from the accusation that he was in any way, shape, or form sympathetic to such extremist Khārijī tendencies. These followers are taught a revisionist understanding of history (in what has been called 'Third-Wave Wahhabism' as we shall discuss later in this chapter),[77] and the claim is made that accusations of *takfīr* against Ibn ʿAbd al-Wahhāb were slanders made by his adversaries, which lacked any shred of credibility or truth. They tend to dismiss, overlook, or reinterpret historical evidence, such as the assassination of Ibn Muʿammar, his constant jihad against fellow professed Muslims, or the explicit declarations of his children and grandchildren that the Ottoman Empire in its totality was pagan and idolatrous. Given this specific paradigm, followers become increasingly convinced that Ibn ʿAbd al-Wahhāb is innocent of the charge of mass-*takfīr*. However, their denials are not rooted in different interpretations of the available evidence but about maintaining a particular portrayal of Ibn ʿAbd al-Wahhāb that suits their worldview.

The second approach assumes that Ibn ʿAbd al-Wahhāb was deceptive and openly lied in his letters to convince his opponents that he was a moderate. The fact that his actions contradicted his letters indicates that he may have been attempting to defend himself by simply denying what he was doing. This is the understanding of many who oppose Ibn ʿAbd al-Wahhāb. Obviously, this approach would mean assuming the worst of such a person: that he was not even sincere in his own message. However, this is too one-sided an explanation to adopt wholesale, and we should consider the other factors at play.

A third way to reconcile his statements with his actions is by reminding ourselves of the political developments in his own life. One could argue that his thought on *takfir* evolved within his lifetime; so at an earlier stage he did not consider his opponents outside the fold of Islam. This is how the earliest wave of Wahhabi clerics, who were very vocal in their excommunication of the 'pagan' Ottoman Empire, understood the cited passages. It is ironic, to say the least, that First-Wave clerics of the eighteenth century found his quotes in which he *excuses* other Muslims to be problematic and had to explain those in light of his actions and other statements. In contrast, modern Third-Wave clerics find his actions and other statements of blanket *takfīr* problematic and need to interpret those vis-à-vis their own views of the faith.

One of the most explicit quotes to buttress this argument of reconciling Ibn ʿAbd al-Wahhāb's apparent contradictions is found in the writings of a senior cleric of the First Saudi State, ʿAbd Allāh Abā Buṭayn (d. 1865), a student of the sons of Ibn ʿAbd al-Wahhāb, and a chief judge of the First Saudi State. In one of his treatises, he writes:

> And as for the claim that Shaykh Muḥammad [b. ʿAbd al-Wahhāb] did not excommunicate those who were upon [the worship] of the mausoleum of al-Kuwāz, and others like them, and the claim that he would not excommunicate such idolators until the evidence had been established against them (*iqāmat al-ḥujja*), this can be answered as yes, this was in fact the case in the beginning part [of his call] ... because they were at that time living in a period in-between messages (*zamān fatra*), and not having access to the teachings of the Prophet. That is why he himself pointed out that they were ignorant and had no one to teach them. However, once the evidence has been established, there is no issue in excommunicating them even if they themselves do not understand the evidence.[78]

This passage is quite telling. Abā Buṭayn is refuting the notion that Ibn ʿAbd al-Wahhāb used ignorance as an excuse (*al-ʿudhr bi-l-jahl*) by claiming that such 'idol-worshipers' cannot be excused anymore. Here, he uses *wathanī* – a term exclusively used for those who worship idols – to describe his fellow Muslims who venerated saints. It should be noted that Abā Buṭayn was born in the lifetime of Ibn ʿAbd al-Wahhāb. According to him, Ibn ʿAbd al-Wahhāb only used ignorance as an excuse *before* he had launched and began propagating his mission, believing that any 'Muslim' alive at the time surely could not have known of the teachings of the Prophet due to the lack of any qualified scholars. To underscore this point, he uses the technical term '*fatra*,' commonly employed in theological treatises to demarcate periods during which prophets had not conveyed the message of monotheism, thereby potentially excusing individuals for their adherence to paganism and unbelief due to the absence of prophetic guidance. However, once Ibn ʿAbd al-Wahhāb's political state was established, Abā Buṭayn claims that the onus now shifted to those 'Muslims' who practice 'idolatry.' If they do not understand the message after the evidence has been established by preachers teaching the true message of Islam, that is a shortcoming for which *they* are liable. This testimony from one of the senior intellectual architects of early Wahhabism explicitly explains the apparent contradiction in Ibn ʿAbd al-Wahhāb's teachings by stating that political circumstances caused the founder to modify his views.

There is yet a fourth way to explain this apparent contradiction. This is to claim that he truly believed that he was not excommunicating the Muslim masses. Rather, in his mind, he was only excommunicating pagans, or in other words, those who were not *really* Muslim. While some may view this as circular, in his mind, it made perfect sense. For example, he writes in his letter to the people of Riyadh and Manfuhah, 'We have not excommunicated Muslims; rather, we have only excommunicated polytheists.'[79]

Similarly, in a letter that Ibn ʿAbd al-Wahhāb wrote to some of his followers who questioned him regarding why the people of the city of Qasim were to be fought, he replied:

> The people of Qasim are deluded [into thinking they are Muslim] because they do not have any graves or mausoleums. However, inform them that loving and hating for the sake of God, and showing loyalty and enmity [in a like manner], are an essential part of faith. So as long as they do not cut off ties from the people of Zulfi and their ilk, the fact that they themselves have not worshiped other than God will not benefit them, nor will their testimony of faith: 'There is no god but God.'[80]

In this, there is no clearer indication of the intent of Ibn ʿAbd al-Wahhāb when he writes that *anyone who doubts the faith has left the faith*. Here, by faith, he means anyone who doubts his *own* interpretation of the faith and who potentially questions his preaching, and he excommunicates the entire town of Qasim simply because they had cordial ties with the neighboring town of Zulfi, the latter of whom had refused to give allegiance to him.

By utilizing such doublespeak, Ibn ʿAbd al-Wahhāb was able to present himself as a moderate in his letters while waging jihad against anyone who opposed him or even was ambivalent about his teachings. And, in all likelihood, he did this entirely sincerely. There is no reason to doubt that he genuinely believed that his message was so pure and clear that opposing him was tantamount to a rejection of the religion revealed by God Himself.

It should be noted that the third and fourth interpretations are not mutually exclusive; in fact, it could be argued that both these responses are simultaneously at play.

As for the next generation of Wahhabi clerics, there simply can be no doubt with respect to this issue. Ibn ʿAbd al-Wahhāb's sons and grandsons, and the clerics that led the movement until the founding of the modern Kingdom of Saudi Arabia a century ago, did not suppress their opinions about *takfīr* of the Ottomans, and any who wavered in their disavowal of them. When the Ottomans sent an expedition to fight the Wahhabis in 1811, Sulaymān b. ʿAbd Allāh Āl al-Shaykh (d. 1818) – a grandson of Ibn ʿAbd al-Wahhāb – wrote an epistle entitled *al-Dalāʾil fī ḥukm muwālāt Ahl al-ishrāk* (*Manifest Evidence Regarding Showing Loyalty to the People of Polytheism*) in which he argued, via twenty-one textual proofs, that anyone sympathetic to the invading 'polytheist' forces was an apostate. Tellingly, the treatise did not even feel the need to excommunicate the Ottomans themselves, as it was taken for granted by both the author and his readers that they were 'people of polytheism.'[81]

The founders of the Wahhabi movement and its earliest generations of clerics, therefore, clearly excommunicated all those who disagreed with their interpretation of the religion and considered them to be polytheists. As we shall see, the modern descendants and followers of the movement would have to reassess and change this narrative in order to protect themselves and the movement from accusations of extremism.

### *3.1.4 The Writings of Muḥammad b. ʿAbd al-Wahhāb*

A salient feature of Ibn ʿAbd al-Wahhāb's books is his heavy reliance on the Qurʾan and hadith, without much explanation apart from chapter headings and a few brief comments analyzing or explaining a citation. He rarely quotes any earlier scholars. This is odd, as it is the practice of Muslim scholars to back up their opinions with quotations from their predecessors, especially when they claim to emulate the earliest generations (*salaf*). It seems that he relies on the intelligence of the reader to draw their conclusions and that he considers the quoted sacred texts self-explanatory. His followers considered his trademark lack of commentary to be part of his genius, while his detractors considered it a sign of his lack of academic credentials.

The single most important book in Wahhabi theology is *Kitāb al-Tawhīd* (*The Book of Monotheism*). It is one of the most influential books in Saudi Arabia and is taught in all Saudi universities as a theological primer or, at the very least, relied upon extensively as a reference point. Due to the brief nature of the text, multiple commentaries have been written on it. The most famous commentary is *Fatḥ al-majīd sharḥ Kitāb al-Tawḥīd* (*The Victory of the Exalted: an explanation of the Book of Monotheism*) by Ibn ʿAbd al-Wahhāb's grandson, ʿAbd al-Raḥmān b. Ḥasan Āl al-Shaykh. Another famous commentary is *al-Qawl al-Mufīd ʿala kitāb al-tawḥīd* (*Explanation of the Book of Monotheism*) by Muḥammad b. Ṣaliḥ al-Uthaymin, who was a leading modern Wahhabi-Salafi scholar from Saudi Arabia. The fact that so many commentaries have been written on it by such high-ranking scholars shows its status in the eyes of Wahhabis. No true student of modern Salafism can possibly rise in its ranks and achieve scholarly status without having read and then eventually taught this seminal work numerous times.[82]

The book's core focus is on the concept of worship (*ulūhiyya*) of God and His divine right to be worshiped alone. Ibn ʿAbd al-Wahhāb begins by presenting the importance of monotheism and the dangers of polytheism. He then focuses on several practices that were common in Arabia during his time and provides evidence that each of them is, in fact, a polytheistic act that was condemned in the Prophet's era. Among the practices he categorizes as polytheistic are the use of bracelets, strings, talismans, and amulets as safeguards against misfortunes, seeking blessings from natural elements such as trees, stones, and graves, and the act of sacrificing animals with motivations other than devotion to God. For each of these, he presents verses of the Qurʾan and hadith as evidence for the prohibition.

Another important tract by Ibn ʿAbd al-Wahhāb is *Kashf al-Shubuhāt* (*The Removal of Doubts*), which was written in response to arguments raised by his adversaries. In it, he discusses thirteen of their arguments and refutes each of them in detail. His responses are comprehensive and rely heavily on the Qurʾan, statements from the Prophet, and his own interpretation of these two sources to convince the readers of his position. The main theme of the book is the issue of the 'polytheistic' practices that had become commonplace among Muslims, which his adversaries argued were not in fact polytheism. In a way, *Kashf al-Shubuhāt* is a follow-up to *Kitāb al-Tawḥīd*, supporting the latter's core responses against counterarguments.[83]

*Al-Qawāʿid al-Arbaʿ* (*The Four Fundamentals*) is a popular, short treatise in which Ibn ʿAbd al-Wahhāb discusses four principles regarding polytheism. In this, he argues that:

(1) The pagans of Mecca believed that there was only One Creator, and this was not enough to make them believers.
(2) They only worshiped these idols to get closer to God and did not regard them as gods in and of themselves.
(3) There were various forms of polytheism present in Arabia in the Prophet's era, and he was sent to eradicate them all equally.
(4) Finally, the book's most controversial point: the polytheism of the Muslims of his time was worse than the polytheism of the pagans of Mecca.

The implication was that, just as it was justified against the pagans of Mecca, jihad should be performed against the inhabitants of Najd. After all, their polytheism was more sinister.

His work *al-Uṣūl al-Thalātha* (*The Three Principles*), in which Ibn ʿAbd al-Wahhāb explained the three foundational principles of Islam, emphasizes monotheism in both belief and practice, knowledge of the religion and its laws, and belief in the final Prophet and obedience to him. In all three, the author affirms the importance of monotheism and the dangers of polytheism. When discussing religion, he focuses on Islam being monotheism. When talking about the Prophet, he highlights that his mission was the eradication of polytheism and promoting monotheism.

In addition, Ibn ʿAbd al-Wahhāb wrote many small treatises, letters, and booklets. These include *Uṣūl al-Īmān* (*Principles of Faith*), in which he summarized the core beliefs of Islam. The writing style of this catechism is very similar to *Kitāb al-Tawḥīd* in that it is made up mostly of quotations from the Qurʾan and hadith without much commentary. He also wrote a short booklet detailing the major sins, another about the superiority of Islam over other religions, and various letters on the importance of monotheism. Almost all his writings were collected by a group of Saudi-based scholars and published under a single title *Majmūʿa Muʾallafat al-Shaykh Muḥammad ibn ʿAbd al-Wahhāb* (*The Collected Works of Shaykh Muḥammad ibn ʿAbd al-Wahhāb*). The various books and treatises found in this compilation form the bedrock of elementary Wahhabism.

An essential aspect that merits further attention before proceeding is the discernible emphasis Ibn ʿAbd al-Wahhāb placed on theology and doctrine. His writings and preaching were fundamentally anchored in specific interpretations of crucial tenets of Islamic theology. There are occasional references to Islamic law, but he did not author any specific treatise on *fiqh*. However, an emphasis on social problems, spirituality, and governmental politics appears almost entirely absent from his oeuvre. While many other movements, particularly Sufi ones, emphasized how one should spiritually purify the soul, and others, such as al-Ṣanʿānī in Yemen, were highly critical of the political practices of the rulers, it is as if Ibn ʿAbd al-Wahhāb did not take into consideration any possible issues with Ibn Saʿūd's governance and taxation, nor is there a particular observable concern on the spiritual level of those who answered his call. This lacuna in the founder's intellectual output continued to be reflected in the mainstream of the movement after him. Many critics consider the Wahhabis to care little for the otherwise mainstream Islamic concept of *tazkiyyat al-nafs* (the purification of the soul), and the movement has largely been sympathetic to its rulers and their policies, as shall be discussed below and in the later chapters.

### *3.1.5 Was Ibn ʿAbd al-Wahhāb's Thought Original or Based on Scholarly Precedent?*

A seminal question that both insiders and outsiders of the movement (and even the religion) ask, is the level of originality of Ibn ʿAbd al-Wahhāb's thought. In particular, they ask: Did he derive his entire thought from the works of Ibn Taymiyya and Ibn Qayyim, or did he extrapolate from their teachings and develop unique ideas?

There is no debate that he owes much to Ibn Taymiyya and Ibn Qayyim: the dominant influence of the works of both Mamluk scholars on Ibn ʿAbd al-Wahhāb is established through his writings, by his frequent citations from their works, or repurposing of their ideas into principles and slogans. In terms of the specific topics that are said to have been derived from Ibn Taymiyya, they can be summarized into three main subjects: (1) matters related to the intercession of the Prophet, (2) the notion of waging war against polytheists, and (3) a concerted distinction in monotheism between *rubūbiyya* and *ulūhiyya*. This last point had especially dramatic implications in

Ibn ʿAbd al-Wahhāb's mind and certainly in the minds of his immediate successors.[84]

But the response to the question is not so simple. It is true that most of the followers of the movement view Ibn ʿAbd al-Wahhāb as faithfully conveying not just Ibn Taymiyya's legacy but the correct teachings of the faith itself, hence the Prophetic legacy. However, while key ideas were taken from Ibn Taymiyya, Ibn ʿAbd al-Wahhāb veered away from Taymiyyan thought, inventing doctrines that are not found anywhere in Ibn Taymiyya's works. An argument can be made that while notions of *ulūhiyya* are indeed Taymiyyan in origin, the understanding and application of these concepts by Ibn ʿAbd al-Wahhāb is not.

In fact, there are even hints of this novelty from Ibn ʿAbd al-Wahhāb himself. Writing in a letter dated around 1745, he says:

> I will tell you about myself. By God, apart from Whom there is no god, I sought learning (*ṭalabtu al-ʿilm*), and those who knew me believed that I had [acquired] some; yet at that time, I did not know the meaning of 'There is no god but God,' nor did I know the religion of Islam, before this blessing (*khayr*) which God vouchsafed to me. Likewise, not one among my teachers knew it; if any of the scholars of the ʿĀriḍ [his region in Najd] claims that he knew the meaning of 'There is no god but God,' or knew the meaning of Islam, before this time, or maintains that any of his teachers knew it, he lies, fabricates, leads people astray, and falsely praises himself.[85]

While this statement ostensibly indicates that his theological formulations of the essentials of Islamic monotheism were his alone in the region, a deeper consideration might suggest that Ibn ʿAbd al-Wahhāb might have had an alternative intention behind his assertion.

Followers of the movement point out that Ibn ʿAbd al-Wahhāb was not the first to differentiate between *rubūbiyya* and *ulūhiyya* in divine unity, as some authorities before him, including Ibn Taymiyya, had done likewise. Furthermore, he was not the first theologian to deem certain acts of intercession, such as the calling upon the dead for aid (*istighātha*), as polytheism (*shirk*). For instance, they claim that Ibn Taymiyya had made such a determination in his refutation of a Sufi contemporary, the aforementioned al-Bakrī, who had argued in favor of the propriety of such prevalent forms of *istighātha*.[86] Ibn Taymiyya clearly was no supporter of the exaltation of shrines and the visitation of mausoleums.

Nonetheless, such a seemingly generous interpretation of Ibn ʿAbd al-Wahhāb's words is somewhat undermined by considering how his understanding differed from Ibn Taymiyya's in significant ways on these very points. One of the main aspects is that Ibn Taymiyya did not *categorically* consider each and every invocation to the dead to be *shirk*. Rather, he claimed it was either a reprehensible innovation that leads to *shirk* or is *shirk* itself.[87] He also clearly did not open the door of excommunication (*takfīr*) as casually and easily as Ibn ʿAbd al-Wahhāb did. One could also add to this the criticism of Ibn ʿAbd al-Wahhāb by his contemporaries, including his own brother Sulaymān and by Ibn ʿAfāliq, along with other Ḥanbalīs of his time, who accused Ibn ʿAbd al-Wahhāb of misunderstanding Ibn Taymiyya.

It does appear this criticism is valid. Firstly, Ibn Taymiyya did not excommunicate al-Bakrī and his likes among the Sufis, even though he condemned their practices as polytheistic. He most certainly did not call for jihad against such people, despite the fact that he was not reticent in calling for war or engaging in excommunication when it was concluded to be justified in his understanding – an example of this is his fatwas in which he called for jihad against the Mongols whom he considered to be disbelievers, despite their having ostensibly converted to Islam. However, Ibn Taymiyya not only failed to excommunicate al-Bakrī, but when the latter went into hiding from the authorities, he was afforded shelter by Ibn Taymiyya in Egypt.[88] Clearly, Ibn Taymiyya viewed al-Bakrī as a fellow believer who should be aided in times of need. Modern supporters of Ibn ʿAbd al-Wahhāb who quote Ibn Taymiyya's harsh fatwas against *istighātha* and the cult of saints, as if the two figures are in agreement, do not take into account Ibn Taymiyya's other writings in which more nuance is given, and his actions that clearly contradict al-Wahhāb's positions.

Secondly, Ibn ʿAbd al-Wahhāb placed an unprecedented emphasis on *rubūbiyya* and *ulūhiyya* in his comparison of the Meccan polytheists of the Prophet's time with his contemporaries of the Muslim world, including those in the Ottoman heartlands. Ibn ʿAbd al-Wahhāb had no reservation in claiming that the people of his time who called themselves 'Muslims' were, in fact, *worse* than the polytheists of the Prophet's time. There is simply no equivalent here, as Ibn Taymiyya did not consider his lands of Egypt and Syria to be polytheistic despite the prevalence of actions he considered to be problematic.

Thirdly, the issue of weaponizing a notion of *al-walāʾ wa-l-barāʾ* to mass excommunicate groups of people on the basis of political affiliations – such as recognizing the legitimacy of the Ottoman Empire for example – simply has no precedent in mainstream Islamic thought.

It is fair to conclude, despite the claims that Wahhabis themselves make, that Ibn ʿAbd al-Wahhāb's beliefs are in fact radical departures from Ibn Taymiyya, and lack any precedent in Sunni Islamic tradition.

### *3.1.6 The Reactions to the Wahhabi Movement*

Ibn ʿAbd al-Wahhāb's message did not go unchallenged during his time. As the Wahhabi movement rose to power in Najd, refutations poured in from across the Muslim world. Scholars from the Hijaz, the Ottoman Empire, and even local Ḥanbalī and regional Salafi scholars all wrote refutations directed at Ibn ʿAbd al-Wahhāb and his message.[89] In this section, we will focus on some of the most important of these refutations.

Because the followers of Ibn ʿAbd al-Wahhāb waged war against both the Arabs and the Ottoman Empire, the responses that came were sourced from a mix of Ottoman and Arab Muslim scholarship. Combined, the main objections raised by the Ottomans and their allies against the Wahhabis were the following:

(1) They had excommunicated the majority of Muslims.
(2) They had spilled the blood of innocent Muslims in the name of jihad.
(3) They had labeled mainstream normative practices associated with Sufism as heretical and paganistic.
(4) They had shown disrespect to the status of the Prophet by claiming that his grave was not a source of blessings and that his name should not be invoked during prayers.
(5) They had rebelled against the legitimate Caliph of the Muslims – meaning the Ottoman Sultan.
(6) At times, they had departed from the Ḥanbalī school of law and even the consensus of the 'Four Schools' and brought forth interpretations outside the mainstream of Islamic law.

One of the most outspoken scholars against Wahhabism during this era, particularly during the reign of the Second Saudi State, was the Mufti of Mecca, a direct descendant of the Prophet, Aḥmad b. Zaynī Daḥlān (d. 1886). He wrote various refutations against the Wahhabi movement, targeting its core beliefs and arguments. His most famous work in this regard is his booklet *al-Fitnat al-Wahhābiyya* (*The Wahhabi Tribulation*).[90] In it, he mentioned that the Wahhabis had claimed that there was no difference between the pagans of Mecca worshiping idols to get closer to God at the time of the Prophet and the Muslims seeking to get closer to God through prophets and saints. Daḥlān countered this argument by pointing out fundamental differences between the two, such as:

(1) The pagans attributed powers directly to their idols, independent of God. On the other hand, Muslims believe all power belongs to and originates from God alone. Hence, the pagans intended to worship their gods, whereas no Muslim on earth intends to worship the Prophet or the righteous.
(2) The evidence that Ibn ʿAbd al-Wahhāb used was directed at idolaters. It is a fundamental mistake to ignore the beliefs of fellow Muslims and then find some broad commonality using these verses between the beliefs of Muslims and the practices of idolaters.

(3) The pagans had no evidence for what they were doing, while the Muslim practice of seeking blessings and other Sufi rituals was based on evidence from the Qur᾿an and Sunna.[91]

Daḥlān also argued that Wahhabis had taken many things literally that were meant to be figurative. For example, when a person says, 'This medicine cured me,' Wahhabis consider this a form of disbelief in God. This is because, according to the Wahhabis, the speaker is attributing the ability to cure to the medicine when this ability to cure is exclusively God's. Daḥlān argued that this innocent statement is made metaphorically and is understood to mean, 'All cure is from God, and He cured me through this medicine,' and that nobody understood it in the literal way that the Wahhabis did.[92]

Mainstream Ḥanbalī scholars also opposed the Wahhabi movement. A famous refutation of Wahhabism from al-Ahsa was Ibn ʿAfāliq's *Tahakkum al-muqallidīn* (*The Destruction of Those who Blindly Follow*). Ibn ʿAfāliq's writings argue that not only was Ibn ʿAbd al-Wahhāb hostile to the theology of the majority of Muslims but to their approach to jurisprudence as well.[93] Ibn ʿAfāliq opined that Ibn ʿAbd al-Wahhāb was not qualified to make independent rulings and had overstepped his bounds.[94] Ibn ʿAfāliq's book, although rather brief, shows what appears to be the prevailing attitude of Ḥanbalī scholars of that period towards the message and persona of Ibn ʿAbd al-Wahhāb. He declares Ibn ʿAbd al-Wahhāb incompetent in his scholarship and even challenges him to answer a series of advanced questions about Islam.[95] His challenge received no response from Ibn ʿAbd al-Wahhāb.[96]

Mention must also be made of the famous Ḥanbalī scholar based in Nablus (modern Palestine), the aforementioned al-Saffārīnī,[97] who compared Ibn ʿAbd al-Wahhāb to the Khārijī leader Nāfiʿ b. al-Azraq (d. 65/685).[98] In fact, several scholars compared Ibn ʿAbd al-Wahhāb to the ancient Khārijīs due to his excesses in *takfīr* and declaring jihad against Muslims, including ʿAbd Allāh b. ʿĪsā al-Muways (d. 1175/1761),[99] and Ibn ʿAbd al-Wahhāb's own brother Sulaymān b. Abd al-Wahhāb.[100]

Perhaps the most interesting refutation of Ibn ʿAbd al-Wahhāb came from a former ally, Ibn al-Amīr al-Ṣanʿānī (also mentioned earlier in Chapter 2).[101] Around the time Wahhabism was rising in Najd, al-Ṣanʿānī was promoting a Salafi understanding of Islam in Yemen. Due to the similar natures of their messages, al-Ṣanʿānī initially expressed support for Ibn ʿAbd al-Wahhāb and his message in poems and letters. However, once it became clear to him that Ibn ʿAbd al-Wahhāb was engaged in *takfīr* of the Muslim masses and justifying violence against them in the name of jihad, al-Ṣanʿānī reversed his position and wrote a poem warning people against him.[102] The following lines from his poem are of special significance in showing the change he made upon discovering the extreme nature of the Wahhabi call:

> *I renounce the poem that I wrote concerning the Najdī*
> *For it has been proven true to me that he is not in agreement with me...*
> *Shaykh Mirbad came to us from his land*
> *And verified all the things that he is manifesting;*
> *And he brought epistles written by him*
> *In which he willfully excommunicates the people of the earth knowingly...*
> *He has vied in spilling the blood of every Muslim*
> *Who prays and pays zakāt and withdraws not from the covenant.*[103]

To summarize, we can state that refutations of Ibn ʿAbd al-Wahhāb came from three different paradigms. Firstly, there were those who refuted him from within the paradigm of Ottoman Sufi 'traditionalist' Islam. These would be his theological and political opponents at every single level; Zaynī Daḥlan, the Chief Muftī of Mecca, is the best example of this. Secondly, there were his fellow Ḥanbalīs who felt that he had misunderstood the positions and teachings of Ibn Taymiyya or perhaps disagreed with a particular verdict of Ibn Taymiyya in the first place. Examples of this category include his own brother Sulaymān, Ibn ʿAfāliq – who accused him of blindly following some of Ibn Taymiyya's mistakes or extreme opinions – and Muḥammad b. Fayrūz (d. 1176/1762), who claimed that he completely misunderstood Ibn Taymiyya's positions.[104] A third group of critics consists of Salafi-minded reformers from lands outside of Ottoman control, such as al-Ṣanʿānī and al-Shawkānī, who both were initial admirers of specific theological aspects of the movement, but when they realized the violence and jihad associated with it, became vocal critics. All his critics were united in condemning his view that his group of followers alone were *true* Muslims, and the rest of the Muslim world was misguided.

Ultimately, however, these academic refutations proved, at least politically, unfruitful, as the Wahhabi movement continued to rise in power. Moreover, a growing number of similar movements began appearing elsewhere in the Muslim world, though they were less violent in nature. Eventually, refutations gave way to political involvement, and the Ottomans launched an offensive against the Wahhabi movement, to which we will now turn.[105]

## *3.2 The Influence of the Saudi States on the Development of Wahhabism*

While this work is not intended to elaborate on the history of Saudi Arabia, any meaningful discussion of Wahhabism and its evolutions requires some detail about political events related to the Saudi State. The reason is that specific political events forced the Wahhabi movement to react and modify itself in dramatic ways. Hence, it is not possible to understand these theological developments without contextualizing their historical causes, nor can one understand the implications of Wahhabi theory without seeing how it was implemented when it had the freedom to operate according to its own principles or when it had to be compromised in light of more constrained political circumstances. The waves of Wahhabism are often defined, overall, as amicable to manipulation by the dominant politics of the day, which naturally results in internal Wahhabi divisions between pragmatists (usually the majority) and idealists (a constant and sometimes varied minority).

The Kingdom of Saudi Arabia, as it currently exists, is not a direct continuation of the one established by its founder, Muḥammad b. Saʿūd. Rather, historians identify three distinct Saudi States, which explain certain distinguishing reigns of the Saudi royal family's rule in the region. The initial state was called the First Saudi State (also known as the 'Emirate of Diriyah'), which existed from 1744 until 1818. The Second Saudi State (also known as the 'Emirate of Najd') lasted from 1824 until 1891. The Third Saudi State (later known as the 'Kingdom of Saudi Arabia') came into existence in 1902 and continues today.[106]

In this work, we will highlight what we have called three waves of Wahhabism; each subsequent wave representing a shift and toning down from the previous one. However, the reader should be cautioned in understanding that the three waves of Wahhabism do *not* coincide with the three Saudi states. Rather, 'First-Wave Wahhabism' corresponds timewise to the first two Saudi states through the founding of the third Saudi state; 'Second-Wave Wahhabism' appeared around the founding of the Kingdom of Saudi Arabia in 1932; and 'Third-Wave Wahhabism' appeared after the effects of the oil-boom on Saudi's economy. From 'Third-Wave Wahhabism,' subsequent groups have branched out, such as the *Ṣaḥwa* movement and the Madkhalīs. The emergence of the Jihadi-Salafis, as we shall see, can be viewed (at least one strand among them) as a modern attempt at reviving the militancy of First-Wave Wahhabism. It is to each of these trends that we will now turn.

### *3.2.1 First-Wave Wahhabism*

First-Wave Wahhabism is the original message of the founder, Ibn ʿAbd al-Wahhāb, and his immediate followers, sons, and grandsons after him. Its main tenets have already been summarized in the previous section: (1) a unique understanding of *ulūhiyya* and hence *shirk*, (2) a willingness to excommunicate (*takfīr*) any Muslim who disagrees (including using their doctrine of *al-walāʾ wa-l-baraʾ*, via guilt by association or silence), and (3) an active military engagement against others who professed Islam. This wave was manifested from the inception of the movement in the late eighteenth century until the Battle of Sibilla in 1929.

*The First Saudi State*

The alliance between Muhammad b. ʿAbd al-Wahhāb and Muhammad b. Saʿūd in 1744 is considered the beginning of the First Saudi State. Together, they allied to take back Arabia from the Ottomans and revive 'pure Islam' through military might. During the reigns of Muhammad b. Saʿūd and his son ʿAbd al-Azīz, multiple cities were conquered and brought under the rule of Āl Saʿūd (the Family of Saʿūd). However, it was during the reign of Muhammad b. Saʿūd's grandson, Saʿūd b. ʿAbd al-Azīz (d. 1814), that the Saudi-Wahhabi movement became conspicuous enough to catch the attention of the Ottoman Empire.[107]

During the eighteenth century, despite the constant battles between the Sharif of Mecca and the Wahhabis, the Ottomans were undecided in how to deal with them. This was, for the most part, due to the Ottomans not considering the Wahhabis to be a serious threat to their power. It has also been argued that the Ottomans never directly controlled the Najd region in the interior of Arabia: they acquired nominal control over it from the sixteenth century when they succeeded the Mamluks in ruling Hijaz.[108] Indeed, there is a contention that Najd was not ruled by any foreign force, including the Ottomans, and was left to the infighting of the local leaders who sought control.[109] Whatever the reason, the Ottoman's indecisiveness in dealing with the nascent Saudi-Wahhabi alliance would haunt them in the next century.

The Wahhabi raid on the Shiʿi city of Karbala in 1802 – and the ensuing mass slaughter – was the first event that forced the Ottomans to take notice. The Ottomans risked war with the Shiʿa if they did not take decisive action against the Wahhabis. However, since they were preoccupied with other wars, they chose not to resort to military action. Instead, they sent an Iraqi scholar based in Istanbul named Ahmad Effendi (d. 1854) to challenge the Wahhabis in a series of intellectual debates. The discussions did not go smoothly from the Ottoman point of view, and Ahmad Effendi was ordered back to Istanbul. A few months later, the Wahhabis attacked Mecca.[110]

Saʿūd b. ʿAbd al-Azīz conquered much of the Hijaz region during his reign, starting with the city of Taif. But it was the dual conquests of the holy cities of Mecca and Medina – between 1803 and 1805 – that triggered a full-scale war with the Ottomans.[111] This was significant because it eventually brought the two holiest Muslim cities under Wahhabi rule. Now, it was impossible for the Ottomans to ignore the movement any longer.

Wahhabi doctrine was immediately enforced upon the pilgrims entering the Holy Lands. They closed coffee houses, banned tobacco smoking, destroyed musical instruments, and demolished tombs, deeming all of these to be religiously prohibited.[112] In an effort to purge certain perceived Sufi excesses, there was a prohibition of celebrations of the birth of the Prophet (*mawlid*) and the use of rosaries and the like. But it was the demolition of early Islamic heritage sites, deemed sacred by the bulk of the Muslim world, that was deeply troubling for the Muslim pilgrims and masses.

Swiss traveler Johann Burckhardt (d. 1817) described the effects of these campaigns in his eye-witness travelogue, and we can infer a sense of the anguish that was felt:

> Wherever the Wahabys (*sic.*) carried their arms, they destroyed all the domes and ornamented tombs… The destruction of cupolas and tombs of saints became the favorite taste of the Wahabys. In Hedjaz, Yemen, Mesopotamia, and Syria, this was always the first result of their victory; and as many domes formed the roofs of mosques, they were charged with destroying these also. At Mekka, not a single cupola was suffered to remain over the tomb of any renown Arab; even those covering the birth-place of Mohammed, and of his grandsons, Hasan and Hosseyn, and of his uncle Abou Taleb, and his wife, Khadydje, were all broken down.[113]

This marked the beginning of an ideological and political war between the two nations. The Wahhabis declared the Ottomans to be pagans and not worthy of being considered a Muslim Caliphate. In return, the Ottomans labeled the Wahhabis as apostates and called them modern Khārijīs. They even circulated a fatwa declaring that the pilgrimage was not compulsory as long as the Wahhabis controlled Mecca.[114] During this time, various books were written by both sides in refutation of the other.

On the Wahhabi side, scholarship remained in the custody of the descendants of Ibn ʿAbd al-Wahhāb. His son ʿAbd Allāh (d. 1826) was the head of the Wahhabi movement until the fall of the First Saudi State. He wrote a number of books and letters in reply to all that was written against his father and himself. ʿAbd Allāh's son, Sulaymān, also played an important role in cementing Wahhabi scholarship during this period. He wrote the aforementioned famous and influential book, entitled *al-Dalāʾil fī ḥukm muwālāt Ahl al-ishrāk* (*The Evidences Regarding the Verdict in Allying With People of Polytheism*), in which he declared living outside the Wahhabi lands to be prohibited on the basis that the Ottomans were disbelievers, and that people who defected to the Ottoman side were disbelievers themselves.[115]

The Ottomans could not forsake the Holy Lands and leave them in the hands of the Wahhabis, so they were forced to act militarily. They handed the task of defeating the Saudis to their most powerful general, Muḥammad ʿAlī Pasha (d. 1849), who was the governor of Egypt at the time. (In one of the most ironic twists of late Ottoman history, Muḥammad ʿAlī Pasha would himself end up breaking away from his Ottoman leaders and establishing an independent Egypt, which would be the crucial catalyst in the rise of Egypt as a global Arab power of the next century). In turn, Muḥammad ʿAlī Pasha delegated the task to his sons. This marked the beginning of the Ottoman-Wahhabi War, which lasted from 1811 until 1818.

Eventually, Muḥammad ʿAlī's son Ibrāhīm Pasha (d. 1848) was successful in driving the Saudis out of Mecca and Medina. From the Hijaz, he then went after their base in Diriyah, leveling the city and putting an end to the First Saudi State. The ill-equipped and untrained Bedouin warriors simply could not stand in battle against an organized and militarily superior Ottoman army. Sulaymān, the grandson of Ibn ʿAbd al-Wahhāb, would meet his end aged just thirty-two during the siege of Diriyah in 1818, marking the complete victory of the Ottomans over the Wahhabis. Sulaymān was tied up and led outside the city; according to some reports, he was forced to listen to lute music before being executed, as a mockery of the strict Wahhabi prohibition of music.[116]

The Saudi ruler, ʿAbd Allāh b. Saʿūd (d. 1818) was captured and brought to Cairo, where he was paraded in front of large crowds for days. He was handed over to the Ottomans to be executed in Istanbul, in front of the Hagia Sophia. His head was mounted on a spike (or, according to other reports, publicly thrown into the Bosporus), and his body staked on a pillar, with a warning from the Sultan about the fate of those who transgressed against the Holy Cities. This event sent the remaining members of the Āl Saʿūd into hiding for a number of years. ʿAbd Allāh, the son of Ibn ʿAbd al-Wahhāb, managed to elude capture, eventually going into hiding in Egypt, where he passed away in 1826.[117]

While the rejectionist and exclusivist attitude towards non-Wahhabis – exemplified by Sulaymān, the grandson of Ibn ʿAbd al-Wahhāb – would remain a dominant trend in southern Najd, with the fall of the First State, other Wahhabi voices emerged. The collapse of the State did provoke some tempering of views among clerics in Qasim, al-Ahsa, and Ha'il (although it should be noted that these were not from the actual family members of Ibn ʿAbd al-Wahhāb himself). Part of the critique from the more conciliatory Wahhabis was the notion that the descendants of Ibn ʿAbd al-Wahhāb were to be blamed for bringing about their own destruction through an aggressive policy of making enemies. As such, a nascent push-back against the fanaticism of 'pure' Wahhabism was born. This push-back remained in the community among some scholars from this time, through a civil war during the Second Saudi State, until finally becoming mainstream at the beginning of the twentieth century during the Third Saudi State, when the biological descendants of Ibn ʿAbd al-Wahhāb had to adopt some of these more conciliatory stances.[118]

*The Second Saudi State*

In 1824, the Saudi dynasty formed its second state. A cousin of ʿAbd Allāh b. Saʿūd, Turkī b. ʿAbd Allāh (d. 1834), took over Riyadh with the help of some loyal followers. The Second Saudi State lasted from 1824 until 1891. During this period, the Saudis took over large areas of Najd – in-between a 'Second Egyptian Occupation' from 1837 to 1843 – but were unable to wrest control of the Hijaz from the Ottomans. The religious leadership of the Second Saudi State remained vested in the family of Ibn ʿAbd al-Wahhāb and were by then known by the title 'Family of the Shaykh' (Āl al-Shaykh).

One of Ibn ʿAbd al-Wahhāb's grandsons, ʿAbd al-Raḥmān b. Ḥasan, was the religious leader of the Second Saudi State until his passing in 1869. ʿAbd al-Raḥmān wrote the most famed commentary on his grandfather's book *Kitāb al-Tawḥīd*, titled *Fatḥ al-Majīd* (*The Victory of the Exalted*), in which he exhibited the same rejectionist and exclusivist trends that dominated First Saudi State Wahhabism. Upon the destruction of the First Saudi State in 1818, ʿAbd al-Raḥmān was taken to Cairo, where he spent seven or eight years before returning to Najd around 1825 or 1826. In Cairo, he is said to have studied and taught at al-Azhar University. Later, ʿAbd al-Raḥmān again fled Egyptian-controlled territory between 1837 and 1843 and portrayed his flight as a 'sacred emigration' (*hijra*), urging his community to wage jihad against the Egyptians, whom he characterized as polytheists.[119]

He was succeeded by his son ʿAbd al-Laṭīf (d. 1876), who had also been trained at al-Azhar University in Cairo during his father's initial tenure there after 1818. ʿAbd al-Laṭīf served as the chief scholar until 1876. ʿAbd al-Laṭīf was then succeeded by his son ʿAbd Allāh b. ʿAbd al-Laṭīf (d. 1920), who remained the religious head long after the fall of the Second Saudi State. ʿAbd Allāh b. ʿAbd al-Laṭīf was the tutor of both the future king and founder of the Third Saudi State, ʿAbd al-ʿAzīz b. Saʿūd (also known simply as Ibn Saud), and the future Grand Mufti of the Third Saudi State, his nephew Muḥammad b. Ibrāhīm b. ʿAbd al-Laṭīf (d. 1969). He remained the spiritual leader of the Saudi-Wahhabi movement until his death in 1920. He gave one of his daughters as a bride to the founder of the Third Saudi State, thus making him the grandfather of the most impactful of all modern Saudi kings, namely King Faisal (d. 1975).

It was during this era of the Second Saudi State that direct ties were established between Wahhabi scholars and the Indian subcontinent, particularly the Ahl-e Ḥadīth movement mentioned in the previous chapter. Over twenty Saudi clerics traveled to India to study under its Ahl-e Ḥadīth scholars, in particular Ṣiddīq Ḥasan Khān, and including a great-grandson of Ibn ʿAbd al-Wahhāb, Isḥāq b. ʿAbd al-Rahmān Āl al-Shaykh (d. 1901), and Sa'd b. Hamad b. 'Atīq (d. 1930).[120] Such connections solidified the bonds between these movements and influenced each one in subtle manners of theology and hadith.

Wahhabi theology did not significantly change over these seven decades. This original version is what we have called First-Wave Wahhabism and includes the period of the First and Second Saudi States. To reiterate, this original ideology of Wahhabism pronounced *takfīr* upon its Muslim enemies, waged jihad against Muslims, and forcefully seized the lands of Arabia in the name of Islam. This wave was theologically and ideologically driven to wage war and conquer all who opposed them. It was roundly rejected by all other strands of Islam and condemned for heretical and extremist tendencies. In particular, the Second Saudi State's explicit *takfīr* of the Ottoman Empire and its declaring war against them because they viewed them as polytheists is a factual reality that cannot be denied.[121] The final decades of the First-Wave brought Wahhabism into contact with its first near-equivalent in South Asia, hinting at the movement's move away from its earlier inward-looking orthodoxy. The differences between the Wahhabis and Ahl-e Ḥadīth were few. However, what is important here is the fact that the latter not only did not resort to excommunicating the Ottomans, but many of its members honored Sultan 'Abd al-Ḥamīd (d. 1918).

In contrast, Sulaymān b. 'Abd Allāh Āl al-Shaykh (d. 1818), grandson of Ibn 'Abd al-Wahhāb, wrote an entire work, entitled *al-Dalā'il fī ḥukm muwālāt Ahl al-Ishrāk* (*The Evidences for the Ruling Regarding Alliance with the Infidels*), in which he argued, not that the Ottoman Empire was pagan, as that was already understood, but that loyalty to them turned one into a disbeliever. Another example that illustrates the popularity of mass-*takfiri* tendencies among leading Wahhabi clerics of the time, is an incident that occurred during the power struggle between 'Abd Allāh b. Faisal (d. 1873), who succeeded his father as king, and his rebel brother Sa'ūd b. Faisal (d. 1875). During one civil war between these brothers, Sa'ūd managed to oust his brother, who then turned to the Ottomans for military help. His asking for assistance from the Ottomans generated a controversy among the Wahhabi clerics in his own ranks. While some of his *ulama* gave a fatwa in support of this act – based on necessity and the fact that Sa'ūd did not possess a rightful claim to power – a significant group opposed it and in fact considered such an alliance to be one of 'seeking the assistance of the disbelievers' (*al-isti'ana bi'l-kuffar*).[122] In this context, Hamad b. 'Atīq (d. 1301/1884), the most prominent Wahhabi cleric outside the Āl al-Shaykh family at the time, excommunicated another Wahhabi religious judge, Muhammad b. Ibrahim b. 'Ajlān.[123] Furthermore, Ibn 'Atiq wrote a treatise against such alliances with the Ottomans, entitled *Sabil al-najat wa'l-fikak min muwalat al-murtaddin wa-l-atrak* (*The Path of Success and Fleeing from Loyalty to the Apostates and Turks*), in which he unequivocally affirmed that one must not enter into relationships of loyalty with apostates like the Ottoman Empire, and that doing so jeopardized one's own standing in the faith. This hardline stance was also supported by the most prominent Wahhabi cleric in that era, a great-grandson of the founder, ʿAbd al-Laṭīf b. ʿAbd al-Raḥmān Āl al-Shaykh (d. 1876). In what appears an attempt to remain neutral, he encouraged both brothers to set aside their differences and to unite together so they could engage in jihad against the real enemy: the pagan Ottomans![124]

The sheer number of explicit quotations in this regard, from multiple clerics of the First and Second Saudi states, cannot be misinterpreted or misunderstood. As one final example for this section, the son of ʿAbd al-Laṭīf, ʿAbdullāh b. ʿAbd al-Laṭīf Āl al-Shaykh, the uncle of the future Muftī Muḥammad b. Ibrahīm, and the grandfather of the future King Faisal, was asked about someone who did not consider the Ottomans to be polytheists, preferring their rule over the rule of the Saudi state. He responded:

> Whoever does not know the *kufr* [heresy] of this nation (viz., the Ottomans), and cannot differentiate between them and a rebellious Muslim dynasty (*bughāt*), does not understand the meaning of '*There is no god but Allah.*' And if he further believes that this nation is actually Muslim, then this is a much more severe level, and it is exactly [what Ibn Abd al-Wahhāb taught] '…to doubt the *kufr* of the one who commits *kufr* and *shirk*.' The act of aiding them (viz., the Ottomans) and helping them against the Muslims with any type of help is pure apostasy from the faith (*riddah ṣarīḥa*).[125]

This simple fatwa, written before the turn of the twentieth century, encapsulates First-Wave Wahhabi thought.

The Second Saudi State's rule was roughly seven years shorter than the first. Various civil wars with other tribal leaders slowed its expansion, and the incessant internal struggles between siblings and cousins of the royal family caused the State to grow weak and fall apart. In 1891, the Saudi family lost control of Riyadh to a formidable rival tribe, the Āl Rashīd clan, marking the end of the Second Saudi State. The remaining members of the Family of Saʿūd escaped and dispersed among the Bedouins in the desert, with a small clan making their way further east until they arrived in Kuwait. It would be a member of this clan that would rise up again to make modern history by founding the Third Saudi State.

*The Third Saudi State*

The Third Saudi State has its origins in 1902, when ʿAbd al-Azīz b. Saʿūd (also known as Ibn Saʿūd) led a small group of devotees and relatives from

Kuwait to regain control of his ancestral capital Riyadh. ʿAbd al-Azīz's grandfather was Faisal b. Turkī (d. 1865), one of the more dominant rulers in the Second Saudi State and the great-grandson of the founder Muḥammad b. Saʿūd. His father, ʿAbd al-Raḥmān b. Faisal (d. 1920) was deeply involved in the power struggle between brothers and cousins during the final days of the Second Saudi State before its collapse (although he himself never became a ruler), and he had to flee for his life and seek refuge in Kuwait.

While growing up in exile, Ibn Saʿūd was raised on legendary stories of his noble ancestry and the brave feats of the Saudi dynasties. This fueled his eagerness to regain his rightful kingdom and led to his decision in his twenties to attack and conquer his grandfather's capital. Accompanied by a group of forty men, Ibn Saʿūd was able to infiltrate Riyadh and kill the governor.[126] This incident marks the beginning of the Third Saudi State (although it would be another few decades before the 'Kingdom' was announced to the world).

Over the next two years, almost half of Najd fell to the Saudis as they slowly regained their lost territory. In the meantime, the Rashīdīs allied with the Ottomans to fight off the rising Saudi power and were temporarily successful. However, the Saudis soon regrouped and eventually eliminated the Ottoman presence in Najd completely by 1906. By the end of 1912, Ibn Saʿūd was ruling all of Najd and many surrounding territories. At this critical juncture, he established the *Ikhwān* (*The Brotherhood*),[127] a band of rural religious folk-cum-urbanized paramilitaries whose sole aim was to fight under ʿAbd al-Azīz b. Saʿūd's banner to spread the Wahhabi creed and establish Wahhabi colonies across the Arabian Desert.[128]

World War I was a turning point for the rising Third Saudi State, as they formed an alliance with the British Empire against the Ottomans. This alliance proved fruitful, and when the Ottoman Empire collapsed, Ibn Saʿūd was able to take over the Hijaz with British support – this, despite the fact that they had previously promised the Holy Lands to the Sharif family of Mecca. After the takeover of the Holy Cities of Mecca and Medina, in accordance with Wahhabi doctrine, all of the still standing or reconstructed mausoleums that the Ottomans had built over the graves of the Companions and family members of the Prophet (most famously those in the Baqīʿ cemetery of Medina and the Muʿalla cemetery in Mecca) were demolished.

### *The Ikhwān and the Battle of Sibilla (1929)*

As mentioned previously, the *Ikhwān* was a paramilitary invention of Ibn Saʿūd. Needing an army to establish his power and wishing to co-opt the religious sentiment of the Wahhabis of Arabia, Ibn Saʿūd formed what were religious bonds of brotherhood between the Bedouin Arabs who signed up for his cause. He convinced them to abandon their old nomadic routines and join forces in order to wage jihad like their forefathers had done under Ibn ʿAbd al-Wahhāb. The purpose of this movement was to simultaneously tap into the religious zeal that had served the original founders of the First Saudi State and to rally men to serve as an unofficial army that Ibn Saʿūd could use to conquer the Ottoman and Rashīdī territories.

The *Ikhwān* were brought into the same theology as First-Wave Wahhabism, in which all political opponents were *ipso facto* deemed apostates. One of the clearest examples of this is the capture of the town of Hā'il by Ibn Saʿūd. Even though this city had already been pro-Wahhabi and did not have apparent graves or icons, it was nominally allied with the rival Āl-Rashīd clan, which acknowledged the legitimacy of the Ottoman Sultan. In order to justify invading Ḥā'il, Ibn Saʿūd solicited fatwas from the leading Wahhabi clerics in his ranks, including Saʿd b. ʿAtīq and ʿAbdullāh b. ʿAbd al-Laṭīf Āl al-Shaykh (the uncle of the future Muftī Muḥammad b. Ibrahīm). These clerics claimed that the equivocation of the people of Ḥā'il to the legitimate ruler Ibn Saʿūd and their 'support' of the Ottomans constituted apostasy and legitimized jihad against them or, as one of them wrote, 'fighting against the people of Ḥā'il constitutes the best of jihāds.'[129]

This alliance initially proved successful, and within the first two decades, the Kingdom was established.[130] However, once Ibn Saʿūd had established power, the *Ikhwān* grew restless. They represented Wahhabism in its original form. They were Bedouins who disliked city life and were, to put it bluntly, simple Luddites, considering all technological inventions as religious innovations (*bidʿa*). They also had no tolerance for Sufis or Shiʿis, let alone non-Muslims. Moreover, the *Ikhwān* insisted on raiding lands controlled by the British, and upon conquering cities, they demanded that the conquered be treated in the harshest manner as apostates. They refused Ibn Saʿūd the right to negotiate any treaties with the 'infidels,' arguing that this would amount to tacit approval of their rule. Furthermore, they wished to expel the Shīʿis from conquered lands (Shiʿa today constitute approximately 12% of the country, concentrated in the regions of Najran and Qatif). They pined for a return to the original Saʿūdī-style kingdom of a century and a half earlier.

Ibn Saʿūd could not tolerate such views after he had established the modern kingdom and set its borders. The hardcore Wahhabi beliefs made it impossible for the Saudi family to form the necessary political alliances needed to gain power post-World War I. Predictably, as Ibn Saʿūd tried to carve out a new, modern country, with his pragmatic policies of citizenship for all sects and its well-defined borders, the *Ikhwān*'s trust in Ibn Saʿūd as their leader rapidly deteriorated. They came to view him as betraying the very principles that they held dear and fought for.

In order to maintain peace with the British, Ibn Saʿūd did not allow the *Ikhwān* to attack any of the British allies, which at that time included a significant number of Arab statelets. Ibn Saʿūd's alliance with the British was a primary cause of malcontent among the *Ikhwān*: Wahhabi doctrines clearly taught strict notions of *al-walā wa-l-barā'* and there was no way, in their minds, to reconcile between their theology and the policies of their leader. In all likelihood they were probably unaware of the depth of involvement that Ibn Saʿūd had with the British, or the fact that Ibn Saʿūd had agreed, in 1915, to a protection treaty with the British to protect specific interests, whereby he was to receive a payment of £5,000 a month (which lasted until 1924) and arms[131] – as this relationship would have automatically constituted a fatwa of excommunication.[132] They were further angered by the new Saudi state embracing modern technology which they viewed as the work of the devil. There are many records of their accusations of the gramophone and radio being types of demonic sorcery, and electricity being a manifestation of magic. Frustrated at not being allowed to attack those they deemed to be deviant in the countries dotted around Arabia (in particular Iraq), the *Ikhwān* began to openly rebel against Ibn Saʿūd.[133]

After a few failed attempts to quell the *Ikhwān*, Ibn Saʿūd sensed that it was best to go on the offensive rather than risk a surprise attack, and launched a war against them with the help of the British RAF and army who were stationed in Iraq at the time.[134] In the Battle of Sibilla in March 1929, the *Ikhwān*, on horseback and armed with spears, swords, and primitive guns, faced the modern army of Ibn Saʿūd, powerfully furnished with far superior guns and other modern artillery. Over 500 *Ikhwān* were slaughtered in that battle, along with 200 Saudi troops. The war ended with their leader, Faisal al-Duwaysh (d. 1931), handing himself over to the British in January 1930, in order to protect himself (which, ironically, would have been forbidden in accordance with Wahhabi doctrine; he was eventually handed back to the king and kept in prison until his death). To avoid such a rebellion occurring again, Ibn Saʿūd dismantled the *Ikhwān* permanently and rebranded his personal troops as the Saudi Arabian National Guard. The victory of King Ibn Saʿūd over the *Ikhwān* was the death knell of original First-Wave Wahhabism.

However, the extreme, religiously oriented danger that the *Ikhwān* represented only went underground as they were subsumed into the wider Saudi society. That danger would rear its head in a brutal and sinister fashion just five decades later, in an event that arguably reshaped the course of both the twentieth century and Muslim history, as well as the future of Salafism in particular: the Siege of Mecca in 1979.[135] Furthermore, the rebellion had an unintended but logical consequence. By eradicating the *Ikhwān*, Ibn Saʿūd eliminated their ideological doctrines from the public sphere. It was at this juncture that Wahhabism underwent the most major reform since its inception.

If the Wahhabi movement wished to survive it needed to reform and would have to accommodate the new Kingdom of Saudi Arabia. Survive it did, but only by adopting strategic concessions: these concessions are hereby termed Second-Wave Wahhabism.

### *3.2.2 Second-Wave Wahhabism*

In 1932, Ibn Saʿūd officially declared his state as the Kingdom of Saudi Arabia.[136] But the alliance with the British which assisted to this end would also tarnish the state's reputation, and forever cast a shadow in the eyes of its detractors. It fueled many conspiracy theories and cast doubt on the purity of their motivations. The British relationship with Ibn Saud was 'ambiguous' from 1929 until around 1937 after which he was finally counted as being a 'critical factor in Britain's position in the Arab world.'[137] Nonetheless, the meteoric rise of the Kingdom of Saudi Arabia would be deeply connected to the rise of Wahhabism, and the former functioned as the base of the latter from which Wahhabism would spread across the globe in various forms over the next few decades.

In the decades following its founding, a series of monumental episodes occurred in the Kingdom which shaped the development of modern Wahhabism and its attempts to rebrand their 'authentic' doctrine as Salafi. Many of these challenging historical events – in particular, the modernization of the country, the establishment of the Islamic University of Medina (IUM) and its proselytizing efforts around the world, the Siege of Mecca by militant extremists in 1979, and the *Ṣaḥwa* (Awakening) movement of the 1990s – would impact the direction of Saudi Salafism in completely unprecedented ways. As we mentioned, the catalyst that precipitated this shift was the infamous rebellion of the new King's most loyal followers, the *Ikhwān*.

Saudi Arabia remained a technologically backward and primitive place during the early years of Ibn Saʿūd's reign. Life in the desert kingdom seemed almost the same as it had been for millennia. All of this changed dramatically in 1938 when oil was accidentally discovered in the country. From this point, Saudi Arabia immediately started experiencing the benefits of this discovery. In 1945, Ibn Saʿūd met with the President of the United States, Franklin Roosevelt (d. 1945), resulting in the famous handshake aboard the USS *Quincy* in the Suez. This handshake granted American oil companies extraction access to oil fields, and in exchange, America agreed to protect the Saudi state. The formation of Aramco (Arabian American Oil Company) inaugurated a long-term strategic partnership between the two countries that continues to this day.

The revenue that flowed in from Saudi oil would eventually transform the country, but there were several hurdles to overcome. Ibn Saʿūd's reign was marked with stories of pilgrims being beaten for practicing religious innovations or playing music during their travels. Tobacco was prohibited, graves were leveled, and many long-standing cultural and religious practices were banned. At the same time, oil money was used to begin the global spread of the message of Wahhabism, and ties were established with Rashīd Riḍā and other sympathetic figures in the Arab and wider Muslim world.

Ibn Saʿūd was succeeded in 1953 by his son Saʿūd b. ʿAbd al-ʿAzīz (d. 1969), who ruled for eleven years. His reign was a period of internal strife, palace intrigue, and tension. The Kingdom was in debt, and the national currency (the riyal) was losing value against the dollar. Faisal (d. 1975), Saʿūd's younger brother, opposed him strongly and felt he was more suitable for leadership. Eventually, Saʿūd was forced to abdicate the throne, and Faisal became the third king of Saudi Arabia in 1964. The drawn-out path towards this succession involved the leading clerics, who displayed a long-standing scholarly tradition of giving their support to leaders who demonstrated that they held the best means of maintaining political authority. In January 1964, these clerics, including Ibn Ibrahim, were asked by leading members of the royal family to produce a fatwa on the dispute for the throne. The scholars decided, out of respect for the incumbent king, not to issue an official fatwa against him, but they advised him to step down in favor of Faisal's more powerful faction. As the political tension worsened during 1964, the clerics eventually produced a fatwa endorsing the change of king and the need to offer the allegiance accordingly. The reasoning behind the clerics' advice for a change in monarch was, in the analysis of Nabil Mouline, in keeping with the intention to always maintain the preservation of 'three O's': *orthodoxy*, *orthopraxy*, and political *order*. This illustrates an old and present practice of the Wahhabi clerics in relation to the royal family, whereby they used their religious and theological position for 'sanctifying political action,' but only on the invitation of the House of Saud and as 'strictly religious actors.'[138]

Faisal would also rule for eleven years, during which his reign saw the global ascendancy of Saudi power and the establishment of the Kingdom as a force to be reckoned with. This gave Saudi-backed Salafism a greater prominence and legitimacy in the eyes of many Muslims around the world. Widely perceived as the most religious of all Saudi kings, and the only one whose maternal ancestry went back to Ibn ʿAbd al-Wahhāb, Faisal's reforms were both pragmatic – aimed at modernizing the country – and religious. The latter aspect of his agenda entailed a Salafi-dominated piety, even if it was to mix with other Islamic movements – such as the Muslim Brotherhood from Egypt and Syria – or take on aspects of modern life that Wahhabi clerics were uncomfortable with.

As Crown Prince, Faisal had already begun a program of reform and modernization in the Kingdom during his brother's reign. In 1961, he helped establish the Islamic University of Medina, which became the global center of Wahhabi-Salafi education (as will be discussed later). In 1962, when most Saudi clerics regarded television as prohibited and the devil's handiwork, he established the Kingdom's first television channel. Importantly, during the same year, he abolished slavery in Saudi Arabia. This made Saudi Arabia one of the last countries in the world to officially abolish the practice, relying thereafter on cheap labor from impoverished countries in South and South-East Asia.

Yet, one of the most significant strategies implemented by Faisal was his openness to non-Wahhabi Muslims, and his facilitation of their entry into the Kingdom. Restrictions on Hajj and Umra were eased, and Muslims of various backgrounds were allowed to work and live in the country. Most tellingly, he allowed non-Wahhabi scholars to teach at Islamic schools and universities, although they were prohibited from teaching theology. It was during this time that the Kingdom decided to form a strategic alliance with the Muslim Brotherhood of Egypt, allowing many thousands of them – most of whom were under threat of persecution or exile – safe haven in the Kingdom. Since the members of the Brotherhood were typically highly educated, and the Kingdom needed technical and academic talent, it proved to be a useful alliance at the time, but it was to have profound repercussions (as explored in Chapter 4).

King Faisal actively pursued an agenda of connecting Saudi Islam with global currents, and of situating the Kingdom as an intellectual and political capital of the Muslim faith. He was instrumental in founding the World Assembly of Muslim Youth (known as *al-Nadwa al-ʿālamiyya li-shabāb al-Islāmī*), which published hundreds of books in dozens of languages for free distribution around the globe. He participated in the formation of the Organization of Islamic Conference (OIC), an intergovernmental organization consisting of fifty-seven member countries, with permanent offices and representation at the United Nations. (These reforms will be mentioned again in Chapter 4, where we will explore the ties to the Muslim Brotherhood.)

The pace of modernization was astronomical. Within a decade, the Kingdom was almost unrecognizable from its earlier years. Skyscrapers were being built in all major cities; highways now made travel between Jeddah, Riyadh, and even Dhahran possible. The literacy rate increased exponentially as schools (including, after a fight with the clerics, for girls) were built almost overnight in every neighborhood. Saudi students were allowed to study abroad and would come back with many innovative ideas that would harbinger further change.

In order to expedite this modernization process, hundreds of thousands of non-Muslim foreigners were brought in to create a new 'expatriate' culture that anyone who has lived in the Kingdom is familiar with. For the first time in history, large groups of foreigners from many nationalities and faiths flocked in with the incentive of tax-free, high-paying jobs. Many were willing to live in the harsh conditions in lieu of the salary and other perks and benefits. To further entice foreigners, certain laws were relaxed, television shows came to increasingly flout what were understood to be the traditional norms of modesty, foreign women appeared without the normal *hijab*s and *burqa*s that Saudi society was accustomed to, and anecdotal evidence suggests that even contraband substances were not as contraband as the public perceived them to be.

The swift modernization of the country angered many of its citizens, which caused a split in the Wahhabi movement. There was a growing sentiment – especially because the Royal family, in particular, was increasing exponentially its wealth and being awarded vast allowances of the oil wealth to the exclusion of the regular citizens – that this modernization was not being done for the betterment of the country, but for the enrichment of the Family of Saʿūd alone. The question also arose as to the moral costs of such progress: Was it really worth it to have tall skyscrapers and fast cars if it meant losing one's soul and destroying one's morality? Eventually, in murky circumstances that are still debated to this day, King Faisal was murdered by his own nephew in March 1975. This assassination shocked the Kingdom and heralded the beginning of a period of uncertainty and a simmering, impending rebellion within the Kingdom.[139]

In the midst of these challenges and debates, a Second-Wave Wahhabism emerged and came to eschew the prominent political interpretations of *al-walāʾ waʾl-barāʾ* in lieu of a more socially acceptable presentation.[140] Thus, in this new trend, treaties and commercial transactions with 'infidel' states were to be permitted, but one was obligated to 'dissociate' from all polytheists in one's heart, and express that dissociation in a variety of ways: one's dress code, for to 'resemble the disbeliever' was forbidden; cultural habits, as the celebration of any non-religious festival, such as birthdays or commemorative days, was against the teachings of Islam; and even travel, because traveling to foreign lands was strictly forbidden except for some type of necessity.[141] In addition, the old-school Wahhabī's Luddite-like animosity towards foreign technology and modern culture also held the Kingdom back. So, in the face of the new political pressure, this Second-Wave quietly isolated from their public discourse the original fatwas that declared such technology to be handiwork of the devil and manifestations of magic.

Perhaps the single scholar who best represents this wave is the first Grand Muftī of Saudi Arabia: Muḥammad b. Ibrahīm Āl al-Shaykh (d. 1969), whose grandfather ʿAbd al-Laṭīf b. ʿAbd al-Rahman, and uncle Abdullāh b. ʿAbd al-Laṭīf (both mentioned in the previous section) played prominent roles in the Second Saudi State.

*Muḥammad b. Ibrāhīm and the winds of change in Second-Wave Wahhabism*

It was Muḥammad b. Ibrahīm Āl al-Shaykh who oversaw the entrance of the Kingdom onto the global stage. His significance has been identified as so important that he has been called 'the founder of modern Hanbali-Wahhabism,' and 'a formidable strategist' that 'worked methodically and patiently to establish a global, modern, centralized, and pyramidal organization.' Consequently, his efforts led to the 'institutionalization and routinization of the Najdi tradition.' Of course, such changes only took place as the result of numerous, and at the time tense, back-and-forths between the policies of the king and clerical oppositions to those policies, which inevitably resulted in some compromise.[142]

Ibn Ibrahim was born in 1893 and lost his eyesight due to an illness as a teenager. He studied with his uncle Abdullāh b. ʿAbd al-Laṭīf and Saʿd b. Ḥamad b. ʿAtīq, along with many other icons of the Wahhabi clergy, and witnessed the rise of Ibn Saʿūd, finding a place early on in the Third Saudi State when, on his deathbed, his uncle Abdullah advised King Ibn Saʿūd to place his young nephew in a position of religious authority. Thus began a relationship with the Royal Court that would span five decades and three kings, most prominently his cousin King Faisal (as Faisal's mother was his paternal aunt). As the Kingdom created new religious positions, Muḥammad b. Ibrahīm was the perfect person to fill them, becoming the first person to be officially appointed to give fatwas and to decide who was qualified to give them, under the auspices of the Institute of Legal Pronouncements (the *Dār al-Iftā*); then becoming the Chief Judge (*al-Qaḍā al-ʿAlā*); then becoming the first Grand Mufti of the Kingdom; then Minister of Girls' Education; then the first Chair of the World Association of Muslim Youth; then first President of the Islamic University of Medina, and many other titles and responsibilities. Along with his governmental role, he continued teaching classes to students in his local mosque. His most famous pupil, another blind student by the name of ʿAbdul ʿAzīz b. Abdullah Ibn Bāz (d. 1999), would eventually succeed him in most of these positions.[143]

While Ibn Ibrahim had studied with the last batch of clerics of the Second Saudi State, he had never actually lived under that state and came of age when the modern Kingdom was already an established political entity after the Battle of Sibilla. Hence, circumstances forced him to come to terms with the new Kingdom. It was under his watch that the hard-core radicalism of First-Wave Wahhabi doctrine gave way to pragmatic development. There are many examples that can be given here.[144]

One example is his stance towards women's education. He initially opposed the opening of schools for girls, claiming that this would only corrupt them the way that other societies had corrupted their women. Eventually and after pressure from the king, he allowed the opening of a special institute for training female nurses, with the condition that they study with women teachers, and observe proper decorum, and treat female patients exclusively. This small concession was widened in less than a year, when King Faisal announced public high schools for all Saudi girls. Ibn Ibrahim then gave a fatwa stating that the Shariʿa did not restrict the education of females of any age, and as long as proper decorum was observed, education may be administered to females.[145] However, he insisted that he be placed in charge of the Ministry of Girls' Education, in order to maintain its Islamic environment.

One of the thorniest realities of First-Wave Wahhabism was its blatant *takfir* of the rest of the Muslim world, based not just on theology, but on the fact that they were not judging in accordance with God's laws. In addressing this issue, Ibn Ibrahim authored one of his most famous treatises, written in 1960, entitled *Taḥkīm al-Qawānīn* (*A Treatise Regarding the Canonization of Laws*). This was a direct attack on the secularist laws and European codes that were being adopted across the Arab world. In it, he claimed that there are six categories of people vis-à-vis secular laws, and he considered five of them to be apostates without any room for debate.[146] He had no qualms stating that the rest of the Muslim world was 'Islamic in name only' (*islam al-akthar islam ismi*).[147] He explicitly named Egypt – then the most prominent Muslim country – to be 'stripped of Shariʿa' and to be opposing, through its constitutional laws, the testimony of faith (*naqḍ al-shāhadah*).[148] Such wordings, couched in standard First-Wave Wahhabi rhetoric, clearly implied that such entities were outside the fold of Islam. Yet, despite these harsh views, he never once encouraged Ibn Saʿūd to wage war against them.

In fact, as the first Chair of the *Rābiṭa al-ʿAlam al-Islāmī* (WAMY), he regularly welcomed scholars from other countries and persuasions (including from the very land his ancestors fought and declared pagan: the modern Turkish state). But while at times his talks seemed to criticize some of their beliefs, he never accused them of actually being non-Muslims, and he encouraged them to unite for greater Islamic causes.[149] And while he did not allow Shiʿi teachers to be hired as judges even in their own regions, or teachers in the newly-opened public schools, even for non-religious subjects, and explicitly considered their beliefs to expel them from the fold of Islam,[150] he did not force the Shiʿi populations of the Kingdom (estimated to be around 12%) to convert to Wahhabism.

A further example that helps us fully understand Second-Wave Wahhabism was his stance towards the opening of Commercial Courts in the Kingdom. This was the government's alternative to solving disputes with respect to areas of finance that the traditional Shariʿa courts would not or could not handle, such as disputes involving banks and interest-bearing loans, or regarding cinemas and the sale of tobacco and musical products. All such transactions would have been deemed illegitimate and invalid in any traditional court (as interest is forbidden in Islamic law; as is the sale of impermissible products, such as, in accordance with Wahhabi beliefs, music and cinema tickets). However, the Kingdom had to solve business disputes involving such transactions, despite the clerical prohibition against them, because they existed in the society and were recognized by the Saudi State.

The Grand Mufti was extremely harsh in his fatwas against these Commercial Courts and did not mince his words, even as he wrote to other ministers or to the Royal Court itself, claiming that any such system of jurisdiction was 'disbelief' (*kufr*) and that the Shariʿa alone must be the law of the land.[151] It is also known that he would publicly state this in his gatherings and even gave this verdict directly to the king on multiple occasions.[152] Yet, crucially, *he did not claim the government, much less the king, had left the fold of Islam*, and for all practical purposes he continued to work with and under the government on all affairs.

There are numerous other positions and opinions that the Grand Mufti advocated throughout his life which fell on deaf ears before the rulers. While he was not private about his views, he never rallied against the government nor publicly called on the people to rise up. In fact, he never participated in fomenting any political dissent against the government, despite his strong religious disagreements with many of its policies.

In light of the above, the distinction between First-Wave and Second-Wave Wahhabism should be evident, in that the former considered all others outside their movement as enemies and apostates and viewed jihad as obligatory against them, while the latter grudgingly tolerated the existence of others and interacted with them, even while claiming that many or all of them were apostates or innovators.[153] In other words, the FIrst-Wave actually interacted with the rest of the Muslim world as apostates, while the Second-Wave looked at them as *potential* apostates but were willing to deal with many of them as fellow Muslims.

Second-Wave Wahhabism also began to come to terms with differentiating between *theory* and *practice*, realizing that while 'judging by other than God's law' should be deemed as ultimate heresy (*kufr*), in practice there was nothing they should do about it other than claim it was heresy (*kufr*). Ibn Ibrahim served as the primary model for the Wahhabis of his time by enacting that one did not have to modify the beliefs or practices of First-Wave Wahhabism in order to live in the modern Kingdom as an authentic Muslim.

The policies of the Royal Court in allowing such harsh criticism is also noteworthy – after all, King Faisal had no qualms banning multiple socialist and communist organizations and imprisoning or exiling numerous political agitators, even forcing his own brother Talal into exile for his attempts at reform. The fact that he tolerated his cousin the Mufti to such an extent, despite accusations of allowing *kufr*, clearly indicates he understood he needed the tacit support of the religious establishment in order to maintain his own legitimacy. As long as the Mufti did not call for rebellion, letting off some steam in his writings was tolerable.

However, the power that Ibn Ibrahim wielded was also dangerous, and King Faisal clearly understood that it could easily become a threat. Hence, upon the death of his cousin, the king attempted to remove 'the establishment's centralized and monocephalic leadership' by diversifying and diluting it with the creation of a number of bodies, without leadership positions within them. One of these was the formation of the Council of Senior Religious Scholars (*Hay'at Kibār al-ʿUlamā*) which is still an active clerical body. However, over time, this council managed to become 'the heart of the corporation and the focus of the ulama's ideological authority as a collective actor' and presented some challenges to subsequent rulers.[154]

All of these changes were necessary, but not sufficient for the flourishing of Wahhabism. Second-Wave Wahhabism allowed the group to live peacefully in the modern world, but it clearly had plenty of internal contradictions that had yet to be resolved. Part of the unease was caused by the memory of the violence of early Wahhabi history, and the explicit *takfīrī* tendencies of its founder and all earlier clerics. Thus, one sees the seeds of Third-Wave Wahhabism being sown in response to this seeming contradiction, so as to eliminate the uncomfortable dichotomy between theory and practice. However, the final event that signaled the crisis of Second-Wave Wahhabism and the need for its reform was the Siege of Mecca in 1979. It was the attempt to resolve those internal realities that resulted in Third-Wave Wahhabism.[155]

### *The Siege of Mecca in 1979*

The modernization of Saudi Arabia reached a rapid pace as the twentieth century came to a close. Upon the assassination of King Faisal, his half-brother, Khālid, ascended the throne. The latter is generally recognized as a genial, almost ineffective leader, who suffered from a number of medical ailments, until his death in 1982. However, his reign did see the exponential rise of the country's GDP, which allowed Saudi Arabia to become one of the wealthiest countries in the world. This influx of wealth and the rapid pace of modernization continued to exacerbate the tensions between the conservative clerics and the elites, as well as within the population and their perceptions of the rulers.

Much of the scholarly backlash was directed at the people and their adoption of the culture of 'foreigners,' not at the political rulers who allowed those foreigners free rein within the Kingdom. Perhaps the most prominent of such scholars was ʿAbd al-ʿAzīz b. ʿAbd Allāh b. Bāz,[156] as the leading scholar of Third-Wave Wahhabism.[157] Ibn Bāz was one of the tripartite-leadership that unofficially dictated mainstream Salafi doctrine at the end of the twentieth century, along with Nasir al-Din al-Albānī,[158] and

Muḥammad b. Ṣālih al-Uthaymin.[159] Ibn Bāz's position as the Grand Mufti of the Kingdom from 1992 until his death in 1999 made him one of the most prominent Muslim clerics of the twentieth century, and the only Grand Mufti of the country to date that was not a direct descendant of Ibn ʿAbd al-Wahhāb. He also played the seminal role in propagating Third-Wave Wahhabism, as we shall see. Nonetheless, the preaching of the Wahhabi clerical class to the generality of society would lead to a dramatic incident which brought to the forefront the simmering tensions in understanding Wahhabism during this period.

In the early 1970s, long before reaching the prime of his career, Ibn Bāz had inherited the Second-Wave Wahhabism of his teacher, Muḥammad b. Ibrāhīm, and attempted to balance what he viewed as the religious obligation of obeying the rulers with the clear proliferation of un-Islamic practices allowed by the regime. Even in the holy city of Medina, where he was the rector of the Islamic University of Medina (IUM) at the time, music shops had appeared, and magazines with pictures of women without appropriate *hijab*s were to be found everywhere. As a result of these societal developments a group of fiery students formed, around 1965, a collective known as *al-Jamaʿa al-Salafiyya al-Muḥtasiba* (The Salafi Group That Commands Right and Forbids Wrong, or JSM). Many of them had studied under Ibn Baz and al-Albānī and were associated with IUM. They began publicly preaching, particularly in poorer communities, against what they perceived as this modern hedonism. In time, they resorted to vigilante justice, vandalizing music stores and disposing of magazines that were deemed obscene. The purpose of this group was to call people back to piety and the austere doctrines of Wahhabism. Although Ibn Bāz did not officially join the movement, he supported many of their activities, and some of its main leaders were his students.

While the group saw Ibn Bāz as their spiritual leader, they were also taking instruction from the teachings of prominent non-Saudi Salafis like al-Albānī (from whom the term '*Salafi*' had come), Muqbil al-Wadiʿī (d. 2001) and Abū Bakr al-Jazāʾirī (d. 2018) – the latter of whom was a member of the group's consultative committee (*majlis al-shura*) and became their deputy. When al-Albānī visited Mecca, they arranged teaching sessions with him, and adopted his radical opposition to blind-following (*taqlid*) whereby they did not see themselves as following any scholar or legal school but rather the primary, scriptural sources. They also had links to the Pakistani *Ahl-e-Hadith* and the Egyptian *Ansar al-Sunna al-Muhammadiyya* (Helpers of the Prophetic Sunna) – two groups with similar radical opposition to *taqlīd*. The group's hard-edged Salafi message and method became quite popular by around 1976, to the extent that they had branches in Mecca, Riyadh, Taif, Buraydah, Jeddah and Dammam, among others. From a sociological perspective, the group could be seen as largely lower class (from groups that had not benefitted from modernization), Bedouin in tribal origin (and hence marginalized) and young, with most members in their mid-twenties and often unmarried.[160] Many of them were students at the IUM, who found purpose in this group's call to austerity and public morality.[161]

One of the founders of this group was known personally to Ibn Bāz, a certain Juhaymān al-ʿUtaybī (d. 1980).[162] Juhaymān was from a family of the *Ikhwān* paramilitary rebels, with his father participating in the Battle of Sibilla, but surviving until 1972. Following the urbanization program of the defeated *Ikhwān*, the religious outlook they harbored penetrated Saudi society. As the son of a soldier involved in the Battle of Sibilla, Juhaymān possessed the complex mentality that came from originating from this tribal society, and as a member of the Saudi Arabia National Guard (until around the mid-1970s). He had moved to Medina to informally study Islam, despite having not reached the fifth year of primary school and seemingly having language difficulties. He subsequently lived a very simple lifestyle and was not able to officially enter IUM as he possessed no formal educational qualifications. Juhaymān became more vocal in his dislike for the modernizations taking place, and eventually a rift grew between him and his teachers, whom he saw as sellouts. The tensions came to a head in 1977 when they had a meeting with al-Jaza'irī, who wanted to resolve some of their concerns. However, the meeting ended with the group splitting, with a minority siding with al-Jaza'irī and the majority siding with Juhaymān.[163] Thereafter, unbeknown to the Saudi authorities, Juhaymān slowly developed his own following among some Bedouins of Najd who shared his dislike for modernity. It was at this stage that he took a smaller group of more dedicated followers and began doing military training with them in the desert.[164]

Although the security forces had been aware of some of the rebellious talk occurring in the Kingdom, major steps to counter it had not been taken. At one point, some of Juhaymān's followers were imprisoned and questioned in Riyadh. However, Ibn Bāz oversaw the questioning and did not see anything wrong with their beliefs, so they were released without charge.[165] This apparent sloppiness would come back to haunt him a decade later, during the crisis of the First Gulf War, and had further consequences for the state of Salafism.

Among the followers of Juhaymān was a young man named Muḥammad b. ʿAbd Allāh al-Qaḥṭānī (d. 1979). Juhaymān was convinced that he was living at the end of times, and he came to believe that Muhammad – who happened to be his brother-in-law – resembled the awaited Mahdī[166] and subsequently began to persuade his followers that he had arrived.[167] He then decided to force the Muslim world to give their allegiance to the Mahdī at the Kaaba in Mecca. In order to accomplish this, he planned a hostile takeover of Islam's most sacred site. Juhaymān and his loyalists continued to operate in relative secrecy, planning a daring and unprecedented mechanism to publicize the arrival of the Mahdī. It was the year 1399 AH, and hadith literature mentioned the concept of the 'Reviver of the Century.'[168]

On 1 Muharram 1400 AH/20 November 1979 the turn of the century according to the Muslim Hijri calendar, in the early hours of dawn, Juhaymān and around 400 of his followers seized the Grand Mosque in Mecca and held it hostage. The mosque contained many worshipers who had attended the early morning (*fajr*) congregational prayer. After the prayer, Juhaymān had his guards subdue the minimal security in place, and took control of the microphone, where he symbolically brought al-Qahtani into the central open-air courtyard where the Ka'ba is situated, and publicly declared him the Mahdī. He urged all Muslims to pledge allegiance to the Mahdī and abandon the Saudi government and their scholars. Here, he announced in front of the House of God his long-held belief about the government being the enemies of Islam and the scholars who supported them being sellouts. He listed a long litany of grievances against the Royal Family, including their alliances with America, the corruption they had allowed, the licentious lifestyles they were known for (the governor of Mecca, a half-brother of the king, was rumored to be a frequent drinker and gambler), and the overall abandonment of the teachings of Islam. In his eyes, they had lost all legitimacy as rulers, and he called on the people present, and through them the entire world, to pledge allegiance to the awaited Mahdī and to then overthrow the government and establish a new Islamic Caliphate. He asserted that all modern governments were illegitimate according to Islamic law, and that the Saudi dynasty was likewise illegitimate from the time it refused to join Sharif Husain in his rebellion against the Ottomans at the beginning of the twentieth century.[169]

The siege lasted two weeks before the Saudi forces could break through and regain control of the mosque, with the help of French special forces. Al-Qahtani died during the battle in a grenade explosion. This was witnessed by several rebels, who immediately lost faith in Juhaymān's cause, as his untimely death did not fit with the Muslim scriptural narrative prophesized for the Mahdī. The battle resulted in severe casualties on both sides, and dozens of worshipers and pilgrims were killed in the crossfire. In the end, Juhaymān, along with hundreds of his followers, was captured and publicly executed on 9 January 1980.[170]

The hostage crisis became a public scandal of the highest order. Not only did it show the incompetence of the Saudi government (both at an intelligence and tactical level, as they had to bring in foreign help to battle the rebels), but it also demonstrated the deep public discontent that many religious segments felt against the government. While hardly anyone would agree with the *tactics* of the group, the awkward reality is that many among the population agreed with its *grievances*. The siege was to have a long-term impact; and in an ironic twist of events, in a bid to placate the religious clergy, the government ended up silently caving in to many of the demands that Juhaymān had made, which came to benefit the Wahhabi-Salafi scholars.[171]

As a result of the uprising, the Saudi government backtracked on some of its more liberal changes and returned the country to a semi-conservative Wahhabi state. In the period shortly thereafter, women were excluded from the workplace and media, the religious police were given stronger authority, cinemas were banned, and religious scholars started to play a bigger role in public life, and in framing policy.

Here, it is important to stress that Juhaymān and his band of fanatical followers were tapping into mainstream First-Wave Wahhabism. He considered obedience to the rulers as forfeit *because* they had formed alliances with America and other non-Muslim countries and judged by other than God's law; he also criticized them for their allowance of immorality in the Kingdom. However, his views were a distortion and evolution into something unique: a jihadist-messianic apocalyptic First-Wave Wahhabism, wherein he believed he was witnessing the end of times, and that God would send the promised and awaited Mahdī to overthrow the evil rulers and establish God's law on earth one last time before Judgment Day.[172]

The Siege of Mecca affected the future of Saudi Arabia in multiple ways. Juhaymān's band of fanatics was the first manifestation of what would later evolve into a Jihadi-Salafi mindset that would emerge and gain popularity in the coming years. (Incidentally, Juhaymān's public confrontation with the government was what sparked a political and religious zeal in a young, wealthy socialite by the name of Usama b. Laden – his story will be mentioned in a future chapter.) It was also the first time since the inception of Saudi Arabia and the Battle of Sibilla that a fault line was exposed between the ideals of the Wahhabi religious establishment – which had directly inspired Juhaymān's thoughts – and the Saudi government. Until this time, besides the *Ikhwān* revolt in 1927, there was always a public solidarity and an apparent congruence between the Wahhabi clerics and the Saudi government. Yet the idea that the Saudi government could be opposed on the grounds of violating Wahhabi principles would only grow over time.

The hyper-modernization of Saudi Arabia up to 1979 had created a chasm in the seemingly harmonious relationship between the Wahhabis and Āl Saʿūd. With the fault line exposed, this invariably led to a fracturing of the Wahhabis within themselves and the emergence of various strands within the movement, differing on the level and mechanism of political participation and engagement. But before we mention these splinter movements that would fracture Saudi Wahhabism and forever break its unity, we must now pause and assess what changes took place during this time frame, as it is these changes that can be considered to be Third-Wave Wahhabism.

### *3.2.3 Third-Wave Wahhabism*

The main problem with Second-Wave Wahhabism was the clear internal contradiction between its *theory* and its *practice*. If indeed non-Wahhabi sects, like Sufis and Shiʿi, allowed the worship of other than God, and if abandoning the Shariʿa in judgment meant abandoning the religion, then on what basis could such people who claimed to be Muslims not be treated as *murtad*s, or apostates, as First-Wave Wahhabism taught? While the Second-Wave had tempered the original teachings in *action*, it had not tempered those teachings in *thought*. Another conundrum faced by this generation was the history of its origins, and particularly, the seemingly blatant fanaticism of the founder.

To save the movement, a complete overhaul was required, and there was a clear need to rehabilitate the image of Ibn ʿAbd al-Wahhāb. With the advent of modernity, and the entrance of Saudi Arabia into global politics, the image of the founder of the movement – as an extreme fanatic who considered anyone who opposed him to be an apostate, viewing himself as the only one representing the religion of God – would not be appropriate. Ibn ʿAbd al-Wahhāb was thus heralded as 'a Salafi imam': this was first time the term 'Salafi' would be used as the main identifying adjective of the movement, a term that was completely absent from First-Wave and rarely mentioned in Second.

Third-Wave Wahhabism began interpreting classical Wahhabi texts in an unprecedented manner, taking great pains to ensure that no phrase of the founder would possibly insinuate blanket *takfīr*. Such phrases, Third-Wave clerics argued, must be understood in light of other treatises and statements which clearly indicated that *theoretically*, Ibn ʿAbd al-Wahhāb might consider certain people to be apostates, but *in practice* he never declared a Muslim to be one; rather, he afforded him the excuse of being ignorant of the reality of Islam (*al-ʿudhr bi-l-jahl*).[173] Such ignorance could only be lifted by a qualified person, having engaged with this mistaken Muslim and explaining the evidence in a proper manner, such that they could claim with certainty that the 'evidence was established' against him. Or, to phrase it as a jurist would: Only after 'the evidence had been established' (*iqamat al-ḥujja*) could the 'excuse from ignorance' be lifted; in the absence of *iqamat al-ḥujja*, one must remain on the default of excusing a Muslim because of his potential ignorance.

This notion, of 'excusing the Muslim because of ignorance' (*al-ʿudhr bi-l-jahl*), became a key doctrine of Third-Wave Wahhabism, and was used to soften the movement's interactions with outsiders. In technical language, the Third-Wave taught that *takfir* is to be made by description (*takfir bi-l-waṣf*), but not on a specific individual (*takfir al-mu ʿayyan*), until it could be confirmed that the evidence was established against him (*iqamat al-ḥujja*). To put it simply, the Third-Wave argued that, in practice, one should not carelessly declare other Muslims to be apostates, but rather should say that they are committing *actions* that could potentially lead to apostasy, but because it was assumed that such Muslims were *ignorant* of Islam's beliefs on monotheism, they should be *excused* as a rule. They then back projected this interpretation on to Ibn ʿAbd al-Wahhāb himself.

The concept of *al-ʿudhr bi-l-jahl*, and hence by extension *iqamat al-ḥujja*, is a standard doctrine of the faith, found in numerous Sunni classical theological and legal textbooks. As mentioned earlier, even Ibn ʿAbd al-Wahhāb himself invoked it in a number of his early treatises. This notion, as understood by mainstream scholars, gave an excuse to someone who might otherwise not be excused *if he did not know any better*. For example, the Egyptian polymath al-Suyūṭī (d. 911/1505) mentions that if someone is guilty of claiming that murder or alcohol or illicit sex are permitted by God, then this constitutes disbelief (*kufr*) and would typically deem one an apostate, 'unless he newly embraced Islam, or grew up in some wilderness far from city-life, such that these rulings were not known to him.'[174] Ibn Taymiyya also used this principle multiple times in his works.

It was not in the invention of this principle that Third-Wave Wahhabism broke away from its predecessors, but rather in its application. The claim was made that Ibn ʿAbd al-Wahhāb was only speaking *theoretically* about who becomes an apostate, and that he never considered the rest of the world as actual apostates. In order to validate this claim, a revisionist history needed to be taught, one in which the actual teachings of First-Wave Wahhabism were reinterpreted in a less *takfīrī* manner, with the history of the movement simply glossed over and excised from public discourse.

The Third-Wave was led by the most famous student of Muḥammad b. Ibrahīm, Ibn Bāz, the senior-most cleric of the movement for many decades who served as the Grand Mufti towards the end of his life. He was by no means the only reformist voice, as attested to by the careers of Muhammad ibn Salih al-ʻUthaymin and Salih b. Fawzan al-Fawzan, to mention two of the more prominent scholars of that era (further discussed below).

*ʿAbd al-ʿAzīz b. ʿAbd Allāh b. Bāz (d. 1999)*

ʿAbd al-ʿAzīz b. ʿAbd Allāh, from the tribe of Āl Bāz, was born in Riyadh in 1912.[175] At a young age, he lost his eyesight due to illness but was known for his sharp memory and ability to quote religious texts. He studied with many famous scholars, most importantly with Muḥammad b. Ibrahīm, who considered him his main student, and with Saʿd b. Ḥamad b. ʿAtīq. His teacher Muḥammad b. Ibrahīm would use him for many tasks, including governmental responsibilities, which facilitated his exposure to many fields. He was appointed initially as a judge in one of the provinces of the Kingdom, after which he returned to Riyadh and was given responsibility to be the Chair of the 'Fatwa and Research Academy' (*Idārah al-Buḥūth al-ʿIlmiyya wa-l-Iftā'*), a position he held for two decades, until he was appointed by Royal Decree as the Grand Mufti of the Kingdom. He was also appointed first as the Vice-President of the Islamic University of Medina (IUM), and then President; his association with the IUM lasted almost twenty years, during which he taught classes while assuming administrative responsibilities. He maintained a scholarly life, teaching and interacting with students, and corresponded with global leaders and non-Wahhabi clerics and leaders, even writing a letter to Gamal Abdel Nasser asking for clemency in his decision to execute Sayyid Qutb (d. 1966) (although the letter was ignored).

One of the first treatises that earned him international fame was his attack on the rising trend of pan-Arab nationalism, a long epistle entitled *Naqd al-qawmiyya al-'Arabiyyh 'ala daw' al-Islam wa'l-waqi'* (*Critique of Arab Nationalism in the Light of Islam and Reality*). First released in 1961, it had been requested by the Grand Mufti of Saudi Arabia and was funded by the Saudi regime. It was a time when socialist pan-Arab movements were sweeping the Middle East, from Libya to Iraq and Egypt, and popular dictators were fueling anti-Western sentiment.

In what was the first religious critique of this new trend by a Wahhabi, Ibn Bāz was forced to widen the discourse beyond the terms of traditional Wahhabism, and even resorted to scholars affiliated with schools of thought that Salafis rebuked. Thus, the author condemned pan-Arabism by quoting extensively from Muhammad al-Ghazali al-Saqqa (d. 1996), a contemporary Egyptian Azhari scholar who was Ashʿarī in theology and aligned with the Muslim Brotherhood in thought, and Abul Hasan Ali Nadwi (d. 1999), a leading Indian scholar, who was a Māturīdī in theology and a Sufi. In a decidedly non-Wahhabi voice of Islamic ecumenism, Ibn Bāz urged all those who proclaimed the testimony of faith to unite against this imperialist plot to rob the Muslim world of its true identity, that of Islam. He claimed that boasting of one's ancestry was nothing short of pre-Islamic ignorance (*jāhiliyya*). He challenged his readers: Who were the Arabs except a bunch of unknown disparate nomadic Bedouins before the coming of Islam? Clearly, Islam gave the Arabs their honor and strength, and through Islam, all Muslims, black and white, Arab and non-Arab, were equal.[176]

Ibn Bāz also played an active role in establishing the Muslim World League (the *Rābiṭah*), and World Assembly of Muslim Youth (WAMY) – which will be discussed further in Chapter 4 – and participated in many conferences with scholars from diverse backgrounds, without objecting to their strands of Islam during that time. This led to Ibn Bāz's famous interaction with leading clerics of other strands of Islam, not merely tolerating their presence but rubbing shoulders with them at conferences and speaking on the same podiums. He inculcated an aura of tolerance and respect that had been initiated in the Second-Wave but was now coming to fruition under his watch. Prominent non-Wahhabi scholars of Egypt, India, Morocco, and other lands were invited to conferences in the Kingdom under the auspices of Ibn Bāz.

He authored over forty works and released many thousands of fatwas; he was also a regular guest and the primary scholar on the Saudi Radio's 'Ask a fatwa' program called '*Nūr ʿala al-darb*,' in which listeners would call in live and receive a fatwa. His opinions and views embodied Third-Wave thought. His fatwas regarding cultural or theological issues typically were in conformity with Wahhabi thought and in disagreement with other strands of Islam, but in a language and style that was markedly different from that of his predecessors. Instead of engaging in excommunication (*takfir*) of those who disagreed with his notions of Salafism, it was now possible to simply label non-Wahhabis as astray (*tabdīʿ*) – declaring a fellow Muslim a 'deviant' implied they were still Muslim but not fully guided. At times, he argued that a person might be a disbeliever (*kāfir*) in the eyes of God, or treated as a disbeliever but, still, it was not the job of another person to execute or even declare such a person to be a disbeliever.

As an example, in one fatwa, he was asked regarding the verdict of the one who called out to the dead saints as a Muslim. He replied:

> The verdict here is that his deed is a deed of *kufr*. Whoever calls out to the dead and asks help (*istighātha*) of them has done a deed of *kufr*. But the scholars differ: does he immediately become a *kāfir* by this deed, or must he first be taught (that this is *kufr*). There are two opinions. The first opinion is that he must be taught this fact, because the matter might be confusing for him, as he might have been exposed to misguided preachers, or evil scholars, and so he is confused about this matter. And hence, he must be taught, and he must be warned, before one can pronounce a verdict of *kufr* on him. And this is the position of a group of scholars.
>
> The second opinion is that no clarification is needed, since this matter is clear, as the Qurʾan in its entirety clarifies that this is *shirk*, as does the Sunna, and the statements of the scholars. Hence, [according to this opinion] there is no need to clarify anything to him, and this very deed of his would make him a *kāfir*. However, [even in this case] he must be asked to repent before he is executed, if there is an actual Islamic state that will hold him to account – he cannot be executed until he is asked to repent and told to leave *shirk*. And if he does so, and repents, and desists, then that is well

> and good! But if he does not, and persists [in his deed], then he should be executed.
>
> And no doubt this is a severe matter, and the [second] opinion that he is a *kāfir* merely by this deed is a strong opinion, but the safer opinion is that this should not be done [i.e., he should not be declared a *kāfir*] until he is taught, and until good guidance is given to him, perchance he would then be rightly guided. But no doubt his verdict in this world is that of a *kāfir* as long as he continues to do the deeds of a *kāfir*, so his funeral should not be done, nor should he be washed [ritually], nor should Muslims inherit from him.[177]

This fatwa, and many similar, precisely encapsulate Third-Wave Wahhabism. Whereas no First or Second-Wave Wahhabi cleric would have hesitated in declaring the disbelief of such a person, and even *doubting* the verdict on such a person would be considered automatic heresy (*kufr*) and apostasy (*ridda*), Ibn Bāz gives the novel and unprecedented view – for Wahhabis, at least – that there are in fact two opinions! The first opinion would itself be deemed heresy by First-Wave Wahhabi clerics, but it is the one that Ibn Bāz essentially adopted in practice. Even the second, harsher opinion was a mitigated version, encapsulating a type of Second-Wave Wahhabism, in that such a person should not be physically harmed, *even in an ideal Islamic state*, without a formal trial and an opportunity to repent. It would be pertinent to recall here that no First-Wave Wahhabi cleric, much less Ibn ʿAbd al-Wahhāb himself, *ever* afforded any opponent a trial and an opportunity to defend themselves before attacking and executing them: jihad was declared merely because they refused to politically join the First State. In this fatwa, and in his similar verdicts, there is essentially no indication of original, First-Wave Wahhabi thought, much less their practice, vis-à-vis those who invoke saints.

In another clear indication of Third-Wave Wahhabism, Ibn Bāz famously and publicly disagreed with his mentor Muḥammad b. Ibrahīm regarding excommunicating other Muslim lands that had systems of governments not in line with the shariah. Rather, he claimed that one should not declare these lands as *kāfir*, as long as they did not deem such a contravention of the rulings of God and His Prophet to be valid.[178]

Under his watch, Wahhabi thought gradually shifted from a fringe *takfir*-movement to a slightly radical, yet right-of-center mainstream, of a generally acceptable nature to other leading conventional Islamic groups. His frequent usage of the term 'Salafi,' or the ascription to '*al-salaf al-ṣāliḥ*,' also helped in this shift. This coincided with modern means of communication, beginning with the radio and cassette tape and ending with the internet, and bolstered the pivotal role that the IUM would play globally (as discussed below at 3.3). This version of Wahhabism would spread around the globe. While it was still hostile to other strands of Islam, it did not openly excommunicate them, much less call for jihad against them.

This version of Wahhabism was far closer to Taymiyyan Salafism than to the original version of Wahhabism. Hence, it could claim more legitimacy and acceptability in the esteem of non-Salafis and non-Wahhabis. The country's leading institution for issuing legal edicts, the *Dār al-Iftā'*, can be seen, during the period between 1971 and 1999, to have been liberal and open in relation to technological progress and the politics of the country's leadership. However, it was conservative in relation to social practice – and this remained the case when Ibn Bāz was the leading figure of the institution. Ibn Bāz's openness was evident in many of his political opinions, most famously in his endorsement of the American troops and presence in the Kingdom during the First Gulf War; and in his claim that a peace treaty (*sulḥ*) with Israel, and the exchange of ambassadors was not contrary to the principles of *al-walā' wa-l-barā'*, as such a practice did not entail friendship (*mawadda*) and loyalty (*muwalat*).[179] It does not need to be pointed out that such opinions would themselves have been anathematized by First-Wave clerics.

Ibn Bāz passed away in 1999, the first of the 'three pillars' of modern Salafi thought to do so. He remains one of the most esteemed scholars among all Salafis, not just because of his thought, but also because of his austere lifestyle, his generosity, and his kindness.

*Muḥammad b. Salih al-Uthaymīn (d. 2001)*

The second most prominent scholar of the Third-Wave school was Muḥammad b. Salih al-Uthaymīn, commonly known as Shaykh Ibn 'Uthaymīn. He was from the Muqbil branch of the Tamīm tribe. He was born in the Saudi Arabian city of 'Unayza in 1929 and began his Islamic studies at an early age. 'Unayza, in the province of Qaṣīm had, and continues to have, a reputation of independent Wahhabi thought. Its most famous scholar, 'Abd al-Raḥmān b. Nāṣir, commonly called Ibn al-Sa'dī (d. 1957), took Ibn 'Uthaymīn under his tutelage and had a profound impact on him. At a time when most scholars of the Arabian Peninsula were staunch Ḥanbalis, Ibn al-Sa'dī was known for his stance on rejecting strict adherence to one *madhhab*, and instead taking the legal positions that seemed more in line with the texts of the Qur'an and Sunna. Typically (but not always) those positions reflected the verdicts of Ibn Taymiyya. Ibn 'Uthaymīn was influenced by his teacher Ibn al-Sa'dī and became one of the main proponents of this strand of legal thought within the Wahhabī school, in contrast to Ibn Bāz who rarely opposed the rulings of the Ḥanbali school.

After the death of his teacher Ibn al-Sa'dī in 1957, Ibn 'Uthaymīn took over the position of the Imam of the Grand Mosque of 'Unayza. In 1978, he was offered a Professorship in Islamic Studies at the Imam Muḥammad

b. Saʿūd University in Qaṣīm. He continued in both these positions until his death. Ibn ʿUthaymīn also lectured at the Grand Mosque in Mecca during the month of Ramadan, where a special honorary chair would be placed for him for the duration of the holy month. He occupied this chair for thirty-five years.

Although he had been teaching local students in the Grand Mosque of ʿUnayza since the death of Ibn al-Saʿdī, it was during the early part of the 1980s that his reputation began to grow, and students from across the Arab and Muslim world began to flock to his mosque. Eventually, a separate dormitory had to be built to accommodate them. These students were not typically affiliated with any accredited university, preferring to study with Ibn ʿUthaymīn in the traditional, mosque-centered method of Islamic scholarship. It is impossible to estimate the number of students who studied with him in this manner, but they are in the thousands.[180] Additionally, his lectures were recorded and distributed across the world, which brought him international fame. His erudite scholarship, eloquent speech, and cogent manner of explaining *fiqh*, endeared him to many followers of the wider Salafi movement.

In 1987, he was appointed as a member of the 'Committee of Senior Scholars,' an official body of the senior-most clergy of Saudi Arabia, and the only committee whose religious verdicts (fatwas) carry official weight and are authorized to be distributed within the Kingdom. Along with his academic credentials, Ibn ʿUthaymīn was revered by his admirers for his extreme asceticism and simple lifestyle. He was awarded the King Faisal Prize for Contributions to Islamic Studies in 1994. In awarding the prize, the committee noted, in addition to his lengthy academic accomplishments, the fact that 'he embodied the mannerisms that befit a scholar of Islam.'[181] He died of colon cancer in January 2001. He never traveled outside Saudi Arabia except for a brief ten-day trip to Boston in an unsuccessful attempt to treat his cancer a few months before his death.

Along with Ibn Bāz and al-Albānī, he is widely considered among the three most influential scholars of the modern Salafi movement. He was a prolific writer, authoring over fifty works, and authorizing some of his closest students to transcribe and edit his recorded lectures for publication, boosting the number of his publications to over a hundred. He particularly emphasized the importance of the *fiqh* text of *Zād al-Mustaqniʿ* (*The Provision of the One Who is Satiated*) by Mūsā al-Ḥajjāwī (d. 968/1561), which is a concise and popular intermediate-level treatise of Islamic law according to the Ḥanbalī school. His most popular work is his explanation of this text, entitled *al-Sharḥ al-Mumtiʿ ʿalā Zād al-Mustaqniʿ* (*The Pleasing Commentary of Zād al-Mustaqniʿ*), which was printed in fifteen large volumes. In this work, he regularly disagreed with the standard Ḥanbalī school and generally preferred the opinions of Ibn Taymiyya, although at times he also offered his own legal opinions that differed from both of them.

On the political front, he remained relatively neutral, keeping aloof from the kings and princes, and pointedly refraining from either praising or criticizing the *Ṣaḥwa* or Madkhalī strands (discussed in section 3.2.5). Like Ibn Bāz, he retained the admiration of the entire spectrum of Salafi movements.

He categorically forbade suicide bombing operations against civilian targets, not only because he considered it prohibited to target civilians, but also because he viewed this tactic as a clear case of suicide, which Islam forbids. He also gave a somewhat ambiguous fatwa regarding those Muslim rulers who institute or implement legal regimes other than God's law: while he did consider such rulers to be potential apostates (echoing similar sentiments from Ibn Taymiyya), he stressed that people should leave this judgment to God, and not rebel against their rulers.

He also wrote many popular works on theology, summarizing and explaining the works of Ibn Taymiyya and Ibn ʿAbd al-Wahhāb. Yet it is in these essentially theological works that clear and unequivocal examples emerge, exemplifying Ibn ʿUthaymīn's adoption of Third-Wave thought. For example, Ibn ʿAbd al-Wahhāb's *Kashf al-Shubuhāt* (*The Removal of Doubts*) clearly demonstrates, on a number of occasions, his explicit *takfir* of all of his opponents. Most explicitly, he writes, 'a person can become a disbeliever (*kāfir*) because of a word that comes from his mouth, even though he is ignorant [of its implications], and his ignorance is not a valid excuse.'[182] This phrase categorically demonstrates that Ibn ʿAbd al-Wahhāb, in this work at least, did not view ignorance as a legitimate excuse for making certain heretical statements (i.e., *ʿudhr bi-l-jahl* in such cases was not valid in his eyes).

However, in commenting on this phrase, Ibn ʿUthaymīn says, 'I do not think the Shaykh [meaning Ibn ʿAbd al-Wahhāb] actually believes that ignorance cannot be an excuse. Perhaps it means someone fell short of learning obligatory matters due to laziness, then yes in this case. Otherwise [ignorance is an excuse], and we know this because the Shaykh has explicit texts in other places that show that he did excuse based on ignorance.'[183] In another example, he was asked whether someone who invokes the dead should be considered a *mushrik* because of that act, and whether *takfir* should be made immediately upon such an individual. He replied that while this person was a *mushrik* in light of this act, it would not be permissible for anyone to declare him a *kāfir* without the evidence being established against him (i.e., *iqamat al-ḥujja*), for he could be ignorant. The questioner then quotes the famous treatise of the grandson of the founder, ʿAbd al-Raḥmān b. Ḥasan, in which he makes *takfir* of the one who invokes other than God and says that there is no excuse in such matters – the mere fact that he utters the testimony of faith and lives among Muslims means that the proof has been established. Ibn `Uthaymīn replies, 'It is understood that *shirk* is forbidden, and that it necessitates eternal damnation in the fire of Hell and forbids one from entering Paradise. However, this person might not know that this particular act (that he does) constitutes *shirk*, and this is indeed a possibility.'[184] This last example is extremely telling in that Ibn ʿUthaymīn is presented with an explicit First-Wave cleric and verdict that seems to contradict his opinion, and rather than addressing the contradiction, he simply evades it and reiterates that ignorance is indeed an excuse.

*Salih b. Fawzan al-Fawzan (b. 1933)*

Although Salih b. Fawzan al-Fawzan is incomparable to Ibn Bāz and al-'Uthaymin in scholarly terms and social prestige, he is a key figure in Third-Wave Wahhabism, and perhaps the senior-most figure still alive (at the time of writing) of that generation. He is a member of the Council of Senior Scholars, and was a close student and associate of Ibn Bāz.

Almost all of his writings consist of Third-Wave thought. For example, he wrote a commentary on Sulaymān b. ʿAbdillah Āl al-Shaykh's infamous work against the Ottomans, *al-Dalā'il fī ḥukm muwālāt Ahl al-Ishrāk* (*The Evidences for the Ruling Regarding Alliance with the Infidels*). As mentioned earlier, this entire work, written during the Second Saudi Emirate in the nineteenth century, is crystal clear in expressing the standard Wahhabi unconditional excommunication (*takfir*) of the Ottomans and all those who support them. The title itself announces that the Ottomans are 'people of paganism.' However, in his commentary, written *after* the Kingdom enlisted the help of America in fighting Saddam Hussein, al-Fawzan argues that this work does not condemn the seeking of military aid from polytheists, but rather it censures the support of a particular army only, namely that of Muhammad Ali Pasha, which was intending to destroy Islam through its opposition to pure monotheism and its support of grave-worship (*quburiyya*).[185]

*Conclusion*

Before we move on to other strands of Wahhabism, let us summarize the key takeaways regarding the Three Waves of Wahhabi thought. First-Wave Wahhabism stood upon the original teachings of its founder, managing to last almost a century and a half: through two Saudi states, and helping in the establishment of the third, and current, Kingdom. But its teachings were simply incompatible with a modern nation-state, and hence changes were inevitable if the movement wished to survive. And survive it did, by compromising *in practice* and allowing the government to not live up to Wahhabi ideals – this was the net result of Second-Wave thought. Not much changed in theory, but an awkward modus vivendi was carved out where both sides – the government and the clergy – tolerated the existence of the other, as long as they continued to validate one another's legitimacy.

As a new generation of Wahhabis grew up disconnected from the past, it was then possible, as a Third-Wave project, to introduce new doctrines that would have been rejected by the founders. An organic historical revisionism developed that was then back projected onto the community's understanding of their history. The net result was that Third-Wave Wahhabism was more similar to a Taymiyyan understanding of Salafism than Ibn ʿAbd al-Wahhāb's original ideas. This era also witnessed the active engagement with, and adoption of, the term 'Salafi,' which was unknown among the first two waves. Undoubtedly, the discovery, critical review, and publication of Ibn Taymiyya's scattered works, not cited by Ibn Abd al-Wahhāb, contributed to a greater understanding of the Mamluk scholar's thought and a more direct affinity with him.

Modern Wahhabis have dismissed numerous critical works written about Ibn ʿAbd al-Wahhāb and his early movement as being the works of mere enemies, whose aim was simply to smear, malign, and besmirch the doctrines of the founder, by falsely claiming that Ibn ʿAbd al-Wahhāb was a *takfīrī* fanatic. An entire new generation of defenders constantly reiterated that this was a blatant lie. The standard tactic was to quote directly from the writings of Ibn ʿAbd al-Wahhāb, where he explicitly claimed that he did not make mass *takfir*, and that he believed that ignorance was an excuse (these quotations, and their explanation in their historic contexts, have been mentioned in Section 3.1.3).[186] In all of these defenses, no mention is ever made of the early history of the movement, or its explicit stances towards the Ottoman Empire and those tribes who gave allegiance to them, or of the other quotations of the first generation of Wahhabi clerics (students of the founder) that clearly demonstrated their *takfīrī* stances. In other words, the early history of the movement was simply ignored. Those quotations that portrayed the founder in a more mainstream light were constantly quoted, and used to interpret away the more problematic ones.

Hence, the Third-Wave Wahhabism that is now taught in schools and universities in Saudi Arabia is an expunged and distorted version of the original. The original expansionist history is sanitized, and the more extreme statements – if they are ever read – are conveniently explained away. Current Wahhabis are taught that Ibn ʿAbd al-Wahhāb was a reviver of Islam who did not make *takfīr* of the masses, and only waged jihad against disbelievers, or those who attacked him, and who protected Salafism against external forces who posed an existential threat. As he is held up as a hero, his extreme views and actions are glossed over, unaddressed or explained away through capricious use of the evidence. This allows many modern Wahhabis to live in peace with other communities without feeling any disconnect from their tradition.

Those who, by chance, or extensive personal reading, come across the reality of early Wahhabi history are genuinely shocked to discover the real nature of the movement. Some may develop a type of cognitive dissonance, choosing to believe contradictory stances at once. Others choose to abandon the movement altogether. Still others, admittedly a small fringe, embrace the attitudes represented by First-Wave Wahhabism perhaps becoming sympathetic to Jihadi-Salafism.

In essence, both Second- and Third-Wave Wahhabism are products of the tempering of First-Wave views in light of political changes, and attempts to coordinate a reasonable position in the modern world. Therefore, one can agree with the conclusion of Nabil Mouline 'that Hanbali-Wahhabism,' of all three waves in our demonstration, 'is not the monolithic entity described by others, but is in fact a living tradition that interacts with social facts and responds to historical contingencies.' This is part of what Mouline describes as the 'ethic of responsibility' that the Wahhabis have maintained to uphold the 'three O's' of orthodoxy, orthopraxy, and political order. Furthermore, the clerics have had to remain politically pragmatic in pursuit of their goals, as numerous Saudi kings, from Ibn Saud to Faisal, attempted to ensure that the Wahhabi clerics would remain subordinate to their political will. Monarchical attempts to totally control the religious scholars only led to the latter demonstrating a significant flexibility and ingenuity to remain powerful and highly relevant in the society, albeit always under the royal power and prerogative.[187]

Nonetheless, there would still be discontent and internal inconsistencies, and Third-Wave Wahhabism could not remain stagnant in the face of other changes. Rather, it continued to evolve and splinter into many sub-strands, even while retaining a core base. It is to these sub-strands that we now turn. Given that it is specific to Saudi Arabia during a particular moment in its history (1990s–2010s), it is possible to frame our discussion using Wagemaker's revised tripartite typology of *quietist*, *politico*, and *jihadi* (see Chapter 1).

### *3.2.4 The Ṣaḥwa Movement*

The next phase of the Kingdom would prove to be its most significant in terms of the fractionalization of the Wahhabi movement: political events forced the movement to split. This phase begins with the crowning of King Fahd, who became king after the death of Khalid in 1982. He was the fourth son of ʿAbd al-Azīz to take the crown, and the first of the famous 'Sudayrī Seven,' a powerful group of seven full-brothers who shared the same mother (a woman from the Sudayri tribe) and who would become prominent for helping one another against the other half-brothers in the Āl Saʿūd intra-civil disputes. King Fahd ruled for over two decades until he passed away in 2005. He was technically the de facto ruler for most of King Khalid's reign as well due to the latter's poor health. Hence, his impact has been profound. The most significant event during King Fahd's reign was the Gulf War of 1990–91 and the events it set in motion. The war would end up dividing not just Wahhabism, but the entire global Salafi movement, in unprecedented ways.

In order to understand this split, we need to look at the roots of what is called the *Ṣaḥwa* movement. (It should be noted that there will be some overlapping discussion in this section and in Chapter 4, which deals with the Muslim Brotherhood and its relationship to Salafism.) '*Ṣaḥwa*' is an Arabic word that translates as 'awakening,' and is the short form of the term *al–Ṣaḥwa al-Islāmiyya*, which means 'The Islamic Awakening.' Although the *Ṣaḥwa* movement as a socio-political religious phenomenon only crystalized in the 1990s, the roots of the movement can be traced to the impact of Egyptian affairs on Saudi Arabia three decades earlier. During the 1960s, Gamal Abdel Nasser (d. 1970), the president of Egypt, began a harsh crackdown on the Muslim Brotherhood (*al-Ikhwān al-Muslimūn*) which was partially responsible for his own rise. Senior members of the party were executed, imprisoned, or exiled. Many of these exiles found their way to Saudi Arabia. Despite the fact that the Muslim Brotherhood was not Salafi, Saudi Arabia welcomed these exiles as forward-thinking intellectuals dedicated to Islam.

The arrival of the leadership of the Muslim Brotherhood into Saudi Arabia led to a cross-pollination of ideas. The Brotherhood interacted with the local Wahhabi clerics, and both parties influenced each other's understanding of Islam and politics. This led to the creation of various sub-strands within both the Muslim Brotherhood and the Wahhabis.

The *Ṣaḥwa* movement is undoubtedly the largest and most significant movement that arose from this exchange of ideas. It focused primarily on increasing the role of religious scholars in politics while assisting the average Muslim to gain a stronger understanding of Islam. They established various schools and circles of study across Saudi Arabia and attracted thousands of youths. Initially, the Saudi government remained ambivalent about the movement, and even engaged with it when necessary. In its early phase, it did not openly challenge the government or criticize them by name. Instead, they concentrated on bringing political discourse into religious circles and appealing to a younger, more educated audience. Their stance was that if the government needed to be engaged, it would be through dialogue and letters.[188] While the revivalist trend, represented by Juhaymān, has been seen as 'isolationist, pietistic, and lower-class,' and on the margins, the *Ṣaḥwa* movement has been viewed as 'pragmatic, political, and elitist,' and mainly on university campuses.[189]

Like other similar movements, the *Ṣaḥwa* has never been a neatly demarcated group with precise points of definition. Rather, one can pinpoint various sub-trends within it. For instance, one group followed the Muslim

Brotherhood in their ideology, with a slight dose of Wahhabi-infused theology and religiosity. Another group merged Wahhabism with Muslim Brotherhood political aspiration and promoted a new politically conscious form of Wahhabism. This group was derided as 'Sururis' by its opponents, taking this moniker from one of the key figures of the *Ṣaḥwa* movement, the Syrian scholar Muhammad Surur Zayn al-ʿAbidīn (d. 2016). He was a member of the Muslim Brotherhood in Syria, considered to favor the thought of Sayyid Qutb,[190] who fled Syria for Saudi Arabia in 1965, where he taught from then until the 1970s, including in Burayda, a scholarly Wahhabi hub.[191] He was forced to leave Saudi Arabia in 1973 and went to Kuwait before he was exiled to England in 1984. He had formed a Salafi group with a Muslim Brotherhood political orientation in the 1970s, but he rejected armed rebellion as a means of political change. Yet he advocated political activism and did not propose the sort of loyalty to the Muslim regimes which was a dominant trait of quietist Salafism.[192]

The most famous scholars of this *Ṣaḥwa* trend at the time were two young, dynamic Saudi clerics by the names of Safar al-Hawali and Salman al-Oudah (the latter is discussed in section 6.6.3). By the late 1980s, these clerics had carved out a relatively large following, preaching Wahhabi ideals with a more modern rhetoric conducive to a younger generation.[193] The Saudi academic Madawi Al-Rasheed has pointed to the indigenousness of the *Ṣaḥwa* movement, in which the link with the Muslim Brotherhood ideology is possible or even probable, but that must not detract from the fact that 'Sahwi thought is a hybrid tradition that rediscovered the revolutionary potential of Wahhabi religio-political discourse and rearticulated it in a modern language accessible to all. This rediscovery was *perhaps* [italics mine] assisted by various outside influences that arrived in Saudi Arabia in the second half of the twentieth century.'[194] Nonetheless, the importance of the *Ṣaḥwa* movement would become more prominent with the events of 1990 onwards.

In 1990, Saddam Hussein (d. 2006) invaded Kuwait, sparking a pan-Arab crisis. King Fahd had already felt that Saudi Arabia was deeply vulnerable through the 1980s, and under the threat of Iran and the Soviet Union; he expended perhaps more effort than any previous king in deepening Saudi's military, political, and economic relations with the USA. It was therefore completely natural for him, fearing that Saddam Hussein would advance and attack the border with Saudi Arabia, to invite American troops into the country – with the religious blessing and acquiescence of the post-Juhaymān chastened and politically-pressured Ibn Bāz – to protect Saudi Arabia and launch attacks on Saddam Hussein's forces from Saudi soil. With this, Fahd dispensed with the caution that defined the special relationship between Saudi and the USA, whereby the latter maintained 'minimal visibility.'[195] Consequently, the Iraqi army was swiftly defeated by the Americans and their allies, with the Americans having sent more than 500,000 soldiers.[196] After the war was over, Saudi Arabia allowed the US to keep its army bases in the Kingdom as a deterrent to potential large-scale future attacks.

This whole saga sparked outrage among the population, and it was the *Ṣaḥwa* clerics who led the religious opposition. Not for the first time, opposition to the Āl Saʿūd came from its own people and was based on religious matters. However, rather than base their primary criticism on ancient Wahhabi doctrine, Safar al-Ḥawālī led the charge by accusing the royal family of being used by the Americans for their own interests. He wrote a treatise entitled *Waʿd Kissinjar* (*The Promise of Kissinger*), in which he made the argument that what was transpiring was, in fact, all a part of Henry Kissinger's foreign policies that would benefit Israel and harm the Muslim world. By interweaving quotes from Kissinger's speeches with Islamic prohibitions regarding the impermissibility of allying with non-Muslims against other Muslims (much of which was used two centuries earlier by the first generation of Wahhabi clerics against those tribes who allied with the Ottomans), al-Ḥawālī demonstrated, perhaps for the first time, the ideological paradigms of this movement: a unique blend of politically-active Wahhabism that wanted to challenge the West directly, and the Family of Saʿūd indirectly. Understandably, this book, along with other critical lectures and activities from figures associated with the movement, sent shock waves through Saudi society. It also pitted these younger, more internationally suave clerics against the old guard who were part of the establishment. Thus, Ibn Bāz and other senior clerics were forced to denounce the 'radicalism' of this new trend as a contravention of Salafi principles.

Yet Ibn Bāz became embroiled with the *Ṣaḥwa* scholars after a petition, in December 1990, from liberal tendencies in Saudi Arabia, called for governmental reform along distinctly liberal lines. The response of the religious scholars, whose authority was challenged by the initiative, was to submit a counter petition with signatures in May 1991. It was entitled 'The Letter of Demands' (*khitab al-matalib*), and was signed by 400 clergy, including *Sahwi* scholars and intellectuals and royalists like Ibn Bāz, al-'Uthaymin, Salih al-Fawzan, Abd al-Raḥman al-Sudais, and Rabiʿ al-Madkhali; it called for reforms which were in accordance with their broad principles, but in a manner that opposed the liberal submission. It also demanded that all political alliances that were not in accordance with Islam be abolished – a reference to Saudi's alliance with America. However, when challenged, Ibn Bāz claimed that his signature was obtained on the condition that the letter would remain private, and he did not publicly support the letter; many others appear to have signed because Ibn Bāz had done so. Yet, the *Ṣaḥwa* contingent pushed on with their public drive for reform, which led, among other things, to 'The Memorandum of Advice' (*Mudhakkirat al-nasiha*) in

1992, which expanded upon the general points of The Letter of Demands, but had only 110 signatories, none of whom were senior.[197]

In response, the king announced, in March 1992, that three reforms would take place: the Basic Law of Government, the Law of the Consultative Council, and the Law of the Provinces. One of the stipulations of the Law of the Consultative Council was the creation of a council consisting of sixty members, who would, in part, interpret laws and ministerial reports. What was significant for the Wahhabi scholars in this regard was that the appointments highlighted a government intention to work more closely with, and empower, what has been called the 'professional elite.' Only nine members were experts in Islamic law. While most held doctorates and masters in non-religious fields – often from Western universities – 40% of the appointments were from Najd, establishing a crucial representation of the royal family's tribal links. Furthermore, the Saudi government enforced stricter restrictions on social, religious, and political movements in the country, and implemented a massive political crackdown between 1992 and 1994.[198]

In 1994, they imprisoned the leaders of the *Ṣaḥwa* movement, further alienating large segments of the society from the ruling class. These clerics were revered and admired by politically-minded Salafis around the globe, and their teachings – disseminated primarily through cassette recordings – were eagerly absorbed by audiences from America to Central Asia. They were intellectually sophisticated and tapped into popular sentiments about the misguided political stances of Saudi Arabia. Although they were released in 1999, both al-Ḥawālī and al-Oudah would eventually be imprisoned again (as this book goes to print, both are still political prisoners). The movement soon lost steam as its leaders, after being released, were forcibly muted in the public sphere unless they recanted their former views. The *Ṣaḥwa* movement still exists, but it has evolved from its original iteration, and it appears that its activism heydays of the '90s will not be seen again.

The main group that led the campaign *against* the scholars of the *Ṣahwa* movement, eventually causing a further splintering among the Wahhabis, came to be called 'Madkhalism.' [199]

### *3.2.5 Madkhalism*

As a reaction to the *Ṣaḥwa*'s criticism of the government and the corresponding political crackdown against them in Saudi Arabia, a new strand of Salafism emerged. The adherents of this strand were pejoratively called the 'Jāmis' by their *Ṣaḥwa* opponents, after its founder, an African émigré to Medina and a professor at the IUM, Muhammad b. Amān al-Jamī (d. 1996). This countermovement seems to have begun in the early half of the 1990s and is viewed as the most effective opposition to the *Ṣaḥwa*. The underlying philosophy of this trend is the belief that maintaining loyalty to the ruler is a necessary part of one's piety and orthodoxy. They argue that it is *religiously prohibited* to publicly disagree with the ruler, and doing so jeopardizes one's orthodoxy and standing with Salafism. They emphasized not just theology (*`aqidah*), but also a concept that they called '*manhaj*' which indicates methodology. They differentiated themselves from scholars like Ibn Bāz because their entire premise of showing loyalty to the ruler was drawn from the works of proto-Salafis who largely eschewed rebellions.

The people associated with this group are now more commonly known today, especially outside Saudi Arabia, as the 'Madkhalis,' named after its most influential Saudi scholar, Rabīʿ b. Hādi al-Madkhalī (b. 1931). As a movement it is called 'Madkhalism,' 'the Madkhali school,' or the 'Madkhali movement' by outsiders.[200] Al-Madkhalī was an early graduate of IUM, having joined when the university first opened in the early 1960s. He had a fleeting association with Juhaymān's JSM movement in the 1970s, although he was never imprisoned with fellow members. Al-Madkhalī himself was a part of the Muslim Brotherhood in his younger days; but in later life, he became the most vocal critic of the Brotherhood and the *Ṣaḥwa* movement, going so far as to claim that the teachings of the Muslim Brotherhood were the single greatest disaster to have been inflicted upon the religion of Islam in all of its history, and that each calamity upon the Muslim world, or deviation in modern Islam, could be directly attributed to the Brotherhood.[201] Al-Madkhalī came to prominence in the late 1980s when he authored *Manhaj al-Anbiyā fi-l-daʿwah ilā Allah fihī al-Ḥikmah wa-l-ʿaql* (*The Method Followed by the Prophets in Religious Preaching Contains Wisdom and Reason*), which contained a stern critique of Sayyid Abu al-A'la Mawdudi (d. 1979) for seeking to establish an Islamic state in Pakistan before the creed of the people was purified. In later years he concentrated more heavily on delegitimizing the authority of Sayyid Qutb (d. 1966).

He also maintained a prominent role by directing the hadith faculty of IUM for many decades, which partially explains his popularity around the world, due to its focus on non-Saudi students. However, al-Madkhalī was not, and has never been, a member of the senior scholarly collectives administered under state control in Saudi Arabia: the Permanent Committee for Scientific Research and Legal Rulings (*al-Lajna al-Dāʾima li-l-Buḥūth al-ʿIlmiyya wa-l-Iftāʾ*) and the Council of Senior Religious Scholars (*Hayʾat al-Kibār al-ʿUlamāʾ*).[202] Such a lack of official recognition has not stopped his followers from elevating some rather nebulous words of al-Albānī in praise of al-Madkhalī to mean that he is, without question, 'the standard-bearer of disparagement and praise in this era' (*ḥāmil rāyat al-jarḥ wa-l-taʿdīl fī hādha l-ʿaṣr*). This is despite the fact that there has been scholarly opposition to how Madkhalis interpreted the words of al-Albānī in this matter.[203]

The Madkhalis adopted the position of absolute support for the Saudi government, regardless of their policies and source of legislation; and in return, they apparently received generous financial patronage and support for their work from the regime. Additionally, connections to the movement were known to benefit a student in obtaining a place at the IUM or progressing in the institute. This potential for social mobility extended to groups that would ordinarily find themselves disadvantaged, such as non-Saudis or even Saudis from more obscure areas. This includes both Jami, who was Ethiopian in origin having come to Saudi Arabia in his twenties, and al-Madkhalī who was from the Jizan area in Saudi near to Yemen (a region that is generally not viewed favorably by those in Najd, and not known for producing notable Wahhabi-Salafi clerics).

In time, this group became favored by the regime and even Najdis without any previous scholarly fame joined the ranks and quickly earned reputable university posts, including Abd al-Aziz al-ʿAskar (who was regularly promoted by Saudi news and media for religious affairs) and Sulayman Aba al-Khayl (who was appointed Minister of Islamic Affairs, and President of Muhammad b. Saud University in Riyad). Even some *Ṣaḥwa* scholars such as Abd al-Muhsin al-ʿUbaykan, Aid al-Qarni, and ʿIsa al-Sinani would renounce their previous politics and align with the apolitical and royalist Madkhalis.

As mentioned earlier, the *Ṣaḥwa* movement was extremely active in universities across the country. To counter this trend, the Madkhalis started to replace *Ṣaḥwa* professors in prominent universities and other administrative positions, including posts in the IUM, from the 1990s onwards.

As a demonstration of their adoption of an attitude to Salafi methodology derived from al-Albānī, they would accept that many members of the *Ṣaḥwa* had a Salafi creed (*aqidah*), but they had departed from the Salafi methodology (*manhaj*) in politics. In addition, they developed an obsession with a concept developed by Yemeni scholar Muqbil al-Wadiʿī, whereby the *Ṣaḥwa* and other politicos were, in their reasoning, guilty of 'factionalism' (*hizbiyya*) in their arranging of political organizations, and blameworthy innovation in their methods, which were deemed to be a contravention of this notion of a comprehensive Salafi methodology (*manhaj*). The group also has a reputation for cooperating with state agents and working with the secret police in an effort to undermine politicos. They vied with the *Ṣaḥwa* to prove that they had the support of elders like Ibn Bāz, al-ʿUthaymin and al-Albānī.[204] However, in 2001, al-Madkhalī would demonstrate his disagreement with Ibn Bāz and al-Albānī for supporting the *mujahideen* going from Saudi Arabia to fight the Soviets in Afghanistan in the 1980s.

Madkhalis taught that obedience to the rulers was a *religious obligation* and a part of true Salafi doctrine, not just to the Saudi king, but to any Muslim country in which one lived. In line with their application of accommodationist Third-Wave Wahhabism, they adhered to the doctrine that it is not disbelief (*kufr*) for a ruler to abandon Islamic law on the state level, as long as they did not claim that this abandonment was religiously sanctioned.[205] Accordingly, they argued that it was obligatory to quietly and tacitly obey the Muslim ruler and not question his actions publicly. Any criticism, they maintained, must happen in private, directly to the ruler, and not in public where it might lead to chaos and civil disorder (*fitna*). As a result, they spread out from their base in Saudi Arabia, and started to earn a favorable place in the eyes of Arab rulers. Not surprisingly, their critics allege – sometimes with proof – they have been directly supported by numerous political authorities in an effort to mainstream such views.

As perceptibly noted by Bernard Haykel, while they adopt a 'quietist posture' demanding full obedience to rulers – both just and unjust – they are not 'pacifists…but rather obedience-minded people who would not hesitate to engage in armed warfare if given the order to do so by the ruler (*wali al-amr*).'[206] Therefore, Madkhalis have engaged in the taking up of arms in political causes, such as the civil war in Yemen in 1994, with the government of Yemen since 2004,[207] and in Libya shortly after the Arab Spring in 2011 (see the sections on Libya and Yemen in Chapter 6).

Nonetheless, concerns about al-Madkhalī's harshness were raised by al-Albānī, who advised him to 'soften in his manners; that would be more beneficial for the masses of the people.'[208] Furthermore, critics, including fellow Salafis, have also criticized their principles and accused them of engaging in McCarthyite and cultish behavior, whereby anyone whose loyalty to the ruler is doubted is condemned. Once one is condemned, anyone who convenes with such a person is *guilty by association*, and so forth. Madkhalism became infamous for what were called the '*manhaj*-wars' of the 1990s: people were put 'on' or 'off' the proverbial *manhaj* by the leaders of the movement. Followers had to scramble to continuously update themselves on the names on either side, lest their own associations cause a change in their position on these lists. For a period, especially in the mid-to-late 1990s, the Kingdom gave this trend its complete support. Key positions in many jobs, particularly at the IUM, were stripped away at the mere whisperings of associations with those on the 'off-list,' while some of the most powerful spokespersons for this trend were promoted to important posts.[209] The Madkhalī/Sūrurī clash of the 1990s became the single greatest cause of division between Salafis across the world, including in America and England. Individuals and organizations were forced to choose between two camps of scholars, typically with much acrimonious sentiment expressed by the opposing camp. While this division continues until this day, the events of the last two decades have caused other strands to emerge, and 'pure' Madkhalism remains an ever-dwindling phenomenon.

On the decline of Madkhalism after its meteoric rise, subsequent state support or tacit approval for its activities, and growing popularity, R. Meijer wrote in 2011 that 'al-Madkhalī has become controversial in recent years and that his influence in Saudi Arabia has waned to such an extent that "Madkhalism" is now largely a European phenomenon. Members of the Council of Senior Religious Scholars [including the current Grand Mufti of Saudi Arabia, 'Abd al-Azīz b. 'Abdallāh Āl al-Shaykh] have denounced him for sowing dissension (*fitna*) and for his stridency. As a result, Madkhalism has become a transnational phenomenon without a real base in Saudi Arabia.'[210] Despite being seemingly paltry in demographic terms, it continues to persist around the world, and has an especially strong online influence on social media. One could argue that we are seeing a post-Madkhali strand of the same thought under the current ruler and controversial reforms, albeit one in which the names and specific thoughts of the founders has been sidelined, while the theological underpinnings remain (more on this in section 3.2.7).

During this time frame, yet another strand would emerge, which, although statistically extremely small, would take center stage and eclipse the bickering between these two, at least in the eyes of the world. This strand was that of Jihadi-Salafis.

### *3.2.6 Jihadi-Salafism and the Wahhabi-Jihadi-Salafi Strand*

The topic of Jihadi-Salafism is complex and is fully explored in Chapter 5. However, there is one strand that is especially relevant to us in this chapter, hence a summary is warranted here.

There are numerous movements around the globe that claim they are engaged in legitimate jihad. How one categorizes and views each of them is highly contested. For now, we will differentiate between *defensive* movements that are *regional* and *reacting* to an invading or occupying power and *offensive* movements that target what can reasonably be defined as civilian targets. We are more concerned with the latter here.

Within these jihadist movements, we can label Jihadi-Salafi movements as those that have been directly and explicitly influenced by Salafi thought, and which believe that jihad is the principal mechanism by which to achieve their aims. Jihadi-Salafism is not a unitary category – there is plenty of diversity. For the purposes of this chapter, we are primarily interested in one sub-strand of Jihadi-Salafis: the Wahhabi-Jihadi-Salafis (WJS). WJS began to emerge out of a more general Saudi-Jihadi-Salafism (SJS), which had some doctrinal Wahhabi roots, but was not overtly Wahhabi in justifying its tactics. To further complicate matters, SJS began chronologically after the first Jihadi-Salafi manifestations in Egypt: since Jihadi-Salafism began in Egypt, its first strand can be called Egyptian-Jihadi-Salafism (EJS).

In the Saudi context, the catalyst for Saudi-Jihadi-Salafism (SJS) can be traced to four major political events: the Siege of Mecca (1979), the Soviet–Afghan War (1979–89), the First Gulf War (1990–91), and the Al-Qaeda attack on the USA (2001).

Saudi-Jihadi-Salafism first emerged in large part from Saudis who traveled to Afghanistan in the 1980s, and interacted with, or joined, jihadist movements there. WJS, on the other hand, emerged directly from within the clerics of the Kingdom, who were prompted by global events to reconnect with First-Wave Wahhabism, to justify, support, and find direct inspiration for, the practical methodology of violence, without a seeming need for EJS influence.

The Siege of Mecca was the first modern movement that demonstrated military opposition to, and *takfir* of, the Saudi milieu. However, it was atypical of other movements insofar as it had messianic and apocalyptic beliefs. Hence, after the unsuccessful siege of the Grand Mosque, it fizzled out of existence. The jihadi movement that emerged in the 1980s would look back at Juhaymān and his followers as an inspiration and role model. Although they would make clear that he was mistaken in his claims regarding the promised Mahdī, they agreed with his overall ideology of opposing the government with military force and considering them to be traitors to the faith (although they disagreed with his choice of target, the Grand Mosque of Mecca, as his attack violated the sanctity of the mosques and the blood of innocent worshipers).[211]

The Soviet invasion of Afghanistan led to a host of allies, including the United States and Saudi Arabia, supporting the locals to repel the foreign occupiers. Consequently, young Saudi citizens flocked to Afghanistan to join the jihad against the communists. One of these young soldiers was Osama bin Laden.[212] In Afghanistan, Bin Laden met and exchanged ideas with jihadi movements from other parts of the world. In these exchanges, one jihadi version of Salafism began to take shape, and in 1988, Bin Laden co-founded Al-Qaeda, the first transnational jihadi organization with a clear Wahhabi influence, married to Muslim Brotherhood ideals.[213]

With the return of Saudi Afghan fighters, SJS emerged in Saudi Arabia. Until 1990, SJS was not openly critical of the government, but its existence led to a government crackdown on members by the mid-1990s. This coincided with Osama bin Laden and other adherents to SJS deciding that the American presence in the region had to be opposed violently. In 1994, King Fahd stripped Bin Laden of his Saudi citizenship.[214] On 13 November 1995, four members of this radical network set off a 100 kg car bomb in Riyadh, which killed five Americans and two Indians, and injured six others, seemingly in retaliation for the execution of one of their members in August 1995. This was the first major terrorist bombing on Saudi soil. Three of the four bombers had fought in the Afghan–Soviet war and were said to be passionate readers of Osama bin Laden; the fourth was reported to be a close friend of the Jihadi-Salafi ideologue Abu Muhammad al-Maqdisi (discussed in section 5.4.3).

Over the next five years, the government made thousands of arrests, which consisted mainly of Shiites, but included those associated with SJS, such as Yusuf al-Uyayri, an important associate of Bin Laden.[215] Such arrests were traumatizing, as there was widespread torture of prisoners, many of whom were innocent or 'guilty by association,' as was later reported. This cruel mistreatment is seen as contributing to the further radicalization of those in the movement and contributed to SJS retaliating in kind.[216]

What is of particular interest to us in this section is that the 9/11 attacks in New York, which clearly did have a Jihadi-Salafi basis, would lead to the emergence of a new group, which can be viewed as being distinctly Wahhabi-Jihadi-Salafi (WJS). The main clerics of this movement have had no influence from outside thinkers and strands (in particular, the jihadi movements of Egypt), and are Wahhabi clerics who took their inspiration from the radicalism and violence of First-Wave Wahhabism directly. While the broader Jihadi-Salafi rhetoric and actions *triggered* this movement and acted as a catalyst, most of its clerics never joined Al-Qaeda, nor did they have any affiliations with transnational jihadi actors and thinkers. Instead, they were inspired to rediscover and reclaim the original message of Ibn ʿAbd al-Wahhāb, and interpret it in light of current circumstances, to justify and legitimize broader Jihadi-Salafi actions.

Between September 2001 and May 2003, SJS operated primarily in the form of Al-Qaeda on the Arabian Peninsula (AQAP). It indirectly benefitted from the dispute between the so-called 'Shuʿaybi school' and the Ṣaḥwa scholars. The Shuʿaybi school was led by three main ideologues: Ḥamūd b. ʿAbd Allah al-ʿUqla al-Shuʿaybi (d. 2002), Nasir b. Ḥamad al-Fahd (b. 1969), and ʿAli b. Khuḍayr al-Khuḍayr (b. 1955), together with lesser figures, including Sulayman al-ʿUlwān (b. 1969), all of whom cooperated between 1999 and 2002. In essence, these figures wrote treatises and fatwas that justified acts of terrorism which afflicted large numbers of civilians at the hands of Jihadi-Salafis. The movement was almost completely wiped out in Saudi Arabia by 2006, and many of the Shuʿaybī school leaders repented of their extreme doctrines.[217] The WJS phenomenon continues to exist, but in a much-reduced capacity. We shall return to discuss Jihadi-Salafism in more detail in a later chapter.

### *3.2.7 Fourth-Wave Wahhabism?*

At the time of writing, Saudi Arabia is currently ruled by King Salman, who came to power in 2015.[218] He succeeded his brother Abdullah, who ruled from 2005 until 2015. The next in line for the throne is Crown Prince

Muhammad b. Salman (popularly known as 'MBS'), who is slated to become the first third-generation king of Saudi Arabia. Since becoming the crown prince in 2015, MBS has become the most influential policymaker in Saudi Arabia.

MBS is in the process of modernizing Saudi Arabia under his brainchild Vision 2030, designed to diversify the country's revenue streams and halt its dependency on oil revenue, as well as other social and educational programs. He has introduced fresh taxes on goods and services, cut state subsidies, presided over a 'Saudization' program for the workforce, introduced austerity, and privatized a small share of Aramco. Sovereign wealth funds in the country are targeting assets worldwide such as the purchase of Newcastle United Football Club in England in 2021, emulating Qatar and the UAE. Moreover, events that were unthinkable just a few years ago are happening in the Kingdom, such as female wrestlers from World Wrestling Entertainment performing for a Saudi audience, public music concerts featuring scantily dressed female singers and dancers, photoshoots of supermodels in the desert, the first steps to normalizing relations with Israel, and Saudis openly celebrating Valentine's Day and Halloween.[219]

Under his watch, the Kingdom has rolled back several conservative rulings from the past few decades. This includes the prohibition of women driving, the ban on cinemas, the ban on women attending stadia to witness sporting events, restrictions on the female dress code, and restrictions in business and employment related to women. Furthermore, the religious police have been stripped of their power. In effect, MBS is seeking to renegotiate the deal with the Wahhabi clerics that was struck with the royal family after the 1979 hostage crisis.

Although MBS is portrayed as a reformer of Saudi Arabia, he is not free from controversy, especially in geopolitics and ethics. His overtures to Israel to unite against Iran altered Saudi foreign policy and would be widely opposed in the Arab world.[220] He was also responsible for the blockade and boycott of Qatar, which included an air travel ban, a media ban on Qatar's pay-TV broadcaster beIN Sports and news broadcaster Al Jazeera, and developed a counterfeit pirate TV operation designed to weaken beIN as a serious TV player and content rights holder in the Arab world. In addition, religious critics of MBS have been imprisoned, including – but not limited to – the 1990s' Ṣaḥwa figures Salman al-Oudah and Safar al-Hawali; this crackdown has extended to prominent imams, including one of the imams who led prayers in Masjid al-Haram in Makkah, for having subtly criticized the rise of liberalism in the Kingdom. Various women's rights activists are also currently in prison for opposing Saudi policy, despite the policies they had campaigned for now being enacted. The Saudi-led war with Yemeni Houthis intensified as MBS became Crown Prince – millions of Yemenis have faced starvation and instability.

To make matters worse, many of the goals MBS set for himself have not yet been achieved. In 2017, he ordered the 'imprisonment and shake-down' of princes and prominent businessmen in the Ritz-Carlton in Riyadh. Prominent figures who were taken in included Waleed b. Talal (businessman and part of the extended royal family), Mutʿab b. ʿAbd Allāh (son of the late King Abdullah), Walīd b. Ibrāhīm (chairman, MBC), Bakr b. Laden (chairman of the Bin Laden Group; half-brother of Osama), and at least a dozen others. But perhaps the most infamous individual incident associated with MBS relates to the Saudi *Washington Post* journalist Jamal Khashoggi (d. 2018), who was last seen entering the Saudi Embassy in Istanbul, never to re-emerge. The CIA suspects – with great certainty – that he was murdered by assassins within the Embassy, on the orders of MBS, and that his body was dismembered and smuggled away. Officially, Saudi authorities have blamed rogue elements within their security forces, claiming they were not acting under the official orders of MBS. Understandably, not many, besides hardcore loyalists, find that narrative plausible.[221]

As MBS focuses on modernizing the country while also violently opposing his critics and enemies, the culture of Saudi Arabia seems to be drifting away from traditional Wahhabism. To cement this reality, two significant acts were passed which officially began distancing the regime from Wahhabism and redefining the nature of the relationship for the future. Firstly, in 2021, during Ramadan, MBS declared on television that the Saudi state should not be tied to one man or movement, as this would be 'deifying human beings.' He added,

> If Sheikh Muhammad ibn Abd al-Wahhāb were with us today, and he found us committed blindly to his texts, and closing our minds to interpretation and jurisprudence, while deifying and sanctifying him, he would be the first to object to this. There are no fixed schools of thought and there is no infallible person. We should engage in continuous interpretation of Qurʾanic texts, and the same goes for the traditions of the Prophet.[222]

Secondly, in 2022 a new state holiday, Founding Day (*yawm al-taʾsīs*), commemorating the royal family's capture of Diriyah in 1727 was fixed, in addition to the already celebrated National Day (*al-yawm al-watani*), marking the establishment of Saudi Arabia in 1932. This new date is significant because it predates the Wahhabi alliance, thus diminishing the Wahhabi significance and giving greater prominence to the royal family *sans* Ibn ʿAbd al-Wahhāb in the national story.

One can, therefore, assume that MBS has actively succeeded in undermining the Wahhabi establishment. This was especially evident when he legalized driving for women in 2018. For decades, all Wahhabi clerics had united in prohibiting women's driving on religious grounds. Two previous kings, Fahd and Abdullah, had multiple times tried their best to nudge the Council of Senior Religious Scholars, led by Ibn Bāz, to allow some leeway in this regard, but the clerics refused to acquiesce. Previous kings had shown deference to senior scholars and did not feel it wise to challenge the clerical ban. MBS, on the other hand, simply did not bother to get clerical approval, and announced his decision directly to the public, bypassing the customary protocol of religious approval for such matters. As if to add insult to injury, he has directly sponsored music festivals where Saudis of both genders participate and dance, and international female musicians, hitherto banned even from mainstream TV, are brought in for public raves, in what would have been deemed debaucherously provocative circumstances by a previous generation of clerics. Ironically, these changes have been introduced at the hands of the Kingdom's Chairman of General Entertainment Authority, Turki Al-Sheikh, a direct descendant of Ibn ʿAbd al-Wahhāb.

One can only surmise the underlying simmering tensions between MBS and the Wahhabi clerics, or the private murmurings and reservations that the scholars of Saudi Arabia, faithful to their roots, have regarding MBS. Anecdotal evidence suggests a deep resentment among many of the senior hardline clerics. However, some famous clerics have openly endorsed MBS's policies in astounding about-turns. Video clips of clerics who used to vehemently oppose women's driving went viral, juxtaposed with their endorsements of MBS's announcement. There has also been a clear rise of a new Fourth-Wave Madkhalism, where the same unconditional loyalty to the rulers is made a key doctrine of theology, but the 'old-guard' clerics of original Madhkahlism have been sidelined, and attacks on the Muslim Brotherhood and its leaders become even more pronounced. This trend is given increasing prominence, as almost *all* public clerics given a platform and propped up by the Ministry are considered part of this new Fourth-Wave Madkhalism. Meanwhile standard theological issues that used to define Wahhabism are no longer of primary concern. One can see such trends in clerics like Saleh al-Maghamisi (b. 1963), the imam of the famous historic Quba Mosque in Medina who, among other infamous interviews, attempted to religiously excuse the assassination of Khashoggi,[223] and of course the imam of Mecca, Abd al-Raḥman al-Sudais (b. 1962), whose explicit sermons in praise of the ruler and disparaging other movements during and after the Arab Spring have, to put it mildly, raised many millions of eyebrows around the world. Also of interest is the famous cleric Aid al-Qarni, who was an integral part of the *Ṣaḥwa* movement in the early '90s, but after a stint in jail, transformed into a very different cleric, and is now one of the most prominent public figures in the Kingdom, and a close associate of MBS.

MBS will, if things progress as they are now, most likely be the first grandson of Ibn Sa'ūd to be king. And with the privilege of being the first monarch hailing from his own generation, he will play an even more pivotal role in shaping Saudi Arabia. Given the current trajectory, these new waves may well be unrecognizable as Wahhabism.

## *3.3 The Islamic University of Medina (IUM)*

Arguably the most important institution that helped Saudi Arabia spread Salafism internationally is the Islamic University of Medina,[224] with the most significant intake of foreign students among all the universities of the Kingdom.[225] The IUM exemplified the drive of Third-Wave Wahhabism to refine their proselytization efforts, through the acceptance of the modern educational model rather than relying on the traditional seminary system. It quickly grew into the most prestigious center of Salafi education in the world, attracting both Arab and non-Arab students.[226] Its prominence and significance warrant further elaboration, as it has been a primary mechanism for the global spread of Third-Wave Wahhabi-Salafism.

It should be noted however, that when it comes to the training of the senior scholars of Saudi Arabia, the IUM is not the most significant institute, educating only 2% of the members of the Committee of Grand Scholars between 1971 and 2010. The most significant institution in this regard is the Imam Muhammad ibn Saud Islamic University, founded in Riyadh in 1974, which has provided education for around 50% of the members of the Committee of Grand Scholars during the same period.[227]

### *3.3.1 The Founding of the IUM*

The IUM was established by a Royal Decree issued by King Sa'ūd b. 'Abd al-Azīz in 1961, which allocated land owned by the Royal Palace for the sake of establishing a university for Islamic studies, primarily for international students. This was part of a broader strategy to build alliances with other Muslim lands and situate Saudi Arabia as an intellectual and religious capital of the Muslim world.[228] From its very inception, the goal was to establish credibility among a broad spectrum of movements and orientations, with as little departure from Wahhabi thought as possible.

At the invitation of the king, an international council of scholars was established to develop plans for the university, utilizing a proposal made by Sayyid Abu al-A'la Mawdudi (d. 1979), the founder of the Islamist *Jamaat-e-Islami* party of Pakistan. The council of IUM included scholars from diverse backgrounds and represented many of the most important movements and institutes of the time, with a strong Islamist influence (discussed further in Chapter 4).[229] This diversity would be an important step for the progression, and eventual acceptance, of Third-Wave Wahhabism internationally.

When the IUM was founded, Saudi Arabia lacked qualified teachers to run the Islamic Studies program. Most Wahhabi scholars focused on theology, with many also being advanced in their familiarity with the Ḥanbali school of Islamic law. However, very few had mastered the more intricate Islamic subjects like Islamic jurisprudence (*usūl al-fiqh*), Qur'anic exegesis (*tafsīr*), the hadith sciences, or Islamic history. As a result, the IUM was forced to recruit its teachers from outside the Wahhabi circle, including *Ahl-e-Hadith* scholars from India and Pakistan, Salafi scholars from Egypt, and even Ashʿarī scholars from al-Azhar University.[230] While the *Ahl-e-Hadith* and Salafi scholars influenced the direction of the university, Ashʿarī teachers were more restricted. They were hired to teach various technical Islamic sciences, such as Arabic morphology, grammar, and Qur'anic exegesis, but were not allowed to teach the most important subject: theology. This was only taught by known Salafis, whether Saudis or, in limited cases, Egyptian Salafis from *Ansar al-Sunna* (*Helpers of the Sunna*).[231] Slowly, as the IUM produced its own graduates, many non-Salafi teachers were phased out and replaced with alumni from the IUM, as well as other Saudi universities.

The biggest influence that the *Ahl-e-Hadith* and non-Saudi Salafi teachers had at the IUM was in the field of Islamic law (*fiqh*). Through these teachers, it adopted an approach to Islamic law that was more familiar to non-Saudi Salafis. Until the founding of the IUM, the Wahhabis had been, overall, staunch adherents to the Ḥanbalī school of law and its normative tradition. In contrast, other Salafi movements such as the *Ahl-e-Hadith* rejected the notion of strictly following one school of thought and derived their legal rulings directly from the Qur'an and Sunna.

At its inception, the IUM Islamic law curriculum was to be purely Ḥanbali in nature.[232] This drew criticism from intellectuals and scholars from both within, and outside the Kingdom, who wanted all four established Sunni legal schools to be taught, forcing Ibn Bāz – a member of the Advisory Council and effectively its President – to publicly respond.[233] The sense of discontent was also felt by the IUM's international student body, who came from a variety of legal backgrounds, and did not want to be taught Ḥanbali law. To solve this problem, the IUM adopted a more open Salafi approach at the undergraduate level and began to teach comparative law, in which the opinions of the various legal schools were discussed and judged based on the primary sources. In every other madrasa around the world, a student would be taught only one of the four schools of law (with the odd seminary adding some basic overviews of the others). At the IUM, the entire curriculum consisted of a comparative, evidence-based approach, which trained students to view the legal schools not as an end, but as a means to derive 'the correct position' on any issue.

This method was innovative and unique, and it had a global impact that can still be seen in many modern Islamic institutions to this day. Dozens of institutes around the world now focus on comparative law, instead of having students focus on one school. In this, we see how the IUM played a vital role in the creation, and perpetuation, of Third-Wave Wahhabism. Never before had Wahhabi clerics taught alongside scholars from other backgrounds, and never had such diverse strands of Islamic thought come together for a project on such a grand scale.

### *3.3.2 Departments, Pedagogy, and Student Life*

In its early years, the IUM consisted of both a secondary school and a university, and both curriculums covered Arabic, theology (*ʿaqida*) and sectarianism (*al-firaq al-Islamiyya*), Islamic law and jurisprudence, Qurʾanic exegesis and recitation (*tajwīd*), hadith, and Islamic history, to different levels. When the university opened its doors in 1962, it consisted of only one department. But the oil booms of the 1970s enabled the Kingdom to finance the IUM's expansion. The original department became five separate colleges: Islamic Law (*shariʿa*); Preaching (*daʿwa*); Qurʾanic Sciences; Arabic Language; and Hadith Sciences. For the next thirty years, these Islamic colleges would form the backbone of the university, attracting a constellation of specialists in different fields from all over the world.

The university was steered, from its founding, by the Kingdom's religious establishment headed by the Grand Mufti, Muhammad b. Ibrahīm, with his protégé Ibn Bāz. Perhaps the most prominent professor of this formative period was Muhammad Nasir al-Din al-Albānī, who was brought in to teach hadith. His ideas and philosophy would have a marked impact on the university and help shape Wahhabism in line with his own version of Salafism. The most salient aspect of his legacy was cultivating a culture in which great care was taken to only quote authentic traditions from the Prophet. In addition, his attack on following the legal schools led to increasing numbers of Salafis moving away from *fiqh*-based law into comparative law, and seeking the evidence directly from the sacred texts.

There were also several prominent teachers from the African Sahel, including Mali, Nigeria, and Mauritania. Foremost among this group was Muḥammad al-Amīn Al-Shinqīṭī (d. 1973). Born in Mauritania's Kiffa region, he came to Mecca in 1947 as part of a Hajj group and stayed, with two of his sons following in his footsteps to become professors at the university. Also represented among the faculty and administrators were those associated with the Egyptian and Syrian Muslim Brotherhoods, and the South

Asian *Ahl-e-Hadith* movement.[234] The IUM's founding charter stated that Advisory Council members – who were tasked with supervising syllabi, setting and amending university administration and statutes, and overseeing the establishment of new faculties and departments – were to be multinational, and represent an array of areas of expertise, as well as ensure a global reach.

The IUM's language of instruction has always been Arabic, so while the teaching faculty has been multinational, it has historically been drawn primarily from the Middle East and North Africa. Until the late 1980s, non-Saudi faculty occupied many prominent positions within the university – many from the Egyptian Muslim Brotherhood and some from the *Ahl-e-Hadith* movement in the subcontinent. In addition, there were a handful of African scholars who had trained in their local lands but, upon coming to Saudi Arabia, had embraced Wahhabism, and come to be accepted among the local clerics.

Established as a free university, the IUM provided travel costs, a modest stipend and health care for young Muslim men from across the world.[235] Students came from various backgrounds, with some attracted to the Salafi mindset and Wahhabi roots; others may not have subscribed to this theology but were attracted by the chance to study in the Holy Lands and pray in the Prophet's Mosque.

Following the First Gulf War in 1991, the Saudi monarchy moved to replace members of the faculty seen as being too sympathetic to Islamist movements, including the Muslim Brotherhood. They came to promote Salafi voices that were seen as being politically 'quietist' – or at least pliant to the government – like that of Dr Rabīʿ al-Madkhalī. From the early 1990s onward, the university began an aggressive policy of 'Saudiazation' among the faculty, purging almost the entirety of non-Saudi teaching staff.[236] By the end of the 1990s, politically active scholars who were seen as unsupportive of the royal family were either let go or quietly shuffled into administrative positions, while those of whom Dr al-Madkhalī and his supporters approved were given prominent posts and positions within all departments.[237]

The IUM's pedagogy was influenced by major shifts in religious education, including: the adoption of more fixed schedules for students and faculty; examinations to determine knowledge acquisition and advancement; the modernization of the Saudi state; and counter-reactions to European colonialism and the infiltration of 'un-Islamic' ideas into the education systems and social spheres of Muslim-majority countries.[238] One senior cleric, Shaykh ʿAbd al-Muḥsin al-ʿAbbād (b. 1934), described the mission of graduates as 'the stage of struggle' (*marhalat al-jihad*) and graduates collectively as 'lions of the [Wahhabi/Salafi] call (*daʿwa*).'[239]

Given that the campus was located just outside the sacred city of Medina, all students resided within its premises, surrounded by religious clergy. It is difficult to describe the mesmerizing atmosphere and spiritual impact that such an ambiance had on a student, especially one coming from a non-Muslim land. At all times of the day and night, one could hear discussions in the campus mosque, street corners, dormitories, or in front of the campus cafes, regarding arcane issues and abstract theological or spiritual concepts. Moreover, the ethnic diversity of the student body created a multicultural environment, where the one thing in common was faith – and only *one* public interpretation.

The university provided free daily transportation to the Prophet's Mosque where every evening some of the most prestigious scholars would deliver free open seminars on miscellaneous topics, following the traditional *ḥalaqa* (open learning) system of the past. Studious students would supplement their university classes with regular attendance at these public seminars, as well as private classes that scholars hosted at their houses, thus creating a complex web of interrelated cliques and persuasions. Students who might sympathize with one trend (say, the Madkhalis or the *Ṣaḥwa* scholars) would invariably find teachers of a similar persuasion.

At times, the partisan politics of such divisions would become fraught, with divisive factions 'warning' other students of the 'deviations' of other strands – with familiar Salafi splits being discernible, along quietist, politico, and jihadi lines.[240] The university administration generally tolerated such differences if no violence ensued – a rare, but not unheard of, occurrence on campus – although occasionally university authorities did have to intervene.

Despite being the foremost Salafi university in the world, the student body possessed numerous students who did not sympathize with the religious sentiments of the Wahhabi trend, which they generally kept to themselves, because publicly criticizing Salafi theology would be grounds for expulsion, although this only seldom happened.[241]

Together with divisions based on religious trends, there were also natural divisions based on ethnicities and nationalities. As students were admitted based on a quota system, and the number of applicants varied significantly from country to country, some nationalities – like Nigerians and Indonesians – had far more students than others. However, by the 2000s, the number of students from different countries increased, and social gatherings became more politically demarcated along various factions of Wahhabi trends.

After the incidents of 11 September 2001, pressure was placed on the Kingdom by the US State Department to update its religious curriculum, and from around 2004, the IUM undertook a complete and radical revision of both its curriculum and teaching style. The next few years would see the addition of three new colleges – Engineering, Computer Science, and Natural Science – and a sharp increase in the number of Saudi students, resulting in a change of the dynamics of student life, and a quadrupling of the number of the student body. The IUM now has more than 22,000 students from over 170 countries, making it the most diverse student body in the world.[242]

The IUM alumni who embraced the Salafi message of their teachers became propagators of this message in their home countries and this led to Wahhabi-Salafism spreading outside Saudi Arabia and across the globe for the first time. Taking their cue from al-Albānī, and their exposure to other international Salafi movements, these proselytizers came to forthrightly declare themselves as 'Salafis,' and not mere adherents to the teachings of Ibn ʿAbd al-Wahhāb. This was intended to illustrate, in the clearest terms, their unique claim to Islamic authenticity. They wanted to distinguish themselves from other groups who asserted they held a 'Qurʾan and Sunna' understanding, which Salafis rejected as inauthentic, as it was not qualified with 'according to the understanding of the *salaf*.'

The spread of the IUM graduates across the globe coincided with the Saudi government aiding the establishment of schools, mosques, and colleges around the world, and the mass printing of Wahhabi literature in various languages, though organizations such as WAMY (World Assembly of Muslim Youth). IUM alumni were generally chosen to run these new projects, ensuring that the Wahhabi mission spread far and wide. Graduates also became prominent figures in the *daʿwa* (proselytization) field as well as serving their communities as imams, and working in legal, educational or academic roles. The following section will highlight some of the work of IUM graduates around the globe.

### *3.3.3 Brief Survey of the Impact of the Alumni of IUM*

The total number of graduates from the IUM, including its undergraduate and post-graduate colleges, was 97,578 up until 2023.[243] While a significant percentage of these return to an ordinary life, the majority become preachers, teachers, clerics, and academics, establishing footholds for the Salafi movement in countries all around the world. Some have even entered politics, becoming ministers and government leaders, while others have established charitable foundations with an international reach. Those who attended the IUM but did not complete their studies number in the hundreds of thousands, and many of them have gone on to be effective clerics and preachers in their respective lands as well.

A graduate from the IUM is typically treated with the utmost respect by their community, regardless of their theological leanings. The fact that a student has lived in the holy city of Medina, become fluent in Arabic, and trained with the most renowned clerics, virtually guarantees a level of respect among many Muslims, Salafi or not. For Salafi Muslims in particular, the IUM is, without a doubt, the Oxford or Cambridge equivalent. It would be impossible to do a thorough survey of the impact of all IUM graduates; here, I will illustrate its global reach through zooming in on a selection of its alumni.

Among the graduates of the IUM who have served their countries in governmental roles is Dr Zulkifli Mohamad Al-Bakri of Malaysia, who graduated in 1993[244] and went on to become Mufti of the Federal Territories before joining the government as Minister of Religious Affairs. From the Maldives, Dr Mohamed Shaheem Ali Saeed graduated in 2004,[245] going on to gain a PhD from the Islamic University of Malaysia and serving as Minister of Islamic Affairs in the Maldivian parliament and Chancellor of the Islamic University of the Maldives. Having joined the IUM as a high school student in 1981, Dr Mohammad Ahmed Lo of Senegal went on to graduate with a PhD in 1997 and served as the Senegalese Minister of Higher Education, Dean of the African College of Studies and President of the Board of Directors of the Union of African Scholars.[246] Graduating with a PhD in 1993, Dr Ali Sheikh Ahmed Abubakar returned to Somalia and established Mogadishu University.[247] Dr Ibrahim Jallow from Sierra Leone completed his PhD at the IUM in 2001[248] and is currently Ambassador of the Republic of Sierra Leone to the Kingdom of Saudi Arabia.[249]

Holding the revered position of Imam at *al-Masjid al-Ḥarām* (The Sacred Mosque) in Mecca is Saudi graduate Abdullah Awad Al Juhany.[250] Kuwaiti Mishary bin Rashid Alafasy, arguably the most famous reciter alive, specialized in the ten *qirā'āt* (recitations) and *tafsīr* (explanations) of Qur'an at IUM, currently serves as Imam of Masjid Al-Kabīr (Grand Mosque) in Kuwait City and tours internationally.[251] Popularly known as 'Mufti Menk,' Zimbabwean Ismail Ibn Musa Menk has acquired a large global following and been listed as one of the 500 Most Influential Muslims in the world.[252] He studied sharīʿa at the IUM and became the Grand Mufti of Zimbabwe and Head of the Fatwa Department for the Council of Islamic Scholars of Zimbabwe.[253] Polish graduate Tomasz Miśkiewicz became Mufti of the *Muzułmański Związek Religijny* (Muslim Religious Union) after graduating in 2000.[254] Professor Hamid Choi Yeong-Kil of South Korea graduated in 1980, worked as an academic and was the first to translate the Qur'an into Korean.[255] Professor of Islamic Law in Nigeria, Dr Abdul Razzaq Abdul Majeed Alaro graduated in 1993[256] and is now a Barrister at the Supreme Court of Nigeria. Dr Khalil-ur-Rahman Sajjad Nomani of India completed his PhD in Qur'anic Studies at IUM and is currently spokesperson for the All India Muslim Personal Law Board[257] and a Sufi spiritual teacher. From Pakistan, Dr Abdur Razzaq Iskander (d. 2021), considered to be one of the country's most influential scholars, was an alumnus of Darul Uloom

Karachi, the IUM and Al-Azhar University. He served as Chancellor of *Jamia Uloom-ul-Islamia* and President of *Wifaq-ul-Madaris ul-Arabia*[258] among other roles. Dr Suhaib Hasan, originally from Pakistan but now resident in the UK, is a founding member and General Secretary of The Islamic Shariah Council,[259] a member of The European Council for Fatwa and Research[260] and the Assembly of Muslim Jurists in America (AMJA).[261] Having graduated with an MA from the IUM and PhD from Yale, this author currently serves as Chairman of the Fiqh Council of North America,[262] Dean of Academic Affairs at the Islamic Seminary of North America[263] and Resident Scholar at the East Plano Islamic Center in Texas.[264] These examples, and many more like them, illustrate the level of commitment, and depth and breadth of influence of the IUM Alumni on the international Islamic community.

## *3.4 Conclusion*

Wahhabism is the most widespread manifestation of Salafism, probably in the entire history of the movement. The primary factor for this is the political support given by the modern Kingdom of Saudi Arabia, bolstering claims of legitimacy and supporting institutions, scholars, and organizations that champion it.

However, Wahhabism is not 'pure' Salafism, if there is in fact, any such thing. It is without a doubt based on the teachings of Ibn Taymiyya, and his student Ibn al-Qayyim, and no other post-Taymiyyan movement is as clearly indebted to Ibn Taymiyya as that of Ibn ʿAbd al-Wahhāb. Wahhabis, especially those in the sanitized and reformed Third-Wave iteration, can easily find copious quotes from Ibn Taymiyya and Ibn al-Qayyim that give the illusion of a direct continuity of thought. But Ibn ʿAbd al-Wahhāb was no Ibn Taymiyya, neither in his breadth of scholarship, nor in his application of knowledge. Put bluntly: Wahhabism, while recognizable as Taymiyyan in origin, is an aberration of the teachings of Ibn Taymiyya. The brazenness of mass *takfir*, the presumptuousness of being the only legitimate Muslim group, the blithe acceptance of going to war and killing thousands of fellow Muslims, simply have no parallel in Sunni history (although there are parallels, critics point out, to Khārijī movements of the past). While Ibn Taymiyya might have been harsh in principle, and uncompromising in theory, towards non-Sunni groups, in real life, and in his dealings with people and interactions with his opponents, he clearly demonstrated a compassionate and humane side.

Studying Wahhabism in detail reveals a clear incongruity that threatens the very foundation of Salafism: the Salafi belief that it is an uncorrupted, pristine, flawless system that has been handed down generation to generation in its original form. Wahhabism has *demonstrably* evolved – multiple times – over the course of its three-hundred-and-fifty-year existence and has fractured into a veritable chromatic spectrum of splinter movements.

History teaches us that this is the case with all movements, groups, and ideas. To effect change, and be affected by change, is a social phenomenon that all peoples and groups exhibit; Salafism, and in particular Wahhabism, cannot escape this fate. We saw this phenomenon in the historical overview of the previous chapter, but because the figures and movements were spread across different regions and eras, the continuity was not as clear; the evolution easier to ignore. The same cannot be said of Wahhabism and, as Wahhabis should know, '*ignorance is not an excuse.*'

First-Wave Wahhabism had to be toned down and reined in in order to enter the modern world; this defanging process took over a century and had at least two recognizable phases. Second-Wave Wahhabism had to adapt itself to the new political reality of the establishment of the Kingdom of Saudi Arabia, the coming of oil wealth, and the inevitable modernization of the country. The establishment of the Islamic University of Medina, with its international focus and innovative approach, led to the global spread of Third-Wave Wahhabism, the impact of which is still being felt today. But the bitter reality is that the original batch of Wahhabis, and even Ibn ʿAbd al-Wahhāb himself, would not have recognized, much less aligned themselves with, the bulk of those who identify as his followers today. This includes the founder's own descendants, who claim to carry his mantle, and speak on his behalf. There are a myriad of issues – theological, methodological, and political – that they would have deemed to be problematic, and indeed, outside the fold of Islam. To put it in Wahhabi terms, First-Wave Wahhabism would require itself to dissociate completely from its own Third-Wave descendants.

Some Wahhabis were influenced by the teachings of the Muslim Brotherhood, and the two strands have had a complicated and colorful interplay over the last seventy years. Let us now look at this interaction in more detail.

# 4

# SALAFISM AND ISLAMISM: A CASE STUDY OF THE MUSLIM BROTHERHOOD

*'The closest groups to the truth, and the most eager of them to apply Islam, are: Ahl al-Sunna, and they are the Ahl al-Ḥadīth, and then the Anṣār al-Sunna [of Egypt], and then the Muslim Brotherhood. All of these groups, and others, have errors and truths, so you should cooperate with them in their good, and avoid their mistakes...'*
*~ Fatwa of the Senior Council of Scholars, Chaired by the Grand Mufti Ibn Bāz*[1]

*'This group known as the Muslim Brotherhood has absolutely no relationship with Islam, and they are a misguided, deviant group...'*
*~ Fatwa of the Grand Mufti 'Abd al-Azīz Āl-Shaykh*[2]

In terms of major global impact, Salafism's rise in the twentieth century has only been matched by the emergence of what has been called 'political Islam' or 'Islamism' (with an advocate called 'Islamist').[3] The archetypal form of political Islam is the Muslim Brotherhood (al-Ikhwān al-Muslimūn), which was founded in Egypt in 1928 under the leadership of Ḥasan al-Bannā.[4] Due to the dynamic message and activism of the Muslim Brotherhood, the movement quickly became well supported throughout Egyptian society – four branches in 1929 became fifteen in 1932, then 300 by 1938 and in excess of 2,000 in 1948[5] – and developed branches outside Egypt, as well as inspiring other political movements that were near replicas of it (such as al-Naḥda in Tunisia).[6]

As the Muslim Brotherhood is the first, and most prominent, Islamist tradition, this chapter will use the group as a means of illustrating how quietist and political forms of Salafism have responded to the Muslim Brotherhood in the Middle East, as a general indication of the political implications of such Salafism in the modern age. It should also be noted that the Muslim Brotherhood can be seen as a product of 'Enlightenment Salafism,' since its founder Ḥasan al-Bannā was a direct student and close associate of Rashīd Riḍā. Hence, this chapter will demonstrate that 'Enlightenment Salafism' and 'puritan Salafism' are two different ideologies.

While Salafism and Islamism are distinct methodologies, we have seen earlier (in section 3.2.4) that there has been some common ground between the Muslim Brotherhood and elements of Salafism in Saudi Arabia. However, there has been a varied history between the Muslim Brotherhood and various strands of Salafism, in different countries, throughout the twentieth century and leading into the twenty-first, with moments of both conflict and cooperation. The main focal points for this historic relationship are Saudi Arabia and Egypt, the bases of modern Salafism (for the purposes of this chapter we shall revert to this term to describe the Wahhabi movement) and Islamism, respectively. Their critical engagements have had major global implications, also impacting other countries such as Syria, Jordan, and Kuwait.

This chapter demonstrates that quietist and political forms of Salafism lead to surprisingly conservative results, despite the radical picture that is painted in the mainstream media. They have never called for revolution against autocratic regimes in the Middle East. In the case of Egypt, political Salafism can be seen to move from embracing a pro-democracy stance like the Muslim Brotherhood, to aligning themselves with the army junta in suppressing the call for Islamic law, democracy, and political freedom, and endorsing the suppression of the Muslim Brotherhood. Quietist Salafism, on the other hand, can be seen, on the whole, to be a historic foe to the Muslim Brotherhood (with occasional exceptions), but a full supporter of autocratic political regimes.

## *4.1 Al-Bannā, Qutb, and Salafism*

Ḥasan al-Bannā (d. 1949), the founder of the Muslim Brotherhood, was raised in a modest household. His father was a religious scholar who trained in al-Azhar University during the time of Muḥammad ʿAbduh.[7] Although heavily influenced by the Sufi tradition, his father was also dedicated to the science of hadith and drew international acclaim for an erudite re-editing and brief commentary of the massive hadith collection of Ibn Ḥanbal, entitled the *Musnad.*[8]

Al-Bannā had trained as a schoolteacher at the Dār al-ʿUlūm institute in Cairo. While in the Egyptian capital, he attended the circles of Rashīd Riḍā, and socialized with the Syrian Salafi writer Muḥibb al-Dīn al-Khaṭīb. In addition, he frequented the Salafiyya Bookstore which was headed by al-Khaṭīb.[9] While al-Bannā was not a bona fide Islamic scholar, he was certainly no mere activist. After being raised in a scholarly home and dedicating himself to ongoing Islamic learning, he was able to provide sophisticated pronouncements on numerous religious issues in his small booklets and speeches. Accordingly, his call was able to attract some Azhari scholars from the very beginning, although the number was quite negligible.[10]

A significant part of the Muslim Brotherhood's appeal lay in al-Bannā making use of his own Sufi heritage, which was shared by the general public, while infusing his discourse with elements of the 'Salafi' call. The wide-ranging nature of the founding principles of the early Muslim Brotherhood were outlined by al-Bannā in the Fifth Conference of the organization in January 1939, by which time it had experienced an exponential rise and was one of the major political actors in Egypt. Firstly, as al-Bannā outlined to an audience of thousands, the Muslim Brotherhood was 'a Salafi message,' in which they sought to rely on the Qurʾan and the Sunna as their foundation (al-Bannā's 'Salafism' is explored further below). Secondly, the organization was 'a Sunni way' in its tradition. Thirdly, it was 'a Sufi truth,' in which it sought to bring about spiritual rectification as well as consistency on the path of virtuous behavior. Fourthly, the movement was 'a political organization,' calling for a reform of the government and foreign policy, so that the nation could be protected. Fifthly, it was 'an athletic group,' in order to strengthen the body and soul in order to best perform the duties laid down by religion. Sixthly, it was 'an institution of culture and knowledge.' Seventhly, 'an economic company' that sought to bring matters of trade and earning of money under Islamic rules. Lastly, it was 'a social idea' that sought to identify the weaknesses and wrongs of society and provide the means of alleviating those ills in order to bring about the restoration and health of the nation. As such, it is clear to observe an ambitious comprehensiveness, or *shumuliyya.*[11] Al-Bannā summarized the method for the ultimate revival of the Muslim nation as a combination of three powers: firstly, the knowledge of al-Azhar University; secondly, the spirituality of the Sufi orders; and thirdly, material strength.[12] Such a broad and ambitious methodology appealed to many people, over numerous lands, and explains the group's meteoric rise and longevity.

What concerns us here is the relationship between al-Bannā and Salafism. In particular, the question: Can al-Bannā be classified as a 'Salafi'? He described his own vision of Islam as: 'a *salafī* call, because they call to returning to the correct understanding of the Book of Allah and Way of the Messenger.'[13] Nonetheless, a critical reading of al-Bannā's works, and his relationship with the primary concepts and figures of the Salafi movement, show that while they shared some broad similarities with Riḍā's program of revival, he cannot be considered a part of Salafism in the technical sense (meaning, he was not a 'puritanical Salafi' but rather an 'Enlightened Salafi'). This is demonstrated via an explication of several points concerning his thought.

Firstly, al-Bannā clearly was not advocating Ḥanbalī or Taymiyyan theology. While at some level he did appear to have been influenced by Riḍā's admiration of Ibn Taymiyya, it is important to note that he never made theological issues a priority. Regarding the divine attributes, he states, 'We believe that the methodology of the *salaf* in remaining silent and leaving the intended meanings of words to God is safer and more preferable.'[14] This is clearly a nod in Ibn Taymiyya's direction, but he then goes on to say, 'The differences between them were limited to explaining the meaning of certain words which were allowed to be explained, making it a petty issue.'[15] He also stated in his conclusion of *A Treatise on the Islamic Faith* that 'the most important thing that the Muslims should focus on now is unifying their ranks.'[16] Throughout his life, he made it a point not to get involved in theological or legal controversies, including those that are considered key to Wahhabism. In fact, when asked about invoking the saints, he replied that these matters should be left to the scholars of theology and that lay-Muslims should not dispute such abstruse issues among themselves.[17] Such an answer would have resulted in a verdict of heresy from any Wahhabi cleric of that era.

Al-Bannā's life and writings show an admiration for Sufism, and his description of his movement acknowledges the 'Sufī reality,' which he describes as having good character, loving God, and encouraging people to do good deeds. His association with Sufism and his frequenting of their monasteries and festivals was an essential part of his life, from his childhood until his death.[18] He would regularly participate in the *mawlid* – the celebration of the Prophet's birthday.

Hence, *theologically*, al-Bannā has little to do with Salafism, and in fact would not be viewed as an adherent to either *ahl al-hadith* theology or Wahhabism.

Secondly, he wished to cast as broad a net as possible in terms of cooperation. He explicitly wanted to overlook theological and legal differences, and aimed to look at the greater good of unity against what he viewed as common threats to the entire umma. Throughout his writings, he emphasizes that members of the Brotherhood do not belong to any sect or school, and that differences of opinion have always existed and should be tolerated to the greatest extent possible. One of his most oft-quoted phrases, which is still invoked by the group to this day, is, 'Let us cooperate in those things on which we can agree and be lenient and excuse one another in those things which we cannot.'[19] Once again, such sentiments clash directly with the hardline theological stances of the classical Atharī and modern Wahhabi strands of Islam.

Therefore, *methodologically*, al-Bannā was at odds with the icons of the Salafi movement, such as Ibn Taymiyya and Ibn ʿAbd al-Wahhāb.

Thirdly, it is important to remember that al-Bannā was active during the same period as the Salafi cleric al-Fiqī (see section 2.9.1), and witnessed the formation, and activities, of the *Anṣār al-Sunna* group that the latter founded. Yet, there is no indication that al-Bannā was ever involved with that organization, or even on good terms with al-Fiqī. In fact, it does not appear that al-Bannā was involved with any of the Salafi movements of Egypt.

Hence, *historically*, al-Bannā was not attached to the Salafi movements and their agenda in Egypt. Nonetheless, al-Bannā was sufficiently aware of where his vision could align with the Salafis and the Saudis (as explored below in section 4.2.1).

So, what do we make of al-Bannā's use of the term '*salafi*' to describe his vision of Islam? Quite simply, what al-Bannā meant by this term is not what Wahhabis or puritan Salafis meant when they used it. In fact, al-Bannā's understanding of Salafism was taken from his mentor, Rashīd Riḍā. He believed that people had strayed from the purpose of life and understanding of the early Muslims, and that returning to their way was what was best for the Muslim community. For al-Bannā, a return to the way of the early Muslims meant a return to Islamic dynamism and a political and legal revival: it was not primarily related to theology. Rather, it was more concerned with opposing the dogmatism of the legal schools and embracing a rethinking of Islamic law in light of modern issues, as the original *salaf* were forced to do when they extrapolated Islamic law from its actual sources – in other words, the 'Enlightenment Salafis' of the Riḍā school.

This type of broad-based Islamic approach has historically made the group attractive to a wide variety of sections in society – from the Sufi to the Salafi – as it has not strayed greatly from these founding principles, even if it has become increasingly more Salafi, and less Sufi, in later times. Naturally, this type of ecumenical behavior has not endeared it to hardline Salafi factions.

The second major leader of the Muslim Brotherhood, who came to influence political Salafism with his notions of ignorance and justice, was Sayyid Qutb. Qutb had memorized the Qur'an at an early age and had trained at the Dār al-ʿUlum of Cairo.[20] He went on to become an acclaimed writer, poet and art critic, who worked for the government in the early part of his career. He joined the Muslim Brotherhood later in life in 1953, rising up in its ranks, and becoming editor in chief of their magazine. For many, he became the public face of the movement. After a sham trial, Qutb was sentenced to death by the Egyptian government in 1966 for his activism with the Brotherhood. In posterity, Qutb has had an ambiguous legacy, even within the Muslim Brotherhood; while the majority admire him greatly and call him 'The Martyr' (*al-Shahīd*), some claim he has been misrepresented through extreme readings, and others embrace a radical reading of his thought (as in the case of Jihadi-Salafis).[21]

Qutb was not formally a Salafi in his thought. He was uncomfortable with the formalities and traditions of the Muslim clerics – exemplified in his dismissal of the detailed explanations of Azhari scholars – and stressed the importance and sufficiency of relying directly on the Qur'an and Sunna.[22] Furthermore, al-Albānī initially spoke of how unjust Qutb's execution was, and how Qutb was not a Salafi, but had 'a strong tendency towards the Salafi *manhaj* [methodology] at the end of his life.'[23] Qutb would become the most influential figurehead of the Brotherhood regarding Salafism, despite his own lack of formal identification with the movement. It was his sense of political authenticity and standing up to the injustices of government that would make him an inspirational reference for many Salafis, both political Salafis (who are dealt with in this chapter) and Jihadi-Salafis (who are dealt with in the next chapter). These trends were inspired by Qutb's synthesis of belief in divine oneness (*tawḥīd*) and Islamic governance (*ḥākimiyya*) in its widest sense, and the claim that one cannot be a true believer in God's unity without also striving to apply God's laws in the political realm.

## *4.2 The Salafi–Brotherhood Relationship in the Kingdom and Egypt*

In outlining the critical historic relationship between these pivotal nations, one encounters contrasting phases of mutual interest, cooperation, and conflict. These phases can be categorized into five distinct chronological stages, with each stage marked by clearly discernible shifts that can be likened to a marital relationship: (1) the initial mutual attraction, (2) the courting, (3) the marriage (of convenience?), (4) the child, (5) the bitter divorce, and finally (6) the post-divorce hostility.

### *4.2.1 The Initial Mutual Attraction (Mid-1930s to 1949)*

The first stage of their relationship spans the period of the founding of the Brotherhood and the rise of the Third Saudi Kingdom, from the 1930s to

1949, concluding with the assassination of al-Bannā. During this phase, the Egyptian Muslim Brotherhood and the Saudis established their initial contacts, marked by a mutual acknowledgment of similarities and common ground.

By the mid-1930s, the Brotherhood had formulated a strategic decision to extend its ideological and financial support to influential individuals beyond the borders of Egypt, with a particular focus on Saudi Arabia. In pursuit of this goal, al-Bannā initiated efforts to engage with prominent Saudi officials towards the end of 1934. During the visit of the Governor of Hijaz to Cairo, al-Bannā arranged a meeting with him, accompanied by a group of Brotherhood members. Subsequently, the Governor briefly visited the Brotherhood's headquarters and even offered certain privileges to the Brotherhood members in relation to performing the Hajj. Following these interactions, the Brotherhood demonstrated their commitment to their burgeoning relationship with Saudi Arabia through several notable actions. They dedicated an entire edition of their journal to the city of Medina, orchestrated a charity campaign to assist the needy residents of the city, and launched an initiative to encourage their organization's members to fulfill the Islamic duty of performing the Hajj pilgrimage.[24]

These relations were further fostered in the 1930s, establishing the Brotherhood's working relationship with the Egyptian and Saudi Salafis. The first volumes of Ahmad al-Bannā's work on the *Musnad* of Ibn Ḥanbal were published by the Muslim Brotherhood's publishing house, with the first volume being prepared around 1934. Further volumes were published with the patronage of Ibn Saʿūd, following the entreaties of the Egyptian Salafi ʿAbd al-Ẓāhir Abū al-Samḥ (d. 1951).[25] The latter had established the Alexandrian chapter of *Jamāʿat Ansar al-Sunna al-Muhammadiyya* (The Helpers of the Sunna of Muhammad) shortly after al-Fiqī had founded the group in Cairo in 1926. Abu al-Samh was an older member of Riḍā's group, who had attended the sessions conducted by Muhammad 'Abduh. Abu al-Samh would eventually move to Saudi Arabia after the Hajj of 1926, due to Ibn Saʿūd accepting the recommendation of Abu al-Samh by Riḍā. Abu al-Samh was then appointed the head imam at the Sacred Mosque in Mecca, and as a teacher and supervisor of the Sacred Mosque's educational facility. He would remain a senior scholarly figure in Mecca who enjoyed a close relationship with the king – remaining in Saudi Arabia for the rest of his life, but passing away in Paris, on his way to the USA to have treatment for kidney disease.[26] Furthermore, it is reported that al-Bannā had established good relations with Ibn Saud from 1932, and had provided the king with advisors on how the Kingdom could react to the modernizing process, with the Brotherhood receiving financial support in return.[27]

Nonetheless, as a forewarning of tensions that would emerge between Salafis and the Brotherhood, the Brotherhood would soon show its relative independence and growing strength when it published, in May 1939, a clear criticism of the Saudi ruling class by one of Abu al-Samh's sons. In this work, they accused the Saudi ruling class of flagrantly disobeying Islamic law in their lives, particularly through their trips to Europe and Egypt where they resided in luxury hotels. By publishing this type of article and then refraining from any retraction, the Brotherhood exhibited its highest ideals of encapsulating the Islamic duty to enjoin the good and forbid evil (*amr bi-l-ma'rūf wa-l-nahī 'ani-l-munkar*). This drew an angry response from Abu al-Samh, who complained directly to Ḥasan al-Bannā's father, but the Brotherhood refused to retract the article.[28]

Despite this, the relationship with the Saudi authorities remained multi-faceted. On the one hand, the movement's commitment to Islamic ethos and progressive approach to engaging with the modern world held significant appeal for the king. The educated class of the Brotherhood offered him guidance and assistance, providing much-needed advice on how to handle the country's rapid modernization.[29] However, at the same time, Egyptian members of the Brotherhood operating in this capacity only spent limited periods in the Saudi kingdom, returning to Egypt after a short while. This would change dramatically in the 1950s, after the murder of al-Bannā in 1949 and the Egyptian government's repression of the Brotherhood.[30]

During this period, the Egyptian Salafi community was on what seemed to be relatively good terms with the Muslim Brotherhood. Members of the Salafi organization *Jama'at Ansar al-Sunna al-Muhammadiyya* would write articles in the Muslim Brotherhood's journal. Indeed, the Salafi pioneer Taqi al-Din al-Hilali (d. 1987) wrote for both organizations by the late 1930s and mid-1940s. This highlighted that the early twentieth-century definition of 'Salafi' was not fixed, as opposed to the more rigid and distinct definition and methodology the term acquired by the 1980s. Furthermore, during the colonial period, these groups saw themselves as allies within the broader political context, although they held on to their own particular religious differences.[31]

While the *Ansar* were pro-Saudi, they were also pro-government in general; hence, they praised the Egyptian kings from 1936 until 1952. After that, they praised the Free Officers upon Nasser's revolution in 1952. As a result, the government did not persecute the Salafis in the same way that they viciously repressed the Brotherhood.[32] As loyalists, it is unsurprising that al-Fiqī would be highly critical of the Muslim Brotherhood's committed political agenda, which would not conform to the policies of the ruler of the day. Indeed, al-Fiqi went so far as to say that the Muslim Brotherhood did not really call to Islam as they were more 'Muslim traitors rather than Muslim brothers.'[33]

The fact that the Brotherhood was not Salafi in the strictest sense naturally created some distrust with the Salafis, a sentiment consistent with the elitist attitude exhibited by Salafis towards their non-Salafi co-religionists. Historically, this attitude has hindered their ability to collaborate effectively with other Islamic groups. Indeed, anecdotal evidence seems to suggest that al-Fiqi viewed al-Bannā in a very negative light. Several works claim that al-Bannā visited al-Fiqi in the *Ansar al-Sunna* office, and a seemingly tense conversation ensued. Al-Fiqi wanted the Brotherhood to emphasize Divine Unity (*tawḥīd*) as Salafis understood it, whereas al-Bannā wanted to gather people upon the 'general Islam as understood by all.' Al-Fiqi was not impressed and accused him of being a *ḥātib al-layl* – literally 'wood gatherer at night,' i.e., someone with no discernment, picking up right and wrong alike.[34]

The nature of the Salafi movement in Egypt in relation to the Muslim Brotherhood remained this way until the mid-1960s (a period corresponding to Stage 3 within our classification). Subsequently, internal developments emerged that initiated a process of disunity, which will be discussed in the following sections.

### *4.2.2 The Engagement: Brotherhood Migration and Exile to Saudi Arabia (1950s to 1961)*

The second stage is the one in which the members of the Brotherhood started to move to Saudi Arabia to set down roots within the country. Such a migration led to a closer relationship just before Faisal was to assume effective control in 1962. It was, in some ways, a testing of waters for both strands and a gradual realization that they had much in common, especially against their socialist and nationalist opponents.

By 1953, the Saudi regime had to contend with a growing body of Saudis who were Nasserites, Arab nationalists, and communists. Many of these individuals had been born in the oil fields and in the Saudi camps of such workforces. Yet it was not only the latter who found intellectual comfort and direction from these related forces gathering momentum throughout the Middle East, but also individuals from privileged backgrounds – including teachers and students who had studied abroad in intellectual centers such as Baghdad, Beirut, and Cairo – who were influenced by these ideologies. Moreover, there existed an international network of radical thinkers and activists who played a significant role in disseminating these ideas, with the Gulf region serving as a key focal point for these intellectual exchanges. Additionally, the foreign, semi-skilled workforce that came to work in the Saudi oil fields hailed from countries like Palestine, Syria, Egypt, Lebanon, Italy, Sudan, and India with deep-rooted histories in leftist ideology, and actively propagated these ideas within the region. However, it is essential to note that detailed accounts of these movements are limited due to the brutal suppression they endured. The threat of the death penalty and severe prison sentences loomed over their activities, and even the government amnesty offered in 1975 was contingent on members remaining silent about the history of the underground movement, although some exceptions exist.[35]

The political instability of Saudi Arabia in the 1950s was underscored by a fierce power struggle between two of Ibn Saʿūd's sons – Saʿūd and Faisal – following Ibn Saʿūd's death in 1953. The very real threat that this trend posed to the ruler of Saudi Arabia was demonstrated in 1955, when a planned coup by Egyptian-trained Saudi army officers was uncovered days before it was to occur. This discovery deeply disturbed Saʿūd and the Saudi royal family. In addition, this current of political dissent had an impact that extended to the power struggle between Saʿūd and Faisal when their brother Talal (d. 2018) moved to Cairo and Beirut after being dismissed from the Saudi government in 1961, and formed a royal opposition group named the 'Free Princes' (*al-Umarāʾ al-Aḥrār*), along with some of his full brothers.[36]

The Saudi rulers felt the need to find Islamic forces that would speak to the concerns that such nationalist and leftist trends spoke to, as the period was still tempestuous. In this context, they turned to the Muslim Brotherhood, given their relatively higher levels of education, cognizance, and adaptability to the modern world in comparison to the favored religious group of the rulers, the strictly Wahhabi scholars and preachers, who lacked the intellectual capacity to effectively counter Nasser's political appeal. In addition, the Brotherhood was already actively engaging and opposing these nationalist and leftist forces in Egypt, so they were trained and well-equipped to encounter such groups in Saudi Arabia – in a way that would benefit the rulers.[37]

The significance of pro-Brotherhood scholars to the Saudi Wahhabi scholars in their efforts to counteract Pan-Arabism was illustrated in Chapter 3, with reference to Ibn Bāz's treatise entitled *Naqd al-Qawmiyya al-ʿArabiyya ʿala dawʾ al-Islām wa-l-Waqiʿ* (*Critique of Arab Nationalism in the Light of Islam and Reality*), which quoted freely from non-Salafis and had government sponsorship. Moreover, the establishment of the Islamic University of Medina was not just a Salafi venture, but one keenly and logistically supported by the Brotherhood. When inaugurating the university, King Saʿūd made a clear reference to the members of the Brotherhood, indicating a reliance on individuals 'who have been driven from their country after having been robbed, abused, and tortured.'[38] Furthermore, the first Advisory Council of the Islamic University of Medina included those who either had close ties with the Brotherhood or were formal members. Among them were Mawdudi and Abul Hasan Ali Nadwi, who shared ideological similarities with Qutb during this period. The actual Brotherhood members included Muhammad Mahmud al-Sawwaf (d. 1992), an Iraqi immigrant to the Kingdom, and Muhammad al-Mubarak (d. 1981), a co-founder of the Syrian branch of the Muslim Brotherhood.[39]

Building upon the initial favorable interactions initiated during the lifetime of al-Bannā, the Muslim Brotherhood successfully established a network of supporters within Saudi Arabia by the early 1950s, thereby enhancing the significance and stability of the movement within the Kingdom. In 1953, a pivotal development occurred when Manna al-Qattan (d. 1999), one of the most influential clerics of the Brotherhood, relocated from Egypt to Saudi Arabia to mediate a dispute between a Saudi branch of the Brotherhood and the central Guidance Office in Egypt. Al-Qattan would later emerge as a highly influential figure in recruiting Saudis into the Brotherhood's ranks. Backed by support from the Saudi government, he established additional branches of the Brotherhood within Saudi Arabia, including in the Hijaz region.[40] Even as Saudi attempted to develop closer ties with Nasser until the late 1950s – a period marked by Nasser's antagonism toward the Muslim Brotherhood within Egypt – the Saudi leadership continued cultivating its relationship with the Brotherhood. This commitment was evident when, during his visit in March 1954, Saʿūd's intervention secured the release of al-Hudaybi from imprisonment by Nasser, after the dissolution of the Brotherhood by the Revolutionary Command Council (RCC) on 14 January 1954.[41] Subsequently, in May 1954, al-Hudaybi traveled to Saudi Arabia, among other countries, seeking to garner increased support for the Brotherhood's cause.[42] As time passed, the Saudi supporters of the Brotherhood would become a crucial source of financial support.[43]

The high esteem in which the Saudi rulers held the Brotherhood can be seen in the genesis of what would eventually become the Muslim World League (*Rabitat al-ʿAlam al-Islami*) in 1962. This organization was first conceived by Amjad al-Zahhawi (d. 1967), a religious scholar and one of the founding members of the Muslim Brotherhood in Iraq. In 1957, he advised Saʿud to establish an institute that would encompass various Muslim groups, whose purpose was the study of religious matters that affected the Muslim world. The king found the idea compelling and sought counsel from the Grand Mufti of Saudi Arabia, who outlined certain conditions for its formation, and the organization was eventually established. It is noteworthy that this initiative, which the Brotherhood inspired, was eventually adopted by the ruling authority. Moreover, the Muslim World League was founded with a Constituent Assembly in which the Saudi Wahhabis constituted a minority, coexisting with Ashʿarīs, Māturīdīs, and Sufis. Additionally, the inaugural session of this organization was presided over by Abul Hasan Ali Nadwi (another prominent non-Salafi cleric), as the Grand Mufti of Saudi Arabia delegated this responsibility to him.[44]

Now that this solid foundation had been laid, with the two strands of the Brotherhood and Salafism having been united to fight against a common threat, it was inevitable that the relationship would be strengthened considerably, and in the process, each strand would influence the other.

### *4.2.3 The Marriage (of Convenience?): Support for the Muslim Brotherhood (1962 to 1978)*

The third stage was marked by the leadership of Ibn Saʿud's son Faisal, who would formally reign as king from 1964 until 1975, and ended just before the tumultuous political events of 1979. It was a period in which the Muslim Brotherhood was given substantial support to occupy distinguished positions within Saudi Arabia. This provided the foundation for the Brotherhood to influence certain Salafi factions. During this stage, in some arenas, the Brotherhood played a more prominent role in the Kingdom's Islamic activities than the Salafi clerics did, especially in forming organizations with a more global reach.

The question mark appended to the term 'convenience' in the title of this sub-section underscores the ongoing debate regarding the nature of support for the Brotherhood during this time. Specifically, scholars discuss whether this support stemmed from a sincere religious commitment on the part of Faisal, whether it was dictated by *realpolitik* considerations aimed at consolidating his own power, or whether it evolved from the latter into the former over time. In truth, this question about the sincerity or otherwise behind supporting the Brotherhood can never be satisfactorily answered.

Faisal's backing of the Brotherhood as king, together with what can be described as the silent acquiescence of the Wahhabi-Salafi establishment (in the form of Second-Wave Wahhabism), is demonstrated by their support for Sayyid Qutb. Firstly, selections from Qutb's commentary on the Qurʾan were broadcast on Saudi radio.[45] Secondly, in 1966, when Qutb was sentenced to death by the Egyptian government, Faisal and Ibn Bāz both publicly expressed their condemnation of the sentence, and directly appealed for clemency to President Nasser.[46] While one could be cynical about such publicly announced outrage, seeing it as merely a continuation of the propaganda against the ungodly Nasserite nationalists, the fact of the matter is that the Saudi regime and the Salafi movement – here represented by Ibn Bāz – were willing to support a leading member of the Brotherhood.

The creation, in 1972, of the World Assembly of Muslim Youth (*al-Nadwa al-ʿAlamiyya liʾl-Shabab al-Islami*), or WAMY, played a pivotal role in forging a nexus between the Brotherhood and Salafism, disseminating a message that incorporated elements of both movements. While the charitable organization was officially under the auspices of the Saudi Ministry of Social Affairs, WAMY directed its efforts towards propagating Salafism within schools and mosques in the region, encompassing the distribution of religious literature and the construction of mosques. However, as the Brotherhood in Hijaz secured control of the organization and its network and resources, the organization became the primary tool for Brotherhood recruitment, achieving notable success in the Eastern Provinces. Through

WAMY's initiatives, Brotherhood activists closely collaborated with Salafi clerics, and this mutual engagement resulted in a reciprocal influence: Brotherhood members underwent a gradual cultural assimilation into Salafism, while some Salafis were influenced by the Brotherhood to become more politicized, instead of quietist.[47]

The social impact of WAMY is exemplified through the activities of Kamal El-Helbawy (d. 2023), an Egyptian Brotherhood member (who later left on acrimonious terms). El-Helbawy relocated to Saudi Arabia in 1972 and assumed a pivotal role as one of WAMY's founding members, serving as its director from 1973. As the director, with the support of the current King Salman b. Abd al-ʿAziz, who at that time held the position of governor of Riyadh before ascending to the throne in 2015, El-Helbawy organized conferences and youth camps within the Kingdom. Additionally, another Egyptian Brotherhood member, Mohammed Mahdī Akef (d. 2022), upon being released from two decades of imprisonment in 1974, was able to arrange seminars in Saudi Arabia and worldwide.[48]

For the purposes of our study of the relationship between Salafism and the Brotherhood, the most important field that the Brotherhood populated in Saudi Arabia was in higher education, particularly at institutions such as King Abd al-Aziz University in Jeddah, the Islamic University of Medina, and King Saʿud University in Riyadh, which were meant to be ostensibly Salafi.[49] Notably, at King ʿAbd al-ʿAziz University and its annex Umm al-Qura, established in Mecca in 1981, the Brotherhood held a prominent position among the faculty from the outset. Three notable Brotherhood figures – all Syrian – namely, the aforementioned Muhammad al-Mubarak, who headed the Shariʿa department from 1969 to 1973, Abd al-Rahman Habannaka (d. 2004), and ʿAli al-Tantawi (d. 1999), played key roles in shaping the university's academic landscape.[50]

Of particular significance is al-Tantawi, as his time in Saudi Arabia was to be highly influential. He was educated in Damascus and came from a learned family with connections to the reformist Salafis of that time. He had engaged in defending Syria against French colonialization and was active in his support for the Palestinian cause following the 1948 occupation of their land. Having served as a judge in Syria until his forced departure in 1963, al-Tantawi spent four decades in Saudi Arabia, leaving an enduring imprint on the culture through his widely popular radio and television broadcasts spanning twenty-five years. For many Saudis of that generation, he was *the* face of Islamic lectures, as he was broadcast weekly on Friday evenings (prime religious time), and daily during the holy month of Ramadan. In recognition of his contributions, he was honored with the King Faisal Prize for Service to Islam in 1990.[51]

At the Islamic University of Medina, the Brotherhood's presence among the faculty expanded during the 1960s, with figures like Muhammad al-Majdhub (d. 1999), a senior Syrian Brotherhood member who arrived at the university soon after it opened, in 1963, and served on the advisory board of the university journal for fifteen years.[52] Additionally, the faculty included Ali Juraysha (d. 2011), an Egyptian Brotherhood member who had been imprisoned and exiled by Nasser's government during this period.[53]

Perhaps the most famous figure from the Brotherhood was Muhammad Qutb (d. 2014), Sayyid Qutb's brother, who moved to the Kingdom after his release from prison in 1972 – in what was a monumental moment in the relations between the Brotherhood and Salafism in Saudi Arabia – and took an academic post at the Mecca campus of King 'Abd al-'Aziz University (later called Umm al-Qura University). As a university lecturer, he introduced his brother's thought to the students, in which he equated the concept of divine sovereignty (*al-hākimiyya*) with the Salafi emphasis on divine unity (*tawḥīd*) and the dichotomy of *Ḥizb Allāh* (Party of God) and *Ḥizb al-Shayṭān* (Party of Satan) with the Salafi doctrine of loyalty to the Muslims and opposition to disbelievers (*al-walāʾ wa-l-barāʾ*). He also endorsed Saudi Arabia as the only modern nation-state with aspects of Islam. Although Muhammad Qutb was never an official member of the Brotherhood, he had been the 'primary custodian and official interpreter of his brother's legacy.'[54] He was seen as the most critical transmitter of Qutbian theory to those who would be identified as political Salafis, especially the *Ṣaḥwa* movement, as he was the supervisor for Safar al-Hawali's masters and doctorate degrees at Umm al-Qura University.

Initially, this accommodation of the Brotherhood was conceived as an unofficial component of Saudi Arabia's foreign policy, a strategy employed in the confrontation with Arab nationalists and socialists, and it persisted through the reign of the subsequent king, Khalid (d. 1982), who ascended the throne in 1975. However, the unearthing of radical Arab nationalist cells within major Saudi cities in the mid-1960s prompted Faisal to utilize the Brotherhood for external propaganda and harness them as a tool for internal propaganda directed at Saudi citizens. Hence, they assumed an augmented role, notably within the media.[55] Nevertheless, this approach carried inherent risks for the royal family, exemplified by the case of Muhammad Surur, who resided in Saudi Arabia between 1965 and 1974, and later critiqued the royal family for contravening Islam, eventually inspiring a faction that followed his path (as discussed in Chapter 3).

Naturally, this elevation of the Brotherhood within Saudi society was, to a certain extent, at the expense of the Salafi movement – with the implicit notion that the Wahhabi-Salafis were ill-equipped to lead a program of modernization in the country, especially in the realm of education. Hence, there were moves to counter the Brotherhood by Salafis in the region, which gained momentum after Stage 4, as will be discussed below. One manifestation of this Salafi response to the Brotherhood, as mentioned earlier regarding the Juhaymān incident, was the establishment in the mid-1960s of *al-Jama'a al-Salafiyya al-Muhtasiba* (The Salafi Group that Promotes Virtue and Prevents Vice). They took from their mentor al-Albānī an impassioned anti-Brotherhood stance, fueled by an obsession with legalistic minutiae and the belief that the theology of the people had to be purified before any political action.

Salafi disquiet at the mission of the Brotherhood was widespread among their ranks; but, at the time, Salafis were too powerless politically to vigorously spread their antipathy. This would change in a few decades when the regime would need them to counter what would be bequeathed by the mixing of the Brotherhood with Salafism, namely Juhaymān's *al-Jama'ah al-Salafiyyah al-Muhtasibah* movement (JSM), which would be a means of uniting Egyptian Salafis with Saudi Salafis, as members of *Ansar al-Sunna* in Egypt came to lecture in the JSM's base when they visited Medina.

What would become an overt and developed Salafi influence on the Muslim Brotherhood in Egypt began in Cairo in 1973. These developments witnessed the launch of annual Islamic summer camps led by the Islamically-oriented student body. These gatherings facilitated the convergence of leaders from diverse Islamic groups, encompassing Muslim Brotherhood figures such as 'Umar al-Tilmisani (d. 1986) who succeeded al-Hudaybi as the Supreme Guide of the Brotherhood, prominent Salafis like al-Albānī, and Azhari scholars with sympathies toward the Brotherhood, exemplified by individuals like Yusuf al-Qaradawi and Muhammad al-Ghazali.[56]

Notably, the camp activities encompassed an organized pilgrimage to Saudi Arabia for *'umra* in 1974. Such meetings led to passionate debates among the students on issues the competing Islamic groups raised – yet the Salafi call was the most strongly held among the young activists. The Salafi-inclined youth attacked the Brotherhood for not growing beards, or enforcing the face veil (*niqāb*) on their wives and for claiming that the head-covering alone (*hijāb*) was sufficient. In response, the Brotherhood attempted to convey to their interlocutors that it was the only movement that had a methodology that could unite Muslims and lead to a victory, as opposed to the narrow and parochial approach of the Salafis. The Salafis, they argued, predominantly focused on minor issues of ritual and prompted widespread argumentation on matters that were legitimately differed upon by religious scholars. Subsequently, the Brotherhood would score a number of victories over the Salafis as they convinced leading groups of student activists in Cairo University and Alexandria to choose allegiance to their ranks in 1974.[57]

However, the Brotherhood struggled to replicate its success among students in Upper and Middle Egypt. A key factor contributing to this challenge was the widespread dissemination of Saudi-funded Wahhabi-Salafi literature during the 1970s, which led to the adoption of Wahhabi-Salafi doctrines in the Upper and Middle regions. These areas became predominantly conservative and harbored suspicions toward the Brotherhood, which was perceived as advocating modernist principles. Southern students, echoing concerns from their northern counterparts, voiced complaints regarding the presence of beards and face veils among Brotherhood members.[58]

The 1970s marked the first of three phases that defined the relationship between the Muslim Brotherhood and Salafis in Egypt. This phase, triggered by the emergence of the 'Salafi Call' (*al-Daʿwah al-Salafiyya*) in Alexandria during that period (although the formal naming of this movement occurred in the early 1980s), was characterized by underlying tension and mutual criticism, though not outright hostility. The Salafi Call was born out of dissenters among the Islamic Group (*Gamaʿa Islamiyya*) who refused to follow their leaders in officially aligning themselves with the Muslim Brotherhood, but retained their activist spirit and methodology.[59] The acrimony persisted until the onset of the 2011 revolution.[60] Phases 2 and 3 of this intricate relationship will be examined in detail in the discussion of Stage 5 in Brotherhood–Salafi relations.

#### *4.2.4 The Child: Political Salafism (1979 to 2000)*

Whether one interprets the increased presence of the Muslim Brotherhood in Saudi Arabia as a catalyst or the sole driving force behind the emergence of a distinctively political form of Salafism in the 1980s, it is undeniable that the Brotherhood played a significant role in shaping this political phenomenon. The period between 1979 and 1980 witnessed a series of pivotal political events that compelled the Saudi regime to actively manage various competing Islamic political currents in order to maintain control over society. As a result, political Salafism had to be both nurtured and controlled, serving as a counterforce to both Jihadi-Salafism and Shiʿism. Simultaneously, the regime had to take measures to temper the influence and appeal of political Salafism by promoting apolitical Salafism. Furthermore, there was a need to display some degree of support for nascent Jihadi-Salafism, to appease public sentiment, and align with American foreign policy, particularly in the context of the Afghan war against the Soviet Union. This complex dynamic led to a turbulent period in the relationship between the Muslim Brotherhood and Salafism within Saudi Arabia. The Saudi regime strategically played these groups against each other, and against external forces. Meanwhile, in Egypt, the Salafi movement expanded its outreach and, in turn, exerted its influence on the grassroots of the Muslim Brotherhood.

The first major political event of this period that would cast a long shadow over the relationship of the Brotherhood with Saudi Salafism was the Iranian Revolution at the start of 1979. Within a few short months, the

Shah was deposed and an Islamic republic was established. More events changing the geopolitical landscape swiftly followed; in November 1979, Saudi Arabia witnessed the siege of al-Masjid al-Ḥarām by six hundred religious militants under the leadership of Juhaymān al-'Utaybi. A month later, the Soviets invaded Afghanistan. In September the following year, the Iran–Iraq War commenced, a devastating display of the military capabilities of Saudi Arabia's regional neighbors. These events shaped Saudi Arabia's concerns in the 1980s: it perceived a threat to its regime, both from internal turmoil, and from the shifts in the geopolitical landscape. The Iranian Revolution not only highlighted how easily a modern monarchy could be toppled but also established the country, led by the austere and mystic figure Ayatollah Khomeini (d. 1989), as a rival claimant to Saudi Arabia's mantle of being leaders of the Islamic world. The presence of a substantial Shiʿi population within Saudi Arabia, particularly in the Eastern Province, further compounded the challenge posed by the Iranian Revolution.

The Soviet invasion of Afghanistan would play an important role in the relationship between the Muslim Brotherhood and Salafism. It marked a pivotal moment, as Saudi Arabia, with full support from the United States, threw its weight behind the anti-Soviet factions, comprising both Brotherhood and Salafi elements, who stood together in their fight. The Saudi government not only provided substantial financial assistance, but also actively encouraged its citizens to participate in the battle against the communists.

The Iran–Iraq war exacerbated Saudi Arabia's apprehensions regarding Iran, given that Iraq's Ba'athist regime was perceived as an additional security threat to the Kingdom. Both Iran and Iraq were seen as having expansionist designs along Saudi Arabia's borders. Despite this, Saudi Arabia displayed a clear preference for Iraq over Iran during their conflict, extending substantial assistance totaling approximately US$25.7 billion to Iraq. This support was provided despite Saddam Hussein's pan-Arab agenda possessing the potential to undermine Saudi Arabia's credibility.[61]

Thus, the Saudi regime's method of countering such multifarious politico-religious opposition – comprising Jihadi-Salafis, Shiʿis, and socialists – was to turn, primarily, to its historical ally of the establishment of Wahhabi-Salafi scholars. The latter could be counted upon to vehemently denounce these adversaries, whether engaging in a primarily theological dispute with Shiʿism, or a broader ideological struggle against political iterations of Salafism. To them, both the Jihadi-Salafis and Shiʿis were methodologically deviant. On the other hand, dealing with the socialists merely required a repeat of the earlier campaign waged against Nasserites in the 1960s, emphasizing the allegedly 'godless' nature of their ideology. The Saudi regime also emboldened politicized Salafism fueled by the Brotherhood's influence, namely the *Ṣaḥwis*, to counter Jihadi-Salafism. This was because the *Ṣaḥwis* were more inclined to maintain the political status quo and were dedicated to pursuing peaceful dialogue with the regime rather than advocating violent revolution.

This reliance upon the establishment Salafis had, in fact, a twofold effect on Brotherhood–Salafi relations in Saudi Arabia. Any support for authentic Islamic piety would strengthen Sunni groups like the Brotherhood or Brotherhood-influenced groups like the *Ṣaḥwis*. Nonetheless, the establishment Salafis were, at the same time, emboldened to attack such politically orientated groups, by reference to perceived contraventions of a Salafi methodology. While it would take a later political event – namely the First Gulf War in 1990 – to make the establishment Salafis fully turn on the *Ṣaḥwis*, they were given more permission to directly attack the Brotherhood.

During this period, there still existed a diversity of opinions among Salafis about the Brotherhood. Some of the leading Salafi scholars openly rebuked the Brotherhood or its leaders on specific questions of doctrine, with others going so far as to declare the Brotherhood to be a deviant sect. In the latter group, one sees the likes of Ibn Bāz, Ibn al-Uthaymin, and Saleh al-Fawzan, all criticizing Qutb's knowledge of Islamic jurisprudence (*uṣūl al-fiqh*) as a basis to explain his mistakes in matters of Islamic law. In addition, Ibn Bāz considered Qutb to have made comments in his works that amounted to unlawfully disrespecting the Prophets and Companions, being severely extreme on Muslims who did not fulfill his position on correct behavior and espousing the pantheistic Sufi heresy of the Unity of Being.[62] Yet, despite this specific criticism, many of them, including Ibn Bāz, publicly cooperated with the Brotherhood and regularly invited their leaders (for example, al-Qaradawi) to conferences in the Kingdom.

During this phase therefore, one finds contradictory fatwas given by Salafi clerics regarding the Brotherhood. While the relationship was officially intact, it was clear that trouble was brewing.

One of those who gave comprehensive denunciations of the Brotherhood was Salih al-Fawzan, who, when asked, 'Do these groups (Muslim Brotherhood and other groups) enter into the seventy-two destroyed sects?' responded, 'Yes, everyone, from those who ascribe to Islam, who opposes the people of the Sunna in *da'wa* or theology or in anything from the foundations of faith, enters into the seventy-two sects.' Salih al-Luhaydan (d. 2022), another senior Saudi Wahhabi cleric, similarly asserted, 'The Brotherhood…are not from the people of sound methodologies, and all of these groups and labels (they assume) do not have any basis from the early generations of this umma.'[63] Salih Āl al-Shaykh, the grandson of the previous Mufti Muḥammad b. Ibrahīm and twice Minister of Islamic Affairs, also remarked, 'As for the group of the Muslim Brotherhood, then from the greatest manifestations of *da'wa* with them is concealment, secrecy, changing colors (i.e., changing views, opinions, allegiances, and so on), seeking closeness to whomever they believe will benefit them, and not revealing the true reality of their affair.' [64] There are many more fatwas like the aforementioned from the senior scholars of Saudi Arabia condemning the Muslim Brotherhood.

Yet, in contrast to this, one also finds fatwas were passed declaring it permissible to work alongside the Muslim Brotherhood towards common mutual goals. An example of a fatwa that speaks favorably of working alongside them is found in the compendium of verdicts by the Senior Fatwa Committee of Saudi Arabia: 'The closest Islamic groups towards the truth are the *Ahl al-Hadith* [of India], the *Ansar al-Sunna* [of Eygpt] group, and then the Muslim Brotherhood. In general, every group, these and others, are correct on some issues and mistaken on others. So, assist them in that which they are correct, and refrain from assisting them with their mistakes. Offer them advice and assist them in righteousness and piety.'[65] Another fatwa confirms this and states, 'Each of these groups (Muslim Brotherhood and other movements) are correct on some issues and mistaken on others. So, assist them in that which you recognize from the truth, offer them advice regarding the issues they are wrong about, and avoid that which makes you doubt.'[66]

It does seem that all of these fatwas were influenced by the political climate, and the government's stance towards the Brotherhood at particular points in time. Hence, during times when the Saudi regime wanted to encourage alliance, one finds fatwas of a conciliatory nature, yet during times when the regime favored a clash between the two sides, like during the high popularity of the *Ṣaḥwa*, the fatwas seem to condemn the Muslim Brotherhood as rebels and troublemakers.

This complex relationship between the Muslim Brotherhood and Salafism would persist throughout the fourth stage of their mutual history in Saudi Arabia. Such ambiguity indicated that the marriage of convenience between them was beginning to become more turbulent, and it would lead to the rupture, or divorce, in the fifth stage. So, while the major Salafi scholars had welcomed the Brotherhood into the Saudi kingdom at an earlier stage, the Brotherhood would come to be held responsible for influencing, if not creating, manifestations of political Salafism. Hence, mainstream quietist Salafi voices came to consider the Brotherhood ideology an unsettling influence on society and the political establishment.

Although it can be contended that the Brotherhood had a more influential effect on Salafism in Saudi Arabia during the period under discussion than Salafism had on it, the picture in Egypt between 1991 and 2001 appears to show the opposite, indicating a strengthening of the Salafi movement during that time. This was despite the fact that the Brotherhood's intellectual leadership – as seen in the theological writings of Muhammad al-Ghazali, al-Qaradawi, and 'Umar al-Tilmisani – did not adhere to an overt Salafi theology and, in fact, seemed closer to the Ashʿarī school.[67] Yet the social base of the Brotherhood became increasingly Salafi, which led to a change in their values and practices in accordance with popular Wahhabi-Salafi doctrine.

A number of factors led to this enhanced Salafi identity among many of the Brotherhood's grassroots members in Egypt. Firstly, the Brotherhood led a successful concerted campaign in the 1990s and early 2000s among the recently mobile rural-to-urban migrants. These individuals had left their homes in Upper and Middle Egypt, relocating to the outskirts of major cities such as Cairo, Alexandria, and various Delta cities. Their migration was a response to the declining agricultural economy in favor of secondary and tertiary economic sectors. Nonetheless, a cultural clash occurred within the Brotherhood between the new rural recruits and the urban elites. Consequently, leadership positions were recalibrated within the organization, with a notable shift towards rural and semi-urban classes. Secondly, this newly migrated semi-urban class was heavily influenced in their religious outlook by Wahhabi-Salafis, as discussed above. In this regard, one result of the First Gulf War was to undermine the internationalist vision of the Brotherhood.

This created a space to be occupied by Salafi-trained or inspired preachers, some of whom had been Brotherhood affiliated, who managed to utilize the new access to satellite television as a means of expanding their impact and call. This group included Ahmad Farid (b. 1952), who had past affiliations with the Brotherhood during his student years, and Yasir Burhami (b. 1958), whose father and uncle were former Brotherhood members detained under Nasser's regime, even though Burhami himself was not directly associated with the Brotherhood.[68] From the 1980s, the Mubarak regime gave the Salafis more freedom than other Islamic groups because they were apolitical, preaching on issues that were of no concern to the regime. In addition, their doctrine acted as a counter to the Muslim Brotherhood, which was an actual threat to the regime, due to its popularity among the population, and the skill of its educated and affluent leadership. In fact, it has been said that the quietist and authoritarian Salafi currents were positive allies of the Mubarak regime during the 1980s.[69] Indeed, very few members of the Salafi Call of Alexandria were arrested after the assassination of President Anwar Sadat in 1981, despite Mubarak's regime making general arrests of Islamic activists, regardless of whether they were involved in the assassination or not.[70] Moreover, Salafi preachers, such as Muhammad Hassan (b. 1962) of Mansoura and Muhammad Isma'il al-Muqaddam (b. 1952), were also to grow in popularity as their cassette lectures became increasingly popular in the 1980s and 1990s, and their social services network provided food and essential education to poor sections of society.[71]

Despite the Brotherhood rank and file being influenced by Salafi discourse, this period was one of mutual tension at the institutional level between the Brotherhood and the leading Salafi organization in Egypt, namely the Salafi Call, which was formally named in 1982 and established in Alexandria. During this period, the Salafi Call condemned the Brotherhood on several counts. This included accusing them of pursuing political advantage at the expense of their core principles by participating in every parliamentary election from 1984 onwards, in contrast to the Salafi Call, which was barred from political engagement. The Brotherhood was also chastised for their perceived lack of genuine commitment to the comprehensive implementation of Islamic law across society, by prioritizing politics over theology in their willingness to put forming alliances above religious principles. Furthermore, they were labeled as inadequate guardians of the Islamic message.

In response, the Brotherhood contended that the Egyptian regime allowed the Salafi Call to operate openly with relative ease, viewing them as a competitor for the Brotherhood's support base, essentially a tool of divide and rule. The Brotherhood also accused Egyptian Salafis of excessive subservience to the regime and failing to hold it accountable, which mirrored the traditional deference exhibited by Salafis toward national leadership in Egypt and Saudi Arabia, as discussed throughout this chapter.[72] It is, therefore, accurate to point out that the tensions between Salafis and the Brotherhood in Egypt during this time were slightly more acrimonious than those in the Kingdom during the same period.

Nonetheless, the Egyptian Salafis in general, and the Salafi Call in Alexandria in particular, came under general security restrictions imposed on religious preachers between 1994 and 2002, even though their message was apolitical. The state's concern was aroused as the *Ansar al-Sunna* had grown from less than 1,000 members before 1939 to around 10,000 members with a thousand mosques by the 2000s.[73] Some of the Salafi Call preachers were even arrested and beaten during this time, with their institute and magazine shut down.[74]

During this period, despite being deeply divided, Salafism in Egypt retained a distinctly Egyptian coloring, with the production of their own literature, and centers in Cairo and Alexandria.[75] The Salafi Call was not particularly tied to Saudi Arabia and was proud of its Egyptian heritage, believing that Egyptian Salafis influenced Saudi Salafis more than vice versa, and even opposing certain Saudi-Salafi legal positions (like deeming the face veil as *not* obligatory for women).[76]

Up to the mid-1970s, the Saudi influence on Egyptian Salafism was quite minimal, although they did support *Ansar al-Sunna*, but not with vast sums of money. However, as the century went on, *Ansar al-Sunna* would receive substantial financial aid from the Saudis, the Qatari Eid Charity Foundation and the Kuwaiti Association for the Revival of Islamic Heritage.[77] Furthermore, the Saudis flooded the Egyptian market with free or cheap Salafi books from the mid-to-late 1970s, and Egyptian students would have increasing links with Wahhabi scholars, after a movement emerged which provided heavily subsidized pilgrimage trips to Saudi for Egyptian students.[78] Eventually, a Saudi-influenced form of Salafism came to be attractive to Cairenes in upper and middle-class areas like al-Muhandisin and Madinat Nasr, as well as working class areas like Shubra, Faisal and Dar al-Salam/Ma'di.[79]

This move towards a Saudi-type of Salafism was also apparent in the *Ansar al-Sunna*. The first three leaders – al-Fiqi, Abd al-Razzaq Afifi (who also taught in Saudi Arabia at the behest of the country's Mufti and went on to rise to a senior bureaucratic position in the country), and 'Abd al-Rahman al-Wakil – were all Azharis. Moreover, numerous Azharis contributed to the organization and/or their publications, including the highly polemical *al-Hadi al-Nabawi* (*The Guidance of the Prophet*) (which targeted all non-Salafi groups, but with a focus on Sufi opponents). Some were not seen as strict Salafis, like Ahmad Shakir (who had a complex relationship and rivalry with al-Fiqi), and Mahmud Shaltut (*Shaykh al-Azhar* from 1958 until 1963). However, the leadership became increasingly Saudi-trained, and less Azhari, but Azhari training still persisted among their ranks in a significant way. Indeed, it is widely held that Al-Azhar became increasingly Salafi, with a number of Salafi scholars gaining official Azhari stamps of approval for their work. This relationship between the *Ansar al-Sunna* and al-Azhar continued despite the leadership of Al-Azhar under Muhammad Sayyid al-Tantawi (*Shaykh al-Azhar* from 1996 to 2010), who was not pro-Salafi, and then the overtly Sufi Ali Gomaa (Grand Mufti from 2002 to 2013).[80]

### *4.2.5 The Bitter Divorce (2001 to 2010)*

A struggling relationship can crumble in the best of circumstances. However, the terrorist attack on the United States in September 2001 put in motion a series of actions that dramatically ended the marriage of the Brotherhood and Salafism, and this is what characterizes the fifth and penultimate stage of this relationship. It also brought about a stern disavowal of the child of political Salafism by establishment Salafism. The bitterness of this divorce was exacerbated by the events of the Arab Spring in 2011, where the Egyptian part of the story was brought to the forefront.

The significance of 9/11 for Saudi Arabia emerged when it became known that fifteen of the nineteen hijackers were Saudi nationals. Although the Bush government in the United States did not directly blame Saudi Arabia, the American press certainly did, and launched an attack on Wahhabi-Salafi doctrines and activities, both educational and charitable. Even when the 9/11 Commission exonerated Saudi Arabia of blame, its reputation was still tainted. Thus, Saudi Arabia engaged in a sustained and widespread campaign, entailing media appearances and sponsorship of important seminars, especially in the United States, to rescue its global image.[81]

In response to the events of 9/11, the United States initiated its 'war on terror' and conducted military operations against Afghanistan and its Taliban government for harboring those individuals deemed responsible for the terrorist attacks. This included the Jihadi-Salafi organization Al-Qaeda and its prominent figure, Saudi national Osama bin Laden, who had allegedly orchestrated the attack. After the American onslaught had destroyed Al-Qaeda training camps and Taliban rule in Afghanistan by 2002, a number of Al-Qaeda's Arab fighters made their way back to Saudi Arabia. These operatives would replicate the Al-Qaeda of Afghanistan in the Arabian Peninsula (discussed further in Chapter 5).

Needless to say, this terrifying threat from internal forces led to a questioning of what was responsible for such mayhem which, naturally, pointed in the direction of the Saudi regime and, in particular, its cultivation of Wahhabism throughout its history. Unsurprisingly, the Saudi regime would not disavow its longest and perhaps most significant ally. Indeed, the grand narrative of Saudi Arabia was that it rested on a foundation that had Wahhabism as one of two cores, as King Fahd said in a speech announcing reforms in the aftermath of the First Gulf War: 'In modern history, the first Saudi state was established on the basis of Islam more than two and a half centuries ago, when two pious reformists – Imam Muhammad Ibn Saʿūd and Shaykh Muhammad Ibn ʿAbd al-Wahhāb, may God have mercy on their souls – agreed on that. This state was established on a clear program of politics, rule, and sociology: this program is Islam-belief and shariʿa.'[82] In fact, the speech identified the 1744 Saudi–Wahhabi pact as the moment that made the emergence of the modern Saudi state possible.[83]

Yet, the Saudi government refrained from attributing any culpability to Wahhabism in connection with the intellectual orientation of the hijackers involved. Instead, the decision was made to scapegoat the Muslim Brotherhood and insinuate that they held at least some responsibility for these acts. The primary advocate of this viewpoint within the Saudi leadership, who also publicly endorsed this theory, was Prince Nayef ibn ʿAbd al-ʿAziz (d. 2012), one of the famous 'Sudayri Seven' princes, who held the position of Minister of the Interior in the initial post-9/11 period (and subsequently briefly served as Crown Prince until his demise). In 2002, in a widely publicized interview on Saudi TV, Nayef attributed responsibility for the terrorism to the 'radical Muslim Brotherhood ideology,' alleging that it had taken undue advantage of Saudi hospitality and charity when the Saudi government had offered them refuge from Egypt in the 1960s and later from Syria in the 1980s.[84]

This perspective was, to some extent, supported by Salafi fatwas condemning the Brotherhood (as discussed above). However, as evidence emerged linking the 2003–5 wave of violence in Saudi Arabia to Saudi nationals who had drawn direct inspiration from Wahhabi scholars (the Wahhabi-Jihadi-Salafis discussed in section 3.2.6), it became clear that their inspiration was more closely aligned with the teachings of Ibn ʿAbd al-Wahhāb than with those of Sayyid Qutb. Consequently, accusations against the Muslim Brotherhood diminished, and the terrorists were categorized as contemporary Khārijīs, invoking the historical analogy of the murderous sect of early Islamic history.[85]

Meanwhile, in Egypt, a similar fallout occurred. As noted earlier, apolitical Egyptian Salafis faced imprisonment and harassment by the Egyptian regime from 1994 until 2002, just after 9/11. However, by 2004, all imprisoned Salafi leaders and activists had been released. The greater electoral freedom surrounding the 2005 Egyptian elections led to the Muslim Brotherhood candidates – who had to run as independents – securing around 20% of the parliamentary seats, making them by far the largest opposition. Consequently, the regime launched a renewed attack on the Muslim Brotherhood,[86] and as a repeat of the tactics of the 1980s, the Mubarak regime seemingly encouraged the apolitical Salafis, who were able to effectively network and preach between 2004 and 2011.

The case of the *Ansar al-Sunna* during this time was illustrative of the struggles of retaining a relatively neutral Salafism in Egypt as a result of government interference. There was the notion that Mubarak had ensured that most of the chapters of the *Ansar al-Sunna* were controlled by 'Madkhalis' (i.e., those who repudiated any criticism of the rulers, even mildly, and were of the utmost loyalist nature, as discussed in section 3.2.5). The naming of such loyalists as 'Madkhalis' had become a norm by this stage, even if such figures did not have a direct link to Rabiʿ al-Madkhalī in Saudi Arabia; rather, it was a name to simply indicate a state of mind and methodology. In addition, there were indications that certain leaders in *Ansar al-Sunna* received extra assistance from the government on the basis of increasing their rebuttal of the Muslim Brotherhood and Salafis critical of the regime. Indeed, Muhammad ʿAbd al-Maqsud (b. 1947) claimed in an interview in *al-Ahram* that this Egyptian governmental support was true, and that it also included finances from Saudi Arabia. Hence it was not surprising to see the 2009 publication of *al-Hakimiyya wa'l-siyasa al-sharʿiyya* (*God's Rule and Political Rule*) by ʿAdl Sayyid, vice-president of the ʿAbdin *Ansar al-Sunna* chapter, in which he argued that *Ansar al-Sunna* had 'modern-day Khawarij' in its ranks who would bring about its own destruction with their disobedience to the rulers – all standard Madkhali tropes, even though Madkhali is not actually quoted in the text itself. However, in an indication of how the *Ansar al-Sunna* were disunited on presenting a subservient loyalist stance to the current rulers, the book was shunned by leading members such as Gamal Saʿd (editor of Ansar al-Sunna's publication *al-Tawḥīd*),

'Abdullah Shakir (who was the current leader at the time), and al Marakbi (the previous leader).[87]

Yet, in 2006, the government laid strong foundations for the strengthening of Salafi proselytizing, when a number of Salafi satellite channels were granted licenses by the government to preach. Consequently, NileSat, the satellite provider in Egypt, started broadcasting twelve Salafi channels by 2009.[88] These channels not only influenced Egyptians, but also others in the region, including Tunisians. The first station to attain popularity as a Salafi channel was *Al-Nas* (The People), which was not Salafi originally, but soon became so in a bid to attract more viewers. In order to accomplish the latter goal, it invited Salafi preachers to present, such as Muhammad Hassan, Abu Ishaq al-Huwayni (b. 1956),[89] and Muhammad Husayn Yaʿqub (b. 1956), demonstrating the attractiveness of Salafism to an Egyptian audience. Nonetheless, the three aforementioned Salafi clerics soon left in 2006, when the station would not remove the Sufi preacher Ahmed Abduh Awid, or the popular religious televangelist Amr Khalid. Al-Nas retained a more open policy across different groups, eventually becoming aligned with the neo-traditionalist Sufi movement and the state by 2020.[90]

*Al-Rahma* (Mercy), started in 2007 by Muhammad Hassan after he left Al-Nas, would become an influential Salafi satellite channel. The channel was wholly Salafi in its output, with financial backing from a wealthy Saudi national.[91] Hassan had studied at Al-Azhar and Cairo University, before studying in Saudi Arabia, most notably with Ibn 'Uthaymin. He was perhaps the most popular Salafi preacher as a result of his work. The programs on these stations concentrated on beliefs and ethics, and stayed away from politics,[92] although the channel would also invite the Kuwaiti Salafi activist Nabil al-'Awadhi to present.[93] Salafis would again fall foul of the authorities in 2009 when certain Salafi preachers rejoined public religious gatherings upon security arrests subsiding. The regime started to crack down on the apolitical Salafis, including a suspension of their satellite channels in 2010, but their tactics were interrupted by the uprising of 25 January 2011.

#### *4.2.6 The Post-Divorce Hostility (2011 to the Present)*

Although the relations between the Brotherhood and the Salafis were fraught with disputes until 2010, the Arab Spring of 2011 would have momentous consequences for the relationship between the two movements, especially in Egypt and Saudi Arabia. While there were some initial patterns of cooperation, the eventual settling of the tumultuous Arab Spring would lead to unprecedented acrimony between the Brotherhood and the generality of Salafis, especially Salafi leaders, with the latter, and others (like leading 'neo-traditionalist Sufis') being seemingly driven by governmental forces. In this context, Usaama al-Azami has characterized Saudi Arabia and the UAE as 'counter-revolutionary, anti-democratic, and anti-Islamist,' with Egypt as a 'junior partner' to Saudi Arabia and the UAE, while Qatar was deemed to be 'pro-revolutionary and pro-Islamist.'[94]

Behind these far-reaching political events with their geopolitical factors were important contestations about Islamic theology, with the Brotherhood and loyalist Salafis defined within competing sub-traditions. In terms of personalities, this conflict was epitomized in the persons of Yusuf al-Qaradawi (d. 2022) and Ali Gomaa (or al-Jumʿa, b. 1952), the latter being an establishment Sufi who was Egypt's Grand Mufti for a decade until February 2013, and the former the Brotherhood's spiritual leader. The Brotherhood was identified with Qaradawi, and the loyalist Salafis with Gomaa (in practice, but not in theory or declared allegiance).[95] Mohammad Fadel has argued that Qaradawi represents a *republican* sub-tradition going back to reformers from the nineteenth century onwards such as Rashīd Riḍā, who argued for pluralism and Islamic values in the political sphere, whereby the general public could have independent political agency. Whereas Gomaa represents a *traditionalist* sub-tradition, going back to medieval scholarly norms which, aside from its theories of hierarchy and supporting those who held power, simply manifested as a general societal acquiescence with authoritarian regimes, with a view to religious scholars simply trying to *influence* such rulers without *contesting legitimacy*.[96] However, David H. Warren added that Gomaa's siding with the authoritarian state could also be seen more in terms of a 'proto-nationalist twist' to the classical understanding of such relations, derived from the reformist Rifaʿa al-Tahtawi (d. 1873), and attitudes derived as a consequence of the emergence of the nation-state and what it entails.[97]

The revolution came at a time when the Egyptian middle class had shrunk from being 45% of the population in 1991 to 20% in 2010, as economic inequality began to be deeply felt by much of the country. President Mubarak's neoliberal economic reforms had stretched the gap between the rich and the poor, and social services and transport provision were eroded in similar measure. Unemployment rose from 5.2% in 1980 to 13.2% in 2011, with the youth comprising 90% of that total, despite being 60% of the population; 20% of the population lived in poverty.[98]

When the demonstrations that led to the 2011 revolution began, the Salafis maintained their historic stance of supporting the ruler. Hence the Salafi Call of Alexandria and the popular Salafi cleric Muhammad Hassan were unsupportive of the activism, as they publicly condemned the demonstrations from a national-strategic and Islamic perspective. This fitted in with the apolitical Salafis' suspiciousness of such protests as being unlawful rebellion against the ruler (*khurūj*), as explicitly stated by Saudi Salafi clerics at the time.[99] Moreover, the Salafi Call, before the revolution, had a negative view of the trappings of liberal democracy, including human rights and political pluralism.

However, when the protests gained momentum, many quietist Salafis, including Muhammad Hassan, came out in support of the protestors. This change of attitude was perhaps most apparent in the character of Yasir Burhami, the leading member of the Salafi Call. After initially calling for the protestors to stop demonstrating, he then spoke of their heroism and called for Salafis to engage in the political process. He explained this radical about-turn as overcoming his fear of Mubarak and his regime.[100]

Then the Salafi Call made a decisive break from their historic apolitical-loyalist Salafis and set about forming a political party to contest the upcoming parliamentary elections – after itself becoming officially recognized in Alexandria by the state, under national social association laws, in April 2011. This was a revision of their previous stance on political parties being corrupt and tainted. Yet it reflected the recognition of the new potential for driving the country towards a more Islamic path, as well as a historic distrust of the Muslim Brotherhood by the Salafi Call, who emerged in the 1980s in Alexandria in passionate opposition to the Brotherhood.

From within the Salafi Call emerged the Nour Party (*Ḥizb al-Nūr*) in June 2011, under the leadership of the main architect Emad Abdel Ghaffour (b. 1960), who was a founding member of the Salafi Call (although he would later leave). This political party was deemed to be separate to the religious side of the movement, which was to continue concentrating on teaching and propagation, under the effective leadership of Yasir Burhami (although he was not the official leader).[101] While there did emerge other Salafi political actors, none of them replicated Nour's ascent, with its membership soon reaching 220,000. During the summer of 2011, the Salafi groups struggled to remain together, and eventually separated. There were tensions between Abdel Ghaffour and Burhami from the beginning, due to differences in their approach to politics and how they conceived of the relationship between the political party and the religious entity. Abdel Ghaffour saw the two as related but he perceived of the Nour Party as being a distinct, independent political entity, which was to benefit Salafism; but Burhami saw the party as being subservient to the Salafi Call and its theological agenda, and not as a mere political party.[102]

The period after the fall of Hosni Mubarak, one of Egypt's longest-serving presidents, can be divided into three distinct phases in the relationship between the Brotherhood and the Salafi Call – the most prominent Salafi force at the time – who were represented by their political party, the Nour Party. The first of these three phases, spanning from February 2011 to December 2012, began with Mubarak's resignation. Alaa Al-Din Arafat characterized this phase as one marked 'by mistrust but also circumspect cooperation,' although he noted that in the first few months following Mubarak's departure 'there was a genuine thawing of relations between the two groups.'[103] The reason for this cooperation was obvious: Salafis and the Brotherhood understood that in a democracy, numbers mattered, and that they would both benefit each other by forming strategic alliances and cross-endorsements against liberal and secular parties and candidates.

Hence, mainstream Salafi leaders in Egypt started to make statements about the Brotherhood that were uncharacteristic endorsements. For example, the quietist Salafi preacher Mohamed Hassan spoke of the Brotherhood as 'those who most deserve and are the most competent to enter parliament,' and Yasir Burhami argued that Salafis should support Brotherhood candidates in the parliamentary elections. This was reciprocated by the Brotherhood, who indicated that they would work with the Salafis in order to achieve their common political objectives, as they both had widespread support through the country, so a united movement could be a major force in securing electoral support against the non-religious parties.[104]

Further support for this emerging political Salafism came from the quietist *Ansar al-Sunna* when their leader, Abdullah Shakir, said regarding political participation, 'There is no wrongdoing in this. [...] There is no objection to whoever wishes to be nominated for the People's Assembly. This is work within the state and even if it is as a leader, there is no wrongdoing in this if they accept him.'[105] Yet, Nour received criticism, unsurprisingly, from non-Egyptian quietists, such as the Saudi scholars Rabi' al-Madkhalī and Salih al-Fawzan,[106] and the Jordanian al-Halabi (see section 4.3.2). These hardline apolitical and pro-government Salafis stayed aloof from political activism, which accorded with their pre-2011 stance.[107]

At this point, the traditional typology of Egyptian Salafis became frayed. Traditionally, a clear distinction between *quietist/apolitical* and *activist* Salafis could be made, with both groups being further divided. In the apolitical group, one could previously include: firstly, the traditional quietists with a certain loose organizational structure, such as *Ansar al-Sunna* and the Salafi Call; secondly, the popular preachers who maintained an essential independence and focus on teaching, such as Abu Ishaq al-Huwayni, Muhammad Husayn Yaq'ub, Muhammad Hassan (although the latter two have *Ansar al-Sunna* links), and Mustafa al-Adawi; and thirdly, the Jami-Madkhali faction with their cult-like focus on their small, and ever-shrinking, group of leaders, who rejected the Salafi authenticity of the apolitical Salafi groups in Egypt, with the vocal support of existing rulers; they included Muhammad Sa'id Raslan, Hisham al-Beyali, Mahmud 'Amr and Usama al-Qusi.[108] The activist Salafis could traditionally be identified with the Muslim Brotherhood or Jihadi-Salafi groups, or even those associated with the more politically-orientated Salafis of Kuwait. Yet, for the Madkhalis, any divergence from their political stance of absolute loyalty to the rulers could get a Salafi labeled as a 'Qutbi' (i.e., a follower of

Sayyid Qutb) even if such a Salafi seemed quietist, which is the case with Huwayni and Muhammad Hassan, who were deemed by Madkhalī-types to be slightly Quṭbī; but then the Salafi Call were also deemed to be 'Qutbi' by the Madkhalis.[109] However, the emergence of a political party from the Salafi Call, with support from the hierarchy of *Ansar al-Sunna*, as well as Hassan's support for demonstrators, blurred such a demarcation between *quietist* and *activist* at this time. Nonetheless, the Madkhalis remained aloof from politics, as they would throughout.

Furthermore, there was a number of what could be termed 'Cairene Salafis' who did not form political parties, due to pragmatic reasons or fear, but they belonged to a Cairene Salafi tradition of being quite pro-Brotherhood since the time of Nasser. These included, for example, Muhammad 'Abd al-Maqsud,[110] Sayyid Abd al-Azim, Muhammad Yusri, and Fawzi al-Sa'id, in addition to the overtly independent political stance of the Ṣaḥwa-types, such as Hazim Abu Ismail. The 'activist Salafism' (*al-salafiyya al-harakiyya*) of people like Muhammad 'Abd al-Maqsud and Fawzi al-Sa'id has even been called 'the Shubra Salafi School,' in reference to their suburb of Cairo. Although they did not form political parties, they were highly political, condemning governments not applying Islamic law as falling into disbelief (*kufr*), and actively campaigning and raising funds for Palestine, without calling for revolution. Moreover, Muhammad 'Abd al-Maqsud did involve himself in the emerging political Salafi scene, such as the newly formed Salafi political party *Ḥizb al-Faḍīla* (*The Party of Virtue*), which was established by his elder brother 'Adl 'Abd al-Maqsud. When that party seemed to veer too close to the jihadi side, Muhammad 'Abd al-Maqsud was then reported to have moved to work with another political entity called *Ḥizb al-Asala* (The Authenticity Party) – incidentally, Muhammad Hassan was also said to have gone to *al-Fadila* and then *al-Asala*.[111]

When the Brotherhood and the Nour Party jointly led the campaign to vote 'Yes' in the March 2011 referendum to amend the constitution, this marked the first occasion in which they had united, and the result was a substantial 77% majority in favor of the proposed amendments (with more than 14 million votes, compared to around 4 million against).[112] However, tensions between the Brotherhood and the Salafis emerged before the elections at the end of 2011. These revolved around the specifics of constitutional amendments, their Islamic wording, and the use of Islamic slogans during demonstrations. During this time, the Brotherhood wanted to proceed cautiously so as not to alarm the public of any Islamic takeover. In the media, numerous Brotherhood spokespeople stated that the revolution was not Islamic but Egyptian, and was supported by Egyptians across the religious spectrum.[113]

Meanwhile, the Salafi influence gained momentum, prompting the Brotherhood to maintain a delicate balance. Rejecting the Salafis risked accusations of transgressing Islamic principles, while full support could undermine their already fragile relationship with secular parties and their commitment to the democratic process. Yet the Brotherhood, through its political party *Ḥizb al-Ḥurriyyah wa-l-ʿAdālah* (Freedom and Justice Party or FJP), was able to put together a Democratic Alliance in June 2011, which included secular parties and Salafis. This quickly disintegrated by October 2011, and the Nour Party left the group. Then three Salafi parties, led by the Nour Party, ran a coalition called the Islamic Alliance.[114]

The elections for the People's Assembly, conducted from November 2011 to January 2012, yielded a resounding victory for both the Muslim Brotherhood's FJP, which secured 47.3% of the vote, and the Salafi Call's Nour Party, with 24.3% of the vote. Together, these results accounted for two-thirds of the seats in the assembly.[115] This translated to the Brotherhood-dominated Democratic Alliance receiving over a third of the total, with over 10 million votes, and the Islamic Alliance securing the second position with over 7 million votes. Consequently, the FJP claimed the majority of seats in the parliament, with 216 seats, equivalent to 43.4%, while the Islamic Alliance followed closely with 125 seats, representing around 25%.[116] Indeed, the Brotherhood and the Salafis had cooperated in some districts against secularists.[117] Such pragmatism is what defined the leadership of the Nour Party under Abdel Ghaffour, as he refrained from using the 'Salafi' label as it was a 'party for all Egyptians,' while calling for a gradual path towards a full implementation of Islamic law, yet avoiding discussions regarding theology. Abdel Ghaffour came under attack from Burhami for entertaining the idea of cooperation with non-Islamist political parties.[118]

On 24 June 2012, the Brotherhood's Mohamed Morsi (d. 2019) was elected President of Egypt with 13.2 million votes or around 52% of the vote.[119] This was after the Nour Party, with support from the Salafi Call, did not field a presidential candidate, but supported the more progressive Islamist candidate, Abdel Moneim Aboul Fotouh, who had recently left the Brotherhood. Yet this Salafi unity masked contrary agendas: Abdel Ghaffour saw Aboul Fotouh as a mainstream Islamist who could further their own political agenda and thwart the return of the security state, whereas the Burhami group simply wanted to oppose the Brotherhood's candidate, as they feared that the political triumph of the latter would lead to their theological dominance.[120] This caused animosity between the Brotherhood and the Nour Party, although rank-and-file Salafis were not impressed with the liberal Aboul Fotouh. Many either abstained from voting or even cast their votes for Morsi.[121] Yet, in the final run-off for the presidency between the Muslim Brotherhood's Mohamed Morsi and the old regime's Ahmed Shafiq (Mubarak's last prime minister), Nour supported Morsi.[122]

The FJP quickly secured the most significant leadership roles in the parliamentary assembly, including Speaker of the House, and assumed leadership of twelve of the nineteen parliamentary committees. These committees included vital areas such as Foreign Affairs, Defense and National Security, Budget and Planning, and Religious Affairs. Deputies from the Nour Party got the leadership of a further three parliamentary committees, resulting in the Brotherhood and the Salafis controlling fifteen out of the nineteen committees, equivalent to nearly 80% of the total. Moreover, the FJP and Nour led the selection of the one-hundred-member Constituent Assembly, which was to rewrite the constitution. However, the dominance of members backed by the two Islamic blocs, which numbered sixty-three out of the hundred, led to major administrative problems, with numerous boycotts by other members. On 12 June 2011, a new Constituent Assembly was elected. It included twenty Brotherhood members and ten Nour members, which helped bolster the Islamic bloc to fifty-seven, giving them a slight majority.[123]

During the 2011–12 parliamentary elections, the Salafi Call had accused the Brotherhood of colluding with the military in an attempt to repress them.[124] Furthermore, the Brotherhood quickly encountered constitutional and political crises in the spring and summer of 2012. Notably, the Egyptian Salafis had historically been cautious of the Brotherhood and had agreed with the military to safeguard their interests.[125] Then, in December 2012, the new constitution was approved through a referendum. This development highlighted how the Salafis had managed to get the Brotherhood to capitulate to several key demands. This conciliation stemmed from the Brotherhood's concerns that the Salafi opposition could imperil the success of the 'Yes' vote. As part of this compromise, Morsi appointed three Nour Party members as his advisors.[126]

Yet, while the Nour Party almost immediately turned on the Brotherhood over the new constitution, the second phase in their relationship was only truly entered at the end of December 2012. This was when Abd al-Ghaffour was forced to resign the leadership of the Nour Party, with control being grasped by Burhami, as his close ally Younes Makhioun (b. 1955) was elected as leader – denoting a switch for the party from the *political* to the *clerical*. This change in leadership direction marked a turning away from the path of an Islamist party to taking a 'a purely instrumental approach to politics,' whereby the goal of bringing about an Islamic state was replaced with simply trying to protect and further the freedom of the Salafi movement in narrow social terms. Hence one understands the future approach of the clerical-led Nour Party in siding with opponents of Islamism, as it truly became a political extension of the Salafi Call.[127] During this time, the Nour

Party forged an alliance with the National Salvation Front (NSF), a coalition comprising various elements such as 'young secular liberal and revolutionary forces, Mubarak loyalist opposition parties like the New Wafd Party, the dissolved NDP, and *feloul* [Mubarak-era holdovers and Mubarak regime loyalists],'[128] in addition to receiving support from security and military quarters. Part of the agenda of this coalition was to call for early presidential elections.[129]

Unsurprisingly, this led to a third phase in Brotherhood–Salafi relations defined by Arafat as one of 'open enmity' based on seven factors. Firstly, Salafis harbored resentment towards the Brotherhood. Secondly, despite the Salafi Call openly expressing its desire to join the new government, the Brotherhood excluded them, instead awarding seven ministries and the vice presidency to its own members. Thirdly, the Salafis were deeply outraged by Morsi's overtures to the Iranians, whom they despised for their Shīʿism, a sentiment rooted in modern Salafism influenced by the Wahhabi movement's stance. Fourthly, Younes Makhioun was elected the Nour Party chairperson in January 2013, and he declared that the alliance with the Brotherhood did 'more harm than good.'[130] Fifthly, in mid-February 2013, the Salafi Call released a scathing report criticizing what they saw as a Brotherhood takeover of the state and the provision of 13,000 state jobs to Brotherhood members. Sixthly, the Salafi Call were angry when Morsi dismissed their long-standing member Khalid ʿAlim al-Din as an advisor. And seventhly, the Salafi Call formed an alliance with secularists through the NSF, viewing it as the 'lesser of two evils.' They feared that the Brotherhood would dominate the country and eradicate the Salafi Call, so it was better, in their view, to join with 'infidels.' Wagdy Ghoneim (b. 1951) of the Brotherhood responded with a fatwa prohibiting people from voting for a party that aligned itself with secularists, which is somewhat strange considering the Brotherhood's historical cooperation with secularists within the post-Arab Spring political scene in Egypt.[131] However, while Morsi's relations with Nour had become strained, he had retained a separate relationship with more independent Salafis, like Muhammad ʿAbd al-Maqsud and Muhammad Hassan, who were both invited to the 'Support for Syria Conference' in 2013 and spoke at the event arranged by Morsi's government. Nour representatives were not invited.[132]

During the power struggle that occurred between the Morsi government and the apparatus of the state, especially the military, from June 2012 until 3 July 2013 when the army junta removed Morsi from power, there was widespread unrest in the country. This was especially so after Morsi's Constitutional Declaration on 22 November 2012, in which he declared the protection of presidential decrees and the bodies drafting the new constitution. The consequence of such an attempted show of force was that opposition groups to the Brotherhood became unified, leading to civilian protests from December 2012. Moreover, the perception of Brotherhood aggression in suppressing such protests led Morsi's relationship with his newly appointed Defense Minister, General Abdel Fattah al-Sisi (b. 1954), to deteriorate, as the latter voiced the military's unease with the civil unrest.

By April or May 2013, the Morsi regime was widely unpopular, and the military had gained widespread endorsement. On 17 June 2013, Morsi responded to his weakened political position by appointing a number of new governors, mainly from the Brotherhood, which only worsened the unrest. The protests of 30 June 2013 drew millions of people on to the streets, opposing the Morsi government. Afterwards, Morsi sought official support from the political Salafis, as well as from the military, the Interior Ministry, al-Azhar University, and the Coptic Church; but none would support him and his Brotherhood regime. The Salafis were divided: the leadership supported the demonstrations to remove Morsi, but the regular members supported him retaining power. Both the Nour Party and the Salafi Call made it known to the Americans and the Egyptian military that they were a viable alternative to the Brotherhood.[133]

On 3 July 2013, General Sisi removed Morsi as president, arrested him and suspended the constitution. His coup d'état immediately attracted billions of dollars from countries such as Saudi Arabia and the UAE. The Secretary General of the Nour Party, Galal Murra, was seated alongside a select group of others as General Sisi made the announcement of the regime change.[134] Even though the Nour Party opposed the dissolution of the Shura Council on 5 July 2013, and the secularist ElBaradei (b. 1942) assuming the position of vice president, they would soon make public declarations of support for the military and Sisi if he was to run for president.[135] In the end, the Nour Party was the sole Islamic party to endorse the military coup and consequently took measures to prohibit its members from participating in public protests against it, although not all followed this instruction. An internal opinion poll revealed that 60% of party members opposed the ousting of Morsi and disagreed with the party's position on the matter. As a result, many Salafis redirected their focus away from the Salafi Call's political involvement, instead choosing to concentrate on religious preaching activities.[136]

Thereafter, the Salafi leadership supported the military's violent suppression of pro-Morsi demonstrations in July and August 2013, in which the army killed around 1,150 demonstrators across five sites. The worst atrocities occurred at Rabaa Square, where Human Rights Watch estimated that 817 protestors were killed by the security forces (while many present claimed the number was exponentially higher), although only a small number of the protestors were reported to be armed.[137] While Salafi leaders supported the military in taking down pro-Morsi marches and denied the Human Rights Watch report and any foreign interference, they did not actively encourage violence on the part of state with the sort of inflammatory language used by some clerics. Ali Gomaa on the other hand not only called protestors *khawarij* (a typical Salafi slight for modern activists) in lectures to the army, but also called them the 'Dogs of Hell' (*kilab al-nar*), quoting a hadith that is seen as advising people on how to deal with the *khawarij* when they cause disunity.[138] This was viewed as giving the army encouragement to murder protestors.[139] Yet, such support for the regime in these dire circumstances was not universal. For instance, Emad Abdel Ghaffour and other leading Salafis addressed the Rabaa protest; and the popular Salafi preachers Muhammad Hassan and Muhammad ʿAbd al-Maqsud directly criticized Sisi's regime for killing the unarmed protestors. However, as the violence increased, Hassan chose to go mute on the matter,[140] and later came to criticize the Muslim Brotherhood and even Muhammad ʿAbd al-Maqsud.[141]

Although the Salafi Call had taken the Brotherhood as their main religious opposition, they were to lose the religious domain to the revitalized al-Azhar which, after decades of losing credibility in the public mind because of being pro-Mubarak, became the favored religious institution of the military. Through the Ministry of Religious Affairs, dominated by non-Salafi Azharis, it became necessary for imams to be Azhari graduates, or sit an exam to obtain a license (*tarkhis*), and Friday sermons had to be obtained from the Ministry rather than given individually. All of these rulings hit the Salafis negatively, as they were often outside the Azhari system, although the government did not strictly enforce these rules.[142]

In the midst of this, there was also individual Salafi members' condemnations of the actions of the Salafi Call and the Nour Party, and not just from the expected apolitical quarters, but also from within their own ranks and political Salafis. For instance, two leading members of the administrative council of the Salafi Call, Saʿid Abd al-Azim (a founding member) and Mohammed Ismail al-Muqaddam (their leading scholarly figure), were to oppose the developments. Abd al-Azim had supported Morsi and left the country by December 2013, and al-Muqaddam simply fell from the public eye; neither is listed as a member of the administrative council. However, the most vehement condemnation came from the Islamic University of Medina trained, Egyptian-Kuwaiti Abd al-Rahman Abd al-Khaliq (d. 2020). The latter had a major impact on the Salafi Call in the 1980s, but wrote to Burhami, 'You were one of Satan's soldiers, but you have advanced in evil, and you are now his teacher.'[143]

Despite their overt show of loyalty to the army junta, the Nour Party Salafis were immediately sidelined by the military: they were excluded from the transitional government and given only one seat from the fifty in the constitutional assembly that was convened in the summer of 2013.

Despite some calls from secularists to have them banned as the new constitution prohibited 'religious parties,' the military regime allowed them to maintain their legality, but let them know how restricted their activities were going to be.[144]

The culmination of these factors was observable in the Nour Party's poor performance in the 2015 elections. Despite being the sole Islamic party permitted to participate, the Nour Party secured only 12 of 596 seats (a mere 2% of the total), in stark contrast to their 2011 performance when they won 128 seats (equivalent to 26% of the total). Furthermore, the continued harassment of some of its members by the regime due to their religious beliefs underscored the challenges they faced. However, perhaps the most glaring sign of their extended political pragmatism was seen in the fact that they fielded non-Muslim candidates, as required by the electoral law, for this had been one of Burhami's attacks upon Abdel Ghaffour, during the latter's reign.[145]

The Salafi Call ultimately suffered for its seemingly inexplicable political opportunism, particularly their outreach to the military and the United States as an alternative to the Brotherhood. In the eyes of religiously inclined Egyptians and others, these actions compromised their religious integrity, and they are unlikely to reap future benefits with the support of liberal or secularist factions, or even from the former Brotherhood constituency, which has been effectively marginalized in Egypt's new political landscape. Hence one fails to see how the Salafi Call and the Nour Party benefitted from their calculated adherence to a 'paradox of the party's extreme political pragmatism and its rigidity and sectarianism at the doctrinal level,' although it appears that there is still some longevity in this approach.[146] Perhaps the sustainability is due to the usual pattern of autocratic regimes seeing a benefit in allowing, and even clandestinely supporting, apolitical Salafism to maintain a healthy presence in the public sphere to counteract more serious challenges to authority from committed Islamists or even political Salafis.

In addition, one observes the widespread pressure placed on Madkhalis and non-revolutionary Salafis, despite such loyalty to the state and their making major political concessions. The restrictions on having to adhere to state-sanctioned Friday sermons were monitored sufficiently by the authorities so that even Madkhalis could fall foul of not abiding by them fully. For example, the Madkhali preacher Muhammad Raslan (b. 1955) was banned from preaching in 2018 when he slightly diverted from a scripted Friday sermon, despite the fact that he was known for praising Sisi,[147] and – shockingly – justifying the murder of Muslim Brothers.[148] Perhaps the most striking example of the pressure faced by relatively apolitical Salafis was seen in 2021 during the so-called 'ISIS Imbala cell' case. This was a prosecution in which twelve men stood accused of being Jihadi-Salafis linked to terrorist attacks and ISIS. But the defendants claimed to have been taught by famous apolitical Salafi preachers Muhammad Husayn Ya'qub and Muhammad Hassan. Not only did Ya'qub's court testimony in June 2021 dismiss the accused and their doctrine, but he inexplicably claimed 'I do not know anything about Salafism,' for 'I am Hanbali.'[149] If leading apolitical Salafis feel such pressure to publicly disavow the movement, then one can safely conclude that the future of Salafism in Egypt is shrouded in mystery, although its historic usefulness for autocratic authorities is highly unlikely to make it obsolete.

While the Salafi Call and the Nour Party were often seen as being Saudi backed, this does not appear to be the case, in large part because the Saudi regime preferred to support the army and the remaining apparatus of the Mubarak state.[150] Nonetheless, the Nour Party seems to see no alternative way out of its predicament, and maintained their full allegiance to the military rule of Sisi by endorsing his candidacy for the 2023 presidential elections, which he won with an 89.6% share of the vote. This was of course marred with accusations of repressing dissent by the military regime.[151]

The consequence of the Arab Spring in Saudi Arabia was that certain factions with ties to the Muslim Brotherhood advocated for political reforms, which led to a hardening of the Kingdom's stance against them. In 2017, this intensification in opposition to the Brotherhood was heightened when the latest Crown Prince, Muhammad b. Salman publicized his vision to take Saudi Arabia in a modern, liberal direction, described as 'a return to moderation.'[152] In his briefings to domestic and foreign journalists, he argued that the Brotherhood was responsible for weakening ties between Egypt and Saudi, stating that they had assassinated his uncle King Faisal, and were behind the Jihadi-Salafism of Bin Laden and Abu Bakr al-Baghdadi (d. 2019) of ISIS. The Brotherhood responded to these accusations, dismissing them as lies intended to earn the favor of American Zionism.[153]

By 2020, the Muslim Brotherhood had been declared a terrorist organization by Saudi Arabia, with a number of the country's regional allies, including the United Arab Emirates (UAE), Bahrain, and Egypt, following suit. The UAE's Crown Prince, Mohammed b. Zayed (referred to as MBZ), is a particularly passionate advocate of portraying the Brotherhood as being the most evil force in the Middle East. In fact, Qatar's support for the Muslim Brotherhood led to a temporary severance of diplomatic ties by the Saudis in 2017. These ties however, were mended by 2020, signifying the conclusion of the blockade that had earlier been initiated in collaboration with Egypt, UAE, and Bahrain on 5 June 2017. Then, in November 2020, the current Grand Mufti of Saudi Arabia, 'Abd al-'Aziz Āl al-Shaykh, declared that the Brotherhood was a 'deviant group' that 'had no links to Islam whatsoever.'[154] Similarly, the Council of Senior Religious Scholars (*Hay'at Kibār al-'Ulamā'*), the highest religious body in Saudi Arabia, issued a warning against affiliating or sympathizing with the Muslim Brotherhood – a message that was disseminated throughout the region during Friday sermons delivered in mosques, including, infamously, one by the imam of the Grand Mosque in Mecca, Abd al-Raḥman al-Sudais, when he atypically mentioned the Brotherhood by name and called them a terrorist organization.[155] Indeed, the Saudi government had previously attempted, in 2014, albeit without success, to persuade the United States and the United Kingdom to declare the Muslim Brotherhood a terrorist organization, and had campaigned unsuccessfully to ban charities and Muslim civil rights organizations linked to it to be shut down.

Interestingly, the Saudi-led campaign for liberalization not only targeted the Muslim Brotherhood, but also resulted in the marginalization of Salafis. The quietist Salafis were instructed to adopt a more moderate tone, to avoid causing disruption, and even publicly express views that contradicted their previously held positions. This process eroded the influence of establishment Saudi-Salafi scholars among the public. Naturally, the shift in stance led to a loss of prestige in the eyes of some of their followers. However, this mutual rejection did not bring the Brotherhood and the Salafis closer together, as each group perhaps hoped to exploit the other's unpopularity with the regime to their own advantage. If this was the case, then neither the Brotherhood-influenced factions nor the establishment Salafis were to attain success.

## *4.3 Salafism and the Muslim Brotherhood in Other Middle Eastern Countries*

While Egypt and Saudi Arabia represent the focal points in the narrative of the interplay between Salafism and the Muslim Brotherhood, noteworthy interactions have also transpired in various Middle Eastern nations and in Western lands. For the purposes of this work, we will summarize three notable areas: Syria, Jordan, and Kuwait.[156]

### *4.3.1 Syria*

The Syrian Muslim Brotherhood (SMB) was founded around the mid-1940s and immediately charted its own course, separate from its Egyptian counterpart. The SMB was heavily involved in the political process of Syria, standing for elections from the 1940s, and even had members successfully enter parliament.

Early in its history, the SMB experienced internal divisions that can be aptly categorized as a schism between Ashʿarī-Sufi and Salafi factions, with the latter encompassing both reformist and traditional Salafis. This division manifested itself prominently in the distinction between the Aleppo and Damascus branches. The Damascene branch was led by Mustafa al-Sibaʿi (d. 1964), Issam al-Attar (d. 2024), and Zuhayr al-Shawish (d. 2013). Al-Sibaʿi and al-Attar were not only leaders of the SMB but also members of the Syrian parliament. Al-Attar and al-Shawish were both traditional Salafis, however the branch also had leading members who were Sufis, such as Mohammed Hawari and Hassan al-Houeidi (d. 2009). The Aleppo wing was led by ʿAbd al-Fattāḥ Abū Ghudda (d. 1997) – who served as the superintendent of the SMB on three separate occasions in 1955, 1973, and 1986 – and Saʿid Hawwa (d. 1989), who were both traditionalist Sufis in their outlook.[157] In fact, both of these figures also had some acrimonious refutations against Salafis.

A Sufi-Salafi rapprochement was attempted in the Syrian city of Hama by the SMB leader Muhammad al-Hamid (d. 1969), also a leader of the Naqshbandi Sufi order. Al-Hamid was a class fellow of al-Sibaʿi at Al-Azhar University in Cairo, and it was during this period he met and became deeply influenced by al-Bannā. These experiences had led al-Hamid to establish the Hama branch of the SMB upon his return to Syria. Despite his formal departure from the SMB in the early 1950s, al-Hamid continued to serve as a source of inspiration and an informal guide to its members. Saʿid Hawwa – who would go on to assume leadership of the Aleppo branch – held his teacher al-Hamid in the highest regard. He emphasized how al-Hamid served as a shining example of how individuals from diverse backgrounds, including Sufis, Salafis, and members of the Brotherhood, could collaborate harmoniously, transcending their religious differences:

> [Al-Hamid] molded his town Hamah in such a way that he made it capable of every good. From here there emerged in Hamah a generation that is an example of how the people all over the Muslim world should be... [H]e educated his brothers to adhere to the Scriptures, to respect the religious scholars and the jurists, and to follow the Sufis while adhering to the Scriptures and to the precepts of the Law. He educated his brothers to love Ḥasan al-Bannā, to love the Muslim Brothers, and to love all the Muslims... He believed that in order to stop the apostasy (*ridda*) the Muslims must join hands despite their many controversies. And although he was a Hanafī Sufi, he had always declared his readiness to put his hand in the hand of the fiercest Salafi to stop this apostasy. His chief preoccupations were *dhikr* [spiritual invocation], *ʿilm* [knowledge], and counsel.[158]

Nevertheless, the period of al-Attar's leadership within the SMB, spanning 1957 to 1969, was characterized by an overarching Salafi influence.

This resulted in a division between the SMB factions located in Hama, Aleppo, Latakia, and other cities. However, it's important to acknowledge that several other factors also contributed to the schism between these groups that came to be settled in 1972. One pivotal point of contention concerned the use of violence against the state. Notably, figures like Hawwa and others within the SMB advocated for more militant methods, while the Damascene leadership under al-Attar's guidance remained committed to principles of democracy and non-violence – a stance supported by al-Hamid.[159] Abu Ghudda, a leading scholar of the twentieth century, engaged in impassioned scholarly debates, primarily on matters of religion rather than politics. Particularly notable were his interactions with Salafi scholars like al-Albānī, during his tenure as a university lecturer in Saudi Arabia, a position he held from 1963 until his passing.[160] In contrast to the SMB, the leading Syrian Salafis predominantly adopted an apolitical stance and maintained a strong anti-Muslim Brotherhood position, although the Salafi leader ʿAbd al-Qadir al-Arnaʾut (d. 2004) maintained positive relations with Sufi circles in Syria, in contrast to the approach of al-Albānī.[161]

It is worth noting that during the 1960s, al-Albānī was present at meetings of the SMB and maintained positive relations with them during his early years. They played a pivotal role in facilitating many of his teaching sessions around that period.[162] Furthermore, his early editor and employer was al-Shawish, the leading Salafi member of the Damascene SMB before his move to Lebanon. There, al-Shawish ran the publishing house *al-Maktab al-Islami*, which published many of al-Albānī's early works before they fell out (as mentioned in Chapter 3).[163] Al-Albānī's willingness to keep close contact with the Damascene SMB is easily explained by the fact that they were historically Salafi. However, from the 1960s and 1970s, he was openly critical of Qutb and al-Bannā.

As we've seen, numerous SMB members were exiled to Saudi Arabia in the 1980s and, in turn, influenced Salafism through the university system (most prominently ʿAli al-Tantawi). The Brotherhood's base was the city of Hama, and multiple clashes with the army took place there. In 1982, after mass protests and an uprising, the government sent in the army and tens of thousands of people were massacred.[164] This brutal crackdown caused a frantic exile of many Brotherhood and Salafi members. Both were targeted by the Baʿath regime and faced harsh political repression, leading to their decline and rendering discussions about their relations somewhat moot. It is interesting to note that according to Abdullah Azzam (d. 1989), Ibn Bāz himself issued a fatwa in support of the SMB during their uprising in Syria at that time.[165]

The eruption of the 2011 Arab Spring caused the government to crack down and massacre hundreds of thousands of its own citizens, resulting in an all-out civil war lasting over a decade. Syria remains in an acute humanitarian crisis – there is no scope for these movements to pursue activity in civil society. However, in the power vacuum, new jihadist movements entered the public eye, some Brotherhood-affiliated and others Jihadi-Salafi.[166]

### *4.3.2 Jordan*

The Jordanian Muslim Brotherhood (JMB) was formed in 1945 and enjoyed a lengthy presence in the Jordanian parliament. In recent history it has been most influenced by the Brotherhood scholar Yusuf al-Qaradawi. In accordance with general Brotherhood methodology, the JMB is not Salafi, but nor is it a vehement opponent of Salafism.[167]

The emergence of apolitical or quietist Salafism, and the arrival of al-Albānī in Amman in the early 1980s, significantly impacted the relationship between JMB and Salafism, and al-Albānī Salafism became dominant.[168] The quietist Salafis in Jordan criticized the JMB for being 'partisan' (*ḥizbī*) and for being disloyal to the methodology (*manhaj*) of the *Salaf* in favor of adherence to their own group. They accused the JMB of subscribing to flawed theology and supporting blameworthy religious innovations (*bidʿa*). Consequently, Salafi attitudes towards the JMB have been marked by condemnation and mockery, with Jordanian Salafis perceiving the JMB as superficial, overtly politically inclined, and lacking in scholarly depth.[169]

Nonetheless, many JMB members were impressed with al-Albānī's teachings and studied with him in the 1970s, although most did not leave the Brotherhood for Salafism. There are, however, a few exceptions including individuals like Mashhur b. Salman, who was a prominent member of the JMB but is now a leading scholar of the al-Albānī school (if such a thing can be said to exist). This led to the JMB eventually boycotting al-Albānī and banning its members from studying with him.[170]

In an interesting turn of events in 1982, certain JMB members attempted, unsuccessfully, to have al-Albānī extradited. This was primarily due to al-Albānī's vocal anti-JMB rhetoric and the subsequent disturbances it caused within the community. A close associate of al-Albānī with favorable government connections managed to thwart the extradition efforts. However, al-Albānī was only permitted to remain in the country on the condition that he refrain from conducting public teaching activities.[171]

A further indication of the ambiguity between the two movements is the Jordanian Salafis' somewhat fluctuating approaches to Sayyid Qutb, which appears to mirror the way their Saudi associates swayed with the political direction of the day. Hence, as mentioned earlier, al-Albānī initially spoke of the injustice of Qutb's execution and his being close to Salafism at the end of his life, despite maintaining a relatively restrained critique of Qutb's scholarly mistakes (which consistently upset followers of the Brotherhood).

Furthermore, al-Albānī's student al-Halabi had, in a book released in 1985, approvingly quoted from Qutb's commentary on the Qur'an and prayed for mercy upon him. However, this approach changed after the First Gulf War, when the QSJ joined their establishment Saudi counterparts in condemning Qutb in forthright terms. This is evident in the later writings of al-Halabi and others, and it appeared as something of an unhealthy obsession for them.[172]

Moreover, like their Saudi counterparts, the quietist Salafis became increasingly close to the Jordanian regime. By the 1990s, they had occupied the position of loyalty to the regime that the JMB had possessed before 1989, as the regime became increasingly critical of the JMB.[173] This shift raised concerns among Jordanian Salafis, as they believed it fostered allegiance to the Jordanian monarch at the expense of the kind of political autonomy advocated by figures like al-Albānī, well known for his apolitical disposition of aloofness. It appeared to many that this faction of Salafis were compromising their principles to pursue wealth and influence. Indeed, this is a consistent theme throughout this chapter when it comes to quietist Salafism and the dominant political regimes, with a notable exception being the Salafi efforts to undermine Morsi's government in Egypt.[174]

Nonetheless, in the wake of the Arab Spring in 2011, a more Salafi-inclined version of the JMB began to emerge. This development caused anxiety for both the Jordanian regime and the quietist Salafis, who responded negatively to this phenomenon. The quietist Salafis firmly rejected the Arab Spring, considering it 'social discord' (*fitna*), in favor of the political status quo that prevailed before the revolution. It is important to note that quietist Salafis adherents, such as al-Halabi, expressed their disgust not only towards the Brotherhood but also towards Salafis who engaged in politics, exemplified by the Nour Party in Egypt – which became active in the political arena as a result of the Arab Spring.[175]

### *4.3.3 Kuwait*

The Muslim Brotherhood established a local branch in Kuwait in 1951 and in the 1960s participated in elections as individual candidates, because Kuwait – despite a relatively liberal political climate that allows religious groups to participate in elections – does not officially recognize political parties. Although the Brotherhood's political successes were sparse during this period, they became increasingly influential during the 1960s and the 1970s as they occupied important governmental posts, especially in education. It was, however, in the 1980s that they began to contest elections explicitly as members of the Muslim Brotherhood, and it was during this time that political Salafis emerged in the country.[176] In March 1991, after the liberation of Kuwait, the Brotherhood established the Islamic Constitutional

Movement (ICM). This political bloc has been very successful in steering the direction of governmental legislation in an Islamic direction, which has, in turn, encouraged the growth of the Salafi movement, including an effective presence in parliament.

The Kuwaiti Salafi movement began in the 1960s and concentrated on religious matters, not politics. Political Salafism took a foothold in 1981 when the Society for the Revival of Islamic Heritage (*Jam'iyyat Ihya' al-Turath al-Islami* or RIHS) was established. This organization was founded under the guidance of the Kuwaiti-based Egyptian 'Abd al-Rahman 'Abd al-Khaliq, a student of al-Albānī and a staunch Salafi in almost every regard. It is noteworthy that despite his Salafi stance, 'Abd al-Khaliq had a previous affiliation with the Brotherhood, which perhaps explains his political orientation at this time.

Following the dissolution of the Kuwaiti parliament in July 1986, Salafi Members of Parliament and the ICM came together to form the Constitutional Movement to restore the parliament. However, the politicized Salafism of 'Abd al-Khaliq came under attack from al-Albānī and his quietist Salafi followers. They refuted this apparently Muslim Brotherhood-inspired foray into politics, deeming it premature. In their view, society needed to first purify its religious doctrine before becoming involved in the political arena. Consequently, RIHS suffered splits in the 1990s and early 2000s, the leadership fell into the hands of loyalist Salafis and 'Abd al-Khaliq was removed.[177] Nonetheless, the participation and social mobilization of such politicized Salafis can be seen as being influenced by the method of the Muslim Brotherhood. RIHS became the most active global manifestation of politico-Salafi thought in the 1990s, as they funded conferences, publications, and even other organizations around the globe, including branches in America and England. This caused tensions globally when clashes occurred between leading clerics of political Salafism and quietist Salafism in Arab lands. An interesting byproduct of this, as shall be discussed in Chapter 6, is the splits between Western Salafis based on these interactions in Kuwait and Jordan.

By the 1990s, other Salafi political groups were emerging. These included the Islamic Salafi Association (*al-Tajammu' al-Islami al-Salafi*) in 1991, followed by the Salafi Movement (*al-Ḥaraka al-Salafiyya*), which separated from the Islamic Salafi Association in 1996, and the Party of the Nation (*Ḥizb al-Umma*). Throughout all of this, the relationship between the Brotherhood and politicized Salafis in Kuwait was quite complex. In parliament, their interactions fluctuated, ranging from moments of collaboration on legislative matters that aligned with their shared religious beliefs, to instances where they disagreed, such as on certain women's issues. There were also occasions when the Salafis accused the ICM of not adhering to Islamic principles. Furthermore, the

ICM at times attempted to serve as a mediating force between the secularists and the Salafis.

Since 2006, the Brotherhood's electoral influence has waned, prompting them to form potential alliances with the Salafis, although the Salafis ultimately backtracked on prior agreements. The Salafis have adjusted their approach upon entering the political arena, adopting a more pragmatic method that has made them appear closer to the consistently pragmatic Brotherhood.[178] It is important to highlight that while Salafis have demonstrated pragmatism, they remain unwilling to emulate the Muslim Brotherhood's readiness to collaborate with Shiʿi groups or engage with Western countries. Nonetheless, it has been argued that the Kuwaiti Brotherhood has been swayed by Salafism more than Brotherhood units in other Middle Eastern countries.

It should be clear from this brief summary that the politico-Salafist groups of Kuwait have demonstrated perhaps the highest level of success of this trend in the Arab world, attaining seats in parliament and clearly demonstrating that they have political clout and popular support. As with all groups, however, they are not a monolithic entity, and their many factions, and players, have diverse tactics when dealing with the Brotherhood, and with their government.

## *4.4 Conclusion*

The Muslim Brotherhood's history is both remarkable and complex. It rose from the ashes of the collapse of the Ottoman Caliphate, evolving into the first modern pan-Islamic organization, eventually acquiring political power in Egypt, catapulted by the events of the Arab Spring. It is the largest religio-political organization in the world, having branches and admirers in every single country where Muslims reside. Hence, its relationship with Salafism, especially in Egypt and Saudi Arabia, is similarly complex. On the one hand, its founders clearly had direct links with the version of Salafism espoused by Rashīd Riḍā, hence some aspects of their creed – such as their aversion to some of the more syncretic practices of Sufism – have a commonality with Salafism. On the other hand, the focus of the Brotherhood extends beyond mere creed. They seek to establish a broader Islamic society rooted in the ethical and moral values of Islam. And in doing so, they are willing to overlook many creedal and legal differences for the greater good of Muslim unity. Their call for unity with Shīʿis, Sufis, and Ashʿarīs has sparked contention with the more mainstream Salafis, who find it difficult to envision any form of unity with these groups. Moreover, their prioritization of political issues over theological ones typically finds push-back from

Salafist clerics, who view the methodology of the Brotherhood as a reversal of religious priorities.

Currently, the relationship between the Brotherhood and mainstream Salafis appears to be at its most strained, especially after the failure of the Brotherhood-led Arab Spring. Egypt has clamped down on the Brotherhood and even Egyptian quietist Salafis have supported these measures, while the Emiratis and Saudis have publicly declared them to be a terrorist organization. Political Salafism, as exemplified by the *Ṣaḥwa* movements, has waned considerably in the last two decades, primarily due to government repression, while quietist strands (with all stripes of Madkhalism) have been supported by almost all Arab regimes. Yet the irony is that the quietist Salafi alignment with government opposition to the Brotherhood in both Egypt and Saudi Arabia has not yielded benefits for the Salafis themselves. Rather, they find themselves increasingly marginalized in both countries – and hence, even globally – not just by outsiders but by many within their own ranks, with the public's perception of them as being government stooges, along with the notion that they primarily focus on ritualistic religiosity and theological argumentation while ignoring far more pressing problems.

However, in light of past historical collaborations between the Brotherhood and the Salafis against common enemies, together with the waning of quietist Salafism, it is highly likely that there will be a future stage of reconciliation and cooperation, especially as Muslim communities come under the increasing pressure of anti-Muslim and anti-Islamic sentiment across the globe.

# 5

# THE PHENOMENON OF JIHADI-SALAFISM

*'God sent me Sayyid Qutb for ideas, Ibn Taymiyya for creed, Ibn Qayyim for spirituality, and al-Nawawī for jurisprudence. These are the four who have influenced me most profoundly in my life.'*
*~ Shaykh al-Mujāhīdīn Abdullah Yusuf Azzam (d. 1989)*[1]

*'Most of the Jihādīs chose Salafi beliefs, jurisprudence, and methodology. Hence, their problems eventually came to us as well.'*
*~ Abū Mus'ab al-Suri*[2]

Islamic political theory – rooted in the Qur'an – demonstrates that Islam's essential conceptualization of relationships between Muslim and non-Muslim political communities is one of peace.[3] Nonetheless, when peace is unachievable, the Shari'a has legislated many clear rulings of warfare that Muslims must adhere to, under a law of military engagement that has been termed *jihad*, based on the Arabic verb meaning 'to strive.' As Muslim lands had to withstand perpetual aggression, the law and practice of jihad remained largely relevant throughout early Islamic history.[4]

During the latter part of the nineteenth century and early twentieth century, in the wake of Western political dominance and colonization of large parts of the Muslim lands, jihad was a somewhat neglected occupation. Nonetheless, some key defenses of Muslim lands did take place under its banner, particularly in Palestine and later during the Afghanistan–Soviet War (1979–89). Around this time, particularly between the 1960s and 1980s, there was renewed theoretical interest in the applicability of jihad to the modern world. The 1980s thus saw the emergence of discernible jihadist groups whose ideological articulations emphasized jihad as a central methodological concern.[5] From this general jihadism emerged a subset defined as Jihadi-Salafism (JS) during the mid-1990s whose intellectual roots can be found in the 1970s in Egypt and Syria, although the actual terminology started to emerge in the 1990s, rising to prominence in the 2000s.[6] This latter phenomenon would have dramatic consequences for the world, particularly after the JS attacks on the USA on 11 September 2001, leading to a major subset of JS called Wahhabi-Jihadi-Salafism (WJS), which we briefly touched upon in a previous chapter (see section 3.2.6). The prominence of Salafism in the jihadist movement has been noted by the major jihadist theorist and practitioner Abu Musʿab al-Suri in his famous book *The Global Resistance Call*, in which he stated: 'Most of the Jihādīs chose Salafi beliefs, jurisprudence, and methodology. Hence, their problems eventually came to us as well.'[7] Over the course of time JS underwent an evolution and there were internal debates over some of the finer details of the methodology.[8] While never jettisoning its Salafi foundations, it came to restrict the Salafi canon in order to justify its use of violence, emphasizing the jihadist outlook over loyalty to theology.[9]

Therefore, in the course of adopting these categorizations, it must be accepted that a certain ambiguity exists due to the overlap between such trends, while acknowledging that a significant proportion of academic and journalistic work on the subject is prone to make distortions based on, in the words of Darryl Li, the 'gravitational pull of the anti-Muslim animus that hangs over all such conversations.' For Li, 'The jihadism discourse has updated the old racist canard "not all Muslims are terrorists, but all terrorists are Muslim" by simply substituting the narrower "Salafi" for "Muslim,"' and only 'usefully reveals how empire thinks, how it structures relations of compliance and enmity.'[10] Hence, we will proceed with such nomenclature, as they can present something of an accurate picture, but with these well-founded cautions and fears in mind.

## *5.1 Defining Jihadi-Salafism*

### *5.1.1 The Concept of Jihad in Islam*

The concept of jihad, which entails the military struggle to protect Islam and expand its borders, is not exclusive to the jihadist movements of the twentieth and twenty-first centuries. It has been a part of mainstream Islam from the earliest times and is held to be an integral part of Islamic law. While some Muslim groups tend to focus on alternative meanings of the word – such as fighting one's desires – the word 'jihad' in Islamic legal texts generally refers to combat and warfare.

Within mainstream Islam, jihad could refer either to combat in defense of an Islamic polity or to further its expansion. Both aspects have been discussed in detail in medieval Islamic texts, with strict rules of engagement laid out – including the prohibition of killing non-combatants and the importance of honoring peace treaties. Notably, the adherence to the principles of honoring peace treaties has rendered expansive jihad historically obsolete for many centuries. Most Muslim nation-states have agreed that the signing of international peace treaties and international border agreements must be upheld by Muslims. Furthermore, the absence of a caliphate means that there is no ruling authority that can declare expansionist jihad. In other words, expansionist jihad has been phased out as it is not relevant to our times. Rashīd Riḍā, for example, argued that religiously legitimate expansionist wars no longer exist. Similar arguments have been made by other scholars like Muhammad Abu Zahra (d. 1974), al-Qaradawi, and Muhammad Qutb.[11] This position has been accepted by the majority of Muslims across the globe and is the reason that many of them rarely talk about, or even think about, offensive jihad as a reality in their lives.

Conversely, the question of defensive jihad remains a subject of contention. These debates have arisen in response to geopolitical realities, such as the occupation of Palestine and the invasions of Iraq and Afghanistan, prompting an examination of whether Muslims bear a religious obligation to defend these territories. While most Muslims took the position that the obligation to defend those lands fell only on the people living in the attacked region, a minority believed it was a global obligation, and migrated to these lands for the sake of jihad. It is within these contexts (and lands) – amid wars and precarious circumstances – that modern jihadism has manifested, as a reaction to the economic and political problems that plague the Muslim world today.

In terms of seeing how non-Muslim academics have understood the causes of JS, the polarized conclusions, from opposite sides of the spectrum, can be cogently epitomized in the academic conflict in the French academy between Olivier Roy and Gilles Kepel: the former places the blame on rogues acting separate to and in contravention of the Islamic religion, while the latter advocates that such terrorism is derived from the sources of Islam by extremist Islamists. Roy's argument is based on the idea that 'jihadism is a nihilist and generational revolt.' Hence the problem is not one of a 'radicalization of Islam' but an 'Islamization of radicalism,' because, in reality, the problem is one of 'the revolt of the youth' who have a penchant for 'a modern violence,' rather than one of subscribing to the norms of traditional jihad. In contrast, Kepel has found great popularity among the French right wing with his emphasis on Islamist groups and their Islam-inspired extremism, which has emerged in such spectacular and cruel violence.[12] For Kepel, as summarized in an interview published in May

2016 in the *Revue des Deux Mondes*, 'radicalization does not come before Islamization.'[13] The truth is probably in between the two positions, with great room for further nuance and diversity among cases, but this author leans more towards Roy than Kepel.

Nonetheless, it should be noted that most analysis found in Western literature overlooks the political causes of jihad and concentrates on the religious. Consequently, this effectively skews the narrative and typically exonerates or sidelines the role that Western countries have played in creating the necessary circumstances to generate both defensive and offensive jihadist movements. Obviously, this is not a justification of such movements, but rather a contextualization, one that is almost inevitably ignored in most analyses.[14] Since this work is not about jihadist movements per se, we will suffice with this general disclaimer: modern jihadist movements are more a reaction to political repression (both from tyrannical governments and from foreign invasions) than a manifestation of perverted fundamentalist religious zeal, although no doubt, (mis)interpretation of Islamic law does have a role to play.

### *5.1.2 Categorizing Jihadi Movements*

How one chooses to distinguish between and categorize these jihadi movements is, of course, very much related to one's own world view and presuppositions. For the purposes of our work, it is important to distinguish between generic Jihadis, Jihadi-Salafis and Salafis engaged in Jihad. This is because, as a result of various warring and violent traditions emerging out of the Afghan–Soviet war, a popular trend has emerged in both academia and the media, in which any soldier who has the outward appearance of a religious person is termed a 'jihadi,' with wholly negative connotations applied. But this overarching use of one label does not allow us to identify the very obvious and critical differences between the many fighting groups. During the Afghan–Soviet war, the USA and her allies happily supported the 'jihadis' (the *mujahidin* in the Arabic plural), as they were a party 'on our side,' and therefore worthy of support in arms and morale. However, when such people were 'not on our side,' they were universally condemned in the West – sometimes justifiably. Still, a lack of nuance and a crass caricature of such movements became the norm. This section seeks to provide the necessary distinctions. We will distinguish between jihadism and Jihadi-Salafism, as well as identifying moderate or strict Salafis who are engaged in military combat – or jihad – in the context of defensive war efforts without being Jihadi-Salafis.

There are, of course, Muslims who prefer not to have the Islamic institution of jihad sullied through an association with terrorist violence that is antithetical to normative jihad or the Pious Predecessors.[15] They consider the phrase 'Jihadi Salafism' to be part of a regime of nefarious propaganda about Islam and terrorism, and would prefer that the groups under discussion are simply called 'terrorists' (*irhabiyyun*), Khārijites, 'deviants' (*munharifun*), or members of 'the misled sect' (*al-fi'a al- dhalla*).[16] However, the term Jihadi-Salafism retains a usefulness and sense of accuracy in describing an aspiration to perform jihad with adherence to Salafi foundations and principles, even if there is an element of imperfection in its use, as is the case with the related term 'Islamism.' People who are often deemed to be Jihadi-Salafis, like Abu Muhammad al-Maqdisi (as mentioned in section 3.1.2), have come to adopt this label for themselves, particularly after 9/11, despite its questionable origins.[17] Furthermore, some respected scholars have suggested that the term should be replaced with 'preference-based typologies,' in order to provide coherence to what is a very complex reality;[18] or to alternatively call it Jihadi-*takfiri* due to the gulf between it and traditional Salafism.[19] Nonetheless, there is a compelling case to maintain the popular term and to identify the key concepts that largely define Jihadi-Salafism, even if there is a wide spectrum of interpretations regarding these concepts between disparate groups.[20]

Jihadism can be understood as one form of 'Islamism,' meaning the belief that the teachings of Islam should be the political definer of a modern state and that Muslims should actively work to achieve this. In its specificity, we shall define 'jihadism' as the belief – and invariably the practice – that advocates the centrality of violent military activism as the means of transforming society and bringing about political change in accordance with Islam. These generic jihadi movements can be subdivided into defensive (or regional), and offensive (or global). The former are those movements that have been formed as a *reaction* to an invading force, and whose goals are the reclaiming of their own lands from the invading army, whereas the latter wish to establish a larger Islamic caliphate with an outlook of global domination.

Some offensive/global jihadist movements can be classified as Jihadi-Salafi. Jihadi-Salafis are that spectrum within jihadi movements that are influenced by specific Salafi doctrines, as shall be discussed below. On the other hand, there will be some Salafis who engage in defensive jihad, whose understanding of jihad is in line with mainstream Sunnism, but they just happen to be Salafi in theology, and are participating in what they view as a legitimate religious battle to defend their country from foreign invasion.

This spectrum is perhaps best illustrated with historical examples. In general, jihadists can be Salafi or non-Salafi. A prominent example of non-Salafi jihadists is the Taliban in late twentieth-century Afghanistan. This group adheres to Deobandī theology within the Ḥanafī-Māturīdī *kalām* tradition; hence, it would not be factually inaccurate to label them

'Jihadi-Sufis.'[21] Examples of jihadists who – despite possessing some Salafi characteristics – remain non-Salafi in terms of methodology, are generals like Marwan Hadid (d. 1976) in Syria during the 1960s and 1970s and the Palestinian-Afghan fighter Abdullah Azzam (discussed in section 5.2.4 below). These figures are known for their broad approach of fostering positive relationships with non-Salafis, and even Sufis, while they are engaged in defensive jihad, demonstrating their roots in the ecumenically orientated Muslim Brotherhood, and marking a departure from the characteristic stance of committed Salafis. Meanwhile, Salafis engaged in jihad, in contrast to Jihadi-Salafis, can be identified as people whose religious foundation and outlook were shaped by modern Salafi scholars, particularly from Saudi Arabia, and who actively participated in defensive jihad efforts, without calling for any offensive jihad.[22]

In the last few decades, three regional conflicts brought diverse groups of peoples, including many Salafis, to fight against invading forces: (1) the Afghan–Soviet War, where figures like Abdulrab Rasul Sayyaf and Jamil al-Rahman (d. 1991) were preaching Salafist doctrines and fighting the invading forces, (2) the events surrounding the dissolution of the former Yugoslavia and its communal war from 1991, especially in Bosnia between 1992 and 1995, in which many Salafis joined, and (3) the Chechen defensive war against the Russians from 1995 to 1999, led by figures such as the Saudi fighter Ibn al-Khattab (real name Samir al-Suwailim, d. 2002). The latter, a veteran of the Afghan war against the Soviets, serves as a notable illustration of the nuanced distinctions between Salafis who fought in jihad versus Jihadi-Salafis. Ibn al-Khattab opposed Bin Laden – who is representative of Jihadi-Salafis – by abstaining from endorsing military engagement with the United States. He and those aligned with him opposed the idea of combatting Muslim governments and adhered to a strategic approach that avoided civilian casualties, defining military targets to be strictly within the context of legitimate military confrontations. This contrast is further underscored by Ibn al-Khattab's rejection of Bin Laden's offer in 1998 to collaborate more closely. Some academics therefore distinguished between what they called 'Khattabists' and 'Bin Ladenists,' but the distinction above seems more precise.[23]

Now that we've explained what Jihadi-Salafism is *not*, let us begin in earnest with the topic of this chapter. Jihadi-Salafism is characterized by several key features. Firstly, there is a direct association with the thought and teachings of both Ibn Taymiyya and Ibn ʿAbd al-Wahhāb, which automatically makes such movements theologically 'Salafi' in every sense of the term. Secondly, one finds the frequent excommunication (*takfīr*) of Muslims who are not associated with the movement – in particular, governments that do not follow a comprehensive program of Islamic law. Thirdly, as a consequence of these ideas, they engage in acts of violence that claim non-combatants as their victims.[24]

Jihadi-Salafism seems to have become a popular term of self-designation among jihad-focused groups in London in the 1990s, despite possibly having some earlier antecedents. For instance, in a 1994 interview for a London-based jihadist magazine, Ayman al-Zawahiri (d. 2022) referred to the 'Jihadi-Salafi movement' (*al-ḥaraka al-jihādiyya al-salafiyya*).[25] Moreover, our utilization of the Jihadi-Salafi term does not intend to deny the occasional crossover between what we call Jihadi-Salafism and the other two popular trends of Salafism – namely, quietist/apolitical and political – nor does it negate the potential theological differences among these branches.[26] As Wiktorowicz notes, 'The most influential and well-known Salafi scholars produce students, followings, and groups representing the entire spectrum of Salafi activism, ranging from pacifists to the extremes of Al Qaeda.'[27] Although this is a somewhat common trend, it can be usefully highlighted in the notable case of al-Albānī. His students in Jordan – following his relocation from Syria in the 1980s – span a spectrum from pacifists/quietists like 'Ali al-Halabi and Salim al-Hilali, to jihadists like Abu Qatada al-Filastini and Hassan Abu Haniyeh.[28] However, moving beyond the initial simplistic assumption that puritan Salafi scholars were merely uninformed about political realities and, therefore, susceptible to manipulation by political authorities – and so excusable to some extent – Jihadi-Salafis, such as Osama bin Laden and Abu Musʿab al-Zarqawi, concluded that puritan Salafis had knowingly aligned themselves with tyrants out of fear. Consequently, they characterized them as 'scholars of the political authority' (*ʿulamāʾ al-sulṭa*) – sometimes pejoratively referred to in English circles as 'scholars for dollars.'[29]

### *5.1.3 Key Doctrines of Jihadi-Salafis*

The central ideas of Jihadi-Salafi groups can be summarized in the following five points: (1) a Salafi conception of Divine Unity, or *tawḥīd*, (2) the concept of *al-ḥākimiyya*, or God's sole right to legislate, as being an integral part of *tawḥīd*, (3) an excessive practice of excommunicating Muslims (*takfīr*), including the rulers of Muslim-majority countries, and often a mass of regular believers who do not share some of their key tenets, (4) using extreme violence that they consider to be jihad, as a means of social change and removing those rulers of Muslim-majority countries whom they deem to be illegitimate – this can often entail hitting ostensibly civilian targets, with non-combatants regularly the victims (again, this is widely debated in JS circles), and (5) a robust theory of loyalty to the Muslims and a disavowal of non-Muslims (*al-walāʾ wa'l-barāʾ*). While it has been rightfully argued by Alexander Thurston that these five concepts can be reduced to 'two goals: the imperative to overthrow rulers seen as tyrants, and the imperative to uphold and enforce Salafi theology,'[30] it is useful for our purposes of achieving clarity to explain this phenomenon under these five separate headings.

It should be noted that while these five concepts are predominant in *most* Jihadi-Salafi groups, their specific interpretation and level of application vary, and there exists numerous disagreements between the sub-strands of this movement (a prominent example is the difference on applying *takfīr* and the level of violence acceptable on the Muslim masses who don't agree with the movement in question, which led to the infamous disagreement between Zarqawi and Al-Qaeda, as shall be discussed later).

*A Salafi conceptualization of Tawḥīd*

As mentioned at the beginning of this chapter, the popular jihadi theorist Abu Musʿab al-Suri argued that most Jihadis adopted the Salafi methodology in doctrine, jurisprudence and methodology.[31] The clearest indication that most Jihadis are Salafi in doctrine is their conceptualization of Divine Unity or *tawḥīd.* They adopt the uniquely Taymiyyan three-category tripartite division outlined earlier (see section 2.4). Many additionally add a fourth category, namely *al-ḥākimiyya*, to justify the excommunication of Muslim governments.[32] Jihadi literature rarely discusses the first three categories of *tawḥīd* as they believe it has been sufficiently discussed by their predecessors; hence their attention is more focused on *al-ḥākimiyya*, which is central to their understanding of the world.

In their circles, they promote and teach the books of Ibn Taymiyya and Muḥammad ibn ʿAbd al-Wahhāb and consider their works sufficient for understanding the essence of *tawḥīd* and other aspects of theology. In many ways, their understanding of these topics is closer to the understanding of Ibn ʿAbd al-Wahhāb (i.e., First-Wave Wahhabism) than that of modern Salafis, as they justify waging jihad against Muslims on the basis that these Muslims are apostates for violating one of the categories of *tawḥīd.*[33]

Another manifestation of the Jihadi-Salafi understanding of *tawḥīd* is the general animosity that these movements display towards Shiʿites. Generally, these movements are quick to excommunicate them based on the notion that they 'deify' their imams, a common trope of Wahhabi thought. Jihadi-Salafis have historically targeted Shiʿite mosques and shrines with the justification that they are not Muslims in the first place.

*Al-ḥākimiyyah as the fourth category of Tawḥīd*

The term *al-ḥākimiyyah* is often translated as 'God's Oneness in legislation.' It was taken from the writings of political activists Sayyid Qutb and Abu al-A'la Mawdudi, the latter of whom coined the term, and was later elevated by jihadi movements to become a part of monotheism – some even made it a 'fourth category' – referring to it as *tawḥīd al-ḥākimiyyah.*[34] It is defined as the belief that God alone has the right to make laws, and that anybody who invents a law contradicting God's law, or follows a law that contradicts God's law, is therefore a disbeliever, as they have not followed pure monotheism. Based on this belief, Jihadis have excommunicated the majority of Muslim leaders for not implementing Islamic law in their lands, and by proxy, they excommunicate the supporters of these rulers and their citizens.[35]

Jihadi-Salafism therefore elevates political concepts into matters of faith and disbelief. While Jihadi-Salafis do see the West as their ultimate enemy, they also see non-Salafi Muslims in general, and secularists and non-Sunni groups in particular, as a more dangerous enemy, the 'enemy from within.'

### *Takfīr*

Jihadi-Salafis are more liberal in their usage of *takfīr* (excommunication) than other Salafis, which is why many critics, Salafis and otherwise, label these movements as Kharijites.[36] Many of those that subscribe to jihadism consider *takfīr* a necessity of our times, in order to differentiate themselves from other groups, as well as permit their supposed jihad against them. This draws parallels with the early Wahhabi movement that made *takfīr* of the Ottomans in order to wage jihad against them. Building on this legacy, the Jihadis of today make *takfīr* of the rulers of Muslim countries, as well as anybody who passively supports them. This gives them a justification for waging jihad against Muslims on the basis that the majority of Muslims are apostates that need to be fought and killed.[37]

Jihadi-Salafis reject the label 'Kharijites,' stating that the Kharijites declared people to be disbelievers for committing sins, while they only declare people to be disbelievers for engaging in acts of disbelief. These 'acts of disbelief' according to the Jihadis include ruling by a law other than Islamic law; supporting a government that rules by man-made laws; working for a government that implements man-made laws; allying with disbelievers; and not supporting their jihad. They declare people to be disbelievers and apostates based on these issues, thus justifying the targeting and murder of such people in the name of jihad.

To justify their *takfīr*, the Jihadi-Salafis developed a concept earlier expounded by Ibn Abd al-Wahhāb for another classical Arabic term: *ṭawāghīt*. This is an Arabic word that traditionally refers to idols or false gods and is rarely used in traditional Islam. In jihadi circles, however, it is very popular and, drawing on Ibn Abd al-Wahhāb's definition, has taken on the meaning of 'tyrant rulers' or 'anyone who rules by other than what Allah revealed.' They view these rulers as apostates, and by proxy, anybody who supports these rulers is also declared to be an apostate.[38] Jihadi-Salafi preacher Abu Basir al-Tartusi has said, 'Everyone who supports, protects, and defends this (Saudi) regime from among the kings, princes and other than them from their associates who carry out their will, are all disbelievers and apostates.'[39] All jihadi preachers who make mass *takfīr* by association justify their violent campaigns in similar terms.

Nonetheless, this is the most contentious aspect of the principles of Jihadi-Salafism that are identified here. As will be seen, there have been some JS groups who engaged in wanton excommunication of masses of Muslims; however, these same groups have also come under direct condemnation for excesses in this regard from fellow Jihadis and even Jihadi-Salafis. Yet, the preponderance of *takfīr* in such groups justifies it being identified as a defining feature of JS, even if there is a spectrum of applicability among Jihadi-Salafis in this regard.

*Violence as the central method for social change*

As stated at the beginning of this chapter, jihad is a known concept in traditional Islam, and is mentioned frequently in the Qur'an. The controversy lies in the central importance Jihadis place on this concept, which manifests in their violent misapplication of it to modern times, and their blatant violation of the rules of engagement that are clearly stated in Islamic legal sources.

Some Jihadis elevate the concept of jihad and treat it as if it were one of the fundamental pillars of the faith (as we shall see, some called it the 'sixth pillar' of Islam). They consider it the most important obligation after belief in *tawḥīd*, and the primary method of defending and propagating *tawḥīd*. Their worldview is that they are now in a state of perpetual jihad against disbelievers and see jihad as the only means to revive Islam and restore the Muslim world to its former glory.[40] The targets for this struggle were initially considered to be 'the near enemy,' which referred to their respective Muslim governments which they considered to be apostates. This was then developed by some Jihadi-Salafis – although contentious with many of the camp – into the necessity of engaging 'the far enemy' in war, namely the United States, who are considered by them to be controlling the un-Islamic agenda of 'the near enemy.'

The problems with the JS understanding of jihad in light of normative formulations of Islamic law are many. Firstly, they elevate it into the greatest act of worship. Secondly, they view it as a perpetual act that must be carried out all the time, with peace not being an option. Thirdly, they view it as an individual obligation on every believer. Fourthly, the killing of citizens and bystanders is deemed by them to be permissible. Fifthly, it is held that their notion of jihad demarcates between faith and disbelief; hence anybody who supports their jihad is a believer, and all those who oppose them are disbelievers. Sixthly, the functions of states, borders, and treaties with non-Muslim lands, allies or otherwise, is altogether disqualified despite modern Muslim jurisprudence in the traditions of the existing legal schools recognizing their legitimacy in the modern world within an Islamic law framework.

This new understanding of jihad did not exist even half a century ago. It is a post-modernist understanding that was invented out of desperation, due to the current tyranny, wars, and oppression that are carried out against Muslims in various parts of the world. Unable to see any way for the Muslim world to overcome its humiliation and oppression, many young people turn to this theory of jihad as a desperate solution. Yet, the results have been catastrophic, causing even more problems for Muslims across the globe than before.

By way of illustration, the following passage by Abu Mus'ab al-Suri is a good example of the understanding of jihad that is keenly taken up by Jihadi-Salafis, many of whom have been directly influenced by him:

> The method of the Global Islamic Resistance considers fighting God's invader enemies and those who help them and fight Muslims along with them, to be an individual duty like prayer and almsgiving [zakat]. The timing of performing this duty under the present conditions is regarded immediate. The only obligation is to embrace Islam. As said by the Prophet Muhammed, peace and blessings upon him: '*Embrace Islam, then fight.*' Thus… everyone who is a Muslim, even if he converted an hour after the occupation forces entered and made jihad an individual duty for every Muslim, has been assigned with this duty.[41]

The author goes on to explain that it is the duty of the leader of the jihad unit to train his new recruits in how to perform this obligation. He explains that new converts need to learn how to wage jihad, just like how they need to learn how to pray. The above passage clearly demonstrates that Jihadis consider jihad to be an individual obligation that becomes compulsory upon a person as soon as they convert to Islam, and as being on the same level as praying and zakat. This understanding of jihad is unique to this fringe movement and is not the belief of mainstream Muslims, who view defensive jihad as an obligation only on those who are under attack.

Another dangerous aspect of jihadi thought is that they consider citizens to be legitimate targets for attack. This contradicts the mainstream understanding of Islam which prohibits attacking any citizens during a legitimate war, as per the strict rules of jihad laid down by the early Muslims. For example, the Prophet's companion Ibn ʿAbbas stated, 'Do not kill women, or children, or old men, or whoever comes to you with peace, and he restrains his hand from fighting, for if you did that you would certainly have transgressed.'[42]

Contrary to this, Jihadis justify attacking and killing any citizen of a state they are at war with on the basis of retribution and equity. Al-Qaeda stated this as a justification for 9/11, claiming: 'It is allowed for Muslims to kill protected ones among unbelievers as an act of reciprocity.'[43] The first to adopt this position was the Armed Islamic Group (*Groupe Islamique Armé* or GIA) in Algeria in the early 1990s who started bombing and massacring civilians in the name of jihad, justifying their aggression through the concept of retribution against the brutal government crackdown.[44] Over time, this became the standard belief of jihadi groups like Al-Qaeda and ISIS.

*Al-Walāʾ waʾl-Barāʾ*

The concept of *al-walāʾ waʾl-barāʾ* has already been introduced in the discussion of Ibn ʿAbd al-Wahhāb's theology in Chapter 3 (see section 3.1.2). Jihadi-Salafis have taken this notion as a central tenet of their ideology, and used it primarily in the context of political allegiance to their movements, versus aiding and abetting those who oppose them.[45] The term was used by Juhaymān al-ʻUtaybi to justify his rebellion against the Saudi government (see section 5.3.2).[46] Interestingly, at this early stage, he did not use this concept to excommunicate the Saudi government or any other Muslims. The elevation of the concept of *al-walāʾ waʾl-barāʾ* into a matter of faith and disbelief, and a primary mechanism of *takfir*, was done by Abu Muhammad al-Maqdisi, in his famous book *Millat Ibrahim* (*The Religion of Abraham*).[47] This book is *the* fundamental book for all Jihadi-Salafi movements, and its importance cannot be overstated.

In this book, al-Maqdisi argues that allying with the believers, and supporting the jihad, is a fundamental of faith and a part of *tawḥīd*. Consequently, he argues that refusing to support the jihad and allying with the disbelievers is an act of disbelief. Utilizing this new definition, al-Maqdisi declared that the rulers of Muslim lands are disbelievers as are anybody who supports them. This became a core justification for violence against Muslims in the name of jihad.[48] Al-Maqdisi borrowed such concepts from Muḥammad ibn ʿAbd al-Wahhāb and his descendants and applied them to the present situation. There are obvious and clear parallels with First-Wave Wahhabism, and copious quotations from Wahhabi scholars, in the writings of al-Maqdisi.

Post 9/11, Al-Qaeda demanded *al-walāʾ* (alliance) from all Muslims and consequently utilized this belief to make *takfīr* of those who refused to ally with them.[49] ISIS did the same thing in 2014 but took it one step further and declared that anybody who did not pledge their allegiance to the Islamic State was an apostate for violating *al-walāʾ waʾl-barāʾ*.[50]

## *5.2 Important Events and Personalities That Influenced Jihadi-Salafism*

### *5.2.1 Wahhabism*

Although it is often argued that Jihadi-Salafism is a new strand of Salafism that emerged in the late twentieth century – and that it is the most dangerous strand of Salafism since early Wahhabism – in many ways, it is actually a revival of Muḥammad b. ʿAbd al-Wahhāb's original methodology. Just as the early Wahhabis declared the Ottomans and other Najdi political opponents to be illegitimate rulers and disbelievers, then waged war against them, so Al-Qaeda and ISIS have taken the same stance against the modern nation-states of the Muslim world, including Saudi Arabia. The one modern element that makes it deserving of the title 'Jihadi-Salafism,' rather than simply being 'neo-Wahhabism,' is the incorporation of Sayyid Qutb's political ideology into Wahhabi theology. This fusion transforms Jihadi-Salafism beyond a mere continuation of Wahhabism, infusing it with a politically driven dimension characterized by violence. This topic will be further explored in subsequent sections of this chapter.

### *5.2.2 The Muslim Brotherhood and Sayyid Qutb*

While one can identify the influence of ideas from the Muslim Brotherhood on Jihadi-Salafism, it must be acknowledged that the resulting doctrine of the latter is peculiar to it and has consistently faced censure from the leadership of the Muslim Brotherhood throughout its historical trajectory. However, the activities and thoughts of the Brotherhood ideologue Qutb in the 1960s would be foundational for modern jihadism. In fact, Qutb was pivotal in the emergence of Jihadi-Salafism. Ayman al-Zawahiri credited him as being the one who ignited the modern jihadist flame,[51] stating that he was 'the most prominent theoretician of the jihadist movement.'[52]

Although Qutb was leader of a special unit that considered overthrowing the government, endorsing the use of force in self-defense against oppressive measures and even seeking to smuggle arms into the country for this purpose, it was his intellectual output on the prevalence of un-Islamic ignorance (*jāhiliyya*) and the imperative of ruling by God's law (*ḥākimiyya*)[53] that greatly shaped Jihadi-Salafism. Under the influence of Abu al-Aʿla Mawdudi, Qutb conceived of the revival of Muslim society through the establishment of a 'vanguard' tasked with struggling against the dominant ignorant society in rebellion against God's laws.[54] Furthermore, Qutb's declaration that the majority of society was in a state of ignorance resulted in him being accused of excommunicating the entire community, although he himself denied this.

Qutb's significance was recognized by Jihadi-Salafis such as al-Zawahiri and Sayyid Imām al-Sharif (also known simply as 'Dr Faḍl'), with Abdullah Azzam effectively conveying it to many, among them Bin Laden. Qutb's writings are so important that jihadists tend to quote him as often as they quote Ibn Taymiyya and Ibn ʿAbd al-Wahhāb. Qutb's books *Maʿālim fī al-Tarīq* (*Milestones on the Path*) and *Fī Ẓilāl al-Qurʾān* (*In the Shade of the Qurʾan*) provide the basic ideas upon which his jihadism is founded, namely (1) the concept of (*takfīr*) excommunication of rulers, (2) ignorance (*jāhiliyya*) of the masses, (3) the central role of jihad in reviving Islam, and (4) the concept of ruling by God's law (*ḥākimiyya*).

Nonetheless, it can be argued that Qutb was not a jihadist himself and had no idea of the kind of carnage and extremism his writings would inspire. This does not, however, negate the important role his writings played in shaping the jihadist school of thought. The fact that the first jihadist movements started in Egypt during his lifetime, and were led by his students, is evidence enough of this.[55]

Hence several concepts which the Jihadi-Salafis adopted from the Brotherhood can be outlined. These notions include (1) the importance of military preparation and participation, (2) the centrality of the caliphate, (3) the need for Muslim governments to rule by Islamic law, (4) the notion that un-Islamic attitudes and practices were widespread throughout the Muslim lands, and lastly (4) that this deviation from correct Islamic practice must be strongly opposed.

Ironically, while Jihadi-Salafis have extolled the virtues of Qutb, they have been stern in their disavowal of the Muslim Brotherhood, whom they saw as being overly pragmatic and compromising in the face of the system of *jāhiliyya*. For example, al-Zawahiri wrote *al-Ḥiṣād al-Murr: al-Ikhwān al-Muslimūn fī Sittīn ʿāmā* (*Bitter Harvest: Sixty Years of the Muslim Brotherhood*) in the early 1990s. He chided the leadership of the Brotherhood for adhering to the law of the land, a system of *jāhiliyya*, and tyrannical rule (*tāghūt*). He accused them of leaving Qutb's legacy and abandoning jihad against the *tāghūt* in favor of reconciliation with the regime. This, according to al-Zawahiri, mirrored the same flawed approach adopted prior to Gamal Abdel Nasser's ascendancy to power. Furthermore, he criticized the Brotherhood for participating in the democratic system while ostensibly upholding the concept of popular sovereignty. Al-Zawahiri also accused the Brotherhood of siding with the regime of Hosni Mubarak in the 1980s against the jihadist groups, as well as historically compromising with King Farouk (d. 1965), Nasser, and Anwar Sadat. In this sweeping accusation, even al-Bannā himself was included. Furthermore, al-Zawahiri sought to rebuff the Brotherhood's claims of glory in the fight for Palestine, minimizing their impact and scope. He portrayed their involvement as mere obedience to official government policy rather than outside its prescriptions, citing how al-Hudaybi opposed fighting the British in the Canal Zone.[56]

Ultimately, Jihadi-Salafism signifies a departure even from Qutb and those who espoused his views at the end of the twentieth century in regard to three core areas: (1) the legitimate realm of jihad, (2) using violence against Western civilians, and (3) the scope of excommunication of fellow Muslims.[57]

### *5.2.3 Afghanistan: The Breeding Ground of Jihadi-Salafism*

The Soviet Union's invasion of Afghanistan at the end of December 1979 would have significant consequences in the Cold War with the United States. In a world where the advances of one of the two leading nations meant the intolerable disadvantage of the other, the Soviet invasion could not be ignored. Moreover, the Soviet decision to assist the weakened communist government in Kabul – which had only recently come to power in April 1978 – made the Soviet Union seem ever-closer as a rival to American interests in the Muslim lands. This perception was exacerbated by events such as the Islamic Revolution in Iran earlier in 1979 and the subsequent seizure of the American Embassy in Tehran in November of the same year.[58] Saudi Arabia was also perturbed by the Soviet invasion, which added to its anxiety about political developments in the region, as well as its growing fear of communism.[59]

By July 1980, the United States and Saudi Arabia both agreed to provide US$300–$500 million a year to the fighters in Afghanistan.[60] Hence, the United States and its primary ally Saudi Arabia, together with the Gulf monarchies, directed billions of dollars to the freedom fighters engaging in military operations against the Soviets in pursuit of liberating Afghanistan. These fighters, known as the *mujāhidīn* or 'those engaged in jihad,' were widely celebrated by anti-Soviet nations as part of the propaganda efforts against the Soviet Union. Even the Hollywood blockbuster *Rambo III* (1988) was 'dedicated to the brave Mujahidin fighters of Afghanistan.'[61] However, prominent mujahidin, like Abdullah Azzam, believed that the United States actually worked to eventually undermine their efforts and goals of creating an Islamic state.[62]

The allocation of these funds was primarily facilitated through the Inter-Services Intelligence (ISI) of the Pakistani military. Yet it was not only military aid that was supplied to these insurgent groups; civil organizations engaged in humanitarian endeavors also received substantial funding – especially from Saudi Arabia and the Gulf states. These sources encouraged aid and volunteers to participate directly in various capacities, whether as doctors, engineers, journalists, teachers, or combatants.[63] Nonetheless, the majority of the *mujahidin* were overwhelmingly Afghani, with only a minority composed of foreign fighters – including Arabs. These foreign fighters only began arriving in larger numbers from the mid-1980s onwards. The numbers of such fighters vary, with some estimating that the Arab fighters ranged between 8,000 and 25,000, most of whom arrived after the Soviet withdrawal.[64] An alternative estimate claims that Arab fighters constituted only around 1% of the overall fighting force – which ranged between 175,000 and 250,000 Afghan fighters, with the Arab fighters before the Soviets left being calculated at 2,000.[65]

The Arabs and Afghans would fight together in three main regions – the eastern, southern, and southeastern border areas of Afghanistan.[66] Among the Saudi citizens who flocked to Afghanistan to join the jihad against the communists – with significant consequences for the rise of Jihadi-Salafism – was a young soldier by the name of Osama bin Laden.[67] However, as per the events recounted by Bin Laden himself in 1986, the Arab fighters remained largely untrained, and Afghan forces hesitated to deploy them in frontline operations, often relegating them to supporting roles. The resulting humiliation of being sidelined prompted the Arabs to establish their own specialized training camps.[68]

In Afghanistan, Muslim aid volunteers and fighters from all over the world came to meet and exchange ideas. For the emergence of JS, the most important ingredient in Afghanistan was the Egyptian jihadists who brought their radical politics and reading of Qutb which would, in turn, influence jihadists from Saudi Arabia like Bin Laden. While Arab fighters had been steadily joining the war effort from the 1980s, and even had an influential leader in Azzam, the important Jihadi-Salafis came to Afghanistan from Egypt from the mid-1980s after serving jail sentences, and would set up somewhat independent camps. Of the significant JS groups to become established in the region were the Egyptian Islamic Jihad (EIJ) which grew from 1986 upon the arrival of al-Zawahiri; and the Egyptian Islamic Group (EIG) which developed from 1987[69] with leaders like Muhammad Shawki al-Islambuli and Rifaʿi Ahmad Taha (d. 2016). It is also documented that their spiritual leader, ʿUmar ʿAbd al-Raḥmān (d. 2017), made a visit to Peshawar in 1988 and then again in 1990.[70] Nonetheless, the jihad against the Soviets was dominated by non-Salafis, including the traditional Sunni Afghans. Salafis who were regular jihadists were a distinct minority, and the JS contingent was even smaller.

As the 1980s progressed, Jihadi-Salafis came to Afghanistan as a means of finding an outlet for their political worldview, after being thwarted from their ambitions in their home countries. One important figure for these Jihadi-Salafis was Abu Musʿab al-Suri, who fled Syria in 1987 for the region after his group was crushed.[71] He came to describe the Peshawar and Afghanistan of the late 1980s and early 1990s as 'a true university' and 'a turning point in Muslim history,' as different jihadist groups came together and debated.[72] Nonetheless, it is difficult to define al-Suri as a Jihadi-Salafi, as his Salafi credentials are weak.[73]

Al-Zawahiri described this time as a 'training course' for engaging in an eventual battle with the United States, whereby it brought together Arabs and non-Arabs (Pakistanis, Turks, and those from Central and East Asia) to acquaint themselves with each other and share their specialist military knowledge.[74] A pivotal moment in the development of JS came in 1988 when Bin Laden founded Al-Qaeda, the first jihadi organization with clear Wahhabi roots, which will be discussed in more detail below.[75] Indeed, it is in light of all the aforementioned that Afghanistan at this time has been described as 'the cradle of the Jihadist movement.'[76]

However, by the late 1980s, the JS presence in the camps of the 'Afghan Arabs' was causing disputes. For example, Sayyid Imām al-Sharif ('Dr Faḍl'),[77] the de facto leader of the EIJ and its supporters, had become divided from Abdullah Azzam and a significant number of those who supported the Muslim Brotherhood, who were more pragmatic about politics and other Islamic issues than the Jihadi-Salafis. Therefore, Afghanistan started to manifest the sort of disputes that pitted these two groups against each other in Egypt. At this time, there were emerging debates about the future direction after the Afghan jihad.

The Jihadi-Salafis would be significantly strengthened when Azzam was assassinated on 24 November 1989. Egyptian Jihadi-Salafis like EIJ, their leader Dr Faḍl, and his close associate al-Zawahiri, rose in prominence in these ranks, and became closer with Osama bin Laden. The most keenly debated topic among these factions was determining the real enemy, and how it was to be engaged within the jihad. While Azzam had seen Afghanistan as a base from which to defend causes around the world, members of EIJ, like al-Zawahiri, concluded that the Afghan war had served its purpose of bringing Jihadis together, away from the limitations imposed in the Arab lands by the autocratic and oppressive harassment of the governments in the region. Thus, in his estimation, it was now necessary to return the battle to the Arab lands and their regimes, as well as beginning to give some consideration to the foreign sponsors of these Arab dictators.[78]

Furthermore, there was a contrast between the Arabs who came to fight in the early 1980s and those that came at the end of the 1980s: the former were very involved with the Afghans and had to respect their ways, which were certainly not Salafi. However, Bin Laden was able to construct an independent camp by the end of the 1980s, so the Arabs there worked separately to the Afghans, which helped to keep them somewhat distant from the Afghan disputes that erupted after the Soviet withdrawal.[79] As the Jihadi-Salafis started to come to the region at the end of the Afghanistan war some, like Abū Muḥammad al-Maqdisi, and al-Zawahiri before the 1990s, were seemingly more interested in taking refuge in the north-west of Pakistan than liberating Afghanistan through jihad.

Certain works that would be particularly significant for JS emerged during this time, including Sayyid Imam al-Sharif's *The Pillar of Military Preparation* (1988); Abū Muḥammad al-Maqdisi's *The Community of Abraham* (1984) and *The Blatant Proof of the Infidel Nature of the Saudi State* (1989); Ayman al-Zawahiri's *The Bitter Harvest: The Muslim Brothers in Sixty Years* (ca. 1991); and Abu Mus'ab al-Suri's *The Jihadi Revolution in Syria: Hopes and Pains* (ca. 1991).[80] Thus the theoretical groundwork for what became identifiable as JS was laid in the background of the Afghan war. Furthermore, the activities of these groups served to shatter Arab unity in the region among the fighters and brought about fragmentation and suspicion.

After the Soviets left in 1989, the Afghan *mujāhidīn* became disunited and began to vigorously oppose one another,[81] with growing tensions between leaders Gulbuddin Hekmatyar and Ahmed Shah Massoud (d. 2001).[82] Consequently, many of the foreign fighters returned to their homelands, such as Sudan, which became a haven for Jihadis under the de facto leader Hassan al-Turabi, as well as Yemen, the Philippines, Indonesia, Malaysia, Europe, and America.[83]

The reception given to the returning fighters varied considerably, from the welcome they received in the United Arab Emirates, with stipends to settle back into society and scholarships for their children, to the suspicion they encountered in countries like Egypt and Saudi Arabia. The unease felt by the authorities in Saudi Arabia, at the prospect of the returning 12,000 men who traveled to Afghanistan between the late 1980s and early 1990s, was justified: on 13 November 1995, a car bomb exploded in the car park outside a US military building in Riyadh.[84]

### *5.2.4 Abdullah Azzam (d. 1989)*

Abdullah Azzam was one of the most influential jihadi writers of the twentieth century, and the most important figure around whom most of the Afghan Arabs would gather.[85] His significance is highlighted by the fact that he has been named the 'Imam of Jihād' and the 'Sayyid Qutb of Jordan.'[86] In this work, we will classify him not as a Jihadi-Salafi, but rather as a Salafi who was engaged in defensive jihad. Nonetheless, he would be highly influential for many Jihadi-Salafis, as this chapter will illustrate.

In 1941, Azzam was born in what was then British Mandatory Palestine, to a moderately religious family, and he was both exceptionally devout and academically gifted. Following the establishment of Israel in 1948, Azzam's village would be annexed by Transjordan. In 1954, he joined the Jordanian Muslim Brotherhood, and started a religious study class in the community. He was particularly keen on the works of the main Brotherhood ideologues, like Ḥasan al-Bannā and Sayyid Qutb. After specializing in agriculture at college and being a schoolteacher for a time, he then traveled, in 1962, to pursue religious studies at Damascus University in Syria, and obtained a diploma in Islamic law, with the highest honors, in 1966.[87]

However, his family was displaced in the Second *Nakba* when Israel seized the West Bank of Palestine in 1967, and he had to move to Jordan, where they settled in a refugee camp in al-Zarqa, a few kilometers northwest of Amman. Between 1967 and 1970, he engaged in military operations against the Israelis, with the *fidāʾiyyīn*. During this time, he obtained a master's degree with high honors in Islamic law from al-Azhar University in Cairo, Egypt, taking up a lectureship post teaching Islamic law at the Jordan University in Amman in 1970. After enrolling in a doctoral program at al-Azhar in 1971, he obtained a PhD in Islamic law in 1973.[88]

While a student in Egypt, he had become a close friend of Sayyid Qutb's family, and other leading members of the Muslim Brotherhood and their families. He also came into contact with some people who were attached to the radical emerging Jihadi-Salafis from Egypt, including one young man who liked Azzam but was linked to the radical Shukrī Muṣṭafā, considering him and all of the Muslim Brotherhood to be disbelievers. Azzam does not appear to have met, at this time, such figures as Muḥammad Faraj, Khalid al-Islambouli, and Ayman al-Zawahiri.[89]

In the late 1970s his preaching started to include criticism of the Jordanian government, which led to him being threatened with jail. After being dismissed from his post in 1980, he moved to Saudi Arabia and started to teach at King ʿAbd al-ʿAzīz University in Jeddah and Mecca. It was upon performing the Hajj in October 1980 that Azzam's life took a dramatic turn, upon meeting Kamāl al-Sanānirī (d. 1981). He was a legendary member of the Muslim Brotherhood who had studied with Ḥasan al-Bannā and spent twenty years in prison in deplorable conditions for being a prominent member of the Brotherhood's secret unit.[90] Al-Sanānirī was married to Sayyid Qutb's sister, Amīnah, and had been among the first delegation sent by the Egyptian Muslim Brotherhood to Afghanistan in November 1980, to investigate the proceedings of the war effort. There he had mediated between competing factions of the *mujahidin* and laid the foundations of the group that would be headed by ʿAbd al-Rasūl Sayyāf. During the course of their meeting, al-Sanānirī convinced Azzam to join the jihad in Afghanistan against the Soviet Union.[91] He was due to join Azzam but was arrested by the Egyptian authorities on returning to Egypt on 4 September 1981, and would be declared dead, seemingly from torture, on 6 November 1981.[92]

Subsequently, in 1981, Azzam transferred to the new International Islamic University in Islamabad. From the beginning of his time in the war effort, he was an important intermediary between the fighters in Afghanistan and those with a similar political persuasion in the Middle East. In 1984, he created the influential Services Bureau (*Maktab al-Khadamāt*) in Peshawar. This was essentially a militarized charity, with military, humanitarian, and educational projects, and from where he produced the influential magazine *al-Jihad* and other publications. The Services Bureau facilitated the entry, hosting, training, and eventual deployment of Arab and foreign fighters against the Soviet forces.

In founding the Services Bureau, he had received the financial backing of the young Osama bin Laden. Azzam met Bin Laden while he was a professor in Saudi Arabia, and eventually Bin Laden would host Azzam and his family, and even visited Azzam's family in Amman in 1984. Bin Laden was to become a member of the Consultative Council (*majlis al-shūrā*) of the Services Bureau by 1986, but he was not very active in the role. One of the colleagues that Azzam directed to work on a humanitarian project at this time was Khalid Sheikh Mohammed, who would later be identified as one of the masterminds behind the 9/11 attacks on the United States. Bin Laden would break from the Bureau when it was deemed to be an insufficient training operation for the fighters. However, the Bureau was, in Azzam's assessment in 1989 – an opinion shared by academia – critical in enlarging the jihad effort from a localized one into a global one.[93]

Among his many writings on the subject of the jihad in Afghanistan, he is most famous for three, which still retain popularity among Jihadis of all kinds: *Signs of the Merciful in the Afghan Jihad, In Defense of Muslim Lands*, and *Join the Caravan.*[94] *Signs of the Merciful in the Afghan Jihad* was published in 1983 and is an analysis of the political and historical factors surrounding the jihad in Afghanistan, as well as a documentation of numerous miracle stories that were narrated to have occurred at the hands of the *mujahidin*.[95] This work was, however, not universally appreciated; for instance, Nabil Na'im, who had led the Jihadi-Salafi Egyptian Islamic Jihad, said that the book was 'mostly myths. We used to read it and laugh.'[96] After Azzam's credentials were questioned by his quoting of Sufis like Abū Yazīd and Suhrawardī in the context of a discussion on miracles – the usual domain of Sufi discourse – Azzam went on to address, somewhat indirectly, such concerns in a later edition, highlighting his mild Salafism:

> The man who writes these words on *karamat* is a person who has spent a quarter-century studying Islam carrying the Salafi creed. He does not believe in superstitions, lives to fight *bid'a* and to establish God's religion on earth, and is influenced most by the books of Ibn Taymiyya and Ibn Qayyim. He doesn't take his beliefs from the delusions of windbags, or even the visions of the pious (*ru'a al-salihin*). His only doctrine comes from the book of God and the sunna of the messengers and from the luminaries of Islamic thought through history, especially the line of Ahmad ibn Hanbal.[97]

*In Defense of Muslim Lands* appeared in early 1984 and was an elaboration of a 1983 fatwa in which he argued that the jihad in Afghanistan was 'personally obligatory' (*farḍ 'ayn*) – like the daily ritual prayers and fasting in Ramadan – for every able-bodied Muslim male across the globe. They were obligated to join, even if their parents, spouses or governmental authorities denied them permission. The uniqueness of the fatwa, and the book, was in expanding the scope of the duty, from what numerous scholars deemed to be a 'communal obligation' (*farḍ kifāyah*) for the Muslims of that region, to the entire world. Moreover, its significance can be seen as opposing the international legal order, by granting the right of individuals to declare war, and not rely on the declarations of nation states.[98]

It is of note that Azzam appeals to the authority of conservative, non-Jihādī Salafi scholars in this work, like Ibn Bāz (whom he dearly loved and personally met a few times) and Ibn ʿUthaymīn, as supposedly supporting the argument espoused by him, which can be disputed by the lack of evidence showing them to believe that jihad in Afghanistan was personally obligatory for every able-bodied Muslim.[99] Yet elsewhere, Ibn Bāz spoke of the 'individual duty of Muslims' to help the Afghan fighters, 'financially and physically or one of the two according to one's capability,'[100] which was subtly different to Azzam's stance, and may have contributed to Azzam misunderstanding Ibn Bāz and Ibn 'Uthaymin. Nonetheless, Azzam's position of the personal obligation of jihad was widely rejected by Salafi scholars, from quietists like Muqbil al-Wadi'i to *Ṣaḥwa* scholars like Salman al-Oudah, Safar al-Hawali, and Muhammad al-Munajjid. Likewise, Azzam was directly opposed in this regard by non-Salafis such as Ḥasan al-Turabi, in an interview with Azzam in the magazine *al-Jihad*, and Taqi Uthmani, as narrated by Afghan veteran Muhammad Yasir.[101]

*Join the Caravan* was published in 1987 and was another impassioned call for the worldwide Muslim community to join the jihad in Afghanistan. It was immediately influential and is hailed as a Jihādī classic to this day. In the work, he lamented the lack of 'real men,' 'men of knowledge,' and 'action,' but that 'Those who go on jihad are fewer still, and those who continue on that path are too few to mention,' and 'tyrants' have come to rule Muslim lands because of the Muslims 'abandoning jihad.' He also disputed those scholars who said that the war effort simply needed aid, and not fighters, complaining that as a result it was only 'young Arabs whose education is rudimentary' who were joining the fight and that they could not even read the Qurʾan properly. The essence of his appeal can be seen in the following words from him: 'A Muslim who is not performing jihad today is just like one who breaks the fast in Ramadan without permission, or a rich person who withholds legal alms [*zakat*]. Indeed, failing to carry out jihad is more serious still.'[102] For Azzam, the only way to fulfill the religious imperative of establishing an Islamic society was through this jihad. Yet, he disavowed a fanatical type of legalist Salafism, as he advised foreigners coming to the jihad to adopt the ritual prayer postures of the Afghans in accordance with the latter's adherence to the Ḥanafī legal school, so as to endear oneself to them.[103]

Azzam's acceptance of Sufis and other non-Salafis earned him the ire of quietist Salafis like Rabiʿ al-Madkhalī, who criticized Azzam in the late

1980s for not opposing Sufis and Shiʿa; and Jihadi-Salafis in Afghanistan and the North-West Frontier province of Pakistan, like Abū Muḥammad al-Maqdisi.[104] This perhaps contributed to his assassination in 1989, which remains one of the most mysterious events in the history of jihadism: no one has ever proven who carried it out.[105] Rumors allege that Jihadi-Salafis themselves, and perhaps even al-Zawahiri, were behind the assassination.

Moreover, his writings did not display any of the defining JS tendencies towards anathematization of Muslims and wanton violence which easily targets civilians, despite the fact that he was well aware of such extremist JS doctrines which had already taken shape in Egypt since the 1970s (as will be discussed). Nonetheless, he was a mentor to a number of significant Jihadi-Salafis due to his passionate advocacy of jihad, and perhaps due to his motivational speaking style and leadership. He was known to be easy-going, charismatic, popular, and austere with regards to food and material things, and to possess a soft heart – he was often given to crying, especially when praying or invoking God. Yet, he was not a co-founder or a member of Al-Qaeda, as is widely assumed.

Therefore, caution should be adopted in identifying Azzam's thought with the clear extremist tendencies that would later define Jihadi-Salafism, such as reckless condemnation of Muslim rulers and others, and unrestrained acts of violence that inevitably harmed civilians and non-combatants. Nonetheless, he wrote, in relation to the secular Arab rulers and leftists, 'He who embraces nationalist principles leaves Islam' and 'let it be clear from the start that those who legislate by something other than God's revelation are infidels [*kuffar*].'[106] But this phrasing is characteristic of Brotherhood scholars, including the moderate Yūsuf al-Qaraḍāwī, and does not gravitate towards the calls for reckless acts of violence upon such governments, as is a JS characteristic. Indeed, Azzam directly criticized the proto-JS leader Shukri Mustafa for his reckless excommunication of Muslims, and the harm it brought with murder and violence.[107]

It has, therefore, been noted that his writings could be contradictory, and some parts could seem to align with what we now identify as Jihadi-Salafism. For instance, he spoke of one having to obey the laws of the land in which one is resident, but elsewhere in a lecture he apparently justified killing supporters of Israel in the United States (although he never articulated such a position in writing).[108] It is possible that there was no contradiction in Azzam's mind, and rather the general position was expressed in the former stance, and the exception was represented in the latter; or maybe he simply changed his mind. There are statements from Azzam which could be interpreted in an extremist JS manner in regard to killing Westerners in Muslim lands, on the basis of those who 'initiate fighting with us' or if they 'spread evil' and refuse warnings to leave the country.[109] Nonetheless, it is such seeming ambiguities which, unsurprisingly, gave rise to disputes about his legacy and opened the door to Jihadi-Salafis arguing that 'Azzam was one of them in thought.'[110] Ultimately, Thomas Hegghammer argues,

> Azzam neither preached nor practiced international terrorism of the kind that secular Palestinian groups had used before him and jihadi groups would use after him. He did not actively prescribe or condone out-of-area attacks on Soviet targets outside Afghanistan, deliberate mass-casualty attacks on civilians, or suicide bombings… Azzam almost certainly disapproved of the most blatant forms of international terrorism, such as hijackings and the bombing of civilians.[111]

Moreover, his *al-Jihad* magazine was not exclusively Salafi, as it often featured prominent people associated with the Muslim Brotherhood and its related organizations (some seen as moderate activists, and not Jihadis). Such people included Yūsuf al-Qaraḍāwī, Zaynab al-Ghazālī (d. 2005), Hasan al-Turābī (d. 2016), Qāzī Hussain Aḥmad (d. 2013), and Rachid Ghannouchi, as well as Salafis like Ibn Bāz and Abū Bakr al-Jazāʾirī (d. 2018), and *mujāhidīn* leaders like Hekmatyar, Sayyāf and Ḥaqqānī (d. 2018). He remained a jihadi of the Muslim Brotherhood, or perhaps a Salafi engaged in jihad, but not a Jihadi-Salafi as defined in this chapter. He declared in 1988, a year before his death, 'My creed has been that of the Muslim Brotherhood for thirty-six years.'[112] Earlier, in the 1980s, he declared that the works of Sayyid Qutb were most influential on him in the realm of ideas (*fikriyyan*), but he was also inspired by Ibn Taymiyya in creedal matters (*ʿaqdiyyan*), Ibn Qayyim in spirituality (*rūḥiyyan*) and Nawawi in Islamic law (*fiqhiyyan*).[113] Nonetheless, Azzam considered al-Albānī to hold strange legal opinions and to be gravely mistaken in his criticism of Sayyid Qutb for holding Sufi notions, and he was highly critical of his quietist political teachings.[114] At the end of his life, Azzam continued to display an anti-factionalist approach, whereby he encouraged one to see the good in various groups including the Muslim Brotherhood, the Tabligh-Deoband movement, and the Salafis. His son-in-law, Abdullah Anas, rejected the idea that he or his father-in-law were Salafis, or that they opposed the Salafis.[115] This, again, makes sense of why his legacy is so contested.

A distinct feature of Azzam's activities in the jihad in Afghanistan is that he never sought to displace the leadership of the native Afghans; hence he merely attempted to unite their ranks and have the Arab fighters accept their leadership and follow their directions. For his part, he worked closely under the leadership of Sayyāf's group, and later built up a close relationship with the Panjshiri commander Ahmed Shah Massoud, who cannot be characterized as a Salafi.[116] This is something of a contrast to the later Jihadi-Salafis who, unsurprisingly, would later seek to strike out on their own path.

At the end of the 1980s, Azzam faced a number of opponents, including, for our purposes, Saudi Salafis who mistrusted him for his link to the Muslim Brotherhood; and militant Jihadi-Salafis who viewed him as too moderate. This latter group had come to be known as *takfīrīs*, due to their laxity in engaging in anathematization of Muslims and the rulers in Muslim lands; and they were known for having their minds set on violently overthrowing the governments of the Muslim world. While these groups differed among themselves, they also differed in their level of antagonism to Azzam. He had the most trouble with the leaders of the EIJ and their people like Ayman al-Zawahiri, but he was on very good terms – despite having contrary views on military tactics – with his fellow Azhari 'Umar 'Abd al-Rahman (d. 2017) ('the blind shaykh' subsequently implicated in the 1993 World Trade Center bombing), known as the spiritual leader of the Egyptian Islamic Group.[117] Yet, these factions also criticized Azzam for other reasons: accommodating the Ḥanafī school of law of the overwhelming majority of Afghans which was markedly different to the Salafi trends; supporting Massoud who was seen as a liberal; and for working with the Gulf states, among other matters that they passionately objected to in their usual zeal.

Azzam has been publicly lauded by Jihadi-Salafis as a hero and beyond suspicion, despite their private discourse about him. For instance, al-Zawahiri said of him, 'Is it possible that the martyr Abdallah Azzam was a US collaborator, when in fact he never stopped inciting young men against the United States and used to back Hamas with all the resources at his disposal?'[118] Even as late as 2008, when al-Zawahiri was writing a refutation of his ex-JS colleague Dr Faḍl – who had repented of jihadism – al-Zawahiri wrote of Azzam: 'We only knew him as the spiritual, worshipping, devout, godly, pious scholar who was one of the people of determination and patience and who upheld this religion to the fullest extent.'[119] Nonetheless, it is also reported that al-Zawahiri had a deep conflict with Azzam, considered him during his lifetime to be an agent for the United States and Saudi Arabia, and urged Bin Laden to stop giving him funds. Furthermore, some of Azzam's family have said that al-Zawahiri considered Azzam to be a disbeliever, and refused to pray behind him; but again, this is refuted by al-Zawahiri's own testimony in 2008 in forthright terms. In fact, one only finds statements by al-Zawahiri praising Azzam. It is difficult to know where the truth actually lies in this matter, although the public face is significant.[120] In addition, by way of illustrating his luminous reputation within JS, the following statement given by Osama bin Laden in 1999 is fully apt: 'Shaykh Abdallah Azzam, may God have mercy on his soul, is a man worth a nation. After his assassination, Muslim women proved to be unable to give birth to a man like him. The people of jihad who lived that epoch know that Islamic Jihad in Afghanistan has not benefitted from anyone as it has from Shaykh Abdallah Azzam.'[121]

In conclusion, Azzam's genuine sincerity, and commitment to defending the Palestinians and Afghans against oppressors, appears to have impressed multiple sections of the Muslim world, including militant Jihadi-Salafi groups who would go on to claim him as their own, even though his teachings and actions belie such an association.

## *5.3 The History of Jihadi-Salafism*

As the ideas of Sayyid Qutb and Salafism inspired Jihadi-Salafis all over the world, it is possible to identify the main areas where this thought developed: Egypt, Morocco, Saudi Arabia, Algeria, Afghanistan, and the Malay Archipelago. It was in these countries that the initial proto-JS groups started to emerge, before the appearance of actual JS groups from the mid-1990s onwards. The following discussion will focus on these key areas, despite the fact that JS has become a global phenomenon, impacting countries as diverse as Mauritania, Mali,[122] and Sweden.[123]

### *5.3.1 Egypt*

*The origins of Jihadi-Salafism*

Egypt is where Jihadi-Salafism was born. The most popular account for its origins starts with the rift that occurred between Gamal Abdel Nasser and the Muslim Brotherhood when Nasser came to power in the 1950s. After a Brotherhood member tried to assassinate him, Nasser began a series of crackdowns that began with shutting down the Muslim Brotherhood. This was followed by the mass imprisonment of Islamists, accompanied by unfair trials and excessive torture. The initial ideas that would eventually morph into jihadism appeared to emerge from deep within these dungeons.[124]

The indignity of being treated this way by their fellow Muslims led to retaliatory thinking, and factions began to form among the inmates, with some being driven to revise part of the ideology of the Muslim Brotherhood. The most influential of these inmates was Sayyid Qutb whose *Milestones on the Path* eventually became the foundational textbook for jihadism.[125] Qutb's theory that humans had regressed back to a state of pre-Islamic ignorance or *jāhiliyyah* led some readers of Qutb to contend that many people who called themselves Muslim were not, in fact, Muslims any longer. This idea influenced some Egyptian Islamists to excommunicate or make *takfīr* of the government, and from this notion the concept of jihadism evolved.[126]

Furthermore, Qutb's use of the concepts *mufāṣalah* (separation) and *ʿuzlah* (withdrawal) would lead to avid readers of his books forming two camps within the prisons. The first group deemed the detachment spoken of to be a spiritual one, but nonetheless excommunicated the general Egyptian population. Naturally, upon release, they concealed their beliefs, while continuing to remain within society, yet hoping for the day that Islamic law could be established within the country. The second group agreed with the first in excommunicating the society of *jāhiliyyah* and had the same appreciation of the dangers that came with publicly espousing such views while they were in such a state of weakness, but they believed in 'total separation' (*mufāṣalah kāmilah*) from society, in a practical sense, whereby they could withdraw from society into their own Islamic community and then cast judgments of excommunication upon the rest of society.

This latter faction came into the Egyptian public eye in 1977, when a group that the media called *al-Takfīr wa'l-Hijrah* (The Party of Excommunication and Emigration), but which called itself *Jamāʿat al-Muslimīin* (The Group of the Muslims), was caught up in a scandal of kidnap and murder.[127] At most, one can identify this group as proto-JS in its renouncing of the legal tradition, and attempting to follow sacred texts themselves, despite being untrained as legal experts. Similarly, their extreme use of excommunication, violence and sense of *al-wala' wa'l-bara'* has echoes in later Jihadi-Salafism. Nonetheless, while more correctly defined Jihadi-Salafis would soon criticize this group, their methodology has perhaps been revived in some sense by neo-Jihadi-Salafis, or *takfiri*s, who have emerged post-Al-Qaeda.

The leader of *al-Takfīr wa'l-Hijrah* was Shukri Mustafa (d. 1978), who had inherited the mantle when its initial leader, 'Ali 'Abduh Isma'il, a young graduate of al-Azhar University was convinced, in 1969, by Hasan al-Hudaybi, the leader of the Muslim Brotherhood, of the error of practicing widespread excommunication of Muslims. Isma'il's dramatic renouncing of the leadership led to the original group collapsing, after which Shukri Mustafa strove to rebuild it.

Mustafa was born in 1942, in a village thirty kilometers from Asyut, in Middle Egypt. His father was mayor of the village, but his parents divorced when he was still a child, and he and his mother left for Asyut. After a mediocre education, he came to study agriculture at Asyut University. While a student there in 1965, he was arrested for distributing Muslim Brotherhood leaflets, at a time when Nasser had announced that he had uncovered a Muslim Brotherhood plot to overthrow him, and mass arrests had ensued as a result. It is this series of events which makes scholars draw the conclusion that Mustafa's group is simply a radical offshoot of the Muslim Brotherhood, especially as Mustafa is said, by some, to have been a member of the Brotherhood's special military wing.[128]

Indeed, the movement has been comprehensively dismissed by leading Jihadi-Salafis in recent times, such as leaders of the EIG and EIJ, who have spoken of their attempts to correct the group,[129] as well as by Ayman al-Zawahiri[130] and Abu Hamza al-Misri (who labels Mustafa's group as a modern version of the deviant early Islamic group called the *Khawārij*).[131]

Yet, due to certain close social bonds, such as some marriage links, and similarities in political thought between Shukri Mustafa's group and some members of the JS group in Asyut who killed President Sadat in 1981, there were members of the Egyptian press reporting on the Sadat assassination who wrongly thought the assassins to be part of *al-Takfir wa'l-Hijrah.*[132]

It should be noted that there are at least two other accounts of the origins of Jihadi-Salafism in Egypt which differ from the aforementioned conveyor-belt theory from Qutb, and the government oppression of the Muslim Brotherhood, to the likes of Shukri Mustafa. The first of these alternative accounts provides a narrative of an indigenous proto-JS developing in Egypt before Shukri Mustafa was arrested, which was independent of the Muslim Brotherhood. It was not created by the writings of Qutb or the oppression of the Brotherhood, even if Qutb and the torture of the Brotherhood was to influence its trajectory. The second account is part of the official account that was pushed during the trial of Shukri Mustafa and his followers. It is useful, if only for academic purposes, to briefly summarize those accounts here.

The first alternative account argues that JS cells developed in Egypt between the end of the 1950s and the beginning of the 1960s, under the leadership of Nabil Bur'i, Isma'il Tantawi and 'Alawi Mustafa, with its formal organization being around 1966 in Cairo. This would be the foundation of what would become the Egyptian Islamic Jihad. Notable new recruits included a teenaged Ayman al-Zawahiri and a young Sayyid Imām al-Sharif (later known as 'Dr Faḍl'), who both became prominent Jihadi-Salafi leaders (as discussed briefly above in the section on Afghanistan). The focus of the group was preparing for jihad, as opposed to planning an armed insurrection and revolution.[133] They formed independently of the Muslim Brotherhood and the prisons, and were recruited through Salafi centers, such as the *Ansar al-Sunna*, and the organization *al-Jam'iyyah al-Shar'iyyah* (The Legitimacy Organization); hence their creedal and jurisprudential outlook was defined by a traditionalist Salafism. Interestingly, the group emphasized that they had no connections to the Muslim Brotherhood, but held Sayyid Qutb in the highest esteem and studied his commentary of the Qur'an and *Milestones*, which were included in the curriculum of study by the *Ansar al-Sunna.*[134] These recruits were instructed by Jihadi-inclined teachers, who believed that the creation of an Islamic state in Egypt would remedy the problems of the Muslim world, including the liberation of Palestine and the establishment of an ideal Islamic society.[135] Nonetheless, the training within the group consisted only of martial arts and wrestling – the idea was that a military coup would be performed by those they recruited in the military academy. For this purpose, those who had graduated from university were expected to then proceed to the military academy as well.[136]

The second alternative account relates to a figure called Sāliḥ Sirriyyah (d. 1976), who led a group that perpetrated the first public act of jihadi violence in the time of President Sadat in Egypt. They unsuccessfully attempted a military coup in 1974 by attacking the Military Technical Academy (*al-Fanniya al-'Askariyya*) in Heliopolis, as a prelude to then attacking the President's cortege as it passed.[137] This episode has relevance for the story of Jihadi-Salafism in Egypt because the official account which emerged in the aftermath of the murder of President Sadat by Jihadi-Salafis in October 1981 attributed the origins of the event to the attempted coup of 1974, and the subsequent regrouping of members of this 1974 mission.[138]

Sirriyyah had spent time in Iraq as a member of the Iraqi Muslim Brotherhood but had left the movement after a disagreement with the leadership, returning to Egypt in 1970. His primary goal was to liberate Palestine from Israeli control, and he saw this as being viable only if an Islamic state was established in Egypt. He also associated with the nascent Jihadi-Salafi group led by Isma'il Tantawi; however, Tantawi rebuffed his plans and refused to cooperate with him. During Sirriyyah's trial for the attempted coup, a document was found to have been written by him entitled *The Treatise on Faith*, where he argued that they were now in a state of *jāhiliyyah*, and that the rulers were unbelievers, as were those who supported them and their system, or participated in an un-Islamic party or displayed obedience to the nation state. Jihad, he argued, was therefore called for to remove such a system.[139] This type of reasoning was certainly Jihadi, and was shared by Jihadi-Salafis, but it was missing the Salafi element.

What is significant in the Tantawi group's rejection of Sirriyah's plan is that it marks the defining moment when Salafism comes to be the central feature of a jihadi movement, over and above any seemingly beneficial alliances between cross-Sunni groups. This is because Tantawi rejected joining forces with Sirriyyah because the latter would not make Salafism the cornerstone of his movement. Sirriyyah's focus was the military action with as many Muslims as possible, and he was willing to cooperate with any and all Muslims who agreed with his aim. On the other hand, Tantawi and his group considered the foundational doctrines of Salafism, including the claim that Ibn Taymiyya was their primary scholarly reference, to be non-negotiable.[140] Hence Tantawi's group did not join the political cause of Sirriyyah, which they believed in, because of theological reasons, and it is this rejection that can be considered to have given birth to a truly Jihadi-Salafi movement.

At this stage, it is difficult, if not impossible, to state which of these three narratives is the most accurate, but all three have factual bases to them, and perhaps all of them contributed in different ways to the mix that eventually became Egyptian Jihadi-Salafism.

*The murder of Sadat as the public announcement of JS in Egypt*

The religious basis for the assassination of Sadat had been set in late 1980 when 'Umar 'Abd al-Rahman – the blind Azhari scholar who was seen as the source of legal edicts (*fatwa*) for the Jihadi-Salafis – ruled that the murder of President Sadat was religiously lawful on account of him failing to implement Islamic law and adhere to the dictates of belief in *al-hakimiyya*.[141] Abd al-Rahman was particularly close to *al-Jama'ah al-Islamiyyah* (The Egyptian Islamic Group or EIG), which had emerged as a student organization in Upper Egypt, and then spread around the country, during the early to mid-1970s, and came to include many professionals, such as doctors, engineers, lawyers, and teachers. Although the late 1970s saw a number of their leadership persuaded by the methodology of the Egyptian Muslim Brotherhood (including the whole Lower Egypt faction[142]) and the early movement divided, the general leadership quickly turned to the path of JS and were instrumental in the plan to assassinate Sadat.

The assassination of Sadat on 6 October 1981, by what was a merger of various JS groups, marks the defining public announcement of JS political violence. Various groups came together to operate under the leadership of Faraj, a twenty-seven-year-old electrical engineer, who was based in Cairo, under the banner *Tanzim al-Jihad* (The Organization of Jihad). Faraj's significance for Jihadi-Salafism is not that he was simply the coordinator of the killing of Sadat, but also that he published a treatise, in 1981, entitled *al-Farīḍah al-Ghā'ibah* (*The Neglected Obligation*).[143] This work marked the true beginning of written, theorized Jihadi-Salafism, as it essentially took the ideas of Qutb and Shukri Mustafa to a further conclusion: the ruler is an apostate and must be fought now, in the present, until Islamic law is restored in accordance with the establishment of a wholly-functioning Islamic state. Furthermore, it was considered to be an 'operational manual' throughout the 1980s in the circles of Jihadis and retained by its leadership through the beginning of the 1990s.[144] In the work, Faraj maximized the utility of Ibn Taymiyya's anti-Mongolian fatwa, where he permitted jihad against an ostensibly Muslim ruler on the basis that he was not actually a Muslim. Faraj applied it to a modern context in its fullest and most violent sense.[145]

The public trials which followed Sadat's murder were illuminating in terms of highlighting the motivations of the perpetrators and the vicious interrogations of the suspects by the police. Egyptian military officer Khalid al-Islambouli's (d. 1982) hostility towards Sadat shocked many secular Egyptians who admired him. During one infamous part of his trial, he equated Sadat with the most despised Qur'anic figure when he said: 'I have killed the Pharaoh, and I don't fear death.' When asked in his trial about why he had committed the murder, al-Islambouli said that Sadat's crimes were making peace with Israel (in the 1978 Camp David Accords, leading to the 1979 Egypt–Israel Peace Treaty), the oppression of 'the sons of Egypt' during the September crackdown (including his brother, which had deeply distressed Khalid), and that the non-implementation of Islamic Law was bringing harm to the people of Egypt.[146] At one point, a young al-Zawahiri appeared in court and addressed the foreign journalists in broken English, declaring that the movement was simply a collective of Muslims seeking to establish 'an Islamic state and an Islamic society,' and that they had been severely tortured in prison, as he and other prisoners revealed the physical signs of harm. He then explained to the journalists:

> We suffered the severest inhuman treatment. They kicked us, they beat us, they whipped us with electric cables, they shocked us with electricity! They shocked us with electricity! And they used the wild dogs! And they used the wild dogs! And they hung us over the edges of the doors with our hands tied at the back! [He bent over to demonstrate.] They arrested the wives, the mothers, the fathers, the sisters, and the sons![147]

Furthermore, he explained the movement's ultimate perception of itself:

> We are here – the real Islamic front and the real Islamic opposition against Zionism, communism, and imperialism… And now, as an answer to the second question: Why did they bring us here? They bring us here for two reasons. First, they are trying to abolish the outstanding Islamic movement… and secondly, to complete the conspiracy of evacuating the area in preparation for the Zionist infiltration.[148]

Although their jihadi and Islamist outlook was clearly in view, the Salafi part of their ideology was more obscure.

After being sentenced by the court, the time spent in prison was to bring the divisions of the jihadi groups to the fore. Before that time, *Tanzim* and the EIG had differed in strategy: the former favored a coup led by military officers, while the latter preferred encouraging the state into a protracted battle. The *Tanzim* were very secretive in their activities, whereas the EIG operated quite openly in the mosques and charitable causes.[149] Furthermore, they disagreed about the leadership of ʿUmar ʿAbd al-Raḥmān, whereby the EIG supported him and the *Tanzim* opposed him; and the EIG held that those who sinned out of ignorance would be pardoned, while the *Tanzim* held that they would not be so excused.[150]

During the reign of Sadat's successor, President Hosni Mubarak, the *Tanzim* faction became extinct, as leaders like al-Zawahiri (released in

1984), left the country after serving relatively short sentences. The next chapter in the story of this faction is told as they resurfaced in Afghanistan and eventually developed into Al-Qaeda (discussed below).

The EIG underwent a radical transformation as a result of the imprisonments for Sadat's murder. Sherman A. Jackson has described this period as marking 'a new phase in the *Gamāʻah*'s organizational infrastructure, a more explicit and formal doctrinal commitment, and an inexorably more confrontational relationship with the Egyptian state and society.'[151] The EIG's violent retaliation against the oppression they suffered at the hands of the government led to increasing levels of violence in society by the late 1980s, with a significant death toll, including EIG members, police and security workers, tourists, and others. The government's rejection of a communiqué from the EIG in 1989 seeking a cessation of violence upon accepting a six-point plan led to a wave of violence, culminating in an unsuccessful attempt on Mubarak's life in 1995 in Addis Ababa.[152]

*The repentance of major Jihadi-Salafis in Egypt*

A momentous event occurred on 5 July 1997 during the trial of Muhammad al-Amin Abd al-Alim, a member of the EIG accused of setting off explosions in banks. He stood and delivered to the court a statement, which had been signed by six of the top imprisoned members of the EIG and, in part, it read:

> The Historical Leadership of *al-Gamāʻah al-Islāmīyah* calls upon their brethren from among the leadership and the rank-and-file to terminate, without stipulation and with no prerequisites, all armed campaigns and all communiqués that call for such, both inside and outside of Egypt, in the interest of Islam and the Muslims.[153]

This marked the official beginning of what would be called the EIG's 'Initiative to Stop the Violence,' which would later lead to the publication, in 2002, of four booklets devoted to renouncing political violence as a means of social change and Islamic revival, as well as denouncing religious extremism (*ghulūw*) and wanton excommunication of Muslims.[154] These publications were composed by two or three members of the Consultative Council, and then accompanied by an endorsement signed by the remaining five or six members. Of most importance among these eight members was the presence of Karam Zuhdi (b. 1953), who had been imprisoned since being convicted of leading the EIG in the planned assassination of Sadat in 1981.[155]

In addition to the EIG's composition of these treatises, and self-endorsing them, they also sent the works to al-Azhar's Council for Islamic Research (*Majmaʻ al-Buhuth al-Islamiyyah*), who noted that they did not contradict normative Islamic teachings, even if they possessed some mistakes. The significance of al-Azhar in this context is that they have constantly been placed in opposition to Jihadis or Jihadi-Salafis in Egypt, as the final authority on what constitutes correct Islamic doctrine and practice; and, in many ways, they have played a role almost indistinguishable from that of the government. Yet the EIG was willing at this juncture to turn to al-Azhar for the final ratification of their new teaching. From the 1980s until the early 1990s, the prominent Azhari scholars who attempted to dissuade the Jihadis included the Rector of al-Azhar University, the Mufti of Egypt, Muhammad al-Ghazali and Muhammad Mutawalli al-Sha'rawi.[156]

In addition to the anarchic thought that besets a Jihadi-Salafi methodology, the utilization of Azhari scholars to re-educate radicals in prison harmed the public relations of such campaigns as the Initiative to Stop the Violence. This was because often reformed prisoners would be released from prison on account of repenting of their violent outlook and operations. Hence, prisoner retractions could be deemed self-serving and insincere in view of the reward offered by the state for such repudiations; and such aspersions were cast by some other Islamist groups and even government officials.

Furthermore, not only were some of the signatories of the manifestoes somewhat reluctant about the Initiative to Stop the Violence, but they also had a battle on their hands to convince the rank-and-file of the probity of this change in direction. For example, a small group of EIG members would soon murder fifty-eight Western tourists and Egyptians in Luxor on 17 November 1997, an act which was endorsed by one member of the Consultative Council, Rifa'i Taha, who headed the Consultative Council outside Egypt, and had left for Afghanistan in order to fight the Soviets. The massacre would deeply distress the members of the Historical Leadership who had just renounced such violence.[157]

Nonetheless, the Historical Leadership continued to pursue their initiative, despite opposition from notables among their ranks; and, to their undoubted relief, the Luxor incident would be the last major act of violence committed by members of the EIG. The Historical Leadership achieved a breakthrough when 'Umar 'Abd al-Rahman ('the blind shaykh') expressed his approval of the initiative in 1999, although he later reneged on such an endorsement upon learning of EIG members being killed by the police. However, the Historical Leadership continued to struggle to achieve something near a consensus in its own ranks. In the aftermath of the September 2001 attacks, the Egyptian government permitted them to undertake a tour of the prisons, so that they could engage with prisoners of all ranks about their new stances on political violence. This tour took ten months and had a profound impact on the members of the EIG which seems to have been of critical importance in making the initiative a success.[158]

There are various accounts which attest to the sincerity of the initiative as a manifestation of a religious conviction and change of heart based on what are considered sound religious principles, as opposed to being a mere self-serving capitulation without any real religious motivation. Firstly, members of the EIG who disagreed with the initiative still gained their freedom, despite such opposition. Secondly, the manifestoes reflect a coherence and argument that is almost universally upheld as being a normative reasoning in accordance with Islamic law, hence the endorsement of al-Azhar attached to the booklets. Thirdly, while sustained torture cannot be discounted in influencing such changes of heart, one must be cautious in casually applying it to veterans of the movement who had been seemingly hardened to the prison regime. Indeed, many of the rank-and-file members stated that they changed their position on the matter simply on the basis that they had full conviction that Zuhdi and his fellow veterans would never succumb to the torture in contravention of their religious certainty.

Of course, there were hardened JS veterans who attacked this retraction in the harshest terms. For example, Hani al-Siba'i, an Egyptian jihadi exiled in London – accused of being a senior member of EIJ for which he was found guilty and given a life sentence *in absentia* – was very forthright in his condemnation. Al-Siba'i argued that such people could not be trusted, as they went from working to kill Sadat as an apostate who was an agent of the United States and Zionism, to considering him a martyr, which is one of the highest ranks articulated in terms of Islamic theology. He added that when they sought to murder Sadat, they claimed the backing of Islamic scholars, and had now backtracked on that position and again justified it as being endorsed by Islamic scholars. He added, 'How do we trust a group that overnight changes its color from black to white and then white to black? How are we to take its revisions seriously? What I want to say is that this initiative was born in a corrupt environment, the prison environment, and what is founded on corruption would be corrupt.'[159]

Al-Siba'i was not alone in his critique, as other exiled Jihadi-Salafis like Osama Rushdi voiced the same concerns. For such people, this type of retreat was simply the work of the Egyptian security services, and not an authentic espousal of Islamic law. Notwithstanding this critique, al-Siba'i and Rushdi supported the EIG ceasefire, but they could not tolerate what they saw as a total surrender to the Egyptian regime and a complete disavowal of their past. As such, they claimed that young Jihadi-Salafis would ignore the stance of these elders and continue their ways as they simply saw the elders humiliated by the regime. This begs the question: Was the complete renunciation of the past by EIG leaders a step too far, when a retraction with more nuances might have been more convincing?[160] Perhaps the continuation of JS until the present time, with groups developing from Al-Qaeda to IS/ISIS, and their many affiliates, is a sign that not only do the same grievances still exist, but that the theology is still far from being categorically refuted.

The renunciation of violence by the EIG demonstrates how their time in prison seemed to enable them to gain a broad grasp of the classical tradition, as they moved on from limiting themselves to one school (which is a distinctly Salafi approach to Islamic law), and from restricting themselves to the articulations of Islamic law claimed by jihadi scholars alone. Their argument was founded on legally-defined notions of benefit (*maslahah*) and the comprehension of current reality (*fiqh al-waqi'*), and they concluded that their violent engagement with the government had not realized the benefits required by the religion; but, rather, brought the opposite, namely harms and detrimental consequences for the EIG and all Islamic groups, as well as Egyptian society as a whole. In addition, they identified that the only ones to benefit from their actions were those associated with opposing Islam: Israel, the United States, the West, the Copts and secularists in general. This result stemmed from the fact that the wanton acts of violence from the Jihadi-Salafis strengthened anti-Islamic rhetoric and forces, while leading people away from the religion.

But they went beyond just considering such acts to be bad publicity and claimed that such wanton acts of violence were actually prohibited according to Islamic law. They went further, in the context of criticizing Al-Qaeda in 2004 (discussed later), to condemn the overextension of violent acts which harm non-combatants. In a very atypical departure from Salafism, the EIG came to recognize that the Egyptian government, or any Muslim government, might suspend the application of a provision of the Islamic law on the basis of some contingent plan or public policy necessity, rather than it being a mere rejection of the Sacred Law, especially in the modern world where there are global pressures on governments to conform to certain trends (as highlighted by Zuhdi, in a 2004 newspaper article).[161] Hence it would not constitute disbelief, as they previously held, when they demanded that every law of the religion be implemented in order for the government to not be considered an apostate one. Moreover, not only did the EIG admit their past mistakes, especially in relation to their violent campaign of the 1990s, but they considered, as stated by Karam Zuhdi, paying blood money to the families of the victims, by raising funds from the sale of their books.[162]

The EIG's renouncing of political violence in 1997 was later replicated in the revised ideology of Dr Faḍl. In 2007, he released a work, from prison, entitled *Wathīqat tarshīd al-ʿamal al-jihādī fī Miṣr wa'l-ʿālam* (*The Document of Right Guidance for Jihad Activity in Egypt and the World*), in which he revised certain important parts of his doctrine, especially in relation to excommunication, violence in civilian contexts, and plunder. He stated that these had all been applied unlawfully according to Islamic law, which had been misunderstood by earlier Jihadi-Salafi leadership due to their ignorance of the complexities in applying pre-modern precepts to modern contexts. His stance therefore was based on jurisprudential and ethical arguments regarding the unlawfulness of killing civilians, rather than a mere statement of pragmatism in the face of the heavy losses which were being suffered by Muslims, in particular the Jihadi-Salafis. In fact, he went as far as to deny violence as a method of social change in Muslim lands and the West, although he maintained support for defensive jihad against invading non-Muslim armies, such as the Americans in Afghanistan and Iraq, as well as Zionism in Palestine.

He was released in 2011, and while he received support from JS activists including the EIG who had renounced political violence in Muslim lands as a religiously unlawful act, he was subjected to very harsh condemnations from those who retained their loyalty to the mass violence that is a hallmark of Jihadi-Salafism. A common argument of such detractors is that he had only had such a change of heart because of the pressures of prison, and his desire to get his sentence lessened by the government. Ayman al-Zawahiri was particularly damning, and in 2008 he penned a lengthy response to his former colleague, whereby he criticized him for renouncing jihad and leaving the Muslim lands at the mercy of invaders and oppressors, as well as dismissing his credentials to provide such guidance as he had been absent from the frontline for many years.

In 2008 Dr Faḍl responded to these criticisms, claiming that Al-Qaeda was not led by informed scholars, but was driven by the 'mentality of blood' (*fikr damawī*) which was destroying the young men who had joined their cause, as well as the Muslim lands, as Western powers came to press home their superior power in retaliation. He added, 'Al Qaeda committed suicide on 9/11 and lost its equilibrium, skilled leaders, and influence,' and accused his former Al-Qaeda colleagues Osama bin Laden and Ayman al-Zawahiri of being 'false prophets' and 'extremely immoral,' as liars and tyrants.[163] However, he came to retain his excommunication of the rulers of Muslim lands, as well as the Muslim Brotherhood, for their involvement in the dominant and prevalent system.

Although such repentances cannot be expected to unite all of the Jihadi-Salafis of Egypt, it is a significant step. The strength of such renunciation is that it comes from originators of this trend, who withstood years of abuse in the Egyptian prison system but were not broken by the torture. The resulting disappearance of the EIG and EIJ decimated the Jihadi-Salafi landscape of Egypt.

### *5.3.2 Saudi Arabia*

The year 1979 is sometimes posited as a significant starting point on the road towards the emergence of Jihadi-Salafism in Saudi Arabia. It was the year of the Salafi inspired storming of the Grand Mosque in Mecca led by Juhaymān al-'Utaybi. Juhaymān has been given a high status in jihadism and is often seen as the father of jihadi thinking, praised as a role model and martyr. Juhaymān was responsible for creating the idea that the Saudi state could be rebelled against based on Salafi theological grounds. His writings were the first conceptualization of the idea of *al-walāʾ wa'l-barāʾ* as a theological concept that could be used against the Saudi state.

This idea was further developed by the important Jihadi-Salafi ideologue Abū Muḥammad al-Maqdisi into its modern manifestation.[164] His formative years, in Kuwait and Saudi Arabia, were shaped by a close association with people who had been part of Juhaymān's group, and his brother-in-law, Abd al-Laṭīf Dirbas, had been a committed member of the movement.[165] However, al-Maqdisi came to develop his own ideas, and excommunicated the Saudi royal family, which is something Juhaymān never did.[166]

The issue of excommunication (*takfīr*), a key feature of the later observable doctrine of JS, had arisen within Juhaymān's movement around 1977, following interactions with followers of Shukri Mustafa's Egyptian *Takfir* group, who had adopted an extreme stance on the matters of excommunication and divine sovereignty (*hakimiyyah*). However, the matter was placed before Nasir al-Din al-Albānī, who demonstrated to Juhaymān and his followers the error of the extreme practice of *takfīr*.[167] As a result, matters of *takfīr* and *hakimiyyah* cannot be said to define Juhaymān's group, which sets it aside from accepted JS doctrine.

The most forthright account that links the Siege of Mecca with Jihadi-Salafism comes from Yaroslav Trofimov, who identifies it as being underpinned by a 'fiery ideology' that 'mutated with time into increasingly more vicious strains, culminating in Al-Qaeda's death cult.' He states that, 'the countdown to September 11, to the terrorist bombings in London and Madrid [in 2005 and 2004 respectively], and to the grisly Islamist violence ravaging Afghanistan and Iraq [around 2007 at the time of writing the book] all began on that warm November morning [in 1979], in the shade of the Kaaba.'[168] The narrative connecting this episode to Jihadi-Salafism is further enhanced by references to Khalid al-Islambouli, the assassin of Sadat, allegedly a keen reader of Juhaymān's teachings.[169] Yet, even while acknowledging Juhaymān's disconnect and dissimilarity to Islamist trends, in general, and JS in particular, the Siege of Mecca is seen by some as the manifestation of ideas developed by people like Mawdudi, Qutb, and Faraj.[170] Nonetheless, Juhaymān's group was quickly disbanded and had very little impact, except a new-found popularity of Juhaymān's thought among some elements of the *Bayt Shubra* network in the early-to-mid-1990s.[171]

The Saudi support for the Afghan war against the Soviets would protect Saudi and the United States from being the target of Sunni militants, and enabled radicals to have an outlet for their political ambitions.[172] The Soviet withdrawal from Afghanistan in 1989 led to fighters returning to Saudi

Arabia, turning their activist attention to their homeland. The combination of their developing extremist political theory and military training would be a disaster for Saudi Arabia, as would the growing discontent of these 'Saudi Afghāns' at the restricted employment opportunities they faced upon their return.[173] Thus there emerged a third type of Saudi Islamism, namely Saudi-Jihadi-Salafism (SJS), after the rejectionist Islamism of Juhaymān and the reformist Islamism of the *Ṣaḥwa* movement.[174]

Until 1990, SJS were not openly critical of the government. In the early 1990s, rejectionists and Jihadis started to mix in Saudi Arabia, and mutually influenced each other. The mid-1990s saw the emergence of a radical and violent Jihadi-Salafism, as an offshoot from the government crackdown on the *Ṣaḥwa* movement, which had convinced Osama bin Laden and others from SJS that the American presence in the region had to be opposed violently. On 13 November 1995, in Riyadh, four members of this radical network set off a 100 kg car bomb, which killed five Americans and two Indians, and injured six, seemingly in retaliation for the execution of one of their members in August 1995. This was the first major bombing on Saudi soil perpetrated by jihadist groups. Three of the four bombers had fought in the Afghan–Soviet war and were said to be passionate readers of Osama bin Laden; and the fourth was reported to be a close friend of the Jihadi-Salafi Abu Muhammad al-Maqdisi.

The bombing seems to have been an independent act, and not on the direct orders of Al-Qaeda: it was never claimed by Bin Laden. Over the next five years, the government made thousands of arrests, which consisted mainly of Shīʿis, but included those associated with SJS, such as Yusuf al-Uyayri, an important associate of Bin Laden.[175] The widespread torture of prisoners, and many innocents caught up by association, is largely seen as contributing to the further radicalization of those in the movement. As happened in Egypt, the security forces' heavy-handedness directly contributed to those in SJS retaliating in kind.[176]

By the late 1990s, some of the rejectionists had become Jihadi-Salafis and left for Afghanistan and other destinations. Khalid Sheikh Mohammed, a senior Al-Qaeda leader, claimed that, by the summer of 2001, 70% of those joining Al-Qaeda's training camp in Afghanistan were Saudis.[177] By the early 2000s, the Saudi Islamist scene had become dominated by reformists and Jihadis, with the rejectionist legacy of Juhaymān almost eclipsed. However, the significance of the Siege of Mecca was far from forgotten, and its horrific violence would soon be replicated.[178] While there were intelligence reports of plans to launch public acts of terrorism in Saudi Arabia, by mid-2001, none of them had materialized.

The 9/11 attacks would lead to Saudi Arabia becoming another node of the global Jihadi-Salafi world between September 2001 and May 2003. At the beginning of this period, SJS, primarily in the form of Al-Qaeda on the Arabian Peninsula (AQAP), indirectly benefitted from the dispute between the Shuʿaybi school[179] and the *Ṣaḥwa* scholars, both politically orientated Salafi groups. Clerics from the Shuʿaybi school issued legal edicts justifying the 9/11 attacks and praising its perpetrators, while *Ṣaḥwa* scholars like Salman al-Oudah and Safar al-Hawali condemned the attacks. As mentioned in Chapter 3 (see section 3.2.6), the Shuʿaybi school was led by Ḥamūd b. ʿAbd Allah al-ʿUqla al-Shuʿaybi, and his students Nasir b. Ḥamad al-Fahd, and ʿAli b. Khuḍayr al-Khuḍayr, with important support from others like Sulayman al-ʿUlwān. While this group ostensibly looks to fit the SJS model, they were not drawing their inspiration from the Egyptian JS movements which had influenced the SJS that had emerged from Afghanistan. Rather, the Shuʿaybi school reached similar conclusions to these groups on the basis of their strict Wahhabism, drawing upon the early movement of Muhammad Ibn ’Abd al-Wahhāb and tapping in to First-Wave Wahhabist thought. Therefore, it is more correct to give them their own designation, namely Wahhabi-Jihadi-Salafism (WJS). In terms of differentiation, the distinguishing feature of WJS is its adherence to the doctrine of *al-walā’ wa’l-barā* in distinctly Wahhabi terms, and the quoting of scholars from the First-Wave era, while disdaining Brotherhood figures like Qutb. WJS scholars also concentrate more on *theological* justifications of jihad than on *political* grievances and causes.

This does not imply that WJS scholars were ignorant of political developments. The invasion of Afghanistan led to the scholars of the Shuʿaybi school giving more support to a rhetoric that bolstered the narrative of those of the SJS movement, while being vaguely critical of the Saudi regime in relation to those events. In the run-up to the invasion of Iraq, the Saudi government tried to arrest the main Shuʿaybi scholars, as a means of gaining control of the public discourse on the matter. However, a number of the clerics evaded arrest and would eventually issue their most radical legal edicts, which indicated (in a First-Wave manner) that assistance to the US invasion was akin to apostasy, and that it was permitted to violently attack Western targets and security forces in Saudi Arabia, as well as ruling that a Saudi visa was not a guarantee of safety. However, the attacks on 12 May 2003 by three suicide bombers on residential compounds in Riyadh – killing 35 people and injuring over 160 – would halt Shuʿaybi support for Al-Qaeda operations in Saudi. The main renegade Shuʿaybi scholars denied knowledge of such domestic operations, and then proceeded to make public repentances of their previous stances on television during November and December 2003. But it appeared too little too late, since by that time the WSJ scholars had indirectly boosted Al-Qaeda’s recruitment drive, especially since Nasir al-Fahd and Ali al-Khudayr were highly respected and deemed to be intelligent and well-trained traditional clerics.[180]

The AQAP campaign in Saudi Arabia between 2003 and 2006 killed around 300 people and injured thousands. Thomas Hegghammer has identified three main reasons for the eventual withering of the AQAP activities: firstly, the power of the state in effectively crushing the movement, by utilizing its immense resources in countering them; secondly, a widespread lack of support for their activities, which were perceived in negative terms, especially when any respected scholarly support dissipated with the abandonment of the Shuʿaybi scholars; and thirdly, the invasion of Iraq in 2003 by the USA and her allies split the SJS movement, and subsequently weakened it. This latter reason is explained through the emergence of 'classical' Jihadis, who called for Jihadis the world over to come to Iraq and engage in a defensive jihad of an invaded Muslim land. 'Global' Jihadis saw Iraq as one of a number of fronts on which the battle of jihad was to be fought; hence, in the fight for increasingly scarce resources and personnel, the AQAP was gradually weakened both in terms of numbers and the resulting ideological battles that ensued as a consequence of the theoretical division.

Although Ayman al-Zawahiri and Osama bin Laden did not engage directly in this debate of whether Iraq or Saudi Arabia should be preferable for focus, they spoke more about Iraq. Furthermore, the continuing flow of Jihadis from Saudi Arabia to foreign war destinations indicates that Al-Qaeda's global jihadi theory was subordinate in the minds of Saudi-Jihadi-Salafis to the classical theory, and Osama bin Laden's call was not as successful among such Jihadis as is widely thought.[181]

Even though AQAP was crushed by 2006,[182] the Saudi authorities still contended with what they claimed were security threats from those holding SJS beliefs. Thus, in April 2007, there was a government sweep of 172 Saudis who were accused of being Al-Qaeda terrorists.[183] Evidence suggests that e-jihad with its various online forums, demonstrates a lurking continuance of SJS ideologies.[184] However, their ability to coordinate acts of mass terror in Saudi has seemingly dissipated. Neither the Arab Spring of 2011, nor the liberal reforms thereafter – with pop music concerts and other anathemas to strict interpretations of traditional Islamic law – brought any sort of SJS violence protesting at any contraventions of the religion. Hence, one can agree with the sentiments expressed in 2008, by CIA Director Michael V. Hayden, stating that Al-Qaeda was defeated in Saudi Arabia, as well as Iraq, and was now defensive all over the world, including the Afghanistan-Pakistan border.[185]

### *5.3.3 Morocco*

*Harakat al-Shabibah al-Islamiyyah: The first public proto-SJ movement*

While the first formative manifestation of Jihadi-Salafism in Egypt is often understood to be the result of the torture of Islamists in the prisons of Nasser's reign after the 1965 arrests,[186] the first significant proto-JS group to emerge on the societal level in Morocco was *Harakat al-Shabibah al-Islamiyyah* (also known as *Jam'iyyat al-Shabibah al-Islamiyyah al-Maghribiyyah*, or the Moroccan Islamic Youth Association).[187] This group was formed in 1969 but would come to infamous prominence in 1975, and academics consider this to be the first organized Islamist group in Morocco.[188] The pioneering nature of this group was demonstrated in 2005 when Abu Mus'ab al-Suri penned his 1,600-page guide to the Jihādī movement and a program for its rejuvenation, entitled *The Call for Global Islamic Resistance*, in which he loaded praise on the Moroccan *Harakat al-Shabibah* as paving the way for later groups.

*Harakat al-Shabibah* was formed in Casablanca by Abdelkrim Mouti and Kamal Ibrahim, and came to consist of teachers, teaching inspectors and university lecturers.[189] Abdelkrim Mouti had previously been an activist for the National Union of Popular Forces – a left-wing party founded in 1959 to call for wide-ranging economic reform and support for anticolonial struggles. Initially, the group's small learning sessions focused on Islamic revivalist thought, but soon expanded into discussions surrounding the need and viability of revolutionary regime change, in line with the principles of revivalist doctrine and Mouti's own focused goal.

The group was essentially proto-JS, according to our contemporary definition, but with an admiration for other groups, especially the Muslim Brotherhood. The jihadi element was derived from their dedicated reading of Sayyid Qutb's works, in particular *Milestones*, which was their main text of inspiration; and entailed developing a strategy to overthrow the government, as well as disseminating the thesis that Moroccan society was now in a state of ignorance (*jahiliyyah*). They were aligned with Wahhabi-Salafism and members attended the classes of the pioneering Salafi Taqi al-Din al-Hilali (see section 6.1.1 for an overview of his life), as well as adopting Salafi creed. Their study sessions also involved reading the works other revivalists such as Ḥasan al-Bannā, Hasan al-Hudaybi, Abu al-A'la Mawdudi, Sa'id Hawwa, and Taqi al-Din al-Nabhani (the founder of the Liberation Party, or *Hizb al-Tahrir*), and they admired the educational philosophy of *Tablighi Jamaat* and their ability to reach the masses. Their eclectic reading and influences all coalesced into one goal: seizing power by overthrowing the regime and re-establishing the Caliphate. Thus one sees how they diverged from others in the Salafi movement, but nevertheless were inspired and linked to it.[190]

Mouti's main work was *The Islamic Revolution is the Destiny of Present-day Morocco*, written in exile, in which economic injustice and inequality was used to call for an Islamic revolution. He identified jihad as the central methodology for removing this injustice, and spoke of the importance of *hijrah*, or emigration from the lands of the disbelievers in order to launch a successful campaign for the cause of Islam. Such notions of jihad and *hijrah* would become defining features of Jihadi-Salafi discourse, from proto-JS leaders like Shukri Mustafa and 'Abd al-Salam Faraj of Egypt and his treatise *The Forgotten Obligation*, to the major Jihadi-Salafi ideologues (see below).[191]

In 1975, the murder of socialist leader Omar Ben Jelloun was blamed on the *Shabibah*, although they denied any part. Nonetheless, Mouti went into exile and was sentenced to death in his absence, destined never to return to Morocco.[192] As the movement was reliant on Mouti for its direction it quickly fragmented, and during the 1980s members would further splinter into various offshoots. The wildest speculation about Mouti's activities in exile include the rumor that he participated in the Siege of Mecca in 1979 with the proto-JS group led by Juhaymān al-'Utaybi.[193] Although essentially ineffectual, *Shabibah* retains its significance as the first proto-JS movement in the region.

*SJ in Morocco from the Afghan–Soviet war to the present*

After the Afghan–Soviet war, a small number of Moroccan war veterans returned with the emerging Jihadi-Salafi doctrine, which they sought to propagate in their homeland. The Moroccan contribution to the war effort had been meager as most had joined in 1989 when the war had almost ended, and very few were soldiers, as most were there on humanitarian duties. The numbers of Moroccans in Afghanistan increased after 1996 when Osama bin Laden and his Al-Qaeda developed a firm footing in the country once the Taliban came to power, although Moroccans did not have significant leadership roles among the Arab fighters.[194]

A small umbrella of JS cells emerged among those who returned from Afghanistan in the early 1990s. Before the 9/11 attacks, the Moroccan authorities had a somewhat nonchalant approach to the existence of such JS groups, on the assumption that they were based in remote areas and did not pose an actual threat.[195] In the immediate aftermath of the terror attack, Morocco was one of the first nation states to join the international coalition to eradicate Al-Qaeda. In addition to engaging in the interrogation of suspects in Guantanamo Bay, the Moroccans also uncovered a small number of JS cells, including one in Casablanca that appeared to have Al-Qaeda links, which was planning a terrorist campaign of attacking NATO ships in the Straits of Gibraltar. On 16 May 2003, twelve Moroccan radicals blew themselves up in Casablanca, killing thirty-three civilians, and investigations led to the arrest of suspected Jihadi-Salafis involved in the attack, whose aim was the violent overthrow of the monarchy.

Consequently, heightened security measures were put in place to prevent such cells emerging again, and over 1,000 arrests had been made by the end of August 2003, mainly of Jihadi-Salafis, or those suspected of being such. Shortly thereafter, an extensive set of social and economic reforms were passed by the government, as a means of cutting the supply chain to Jihadi-Salafis and their method of recruiting from the underprivileged. A further 5,000 people were arrested the following year in relation to the Casablanca attacks. A Moroccan Islamic Combatant Group (GICM) was uncovered, with links to Al-Qaeda, who were to be implicated in the Madrid bombings of 11 March 2004 which killed 201 people and injured around 2,000. Again, the security forces' techniques of prisoner interrogation came under scrutiny and criticism from human rights organizations, after reports of torture being visited upon prisoners and suspects.[196]

One of the early local ideologues for Moroccan Jihadi-Salafis was the preacher Mohammed Fizazi (or al-Fazazi). He had gained notoriety for preaching in Morocco and Germany – including in a mosque in Hamburg that some of the 9/11 perpetrators had attended – and had a public profile that mirrored that of the leading JS ideologue Abu Muhammad al-Maqdisi (see section 5.4.3 below). Fizazi praised Osama bin Laden and justified the 9/11 attacks and the declaration of war upon the United States by Al-Qaeda,[197] and association with him became a criminal offense in the ensuing war on terror.[198] In 2003 he was sentenced to thirty years' imprisonment under anti-terrorism legislation for his alleged influence on the perpetrators of the bombings in Casablanca, although Fizazi condemned the attacks in his trial.

During the Arab Spring in February 2011, the general Salafi endorsement and participation in the protests in Morocco led to the government making overtures to Islamists in general, and Salafis in particular, including some Jihadi-Salafis. Fizazi was one of 194 political prisoners granted pardons by King Mohammed VI, just two months after the unrest – many of whom had been imprisoned without any direct links to violence, but rather an assumed association with radical Salafi thought. Upon his release, Fizazi renounced his radical thought and even embraced democracy, under a guise that he defines as Islamic. In 2014, he led a Friday prayer in which the king participated, even indulging in a photoshoot afterward. Naturally, Fizazi lost support among Salafis, and in particular Jihadi-Salafis, because of his renunciation of violence.[199]

Jihadi-Salafis have continued to exist in Morocco, with some conforming to the worldview of Al-Qaeda. JS literature has been widely available in the country since the 1990s, with Abu Muhammad al-Maqdisi and Abu Mus'ab al-Zarqawi (discussed in section 5.4.4) among the most popular authors.[200] However, adherents focus on social issues and preaching and work for the release of prisoners, as opposed to engaging in battle with the ruling regime. Experts have estimated that around 1,500 Moroccans went to fight in the Syrian revolution after the Arab Spring, but not all of these were Jihadi-Salafis.[201]

### *5.3.4 Algeria*

When it comes to explaining the history of jihadism, the Algerian civil war (1992–2002) is generally overshadowed by the First and Second Gulf Wars, and the invasions of Afghanistan by first the Soviet Union and then the United States and her allies after 9/11. Yet it was in Algeria that some of the first extreme jihadi ideas were practiced for the first time; and a clear outlining of this development is noteworthy. Furthermore, from a jihadi perspective, Algeria took on new meaning from 1994, as it was seen as 'the second step for the Arab-Afghans towards the Arab world after the Afghanistan period,' hence it was supported by Ayman al-Zawahiri, head of the Egyptian Islamic Jihad at the time, and the Libyan Fighting Group, as it was 'the main axis of interest for the Jihadis in that period.'[202]

*The fight for independence and the norm of war*

The path to the emergence of Jihadi-Salafism in Algeria is one that passes through interlinked phases: from the violent resistance to French colonization in 1830 that led to eventual independence in 1962; to the public demand for Islamic governance in the mid-1970s and 1980s,[203] after a period in which religion was relegated in favor of a Third Worldism, where countries non-aligned to the United States or Soviet Union tried to create unity among themselves; to the seemingly inevitable electoral victory for Islamists indicated by the first round of parliamentary elections in December 1991; to the decade-long civil war between 1992 and 2002 which claimed the lives of an estimated 200,000 people.[204] The continuous culture of fighting, from the war of independence to the Islamist demand for power, and the ultimate denial of Islamic rule through the democratic process in 1991; there were decisive reasons for JS launching in Algeria in an almost desperate manner, and being so crucial to the global development of Jihadi-Salafism.

*The Armed Islamic Movement (MIA) and the birth of jihadism*

The emerging Islamic groups of the post-independence period were far from homogenous. In November 1981, the first post-independence jihadi group, the Armed Islamic Movement (*Mouvement islamique armé* or MIA) was formed under the leadership of Mustafa Bouyali (d. 1987), who was not a religious scholar, but an employee of the state electricity company.[205] They would be identified by jihadi ideologue Abu Mus'ab al-Suri to be among his 'paradigmatic jihadi movements' worthy of analysis. Not only did the MIA engage in a violent battle with the Algerian government, seemingly on the pretext of the government being considered non-Muslim and therefore excommunicated, but they also called for an Islamic state as their ultimate goal. They therefore subscribed to *hakimiyyah*, violence and *takfir* (albeit relatively limited in its scope according to the MIA),[206] which perhaps makes the MIA a proto-JS group; or more accurately a proto-jihadi group, in light of its rather weak connections to Salafism.[207]

Upon the murder of Bouyali and three of his associates by government forces in 1987, the Algerian government tried 202 members of the MIA, sentencing five to death, including Mansour Meliani, a senior lieutenant; only fifteen were acquitted of the charges brought against them. However, President Bendjedid would grant a pardon for all members in March 1989, and they were subsequently released. This governmental reprieve would have consequences for the emergence of what has been identified as the first jihadi movement to subscribe to Salafi theology in Algeria – the Armed Islamic Group of Algeria (*Groupe Islamique Armé* or GIA)[208] – with a number of ex-MIA members making a significant contribution.

*The failed path to the Islamization of Algeria*

The context within which Jihadi-Salafism was born in Algeria is crucial. There was an intense and nearly successful movement for the Islamization of Algeria at the end of the 1980s and the early 1990s, much of it in a democratic and open manner. This movement was brutally crushed, with Western powers openly backing the Algerian president and army. Therefore, one cannot understand the rise of jihadist groups without acknowledging the precursors that had laid the ground for jihad's mass appeal.

The fragmentary nature of the Islamist ideology and agenda in Algeria, despite its continuing diversity, became something of a movement by the end of the 1980s. Algeria came to have a reputation as possessing one of the most powerful and well-supported Islamist movements in the world. The diffuse movement was somewhat assuaged with the formation of the Islamic Salvation Front (FIS) between 1988 and 1990,[209] in the immediate aftermath of a large protest, which was joined by Islamists, and ended with bloodshed at the hands of the state security forces. After its formal creation in March 1989, FIS immediately became a formidable political entity under the leadership of Ali Benhadj (a schoolteacher who had accompanied Bouyali, seen as a radical) and Abbassi Madani (a university lecturer, seen as a pragmatist of sorts).[210] It not only represented continuity from the war of independence to the activism of the early 1980s and the Bouyali movement, but it led, directly and indirectly, to the later explosive emergence of JS in Algeria. Some of its more military elements were involved in the first jihadi movement to fully embrace Salafism in an exclusivist manner – the GIA – which in turn indirectly influenced the radically extreme Jihadi-Salafi movements, such as Zarqawi's Iraqi forces after its split with Al-Qaeda and then ISIS (see below). In terms of the Salafism of the FIS's leadership, Madani cannot be categorized as a Salafi in light of his diverse influences; however Benhadj was largely viewed as being Salafi in thought, primarily due to his admiration for Ibn Taymiyya, and was generally understood as being a part of the broader Salafi *Ṣaḥwa* movement.[211] Still, the pragmatism he displayed in dealing with non Salafi groups earned him the ire of many other Salafi leaders around the globe.

The effectiveness of this activism was demonstrated when FIS was victorious in the municipal and regional elections on 12 June 1990, gaining control of over half of the country's communes. A strained relationship with the regime intensified between the December election of 1990 and May 1991, when it was revealed that the regime considered changing electoral boundaries to negatively impact FIS's electorate. A sense of betrayal led Madani to call a general strike, and demonstrations turned violent, with a mass sit-in lasting a full week in one of the major squares of Algiers. With such social unrest, and a legitimate concern about a general uprising, the army took control of the situation, disbanding the protests with tanks, and declaring a state of emergency on 3 June 1991. The army then seized control of the country and put forward a new prime minister. Benhadj called for a general uprising in response and Madani promised a jihad if the army refused to stand down, so the army arrested them, and they remained imprisoned throughout the subsequent civil war.

The first round of the legislative elections on 26 December 1991 would highlight the continued general popularity of FIS. They won easily with over 47% of the vote but had lost around one million votes (25% of its support). Such success for FIS despite all the adverse pressures, and the projections for the second round indicating a resounding victory for FIS with a predicted majority in parliament, led the army to cancel the upcoming elections on 13 January 1992, and the presidency of Chadli Bendjedid on 11 January 1992. The army officially dissolved the FIS on 4 March 1992, effectively decimating the movement. Subsequently, over 40,000 suspected Islamists were arrested and imprisoned in camps in the Sahara, and mosques came under close scrutiny from the regime.[212]

*Opening the road to JS: From the GIA after 1992 until the AQIM*

Even before the annulment of the December 1991 elections, the repression of the FIS and the attempts of the army to negate FIS's electoral success would have a pivotal impact on the emergence of Jihadi-Salafism, supplanting even what the Egyptian Islamic Jihad had achieved with the assassination of President Sadat and their subsequent campaign of terror in Egypt. Upon the imprisonment of the FIS leadership, those factions of the Islamists who had never believed in the validity of the democratic process, instead advocating for a violent overthrow of the system, now had confirmation that the moment had arrived for their method of regime change. They would be joined by military elements of the FIS, and others, especially those who would emerge from the prison camps in the Sahara.[213]

A crucial development on the path towards the ensuing civil war was the emergence of Bouyali's remaining followers and other Algerians returning from military service in Afghanistan. They began to go into hiding and gathered weapons for battle. This new phase of jihad in Algeria commenced in dramatic fashion when a group of 'Afghan-Algerians' stormed a frontier post and ruthlessly slaughtered army conscripts at Guemmar on 28 November 1991 – the date was chosen to commemorate the martyrdom of Abdullah Azzam. This unleashed a vicious cycle of violence in which over 100,000 lives were lost to civil war between 1992 and 1997, as the state and Islamists, including Jihadi-Salafis, fought for control. Various groups contributed to the violence including the FIS's armed wing, the Islamic Salvation Army (AIS). The intense violence of 1994–95 seemed to indicate that the state would lose the battle and an Islamist polity would emerge, but by 1997 the Jihadis had lost popular support amid the carnage of the war, and a ceasefire was announced.[214]

The most infamous Islamist faction of the period was the GIA, whose nucleus consisted of former Bouyali loyalists, 'Afghan Algerians' and home-grown Algerian Jihadi-Salafis.[215] Its formal creation came when Abdelhaq Layada, a mechanic who discovered religious life in the October 1988 riots, brought together a few jihadi groups. Layada's Jihadi-Salafi lineage went back to Mansour Meliani, who had been a member of Bouyali's movement. By the end of 1992, the armed movement consisted of two main groups: the revived MIA led by Chebouti, whose methods extended their Bouyalist roots and consisted of a long-term war effort with a focus aimed at the state's apparatus and people; and Layada's group, with its strategy of immediate attack in order to create widespread insecurity. Furthermore, Layada emphasized that the movement adhered to a 'Sunni methodology' (*minhaj ahl al-sunna wa'l-jama'ah*) and was Salafi (*wa fahm al-salaf al-salih*); thus we see the uniting of all the tenets of Jihadi-Salafism in a most explicit manner.[216]

Layada was arrested in Morocco in June 1993 and succeeded by Mourad Si Ahmed (also known as Seif Allah Djafar or Djafar al-Afghānī, as he had spent two years in Afghanistan with General Hekmatyar), then aged thirty. He only had a primary level education and made his living dealing in contraband goods. Yet Djafar al-Afghānī's reign would see the GIA expand its outreach to various groups within Algeria, as well as developing an international voice with the creation, in July 1993, of the weekly publication *al-Ansar* (*The Partisans*), produced in London under the editorial control of the jihadi ideologue Abu Mus'ab al-Suri and the JS thinker Abu Qatada al-Filastini, who initially supported the GIA's activities. Djafar al-Afghānī's period as leader was marked by increased violence, until he met his death in battle on 26 February 1994.[217]

On 21 September 1993 a GIA-affiliate killed two French surveyors, which marked the beginning of Jihadi-Salafis attacking foreigners, and they would kill twenty-six by the end of the year. Furthermore, November

1993 marked the start of fellow Islamists being at risk of GIA assassination when Mohamed Bouslimani, a prominent member of Nahnah's Hamas party, *Harakat Mujtama' as-Silm* (Movement of Society for Peace), was kidnapped and killed for failing to support a legal edict issued by the GIA. In addition, al-Afghānī's successor, Cherif Gousmi (also known as Abu Abdallah Ahmed), managed to recruit former members of FIS. Gousmi was only twenty-six when he assumed leadership, but was a credible leader as he had been a Salafi imam and a local representative of the FIS, before being imprisoned in the Sahara camps in 1992.[218]

When Gousmi was killed on 26 September 1994, the search for a successor led to an intense battle between competing factions within the movement. He was eventually succeeded by the thirty-year-old Djamel Zitouni, who had only a francophone secondary school education, limited Arabic proficiency, and sold chickens for a living.[219] His ascension to leadership was questioned by many in the group in light of his lack of religious qualification, but he gained notoriety for killing French civilians.[220]

Zitouni was almost fanatical in his commitment to Salafism, and regularly accused other Jihadi-Salafis of compromising in their commitment to it. He exchanged messages with the experienced and pioneering JS leader Ayman al-Zawahiri and cast aspersions on his Salafi co-thinkers for working with other groups, even if they urged the latter toward Salafism.[221] Under his leadership, the GIA began assassinating those who left the movement. As a consequence, many GIA leaders cut ties with Zitouni, and the editorial team of *al-Ansar* wavered in their support.[222]

In March 1996, as many began leaving the group, Zitouni kidnapped seven French Trappist monks from their monastery in Tibhirine and claimed responsibility for their decapitation two months later. This act caused public outrage, especially in light of the explicit prophetic hadiths which order Muslims to respect monks in times of war. After this incident, Zitouni received another blow to his legitimacy when Abu Qatada and al-Suri suspended the publication of *al-Ansar*, withdrawing their support of Zitouni for his 'deviations' in the struggle and for 'shed[ding] forbidden blood' by killing ex-colleagues, as well as other veterans from the Afghanistan–Soviet war who had opposed GIA policies.[223]

The scale of GIA's atrocities shook Jihadi-Salafis to such an extent that even Osama bin Laden was reported to demur at their ferociousness in light of the damage it posed to the public image of the movement – although this sentiment was certainly shed by the time of the 9/11 terrorist attack. So strident were the GIA in their dissociation from other groups that they even accused Bin Laden of possessing a certain weakness by being 'too flexible' with democrats, which led him to sever his support for the movement. The GIA saw democracy as being wholly incompatible with Islam, and therefore the espousal of democracy was worthy of excommunication.[224]

Zitouni's course of destruction was brought to an end when he was killed on 16 July 1996. At this point, the GIA was split, especially in Algiers where the youth were tired of violence. They participated in the presidential elections on 16 November 1995, in which the moderate Islamist Nahnah came second to the former army commander Liamine Zéroual. The GIA would elect the twenty-six-year-old Antar Zouabri as Zitouni's successor. Of very humble origins, he had been an activist since his youth. He continued his predecessor's killing spree with even greater vigor, including those who opposed him. Under his leadership the GIA committed mass atrocities against civilians, the likes of which had never before been done in the name of jihad.[225]

By early 1997, Zouabri's aggression had led to the attainment of a certain level of authority. His position was strengthened when he obtained the backing and services of Abu Hamza al-Misri (discussed in section 5.6.2). Abu Hamza ordered the composition of a document that came to be titled, in short, *The Sharp Sword*, in which Zouabri was endorsed for his Salafi orthodoxy and his purges given justification. Furthermore, the author of *The Sharp Sword* argued that the GIA had never excommunicated the whole of Algerian society, yet it did punish those who failed to back their call to perform jihad against the regime.

The slaughters continued in August and September 1997, with hundreds massacred. Yet, by the end of September, the GIA had ceased to exist, with Zouabri signing a final message when the Islamic Salvation Army declared a unilateral ceasefire (whereby they earned an amnesty upon assuming loyalty to the regime). This final communiqué of the GIA, published by Abu Hamza in the 27 September 1997 issue of *al-Ansar*, claimed responsibility for the mass killings and sought to justify them on the grounds that any Algerian who had not joined the GIA was excommunicated from the faith, and thus punishable by death. Hence the GIA finally came to excommunicate the entire society. As a result, Abu Hamza announced the cessation of *al-Ansar* and support for the GIA, on the intolerable grounds that they now made mass *takfir*, which was a clear breach of Jihadi-Salafi principles.[226] The GIA's final articulation of JS brokered no compromise and fully fused theology with politics.[227]

The jihad movement in Algeria received a further blow when notable scholars of the more puritan Salafi strands – such as Ibn Bāz, Nasir al-Din al-Albānī, and Ibn 'Uthaymin – came to directly refute the Jihadi-Salafis as an aberration and departure from Salafism due to their general excommunication and widespread violence. A compilation of the statements of these three scholars from the 1990s was released in 2001, entitled *Fatāwā al-'Ulamā' al-Akābir fī-mā Uhdira min Dimā' fī al-Jazā'ir* (*The Opinions of Major Scholars on the Blood Spilled in Algeria*), and compiled by 'Abd al-Malik al-Ramdani – an Algerian Salafi leader who had engaged in refuting the Jihadi-Salafi Abu Qatada and FIS's Benhadj during the 1990s.[228] It included Ibn Bāz saying that the only political option that was viable now was the non-violent preaching that characterized the Prophet Muhammad's politically weakened phase in Mecca; and that the public berating of the rulers was a worthless activity that only brought a more violent response. Perhaps most poignantly, al-Albānī was quoted as musing about what would happen if the AIS and the GIA succeeded in removing the rulers, and wondering if they would merely fall into battle against one another as the Afghan *mujahidin* had done upon the Soviets' withdrawal from that land.[229]

Notwithstanding the Algerian state's success in suppressing the Islamist drive for political victory, and the almost complete disappearance of JS violence in the society, Jihadi-Salafism continued to exist on a somewhat smaller scale. An essential element in this initially clandestine persistence developed between 1995 and 1999 with the formation of a breakaway from the GIA called the Salafist Group for Preaching and Combat (GSPC), the direct predecessor organization of Al-Qaeda in the Islamic Maghreb (AQIM).[230] This group was founded by a breakaway GIA commander, Hassan Hattab,[231] and quickly grew from 700 members to 3,000 within a year. The GSPC's endorsement of the GIA ends with its praise for Gousmi.[232]

The GSPC focused its attack on the regime and not civilians and sought to encourage groups not to accept a compromise with the regime. When the GSPC spoke of disbelief, it referred to states, and its accusations of deviance were only aimed at the GIA, with its extremist excommunication. In this regard, they attempted to benefit from the disdain felt by the general populace at the violence of the GIA and the surrender of the AIS. The GSPC categorically stated its Salafi-theological foundation, but it attempted to steer disputes away from theological language, and to discuss differences within the confines of politics and strategy.[233]

Furthermore, the GSPC attempted to repair international links, and their attempts to be more moderate than the GIA was said to have received the encouragement of Osama bin Laden who, as was mentioned earlier, had cut links with the GIA. So it was that in 2003 the GSPC developed links with Al-Qaeda, and the two formally united in 2006–07.[234] The step towards uniting with Al-Qaeda was not universally endorsed within the group – Hassan Hattab left the GSPC and later surrendered to the Algerian authorities and has since worked to encourage other Jihadis to follow his course. In addition to Hattab's earlier objections to the GIA's liberal use of excommunication and mass murders, he feared that joining Al-Qaeda would lead to more suicide operations which he rejected as a legitimate tactic, and more kidnapping of foreigners, which would lead to bad publicity as well as international intervention.[235]

Nonetheless, it has been argued that the GSPC's morphing into AQIM was a desperate move on the part of the former, as a means of maintaining its own existence in the midst of circumstances which pointed to its rapid demise. An alliance with Al-Qaeda would be a way of reassuring the members that their path was an international one and promised a future. Predictably, the new AQIM started to renew violent attacks on the state and its apparatus, including suicide operations on military targets, as well as bombings in Algeria and Morocco in April 2007 and a United Nations building in Algeria in December 2007.[236]

Rather than destabilizing the Algerian regime, these acts actually strengthened the Algerian government as it drew closer to the United States as a consequence, entering into a formalized united front in the 'war against terrorism.' This campaign also benefitted from the Algerian government's utilization of puritan, government-friendly Salafis to preach against the Jihadi-Salafis of the AQIM.[237]

AQIM's most successful period was between January 2012 and January 2013, in particular through their influence in northern Mali as Jihadis took control, with AQIM directing events. As with all affiliates of Al-Qaeda, AQIM categorically rejected Islamic State (IS), who came to prominence in 2014 (discussed in section 5.5.1).[238] Nonetheless, there were some groups that broke away from AQIM and joined IS, such as *Jund al-Khilafah* (Soldiers of the Caliphate) or *Wilayat Jaza'ir* (Guardians of Algeria), connected to Abu Bakr al-Baghdadi's group which operated in Algeria, but they soon became irrelevant.[239] Thus, the continuing existence of AQIM provides an interesting episode to further explore how JS groups can build on the history of the movement and use their Salafi principles to resolve disputes and learn from past mistakes, while also attempting to keep some sort of momentum in a world where their relevance and impact is ever waning.

### *5.3.5 Afghanistan, the North-West Frontier, Al-Qaeda and the Launch of Global Jihadi-Salafism*

*An overview of the path toward global Jihadi-Salafism*

The tale of Jihadi-Salafism in Afghanistan is one about Arabs in Afghanistan, and not Afghani Jihadi-Salafis – although some Afghans did take up the cause much later after its inception.

After the *mujahidin* fell into civil war upon the Soviets leaving Afghanistan, the Taliban emerged around 1994 and had formed a government in Kabul by 1996. This opened the doors to other jihadi movements who migrated and settled in the region. The Taliban was not Salafi in ideology, and this eventually caused a rift with the Jihadi-Salafis. They also differed in methodology, especially on the question of Osama bin Laden giving public declarations of war to the foreign press.[240]

During the late 1990s, there were over a dozen different jihadi camps in Afghanistan, including Al-Qaeda, who would be the most significant.[241] It was in these camps that JS ideology reached its maturity during the discussions, meetings, writings, and training sessions that occurred. The ideas that eventually give birth to ISIS were likely developed in these camps, most notably with the arrival of Abu Musʿab al-Zarqawi (discussed in section 5.4.4).[242] Hence the story of Al-Qaeda is one of how Jihadi-Salafism went global, after its localized beginnings, whether in the Arab heartlands or in the camps defending non-Arab lands from foreign invasion, as was the case in Afghanistan and then Bosnia.

*The history of Al-Qaeda in Afghanistan, leading to Islamic State*

The formation of Al-Qaeda emerged from a series of meetings in Peshawar in 1988, with Arab fighters around Osama bin Laden taking an oath of allegiance.[243] The creation of the organization was simply to provide high-quality military training for Arab fighters, as a sign of disgruntlement at the seemingly 'moderate center' of Azzam's operation.[244] At this point, 'the group was more an idea than a reality as an organization.'[245]

The initial discussions agreed on the imperative to continue the jihad against the Soviets and the idea of creating a vanguard for the umma. However, the participants were vague on the specifics of what would underpin these goals. Yet it was clear that this formation 'was a physical and ideological purge of Muslim Brotherhood elements,'[246] which had been a defining feature of the pioneering jihadi Abdullah Azzam. The Al-Qaeda attack on the Muslim Brotherhood as a whole – although they still thought highly of Sayyid Qutb – was expressly stated with the publication of two works in 1991: Ayman al-Zawahiri's *al-Ḥiṣād al-Murr: al-Ikhwān al-Muslimūn fī Sittīn ʿĀmm* (*The Bitter Harvest: The Muslim Brotherhood in Sixty Years*) and Abū Musʿab al-Sūrī's *al-Thawrah al-Islāmiyyah al-Jihadiyyah fī Sūriyā* (*The Islamic Jihad Revolution in Syria*). This type of hostility to mainstream Islamism would be replicated by the GIA in Algeria.

The early 1990s have been described as Al-Qaeda's 'ideological and operational morass,'[247] with their vision poorly outlined and key figures, like al-Zawahiri, concentrating on other projects such as toppling Mubarak in Egypt. It has been argued by al-Suri that even Bin Laden and al-Zawahiri were not ideologically aligned at this point, with Bin Laden quite a distance from the JS thought of the Egyptian Islamic Jihad group and al-Zawahiri by even 1990.[248] In this unfocused state, the group failed to contribute to current battles besetting Muslim communities in the world in the early 1990s, such as in Bosnia and Tajikistan.[249]

Upon the commencement of the civil war in Afghanistan in 1992, Al-Qaeda ceased frontline action. Their training in the region was compromised by the ISI inhibiting their movement in Pakistan and other Afghan fighters wanted their weapons. The situation was so fraught that Al-Qaeda even considered closing its camps in 1994. But they stayed open, and when their leader, Bin Laden, was forced to leave his residence in Sudan where he had been since 1992, he returned, albeit without Saudi citizenship. Around the same time, al-Zawahiri and other members of the EIJ also returned to Afghanistan after facing a similar expulsion from Sudan for their violent exploits.[250] But Bin Laden and Al-Qaeda had undergone a transformation in Sudan and 'became a relatively structured enterprise with a central leadership, functionally differentiated committees and a salary system,' although their military and political vision was still not finalized.[251]

Bin Laden's return to Afghanistan had not been of concern to the Taliban at the time, as they were focused on the capture of Kabul.[252] He and his associates were able to develop links with local commanders, probably with the benefit of providing financial aid. On 23 August 1996, Bin Laden announced the commencement of his battle against 'the far enemy' by releasing a short document entitled *Declaration of Jihad against the Americans Occupying the Land of the Two Holy Places*. In the tract, he declared the American presence in the holy land to be the most aggressive attack upon the Muslims. His elaboration on the point quoted from the Qur'an and the hadith, but his citation of other authorities is revealing of his influences, which were somewhat varied at this point. His Salafi credentials were highlighted with the citation of Ibn Taymiyya, the venerable pillar of Salafi thought; and he lamented the injustice of the arrests – instigated by what he called 'a Judeo-Christian coalition' – of *Ṣaḥwa* Salafis like Safar al-Hawali and Salman al-Oudah, the Jihadi-Salafi 'Umar 'Abd al-Rahman, and the Palestinian jihadi Ahmad Yassin (d. 2004), and their assassination of his early guide 'Azzam. He also called for Muslims to unite in expelling the Americans from Saudi Arabia, so that Islam could be established, and declared that the battle would not end until the goal was accomplished. This work marked Bin Laden's shift into being a theorist, whereas before he was mainly a financier, fighter, and coordinator.[253]

Shortly after the Taliban took control of Kabul, the Saudi ambassador to Afghanistan urged Mullah Muhammad 'Umar (d. 2013), the leader of the Taliban, to hand Bin Laden over to the Americans. Upon learning that Bin Laden was no longer a Saudi national and the Americans had not accused him of crimes against the United States, Umar refused, in his express terms, 'to surrender a Muslim to a non-believer.' This sentiment would be reiterated after 9/11 with devastating consequences, as the resulting American-led invasion laid violent siege to Afghanistan, soon destroying its infrastructure and occupying the country. Such intransigence and sense of loyalty to the 'guest' was not a universal attitude among all Taliban leaders, even from the beginning of Bin Laden's return to Afghanistan. Mullah Muhammad Khaksar (d. 2006) – Intelligence Minister for the Taliban between 1994 and

1996, and Deputy Minister of the Interior from 1996 until 2001 – met Bin Laden around this time and told him to leave with his people, as they would only bring trouble upon Afghanistan. Khaksar advised Mullah ‘Umar of the danger posed to the country by the Arabs.[254]

Around the middle of 1996 or early 1997, Khalid Sheikh Mohammed, who had worked with Sayyaf in the 1980s, met with Bin Laden and informed him of a variety of strategies for attacking American and other interests, suggesting ‘the planes operation,’ which was the rough idea that would later translate into the 9/11 terror attacks. Bin Laden was not favorably disposed to the idea at this time, but would come around to it two years later, in late 1998 or early 1999, when the plans were further developed by Mohammed Atta. By this time, Bin Laden had not only announced his *Declaration of Jihad against the Americans* in 1996, but he had, in February 1998, already created the *World Islamic Front for Jihad against Jews and Crusaders*, with its chilling argument that ‘every Muslim who is capable of doing so has the personal duty to kill Americans and their allies, whether civilians or military personnel, in every country where this is possible.’[255]

This declaration, with its accompanying media event, greatly angered Mullah ‘Umar, who saw it as a flagrant breach of what he considered to be his order that Bin Laden stay away from the press. It also fueled the anti-Bin Laden faction in the government and led to Mullah ‘Umar being somewhat isolated in his support for Bin Laden, effectively dividing the government. The jihadi Abu Musʿab al-Suri, a staunch defender of the Taliban as ‘a legitimate Islamic Emirate,’ also wrote passionately in opposition to Bin Laden’s antics: ‘In short, our brother [Bin Laden’s] latest troublemaking with the Taliban and the Leader of the Faithful jeopardizes the Arabs, and the Arab presence, today in Afghanistan, for no good reason.’ Al-Suri also said, ‘I think our brother [Bin Laden] has caught the disease of screens, flashes, fans, and applause.’[256]

After the bombing of the United States’ embassies in Nairobi, Kenya, and Dar-es-Salaam in Tanzania on 7 August 1998, Mullah ‘Umar informed Bin Laden that it was best if he and his men left the country, even though they did not accept responsibility for the attacks. Bin Laden warned ‘Umar that bowing to the pressure of a disbelieving country was against Islam. At this, ‘Umar relented, and advised Bin Laden that he would take the approach that the Sudanese government had taken, offering him an eighteen-month amnesty in which he and his family were to find an alternative home. Yet more intriguing is the fact that August 1998 confirmed a significant change of heart on the part of Mullah ‘Umar, as he had agreed to hand Bin Laden over to the Saudis, who would convene a religious panel to judge Bin Laden’s case. Yet, when Prince Turki returned to Afghanistan after the bombings in 1998, presumably on the pretext of collecting Bin Laden, Umar refused to deliver him, and he even declared that the Saudi government was 'illegitimate' on the basis of having allowed American troops to set up bases in the holy lands. There was such discontent with Mullah 'Umar within the Taliban over his rebuke of Saudi Arabia, that there were rumors in Kabul of a coup against him. As a result of the growing hostility to his stance, he began to isolate those who opposed him, such as Mullah Mutawakkil, the Foreign Minister at the time.[257]

Al-Qaeda was able to increase its numbers between 1999 and 2001, thanks to its settled base in Afghanistan under the protection of the Taliban, and the partnership with it. This expansion included the opening of Al-Qaeda's main training camp, named *al-Faruq* in Kandahar in mid-2000, and a large influx of new recruits coming to swell their ranks. Such was the scale of their success that they started to consider themselves a 'government in exile.'[258] The relationship between Al-Qaeda and the Taliban was always fraught; and the popular position of portraying them as a united front in the 'TalQaeda' narrative is one of inattentiveness. Al-Qaeda members were Jihadi-Salafis and the Taliban were Deobandīs, with the latter intellectual and spiritual tradition opposing modern Salafism across the religious disciplines, primarily in their respective methodologies toward theology, law, and spirituality.

Subsequently, the United States-led assault on Afghanistan after 9/11 dismantled Taliban rule and the Al-Qaeda establishment, immediately and comprehensively, such that all were forced to halt plans in order to survive. Not only did Al-Qaeda have to evade death and capture from the rapid and widespread attack, they also had to contend with disagreements among themselves about the attack, such as Abu Muhammad al-Zayyat, head of AQ's Military Committee, and their jihadi affiliates who condemned Bin Laden and al-Zawahiri, in particular, for undertaking such an attack without consultation.[259] Furthermore, Bin Laden was opposed internally within Al-Qaeda by senior figures for his 'catastrophic leadership' and for deludedly believing that the Americans were relatively weak militarily, and not appreciating that the might of America and her allies would obliterate the Taliban's rule – which they all supported, despite differences in ideology – and how this would then weaken Al-Qaeda. Abu al-Walid al-Masri, a member of Al-Qaeda's consultative body at the time, and the author of a document published around 2004 criticizing Bin Laden, said of the group's cult-like docility at the time of the 9/11 attacks, and the immediate aftermath in the face of the American-led onslaught, 'Everyone knew that their leader was leading them to the abyss and even leading the entire country to utter destruction, but they continued to bend to his will and take his orders with suicidal submission.' Abu al-Walid also criticized Bin Laden for 'extreme infatuation' with or 'crazy attraction' to media exposure.[260]

Before the bulk of Al-Qaeda's leadership fled to Pakistan in the face of the American retaliation for 9/11, they still engaged in some significant fighting, such as the battle of Tora Bora in December 2001.[261] They attempted to exploit the sought-after notoriety that they gained with the 9/11 attacks – although they would only admit responsibility in October 2004 – and expanded their operations to other parts of the world, with the formation of Al-Qaeda on the Arabian Peninsula (AQAP) and Al-Qaeda in the Islamic Maghreb (AQIM), as well as the emergence of terrorist acts attributed to Al-Qaeda and its affiliates. Formal affiliates, or those inspired by their example, committed attacks such as: Casablanca in May 2003; suicide bombings in March 2004 in Madrid and in London in July 2005; Sharm al-Sheikh, Egypt, in July 2005; Delhi, India, in October 2005; Amman, Jordan, in November 2005; and others either claimed or attributed to Al-Qaeda during this period in Türkiye, Indonesia, Iraq, Saudi Arabia, and Pakistan. Nonetheless, Bin Laden and al-Zawahiri released statements saying that their focus was Iraq, after the United States-led invasion in late 2002 and early 2003.[262]

Since Al-Qaeda's central command was obliterated by the American-led invasion of Afghanistan, according to a Joint Report by the US State Department and the National Counterterrorism Center in 2004, most of the acts of terrorism committed in their name were carried out by affiliates and those merely inspired by Al-Qaeda's vision, rather than having actual AQ involvement, direction, and leadership. This was most certainly the case with the 2004 bombings in Madrid and the 2005 bombings in London.[263]

However, it was during this period, in the aftermath of 9/11, that Al-Qaeda received a direct and powerful rebuke from repentant Jihadi-Salafi colleagues. As outlined earlier in the section on Egypt, the EIG had embarked on the Initiative to Stop the Violence and, from 2002, they released eight booklets correcting notions of jihad that had become prevalent in such circles, but which were, they now argued, religiously incorrect. Two of the eight treatises composed by imprisoned EIG members dealt with Al-Qaeda directly: *Al Qaeda Strategy: Mistakes and Dangers* (2003) by Mohammed Essam Derbala and *Islam and the Challenges of the Twenty-First Century* (2004) by Nageh Abdullah Ibrahim – both authors serving life sentences in Egypt for their EIG activities. Furthermore, the EIG leader Karam Zuhdi chided Al-Qaeda for failing to grasp how the Cold War world of bipolar power had given way to a unipolar world where the United States was completely dominant, and yet Al-Qaeda, with their meagerness, had the temerity to think they could challenge this superpower. In addition, it was argued that AQ had failed to appreciate that the worldwide Muslim community was altogether incapable of taking on the United States, never mind the fact that they did not, on the whole, even have any desire to do so. As such, Al-Qaeda, in his estimation, was simply bent on killing non-Muslims, lacking any regard for a rational cost-benefit analysis.

Furthermore, the imprisoned EIG leaders denounced Al-Qaeda's entrenched determination about the inevitability of hostile relations between

Muslims and the United States; and they presented a variety of examples to show American assistance to Muslims: backing the Afghan *mujahidin* against the Soviet Union; supporting Saudi Arabia and Kuwait against the Iraqi invasion of Kuwait in 1990 to 1991; helping end the war afflicting Bosnia, and the massacre of her people, in 1995; and leading the NATO intervention in Kosovo in 1999, ending Serbia's ethnic cleansing in the region. Thus the EIG called Al-Qaeda to seek peaceful dialogue, despite the fact that US policies over the last sixty years, as argued by Derbala, had been largely negative towards Muslims; Al-Qaeda's misguided and religiously-reprehensible actions had only exacerbated anti-Islamic sentiments in the United States and the West, and helped the latter wage a most destructive war against Islam and the Muslims, which was wholly unproductive in terms of achieving their goals of Islam's revival. Derbala also posed a telling contrast between the Prophet Muhammad's method of 'neutralizing enemies' and Al-Qaeda's woeful 'art of making enemies'; and they ridiculously declared war on the world then were thoroughly unprepared for such an engagement. In addition, he condemned the group for failing to grasp that 'Jihad is a means, not an end,' stating that such an approach is highly detrimental, bearing huge costs and few benefits. Derbala urged Al-Qaeda to turn back or face the wretched fate of the Algerian GIA: miserably failed, widely hated, and religiously condemned.

Ibrahim then added to Derbala, by condemning conspiracy theories (like believing 9/11 was the work of the Israeli Mossad so the Americans would attack the Muslims), and calling for a renewal in Islamic discourse that went beyond just Al-Qaeda. He accepted that the EIG had made a similar mistake to Al-Qaeda in the 1980s with their document statement entitled *The Inevitability of Confrontation*, and that their armed resistance to the Egyptian regime had caused enormous harm and many unnecessary deaths, resulting in abject failure. Moreover, he criticized the Algerian militants for excommunicating the state and society, which was a perilous road that Al-Qaeda was following, the path of the early deviant *Khawarij* sect, who incorrectly legitimized killing people. Ibrahim posed the following questions, and answered in the negative: 'Is armed conflict the ideal way to apply the Shariah? Is fighting the only way to free prisoners and resolve Islamists' problems? All these inquiries raise one question: Does the justice of a cause imply the inevitability of armed confrontation?' For Ibrahim, patience might be worth more than fighting, and consideration of the current circumstances could outweigh the nobility of fighting in God's cause, especially when such actions harm the achievement of higher goals.[264]

The period around 2005 and 2008 witnessed the strengthening of the forces seeking to repel the foreign invaders and topple the US-endorsed government of Afghanistan, as the Taliban's Mullah Dadullah (d. 2007) achieved numerous military successes, particularly in 2006, and the ranks of the resistance forces swelled as a result of growing disgruntlement at the invaders and the new regime. Before his death in May 2007, Dadullah provided an interesting development in the jihadi outlook of certain parts of the Taliban, which illustrated the growing influence of Al-Qaeda-type JS methods of warfare on certain strands of the Taliban. Most likely inspired by the resistance methods used by forces in the defense of Iraq against the invasion, Dadullah encouraged suicide bombing as a military method, which was not prevalent among the Taliban, and was in fact condemned by most of them. Later it would come to be categorically condemned by the movement, after growing civilian casualties led to the Taliban having to contend with increasing hostility and loss of support. A Taliban newspaper campaign in Kandahar said such missions were religiously unsanctioned and had been carried out by 'foreign fighters.' Dadullah spoke in global-jihadi terms and entertained the notion of attacks in Europe and the United States, while also proudly proclaiming the unity of the Taliban and Al-Qaeda in outlook and working together. However, the Taliban as a whole did not come to accept the Jihadi-Salafi religious outlook, and the leadership acted cautiously in public when it came to discussing Al-Qaeda: it did not offer unquestioning support.[265]

In terms of Jihadi-Salafism's relevance in the region, Al-Qaeda retained some significance in areas of south Asia and the Middle East, as well as the Sahel.[266] Yet, the public relations disaster of their merger in Iraq with Abu Mus'ab al-Zarqawi, with the latter's maverick brutality being too extreme for Al-Qaeda, led Osama bin Laden to admit 'mistakes' were made in Iraq, in a rare public admission of error.[267] Noteworthy as well was Al-Qaeda's almost complete absence from the Arab Spring of 2010 onwards, despite al-Zawahiri trying to adopt the Arab Spring as some sort of continuum from his activism after the event,[268] and then a spate of Al-Qaeda attacks in Syria in 2011 and Yemen in 2012 in an attempt to capitalize on the insecurity of the time.[269] However, the public profile of Al-Qaeda came to be almost fully overshadowed, in time, by Islamic State (IS, discussed in section 5.5.1); and around the summer of 2014, IS expanded into areas of Afghanistan and Pakistan. In January 2015 there was the formal announcement of the Islamic State in Khorasan (IS-K), which was said to include Afghanistan, Pakistan, all of central Asia, Iran and parts of India and Russia, and was a branch of IS-Central.[270]

What problematizes the characterization of IS-K as Jihadi-Salafi is the denial, from some on their part, that they are Salafis, or that their main support is from areas with strong Salafi presences like Nuristan, Kunar, and Nangarhar. In addition, differences have been identified between IS-K and IS-Central, including the fact that IS-K has not utilized mass-excommunication, which raises further questions about IS-K's Salafism. Nonetheless, they have drawn from the Salafi networks and have been widely accused of being

Salafi, displaying Salafi tendencies such as destroying shrines, and imposing Salafi prayer-styles in Kajaki, which angered locals on account of their traditional practice. So, while they might not be as Salafi as IS-Central, they still adhere to core Jihadi-Salafi notions. Initially, IS-K sought co-existence with the Taliban and Al-Qaeda, even as it tried, successfully on occasion, to recruit from within their ranks, and ultimately aimed to supersede them in the region. However, IS-K has been engaged with fighting the Taliban since 2015, starting with military engagement in the eastern, southern, and western parts of Afghanistan, and it did not have good relations with Al-Qaeda. IS-K's bombing campaigns have continued to the present day, but it is nowhere near achieving its goals of governmental rule in the region.

Bin Laden's clandestine terror effort continued until 2 May 2011, when a team of Navy SEALs executed him in Pakistan.[271] The leadership of Al-Qaeda then passed on to Bin Laden's long-time colleague Ayman al-Zawahiri, who countered IS-K by giving greater public support to the Taliban. In 2014, he even portrayed the Taliban's Mullah 'Umar as a proto-Caliph. In 2015, al-Zawahiri made a public display of loyalty to 'Umar's successor, Akhtar Mansur (d. 2016), when it was announced that Mullah 'Umar had been dead for two years. Al-Zawahiri's reign as the leader of Al-Qaeda continued until he was killed on 31 July 2022 by a US drone in Kabul.

The re-establishment of the Taliban rule was achieved by the Doha agreement of 2020 with the United States, in which the Taliban agreed to not shelter terrorist groups who were fighting Americans. Yet, in early 2022, Al-Qaeda leader al-Zawahiri started releasing frequent video messages. Denying that the Taliban had any knowledge of al-Zawahiri returning to Kabul, the Interior Minister, Sirajuddin Haqqani, announced to the world's press that Al-Qaeda was a 'dead' organization which no longer existed. This confirmed what a July 2022 report by the United Nations stated: 'Al-Qaida is not viewed as posing an immediate international threat from its safe haven in Afghanistan because it lacks an external operational capability and does not currently wish to cause the Taliban international difficulty or embarrassment.'[272] On all these fronts, it appears that the Taliban and Al-Qaeda may have learnt a harsh lesson from their political naiveté of the late 1990s until 2001. But while the Taliban seem to have appreciated the benefit of being less harsh in their behavior towards their people, Al-Qaeda showed no repentance for their original ideology, brutality, or the resulting replica spinoffs.

### *5.3.6 The Malay Archipelago*

Jihadism has historical roots in the Malay Archipelago, with Indonesia providing the most striking case study. This phenomenon developed, in some quarters, into a Jihadi-Salafi movement in the 1990s, with its most infamous, devastating manifestation being the Bali bombings of 2002.[273]

*The Darul Islam movement: From jihadism towards Jihadi-Salafism*

The formative jihadi movement in Indonesia was the Darul Islam movement, which was founded by Sekarmadji Maridjan Kartosuwirjo (d. 1962) in 1948. In May 1948, he declared himself to be the leader of an independent state called *Darul Islam* (The Abode of Islam or DI) in the first rebellion against the Indonesian Republic. Then, on 7 August 1949, he announced the Islamic State of Indonesia (*Negara Islam Indonesia* or NII) in Cisampak, West Java. Kartosuwirjo began excommunicating all Muslims who did not pledge loyalty to his state or merely disagreed with his views. On 4 June 1962, he was surrounded by government troops and he and his entourage surrendered. After a quick trial, he was charged with rebellion and sentenced to death, thus marking the end of a rebellion which had destroyed the economy of West Java and led to the death, injury or kidnapping of 22,895 civilians. While Kartosuwirjo was a jihadi, he had no links to Salafism or Wahhabism either theologically or ideologically, despite the fact that he engaged in *takfir* against his political opponents.

Attempts to revive DI in the 1970s led to a growing influence of the ideas of Sayyid Qutb and Mawdudi in their ranks, as more of these books became available in translation. Moreover, it was a period when the people who were recruited brought a distinctly Salafi character to their activism, including Abdullah Sungkar (d. 1999), who was a teacher devoted to the works of Ibn ʿAbd al-Wahhāb, and Abu Bakar Ba'asyir, although the influence of the Muslim Brotherhood was still significant. Excommunication was a prevalent practice; and they robbed Muslims who they felt had apostatized.

A failed bombing attempt by the group in Bali in 1985 led Sungkar and Ba'asyir to flee to Malaysia, after an order was placed for their arrest. While in Malaysia their plan for jihad in Indonesia took another turn as the Afghan–Soviet war provided them with an arena in which to get recruits trained for military action. Thereafter Sungkar and Ba'asyir journeyed to Saudi Arabia and met with Shaykh Ibn Bāz, before traveling on to Pakistan. In Peshawar they met with the Afghan military leader Abdul Rasul Sayyaf and made arrangements for training. Between 1985 and 1994, more than 200 DI members went to the war zone, including three who would go on to conduct the Bali bombings in 2002, namely Mukhlas (d. 2008), Dulmatin (d. 2010), and Umar Patek.

The dispute between the Afghan *mujahidin* around the late 1980s would come to affect the Indonesians. On the one hand was Azzam and his view that Muslims should liberate Muslim lands under occupation – like Palestine, Kashmir, and the Philippines – and on the other was al-Zawahiri with his argument that fighters should return to their homelands and take the fight to the apostate rulers. In 1990, some of the DI Afghan fighters would develop close ties with the Egyptian Islamic Group, the JS organization in the Khowst region. Indeed, many of the stances of DI were not far from the JS views of the EIG.

### Jemaah Islamiyah *and the birth of Jihadi-Salafism*

Yet the gravitation towards Jihadi-Salafism of some of the DI Afghan fighters did not receive universal acceptance. This led to a split and the formal establishment of the breakaway *Jemaah Islamiyah* (JI) in 1992, under Sungkar. Part of Sungkar's disagreement with Masduki, in addition to strategic differences and understandings of DI as a polity, was the fact that Masduki was seen to have developed distinctly Sufi leanings, which were anathema to Sungkar's Salafism.

JI was the first JS movement in the Malay Archipelago, and it was formally based on the EIG, with the same goal of engaging in a war against a government deemed to have apostatized. Some JI members would go on to embrace the global jihadi outlook of Osama bin Laden and seek to engage in military action against the United States and the West. This latter group came to carry out the Bali bombings in 2002.

Sungkar developed the group in Malaysia, with the help of associates like Ba'asyir. The ideological basis of the group was Muslim Brotherhood–Salafi and Jihadi-Salafi, as indicated by the three main books it relied upon for its outlook: the Muslim Brotherhood–Salafi perspective was articulated through Husayn ibn Muhammad ibn 'Ali Jabari's *al-Tariq ila jama'at al-Muslimin* (*The Path to Unify the Community of Muslims*) and Muhammad Munir al-Ghadban's *al-Manhaj al-haraki li'l-sirah al-nabawiyyah* (*The Dynamic Methodology of the Life of the Prophet*), and the Jihadi-Salafi instruction came through the EIG's *Charter of Islamic Action* (*Mīthāq al-'amal al-islāmī*), released in 1984, a hastily arranged treatise penned in prison in the midst of the vicious government crackdown on the movement after the assassination of Sadat in 1981.

By the late 1990s, JI was sending members to train in Afghanistan at Al-Qaeda's *al-Faruq* camp, which consolidated its internationalist JS connections and orientation. Around twenty members trained at the location between 1999 and 2001, mainly from Malaysia.

The divisions in JI would be further tested after Osama bin Laden released his fatwa against the Americans in 1998. Sungkar and Ba'asyir went to Afghanistan and met with Bin Laden then returned with the latter's invitation to the members of DI. DI rejected the offer, as did the JI's jihad section over much of Indonesia, who argued that the main target should remain the Indonesian government, as the principles of jihad dictated that a near enemy should be prioritized over the far. However, Bin Laden's fatwa was supported by leadership in JI's Malaysian and Singapore section, who wanted to wage war on America as the primary enemy of the umma.

Nonetheless, the debate was put on hold as communal violence broke out between Christians and Muslims in Indonesia, lasting for a number of years and costing thousands of lives on each side.

After making meticulous plans, on the Saturday night of 12 October 2002, a group of JI members bombed two popular nightspots in Bali, killing 202 people including 88 Australians and 38 Indonesians, and wounding more than 300.

The Indonesian government made swift progress in tracking down the perpetrators, commencing a widespread and destructive crackdown on JI, with mass imprisonments (including of JI leaders who had opposed the bombing campaign) and the destruction of their networks and general condemnation from all segments of Indonesian society.

While the damage after the Bali bombings was almost terminal, it did not signify the end of such terrorism in Indonesia, with JI members being responsible for the bombing of the Marriott hotel in 2003; the Australian embassy in 2004; a further Bali bombing in 2005; and then the bombing of the Marriott and Ritz-Carlton hotels in 2009. Nonetheless, Jihadi-Salafism in the region accords with the global trends in continuing to splinter, with numerous jihadi groups coming into existence, bombing miscellaneous targets and robbing banks.

The release of Abu Muhammad al-Maqdisi's 2004 work *Waqafāt ma'a Thamarāt al-Jihad* (*An Assessment of the Fruits of Jihadist Efforts*) resulted, a few years later, in a division within Indonesian JS ranks. This work caused controversy as it was a critical reflection on the jihadi movement by a leading Jihadi-Salafi in which he argued that their operations should consider the harms and benefits of their actions, rather than merely focusing on the permissibility of the deeds. He also stated the priority of fighting to establish Islamic rule (*qital tamkin*) over simply weakening the enemy (*qital nikayah*). In practical terms, this was the contrast between forming jihadi *cells* and forming a jihadi *organization* (*tanzim*).

Based on his reflection, *Jamaah Anshorut Tauhid* (Helpers of Tawḥīd Congregation or JAT) was formed in 2008 when Ba'asyir left JI due to his favoring *qital tamkin* over the preference for *qital nikayah* by other JI leaders. But JAT would itself split in 2014, when Ba'asyir came out in support of Islamic State in Iraq and Syria (ISIS), with the breakaway opponents taking on the name *Jamaah Ansharus Syariah* (Community of the Helpers of Shariah or JAS). The ISIS supporters were responsible for a 2016 bombing in Jakarta, a suicide bombing of a police station in Solo in 2016, and an attack in Kampung Melayu, Jakarta in 2017.

The continuing appeal of Jihadi-Salafism in the Malay Archipelago has been minimal, with people often recruited through religious study circles (*pengajian*) or due to kinship ties, without any political gain or serious threat to the governments of the region.

## *5.4 The Main Ideologues of Jihadi-Salafism*

Even though Jihadi-Salafism has historical roots in the 1960s and 1970s, its main ideological expression came from the 1990s. While there were numerous earlier figures who have acted as ideological pioneers for JS, in the modern era, one can identify four main ideologues who determined the direction of Jihadi-Salafism on a global scale. They are, in order of importance: Osama bin Laden, Ayman al-Zawahiri, Abu Muhammad al-Maqdisi, and Abu Musʿab al-Zarqawi. Much of their organizational history, except for al-Zarqawi (whose organization is discussed below), has been recounted earlier, so it will not be repeated, leaving us with their essential biographical details.

### *5.4.1 Osama bin Laden (d. 2011)*

Osama bin Laden is the most infamous Jihadi-Salafi name in the West,[274] yet his role in shaping the doctrine of Jihadi-Salafism is less significant than the other names on this list. In many ways, Bin Laden was more of a student and follower, rather than a leader and innovator. He was highly influenced by the writings of other jihadi authors and followed through on the ideas that many of them had preached, such as the notions developed by Sayyid Qutb and Abu Muhammad al-Maqdisi.

Bin Laden was born in Saudi Arabia into the wealthy Bin Laden family who operate the country's largest construction company. His father was a Yemeni immigrant who became a billionaire upon gaining favor with the royal family, before finally passing away in 1967. He married often, and had twenty-four sons and thirty daughters, with Osama being the seventeenth son. Osama's mother, Alia Ghanem, gave birth to Osama a year after her marriage. She was originally from the Syrian city of Latakia, which is the Alawite capital, and her first name is popular among Shīʿis; hence Osama was beset with rumors about having some close heretical heritage. His mother was divorced when Osama was young, and she remarried and relocated to Jeddah, where Osama was raised.

He grew up in luxury among the elite of Saudi society. His youth was somewhat unspectacular, although his upbringing was strict, and he was very religious from a young age, albeit with a passion for cars and football. He married a cousin in 1974. In 1976 and 1977, as mentioned by his friend Jamal Khalifa, Bin Laden was making a concerted effort to read and understand Sayyid Qutb's *Milestones* and *In the Shade of the Qur'an*; and thereafter took lessons with Muhammad Qutb – the brother of Sayyid Qutb – who was a lecturer at King 'Abd al-'Aziz University in Jeddah.[275] One can surmise that his version of Salafism was relatively mainstream, having studied the standard Saudi curriculum and listening to preachers on national television and radio. He eventually enrolled in King Abdul Aziz University to study civil engineering, perhaps seeing an opportunity to help in the family construction business. However, it was during his time at the University that he took the mandatory Islamic Studies course that was being offered by Abdullah Azzam and a life-long mentorship between the two began. Bin Laden was mesmerized by the stories told by Azzam, of fighting the Soviets with the Afghan *mujahidin*, and at a young age, he aided the jihad in Afghanistan against the Soviets.[276] During the 1980s, he frequently traveled between Saudi Arabia and Afghanistan, and gained a certain level of fame for his activities – being something of a 'poster boy' for the cause after a series of articles were published on him in 1988 by Jamal Khashoggi.[277] Then, he was mainly involved in fundraising rather than combat, perhaps taking part in one battle in Jaji in 1986. He would go to Pakistan to give funds to the Afghan fighters through the *Jamaat-e-Islami*, the Pakistani equivalent of the Muslim Brotherhood.[278] However, by the end of the 1980s he would turn to armed combat.

It was in Afghanistan that he intersected with various other strands of jihadism from around the globe, including, most prominently (apart from Azzam) the proto-JS activists of the Algerian Bouyalists, and the freed Jihadi-Salafis of Egypt who were involved in the assassination of Sadat. Initially, for much of the decade, Bin Laden was close to Azzam, which is unsurprising as he was seen as being linked to the Muslim Brotherhood at the time.[279] Nonetheless, they eventually drifted apart, beginning in around 1986, and Bin Laden's formal support had ended by 1987 or 1988, although some informal links continued for a short while.[280] Azzam does not appear to have possessed any personal animosity towards Bin Laden's independence and organization, as he proposed that Bin Laden should be made the emir of the Arab fighters as a way of maintaining unity among the forces. This however did not materialize.[281]

Some attribute Bin Laden's shift towards radicalism to his coming closer to the Egyptian Jihadi-Salafis like Ayman al-Zawahiri in 1987 and being in part a disgruntlement with the pragmatism of Azzam, in contrast with the radicalism of the Egyptian Jihadi-Salafis who had historically and vehemently opposed the Muslim Brotherhood. Despite the popularity of the theory that Bin Laden was manipulated and perhaps brainwashed by the Egyptian Jihadi-Salafis – namely the 'evil Egyptian' theory – it has been convincingly argued that Bin Laden was highly independent, intelligent, and not easily swayed.[282] If he was of such a persuasive disposition, then his Muslim Brotherhood foundations and his early relationship with Azzam would have held him captive, but they did not. Thus, it can be asserted that Bin Laden's radical turn was his own decision. Indeed, Bin Laden's later declaration of war on the United States in 1996 seems to have been more his thought than anyone else who signed the document.

Upon returning to Saudi, he would soon be faced with the impending Gulf War in 1991. His response was to offer the regime the assistance of *mujahidin* as defenders of the Kingdom against Saddam Hussein's Iraqi forces, rather than permitting the non-Muslim forces of the Americans and her allies on to Saudi soil. Unsurprisingly, this suggestion was rejected by the Saudi rulers, but his offer was indicative of a delusional sense of power which would characterize his later declaration of war upon the United States.

After leaving Saudi in 1992 for Peshawar, then Sudan, before being expelled by the latter, and then being given a safe haven in Afghanistan in 1996, he released his *Declaration of Jihad against the Americans*. By this stage, he had been stripped of his Saudi citizenship.[283] In February 1998, he created the World Islamic Front for Jihad against Jews and Crusaders and became a fugitive after the US embassy bombings on 7 August. He is most infamous for being the mastermind behind the 11 September 2001 attacks, which started the US war on terror. Following an extended period in hiding, with a sporadic release of public statements – which ceased being video recordings and became simple voice messages – Bin Laden was shot and killed by US Navy SEALs on 1 May 2011 in a private residential compound in Abbottabad, Pakistan.[284]

Within the jihadi camp, however, not everybody agreed with Bin Laden's methods and role. As previously mentioned, al-Suri considered Bin Laden to have been smitten by the fame of being the figurehead of jihadism, and thought that this may have made him unbalanced, adversely affecting his policies and strategy. A similar disagreement caused a rift between the Taliban and Bin Laden in later years.[285]

### *5.4.2 Ayman al-Zawahiri (d. 2022)*

Al-Zawahiri was born in Cairo into a wealthy and respected family, on both his maternal and paternal sides.[286] His father was a lecturer in pharmacology at Ayn Shams University, and a prestigious doctor, as were his uncles and cousins. Also on his father's side, his great-uncle had been the Shaykh of al-Azhar University, and his grandfather and great-grandfather had been prominent scholars there. On his mother's side, there were many graduates of al-Azhar, including his maternal grandfather, who then headed the Faculty of Literature at Cairo University and founded King Sa‘ud University in Riyadh. In addition, his maternal grand-uncle was Abdul Rahman Azzam, who was Secretary-General of the Arab League upon its formation in 1948; one of his maternal uncles was Mahfouz Azzam, who was Sayyid Qutb's lawyer and the last person to see Qutb alive before the Egyptian state executed him.[287] Despite being part of upper-class society, which typically veers towards the less religious side of the spectrum, al-Zawahiri's parents seem to have been quite religious and modest in comparison to their social peers.

The young al-Zawahiri was an observantly religious child, and highly intelligent. He was said to be unsociable, dedicated to reading and study, particularly religious books, and would not often play with other children.[288] After Sayyid Qutb was executed in 1966, al-Zawahiri, then aged fifteen, along with four other students, formed an underground cell devoted to overthrowing the government and establishing an Islamic state: his goal was to put Qutb's vision into action. He would later write, in his 2001 work entitled *Knights under the Prophet's Banner*, how Qutb was crucial for the development of the jihadi movement, and how much his work had impacted him. Nonetheless, throughout his career in jihadism, al-Zawahiri remained fiercely in opposition to the Muslim Brotherhood in general, for their pragmatism and surrender to the current governments and systems of rule, like standing for election within the democratic process. Another contributory factor to his aversion to the Muslim Brotherhood is that he was a product of the Salafi scene in Egypt, and Salafis have been historic critics of the Muslim Brotherhood's approach to law and theology.

He studied medicine at Cairo University and in the late 1970s would become a member of the coalition of different jihadi groups – including the Egyptian Islamic Group – who came to be united as *Tanzim al-Jihad* under Faraj. He was imprisoned in the sweep of arrests that followed the assassination of Sadat in 1981, spent three years in prison, and was reportedly severely tortured due to the seniority he held in the movement. Montasser al-Zayyat, an Islamist lawyer and a former colleague of al-Zawahiri, narrates that the torture led al-Zawahiri to betray the location of his long-term friend and colleague ʻIsam al-Qamari. During his trial for his connection to the Sadat conspiracy, he emerged as a leader of the movement and addressed the press in English from his court cage, stating their aims of establishing Islam and how they had been beaten in prison.

Al-Zawahiri was released in 1984 and left for Saudi Arabia, where he practiced medicine. He then traveled with other Jihadis to Peshawar where they reorganized, in 1987, under a new banner, named Egyptian Islamic Jihad (EIJ). Nonetheless, there is little mention of al-Zawahiri's involvement in fighting from the late 1980s to the early 1990s, although this was more a time when the *mujahidin* were fighting among themselves. EIJ was a continuation of Faraj's *al-Jihad* movement, but they developed an even more extreme approach, and did not pay allegiance to Abdullah Azzam who was the leading Arab among the *mujahidin*. The EIJ was initially led by Sayyid Imam al-Sharif, popularly known as 'Dr Faḍl,' who played a prominent role in furthering the development of jihadi theology. Decades later, Dr Faḍl denied his leadership role in the EIJ and retracted his theories, publicly repenting from Jihadhi-Salafism, earning him the ire of his old friend (discussed further below).

Al-Zawahiri impressed those around him, and soon rose up the ranks and became its leader. It was around this time that he formed a close friendship with Bin Laden, joining him in Sudan in 1992 after leaving Kabul, and eventually al-Zawahiri's cell merged with Bin Laden's Al-Qaeda in 1998, with EIJ formally ceasing to exist in June 2001.[289] Before then, he had become increasingly distant from his own Egyptian militants, as some came to agree with the EIG's non-violence initiative which al-Zawahiri passionately opposed. He became Bin Laden's advisor and physician, and eventually took up the role of leader of Al-Qaeda after his death. Al-Zawahiri is noted as being the one who coined the term 'Jihadi-Salafi.'[290]

Al-Zawahiri's initial goal had been the battle against the near enemy, which for him was the Egyptian government. In 1995, he argued that victories in Egypt and Algeria, with the latter experiencing civil war at the time, were crucial for leading an assault that could then recapture Jerusalem. In this, he remained ideologically distant from Bin Laden, who earlier had conceived of the need to launch an attack on the United States: the far enemy. Al-Zawahiri did however come around to Bin Laden's methodology, joining forces with Al-Qaeda and becoming one of the signatories of Bin Laden's World Islamic Front for Jihad against Jews and Crusaders in 1998. The latter move in particular was widely criticized in JS circles, including members of his own group, who opposed taking on the United States; and it was said that al-Zawahiri had 'committed political suicide.'[291] From this point on al-Zawahiri would speak in the same vein as Bin Laden, focusing on the far enemy (*viz.*, America) over the near one.

The most forceful critique of al-Zawahiri would come from his former colleague Dr Faḍl. Faḍl's release from prison in 2007 allowed him to publish his seminal work, *Wathīqat tarshīd al-ʿamal al-jihādī fī Miṣr wa'l-ʿālam* (*The Document of Right Guidance for Jihad Activity in Egypt and the World*), in which Osama bin Laden and al-Zawahiri were subjected to a brutal critique, accused of being unscrupulous, untrustworthy and tyrannical, and charged with being grossly mistaken in the 9/11 attacks. In essence, Dr Faḍl's assessment was that contemporary jihadi movements were operating in opposition to normative understandings of Islamic law, were ineffectual in their methodology, and conducted a deviant course of unbridled violence which included the wrongful targeting of civilians.[292] Dr Faḍl's critique was signed by numerous former associates of al-Zawahiri, which added to its impact.

A year later, al-Zawahiri would respond with vigor in his *Treatise Exonerating the Nation of the Pen and the Sword from the Blemish of the Accusation of Weakness and Fatigue*, accusing Dr Faḍl of being a traitor, in the service of the Americans, and out of touch as he had not been involved in the movement for a number of years. The work, which ran into hundreds of pages, continued to legitimize the clash of civilizations between Islam and the West. Nonetheless, such was the impact of Dr Faḍl's verbal assault, backed with strong arguments derived from the Islamic intellectual tradition, and enhanced by Dr Faḍl's legendary veteran status in Jihadi-Salafism, that al-Zawahiri was forced to respond to internal concerns about killing innocents, which he did in highly defensive terms:

> We have not killed innocents. In fact, we fight those who kill innocents. Those who kill innocents are the Americans, the Jews, the Russians, the French and their agents. Were we insane killers of innocents, it would be possible for us to kill thousands of them in the crowded markets, but we are confronting the enemies of the Muslims and targeting them, and during this, an innocent might fall.[293]

This outwardly intransigent rhetoric belied the discontent that was growing in his own ranks. As the EIG found after its bloody campaign against the Egyptian government in the 1980s and 1990s, and the GIA after its horrific war against the Algerian state, al-Zawahiri and Al-Qaeda were facing unease due to the fact that their methods seemed to kill so many non-combatants. Dr Fadl responded in late 2008, accusing Bin Laden and al-Zawahiri of being ignorant and driven by a 'blood mentality' (*fikr damawī*). However, al-Zawahiri would continue in his role without deviation, becoming leader of Al-Qaeda after Bin Laden's assassination, and remaining in post as one of the most wanted men on earth until he was killed on 31 July 2022 by a US drone strike in Kabul.

### *5.4.3 Abu Muhammad al-Maqdisi (b. 1959)*

Abu Muhammad al-Maqdisi, whose full name is Asim ibn Muhammad ibn Tahir al-Barqawi, is a Jordanian-Palestinian writer who was highly instrumental in the rise and shaping of modern jihadism. He was born in the city of al-Barqa, near al-Nablus; however, his family moved to Kuwait when he was still young. His father narrates that al-Maqdisi led a solitary childhood, without friends, and his later guide, Abu Anas al-Shami, reiterates the notion of an unhappy childhood, but al-Maqdisi talks of having been happy during this time.[294]

Al-Maqdisi's Salafism was honed from an early age. In Kuwait in the early 1980s he joined the company of members of the Kuwaiti branch of *al-Jamāʿah al-Salafiyyah al-Muḥtasibah* (The Salafi Inspection Group or JSM), which had been led by Juhaymān al-ʿUtaybi in Saudi Arabia. Around 1981 or 1982, al-Maqdisi went to study in Saudi Arabia and enhanced his contacts with the JSM, making repeated trips to their base in the Saudi desert in the late 1980s. His brother-in-law, ʿAbd al-Laṭīf al-Dirbas, was one of Juhaymān's most loyal followers, and had been imprisoned in Saudi for a number of years.

In 1985, al-Maqdisi went to Peshawar to join the Afghan jihad against the Soviets. Here his outspoken Salafism openly clashed with the diplomatic Muslim Brotherhood openness of Abdullah Azzam, and it was felt that the Brotherhood and 'Azzam prevented the open espousal of Salafi doctrine.[295] In the early 1990s he settled in Jordan, but continued his militant rhetoric, which led to his eventual imprisonment in 1995. He would continue to go back and forth between prison and freedom for a number of years.

Inspired by the writings and effort of Juhaymān, he has been called the 'most prominent' of Juhaymān's 'intellectual heirs.'[296] He is responsible for formulating many of the concepts that Jihadi-Salafis hold firmly onto,[297] which can be traced back to Juhaymān but expressed in a more extreme manner. These include the particular articulation of concepts such as *al-walāʾ wa'l-barāʾ*, excommunication of the Saudi royal family, and the classification of democracy as a religion. In 1989, he had excommunicated the Saudi royal family, along with the other governments of the Muslim world, in his *al-Kawashif al-jaliyyah fi kufr al-dawlah al-Saʿudiyyah* (*The Obvious Proofs of the Saudi State's Disbelief*), while praising Juhaymān, but lamenting that he had not excommunicated the royal family.

What makes al-Maqdisi particularly unique among the JS ideologues is that he is the primary figure who introduced First-Wave Wahhabi thought into the global JS discourse. Further, he used First-Wave writings to call out Third-Wave reinterpretations as being heretical. Al-Maqdisi is most famous for his seminal work *Millat Ibrahim* (*The Religion of Abraham*), published in 1984, in which he draws from various verses of the Qurʾan the claim that the primary message of the Prophet Abraham was to hate and dissociate from those who opposed him. Developing this point, he argued that hatred of the disbelievers was a religious obligation, and that this enmity must be open and visible. He also stated that those who do not openly show hatred for the disbelievers are guilty of violating *al-walāʾ wa'l-barāʾ* and therefore cannot be considered Muslims.[298] This work became one of the most influential works of Jihadi-Salafi movements.

The entire book was written to prove the legitimacy of *al-walāʾ wa'l-barāʾ* as a basis for *takfīr*. While he refrained from excommunicating the entire Muslim world, unlike Shukri Mustafa's Egyptian group or the later GIA of Algeria, he does excommunicate the Muslim states and those who assist them, such as the police, the army and parliamentarians who support the legislature. The work also cautioned against excessive use of excommunication, which seemed somewhat absurd to many who read it. On the subject of jihad and who to direct the battle towards, he preferred that groups concentrate on the near enemy, but he did not condemn those who sought to engage the far enemy in a violent confrontation, which explains his praise for the 9/11 plane hijackers.[299]

Part of al-Maqdisi's continuing notoriety is that he was the spiritual mentor of Abu Mus'ab al-Zarqawi, the initial leader of Al-Qaeda in Iraq (discussed in section 5.4.4). Although a rift formed between them in 2004 due to their disagreement on the status of Shi'a Muslims and the overzealous engagement in suicide bombings (which al-Maqdisi said should be used sparingly and for a clear military advantage), the ideas propagated by al-Maqdisi were morphed by al-Zarqawi into the group that would eventually become ISIS.[300]

Al-Maqdisi continues to promote JS ideas through his writings and has long-remained relevant to the Jihadi-Salafi movement. A 2004 study by the Saudi government of thousands of young Jihadis or sympathizers found that Abdullah Azzam was the most prominent influence, closely followed by al-Maqdisi.[301] In 2006, when the Combatting Terrorism Center at West Point conducted a study of the online library of jihadi texts called *Minbar al-Tawḥīd wa'l-Jihad*, they found al-Maqdisi's works to be the third most popular, behind Sayyid Qutb and Ahmad Shakir.[302]

In terms of legacy and his matured thought, al-Maqdisi would create a major debate in Jihadi-Salafi circles with the release of his *Waqafāt ma'a Thamarāt al-Jihad* (*Reflections on the Fruits of the Jihad Movements*) in 2004. In this work, he criticized Jihadis who failed to adequately consider the benefits and harms of their violent activity and who, as a consequence, caused more harm than good. He also argued that it was more important to gain control of a territory to rule by Islamic law (*qital tamkin*), rather than concentrating on merely weakening the enemy (*qital nikayah*). In fact, his critique of ISIS was seen as the reason behind his surprise release in 2014, as his opposition could be utilized by the Jordanian government in their drive against ISIS (it was reported that there were around 2,000 ISIS supporters in Jordan at the time). Yet his unexpected discharge from prison was welcomed by Jihadi-Salafis, where he was proclaimed by one leader, Muhammad Shalabi, aka Abu Sayyaf, to be 'the mentor and father of our curriculum,' which highlighted his continuing relevance to Jihadi-Salafism.[303]

### *5.4.4 Abu Mus'ab al-Zarqawi (d. 2006)*

As Romain Caillet noted in 2017, Abu Mus'ab al-Zarqawi is the leader of contemporary jihad, behind Osama bin Laden.[304] His legacy is built upon the attacks that his network coordinated in Iraq between 2003 and 2006, as well as the Sunni-Shi'a conflict that he significantly contributed to. The brutality with which he set about his tasks was to produce horror and disgust across the Muslim world, including within his own Jihadi-Salafi circles. He set the foundations for the most significant Jihadi-Salafi spin-off from Al-Qaeda, namely ISIS (discussed in section 5.5.1). In the Al-Qaeda sphere, al-Zarqawi represented a new type of leader: socially and educationally underprivileged, in contrast to the aristocratic, educated and privileged types defined by Bin Laden, al-Zawahiri, and Dr Faḍl.

Al-Zarqawi was born on 20 October 1966 in Zarqa, Jordan. His family was of an average socio-economic background and consisted of three sons and seven daughters. His father died in 1984, and he left school that same year with a basic education. He was known for having a problem with anger and fighting in the streets, without a religious outlook. After the death of his father, he turned to alcohol and petty crime, eventually ending up in prison on sexual assault and drug possession charges. Upon leaving prison, he had a religious awakening.[305] In 1989, he left for Peshawar where, on arrival, he stayed in accommodation supplied by Osama bin Laden. It was in this city that he met Abu Muhammad al-Maqdisi, who helped him secure work with a jihadi publication. He also participated in the post-Soviet withdrawal fights between the Afghan *mujahidin*, on the side of Gulbuddin Hekmatyar.

He returned to Jordan in 1993, establishing links again with al-Maqdisi's JS group, before being arrested in 1994 and sentenced to fifteen years' imprisonment for possessing firearms and false documents. Even before his arrest he was described as simple and was known to have a poor grasp of classical Arabic. In prison, as is the norm in the Middle East, he was severely tortured, and it is reported by those who knew him that the trauma this caused was the most significant episode in his life, and radically transformed him. As Fawaz A. Gerges has written, 'It is well documented that Arab prisons serve as incubators of future terrorists, and, like numerous Arab Jihadists, Zarqawi was traumatized by his prison years in Jordan.'[306] He is said to have become more ruthless and brutal as a consequence and was hot tempered and rash. In prison, he became a leader who Jihadis gravitated towards, especially as he became known for picking fights with the guards, despite their resulting brutality.

He was released on 29 March 1999 as part of Abdullah II's amnesty that accompanied his coronation ceremonies. Al-Zarqawi swiftly returned to Pakistan and then Afghanistan as, in the explanation of al-Maqdisi, he loved jihad and did not have the patience to be a student, teacher or preacher. He subsequently became close to Bin Laden but was never under his control, and then led a camp in Herat in the west of Afghanistan, in early 2000. Many eyewitnesses recall al-Zarqawi's independent fanaticism causing him to clash with the ideas and leadership of Bin Laden.[307] The situation became so tense that even when both were in Afghanistan fighting the Soviets, they established separate camps, with al-Zarqawi refusing to serve under Bin Laden or his allies the Taliban, whom he considered deviants; a common Salafi belief.[308] Indeed, al-Zarqawi felt that Al-Qaeda were not fierce enough in dealing with their enemy.[309]

After the American invasion of Iraq following 9/11, al-Zarqawi was briefly detained in Iran, but he was soon freed and created, in late 2001, *Ansar al-Islam* (Partisans of Islam), which fought in Kurdistan. He also attempted to coordinate attacks in Jordan, including at tourist locations, but he was often foiled. In addition, the organization was blamed for involvement in acts of terror in Europe, such as the Madrid bombings of 2004, as well as attacks in Germany and Italy where cells were found between 2002 and 2003. In 2003, the US Secretary of State Colin Powell, announced the existence of a terrorist network led by al-Zarqawi in Iraq, which led to al-Zarqawi gaining more popularity, despite the fact that his centrality, at this stage, was likely exaggerated.[310]

With the US-led invasion of Iraq, al-Zarqawi's network set about defending the country in a brutal way, including the kidnapping and slaughter of foreigners, whose deaths were recorded and then released on the internet. But al-Zarqawi soon expanded the range of targets and started killing Shīʿis in Iraq, whether on religious or political grounds (such as working with the new government), which may be indicative of some sort of Wahhabi-Salafism. Al-Zarqawi considered the Shiʿa to be disbelievers and wanted to declare a religious war against them and wipe them out. As a reinforcement of the Salafism of the group, one sees Abu Anas al-Shami (d. 2004) joining their ranks in 2003, as a jurist (*mufti*). Abu Anas had studied at the Islamic University of Medina between 1988 and 1991, where he was influenced by *Ṣaḥwa* scholars like al-Hawali and al-Oudah, before training in Afghanistan and spending some time in Bosnia.

In 2004, al-Maqdisi came out in opposition to al-Zarqawi's killing sprees, criticizing him for his killing of Muslims, including Shiʿa and Christians in their places of worship, rather than concentrating on combatting the invading forces. Al-Maqdisi also harshly lambasted him for his overuse of suicide bombings, claiming that this tactic had little positive effect. This outspoken opposition from his spiritual mentor was a significant blow to al-Zarqawi, in personal terms as well as for his public reputation. Nonetheless, he responded and said that he always believed in the efficacy of suicide bombings when they were planned and utilized, and that he was simply responding to Shiʿi aggression and collaboration with the new government, adding that he attempted to avoid the killing of civilians as much as possible.[311] Al-Zarqawi also mentioned a motto in response: 'A prisoner has no authority.'[312] This was a declaration of al-Maqdisi's compromised position as someone writing from a prison cell, especially in the notorious Arab prison system. Nonetheless, the criticism of al-Zarqawi by Jihadi-Salafis, including al-Zawahiri, would continue through 2005 and 2006, in relation to his attacks on the Shīʿis and liberal use of excommunication.[313]

Eventually, al-Zarqawi grudgingly formed the Iraqi wing of Al-Qaeda on 19 October 2004, after Abu Anas and thirty members of his group were killed by the Americans in an operation at Abu Ghraib prison on 17 September 2004. This affiliate branch did not last long, as Bin Laden himself was reluctant to grant al-Zarqawi formal recognition as an affiliate. Al-Zarqawi separated from Al-Qaeda over theological and strategic differences, such as Al-Qaeda's opposition to starting a theological war with the Shiʿa, which they condemned as detracting from focus on fighting the Americans.[314] He then started his own jihadi movement named *Jama'at Al-Tawhīd wa'l-Jihad* (Congregation of Monotheism and Jihad). He was killed in a US airstrike in 2006 before his vision could be established; having, however, laid the groundwork for the establishment of ISIS.[315]

## *5.5 The Main Jihadi-Salafi Movements After Al-Qaeda*

With the 9/11 terrorist attacks, Al-Qaeda became the symbol for global Jihadi-Salafism. In turn, it would influence the emergence of many similar groups and cells, some formally affiliated to Al-Qaeda and others just inspired by them. These spin-offs have varied in size but have proliferated globally. The three main groups are: ISIS, Boko Haram, and Al-Shabaab. While there was an alarming upturn in such JS movements around 2014 and 2015,[316] there has been a subsequent downturn as they started to receive significant losses at the hands of improved governmental security measures.

### *5.5.1 ISIS in the Middle East*

In 2013, the most extreme manifestation of Jihadi-Salafism came into existence and even managed to establish a state, controlling around a third of Iraq and Syria. This is of course, 'The Islamic State of Iraq and Syria,' or ISIS,[317] also known as IS (Islamic State) or ISIL (Islamic State of Iraq and the Levant) or Daesh (*Dāʿish*, as the acronym of its Arabic title: *al-dawla al-Islamiyya fi-l-ʿIrāq wa'l-Shām*, The State of Islam in Iraq and the Levant). The sudden rise of ISIS shocked the world, particularly as it was able to rapidly and effectively create an operational state apparatus, including around 30,000 soldiers, a territory of around 400,000 square miles, a substantial annual budget of US$2 billion[318] from the sale of oil and gas reserves, and tax revenues of around US$800 million. These achievements made Al-Qaeda look almost insignificant, with its 1,000-plus fighters and lack of a controlled territory. While the eyes of the world were on Al-Qaeda and the Syrian Civil War, ISIS had worked in the shadows to gather power until they were ready to establish their own Islamic state. In the process, they were able to supersede Al-Qaeda as the global leaders of Jihadi-Salafism.[319]

ISIS started out in the mid 2000s as the Iraqi branch of Al-Qaeda headed by Abū Musʿab al-Zarqawi but would eventually split due to ideological differences. The unity of Al-Qaeda in Iraq (AQI) with what were the beginnings of ISIS occurred in October 2006, when AQI allied with Iraqi insurgents and formed Islamic State in Iraq (ISI), although the group continued to be known as AQI. As a precursor of later trouble, ISI was formed without consultation with Al-Qaeda Central (AQC), including its top two leaders, Bin Laden and al-Zawahiri. Initially, Abu ʻUmar al-Baghdadi (d. 2010), who became leader of ISI after al-Zarqawi's death, pledged allegiance to Bin Laden, but continued to act independently of AQC. The top leaders of AQC soon called ISI 'blessed,' and in 2008 al-Zawahiri endorsed the movement as a legitimate Islamic emirate.[320]

After al-Zarqawi's death in 2006, the movement continued to operate in relative secrecy with varying degrees of success, until it slowly began to take over regions of Iraq. In 2011, a relatively unknown Abu Bakr al-Baghdadi (d. 2019) claimed leadership of ISI, after succeeding Abu ʻUmar al-Baghdadi in May 2010. Abu Bakr – whose real name was Ibrahim ibn Awwad Ibrahim ʻAli al-Badri al-Samarrai, also called Abu Awwad or Abu Dua – was born in 1971 in Samarra, Iraq, and grew up in a lower middle-class area. He was known for his pious religious observance and calm character. He had allegedly obtained a PhD in Islamic jurisprudence from a university that was renamed the Islamic University of Baghdad. Upon the American-invasion, Abu Bakr founded a military group to defend the country and was captured by the American forces in February 2004. He was imprisoned in Camp Bucca, with varying reports about the length of time he served there. Regardless of his duration of incarceration, it is reported that he came out intent on brutal revenge, and soon joined al-Zarqawi in 2006.

Abu Bakr al-Baghdadi would receive a scathing appraisal from his former teacher of theology Abu Abdullah Mohamed al-Mansour al-Issawi, the leader of *Jaysh al-Mujahidin* (Army of the Mujahidin). While al-Issawi accepted that al-Baghdadi's captivity in Camp Bucca had transformed him into a violent leader, he was also brutally frank in his assessment of al-Baghdadi's qualities, saying, 'I know him quite well. He has limited intelligence with no leadership skills.'[321] Issawi may have characterized al-Baghdadi as a 'mediocrity' but what he lacked in skill and intelligence he made up for in loyalty, which earned him the trust of the hierarchy of ISI. Others have spoken of his charisma, describing how he could persuade people of his perspective. It is claimed that al-Baghdadi was more ruthless and brutal than his predecessors al-Zarqawi and Abu ʻUmar al-Baghdadi, with al-Issawi describing him as 'a super slaughterer.' He was quick to excommunicate Sunnis in rival jihadi groups, and in this regard Fawaz A. Gerges refers to him as a 'super takfiri' who considered fighting Sunni rivals a more pressing duty than fighting the Americans.[322]

The notion of being radicalized in US-run prisons has been widely explored, as a large proportion of jihadi commanders in Iraq had been imprisoned between 2004 and 2011. Camp Bucca has even been referred to as an 'Al-Qaeda school,' with 24,000 prisoners, including many ex-Baathist officers. An emphasis has been placed on the extreme torture they suffered at the hands of the Americans – with the awful happenings at Abu Ghraib prison, in 2003, being the starkest example[323] – and the resulting psychological trauma. Such considerations may be helpful in explaining radical transformations of character. Many detainees went into these prisons without being members of AQI, or adherents of Jihadi-Salafism, but joined these forces upon their release. Along with similar detention centers, Camp Bucca has been described as 'an incubator of Islamist radicalization and a recruitment center for Jihadists.'[324]

Under Abu Bakr al-Baghdadi, ISI would truly become ISIS, after the group took over several regions of Iraq, and eventually a small portion of Syria. On 4 July 2014 al-Baghdadi declared his land to be an Islamic state and himself the Caliph of the Muslim world. He ordered all Muslims to migrate to his state to defend it and declared that whoever opposed it were apostates who needed to be fought.[325] Ultimately, his achievement was, in the words of Fawaz A. Gerges, 'to transform a fragile organization on the brink of collapse into a mini-professional army, an army capable of waging urban and guerrilla warfare as well as conventional warfare. In this sense, Baghdadi surpassed his two mentors, Osama bin Laden and Abu Mus'ab al-Zarqawi, in strategic cunning, organizational skills, and mobilizational outreach.'[326] While he cannot be considered a pioneering Jihadi-Salafi theorist – like Bin Laden, al-Zawahiri, al-Maqdisi or al-Zarqawi – Abu Bakr al-Baghdadi's military feats set him above these ideologues in terms of practical achievement.

ISIS continued with al-Zarqawi's assault on Shīʿis as a near enemy, in a bloody sectarian battle. AQC and AQI under al-Zarqawi and then Abu 'Umar al-Baghdadi had earlier clashed over the treatment of Shiʿa Muslims, whom the AQI had anathematized as a whole, along with anyone working with the Iraqi authorities. The consequence of AQI's conclusion that the Shiʿa are all disbelievers was that AQI wanted to declare a religious war against them. AQC, however, was against this theological war and condemned it.[327]

During 2013–14 Abu Bakr al-Baghdadi split from al-Zawahiri, when the latter admitted that they had tried, in vain, to convince ISI not to declare themselves an Islamic state. This was after documents surfaced in 2010 in which Bin Laden was shown to hold similar reservations about publicly declaring an Islamic state, on the basis that the United States would destroy such a polity, as they had done Taliban rule after 9/11.[328] AQC would come to support an affiliate in the region called *Jabhat al-Nusrah* (Front for the Conquest of the Levant), which was established in Syria in 2012. IS and *Jabhat* had been allies against the Syrian regime in 2013 but, in time, *Jabhat* was unable to contend with the power and ascension of ISIS which became the dominant force in the area. *Jabhat*'s later animosity towards ISIS was illustrated in the words of Abu Muhammad al-Maqdisi, who supported *Jabhat*, when he said of ISIS that 'they have just discovered Islam, and were until recently Baathists slaughtering Muslims.'[329] It is understood that *Jabhat* and al-Maqdisi were behind the spreading of the notion that al-Baghdadi was just a Baathist front, as a means of discrediting him before the public, as well as an explanation of the group's cruelty. However, apart from the skepticism that arises from such a conspiracy being aired, the evidence is more indicative of Baathists being gradually and increasingly convinced of Jihadi-Salafism.[330]

Muslims across the globe were morally outraged by ISIS's version of an Islamic state and the cruel policies of this polity. Even Al-Qaeda condemned them as extremists and distanced themselves, in 2015 calling on Muslims everywhere to rise up and destroy ISIS, labeling them a deviant sect. Al-Qaeda leader al-Zawahiri is quoted to have said, 'ISIS was struck with madness in *takfīr* and exceeded the limits of extremism.'[331]

ISIS, like other jihadi groups before them, used the internet for their recruitment. However, they were far more organized in their online propaganda than any previous version of jihadism. From forums to videos to magazines, ISIS produced a mass of jihadi propaganda calling for self-radicalization and terrorism.[332] Many confused young Muslims from around the world were convinced by the arguments put forth in ISIS forums and websites. Their arguments utilized the Qur'an and hadith and had a strong Salafi foundation; thousands of youth including hundreds from America and Europe, were convinced by such explanations, and left their homes, jobs and families to migrate and join ISIS.

ISIS seemed to fulfill every negative stereotype about religious zealots: excommunicating anyone and everyone who disagreed with them; mass-murdering their opponents in the most brutal fashion;[333] reviving slavery and raping captured 'slave-women.'[334] In 2016, ISIS went on the offensive against their critics by declaring all Muslim clerics who opposed them apostates who should be killed. Their magazine, *al-Dabiq*, issued a kill list asking members to assassinate anyone on the list; each name was accompanied by a color photograph. The kill list included mainly Arab scholars, along with a handful of Western clerics who ranged from Sufi clerics such as Hamza Yusuf to Salafi scholars such as Dr Bilal Philips. The author of this work has also been placed on their kill list twice, once for delivering a talk in which their theological justifications were deconstructed, and once for delivering a sermon in which their targeting of the Charlie Hebdo offices in Paris was strongly condemned.[335]

In an effort to justify their methodology, ISIS attempted to appropriate quotes and even books from prominent JS authors, such as early work by the then reformed Dr Faḍl and al-Maqdisi, who condemned them for their attempt to utilize their respective works for unintended violent purposes. In addition to the Jihadi-Salafis outlined above who opposed ISIS's stances, with its lack of scholars and intellectuals, there were clear denouncements and global outrage from others, across the spectrum of Islamic groups.

Unsurprisingly, ISIS did not last long. Globally isolated, and without any allies even among other Jihadis, they were easily defeated and lost most of their territory within a few short years. The ISIS phenomenon ended quickly, with Muslim clerics around the globe pointing out that their quick and humiliating defeat was God's punishment for their evil actions in the name of Islam.

In some ways, ISIS resembled the Siege of Mecca by Juhaymān and his forces, as both events had eschatological roots. Just as Juhaymān tried to bring about the Mahdī event that would occur at the end of times, ISIS tried to cause 'the great war' that would occur at the end of time.[336] The first defense minister of ISI after al-Zarqawi's death, an Egyptian called Abu Hamza al-Muhajjer (or Abu Ayyub al-Masri) (d. 2010), declared that they had created a 'podium' for the Mahdī and called his ranks 'the Mahdī's knights.'[337] This apocalyptic attitude can be seen in their seizing of Dabiq in August 2014 and making it their capital, as well as naming their publication after the town in Syria near the Turkish border, to try to fulfill the prophecy stated in the hadith, 'The Last Hour will not come until the Romans land in Dabiq…'[338] History shows, however, that apocalyptic movements, while generating the most zeal and fanaticism, are also the fastest to disappear.

Abu Bakr al-Baghdadi died on 26 October 2019, as a US mission moved in on him in the Idlib province in Syria, and ISIS was shortly destroyed. Nonetheless, one should be cautious in celebrating the removal of the serious JS threat. As many have argued, the grievances and socio-political circumstances which drive people – mainly youngsters – to support such causes, still exist in the Muslim world today: communal strife and conflict zones, non-transparent nation states in need of rebuilding, and the ongoing injustices upon the Palestinians by Israel (which has intensified almost beyond imagination after Israel sought revenge for the Hamas-led attack on 7 October 2023, with Israel coming to be accused by South Africa, in the International Court of Justice, of genocide, in addition to previous charges of apartheid).[339] Indeed, the Palestinian cause is a constant rallying call used by Jihadi-Salafis – most prominently by Al-Qaeda and ISIS – and is expressed as the final destination of their efforts.[340] These concerns are unfortunately not likely to be resolved in the near future. Moreover, ISIS ideology and adherents have persisted until the present time in the Middle East; and are still a group with 'sprawling operations, which stretch across many theaters worldwide. Increasingly resourceful and agile, the Islamic State has morphed from a top-down, centralized caliphate into a decentralized, largely rural, but nonetheless resilient insurgency.'[341]

### *5.5.2 Boko Haram in West Africa*

Boko Haram is the Hausa name for the West African group called *Ahl al-Sunna li-l-Daʿwah wa-l-Jihad* (Sunnis for Proselytization and Jihad). The significance of Boko Haram as a leading Jihadi-Salafi movement is highlighted by the fact that it has been responsible for tens of thousands of deaths, in Nigeria primarily, as well as in Niger, Chad, and Cameroon, which border Nigeria.[342] The movement emerged in the early 2000s, in the city of Maiduguri, in Nigeria. The name relates to the group's hostility to Western-style education (*boko* in Hausa) as religiously forbidden (*haram* in Arabic), which gained it numerous followers in the early days, as many shared similar concerns. However, this developed into a general condemnation of a system which Western-style education was immersed within, such as democracy, constitutionalism, and 'man-made laws.'

Alexander Thurston has helpfully divided the history of Boko Haram into five phases. The first relates to the group's prehistory, from the 1970s until the 1990s, when the founding figures were educated and developed their ideological positions. Most notable among such figures is the founder of Boko Haram, Muhammad Yusuf (d. 2009). The second phase of the movement relates to the period from around 2001 until 2009, when the group was involved in preaching. While a section of Boko Haram had attacked local authorities in 2003–4, in 2009 the group launched an offensive campaign in several Nigerian states. This conflict led to the killing of the group's founder, Muhammad Yusuf by the police, as they successfully put down the rebellion. The third phase occurred between 2010 until 2013, where the group pursued terrorist activities led by Yusuf's companion Abubakar Shekau (d. 2021), which included bombings and assassinations, but was signified by a diminishing emphasis on Salafism and more focus on the theology of aggressive jihad. The fourth phase was between 2013 and 2015 when Boko Haram took control of an area in northeastern Nigeria where they implemented what they understood to be Islamic penal codes, and engaged in brute force, giving people the choice between following them or facing a violent onslaught. This fourth phase also witnessed their most infamous episode when they kidnapped 276 schoolgirls in April 2014, in the town of Chibok. The fifth phase begins with the loss of their territory to the forces of the Nigerian regime and her neighboring partners which led to Boko Haram giving allegiance to ISIS in March 2015. Upon entering into this agreement, Boko Haram's official name became Islamic State of the West Africa Province (*Wilayat Gharb Ifriqiyya*), as a province of ISIS's caliphate.[343] The threat of terrorist acts from Boko Haram, or ISIS sympathizers, was a continuing problem in the area, even in 2022.[344] Notwithstanding its growing tendency not to emphasize its Salafi character, and the difficulty in identifying the rank-and-file as committed Salafis,[345] its focus on jihadi methodology still makes it possible to characterize Boko Haram as a Jihadi-Salafi movement.

The intellectual roots of Boko Haram's founder, Muhammad Yusuf, were in the Nigerian Salafi movement which emerged after Nigerian graduates of the Islamic University of Medina returned to their homeland in the 1990s. Yusuf most likely joined their ranks in the late 1990s, although the details of his development are somewhat obscure. These graduates had a greater appreciation of Salafi doctrine and a more pronounced Salafi perspective than their forefathers in the nascent Nigerian Salafi movement. Hence, they established their own movement of preachers, separate to the first Nigerian Salafi movement associated with the *Izala* organization, which had been established in 1978 by followers of the pioneering Nigerian-Salafi Abubakar Gumi (d. 1992). (See Chapter 6 for more details on them and their Salafism.)[346]

The Jihadi-Salafi philosophy of Boko Haram was clearly articulated, without any ambiguity, in the following words of the founder, Muhammad Yusuf:

> Our religion is Islam, our creed is the creed of the *al-salaf al-sāliḥ Ahlul Sunna Wal Jama'ah*, and our *manhaj* [methodology] is *jihād*. We believe that the *Sharīʿah* is the only truth. The constitution is a lie; it is *Kufr* [disbelief]. Democracy is a lie; it is *Kufr*. Working with the government that does not rule by the *Sharīʿah* is a lie; it is *Kufr*. Working with the security agencies is a lie; it is *Kufr*. For those who are ignorant, let them be aware that it is important for a Muslim to make *hijrah* [migration] from the institutions established by the *ṭawāghīt* [any secular entity derived from the man-made constitution].[347]

Yusuf made similar declarations in his 2009 manifesto entitled *Hādhihi ʿAqīdatunā wa-Manhaj Daʿwatinā* (*This Is Our Creed and the Method of Our Preaching*), together with the expected denouncements of the Shīʿis and Sufis, and adherence to *al-wala' wa'l-bara'*. Such pronouncements of fidelity to Salafism were composed in the midst of puritan Salafi attacks upon Yusuf and his group, when Boko Haram was derided for being unorthodox and thus not Salafi.[348]

Boko Haram and ISIS emphasized how the battle being fought by Boko Haram was one between true Muslims, 'Crusader' Christians, and apostates. Indeed, ISIS declared the Jihadi-Salafi nature of Boko Haram's allegiance and task: 'It was the rejection of nationalism that drove the *mujahidin* in Nigeria to give *bay'ah* (fealty) to the Islamic State, and wage war against the Nigerian *murtaddin* (apostates) fighting for the Nigerian *ṭaghūt* (idolatrous tyrant).'[349]

This religious aspect of Boko Haram's approach continued under Shekau in distinctly jihadi terms and with a large degree of defensiveness:

> We are the *Jama'atu Ahlus-Sunna Lidda'Awati Wal Jihad* that has been maliciously branded Boko Haram. Everybody knows about the gruesome murders of Muslims in different parts of Nigeria. JOS is a testimony to the gruesome killings of our Muslim brethren and the abductions of our women and children whose whereabouts are still unknown. My message to my Muslim brethren is that they should know that this war is a war between Muslims and infidels. This is a religious war.[350]

Even in the midst of impassioned calls for widespread killing, Shekau was alert enough to warn his followers of certain excesses, even if the tone detracted from heeding the cautionary note:

> Today our religion is nothing but killings, killings and killings! Kill and slaughter, but don't eat them. Abstain from killing their elderly, women, the insane, and anyone who repents. Anybody who rebels against Allah, kill him. By Allah, I will kill you. Killing is my job.[351]

Furthermore, Shekau's caution in relation to non-combatants is belied by his own endorsement of the doctrine of Al-Qaeda, which has been explained earlier in terms of its recklessness with regards to non-combatants.

Indeed, Shekau wrote to Al-Qaeda in the following terms in around 2010:

> We have listened to your tapes and heard of your affairs – the tapes of the scholars of al-Qa'ida and its shaykhs, such as Osama bin Laden, may God protect him, and Dr Ayman al-Zawahiri, and Abu Mus'ab al- Zarqawi, may God have mercy on him, and others among its scholars, such as Abu Yahya al-Libi and Abu Qatada al-Filastini, may God protect them and preserve them… Now nothing remains for us except to know [Al-Qaeda's] system and its component organizations, for he who does not know the path he's on until after the journey begins will fail…[352]

While Shekau displays ignorance of Al-Qaeda's modus operandi, he would not have been ignorant of 9/11, nor the sort of slaughter that al-Zarqawi was responsible for. Hence it is unsurprising that Boko Haram later joined

ISIS, presumably after being better informed of the details of their doctrine, which was a more extreme derivation from Al-Qaeda. This may merely have been a desperate attempt at survival, as it came at a time when Boko Haram were experiencing heavy losses in their fight. In fact, Boko Haram's committing of atrocities against civilians, both Muslim and non-Muslim, removes any semblance of a 'just war theory' on their part.[353]

The local nature of Boko Haram was seen in their claim to be carrying on the legacy of 'Uthman dan Fodio (d. 1817), who established the Sokoto Caliphate, which required an armed struggle to reinforce it.[354] This reforming scholar engaged in jihad and opposed religious innovations (*bid'a*) as Jihadi-Salafis would accept, but Dan Fodio was not a Salafi theologian, in fact he was the Sufi master of a Sufi order (*tariqa*) usually abhorred by Salafis. Hence Boko Haram's type of Jihadi-Salafism has a localized personality that cannot be attributed to the global Jihadi-Salafis of the Middle East. This is the case even if it is highly revisionist and reductionist, as in the attempt to appropriate and claim the legacy of Dan Fodio, as though the latter's call to jihad can be coherently extracted from his wider intellectual framework.

Boko Haram's emergence can therefore be seen in very local terms, defined by the interaction of politics (between Muslims and Christians) and religion (including intra-Muslim conflicts) in Nigeria. Their emergence and trajectory cannot be explained as being simply the result of outside forces, such as Al-Qaeda, nor is it merely the consequence of economic factors, like the wealth disparity between the north and south of Nigeria, or 'poor governance.' Ultimately, it is misplaced logic to attribute only one cause for the emergence of a jihadi organization.[355]

### *5.5.3 Al-Shabaab in East Africa*

Al-Shabaab is a pioneering Jihadi-Salafi organization which controlled large areas of central and southern Somalia, in particular in 2008 and 2009, with a strict regime of implementing their reading of Islamic law. It was quickly able to become a key ally of Al-Qaeda in the East African region. The movement's ability to attract a large number of national and international recruits, its establishment of political power and ability to create a serious threat to the central government of Somalia preceded the rise of ISIS, and perhaps, in some ways, paved a way for how ISIS would construct their own functioning state.[356]

The inception of Al-Shabaab is a somewhat contentious issue, however. It has roots in some of the Islamist currents that existed in Somalia from the 1970s, which had an antithetical perspective to the dominant Sufi orders. This trend came to the fore in the mid-1990s when the country descended into civil war, and *al-Ittihad al-Islami* (Islamic Union) managed to create a small polity in Luuq. *Al-Ittihad* had been successful in obtaining support from the Somalian diaspora, especially in Kenya. Nonetheless, the movement would soon face significant losses in the south, together with becoming beset by internal divisions along clan-lines, before the Ethiopian military ended their rule in 1996. It has also been reported – although the details remain sketchy – that some members of *al-Ittihad*, but not the group as a whole, developed links with Al-Qaeda during this time.

After *al-Ittihad*'s experiment with governance, a system of Islamic courts was established around Somalia in an initiative that brought together Sufi groups with Islamist figures, some who had been associated with *al-Ittihad* during the 1990s and into the early 2000s. Eventually, a trend emerged named the Islamic Courts Union (ICU), formed around 2005 and 2006, which brought together Islamic scholars, including members of the Islamic courts and various Islamists, and clan leaders, and won the support – perhaps due to its diversity and previous links – of important members of the Somalian diaspora, including wealthy factions. The ICU came to rival the Transitional Federal Government (TFG), which was notorious for corruption. Consequently, in December 2006, the Ethiopian government invaded Somalia with a force of 10,000 soldiers, supported by US intelligence, and soundly defeated the ICU, dispersing the remaining members and leaders, and strengthening the TFG. The Ethiopian invasion and its dismantling of the ICU left a vacuum from which Al-Shabaab emerged in 2007. After expanding in size, it became the most prominent anti-Ethiopian military force by 2008.

Although Al-Shabaab was originally part of the ICU's military wing, it started to act with increasing independence. After the Ethiopia withdrawal in 2009, Al-Shabaab occupied a number of territories including much of Mogadishu, and constructed the bureaucracy needed to ensure their governance. This was at a time when the Islamic State in Iraq was a mere 'paper state.' Their success was buttressed by their skillful use of Somali nationalism driven by opposition to Ethiopian occupation of the country, as well as benefitting from the Somalian diaspora in Africa, the Middle East, Europe, Australia, and North America.

Their *takfiri* tendencies, an illustration of their Jihadi-Salafi loyalty, were exhibited in 2009 when they declared the new President of the TFG, Sheikh Sharif, to be an apostate for joining the internationally-backed government after being part of the opposition. Their capture of new territories continued throughout 2009 and 2010, and led to a shift in their self-portrayal, from being a military force defending the country to being an Islamic state. In 2008 they declared Islamic rule, including the implementation of Islamic penal punishments, after capturing important economic centers like Baidoa and Kismaayo. Notwithstanding their wide popularity, they began to lose territories during 2011 and 2012 as the Kenyan army intervened in southern

Somalia, and the Ethiopian army converged on western Somalia in October and November 2011. Consequently, Al-Shabaab were forced out of all major urban and economic centers by the autumn of 2012. Then, in October 2014, they were forced out of their last major coastal town of Baraawe.

As they were forced to retreat, they resorted to hit-and-run tactics, including assassinations and the use of car bombings, sometimes in public places like restaurants and hotels. They were also able to carry out a substantial attack on a Kenyan military base in Somalia in January 2016, killing 141 Kenyan soldiers and taking many more captive, after a suicide bomber provided the opening blow.

In retaliation for wider African involvement in their struggle, Al-Shabaab expanded their attacks into other countries deemed to have unjustly meddled in their country, especially in Kenya. The defensive narrative developed by Al-Shabaab, Al-Qaeda, and ISIS of retributive punishment (*qiṣāṣ*) – derived from the famous principle of Islamic law – was repeatedly invoked in their videos. These pointed to the alleged historical genocide of thousands of Somalis by the Kenyan government since the 1980s, and their historical discrimination of Muslims up to the present time. They also released a laudatory video on the attack on off-duty soldier Lee Rigby in Woolwich, London, on 22 May 2013, by Michael Adebolajo and Michael Adebowale.

In identifying Al-Shabaab as Jihadi-Salafi, it is of significance that some of Al-Shabaab's founding figures, such as Hassan Dahir Aweys (who came to leave Al-Shabaab in 2013), Aden Hashi Farah Ayro (d. 2008), Ahmed Godane (d. 2014), and Mukhtar Robow, had been members of earlier Islamist currents such as *al-Ittihad* and the ICU. Furthermore, a number of them had also trained in Afghanistan with Al-Qaeda, such as Ayro, Mukhtar Robow, and Ibrahim al-Afghānī (Ibrahim Hajji Jama Mee'aad) (d. 2013). Indeed, Ayro is reported to have met Osama bin Laden, and would provide Al-Shabaab with a global perspective for its JS methodology.

The movement's attempts to link themselves to the global jihadi movement, including Al-Qaeda, was demonstrated from 2007 and 2008 when Al-Shabaab started to produce video messages and films as part of a sophisticated media recruitment drive, which featured clips of 'Abdullah 'Azzam, Osama bin Laden, Ayman al-Zawahiri, and 'the blind shaykh' 'Umar 'Abd al-Rahman. This media campaign included a September 2009 video message from Al-Shabaab's then-leader, Ahmed Godane, declaring his loyalty to Al-Qaeda's Osama bin Laden. Nonetheless, Bin Laden is reported to have had concerns about Al-Shabaab, such as his opposition to declaring an Islamic state, his concerns about their harsh implementation of Islamic law, and their failure to improve the economy. Hence, he was reluctant to publicly declare an alliance. This was in contrast to the glowing praise that Al-Qaeda supporter Anwar al-Awlaki (discussed in section 5.6.1) gave Al-Shabaab in 2010, when he spoke of them as an ideal jihadi organization that other Jihadis should learn from. Nonetheless, Al-Qaeda Central would undertake a formal alliance with Al-Shabaab in Spring 2012.[357]

A clear indication of Al-Shabaab's JS outlook is provided by the educational program it conducted for its military recruits in 2010. The religious studies aspect of the course included an intense study of a variety of religious texts covering a wide range of subjects, including Qur'an, hadith, Islamic law and theology, and their related theoretical principles, as well as the Arabic language and Islamic ethics (*akhlāq*) and manners (*ādāb*). In terms of Salafi principles, the students were to study works by Ibn Taymiyya, Muhammad Ibn ʿAbd al-Wahhāb (who was referenced in Al-Shabaab media productions from 2008), and Ibn 'Uthaymin. The JS aspects were covered by readings from al-Zawahiri and al-Maqdisi. Furthermore, their Salafi activism was demonstrated in their robust opposition to the Sufism popular in Somalia, including the destruction of graves and shrines, which also had a political dimension as it helped undermine the competing militias associated with certain powerful clans who espoused a loyalty with Sufism.[358]

In 2011, African Union forces regained control of Mogadishu by forcing Al-Shabaab out of the Somalian capital, although Al-Shabaab would continue to control significant areas of the Somalian countryside, up to the present time. When Al-Shabaab lost a significant proportion of their territories, they underwent sweeping changes in their leadership in 2014, and planned devastating attacks in Kenya as revenge for the Kenyan forces intervention in Somalia, as well as attacking African Union peacekeepers.[359]

In the same way that Al-Qaeda's credentials as Jihadi-Salafis were tested by the rise of ISIS between 2012 and 2015, so the reputation of Al-Shabaab was put under scrutiny in the scales of Jihadi-Salafism. This was particularly the case when ISIS declared, in 2014, that they were *the* Islamic state, and all Muslims were obliged to pledge allegiance to them. Understandably, the call of ISIS divided the ranks of Al-Shabaab, including its leadership, and led to intense power struggles within the movement between 2012 and 2013. Godane was on one side, against joining ISIS,[360] while other prominent leaders supported the notion of aligning with ISIS, including founding figures like Aweys, Robow, and Ibrahim al-Afghānī. Godane would win the power struggle, but not before al-Afghānī and others were killed, and Robow and Aweys left the movement in 2013. (Robow would later surrender to the Somali government in 2017.)[361]

In May 2015 ISIS began a media campaign in which they called upon Al-Shabaab to pledge its allegiance to ISIS and Abu Bakr al-Baghdadi. This campaign met with some very limited success, most notably with the defection from Al-Shabaab to ISIS of Shaykh 'Abd al-Qadir Mu'min and his few followers in northern Somalia. Consequently, Al-Shabaab undertook measures to crack down on ISIS supporters in the areas controlled by them in Somalia but made very few official public pronouncements on the matter, which is most likely to have been a tactic dictated by a desire not to inflame the ongoing internal battles over the issue. Notwithstanding this reticence, the prevailing leadership publicly reaffirmed its loyalty to Ayman al-Zawahiri and Al-Qaeda in 2014 and 2015, which was an indirect rejection of ISIS's claim to being an authentic Caliphate that Muslims worldwide had to adhere to.

As with ISIS and Boko Haram, Al-Shabaab has remained a threat in East Africa up to the present time, with continuing attacks carried out by suspected members of the group, including an intensification of battles with government forces and car bombings at the Education Ministry in the capital, Mogadishu. Such is the continuing threat posed by Al-Shabaab, the new President of Somalia Hassan Sheikh Mohamud, upon taking office in May 2022, declared an 'all-out war' against the movement. By way of illustrating the importance placed on capturing and neutralizing them, the US Department of State declared in November 2022 that it would increase the reward for information on Al-Shabaab leaders to US$10 million, as well as giving US$10 million for information that led to undermining their finances.[362] Al-Shabaab's lack of heavy military equipment makes it unlikely to replicate its earlier success, but they are likely to remain a terror threat, despite their inability to effect major political change.

## *5.6 Leading Jihadi-Salafi Preachers in the English-Speaking West*

With the rise of Jihadi-Salafism in the East, and the direct involvement of Western lands in the invasion of Muslim countries post-9/11, it was inevitable that some Western nationals would begin to champion the cause of Jihadi-Salafism. Although such people remain a small minority, with barely any mainstream following, they did act as conduits to bring to an English-speaking world the thought and rhetoric of Jihadi-Salafism and garnered a disproportionate public presence due to the media's thirst for the sensational. As Western Muslims decided to join some of these movements overseas, and terrorist attacks took place on Western soil, some stated that they were inspired by English-speaking preachers.

In this section, we will highlight three of the most prominent Jihadi-Salafi preachers in the West: Anwar al-Awlaki, Abu Hamza al-Misri, and Abdullah al-Faisal al-Jamaiki.[363]

### *5.6.1 Anwar al-Awlaki (d. 2011)*

Anwar al-Awlaki is perhaps the most infamous Western Jihadi-Salafi preacher. His legacy is so significant that he 'might well be considered the Pied Piper of Western jihad.'[364] Due to the overwhelming influence his lectures have had on past and present Jihadis, it is worth elaborating on his life in some detail, as it is indicative of the kind of incongruousness – both intellectual and behavioral – found in a number of Western Jihadi-Salafis. Al-Awlaki and other similar examples show us that middle-class social mobility is not a defense against becoming radicalized, undermining the popular narrative that religious extremism is the result of socio-economic deprivation.[365]

Anwar al-Awlaki was born in 1971 in New Mexico, United States, to parents of Yemeni origin. In 1993, he visited Afghanistan, after the conclusion of the Afghan–Soviet war, and returned to university, where he began to wear an Afghan hat and quote Abdullah Azzam. He started to undertake preaching duties at a local Islamic center in 1994, while studying for a degree in Civil Engineering at Colorado State University (CSU). During his time there he was also active in the university Muslim Students Association (MSA), serving for a time as its president. Upon moving to Denver in 1995, and taking on a part-time imam post, he encouraged a student from Saudi to travel to fight the Russians in Chechnya. Reports about his time in Denver reveal his passion, perhaps somewhat subtly conveyed, for proselytizing about engaging in jihad, which earned the ire of certain elder factions of the community.[366]

His rise to fame occurred in the late 1990s and early 2000s, due to a series of audio lectures on the lives of the Prophets and early Muslims, which were distributed widely through the funding of a wealthy philanthropist, Homaidan al-Turki, who financed Basheer Publications in Colorado. These lectures gained him international fame and became a primary source of historical knowledge for an entire generation of English-speaking Muslims; they were sold all over the globe, from South Africa to Saudi Arabia.[367] Part of the success of these lectures was the impressive marketing that al-Turki systematized at Basheer Publications. The CDs were produced in a professional and attractive manner in contrast to the simple cassette tapes that were generally the norm at the time. This, together with the insertion of a melodic Qur'anic reciter at points where al-Awlaki recited from the Qur'an, added to their appeal. There had never been an English preacher who spoke in such an endearing manner, basing his lectures on Arabic sources and speaking fluently in English, with just enough Arabic words to give it the aura of authenticity: Al-Awlaki took the Western world by storm. It was as if *everyone* was listening to him, and since the topics were neutral and with mass appeal (stories of the prophets and pioneers of Islam), people of all backgrounds found themselves enthralled with his preaching.

Notwithstanding his seemingly private preaching about jihad in Denver, the public persona conveyed in his early life as an imam is in stark contrast with that of his later life. Post 9/11, he rose to further fame in the United States as a role-model moderate imam. He called people to tolerance and claimed that Islam was a peaceful religion. During this period, he preached a moderate, quietist brand of Salafism, and there seemed to be no hint of radicalization in his lifestyle or speeches.[368] The lectures that al-Awlaki delivered during this period are still popular today, even among mainstream Muslims, who tend to ignore his later radical phase.[369] Then suddenly, he left the United States and moved to the UK, leaving his status as a popular imam behind.[370]

It seems that al-Awlaki may have left because he learned that the FBI had built a case against him. The FBI started investigating al-Awlaki due to a seemingly random connection between him and some of the 9/11 hijackers. Two of them – Nawaf al-Hazmi and Khaldi al-Mihdhar – had previously contacted al-Awlaki and consulted him when he was an imam. This could have been a harmless consultation between an imam and his congregants, or it could have been part of a terrorist plot. The FBI needed to investigate further, as there were several other terrorists and suspected terrorists who had contacted al-Awlaki on a number of occasions. These events gave the FBI cause for concern, and they opened up an official investigation against him. What they discovered, however, was something else: a secret life that al-Awlaki was hiding from his followers.[371]

According to FBI records, al-Awlaki had a secret life frequenting prostitutes. The FBI followed him expecting to discover secret meetings with potential terrorists, but instead they discovered that he regularly sought the services of prostitutes, sometimes even during the day in the sacred month of Ramadan – a flagrant contravention of the religious laws demanding sexual abstinence from adult Muslims before sunset.[372] Looking into his criminal record, they discovered that in August 1996, and again in April 1997, al-Awlaki had been arrested in San Diego and charged with soliciting prostitutes. The first time he pleaded guilty to a lesser charge and was fined $400. The second time he pleaded guilty and was fined $240, ordered to perform twelve days of community service, and received three years' probation.[373] He had also been arrested in this regard in Washington D.C.[374]

The FBI was unsure what to do with this information. They discussed whether to blackmail him and make him an informant or to expose him and destroy his credibility. The official report states that neither option was chosen and al-Awlaki learned about the FBI file and fled the country before they could act on the intelligence.[375] But there is a contradictory report that indicates that he did work as an FBI informant for a short while. Ismail Royer, a former Jihadi-Salafi who spent over a decade in prison due to his involvement in what was called the Virginia Jihad Network (VJN), stated that al-Awlaki was responsible for his arrest, as well as the arrest of the mentor of the VJN, Ali al-Timimi, and several other Salafis in the United States. He said that al-Awlaki worked secretly as an informant for the FBI while visiting them, wearing a wire to gather evidence against them, which led to their imprisonment.[376]

Nonetheless, the veracity of this account about al-Awlaki being an FBI informant has been questioned on the basis of what al-Timimi's defense team stated, on 4 November 2004, during the course of his trial against the terrorist charges brought against him. It was argued that al-Awlaki attempted to entrap al-Timimi during the course of a visit in October 2002, when al-Awlaki asked about recruiting Americans for jihad against their own government forces, while al-Timimi did not respond in the affirmative to such questioning. The defense team also buttressed their argument by adding that al-Awlaki was accompanied to the meeting by Nabil Garbeih, a minor figure in the VJN who became a government informant and testified against al-Timimi. Yet, al-Timimi's first account to the FBI of the October 2002 meeting did not mention such questioning by al-Awlaki, and instead recounted that al-Awlaki simply spoke about his plans to relocate to Yemen on account of FBI harassment.[377]

Upon leaving the United States, al-Awlaki spent a few years in the UK where he built a following in the local Salafi community. The war on terror seemed to disillusion him, and his rhetoric became more angry. In 2003, he began to speak out against the victimization of Muslims in the United States, and the unjustified murder of civilians in the Middle East by US troops. In the UK, al-Awlaki found a more receptive audience to his newly found passionate anti-American message and began to preach it more openly. It was during this period that his message took on a clear JS tone. There are three possibilities for what caused this sudden shift, and various researchers have opted for any of these three. Some claim that he was always radical in his understanding of Salafism, and that he slowly revealed his jihadist thoughts as he gained more of a following. Many claim that he was radicalized post-9/11 due to his anger at the US war on terror and the invasions of Afghanistan and Iraq. And some would opine that his circumstances and potential entrapment by the FBI forced him to play his hand and advocate a message that would also serve to rebut any information the FBI might possibly leak. It is, of course, impossible to state with certainty which of these options is correct, but what can be stated is that by 2003, after more than a decade of moderate preaching, he was clearly preaching a vigorous jihadi message, but in a way that was still legal. As an example, he delivered a series of lectures narrating from a fourteenth-century treatise entitled *The Book of Jihad* by the Damascene scholar Ibn Nuhās (d. 814/1411). Before covering material that he knew would be contentious, he added the disclaimer that he was narrating the book for academic purposes only, and not to promote violence.

In 2004, al-Awlaki left the UK fearing that the government may no longer tolerate his increasingly hostile message. He returned to Yemen, whereupon he sought a variety of answers to questions on the topic of jihad. He was arrested by the Yemeni authorities and is reported to have been seriously manhandled in custody. Upon receiving answers from the Salafi scholars that he encountered there, he was left dissatisfied with what he saw as the passive approach of the quietist Salafis. Despite having a few discussions with the *Ṣaḥwa* icon Salman al-Oudah, he was not convinced of the activist-Salafi approach either. His brother, Ammar, has said that 2004 was the turning point when al-Awlaki completely embraced the Jihadi-Salafi ideology.[378] That year, from Yemen, al-Awlaki produced a series of lectures entitled 'Constants on the Path of Jihad,' which became the most influential jihadi lecture series in English. From that point on, al-Awlaki preached a new message: that killing any American citizen was permissible because they voted for their leader, and hence are responsible for his crimes and the crimes of their army. He directly encouraged Westerners to take up arms against their own governments, and to attack all Americans.[379]

On 7 July 2005 the London bombings occurred, and three of the four bombers that attacked the subway were found to have been attendees of his lecture series on *The Book of Jihad* and students of al-Awlaki.[380] Over the next few years, al-Awlaki became the most popular English jihadi preacher in the world. Before this time, Al-Qaeda had found propagation to English-speaking Muslims difficult due to the language barrier, so it was a great boon to them when al-Awlaki became an Al-Qaeda supporter. Whether they ever officially embraced him and gave him a formal position is debatable; it seems more likely that he independently declared an allegiance to them, and that that benefitted them in the Western world. This was because al-Awlaki was not only a native English speaker, he was also a household name. This gave Jihadis an entirely new channel to reach out to possible recruits in the West. He then expanded his media outreach by starting a blog, a YouTube channel, and an online magazine. He also began using the internet to reach out to Muslim youth in the West in order to encourage violence against America and her allies.

His new jihadi focus started to inspire some individuals to commit acts of terror which they had been led to believe was jihad. Such was the direct influence of al-Awlaki upon some of these individuals that they have been termed his 'disciples.' For example, the 2009 Fort Hood shooter Nidal Hasan, a US army psychiatrist, came to be influenced by al-Awlaki after he presided over the funeral after the traumatic passing of Hasan's mother in 2001. This fateful meeting eventually led the grieving and newly religious Hasan – who claimed to have experienced a religious awakening in 2003, after a very non-religious upbringing – to be influenced by al-Awlaki's lectures and blog posts. He consumed al-Awlaki's work with a passion after being mesmerized by the eloquence and apparent command of the religion shown.[381] Hasan re-established contact with al-Awlaki around the end of 2008 and sent a number of messages to him before his attack, with a good proportion of them being connected to political violence. Al-Awlaki rarely replied, but if he did it was in response to more mundane matters like an essay competition and looking for a wife. Hasan's killing of twelve American soldiers and one civilian was subsequently praised by al-Awlaki in his blog – just four days after the attack – where he stated, 'Nidal Hasan is a hero.'[382]

A second 'disciple' was the 'underwear bomber,' Umar Farouk Abdulmutallab, who attempted a terrorist attack on a plane in December 2009, after being inspired to join the jihadi mission by al-Awlaki's lectures. His response to feelings of emptiness and discontent ('I have no friend' and 'I feel depressed and lonely') in his teenage years was to try and fill the void with '*jihad* fantasies.'[383] He traveled to Yemen where he met al-Awlaki and was given his bomb and mission. Abdulmutallab subsequently failed to complete the mission and was sentenced to life in prison. He stated, 'I was greatly inspired to participate in jihad by the lectures of the great and rightly guided mujahideen who is alive, Sheikh Anwar al-Awlaki, may Allah preserve him and his family and give them victory.'[384]

A third example is Zachary Adam Chesser, who after converting to Islam as a young man in 2008, was convicted in 2010 of attempting to supply Al-Shabaab – a designated terrorist organization – with support, and making threats to kill the creators of the animation *South Park* for their depiction of the Prophet Muhammad.[385] Upon conversion, Chesser threw himself into the online jihadi world – especially al-Awlaki's blog – and became an activist for the jihadi cause. He credited al-Awlaki's public proclamations with introducing him to the importance of supporting Al-Shabaab. In addition, two May 2010 terrorist attackers were found to have been inspired by al-Awlaki: Times Square bomber, Faisal Shahzad, and Roshonara Choudhry, who stabbed former British Cabinet Minister Stephen Timms.

The rising number of terrorist cases inspired by al-Awlaki caused the government to take action. In April 2010, he was placed on the CIA kill list by President Barack Obama, leading to his murder by drone on 30 September 2011.[386] Two weeks later, another drone attack killed his sixteen-year-old son, Abdulrahman, who was a US citizen not charged with any crime.[387] The US Department of Justice released a memorandum declaring the killing as an act of war, although this act has been described by several civil liberties as an execution without due process.

The murder of al-Awlaki is a difficult chapter in US history. It was the first time that the American government had conducted a targeted drone strike to kill an American citizen without due process. As I stated in my op-ed published in the *New York Times* the day after his assassination,

> The accusations against him were very serious, but as a citizen, he deserved a fair trial and the chance to face his accusers in a court of law. Whether he deserved any punishment for his speech was a decision that a jury should have made, not the executive branch of our government. The killing of this American citizen is not only unconstitutional but hypocritical and counterproductive.[388]

By way of a double tragic fate, his murder simply gave new life to his message, just as the execution of Sayyid Qutb inspired violent Jihadis before him. Anwar al-Awlaki is now honored as a martyr and role model by Jihadi-Salafis, and the popularity of his lectures actually increased because of his death. A study of the 212 cases charged as jihadi offenses in the United States between 2009 and 2016 found that 66 were inspired or linked to al-Awlaki.[389] A 2017 study of the material on the computers of 44 suspects in ten Jihadi-terrorist cases in the UK between 2004 and 2015 concluded that 'Anwar al-Awlaki dominated the list of most popular authors, in both old and new cases.'[390] A further study of 161 ISIS-related cases of terrorism in the United States up to May 2018 showed that 37 (23%) American Jihadis cited al-Awlaki as an inspiration. Moreover, a study of the online activity of 104 people from the UK who went to join the fight with ISIS found that 24 (23%) spoke of al-Awlaki in positive terms.[391] Any attempts to refute his thought are immediately dismissed as rhetoric designed to appease Western superpowers, and any facts presented about his life that might potentially tarnish his image are viewed as baseless propaganda attempting to slander 'the lion' of Western scholars, as jihadis refer to him. In fact, not only did his murder open the door for the radicalization of more youth, but it also opened the door to violating the Constitution in order to assassinate American citizens without due process.

Al-Awlaki's life was one full of contradiction. He has been portrayed as a motivational speaker who helped thousands of Muslims practice mainstream Islam; an extremist jihadi preacher who called for violence; an adulterer who solicited prostitutes; and an FBI informant. These contradictory narratives explain why Muslims around the world still debate his status. Many countries still sell and promote his history lecture series, choosing to ignore his jihadi phase, while Jihadis elevate him to the status of a martyr and make him a symbol for their struggle. Others look down upon him as a hypocrite and opportunist who lived a double life.

Ultimately, Anwar al-Awlaki's story brought the realities of jihadism home to America. It made Americans realize that even their own preachers could be radicalized. It should be noted though that, just as in the case of al-Faisal (discussed in section 5.6.3), al-Awlaki was not a qualified Islamic scholar, in the sense that he had no formal training of Islam. He rose to fame for his simple eloquence and standard preaching and then, for reasons that are still unclear, turned around and used that fame to incite violence in the name of Islam.

### *5.6.2 Abu Hamza al-Misri*

Abu Hamza is a preacher who came to symbolize the notion of 'Londonistan' (i.e., a London full of radical Muslims) that emerged and was popularized, in certain circles, in the 1990s. He was a crucial figure in the London jihadi movement, and was associated for a period of time with Finsbury Park Mosque in London which became known as a jihadi headquarters where hundreds of Jihadis came to attend, network and operate from.[392] Although he is not considered to be a significant original JS ideologue, he regularly published writings on the subject – including in English – and was a key figure in the recruitment of people to the ranks.[393] He was also responsible for reviving the GIA's publication *al-Ansar* after al-Suri and Abu Qatada had stopped it. Abu Hamza ceased supporting the GIA in 1997 when the leadership came to excommunicate the entire society, which was a step too far for him.

Born Mostafa Kemal Mostafa in 1958 in Alexandria, Egypt, he came to England in 1979 to study engineering. He was not particularly religious, and married an English woman, becoming a British citizen in 1982. He divorced his wife around 1985 or 1986 and had worked as a bouncer in a nightclub.[394] However, he turned to religion in the mid-1980s and is said to have been transformed when he met Abdullah Azzam during the Hajj in 1987. Upon his return to the UK, he declared to a friend that Azzam was 'a great man who represented the future of Islam.' He later went to Afghanistan in the 1990s, and specialized in making bombs, but lost both hands and an eye in an incident with explosives, and returned to England.[395] Not surprisingly, the fact that he wore a pirate-like eyepatch and had metallic hooks in place of his hands only added to his media notoriety.

Back in England he studied with the JS ideologue Abu Qatada al-Filastini and became a preacher in his own right. In 1994, he formed the North-African based organization called Supporters of Shariah (SOS), which supported jihad in Algeria, Bosnia, Yemen, and Chechnya, by organizing rallies and sending people to fight. In 1995, he participated in the Bosnian war, which elevated his standing.

Around 1996 and 1997, he came to lead the Finsbury Park Mosque as imam. The mosque committee had originally wanted Abu Qatada for the post, but it is said that his financial demands for accepting the role were considered too high.[396] This was a monumental moment for Jihadi-Salafis in the UK, as the mosque became a focal point for national and international seekers of global jihad. During his time as head of the institution, the mosque hosted open sermons and lectures on jihad, opened a small bookstore which stocked numerous hard-to-find jihadi publications, and provided a place where seekers of jihad could socialize, network, arrange marriages and get approval and help in reaching troublespots for fighting activity.

Numerous people who were convicted of, or involved in, jihadi plots between 1999 and 2005 have been direct students and associates of Abu Hamza or were found to have frequented Finsbury Park Mosque during his infamous reign. These figures included members of SOS – two of whom were sons of Abu Hamza – for terrorist activities in Yemen between December 1998 and January 1999. Abu Hamza was reported to have come to believe that the establishment of Islamic rule in Yemen would be the starting point from which the other secular Arab regimes of the region would fall, perhaps as part of an apocalyptic vision based on the Prophetic saying about the Mahdī's arrival being heralded by a great fire in Aden.[397] In addition, there was the conviction of the three individuals sent by Abu Hamza to set up the training camp in the United States in 1999; and Siddique Khan and Shehzad Tanweer from the 7/7 terror cell, among others.[398]

During his tenure at Finsbury Park, Abu Hamza was known for being surrounded by a thuggish entourage – reported for using violence against those who opposed them – as well as being linked to an elaborate and extensive operation of financial deception including credit card fraud and false passports. These operations gained legitimacy in his eyes, because, in his words: 'It is theft, but it is theft from non-protected persons. It is like killing a non-protected person, there is nothing in it; it is not protected blood.' This was in addition to his support for state benefit fraud, and non-payment of debts like student loans. Yet he did state that those who had been granted sanctuary in Britain from religious persecution in their own lands were prohibited from engaging in such crime, as they were under a duty of gratitude.[399]

Abu Hamza was ousted from Finsbury Park Mosque in 2003, after a police raid. He was then arrested in 2004 for soliciting murder and supporting terrorism with his 1999 attempt to set up a training camp in the United States and was eventually extradited to the United States in 2012 to face charges. In Jan 2015, he was sentenced to life in prison without the possibility of parole. Although incarcerated since then, he has remained an inspiration for global Jihadis in Europe.[400]

### *5.6.3 Abdullah al-Faisal*

Born Trevor William Forrest in Jamaica in 1963, Abdullah converted to Islam when he was sixteen years old. In the early 1980s, he traveled to Riyadh to study at Ibn Saʿud University, although there is some dispute as to whether he actually graduated. Under his newly acquired name of Abdullah al-Faisal, he established himself as a religious scholar in Brixton, London, in 1992.[401]

Despite the mosque identifying itself as Salafi, his rhetoric was too radical for them, and he was soon expelled in 1993.[402] Yet despite the fact that he lacked any official credentials, he found a small following in London, as well as around the UK, through a series of lectures self-distributed in cassette form in which he expounded on Salafism, in extreme and often jihadi terms. He is one of the first Western preachers to openly propagate Jihadi-Salafism, as he began preaching almost a decade before al-Awlaki. Within a short period of time his preaching influenced a number of terrorists, including, most notably, Zacarias Moussaoui, who was convicted in March 2006 in connection with actions related to the 9/11 terror attacks;[403] Richard Reid ('the shoe bomber' in December 2001);[404] Germaine Lindsey and Siddique Khan of the 7/7 cell in England; and Umar Farouk Abdulmutallab.

His popular lectures were distinguished by the ease with which he declared *takfīr* of those who opposed him, particularly puritan Salafis in Brixton. He also spoke about concepts previously unheard of in the West by the general public, like *Tawḥīd al-ḥākimiyyah* and *al-walāʾ wa'l-barāʾ*. Moreover, he preached violence and vigilantism against non-Muslims and Muslims alike. His aggressive and condemnatory rhetoric included discussions of 'The Devil's Deception of the Saudi Salafis,' and use of inflammatory titles like 'The Devil's Deception of the 21st Century House Niggers,' and the rejection of democracy in favor of 'the bullet.' In his message to 'exterminate unbelievers,' he said, 'You can go to India, and if you see a Hindu down the road, you can kill him and take his money, it is clear, because there is no treaty of peace between us.' He also said, 'Jews should be killed… as by Hitler. People with British passports, if you fly to Israel, it's easy. Fly to Israel and do everything you can. If you die, you are in heaven. How do you fight a Jew? You kill a Jew. In the case of Hindus, bombing their companies.'[405] In relation to Salafis, he said on one occasion, 'If he is a supporter of *kufr* (disbelief), a Saudi Salafi, you have to kill him and chop his head off.'[406] In the midst of his murderous rhetoric was a certain pantomime element which undoubtedly made his performance more entertaining for people with a similarly warped worldview. For instance, after playing a recording of one opponent, he asked the crowd about what should be done with such a person. Members of the audience replied, 'Kill him!' He said, 'I can't hear you.' So the reply came back with more vigor, 'Kill him!' Then, after one more back and forth, with the audience response growing louder, satisfied, he said, 'Okay, that makes sense.'[407]

Eventually, in 2002, he was arrested, sentenced in 2003 to a total of nine years in prison, then deported to Jamaica in 2007.[408] He was the first cleric to be convicted in the UK for terrorist activities after 9/11. After his release, al-Faisal tried to revive his message in various countries, including South Africa and Botswana. Thereafter, he was banned and deported from multiple countries and forced to return to Jamaica. In 2017, he was arrested for conspiracy to recruit for ISIS, and then extradited to the United States in 2020 for trial on these charges. On 26 January 2023, he was convicted at the state Supreme Court in Manhattan on a number of counts, including soliciting or providing support for an act of terrorism, and eventually sentenced to eighteen years in prison.[409]

The case of al-Faisal is an example of extreme jihadi ideology manifesting itself in the West. It should be noted, however, that not only did the majority of Muslims reject al-Faisal and his message, even other Jihadis criticized him and warned against him, and no actual terrorist attack was linked to him. Many viewed him as a fringe figure with an eccentric demeanor and pompous, perhaps even clownish, behavior. His message was not delivered with any level of profundity, and most of his followers were people from lower socio-economic and educational backgrounds.

## *5.7 Conclusion*

The rise of Jihadi-Salafism has been one of the most striking developments of our lifetime. Cults of this nature, especially the likes of ISIS, did not exist at any point in the 1,400-year history of Islam. It is a uniquely modern phenomenon, caused primarily by domestic and international political and socio-economic factors, coupled with the desperation of Muslim youth and the lack of any practical alternatives to achieving political and economic freedom. Jihadi-Salafism is a product of politics as much as it is a product of the merging of ideas. In a better political climate, if peace and stability were to reign in the Middle East, it is inconceivable that such an ideology would ever have materialized or taken root. It is unfortunate that many researchers do not focus on the political and economic context and therefore miss the bigger picture, invariably concentrating on religious beliefs, historical figures, and Islamic texts utilized by such movements.

Our work is not one dedicated to political contexts, hence this chapter was, grudgingly, forced to emphasize the 'Salafi' aspects of the movements more than their socio-political origins. Yet it must be reiterated that before one claims that religious fervor alone, of any persuasion, is the cause of Jihadi-Salafism, it would be wise to contextualize the reality of the world from within which it was formed: a world shaped by colonialist powers carving out nation-states based on the whims of a few superpowers post-World War I, and then planting and nurturing tyrannical dictators that brutally suppressed the freedoms of their own peoples, followed by invading some of those very lands on false pretexts to cause the greatest destabilization those regions have ever seen. This, along with the backdrop of almost a century of Palestinian injustice, coupled with global campaigns of Islamophobia which have demonized the Muslim community and stripped away the political rights of Muslim minorities. There is no justification for Jihadi-Salafism, but if one listens directly to the arguments of Bin Laden, or al-Awlaki, or al-Suri, as they attempt to justify their tactics, it is *always* political grievances that are mentioned, and jihad is their response to those political grievances. It would behoove researchers and politicians to understand the primary appeal of Jihadi-Salafism – an appeal that requires no background in Islamic theology to grasp.

The unique phenomenon of Jihadi-Salafism was born in such circumstances, coalescing ideas from Salafi theology and the Muslim Brotherhood in a desperate socio-economic environment, in the torturous prison-cells of Egypt and bloody battlefields of Afghanistan, Iraq, and Syria. This ideology went on to wreak havoc and cause widespread panic and violence across the globe. Yet the ironic fact remains that all of the bloodshed and terror caused by those jihadist movements pales in comparison to the bloodshed and violence out of which Jihadism was born.

The appeal to JS thought is *not* because Muslims are prone to violence, but rather because many Muslims (like all oppressed minorities) are more politically savvy in remembering the conflicts and grievances inflicted on them; Jihadi-Salafism merely channels that anger and incorrectly justifies for its followers the belief that God has sanctioned the type of warfare that these groups engage in in order to defend their political and religious freedom. To put it simply, ISIS would not exist had it not been for over three decades of American meddling in Iraq, first with the double-game between Iraq and Iran, then the sanctions of the 1990s, followed by both Gulf Wars (under the Bushes), and finally culminating with the complete destabilization of the region in the 2000s beginning with the invasion of Iraq under false pretenses. Oppressed peoples will find a way to justify fighting back; removing the oppression will go a much longer way in countering violent extremism than outlawing the religious beliefs that undergird the justifications of fighting back.

This does not condone JS and their violence. From the very moment it started to emerge in the Muslim world, the movement has been universally condemned by many Muslim scholars, preachers, activists and leaders, who have spoken out, written against, and warned about JS over the past few decades, and this includes Salafis. This began in Egypt in the late 1960s and the 1970s, from not only establishment scholars in al-Azhar, but also moderate Islamists of the Muslim Brotherhood. The latter, in particular, were some of the most forthright in condemning this developing JS trend, from al-Hudaybi in 1969 to Brotherhood publications in 1977 by Mustafa Hilmi and Salim Ali al-Bahnasawi, which labelled such Jihadi-Salafis as

*Khawārij*, while not exonerating those that they saw as scholars operating as mouthpieces for the corrupt Egyptian government.[410]

The leading *Ṣaḥwa*-Salafi scholar Salman al-Oudah appropriately lamented and highlighted the cost of JS in 2007, as the brutal Zarqawian mutation was starting to take shape (later emerging in the even more odious form of ISIS):

> You are responsible – brother Osama [Bin Laden] – for spreading *takfiri* ideology and fostering a culture of suicide bombings that has caused bloodshed and suffering and brought ruin to entire Muslim communities and families... To what end, even if your plan succeeds by marching over the corpses of hundreds of thousands of people? ... Is Islam only about guns and war? Have your means become the end themselves? ... Many of your brethren in Egypt, Algeria and elsewhere have come to see the end road for al-Qaeda's ideology. They now realize how destructive and dangerous it is.[1032]

Salafi authors have produced many books condemning Jihadis as extremists. A notable example was the Saudi author Abd Al-Rahman Luwayhiq, who wrote a detailed refutation of the beliefs of the Jihadis entitled *Extremism in the Religion*, which has been translated into English,[411] and then followed it with a two-volume work entitled *Difficult Questions Regarding Extremism in the Religion*. The titles of these books highlight the Jihadi-Salafi perception of jihadism as an extremist manifestation of Islam, unrelated to Salafism in any way.

Nonetheless, recent examples do exist of Salafi scholars linking jihadism to Salafism, such as Adil al-Kalbani, a former imam at the Holy Mosque in Mecca, who declared in 2014 that '[ISIS] is a Salafi [fundamentalist] offshoot ... a reality we should confront with transparency,'[412] and 'not from other Islamists, including the Muslim Brotherhood or Sayyid Qutb.'[413] Yet, the most significant criticism of Wahhabism as a major contributory factor to the development of the Jihadi-Salafi ISIS came in the aftermath of King Abdullah of Saudi Arabia criticizing the Saudi scholars for not adequately refuting jihadism, in particular the Islamic State. This was when the Salafi cleric Sharif Hatim al-Awni criticized the Wahhabis' extreme understanding of *takfir* and *al-wala wa'l-bara*, and argued that the reason for the Salafi scholars' 'laziness' in tackling Islamic State was because they shared the same skewed notions of *takfir*, as exemplified in Muhammad Ibn ʿAbd al-Wahhāb's *al-Durar al-Saniyyah* – a work which has been an inspiration for Jihadi-Salafis, such as Abu Muhammad al-Maqdisi.[414]

But the voices of people like al-Kalbani and al-Awni are rare among Salafis; and they are more likely to take the line that the Grand Mufti 'Abd al-ʻAzīz Āl al-Shaykh did after King Abdullah's reprimand of the scholars, and suffice with simply labeling the Jihadi-Salafis as Khārijis, thus exonerating Salafism and Wahhabism. Another establishment Salafi scholar, Saad al-Shathri, took a similar approach of denial, but went further, labeling the Jihadi-Salafis of the Islamic State as 'unbelievers,' and went on to say: 'The truth of this organization [Islamic state] is that it has no connection to the mission of Shaykh Muhammad ibn Abd al-Wahhāb.'[415]

The abhorrent nature of JS has led even major jihadist theorists to condemn the phenomenon and attribute its errors to Salafism. For instance, Abu Mus'ab al-Suri blamed Salafism for the extremist direction that jihadism took in recent years, and for introducing *takfīr* into the jihadi ideology: 'Some prominent men from the Salafi-Jihādī current, or at least those scholars and students who followed them, offered interpretations which were either extremist, or were articulated in such a general manner that some ignorant Jihadist took a step further and widened the concept of excommunicating others.'[416] In fact, al-Suri saw Salafism as an argumentative and troublesome methodology which weakened the war movement: 'It [Salafism] causes internal strife among Muslims and within the Resistance movement itself at a time when we are being invaded by the Americans and Zionist Mongols and their war machines…'[417]

Furthermore, the phenomenon of JS cannot be simply defined as the desperate violence of an angry and deprived underclass, although it often is – as certain JS personalities have come from the most privileged sections of society, as in the cases of Osama bin Laden and Ayman al-Zawahiri. Montasser al-Zayyat, in his study of Ayman al-Zawahiri, entitled *The Road to Al-Qaeda*, mentions being imprisoned in Egypt with numerous professionals and well-educated individuals who were part of the movement, including most notably al-Zawahiri himself. The same dismantling of stereotypes occurs when we consider religious education and whether madrasas and centers of religious higher learning cause such outlooks. On this point, we see that surprisingly few Al-Qaeda adherents had religious backgrounds. Sageman's study of the early group, with a sample of 137, showed that only 23 (17%) had an Islamic primary and secondary education, and the rest were educated in secular schools, with a dominance of engineers, and people like al-Zawahiri and Sayyid Imam being professional surgeons.[1031] Likewise, Gambetta and Hertog have found a high proportion of Islamic extremists in the Muslim world with higher education, which were over the tertiary enrolment rates for such countries, even if 'the Western based jihadists have attracted far fewer graduates and fewer qualified individuals and many more from a lower class and lower middle class background.'[418]

Ultimately, the Jihadi-Salafis are an ever-decreasing minority within the Muslim world, and their disunity, quickness to excommunicate and extreme differences have fractured them further and removed any chance of success in completing their mission. It is true that they have a specific understanding of religious texts that might continue to appeal to a small segment of religious adherents. Nonetheless, it is the contention of this author that the elimination of the many ongoing political and social grievances that have plagued the modern Muslim world, and given rise to such extremism, is the best means of taking important steps towards the eradication of this dangerous trend.

# 6

# GLOBAL SALAFISM IN THE CONTEMPORARY WORLD

*'The Salafi message is the message that God sent His Prophet Muhammad (peace be upon him) with... And Wahhabis are callers to the truth, callers to Salafism. They are calling to what the Prophet and his Companions and those after them were upon. And so too are all the scholars who followed this method: in India, and Syria, and Iraq, and Egypt, and all over the world. This call has many followers, in many continents, and in many regions around the globe: they recognized the truth, and they saw this pure message from its books. For it is the Salafi message: calling to the tawḥīd of Allah, and to follow God's Laws, and to follow His Prophet Muhammad – may peace be upon him.'*
~ *Grand Muftī Ibn Bāz (d. 1999)*[1]

*'I say that unfortunately the Salafis are now in disarray, and I attribute the cause of this to the hastiness of many of the Muslim youth who claim knowledge: so he will have the audacity to pass fatwās, and to declare things to be permissible or impermissible before he knows.'*
~ *Muhammad Nasir al-Din al-Albānī (d. 1999)*[2]

From its somewhat humble beginnings in the modern world, Salafism has come to be a truly global phenomenon, expanding out from the Muslim world into majority non-Muslim countries with significant Muslim minorities. Of the three kinds of Salafism that are commonly identified, all have emerged across the world. Since Chapter 5 focused on Jihadi-Salafism as a worldwide movement, this chapter will concentrate, sometimes in a cursory fashion, on the quietist and political forms of Salafism that have formed in different parts of the world.

This chapter must be preceded with some disclaimers. While there have been studies of Salafism in Afghanistan,[3] Ethiopia,[4] Africa in general,[5] France,[6] Netherlands,[7] Sweden[8] and Germany,[9] as well as the impact of African scholars on Salafism in Saudi Arabia,[10] our discussions will only focus, with brevity in mind, on those countries which have an intriguing history of Salafism, with either a transnational impact, such as the major trends in Africa and West Asia; or exemplify the impact of more global trends, such as in the United Kingdom and North America; or have such geo-political importance that it warrants some sort of comment, even if less detailed because their experience is rather narrow, as is the case with India and Pakistan, Nigeria, the Malay Archipelago, Türkiye, and Bosnia and Herzegovina. This chapter is not meant to be exhaustive, and the level of detail for each region will vary (countries with the most complex and significant histories will receive the most elaboration).

The modern aspects of this history that were discussed in sufficient detail in Chapter 2 (such as the 'Enlightenment' project of Riḍā) will not be repeated here. Furthermore, the United Kingdom and North America are elaborated in more detail than many other countries, as this work is aimed at the English-speaking world, and they are noteworthy examples of how the political orientation of major scholars based in the Arab countries can determine the development and division of Salafis in Western countries. In addition, it should be noted that these discussions will contain some personal reflections of the author, especially as I was one of the leading Salafi proponents in the English-speaking world for a relatively extensive period;[11] hence I ask the readers indulgence in including such remarks in light of my intimate insider experience.

This section will not have entries for Saudi Arabia and Egypt.[12] Despite Saudi Arabia and Egypt being the two most important countries for the development of modern Salafism, from its foundations until the present, the phenomenon of Salafism in these countries has been covered in detail in almost every chapter in this book, hence there is no reason to repeat those regions here.

Lastly, as this work is not meant to be an encyclopedia of all global Salafi movements, unfortunately some key regions will not be included. For example, Salafism is growing in popularity in Russia and the countries surrounding it (in particular, Chechnya and Dagestan); and South America, despite its overall small percentage of Muslims, has also seen the rise of popular Salafi preachers and institutional influence. These, and other regions, will have to be overlooked for our purposes.

## *6.1 Africa*

### *6.1.1 Morocco*

During the time of the French protectorate in Morocco, between 1912 and 1956, the emerging form of Salafism was the Riḍā modernist-reformist type. Quite a few clerics were inspired by Riḍā's message, most significantly opposed to the more reformist-modernist movement of Abu Shu'ayb al-Dukkali (d. 1937) and Mohamed Allal al-Fassi (d. 1974), which will not be discussed here.[13] However, after independence, the puritan-traditionalist form began to emerge; and this quietist form became prevalent as a result of the backing of the Moroccan monarchy and Saudi Arabia, until the Arab Spring in 2011. The quietist movement was shaken by the emergence of Jihadi-Salafism in Morocco, especially with the Casablanca terrorist attack in May 2003, and then the pro-democracy movement that accompanied the Arab uprisings of 2011. Consequently, a significant split took place in the movement, with some remaining fixed on a quietist path and others opting for a more politically orientated Salafism.[14]

Nonetheless, Moroccan exposure to Salafism has much longer roots than simply the time of the French protectorate. For instance, Wahhabi traditions were introduced into the country with the approval of rulers Muḥammad ibn ʿAbd Allah (d. 1790) and Sultan Mawlay Sulayman (d. 1822). Wahhabi-type attacks on perceived Sufi excesses helped Sulayman, in particular, in his power struggle with the Sufi brotherhoods, simply as a way of reforming Sufism, rather than rejecting the tradition. The nineteenth century also saw Ibn Taymiyya's thought introduced into Morocco by leading scholars like Muḥammad bin Ja'far al-Kattani (d. 1927) and Abdullah Idris al-Sanusi (d. 1931). But the Salafi drive took on a more defined form in the early twentieth century, as a response to the growing threat from Europe and the growing sense that Morocco had to renew itself in order to maintain its independence. The notable puritan Salafi to emerge in Morocco at this time was Muhammad Taqi al-Din al-Hilali (d. 1987). The latter's fame would be primarily attained due to his joint English translations, with Muhsin Khan (d. 1997), of *The Translation of the Meaning of the Noble Qur'an* and the first entire translation of *Ṣaḥīḥ al-Bukhārī.*

Al-Hilali left Morocco in 1915, and after spending time in Algeria, Egypt (where he spent an extensive period studying under Rashīd Riḍā), India (where he studied with *Ahl-e-Hadith* scholars, taught at the seminary of Nadwat al-Ulama in Lucknow, and studied English as well),[15] Iraq, Saudi Arabia and Germany (for doctoral studies in 1936, and then working with the Nazis), he returned in 1942, remaining until 1947. During this time, he founded a journal, *Lisan al-Din* (*The Language of Religion*), in 1946, and remained the chief editor until 1949, when he was replaced by the important Moroccan reformist Abdullah Gannun, who identified as Salafi in creed, but had a reformist method like ʻAbduh. He started his career as a member of the Tijānī Sufi order. However, after losing a debate to a Salafi scholar, he abandoned Sufism and became a Salafi.[16] Regardless of whether his claim to have turned to Salafism in 1921 is wholly accurate or not, al-Hilali did return to Morocco as a puritan Salafi.

As the reformist interpretation of Salafism then prevailed in Morocco, upon al-Hilali's return, he immediately started to redefine the term according to his puritan understanding by writing articles and preaching in mosques on the subject; hence he spoke of a purified Islam taken from the earliest generations of Muslims, and how it denounced unsanctioned religious innovation. He therefore condemned the Ashʿarī school of theology, the strict adherence to the Mālikī school by Moroccans and prevalent forms of Sufism. In addition, he taught Wahhabi books, such as *Fath al-Majid*, the popular commentary on the *Kitāb al-Tawḥīd* of Muhammad Ibn ʿAbd al-Wahhāb, as well as publishing a fatwa condemning certain forms of visiting graves by Ibn Taymiyya and Muhammad Ibn ʿAbd al-Wahhāb's *Kashf al-shubuhat*.[17]

Naturally, he claimed to encounter a great deal of hostility to his message. Therefore he resorted to creative methods of selling his books in such a hostile environment, by altering the names of the authors; so Muhammad Ibn ʿAbd al-Wahhāb became Muhammad ibn Sulayman al-Dirʻi (ascribing him to the town where he entered into his political alliance with the family of Saʻud), and Ibn Taymiyya became al-Hafiz al-Harrani (referring him to his scholarly eminence and his place of origin). Nonetheless, he maintained his habit of praising non-Salafis for their adherence to Islamic law while rejecting their contraventions of Salafi theology; thus, he condemned Ibn Tumart (d. 524/1130), the leading scholar of the Almohad dynasty, for bringing Ashʿarī theology to Morocco, but he was praised for his piety. Yet, for all his Salafism, he still wore suits and ties and did not grow a beard (hence he was criticized as 'a Europeanized man' *rajul mutafarnij*), which presented something of a paradox, certainly for our conception of Salafism now.[18]

In 1957, al-Hilali visited Rabat and submitted two articles to the new Moroccan Islamic journal entitled *Daʻwat al-Haqq* (*The Call to Truth*). His first article spoke of the Moroccan independence from France being wholly attributable to the workings of God due to the faith of the Moroccans, and he proceeded to define divinity in Salafi terms of His lordship (*Tawḥīd al-rubūbiyyah*) and His sole right to receive worship from the creation (*Tawḥīd al-ulūhiyyah*). The second article was an account of his audience with the king and was followed by al-Hilali composing a poem in praise of the king's religiousness and efforts against French colonialism. With such social ice-breakers, al-Hilali returned to live in Morocco in 1959, having set down markers for his activity: an apolitical social outlook, with loyalty to the monarchy, and his calling to a puritanical Salafism.[19]

Between 1959 and 1968, despite being a general oddity in Morocco due to the content of his apolitical Salafism which was not widely supported, al-Hilali was still able to secure employment as an official preacher (*wa'iz*). He then proceeded to lecture around the country, as well as teaching, primarily as a lecturer in Arabic at the new Muhammad V University in Rabat (after Gannun's recommendation), and writing in *Da'wat al-Haqq* (*Invitation to the Truth*). Yet his attacks on the Moroccan Islamic intellectual tradition led to uproar, and he was subjected to a governmental investigation but was absolved of charges before a commission headed by his old friend Gannun. During this time, he was able to use his contacts with the Saudis to receive free books to aid his Salafi teaching from Wahhabi texts, together with financial aid from Ibn Bāz, as well as providing consultation services to the Saudi establishment.[20]

Al-Hilali was able to maintain an attack on the Moroccan scholars and common Sufi practices, while exonerating the king for endorsing the very same acts, such as saint commemorations (*mawāsim*), even when he was challenged on this obvious contradiction. Nor did al-Hilali criticize the semi-official celebrations that occurred at the tomb of Mulay Idris I (d. 175/791), who founded the first Moroccan dynasty. However, in post-independence Morocco, al-Hilali's critiques of loyal Moroccan subjects caused unease within the government, especially as a result of the ensuing unrest it provoked. The authorities would intervene when al-Hilali's preaching caused too much outrage, and he would be moved on, despite his protests of innocence.[21]

However, the unraveling of al-Hilali's call to Salafism was becoming all the more apparent. Firstly, in 1964, he had only lasted two-and-a-half months teaching at the newly established *Dar al-Hadith al-Hassaniyyah* in Rabat. This was despite his initial enthusiasm for the institute. However, after Sufi students opposed him, and he received no support from the equally Sufi hierarchy, he was seen as intellectually limited and more of a sectarian fanatic. Secondly, his religious polemics in journals, whether against the Baha'is or René Habachi (d. 2003), made him look curiously at odds with his time. He appeared to be a puritan Salafi with little sophisticated knowledge of modern social sciences; his students at Muhammad V University tired of his Salafi approach and increasingly began to criticize him. Then, in 1968, al-Hilali received an offer from Ibn Bāz to go and teach at the

Islamic University of Medina, which al-Hilali readily accepted, especially as it came at a time when his reformist attempts were failing in Morocco. Indeed, from the late 1940s until the late 1960s, Saudi Arabia was a place of retreat for many puritan Salafis.[22]

From the late 1960s onwards, the Islamists came to prominence over the modernist Salafis in Moroccan society, after the latter had achieved substantial political success, including Gannun becoming the governor of Tangier in 1956. But puritan Salafis began to strengthen during this time; with their simple focus and apolitical stance, they did not suffer from the turbulence of socio-political affairs. They focused on providing a strictly devotional service, and the government gave them greater freedom so they could oppose left-wing movements, who were becoming increasingly popular.[23]

The 1970s witnessed the strengthening of puritan Salafism in Morocco, especially with al-Hilali's return in 1974 (he would remain in his homeland until his death in 1987), as Saudi Arabia enlarged its support of the proselytizing of Salafism outside the Kingdom. At this time, puritan, apolitical Salafism was the only version on offer, and the modernist Salafis had come to be eclipsed as not being *Salafis* any longer, but merely *modernists*. While Moroccan Islam was still decidedly Ashʿarī-Mālikī-Sufi, the authorities seemed to welcome the apolitical approach of the puritan Salafis, especially after the failed coups of 1971 and 1972 and the Iranian Revolution of 1979, and the ensuing limits on political activity.[24] Salafism was further aided when hundreds of Moroccans went, in the 1980s and 1990s, to study in Saudi universities, in particular at the IUM, and the availability of Salafi books became widespread.[25]

Al-Hilali's foundation of the popular apolitical Salafi movement was cemented with his student Muhammad ibn ʻAbd al-Rahman al-Maghrawi (b. 1948) who, in 1976, formed the leading puritan Salafi organization, called *al-Daʻwah ila al-Qurʾan waʼl-Sunna* (The Call to the Qurʾan and the Sunna), after his studies at the IUM. This organization benefitted from prominent Saudi links and backing, and al-Hilali requested and managed funds for Salafi activities in Morocco, and for associates of his in other places. In a move that surely favored the Moroccan monarchy and the Saudi royal family, al-Maghrawi's favorite targets for criticism were the Shiʿa and political Islam. With regards to the latter, al-Maghrawi directed his attention towards Abdessalam Yassine (d. 2012), the founder of the proscribed Moroccan Sufi-Islamist party *Al Adl Wal Ihsan* (Justice and Spirituality), which upset al-Maghrawi with its criticisms of the Moroccan king and Sufi influences. Even when a general crackdown on Salafi activities occurred in the country as a result of the May 2003 Casablanca bombings, al-Maghrawi's organization was not targeted or shut down, as he extolled the correctness of the government response to the threat. Naturally, there were

Salafi voices who were not content with the subservient apolitical nature of al-Maghrawi, and not just among the Jihadi-Salafis. Hence in 2007, some of the usually apolitical Salafis supported the Islamist Party of Justice and Development (PJD) in the 2007 legislative elections.[26]

The dominant apolitical Salafism of Morocco was weakened when al-Maghrawi was forced into exile in Saudi Arabia in September 2008, due to taking a legal position on the marriage of youngsters which contravened the national law, and the government closed dozens of his organization's NGOs and schools. Yet, the momentum of the Arab Spring was felt in Morocco when the 20 February Movement (M20F) started to arrange protests throughout the country in the early part of 2011. The government allowed al-Maghrawi to return in April 2011, as part of an arrangement whereby he and his faction would work to calm the protests down. Unsurprisingly, al-Maghrawi first praised the constitutional reforms of the government in July 2011 (which were opposed by *Al Adl Wal Ihsan* and much of the leadership of M20F as insufficient), and quietist Salafis started to request that their closed-down schools should be reopened in the climate of calling for greater freedom.

But al-Maghrawi then, quite unexpectedly, encouraged voting in the upcoming elections for those most advantageous to the faith, which was interpreted as a subtle endorsement of the PJD. Furthermore, Hamad Kabbaj, one of al-Maghrawi's close associates, wrote a work in 2012 entitled *Foresight and Persistence*, which had an introduction by al-Maghrawi and was understood as being a highly political treatise, with an almost favorable treatment of a particular type of democracy, as well as accepting forms of political activism like protests. Democracy, in particular, had historically been condemned by al-Maghrawi and the apolitical Salafis, and explained with little nuance; hence the work understandably met with a quizzical response from the apolitical Salafi audience.

Al-Maghrawi and his people had made their tentative move towards political activism when the circumstances seemed quite pregnant with positivity for change and Islamic sentiment, and it was a door that could not be shut. The consequences of the normally-apolitical Salafis' cautious step towards the political realm were exposed in the midst of the rapidly developing counter-revolution, which would soon cause a deep division among the Moroccan Salafis. There were two factors that led to this rupture: firstly, the conflicting stances taken by Moroccan Salafi factions in the wake of the July 2013 coup in Egypt against the then-President Morsi; and secondly, the differing responses to the growing pressure applied at home by the Moroccan authorities for Salafis to conform to the regime's drive for supporting the political status quo, with Salafi imams marked for removal and authorities closing down four of al-Maghrawi's Qur'anic schools in Marrakesh in July 2013. These draconian measures were seen, in some quarters, as retribution for the Salafis supporting the PJD and not the monarchy-backed parties, as well as opposing the official Moroccan Islam which was Sufi.

Soon, in the face of such hostility, al-Maghrawi reverted to type and backed the coup, in alignment with his Saudi establishment links and many Moroccan followers, and explicitly issued an apolitical message in March 2014. However, two close associates of al-Maghrawi in his organization, Hamad Kabbaj and Adil al-Rafush, immediately condemned the Egyptian coup, as well as the Egyptian Salafi Nour Party and the Saudis for their involvement in the overthrowing of Morsi. Kabbaj and other Salafis participated in the August 2013 demonstrations in Rabat to decry the killing of Egyptian protestors in Rabaa by the military and joined hands with Islamists and members of *Al Adl Wal Ihsan* and the PJD, and others.

During August 2013, al-Rafush issued a poem that criticized the Saudis for their corruption, which led al-Maghrawi to make a concerted effort to distance himself and urge al-Rafush to recant – he was unsuccessful. In the 2016 legislative elections, al-Maghrawi openly endorsed the state-supporting Party of Authenticity and Progress (PAM). Political Salafis criticized al-Maghrawi for such a crass political move, especially for a party led by someone they felt could not be trusted. Kabbaj was particularly scornful, pointing out that al-Maghrawi decided to back a pro-regime party but rejected any compromise with *Al Adl Wal Ihsan*, while Kabbaj himself supported the PJD (and had intended to actually stand for them in Marrakesh, but did not). This, again, highlighted that the Salafi methodology of apolitical Salafis tolerates secular political formulae over religious political doctrine, and such quietists have a tendency, as Kabbaj noted, to lavishly praise dictators yet passionately denounce religious opponents, especially Islamists of various types.

This divide between apolitical Salafis and politically-inclined Salafis has persisted in Morocco, without the latter forming a political party or developing leading political figures (which contrasts with those seen as repentant Jihadi-Salafis in Morocco, such as Muhammad al-Fizazi, Muhammad Rafiki Abu Hafs and Hassan Kettani).[27] Yet the most worrying aspect of the quietist Salafi trend has been pointed out by Kabbaj in relation to the North African Madkhalis, who have displayed an increasingly radical tendency to justify the murder of Islamists and their supporters. Thus al-Rafush likened the Madkhalis' permitting the killing of Muslim Brothers to the methodology of ISIS, stating that their global slogan was now in effect, 'Betraying the Righteous and Supporting the Corrupt.'

One of the most significant aspects to emerge from this split among the historically-apolitical Salafis of Morocco is in the political analysis offered by Kabbaj, which is closely akin to the discourse of the Islamists: discussing the virtue of democracy as a defense against dictatorship and secularism, as well as the notion of political compromise, and doing as much good and benefit as one can by emulating the Prophetic model. On the latter point, he utilized the example of Prophet Joseph (Yusuf) and his offer to serve in the administration of the Pharaoh. Kabbaj writes, 'Yusuf did not condition his entry into government on the banning of alcohol, eating pork, and renunciation of Pharaonic beliefs, but instead he took upon himself the heavy charge of serving the people and relieving their hardships from severe drought and oppressive politics.'[28] The future of such political Salafism is difficult to predict at present, although it seems highly unlikely that it will become a major movement any time soon. However, the growth of educated and middle-class Salafis moving from their roots in the apolitical Salafism of al-Maghrawi in the mid-1990s and taking steps towards making Salafi theology fit the socio-political challenges of the age, is a fascinating one to observe.

### *6.1.2 Algeria*

Algeria's history with Salafism has been largely defined by its relationship with violent Jihadi-Salafism, especially the periods spanning 1982–87 and 1991–99, which were described in Chapter 5. Nonetheless, Algeria, like much of the surrounding Maghreb, has had more historic links with Salafism.

As has been the norm in many parts of the Muslim world, Algeria's first exposure to a Salafism of sorts was its experience of reformist Salafism, whereby certain thinkers saw the need to religiously rejuvenate the Algerian people into a force that could break the yoke of French colonialism which had beset the country since 1830, by reviving the spirit of the predecessors (*salaf*) – although they did not subscribe to something called Salafism (*salafiyya*).[29] Such reformers were, most notably, 'Abd al-Hamid Ben Badis (d. 1940) and Muhammad Bashir al-Ibrahimi (d. 1965). Badis' formation of the Association of Algerian Muslim 'Ulama (AAMU) in 1931 was to prove significant in opening a pathway to the emergence of traditionalist Salafism from its reformist namesake.

Traditionalist Salafis were quite obscure in Algeria for most of the twentieth century, perhaps due to the fact that Algeria was riding a wave of nationalistic sentiment after independence from the French. Apolitical Salafism was something of an irrelevance as political actors set about crafting the future in real terms. With its penchant for arguing about the details of theological doctrine and religious practice, apolitical Salafism didn't seem to have much to offer to the country carving out a new system. Yet the type of social trauma that allows Salafism to thrive in times of uncertainty began to emerge in Algeria in the late 1980s, as the oil prices crashed, the economy suffered, and living conditions got dramatically worse. This led to riots in October 1988, which forced the government to concede to democratic demands and end one-party rule.

The Islamic faction which made the most of this emerging opportunity for political advancement was the Islamist Islamic Salvation Front (FIS). One of the latter's two leaders, Ali Benhadj, had something of a Salafi approach that was heavily based on his admiration for Ibn Taymiyya and its seeming alignment with the *Ṣaḥwa* Salafi movement (as discussed in section 5.3.4). While some Salafi leaders in Algeria – like Mohammed Ali Ferkous and Abdelmalek Ramdani – treated the political moment with caution and remained focused on purely religious affairs and social welfare, there were other Salafi leaders who had supported FIS in their political cause.[30] FIS attracted Salafi supporters in the same way that it was able to draw supporters from numerous religious persuasions. Prior to this, political Salafis in Algeria during the 1980s were not an organized movement, but a disparate grouping involved in activism with Salafi foundations; however, FIS gave people a direction to apply their theories.

Nonetheless, with the military defeat of Islamists and the project of political Islam in the 1990s in Algeria (after the military cancellation of the 1991 elections which FIS looked set to win by a clear margin) two forms of Salafism emerged in a strengthened form: anti-politics Jihadi-Salafism (which has been dealt with in Chapter 5) and apolitical Salafism. The latter group was able to capitalize on the vacuum created by the regime's repression of the Islamists as a consequence of the canceled elections, as well as being able to assert that their doubts about the futility of entering the political fray had been vindicated by the failed Islamist venture, despite its overwhelming support. Furthermore, as the country descended into civil war, with the Jihadi-Salafis and military creating a bloodbath, the quietist Salafis were able to capitalize, in the 1990s and 2000s, on their apolitical stance and their condemnation of the universally-despised killings, as many found solace from the trauma of the civil war in the quietist Salafi emphasis on doctrine and personal worship.[31]

Hence the regime came to utilize the quietist Salafis against their Jihadi-Salafi and Islamist opponents. From the 1990s, Abdelmalek Ramdani was allowed to preach his refutations against Jihadi-Salafis, which he did before moving to Saudi Arabia, as was the quietist Salafi Mohamed Ali Ferkous. In 2007, the Ministry of Religious Affairs organized a campaign for quietist Salafi imams to preach their message in mosques during Ramadan; and in 2008, the government utilized the sermons of apolitical Salafis, like Abdelghani Aouissat and Ramdani, on Radio Qur'an against Jihadi-Salafis. Aouissat had turned to Salafism in the 1970s, after a more traditional religious education, and had links to the Saudi religious establishment, such as to Ibn Bāz. For well over a decade, Aouissat had a significant presence on Algerian television.

Due to these factors, the Madkhali-faction emerged with vigor and its characteristic aggressive intolerance. Furthermore, the Algerian government placed itself in a leading position in aiding the United States' war on terror after 9/11 and opted for the security approach endorsed by such Western powers. This assisted its agenda against political Islam and encouraged support for the apolitical Salafis – although Algeria's relationship with the United States was complicated during this time, probably due to the Algerian desire to maintain their sovereignty and control over their important oil reserves.[32]

When uprisings started to occur across the Arab world during the Arab Spring, the quietist Algerian Salafi leaders condemned the activism and called for respecting the rulers. Thus, for example, Ramdani, then in Saudi, and Ferkous condemned the political awakening and emphasized that the Islamic ruling was to obey the Muslim leader, and that the protests were religiously unacceptable due to the mixing of the genders (*ikhtilat*). Then, in 2014, in the build-up to the presidential elections, Ramdani, Ferkous and Aouissat, along with other quietist Salafis, called for adherence to the status quo, refusing to endorse even Salafis who had taken a political path; yet, at the same time, they called for their followers not to vote.[33]

Naturally, the quietist Salafis in Algeria drew heavy criticism from their politico Salafis in the country. For example, Abdelfattah Hamadache was scathing in his rebuke of Ferkous. Zeraoui was a former member of FIS and the founder in 2013 of the Islamic Ṣaḥwa Front (which has not received recognition from the regime as a legitimate political party, despite their application). For Hamadache, Ferkous was not a legitimate scholar, and he had the dishonor of being against jihad and failing to support those who engaged in it, while never engaging in the liberation of Muslims under oppression. But trouble for the quietist Salafis also came from their own ranks when two members of the Madkhal tribe, Muhammad ibn Hadi al-Madkhalī and Rabi' ibn Hadi al-Makdhali, had a bitter falling out during 2017 and 2018. This dispute shook the loyalist Salafi movement worldwide, and led to splits among the Algerian faction, including relations between Ferkous, Ramdani and Aouissat.[34]

Despite Salafism often being portrayed in the Algerian media, by leading politicians and journalists alike, as a radicalizing and destabilizing force in Algeria, the Algerian quietist Salafis have managed to maintain their position as loyalists to the regime, and useful in opposing the Islamist and political Salafi opponents of the regime. Yet their persistent splits and arguments among themselves constantly destabilize them. The lack of popularity and freedom to politically organize experienced by Islamists (including Ali Belhadj, the original leader of FIS, who left prison in 2006 and unsuccessfully tried to obtain permission to run for president in 2014), Jihadi-Salafis and politico Salafis in Algeria means that quietist Salafis are likely to maintain a strong presence.[35] This is despite their inherent failings, as well as the regime, from time to time, banning their books and restricting their activities, as a political method of containing their growth and ensuring loyalty.

### *6.1.3 Libya*

Libya's turbulent twentieth century history – from Italian occupation in 1911, to independence in 1951, to the military coup in 1969 which led to the leadership of Colonel Muammar Gaddafi – witnessed very little Salafi activity, neither reformist nor traditionalist. Gaddafi adopted a forthright religious approach from the beginning of his reign, in his own idiosyncratic style. As a means of consolidating his religious authority, he attacked and sought control of the shrines, institutions and factions which were associated with the royal family – descendants of the Sufi order called the *Sanusiyyah* that the military had removed in 1969[36] – as well as groups like the Muslim Brotherhood, who he saw as unwittingly supporting colonialism by opposing Arab socialism and nationalism.[37] The new revolutionary regime soon launched a mission to monopolize religious interpretation, by overthrowing sects, groups and clerics, without attempting to present a modernized or secular attitude to the faith. The political and religious opposition was largely quashed, whether with the hard hand of the regime or a growing turning away from politics by increasing parts of the society. This continued until Libya hit serious economic hardship in the late 1980s, after years of being economically sanctioned by the West.[38]

By the 1980s, certain parts of Libyan society came to be influenced by the growing religiosity in the Arab world, and the propagation of Salafism at this time. A trend of apolitical Salafism was allowed to grow in the 1980s in Libya, as the regime did not consider it to be a threat.[39] However, the emergence of jihadi trends made the regime look more closely at even apolitical Salafis, especially from the mid-1990s when Libya joined with the Saudi security forces to tackle Jihadi-Salafism, and expanded their crackdown. In 1998, the Saudis expelled Libyan Salafis of all types, and they were sent back to Libya, many imprisoned upon their return. Nonetheless, this coincided with Gaddafi regime's changing policy with regards to apolitical Salafis, whereby he came to see their usefulness in combatting the more threatening Islamists (who they feared would receive mass support), and Jihadi-Salafis (whose wanton violence they feared). In this respect, the Libyans benefitted from their closer links with the Egyptian secret services who had engaged in their own battles with such opponents over a longer period of time.

In something of a division of labor, which covered all angles for the regime in successfully co-opting the various Salafi movements, two of Gaddafi's sons, Saif al-Islam and Saadi, were reported as developing closer links with different factions. Saif al-Islam focused on combatting

Jihadi-Salafis, so he worked more closely with political Salafis, and even invited Salman al-Oudah and Ayidh al-Qarni to Libya in 2010 to lecture against extremism. Saadi, on the other hand, worked with the loyalist-Madkhali faction, likely from the mid-1990s.[40] Thus Salafism was allowed to spread in Libya, despite the continuing scrutiny of the security forces, with Gaddafi having in 2002 relaxed the rules by letting Libyans study in Saudi and Yemen, and permitting the distribution of Salafi material. Then, in 2003, in a significant move on the part of the government, such Salafi clerics were allowed to become imams in Libyan mosques.[41]

The mainstream Salafi movement continued to grow slowly, even when its elements became embroiled in the global splits between politicos and quietists that beset Salafism in the mid-1990s. This intra-Salafi divide occurred after some Libyan Salafis had gone to study in the Islamic institute of the influential Salafi Muqbil ibn Hadi al-Wadi'i in Yemen. The latter died in 2001, but one of his leading students, Abu al-Hasan al-Ma'ribi, an Egyptian in origin, soon emerged with a political position which closely resembled that of the *Ṣaḥwa* Salafis.[42] This brought the ire of the loyalist-quietists and the condemnation of their leader, Rabi' al-Madkhalī, and split the global movement.[43] During the early-to-middle 2000s, with the regime's backing, the Madkhali faction increased in popularity throughout various parts of the country, and among different classes, both educated and not. The protests and revolution against Gaddafi in early 2011 would profoundly change the landscape and impact the nature of Salafi groups in Libya.[44]

As the uprising began, Gaddafi mobilized the Madkhalis through his son Saadi, with a campaign to deter protests as being prohibited in Islam, as they entailed the illegitimate rebellion (*khuruj*) against the legitimate leader (*wali al-amr*) of the country. The Madkhali leader in Libya, Majdi Hafalah,[45] supplied an endorsing fatwa to this effect, whereby he attributed the demonstrations to the dissension of Al-Qaeda. In March 2011, Gaddafi tried to enlist the support of al-Oudah and al-Qarni, but they refused; and al-Qarni went on to praise the activists and named one who died in the cause as a 'martyr' (*shahid*). Initially, Rabi' al-Madkhalī had urged his supporters not to participate in the rebellion, nor to support Gaddafi; by October 2011, he was recorded calling Gaddafi a 'criminal,' yet he still did not advocate armed rebellion. The fall of Gaddafi in October 2011 presented Libyan Salafis with a number of difficult choices, and dramatically altered the Salafi landscape, perhaps more so than in any other country.[46]

Between late 2011 and early 2012, Madkhali factions became prominent and joined the transitional government forces in a military capacity in Tripoli, contributing to policing crimes such as drug trafficking, alcohol and prostitution; their role in this capacity would increase as the situation in Libya further deteriorated. A significant Salafi policing unit that emerged in Tripoli during the uprising, taking up a base at the Mitiga Airport, was the

Special Deterrence Force, led by ‘Abd al-Ra’uf Kara. Although the latter was a Salafi, he was open to democracy, and stated that his main influences were Salafi clerics like Ibn ‘Uthaymin, al-Albānī, Ibn Bāz and Muqbil, rather than Rabi‘ al-Madkhalī; but it is estimated that the majority of his team were Madkhalis.[47]

In the build-up to the 2012 parliamentary elections. a number of Salafis joined the political process. This trend included the formation of the Salafi party *al-Asala* (Authenticity), with the alleged influence of Kuwait’s *Al-Umma* party. But on the whole, the Madkhalis did not participate in the political process. Yet the Salafis received very little backing from the electorate in the election for the General National Congress (GNC), as the liberal National Forces Alliance (NFA) came first, with the Islamist-leaning Justice and Construction Party (JCP) coming second.[48]

The Salafis were again divided in early 2013 when the Political Isolation Law was debated, which sought to exclude people from government roles based on prior service to the old regime. The bill was broadly supported by Islamists, and it became law in May 2013. An important part of the activist Salafis’ drive to make this act into legislation was the militia called the Libyan Revolutionaries Operations Rooms (LROR), led by Sha‘ban Madud Khalifah Hadiyah, from the western town of Zawiya. Hadiyah had a PhD in Islamic Law from the University of Alexandria, and had spent ten years, from 1993, studying in Muqbil’s Yemeni seminary, before becoming a teacher in the same institute. He is believed to have returned to Libya after the 2011 revolution and joined the armed forces in his home town.[49] In April 2011, the LROR had joined forces with other armed groups from Misrata, Tripoli, and other cities to pressure the GNC over the law, with the lead taken by the LROR, the Coordination for Political Isolation (led by Sami al-Saadi, who had been a leader of the Libyan Islamic Fighting Group or LIFG), and the Supreme Council of Libyan Revolutionaries.[50] However, the Salafis caused local consternation in Tripoli from late 2011 until mid-2013 as they attacked Sufi locations, with the acquiescence or approval of the security authorities; although these appear to have been vigilante operations.[51]

Under the GNC, the situation in Libya worsened with growing violence across the country in 2013 until early 2014, with Salafi militias emerging, especially in Benghazi in the east. In October 2013, an armed wing of the LROR kidnapped Prime Minister Ali Zeidan but later released him. The parliamentary elections of 25 June 2014, with all candidates running as independents, were overshadowed by violence, and there was only a third of the turnout of the 2012 elections, with just a fifth of the electorate voting, as some areas could not even vote for fear of being attacked. The second civil war in Libya was to start in 2014.[52]

In the aftermath of the 4 August 2014 parliamentary elections arranged by the GNC for the new House of Representatives (HoR), and the resulting escalating violence, Libya soon came to be divided. By 2015 the eastern region was allied with General Khalifah Haftar's Libyan National Army (LNA),[53] and backed by the UAE and Egypt. The HoR headquarters was established in Tobruk, after they refused to take the Tripoli buildings from the GNC, and the western region was affiliated with the so-called Libya Dawn, under the National Salvation Government, with backing from Qatar and Türkiye. Amid this chaos, the Salafis were divided. During this time, Hadiyah had, from his position in western Libya, declared his support for the Libya Dawn coalition, and urged Haftar to act honorably for the Libyan nation. In the east, Haftar's militancy had strengthened Salafi armed militias, who increasingly joined the battle against the western Libyans.[54]

These developments seemed to totally skew traditional understandings of Salafi typologies, with the quietist Madkhalis now seemingly becoming jihadi and involved in the political battle. Yet the reports from Rabiʿ al-Madkhalī at the beginning of the conflict only allowed his Salafis to take up arms in a case of necessity where they were directly under attack, and not to venture into other parts of the country and participate in battle. In early 2015, he forbade people to participate in the battle between the Libya Dawn and Haftar's forces but in July 2016 he urged direct action against the Benghazi Defense Brigades, which had Islamist roots and were opposing Haftar. Al-Madkhalī's framing of this exhortation was in terms that identified the Benghazi Defense Brigades as Muslim Brotherhood who were backed by Qatar, which played into the politics of the region at the time which set Qatar against Saudi, the UAE, and Egypt.[55]

In December 2015, the international community secured an agreement between some of the eastern and western Libyan factions, which was signed in Skhirat, Morocco. The agreement formed the Government of National Accord (GNA), but had not included all the relevant parties, such as important armed groups, as well as not clarifying Haftar's role, who still had the backing of important powerbrokers such as Egypt, UAE, France, and Russia. This flawed agreement would further strengthen the Madkhali faction. A number of Madkhali leaders were forced to leave Tripoli in 2014 as they were pressured by the forces controlling the government there at the time; however, the GNA enabled such leaders to return to Tripoli, as the internationally-backed treaty supported and relied upon such Madkhali factions. In particular, there was a dependency on the Special Deterrence Force led by Kara in Tripoli (which also assisted other Madkhali militias in the country, including in southern Libya), to strengthen the GNA in its precarious state. The Special Deterrence Force took on an important role in guarding and servicing the Central Bank for the GNA, as well as engaging in counterterrorist operations against Jihadi-Salafi cells linked to ISIS, together with running their prison with its rehabilitative program for extremists, using a variety of texts from quietist Salafi scholars like Salih al-Fawzan and al-Albānī. Madkhali forces contributed to similar offensives against Jihadi-Salafis around the country, as in the spring 2016 mission in Sirte. Yet it was reported that more aggressive acts of a more doctrinal nature were committed against activists and others by sub-sections of the Special Deterrence Force, without being commanded directly by the hierarchy.[56]

As Haftar tried to declare victory in 2017, the Madkhali militias, along with others, had developed into powerful and wealthy entities, both militarily and socially, in Tripoli and elsewhere in Libya. The Madkhalis had expanded into maintaining religious endowments (*awqāf*) and other aspects of religious life in the region; appointing Salafi mosque imams, controlling businesses engaged in selling media, and establishing schools in Sirte after Madkhalis came to control the city after eliminating the threat from ISIS sympathizers. This was despite tensions with fellow fighters from Misrata, who were distrustful of the Madkhalis' seemingly close relations with Haftar (to whom they were historically opposed), as most of the Madkhalis in this offensive belonged to Haftar's tribe and were not Salafis. In addition to their base in eastern Libya, the Madkhalis expanded into the south and even Misrata itself.[57]

When Haftar's forces attacked Tripoli on 4 April 2019, in an act that undermined the UN-backed plan for a transition from the GNA, the Madkhali and Salafi factions were divided in supporting Haftar across the region, as a number of factors – religious as well as socio-political – began to emerge. The one factor which divided the Madkhalis, including those in Tripoli among the Special Deterrence Force, was who was the legitimate ruler who had to be obeyed, which some considered to be Haftar on the basis of him having compelling power, and others held to be the GNA, with its international support.[58]

In June 2019, a unit of the Special Deterrence Force, under the command of Mahmud Hamzah, attacked Haftar's forces, with Madkhalis believed to be among the forces. The Madkhalis in Misrata were understood to have generally supported the fighters defending the city against Haftar's troops, with the Misratan Madkhali Anwar Faraj al-Swessi publicly declaring that Haftar's assault was a 'betrayal,'[59] even if they did not actually engage in physical fighting in Tripoli. The Madkhalis were likewise split in Zawiya and Zintan. In such troubling circumstances, it is unsurprising that leading Libyan Madkhalis, like Majdi Hafalah and Tariq Durman, chose the path of silence for the most part, even after the former allegedly met the Saudi King Salman at this time, which would be considered a moment when he came to be convinced to support the western Libyan forces. Nonetheless, Durman did eventually oppose Haftar's LNA, under the leadership of Usamah al-Juwayli from Zintan. Consequently, he was lambasted by the Egyptian Madkhali, Khalid ibn 'Uthman al-Masri, who even criticized Saudi clerics, like Salih al-Fawzan, for not firmly rebuking Durman for his actions. Such fanatical Egyptian Madkhalis heaped praise upon Haftar for fighting those they deemed to be *Khawarij* and urged Libyan Salafis to back his efforts.[60]

It remains to be seen how the Libyan civil war, and in particular the Madkhali involvement, alters the typologies of Salafism. To a certain extent there are elements among the Madkhali fighters who distinguish between an unlawful 'political war' (*harb siyasi*) and a lawful religious war against those they deemed to be the *Khawarij* (which, for Madkhalis, includes the Muslim Brotherhood). The general Salafi and particular Madkhali approach to legitimating a ruler based on who has the most power effectively makes the faction a political pendulum, swinging from one powerful grouping to another, while inexplicably claiming a sound theological basis for such inconsistency – thus, for them, yesterday's condemned dissenters (*khawarij*) can become tomorrow's legitimate ruler (*wali al-amr*) deserving of full obedience. In short, for the quietist Salafis, power is its own justification. In Libya the Madkhali factions, in both the eastern and western parts of the country, justified their being co-opted into competing political entities on the basis that they were obeying the most powerful ruler of their province. This naturally led to scholarly divides among them. Hence, when the Saudi Madkhali Usamah al-'Utaybi toured the eastern province in 2017 and praised Haftar and his LNA, al-'Utaybi was prevented from touring in the west by the resident Madkhali Tariq Durman. Thus Madkhalis are left as mere political pawns rather than principled politicians with any program for social reform.[61] Politics is simply decided by force and the role of Madkhalis is to submit.

Nonetheless, even in the course of outlining increasing Madkhali power in Libya, one must acknowledge that the Madkhalis have not always had their own way even in the east. For example, in April 2019, a Madkhali was removed as the director of religious endowments and was replaced by a Sufi, which indicates the surviving vitality of the Sufi tradition throughout the country.[62] This perhaps allays the fears that the Madkhalis could become a unified political force in Libya, as across the globe they cannot remain theologically and politically united among themselves. In the Libyan context, the Madkhalis have not only had to contend with their own divides along numerous lines as indicated in this chapter, but they were also the unfortunate recipients of non-Libyan divides, which have negatively impacted them and split their ranks. For instance, there was first the divide between Rabi' al-Madkhalī and Abu al-Hasan al-Ma'ribi around 2002 and 2003, and then later Rabi' al-Madkhalī with Muhammad ibn Hadi al-Madkhalī around 2017 and 2018. Such trends seem bound to continue. Ultimately, Madkhalis, as illustrated in the Libyan context, are perhaps most like their Wahhabi antecedents: religious foot-soldiers content with obeying a powerful ruler – even a religiously-compromised one – as long as they are allowed to control religious institutions and set the tone for religious discourse in civil society, i.e., to ‘enjoin the good and forbid the evil’ as they narrowly perceive it.

A further complication to the typologies of Salafism is raised by one of the main rivals to the Madkhalis, namely the Grand Mufti of the country, Sadiq al-Ghariani. His apparent Islamist leanings make Madkhalis dismiss his followers as ‘Ma’ribis,’ after their nemesis Abu al-Hasan al-Ma’ribi. Al-Ghariani, from Tripoli, with PhDs in Islamic law from Al-Azhar University and the University of Exeter in England, was a supporter of the 2011 uprising and was made Mufti of the country in 2012 by the transitional government. He has accused the Madkhalis of being spies. Although he is seen as being Mālikī in his legal methodology, albeit a reformist one, he is understood to be Salafi in theology, but favorably disposed to all sorts of activist Islamic groups. Nonetheless, he has a widespread influence in the country, and is an arch-opponent of the Madkhalis. But Madkhali factions, including Kara’s Special Deterrence Force in Tripoli, have dealt a harsh blow to the Islamists and supporters of al-Ghariani, with many killed by the Madkhalis as they deem such people to be Khārijis, whose blood can be lawfully shed. This included the slaying, in 2016, of IUM graduate Nadir al-Umrani, who was the head of al-Ghariani’s research council in Tripoli (with reports indicating that his murder was due to anti-Madkhali statements and was sanctioned by the Egyptian Madkhali Muhammad Sa‘id Raslan).[63] However, after a short crackdown, the Madkhalis were able to return to prominence.[64]

Ultimately, the future of Salafism in Libya looks to have a highly variegated near future. Once stability arrives in Libya, although we do not know by what means, Libyan Salafism is likely to assume a prominent role in the global movement, even if the form of the triumphant tendency remains unclear.

### *6.1.4 Nigeria*

Nigeria is the most populous country in Africa, and the sixth largest Muslim country in the world. With a Muslim majority in the north of the country (although in totality, the country is around 50% Muslim, with the other significant religious group being Christians),[65] Salafism has succeeded in forging a position for itself.[66]

Salafism in Nigeria began as an anti-Sufi movement. Its central figure, Abubakar Gumi, received his legal training in Nigeria and was Grand Khadi, or Chief Religious Judge, in the northern region of Nigeria for a short time in the 1960s.[67] Gumi was the religious advisor to the northern Nigerian Premier Ahmadu Bello (d. 1966), who had a close relationship with Saudi Arabia, and was the founding vice president of the Muslim World League.

Gumi acted as his representative and this position allowed him to develop his own links with Saudi Arabia.[68]

As an anti-Sufi with esteemed political contacts, it is not surprising that Gumi was a member of the Islamic University of Medina's Advisory Council (*al-majlis al-istishārī*), upon its first meeting in 1962, although not all Nigerian students at the IUM were Salafi, and some maintained unease with his criticisms of Sufism, as indicated when Gumi visited the students in 1964. Gumi was on IUM's Advisory Council until about 1974 and was then a member of the IUM's Highest Council (*al-majlis al-aʿlā*) between 1978 and 1987. He also received the sponsorship of the Muslim World League for his Hausa translation of the Qurʾan in 1979 and was awarded the 1989 King Faisal Award for services to Islam. Nonetheless, he was not a subscriber to all aspects of modern Salafism, as he still adhered to the Mālikī school of Islamic law, esteemed the Sufi ʻUthman dan Fodio as his fourth most important African scholar, quoted Sayyid Qutb in his commentary of the Qurʾan, and was not a keen adherent of the Wahhabi canon, or even the works of Muhammad Ibn ʿAbd al-Wahhāb. Moreover, he passionately advocated voting in elections and being a part of the political process (as he himself was for most of his adult life).

The pathway towards full Salafism continued with another proto-Salafi movement, *Jamāʿat Izālat al-Bidʿa wa-Iqāmat al-Sunna* (The Society for Removing Heretical Innovation and Establishing the Sunna). The latter was formed in 1978 in Jos by Ismail Idris (d. 2000) and was popular in the 1980s. The founder was, in many ways, similar to Gumi, in that he received his Islamic training in Nigeria and was a Mālikī, but he was passionately anti-Sufi, despite being inspired by ʻUthman dan Fodio to name and direct the group. As a bastion of anti-Sufi rhetoric, his movement attracted figures who would go on to become popular Salafi preachers in Nigeria, such as Jaʿfar Ādam (d. 2007).[69]

Between 1982 and 1997, the IUM conducted recruitment tours throughout the world, with Nigeria receiving the most attention; hence many Nigerians would go on to study at the IUM and develop into Salafi leaders upon their return. Between 1965 and 2001, 856 Nigerians graduated from IUM, including two with doctorate degrees, and this placed Nigeria behind only Yemen, Pakistan, Indonesia, India, and Eritrea in foreign graduates.[70] IUM graduates who returned to Nigeria in the 1990s and 2000s often came back with a firmer adherence to the Salafi canon and doctrine than their predecessors named above, and did not refer to themselves as members of *Izalah* but rather as icons of *Ahl al-Sunna*. In general, the returning IUM graduates sided with the leading figures of the quietist Salafis, like Ibn Bāz, rather than the politicos, although the global charity *al-Muntada al-Islami* (Islamic Forum), affiliated with the politicos, funded numerous Salafi projects in Nigeria, including those led by Jaʿfar Ādam.

Indeed, by way of further complicating the definition of such Salafis, leaders such as Ādam and Rijiyar Lemo began to differ with the hardline anti-Sufi line of the *Izalah* leadership and took on a more tolerant stance. This was perhaps a way of not replicating the violence which erupted between Salafis and Sufis in the 1980s which led to bloodshed, although they still engaged in critiques of Sufi practices like the celebration of the Prophet Muhammad's birthday (*mawlid*).

In terms of northern Nigerian politics, one finds Salafis who support local politicians and those who do not, and Jaʿfar Ādam positioned himself between the two stances. Thus, it is difficult to neatly demarcate such Salafis in Nigeria into quietist and politico camps. Nonetheless, a major crisis for the Salafi movement in Nigeria was the emergence of Boko Haram from within their Salafi circles (discussed in section 5.5.2), as the founder, Muhammad Yusuf, had been a student of Jaʿfar Ādam before their split. Of course, like all mainstream Salafis, most Nigerian Salafis have rejected such Jihadi-Salafism as a deviation from the correct Salafi methodology.[71]

### *6.1.5 Sudan*

The roots of Salafism in Sudan go back to ʻAbd al-Rahman Abu Hajar (d. 1939), an Algerian who had studied at Al-Azhar University in Egypt.[72] He settled in Sudan and from his study circle in the western city of al-Nahud would emerge students who formed the first Salafi organization in 1939, namely, *Ansar al-Sunna* (Helpers of the Sunnah), which has gone on to become the strongest Salafi organization in the country; it was notably led by Muhammad Hashim al-Hadiyyah from 1952 until his death on 19 September 2007.[73]

*Ansar al-Sunna* was influenced by the organization with the same name founded by al-Fiqi in Egypt but remained independent from them. So, although it was traditional like its Egyptian namesake, it has been characterized as political in orientation with a number of parliamentarians over time (which is not the case with the Egyptian counterpart), despite being more apolitical and focused on preaching before the Islamist coup of 1989. Nonetheless, it is not violent, unlike the perceived notion of the relatively small group called *al-Rabitah al-sharʻiah li'l-ʻulama' wa'l-duʻat* (The Legitimate League for Religious Scholars). The latter was founded in 2004, with some founding fathers trained in Saudi universities, and is understood to be Jihadi-Salafi, as they have been accused of advocating violence and widespread excommunication of other Muslims. However, it is possible that this Jihadi-Salafi definition might be a slightly exaggerated classification in light of them opposing the 2004 peace process which led to the south of Sudan gaining independence in 2011. They criticized the regime in the strongest terms as abandoning Islamic law on the matter and being part of the pre-Islamic ignorance (*jahiliyyah*).[74] Although these two Salafi groups differed in such fundamental ways, while also agreeing on Salafi essentials, they did come together with other Salafis and other Islamic groups by the 2000s, to form the Front for Islamic Constitution (FIC), a movement towards a Salafi reform of the constitution.[75]

As argued by Abdelwahab El-Affendi, traditionalist Salafism, under the influence of Saudi scholars, remained a small and insignificant trend in Sudan until the 1960s and 1970s. Yet the University of Khartoum became a site of gathering intellectual competition between lecturers in the mid-1960s, including the Islamist Hasan al-Turabi and Salafis like Jafar Shaikh Idrees and Jafar Mirghani, with the latter being seen as academically-focused Salafis rather than later 'Sururi' trends among the university faculty which were seen as more political and radical, as discussed below.[76] Nonetheless, such Sudanese Salafis were often aligned with the Islamists in the country, which was sometimes a collective which included Sufi groups.

During this initial period, the Salafi trend was not popular among youth; however, by the end of the 1990s, the Salafis developed an increasing influence among university students, following the Islamist coup in 1989 by the National Islamic Front (NIF). Thus, the Islamic revival led by the Islamists was one that they were unable to retain full control of, and both Salafis and Sufis strengthened their constituencies as a result of benefitting from the establishment of Islam as a social determiner, whereby they could articulate their own competing visions of the religion. In 2006, Hasan al-Turabi, the foremost ideologue of the NIF and long-considered the de facto leader, lamented that the Islamists' entry into government and the focus it required left the social arena, including the mosques, with a void that these other Islamic groupings sought to fill.[77] During this time, the *Ansar al-Sunna* was able to benefit from generous financial support provided by the Sudanese government, Saudi Arabia and Kuwait. Consequently, the Sudanese Salafi landscape is divided by various activist Salafis such as *Ansar al-Sunna*, and university lecturers Yusuf 'Abd al-Hayy and 'Ala al-Din al-Zāki, who are characterized as being heavily influenced by Muhammad al-Surur (and are therefore called 'Sururis') although al-Zāki, a graduate of the IUM, is perhaps to be seen as more radical in light of his being a founding member of the Legitimate League for Religious Scholars.

In the aftermath of Hasan al-Turabi being removed from the government in 1999, *Ansar al-Sunna* aligned with the ruling regime led by President Omar al-Bashir,[78] and rhetoric could be heard in Salafi circles portraying the Muslim Brotherhood as the worst of Islamic trends.[79] This type of behavior put such Sudanese Salafis in line with many of their brethren in Saudi Arabia, UAE, Egypt, and Libya (as discussed throughout this book). The developing political scene led to *Ansar al-Sunna* splitting shortly after this time into a more political wing (Headquarters or *al-Markaz al-'amm*) and a wing (Reform or *al-Islah*) more loyalist to the regime with a limited notion of political activism. Nonetheless, the *Ansar al-Sunna*, past or present, Headquarters or Reform, are unanimous in affording the legitimate leader full obedience and not revolting against him (or her, as the Sudanese constitution of 2005 permits a female head of state).

Ultimately, the lack of despotism in the Sudanese regime, compared to neighbors at the same time in North Africa and the Middle East, explains the dominance of activist Salafism in Sudan, compared to other countries where apolitical or loyalist brands of Salafism have been supported to the point of dominance over other Salafi groupings. Aside from the violence of the small Sudanese Jihadi-Salafis, *Ansar al-Sunna* supporters have been accused of minor acts of violence against Sufis, especially during celebrations of the Prophet's birthday (*mawlid*); but such vigilantism has always been condemned by the group's leadership, despite the hierarchy not being accommodating of such Sufi practices. From the perspective of the regime, they have supported both Sufis and Salafis – who have maintained relatively cordial relations at the top of their groups, notwithstanding their deep theoretical divide – which has been an excellent method of maintaining their own control; these opposing factions stay away from leading government and focus on matters of Islamic ritual, and neither the Salafis nor the Sufis have developed political entities which look capable of upsetting the political status quo.

### *6.1.6 Mauritania*

Although modern Salafism in Mauritania can be traced back to roots in the 1920s, it only significantly emerged during the late 1970s and 1980s as Saudi and Gulf funding came to be directed to the country. This was achieved through the establishment of charities and mosques, and Mauritanians who had studied in Saudi Arabia returned to the country, as well as the availability of printed Salafi works.[80] Nevertheless, the articulation of Salafism in Mauritania has had to maintain a strong connection to the dominant scholarly traditions of the majority non-Salafi scholars, so its critiques are mildly articulated and made to appeal to the existent religious sensibilities. In a country of only around 4 million people, which has undergone long-term economic hardship, and has suffered military political interventions since 1978, together with having to contend with widespread corruption, and deep racial and social divides, Salafism has come to be something of a toxic element in an already volatile situation. This came to a head in the mid-2000s, from 2005 until 2011, with the emergence of attacks by home-grown Jihadi-Salafis, who were then disowned by the mainstream Salafis, who sided with the government.[81]

Due to his work reforming the Mālikī school of law, which dominates Africa, Buddah al-Buṣayrī (d. 2009) is seen as the leading scholar of the Salafi trend. However, from his position as the imam of a Saudi-funded mosque in the capital Nouakchott, he was actually an inspiration to Islamists, Tablighis, and Salafis of all types, from Jihadis to politicos to quietists who were state loyalists, which all exist in Mauritania to a rather limited extent, compared to the dominant Mālikī-Sufi scholarly tradition. Furthermore, while he was Salafi in creed, much of his legal output was within a broad Mālikī legal domain. Another major scholar from Mauritania, Muhammad Salim Ould Addoud (d. 2009) – head of the Supreme Court from 1982 to 1988 and Minister of Culture and Islamic Orientation from 1988 to 1991, and head of Mauritania's Supreme Islamic Council[82] – was also Salafi in creed, but his flexibility in the Mālikī school was still defined by an overall adherence to the school. However, Ould Addoud was a political loyalist to the regime.[83]

It is difficult to define al-Buṣayrī in strict Salafi terms, due to his being largely loyal to the Mālikī school and not known for the sort of Salafi-like polemics against Sufism. However, one can see a more distinct Salafi persuasion in his son-in-law and successor in his Nouakchott Mosque, Ahmad Ould Lembrabott, and al-Buṣayrī's student Muhammad Salim al-Majlisi. Furthermore, the observable Salafi tendencies of Mauritanians' methods of prayer, reading habits and doubtful approach to Sufism have been noted as displaying a Salafi influence.[84]

The importance of Mauritania in discussing the history of Salafism is highlighted in the 'post-Salafi' trajectory of one of her scholars who is seen as Salafi, Muhammad al-Hasan al-Dedew (b. 1963). Al-Dedew is unquestionably one of the most popular global scholars of our times, and one who garners respect not only from mainstream Salafis, but from many in the Brotherhood, and Sufis and non-Salafi movements. Some view him as a successor to Qaradawi, yet without a doubt he comes from Salafism and is now considered post-Salafi (as we shall discuss later in this chapter).

Al-Dedew is Salafi in the same way as his maternal uncle and teacher, Ould Addoud, who was given an official commendation (*tazkiyat*) from 'Abd al-'Aziz Al al-Shaykh, the Grand Mutfi of Saudi Arabia. He had studied in a traditional seminary as well as a modern university in Mauritania, before going on to pursue a master's degree at Imam Muhammad bin Saud University in Saudi Arabia. He has gone on to become a popular religious scholar, with an involvement in Islamist political activism, as well as forming an Islamic university in Mauritania. However, his own personal Salafism has not prevented him from providing a wide definition of Islamic orthodoxy, while also holding a positive attitude towards non-Salafis like Ashʿarīs, Sufis and average Shiʿi believers. As such, al-Dedew places himself in a progressive Salafi light.

## *6.2 The Middle East*

### *6.2.1 Syria*

Only a few Salafi scholars remained active in Syria from the mid-1960s until the late 1970s, after the regime's purge of the Muslim Brotherhood, such that a visiting Saudi scholar noted in 1978 that he only met two Salafi scholars during his visit: al-Albānī and ʻAbd al-Qadir al-Arna'ut (d. 2004). The latter, incidentally, was also a member of the same Damascene immigrant community as al-Albānī and had trained as a Ḥanafī with Salih al-Farfur (d. 1986). He only received a primary school education and was a watchmaker, who would become famous as an editor and hadith specialist. However, in contrast to al-Albānī, al-Arna'ut was a more conciliatory figure and had a good relationship with the traditionalist Sufi scholars.[85]

After al-Albānī's migration to Jordan, ʻAbd al-Qadir al-Arna'ut was considered the Salafi leader within Syria, even though his followers were few; and this reaffirmed the persistence of mainly apolitical Salafism in the country. But the security forces started to harass such quietist Salafis during the mid-1990s, despite the Salafis' lack of political ambition, with ʻAbd al-Qadir al-Arna'ut being banned from public talks. Such scrutiny by the Syrian regime continued until 2001, even though the Salafis were marginal as a social phenomenon and not a political threat. This was the case because the majority of the Syrian scholars followed the traditionalist *kalam-madhhab-tariqa* tripartite approach to the religion and were able to influence the regime against their religious opponents, especially after they sensed that Salafi popularity was starting to grow among the youth.[86]

However, with the 9/11 attacks and the demarcation of Salafism as a global threat to security, the harassment of the Syrian Salafis by security forces increased, especially after the emergence of Jihadi-Salafi elements from 2004. In the same year, Muhammad Saʻid Ramadan al-Buti (d. 2013), a staunch opponent of the Salafis in general, and al-Albānī in particular, as well as being perhaps the primary clerical supporter of the regime, praised the government crackdown on Salafism. There were reports of suspected Salafis in traditional Sunni seminaries being questioned by the secret police, and then expelled even if they simply failed to convince the authorities of their sectarian persuasion.[87]

The leadership of the Salafis was further weakened by ʻAbd al-Qadir al-Arna'ut's passing in 2004, while under a partial house arrest, without a discernible leader left after him in Damascus, and leading Salafis from Aleppo having moved to the Gulf. Nonetheless, Salafis continued to propagate their stances against the old orthodoxy, especially the perceived excesses of the Sufis, including sober ones like al-Buti, and were aided by internet websites and satellite channels that beamed into Syria from outside. Also, not all upholders of the old orthodoxy against Salafism were as aggressive as al-Buti, hence Usama al-Rifa'i, the leader of the traditionalist group *Jama'at Zayd*, performed the eulogy at 'Abd al-Qadir al-Arna'ut's funeral and spoke of his 'Salafi brothers.'[88]

Salafism was not, in numerical terms, a major movement in Syria, but it still impacted governmental policy in significant ways. Although its adherents could be found among the politically-orientated Syrian Muslim Brotherhood (SMB) in the middle of the twentieth century, the quietist form of Salafism came to be dominant, as the Syrian government successfully oppressed and eliminated the SMB presence in the country, after the brutal quelling of the Hama uprising in 1982 – in which two thirds of the mainly Sunni city was demolished, and over ten thousand people were killed. Despite the near removal of Salafism from the Syrian landscape by the end of the twentieth century, Salafism played a major part in galvanizing the old orthodoxy before this time. Not only did it force some quarters to revise certain Sufi practices and revive hadith studies in Damascus, but it also led to major Syrian scholars becoming part of what has been called an 'anti-Salafi international,' buttressed by the Jordanian Royal Aal al-Bayt Institute for Islamic Thought[89] and the Al-Azhar University hierarchy in Egypt.[90]

However, the attempted Syrian revolution since 2011 has given Salafism a renewed impetus in Syria, with a significant attraction to Salafis engaged in jihad,[91] and Jihadi-Salafism[92], especially in the non-urban centers – although the Jihadi-Salafis would emerge dominant over the other Salafi fighters by the end of 2014, with the rise of ISIS.[93] This development of a newly-found openness to Salafism among the populace could perhaps be attributable to the notion that much of the old orthodoxy was aligned with, or perceived to be aligned with, the regime, and hence seen as tolerant of, or even complicit in, the repression many ordinary Syrians suffered.[94] The Syrian Civil War further complicated the more common ways of categorizing Salafis, as ostensibly quietist Salafis like Saudi-based 'Adnan al-'A'rur supported the uprising, while not supporting uprisings against Sunni regimes in the region. Al-'A'rur support for rebellion against Assad can be explained by the fact that Assad is an Alawite, hence not a legitimate leader, unlike Sunni Muslim dictators who are similarly repressive. Although the civil war in Syria is grinding to a slow halt, after over a decade of devastation, the country remains in an acute humanitarian crisis. We do not know what role Salafism will play once civil society emerges from the ashes.*

* As this book was going to press, President Assad fled to Russia as one of the Salafi-Jihadist groups, *Hay'at Tahrir al-Sham*, succeeded in overthrowing the remnants of the Syrian regime and installing a new government. This is undoubtedly an astonishing turn of events and will most definitely have multiple repercussions at the political and ideological levels. It remains to be seen how this Salafi-Jihadist movement will itself change and adapt, and whether it will succeed in forming a modern government and be accepted by other regional and global powers.

### *6.2.2 Jordan*

Salafism has roots in Jordan that precede al-Albānī, although it is true that the latter's settling in Jordan led to a quietist Salafi revival in the country.[95] In terms of Salafi beginnings, one can point to the Salafi theology of the Kingdom's first supreme judge, Muhammad al-Khadir al-Shinqiti (d. 1935). Furthermore, 'Ali al-Halabi has identified the Salafi roots with the influence of reformist-Salafis like Rashīd Riḍā and Muḥibb al-Dīn al-Khaṭīb (d. 1969) upon the country's founders, and then the importance of ʿAbdallah al-Qalqili (d. 1969), who served as the Mufti of Jordan, and Ibrahim al-Qattan (d. 1984), who was the country's supreme judge. Nonetheless, one cannot dismiss the fact that these people were anomalies in a country where the scholars were overwhelmingly non-Salafi. However, Salafism did start to gain prominence in Jordan from the 1950s. This trend started with two Jordanians who returned from studying at Al-Azhar University in Egypt and taught a Salafi Islam: Ahmad al-Salik (d. 2010) and Muhammad Ibrahim Shaqra (b. 1933).[96]

Ahmad al-Salik was born in Türkiye, to a scholarly father, who left Türkiye when Ahmad was six, concerned that Türkiye's growing secularism would harm his family's religiosity. Ahmad's father was a Sufi and became a prominent preacher in Amman, Jordan. In 1952, Ahmad went to study at Al-Azhar University; and he returned to Jordan in 1956 and began teaching, having been influenced by elements outside the Azhari curriculum, such as the works of Muhammad Ibn ʿAbd al-Wahhāb.

Shaqrah was a Palestinian who was forced to relocate to Jordan with his family in 1948, and he and Ahmad al-Salik would be close associates, going to Al-Azhar University together.[97] Shaqrah also became a Salafi while in Egypt, and the two friends would return and teach in two different mosques in the same area of Amman. Shaqrah would deepen his Salafi affiliation when he went to teach at the Islamic University of Medina in the early 1960s. Upon his return to Jordan, he and Ahmad al-Salik became prominent Salafi teachers, with Shaqrah the most significant Salafi in Jordan during the 1960s and the 1970s. Then these two prominent Salafi teachers were joined in 1976 by Muhammad Nasib al-Rifaʿi (d. 1992), from a leading Sufi family in Aleppo, Syria, who had been forced to leave Syria after being arrested and suspected by the Syrian regime of being a Wahhabi spy on behalf of the Saudis. In addition, the quietist Salafis like 'Ali al-Halabi would recognize Yusuf al-Barqawi (d. 2009), a mufti from Zarqa, as an important Jordanian Salafi, even though al-Barqawi was said to be deeply attached to the Ḥanbalī school of law, and clashed with al-Albānī about the issue of following schools – which is further indication that the following, or not following, of a legal school remained one of the enduring disputes among modern Salafis, unlike matters of theological essentials.[98]

Shaqrah and Ahmad al-Salik would be instrumental in al-Albānī coming to Jordan, after each had visited him in Damascus and invited him to come and teach. Indeed, as mentioned earlier, a number of the Jordanian Muslim Brotherhood (JMB) were attracted to al-Albānī's lessons in Jordan in the 1970s, but the relationship ended in the 1980s.[99] JMB members were soon to be banned by the hierarchy from attending al-Albānī's sessions as he openly criticized Muslim Brotherhood luminaries like Ḥasan al-Bannā and Sayyid Qutb. Increasing numbers of members were attracted to al-Albānī's alternative philosophy, such as Mashhur Hasan Salman, who became one of the leading quietist Salafis in Jordan. In many ways, such a divide between Islamists like the JMB and apolitical Salafis like al-Albānī is understandable, especially when one considers how the Salafis in the region, including the West Bank and Gaza Strip, have not contributed to a discourse that seeks to liberate Palestine (as they are accused of a 'de-Palestinized discourse'), which is the objective of the Islamists. Apolitical Salafism's emphasis on doctrine and personal ritual seems wholly at odds with the wider concerns of the region.[100]

Yet, while al-Albānī's message would reach throughout the country as a result of taped recordings of his sessions being spread and his informal visits around various parts of the Kingdom, his main influence was in Amman, where he was based. Furthermore, many of his followers were from lower economic classes and did not have university qualifications, like al-Albānī himself, and other leading associates of his, like 'Ali al-Halabi (although some did possess university PhDs, like Muhammad Musa Nasr, Husayn al-ʿAwayisha, and Basim al-Jawabira). A large number of his followers were also converts to Salafism from other Sunni groupings, like the Muslim Brotherhood and *Jama'at al-Tabligh*.[101]

Yet, in a short time, the prominent and quietist Salafis of Jordan would become embroiled in the international disputes that beset the global Salafi community. One such development was the *Ṣaḥwa* movement, which brought the Saudi Rabi' al-Madkhalī and the Jordanian 'Ali al-Halabi closer together, as they sought to counter and condemn it. Al-Halabi's attempts to co-opt his teacher al-Albānī initially failed, as the latter refused to proclaim a condemnation without being fully convinced of the evidence on the matter. However, this would change when al-Albānī was made aware of the disparaging comments made by the leading *Ṣaḥwa* scholar Safar al-Hawali in his PhD thesis, about al-Albānī's embrace of deviant principles of *irja'*, namely that the judgment of sinners can only be deferred to God on the Day of Judgment. This led al-Albānī to condemn al-Hawali, and al-Halabi apparently swiftly reported back to al-Madkhalī.[102] The apolitical Jordanian Salafis consequently launched into passionate condemnations of the *Ṣaḥwa* leaders, as well as the supposed cause of their fellow theological Salafis going astray: namely, the Muslim Brotherhood. While al-Albānī had always spoken of Qutb's mistakes, he was gentle with his refutations, for he admired the fact that Qutb had died for the faith at the hands of those he saw as enemies. He even saw Qutb as becoming closer to the Salafi methodology near the end of his life. But al-Albānī's Jordanian associates, like al-Halabi, would abandon such subtleties, especially after the First Gulf War, as the rise of the *Ṣaḥwa* threatened their very idea of Salafism.[103]

Initially, the unease on the part of the Jordanian quietist Salafis towards the *Ṣaḥwa* was a reflection of global or regional concerns, as the *Ṣaḥwa* were not a strong force in Jordan at the time. However, the ejection of 400,000 Palestinians from Kuwait after the Palestine Liberation Organization (PLO) backed Iraq in the beginning of the First Gulf War would impact the Salafi movement in Jordan. Many of them returned to Jordan as they were Jordanian citizens who had gone to work in Kuwait from the 1940s until the early 1960s. A number of these returning Palestinians were activist Salafis, with some having been influenced by the political Salafi movement in Kuwait. This was led by 'Abd al-Rahman 'Abd al-Khaliq (d. 2020) with his *Jam'iyyat Ihya' al-Turath al-Islami* (Revival of the Islamic Heritage Society), which was a political Salafi organization in Kuwait at the time, but would later become increasingly quietist after the First Gulf War in the 1990s, in the aftermath of 'Abd al-Rahman 'Abd al-Khaliq being expelled from the organization.[104] Two of the leading activist Salafis who returned to Jordan from Kuwait were Usamah Shahadah and Ihsan al-'Utaybi, with the former being based in Amman and the latter in Irbid.[105] The activists' vision of Salafism as more than the mere teaching of doctrine and personal worship of the quietists caused divisions in the Jordanian Salafi movement, but the quietist strand remained by far the dominant one.

The essence of political Salafism is to publicly challenge the rulers for their wrongdoing through peaceful means, and not through violence, but, at the same time, rejecting the quietist Salafi approaches of silence, aloofness or loyalist behavior. As articulated by 'Abd al-Rahman 'Abd al-Khaliq, this striving for the implementation of Islam did not preclude standing in elections, if one's goal was to adhere to and work for the establishment of Islamic law. Usamah Shahadah even argued that al-Albānī had been misrepresented by quietists, who simply quoted the latter saying, 'In the present circumstances, the good policy is to stay away from politics' (*min al-siyasa tark al-siyasa*). These words had been spoken in the context of the Syrian regime's oppression of Islamic currents, however, and that al-Albānī had actually supported the notion of Islamic politics and Islamic political parties if the circumstances warranted it as a better option. Furthermore, such activist Salafis engaged in wider economic and socio-political issues which were not directly linked to Salafi doctrine.[106]

Until al-Albānī's death in 1999, the quietist Salafis had maintained a unified public face, despite tensions emerging in his final years; however, the passing of their leader would lead to chaos in their ranks, and the emergence of, in the words of Mashhur Hasan Salman, 'the tribulation' (*fitna*).[107] 'Ali al-Halabi would be, in many ways, at the center of these controversies and ensuing divides, for he was accused of plagiarism, which started in al-Albānī's lifetime when he privately rebuked al-Halabi for plagiarizing a book by 'Abd al-Rahman 'Abd al-Khaliq. In 1994, al-Halabi endorsed a book[108] by Murad Shukri relating to faith and excommunication which was condemned for *irja'* by the Permanent Committee for Scientific Research and Legal Rulings (*al-Lajna al-Da'ima li'l-Buhuth al-'Ilmiyya wa'l-Ifta'*). Al-Halabi even had his name printed on the front of the book when he was not involved in its composition. Furthermore, he became embroiled in a leadership struggle with Muhammad Ibrahim Shaqra. However, the plagiarism accusations would be extended to Mashhur Hasan Salman and Salim al-Hilali.

Although 'Ali al-Halabi and his associates would appear to emerge victorious in this leadership battle, and went on to form the Imam al-Albānī Centre in 2001 in Amman,[109] the latter would also come into disrepute when the director, Salim al-Hilali, was accused of theft and fraud around 2006 and 2007. (Despite al-Hilali's pleas of innocence, he failed to hold on to his position.) Such disputes removed any utopian misconceptions that the quietist Salafis might have had. But the victory of the Halabites led to the dominant group being incorporated into the regime, certainly as a response to survive in the 'age of terror' wherein Salafis fell under suspicion as 'extremists' and 'terrorists.' This political move might not have emerged if the more independent-minded Shaqrah and his allies had gained prominence. In addition, such closeness to the Jordanian royal family appeared to oppose the apolitical 'aloofness' that characterized al-Albānī's approach to rulers. Indeed, from 2003, the quietists had managed to become part of the 'official Islam' of the Kingdom, as seen by the endorsement of 'moderate Salafi Islamic thought' under the Amman Interfaith Message arranged by the Jordanian regime in 2005, and the Minister for Religious Endowments claiming in 2014 that most Salafi imams in the Kingdom were the 'moderate' type. The quietists further endeared themselves to the regime by countering Jihadi-Salafism and labeling the adherents as modern-day *Khāwarij*.[110] Nonetheless, the regime retains its skepticism about the quietist movement in light of their retention of staunch beliefs and the implications of those in the future if the right socio-political factors were to favor such Salafis.[111]

The beginning of the Arab Spring of 2010, with the removal, most notably, of long-term Arab dictators in Tunisia, Libya, and Egypt in 2011, was welcomed in activist Salafi circles in Jordan. Usamah Shahadah praised the work of the Muslim Brotherhood and the Salafi Al-Nour Party in Egypt, with their success in the democratic elections after the Arab Spring. He also spoke of how such developments had led to Salafis in Jordan analyzing these events and seeing how they could better organize themselves in their own country, even giving consideration to forming a political party, although the latter failed to materialize due to the undeveloped state of Jordanian Salafism.

Of course, such a developing political Salafism, with its apparent commonality with the Muslim Brotherhood, has caused unease on the part of the regime and quietist Salafis. Indeed, the latter viewed the Arab Spring with distrust, and they did not endorse measures that entailed public protests and the like, in accordance with quietist Salafis throughout the region. Al-Halabi even criticized the Egyptian Salafis for joining the political process, in what he saw as a contravention of al-Albānī's directive to avoid all politics (in his understanding of the statement which Shahadah interpreted differently, as discussed above). For the loyalists like al-Halabi, Shahadah and the like were not really Salafi, and were influenced by Sufism and secularism. Consequently, one sees quietist Salafism as one of the main supporters of the old order.[112]

### *6.2.3 Lebanon*

The roots of Salafism in Lebanon are seen in the 1930s, with the influence of Saudi Wahhabism emerging, particularly in Tripoli. However, the first Salafi organization was established in the country in 1946 by Salim al-Shahal (b. 1922), called *Shabab Muhammad* (Muhammad's Youth) and later *Muslimūn* (Muslims).[113] Al-Shahal was a self-taught man who had turned to Salafism after initially being influenced by Rashīd Riḍā's *al-Manar*,[114] and developed good links with Ibn Bāz in Saudi Arabia and al-Albānī. Hence two of his sons, Da'i al-Islam and Radi al-Islam, and numerous other Lebanese Salafis went to study at Saudi universities, in particular the Islamic University of Medina, during al-Shahal's time as a Salafi leader in Lebanon.[115]

In the late 1980s, al-Shahal formed the *Jam'iyyat al-Hidayah wa'l-Ihsan al-Islamiyyah* (Islamic Association of Guidance and Charity), which was Saudi funded and Salafi in its ideology, and established mosques, schools, charities, and orphanages during the 1990s, but remained peripheral to Lebanese society, despite being the leading Salafi group in Tripoli.[116] Primarily, this movement has been quietist, notwithstanding al-Shahal's unsuccessful standing for parliament in 1992, although it came under a general crackdown on Salafis in the country following the murder of a leading pro-Syria politician in 1995, as al-Shahal's movement taught that the Alawites who ruled Syria were heretics. The situation did not change as Jihadi-Salafi forces clashed with the Lebanese authorities through the late 1990s into the 2000s. Indeed, in such a climate, *Jam'iyyat al-Hidayha wa'l-Ihsan al-Islamiyyah* was closed down by the government in 1996 and al-Shahal was imprisoned until the Syrians left Lebanon in 2005, after an occupation of close to thirty years. Yet this movement became more involved in politics following the murder of the former prime minister Rafiq Hariri in 2005.[117]

The most notable Salafi seminary in Lebanon was established in 1993 by Sa'd al-Din ibn Muhammad al-Kibbi (b. 1960) in Akkar, named the Bukhari Institute (*Ma'had al-Bukhari*), with a strong influence of al-Albānī in its teaching methodology, and is quietist by nature. Many of those who graduate from this institution go on to further studies in Saudi Arabia.[118] In addition, there are many more Salafi institutions which run in Lebanon, without official recognition. Furthermore, a number of international Salafi charities have made important contributions to Salafi institutions in Lebabon, namely the Kuwaiti *Jam'iyyat Ihya' al-Turath al-Islami* (The Society for the Revival of Islamic Heritage), the Saudi *Mu'assassat al-Haramayn al-Khayriyyah* (Haramayn Charity Foundation) and the Saudi Ministry of Religious Endowments (*awqaf*), and Qatar's *Mu'assassat Shaykh Eid al-Thani al-Khayriyah* (Shaykh Eid al-Thani Charitable Organization).[119]

The Salafi community in Tripoli would remain largely united until the late 1990s.[120] Being a new phenomenon in the country, Salafis are often converts to the movement, with a fair proportion coming from the Muslim Brotherhood (like al-Kibbi) and Sufis (including from the controversial al-Ahbash, whose Ethiopian leader, 'Abdullah al-Harawi, had based himself in Lebanon and had the support of the Syrian occupiers).[121]

With the withdrawal of Syria from Lebanon in 2005, Salafism in Lebanon received significant funding from Kuwait and UAE; and *Jam'iyyat al-Hidayah wa'l-Ihsan al-Islamiyyah* was reopened shortly thereafter. Then, with the emergence of Egyptian Salafi satellite channels from 2006, which could be viewed in Lebanon, Lebanese Salafi leaders perceived an increased popularity for Salafism as a result of the viewing of these apolitical Salafi preachers.[122]

However, the rise of the Iran-backed Shi'i Hezbollah, as well as the Syrian war from 2011, led to a growing political Salafism in the country, such as that of the Salafi cleric Zakariya 'Abd al-Razzaq al-Masri (the first Lebanese to attain a PhD at IUM), and the circle around Da'i al-Islam (the son of Salim al-Shahal), together with the emergence of powerful Jihadi-Salafi groups in areas of crisis and heightened sectarian tensions. But this political awakening did not lead to mobilized Salafi organization, and certainly no Salafi political party; even the Arab Spring did not inspire a coherent political agenda and methodology, despite events awakening a greater political awareness and voice among many Salafis. This lack of impact and structure is perhaps not surprising considering that they form under 4% of the influential northern population. Salafis in Lebanon, as the world over, are also divided among themselves, perhaps as a result of the varied sources that fund Salafi projects – Saudi Arabia, Kuwait, UAE, and Qatar – a situation which brings with it a host of political complications, leading to political lethargy. The crux of their political agenda revolves around the Sunni community receiving due protection, with the expanse of Hezbollah curtailed, while they have freedom to preach their self-defined version of a purified faith.[123]

### *6.2.4 Kuwait*

Kuwait's political system, with its constitutional monarchy, free press and democratically-elected parliament (candidates must stand as independents because political parties are not legalized in Kuwait), has impacted the nature of Salafism in the country, and has presented a more open, politically-orientated version that has troubled the dominant apolitical forms of Salafism which are most popular around the world. Although Salafism is likely to have arrived in Kuwait in the beginning of the twentieth century via links with Saudi Arabia, it only started to become a significant presence in the late 1960s. This growth was through the arrival of three foreign Salafi leaders into the country at this time: 'Abd al-Rahman 'Abd al-Khaliq from Egypt (although he graduated from the IUM); Abdullah al-Sabt from Palestine; and Umar al-Ashqar, a Palestinian who studied at the IUM, obtained a PhD at Al-Azhar in Egypt, and who was a Salafi but also aligned with the Muslim Brotherhood.

Salafism in Kuwait, as with much of the Arab world, was aided by the 1967 defeat of the Arabs by Israel, which dented faith in Arab nationalism and turned more people towards religion as they engaged in soul-searching as to the causes of such a disastrous and humiliating event. Then, in the early 1970s, Salafism was able to penetrate the merchant and political classes in the country, with the Salafi-inclined politician Khalid Sultan being crucial in this regard, and the merchant class being the means towards the political class, in general, due to their powerful political contacts and position. It was during the 1970s that some Kuwaiti Salafis joined the Muslim Brotherhood, while others debated with the Muslim Brotherhood over correct doctrine and methodology. Then, with the Iranian Revolution in 1979, Salafism received a boost in Kuwait due to a number of factors. Firstly, the Iranian state posed a military threat, and militant Shiʿi cells started to emerge in Kuwait, a country with a Shiʿi population that consisted of around a third of the total, as Khomeini looked to export his revolution. Secondly, the Iranian Revolution boosted the political aspirations of the Muslim Brotherhood, so the royal family took to supporting Salafism as a counter to the Brotherhood's growing popularity. Thirdly, as the royal family backed Saddam Hussein's Iraq in its war with Iran between 1980 and 1988, it used its support of local Salafism as a means of achieving some level of Islamic legitimacy.[124]

Salafism emerged in the early 1980s as a rival to the Muslim Brotherhood in Kuwait and was able to penetrate the labor organizations and student bodies. However, its most significant development was the formation, in

1981, of the *Jam'iyyat Ihya' al-Turath al-Islami* (The Revival of Islamic Heritage Society, or RIHS). This was founded as a charitable organization which eventually expanded into education and proselytization in more than fifty countries, including non-Arab countries like Indonesia, Yemen, Lebanon, and Bosnia.[125] Furthermore, RIHS assisted in supporting Kuwaiti Salafis move into conventional politics, and aided the *al-Tajammu' al-Salafi al-Islami* (Salafi Islamic Gathering), which was formed in 1981 and became the biggest Salafi parliamentary grouping.[126]

This break with the dominant apolitical Salafism which opposed democratic politics was the result of 'Abd al-Rahman 'Abd al-Khaliq's role as the pioneering ideologue of activist Salafism, whose writings, such as those in his weekly-publication *al-Watan* (*The Homeland*), concentrated on political affairs – he had even used his publishing space, in late 1978, to refute the notions of the Saudi Juhaymān al-'Utaybi, whose group would go on to embark on the Siege of Mecca in 1979.[127] His argument against apolitical voices was that the Prophet had engaged in political activities for the good of his community, and that the failure of religious people to join the political process had contributed to weak leaders in the Muslim world, which in turn resulted in the domination of Muslims by Western powers. Hence, he argued in favor of creating political parties to operate within the democratic process, which was preferable to dictatorships in preserving the rights of Muslims. So as to buttress his point, he highlighted how the early Muslims under the leadership of Ja'far ibn Abi Talib, the Prophet's cousin, had forged political ties with Christians in Abyssinia as they fled the persecution of Muslims in Mecca at the beginning of the Prophetic ministry.[128]

The Kuwaiti Salafi movement was a central component of the Salafi divisions that emerged in the 1990s, especially with the First Gulf War, as many Kuwaiti Salafis fled to Saudi Arabia, and their brand of Salafism came to create discord with the dominant apolitical form of Salafism, although it was understandably well received by the *Ṣaḥwa* Salafis in Saudi. After the Gulf War, some Kuwaiti Salafis such as Hakim al-Mutairi (who studied at Umm al-Qura University in Saudi Arabia), Hamid al-'Ali and 'Abd al-Razzaq al-Shayiji, returned to Kuwait after having sided with the *Ṣaḥwa*, and further propagated activist Salafism.[129] Naturally, this led to a split among Kuwaiti Salafis, with the politicos being condemned by the apolitical Salafis for their methodology resembling the Muslim Brotherhood.

Indeed, RIHS removed 'Abd al-Rahman 'Abd al-Khaliq and withdrew from politics in the early 1990s, as it took a more puritan and apolitical course from 'Abdullah al-Sabt and Hayy al-Hayy, who were influenced by the apolitical leader Rabi' al-Madkhalī.[130] Al-Sabt would write in refutation of 'Abd al-Rahman 'Abd al-Khaliq, criticizing him for subtly calling for rebellion against the ruler and his conceptualization of Islamic politics.

Despite 'Abd al-Rahman 'Abd al-Khaliq's attempts at defending himself against such critics, the Kuwaiti authorities backed the puritans, and the majority of his followers left RIHS by around 1997[131] and formed a new organization called *al-Harakah al-Salafiyyah* (The Salafi Movement), under the leadership of al-Mutairi. However this movement also split, when al-Mutairi returned from England after pursuing a PhD at the University of Birmingham (completed in 2000), disagreed with the direction of his deputy, Hamid al-'Ali, and proceeded to form a political party *Hizb al-Umma* (Umma Party). The change in direction taken by the RIHS led to certain Kuwaiti critics saying that it was a Saudi puppet. Nonetheless, most Kuwaiti Salafis have been puritans, and even the political Salafis have only managed a limited parliamentarian presence, in part due to the existence of the more popular Muslim Brotherhood.[132]

Up until the Arab Spring in 2011, Kuwait had the most tolerant approach to Salafis in the region. However, quietist Salafis in Kuwait would become divided with the emergence of the Arab Spring. While the Madkhalis remained firmly opposed to any political revolt or protest, members of the RIHS, which had been quietist since the 1990s, initially opposed the uprisings in Libya and Syria, but then came to support them as the regimes engaged in killing their citizens. Of course, Madkhalis criticized such awakened political voices in RIHS, and the leading Kuwaiti Madkhali Salim al-Tawil called the Syrian President Assad the 'legitimate ruler' (*wali al-amr*).[133]

The Arab Spring did not divide activist Salafis, who all agreed with the demonstrations and revolts. If anything, it galvanized their activities, and even widened some of their approaches. For instance, in January 2012, the *Rabitat al-Du'at al-Kuwaitiyyah* (League of Islamic Preachers of Kuwait or LDK) was formed and came under the leadership of the notable activist Salafi scholar Nabil al-'Awadhi. This collective has sought to bring Salafi and Muslim Brotherhood factions together in Kuwait, but the leadership has been mainly Salafi and has attracted Salafis who left the SIG. Furthermore, al-Mutairi has spoken of how the move of Egyptian Salafis into politics after the revolution of 2011 was an idea born in his presence in Kuwait, showing how the Arab Spring enabled Kuwaiti politicos to expand their political purview beyond its borders.[134] The events in Egypt also led to some renewed international celebrity for 'Abd al-Rahman 'Abd al-Khaliq, as he was invited to visit in 2012 and was warmly welcomed by Egyptian Salafis, including Abu Ishaq al-Huwayni. 'Abd al-Rahman 'Abd al-Khaliq reciprocated the cordiality by inviting al-Huwayni and Muhammad Hassan back to Kuwait later in 2012.[135]

Ultimately, in the Kuwaiti context, the Arab Spring did not profoundly affect the existent varieties of Salafism, although it did worsen cracks which were already largely present. It is possible that the scale of the impact was less severe due to the fact that the demonstrations which took place in Kuwait around 2011 and 2012 did not undermine the entirety of the Kuwaiti political system, with its historic openness and free democracy, unlike the popular protests against dictatorships in Tunisia, Libya, Egypt, and Syria. However, the demonstrations did bring a political crisis to Kuwait, which led, nevertheless, to political changes in light of tensions and criticisms of the regime.[136]

### *6.2.5 Yemen*

Yemen has a strong history linking it to major pre-twentieth century antecedents for the Salafi movement, in particular the towering scholarly figure of Muhammad ibn ʻAli al-Shawkānī (d. 1834). However, the Salafi movement only emerged in Yemen in a meaningful way in the early 1980s with the leadership of Muqbil ibn Hadi al-Wadiʻī (d. 2001), who embodied quietist al-Albānī Salafism. The emergence of activist Salafism in Yemen occurred in the early 1990s and received criticism from Muqbil's faction. But shortly after Muqbil's passing in 2001, some of his students became embroiled in a dispute with other quietists. Then, the Arab Spring and the Yemeni civil war from 2014 would further divide politico and quietist Salafis, as well as embroiling the quietists in military action and attack. Nonetheless, Salafism has grown in all parts of Yemen, and is now able to compete with the other popular Islamic groups, namely the Zaydis, the Sufis and the Muslim Brotherhood.[137]

Muqbil was from northern Yemen, in the Zaydi-dominated area of Saada, and was born in the late 1920s or early 1930s (he was himself unsure of the dating). His family background was Zaydi and his social status was that of tribesmen, a lowly rank, hence his access to only a limited early education. After his initial basic studies, he moved to Saudi Arabia and worked as a doorkeeper (*bawwāb*), where he seems to have come across Salafism and its correctives of Zaydism. He returned to Yemen and undertook some religious instruction before returning to Saudi in the 1960s, coming to study at the institute developed by Ibn ʻUthaymin and then graduating from the IUM in 1976.[138] He gained notoriety in 1979 when he was removed from Saudi Arabia because of his close involvement with Juhaymān al-ʻUtaybi and the latter's *al-Jamaʻah al-Salafiyyah al-Muhtasibah* (JSM), who would go on to conduct the Siege of Mecca in 1979. Muqbil had been one of the main teachers of Juhaymān's group,[139] accompanying them on Hajj from Medina in 1976,[140] and was suspected by the Saudi authorities of being an author of the letters produced by JSM around the end of 1978 and the beginning of 1979, which criticized the Saudi royal family (although Muqbil denied being the author). Due to this suspicion, Muqbil was arrested and imprisoned for three months before being extradited to Yemen,[141] but not before he was allowed to defend his master's degree thesis at the IUM.[142]

Upon returning to Yemen, he established an Islamic seminary, *Dar al-Hadith*, in Dammaj, in northern Yemen, which would become the most influential Salafi institution in Yemen.[143] Muqbil and his followers were quietists, and critical of politicos in general, from the early 1990s, as well as being disapproving of democracy. However, Muqbil was not distinctly pro-Saudi,[144] perhaps as a result of his early harsh experience in the country, and he did not encourage his students to study at the IUM. Throughout the 1980s he criticized the royal family, and in 1994 he attacked the Saudis for supporting the socialist succession in South Yemen. Furthermore, he criticized Ibn Bāz for allowing the foreign troops to base themselves in Saudi during the First Gulf War, and he disagreed that all criticism of the ruler should be kept private. But he still retained the patronage for his institutions in Yemen from the Holy Mosque Establishment and the Haramayn Charity Foundation (*Mu'assasat al-Haramayn al-Khayriyyah*), with their Saudi backing – although Muqbil stopped receiving funds from the Haramayn Charity in the mid-1990s when the latter started funding more politically-inclined Salafi organizations in Yemen like *al-Hikmah* and *al-Ihsan*.[145] When Muqbil became ill and neared death, he reconciled with the Saudis, and Prince Nayef met him and paid for his medical treatment in Germany, Saudi, and the United States.[146]

After Muqbil's passing and burial in Mecca, his intellectual heirs came to dispute with one another. Two of the main heirs, Muhammad al-Imam (who directed an institute in Ma'bar) and Yahya al-Hajuri (who took over the directorship of the institute in Dammaj), are seen as having continued Muqbil's methodology. But a third major student, Abu al-Hasan al-Misri (called al-Ma'ribi, with Ma'rib being the town where he headed an Islamic seminary), is considered to have deviated from the path towards a more political methodology.[147] Hence, al-Ma'ribi – who became close to Muqbil after fleeing Egypt due to his association with the extremist *al-Takfir wa'l-Hijrah* group (discussed in section 5.3.1) – has come under intense criticism from quietists, especially fiercely apolitical ones like Rabi' al-Madkhalī, a dispute which has had global ramifications.[148]

A further falling out occurred in the late 2000s among Yemeni quietist Salafis when al-Hajuri came to dispute with the al-'Adani brothers, 'Abd al-Rahman and 'Abdullah, in Aden, with the brothers being accused of departing from Muqbil's methodology. The crisis reached the point where Rabi' al-Madkhalī attempted to reconcile the parties in 2008 and 2009. This dispute further weakened quietist ranks as well as diminished the prestige of *Dar al-Hadith* in Dammaj, as al-Hajuri's conduct was seen by many as odious due to its harshness.[149]

The quietist Salafis have been useful to the Yemeni government over time, and puritan elements have benefitted from the government allowing them to express themselves in violence. For instance, militant Salafi violence against Sufis in Aden and Hadramawt in 1994 and 1995 was not curtailed by the authorities.[150] After 9/11, as Salafis were first treated with deep suspicion, the quietist Salafis came to the forefront of refuting Jihadi-Salafism, as seen especially in the work of Muqbil's student Muhammad al-Imam. Such Salafi elements have also been drawn into fighting alongside the government in the Saada region since 2004 against the Zaydi Houthis.[151] The usefulness of the puritan Salafis has been explained as aiding the government to oppose religious political rivals, like the Zaydis and the Muslim Brotherhood.[152]

Furthermore, these puritan Salafis have deterred the populace from political participation, which aided continuity of rule, with Ali Abdullah Salih remaining in power from 1978 until being forced out in 2012 as a result of the Arab uprising. When the pressure started to mount on Salih's regime in the summer of 2011, Yahya al-Hajuri published a letter in which he explained why the leader was loved by the people. However, such proclamations must be seen in the wider Yemeni context, in which a weakened Sunni regime would open up the political landscape for the march of the Houthis in the Saada province, rather than merely demonstrating spinelessness. This understanding is further evidenced by the violent fighting that broke out between the students of the Salafi institute in Dammaj and the Houthis in early 2011, with *Dar al-Hadith* being attacked between October and November 2011.[153]

The Yemeni tradition of activist Salafism emerged in the 1990s, with North and South Yemen uniting in 1990 and presenting a number of political and social challenges, and the increasing influence of the *Ṣaḥwa* movement. A notable activist Salafi organization was the charity *Jam'iyyat al-Khayriyyah al-Hikmah al-Yamaniyyah* (Yemeni Wisdom Charity Association, known simply as *al-Hikmah*), formed by former students of Muqbil, who maintained reverence for their teacher, despite his criticism of such organizations and their electoral systems. A short while later some members formed *al-Ihsan*, seemingly due to personal disagreements rather than conflicts over Salafi methodology. However, *al-Ihsan* concentrated on teaching and charity, and *al-Hikmah* was more political.[154]

Soon after *al-Hikmah* was formed, members started to involve themselves in the political process, despite the organization not officially participating. They voted for a variety of groups in local and national elections, from the Muslim Brotherhood's *al-Islah* to the ruling General People's Congress (GPC). Members even stood for local elections in 1997 in Aden, and won offices for Hadramawt in 2006, as well as running extensive political campaigns in 2009. The overt references by the *al-Hikmah* hierarchy to Kuwaiti activist Salafis was made around 2008 when there were discussions about forming a Salafi political party. But caution restrained them from doing so, as it was believed that they were still politically immature, with many of the Salafi youth having been raised on the idea of politics being forbidden by the religion, as well as fear of violent repression from the regime. Therefore, activist Salafi groups like *al-Hikmah*, who had historic links to, and were influenced by, the Egyptian-Kuwaiti 'Abd al-Rahman 'Abd al-Khaliq, developed closer relations with the Muslim Brotherhood and *al-Islah*.[155] Furthermore, by way of illustrating greater activist Salafi cooperation in Yemen, *al-Hikmah* and al-Ma'ribi reconciled and collaborated with one another by participating in a conference together in August 2004 in Hadramawt.[156]

Numerous Salafis of various types then participated in the Arab uprising in Yemen. This led to the formation of *al-Rabitah al-Nahdhah wa'l-Taghiyir* (The League of Revival and Change or LRC), so that this coalition of various Salafis, including members from both *al-Hikmah* and *al-Ihsan*, could be better coordinated. This movement eventually progressed to the formation of a political party on 14 March 2012, the *Ittihad al-Rashad* (*Rashad Union*), which was seen as a necessity of the time, so that the historical moment, with its expanding horizons, could be seized and the country directed in a religious manner. As this was a time when Al-Qaeda in the Arabian Peninsula (AQAP) was emerging in Yemen, the Rashad Union were vocal in showing how their Salafism was unlike the indiscriminately violent methodology of the AQAP, but rather was conciliatory and respectful of the wishes of the country. Nonetheless, the Rashad leadership also pointed to the fact that many of the recruits in AQAP had been brutally tortured, and that there must be an acknowledgment of that injustice. Furthermore, Rashad leaders called for AQAP to be brought into peaceful dialogue with the authorities, as the violent Houthis had been allowed to participate in political negotiations; but, of course, this attempt failed.

Naturally, quietist Salafis in Yemen, in particular Yahya al-Hajuri, from his position as the successor leader of Muqbil's institute in Dammaj, called such political efforts an affront to what he defined as true Salafism. The Rashad leadership maintained a cordial disagreement with the quietists, which allowed them to maintain a moral high ground and more charming etiquette of disagreement in the public sphere. Rashad used this same soft criticism of *al-Islah*, as leaders pointed out that they agreed over more than they disagreed with the Muslim Brotherhood; but still they claimed to have a clearer Islamic methodology, whereas the Muslim Brotherhood were too willing to compromise on fixed Islamic principles in order to reach a purely political settlement. Furthermore, Rashad spokesmen were cautious to overemphasize the term 'Salafi' in describing the party, perhaps in acknowledgment of the difficulty it can cause in the public mind in terms of its lack of clear meaning, and excluding potential supporters.[157]

By late 2013, the Salafis in Dammaj were under enormous pressure from Houthi forces. The community was blockaded for three months, with one of al-Hajuri's sons killed in the process, and the government had to seek mediation between the parties in early 2014. But the agreement led to between 10,000 and 15,000 people having to leave Dammaj, including many Salafis, with the families struggling to find welcoming areas in the country, although many eventually went to Sanaa (including al-Hajuri). Jihadi-Salafis pointed to such a humanitarian crisis as a sign that quietist Salafism was ill-equipped to counter the challenges presented by the modern world, and that their suffering was due to abandoning jihad. Al-Hajuri had rejected assistance from Jihadi-Salafis, but he did accept help from the Hashid tribe, which maintained a level of integrity on the part of his community. Furthermore, Islamists and activist Salafis (like Rashad) condemned the oppression of the Salafis in Dammaj. In a strange way, these events gave the apolitical Salafis a certain level of popularity with the increased publicity and sympathy for their plight, so that when al-Hajuri spoke in Sanaa in January 2014 it was attended by thousands.[158]

Nonetheless, the civil war was about to erupt in Yemen in 2014, and the Houthi factions proceeded to seize Sanaa that year. The Saudis and UAE then backed Sunni fighters to contend with the Zaydi forces, and they funded Salafis and Islamists to fend off the attack on the capital. AQAP managed to secure the area of Mukalla after 2015, but they were soon forced out in April 2016, with help from the Saudis and UAE. The intensified fighting led to talks of the north and south again splitting, and in April 2017, Sufis and Salafis participated in a conference in Hadramawt to discuss this matter, with the Salafi Salih al-Sharifi attending.[159]

With the continuation of the civil war until the present time, with Houthi control of Sanaa and much of the north, it is hard to maintain traditional typologies for Salafis in Yemen, as so many of those previously called apolitical or quietist Salafis have had to engage in warfare to protect their region; and the activists have maintained a relative solidarity with those termed quietist, who have been passive victims of events. It will take a long time for matters to become normalized to the point that the branches of Salafism can be meaningfully reinterpreted, except for the case with the easily identifiable Jihadi-Salafism in the region.

## *6.3 Asia and the Far East*

### *6.3.1 India and Pakistan*

The *Ahl-e-Hadith* movement that developed in the Indian subcontinent during the time of British rule (discussed in section 2.8) is the most important part of the history of Salafism and its emergence in the twentieth century in India and Pakistan. Whether the movement is considered proto-Salafi or genuinely Salafi in its inception is a matter of debate. However, what is not disputed is that it came to be a Salafi partner around the mid-twentieth century, and the leading representative of Salafism in the region, albeit with its distinctive characteristics which exemplified its independent development, with its own scholars and literary authorities.

The *Ahl-e-Hadith* developed relations with the Saudis from the 1920s, with a Salafiyyah Bookstore being opened in Multan in 1921 by Abd al-Wahhāb al-Multani, who was linked to *Ahl-e-Hadith* and had connections to Najd.[160] This interaction between *Ahl-e-Hadith* and the Saudis increased in the 1970s, after King Sa'ud contributed to the establishment of the *Jamiah Salafiyyah* seminary in Benares, India, in 1966.[161] Furthermore, important links were established between the *Ahl-e-Hadith* and the Salafi movement in the 1960s when leading members in the Indian subcontinent, namely Abd al-Ghaffar Hasan (d. 2007) and Muhammad Gondalavi (d. 1985), were recruited by the Islamic University of Medina to teach hadith. Hasan would remain at the IUM for sixteen years, and came to teach leading Salafi ideologues like Safar al-Hawali and Muqbil al-Wadi'i, while also building close links with Ibn Bāz.

Since the 1980s, graduates of the IUM have returned to India and Pakistan and disseminated Salafi doctrines. Between 1965 and 2001, Pakistan had the second largest number of foreign graduates of the IUM, with 1,560, and India ranked fourth, with 952.[162] Moreover, a number of the *Ahl-e-Hadith*'s leading institutions are affiliated with Saudi universities: *Jamaa Salafiyyah* in Islamabad is linked to IUM and Umm al-Qura in Mecca, and their main seminary in Quetta (Baluchistan) is linked to the IUM, with teachers who graduated from Saudi universities and courses taught in Arabic. Due to financial backing from Saudi, Qatar, and Kuwait, the fees for studying at the *Ahl-e-Hadith* seminary in Peshawar, *Jamaa Asariah*, were kept very low.[163]

The *Ahl-e-Hadith* in Pakistan gained increased funds from Saudi Arabia after the First Gulf War in 1991, as the regime came to favor them over the more politically-conscious *Jamaat-e-Islami* (*Islamic Party*, which can be viewed as a sister-organization to the Muslim Brotherhood). Nonetheless, as military activity increased in the region, the *Lashkar-e-Taiba* (*Army of the Good*) military outfit, active primarily in Afghanistan and Kashmir, came to be associated with the *Ahl-e-Hadith*, but the official link between the two remains unproven. However, the *Tehrik-e-Mujahidin* (*Movement of Mujahidin*) military outfit, again in Kashmir, is understood to be affiliated with the *Ahl-e-Hadith*. The political orientation of the *Ahl-e-Hadith* is further confirmed by their forming a political party and joining, in 2001, the religious coalition called *Muttahidat Majlis-e-Amal* (United Assembly of Action or MMA).

Yet, one cannot discount Salafi influences in the Indian subcontinent which were independent of *Ahl-e-Hadith*. For example, the Moroccan Taqi al-Din al-Hilali had traveled to India in 1923 to study hadith, and spent over a year studying with leading *Ahl-e-Hadith* scholars including Husayn ibn Muhsin al-Ansari al-Yamani (d. 1925) and Abd al-Rahman al-Mubarakpuri (d. 1935). Al-Hilali then returned to India in 1930, after he left Saudi Arabia in anger after being dismissed from the Saudi Scientific Institute in Mecca, for being non-Saudi. The rector of the ecumenical *Nadwat al-'Ulama* (Council of Scholars) in Lucknow, Sulaymán al-Nadwi (d. 1953), had invited al-Hilali to come and teach Arabic, and he accepted the invitation and stayed at the institution until 1933. Sulayman al-Nadwi requested al-Hilali to establish an Arabic periodical at the seminary; and he did so with the publication in 1932 of the journal *al-Diya'* (*The Light*), which would continue until 1935. The journal was founded and edited by Mas'ud 'Alam al-Nadwi (d. 1954), a student of al-Hilali, who would later become a Salafi in the late 1940s, after *al-Diya'* achieved a respectable status among reformists in North Africa and the Levant. Mas'ud 'Alam al-Nadwi also came to develop close links with the Wahhabis, and even wrote an apologetic defense of Muhammad Ibn ʿAbd al-Wahhāb in Urdu, which was later translated into Arabic with a preface by al-Hilali. In 1947, he moved to the newly-created state of Pakistan and worked on Arabic works propagating the reformist thought of Abu al-A'la Mawdudi.[164]

Mawdudi criticized *Ahl-e-Hadith* for not sufficiently considering the schools of law as valid, while in return their senior figures criticized Mawdudi for being too political and for holding specific views (especially about the Companions) that were deemed unorthodox.[165] As with the Egyptian counterpart, the relationship between *Jamaat-e-Islami* and *Ahl-e-Hadith* is extremely fluid, with some attempting to build bridges and others fostering isolationism from each other. At present, both Indian and Pakistani *Ahl-e-Hadith* maintain a strong affinity with Saudi religious scholars and institutes and are among the strongest supporters of the Saudi government outside the Kingdom.

### *6.3.2 Malaysia*

While there was a reformist Salafi tradition in the Malay region in the early twentieth century, known as *Kaum Muda* (Young People) in local languages, as students studied in Al-Azhar University in Egypt and returned to the region, traditional Salafism became more popular in the 1980s as some Malaysians returned from studying in universities in Saudi Arabia. The work of Abdullah al-Qari Haji Salleh (b. 1937) is also significant – he translated numerous Salafi works in the 1980s, and eventually produced the first Bahasa Melayu translation of al-Albānī's *The Prophet's Prayer*.

The Islamic revival of the 1970s and 1980s also assisted the rise of Salafism as a number of Muslim Brotherhood organizations, such as the *Angkatan Belia Islam Malaysia* (Muslim Youth Movement or ABIM) and the Islamic Representative Group (IRC) which operated in the UK for Malaysian students, founded in 1971 and 1975, respectively, propagated Salafi theology in Malaysia and for Malaysians.[166]

The most notable Salafi preachers to emerge after studying in Saudi Arabia were Rasul Dahri, Ismail Omar, Sulaiman Nordin, Johari Mat, and Hussein Yee, although returning Malaysian students from Jordan also contributed to the spread of Salafism, especially as al-Albānī's presence seemed to inspire a number of them to commit to it. Furthermore, the popular Salafi scene in the UK in the 1990s also influenced a number of Malaysian students to move towards Salafism, before returning to Malaysia. Then in the late 1990s and early 2000s, Salafi publishing houses emerged to spur on the growth of Salafism in Malaysia, allied with the popularity of Salafi internet sites. The publisher *Jahabersa* was seen as particularly pioneering, and produced Malay translations of works by Ibn Bāz, Ibn 'Uthaymin, al-Albānī, Salih al-Fawzan and others, although the publisher also produced non-Salafi works.

As is the case with global Salafism, Malaysia possesses the full spectrum of Salafi approaches, from the apolitical to the radically-violent and everything in between. Likewise, traditionalist currents in Malaysia have responded to the emergence of Salafism by vigorously defending many intellectual aspects of speculative theology and Sufism, and they have often been able to successfully appeal to the authorities to support them against Salafi organizations. However, the federal government has maintained a neutral stance towards non-violent Salafi strands, and that bodes well for the continuation of Salafism in the country.

### *6.3.3 Indonesia*

The creation of the *Dewan Dakwah Islamiyah Indonesia* (Indonesian Council for Islamic Propagation or DDII) in 1967 heralded the beginnings of Salafism in Indonesia. It received financial and educational support from Saudi Arabia (who funded a number of non-Salafi projects in Indonesia as well). Subsequently, due to Saudi concerns about Shīʿis in the wake of the Iranian Revolution in 1979, Saudi Arabia founded the *Lembaga Ilmu Pengetahuan Islam dan Bahasa Arab* (Institute of Islamic and Arabic Studies or LIPIA) in Jakarta in 1980, which focused on the study of Arabic and came to host a number of notable members of the Saudi royal family in the 1980s and 1990s. Indonesians were also offered the opportunity to study in Saudi Arabia, with LIPIA offering thirty scholarships a year. Between 1965 and 2001, 1,238 Indonesians graduated from the Islamic University of

Medina, which placed them third on the international list of those with such graduates, behind only Yemen and Pakistan. Some Indonesians traveled to Afghanistan to fight the Soviet Union, which also brought them into contact with Salafi doctrines.[167] With such activities, the first emergence of staunch and committed Salafis appeared in Indonesia in the 1980s, together with the opening of Salafi *pesantren*s (rural Islamic schools) and madrasas in the late 1980s.[168] The importance of Saudi patronage for the development of Salafism in Indonesia has continued until the time of writing.[169]

The Indonesian Ja'far 'Umar Thalib (d. 2019) became the most prominent Salafi preacher in Indonesia and helped another leading Salafi activist, Abu Nida (who had graduated in Saudi), create the first major Salafi madrasa in Indonesia, called *Ihya al-Sunna* (The Revival of the Sunna), in 1994. From this base, Abu Nida was successful in propagating Salafism among university students around Yogyakarta, and many Salafi madrasas followed between 1995 and 2000. These leaders took a more apolitical approach to Salafism than the earlier graduates from Saudi universities in the 1970s, through the DDII network, who were more politically orientated. Abu Nida had networked his way into gaining the patronage of the *Mu'assasat al-Haramayn al-Khayriyyah* (Haramayn Charitable Foundation) from Saudi and *Jam'iyyat Ihya al-Turath al-Islami* (Reviving of Islamic Heritage Society) from Kuwait.

As the Indonesian Salafi trend was closely related to the Salafi trends in Saudi Arabia and Yemen, when disputes broke out between quietists and politicos in the early 1990s Indonesian Salafis, whether studying in Saudi or at home in Indonesia, were dragged into the dispute, and split along group lines, especially as the Kuwaiti *Jam'iyyat Ihya' al-Turath* (see section 6.2.4) had sent teachers to Islamic schools in Indonesia. Thalib, an Afghan veteran (working under Sayyaf and then Jamil al-Rahman and the latter's Salafi faction) and the first Indonesian student of Muqbil in Yemen, received the backing of Saudis such as Rabi' al-Madkhalī, 'Abd al-Razzaq ibn 'Abd al-Muhsin al-'Abbad, and Zayd ibn Muhammad ibn al-Hadi al-Madkhalī; and an Indonesian Salafi rival, Yusuf Baysa, was emblematic of the activist side. Thalib's antics and tirades against 'Sururis' brought him into conflict with *Negara Islam Indonesia* (Indonesian Islamic State or NII) led by 'Abdullah Sungkar and Abu Bakar Ba'asyir (see section 5.3.6), who were deeply sensitive to attacks on Sayyid Qutb from quietist Salafis.

Later, the Salafi madrasas became divided as Thalib and Abu Nida parted ways with one another, with Thalib accusing Abu Nida of being a 'Sururi.' However, Abu Nida's network retained stronger ties with Saudi backers, as well as returning students, so his madrasas have tended to be better financed, while Thalib's headquarters at *Ihya al-Sunna* and other madrasas had an almost impoverished appearance, and were based more on the Yemeni model of Muqbil al-Wadi'i. A further difference in the schools of these two leaders is that those linked to Abu Nida incorporated the government guidelines for subjects and engaged in national exams, so they received diplomas which gave them access to higher education, whereas those linked to Thalib only studied religious subjects, and rejected the national curriculum.

Then, when Indonesia suffered from inter-religious and inter-ethnic conflicts in the wake of the 1997 Asian economic crisis, Indonesian Salafis caught up in the violence in the Moluccas turned to their Arab guides, through the request of the *Forum Komunikasi Ahlus Sunna wal Jama'ah* (Forum for Followers of the Sunna and the Community of the Prophet or FKASWJ). In 2000, they received fatwas from, among others, Rabi' al-Madkhalī, 'Abd al-Razzaq ibn 'Abd al-Muhsin al-'Abbad, Salih al-Fawzan, and Muqbil al-Wadi'i, which all justified the assailed to wage jihad against those who were attacking them. Thus the FKASWJ formed a military wing, called *Laskar Jihad Ahlus Sunna Wal Jama'ah* (Warriors of Jihad of the People of the Sunnah), under the leadership of Ja'far 'Umar Thalib (but the wing only lasted until 2002, with Thalib the object of Salafi-testing that he had utilized against activists).[170] This illustrated the military dynamism that apolitical Salafism can provide Muslims under attack by non-Muslims – especially when no pressure is applied by Arab governments to oppose such military responses – despite the fact that the Indonesian president did not give his approval to such militias. In fact, the existence of the Indonesian government is what led Abu Nida not to support the jihad, as the legitimate leader had the right and means to declare war, rather than vigilante groups forming themselves.

Nonetheless, Salafism, in its various guises, has continued in Indonesia and expanded its appeal to non-Salafis through its educational methods (such as its tripartite presentation of *Tawḥīd*, which has become increasingly popular in Indonesian schools); and their social media outreach which has, generally, assumed a more broadly appealing nature (perhaps even taking on, as stated by Noorhaidi Hasan, a 'post-Salafi' character). For example, there is the celebrity-preacher style of Firanda Andirja, a graduate of the IUM, whose colorful approach expanded into forming two Salafi television channels: Rodja TV and Yufid TV. Unsurprisingly, Andirja's methods have been reproached by older and more conservative Salafis as well as Madkhalis like Lukman Ba'abduh, since he appeals to the masses with a softer style, especially against what mainstream Salafis would view as deviations.[171]

The relevance of Salafism in Indonesia – no matter how reformed it is in some respects – continues despite the fact that the movement is very much beleaguered. Firstly, internal divisions have weakened it – with a Madkhali faction developing recently, under Luqman Ba'abduh, now competing with the existing tendencies. Secondly, coming under greater scrutiny due to the

9/11 terror attacks and growing Jihadi-Salafi tendencies[172] led some of the Salafi madrasas to revise their curricula. Thirdly, it has encountered the opposition of the largest Islamic organization in Indonesia, the *Nahdlatul Ulama* (Revival of the Umma), who have accused Salafis in the country of spreading intolerance and opposing the Islamic traditions of South-East Asia.[173]

Indonesia, like the United States and United Kingdom, exemplifies how post-Salafism has started to emerge out of the traditional overtly Salafi groupings, adapting to remain relevant. Beneath this lies an unspoken rejection of the historic idealism and resultant splintering of Salafi groups. This has led to a greater accommodation of the Salafi Other, and made its appeal, in some respects, more widespread and mainstream.[174]

## 6.4 Europe

### 6.4.1 The United Kingdom

The development of Salafism in the UK has an extensive history, interacting with significant global Salafi trends.[175] It rewards a detailed examination, as it demonstrates how trends in Salafism can lead to fragmentation of the movement.

#### *First phase: The activism of the* Ahl-e-Hadith

The first phase of Salafism in the UK was initially through those influenced by the proto-Salafi *Ahl-e-Hadith* movement of the Indian subcontinent (discussed in Chapter 2). This led to the first Salafi youth organizations, including *Harakat Islah al-Shabab al-Muslim* (The Movement to Reform Muslim Youth or HISAM), although they are not credited as such.

In early 1975, the *Markaz Jamiat Ahl-e-Hadith* UK or (MJAH) was formally established through the leadership of Fazal Karim Asim – he would remain leader of the organization until 1991, passing away in 2003.[176] Asim was a trained religious scholar and an adherent of the *Ahl-e-Hadith* movement from Pakistan, who had migrated to England in 1962 in order to undertake factory work. As a religious teacher, he joined already existent religious projects in his new city of Birmingham, and eventually became a very active member of the UK Islamic Mission (linked to the political party *Jamaat-e-Islami*) that was created in Birmingham in 1963 (after the organization was formed in London in 1962). However, emerging sectarian trends in Birmingham, which mirrored those found in the Indian subcontinent, convinced Asim that it was time to solidify an *Ahl-e-Hadith* contingent in the UK.[177]

Within months of being formed, the MJAH received a delegation from the Islamic University of Medina (IUM), in August 1975. This delegation was led by two scholars, ʻAbd al-Wahhāb al-Bannā and Nasir al-Din al-Albānī, and three students, Sharif Ahmad Hafiz, Mahmud Ahmad Mirpuri, and Major Muhammad Aslam. The task of the delegation had been to study the conditions of the UK for potential projects and allies to support with their Salafi missionary activities. The delegation spent a month and a half in Birmingham, and after a number of meetings and interactions found the MJAH to fit their ideological model. Indeed, *Ahl-e-Hadith* scholars from the Indian subcontinent had worked closely with the IUM since its inception in 1961. After Asim sought financial and educational assistance from the delegation, he was encouraged to make the Hajj and seek an audience with Ibn Bāz, who was President of the IUM from 1969 until October 1975, when he became head of the Permanent Committee for Scientific Research and Legal Rulings.[178]

Upon attending the Hajj in December 1975, Asim was able to have a meeting with Ibn Bāz, where Asim requested financial assistance to purchase a suitable property for the organization, and for Ibn Bāz to send teachers to aid their educational program. Ibn Bāz had good links with the Indian *Ahl-e-Hadith* and had inaugurated their publishing house in Varanasi in 1966 when he was the vice-chancellor of the IUM. The financial request was affirmed but did not materialize, despite a reminder on behalf of MJAH, although they were able to purchase, through a generous, independent donor (a Kuwaiti philanthropist and member of the Muslim Brotherhood) and community fundraising, a council property in 1979, which would be developed into the Green Lane Masjid – the latter becoming so mainstream and generally lauded that it won the 'Mosque of the Year' award at the British Muslim Awards in 2020, for a variety of general community services.[179]

However, Ibn Bāz did send two students, Hafiz and Mirpuri from the initial delegation, upon their graduation from the IUM in 1976. A further graduate of IUM, Abdul Karim Saqib, was also assigned to the project by the Saudis. Saqib had migrated to England from Pakistan and, on his own accord, had independently joined Asim and others before his formal appointment.[180] The lack of significant Saudi financial support, yet educational aid through the arrival of IUM graduates, is a recurring theme from this early period until today. This belies the popular notion that the rise of Salafism in the UK, whether it was the MJAH or later JIMAS, was due to 'Saudi petrodollars.'[181] Indeed, JIMAS refused Saudi government funding, and their early activities were largely funded from the pockets of the early leaders.[182] Recent theses confirm that Saudi funding of Salafi activism in Britain has been largely limited and that instead, the movement has grown organically thanks to its harnessing of media and appealing to the religious sensibilities of ordinary Muslims.[183]

MJAH soon developed into a national organization, with over fifty mosques affiliated to it around the UK. One of the most prominent, Masjid al-Tawhid, was established in Leyton, London, in 1984, by Suhaib Hasan, whose father, 'Abd al-Ghaffar Hasan, had taught at IUM. Suhaib Hasan himself was among the first Pakistanis to graduate from the IUM in 1966. He worked on behalf of the *Dar al-Ifta* of Saudi Arabia, run by Ibn Bāz, and after nine years of service in Kenya, eventually migrated to the UK after requesting Ibn Bāz to send him to work in England to enable him to pursue a PhD.[184] Suhaib Hasan would translate for Ibn Bāz during telephone phone-ins at conferences, and it was Ibn Bāz who arranged significant financial support for purchasing Masjid al-Tawhid.[185] Moreover, Mirpuri also received permission, upon request, of the Grand Mufti of Saudi Arabia, 'Abd al-'Aziz Āl al-Shaykh, to translate fatwas from the official Saudi Arabian fatwa council.[186]

While MJAH wrote in their publications that they were Salafi, they maintained independence from Arabian currents, and continued their own individual orientation. Yet these connections with Arab Salafis helped develop Salafism in the UK at the hands of the *Ahl-e-Hadith*. In addition to their denouncement of rigidly adhering to one of the four Sunni schools of law in favor of simply 'following the Qur'an and Sunna,' they were also vocal opponents of Sufism and the celebration of the birth of the Prophet (*mawlid* or *milad*), which highlighted their Salafi credentials. Therefore, MJAH was Salafi in doctrine and practice without initially making 'Salafi' an important label of self-identification (although in the 1980s they identified themselves as part of the global Salafi movement and did run evening Qur'an schools for children using the name *Madrasah Salafia*); rather, they focused merely on teaching an Islam 'based on the Qur'an and Sunna.'[187]

MJAH exhibited a distinctly political interest, such as in the ongoing troubles in Kashmir, Palestine, Afghanistan, and the Philippines, which they actively called to be freed from non-Muslim control. In 1992, they even called for the Islamist Islamic Salvation Front (FIS) to be free in Algeria after restrictions were placed on them after the elections that were annulled by the army when FIS appeared on course to win comfortably. Moreover, the MJAH publication would also extol the virtue of Islamists such as Ḥasan al-Bannā, Sayyid Qutb, and Sayyid Mawdudi.[188]

Despite developing their message in English through the 1980s, the activities of Asim, Mirpuri, Saqib, Hasan and the MJAH in general were not seen as effectively English-focused. Later they were considered to be only lukewarm Salafis by rather robust converts to Salafism who wholeheartedly followed more outspoken Arab representatives of *true* Salafism. The latter condemned MJAH, in general, and Suhaib Hasan, in particular, for cordial links with the UK-based *Jamaat-e-Islami* at the Islamic Foundation, Leicester.[189]

*Second phase: The rise of JIMAS*

The initial divide among these early proto-Salafis led to the emergence *of Jam'iat Ihyaa' Minhaaj-al-Sunna* (The Society for the Revival of the

Prophetic Way or JIMAS) in the late 1980s, which would become the most prominent Salafi organization of the time in the UK.[190] Under the forthright and domineering leadership of activist Abu Muntasir (Manwar Ali) – whose father Dr Muhammad Mohar Ali had lectured in Islamic History at the IUM in the late 1980s and early '90s – not only did JIMAS succeed in attracting British Muslims with a South Asian heritage, they also gained the following of Muslim converts, both white and Black, most prominently in Brixton, London.

However, as they emerged out of the MJAH milieu, they did not use the 'Salafi' label at first, and they displayed the same political orientation as MJAH had done.[191] Indeed, Abu Muntasir and others from JIMAS (like Usama Hasan and Abdur Raheem Green) had attended the training camps of the Afghan *mujahidin*, and some of them would wear the attire of the fighters in that region: army boots, Afghan hat, *shalwar khamis* and waistcoat.[192] It has been argued that the self-identification of JIMAS as 'Salafis' emerged in the early 1990s as they developed closer ties with certain Jordanian students of al-Albānī, who emphasized the term and the necessity of conforming to the 'Salafi methodology' (*al-manhaj al-salafi*).[193] Nonetheless, the foundations of this JIMAS turn towards al-Albānī was started previously, when early member Daawood Burbank returned from studying in Medina – although he failed to complete his degree at IUM – with an interest in translating and teaching from al-Albānī's works. These were received in awe-inspiring terms by members, in particular Abu Aaliyah; and early, influential JIMAS member Abdul-Kareem McDowell (known as Abu Sufyaan) traveled to Jordan to meet al-Albānī and brought back the latter's question and answer cassettes, which passionately espoused the necessity of adhering to the Salafi methodology.[194]

With JIMAS the overtly-Salafi identification became more pronounced into the 1990s, as did an upholding of the three main Salafi scholars of the time: Ibn Bāz, Ibn 'Uthaymin, and al-Albānī. This unified approach managed to maintain the political dimension of the movement, even after the First Gulf War and its accompanying Salafi divisions. They also developed strong links with Salafis in the United States, who were developing along similar lines; and one sees their utilization of speakers such as Bilal Philips, Jamaal al-Din Zarabozo, and Ali al-Timimi (who continued to speak at JIMAS conferences until 2002), among others, from North America.[195]

While the strands of Salafism were developing in the UK from MJAH to JIMAS to further splits, there was a highly-politicized form of Salafism that was also forming a strong foundation and providing an additional contribution to the growing Salafi identity, and that was through the work of Muhammad Surur (mentioned in Chapters 3 and 4). Upon settling in England, he established the organization entitled *Markaz Dirasat al-Sunna al-Nabawwiyah* (Centre for the Teaching of the Sunnah of the Prophet) in Birmingham and the *Al Muntada al-Islami* in London, which became highly influential upon UK Salafism (from the 1990s and then from 2001 when it appointed Haitham al-Haddad).[196] MJAH's acceptance or acquiescence of the Sururis, and their publication *al-Sunna* (first released in 1989), would, unsurprisingly, arouse the hostility of the UK quietist Salafis, as it regularly criticized the pro-Western bias of the Saudi regime, in particular in relation to the Saudi seeking of Western support in the First Gulf War in 1990. Surur's willingness to oppose the perceived political wrongs of the Saudi regime were exemplified in 1994 when he offered the use of his UK network to the Saudi dissidents Sa'd al-Faqih and Muhammad al-Mas'ari.[197]

*Third phase: JIMAS and UK Salafism splinters*

Abu Muntasir's continuing political interests and attempts at balancing, by way of illustration, the jihad-advocates of the Kashmiri military outfit *Laskar-e-Taiba* and the apolitical al-Albānī types came to a head at the JIMAS's annual conferences in Leicester, England, in 1995 and 1996.[198] This moment was emblematic of how the various factions could no longer be contained within the same organization, with each one's Salafism taking on an increasingly distinct form from the other. The quietist/apolitical elements came to feel that JIMAS was incorrectly influenced by Muslim Brotherhood ideas under the leadership of Abu Muntasir. As time progressed, such quietist elements, with complete loyalty to the Saudi royal family, would become influenced by the Saudi cleric Rabi' al-Madkhalī[199] (who inherited the mantle of the *Jamiyyah*[200]) and break with JIMAS completely, setting up their own organizations, mosques, and bookshops, and denouncing people they saw as inauthentic Salafis.

JIMAS would be severely weakened as a consequence and has ceased to be a Salafi organization. The MJAH and Green Lane Masjid, and those of a similar nature, have continued to walk a path close to the 'Madkhalis' (also mockingly called 'Super Salafis'), as self-identified Salafis,[201] but are still maligned by the Madkhalis for seemingly contradicting the Salafi path, which really just entails not following Rabi' al-Madkhalī's endorsements of people, groups, and opinions, which are known to change. There was an attempt in 1999 to maintain unity between the Birmingham Madkhalis and the Brixton Mosque faction who favored the Jordanian scholars associated with al-Albānī, in particular 'Ali Hasan al-Halabi, through the mediation of Abu al-Hasan al-Misri (or al-Ma'ribi), but the divide could not be healed, and the animosity between al-Halabi and al-Madkhalī would continue to grow in intensity until the mid-2000s. Consequently, these continuing Salafi factions uphold various Arab authorities for their own Salafi methodologies, with the quietist community split between the Brixton Mosque and Luton Islamic Centre factions on one side and the Birmingham Madkhalis of Salafi Publications on the other,[202] and still other Salafi groups toeing a line somewhere between the quietists and the activists.

Around this time, a further palatable form of Salafism emerged in the UK with the North American AlMaghrib Institute[203] and the Australian AlKauthar Institute[204] launching courses in the UK in the early 2000s. They both taught Salafi theology in a more commercialized form, which was highly attractive and seemed less combative or even 'Salafi,' hence its attraction to those who could not be easily identified or even self-identified as Salafi. The latter two organizations would start to dwindle in momentum by the late 2010s in the UK, with both becoming increasingly online, especially after the COVID pandemic after 2020. However, as though to confirm the evolving nature of Green Lane Masjid, it has hosted speakers from AlMaghrib and AlKauthar, who are not considered to be real Salafis by puritan factions who still try to hold on to Salafism, despite their dwindling numbers and weakening ideological position.[205]

After Green Lane Masjid, the next significant Salafi mosque in the UK is perhaps the Brixton Mosque (later named Masjid Ibn Taymeeyah), which was a general Sunni mosque until a Salafi leadership was elected in 1993.[206] By 2015, Salafi mosques were the fastest growing in the UK, with a 28% increase between 2014 and 2015; however, even with that rate of growth, their 155 mosques only accounted for 9% of the total. Yet 95% of Salafi mosques in the UK have facilities for women,[207] compared to the two largest groups in the UK, namely the Deobandīs, with around 50%, and Barelwis, with 83%. The Islamic University of Medina has held an important place for Salafi identification among UK Salafis. However, only seven students from the UK had graduated from IUM by 1993, and only twenty-one had graduated a decade later, after the IUM had offered 251 scholarships to applicants in the UK by this time.[208] Both sets of numbers have continued to grow, but have not become academically qualified at the time of writing.

*A note on Salafi literature in the UK*

The MJAH–JIMAS connection would produce some of the first significant Salafi publications in English. This started with the Saqib-led production of the periodical *The Straight Path*, then developed into the publication of books, either by Suhaib Hasan's Al-Quran Society, JIMAS itself or its publishing division, at first named Al-Haneef Publications, then Al-Hidaayah Publishing & Distribution (established in 1993) and Salafi Publications (established in 1996) – the latter two being in Birmingham close to Green Lane Masjid. The mid-1990s until the beginning of the 2000s saw these publishing houses and others produce the most monumental treatises, which had a major impact in supporting the Salafi call throughout the UK and the wider Anglosphere.

Al-Haneef Publications released al-Albānī's *The Prophet's Prayer* (1993) and al-Barbahari's supposed *Explanation of the Creed* (1995).[209] The former text, translated by Usama Hasan, the son of Suhaib Hasan, was nothing short of a phenomenon, and caused shockwaves in the religious community in the UK, cementing al-Albānī's fame and notoriety, in equal measure, among his supporters and opponents, respectively. Due to the generous funding of Usama's brother-in-law's father, 40,000 copies of the first edition were produced in Malaysia, with 20,000 to remain in the region of the printing, and 20,000 for the West.[210] The text falsely attributed to al-Barbahari, meanwhile, aided the extreme-minded Salafis who would later become known as 'Madkhalis,' which is unsurprising as it was translated by Daawood Burbank, who would be, perhaps, the intellectual driving force behind the group who broke with JIMAS along Madkhali-lines. Two other English-Salafi works were pivotal at this time in buttressing this pioneering drive along the terms of al-Albānī: the North American Bilal Philips's *The Evolution of Fiqh* and *The Fundamentals of Tawheed* – both published in 1990 and very popular in the UK by the mid-1990s. The latter two books were not published originally from the UK, although a future edition of *Fundamentals* would be published by al-Hidaayah.

The UK Salafi assault on Ashʿarī-Sufis was established by a number of al-Hidaayah publications: al-Albānī's *Tawassul – Seeking a Means of Nearness to Allaah: its Types and its Rulings* (1996) and Ibn 'Uthaymin's *Explanation of the Three Fundamental Principles of Islaam* (1997), both translated by Burbank; and two studies by this author expounding upon the theology of Muhammad Ibn ʿAbd al-Wahhāb: *An Explanation of Muḥammad Ibn ʿAbdul Wahhāb's Four Principles of Shirk* (2002) and *A Critical Study of Shirk: An Explanation of Muḥammad ibn ʿAbd al-Wahhāb's Kashf al-Shubuhāt* (2003). Saudi-based English publisher Darussalam was equally instrumental in distributing its Khan-Hilali translation of the Qur'an, *Kitāb al-Tawḥīd* by Ibn Abd al-Wahhāb, and many other Salafi titles through franchises based in London and Birmingham during the 1990s and 2000s.

### *UK Salafism and the war on terror*

The terrorist attacks of 9/11 would bring differing attitudes towards Salafism at the British governmental level. After the London bombings in 2005, the Prevent counter-terrorism policy came into existence under Labour in 2007, with an annual budget of £40 million. It was limited in its ability to connect with Muslims, as it failed to see how aggressive foreign policy, such as the invasions of Iraq and Afghanistan, contributed to the sense of grievances felt by British Muslims. Initially, there was governmental support under the scheme for quietist Salafis to tackle Islamic extremism in the community; hence the backing that was given to Strategy to Reach, Empower, and Educate Teenagers (STREET), led by Abdul Haqq

Baker at Brixton Mosque – shortly after converting, Baker had become one of JIMAS's leading speakers in the 1990s. However, this favoring of the 'street cred' or 'street skills' of the quietist Salafis waned by 2009 as governmental voices called for Prevent to support Muslim groups who shared Western, liberal values, which would exclude even quietist Salafis. The disavowal of 'non-violent extremists' became governmental policy under the Conservative government of David Cameron, when the Prevent policy was revised in 2011. This reversal saw STREET lose its funding in 2011, on the basis that its outlook was considered to fall under extreme guidelines.[211]

A review of the Prevent program was announced in February 2019 by the Conservative government of Theresa May, with William Shawcross appointed in January 2021 by the then-Conservative prime minister Boris Johnson to lead the investigation. However, media reports in December 2022 about the delays in releasing the report indicated an internal government dispute between those who wanted to take an aggressive approach towards Muslim extremism, in a time when far-right extremism was highlighted as a greater threat in the UK,[212] and those in the Home Office who did not want to take a widespread name-and-shame approach, in fear of being successfully prosecuted for libel.[213] For instance, Salman Butt, editor of the website Islam21C, which has strong Salafi connections (especially with its links to Haitham al-Haddad), received an apology from the Secretary of State for the Home Department, who had to read an apology to Butt in court in August 2021. This occurred after the government issued a press release on 17 September 2015 in which they identified Butt as an extremist hate preacher who endorsed terrorism, and therefore should be prevented from addressing students. After Butt brought charges against the government for libel, the government had to accept their wrongdoing, pay compensation for damages and libel and pay Butt's legal fees.[214] Nonetheless, when the report on Prevent by Shawcross was released in February 2023 without an explicit, sustained attack on Salafism, there was still enough hawkish analysis to increase the unease of Salafis in the UK, both quietists and activists.[215]

*Looking to the future*

In conclusion, Salafism has had a significant impact on the UK Muslim population. Yet, aside from its polemical and harsh nature, it has been hindered by disputes among its own ranks. As such, there are now a number of Salafisms operating in the UK, defined largely around the typical typology of (1) puritans/quietists/apolitical, (2) politicos/activists, and (3) Jihadis defined by Wiktorowicz. The main fault-lines were political activism and loyalty to rulers, in particular the Saudi royal family; yet while some are divided neatly into such respective camps, others (like the Brixton Mosque) are a mixture of the two, even though the latter is arguably the dominant trend, whether intentional or not.

While there was a successful flourishing of Salafism in the UK during the 1990s, this has dwindled to a large extent, in part due to the weakening of the Salafi call through its own fractionalization. Their initial success also triggered an intellectual backlash from other Sunni groups, especially from the Deobandī-Ḥanafīs, and the resulting onslaught, along with the internal sectarianism, has seen the exponential dwindling of Salafi conferences and mosques to an almost negligible presence compared to the heydays of the mid-1990s.

A further significant factor in the weakening of adherents in the UK was a spiritual crisis that many felt they were experiencing in Salafism. One of the earliest and most famous preachers to Salafism in the UK, Abu Aaliyah, publicly renounced Salafism primarily on this issue. Furthermore, some of the early leaders of JIMAS, like Abdur Raheem Green, came to perceive that their agendas as Salafis had been dictated by the political expediencies of the Saudi regime, and Green characterized their dogma then as 'really just Wahhabism,' which belied the idea that Salafism was some pristine extraction from the primary sources of Islam.[216]

The rise and eventual fall of British Salafism has yet to be fully documented and studied. As the Muslim population in the UK at the time of writing nears four million, and is increasingly young, it remains to be seen what role Salafism or post-Salafism might play in the future.

### *6.4.2 Türkiye*

Wahhabi-Salafism has probably had the least amount of impact on Turkish religious life. Of course, there was academic Ottoman engagement with Wahhabism from the seventeenth to the twentieth century, and the infamous polemics of one of the last grand scholars of the Ottomans, Muhammad Zahit Kevseri (Ar. Muhammad Zahid al-Kawthari, d. 1952) against the Salafi doctrines of Ibn Taymiyya in particular. But it was only in the 1980s that Salafism developed a presence, with some Salafi preachers emerging after training in Saudi Arabia, and the opening of a number of Salafi publishing houses. Perhaps the political ambience also helped in this regard, as the 1980s was an era in which the Turkish state sought to fend off the political competition posed by the Iranian Revolution and Turkish Islamists by developing the Turkish-Islamic Synthesis (*Türk İslam Sentezi*).[217]

A prominent example of the growing Salafi trend is Abdullah Yolcu (b. 1958), who is Iraqi in origin and settled in Türkiye in 1986, and then launched Guraba Publishing in Istanbul in 1992, as a venture of the Izmir-based charity *İlim Der*. Among the publications of this organization are translations into Turkish from Arabic of works by Salafi leaders such as Ibn Bāz, Ibn 'Uthaymin, al-Albānī, and Salih al-Fawzan, covering issues of theology and law favored by the Salafis. Another prominent Turkish cleric is

Nureddin Yildiz (b. 1960), who was born and raised in the city of Trabzon, then traveled in the 1980s to study in Saudi Arabia, before returning and becoming one of the most popular preachers in the country.[218] After a few years of preaching what can be considered mainstream Salafism, during the last few years his discourse has matured and he may now be viewed as post-Salafi.

In an interesting development, Salafism has come to be officially recognized by the Diyanet of the country as a valid school of theology, along with the Ashʿarī and Māturīdī schools. Nonetheless, the religious institutions of Türkiye remain very much aligned to their historic trajectory, and this has been aided by the migration of scholars from Syria, fleeing from the civil war, who have settled in Türkiye and disseminated their teachings, which are decidedly non-Salafi.

### *6.4.3 Bosnia and Herzegovina*

While there are a number of positions held by academics regarding how Salafism arrived in Bosnia and Herzegovina, what is an unmistakable fact is that in the twenty-first century it has a noticeable presence in the country, in particular in the capital, Sarajevo.[219] The pivotal moment in the country's opening to Salafism was the outbreak of civil war between 1992 and 1995, which pitted Bosnians against Serbs and Croats, as the former Yugoslavia disintegrated into ethnic conflicts. Before this time, Salafism was something almost wholly unknown as the Bosnians had their traditional Islam, which aligned with much of the region in its adherence to the Ḥanafī legal school and Sufi tradition.

Salafism would arrive in Bosnia via the humanitarian aid that came to help the war effort, as well as the foreign fighters who sought to defend the besieged Muslim population. A crucial element of the humanitarian and financial assistance offered to the Bosnians came from Saudi Arabia, with official figures between 1992 and 2011 estimating US$600 million, whereas the unofficial figure, with so many independent contributions, is likely to be far in excess of that total. Along with charitable aid, the Saudis also provided free Islamic literature, which contributed to the dissemination of Salafi doctrines, including *Take Your Belief from the Qurʾan and Sunna* by Muhammad Bin Jamil Zeno, Muhammad ibn ʿAbd al-Wahhāb's *Three Foundational Principles*, and Ibn Bāz's *The Prophet's Prayer* and some of his fatwas. Although the impact of this literature was significant, it did not lead to a Salafi revolution sweeping the country.[220]

The most interesting aspect of the Salafi arrival in Bosnia was the foreign *mujahidin* who started to arrive in greater numbers when the Pakistani government closed down the training camps near the Afghan-Pakistan border in 1993 and sought to deport foreigners from the area.

The Bosnian army had an *al Mujahid* unit, which only ever had a maximum of 700 foreign fighters, although most subscribed to Salafism. Almost immediately, such Salafi fighters were causing disruption among the local people, as seen in the example of the Egyptian Imad al-Misri, who came primarily to engage in combat against the Serbs but also published a book at the end of 1993 entitled *Notions That Must Be Corrected*, printed with the stamp of the Kuwaiti-Salafi *Jam'iyyat Ihya' al-Turath al-Islami*. This booklet critiqued local Sufi religious practice and caused the local Bosnian scholars and politicians to refute its contents, while also condemning its poor timing. Salafis were at the center of another controversy owing to their push to make people change their method of ritual prayer, while the Bosnian scholars called for their people to adhere to the Ḥanafī school. Nevertheless, the Salafi impact was minimal in changing the religious ideas and practice of Bosnians; and some Bosnians joined the foreign Salafi ranks in order to simply fight, rather than out of an attraction to Salafi principles.[221]

The question of whether these foreign Arab fighters were merely Salafis or Jihadi-Salafis, a distinction made earlier in Chapter 5, is a question of debate. Analysis has concluded that most were attracted to the Muslim Brotherhood (which is not wholly Salafi and is certainly not Jihadi-Salafi); and some were Salafis aligned with the Saudi establishment scholars like Ibn Bāz and Ibn al-Uthaymin. Only a small minority were Jihadi-Salafi, linked to the Jihadi-Salafi Egyptian Islamic Group (EIG) who were involved in a violent confrontation with the Egyptian government at the time, although figures like Anwar Sha'ban denied any connection to EIG.[222]

After the war, the Saudis and other Gulf countries contributed to the rebuilding of the country, including the building of homes for displaced people, and mosques. Of the latter, the Saudi-financed King Fahd Mosque was established in Sarajevo in 2000; but Saudi financing of such mosques slowed between 2011 and 2020. Saudi-financed organizations, like the Active Islamic Youth (AIY), were shut down shortly after 9/11.[223]

During the conflict, the Islamic University of Medina also greatly increased its quotas for Bosnian students on humanitarian grounds (as thousands were being massacred, hence a visa to Saudi provided a way out), and hundreds of Bosnians subsequently graduated from the IUM. Many others went to other regions, such as Kuwait and Jordan, but again there is little official documentation of their numbers. These graduates returned to Bosnia and helped spearhead a Salafi revivalist movement that has attracted a sizeable group of locals. Predictably, this generated a backlash from the religious establishment, and in 2017, the authorities raided several Salafi organizations who did not recognize the leadership of the official religious organization of the country. In such circumstances, it seems fair to say that Salafism will remain a visible yet marginal presence in Bosnia.

### *6.4.4 France*

While it is difficult to locate in specific detail the origins of Salafism in France, one can identify a rapid increase in the adoption of Salafism there from the 1990s,[224] which equates to when its exportation became global. Salafism in France is dominated by the quietist version, although there are some political and jihadi currents, and has its roots in the working-class communities of the French suburbs of prominent cities like Paris and Lyon.[225] The Salafi community is dominated by descendants from people with Maghrebi and North African heritage (especially Algerians), as well as a good number from sub-Saharan Africa (like Mali and Senegal) and even converts to the faith. In terms of background, some members have come from other Islamic groups like the Indian-based *Jamā'at al-Tablīgh*, or have traditional non-Salafi backgrounds – but very few are of Turkish origin.[226] Politically, many of the quietist Salafis have taken advice from Salafi religious authorities who prohibit them from participating in the political system. With this rejectionism there is a strong emphasis on detaching one's self from mainstream French society (perhaps understandable, to a certain extent, in light of the harsh political climate against Muslims) and even making migration to a Muslim land, in pursuit of a purer Islamic existence. So, 'the consequence of following the Salafi method,' in the analysis of Mohamed-Ali Adraoui, 'is that the young [French Salafi] Muslim becomes estranged from his newly found homeland.'[227] Any such estrangement is a serious cause for concern, if one considers that estimates put the French Salafi community at between 10,000 and 20,000 in 2014,[228] with around 140 mosques out of roughly 2,500 in 2016 and popular Salafi preachers, like Nader Abou Anas, who founded the D'Clic association.[229]

After the January 2015 attack on the premises of the *Charlie Hebdo* satirical publication, pursuant to their publishing satirical cartoons of the Prophet Muhammad in 2011,[230] the French government expanded its anti-terror laws, which came to have a severe impact on the Salafi community. If a Salafi center or preacher was found to have contravened these laws, they were punished. For instance, the Salafi preacher El Hadi Doudi, formerly an imam of the as-Sounna mosque in Marseille, was deported to Algeria in 2018 on account of provoking 'discrimination, hatred and violence' in his sermons, after the mosque had been closed down in 2017, as were others,[231] such as the Salafi preacher Abderrahim Sayah who was deported to Algeria in 2023.[232]

Within the French context, another innovative and popular development of the Salafi label emerged in the 1990s through the writings and lectures of Tariq Ramadan, who came to label himself as a 'Salafi reformist.'[233] This grandson of Ḥasan al-Bannā, the founder of the Muslim Brotherhood, was born and raised in Switzerland where his family were exiled from Egypt due to their leading roles in the Muslim Brotherhood. While Tariq Ramadan calls for a Salafism returning to the primary sources of the religion, and embraces the Salafi title, his Salafism is more akin to the liberal reform of Rashīd Riḍā. Nonetheless, his writings in French have contributed significantly to the debates about Islam and its place in France and the world, such as in England (for he has written extensively in English, and was a Professor in Islamic Studies at the University of Oxford until 2021)[234] and Morocco.[235] Ultimately, his intellectual contribution places him in the post-Salafi category (which is discussed further in section 6.6.3).

## 6.5 North America

The American Muslim scene began forming its first national and local organizations in the 1960s, as activists associated with the Muslim Brotherhood came to pursue higher studies. The Muslim Students Association (MSA), founded in 1963, which eventually evolved into the larger Islamic Society of North America (ISNA) in 1981, are two such umbrella organizations that have nominal roots in the Brotherhood, but no longer subscribe to its views. In this timeframe, students who had been more directly associated with the 'Enlightenment' Salafism of Riḍā also started organizing activities. In 1981, a group of such thinkers, including Maher Hathhout (d. 2015), Taha Jabir al-Alwani (d. 2016), Ismail Raja Faruqi (d. 1986), and Anwar Ibrahim (b. 1947) the current Prime Minister of Malaysia, formed the International Institute for Islamic Thought, or IIIT. While they were not, of course, puritanical Salafis, the Enlightenment Salafism of Riḍā was clearly demonstrated in their thought, and hence it was Ismail Raja Faruqi who first translated Ibn ʿAbd al-Wahhāb's *Kitāb al-Tawḥīd* into English, which was published in 1980 as part of WAMY's outreach to the Western world (referenced in section 4.2.3).

Salafism in North America emerged as a distinct phenomenon in the mid-1980s, but its roots go back to the 1970s. From the mid-1980s, Salafi organizations started to emerge in North America and became influential and popular, but by the mid-1990s they became fractured, as we've seen in countless other countries.[236] The trend of students from North America going to study at the IUM and other universities in Saudi Arabia and returning to proselytize in the region significantly increased the establishment of Salafism. By 1993, thirteen Americans had received undergraduate degrees from IUM, which increased to twenty by around 2003, after 285 scholarships had been offered by the university to American students.[237] Some of those IUM graduates have had a significant impact on Salafism in North America, as will be discussed. Although Salafism in the United States has been described as 'largely an East Coast phenomenon,' with a particular 'protestant' approach which appeals to 'the generality of Blackamerican Muslims,'[238] it has had influential centers in the south of the United States, particularly in Texas, as well as among non-Black Americans.

The first graduate of the IUM from North America to make a significant impact on Salafism around the world, and not merely in North America, was Bilal Philips.[239] He was born in 1947 in Jamaica and then lived in Canada, where he converted in 1972 – after having been an active communist in the United States and Canada – at the hands of another convert who would also go on to graduate from IUM, the American Abdullah Hakim Quick.[240] After conversion, Philips spent time with the *Tablighi Jama'at* (Society for Spreading Faith), who originate with the Ḥanafī Deobandī tradition of the Indian subcontinent,[241] and even went to England to study. However, after returning to Canada and studying Sayyid Sabiq's comparative legal manual *Fiqh al-Sunna* with an Egyptian imam in Toronto, he became more cognizant of the differences between the various Islamic schools of law. He took the opportunity to study at the IUM when he became aware of scholarship offers for Canadians, as a means of undertaking a path towards a study of the primary sources of the religion.[242] Philips subsequently acquired an undergraduate degree from the IUM in 1979, and then a master's degree in education from the University of Riyadh in 1985, before completing a PhD at the University of Wales in 1994.[243]

Philips' expansive writing career, in which he mostly composed original works rather than mere translations, developed soon after he graduated from the IUM when he began to produce a full school syllabus in Riyadh: his published works now total in excess of fifty. His *Fundamentals of Tawheed* (based on Ibn ʿAbd al-Wahhāb's *Kitāb al-Tawḥīd* and its commentary *Fath al-Majid*) and *The Evolution of Fiqh* (championing al-Albānī's understandings of the Islamic legal schools) in 1990 would be considered modern Salafi classics by the mid-1990s.

His additional achievements include leading a team of proselytizers who engaged the American military in Saudi Arabia in 1991–92, after the First Gulf War, in which 3,000 troops (according to his claims) converted to Islam. He also taught at a variety of universities, and led and founded a number of institutions, including the International Open University (IOU) from Doha, Qatar (2007 until the time of writing).[244]

As perhaps the foremost Salafi intellectual in the mid-1990s writing and speaking in English, Philips was naturally embroiled in the divisions which beset the movement at that time; and the Madkhali faction came to dismiss his Salafism as being politically tainted. In 2001, he expressly replied to critics in an article where he reaffirmed his Salafism, and even spoke of his historical roots in the movement, unlike the new Madkhalis who had no comparative intellectual pedigree. However, by 2018, he was quoted as saying that he no longer used the term 'Salafi' to describe himself, and simply concentrated on conveying the 'concept' without the title. Furthermore, his Salafism came to be further refined, now accommodating Ashʿarīs within the definition of the orthodox community (*ahl al-Sunna wa'l-Jamaʿah*) on the basis that it was merely a mistaken position that they had formed, which was not so serious that it would lead to deviation from the community.[245]

The first significant strand of Salafism to emerge in North America was the quietist and apolitical variety inspired by the thought and methodology of al-Albānī. Institutionally, this took the form of the *al-Qur'an was-Sunnah Society* (QSS) in the 1980s, which was officially formed in Arlington, Texas. The first chair was Mahmud Murad, followed by Muhammad al-Jibaly from the early 1990s. The organization was deeply committed to the Salafism of al-Albānī and his direct students, and disseminated newsletters, publications, and cassettes that were the first of their kind in America. Al-Jibaly, who was from Lebanon originally and a university lecturer with a PhD in physics from the University of Texas at Arlington,[246] was a prolific author of Islamic books in English, composing works on articles of faith and Islamic law, including marriage and inheritance. Eventually by the early 1990s, QSS had adopted a tacit Saudi loyalty, and would oppose Islamic currents in North America that censured the Saudi royal family or the Saudi clerical establishment. Furthermore, QSS was responsible for creating a discourse which was harmful and prone to cultish extremism, and focused on small details of law and dogma without giving enough attention to developing a holistic program.

QSS attracted a large supporter base in the African-American community, including in disadvantaged areas, and was able to maintain its activities publishing Salafi works and holding conferences and lectures until the mid-1990s, whereupon the Western Salafi squabbles led to irreconcilable divides, weakening the organization in particular, and the movement in general – with the developing cultish-Madkhali faction in North America, primarily The Reign of Islamic Daʿwah (TROID), casting QSS and others such as North American Salafi pioneers Jamaal Zarabozo (a largely self-trained scholar and translator) and Bilal Philips as astray (with the common phrase being that they were 'off the *manhaj*'). Muhammad Syed Adly, an early lecturer for QSS, but one who always refused the Salafi labeling, pinpointed the start of the factionalism as the deaths of Ibn Bāz, al-Albānī and Ibn 'Uthaymin, where, in his words, 'everyone tried to become a big shot, like [Rabi'] Madkhali.'[247] Nonetheless, in the aftermath of this factionalism, apolitical and quietist currents persisted, with the main centers being Philadelphia and New Jersey. The latter community had its roots in the community center founded in 1981 by an American convert, Ahmad Burhani, in East Orange, which was then developed by Dawud Adib, a convert who spent some time studying in IUM, and Abu Muslimah, another convert and graduate of the IUM – both Abu Muslimah and Adib had been involved in QSS.[248]

QSS's lack of political engagement in the 1990s led to the first noticeable schism within North America Salafism when the Islamic Assembly of North America (IANA) emerged as a forceful alternative to QSS. IANA was founded in Michigan in 1993 by a non-Salafi, Bassem Khafagi, who was also a member of the Council on American Islamic Relations (CAIR), which is more Islamist in origin and method. Nonetheless, IANA came to be dominated by Salafis with a more political activist agenda and discourse, influenced as they were by the Salafi scholars of the Saudi *Ṣaḥwa* movement.

IANA's political pronouncements attracted a spectrum of American Muslims, and surpassed QSS in popularity, as the doctrine-focused approach of QSS made it seem largely irrelevant to the real world. Yet a large number of Salafis or Salafi-inclined people would continue to attend conferences hosted by both QSS and IANA, and quietist Salafi preachers, like Zarabozo and Philips, would appear as speakers at both organizations. Furthermore, IANA's Arabic publication, *al-Manar al-jadid* (*The New Lighthouse*), would feature Muslim Brotherhood scholars like Shaykh Yusuf al-Qaradawi, and activist Salafis like Jafar Shaikh Idrees, and it referred honorably to Ḥasan al-Bannā and reprinted articles by Sayyid Qutb and Sayyid Mawdudi. Yet the more militant focus of IANA was observable in 1993 when they hosted the Saudi veteran of the war in Bosnia Abd al-Rahman al-Dosari, who delivered a lecture on 'Jihad and Revival'; and in May 2001 their publication, *al-'Asr* (*The Era*), included articles permitting suicide bombs as a military tactic by *Ṣaḥwa* scholar Salman al-Oudah. IANA's demise began when some of its members were targeted after 9/11 for supporting jihad. IANA ceased to function in a meaningful way from 2003.

In 2005, Ali al-Timimi, seen as the leading intellectual in IANA, was convicted of terrorist charges and given a life sentence, as he was considered to be the spiritual leader of what became known as 'the Virginia Jihad Network.' Al-Timimi was a dynamic speaker who had emerged through the Salafi circles of North America and became a leading lecturer during the late 1990s and early 2000s. Al-Timimi was born in Washington DC in 1963, to parents who would have successful professional careers after immigrating to the United States from Iraq in 1962. After a fairly non-religious upbringing in America, his parents moved the family to Saudi Arabia, where al-Timimi received a secular and religious education. His religious instruction was unsurprisingly Salafi, and one of his teachers in his private school in Riyadh was a recently-graduated Bilal Philips.[249] After returning to the United States and obtaining a biology degree from George Washington University, he briefly studied at the IUM in 1987, and developed a good relationship with the quietist-loyalist Salafi scholar Ibn Bāz, but had to return to the United States shortly thereafter due to family issues. While his formal religious education was quite limited, he excelled in his career; and after first obtaining a second undergraduate degree in computer science, he worked successfully in the IT field. Nonetheless, he had maintained his private Islamic studies and began to regularly lecture, rising through the QSS ranks and then coming to prominence in IANA with a number of lecture series which were scholarly and popular on both sides of the Atlantic. Unlike QSS scholars, al-Timimi utilized the works of *Ṣaḥwa* scholars as a basis for his lecture material and would, as early as 1996, support rebuffing invading Western forces in the Middle East using military means. In 1995, al-Timimi had contacts with the activist-Salafi scholar Abd al-Rahman Abd al-Khaliq in Kuwait, as al-Timimi convinced IANA to send him as the head of a delegation to speak at the World Conference on Women in Beijing, which he did in response to learning that the Clinton administration intended to send secular Muslims to represent the United States.[250] Then in 2002, before the Western invasion of Iraq in 2003, he worked with Safar al-Hawali from Saudi in drafting a letter to the American Congress, seeking to dissuade them from violence against Iraq.[251]

In the United States, al-Timimi developed a close relationship with Jafar Shaikh Idrees (b. 1931), a notable activist-Salafi scholar operating in the United States. Idrees was a Saudi national of Sudanese origin, with a PhD from the University of London (his 1970 doctorate thesis was entitled 'The Concept of the Causality in Islam'). He was the founding chairman of the American Open University in Alexandria, Virginia, and director at the Institute of Islamic and Arabic Sciences in America (IIASA) in Fairfax, Virginia, which was founded in 1988 as an affiliate of the Imam Ibn Saʿud University in Riyadh, Saudi Arabia. He had also taught at the latter university in Saudi Arabia.

The relationship between al-Timimi and Idrees was formalized in the mid-1990s when they co-founded the Center for Islamic Information and Education (CIIE), which was also known as *Dar al-Arqam*, and was activist Salafi in orientation. The latter location became very popular with youth in the area and would later be the meeting place for the so-called Virginia Jihad Network, which would lead to al-Timimi being convicted and sentenced to life imprisonment on terrorist charges. Just after being arrested on the charges that would lead to his incarceration, he was able to obtain his PhD in computational biology, related to the study of cancer, at George Mason University, in northern Virginia, in December 2004, after authoring or co-authoring around half a dozen academic papers during his doctoral research.[252] He was released from prison under house arrest in August 2020, as his appeal fight made significant progress. This author had a close relationship with al-Timimi as his student before leaving the United States to study in Saudi Arabia, and the personal assessment of this author is that he never advocated violence. His indictment seems more in line with the well-documented overzealous treatment of Muslims by law enforcement after 9/11 than any actual crime, and the emerging success of his appeal process seems to indicate how he was unjustly treated through his prosecution.

The overarching effects of the America government after 9/11 effectively shut down all Salafi organizations and conferences as they had existed pre-9/11. It would take a few years for the North American trajectory of Salafism to return as the 'post-Salafism' or 'Americanized Salafism' of the AlMaghrib Institute. The latter emerged from these prior Salafi roots, but managed to craft its public presentation to such an extent that many students failed to perceive it as Salafi and saw its methodology as simply mainstream Sunni.[253] AlMaghrib was founded in 2002, with its headquarters in Houston, Texas, by the dynamic and visionary Muhammad Alshareef (d. 2022), a dear friend of this author, and a Canadian who attained an Islamic studies undergraduate degree from the IUM in 1999. The institute would eventually expand to teach over fifty core subjects to over 250,000 students in over forty cities across the world, with the main locations being in the United States and Canada, but also including the UK, Scandinavia, and Australia. In the face of Salafism waning in North America after 9/11 due to its doctrine being associated, in the general public perception, with all sorts of nefarious activities and inclinations, AlMaghrib was described as 'having almost single-handedly revived the Salafi movement in the US among Sunni American Muslim college students.'[254]

AlMaghrib instructors were almost invariably Salafi-trained, and mostly graduates of the IUM, but its declared methodology only speaks of 'Islamic learning,' without using 'Salafi' or even 'the Qurʾan and Sunna' as motifs. This author served for many years, from almost the inception of the institute until 2019, as the Dean of Academic Affairs and was seen to be 'the face' of the organization,[255] teaching the most popular theological seminars offered by AlMaghrib – entitled 'Light of Guidance' and 'Light Upon Light' – for over a decade and a half in numerous cities. In speaking about me, Christopher Pooya Razavian wrote, 'Qadhi is arguably the most famous foreign graduate of the Islamic University of Medinah (IUM), and one of America's most influential Muslims.'[256] These courses were interactive and modernized presentations of the Najdi theology of Muhammad Ibn ʿAbd al-Wahhāb and the Salafi theology of Ibn Taymiyya, and audiences warmly embraced the delivery and concepts; and, in that sense, such students could be fairly described as 'Salafi,' whether they wholeheartedly knew it or not.

Nonetheless, the Salafism of AlMaghrib was so subtle that committed Salafis would reject the notion that AlMaghrib was Salafi and would view it as too liberal for their liking. Furthermore, with my leadership as the Dean of Academic Affairs, AlMaghrib pushed the boundaries of traditional Salafism in North America, by having a leading Sufi, namely Zaid Shakir, attend and speak at an AlMaghrib class, and a woman, Dalia Mogahed, address an audience by around 2009. The success of AlMaghrib, and with it the rise of this author's prominence, helped spearhead a new wave of a more mature, non-confrontational Salafism.

Such moves did lead to more conservative students distancing themselves from AlMaghrib but, in general, these steps were accepted and were developed, to the point that there is now greater tolerance of gender interaction and cooperation with patently non-Salafi groups and instructors. AlMaghrib continues to operate in-person classes and maintains a popular online presence, despite the sudden and tragic passing in 2022 of its founder Muhammad Alshareef, whose foresight and warmth are sadly missed by this author and many others.

Of course, in the post-9/11 world, American security forces targeted not just Jihadi-Salafi trends but also moderate and non-violent Salafi groupings such as AlMaghrib. One response of AlMaghrib, when this author was Dean of Academic Affairs, was to invite the FBI to a seminar in order to address the students. Furthermore, in a move reminiscent of STREET in the UK, and in collaboration with Abdul Haqq Baker and STREET, some quietist Salafis in the United States formed a similar organization, *Tashih ul-Afkar al-Mutatarrifah* (Rectifying Extremist Ideologies or TAM), under the leadership of an American convert, Tahir Wyatt, an IUM doctoral graduate, with the task of combatting extremist ideology, especially for those who misunderstood Salafi teachings in this regard. Towards this aim, TAM sought to work with governmental authorities. It is difficult to verify whether these attempts have changed the negative public perception of Salafism in North America or not, but it is hoped that they will further reduce the social isolation that Salafism has bred, especially in poorer communities in the region.

While quietist Salafism has persisted in small measure in North America, and the post-Salafism of AlMaghrib has become a mainstream Islamic expression, scholarly Salafism has also continued with the Assembly of Muslim Jurists of America (AMJA), based in California, in a form that incorporates the history of QSS, IANA, IIASA and AlMaghrib, among other Salafi currents (except, of course, apolitical quietists whose intellectual output is aimed at polemics). This organization arranges high-level academic conferences and has papers delivered that seek to provide profound scholarly responses (*fatwas*) to the challenges of being Muslim in modern-day North America. By way of illustrating the continuity with the Salafi past in North America, one observes that AMJA's General Secretary, co-founder and member of the Resident Fatwa Committee is Dr Salah Alsawy, an Egyptian with a PhD from Al-Azhar University. He is a former lecturer at Al-Azhar University and Umm al-Qura University in Mecca, and he also taught at IIASA from 1992 to 1995; from 1995 to 2004 he was president and co-founder of the American Open University, where Jafar Shaikh Idrees also taught. In addition, Waleed Basyouni, a member of AMJA's Resident Fatwa Committee and a graduate of Riyad's Imam Saʿud University, is President of the AlMaghrib Institute; and AMJA's 'experts' include Jamaal Zarabozo (who has written many works from a Salafi paradigm, including a 400-page defense of Ibn ʿAbd al-Wahhāb), Muhammad Syed Adly, and many others.

In 2004, Alsawy and AMJA founded an academic institution in Texas which would eventually be named Mishkah University. AMJA shows potential for how scholarly Salafism can still endure, evolve and be productively beneficial for Muslims by embracing the very highest intellectual principles of the faith and not falling victim to the sectarianism rampant in earlier iterations of the movement. Of course, this is not to say that AMJA is devoid of the need for improvement, as its fatwas still tend to be on the ultra-conservative side, but its progress is a welcome development.

Nevertheless, the continuing relevance and relative success of a scholarly Salafism, or even the struggling persistence of quietist and even cultish Salafism, pales in comparison to the appeal of post-Salafism. A somewhat ultimate and progressive step of this American journey of Salafism, perhaps even further than AlMaghrib, can be seen in the highly active and popular Yaqeen Institute, which was founded in 2016 in Irving, Texas. The founder and president (CEO) of Yaqeen is Omar Suleiman, who was a product of the QSS and IANA era. Suleiman studied with Dr al-Ashqar (from the first batch of graduates of the IUM) and has ties with AMJA's Dr Salah Alsawy. Yaqeen is primarily educational, with a distinctive embrace of academia as well as traditional learning, and aims at addressing pressing concerns of faith in the modern world. Thus, rather than focusing on abstract theology, Yaqeen produces videos and written material on questions such as the proofs of Prophethood and the pillars of the faith, as well as more technical articles on the preservation of the Qurʾan and various readings of the Qurʾan, and the belief in evolution. On the academic front, they have collaborations with non-Salafi intellectuals like Jonathan A.C. Brown (who is Yaqeen's Director of History and Islamic Thought, and one of their associate editors), Hatem Bazian (an advisor), and Shabbir Akhtar.[257] A former Salafi, Surkheel Sharif (aka Abu Aaliyah), has written a paper for them;[258] and one of their advisors and associate editors, Abdul Rahman Waheed, studied in Deobandī seminaries, and there are many non-Salafi collaborators. However, the continuing influence of Salafi training is palpable in key positions, especially in theology, even if not doctrinally obvious. For instance, Tahir Wyatt is Director of Systematic Theology and associate editor; Mohammad Elshinawy, a one-time IUM student, and graduate and instructor of Mishkah, is Associate Director of Systematic Theology; and IUM alumni like Yaser Birjas (advisor) and Abdullah Oduro (Head of Convert Resources) are key members. Therefore, it is unsurprising that Yaqeen has never become involved in sectarian issues nor overtly propagated the theological positions of Ibn Abd al-Wahhāb or Ibn Taymiyya; yet its overall research methodology and ecumenical outlook is most certainly not traditionalist Ashʿari or Sufi. As such, Yaqeen's growing popularity, among all sections of society, demonstrates how successful post-Salafism has been, and the appeal it has within the wider Muslim community.

All of this popularity has generated a more robust response from the establishment Salafism icons. While very few have directly challenged the most popular icons and institutes, fearing that it will result in a backlash against them, there have been renewed attempts to 'purify' what puritanical Salafis view as the liberalization of the teachings of Islam. Recently, conventions have also been attempted, led by an Egyptian-American cleric Kareem Abu Zaid, in which figures like Bilal Philips and Dr Zakir Naik are broadcast live via tele-link, and local Salafi preachers (some of whom are graduates of the IUM) are showcased. Still, if one looks at the number of attendees, the impact that such conferences have had is extremely minimal, and in all likelihood, the establishment of Salafism has seen its heyday in the North American context, and the future appears to be for other movements, in particular post-Salafism.

## 6.6 The Phenomenon of Post-Salafism

The term 'post-Salafism' has been used several times throughout this chapter. In this section, we shall define this term and mention its key characteristics and iconic figures.

### 6.6.1 Definitions and Trajectory

Post-Salafism is an observable contemporary global phenomenon that emerged from key actors within the Salafi movement as a critical response to Salafism, reflecting broader socio-political and theological shifts.[259] One academic explains it in the following terms:

> [Post-Salafi refers to] an emerging, amorphous category of Muslim scholars who seem to find Salafi theology and activism too narrow when it comes to confronting complex social and political arenas, and especially in terms of interacting with Sufis. If a core part of Salafism is … a 'muscular discourse that is directed at reforming other non-Salafi Muslims,' then post-Salafism downplays this element in favor of postures that facilitate political and social coalitions with other Muslims. Other variants of post-Salafism, finally, are working to pair Salafi theology with a more wide-ranging view of Muslim spirituality.[260]

Post-Salafism, therefore, can be defined as a reformist and critical strand that emerged from within Salafism and attempts to reconcile aspects of Salafism with contemporary issues and modernity. Unlike traditional Salafism, which emphasizes a strict adherence to the practices of the *salaf* and a literal interpretation of the Qur'an and Sunna, post-Salafism advocates for a more nuanced and contextual understanding of Islamic texts. It represents a significant shift in the approaches of some leading Salafi voices who, for a period of time, represented mainstream Salafism, but then abandoned puritanical Salafism and began to address its perceived limitations while adapting at least some of its principles to modern contexts.

Post-Salafis are often involved in socio-political activism, advocating for justice, human rights, and social welfare, rather than simply focusing on dogma and acts of worship. They believe that Islam should play a constructive role in addressing contemporary issues such as democracy, gender equality, and economic justice, challenging both secular and authoritarian interpretations that marginalize these concerns, while avoiding simplistic fundamentalist responses to these problems that are commonly found in mainstream movements. Such activism typically involves forming alliances with other Muslim groups and participating in political processes, which contrasts with the earlier Salafi stance of political quietism or outright opposition to non-Islamic governance systems.

There are a number of key factors that one can state permeate through all strands of post-Salafism. One of them is a critical engagement with traditional Salafi and Wahhabi doctrines: they emphasize the contextual interpretation of the Qur'an and hadith and scrutinize the methodologies and interpretations of classical Salafi scholars, advocating for a reinterpretation of texts that considers the socio-historical context of earlier interpreters. This approach often leads to more flexible and adaptive religious rulings that align with contemporary realities, hence signaling a withdrawal of their previous support of Salafi authority.

Another feature is the lack of emphasis on theological doctrines typically associated with Salafism, such as a particular understanding of God's Attributes. Unlike the exclusivist stance of traditional Salafism, post-Salafism embraces intellectual pluralism. Post-Salafis are open to engaging with various Islamic schools of thought and even non-Islamic philosophies. This pluralistic approach allows for a more inclusive and dynamic discourse, fostering a more diverse understanding of Islam. Invariably, one finds a softening of sectarian rhetoric and a willingness to embrace a larger group of diverse actors for the greater good.

Post-Salafis argue that the rigidity of traditional Salafism fails to address the complexities of modern life. Therefore, they promote *ijtihad* (independent reasoning) and the application of *maqāsid al-sharīʿa* (objectives of Islamic law) to ensure that Islamic principles serve the welfare of society.

Post-Salafism also places a strong emphasis on the ethical and moral dimensions of Islam rather than prioritizing abstract theological beliefs or a mere literal compliance with specific rituals. Post-Salafis believe that the essence of Islam lies more in its moral teachings than in a narrowly defined 'orthodoxy' and 'orthopraxy.'

Post-Salafism has the potential to transform Islamic education by encouraging critical thinking and intellectual exploration. Incorporating contemporary issues and fresh methodologies into the curriculum can produce a new generation of Muslim scholars who are well-equipped to address the challenges of the modern world.[261]

In the words of one academic, 'Post-Salafism, then, is on one level an argument that the intra-Muslim theological debates of the late twentieth century have partly run their course. The changing atmosphere is giving rise to new conversations and new postures, as the twenty-first century brings surprising rapprochements between post-Salafis and Sufis.'[262]

### *6.6.2 History and Origins*

A number of factors have led to this interesting phenomenon, first and foremost the death of leading Salafi scholars who had garnered universal respect and support among all strands of Salafis – namely Ibn Bāz, Ibn ʿUthaymin, and al-Albānī. The vacuum that was created with their successive deaths (within the span of a year and a half) could not be filled with any other revered cleric and led to an almost complete fragmentation of the movement and a decentralized discourse (as has been discussed in Chapters 3 and 5). Secondly, the massive spread of the movement in the 1990s succeeded in attracting many diverse voices, some of whom came to realize, as they matured, that they fundamentally disagreed with key tenets of the movement. Thirdly, the rise of fanatical groups like ISIS, which were clearly tapping into mainstream Wahhabi beliefs, triggered a backlash from many intellectuals who felt compelled to point out the inherent potential for fanaticism from the movement (figures like Sharif Hatim al-Awni and Adil al-Kalbani, to be discussed in the next section, are examples of this). Fourthly, events of the post-Arab Spring in Egypt, the UAE, and Saudi demonstrated the complete political failure of quietist, Madkhalī, and even *Ṣaḥwa* strands. This failure was then followed by attempts, many of which were highly successful, from the Emirates and Saudi to 'steer' quietist Salafism into being compliant to state interests. Such pliability has understandably led to a growing discontent with the shallowness of the movement as a whole. There is a growing perception among many of its own adherents that the movement – across all of its strands – lacks the capacity to respond to crises Muslims face in the modern world, from systemic injustice and oppression to maintaining Islamic spirituality in a rapidly secularizing society.

Post-Salafism should not be confused with two other common phenomena: firstly, those who left Salafism by simply abandoning religiosity altogether (a phenomenon so common that the phrase 'Salafi burnout' was coined to describe it); and secondly, those who move to adopt another trend (typically, the Ashʿari-Sufi paradigm known as 'traditionalist Islam'). Instead, post-Salafism discards key Salafi beliefs and practices that it sees as irrelevant while retaining a semblance of others, and then adapting those retained principles to local cultures and political realities. This 'indigenization' reflects the pragmatic engagement of post-Salafis with their socio-political environments, resulting in a diverse range of practices and beliefs that deviate from orthodox, puritanical Salafism. One of the problems with this definition, it should be pointed out, is that the level of 'retainment' varies from individual to individual, and hence what exactly remains of puritanical Salafism is not quantifiable. Nevertheless, almost all post-Salafi figures have demonstrated that they do not adopt beliefs from other strands (like, for example, Sufism), and retain an open-mindedness to Islamic law that is more akin to 'Enlightenment Salafism' rather than *madhhab*-based law.

### *6.6.3 Key Figures*

Several key figures have been influential in the development and propagation of post-Salafi thought. The following are, perhaps, the most important.

*Salman al-Oudah*

If post-Salafism has one key figure that can be credited with its spearheading, that figure is Salman al-Oudah (one of the founders of the *Ṣaḥwa* movement, discussed in 3.2.4). Al-Oudah's journey within the realm of Islamic scholarship offers a compelling narrative of post-Salafi evolution, characterized by a departure from rigid orthodoxy towards a more nuanced and reformist approach.

Born in 1956 in Burayda, Saudi Arabia, to an established Najdi religious family, al-Oudah was educated in the central religious institute of Burayda, and became a lecturer at Imam Muhammad ibn Saud University. He emerged as a prominent Salafi figure, deeply involved in Islamist activism as part of the Saudi *Ṣaḥwa* movement, and came to national prominence because of his opposition to the American presence in Saudi Arabia during the First Gulf War in 1990. He was eventually dismissed from his university post in 1993 and jailed for a number of years.[263]

After his release in 1999, al-Oudah's trajectory took a significant turn as he began to engage in more contemplative discourse. From 2001, he publicly attended meetings with Saudi-Shiʿite clerics, which were held under the Saudi regime's initiative called the Dialogue Forums, where he stressed the common values of Islam.[264] These actions led to widespread private criticism of al-Oudah by establishment Salafi clerics, as they deemed it to be too conciliatory towards a heretical group; however, the public announcement of such concerns was avoided, as al-Oudah was working under the sponsorship of the government. Indeed, al-Oudah's involvement in the national dialogue program could be interpreted as him moving closer to more liberal groupings or simply that he was being used as an instrument of the government.[265]

Furthermore, he released a series of videos entitled 'Signs' (*Ar. 'Wasam'*) in which he tackled common social issues, like racism, family violence, harsh treatment of laborers, and arrogance. The series was completely unprecedented for a Salafi audience, and garnered wide praise due to the fact that it tackled issues that were endemic but typically neglected in Salafi discourse. In addition, in 2005 he began to regularly appear on Saudi television, and eventually was given his own weekly program, entitled *Hajar al-Zawiya* (*Corner Stone*), which ran for 150 episodes until being stopped in 2011. Again, al-Oudah's discourse illustrated his reformist and pragmatic development from his earlier work.[266]

In 2012, in the immediate aftermath of the Arab Spring, he released the work *As'ilat al-Thawra* (*Questions on the Arab Spring*), which represents a foundational text for post-Salafi thought, in which he explores complex topics, particularly regarding rebellion, protest, and obedience within Islam, acknowledging the nuances inherent in interpreting scriptural sources and historical context.[267] Contrary to the prevalent narrative of absolute obedience to rulers, al-Oudah highlights the contractual nature of allegiance, emphasizing voluntary compliance and the duty of the ruled to advise the ruler. Central to al-Oudah's discourse is the concept of obedience tempered by moral responsibility and adherence to higher principles. Drawing upon Qur'anic verses and canonical hadiths, he argues for a balanced approach that prioritizes adherence to God's law over blind obedience to authority. His critique extends to problematic hadiths, such as those advocating obedience even in the face of oppression, which he deems unsound based on scholarly analysis. The popularity of this work has been explained by Madawi Al-Rasheed in the following terms:

> His reflections on revolution remain an indigenous attempt to reinterpret political and social history within the normative framework of Salafi thought. His fusion of this Salafi heritage with western political theory and historical case studies makes him appeal to a wider, non-Salafi audience, thus bridging the divide between the so-called authentic Islamic tradition and imported liberal concepts, often pejoratively conceived as *taghrib* (westernisation).[268]

Nonetheless, this book was immediately banned in Saudi Arabia, so the author bravely released a free PDF of it on his social media. Subsequently, his movements were restricted by the Saudi regime, and he was banned from traveling abroad.[269]

In the wake of the Arab revolutions, al-Oudah's perspective gained renewed relevance as he advocated for reform and social justice within the framework of Islamic principles. However, his outspoken views led to his imprisonment in Saudi Arabia in 2017 as part of a crackdown on dissenting voices; he remains in jail as of the writing of this work. Despite facing torture and the threat of the death penalty, al-Oudah remains steadfast in his commitment to a more inclusive and socially conscious interpretation of Islam, embodying the spirit of post-Salafi thought in the contemporary Muslim world.[270]

*al-Sharif Hatim al-Awni*

Another key figure, especially among Wahhabi post-Salafists, is Dr al-Sharif Hatim al-Awni (b. 1966). Dr al-Awni is from a non-Najdi Hijazi Sharifian background, and has always stood somewhat apart from the Wahhabi establishment, despite his upbringing in an activist Salafi environment and in light of his acclaim as a hadith scholar. During the last decades, he gained recognition beyond hadith studies in theology and jurisprudence.

After tentatively beginning a critique of Salafism, he eventually began to directly target Wahhabi theology for criticism, particularly its tendencies toward *takfīr* and violence against fellow Muslims, which became even more pertinent with the rise of ISIS.[271] In this regard, he opposed the Grand Mufti of Saudi Arabia and said, 'ISIS militants and theoreticians refer to Ibn ʿAbd al-Wahhab, and not to Sayyid Qutub or other Muslim Brotherhood figures, precisely because Muslim Brotherhood ideologues and activists are not doctrinally inspired by, or attached to, Salafism.'[272] Over time, his critiques have evolved into severe condemnations of Salafi-Wahhabism, challenging the unquestioning loyalty to figures like Ibn Taymiyya, accusing Ibn ʿAbd al-Wahhāb of outright fanaticism, and highlighting the lack of qualifications among many Salafi scholars.[273] One academic writes of his work, 'In his critique of Salafism, al-Awni has provided the building blocks for a theological outlook that could enable a restructuring of Salafism in the contemporary world. It is based on foundations selected from classical sources that are accepted in contemporary Salafi thought, while it abandons some of its most problematic features. Al-Awni's post-Salafism is primarily post-sectarian.'[274] Al-Awni represents what post-Salafism looks like theologically – a response against the 'salvific exclusivism' characteristic of Wahhabi and Salafi thought.

Critics from within the Salafi movement, both the establishment/quietist and the *Ṣaḥwa* strand, accuse al-Awni of providing fodder to liberal secular forces seeking to undermine Saudi society's Islamic character. However, his supporters argue that such accusations are mere deflections to avoid addressing his substantive critiques.[275] Al-Awni's insider perspective and rigorous scholarly approach have made his critiques arguably the most substantial challenge traditional Wahhabism has faced for the last two centuries. Despite launching scathing attacks on Salafism, his background and status within Saudi Arabia's Salafi scholarly class have led some to view his stance as a form of post-Salafism.

*Adil al-Kalbani*

One more Saudi post-Salafi figure worthy of mention is Adil al-Kalbani (b. 1959). He was initially renowned as a Qur'an reciter and a prayer leader in the Grand Mosque of Mecca, but he has transitioned into more of a social media figure, attracting attention for his revisionist viewpoints. Previously, he was a hardline Salafi, and very anti-Shia, but he has come to modify his stance, under the influence of Hatim al-Awni.[276] While some view his rise as partly fueled by self-promotion, he has also been given a platform by official state media in Saudi Arabia and the Arab world, presenting a seemingly 'liberal' image, especially to Western audiences; for instance, he tweeted a photo of himself driving a Harley Davidson in Western attire – hardly the stereotypical image of a Saudi cleric and prayer leader. He has been highly critical of Wahhabi theology, by claiming that ISIS is fully Wahhabi, and of many Salafi legal rulings that he claims distort the message and spirit of Islam. However, his lack of scholarly credentials limits his influence among the more academic Salafis.[277]

*Post-Salafism as maqāsid al-sharīʿa discourse*

In the broader Arab world, a number of figures can be viewed as representing post-Salafism within the framing of the *maqāsid al-sharīʿa* (the goals of Islamic Law) discourse, even if they do not discuss it as such. Ahmad Raysuni (b. 1953) is a Moroccan scholar known for his contributions to the field of *maqāsid al-sharīʿa* whose approach aligns with the post-Salafist emphasis on contextual interpretation and ethical considerations.[278] Another thinker associated within this trend is Jasser Auda (b. 1966), who has authored notable works in English on the theory of *maqāṣid al-sharīʿa*.[279] Auda advocates for a holistic understanding of Islamic law that goes beyond literalism to consider the intentions and purposes behind the laws. His work promotes a flexible and pragmatic approach to Islamic jurisprudence.

*Post-Salafis in the English-speaking West*

In the Western world, Tariq Ramadan (b. 1962) is a prominent scholar and public intellectual who has been a leading voice in post-Salafism. His works emphasize the need for European Muslims to integrate Islamic values with European cultural norms, advocating for a contextual and dynamic interpretation of Islam. Ramadan has called for a 'European Islam' and reflects the post-Salafist ethos of adapting Islamic principles to contemporary contexts, stating that the 'Salafi Reformism' of the West aims to 'protect the Muslim identity and religious practice, to recognize the Western constitutional structure, to become involved as a citizen at the societal level, and to live with true loyalty to the country to which one belongs.'[280] In his conceptualization of reform, it is '*salafi*' in that it seeks to 'recapture the energy, creativity, and boldness of early scholars'; hence his reform Salafism contrasts with his depiction of 'literalist *salafi trends*,' which 'implies freezing the text beyond time and environment.' His call for a 'radical reform' urges Islamic scholars to 'reconsider the very sources of the fundamentals of Islamic law and jurisprudence (*usul al-fiqh*) rather than keeping to context-related adaptations of law and jurisprudence (*fiqh*).'[281] These type of elaborations on a European Islam have been interpreted as making possible 'an overlapping consensus between the core elements of political liberalism and a form of Islam that might be appealing even to conservative, traditionally minded Muslims.'[282]

Many of the original callers of Western Salafism have also, in their own ways, demonstrated post-Salafi tendencies, such as Abdur Raheem Green (b. 1964), Abu Muntasir Manwar Ali,[283] and this author as well.[284] My own post-Salafi beginnings can perhaps be traced to 2007 when, even as I associated with the movement, I initiated a unity pledge between leaders from various Islamic groups, including Salafis, Sufis, and Islamists, whereby the Sunni nature of each group was to be acknowledged by the others.[285] Despite considering myself to be a loyal Salafi, and such acts of unity being frowned upon or fully condemned by leading Salafi clerics, I still felt that it was a religious obligation for Muslims to work together for the common good.

In addition, another pioneer of British Salafism, Abu Aliyah Surkheel Sharif, writes that contemporary Salafism is the product of 'the many forces that gave rise to various other twentieth century *isms*… Whilst respect for the *salaf* is wholly warranted among Muslims, respecting today's Salafism is a different matter… Salafism, today, for maybe the most part, is fixated on externals; lacking the spiritual or intellectual depth which historically typified orthodoxy.'[286]

The emergence of post-Salafism has significant implications for the Muslim world and beyond. It represents a critical juncture in Islamic thought, challenging the status quo and offering alternative pathways for religious and social reform.

### *6.6.4 Post-Salafi Jihadism?*

Post-Salafism has not just affected academic Salafis but, surprisingly, even Jihadi-Salafis have been swept up in its current.

The battleground of Syria after the Arab Spring, whereby the Assad regime responded with a brutal crackdown which caused the deaths of hundreds of thousands of its own citizens and resulted in over a million refugees, has witnessed the birth of many opposition groups. In a previous chapter, Jihadi-Salafi groups such as ISIS were discussed in detail, and while they have dominated the narrative, another group also emerged: the *Aḥrar al-Sham* (The Freedom Fighters of Syria), a populist revolutionary force challenging ISIS's claims to represent the Syrian revolution.[287] Interviews conducted in 2015 revealed *Aḥrar al-Sham's* roots in Jihadi-Salafism, stemming from founders associated with Syria's Islamist wing; however, *Aḥrar al-Sham*'s subsequent divergence from this ideology marked a critical shift as it distanced itself from the extreme exclusivism of Jihadi-Salafism, its *takfir*, and its extreme militancy. Its leaders, influenced by their experiences in Iraq and the Syrian revolution, formulated a revisionist program emphasizing restraint, political savvy, and collaboration with local communities and rebel factions. While their aim is to overthrow the regime of Bashar al-Assad, they have clearly distanced themselves from claims of establishing a global caliphate, and state that they wish to establish a representative Syrian government based on Islamic principles. The revisionist stance taken by *Aḥrar al-Sham* represents a broader critique of Jihadi-Salafism from within the jihadist movement.

As *Aḥrar al-Sham* navigates diplomatic engagement with the US government (as of yet, the State Department has not designated it as a terrorist organization) and seeks to alleviate pressure on its people, its reformist agenda presents a unique challenge and opportunity for the future of Syria and the broader jihadist movement. The extent to which *Aḥrar al-Sham*'s revisionism resonates beyond Syria's borders remains uncertain, but its diplomatic role and ideological evolution have already cast a shadow on Islamic trends worldwide. In the complex landscape of Syrian politics, finding common ground between *Aḥrar al-Sham*'s reformists and international stakeholders may be crucial for achieving a sustainable political settlement.

### *6.7 Conclusion*

Salafism is now a global phenomenon: where Muslims reside, one will find Salafis, from Alaska to Japan and from Norway to South Africa. As this chapter has shown, however, the regional flavors of the movement are different, and one finds a wide spectrum of interpretation with respect to internal and external issues and methodologies. Just as in a previous chapter we saw how, historically, Salafi movements adapted to their circumstances and had their unique iterations, so too geographically the movement maintains an unspoken flexibility and is shaped by its surroundings.

Almost all modern Salafi movements around the globe are directly or indirectly linked to Saudi Arabia – perhaps the one major exception are the *Ahl-e-Hadith* of the Indian subcontinent, whose birth and trajectory predate that of the modern Kingdom. The Kingdom, through its preachers, publications and institutions, has been a primary catalyst for the transplanting of Salafi thought into indigenous populations. Once the initial seed was planted, local followers accelerated the organic growth of the movement with minor indigenous characteristics.

Perhaps not surprisingly, not all countries are equally weighted, and there is clearly a hierarchical ladder of influence. A dispute between Salafi factions in Senegal will in all likelihood not even register as a ripple at the global level, yet a rift in Saudi Salafism typically creates a cataclysmic wave that splits movements and rocks the proverbial boat of Salafism in almost all other regions. At times, the conflict might begin in another land (as, for example, the dispute that occurred among Yemeni factions), but then be transported back to Saudi Arabia, where the controversy is amplified and then projected onto the global movement.

As the quantity of Salafis in any region grows, so too does the diversity within them, resulting in the fractionalization of the movement. Not surprisingly, one finds the quietist/puritanical strand in all regions of the world, whereas the more political-minded *Ṣaḥwa* types vary from region to region: in some lands, like Kuwait, they dominate, whereas in other regions, like Bosnia, they are marginal. And where there are *Ṣaḥwīs*, there are invariably Madkhalīs, as the two need each other to thrive. Jihadi-Salafis remain in almost all areas and regions a negligible percentage, although due to their potential danger, they cannot be ignored. In some regions, such as in Libya, the fluidity between these strands becomes increasingly difficult to navigate, and one finds the birth of altogether novel phenomena, such as Madkhali-Jihadi-Salafism.

Interestingly, apart from the region of Wahhabism's birth (the Gulf countries – although the Emirates is a more complicated reality), Salafism has never become a majority trend among Muslims. Dominant understandings of traditionalism, from earlier Ottoman or Mughal times, continue to influence modern religious sentiment and form the bulk of clerical scholarship in all other Muslim-majority lands. In contrast, in the Western world where no previous 'traditionalism' dominated, Salafism has been an extremely popular alternative for a newer generation, who find it to be an empowering and authentic manifestation of the faith. While surveys are difficult to conduct, anecdotally, Western Muslims are far more drawn to Salafi thought than their Eastern counterparts.

The rise of Salafism has, undoubtedly, contributed to the wider Islamic revival of the last couple of centuries, along with other Islamic currents such as Islamism and various forms of Sufi and madrasa trends, primarily the Deobandī and the Tablighi movements. However, Salafism's successful call to faith and its many virtues has been largely undermined by its own almost inherent nature of unsettling Muslim communities, and by its propensity to splinter and cannibalize even its own. Across the world, Salafism has clearly waned from its heyday two decades ago.

The phenomenon of 'post-Salafism' is perhaps the most exciting of the global trends that will undoubtedly play a major role in the foreseeable future, especially in the Western world. As post-Salafism continues to develop, it holds the promise of fostering a more inclusive, dynamic, and relevant understanding of Islam in the modern world.

# EPILOGUE

*'The man who views the world at fifty the same as he did at twenty has wasted thirty years of his life.'*
*~ Muhammad Ali*

The subject of this work is one that has been at the forefront of my two vocations as a cleric-preacher and an academic. Since the book is intended as a scholarly work, I've attempted to present the facts and analyze the dynamics of Salafism as objectively as possible. In this final section, however, I ask the reader's indulgence to speak directly and forthrightly on the topic that has preoccupied much of my own personal life and has been at the core of my identity as a cleric. I was a committed adherent of Salafism for more than twenty years of my life; for a period of time, I was among the most active propagators of Salafism in the English-speaking world.

In many ways, my dissemination of Salafism was pioneering, and met with great success. I was one of the first to explain Ibn ʿAbd al-Wahhāb's *Kitāb al-Tawḥīd* in English (the audio files of these lectures, back in 1997, were uploaded to the nascent Internet and became extremely popular among many circles in America and England). I also did an extensive lecture series on Ibn Taymiyya's seminal works on God's divine attributes. Eventually, I translated and published some of Ibn ʿAbd al-Wahhāb's treatises (to this day, I would argue that my *A Critical Study of Shirk* remains the most in-depth discussion and defense of the theological doctrines of Ibn ʿAbd al-Wahhāb); and after my return from studying at the IUM, I began championing what I thought would be a mature, modern, and culturally-relevant version of the doctrines of Ibn Taymiyya. Through my lectures and teachings with various institutes, I directly taught close to 200,000 students in intensive seminars, and many millions more via the Internet and social media. I gained a global reputation as being an almost unofficial spokesperson in English for mainstream Salafism. This perception was bolstered by a 10,000 word cover story about me in *The New York Times Magazine* in 2011, where the author, after spending many months observing my preaching, described me as a 'rock star' of Western Salafism.[1]

Yet, the claim of Salafi-Wahhabis that all those who disagree with their specific understanding of *tawḥīd* are guilty of *shirk* – even if Third-Wave Wahhabism toned that down to claim that an individual non-Wahhabi may be 'excused due to ignorance' – simply proved too troubling for my conscience. It made no sense to me that so many clerics from all other strands could have gotten something so fundamental wrong – after all, *tawḥīd* is the essence of what it means to be a Muslim! This deep uncertainty – along with the rise of ISIS and the fact that I fully understood it was tapping into original Wahhabi teachings (the 'First-Wave') – forced me to rethink and research this topic until I realized that I could no longer subscribe to core ideas of the movement. I would eventually renounce Salafism as my religious identity, and embrace a broader, more accepted understanding of Islamic normativity, which eschewed a parochialism that defines Salafism (and in fact any other human endeavor to understand the faith of Islam that elevates its conclusions into absolutist understandings).

This is not to say that I embraced a form of religious relativism. Indeed, much of Salafism fits well within general notions of the faith. What I actually renounced were certain extreme religious interpretations which not only seemed somewhat idiosyncratic, but were inauthentic when weighed in the scales of the sources of the religion and its intellectual tradition, and could be obsessive and cultish. In the worst cases they created civil disharmony among Muslims and with non-Muslims in ways which seemed to be avoidable according to the principles of the faith.

I don't view myself as having lurched from one extreme to another, nor do I feel that I am embracing a fanatical rejection of everything that defines Salafism. Rather, I phrase it as having 'moved on,' and my shift was one of a few degrees (hence, perhaps 'post-Salafism' is indeed an apt term for it), even if I would be faced with outrage from Salafis that would indicate some complete religious reorientation (a simple Google search will yield hundreds of 'refutations' on the 'deviancy' of this author, almost all of them from Salafis). Indeed, one of my closest mentors and teachers – a primary influence during my teenage years who introduced me to Salafism – refuses to engage in any polite conversation with me beyond returning my greetings, believing religiously that this is a mark of piety on his part by not associating with *ahl al-bidʿa* (people of heresy).

Even now, after amending my religious understanding, I see why Salafism would hold a reasonable appeal for many fair-minded people seeking an authentic experience of Islam, as it did for me. The most significant reason is Salafism's claim to give absolute priority to the sacred texts of the Qurʾan and the traditions of the Prophet, in a manner which does not seem to be replicated in any other movement to the same extent. Hence, Salafism appears to liberate a person from the shackles of an ossified and man-made version of the faith and holds the promise of an absolute rejection of superstition and corruption of the 'original Islam' divinely revealed to the Prophet. Therefore, Salafism prides itself as being the only movement to give emphasis to the direct worship of God, without any syncretic practices. Moreover, no one can doubt the overall academic emphasis that the movement has on studying the various sciences of the faith; while other movements exchange rigorous study with mystic experiences or singing poems, Salafis will typically read classical works on a myriad of subjects and obtain scholastic literacy of the faith. And lastly, at least for Sunnis, it is obvious that the *ahl al-ḥadīth* were the original icons of Sunnism and that *kalām*-based Sunni trends came after them. Hence, there is a legitimate claim that Salafi theology, in its broadest sense, is an appeal to an 'orthodox' historical manifestation of Sunnism.

Yet to simply adopt these claims without scrutinizing them is a major error that most subscribers fall into; a closer inspection will reveal a level of reductionism that can even be accused of being largely false and misrepresentative. Many of the claims of Salafism are no more than simplistic slogans which hide a certain selective choosing of texts and historical incidents to fit a rather utopian picture. The fact of the matter is that 'the *salaf*' is a phrase Salafis invoke – many of whom might very well be sincere – to make claims and justify opinions that have actually originated with them and are conveniently back-projected to the *salaf*. In almost every single issue of theology and law, one will find a healthy diversity of thought within the first few generations of Islam. And as for modern issues, the truth is that there is no definitive opinion from the *salaf* on how one should live in our times, under secular democratic systems, or how – and to what level – one should participate in civil and political life in the current context(s). Likewise, the claim of 'following the *dalīl* (evidence)' is effectively just replacing one set of scholars and their interpretation with another. This is because how the '*dalīl*' is interpreted is almost invariably subject to human biases and, just like other frameworks and hermeneutics, is developed and contested.

Like all fundamentalist movements, Salafism picks – and somewhat arbitrarily chooses – aspects of their interpretation that it then raises to constitute an 'authentic identity' of an imagined past that must be retained for the future. The religion of Islam is more than one selection of points, and faith is more than just specific doctrines about God's attributes. One can easily derive from the Qurʾan that humility and compassion are far more important for one's religion than arguing over God's rising over the throne, to cite but one point of contention. Furthermore, Salafism is largely unable and unwilling to deal with modern challenges. Instead, it prefers to retreat to the arena of past controversies and debates, finding comfort in the known yet irrelevant quibbles of a bygone era, and lacks focus on solving actual problems that the Muslim community faces, like Islamophobia, hostile surveillance in the West, attrition of the younger generation from the faith, and other issues.

Along with these *intellectual* flaws, Salafism is beset by major *social* ills which compound the problem. For instance, Salafism has a major problem with intolerance and exclusivism, with cultish behavior and a clear demarcation of an 'us-versus-them' mentality. Bigotry over petty issues is never a praiseworthy trait, and most certainly not taken from the Prophetic model. Likewise, there is the rampant problem with arrogance towards others, with a repellent 'holier-than-thou' attitude, together with a culture of fault-finding against fellow Muslims.

However, its main problems are what made me finally renounce my association with the movement: extremism in *takfīr* (excommunication) and *tabdīʿ* (hereticization). This has been a historically observed phenomenon in the movement since its inception. There is hardly any other movement in which a neophyte, barely trained in the basics, will feel confident passing verdicts of *kufr* or *bidʿa* on scholars far senior and more knowledgable than themselves. One only needs to see the reality of the 'refutation culture' that is rampant within Salafism (and especially on social media) to understand this point. Salafis can barely tolerate each other, much less other believers! In all such instances, such an attitude breaks an already marginalized community of believers apart; and in rare but significant instances, given the right level of political chaos, it creates fertile ground for violence.

Ultimately, Salafism is a human development – one of many competing strands that attempted to make sense of the Prophetic message. Salafism, like all other movements, is an organic social phenomenon, and there is nothing Divine about it. All movements and sects are historical developments, and there is no reason to bind oneself to how one group of scholars dealt with specific problems of their time (and, as this book has shown, even 'Salafi' scholars have always had a variety of methodologies and views throughout the ages). My advice to those who choose to remain in the movement is to understand that others whom they oppose can be just as sincere and just as certain of their interpretation and can have just as solid and well-constructed arguments as Salafis themselves believe they do. A little compassion and kindness will go much further than a selective 'refutation' that will most likely fall on deaf ears anyway (just as refutations of Salafism fall on deaf ears by those within the movement).

To those believers outside the movement, I ask them to view the positives and consider why so many people are attracted to Salafism. Surely, no true believer would oppose the call to worship and invoke God alone and take the Prophet as a perfect role model? There is, no doubt, an element of appeal to the claim that too many syncretic beliefs and practices have been added to the religion and that one should 'return' to the purity of the 'original beliefs and practices' of the best of generations. Empathy from those on the outside will go a long way in attempting to curb some of the problems of the movement.

To those outside the faith who see Salafism as crossing many 'red lines' of liberal society, I urge restraint in criminalizing or vilifying the vast majority of Salafi strands that exhibit non-violent tendencies – of course, violent elements cannot be tolerated in Muslim or non-Muslim countries. A far more effective way of countering non-violent Salafi tendencies is to freely allow other authentic Islamic voices to temper some of Salafism's more obscurantist and unsavory characteristics. As we cannot realistically expect social uniformity, we must be willing to tolerate Salafi idiosyncrasies that do not cause harm to anyone else (just as, it must be added, Western societies tolerate Jewish and Christian fundamentalist groups with similar, or perhaps even more conservative, views). Those who espouse ideals of secular liberalism cannot then begin to act like religious fundamentalists, banning and proscribing ideas and views outside their spectrum of 'moral orthodoxy.' In fact, this book has demonstrated that Salafi interaction with other segments of society will lead most Salafis (just like the various waves of Wahhabism before them) to naturally accommodate, adapt, and rethink issues organically from within.

***

The world is a very confusing place, and our species is struggling to make sense of it all while answering the perplexing questions of our existence and purpose on this planet. Religion, for so many people, helps provide comforting and concrete answers to these questions. If done right, faith has the potential to transform even those who might have been wandering aimlessly into the best and most productive of people, and some strands of Salafism have indeed accomplished this noble goal. But if wrongly understood, religion can also bring out the worst in mankind and lead to terrifying, evil, and cruel consequences. Sadly, the culture of the Salafi movement, and some of its doctrines, can potentially lead to social alienation, injustices and, in particular contexts, violence against innocents.

However one views the first generations of those who believed in the Prophetic message (i.e., the actual *salaf*), it is historically indisputable that there was a vast spectrum of interpretations present among them in almost all aspects of creed, law, politics, methodology, and spirituality. Collectively, they all formed a part of the fabric of a broader civilization that eventually became one of the most powerful and influential in world history, perhaps in part because of that diversity. It is as if they tacitly understood that even if one arrives at a personal truth, some measure of pluralism is required for society to function, that no single human being or school will be the repository of the absolute truth. In that spirit of the *salaf* – of tolerating difference while working together for greater communal and religious good – one can, and should, aspire to a *'Salafi'* ideal.

# NOTES

## 1 INTRODUCTION

1 Muḥammad Nāṣir al-Dīn al-Albānī, *Durūs li-Shaykh Muḥammad Nāṣir al-Dīn al-Albānī*, audio lessons transcribed by the Islamic Network website http://www.islamweb.net, made available on Shāmila at https://shamela.ws/book/7682, pt. 8:20, accessed May 8, 2024.

2 *Ṣaḥīḥ al-Bukhārī: kitāb al-shahādāt, bāb lā yushhad 'alā shahādat jawr idhā ushida.*

3 See, for example, Muḥammad Sa'īd Ramaḍān al-Būṭī, *al-Salafiyya: Marḥala zamanīyya mubārakah lā madhhab Islāmī* (Damascus: Dār al-Fikr, 1988).

4 Henri Lauzière, 'The Construction of Salafiyya: Reconsidering Salafism from the Perspective of Conceptual History,' *International Journal of Middle East Studies* 42, no. 3 (August 2010): 369–89.

5 For a discussion on the evolution of the term Salafism, see, in particular, Henri Lauzière, *The Making of Salafism: Islamic Reform in the Twentieth Century*, Religion, Culture, and Public Life (New York: Columbia University Press, 2016), 10–23. The following article on the dispute about this term is also instructive: Henri Lauzière, 'Rejoinder: What We Mean Versus What They Meant by "Salafi": A Reply to Frank Griffel,' *Die Welt Des Islams* 56, no. 1 (April 19, 2016): 89–96.

6 Islamism is a term that has recently come into vogue to describe political movements that seek to establish Islamic principles and laws as the foundation of governance and society in the modern world. These movements advocate for the implementation of the Shari'a (Islamic law) in public and private life. While Islamism is rooted in Islamic beliefs and values, the term itself is contested as it encompasses diverse interpretations and approaches, ranging from moderate to radical perspectives. However, for the purposes of this book, we will use the term to refer to non-violent movements like the Muslim Brotherhood without intending any negative connotations. For a brief overview of Islamism, see Gerhard Böwering, ed., 'Fundamentalism,' in *The Princeton Encyclopedia of Islamic Political Thought* (Princeton, NJ: Princeton University Press, 2013).

7 Sunna, literally tradition or precedent, refers to the normative precedent of the Prophet Muhammad, and in early Islam, it also means the precedent of the early Muslim community as a whole. For the understanding of Sunna in Islamic history, and particularly within Sunni Islam and its relation to the hadith literature, see Jonathan A. C. Brown, *Hadith: Muhammad's Legacy in the Medieval and Modern World*, 2nd reprint ed., Foundations of Islam (London: Oneworld Academic, 2020).

8 Hadith (pl. *aḥādīth*), or more generally, the hadith literature, refers to the reports describing the words, actions, or habits of the Prophet and the early Islamic community. For much of Islamic history, it was the primary means through which the Sunna was preserved and transmitted. For a comprehensive treatment on the hadith literature within Islamic history, see Brown, *Hadith*.

9 Khalil al-Anani, 'Unpacking the Sacred Canopy: Egypt's Salafis between Religion and Politics,' in *Salafism After the Arab Awakening: Contending with People's Power*, ed. Francesco Cavatorta and Fabio Merone (London: Oxford University Press, 2017), 25.

10 See Edward W. Said, *Orientalism*, 25th anniversary ed. with a new preface by the author (New York: Vintage Books Edition, 2014).

11 *Ṣaḥīḥ al-Bukhārī: kitāb al-īmān, bāb su'āl Jibrīl al-Nabī ṣallā-llāhu 'alayhi wa-sallam 'an al-īmān wa-l-islām wa-l-iḥsān wa 'ilm al-sā'a; Ṣaḥīḥ Muslim: kitāb al-īmān, bāb bayān al-īmān wa-l-islām wa-l-iḥsān wa-wujūb al-īmīn bi-ithbāt qadar Allāh subḥānahu wa-ta'ālā wa bayān al-dalīl 'ala al-tabarrī mimman la yu'min bi-l-qadar wa ighlāẓ al-qawl fī ḥaqqihi.*

12 Ibn Taymiyya, *al-Īmān*, ed. Muḥammad Nāṣir al-Dīn al-Albānī, 5th ed. (Amman, Jordan: al-Maktab al-Islāmī, 1996), 8.

13 For a discussion that indirectly points to how Salafi theology has come to a tripartite division of monotheism from the works of Ibn Taymiyya and Ibn 'Abd al-Wahhāb, as well as a discussion of the diverse trends within Ḥanbalī theology, see Jon Hoover, 'Hanbali Theology,' in *The Oxford Handbook of Islamic Theology*, ed. Sabine Schmidtke, Oxford Handbooks (Oxford, UK: Oxford University Press, 2016), 626–46.

14 Such phrases are popular in the English-Salafi lexicon, as seen, for example, in the immensely popular treatise by Abu Ameenah Bilal Philips, *The Fundamentals of Tawḥeed: Islamic Monotheism*, 2nd ed. (Riyadh: International Islamic Publ. House, 2006), in particular, chaps. 10–11.

15 In recent years, I have presented at academic conferences on the thought of the contemporary Saudi scholar Sharīf Hatim al-Awni and his rebuttal of Salafi excommunication (*takfīr*) on these related matters. See Sharīf Ḥātim b. 'Ārif al-Awni, *Takfīr ahl al-shahādatayn mawāni'ūhu wa manāṭatuhu*, 1st ed. (Riyadh: Markaz namā' li-l-buḥūthī wa-l-dirāsāt, 2015); al-Sharīf Ḥātim b. 'Ārif al-Awni, *al-'Ibāda: bawābat al-tawḥīd wa-bawābat al-takfīr* (Riyadh: Markaz namā' li-l-buḥūthī wa-l-dirāsāt, 2012). See also Masooda Bano, 'In Today's Saudi Arabia: The State, the Society and the Scholars,' in *Salafi Social and Political Movements: National and Transnational Contexts*, ed. Masooda Bano (Edinburgh: Edinburgh University Press, 2021), 51–55; Christopher Pooya Razavian, 'Post-Salafism: Salman al-Ouda and Hatim al-Awni,' in *Modern Islamic Authority and Social Change, Volume 1*, ed. Masooda Bano, Evolving Debates in Muslim Majority Countries (Edinburgh: Edinburgh University Press, 2018), 172–92; Christopher Pooya Razavian, 'Yasir Qadhi and the Development of Reasonable Salafism,' in *Modern Islamic Authority and Social Change, Volume 2: Evolving Debates in the West*, ed. In essence, al-Awni's argument is that idolatry (*shirk*) must entail the intention to worship an object as a lord and consider it to have a power of lordship and divinity that is independent of God.

16 In a previous phase of my life, shortly after commencing my studies at the Islamic University of Medina, I translated some books by Ibn 'Abd al-Wahhāb, including Ibn 'Abd al-Wahhāb's *Kashf al-Shubuhāt*. See Yasir Qadhi, *An Explanation of Muhammad Ibn 'Abd al-Wahhab's Kashf al-Shubuhat: A Critical Study of Shirk* (Birmingham, UK: Al-Hidaayah Publishing, 2003). To date, this remains one of the most thorough elucidations and defenses of the doctrines of Ibn 'Abd al-Wahhāb in the English language.

17 For a study of excommunication (*takfīr*) in Islam through the centuries and in various lands, see Camilla Adang et al., eds, *Accusations of Unbelief in Islam: A Diachronic Perspective on Takfīr* (Leiden, The Netherlands: Brill, 2015).

18 For an introduction to these schools, see numerous entries in Sabine Schmidtke, ed., *The Oxford Handbook of Islamic Theology*, Reprinted ed. (Oxford, United Kingdom: Oxford University Press, 2018). While the Ash'arī school has historically received more attention in Western academic study, the Māturīdī school has come under greater scrutiny in recent years, see, for example, Ulrich Rudolph, *Al-Maturidi and the Development of Sunni Theology in Samarqand*, trans. Rodrigo Adem, Translated ed. (Leiden; Boston: Brill, 2014); Lejla Demiri, Philip Dorroll, and Dale J. Correa, eds., *Maturidi Theology: A Bilingual Reader*, Bilingual ed. (Tübingen: Mohr Siebrek Ek, 2022).

19 *ʿIlm al-kalām* (the science of discourse) – generally shortened as simply *kalām* – refers to Islamic dialectical, speculative, or rationalist theology. It derives from the Arabic word '*kalām*,' meaning word, speech, or discourse. Within this context, it refers to the discourse on theology and creedal matters by way of a particular style of theological argumentation in which one talks (*kallama*) with one's opponents by asking questions and, subsequently, reducing their position to meaningless alternatives. Practitioners of *kalām* are known as *mutakallimūn*. Despite the general translation of *mutakallimūn* as 'theologians,' it is imperative to recognize that *kalām* is not theology in a general sense but refers to a very specific form of theology that seeks to systematize the Islamic creed and rationally defend the faith based on a very particular set of methodological and epistemic paradigm and covers both the theological and non-theological areas of inquiry (e.g., epistemology and physics). See Alexander Treiger, 'Origins of Kalām,' in *The Oxford Handbook of Islamic Theology*, ed. Sabine Schmidtke, Oxford Handbooks (Oxford, United Kingdom: Oxford University Press, 2016), 28–44; M Abdel Haleem, 'Early Kalām,' in *History of Islamic Philosophy*, ed. Oliver Leaman and Seyyed Hossein Nasr, 1st ed. (London: Routledge, 2001), 71–88; and see also Hanne (Halle/Saale) Schönig, 'Kalam,' in *Brill's New Pauly* (Brill, October 1, 2006), https://referenceworks.brillonline.com/entries/brill-s-new-pauly/*-e605450.

20 For a helpful guide to see where Salafis derive some of their understandings in these matters – although they tend not to possess the same level of sophistication as those they seek to emulate – see *Ibn Taymiyya and the Attributes of God*, trans. Carl Sharif El-Tobgui, Islamic Philosophy, Theology and Science, vol. 125 (Leiden; Boston: Brill, 2023), 81–91, especially Chapter 5 (in relation to the understanding of *ḥaqīqa* and *majāz*) and Chapter 6 (in relation to figurative interpretation [*taʾwīl*]). The Ashʿarī/Māturīdī approach, as explained by Mullā ʿAlī al-Qarī (d. 1014), advocates following the path of the predecessors (*salaf*) as illustrated in an anecdote attributed to Mālik b. Anas, the eponymous founder of the Mālīkī schools of law (which is quoted below in Chapter 2, section 2.1.2). According to this view – which is the "safer" (*aslam*) – one simply affirms all divine attributes without inquiring about their nature. However, if people struggle with such vagueness, then there is limited scope for providing metaphorical interpretations. See Mullā ʿAlī al-Qarī, *Sharḥ Kitāb Al-Fiqh al-Akbar* (Beirut: Dār al-Kutūb al-ʿIlmiyya, n.d.), 70.

21 See Jon Hoover, *Ibn Taymiyya* (London: Oneworld Academic, 2020), 10–11 and 26–29; Livnat Holtzman, *Anthropomorphism in Islam: The Challenge of Traditionalism*, 1st ed. (Edinburgh: Edinburgh University Press, 2019), 313–28.

22 Muḥammad b. Ṣāliḥ al-ʿUthaymīn, *ʿAqīdat ahl al-Sunna wa-l-jamāʿa*, 4th ed. (Riyadh: al-Maktab al-Taʿawunī, 2001), 14.

23 For a detailed treatment of this doctrine, see Mohamed Bin Ali, *The Roots of Religious Extremism: Understanding the Salafi Doctrine of Al-Wala' Wal Bara'*, vol. 9, Insurgency and Terrorism Series (Imperial College Press, 2015), vol. 9; Cole M. Bunzel, *Wahhābism: The History of a Militant Islamic Movement* (Princeton: Princeton University Press, 2023), 162–73.

24 Ibn Taymiyya does discuss generically about being loyal for the sake of God and, consequently, dissociating from the enemies of God. However, it is clear that he does not apply this generic doctrine against fellow Muslims. Ibn ʿAbd al-Wahhāb, on the other hand, made it a point of creed and considered anyone who disagreed with his assessment of specific tribes as non-Muslims to be themselves non-Muslims. This is because, in his eyes, they are showing support for the enemies of God by not agreeing with his assessment. For a more detailed discussion on this and the differences between these two figures, see Bunzel, *Wahhābism*, 162–66.

25 *Sunan Abī Dawūd: kitāb al-sunna, bāb sharḥ al-sunna.*

26 *Jāmiʿ al-Timidhī: kitāb al-īmān, bāb mā jāʾa fī iftirāqi hadhihi al-umma.*

27 *Ṣaḥīḥ Muslim; kitāb al-imāra, bāb qawlihi ṣallā Allāh ʿalayhi wa sallam lā tazālu ṭāʾifatu min ummatī ẓāhirīna ʿalā al-ḥaqq lā yaḍurruhum man khālafahum.*

28 For a discussion on all of the variants of this hadith and the verdicts of scholars both in favor of its authenticity and against it, see ʿAbd Allāh b. Yūsuf al-Judaiʿ, *Aḍwāʿ ʿalā ḥadīth al-iftirāq* (Beirut: Muʾassasat al-Rayyān, 2007); Muḥammad Nāṣir al-Dīn al-Albānī, *Silsilat al-aḥādīth al-ṣaḥīḥah wa-shayʾ min fiqhihā wa-fawā idihā* (Riyadh: Maktabat al-Maʿārif, 1995), 1:539 and 4:597–602. The hadith has been problematized in the past by, inter alia, Ibn Khaldūn (d. 808/1406) and in modern times by Yūsuf al-Qaraḍāwī (d. 2022). See: Yūsuf al-Qaraḍāwī, *Fatāwa Muʿāṣara* (Kuwait: Dar al-Qalam, 2011), vol. 2, 345–6.

29 For the notion and the development of the term '*ahl al-sunna*,' see John B. Henderson, *The Construction of Orthodoxy and Heresy: Neo-Confucian, Islamic, Jewish, and Early Christian Patterns* (Albany, NY: State University of New York Press, 1998), 51–53; Marshall G. S. Hodgson, *The Venture of Islam: Conscience and History in a World Civilization* (Chicago: University of Chicago Press, 1974), 1:276–9; and Josef van Ess, *Theology and Society in the Second and Third Centuries of the Hijra.*, trans. Gwendolin Goldbloom, vol. 4 (Leiden: Brill, 2018), 761–63. For a brief account on the formation of the Sunni movement in early Islam, see W. Montgomery Watt, *The Formative Period of Islamic Thought*, New ed. (Oxford: Oneworld Publications, 1998), 253–71.

30 For Ibn Taymiyya's views, see Ibn Taymiyya, *Minhāj al-sunna al-nabawiyya fī naqḍ kalām al-Shīʿa al-qadariyya*, ed. Muḥammad Rashād Sālim (Riyadh: Jāmiʿat al-Imām Muḥammad ibn Suʿūd al-Islāmiyya, 1986), 2:221.

31 See Ibn al-ʿUthaymīn, *ʿAqīdat ahl al-Sunna wa-l-jamāʿa*, 11:306. The Muʿtazila are the early Muslim rationalists. For a discussion on the group, see section 2.1.2.

32 ʿAmr ʿAbd al-Munʿim Salīm, *al-Manhaj al-Salafī ʿinda al-Shaykh Nāṣir al-Dīn al-Albānī* (Tanta, Egypt: Dār al-Ḍiyāʾ, n.d.), 13.

33 See Muḥammad b. Ṣāliḥ al-ʿUthaymīn, *Liqāʾ al-bāb al-maftūḥ*, transcribed by the Islamic Network website http://www.islamweb.net, made available on Shāmila at https://shamela.ws/book/7687, (Liqāʾ al-bāb, 1992), 57:15.

34 For a comprehensive introduction to Islamic law and its practice, see Wael B. Hallaq, *Sharīʻa: Theory, Practice, Transformations* (Cambridge, UK; New York: Cambridge University Press, 2009).

35 Bernard Weiss, 'Interpretation in Islamic Law: The Theory of Ijtihad,' *The American Journal of Comparative Law* 26, no. 2 (1978): 199–200.

36 Wael B. Hallaq, *The Origins and Evolution of Islamic Law*, Themes in Islamic Law 1 (Cambridge, UK; New York: Cambridge University Press, 2005), 131.

37 Hallaq, 130–32.

38 Aron Zysow, *The Economy of Certainty: An Introduction to the Typology of Islamic Legal Theory*, Resources in Arabic and Islamic Studies 2 (Atlanta, GA: Lockwood Press, 2013), 1.

39 For an overview of the development of these four schools, see Christopher Melchert, *The Formation of the Sunni Schools of Law, 9th–10th Centuries CE* (Leiden; New York: Brill, 1997).

40 For a study of what can be anachronistically called Salafi Islam and its approaches to Islamic law, from the early centuries of Islam through the *madhhab* period, see Scott C. Lucas, 'The Legal Principles of Muhammad b. Isma'il al-Bukhari and their relationship to Classical Salafi Islam,' *Islamic Law and Society*, 13.3 (2006): 289–324.

41 Abdul Hakim al-Matroudi, *The Ḥanbalī School of Law and Ibn Taymiyyah: Conflict or Conciliation*, Culture and Civilization in the Middle East 5 (New York: Routledge, 2006), 40–44.

42 This work is titled *al-Sharḥ al-mumtiʿ ʿalā zād al-mustaqniʿ (The Excellent Commentary of the Provision of the Seeker)* and is published in fifteen volumes. See

Muḥammad b. Ṣāliḥ al-ʿUthaymīn, *al-Sharḥ al-mumtiʿ ʿalā zād al-mustaqniʿ*, ed. Abū Ayyūb al-Sulaymān, 15 vols (Dammam, Saudi Arabia: Dār Ibn al-Jawzī, 2008).

43 One of the students of Ibn al-ʿUthaymīn wrote a monograph in which he listed over 150 examples of issues that his teacher opposed the school on. See ʿAbd Allāh b. Yūsuf al-Ḥāfī, *al-Ikhtiyārāt wa-l-tarjīḥāt li-Shaykh Ibn ʿUthaymīn fī kitābihī al-sharḥ al-mumtiʿ* (Kuwait: Dār al-Ilāf, 1999).

44 The Ẓāhirī school of law, often termed 'the fifth madhhab' of Sunni Islam, was founded in the third/ninth century by Dāwūd al-Ẓāhirī (d. 270/884) in Iraq. The school received its name because of its primary emphasis on the literal (*ẓāhir*) meaning of the revelation and the rejection of individual judgment (*raʾy*) and analogical reasoning (*qiyās*) in its legal method and derivation. The school, under Ibn Ḥazm, became especially influential in Andalus, with its peak during the fifth–sixth/twelfth–thirteenth centuries. However, it declined and practically died out in the tenth/sixteenth century. For a thorough treatment of the school and its development, see Ignaz Goldziher, 'The Ẓāhirīs: Their Doctrine and Their History. A Contribution to the History of Islamic Theology,' in *The Ẓāhirīs* (Brill, 2007); and Camilla Adang, 'The Beginnings of the Zahiri Madhhab in Al-Andalus,' in *The Islamic School of Law: Evolution, Devolution, and Progress*, ed. Peri Bearman, Rudolph Peters, and Frank E. Vogel, Harvard Series in Islamic Law 2 (International Conference on Islamic Legal Studies, Cambridge, Mass.: Harvard Univ. Press, 2005), 117–25. On the eponymous founder, Dāwūd al-Ẓāhirī, see Christopher Melchert, 'Dawud b. Khalaf,' in *Encyclopaedia of Islam Three Online*, ed. Kate Fleet et al. (Brill, 2011), https://referenceworks.brill.com/doi/10.1163/1573-3912_ei3_COM_25936. It should be noted here that in a recent study, Amr Osman argued, contrary to popular presumption, that the Ẓāhirīs occupy a middle position between the two methodological orientations in early Islam: (1) *ahl al-raʾy* (Partisans of Legal Reasoning) – those who use analogical reasoning in their hermeneutical method – and *ahl al-ḥadīth* (Partisans of Hadith) with an affinity to the former. See Amr Osman, *The Ẓāhirī Madhhab (3rd/9th–10th/16th Century): A Textualist Theory of Islamic Law* (Brill, 2014).

45 Bernard Haykel, 'On the Nature of Salafi Thought and Action,' in *Global Salafism*, ed. Roel Meijer (Oxford University Press, 2014), 34–57.

46 Transcript of al-Albānī's *Ittibāʿ sayyid al-umma ṣallā ʿalay-hi wa sallam* 1 lecture, transcribed and translated into English by Emad Hamdeh in Emad Hamdeh, *Salafism and Traditionalism: Scholarly Authority in Modern Islam* (New York: Cambridge University Press, 2020), 133.

47 Hamdeh, 133–34.

48 *The Salafi Fallacy*, 2012, https://www.youtube.com/watch?v=1MRXs5fqlXQ.

49 Jonathan A. C. Brown, 'Is Islam Easy to Understand or Not?: Salafis, the Democratization of Interpretation and the Need for the Ulema,' *Journal of Islamic Studies* 26, no. 2 (2015): 117–44.

50 *Ṣaḥīḥ Muslim: kitāb al-jumuʿa, bāb takhfīf al-ṣalāt wa-l-khuṭba.*

51 For a comprehensive study of the origins and development of the *mawlid*, including modern Salafi objections, see Marion Holmes Katz, *The Birth of the Prophet Muhammad: Devotional Piety in Sunni Islam*, Culture and Civilization in the Middle East, 11 (London: Routledge, 2009). Also, see Raquel Margalit Ukeles, 'Innovation or Deviation: Exploring the Boundaries of Islamic Devotional Law' (PhD, Cambridge, MA, Harvard University, 2006), chap. 3. For numerous instances, in different places where condemnation of the *mawlid* has been a common feature of Salafi polemics against popular Muslim practices, see Roel Meijer, ed., *Global Salafism: Islam's New Religious Movement* (Oxford University Press, 2014).

52 Ukeles, 'Innovation or Deviation: Exploring the Boundaries of Islamic Devotional Law,' 56–82 and also, chap. 2.

53 Ukeles, 'Innovation or Deviation,' 227–32.

54 For a comprehensive introduction to the history and development of Sufism, see Alexander Knysh, *Islamic Mysticism: A Short History* (Leiden, The Netherlands; Boston: Brill, 2000).

55 The Salafi understanding can be depicted as believing in 'spirituality without mysticism,' based on the methodology of spirituality among the early Muslims 'before Sufism.' See Ahmet T. Karamustafa, *Sufism: The Formative Period* (Berkeley: University of California Press, 2007); and also Christopher Melchert, *Before Sufism: Early Islamic Renunciant Piety*, Islam – Thought, Culture, and Society, vol. 4 (Berlin; Boston: De Gruyter, 2020).

56 William C. Chittick defines 'union' as 'the full realization of human perfection, or actualization of the divine image in which human beings were created. Once perfection is achieved, the separation between the divine and the human that was envisaged in the original discernment has been overcome, at least from a certain point of view. The west has disappeared because the Sun has risen.' William C. Chittick, *Sufism: A Beginner's Guide* (London: Oneworld Publications, 2007), 20–21.

57 Gnosticism refers to a collection of religious ideas that emerged in the late first century CE among Jewish and early Christian sects. These various groups emphasized personal spiritual knowledge (*gnosis*) above the proto-orthodox teachings, traditions, and authority of religious institutions. Gnostic cosmology is generally characterized by a distinction between a hidden supreme God and a lesser, malevolent divinity responsible for creating the material universe. Hence, the Gnostics view the material world as flawed and evil and believe that the primary means of salvation is via recognizing one's divine inner 'spark' which connects one to the higher divine force. For a general survey and overview of Gnosticism, see Giovanni Filoramo, *A History of Gnosticism*, Reprinted ed. (Cambridge, MA: Blackwell, 1994). For the Gnostic influence on Sufism, see Willis Barnstone and Marvin W. Meyer, eds., 'Islamic Mystical Literature,' in *The Gnostic Bible*, Revised ed. (Boulder: Shambhala, 2009), 667–759; and Marek Vinklát, 'Sufism and Gnosticism: A Comparison,' accessed March 17, 2024, https://www.academia.edu/428804/Sufism_and_Gnosticism_A_Comparison.

58 Neoplatonism is a version of Platonic philosophy that emerged in the third century CE. It seeks to revive and (re)interpret the teachings of Plato (d. 348 BCE) while incorporating elements from other Hellenistic philosophical traditions, particularly those of Aristotle (d. 322 BCE) and the Stoics. This tradition was pioneered by the philosopher Plotinus (d. 270 CE) and later developed by Porphyry (d. 305 CE) and Proclus (d. 485 CE). At its core, Neoplatonism posits a monist worldview in which existence consists of a hierarchical structure of reality, with an ultimate, ineffable source or principle often referred to as 'the One' or 'the Good.' From this transcendent principle emanate successive levels of reality, including the universal intellect (*nous*) and the universal soul (*psyché*), which in turn give rise to the material world. For a concise overview of Neoplatonism, see Christian Wildberg, 'Neoplatonism,' in *The Stanford Encyclopedia of Philosophy*, ed. Edward N. Zalta, Winter 2021 (Metaphysics Research Lab, Stanford University, 2021), https://plato.stanford.edu/archives/win2021/entries/neoplatonism/. On the Neoplatonic underpinnings of Sufi thought and cosmology, see Milad Milani, 'Mysticism in the Islamicate World: The Question of Neoplatonic Influence in Sufi Thought,' in *Later Platonists and Their Heirs among Christians, Jews, and Muslims*, ed. Eva Anagnostou and Ken Parry (Brill, 2022), 513–44; Kamuran Godelek, 'The Neoplatonist Roots of Sufi Philosophy,' *The Paideia Archive: Twentieth World Congress of Philosophy* 5 (1998): 57–60; and Mehdi Aminrazavi, 'Mysticism in Arabic and Islamic Philosophy,' in *The Stanford Encyclopedia of Philosophy*, ed. Edward N. Zalta, Spring 2021 (Metaphysics Research Lab, Stanford University, 2021), https://plato.stanford.edu/archives/spr2021/entries/arabic-islamic-mysticism/.

59 The doctrine of *waḥdat al-wujūd* (also translated as 'ontological monism') itself – and what it really means and entails – is a highly contested topic. The notion has been ascribed to the famous Andalusian Sufi mystic Muḥyī al-Dīn b. al-ʿArabī (d. 638/1240), the founder of the Akbarian school of Sufism. Although he did express this doctrine throughout his writings, he never seemed to have used this precise terminology himself. For a detailed discussion of Ibn ʿArabī and the notion of *waḥdat al-wujūd*, see William Chittick, 'Rûmî and Wahdat al-Wujûd,' in *Poetry and Mysticism in Islam: The Heritage of Rūmī*, ed. Amin Banani, Richard G. Hovannisian, and Georges Sabagh, Giorgio Levi Della Vida Conferences, 11th conference (Giorgio Levi Della Vida Conference, New York: Cambridge University Press, 1994), 70–111; and Abdul Haq Ansari, 'Ibn 'Arabī: The Doctrine of Waḥdat al-Wujūd,' *Islamic Studies* 38, no. 2 (1999): 149–92. In fact, it is said that Ibn Taymiyya, in his staunch critique of Ibn ʿArabī, was the first one to ascribe him the exact terminology of '*waḥdat al-wujūd*,' calling the doctrine worse than unbelief (*kufr*). See William Chittick, 'Ibn 'Arabî,' in *The Stanford Encyclopedia of Philosophy*, ed. Edward N. Zalta, Spring 2020 (Metaphysics Research Lab, Stanford University, 2020), https://plato.stanford.edu/archives/spr2020/entries/ibn-arabi/. It should, however, be noted here that not all Sufis subscribe to this doctrine, and even when they do, they might disagree with its monistic entailment. For instance, later Sufi thinkers like Aḥmad Sirhindī (d. 1034/1624) interpreted the doctrine – maybe attempting to give it more orthodox undertones – by positing that 'the focus was on the subjective "witnessing" of the spiritual adept rather than on any perceived impingement of the existential transience of God,' – what is called *waḥdat al-shuhūd* (unity of witnessing); see Martin Nguyen, 'Sufi Theological Thought,' in *The Oxford Handbook of Islamic Theology*, ed. Sabine Schmidtke, Reprinted ed. (Oxford, United Kingdom: Oxford University Press, 2018), 325–43. Chittick also provides a non-monistic reading: 'Simply stated, there is only one Being, and all existence is nothing but the manifestation or outward radiance of that One Being. Hence, "everything other than the One Being" – that is, the whole cosmos in all its spatial and temporal extension – is non-existent in itself, though it may be considered to exist through Being.' William C. Chittick, *The Sufi Path of Knowledge: Ibn al-ʿArabi's Metaphysics of Imagination* (Albany, NY: State University of New York Press, 1989), 79.

60 This notion of an unbroken chain of transmission to the Prophet is contested in Islamic scholarship. The earliest chain (*silsila*) on record is narrated from the fourth/tenth centuries, from Jaʿfar al-Khuldī (d. 348/959), back to al-Ḥasan al-Baṣrī (d. 110/728), from the Companion Anas b. Mālik (d. 93/711), from the Prophet. Other popular chains go back to major senior companions like the Prophet's father-in-law Abū Bakr (d. 13/634) or his cousin and son-in-law ʿAlī b. Abī Ṭālib (d. 40/661, who is first mentioned in the chains in the fifth/eleventh century), with one famous chain for the latter going through al-Ḥasan. Classical hadith authorities like Ibn al-Ṣalāḥ (d. 643/1245), Ibn Ḥajar al-ʿAsqalānī (d. 852/1449) and al-Sakhāwī (d. 897/1402) held the position that al-Ḥasan neither met nor narrated from ʿAlī, although al-Suyūṭī (d. 911/1505) argued that al-Ḥasan did narrate from ʿAlī and had sufficient time to learn from him before ʿAlī left Medina. Al-Ḥasan resided in Medina, and by the time ʿAlī left Medina, al-Ḥasan would have been fourteen years old. Ibn al-Jawzī (d. 597/1201), for instance, categorically rejected the claim that the Companions and even later scholars like al-Ḥasan or Aḥmad b. Ḥanbal were Sufis. See J. Spencer Trimingham, *The Sufi Orders in Islam* (New York; Oxford: Oxford University Press, 1998), 261–62; Brown, *Hadith*, 203–4; and also Ibn al-Jawzī, *Naqd al-ʿilm wa-l-ʿulamāʾ ww talbīs Iblīs* (Cairo: Maṭbaʿat al-Saʿāda, 1921), 175.

61 To understand the Salafi understanding of spirituality and their differences with what they commonly understand to be Sufism, see Jamaal al-Din M. Zarabozo, *Purification of the Soul: Concept, Process and Means* (Denver, CO: Al-Basheer Publications & Translations, 2002).

62 For a study of Salafism's historical attitude towards graves and shrine visitations, see Ondřej Beránek and Pavel Ťupek, *The Temptation of Graves in Salafi Islam: Iconoclasm, Destruction and Idolatry*, Paperback ed. (Edinburgh: Edinburgh University Press, 2019).

63 Hoover, *Ibn Taymiyya*, 2020, 68–70. There is great debate about Ibn Taymiyya's attitude towards Sufism, but he seems to have appreciated some aspects while being critical of others. See Hoover, 70–73.

64 Although there are numerous works by Ibn ʿAbd al-Wahhāb on the subject, like, Muḥammad b. ʿAbd al-Wahhāb, *Kitāb al-Tawḥīd alladhī huwa ḥaqq Allāh ʿalā al-ʿabīd*, ed. Daghash b. Shabīb al-ʿAjmī (Kuwait: Maktabat Ahl al-Athar, 2014); Salafis have a modern work on the topic by one of their luminaries, which they utilize, see Muḥammad Nāṣir al-Dīn al-Albānī, *al-Tawassul: Anwāʾuhu wa-aḥkāmuhu* (Riyadh: Maktabat al-Maʿārif, 2001).

65 See Ibn Taymiyya, *Qāʿida jalīla fī al-tawassul wa-l-wasīla*, ed. Shuʿayb al-Arna'ūṭ (Beirut: Ri'āsah ʿIlmiyya, 1999).

66 Muḥammad b. ʿAlawī al-Mālikī al-Ḥasanī, *Notions That Must Be Corrected [Mafāhim Yajib an Tuṣāhhah]*, trans. Suraqah Abdul Aziz (The Netherlands: Sunni Publications, n.d.), 156.

67 For Ibn Taymiyya's attitude towards Sufism, whereby he appreciated some aspects while being critical of others, see Hoover, *Ibn Taymiyya*, 2020, 70–73. On a similar approach of his student Ibn Qayyim and also an overview of Ḥanbalī-Sufi interaction and intersection in early and medieval Islam, see the Translator's Introduction in Ibn Qayyim al-Jawziyya, *Ranks of the Divine Seekers: A Parallel English-Arabic Text*, trans. Ovamir Anjum, vol. 1, 2 vols, Islamic Translation Series, vol. 14 (Leiden; Boston, Mass.: Brill, 2020).

68 For a brief discussion of Salafi spirituality, without Sufism, see Besnik Sinani, 'Normative Spirituality in Wahhabi Prophetology: Saʿīd b. Wahf al-Qaḥṭānī's (d. 2018) Raḥmatan li-l-ʿĀlamīn as Reparatory Theology,' *Religions* 15, no. 5 (April 28, 2024): 543.

69 Zarabozo, *Purification of the Soul*, 3–4, emphasis in the original. This fragmentation among the Salafi movement in North America, which has been popularly named as the 'Salafi burnout,' i.e., a rapid enthusiasm that quite quickly dissipates, sometimes descending to complete abandonment, has been recounted in Umar Lee, *The Rise and Fall of the Salafi Dawah in America*, Kindle ed., n.d.

70 The audio recordings of al-Albānī were compiled by his students and released; they are now available online. This phrase and his explanation of it can be found in Muḥammad Nāṣir al-Dīn al-Albānī, *Silsilat al-hudā wa-l-nūr*, n.d., no. 200. As al-Albānī himself notes, these words were first said by the Muslim Brotherhood's founder, and while the two disagreed on many things, this idea was not one of them.

71 Stéphane Lacroix, *Awakening Islam: The Politics of Religious Dissent in Contemporary Saudi Arabia*, trans. George Holoch (Cambridge, Mass.: Harvard University Press, 2011).

72 Gregory D. Johnsen, 'The Rise of ISIS,' *Great Decisions*, 2016, 16.

73 These studies include the ones discussed below, and recent works such as Azmi Bishara, *On Salafism: Concepts and Contexts* (Stanford, California: Stanford University Press, 2022).

74 Quintan Wiktorowicz, 'Anatomy of the Salafi Movement,' *Studies in Conflict & Terrorism* 29, no. 3 (May 2006): 207–39.

75 Wiktorowicz, 208.

76 Wiktorowicz, 217.

77 Wiktorowicz, 208.

78 Wiktorowicz, 208.

79 Zoltan Pall, *Salafism in Lebanon: Local and Transnational Movements*, 1st ed. (New York: Cambridge University Press, 2018), 19.
80 Zoltan Pall, *Lebanese Salafis Between the Gulf and Europe: Development, Fractionalization and Transnational Networks of Salafism in Lebanon*, Forum Publications (Amsterdam: Amsterdam University Press, 2013), 24.
81 Pall, 25.
82 Pall, 26.
83 Pall, *Salafism in Lebanon*, 21.
84 Joas Wagemakers, 'Salafism: Generalisation, Conceptualisation and Categorisation,' ed. Magnus Ranstorp, *Contextualising Salafism and Salafi Jihadism*, March 2020, 33.
85 Joas Wagemakers, 'Revisiting Wiktorowicz,' in *Salafism After the Arab Awakening*, ed. Francesco Cavatorta and Fabio Merone (Oxford University Press, 2017), 7–24.
86 See Wagemakers, 'Salafism: Generalisation, Conceptualisation and Categorisation.'
87 For a challenge to the normalized academic contrast between activists and quietists in the analysis of Salafi groups, see Jan-Peter Hartung, 'Making Sense of "Political Quietism": An Analytical Intervention,' in *Political Quietism in Islam: Sunni and Shi'i Practice and Thought*, ed. Saud al-Sarhan, King Faisal Center for Research and Islamic Studies Series (London; New York, NY: I.B. Tauris, 2020), 15–32.
88 Wagemakers, 'Revisiting Wiktorowicz: Categorising and Defining the Branches of Salafism,' 18.
89 Wagemakers, 18.
90 Wagemakers, 'Salafism: Generalisation, Conceptualisation and Categorisation.'
91 Wagemakers, 36.
92 Wagemakers, 37.
93 Joas Wagemakers, *Salafism in Jordan: Political Islam in a Quietist Community* (Cambridge: Cambridge University Press, 2016), 118–43.

## 2 A COMPREHENSIVE HISTORY OF SALAFI THOUGHT

1 Taqī al-Dīn b. Taymiyya, *Dar' taʿāruḍ al-ʿaql wa-l-naql*, ed. Muḥammad Rashād Sālim, 2nd ed. (Riyadh: Jāmiʿat al-Imām Muḥammad ibn Suʿūd al-Islāmiyya, 1991), 3:146.
2 For a brief discussion on *kalām* theology, see section 1.2.1.
3 On the development of Sufism and its reception within Salafism, see section 1.1.4 of this work.
4 For more on the history of these three earliest generations of Muslims, see Asma Afsaruddin, *The First Muslims: History and Memory* (Oxford: Oneworld, 2008).
5 See, for example, Qur'an 5:119, 9:100, and 58:22.
6 Khārijīs (also called Khārijites) are the adherents of Khārijism, an early Islamic sect associated with militancy, rebellion, and excessive excommunication (*takfīr*) of fellow Muslims. For an overview of the movement, see Watt, *The Formative Period of Islamic Thought*, 9–37. For the moderate subsect of the group, known as the Ibāḍīyya, see Wilfred Madelung, 'Early Ibāḍī Theology,' in *The Oxford Handbook of Islamic Theology*, ed. Sabine Schmidtke, Reprinted ed. (Oxford, United Kingdom: Oxford University Press, 2018), 242–51.
7 Ibn Saba' is portrayed in early sources as a Yemeni Jew who embraced Islam during the reign of the third Caliph ʿUthmān b. ʿAffān (r. 23–35/644–656), and then went on to 'found' Shiʿism via the Saba'iyya sect known for their excessive veneration of the cousin and son-in-law of the Prophet, ʿAlī b. Abī Ṭālib (r. 35–40/656–661). In this regard, he and his followers are seen as belonging to the *ghulāt* (exaggerators) – a group known for their extreme beliefs in early Shi'ism. For the figure of Ibn Saba' and his reception in early and medieval Islam, see Sean W. Anthony, *The Caliph and*

*the Heretic: Ibn Saba' and the Origins of Shī'ism* (Leiden; Boston: Brill, 2011); and Abbas Barzegar, 'The Persistence of Heresy: Paul of Tarsus, Ibn Saba, and Historical Narrative in Sunni Identity Formation,' *Numen* 58, no. 2–3 (January 1, 2011): 207–31.

8 For a brief survey of early and proto-Shi'ism, see Mohammad Ali Amir-Moezzi, 'Early Shī'ī Theology,' in *The Oxford Handbook of Islamic Theology*, ed. Sabine Schmidtke, Reprinted ed. (Oxford, United Kingdom: Oxford University Press, 2018), 81–90; Watt, *The Formative Period of Islamic Thought*, 38–62.

9 Jahmism (also called the Jahmiyya) is an early Islamic sect founded by one Jahm b. Ṣafwan (d. 128/745–6). Although very little is known about Jahm, he (and his movement) was known to have advocated for an extreme transcendentalist understanding of God's nature and attributes. For an overview of Jahm and Jahmism, see Cornelia Schöck, 'Jahm b. Ṣafwān (d. 128/745–6) and the "Jahmiyya" and Ḍirār b.'Amr (d. 200/815),' in *The Oxford Handbook of Islamic Theology*, ed. Sabine Schmidtke, Reprint ed. (Oxford, United Kingdom: Oxford University Press, 2018), 55–80. It should be noted here that the term '*jahmiyya*' in later Islamic literature is not used to necessarily refer to this early movement but as a pejorative umbrella term for all those who nullify and deny the reality of the divine attributes.

10 For an overview of how the definition of a 'Companion' played a controversial role in early Islam, see Maya Yazigi, 'Ḥadīth Al-'Ashara or the Political Uses of a Tradition,' *Studia Islamica*, no. 86 (1997): 159–67; Scott C. Lucas, *Constructive Critics, Hadith Literature, and the Articulation of Sunni Islam: The Legacy of the Generation of Ibn Sa'd, Ibn Ma'īn, and Ibn Ḥanbal* (Leiden; Boston: Brill, 2004).

11 For the ways in which the chain of transmission is used for hadith authentication in classical hadith scholarship, see Brown, *Hadith*, 79–99.

12 The 'Partisans of Hadith' (*ahl al-ḥadīth*) moniker began to be used to describe this group since they primarily associated themselves with narrating and collecting the hadith of the Prophet. In contradistinction, the 'Partisans of Legal Reasoning' (*ahl al-ra'y*) were denoted by their excessive use of rational tools of interpretation (like analogical reasoning). See W. Montgomery Watt, *Islamic Philosophy and Theology: An Extended Survey*, 2nd ed. (Edinburgh: Edinburgh University Press, 1995), chap. 9; and Joas Wagemakers, 'The Citadel of Salafism,' in *Handbook of Islamic Sects and Movements* (Brill, 2021), 333–47. See also, Ahmad Khan, *Heresy and the Formation of Medieval Islamic Orthodoxy: The Making of Sunnism, from the Eighth to the Eleventh Century* (Cambridge: Cambridge University Press, 2023).

13 It should be noted that the Shi'i trends, at this early stage, were not concerned with notions of God's attributes. Their primary focus was political-cum-theological: *who had the right to rule over men? Was it a caliph chosen by men (as held by mainstream Sunni theology), or was it a descendant of the Family of the Prophet (ahl al-bayt), appointed and hence made infallible by God Himself?* Maria Dakake offers a more nuanced view of the formation of Shi'i identity. While recognizing its political aspects, she argues that it went beyond the leadership dispute(s) and the oft-cited Husaynid 'Karbala paradigm.' See Maria Massi Dakake, *The Charismatic Community: Shi'ite Identity in Early Islam* (Albany: State University of New York Press, 2007); Abū al-Ḥasan al-Ash'arī, *Maqālāt al-Islāmiyyīn*, ed. Helmut Ritter (Beirut: Dār al-Nashr, 1980), 5–10.

14 On Neoplatonism and its influence on early Islam, see Chapter 1, note 58 above.

15 For a discussion on Wāṣil b. 'Aṭā' and the development of the early Mu'tazīlī movement, see Racha El-Omari, 'The Mu'tazilite Movement (I): The Origins of the Mu'tazila,' in *The Oxford Handbook of Islamic Theology*, ed. Sabine Schmidtke, Reprint ed. (Oxford, United Kingdom: Oxford University Press, 2018), 131–41.

16 Rodrigo Adem, 'The Intellectual Genealogy of Ibn Taymīya' (PhD, Illinois, The University of Chicago), 86.

17 Jan Thiele, 'Abū Hāshim al-Jubbā'ī's (d. 321/933) Theory of "States" (Aḥwāl) and Its Adaption by Ash'arite Theologians,' in *The Oxford Handbook of Islamic Theology*, ed.

Sabine Schmidtke, Reprint ed. (Oxford, United Kingdom: Oxford University Press, 2018), 364–85.

18 The five principles (*uṣūl al-khamsa*) are: (1) God's perfect unicity (*tawḥīd*), (2) divine justice (*ʿadl*), (3) the doctrine of the divine promise and threat (*al-waʿd wa-l-waʿīd*), (4) the intermediate station of the grave sinner between that of a believer and disbeliever (*al-manzila bayna al-manzilatayn*), and (5) commanding the good and forbidding the evil (*al-amr bi-l-maʿrūf wa-l-nahy ʿan al-munkar*). For a summary of these five principles, see Sabine Schmidtke, 'Neuere Forschungen Zur Muʿtazila Unter Besonderer Berücksichtigung Der Späteren Muʿtazila Ab Dem 4./10. Jahrhundert,' *Arabica* 45, no. 4 (1998): 382–3.

19 For a brief overview of the development of the Muʿtazilī conception(s) of God, see Suleiman, *Ibn Taymiyya and the Attributes of God*, 41–49; Richard M. Frank, *Beings and Their Attributes: The Teaching of the Basrian School of the Muʿtazila in the Classical Period*, Studies in Islamic Philosophy and Science (Albany: State University of New York Press, 1978); Racha El-Omari, *The Theology of Abū l-Qāsim al-Balkhī/al-Kaʿbī (d. 319/931)*, Islamic Philosophy, Theology and Science 99 (Boston; Leiden: Brill, 2016), chap. 2. For a thorough treatment of the Muʿtazilī school and its aftermath in Islamic thought, see chapters 7–11, by various authors, in Schmidtke, *The Oxford Handbook of Islamic Theology*, 130–214; and also, Schmidtke, 'Neuere Forschungen.'

20 See Binyamin Abrahamov, 'Scripturalist and Traditionalist Theology,' in *The Oxford Handbook of Islamic Theology*, ed. Sabine Schmidtke, Reprint ed. (Oxford, United Kingdom: Oxford University Press, 2018), 263–80.

21 Shams al-Dīn al-Dhahabī, *Mukhtaṣar al-ʿulūw li-l-ʿAlī al-Ghaffār*, ed. Muhammad Nāṣir al-Dīn al-Albānī, 1st ed. (Damascus: al-Maktab al-Islāmī, 1981), 185.

22 Holtzman, *Anthropomorphism in Islam,* 191.

23 ʿUthmān b. Saʿīd al-Dārimī, *al-Radd ʿalā al-Jahmiyya*, ed. Badr b. ʿAbd Allāh al-Badr (Kuwait: Dār ibn al-Athīr, 1995), 66.

24 Abū Bakr al-Bayhaqī, *al-Asmāʾ wa-l-ṣifāt*, ed. ʿAbd Allāh al-Ḥāshīdī, 1st ed. (Jeddah: Maktab al-Sawādī, 1993), 538.

25 Muḥammad b. Ismāʿīl al-Bukhārī, *Khalq afʿāl al-ʿibād wa-l-radd ʿalā al-jahmiyya wa-aṣḥāb al-taʿṭīl* (Cairo: Maktab al-Turāth al-Islāmī, n.d.), 137.

26 Abū Ḥātim al-Rāzī, *Kitāb aṣl al-sunna wa iʿtiqād al-dīn*, ed. Ibrāhīm al-Ḥāzimī (Riyadh: Dār al-Sharīf, 1992), 15–19.

27 Jonathan A. C. Brown, *The Canonization of al-Bukhārī and Muslim: The Formation and Function of the Sunnī Ḥadīth Canon* (Leiden; Boston: Brill, 2011), 74–81 and 270–71; Holtzman, *Anthropomorphism in Islam*, 13.

28 Al-Ṭaḥāwī's famous creed, *al-ʿAqīda al-Ṭaḥāwiyya*, which is the standard creed studied in almost all seminaries of the Sunni world, contains phrases that contradict later Salafi thought (for example, his definition of faith [*īmān*] and his conceptualization of the divine attributes).

29 See for example, Azhar Majothi, 'Translating Salafism into English: Anglo–Salafi Print Culture in Britain' (PhD thesis, Nottingham, England, University of Nottingham, 2023), 83.

30 For a short overview of the term *ḥashwiyya* and how it has been used across Islamic history, see Jon Hoover, 'Ḥashwiyya,' in *Encyclopaedia of Islam Three Online* (Brill, 2016), https://doi.org/10.1163/1573-3912_ei3_COM_30377.

31 Abū Muḥammad b. Qutayba, *Taʾwīl mukhtalif al-ḥadīth*, ed. Salīm b. ʿĪd al-Hilālī, Annotated by ʿUmar b. Maḥmūd Abū ʿUmar (Riyadh: Dār Ibn al-Qayyim, 2009).

32 Ibn Qutayba, *al-Ikhtilāf fī al-lafẓ wa-l-radd ʿalā al-Jahmiyya wa-l-mushabbiha*, ed. ʿUmar b. Maḥmūd Abū ʿUmar (Riyadh: Dār al-Rāya, 1991).

33 Ibn Qutayba, *al-Ikhtilāf fī al-lafẓ,* 41. It should be noted that non-Salafis interpret the final phrase to indicate *tafwīḍ al-maʿnā*, or that the meaning of the Attribute is not known.

34 For a more detailed description of Ibn Qutayba's writings, see Holtzman, *Anthropomorphism in Islam*, 196–206.

35 See Christopher Melchert, *Ahmad ibn Hanbal* (Oxford: Oneworld Academic, 2006); Nimrod Hurvitz, *The Formation of Hanbalism: Piety into Power*, 1st ed. (New York: Routledge, 2011); Binyamin Abrahamov, *Islamic Theology: Traditionalism and Rationalism*, 1st ed. (Edinburgh: Edinburgh University Press, 1998); Abdul Hakim I. Al-Matroudi, *The Hanbali School of Law and Ibn Taymiyyah: Conflict or Conciliation*, 1st ed. (Routledge, 2006); Ibn al-Jawzī, *The Life of Ibn Ḥanbal*, trans. Michael Cooperson, Abridged ed. (New York: NYU Press, 2016).

36 A *Musnad* is a hadith collection that is traditionally organized by the names of the original Companions who transmitted each tradition, and the *Musnad* of Ibn Ḥanbal is one of the largest hadith collections available. In modern print, it extends to fifty-two volumes. See Aḥmad b. Ḥanbal, *Musnad al-Imām Aḥmad Ibn Ḥanbal*, ed. Shuʿayb al-Arnaʾūṭ and ʿĀdil Murshid, 52 vols (Beirut: Muʾassasat al-Risāla, 1993).

37 Christopher Melchert, 'Aḥmad ibn Ḥanbal and the Qur'an,' *Journal of Qur'anic Studies* 6, no. 2 (October 2004): 22–34.

38 See, for example, ʿAbd Allāh b. Aḥmad, *Kitāb al-Sunna*, ed. Muḥammad b. Saʿīd b. Sālim al-Qaḥṭānī (Dammam: Dār Ibn al-Qayyim, 1986), 2:483–85.

39 For a discussion on the nature of the Qurʿan and the doctrine of internal divine speech in Ashʿarism, see Nader El-Bizri, 'God: Essence and Attribute,' in *The Cambridge Companion to Classical Islamic Theology*, ed. T. J. Winter, Cambridge Companions to Religion (Cambridge; New York: Cambridge University Press, 2008), 121–40.

40 [pseduo-]Aḥmad b. Ḥanbal, *Uṣūl al-Sunna*, 1st ed. (Al-Kharj, Saudi Arabia: Dār al-Manār, 1990), 18. It should be noted that the attribution of this book to Ibn Ḥanbal is contested; it was likely written at a later date and then ascribed to him. Nonetheless, it is a part of Salafi thought and represents how Ibn Ḥanbal is portrayed by his own followers. See Saud Saleh AlSarhan, 'Early Muslim Traditionalism: A Critical Study of the Works and Political Theology of Aḥmad Ibn Ḥanbal' (PhD thesis, Exeter, UK, University of Exeter, 2011), 26–30.

41 See Ibn Aḥmad, *Kitāb al-Sunna*, 1:267–9.

42 For a discussion on the conflict between Ibn Ḥanbal and al-Muḥāsibī, see Gavin Picken, 'Ibn Ḥanbal and Al-Muḥāsibī: A Study of Early Conflicting Scholarly Methodologies,' *Arabica* 55, no. 3/4 (2008): 337–61.

43 For the application of the doctrine of *al-walāʾ wa-l-barāʾ as employed by Ibn ʿAbd al-Wahhāb to excommunicate (takfīr) the Ottomans, see Chapters 2 and 3.*

44 For the biography of al-Dārimī, see Tāj al-Dīn al-Subkī, *Ṭabaqāt al-Shāfiʿiyya al-kubrā*, ed. Maḥmūd al-Ṭanāḥī and ʿAbd al-Fattāḥ al-Ḥulw, 2nd ed. (Cairo: Dār Hajr, 1992), 2:302–6; Shams al-Dīn al-Dhahabī, *Siyar aʿlām al-nubalāʾ*, ed. Bashshār ʿAwwād Maʿrūf, 3rd ed. (Beirut: Muʾassasat al-Risāla, 1985), 13:319–26. It should also be noted here that ʿUthmān b. Saʿīd al-Dārimī is not to be confused with ʿAbd Allāh b. ʿAbd al-Raḥmān al-Dārimī (d. 255/869), the compiler of the famous hadith collection *Sunan al-Dārimī*.

45 Abū ʿAbd Allāh Muḥammad b. Karrām, the eponymous founder of the Karrāmiyya school, lived primarily in the eastern region of Sijistān. Although he was a student of Ibn Ḥanbal, he and his school were widely accused and criticized for their excessive literalism and subsequent anthropomorphic understanding of God. The Karrāmiyya school flourished from the third/ninth to the seventh/thirteenth century until the Mongol invasion. The designated label 'Karrāmī' refers not only to a theological but also an ascetic and legal orientation, with many Karrāmīs subscribing to the Ḥanafī school of law. It should, however, be noted that none of their theological works are extant and as such, we are unable to verify any of their beliefs. For an overview of the Karrāmiyya, see Aron Zysow, 'Karrāmiyya,' in *The Oxford Handbook of Islamic Theology*, ed. Sabine Schmidtke, Reprint ed. (Oxford, United Kingdom: Oxford

University Press, 2018), 252–62; Aron Zysow, 'Two Unrecognized Karrāmī Texts,' *Journal of the American Oriental Society* 108, no. 4 (1988): 577–87.

46 Shams al-Dīn b. Qayyim al-Jawziyya, *Ijtimāʿ al-juyūsh al-islāmiyya*, ed. ʿAwwād b. ʿAbd Allāh al-Muʿtiq (Riyadh: Maktabat al-Rushd, 1995), 231.

47 al-Dārimī, *al-Radd ʻalā al-Jahmiyya*.

48 al-Dārimī, *al-Radd ʻalā al-Jahmiyya,* 21–25.

49 There are a number of colorful variants to this title. See the editor's introduction of the work in ʿUthmān b. Saʿīd al-Dārimī, *Naqḍ ʿUthmān ibn Saʿīd ʿalā al-Marīsī al-Jahmī al-ʿanīd fī mā aftara ʿalā Allāh al-tawḥīd*, ed. Manṣūr b. ʿAbd al-ʿAzīz al-Simārī (Riyadh: Maktabat Aḍwāʾ al-Salaf, 1999), iv.

50 For a brief overview of Bishr al-Marīsī and his thought, see Josef van Ess, *Theology and Society in the Second and Third Centuries of the Hijra*, trans. Gwendolin Goldbloom, vol. 3 (Leiden: Brill, 2017), 189–202.

51 ʿUthmān b. Saʿīd al-Dārimī, *Radd al-Imām al-Dārimī ʿUthman ibn Saʿīd ʿalā Bishr al-Marīsī al-ʿanīd*, ed. Muḥammad Ḥamīd al-Faqqī (Beirut: Dār al-Kutūb al-ʿIlmiyya, 2004), 13–19.

52 al-Dārimī, *Naqḍ ʿUthmān ibn Saʿīd*, 175.

53 al-Dārimī, 162.

54 al-Dārimī, 188.

55 See, for example, Ibn Taymiyya's lengthy discussion on the issue of whether God can be described as having motion (*ḥaraka*) in Ibn Taymiyya, *Majmūʿ fatāwā Shaykh al-Islām Aḥmad ibn Taymiyya*, ed. ʿAbd al-Raḥmān b. Muḥammad ibn Qāsim and Muḥammad b. ʿAbd al-Raḥmān ibn Qāsim (Riyadh: Maṭābiʿ al-Riyāḍ, 1962), 4:566–75. While he admits that al-Dārimī and other early authorities affirmed this as an attribute, he himself argues that this word should not be used since the sacred texts do not mention it.

56 Abū Bakr b. Khuzayma, *Kitāb al-Tawḥīd wa-ithbāt ṣifāt al-Rabb ʿazza wa-jalla*, ed. ʿAbd al-ʿAzīz al-Shahwān, 2 vols. (Riyadh: Dār al-Rushd, 1994).

57 Khuzayma, *Ṣaḥīḥ Ibn Khuzayma*, ed. Muṣṭafā al-Aʿẓamī (Beirut: al-Maktab al-Islāmī, 1970).

58 Since Ibn Khuzayma lived for almost ninety years, he studied with some of the luminaries of the Golden Age of Hadith, such as al-Bukhārī, Muslim b. al-Ḥajjāj (d. 261/875), Ibn Rāhawayh, among others.

59 Richard Bulliet calls Ibn Khuzayma 'the most prominent Shāfiʿī in Nishapur,' see Richard W. Bulliet, *The Patricians of Nishapur; a Study in Medieval Islamic Social History* (Cambridge, Mass.: Harvard University Press, 1972). See also the high praise that the famous Shāfiʿī scholar Tāj al-Dīn al-Subkī (d. 771/1370) lavishes on him in al-Subkī, *Ṭabaqāt al-Shāfiʿiyya*, 3:109–19.

60 Ibn Khuzayma, *Kitāb al-Tawḥīd*, 1:10.

61 Ibn Khuzayma, *Kitāb al-Tawḥīd*, 1:10–11.

62 Ibn Khuzayma, *Kitāb al-Tawḥīd*, 26–7.

63 Abū al-Ḥusayn Muḥammad b. Abī Yaʿlā al-Farrāʾ, *Ṭabaqāt al-Ḥanābila*, ed. ʿAbd al-Raḥmān b. Sulaymān al-ʿUthaymīn (Riyadh: al-Amāna al-ʿĀmma li-l-Iḥtifāl bi-Murūr Miʾat ʿĀmʿalā Taʾsīs al-Mamlaka, 1999), 2:43.

64 Michael Cook, *Commanding Right and Forbidding Wrong in Islamic Thought* (Cambridge, UK; New York: Cambridge University Press, 2000), 144. For the influence of al-Barbahārī and his control of the theological scene in Baghdad, see Tariq al-Jamil, *Power and Knowledge in Medieval Islam: Shi'i and Sunni Encounters in Baghdad* (I.B. Tauris, 2025); Françoise Micheau, 'Baghdad In The Abbasid Era: A Cosmopolitan And Multi-Confessional Capital,' in *The City in the Islamic World* (2 vols), ed. Salma Khadra Jayyusi et al. (Brill, 2008), 219–45.

65 Ibn Abī Yaʿlā, *Ṭabaqāt*, 2:44.

66 Al-Ḥasan b. ʿAlī al-Barbahārī [or Ghulām Khalīl], *Sharḥ al-Sunna*, ed. Muḥammad b. Saʿīd al-Qaḥṭānī (Cairo: Maktabat al-Sunna, 1996).

67 See al-Hasan ibn Alee ibn Khalf al-Barbahaaree, *Explanation of the Creed*, trans. Dawood Burbank, 1st ed. (Al-Hidaayah, 1995).
68 The work was actually authored by Ghulām Khalīl (d. 275/888), a populist and somewhat bombastic preacher nominally associated with the Ḥanbalī school. See Maher Jarrar and Sebastian Günther, eds, 'Doctrinal Instruction in Early Islam: The Book of the Explanation of the Sunna by Ghulām Khalīl (d. 275/888),' in *Doctrinal Instruction in Early Islam* (Brill, 2020).
69 al-Barbahārī [or Ghulām Khalīl], *Sharḥ al-Sunna*, 26–60.
70 al-Barbahārī [or Ghulām Khalīl], *Sharḥ al-Sunna*, 68.
71 Khan, *Heresy and the Formation of Medieval Islamic Orthodoxy*, 132.
72 Ibn Abī Yaʿlā, *Ṭabaqāt*, 2:18.
73 Abū al-Ḥasan al-Ashʿarī, *al-Ibāna ʿan uṣūl al-Diyāna*, ed. Fawqiyya Ḥusayn Maḥmūd (Cairo: Dār al-Anṣār, 1977).
74 Ibn Abī Yaʿlā, *Ṭabaqāt*, 2:18. It is also reported by the renowned historian Shams al-Dīn al-Dhahabī but he alludes to its weakness by narrating it in the passive, 'It has been said…,' see al-Dhahabī, *Siyar aʿlām al-nubalāʾ*, 13:18. For a classic discussion of the controversy of whether *al-Ibāna* is actually the work of al-Ashʿarī, and if so, whether it is perhaps his last work or one of his early works after leaving the Muʿtaliza – and an elaboration of its creedal contents – see Richard J. McCarthy, *The Theology of Al-Ashʿarī: The Arabic Texts of Al-Ashʿarī's Kitāb al-Lumaʿ and Risālat Istiḥsān al-Khawḍ fī ʿilm al-Kalām, with Briefly Annotated Translations, and Appendices Containing Material Pertinent to the Study of Al-Ashʿarī* (Beyrouth: Impr. catholique, 1953).
75 Ibn Taymiyya, *al-Fatwā al-kubrā*, ed. Ismā'īl al-Khaṭīb (Beirut: Dār al-Qalam, 1987), 5:289.
76 Ibn Abī Yaʿlā attributes this story to a work authored by a certain Abū ʿAlī al-Ahwāzī (d. 446/1055), which was written as a disparagement of al-Ashʿarī. See Ibn Abī Yaʿlā al-Farrāʾ, *Ṭabaqāt*, 2:18.
77 Abū ʿAbd Allāh b. Baṭṭa al-ʿUkbarī, *al-Ibāna ʿan sharīʿat al-firaq al-nājiya wa-l-mujānabat al-firaq al-madhmūma [also: al-Ibāna al-kubrā]*, ed. Riḍā b. Naʿsān Muʿṭī, 2nd ed., 7 vols (Riyadh: Dār al-Rāya, 1994).
78 Ibn Baṭṭa al-ʿUkbarī, *al-Sharḥ wa-l-ibāna ʿalā uṣūl al-sunna wa-l-diyāna [also: al-Ibāna al-ṣughrā]*, ed. Riḍā b. Naʿsān Muʿṭī, 1st ed. (Maktabat al-ʿUlūm wa-l-Ḥikam, 2002).
79 Ibn Baṭṭa, *al-Ibāna al-ṣughrā,* 2:317.
80 For an overview on Ibn Baṭṭa, see Jon Hoover, 'Ḥanbali Theology,' in *The Oxford Handbook of Islamic Theology*, ed. Sabine Schmidtke (Oxford, United Kingdom: Oxford University Press, 2018), 625–46.
81 For an overview of the life and works of al-Lālakāʾī, see Livnat Holtzman, 'Al-Lālakāʾī, Abū l-Qāsim,' in *Encyclopaedia of Islam Three Online*, ed. Kate Fleet et al. (Brill, 2020), https://doi.org/10.1163/1573-3912_ei3_COM_35783.
82 Abū al-Qāsim Ḥibat Allāh al-Lālakāʾī, *Sharḥ uṣūl iʿtiqād ahl al-Sunna wa-l-jamāʿa*, ed. Aḥmad b. Saʿd b. Ḥamdān, 8th ed., 4 vols (Riyadh: Dār Ṭayba, 2003).
83 Abū ʿUthmān Ismāʿīl b. ʿAbd al-Raḥmān al-Ṣābūnī, *ʿAqīdat al-Ṣalaf wa aṣḥāb al-ḥadīth [also: al-Risāla fī iʿtiqād ahl al-Sunna wa aṣḥāb al-ḥadīth wa-l-Aʾimma]*, ed. Nāṣir b. ʿAbd al-Raḥmān al-Judaiʿ (Riyadh: Dār al-ʿĀṣima, 1998).
84 Al-Qādir bi-llāh, also known as Aḥmad b. Isḥāq b. Jaʿfar al-Muqtadir bi-llāh, was the twenty-fifth Abbasid Caliph who reigned for approximately four decades from 81/991 to 422/1031. He ruled in a period in which the status of the Abbasid Caliphate was in decline, and similar to his immediate predecessors, he ruled under the tutelage of the Buyids – a Shiʿi dynasty of Iranian descent who assumed control of Baghdad and ruled the Caliphate de facto from 334/945 to 447/1055. Al-Qādir was appointed as the Caliph

only after his uncle al-Ṭāʾiʿ bi-llāh (d. 393/1003) was deposed by the Buyid *amīr* Bahāʾ al-Dawla (d. 403/1012). However, after the death of Bahāʾ al-Dawla, al-Qādir allied with Maḥmūd b. Sabuktigīn (d. 421/1030) – the powerful sultan of the Ghaznavid dynasty. Under the support of the latter, al-Qādir was able to act without opposition on behalf of Ḥanbalīs against the Muʿtazila and the Shiʿa. Of course, it should be noted here that in later Sunni sources, he is portrayed as a pious and religious individual. For a study on the reign of al-Qādir, see Udjang Tholib, 'The Reign of the Caliph Al-Qādir Billāh (381/991-422/1031)' (Montreal, McGill University, 2002); Livnat Holtzman, 'The Caliph Al-Qādir Bi-llāh and the Qādirī Creed,' in *Rulers as Authors in the Islamic World*, ed. Maribel Fierro, Sonja Brentjes, and Tilman Seidensticker (Leiden: Brill, 2024), 143–209.

85 According to Livnat Holtzman, the Qādirī creed is not one brief text but a series of documents and books issued by al-Qādir from 408/1017–1018 to 420/1209. In fact Holtzman argues that one of these documents issued was a voluminous book. See Holtzman, 'The Caliph Al-Qādir Bi-Llāh and the Qādirī Creed,' 143. However, none of these documents survived except for the concise text of 770 words, also called the *al-Iʿitiqād al-Qādiri wa-l-Qāʾimī (The Qādirī-Qāʾimī Creed)*, found in Ibn al-Jawzī's *al-Muntaẓam fī taʾrikh al-mulūk wa-l-umam (The Chronicle of Kings and Nations).* See Abū al-Faraj ʿAbd al-Raḥmān b. al-Jawzī, *al-Muntaẓam fī taʾrīkh al-mulūk wa-l-umam*, ed. Muḥammad ʿAbd al-Qādir ʿAṭā and Muṣṭafā ʿAbd al-Qādir ʿAṭā (Beirut: Dār al-Kutūb al-ʿIlmiyya, 1992), 15:279–82. The text in its entirety has been recently translated into English by Holtzman, see Appendix C in Holtzman, 'The Caliph Al-Qādir Bi-Llāh and the Qādirī Creed,' 199–203. A partial version of this text (with no additional details) is also found in *Mirʾāt al-zamān (Mirror of Time)* by Shams al-Dīn Abu l-Maẓaffar Yūsuf b. Qizoghulu (d. 654/1256) – more commonly known as Sibṭ Ibn al-Jawzī – the grandson of Ibn al-Jawzī. See Sibṭ b. al-Jawzī, *Mirʾāt al-zamān fī tawārīkh al-aʿyān*, ed. Muḥammad Barakāt et al., vol. 23 (Damascus: Dār al-Risālāt al-ʿĀlamiyya, 2013), 18:422.

86 For a thorough study of the Qādirī creed, see Holtzman, 'The Caliph Al-Qādir Bi-Llāh and the Qādirī Creed.' For earlier studies, see George Makdisi, *Ibn ʿAqil: Religion and Culture in Classical Islam*, 1st ed. (Edinburgh: Edinburgh University Press, 1997), 8–16; Holtzman, *Anthropomorphism in Islam*, 272–78.

87 Ibn al-Jawzī, *al-Muntaẓam*, 15:280; Eng. trans., Holtzman, 'The Caliph Al-Qādir Bi-Llāh and the Qādirī Creed,' 201.

88 Ibn al-Jawzī, *al-Muntaẓam*, 15:280; Eng. trans., Holtzman, 'The Caliph Al-Qādir Bi-Llāh and the Qādirī Creed,' 201.

89 See Ibn al-Jawzī, *al-Muntaẓam*, 15:280; Eng. trans., Holtzman, 'The Caliph Al-Qādir Bi-Llāh and the Qādirī Creed,' 201.

90 Ibid., 201.

91 Makdisi, *Ibn ʿAqil*, 10.

92 Hoover, 'Ḥanbali Theology,' 629. See also Roy Mottahedeh, *Loyalty and Leadership in An Early Islamic Society*, 2nd ed. (London; New York: New York: I.B. Tauris, 2001); A. C. S. Peacock, *The Great Seljuk Empire*, 1st ed. (Edinburgh: Edinburgh University Press, 2015).

93 A. R. Azzam, *Saladin: The Triumph of the Sunni Revival*, 2nd ed. (Cambridge, UK: Islamic Texts Society, 2014), 7.

94 For a brief discussion on the Karrāmīs, see footnote 45 above.

95 See Zysow, 'Two Unrecognized Karrāmī Texts'; Zysow, 'Karrāmiyya.'

96 The aforementioned persona of al-Ṣabūnī is illustrative in this regard. He was the most prominent Ḥanbalī preacher in the city and the chief sermonizer (*khaṭīb*) of the Grand Mosque of Nishapur. Yet, during the Inquisition, other than being officially removed from his post, he was not banned from preaching nor expelled from the city.

See ʿAlī b. al-Ḥasan b. ʿAsākir, *Tabyīn kadhib al-Muftarī fī-mā nusiba ilā al-imām Abī al-Ḥasan al-Ashʿarī*, 2nd ed. (Damascus: Dār al-Fikr, 1979), 108; and Yasir Kazi, 'Reconciling Reason and Revelation in the Writings of Ibn Taymiyya (d. 728/1328): An Analytical Study of Ibn Taymiyya's "Dar' al-Ta'arud"' (PhD, Connecticut, USA, Yale University), 40–45, accessed August 14, 2023.

97 The exact nature and version of Shiʿism that was practiced by this dynasty is the subject of some controversy. See Heinz Halm, *Shi'ism*, trans. Janet Watson and Marian Hill, 2nd ed. (New York: Columbia University Press, 2004), chap. 2.

98 ʿIzz-ad-Dīn Abū-l-Ḥasan ʿAlī Ibn-al-Aṯīr, *The Annals of the Saljuq Turks: Selections from al-Kāmil Fī 'l-Taʾrīkh of ʿIzz al-Dīn Ibn al-Athīr*, trans. Donald S. Richards, Studies in the History of Iran and Turkey (London: RoutledgeCurzon, 2002), 196–7.

99 Ibn al-Jawzī, *al-Muntaẓam*, 9:545; For a more thorough study of this letter and its implications, see Kazi, 'Reconciling Reason and Revelation in the Writings of Ibn Taymiyya (d. 728/1328),' 60–64.

100 Ignác Goldziher, *Le dogme et la loi de l'Islam; Histoire du développement Dogmatique et Juridique de La Religion Musulmane* (Paris: Geuthner, 1920), 98. English translation taken from George Makdisi, 'Muslim Institutions of Learning in Eleventh-Century Baghdad,' *Bulletin of the School of Oriental and African Studies, University of London* 24, no. 1 (1961): 3.

101 Azzam, *Saladin*, 97–98 and 128–9.

102 One of Ibn al-Zāghūnī's works was published and is worthy of further study. See Abū al-Ḥasan b. al-Zāghūnī, *al-Īḍāḥ fī uṣūl al-dīn*, ed. ʿIṣām Sayyid Maḥmūd (Riyadh: Markaz al-Malik Fayṣal li-l-Buḥūth wa-l-Dirāsāt al-Islāmiyya, 2003).

103 Abū Yaʿlā b. al-Farrāʾ, *Ibṭāl al-taʾwīlat li-akhbār al-ṣifāt*, ed. Abū ʿAbd Allāh Muḥammad b. Ḥamad al-Ḥamūd al-Najdī (Kuwait: Ghirās li-l-Nashr wa-l-Tawzīʿ, 2013).

104 Hoover, 'Ḥanbali Theology,' 632.

105 See Adem, 'The Intellectual Genealogy of Ibn Taymīya,' 244–56 and 259–66.

106 For an in-depth study on Ibn ʿAqīl, see Makdisi, *Ibn ʿAqil*.

107 Ibn al-Jawzī, *The Life of Ibn Ḥanbal*, 81.

108 Abū al-Faraj ʿAbd al-Raḥmān b. al-Jawzī, *Dafʿ shubah al-tashbīh bi-akuff al-tanzīh fī al-radd ʿalā al-mujassima wa-l-mushabbiha*, ed. Muḥammad Zāhid al-Kawtharī (Cairo: al-Maktaba al-Tawfīqiyya, 1977). The text has been translated into English by Abdullah bin Hamid 'Ali, see Ibn al-Jawzī, *The Attributes of God: Ibn al-Jawzi's Daf' Shubah al-Tashbih Bi-Akaff al-Tanzih*, trans. Abdullah bin Hamid 'Ali, 1st ed. (Amal Press, 2006). Due to its critique of crass literalism, this relatively short work has gained favor within the Ashʿarī school. They attempt to present Ibn al-Jawzī as an icon of 'true' Ḥanbalī theology. The text was edited and annotated by the erudite Muḥammad Zāhid al-Kawtharī (d. 1952). Al-Kawtharī was notably preoccupied with countering reformist and literalist theological currents, including those associated with the Taymiyyan thought. However, his endeavors occasionally yielded flawed results. For al-Kawthari's important career as 'the most learned manuscript expert in the generation after Ṭāhir al-Jazāʾirī (d. 1920),' see Ahmed El Shamsy, *Rediscovering the Islamic Classics: How Editors and Print Culture Transformed an Intellectual Tradition* (Princeton University Press, 2022), 212–17.

109 Merlin Swartz studied *Kitāb akhbār al-ṣifāt* in detail and translated it in its entirety into English, with important biographical details of the author. See Ibn al-Jawzī, *A Medieval Critique of Anthropomorphism: Ibn Al-Jawzī's Kitāb Akhbār Aṣ-Ṣifāt*, trans. Merlin L. Swartz (Leiden: Brill, 2002).

110 Ibn al-Jawzī, *A Medieval Critique,* 3–32.

111 Ibn al-Jawzī, *A Medieval Critique,* 19–20.

112 Holtzman, 'Al-Lālakāʾī,' 2020.

113 Ibn al-Jawzī, *The Attributes of God*, xviii.

114 For an introduction to the Maqdisī family, see Adem, 'The Intellectual Genealogy of Ibn Taymīya,' 43–48.

115 For an overview on ʿAbd al-Ghanī al-Maqdisi, see Daniella Talmon-Heller, 'ʿAbd Al-Ghanī al-Maqdisi,' in *Encyclopaedia of Islam Three Online*, ed. Kate Fleet et al. (Brill, 2022), https://doi.org/10.1163/1573-3912_ei3_COM_46424.

116 For an overview on the life and works of Ibn Qudāma, see Mustafa Shah, 'Ibn Qudāma, al-Maqdisi,' in *Encyclopaedia of Islam Three Online*, ed. Kate Fleet et al. (Brill, 2018), https://doi.org/10.1163/1573-3912_ei3_COM_32175.

117 Adem, 'The Intellectual Genealogy of Ibn Taymīya,' 3635–72.

118 Muwaffaq al-Dīn b. Qudāma, *al-Mughnī sharḥ mukhtaṣar al-Khiraqī*, ed. ʿAbd Allāh b. ʿAbd al-Muḥsin al-Turkī and ʿAbd al-Fattāḥ Muḥammad al-Ḥilū, 3rd ed., 15 vols. (Riyadh: Dār ʿĀlam al-Kutub, 1997).

119 Hoover, 'Ḥanbali Theology,' 633.

120 Azzam, *Saladin*, 178–79.

121 Carl Sharif El-Tobgui, *Ibn Taymiyya on Reason and Revelation: A Study of Darʾ taʿāruḍ al-ʿaql wa-l-naql* (Leiden; Boston: Brill, 2019), 72.

122 See Ibn Taymiyya, *Against Extremisms*, trans. Yahya Michot (Beirut: Albouraq Editions, 2012).

123 The modern printing of Ibn Taymiyya's works began in the 1900s, and the keen interest in his thought led to the publication, in Egypt, of over 130 works attributed to him by the middle of the century. See Shamsy, *Rediscovering the Islamic Classics*, chap. 7.

124 There are now a vast number of studies on Ibn Taymiyya, so it is not possible to provide a comprehensive bibliography on him. However, the following are some of the more well-known introductory references: Jon Hoover, 'Ibn Taymiyya,' in *The Stanford Encyclopedia of Philosophy*, ed. Edward N. Zalta and Uri Nodelman, Summer 2024 (Metaphysics Research Lab, Stanford University, 2024), https://plato.stanford.edu/archives/sum2024/entries/ibn-taymiyya/; Jon Hoover, *Ibn Taymiyya* (London: Oneworld Academic, 2020); Ovamir Anjum, *Politics, Law and Community in Islamic Thought: The Taymiyyan Moment*, Cambridge Studies in Islamic Civilization (Cambridge; New York: Cambridge University Press, 2012); El-Tobgui, *Ibn Taymiyya on Reason and Revelation: A Study of Darʾ Taʿāruḍ al-ʿaql Wa-l-Naql*; Suleiman, *Ibn Taymiyya and the Attributes of God*; Taqī al-Dīn b. Taymiyya, *Ibn Taymiyya Against the Greek Logicians*, trans. Wael B. Hallaq, 1st ed. (Oxford: New York: Clarendon Press, 1993); Youssef Rapoport and Shahab Ahmed, eds., *Ibn Taymiyya and His Times* (Karachi: Oxford University Press, 2010); Birgit Krawietz and Georges Tamer, eds., *Islamic Theology, Philosophy and Law: Debating Ibn Taymiyya and Ibn Qayyim Al-Jawziyya* (Berlin; Boston: De Gruyter, 2013); Caterina Bori, 'A New Source for the Biography of Ibn Taymiyya,' *Bulletin of the School of Oriental and African Studies, University of London* 67, no. 3 (2004): 321–48; Donald P. Little, 'The Historical and Historiographical Significance of the Detention of Ibn Taymiyya,' *International Journal of Middle East Studies* 4, no. 3 (1973): 311–27; Donald P. Little, 'Did Ibn Taymiyya Have a Screw Loose?' *Studia Islamica*, no. 41 (1975): 93–111. Jon Hoover maintains a comprehensive online bibliography of articles and monographs on Ibn Taymiyya, see Jon Hoover, 'Ibn Taymiyya,' accessed August 14, 2023, https://sites.google.com/site/jhoover363/taymiyyan-studies/ibn-taymiyya.

125 Caterina Bori, 'Ibn Taymiyya wa-Jamaʿatuhu: Authority, Conflict and Consensus in Ibn Taymiyya's Circle,' in *Ibn Taymiyya and His Times*, ed. Youssef Rapoport and Shahab Ahmed (Karachi: Oxford University Press, 2010), 33–36.

126 For an overview of the reasons and their respective dates for his imprisonment, see Suleiman, *Ibn Taymiyya and the Attributes of God*, 64.

127 al-Dhahabī, 'Dhayl Tārīkh al-Islām,' in *al-Jāmiʿ li-sīrat Shaykh al-Islām Ibn Taymiyya khilāla sabʿat qurūn*, ed. Muḥammad ʿUzayr Shams and ʿAlī b. Muḥammad al-ʿImrān, 2nd ed. (Riyadh: Dār ʿĀlam al-Fawāʾid, 2001), 606.

128 Ibn Taymiyya was not the first to invent this categorization; a rudimentary version of it exists in the writings of Ibn Batta. However, it is undeniable that Ibn Taymiyya was the first to establish it as a mainstream notion, and it is his efforts that led to the tripartite division of monotheism becoming a pillar of all later Ḥanbalī and Salafi thought. See: Ibn Baṭṭa al-ʿUkbarī, *al-Ibāna*, vol. 6, 149.

129 For a study on the writings of Ibn Qayyim, see Caterina Bori and Livnat Holtzman, eds., *A Scholar in the Shadow: Essays in the Legal and Theological Thought of Ibn Qayyim Aal-Jawziyya*, Oriente Moderno, nuova serie, anno 90, 1, 2010 (Roma: Istituto per l'Oriente C.A. Nallino, 2010).

130 Ibn Taymiyya, *al-Tadmuriyya: Taḥqīq al-ithbāt fī al-asmāʾ wa-l-ṣifāt wa-l-ḥaqīqat al-jamʿ bayna al-qadar wa-l-sharʿ*, ed. Muḥammad b. ʿAwda al-Saʿawī, 6th ed. (Riyadh: Maktabat al-ʿUbaykān, 2000). Also found in Ibn Taymiyya, *Majmūʿ fatāwā*, 3:1–128.

131 Ibn Taymiyya, *al-Fatwā al-Ḥamawiyya al-kubrā*, ed. Ḥamad b. ʿAbd al-Muḥsin al-Tuwayjirī (Riyadh: Dār al-Ṣumayʿī, 2004). Also found in Ibn Taymiyya, *Majmūʿ fatāwā*, 5:5–120.

132 This creed is found in Ibn Taymiyya, *Majmūʿ fatāwā*, 3:129–59.

133 For a detailed discussion of Ibn Taymiyya's linguistic views, see Suleiman, *Ibn Taymiyya and the Attributes of God*, chap. 5.

134 Ibn Taymiyya, *Ibn Taymiyya Against the Greek Logicians*, 34.

135 For an introductory overview of Fakhr al-Dīn al-Rāzī, see Peter Adamson and Fedor Benevich, 'Fakhr Al-Din al-Razi,' in *The Stanford Encyclopedia of Philosophy*, ed. Edward N. Zalta and Uri Nodelman, Spring 2023 (Metaphysics Research Lab, Stanford University, 2023), https://plato.stanford.edu/archives/spr2023/entries/al-din-al-razi/.

136 Ibn Taymiyya, *Bayān talbīs al-jahmiyya fī taʾsīs bidaʿihim al-kalāmiyya*, ed. Yaḥyā b. Muḥammad al-Hunaydī et al., 10 vols (Medina: Mujammaʿ al-Malik Fahd li-Ṭibāʿat al-Muṣḥaf al-Sharīf, 2005). This treatise was previously published in an incomplete form under another title, see Ibn Taymiyya, *Naqḍ Asās al-taqdīs*, ed. Mūsā b. Sulaymān al-Duwaysh (Medina: Maktabat al-ʿUlūm wa-l-Ḥikam, 2004).

137 Ibn Taymiyya, *Darʾ taʿāruḍ al-ʿaql wa-l-naql*, ed. Muḥammad Rashād Sālim, 2nd ed., 10 vols (Riyadh: Jāmiʿat al-Imām Muḥammad ibn Suʿūd al-Islāmiyya, 1991).

138 For studies on this work, see Kazi, 'Reconciling Reason and Revelation in the Writings of Ibn Taymiyya (d. 728/1328)'; El-Tobgui, *Ibn Taymiyya on Reason and Revelation: A Study of Darʾ taʿāruḍ al-ʿaql wa-l-naql*.

139 For a discussion on the debate between Ibn Taymiyya and the Ashʿarīs on the divine attributes, see Frank Griffel, 'Ibn Taymiyya and His Ash'arite Opponents on Reason and Revelation: Similarities, Differences, and a Vicious Circle,' *Muslim World* 108, no. 1 (January 1, 2018): 11–39.

140 Ibn Taymiyya, *Minhāj al-sunna al-nabawiyya fī naqḍ kalām al-Shīʿa al-qadariyya*, ed. Rashād Sālim, 8 vols (Riyadh: Muʾassasat al-Rayyān, 2003).

141 Ibn Muṭahhar al-Ḥillī, *Minhāj al-karāma fī ithbāt al-Imāma*, Lithographic reprint of a manuscript ([Iran], 1877).

142 Tariq al-Jamil, 'Ibn Taymiyya and Ibn Al-Muṭahhar al-Ḥillī: Shiʿī Polemics and the Struggle for Religious Authority in Medieval Islam,' in *Ibn Taymiyya and His Times*, ed. Youssef Rapoport and Shahab Ahmed (Karachi: Oxford University Press, 2010), 229–46.

143 Yaron Friedman, 'Ibn Taymiyya's Fatāwā against the Nuṣayrī-ʿAlawī Sect' 82, no. 2 (December 12, 2005): 349–63. It is important to note that the Alawis are not, and have never been, universally accepted by Twelver Shīʿi scholars as being part of Shīʿism. On this, see Yaron Friedman, *The Nuṣayrī-ʿalawīs: An Introduction to the Religion, History, and Identity of the Leading Minority in Syria* (Leiden; Boston: Brill, 2010); Martin Kramer, 'Syria's Alawis and Shi'ism,' in *Shi'ism, Resistance and Revolution*, ed. Martin Kramer, 1st ed. (Routledge, 2019), 237–54.

144 Ibn Taymiyya, *al-Jawāb al-ṣaḥīḥ li-man baddala dīn al-Masīḥ*, ed. ʿAlī b. Ḥasan, ʿAbd al-ʿAzīz b. Ibrāhīm al-ʿAskar, and Ḥamdān b. Muḥammad al-Ḥamdān, 7 vols (Riyadh: Dār al-ʿĀṣima, 1999).

145 For a study of Ibn Taymiyya's *al-Jawāb al-ṣaḥīḥ* and his polemics against Christianity, see Thomas F. Michel, ed., *A Muslim Theologian's Response to Christianity: Ibn Taymiyya's Al-Jawab Al-Sahih* (Delmar, NY: Caravan Books, 1656).

146 Ibn Taymiyya, *Iqtiḍāʾ al-ṣirāṭ al-mustaqīm li-mukhālafat aṣḥāb al-jaḥīm*, ed. Nāṣir b. ʿAbd al-Karīm al-ʿAql, 2 vols (Riyadh: Dār al-ʿĀṣima, 1998); Eng. trans. Muhammad Umar Memon, *Ibn Taimiya's Struggle Against Popular Religion: With an Annotated Translation of His Kitab Iqtida as-Sirat al-Mustaqim Mukhalafat Ashab al-Jahim* (De Gruyter, 2013).

147 The main reference of his writings is the compilation that was done by ʿAbd al-Raḥmān b. Qāsim in 1960, in which many of his smaller treatises were compiled in thirty-seven volumes and printed under the title, *Majmūʿ fatāwā*. See Ibn Taymiyya, Ibn Taymiyya, *Majmūʿ fatāwā Shaykh al-Islām Aḥmad ibn Taymiyya*, ed. ʿAbd al-Raḥmān b. Muḥammad b. Qāsim and Muḥammad b. ʿAbd al-Raḥmān b. Qāsim, 37 vols (Riyadh: Maṭābiʿ al-Riyāḍ, 1962). This large collection has been printed and reprinted many times, and for a period of time, it was freely distributed by Saudi authorities and philanthropists for anyone who asked for a copy.

148 For a discussion of Ibn Taymiyya's rationale for his triple-divorce fatwa, see Hoover, *Ibn Taymiyya*, 2020, 84–8. For a discussion of the fatwa within the Ḥanbalī school and the Islamic legal tradition in general, see Al-Matroudi, *The Hanbali School of Law and Ibn Taymiyyah*, 171–85. In relation to the modern embrace of this fatwa by certain reformist scholars, see Shamsy, *Rediscovering the Islamic Classics*, 189.

149 For the normative doctrine of the eternality of the hellfire in Sunni and Shiʿi Islam, see Hoover, *Ibn Taymiyya*, 2020, 137–9; Suleiman, *Ibn Taymiyya and the Attributes of God*, 291–2; Ayatollah Jafar Sobhani, *Doctrines of Shiʿi Islam: A Compendium of Imami Beliefs and Practices*, trans. Reza Shah Kazemi (London: I.B.Tauris, 2001), 138–41.

150 Ibn Taymiyya, *Majmūʿ fatāwā*, 10:82. English translation by M. Abdul Haq Anṣārī, see M. Abdul Haq Anṣārī, 'Ibn Taymiyyah and Sufism,' *Islamic Studies* 24, no. 1 (1985): 1.

151 For a short discussion on the monistic doctrine of Ibn ʿArabī known as *waḥdat al-wujūd* (the unity of being), see Chapter 1, footnote 59.

152 Anṣārī, 'Ibn Taymiyyah and Sufism,' 1–3.

153 For a brief discussion on the doctrine of *istighātha*, see section 1.4.

154 Ibn Taymiyya, *Majmūʿ fatāwā*. Translated into English by Cole Bunzel in Bunzel, *Wahhābism*, 146.

155 Ibn Taymiyya, *al-Istighātha fi al-radd ʿalā al-Bakrī*, ed. ʿAbdallāh b. Dujayn al-Sahlī (Riyadh: Maktabat Dār al-Minhāj, 2014).

156 Abū al-Fidāʾ Ismāʿīl b. Kathīr, *al-Bidāya wa-l-Nihāya*, ed. ʿAbd al-Rahmān al-Lādqī and Muḥammad Ghāzī Bayḍūn (Beirut: Dār al-Maʿarifa, 2010), 13:186.

157 Yahya Michot, the justly famed Taymiyyan expert, has queried the extreme readings of Ibn Taymiyya as a political thinker. These include the overemphasis on the political aspect within his entire oeuvre and life (as seen in his mild criticism of Henri Laoust) and the misreading characterized by 'class dunce neo-orientalism and breezy confidence' combined with mediocre Arabic (as seen in his harsh criticism of Gilles Kepel). See Yahya Michot, *Muslims Under Non-Muslim Rule: Ibn Taymiyya* (Oxford: Interface Publications, 2006), 35–36 and 58–61. For an analysis of Michot's study of the political relevance and application of Ibn Taymiyya by Muslim scholars and activists, see Jon Hoover, 'Ibn Taymiyya Between Moderation and Radicalism,' in *Reclaiming Islamic Tradition: Modern Interpretations of the Classical Heritage*, ed.

Elisabeth Kendall and Ahmad Khan (Edinburgh: Edinburgh University Press, 2016), 177–203.

158 National Commission on Terrorist Attacks upon the United States, ed., *The 9/11 Commission Report: Final Report of the National Commission on Terrorist Attacks Upon the United States*, Authorized ed., 1st ed. (New York: Norton, 2004), 362. See also Yahya Michot, *Ibn Taymiyya: Against Extremism* (Paris: Albouraq, 2012), xx–xxi.

159 Anjum, *Politics, Law and Community in Islamic Thought*, 268.

160 Anjum, *Politics, Law and Community in Islamic Thought,* 268–69.

161 Anjum, *Politics, Law and Community in Islamic Thought*. 269.

162 Cook, *Commanding Right and Forbidding Wrong in Islamic Thought*, 149–57; Hoover, *Ibn Taymiyya*, 2020, 12–18 and 89–105.

163 Michot, *Ibn Taymiyya: Against Extremism*, 257–69.

164 Ibn Taymiyya, *Majmūʿ fatāwā*, 28:146. Passage translated into English and cited by Jon Hoover in Hoover, *Ibn Taymiyya*, 2020, 97.

165 Taqī al-Dīn Abū Bakr b. Aḥmad b. Qāḍī Shuhba, *Tārīkh Ibn Qāḍī Shuhba*, ed. Adnān Darwīsh (Damascus: Institut Français de Damas, 1977), 1:89; and also found in Aḥmad b. ʿAlī b. Ḥajar ʿAsqalānī, *Inabāʾ al-ghumr bi-abānaʾ al-ʿumr fī al-tārīkh* (Hyderabad: Maṭbaʿat Majlis Dāʾirat al-Maʿārif al-ʿUthmāniyya, 1967), 2:96, but with the addition of the phrase '*madhhab Ibn Taymiyya*.' Translated into English and cited by Caterina Bori in Caterina Bori, 'Ibn Taymiyya (14th to 17th Century): Transregional Spaces of Reading and Reception,' *The Muslim World* 108, no. 1 (2018): 93.

166 This is a reference to a hadith found in *Ṣāḥīḥ Muslim*: *kitāb al-masājid wa mawaḍīʿ al-ṣalah, bāb taḥrīm al-kalām fī al-ṣalah wa naskh ma kāna min ibāḥatihī*. In the hadith, a slave girl is asked by the Prophet, 'Where is God?' She replies, 'In the sky,' and she is then freed upon the Prophet, declaring that she is a believer. In keeping with the Ashʿarī principles, al-Nawawī declared this to be 'a hadith from the hadiths of the [divine] attributes,' so there are two approaches to be taken. Firstly, one can believe in it without delving into the meaning while knowing that God does not have the attributes of His creation. Or, secondly, to give it a figurative interpretation, as though the slave girl was affirming God's exaltation and transcendency above the idols of the world – just as people supplicate towards the sky as they pray towards the Kaaba. However, in neither case do people think that God is literally in the Kaaba or the sky. See Yaḥyā b. Sharaf al-Nawawī, *Ṣāḥīḥ Muslim bi-sharḥ al-Nawawī*, 2nd ed. (Cairo: Muʾassasat Qurṭuba, 1994), 5:33. However, Salafis have taken this narration as an article of faith in its literalness, meaning that they affirm verbally that 'God is above us' and not that God necessarily dwells within the created space of the heavens.

167 Bori, 'Ibn Taymiyya (14th to 17th Century),' 91–96.

168 For the most prominent proposal of this view, see Khaled El-Rouayheb, 'From Ibn Hajar Al-Haytami (d. 1566) to Khayr al-Din al-Alusi (d. 1899): Changing Views of Ibn Taymiyya amongst Sunni Islamic Scholars,' in *Ibn Taymiyya and His Times*, ed. Youssef Rapoport and Shahab Ahmed (Karachi: Oxford University Press, 2010), 269–318. I, however, believe the author attempted to find mini-replicas of Ibn Taymiyya rather than examine those who might have taken a seminal aspect or two from his thought. As this section shows, it is clear that further research is warranted, and there is much more to be done to see the full impact of Ibn Taymiyya during this time frame.

169 For studies on the Qāḍīzādelī movement, see Marinos Sariyannis, 'The Kadizeli Movement as a Social and Political Phenomenon: The Rise of a "Mercantile Ethic"?' in *Political Initiatives 'from the Bottom up' in the Ottoman Empire*, ed. Antonis Anastasopoulos (Rethymno: Crete University Press, 2012), 263–89; Ahya Ulumiddin, 'Socio-Political Turbulence of the Ottoman Empire: Reconsidering Sufi and Kadizadeli Hostility in 17th Century,' *Ulumuna* 20, no. 2 (December 1, 2016): 319–52; Madeline C. Zilfi, 'The Kadizadelis: Discordant Revivalism in Seventeenth-Century Istanbul,' *Journal of Near Eastern Studies* 45, no. 4 (1986): 251–69; Semiramis Çavuşoğlu, 'The

Ḳāḍīzādeli Movement: An Attempt of Seri'at-Minded Reform in the Ottoman Empire' (Princeton University, 1990).

170 The pioneering and thorough scholarship of Yahya Michot has helped lead to the uncovering of Taymiyyan influences on the work of a somewhat obscure, yet fascinating, Western Anatolian scholar called Aḥmad al-Rūmī al-Āqḥiṣārī. He may well have been connected with the Qāḍīzādelī movement rather than the Khalwatī Sufi order (whom the Qāḍīzādelīs opposed), as previously thought. See Aḥmad al-Rūmī al-Āqḥiṣārī, *Against Smoking: An Ottoman Manifesto*, trans. Yahya Michot (Markfield: Kube Publishing Ltd, 2011); Mustapha Sheikh, *Ottoman Puritanism and Its Discontents: Ahmad al-Rumi al-Aqhisari and the Qadizadelis*, 1st ed. (Oxford: Oxford University Press, 2017).

171 James Muhammad Dawud Currie, 'Kadizadeli Ottoman Scholarship, Muḥammad Ibn ʿAbd Al-Wahhāb, and the Rise of the Saudi State,' *Journal of Islamic Studies* 26, no. 3 (2015): 2.

172 Muḥammad Dāwūd Kūrī, *Daʿwa jamāʿa Qāḍīzādah al-iṣlāḥiyya fī al-dawla al-ʿUthmāniyya* (Cairo: Dār al-Luʾluʾa li-l-Nashr wa-l-Tawzīʿ, 2018), 44.

173 Currie, 'Kadizadeli Ottoman Scholarship,' 3.

174 Muḥammad b. ʿAlī al-Birkawī (al-Birkalī), *al-Ṭarīqa al-Muḥammadiyya wa-l-sīra al-Aḥmadiyya*, ed. Muḥammad Raḥmat Allāh Ḥāfiẓ Muḥammad Nāẓim al-Nadawī, 1st ed. (Damascus: Dār al-Qalam, 2011). For a critical study of the work, see Katharina A. Ivanyi, *Virtue, Piety and the Law: A Study of Birgivī Meḥmed Efendī's al-Ṭarīqa al-Muḥammadīyya*, The Ottoman Empire and Its Heritage 72 (Leiden, The Netherlands: Koninklijke Brill NV, 2021).

175 B. R. von Schlegell, *Sufism in the Ottoman Arab World: Shaykh 'Abd Al-Ghanī Al-Nābulusī (d.1143/1731)* (University of California, Berkeley, 1997), 85.

176 Al-Āqḥiṣārī may have been a Khalwatī Sufi or was influenced by the Naqshbandī Sufis. This is, however, speculative at present and requires further research.

177 Aḥmad b. Muḥammad al-Rūmī al-Ḥanafī [al-Āqḥiṣārī], *Majālis al-abrār wa masālik al-akhbār*, ed. Irshād al-Ḥaqq al-Atharī (Alexandria: Dār al-Kutub al-ʿArabiyya, 2009).

178 al-Āqḥiṣārī, *Against Smoking*, 1–3. See also Bori, 'Ibn Taymiyya (14th to 17th century).'

179 al-Āqḥiṣārī, *Against Smoking*, 4–5.

180 al-Āqḥiṣārī, *Against Smoking*, 5–7.

181 Caroline Finkel, *Osman's Dream: The Story of the Ottoman Empire, 1300–1923* (New York: Basic Books, 2007), 212–13.

182 Currie, 'Kadizadeli Ottoman Scholarship,' 14.

183 von Schlegell, *Sufism in the Ottoman Arab World*, 84.

184 von Schlegell, 80.

185 Currie, 'Kadizadeli Ottoman Scholarship,' 22–24.

186 Muḥammad b. ʿAbd Allāh b. Nāsir al-Dīn al-Dimashqī, *Al-Radd al-wāfir ʿalā man zaʿam bi-anna man sammā Ibn Taymiyya shaykh al-Islām kāfir*, ed. Zuhyar al-Shāwīsh, 3rd ed. (Beirut: al-Maktab al-Islāmī, 1991).

187 For a discussion of the embrace of Taymiyyan thought in Yemen, see section 2.7.

188 Bori, 'Ibn Taymiyya (14th to 17th century),' 102–12. See also Ibn Taymiyya, *Ibn Taymiyya Against the Greek Logicians*, 3.

189 For the most thorough study to date on al-Kūrānī, see Naser Dumairieh, *Intellectual Life in the Ḥijāz before Wahhabism: Ibrāhīm al-Kūrānī's (d. 1101/1690) Theology of Sufism*, Islamicate Intellectual History, vol. 9 (Leiden; Boston Mass.: Brill, 2022).

190 Basheer M. Nafi, 'Taṣawwuf and Reform in Pre-Modern Islamic Culture: In Search of Ibrāhīm al-Kūrānī,' *Die Welt Des Islams* 42, no. 3 (2002): 332.

191 El-Rouayheb, 'From Ibn Hajar Al-Haytami (d. 1566) to Khayr al-Din al-Alusi (d. 1899): Changing Views of Ibn Taymiyya amongst Sunni Islamic Scholars,' 24.

192 Alexander Knysh, 'Ibrāhīm Al-Kūrānī (d. 1101/1690), an Apologist for "Waḥdat al-Wujūd"', *Journal of the Royal Asiatic Society* 5, no. 1 (1995): 39–47.
193 Nafi, 'Taṣawwuf and Reform in Pre-Modern Islamic Culture,' 338.
194 Shāh Walī Allāh al-Dihlawī, 'Risāla fī nanāqib Ibn Taymiyya wa-l-difāʿ ʿanhu,' in *al-Jāmiʿ li-sīrat shaykh al-Islām Ibn Taymiyya khilāla sabʿat qurūn*, ed. Muḥammad ʿUzayr Shams and ʿAlī b. Muḥammad al-ʿImrān, 2nd ed. (Riyadh: Dār ʿĀlam al-Fawāʾid, 2001), 641–46. This has recently been translated in Muzzammil Ahmad and Ian Greer, 'Shāh Walī Allāh in Defence of Ibn Taymiyyah,' *Islamic Studies* 61, no. 1 (March 31, 2022): 25–44.
195 For studies on Shāh Walī Allāh, see J. M. S. Baljon, *Religion and Thought of Shāh Walī Allāh Dihlawī, 1703–1762* (Leiden: Brill, 1986); Saiyid Athar Abbas Rizvi, *Shāh Walī-Allāh and His Times: A Study of Eighteenth Century Islām, Politics, and Society in India* (Ma'rifat Publishing, 1980).
196 On the Ahl-e Ḥadīth movement, see section 2.8.
197 See SherAli K. Tareen, *Defending Muḥammad in Modernity* (Notre Dame, Indiana: University of Notre Dame Press, 2020), 90.
198 Tareen, *Defending Muḥammad in Modernity,* 65–66.
199 See Muhammad Taqi Usmani, *The Legal Status of Following a Madhab*, trans. Mohammed Amin Kholwadia (Karachi: Zam Zam Publishing, 2009), 58–59.
200 For studies on Muḥammad Ḥayāt al-Sindī, see: Basheer M. Nafi, 'A Teacher of Ibn ʿAbd Al-Wahhāb: Muḥammad Ḥayāt al-Sindī and the Revival of Aṣḥāb al-Ḥadīth's Methodology,' *Islamic Law and Society* 13, no. 2 (2006): 208–41; John Voll, 'Muḥammad Ḥayyā Al-Sindī and Muḥammad Ibn 'Abd al-Wahhāb: An Analysis of an Intellectual Group in Eighteenth-Century Madīna,' *Bulletin of the School of Oriental and African Studies* 38, no. 1 (February 1975): 32–39.
201 See, in particular, Muḥammad Ḥayāt al-Sindī, *al-Īqāf ʿalā asbāb al-ikhtilāf*, ed. Aḥmad ʿAbd al-Mālik ʿAbd al-Raḥman al-Saʿadī (Damascus: Dār Saʿad al-Dīn, 2012); and Muḥammad Ḥayāt al-Sindī, *Tuḥfat al-anām fī al-'amal bi-ḥadīth al-Nabī 'alayhi al-ṣalāh wa-l-salām*, 1st ed. (Beirut: Dār Ibn Ḥazm li-l-Nashr wa-l-Tawzīʿ, 1993).
202 Muḥammad b. Aḥmad al-Saffārīnī, *al-Ḍurra al-muḍiyya fī ʿaqd al-firqa al-marḍiyya*, ed. Abū Muḥammad Ashraf b. ʿAbd al-Maqṣūd, 1st ed. (Riyadh: Maktabat Aḍwāʾ al-Salaf, 1998).
203 al-Saffārīnī, *Lawāmiʿ al-anwār al-bahiyya wa-l-sawāṭiʿ al-asrār al-athariyya*, ed. ʿAbd al-Raḥmān Abā Buṭayn and Sulaymān b. Suḥmān [also: Siḥmān], 3rd ed. (Beirut: al-Maktab al-Islāmī; Riyadh: Dār al-Khānī, 1991).
204 al-Saffārīnī, *Lawāmiʿ al-anwār*, 1:73.
205 The impact of al-Ṣanʿānī is discussed in more detail in section 3.1.6.
206 For studies on al-Shawkānī, see Bernard Haykel, *Revival and Reform in Islam: The Legacy of Muhammad al-Shawkani*, Illustrated ed. (Cambridge, UK; New York: Cambridge University Press, 2003); 'Indian Wahhabism: The Case of the Ahl-i-Ḥadīth In Colonial India' (University of Wales Trinity Saint David, 2017).
207 Ibn ʿAbd al-Wahhāb, *Kitāb al-tawḥīd alladhī huwa ḥaqq Allāh ʿalā al-ʿabīd*, ed. Daghash b. Shabīb al-ʿAjmī (Kuwait: Maktabat Ahl al-Athar, 2014).
208 Due to the significance of this movement and its lasting impact, Chapter 3 will examine its theological underpinnings, the trajectory of its political ascension, the dynamics of its internal schisms, the mechanisms underpinning its establishment, and pertinent ancillary factors.
209 For a study on Zaydism, see Najam Haider, 'Zaydism,' in *Handbook of Islamic Sects and Movements*, ed. Muhammad Afzal Upal and Carole M. Cusack, Brill Handbooks on Contemporary Religion, vol. 21 (Leiden; Boston: Brill, 2021), 203–34.
210 For studies on Ibn al-Wazīr, see Jon Hoover, 'Withholding Judgment on Islamic Universalism: Ibn al-Wazīr (d. 840/1436) on the Duration and Purpose of Hell-Fire,'

in *Locating Hell in Islamic Traditions*, ed. Christian Lange (Brill, 2016), 211; Haykel, *Revival and Reform in Islam*, 338.

211 Muḥammad b. Ibrāhīm Ibn al-Wazīr, *al-ʿAwāṣim wa al-qawāṣim fī al-dhabb ʿan sunna Abī al-Qāsim*, ed. Shuʿayb al-Arna'ūṭ, 3rd ed., 9 vols (Beirut: Muʾassasat al-Risāla li-al-Ṭibāʿa wa-l-Nashr wa-l-Tawzīʿ, 1994).

212 Hoover, 'Withholding Judgment on Islamic Universalism,' 218–28.

213 Muḥammad b. Ismāʿīl al-Amīr al-Ṣanʿānī, *Irshād dhawī al-albāb ilā ḥaqīqat aqwāl Ibn ʿAbd al-Wahhāb*, ed. ʿAbd al-Karīm Aḥmad Jadbān (Majālis Āl Muḥammad, 2008), 108–10. These writings and his stance on the Wahhabi movement will be discussed in more detail in section 3.1.6.

214 Ibn Ḥajar ʿAsqalānī, *Bulūgh al-marām min adillat al-aḥkām*, ed. Samīr b. Amīn al-Zuhrī, 7th ed. (Riyadh: Dār al-Falaq, 2003).

215 al-Ṣanʿānī, *Subul al-salām sharḥ bulūgh al-marām*, ed. ʿIṣām al-Ṣabbābīṭī and ʿImād al-Sayyid, 5th ed., 4 vols (Cairo: Dār al-Ḥadīth, 1997).

216 Muḥammad b. ʿAlī al-Shawkānī, *-Qawl all* ed. ʿAbd al-Raḥmān ʿAbd al-Khāliq, 1st ed. (Kuwait: Dār al-Qalam, 1976 For the English translation, see Muḥammad b. ʿAlī al-Shawkānī, *A Critique of the Ruling of Al-Taqlid*, trans. Adnan Karim (Dar al-Arqam, 2020).

217 Mariam Abou Zahab, 'Salafism in Pakistan: The Ahl-e Ḥadīth Movement,' in *Global Salafism: Islam's New Religious Movement*, ed. Roel Meijer, 1st ed. (New York: Oxford University Press, 2014), 126. See also Haykel, *Revival and Reform in Islam.*

218 Haykel, *Revival and Reform in Islam*, 225.

219 Laurent Bonnefoy, *Salafism in Yemen: Transnationalism and Religious Identity* (Oxford University Press, 2012), 242–44.

220 Zahab, 'Salafism in Pakistan: The Ahl-e Ḥadīth Movement,' 128–29. For a broad introduction to the beginnings of these movements, see Barbara Daly Metcalf, *Islamic Revival in British India: Deoband, 1860–1900* (Princeton, NJ: Princeton University Press, 1982).

221 The Barelwīs and Deobandīs adhere to Shāh Walī Allāh's highly mystical Sufism. The Barelwīs came to consider one of Shāh Walī Allāh's sons and his successor at his madrasa, Shāh ʿAbd al-ʿAzīz (d. 1824), to be the Reviver of Islam (*mujaddid*) in the thirteenth Islamic century. The Deobandī movement proudly possesses and continues to convey Shāh Walī Allāh's hadith chains of transmission, as well as maintaining his endorsement of the four Sunni legal schools. See Metcalf, *Islamic Revival in British India*, 276; 'Intention and Implication: The Disputed Legacy of Shah Wall Allah.' *Journal of Islamic and Muslim Studies* 5, no. 2 (November 1, 2020): 30–31; Mohammad Akram Nadwi, *Shaykh ʾAbū Al-Ḥasan ʿAlī Nadwī*, trans. Mahomed Mahomedy, n.d.; Zeeshan Chaudri, 'Demarcating the Contours of the Deobandi Tradition via a Study of the "Akābirīn"' (PhD, SOAS University of London, 2022), 57–61.

222 In order to see the complexity in establishing a definitive Deobandī position on the question of independent legal reasoning (*ijtihād*) and following a legal school (*taqlīd*), see Chaudri, 'Demarcating the Contours of the Deobandi Tradition via a Study of the "Akābirīn,"' 61–88.

223 For a discussion on these distinctive practices unique to the movement, see Metcalf, *Islamic Revival in British India*, 275. For a study of Shāh Walī Allāh's life and thought on these points, see Abul Hasan Alī Nadwi, *Saviours of Islamic Spirit*, trans. S. Mohiuddin Ahmad, vol. 4, 5 vols (Lucknow: Academy of Islamic Research and Publications, 1993).

224 Zahab, 'Salafism in Pakistan: The Ahl-e Ḥadīth Movement,' 128–29.

225 For a broad overview of the movement's origins, see Metcalf, *Islamic Revival in British India*, 264–69.

226 Martin Riexinger, 'Ibn Taymiyya's Worldview and the Challenge of Modernity: A Conflict Among the Ahl-i Ḥadīth in British India,' in *Islamic Theology, Philosophy*

*and Law: Debating Ibn Taymiyya and Ibn Qayyim Al-Jawziyya*, ed. Birgit Krawietz and Georges Tamer (Berlin ; Boston: De Gruyter, 2013), 499.

227 Metcalf, *Islamic Revival in British India*, 268.

228 For a discussion of these figures, see Saiyid Athar Abbas Rizvi, *Shāh ʿAbd Al-ʿAzīz: Puritanism, Sectarian Polemics and Jihād* (Canberra, Australia: Ma'rifat Pub. House, 1982).

229 Speaking on Sayyid Aḥmad's attainment of gnosis (*maʿrifa*), Shāh ʿAbd al-ʿAzīz said, 'This angelic Saiyid is so clear witted in spiritual apprehension of truth that a mere suggestion is sufficient for him to understand and attain that stage.' Mohiuddin Ahmad, *Saiyid Ahmad Shahid: His Life and Mission*, Academy of Islamic Research and Publications Series; No. 93 (Lucknow: Academy of Islamic Research and Publications, 1975), 40.

230 Ahmad, *Saiyid Ahmad Shahid,* 40 and 95.

231 Ahmad, *Saiyid Ahmad Shahid,* 50.

232 Ahmad, *Saiyid Ahmad Shahid,* 39.

233 On such legal categories of political entities according to classical Islamic law, see Muhammad Taqi Usmani, *Islam and Politics: A Translation of Islam Awr Siyasi Nazariyat*, trans. Z. Baintner (Turath Publishing, 2017), chap. 5.

234 Ahmad, *Saiyid Ahmad Shahid,* 43.

235 The first half of this treatise was later enriched with a commentary in layman's Urdu by the same author and entitled *Taqwiyyat al-īmān (Support of the Faith)* in or around 1825–1826. See Shāh Muḥammad Ismāʿīl, *Radd al-ishrāk*, ed. Ismāʿīl b. ʿAbd al-Ghanī and Muḥammad ʿUzair Shams (Lahore: al-Maktaba al-Salafiyya, 1988); Barbara Daly Metcalf, 'The Taqwiyyat Al-Iman (Support of the Faith) by Shah Ismaʿil Shahid,' in *Islam in South Asia in Practice*, ed. Barbara Daly Metcalf, Princeton Readings in Religions (Princeton: Princeton University Press, 2009), 201–11; Seema Alavi, *Muslim Cosmopolitanism in the Age of Empire* (Cambridge, Mass.; London, England: Harvard University Press, 2015), 36.

236 Barbara Daly Metcalf and Thomas R. Metcalf, *A Concise History of Modern India*, 3rd ed. (Cambridge: Cambridge University Press, 2012), 85.

237 Olivier Roy, *Islam and Resistance in Afghanistan*, 1st ed. (Cambridge; New York: Cambridge University Press, 1986), 56–57.

238 Sayyid Abū al-Aʿlā al-Mawdūdī, *A Short History of the Revivalist Movement in Islam*, trans. Al-Ash'ari (Lahore: Islamic Publications, 1963), 66.

239 Majothi, 'Indian Wahhabism: The Case of the Ahl-i-Ḥadīth In Colonial India,' 27–28.

240 For a discussion on the Wahhabi trials, see Muin-ud-din Ahmad Khan, *Selections from Bengal Government Records on Wahhabi Trials (1863–1870)* (Asiatic Society of Pakistan, 1961).

241 Zahab, 'Salafism in Pakistan: The Ahl-e Ḥadīth Movement,' 129.

242 Metcalf, *Islamic Revival in British India*, 272.

243 Metcalf, *Islamic Revival in British India*, 268.

244 Shāh Muḥammad Isḥāq taught at the family's Delhi madrasa from 1824 until 1842, then moved to Mecca and taught there, and eventually died in Mecca. Rashīd Aḥmad Gangohī (d. 1905), one of the co-founders of the Deoband seminary, considered Shāh Muḥammad Isḥāq to be the teacher of all the 'ulama of Hindustan.' Nadwi, *Saviours of Islamic Spirit*, 4:273. See also Metcalf, *Islamic Revival in British India*, 143–44.

245 Aḥmad Shāgif, *Qurrat al-ʿayn fī tarjama al-Sayyid Nadhīr Ḥusayn* (Lahore: al-Maktaba al-Salafiyya, 2002), 30–31.

246 Muhammad Afzal Upal, 'The Cultural Genetics of the Aḥmadiyya Muslim Jamāʿat,' in *Handbook of Islamic Sects and Movements*, ed. Muhammad Afzal Upal and Carole M. Cusack, Brill Handbooks on Contemporary Religion, vol. 21 (Leiden; Boston: Brill, 2021), 641.

247 M. Naeem Qureshi, *Pan-Islam in British Indian Politics: A Study of the Khilafat Movement, 1918–1924* (Leiden; Boston: Brill, 1999), 178.
248 Daniel W. Brown, *Rethinking Tradition in Modern Islamic Thought*, 1st paperback ed. (Cambridge: Cambridge University Press, 1999), 27.
249 For an exhaustive list of his students according to their country of origin, see Faḍl Ḥusain Muzaffarpūrī, *al-Ḥayāt ba'd al-mamāt* (Agra: Akbari Press, 1908), 322–67.
250 Metcalf, *Islamic Revival in British India*, 276.
251 Siobhan Lambert-Hurley, *Muslim Women, Reform and Princely Patronage: Nawab Sultan Jahan Begam of Bhopal*, Royal Asiatic Society Books (London; New York: Routledge, 2007), 37.
252 Brown, *Rethinking Tradition in Modern Islamic Thought*, 27–28.
253 Alavi, *Muslim Cosmopolitanism in the Age of Empire*, 268.
254 Ahmad, *Saiyid Ahmad Shahid*, 200.
255 Ahmad, *Saiyid Ahmad Shahid*, 256.
256 For brief biographical sketches of Wilayat ʿAlī and his younger brother Enayat ʿAlī (d. 1858), who both received traditional religious instruction under Islamic scholars and joined and continued the mission of Sayyid Aḥmad until the ends of their lives, see Qeyamuddin Ahmad, *The Wahhabi Movement in India*, 2nd rev. ed. (New Delhi: Manohar, 1994), chap. 4.
257 Ahmad, 257. Although Ibn Ḥajar himself was a Shāfiʿī and composed this short hadith work along Shāfiʿī lines, it has become a popular work with *Ahl-e Ḥadīth* and Salafis as being indicative of a hadith-orientated *fiqh*, with the hidden implication being that a school like the Ḥanafī one is somewhat compromised in its loyalty to the hadith corpus. The accusation of the *Ahl-e Ḥadīth* being unwittingly pseudo-Shāfiʿī was advocated by Rashīd Aḥmad Gangohī, who accused them of adopting Shāfiʿī stances, sometimes on the basis of a superficial reading of a relatively simple hadith collection like *Mishkāt al-maṣābīḥ (Niche of Lanterns)*, which was also Shāfiʿī-orientated. Metcalf, *Islamic Revival in British India*, 284.
258 Lambert-Hurley, *Muslim Women, Reform and Princely Patronage*, 37.
259 Seema Alavi, 'Siddiq Hasan Khan (1832–90) and the Creation of a Muslim Cosmopolitanism in the 19th Century,' *Journal of the Economic and Social History of the Orient* 54, no. 1 (January 1, 2011): 5.
260 Ṣiddīq Ḥasan Khān, *Tarjumān-e-Wahhābīyya* (Agra: Mufīd-e-ʿĀm Press, 1884).
261 Alavi, 'Siddiq Hasan Khan,' 8–12.
262 Metcalf, *Islamic Revival in British India*, 279.
263 Lambert-Hurley, *Muslim Women, Reform and Princely Patronage*, 30–34.
264 For a study on the influence of al-Shawkānī and Ḥanbalism on Ṣiddīq Ḥasan, see Claudia Preckel, 'Screening Ṣiddīq Ḥasan Khān's Library: The Use of Ḥanbalī Literature in 19th-Century Bhopal,' in *Islamic Theology, Philosophy and Law*, ed. Birgit Krawietz and Georges Tamer (De Gruyter, 2013), 162–219.
265 Alavi, 'Siddiq Hasan Khan,' 5.
266 Metcalf, *Islamic Revival in British India*, 278.
267 Shamsy, *Rediscovering the Islamic Classics*, 174.
268 Alavi, *Muslim Cosmopolitanism in the Age of Empire*, 28 and 268–320.
269 Metcalf, *Islamic Revival in British India*, 283–84.
270 Metcalf, *Islamic Revival in British India*, 293; Lambert-Hurley, *Muslim Women, Reform and Princely Patronage*, 37–38.
271 Alavi, *Muslim Cosmopolitanism in the Age of Empire*, 268–69.
272 Shams al-Dīn b. Qayyim al-Jawziyya, *Matn al-Qaṣīda al-nūniyya*, 2nd ed. (Cairo: Maktabat Ibn Taymiyya, 1996).
273 The letter is reproduced in Ṣiddīq Ḥasan Khān, *Qiṭf al-thamar fī bayān ʿaqīdat ahl al-athar*, ed. ʿĀṣim al-Qaryūtī (Riyadh: Jāmiʿat al-Imām Muḥammad ibn Suʿūd al-Islāmiyya, 2011), 51–62.

274 On the Wahhabi clerics studying under *Ahl-e Ḥadīth* scholars, see Ibrāhīm b. ʿAbd Allāh al-Mudīhish, *al-Najdiyyūn fī al-Hind: ʿulamāʾ Najd al-ladhīn raḥalū ilā al-Hind li-l-Istiẓādat min al-ḥadīth al-Nabawī,* 1st ed. (Riyadh: Dār al-Thuluthiyya, 2019).

275 Qureshi, *Pan-Islam in British Indian Politics*, 178.

276 Riexinger, 'Ibn Taymiyya's Worldview,' 499; Majothi, 'Indian Wahhabism: The Case of the Ahl-i-Ḥadīth In Colonial India,' 41–43.

277 On the Kilafat movement, see Gail Minault, *The Khilafat Movement Religious Symbolism and Political Mobilization in India*, 1st ed. (New York: Columbia University Press, 1982).

278 Lambert-Hurley, *Muslim Women, Reform and Princely Patronage*, 39.

279 Riexinger, 'Ibn Taymiyya's Worldview,' 511–12.

280 Riexinger, 'Ibn Taymiyya's Worldview,' 501–14.

281 Notable among these was the Ahl-e Qurʾān movement, led by ʿAbdullah Chakralawi (d. 1916) in Lahore. This movement emerged from an internal division within the *Ahl-e Ḥadīth* ranks. It centered on a reliance solely on the Qurʾan as divine guidance while rejecting the validity of the hadith corpus. It is also argued that the Ahmadiyya sect and the modernist movement also found inspiration in this atmosphere of reformist thought that the *Ahl-e Ḥadīth* movement helped foster. Clearly, none of the clerics of the Ahl-e Ḥadīth school would approve of these non-conformist movements, and a number of prominent clerics actually refuted these sects. See Metcalf, *Islamic Revival in British India*, 289 and 295. On Chakralawi's path from *Ahl-e Ḥadīth* to Ahl-e Qurʾān, although his son and grandson remained committed to the *Ahl-e Ḥadīth*, see Ali Usman Qasmi, *Questioning the Authority of the Past: The Ahl al-Qur'an Movements in the Punjab*, 1st ed. (Karachi: Oxford University Press, 2012), 124–45.

The founder of the Ahmadiyya sect, Mirzā Ghulām Aḥmad (d. 1908), was trained as a boy under an *Ahl-e Ḥadīth* teacher among teachers from other groups. Before Mirzā Aḥmad's claims to prophethood, there were also links between the Ahmadiyya founders and prominent early leaders of the *Ahl-e Ḥadīth*, particularly Sayyid Nadhīr (who conducted the Ahmadiyya founder's second marriage), Batalwī (who had been a fellow classmate and close friend of Mirza Ahmad), and ʿAbd Allāh al-Ghaznawī (d. 1881; who might have been the spiritual guide of the Ahmadiyya founder, and whose son was married to the daughter of the second Ahmadiyya leader, before the prophecy controversy). Later, Sayyid Nadhīr, Batalwī, and other *Ahl-e Ḥadīth* leaders led the opposition against Mirzā Aḥmad's declaration of prophecy, declaring it to be disbelief (*kufr*). The second leader of the Ahmadiyya movement, Hakim Nur-ud-Din (d. 1914), had previously pledged spiritual allegiance to one of Shāh Walī Allāh's sons, ʿAbd al-Ghanī, as well as having studied with Sayyid Nadhīr and a student of Sayyid Aḥmad Shahīdī. See Adil Hussain Khan, *From Sufism to Ahmadiyya: A Muslim Minority Movement in South Asia* (Bloomington: Indiana University Press, 2015), 24–25, 30–33, 171–73, 180, and 192n26. On the influence of the *Ahl-e Ḥadīth* methodology on the modernist Sayyid Aḥmad Khān (d. 1898) and the latter's belief that he influenced Sayyid Nadhīr to publicly perform *rafʿ al-yadayn*, which is perhaps the dominant defining act of the *Ahl-e Ḥadīth*, see Muhammad Afzal Upal, 'The Cultural Genetics of the Aḥmadiyya Muslim Jamāʿat,' in *Handbook of Islamic Sects and Movements*, ed. Muhammad Afzal Upal and Carole M. Cusack, Brill Handbooks on Contemporary Religion, vol. 21 (Leiden; Boston: Brill, 2021), 640–41.

282 See, in particular, Majothi, 'Translating Salafism into English,' chap. 2; Hira Amin and Azhar Majothi, 'The Ahl-e-Hadith: From British India to Britain,' *Modern Asian Studies* 56, no. 1 (January 2022): 176–206.

283 Although al-Afghānī was not himself Egyptian, his biography is mentioned here due to his influence on the next two figures we will discuss: Muḥammad ʿAbduh and Rashīd Riḍā.

284 Ahab Bdaiwi, 'Jamāl Al-Dīn al-Afghānī,' in *Christian Muslim Relations Online II* (Leiden: Brill, March 1, 2018), https://referenceworks.brill.com/doi/10.1163/2451-9537_cmrii_COM_31239.

285 Mahmoud Esma'il Sieny, *Heroes of Islam* (Dar-us-Salam Publications, 2000), 303.

286 Masudul Hasan, *History of Islam*, 1st ed. (Lahore, Pakistan: Islamic Publications, 1987), 703.

287 While this is perhaps the most famous quote attributed to ʿAbduh, allegedly after he returned from a trip to Paris, it should be noted that its authenticity is not established. See Aḥmad al-Ṣarāf, 'Hal maqūlat ʿAbduh kādhība?' *Al-Qabas*, 2018, https://www.alqabas.com/article/558966-%D9%87%D9%84-%D9%85%D9%82%D9%88%D9%84%D8%A9-%D8%B9%D8%A8%D8%AF%D9%87-%D9%83%D8%A7%D8%B0%D8%A8%D8%A9%D8%9F.

288 Khaled El-Rouayheb, *Islamic Intellectual History in the Seventeenth Century: Scholarly Currents in the Ottoman Empire and the Maghreb*, 1st ed. (Cambridge University Press, 2015), 202.

289 Oliver Scharbrodt, *Muhammad 'Abduh: Modern Islam and the Culture of Ambiguity* (London; New York; Oxford: I.B. Tauris, 2022), 178.

290 See Shamsy, *Rediscovering the Islamic Classics*, 24–25, 29, 34, 107, 147–51, and 153–58.

291 Lauzière, 'The Construction of Salafiyya,' 374.

292 Muḥammad ʿAbduh, *Risālat Al-Tawḥīd* (Beirut: Dār Ibn Ḥazm, 2001), 78.

293 For studies on Rashīd Riḍā, see Leor Halevi, *Modern Things on Trial: Islam's Global and Material Reformation in the Age of Rida, 1865–1935* (New York: Columbia University Press, 2019); Emad Eldin Shahin, *Through Muslim Eyes: M. Rashid Rida and the West* (Herndon, Va., USA, 1993); Ryad, *Islamic Reformism and Christianity*, Illustrated ed. (Leiden; Boston: Brill, 2009); Elizabeth Sirriyeh, 'Rashid Rida's Autobiography of the Syrian Years, 1865–1897,' *Arabic & Middle Eastern Literature* 3, no. 2 (July 1, 2000): 179–94; Assad Nimer Busool, 'Shaykh Muhammad Rashid Rida's Relations with Jamal Al-Din Al-Afghani and Muhammad 'Abduh,' *The Muslim World (Hartford)* 66, no. 4 (1976): 272.

294 Albert Hourani, 'Rashid Rida and the Sufi Orders: A Footnote to Laoust,' *Bulletin d'études Orientales* 29 (1977): 231–41, 232 and 236.

295 Scharbrodt, *Muhammad 'Abduh*, 149.

296 Albert Hourani, *Arabic Thought in the Liberal Age 1798–1939* (Cambridge: Cambridge University Press, 1983), 222–45; Umar Ryad, 'A Printed Muslim 'Lighthouse' in Cairo al-Manār's Early Years, Religious Aspiration and Reception (1898–1903),' January 1, 2009, 27–60.

297 For a study of Riḍā's adoption of a more politicized understanding of Islam, see Mahmoud Haddad, 'Arab Religious Nationalism in the Colonial Era: Rereading Rashid Rida's Ideas on the Caliphate,' *Journal of the American Oriental Society* 117, no. 2 (June 1997): 253–77. See also Mona Hassan, *Longing for the Lost Caliphate: A Transregional History* (Princeton and Oxford: Princeton University Press, 2016), 204–205, 228 and 327n75.

298 See Henri Lauzière, *The Making of Salafism: Islamic Reform in the Twentieth Century* (Columbia University Press, 2015), chap. 2.

299 Lauzière, 60–94.

300 Lauzière, 'The Construction of Salafiyya,' 8.

301 Khālid b. Fawzī b. ʿAbd al-Ḥamīd Āl Ḥamza, *Muḥammad Rashīd Riḍā: Ṭūd wa-iṣlāḥ daʿwa wa-dāʿiya*, 2nd ed. (Dār ʿUlamāʾ al-Salaf, 1994), 52–61.

302 Āl Ḥamza, *Muḥammad Rashīd Riḍā*, 75–76.

303 Cole M. Bunzel, 'Manifest Enmity: The Origins, Development, and Persistence of Classical Wahhābism (1153–1351/1741–1932)' (Princeton, NJ: Princeton University, 2018), 361.

304 Bunzel, 'Manifest Enmity,' 362.
305 Haykel, 'On the Nature of Salafi Thought and Action,' 47.
306 For the Muslim Brotherhood and its founder, Ḥassan al-Bannā, see Chapter 1.
307 In his own writings, al-Fiqī mentions a rather strange story of coming across a farmer on his return to his village after studying in al-Azhar; this farmer was reading Ibn Qayyim's work *Ijtimāʿ al-juyūsh al-islāmiyya (The Gathering of the Islamic Armies)*, a very technical work that was intended to refute the Ashʿarī school and its positions on the divine attributes. After questioning the farmer, he was informed that as an al-Azhar graduate, al-Fiqī should study the works of the great scholars of Ḥanbalism, like Ibn Taymiyya, Ibn Khuzayma, and others. Inspired by this, he returned to the libraries of al-Azhar and read these authors, which prompted his conversion to Ḥanbalism and inspired a life-long commitment to the teachings of Ibn Taymiyya. The story seems bizarre, but it is oft-cited in his biographies. For his biography, see Lauzière, *The Making of Salafism*, 2015, 73 and 92–93.
308 On Muḥibb al-Dīn al-Khaṭīb, see section 2.9.2.
309 For an overview of the Jamāʿat Anṣār al-Sunna al-Muḥammadiyya and their early activities, especially in relation to the printed works they produced, see Aaron Rock-Singer, *In the Shade of the Sunna: Salafi Piety in the Twentieth-Century Middle East* (Oakland (Calif.): University of California press, 2022), 44–52.
310 See Abdelmonem Moneep, *Islamic Movements in Egypt: A Map and Guidance*, 2nd ed., 2018, 42–45.
311 See Stéphane Lacroix, 'Egypt's Salafi Awakening in the 1970s: Revisiting the History of a Crucial Decade for Egyptian Islamic Activism,' *Religions* 13, no. 4 (April 2, 2022): 316.
312 From the journal *al-Hadī al-nabawī* 18 (1954): 303 as cited and translated into in Lauzière, *The Making of Salafism*, 2015, 89.
313 Ibn Qayyim al-Jawziyya and Shams al-Dīn Muḥammad b. al-Mawṣilī, *Mukhtaṣar al-Ṣawāʿiq al-mursala ʿalā al-jahmiyya wa-l-muʿaṭṭila*, ed. Muḥammad Ḥamīd al-Fiqī and Muḥammad ʿAbd al-Razzāq Ḥamza (al-Maṭbaʿa al-Salafiyya wa-Maktabatuhā, 1929). This is an abridgment of a work by Ibn Qayyim, printed in 1929. Al-Fiqī edited al-Mawṣilī's work with Muḥammad ʿAbd al-Razzāq Ḥamza, an important figure in the emerging Salafi movement in Egypt at the time and a senior deputy to al-Fiqī in Anṣār al-Sunna, after having been an editor of al-Manār for Riḍā. He had been educated at Al-Azhar and Riḍā's Dār al-Daʿwa wa-l-Irshād. He was also part of Riḍā's Hajj party in 1926, whereupon Riḍā recommended him to Ibn Saud. Soon thereafter, Ḥamza moved to Saudi Arabia, where he became an imam at the Prophet's Mosque in Medina before moving to the Sacred Mosque in Mecca and then acting as an educational supervisor in the latter's institute. He would spend the rest of his life in Saudi Arabia and died in Mecca. See Ahmad Khan, 'Islamic Tradition in an Age of Print: Editing, Printing and Publishing the Classical Heritage,' in *Reclaiming Islamic Tradition: Modern Interpretations of the Classical Heritage*, ed. Elisabeth Kendall and Ahmad Khan (Edinburgh: Edinburgh University Press, 2016), 68–69; Lauzière, *The Making of Salafism*, 2016, 73–74. In producing this abridgment, the editors received the patronage of Ibn Saud, who had the work published in Mecca. However, they only relied on one manuscript, which had been produced in the eighteenth century and contained numerous errors. A new critical edition, based on numerous medieval manuscripts and submitted to the Islamic University of Medina for a doctoral dissertation, has recently been published. See Ibn Qayyim al-Jawziyya and Ibn al-Mawṣilī, *Mukhtaṣar al-ṣawāʿiq al-mursala ʿalā al-jahmiyya wa-l-muʿaṭṭila*, ed. al-Ḥasan b. ʿAbd al-Raḥman al-ʿAlawī, 1st ed., 4 vols (Riyadh: Aḍwāʾ al-Salaf, 2004). For a study of the work, see Yasir Qadhi, '"The Unleashed Thunderbolts" of Ibn Qayyim al-Ğawziyyah: An Introductory Essay,' August 12, 2010.

314 For al-Albānī's analysis of Ibn ʿAbd al-Wahhāb's stance in adhering to a legal school, see section 2.9.4.
315 Richard Gauvain, 'Salafism in Modern Egypt: Panacea or Pest?' *Political Theology* 11, no. 6 (December 15, 2010): 813.
316 Abū Bakr Aḥmad b. ʿAlī b. Thābit al-Khaṭīb al-Baghdādī, *Tārīkh madīnat al-salām wa-dhayluh wa-l-mustafād (Tārīkh Baghdād)*, ed. Bashār ʿAwwād Maʿrūf, 1st ed., 21 vols (Beirut: Dār al-Gharb al-Islāmī, 2001).
317 Khan, 'Islamic Tradition in an Age of Print,' 63–65.
318 Most prominent among them are: (1) ʿAbd al-Razzāq ʿAfīfī (d. 1994), who eventually became a permanent member of the Council of Senior Scholars of Saudi Arabia; (2) Muḥammad Khalīl Harrās (d. 1975), who authored seminal works defending Ibn Taymiyya and the Atharī creed; (3) ʿAbd al-Dhāhir Abu al-Samḥ (d. 1950), who would become the first foreign Imam appointed to the Grand Mosque of Mecca – and a key figure in the establishment of one of Mecca's most famous seminaries, the Dār al-Ḥadīth; and (4) Muḥammad Ṣafwat Nūr al-Dīn (d. 2002), the most prominent Egyptian Salafi scholar of his generation.
319 Lauzière, *The Making of Salafism*, 2015, 80.
320 The entry for al-Qāsimī is lengthier as his immediate impact and subsequent legacy are far greater than those of the other two. Hence, the complexities of his thought and actions justify a more elaborate exploration.
321 David Commins, *Islamic Reform: Politics and Social Change in Late Ottoman Syria*, Studies in Middle Eastern History (Oxford; New York: Oxford University Press, 1990), 49.
322 Commins, *Islamic Reform,* 51.
323 Commins, *Islamic Reform,* 56.
324 Issam Eido, 'The Rise of Syrian Salafism: From Denial to Recognition,' in *The Syrian Uprising*, ed. Raymond Hinnebusch and Omar Imady, 1st ed. (London: Routledge, 2018), 260–61.
325 On al-Qāsimī and al-Biṭār and their trials at the hands of the scholars and authorities over their drive for freedom of thought, see Itzchak Weismann, *Taste of Modernity: Sufism, Salafiyya and Arabism in Late Ottoman Damascus*, 2nd unrevised edition, Islamic History and Civilization 34 (Leiden: Brill, 2004), 275–82.
326 For a study of al-Qāsimī's Salafi legal methodology, as well as his relevance for al-Albānī, see Pieter Coppens, 'Jamāl Al-Dīn al-Qāsimī's Treatise on Wiping over Socks and the Rise of a Distinct Salafi Method,' *Die Welt Des Islams* 62, no. 2 (October 28, 2021): 154–87.
327 Coppens, 'Jamāl Al-Dīn al-Qāsimī's Treatise,' 61.
328 Jamāl al-Dīn al-Qāsimī, *Irshād al-khalq ilā al-ʿamal bi-khabar al-barq, wa-yalīhi ʿudda min fatāwā al-ishrāf fī al-ʿamal bi-l-tilighrāf* (Damascus: Maṭbaʿat al-Muqtabis, 1911).
329 For a discussion on al-Qāsimī's view of Ibn ʿArabī within the context of ongoing debate about the relationship between Salafism and Sufism, see Mun'im Sirry, 'Jamāl Al-Dīn al-Qāsimī and the Salafi Approach to Sufism,' *Die Welt Des Islams* 51, no. 1 (2011): 75–108.
330 Jamāl al-Dīn al-Qāsimī, *Al-Jahmiyya Wa-l-Muʿtazila* (Beirut: Muʾassasat al-Risāla, 1979).
331 For al-Qāsimī's approach to Sufism via his Salafism, see Itzchak Weismann, 'Between Ṣūfī Reformism and Modernist Rationalism: A Reappraisal of the Origins of the Salafiyya from the Damascene Angle,' *Die Welt Des Islams* 41, no. 2 (2001): 207–8.
332 Sirry, 'Jamāl Al-Dīn al-Qāsimī and the Salafi Approach to Sufism,' 98–104.
333 For a short discussion on the various condemnations, see David Commins, 'Wahhabis, Sufis and Salafis in Early Twentieth Century Damascus,' in *Guardians of Faith in Modern Times: ʿUlamaʾ in the Middle East*, ed. Meir Hatina (Brill, 2009), 231–46.

334 See Itzchak Weismann, 'The Politics of Popular Religion: Sufis, Salafis, and Muslim Brothers in 20th-Century Hamah,' *International Journal of Middle East Studies* 37, no. 1 (February 2005): 39–58.
335 On Maḥmūd Shukrī al-Ālūsī, see section 2.9.3.
336 Commins, 'Wahhābis, Sufis and Salafis in Early Twentieth Century Damascus,' 233.
337 Weismann, *Taste of Modernity*, 279 n.13.
338 Shamsy, *Rediscovering the Islamic Classics*, 177–91.
339 On al-Albānī and his brand of Salafism, see section 2.9.4.
340 ʿAlī al-Ḥalabī, *Maʿa shaykhinā nāṣir al-sunna wa-l-dīn Muḥammad Nāṣir al-Dīn al-Albānī mujaddid al-qarn wa-muḥaddith al-ʿaṣr fī shuhūr ḥayātihi al-akhīra* (Ras al-Khaimah, UAE: Maktabat Dār al-Ḥadīth, 1999), 12; cited and translated into English in Jacob Olidort, 'In Defense of Tradition: Muḥammad Nāṣir Al-Dīn al-Albānī and the Salafī Method' (PhD, Princeton, NJ, Princeton University, 2015), 79.
341 Sayyid Muhammad Rizvi, 'Muhibb Al-Din al-Khatib: A Portrait of a Salafi-Arabist' (Simon Fraser University, 1991), 61.
342 Lauzière, *The Making of Salafism*, 2015, 47.
343 Maḥmūd al-Ālūsī, *Rūh al-maʿānī fī tafsīr al-Qurʾān al-ʿaẓīm wa sabʿ al-mathānī*, ed. ʿAlī ʿAbd al-Bārī ʿAṭiyya, 1st ed., 15 vols (Beirut: Dār al-Kutub al-ʿIlmiyya, 1994). For a short overview on this *tafsīr*, see Basheer M. Nafi, 'Abu Al-Thana' al-Alusi: An Alim, Ottoman Mufti, and Exegete of the Qur'an,' *International Journal of Middle East Studies* 34, no. 3 (2002): 482–86.
344 Nafi, 'Abu Al-Thana' al-Alusi,' 462–82.
345 Shamsy, *Rediscovering the Islamic Classics*, 215–16. On al-Kawthari's 'prolonged engagement with the discourse of Salafism' and the Salafi response, particularly from al-Albānī, see Andrew Hammond, 'Salafi Publishing and Contestation over Orthodoxy and Leadership in Sunni Islam,' in *Wahhabism and the World: Understanding Saudi Arabia's Global Influence on Islam*, ed. Peter Mandaville, Religion and Global Politics (Oxford; New York: Oxford University Press, 2022), 80–84.
346 Nafi, 'Abu Al-Thana' al-Alusi,' 470.
347 Nafi, 'Abu Al-Thana' al-Alusi,' 472. Maulānā Khālid is an interesting figure and deserves more study. One of his students was Dāwūd b. Jirjīs (d. 1881) – one of the iconic opponents of the Second Saudi Wahhabi state – and also the famous Ḥanafī jurist Ibn ʿĀbidīn (d. 1836). On Ibn Jijīs, see Itzchak Weismann, 'Dāwūd b. Jirjīs,' in *Encyclopaedia of Islam Three Online* (Leiden: Brill, 2012), https://referenceworks.brill.com/doi/10.1163/1573-3912_ei3_COM_25935.
348 Nafi, 'Abu Al-Thana' al-Alusi,' 482–86.
349 Nafi, 'Abu Al-Thana' al-Alusi,' 465.
350 Nuʿmān al-Ālūsī, *Jalāʾ al-ʿaynayn fī muḥākamat al-Aḥmadayn* (Cairo: Maṭbaʿat Būlāq, 1880).
351 Basheer M. Nafi, 'Salafism Revived: Nu'mān al-Alūsī and the Trial of Two Ahmads,' *Die Welt Des Islams* 49, no. 1 (January 1, 2009): 50.
352 Nafi, 'Salafism Revived,' 50–51.
353 Shamsy, *Rediscovering the Islamic Classics*, 182–83.
354 Nafi, 'Salafism Revived,' 50.
355 Shamsy, *Rediscovering the Islamic Classics*, 174–77.
356 For a study of al-Albānī's main area of study, see Kamaruddin Amin, 'Nāṣiruddīn Al-Albānī on Muslim's Ṣaḥīḥ: A Critical Study of His Method,' *Islamic Law and Society* 11, no. 2 (2004): 149–76; Brown, *The Canonization of Al-Bukhārī and Muslim*, 321–34; Christopher Melchert, 'Muḥammad Nāṣir Al-Dīn Al-Albānī and Traditional Hadith Criticism,' in *Reclaiming Islamic Tradition: Modern Interpretations of the Classical Heritage*, ed. Elisabeth Kendall and Ahmad Khan (Edinburgh: Edinburgh University Press, 2016), 33–51.

357 For an autobiographical account of al-Albānī, see Emad Hamdeh, 'The Formative Years of an Iconoclastic Salafi Scholar,' *The Muslim World* 106, no. 3 (July 2016): 411–32. For a review of his life and thought, see Hamdeh, *Salafism and Traditionalism*; Stéphane Lacroix, 'Between Revolution and Apoliticism: Nasir al-Din al-Albānī and His Impact on the Shaping of Contemporary Salafism,' in *Global Salafism: Islam's New Religious Movement*, ed. Roel Meijer (Oxford University Press, 2014).

358 Wagemakers, *Salafism in Jordan*, 108.

359 From al-Albānī's autobiographical interview as reproduced and translated into English in Hamdeh, 'The Formative Years of an Iconoclastic Salafi Scholar,' 425.

360 The Ẓāhiriyya Library emerged in the late nineteenth century through the efforts of the Ottoman governor of Syria, Midhat Pasha (d. 1883), and his educational reforms, which included the formation of a public national library. In the latter task, he utilized the help of the reformist-Salafi scholar Ṭāhir al-Jazāʾirī (d. 1920), who gathered the holdings of the ten most important libraries in Damascus into what became the Ẓāhiriyya Library. Al-Jazāʾirī would then travel through the region on similar missions and founded similar libraries in Hama, Homs, Tripoli, and Jerusalem. See Shamsy, *Rediscovering the Islamic Classics*, 27–28 and 158–70.

361 From al-Albānī's autobiographical interview, see Hamdeh, 'The Formative Years of an Iconoclastic Salafi Scholar,' 425.

362 ʿAṭṭār became the leader of the Syrian Muslim Brotherhood from 1957 until 1969 and was exiled from Syria in 1964. See Dara Conduit, *The Muslim Brotherhood in Syria*, Cambridge Middle East Studies (New York, NY: Cambridge University Press, 2019), xiii. He married the daughter of ʿAli al-Tantawi (d. 1999), one of the most famous Brotherhood leaders of Syria. She was tragically assassinated in 1981 in Germany in a botched attempt on his life launched by Syria.

363 When al-Shāwīsh passed away, Yusuf al-Qaradawi (d. 2022), as President of the International Union of Muslim Scholars (IUMS), wrote an obituary in honor of al-Shāwīsh, in which he spoke of his life-long connection with the Muslim Brotherhood and their leading figures, in particular from Syria, and how he was 'one of the major scholars of the Levant, a preacher and struggler, who has a history of defending the truth, calling for good, and standing up against falsehood.' See 'IUMS Mourns the Death of Sheikh Zuhair Al-Shawish,' International Union of Muslim Scholars, 2013, https://www.iumsonline.org/en/ContentDetails.aspx?ID=2251 (last accessed 30 December 2022).

364 See Thomas Pierret, *Religion and State in Syria: The Sunni Ulama from Coup to Revolution*, Cambridge Middle East Studies (Cambridge: Cambridge University Press, 2013), 107; Olidort, 'In Defense of Tradition,' 221–23.

365 Olidort, 'In Defense of Tradition,' 83.

366 Pierret, *Religion and State in Syria*, 104.

367 Hamdeh, *Salafism and Traditionalism*, 49.

368 Olidort, 'In Defense of Tradition,' 83.

369 Pierret, *Religion and State in Syria*, 106–7; Olidort, 'In Defense of Tradition,' 203; For a study of al-Būṭī, see Andreas Christmann, 'Islamic Scholar and Religious Leader: A Portrait of Shaykh Muhammad Sa Id Ramadan Al-Buti,' *Islam & Christian Muslim Relations* 9, no. 2 (July 1998): 149–69.

370 Pierret, *Religion and State in Syria*, 115.

371 Pierret, 105; Olidort, 'In Defense of Tradition,' 218.

372 Olidort, 'In Defense of Tradition,' 219.

373 Olidort, 'In Defense of Tradition,' 112 and 120.

374 Emad Hamdeh, 'Shaykh Google as Ḥāfiẓ Al-ʿAṣr: The Internet, Traditional ʿUlamāʾ, and Self Learning,' *American Journal of Islam and Society* 37, no. 1–2 (May 15, 2020): 83. This quotation is reproduced and cited by Hamdeh from Jawad Qureshi, 'Zuhayr

Al-Shāwīsh (1925–2013) and al-Maktab al-Islāmī: Print, Hadith Verification, and Authenticated Islam,' presentation of an unpublished paper at the American Academy of Religion, November 21, 2016. See Hamdeh, 'Shaykh Google as Ḥāfiẓ Al-ʿAṣr,' 99 n79.

375 Lacroix, 'Between Revolution and Apoliticism,' 66.

376 Hamdeh, *Salafism and Traditionalism*, 43; Olidort, 'In Defense of Tradition,' 217.

377 Pierret, *Religion and State in Syria*, 107.

378 Wagemakers, *Salafism in Jordan*, 108.

379 Wagemakers, *Salafism in Jordan*, 108–9.

380 Wagemakers, *Salafism in Jordan*, 169.

381 Olidort, 'In Defense of Tradition,' 249–50.

382 This was a common theme in many of his speeches and articles. As one reference, see his article Muḥammad Nāṣir al-Dīn al-Albānī, 'Hadhihī Hiya Al-Salafiyya [This Is Salafism],' *Majalla al-āṣāla* 54 (1993): 54–55. It should be noted that the phrase 'Salafi' as a descriptive adjective to describe a theological school is not unprecedented: al-Dhahabī identified a number of scholars between the ninth and thirteenth centuries as being 'Salafi in creed (*ʿaqīda*).'

383 Hamdeh, *Salafism and Traditionalism*, 43–44; Olidort, 'In Defense of Tradition,' 219–20.

384 Such quietist associates of al-Albānī include the following: ʿAlī al-Ḥalabī, Mashhur b. Hasan, Muhammad Musa al-Nasr (d. 2017), Ḥusayn al-ʿAwāyisha, Bāsim b. Fāyṣal al-Jawābira, and Akram Ziyāda. See Wagemakers, *Salafism in Jordan*, 114–16.

385 The entire series has been uploaded to the internet and can be found on multiple sites, including YouTube.

386 Since he viewed Islamic law as derived straight from hadiths that he considered authentic, he had few qualms about bringing forth either extremely minor opinions or even unprecedented ones. Most of his discourse dealt with the specifics of rituals. Hence, it is not easy to explain to a reader who is not aware of the intricacies of Islamic law.

387 The entire repository of these journals is now online, at https://www.alalbany.org/asala/ (last accessed March 2024).

388 For historical reasons, six works of hadith are considered to be the most seminal by all Sunni groups – in addition to these four, there are the two *ṣaḥīḥ* works of al-Bukhārī and Muslim. See Brown, *The Canonization of Al-Bukhārī and Muslim*.

389 Lacroix, 'Between Revolution and Apoliticism,' 72; Majothi, 'Translating Salafism into English,' 130–31.

390 Nāṣir al-Dīn al-Albānī, *Ṣifat ṣalāt al-Nabī ṣalallahu ʿalaihi wa sallam min al-takbīr ilā-l-taslīm kaʾannaka tarāhā*, 10th ed. (Riyadh: Maktabat al-Maʿārif, 1990).

391 Muḥammad Nāṣir al-Dīn al-Albānī, *Ḥukm tārik al-ṣalāt*, ed. ʿAlī al-Ḥalabī (Jordan: al-Maktab al-Islāmyya, 1992).

392 Muhammad b. Sālim al-Dawsirī, *Rafʿ al-lāʾima ʿan fatwā al-lajna al-dāʾima*, 2nd ed. (Riyadh: Dār ʿĀlam al-Fawāʾid, 2001).

## 3 WAHHABISM AND SALAFISM

1 Muḥammad b. ʿAbd al-Wahhāb, *Kashf Al-Shubuhāt* (Maktabat al-Himma, 2016). For the English translation, see Yasir Qadhi, *An Explanation of Muhammad Ibn 'Abd al-Wahhab's Kashf al-Shubuhat: A Critical Study of Shirk* (Birmingham, UK: Al-Hidaayah Publishing, 2003), 19.

2 Adapted, faithful to the meaning, from a letter written by Ibn ʿAbd al-Wahhāb around 1745. See ʿAbd al-Raḥmān b. Muḥammad b. Qāsim, *al-Durar al-saniyya fī al-ajwiba al-najdiyya*, 6th ed., 1996, 10:51.

3 The first source I came across in any Western language dates back to 1796 when the naturalist Guillaume Antoine Olivier (d. 1814) was visiting Baghdad and heard of a formidable Arab tribe, numbering over 100,000 men, known as the 'Ouhabis' (sic.). The fact that he heard this from his Arab hosts indicates that the term was in vogue from the movement's inception. See Giovanni Bonacina, *The Wahhabis Seen Through European Eyes 1772–1830: Deists and Puritans of Islam* (Leiden; Boston: Brill Academic Pub, 2015), 36; Also see the very interesting article by Mu'Īnuddīn Aḥmad Khan, 'A Diplomat's Report on Wahhabism of Arabia,' *Islamic Studies* 7, no. 1 (1968): 33–46 which analyses a dispatch sent to the British Office in 1799 and describes the 'Whabee (sic.)' movement. Lastly, there is an entry entitled 'The Wahabees (sic.): A New Sect' in Asiatic Annual Register, 'Bengal Occurrences for May 1803,' 47 (1804).

4 Nabil Mouline, *The Clerics of Islam: Religious Authority and Political Power in Saudi Arabia*, trans. Ethan S. Rundell (New Haven/Conn: Yale University Press, 2014), 8–9; Jamaal Al-Din M. Zarabozo, *The Life, Teachings And Influence Of Muhammad Ibn Abdul Wahhaab* (Ministry of Islamic Affairs, 2003), 158–59; David Commins, 'From Wahhabi to Salafi,' in *Saudi Arabia in Transition: Insights on Social, Political, Economic and Religious Change*, ed. Bernard Haykel, Stéphane Lacroix, and Thomas Hegghammer (Cambridge: Cambridge University Press, 2015), 151–66.

5 Ṣiddīq Ḥasan Khān, *An Interpreter of Wahabiism* (Calcutta, 1884), 19.

6 I have written extensively about this movement since I was affiliated with it for a period of my life, and when writing or talking for predominantly Muslim audiences, I generally prefer the term 'Najdī,' as this term describes a geographic-centered movement without any negative connotations. However, this term is simply not in vogue, and hence not suitable for our present discussion.

7 Mouline, *The Clerics of Islam*, 52.

8 Resources used for this narrative include Muḥammad Ibn ʿAbd al-Wahhāb, *Uṣūl Al-Īmān*, ed. Bāsam Fayṣal al-Jawābira, 5th ed. (Medina: Wizārat al-Shuʾūn al-Islāmiyya wa-l-Awqāf wa-l-Daʿwa wa-l-Irshād, 1999), 8–26; Zarabozo, *The Life, Teachings And Influence Of Muhammad Ibn Abdul Wahhaab*, 10–63; Masudul Hasan, *History of Islam*, vol. 2 (Adam Publishers, 1998), 470–71.

9 Zarabozo, *The Life, Teachings And Influence Of Muhammad Ibn Abdul Wahhaab*, 16–17.

10 On Muḥammad Hayāt al-Sindī, see section 2.5.2.

11 Zarabozo, *The Life, Teachings And Influence Of Muhammad Ibn Abdul Wahhaab*, 28–29.

12 Zarabozo, 40; Peter Mandaville, ed., *Wahhabism and the World: Understanding Saudi Arabia's Global Influence on Islam*, Religion and Global Politics (Oxford; New York: Oxford University Press, 2022), 28–30.

13 Bunzel, *Wahhābism*, 199–200.

14 Mouline, *The Clerics of Islam*, 259.

15 Bunzel, *Wahhābism*, 202–3.

16 Muḥammad b. ʿAbd al-Wahhāb, *Muʾallafāt al-Shaykh al-Imām Muḥammad Ibn ʿAbd al-Wahhāb*, ed. ʿAbd al-ʿAzīz b. Zayd al-Rūmī, Muḥammad Baltājī, and Sayyid Ḥijāb (Riyadh: Jāmiʿat al-Imām Muḥammad ibn Suʿūd al-Islāmiyya, 1976), 212.

17 Some later historical sources claim that Sulaymān eventually repented and joined his brother many decades later. However, these reports are very suspicious, and even leading Wahhabi scholars have rejected them. The alternative version of the story states that Muḥammad b. ʿAbd al-Wahhāb eventually captured his brother and kept him under house arrest until he passed away.

18 Bunzel, *Wahhābism*, 205.

19 The adversarial narrative is primarily taken from the following works: Hamid Algar, *Wahhabism: A Critical Essay*, 1st ed (Oneonta, NY: Islamic Publications International,

2002), 6–24; Stephen Schwartz, *The Two Faces of Islam: The House of Sa'ud from Tradition to Terror*, 1 ed. (New York: Doubleday, 2003), 64–74. The aforementioned work by Hamid Algar capitalized on the events of 9/11 and was highly critical of the movement. The work makes no attempt to hide the author's extreme disdain for the movement and blames the power of the Saudi petrodollar for the spread of Wahhabism at the expense of local, more authentic Islamic traditions. Firas Alkhateeb, *Lost Islamic History: Reclaiming Muslim Civilisation from the Past*, Revised and updated edition (London: Hurst & Company, 2017), 201–2.

Wahhābism has many other critics who have reported its history in a hostile manner. One such critic is Khaled Abou El Fadl, a leading voice of the Progressive Muslim trend. In his work *The Great Theft: Wrestling Islam from the Extremists*, he argues that Wahhabism, and its parent branch of Salafism, are literalist trends, or 'Bedouin Islam' as he puts it, which attract simple-minded devotees devoid of intellectual reflection. He claims that Salafism is nearly identical to Wahhābism, with the primary exception being that Salafism was marginally more tolerant of diversity. Along with Algar, he points to the sinister role of Saudi petrodollars in the rise and popularity of what he considers to be this lethal puritanical movement. See Khaled Abou El Fadl, *The Great Theft: Wrestling Islam from the Extremists*, 1. HarperCollins paperback ed. (New York, NY: HarperOne, 2007), 74, 79, 87, 91–94. For an academic study of this time frame, directly from the sources, the best resource to date is Cole M. Bunzel, *Wahhābism: The History of a Militant Islamic Movement* (Princeton: Princeton University Press, 2023), 191–277.

20 *Ṣaḥīḥ al-Bukhārī: kitāb al-fitan, bāb qawl al-nabī ṣallā-llāhu ʿalayhi wa-sallam al-fitnatu min qibali al-mashriq.*

21 Of course, sympathizers have a different interpretation of this tradition. Typically, they will deflect this by quoting earlier authorities, such as Abū Sulaymān al-Khaṭṭābī (d. 388/988), Ibn Ḥajar al-ʿAsqalānī, Badr al-Dīn al-ʿAynī (d. 855/1453), and Shams al-Dīn al-Kirmānī (d. 786/1384), who claimed that the term 'Najd' used to apply in that time frame to the modern region of Iraq. See Zarabozo, *The Life, Teachings And Influence Of Muhammad Ibn Abdul Wahhaab*, 236–38.

22 Madawi Al-Rasheed, *A History of Saudi Arabia*, 2nd ed. (New York: Cambridge University Press, 2010), 13.

23 See Sulaymān b. ʿAbd al-Wahhāb, *The Divine Lightning* (London: Lulu Press, 2003), 32, 45–50, 67–80.

24 The theory of a British Spy named Hempher tricking Ibn ʿAbd al-Wahhāb into becoming an extremist was made popular by Turkish scholar Ayyūb Ṣabrī Pasha (d. 1890) in his book *Mirʾāt al-Ḥaramayn (The Mirror of the Two Holy Sanctuaries)*. Since then, an English translation of Hempher's alleged journal, entitled 'Confessions of a British Spy,' has been circulated. However, academics consider it an obvious forgery from pro-Sufi Ottoman sources that was meant to discredit the movement. See Bernard Haykel, 'Anti-Wahhabism: A Footnote,' *Middle East Strategy at Harvard* (blog), March 27, 2008, https://archive.blogs.harvard.edu/mesh/2008/03/anti_wahhabism_a_footnote/.

25 The deaths were also estimated to be 4,500, as reported by a French diplomat stationed in Iraq. See Bunzel, 'Manifest Enmity,' 219.

26 Algar, *Wahhabism*, 19–22.

27 The majority of his letters referenced throughout this section can be found in the first three volumes of *al-Durar al-saniyya*, which is the most encyclopaedic collection of early Wahhabi treatises. See Ibn Qāsim, *Al-Durar al-saniyya*, vols. 1–3.

28 These four points are taken from Bunzel, *Wahhābism*, 142.

29 See *'Indeed, God does not forgive associating others with Him in worship, but forgives anything else of whoever He wills. And whoever associates others with God has indeed committed a grave sin.'* (Q 4:48)

30 ʿAbd al-Raḥmān b. Ḥasan Āl al-Shaykh, *Fatḥ al-majīd li-Sharḥ Kitāb al-Tawḥīd*, ed. al-Walīd b. ʿAbd al-Raḥmān Āl Furayyān (Riyadh: Dār al-Ṣumayʿī, n.d.), 1:405–10.
31 Āl al-Shaykh, *Fatḥ al-majīd*, 1:371–79.
32 Āl al-Shaykh, *Fatḥ al-majīd*, 1:325–27.
33 Āl al-Shaykh, *Fatḥ al-majīd*, 1:229–49.
34 Āl al-Shaykh, *Fatḥ al-majīd*, 1:229–49.
35 Āl al-Shaykh, *Fatḥ al-majīd*, 1:253–64.
36 Āl al-Shaykh, *Fatḥ al-majīd*, 1:279–93.
37 Āl al-Shaykh, *Fatḥ al-majīd*, 1:265–93.
38 Āl al-Shaykh, *Fatḥ al-majīd*, 2:505–14.
39 Āl al-Shaykh, *Fatḥ al-majīd*, 1:295–301.
40 Āl al-Shaykh, *Fatḥ al-majīd*, 2:797–808.
41 Āl al-Shaykh, *Fatḥ al-majīd*, 2:463–515.
42 Āl al-Shaykh, *Fatḥ al-majīd*, 2:463–515. The hadith is narrated in *Jāmīʿ al-Tirmidhī: kitāb al-daʿwāt ʿan rasūl Allāh ṣallā-llāhu ʿalayhi wa-sallam, bāb mā jāʾa fī faḍl al-duʿāʾ*.
43 In particular, Q. 39:3: *'Indeed, sincere devotion is due only to God. As for those who take other lords besides Him, saying, "We worship them only so they may bring us closer to God," surely God will judge between all regarding what they differed about,' and Q. 10:18: 'They worship besides God others who can neither harm nor benefit them, and say, "These are our intercessors with God." (But) ask them: Are you informing God of something He does not know in the heavens or the earth? Glorified and Exalted is He above what they associate with Him!'*
44 See, in particular, his first four arguments in *Kashf al-Shubuhāt*, in Qadhi, *Kashf Al-Shubuhat*, 81–97.
45 The counterargument that his opponents made was that this was an egregiously false comparison. The Meccan idolaters believed their gods were powerful and independent of God (as numerous evidences show). They viewed them as being worthy of worship and veneration because of their inherent powers. Like all pantheistic belief systems, the Meccans believed in One Supreme God, Allah. But they also believed in many lesser deities who were able to create, sustain, heal, and answer prayers independently of God the Almighty. Those who justified these actions claimed that the Prophet or saints are blessed by God Himself and not independently powerful. They claimed that no Muslim would believe the Prophet to be a god, and that it is understood that they are only approaching God through a means and mechanism that He Himself legislated and is pleased with. See, for example, Aḥmad Zaynī Daḥlān, *Fitnat al-Wahhābiyya* (Istanbul: Işık Kitabevi, 1974), 13–25. We shall return to this point later.
46 See Āl al-Shaykh, *Fatḥ Al-Majīd*, 1:388–94.
47 This caution is derived from a number of hadiths, like the following: 'If a man calls his brother an unbeliever, this applies to one of them.' See Adil Salahi, trans., *Ṣaḥīḥ Muslim: With the Full Commentary by Imam Al-Nawawi*, vol. 2 (London: Islamic Foundation, 2019), 51–53.
48 Ibn Qāsim, *al-Durar al-saniyya*, 1:409.
49 Ibn Qāsim, *al-Durar al-saniyya*, 1:159.
50 Ibn Qāsim, *al-Durar al-saniyya*, 1:160.
51 Ibn Qāsim, *al-Durar al-saniyya*, 10:91.
52 See, for example, Ibn Taymiyya, *Majmūʿ fatāwā Shaykh al-Islām Aḥmad ibn Taymiyya*, ed. ʿAbd al-Raḥmān b. Muḥammad b. Qāsim and Muḥammad b. ʿAbd al-Raḥmān b. Qāsim (Riyadh: Maṭābiʿ al-Riyāḍ, 1962), 28:209; Ibn Taymiyya, *al-Īmān*, ed. Muḥammad Nāṣir al-Dīn al-Albānī, 5th ed. (Amman, Jordan: al-Maktab al-Islāmī, 1996), 14. To be clear, Ibn Taymiyya indeed uses this concept, and one can detect later Wahhabi sentiments in his writings. However, it can be argued that

the context within which Ibn Taymiyya talks is clearly about enemies of God versus the righteous believer; Ibn ʿAbd al-Wahhāb would use this concept against fellow believers, claiming that other non-Wahhabi groups deserved 'dissociation.' It is also interesting to note that Ibn Taymiyya did not write any separate treatise on this topic but rather discussed it generically when he commented on specific Qur'anic verses or hadiths.

53 Interestingly, this notion is actually found as a pillar of early Khārijī theology under the terms '*muwāla*' and '*mu ʿādah*.' Further research remains to be done on whether Ibn ʿAbd al-Wahhāb took this notion from perhaps Ibāḍī literature. See Madelung, 'Early Ibāḍī Theology.'

54 See Ibn Qāsim, *Al-Durar al-saniyya*, 8:113; Muḥammad Ibn ʿAbd al-Wahhāb, *Majmūʿat -l-*, ed. Ismāʿīl b. Muḥammad al-Anṣārī (Riyadh: Jāmiʿat al-Imām Muḥammad ibn Suʿūd al-Islāmiyya, n.d.), 117.

55 Ibn Qāsim, *al-Durar al-Saniyya*, 1:153 and 2:202–5.

56 Ibn Qāsim, *al-Durar al-Saniyya*, 1:109.

57 Bunzel, *Wahhābism*, 162–73.

58 Joas Wagemakers, 'The Transformation of a Radical Concept: Al-Wala' Wa-l-Bara' in the Ideology of Abu Muhammad Al-Maqdisi,' in *Global Salafism: Islam's New Religious Movement*, ed. Roel Meijer (Oxford University Press, 2014), 87–88, https://doi.org/10.1093/acprof:oso/9780199333431.003.0004.

59 Ibid., 88.

60 For a discussion of *hijra* in relation to the movement, see Bunzel, *Wahhābism*, 170–72.

61 See, for example, Abū Muḥammad al-Maqdisi, *Millat Ibrāhīm* (Minbar al-Tawḥīd wa-l-Jihād, n.d.), 51–113.

62 Wagemakers, 'The Transformation of a Radical Concept,' 91–92.

63 See Bunzel, *Wahhābism*, 173–85.

64 Ḥusayn b. Abī Bakr Ibn Ghannām, *Tārīkh Ibn Ghannām al-musammạ rawḍat al-afkār wa-l-afhām li-murtād ḥāl al-imām wa-ta ʿdād ghazawāt dhawī-l-Islām*, ed. Sulaymān b. Ṣāliḥ al-Kharāshī, 2 vols. (Riyadh: Dār al-Thulūthiyya, 2010).

65 Bunzel, *Wahhābism*, 75.

66 Bunzel, *Wahhābism*, 70.

67 Bunzel, *Wahhābism*, 69.

68 Sulaymān b. ʿAbd al-Wahhāb, *al-Ṣawāʿiq al-ilāhiyya fī al-radd ʿalā al-Wahhābiyya*, ed. al-Sarrājī, 1st ed. (Beirut: Dār Dhū al-Qarnayn, 1998), 11.

69 Sulaymān b. ʿAbd al-Wahhāb, *al-Ṣawāʿiq al-ilāhiyya,* 98.

70 All apologetic works written in defense of the founder – or the movement itself – concentrated on this issue since it is the primary difference between Wahhabism and other strands of Islam. See, for example, the entire chapter dedicated to this issue in the seminal dissertation written in defense of the founder, ʿAbd al-ʿAzīz b. Muḥammad Āl ʿAbd al-Laṭīf, *Daʿāwā al-munāwiʾīn li-daʿwat al-shaykh Muḥammad ibn ʿAbd al-Wahhāb* (Riyadh: Dār Ṭayba, 1989), 157–210.

71 Ibn Qāsim, *al-Durar al-saniyya*, 2:20–21.

72 Ibn ʿAbd al-Wahhāb, *Muʾallafāt Al-Shaykh al-Imām Muḥammad Ibn ʿAbd al-Wahhāb*, ed. ʿAbd al-ʿAzīz b. Zayd al-Rūmī, Muḥammad Baltājī, and Sayyid Ḥijāb (Riyadh: Jāmiʿat al-Imām Muḥammad ibn Suʿūd al-Islāmiyya, 1976), 7:25.

73 Ibn Qāsim, *al-Durar al-saniyya*, 1:73.

74 Some of these quotations, for example, can be found here along with many other similar quotations from his letters, see 'Muhammad Bin Abd Al-Wahhab and the Excuse of Ignorance for Muslims Who Fall Into Affairs of Shirk,' Wahhabis.com, accessed June 7, 2024, http://www.wahhabis.com/articles/lxygyii-muhammad-bin-abd-al-wahhab-and-the-

excuse-of-ignorance-for-muslims-who-fall-into-affairs-of-shirk.cfm; the most thorough study and theological defense of the founder to date is Āl ʿAbd al-Laṭīf, *Daʿāwā al-Munāwiʾīn*.

75 For quotations of this genre, see the first point in his work *Kashf al-Shubuhāt*, in Qadhi, *Kashf al-Shubuhat,* 99–101.

76 Ibn Ghannām, *Tārīkh Ibn Ghannām*, 2:687–88.

77 On Third-Wave Wahhabism, see section 3.23.

78 Ibn Qāsim, *al-Durar al-saniyya*, 10:343-44.

79 Ḥusayn b. Abī Bakr Ibn Ghannām, *Tārīkh Ibn Ghannām Al-Musammā Rawḍat al-Afkār Wa-l-Afhām Li-Murtād Ḥāl al-Imām Wa-Ta ʿdād Ghazawāt Dhawī-l-Islām*, ed. Sulaymān b. Ṣāliḥ al-Kharāshī (Riyadh: Dār al-Thulūthiyya, 2010), 1:404. Translated into English and cited in Cole M. Bunzel, *Wahhābism: The History of a Militant Islamic Movement* (Princeton: Princeton University Press, 2023), 161.

80 Ibn ʿAbd al-Wahhāb, *Muʾallafāt al-Shaykh*, 6:322.

81 The treatise can be read in Ibn Qāsim, *al-Durar al-saniyya*, 8:121–23.

82 On a personal note, as a freshman at the Islamic University of Medina I, too, studied this work cover to cover and, in the summer of 1996, taught the entire book in English in America. This detailed audio series, with the explanation of the text in a manner that had perhaps not been done before in English, was one of the main factors that contributed to my own popularity among some circles in the English-speaking world. These lectures were uploaded a year later onto the new technology known as the internet, where tens of thousands of people downloaded and heard them. This series would be the first milestone in my own public prominence within the movement.

83 See my work, Yasir Qadhi, *An Explanation of Muhammad Ibn ʿAbd al-Wahhab's Kashf al-Shubuhat: A Critical Study of Shirk* (Birmingham, UK: Al-Hidaayah Publishing, 2003). To date, this remains one of the most thorough elucidations and defenses of the doctrines of Ibn ʿAbd al-Wahhāb in the English language.

84 See the analysis of Michael Cook and Henri Laoust in Michael Cook, 'On the Origins of Wahhābism,' *Journal of the Royal Asiatic Society* 2, no. 2 (July 1992): 199–200.

85 Ibn Qāsim, *Al-Durar al-saniyya*, 10:51.

86 For Ibn Taymiyya's condemnation of such acts as polytheism, see Ibn Taymiyya, *al-Istighātha fi al-radd ʿalā al-Bakrī*, ed. ʿAbdallāh b. Dujayn al-Sahlī, 4th ed. (Riyadh: Maktabat Dār al-Minhāj, 2014); and for similar writings from him, see Abul Hasan Alī Nadwi, *Saviours of Islamic Spirit*, trans. S. Mohiuddin Ahmad, vol. 4 (Lucknow: Academy of Islamic Research and Publications, 1993), 81–91.

87 See, for example, Ibn Taymiyya's discussion in Ibn Taymiyya, *Iqtiḍāʾ Al-Ṣirāṭ al-Mustaqīm Li-Mukhālafat Aṣḥāb al-Jaḥīm*, ed. Nāṣir b. ʿAbd al-Karīm al-ʿAql (Riyadh: Dār al-ʿĀṣima, 1998), 2:224–250; and Ibn Taymiyya, *al-Istighātha fi al-radd ʿalā al-Bakrī*, ed. ʿAbdallāh b. Dujayn al-Sahlī, 4th ed. (Riyadh: Maktabat Dār al-Minhāj, 2014), 95.

88 Ibn Kathir, *Al-Bidayah wa'l-nihayah* (Qatar: Wizarat al-Awqaf wa'l-Shu'un al-Islamiyyah, 2015), vol. 16, 177–78.

89 For the study of an early refutation of that sort – although one that is somewhat obscure – see Samer Traboulsi, 'An Early Refutation of Muḥammad Ibn ʿAbd Al-Wahhāb's Reformist Views,' *Die Welt Des Islams* 42, no. 3 (2002): 373–415.

90 Aḥmad b. Zaynī Daḥlān, *Fitnat al-Wahhābiyya* (Istanbul: Işık Kitabevi, 1974).

91 Aḥmad b. Zaynī Daḥlān, *Fitnat Al-Wahhābiyya* (Istanbul: Işık Kitabevi, 1974). See also, 5–8; Cole M. Bunzel, *Wahhābism: The History of a Militant Islamic Movement* (Princeton: Princeton University Press, 2023), 270.

92 Aḥmad b. Zaynī Daḥlān, *Fitnat Al-Wahhābiyya* (Istanbul: Işık Kitabevi, 1974), 9–10.

93 Bunzel, 'Manifest Enmity,' 38.

94 Muḥammad b. ʿAbd al-Raḥmān b. ʿAfāliq, *Tahakkum al-muqallidīn fī muddaʿī tajdīd al-dīn*, n.d., 17–18, https://dn790009.ca.archive.org/0/items/lionsunna TAHAKKOMU_ALMUKALLEDIN/lmlkmltkmrl.pdf.
95 Ibn ʿAfāliq, 21.
96 Bunzel, *Wahhābism*, 54.
97 For a brief discussion on al-Saffārīnī, see section 2.5.2.
98 Bunzel, *Wahhābism*, 70.
99 Bunzel, 71.
100 Ibn ʿAbd al-Wahhāb, *al-Ṣawāʿiq al-ilāhiyya*, 11.
101 For a brief discussion on al-Ṣanʿānī, see section 2.5.2.
102 al-Ṣanʿānī, *Irshād dhawī al-albāb*, 108–10.
103 al-Ṣanʿānī, *Irshād dhawī al-albāb*, 111. Translated into English and cited in Bunzel, *Wahhābism*, 82.
104 Bunzel, *Wahhābism*, 75–78.
105 Bunzel, *Wahhābism*, 84–90.
106 Meijer, *Global Salafism*, 7–8.
107 Emine Ö. Evered, 'Rereading Ottoman Accounts of Wahhabism as Alternative Narratives: Ahmed Cevdet Paşa's Historical Survey of the Movement,' *Comparative Studies of South Asia, Africa and the Middle East* 32, no. 3 (December 1, 2012): 627, https://doi.org/10.1215/1089201X-1891615.
108 It should be noted that they did relinquish their control in some areas of the east after a rebellion in 1670 and did not return until the 1870s. See Al-Rasheed, *A History of Saudi Arabia*, 13.
109 Bunzel, *Wahhābism*, 191–92.
110 Bunzel, *Wahhābism*, 192.
111 Bunzel, *Wahhābism*, 217.
112 Evered, 'Rereading Ottoman Accounts of Wahhabism as Alternative Narratives,' 630.
113 John Lewis Burckhardt, *Notes on the Bedouins and Wahabys* (London: Henry Colburn Press, 1831), 103.
114 Ibid., 103.
115 Abdulaziz H. Al-Fahad, 'From Exclusivism to Accommodation: Doctrinal and Legal Evolution of Wahhabism,' *New York University Law Review* 79, no. 2 (519 485AD): 496–97.
116 Al-Fahad, 'From Exclusivism to Accommodation,' 631.
117 Bunzel, 'Manifest Enmity,' 275.
118 Al-Fahad, 'From Exclusivism to Accommodation,' 497–98.
119 Bunzel, *Wahhābism*, 228–31; Mouline, *The Clerics of Islam*, 90.
120 Mudayhish, *Al-Najdiyyūn Fī al-Hind: ʿUlamāʾ Najd al-Ladhīn Raḥalū Ilā al-Hind Li-l-Istiẓādat Min al-Ḥadīth al-Nabawī*, 317–18.
121 Bunzel, 'Manifest Enmity,' 226–74.
122 Abdulaziz H. Al-Fahad argues that the dissenting group against ʿAbd Allāh was actually 'most scholars.' See Al-Fahad, 'From Exclusivism to Accommodation,' 487; Yet Wagemakers considers 'most ulama' to have backed ʿAbd Allāh and 'a powerful minority' to have opposed the stance. See Joas Wagemakers, 'The Enduring Legacy of the Second Saudi State: Quietist and Radical Wahhabi Contestations of Al-Walāʾ Wa-L-Barāʾ,' *International Journal of Middle East Studies* 44, no. 1 (2012): 96; However, ʿAbd Allāh would later change his mind about utilizing Ottoman support and later turned to rely solely on local forces. See Al-Fahad, 'From Exclusivism to Accommodation,' 501.
123 The fact that King Faisal (d. 1865) himself endorsed Ottoman sovereignty when he required support for his rule was a point that Wahhabi clerics in his time did not stress to point out. Furthermore, one should not see Ibn ʿAjlān as having a soft

stance on the matter. In fact, Ibn ʿAjlān seems to have had an almost equally stern position by arguing that the Ottomans were disbelievers, but Ibn Taymiyya had likewise enlisted the help of similar disbelievers during his time, from Egypt and Syria, to fight the Mongols. See Al-Fahad, 'From Exclusivism to Accommodation,' 497n36 and 503.

124 At the same time, this incident also demonstrates the differences between Ibn Taymiyya and the early Wahhābis, including Ibn ʿAbd al-Wahhāb, namely the identification of people as disbelievers. For instance, where Ibn ʿAjlān seems to have argued that it was permissible to enlist the help of disbelieving Ottomans as Ibn Taymiyya had done likewise to fight the Mongols, ʿAbd al-Laṭīf b. ʿAbd al-Raḥmān Āl al-Shaykh rejected Ibn ʿAjlān's argument on the basis that Ibn Taymiyya considered his land to be from the lands of Islam and did not consider the contemporary society to be defined as polytheistic and disbelieving, despite the fact that the cult of saints and calling upon the dead was just as prevalent as in the time of Ibn ʿAbd al-Wahhāb. See Wagemakers, 'The Enduring Legacy of the Second Saudi State,' 94–97; However, ʿAbd al-Laṭīf b. ʿAbd al-Raḥmān Āl al-Shaykh criticized Ḥamad for declaring Ibn ʿAjlān to be an apostate. Al-Fahad, 'From Exclusivism to Accommodation,' 503–4.

125 Ibn Qāsim, *al-Durar al-saniyya*, 10:429.

126 Schwartz, *The Two Faces of Islam*, 81.

127 This group is not to be confused with the 'Muslim Brotherhood' (al-Ikhwān al-Muslimūn) that would be founded in Egypt a few decades later. On the Muslim Brotherhood, see Chapter 4.

128 Schwartz, *The Two Faces of Islam*, 82–84.

129 Ibn Qāsim, *al-Durar al-saniyya*, 9:292; Also, see Bunzel, 'Manifest Enmity,' 345.

130 Bunzel, 'Manifest Enmity,' 348.

131 Al-Rasheed, *A History of Saudi Arabia*, 40.

132 This support for Ibn Saud must be seen in the context of what has been called Britain's 'imperial divide and rule' and a longstanding attitude (even to the present day) of 'expediency' in pursuit of certain political and economic interests. In the Arabian context, the British were, at the same time, supporting Ibn Saud's rival in the Hijaz, Sharīf Ḥusayn. The latter received £12,000 a month from the British; in 1919, he provided aircraft support to Husayn in his battle with Ibn Saud. See Mark Curtis, *Secret Affairs: Britain's Collusion with Radical Islam*, New updated version (London: Serpent's Tail, 2012), 5-14 and 168.

133 Bunzel, 'Manifest Enmity,' 348–54.

134 Curtis, *Secret Affairs*, 13.

135 Curtis, *Secret Affairs*, 353–54. For the Siege of Mecca in 1979, see section 3.2.2.

136 Curtis, *Secret Affairs*, 93.

137 al-Rasheed, *A History of Saudi Arabia*, 46. British-Saudi relations would undergo a tense period later, at the end of Ibn Saud's reign, when a dispute over the oasis Buraimi occurred between them from 1952 until 1955. The Saudis cut diplomatic relations in 1956 when the British invaded Egypt over the Suez Canal. Diplomatic relations were restored between the two countries in 1963. See Curtis, *Secret Affairs*, 68–69.

138 Mouline, *The Clerics of Islam*, 10 and 120–25.

139 Yaroslav Trofimov, *The Siege of Mecca: The 1979 Uprising at Islam's Holiest Shrine*, 1st Anchor Books ed. (New York: Anchor Books, 2007), 21–23.

140 Excommunication of the Ottomans would persist, however, in some, not all, Wahhabi circles until just before the Second Wave of Wahhabism. This is seen in the work of Sulaymān b. Siḥmān (d. 1930), who was a leading Wahhabi cleric from the western Arabian area of ʿAsīr. See Bunzel, *Wahhābism,* 83.

141 See examples of these fatwas in Wagemakers, 'The Enduring Legacy of the Second Saudi State,' 98–100.
142 Mouline, *The Clerics of Islam*, 261.
143 For his biography, see the Introductory section in Muḥammad b. Ibrāhīm Āl al-Shaykh, *Fatāwā Wa-Rasā'il Samāḥat al-Shaykh Muḥammad Ibn Ibrāhīm Ibn 'Abd al-Laṭīf Āl al-Shaykh*, ed. Muḥammad b. 'Abd al-Raḥmān Ibn Qāsim (Mecca: Maṭba'at al-Ḥukūma, 1978), 1:15–22.
144 These examples are culled from his works, and from my own interactions with the clerics of the Kingdom who have preserved this history. There is no doubt that the persona of this fascinating cleric deserves much more attention, and this time frame specifically, and the overall trajectory of Wahhabism, is most definitely worthy of more intensive study.
145 See various fatwas over the course of the late 1950s and early 1960s, in Muḥammad b. Ibrāhīm Āl al-Shaykh, *Fatāwā Wa-Rasā'il Samāḥat al-Shaykh Muḥammad Ibn Ibrāhīm Ibn 'Abd al-Laṭīf Āl al-Shaykh*, ed. Muḥammad b. 'Abd al-Raḥmān Ibn Qāsim (Mecca: Maṭba'at al-Ḥukūma, 1978), 13:220–25.
146 Muḥammad b. Ibrāhīm Āl al-Shaykh, *Risālat Taḥkīm Al-Qawānīn*, n.d., 13. This work has caused some embarrassment to some contemporary apolitical/loyalist Salafis, who have come to argue that the shaykh changed his position from the one expressed in this work, as the argument therein compromises their stance. But there is no evidence of a retraction.
147 Āl al-Shaykh, *Fatāwā wa-rasā'il*, 1:77.
148 Āl al-Shaykh, *Fatāwā wa-rasā'il*, 11:40.
149 See his entire selection of written speeches, recorded in Āl al-Shaykh, *Fatāwā wa-rasā'il*, 13:188–203.
150 See Āl al-Shaykh, *Fatāwā wa-rasā'il*, 12:319 and also, 1:249–255.
151 Āl al-Shaykh, *Fatāwā wa-rasā'il*, 12:261–275.
152 This was mentioned to me by a number of my teachers, at least one of whom claimed to be a student and eyewitness on the occasion of King Faisal's visit to the Islamic University of Medina, probably in the early 1970s, accompanied by the Grand Mufti; an impromptu lecture was given in front of the students and professors at the University, in which the king apparently paid attention and did not say anything in response.
153 Bunzel, 'Manifest Enmity,' 277–344; Wagemakers, 'The Enduring Legacy of the Second Saudi State,' 93–110.
154 Mouline, *The Clerics of Islam*, 262.
155 Bunzel, 'Manifest Enmity,' 344.
156 On Ibn Bāz, see section 3.2.3.
157 Trofimov, *The Siege of Mecca*, 19.
158 On al-Albānī, see section 2.9.4.
159 On Ibn al-'Uthaymīn, see section 3.2.3.
160 Thomas Hegghammer and Stéphane Lacroix, 'Rejectionist Islamism in Saudi Arabia: The Story of Juhayman al-'Utaybi Revisited,' *International Journal of Middle East Studies* 39, no. 1 (2007): 105–8.
161 During my years at IUM, I developed a fascination for this group and informally interviewed dozens of my professors and others who were students at the time of this incident. The impression that many had was that this was a pious group with positive aims – albeit perhaps a bit harsh at times. The public call was open to any who joined; from those who joined, the leaders would decide which to take aside and attempt to persuade to their secret mission, which involved military training and withdrawing from society. A number of my own teachers joined the public side of this movement and informed me that while they were vaguely aware there was a special group doing other activities, they themselves were never in the loop as to the reality of the goals of

Juhaymān and were not – like most of the other members of the group – involved in military activities. For them, it was about preaching a particular interpretation of the religion to the broader public and raising public morality.

162 Trofimov, *The Siege of Mecca*, 29.

163 Hegghammer and Lacroix, 'Rejectionist Islamism in Saudi Arabia,' 108–9.

164 Trofimov, *The Siege of Mecca*, 31–34.

165 Trofimov, 40–41; David Commins, *The Wahhabi Mission and Saudi Arabia* (London ; New York: I.B. Tauris, 2006), 164.

166 The Mahdī is a figure in Islamic eschatology that both mainstream Sunni and Shiʿi believe in, but with fundamental differences between the two. Sunnis believe that this figure will appear towards the end of time as a forerunner to Jesus Christ's return. It is said in the hadith corpus that when the Muslims are in dire need of a spiritual leader, a leader from the descendants of the Prophet named Muḥammad b. ʿAbd Allāh will arise. The Mahdī will be found and formally identified by Muslims while he ritually circumambulates the Kaaba, and an oath of allegiance will be given to him immediately. The Mahdī will subsequently steer the Muslims to victory by defeating the Antichrist, with Jesus – having recently descended back to earth from the heavens – operating under his banner. On the Mahdī, see Marcia Hermansen, 'Eschatology,' in *The Cambridge Companion to Classical Islamic Theology*, ed. T. J. Winter, Cambridge Companions to Religion (Cambridge; New York: Cambridge University Press, 2008), 315–16; Suhaib Hasan, *The Concept of the Mahdi Among Ahl Al-Sunna* (London: Al-Qurʾan Society, 2019).

167 Trofimov, *The Siege of Mecca*, 45–52.

168 As per the hadith corpus, Muslims believe that God sends someone to 'revive' Islam every lunar century. Although it is not necessary that the reviver be present and identified on the first day of the new century, Juhaymān found the date irresistible and capitalized on it for the purposes of his attack.

169 Commins, *The Wahhabi Mission and Saudi Arabia*, 165.

170 Trofimov, *The Siege of Mecca*, 90–100.

171 There are unsubstantiated rumors spread by critics of the establishment that the Senior Council of Scholars, led by Ibn Bāz, took this opportunity to bargain with the government to establish a more conservative culture. In what was assumed to be *a quid pro quo*, they then issued a verdict allowing soldiers to enter the Grand Mosque and fight – considered to be a heinous sin in Islam under usual circumstances – in exchange for a promise from the monarch for the Kingdom to implement a stricter form of Islamic law. This anecdote seems highly unlikely and is not found in any credible source.

172 I have read the entire writings of Juhaymān, presented papers on his thoughts and views, and also interviewed dozens of his contemporaries and even one-time followers of his. For a similar assessment, see Hegghammer and Lacroix, 'Rejectionist Islamism in Saudi Arabia.'

173 For an example of this, see my own work that was written while I was sympathetic to (Third-Wave) Wahhabism: Qadhi, *Kashf Al-Shubuhat*, 70 and 82. Here, the entire problematic sections of this work, with their clear context and explicit statements, are ignored or reinterpreted, based on the explanations of the original work by modern scholars.

174 Jalāl al-Dīn ʿAbd al-Raḥmān al-Suyūṭī, *Al-Ashbāh Wa-l-Naẓāʾir Fī Qawāʿid Wa-Furūʿ Fiqh al-Shāfiʿiyya*, 1st ed. (Beirut: Dār al-Kutub al-ʿIlmiyya, 1983), 200.

175 His biography may be accessed from his official website: 'Al-Mawqiʿ al-Rasmī Li-Shaykh ʿAbd al-ʿAzīz Bin Bāz,' accessed May 15, 2024, https://binbaz.org.sa/.

176 ʿAbd al-ʿAzīz Ibn Bāz, *Naqd Al-Qawmiyya al-ʿArabiyya ʿalā Ḍawʾ al-Islām Wa-l-Wāqiʿ*, 6th ed. (Riyadh: al-Riʾāsa al-ʿĀmma li-Idārāt al-Buḥūth al-ʿIlmiyya wa-l-Iftā, 1991), 12–15.

177 ʿAbd al-ʿAzīz Ibn Bāz, 'Ḥukm Duʿāʾ Ghayr Allāh ʿan Jahl bi-al-Tawḥīd (Fatwa No. 1210),' *al-Mawqiʿ al-Rasmī li-Shaykh ʿAbd al-ʿAzīz bin Bāz*, accessed May 15, 2024, https://binbaz.org.sa/fatwas/1210/%D8%AD%D9%83%D9%85-%D8%AF%D8%B9%D8%A7%D8%A1-%D8%BA%D9%8A%D8%B1-%D8%A7%D9%84%D9%84%D9%87-%D8%B9%D9%86-%D8%AC%D9%87%D9%84-%D8%A8%D8%A7%D9%84%D8%AA%D9%88%D8%AD%D9%8A%D8%AF.

178 ʿAbd al-ʿAzīz Ibn Bāz, *Majmūʿ Fatāwā Wa-Maqālāt Mutanawwiʿa*, ed. Muḥammad b. Saʿd al-Shuwayʿir (Saudi Arabia: Riʾāsat Idārat al-Buḥūth al-ʿIlmiyya wa-l-Iftāʾ, n.d.), 5:355.

179 Wagemakers, 'The Enduring Legacy of the Second Saudi State,' 98.

180 On a personal note, I was fortunate to study with him during one of his intensive summer sessions, in July–August of 2000, a few months before he passed away. There are still audio tapes of private Q&A sessions I had with the Shaykh (in the presence of some other Western students), and I still retain the handwritten testimony (*tazkiya*) that he wrote for me.

181 See Yusuf al-ʿĪsā, 'Kayfa Munḥa Al-Shaykh Ibn ʿUthaymīn Jāʾizat al-Malik Fayṣal al-ʿĀlamiyya,' *Al-Jazirah*, January 13, 2001, https://www.al-jazirah.com/2001/20010113/ln6.htm.

182 Qadhi, *Kashf Al-Shubuhat*, 98. Here, at the time even I reinterpreted this phrase following Third-Wave rhetoric.

183 Muḥammad b. Ṣāliḥ al-ʿUthaymīn, *Sharḥ Kitāb Kashf Al-Shubuhāt Wa-Yalīhi Sharḥ al-Uṣūl al-Sittah*, ed. Fahd b. Nāṣir b. Ibrāhīm al-Sulaymān, 1st ed. (Riyadh: Dār al-Thurayyā li-l-Nashr, 1996), 35.

184 al-ʿUthaymīn, *Liqāʾ al-bāb al-maftūḥ*, no. 195. This is from an audio recording of Ibn ʿUthaymīn's Q&A sessions, transcribed and printed online.

185 Wagemakers, 'The Enduring Legacy of the Second Saudi State,' 99.

186 For examples of such defenses, see Āl ʿAbd al-Laṭīf, *Daʿāwā al-Munāwiʾīn*, 162–77; Aḥmad b. ʿAbd al-ʿAzīz al-Ḥusayn, *Daʿwat Al-Imām Muḥammad Ibn ʿAbd al-Wahhāb Salafiyya Lā Wahhābiyya*, 1st ed. (Riyadh: Dār ʿĀlam al-Kutub, 1999), 282–85; Ṣāliḥ b. ʿAbd Allāh al-ʿAbūd, *Aqīdat Al-Shaykh Muḥammad Ibn ʿAbd al-Wahhāb al-Salafiyya Wa-Atharuhā Fī al-ʿĀlam al-Islāmī* (Medina: Maktabat al-Ghurabāʾ, 1996), 1:293–5.

187 Mouline, *The Clerics of Islam*, 257 and 260–62. It should be noted here that the model presented above, of a Three-Wave gradual shift, is but one analysis of the phenomenon of Wahhabi development. A more cynical view would be to claim that there were no waves at all. Rather, it can be argued that 'First-Wave' original Wahhabism is and always has been the default and that what have been termed the Second- and Third-Waves were merely politically expedient attempts to pacify the demands placed on the clerical establishment by the Royal Courts of their times. Hence, original Wahhabism is alive and well, tempered only by a doublespeak meant to either curry favor with the ruling authorities or placate the harsh criticism of external critics. While such a harsh view is understandable – and perhaps at some level retains an element of truth – I contend that the evolution of Wahhabi doctrines, as demonstrated in this section, is an undeniable fact. Admittedly, the 'Three Waves' are an organic and fluid continuum and do not have a clear demarcation or explicit break between one and the other. Hence, one will easily find statements and fatwas in all eras that seem to conform to original Wahhabi thought.

188 Lacroix, *Awakening Islam*, 51–62.

189 Hegghammer and Lacroix, 'Rejectionist Islamism in Saudi Arabia,' 105.

190 See Lacroix, *Awakening Islam*, 123.

191 Madawi Al-Rasheed, *Contesting the Saudi State: Islamic Voices from a New Generation*, Cambridge Middle East Studies (Cambridge: Cambridge University Press, 2006), 73, https://doi.org/10.1017/CBO9780511492181.

192 Madawi Al-Rasheed, *Contesting the Saudi State: Islamic Voices from a New Generation*, Cambridge Middle East Studies (Cambridge: Cambridge University Press, 2006), 63, https://doi.org/10.1017/CBO9780511492181. See also Ahmad Kindawi, 'A New Synthesis: Saudi Salafism and the Contested Ideologies of Muhammad Surur' (MA Thesis, Glassboro, NJ, Rowan University, 2020), https://rdw.rowan.edu/etd/2784.
193 Lacroix, *Awakening Islam*; Mamoun Fandy, *Saudi Arabia and the Politics of Dissent*, 1st ed. (Basingstoke: Palgrave, 2001), chaps. 2 and 3. At the time of this writing, both al-Ḥawāli and al-Oudah are imprisoned in Saudi Arabia.
194 Al-Rasheed, *Contesting the Saudi State*, 67.
195 Al-Rasheed, *A History of Saudi Arabia*, 156–57.
196 Al-Rasheed, 156–59.
197 Commins, *The Wahhabi Mission and Saudi Arabia*, 178–82; Lacroix, *Awakening Islam*, 179–93.
198 Al-Rasheed, *A History of Saudi Arabia*, 166–70.
199 Stéphane Lacroix, *Awakening Islam: The Politics of Religious Dissent in Contemporary Saudi Arabia*, trans. George Holoch (Cambridge, Mass.: Harvard University Press, 2011), 164–211.
200 Ahmed Zaghloul Shalata, 'The Salafist Call in Alexandria: The Trajectory of the Organization and Outcomes of Its Politics,' *Contemporary Arab Affairs* 9, no. 3 (2016): 362n2.
201 I heard this claim, in many different settings, directly from al-Madkhalī himself – both in public lectures at the IUM and in private gatherings in his house. In almost any lecture that he was asked to deliver during my time at the IUM, regardless of the topic, he would invariably go on a tangent regarding his thoughts on how sinister the Brotherhood was and the heretical natures of its founder, Ḥasan al-Bannā, and its main propagator, Sayyid Qutb. During these tangents, he would become extremely passionate and emotional, raising his voice to shouting levels as he railed against their influence.
202 A. Sunarwoto, 'Negotiating Salafī Islam and the State: The Madkhaliyya in Indonesia,' May 27, 2020, 206, https://doi.org/10.1163/15700607-06023P03.
203 See Roel Meijer, 'Politicising Al-Jarḥ Wa-l-Taʿdīl: Rabīʿ b. Hādī al-Madkhalī and the Transnational Battle for Religious Authority,' in *The Transmission and Dynamics of the Textual Sources of Islam*, ed. Nicolet Boekhoff-van Der Voort, Kees Versteegh, and Joas Wagemakers (Brill, 2011), 376, 380–81, and 393–95, https://doi.org/10.1163/9789004206786_019.
204 Bonnefoy, *Salafism in Yemen*, 95–96.
205 Sunarwoto, 'Negotiating Salafī Islam and the State,' 219–220.
206 Haykel, 'On the Nature of Salafi Thought and Action,' 50.
207 Haykel, 51.
208 Meijer, 'Politicising Al-Jarḥ Wa-l-Taʿdīl,' 394.
209 Lacroix, 'Egypt's Salafi Awakening in the 1970s,' 211–21. For the sake of full disclosure, it is pertinent to point out that I myself was also the subject of an infamous and fairly well-known (at the time) 'witch-hunt' by this strand and its leaders after being admitted and then, due to the efforts of this strand, expelled, from the graduate program at IUM. The sordid details of that debacle are not worthy of being printed in an academic monograph, but it inevitably caused emotional stress and damage to both myself and my family. In the end, thankfully, the hidden hand of divine justice allowed me to be reinstated and complete the graduate program, after which I graduated with honors and willingly chose to leave and pursue my doctorate elsewhere. Despite this personal grievance, it is hoped that the portrayal of this strand will be assessed as fair and accurate by all those outside the strand.
210 Meijer, 'Politicising Al-Jarḥ Wa-l-Taʿdīl,' 382.
211 Trofimov, *The Siege of Mecca*, 246–47.

212 Trofimov, 245.
213 Lacroix, *Awakening Islam*, 115.
214 Lacroix, 194–200.
215 For more on al-ʿUyayrī, see Roel Meijer, 'Yūsuf Al-ʿUwayrī and the Making of a Salafi Praxis,' in *Kingdom Without Borders: Saudi Arabia's Political, Religious, and Media Frontiers*, ed. Madawi Al-Rasheed (New York: Columbia University Press, 2008), 221–43.
216 See Thomas Hegghammer, *Jihad in Saudi Arabia: Violence and Pan-Islamism Since 1979*, Cambridge Middle East Studies 33 (Cambridge, UK; New York: Cambridge University Press, 2010), 71–76 and 117.
217 On the Shuʿaybī school, see Hegghammer, 83–87; Saud Al-Sarhan, 'The Struggle for Authority: The Shaykhs of Jihadi-Salafism in Saudi Arabia, 1997–2003,' in *Saudi Arabia in Transition: Insights on Social, Political, Economic and Religious Change*, ed. Bernard Haykel, Stéphane Lacroix, and Thomas Hegghammer (Cambridge: Cambridge University Press, 2015), 181–206, https://doi.org/10.1017/CBO9781139047586.013.
218 For an overview of King Salman's reign, see Madawi Al-Rasheed, ed., *Salman's Legacy: The Dilemmas of a New Era in Saudi Arabia* (Oxford; New York, NY: Oxford University Press, 2018).
219 Nicolas Pelham, 'MBS: Despot in the Desert,' *The Economist*, accessed May 10, 2024, https://www.economist.com/1843/2022/07/28/mbs-despot-in-the-desert.
220 See Madawi Al-Rasheed, 'Introduction: The Dilemas of a New Era,' in *Salman's Legacy: The Dilemmas of a New Era in Saudi Arabia*, ed. Madawi Al-Rasheed (Oxford; New York, NY: Oxford University Press, 2018), 19; Madawi Al-Rasheed, 'King Salman and His Son: Winning the United States, Losing the Rest,' in *Salman's Legacy: The Dilemmas of a New Era in Saudi Arabia*, ed. Madawi Al-Rasheed (Oxford; New York, NY: Oxford University Press, 2018), 248–49.
221 This incident became the subject of a documentary in 2020, see *The Dissident*, Documentary, Crime, Thriller (Orwell Productions, Diamond Docs, Human Rights Foundation, 2021).
222 Hassan Hassan, 'The "Conscious Uncoupling" of Wahhabism and Saudi Arabia.' New Lines Magazine, February 22, 2022, https://newlinesmag.com/argument/the-conscious-uncoupling-of-wahhabism-and-saudi-arabia/. However, it must be noted that this is a traditional Saudi attitude and was expressed in similar terms by King Ibn Saud in 1934: 'We obey neither Ibn ʿAbd al-Wahhāb nor any other person, unless what they say is clearly endorsed by God's Book and the Prophet's Sunna. God made us – me, my fathers and my ancestors, preachers, and teachers, according to the Qurʾān and the Sunna... Wherever we find strong evidence in any of the four madhhabs, we refer and hold to it. Otherwise, whenever strong evidence is lacking, we adopt the opinion of Imām Aḥmad [Ibn Ḥanbal].' Cited in Muhammad K. Al-Atawneh, *Wahhabi Islam Facing the Challenges of Modernity: Dar Al-Ifta in the Modern Saudi State*, Studies in Islamic Law and Society 32 (Leiden; Boston: Brill, 2010), 74. The difference is not in the expressed sentiment but in the intent and effects: the founder was trying to claim that Wahhābism is, in reality, true Islam that is in accordance with the Qurʾan and hadith, whereas the current prince is actively promoting alternative authorities.
223 See his response at *Tawḍīḥ Min Al-Shaykh Ṣāliḥ al-Mughāmisī Ḥawla Tashbīhih Qiṣṣat Jamāl Khāshuqjī Bi-Qiṣṣat Khālid Ibn al-Walīd*, 2018, https://www.youtube.com/watch?v=R6LeKnAvO-Y. Here, he said that even if this occurred, the Companions of the Prophet made similar or worse mistakes for which they were excused.
224 For a detailed discussion on the rise of the Islamic University of Medina and the role it played in spreading the Wahhabi message across the globe, see Michael Farquhar, *Circuits of Faith: Migration, Education, and the Wahhabi Mission* (Stanford: Stanford University Press, 2016); there are, of course, other universities, in particular the Imam Muḥammad ibn Saʿūd University in Riyadh. However, all other universities in the

country are primarily meant for Saudis; any foreigners in such universities are exceptions to the norm. For an overview of the impact of IUM and other Saudi universities in the spread of Wahhabi-Salafism, see Christopher Anzalone and Yasir Qadhi, 'From Dir'iyya to Riyadh: The History and Global Impact of Saudi Religious Propagation and Education,' in *Wahhabism and the World: Understanding Saudi Arabia's Global Influence on Islam*, ed. Peter Mandaville, Religion and Global Politics (Oxford; New York: Oxford University Press, 2022), 53–75.

225 Mouline, *The Clerics of Islam*, 188.

226 Disclaimer: As has been noted in the Introduction, I am a graduate of this university, having spent over a decade there from 1995 to 2005. I did one year of the Arabic diploma, a four-year BA from the College of Hadith and Islamic Sciences (completed in 2000), and an MA in Islamic Theology (*ʿaqīda*) from the College of Daʿwa (Homiletics) for four-and-a-half years (completed in 2005). Much of the reflections here will, therefore, also be anecdotal and based on my own studies and interactions. While, understandably, some will find my assessments or opinions problematic, there is no intent to disparage or denigrate either the University or any of its professors. I am grateful for my time spent there, and I have deep respect for many of its professors and my fellow students.

227 Mouline, *The Clerics of Islam*, 188–90.

228 Farquhar, *Circuits of Faith*, 77.

229 See also Farquhar, 87–88.

230 Farquhar, 88–91.

231 Lacroix, *Awakening Islam*, 47.

232 Lacroix, 148.

233 Farquhar, *Circuits of Faith*, 92–93.

234 Mike Farquhar, 'The Islamic University of Medina since 1961: The Politics of Religious Mission and the Making of a Modern Salafi Pedagogy1,' in *Shaping Global Islamic Discourses: The Role of al-Azhar, al-Medina and al-Mustafa*, ed. Masooda Bano and Keiko Sakurai (Edinburgh University Press, 2015), 24–25, https://doi.org/10.3366/edinburgh/9780748696857.003.0002. See also Michael Farquhar, *Circuits of Faith: Migration, Education, and the Wahhabi Mission* (Stanford: Stanford University Press, 2016), chaps. 3 and 4; Stéphane Lacroix, *Awakening Islam: The Politics of Religious Dissent in Contemporary Saudi Arabia*, trans. George Holoch (Cambridge, Mass.: Harvard University Press, 2011); Jacob Olidort, 'In Defense of Tradition: Muḥammad Nāṣir Al-Dīn al-Albānī and the Salafī Method' (PhD, Princeton, NJ, Princeton University, 2015), http://arks.princeton.edu/ark:/88435/dsp01nz8062003.

235 Initially, they only accepted those under the age of thirty-five, but this was later reduced to twenty-five. See Farquhar, *Circuits of Faith*, 160.

236 During my time as a student, from 1995 until 2005, I had over a hundred professors who taught me in my diploma, undergraduate, and graduate studies – and precisely two were from a non-Saudi background. Contrast this with what I was told by the first Western graduates of the late 1970s and early '80s, who told me that all of their professors were non-Saudis, except those who taught theology (*ʿaqida*).

237 Lacroix, *Awakening Islam*, 214. This was also an observable and well-known phenomenon during my ten years at IUM.

238 Farquhar, *Circuits of Faith*, 70–71.

239 Farquhar, 70–71.

240 Farquhar, 162–69.

241 I remember a particularly sad incident during my time at the IUM, where a student who was one semester away from graduating confessed to a fellow student, whom he thought to be a friend, that he was not a fan of Salafi theology and did not admire Ibn Taymiyya and Ibn ʿAbd al-Wahhāb, and instead, that he was sympathetic to Deobandīsm and Maturidī theology. The other student filed an official complaint with

Student Affairs. The first student was called in for questioning, interrogated, and then expelled. Nevertheless, it is only fair to mention that, during the course of my decade studying there, such incidents were rare, and I personally knew of many students who did not subscribe to Salafi theology but were private about their beliefs and wished to study in the Holy City and benefit from the other subjects taught.

242 See 'Islamic University of Madinah Joins Guinness World Records,' accessed May 9, 2024, https://www.spa.gov.sa/2364981.

243 Taken from the official website of the University, see 'Al-Jāmiʿa al-Islāmiyya Bi-l-Madīna al-Munawwara,' accessed June 9, 2024, https://www.iu.edu.sa/.

244 'Islamic University of Medinah,' accessed May 9, 2024, https://iu.edu.sa/Postgraduates.

245 Ibid.

246 'Board of Directors | Union of African Muslim Schollars,' accessed May 9, 2024, http://africanulama.org/en/membre-admin/.

247 'Mogadishu University,' accessed June 9, 2024, https://mu.edu.so/.

248 'Islamic University of Medinah.'

249 'Ambassador – Embassy of Sierra Leone, Saudi Arabia,' accessed May 9, 2024, https://sa.slembassy.gov.sl/ambassador-2/.

250 'Sheikh Abdullah Awad Al Juhany Biography – Inside the Haramain,' accessed May 9, 2024, https://www.haramainsharifain.com/sheikh-abdullah-awad-al-juhany-biography/.

251 'Al-Masjid al-Kabīr,' accessed June 9, 2024, https://thegrandmosque.awqaf.gov.kw/ar.

252 'Mufti Ismail Musa Menk | The Muslim 500,' accessed May 9, 2024, https://themuslim500.com/profiles/mufti-ismail-musa-menk/.

253 'Majlisul Ulama Zimbabwe,' accessed June 9, 2024, https://majlis.org.zw/index.html.

254 'Tomasz Miśkiewicz,' accessed June 9, 2024, https://mzr.pl/zyciorys/.

255 'Professor Choi Young Kil-Hamed – King Faisal Foundation,' accessed May 9, 2024, https://www.kff.com/king-faisal-prize/professor-choi-young-kil-hamed/.

256 'Islamic University of Medinah.'

257 'Executive Member – All India Muslim Personal Law Board,' accessed May 9, 2024, https://aimplb.org/executive-members/.

258 'Wifaq Ul Madaris Al Arabia Pakistan,' accessed May 9, 2024, https://www.wifaqulmadaris.org/.

259 'The Islamic Sharia Council,' accessed May 9, 2024, https://www.islamic-sharia.org/.

260 'European Council For Fatwa And Research,' accessed May 9, 2024, https://www.e-cfr.org/en/.

261 'AMJA Members | AMJA Online,' accessed May 9, 2024, https://www.amjaonline.org/about/amja-members/.

262 'About – Fiqh Council of North America,' accessed May 9, 2024, https://fiqhcouncil.org/about/.

263 'The Islamic Seminary of America,' accessed May 9, 2024, https://islamicseminary.us/about-us/.

264 'EPIC's Team – EPIC Masjid,' accessed June 9, 2024, https://epicmasjid.org/epics-team/.

## 4 SALAFISM AND ISLAMISM

1 Aḥmad b. ʿAbd al-Razzāq al-Duwaysh, *Fatāwā Al-Lajna al-Dāʾima Li-l-Buḥūth al-ʿIlmiyya Wa-l-Iftā* (Riyahd: Dār al-Muʾayyad, 2003), 2:237.

2 https://arabic.cnn.com/middle-east/article/2020/11/16/saudi-ifta-muslim-brotherhood (last accessed Apr 2024).

3 On the term Islamism, see Chapter 1, note 6.

4 For the history and study of the Muslim Brotherhood, see Richard P. Mitchell, *The Society of the Muslim Brothers* (New York: Oxford University Press, 1993) which

was first published in 1969; Brynjar Lia, *The Society of the Muslim Brothers in Egypt: The Rise of an Islamic Mass Movement 1928–1942*, 1st ed. (Reading, England: Ithaca Press, 1999); Alison Pargeter, *The Muslim Brotherhood: From Opposition to Power*, New ed. (London: Saqi, 2013); Carrie Rosefsky Wickham, *The Muslim Brotherhood: Evolution of an Islamist Movement*, 1st ed. (Princeton: Princeton University Press, 2013); Victor J. Willi, *The Fourth Ordeal: A History of the Muslim Brotherhood in Egypt, 1968–2018* (Cambridge, UK; New York, NY: Cambridge University Press, 2021); for an introduction to the life of Ḥasan al-Bannā, see Gudrun Krämer, *Hasan Al-Banna* (Oxford: Oneworld Academic, 2009).

5 Mitchell, *The Society of the Muslim Brothers*, 328.

6 For a study of al-Naḥda, see Mohamed Elhachmi Hamdi, *The Politicisation of Islam: A Case Study of Tunisia*, State, Culture & Society in Arab North Africa (Boulder, Colo.: Westview Press, 1998).

7 Mitchell, *The Society of the Muslim Brothers*, 1.

8 The *musnad* is a hadith collection that is traditionally organized by the names of the original Companions who transmitted each tradition, making it inherently challenging to locate specific traditions based on the subject matter. In response to this challenge, al-Saʿati spent decades sifting over each tradition and placing it in a thematic, chapter-based format, greatly enhancing its accessibility for reference purposes. This substantial undertaking culminated in the creation of a comprehensive work titled *Fatḥ al-Rabbānī fī Tartīb Musnad al-Imam Aḥmad ibn Ḥanbal al-Shaybānī (The Divine Victory in Arranging the Musnad of Imam Ahmad ibn Ḥanbal al-Shaybānī)*, spanning twenty-four volumes.

9 Wickham, *The Muslim Brotherhood*, 21; Mitchell, *The Society of the Muslim Brothers*, 2.

10 Lia, *The Society of the Muslim Brothers in Egypt*, 224.

11 Victor J. Willi, *The Fourth Ordeal: A History of the Muslim Brotherhood in Egypt, 1968–2018* (Cambridge, UK; New York, NY: Cambridge University Press, 2021), 17–18.

12 Lia, *The Society of the Muslim Brothers in Egypt*, 38.

13 Ḥasan al-Bannā, *Five Tracts of Ḥasan Al-Bannā (1906–1949): A Selection from the Majmūʿat Rasāʾil Al-Imām Al-Shahīd Ḥasan Al-Bannā*, trans. Charles Wendell, University of California Publications : Near Eastern Studies ; v. 20 (Berkeley: University of California Press, 1978), 5.

14 Hasan al-Bannā, *A Treatise on the Islamic Faith*, ed. Uwais Namazi Nadwi, trans. Mustafa Umar, n.d., 87.

15 al-Bannā, 88.

16 al-Bannā, 88.

17 Krämer, *Hasan Al-Banna*, 54.

18 Krämer, 5.

19 Mitchell, *The Society of the Muslim Brothers*, 217.

20 For a study of Sayyid Qutb's life and thought, see John Calvert, *Sayyid Qutb and the Origins of Radical Islamism*, 1st ed. (New York, NY: Oxford University Press, 2018).

21 Pargeter, *The Muslim Brotherhood*, 187–88; Hasan al-Hudaybi, the second leader of the Muslim Brotherhood, defended Qutb against charges of extremism, but even he had to write a treatise, entitled *Duʿat wa la Qudat* (*Preachers, Not Judges*), which indirectly refuted egregious meanings being found in Qutb's work. For a study of this work by al-Hudaybi, see Barbara Zollner, *The Muslim Brotherhood: Hasan Al-Hudaybi and Ideology*, 1st ed. (London; New York: Routledge, 2008).

22 Calvert, *Sayyid Qutb and the Origins of Radical Islamism*, 160.

23 Wagemakers, *Salafism in Jordan*, 111.

24 Lia, *The Society of the Muslim Brothers in Egypt*, 140–42.

25 Lia, 142–43.
26 Lauzière, *The Making of Salafism*, 2016, 73.
27 Willi, *The Fourth Ordeal*, 115.
28 Lia, *The Society of the Muslim Brothers in Egypt*, 143–44.
29 Willi, *The Fourth Ordeal*, 115–16.
30 Lacroix, *Awakening Islam*, 39–40.
31 Lauzière, *The Making of Salafism*, 2016, 126–27.
32 Stéphane Lacroix, 'Unpacking the Saudi-Salafi Connection in Egypt,' in *Wahhabism and the World: Understanding Saudi Arabia's Global Influence on Islam*, ed. Peter Mandaville, Religion and Global Politics (Oxford; New York: Oxford University Press, 2022), 258.
33 Cited in Hebatullah Nazy Sayed Selim, 'Religionizing Politics: Salafis and Social Change in Egypt' (PhD, University of Birmingham, 2017), 77, https://etheses.bham.ac.uk/id/eprint/7636/.
34 See http://m-noor.com/showthread.php?p=29312 (last accessed Jun, 2021).
35 See Al-Rasheed, *A History of Saudi Arabia*, 92–96; Toby Matthiesen, 'Migration, Minorities, and Radical Networks: Labour Movements and Opposition Groups in Saudi Arabia, 1950–1975,' *International Review of Social History* 59, no. 3 (2014): 473–504.
36 Al-Rasheed, *A History of Saudi Arabia*, 102–8.
37 Mouline, *The Clerics of Islam*, 126–28.
38 Lacroix, *Awakening Islam*, 41–42.
39 Farquhar, *Circuits of Faith*, 87–88 and 92–93.
40 See Willi, *The Fourth Ordeal*, 116; Calvert, *Sayyid Qutb and the Origins of Radical Islamism*, 233.
41 Zollner, *The Muslim Brotherhood*, 34.
42 Calvert, *Sayyid Qutb and the Origins of Radical Islamism*, 191.
43 Zollner, *The Muslim Brotherhood*, 41.
44 Mouline, *The Clerics of Islam*, 130–32.
45 Calvert, *Sayyid Qutb and the Origins of Radical Islamism*, 238.
46 Calvert, 261.
47 Willi, *The Fourth Ordeal*, 116–17.
48 See Willi, 117–20 and 128.
49 Robert G. Rabil, *Salafism in Lebanon: From Apoliticism to Transnational Jihadism* (Washington, DC: Georgetown University Press, 2014), 41–42; Lacroix, *Awakening Islam*, 43.
50 Lacroix, *Awakening Islam*, 43–44.
51 See Adil Salahi, 'Scholar of Renown Sheikh Ali Al-Tantawi,' *Arab News*, June 19, 2001, https://www.arabnews.com/node/212775; Adil Salahi, 'Scholar of Renown: Sheikh Ali Al-Tantawi: II,' *Arab News*, June 25, 2001, https://www.arabnews.com/node/213339.
52 Farquhar, *Circuits of Faith*, 94.
53 Lacroix, *Awakening Islam*, 43.
54 Calvert, *Sayyid Qutb and the Origins of Radical Islamism*, 308.
55 Lacroix, *Awakening Islam*, 42.
56 It has been argued by Husam Tammam that Qaradawi 'was the most influential dāʿī [preacher] in the history of the Muslim Brothers' who came to possess a certain independent seniority 'in the orbit of the Muslim Brothers,' without a known official position within the group. Qaradawi was also able to have a relatively good relationship with political Salafis like Salman Oudah. Ghazali was one of the earliest Azharis to join the Brotherhood; but he was expelled, along with Sayyid Sabiq, another prominent Azhari in the Brotherhood, because of their attempt to replace Hudaybi as leader of the Brotherhood in 1952. Nonetheless, Ghazali remained a symbol of Brotherhood

thought, despite him going on to work with the Nasser regime. See Calvert, *Sayyid Qutb and the Origins of Radical Islamism*, 204–5; Husam Tammam, 'Yūsuf Qaraḍāwī and the Muslim Brothers: The Nature of a Special Relationship,' in *Global Mufti: The Phenomenon of Yūsuf al-Qaraḍāwī*, ed. Bettina Gräf and Jakob Skovgaard-Petersen (London: C. Hurst & Company, 2009), 55, 59, 73–74, 77, and 82; Mitchell, *The Society of the Muslim Brothers*, 124.

57 Willi, *The Fourth Ordeal*, 69 and 74–75.

58 Willi, 85–86 and 165.

59 Stéphane Lacroix, 'Egypt's Pragmatic Salafis: The Politics of Hizb Al-Nour,' *Carnegie Endowment for International Peace.*, November 1, 2016, 4–5, https://carnegieendowment.org/research/2016/11/egypts-pragmatic-salafis-the-politics-of-hizb-al-nour?lang=en.

60 Alaa Al-Din Arafat, *Egypt in Crisis: The Fall of Islamism and Prospects of Democratization*, 1st ed. (Cham: Palgrave Macmillan, 2017), 69.

61 Al-Rasheed, *A History of Saudi Arabia*, 151–52.

62 Calvert, *Sayyid Qutb and the Origins of Radical Islamism*, 287.

63 Abu Iyaad, 'Al-Fawzan, Al-Luhaydan, Aal Al-Shaykh: The Ikhwan (Muslim Brotherhood) Are From the 72 Sects, Use Secrecy and Aim Only to Seek Power,' *Ikhwanis.Com* (blog), accessed August 10, 2019, http://www.ikhwanis.com/articles/lwakzes-the-ikhwan-muslim-brotherhood-are-from-the-72-sects.cfm.

64 Abu Iyaad.

65 Fatāwā al-lajna al-dāʾima, Senior Fatwa Committee of Saudi Arabia, vol. 2, 237, no. 6250.

66 Fatāwā al-lajna al-dāʾima, Senior Fatwa Committee of Saudi Arabia, vol. 2, 238, no. 6280.

67 Jeffry R. Halverson, *Theology and Creed in Sunni Islam: The Muslim Brotherhood, Ash'arism, and Political Sunnism* (New York, NY: Palgrave Macmillan, 2010), chap. 3.

68 Willi, *The Fourth Ordeal*, 163–65; Shalata, 'The Salafist Call in Alexandria,' 351–64.

69 John Chalcraft, 'Egypt's 25 January Uprising, Hegemonic Contestation, and the Explosion of the Poor,' in *The New Middle East: Protest and Revolution in the Arab World*, ed. Fawaz A. Gerges (Cambridge: Cambridge University Press, 2013), 155–79, https://doi.org/10.1017/CBO9781139236737.009.

70 Lacroix, 'Egypt's Pragmatic Salafis,' 5.

71 Jacob Høigilt and Frida Nome, 'Egyptian Salafism in Revolution,' *Journal of Islamic Studies* 25 (January 8, 2014): 33–54, https://doi.org/10.1093/jis/ett056.

72 Arafat, *Egypt in Crisis*, 68–69.

73 Lacroix, 'Unpacking the Saudi-Salafi Connection in Egypt,' 257.

74 Ashraf El-Sherif, 'Egypt's Salafists at a Crossroads,' *Carnegie Endowment for International Peace*, 2015, 9.

75 See Richard Gauvain, *Salafi Ritual Purity: In the Presence of God*, 1st ed., Routledge Islamic Studies Series (New York, NY: Routledge, 2017), chap. 2.

76 See Lacroix, 'Unpacking the Saudi-Salafi Connection in Egypt.'

77 Lacroix, 258.

78 Abdullah A. Al-Arian, *Answering the Call: Popular Islamic Activism in Sadat's Egypt*, Religion and Global Politics (Oxford ; New York: Oxford University Press, 2014), 132–33.

79 These are the views attributed to Cherif Abdel-Meguid and Anas Abdel Fattah Abou Shadi, co-founders of the Azhari telephone-fatwa service called el-Hatef el-Islami in the UK in 2009. See Gauvain, 'Salafism in Modern Egypt.'

80 Gauvain, 811–14; for a study of Gomaa's position in Egypt in relation to the Arab Spring and the anti-Morsi coup, see Usaama Al-Azami, *Islam and the Arab Revolutions: The Ulama Between Democracy and Autocracy* (Oxford: Oxford University Press, 2022).

81 Al-Rasheed, *A History of Saudi Arabia*, 222–23.
82 See 'King Fahd's Speech on the Issuance of the Basic Law of Governance,' The Embassy of The Kingdom of Saudi Arabia, accessed March 10, 2024, https://www.saudiembassy.net/king-fahds-speech-issuance-basic-law-governance.
83 Al-Rasheed, *A History of Saudi Arabia*, 190–91 and 226.
84 'Naif Says Muslim Brotherhood Cause of Most Arab Problems,' *Arab News*, November 28, 2002, https://www.arabnews.com/node/226291; Al-Rasheed, *A History of Saudi Arabia*, 226–27.
85 Al-Rasheed, *A History of Saudi Arabia*, 227.
86 Wickham, *The Muslim Brotherhood*, 117–19.
87 Gauvain, *Salafi Ritual Purity:*, 41–43 and 287–88n47.
88 These were al-Nass, al-Hafith, al-Baraka, al-Rahma, al-Hekma, al-Majd TV, al-Fajr, al-Huda, al-Efasi, al-Madinah, al-Ummah, and Tiba.
89 He was seen as Nāṣir al-Diī al-Albānī's foremost student in Egypt, but he came to be linked to the activist Salafi ʿAbd al-Raḥmān ʿAbd al-Khāliq after the 2011 revolution.
90 Tarek Ghanem, 'Muslim Media in the Post-Arab Spring: The Curious Case of Egypt,' March 18, 2020, *Maydan* (blog), accessed January 14, 2023, https://themaydan.com/2020/03/muslim-media-in-the-post-arab-spring-the-curious-case-of-egypt/.
91 Raihan Ismail, *Rethinking Salafism: The Transnational Networks of Salafi 'Ulama in Egypt, Kuwait, and Saudi Arabia* (Oxford; New York: Oxford University Press, 2021), 47.
92 Nathan Field and Ahmed Hamam, 'Salafi Satellite Tv in Egypt,' *Arab Media & Society* Spring (January 1, 2009).
93 Ismail, *Rethinking Salafism*, 47.
94 Usaama al-Azami, 'Neo-Traditionalist Sufis and Arab Politics: A Preliminary Mapping of the Transnational Networks of Counter-Revolutionary Scholars after the Arab Revolutions,' in *Global Sufism: Boundaries, Structures, and Politics*, ed. Mark Sedgwick and Francesco Piraino (London: Hurst, 2019), 225–36 and 278–83.
95 For an elaboration of the events surrounding Qaradawi and Gomaa, and the related geopolitical factors, see Al-Azami, *Islam and the Arab Revolutions*; the dispute can also be epitomized with Qaradawi against Abdullah bin Bayyah, with each representing the positions taken up by Qatar and UAE, respectively. See David H. Warren, *Rivals in the Gulf: Yusuf al-Qaradawi, Abdullah Bin Bayyah, and the Qatar-Uae Contest Over the Arab Spring and the Gulf Crisis*, Islam in the World (London New York: Routledge, Taylor & Francis Group, 2021).
96 See Mohammad Fadel, 'Islamic Law and Constitution-Making: The Authoritarian Temptation and the Arab Spring,' *Osgoode Hall Law Journal* 53, no. 2 (January 1, 2016): 472–507, https://doi.org/10.60082/2817-5069.2994.
97 See David H. Warren, 'Cleansing the Nation of the "Dogs of Hell": ʿAli Jumʿa's Nationalist Legal Reasoning in Support of the 2013 Egyptian Coup and Its Bloody Aftermath,' *International Journal of Middle East Studies* 49, no. 3 (2017): 457–77.
98 Arafat, *Egypt in Crisis*, 13–14.
99 Jonathan A. C. Brown, 'Salafis and Sufis in Egypt,' *Carnegie Endowment for International Peace*, December 20, 2011, 1–16.
100 al-Anani, 'Unpacking the Sacred Canopy,' 25–42.
101 Jonathan A. C. Brown, 'The Rise and Fall of the Salafi Al-Nour Party in Egypt,' *Jadaliyya* (blog), November 14, 2013, https://www.jadaliyya.com/Details/29813.
102 Lacroix, 'Egypt's Pragmatic Salafis,' 6–8.
103 Arafat, *Egypt in Crisis*, 69–70.
104 Arafat, 69–70.
105 Ctied in Shalata, 'The Salafist Call in Alexandria,' 359.
106 Ismail, *Rethinking Salafism*, 51.
107 El-Sherif, 'Egypt's Salafists at a Crossroads.'

108 For a breakdown of the names attributed to these factions, see El-Sherif, 23; Al-Qusi was a 'Quṭbī' in the 1970s before studying in Saudi Arabia and shedding his political orientation, see Ismail, *Rethinking Salafism*, 46.
109 Gauvain, *Salafi Ritual Purity*, 39–47.
110 For 'Abd al-Maqsud's views on the demonstrations of the Arab Spring, see Abdul Maqsood, 'Shaykh Abdul Maqsood's Ruling on the Events in Egypt,' *Virtual Mosque* (blog), February 5, 2011, https://www.virtualmosque.com/society/international/shaykh-abdul-maqsoods-ruling-on-the-events-in-egypt/.
111 Gauvain, *Salafi Ritual Purity*, 239 and 287n45.
112 Arafat, *Egypt in Crisis*, 70; Wickham, *The Muslim Brotherhood*, 171.
113 Wickham, *The Muslim Brotherhood*, 194.
114 Wickham, 249.
115 Wickham, 195.
116 Wickham, 251–52.
117 Arafat, *Egypt in Crisis*, 70.
118 Lacroix, 'Egypt's Pragmatic Salafis,' 5–9.
119 Wickham, *The Muslim Brotherhood*, 251–64.
120 Lacroix, 'Egypt's Pragmatic Salafis,' 9.
121 See El-Sherif, 'Egypt's Salafists at a Crossroads.'
122 Brown, 'The Rise and Fall of the Salafi Al-Nour Party.'
123 Wickham, *The Muslim Brotherhood*, 252–53 and 265.
124 Arafat, *Egypt in Crisis*, 70.
125 Arafat, 71.
126 Arafat, 71.
127 Lacroix, 'Egypt's Pragmatic Salafis.'
128 Arafat, *Egypt in Crisis*, 4 and 20.
129 Arafat, 71.
130 Arafat, 72.
131 Arafat, 73.
132 Ismail, *Rethinking Salafism*, 54.
133 Arafat, *Egypt in Crisis*, 117–25.
134 Lacroix, 'Egypt's Pragmatic Salafis,' 12; See also 'Ṣūra 'Miṣr 3 Yūliyū 2013': Taʿarraf ʿalā Man Taraqā.. Wa-Man Ẓalla Fī Manṣibih.. Wa-Man Yugharrid Khārij al-Kādir,' *CNN*, July 3, 2015, https://arabic.cnn.com/middleeast/2015/07/03/egypt-memory-picture.
135 Arafat, *Egypt in Crisis*, 126.
136 Arafat, 118; El-Sherif, 'Egypt's Salafists at a Crossroads.'
137 Patrick Kingsley, 'Egypt Massacre Was Premeditated, Says Human Rights Watch,' *The Guardian*, August 12, 2014, https://www.theguardian.com/world/2014/aug/12/egypt-massacre-rabaa-intentional-human-rights-watch; Arafat, *Egypt in Crisis*, 129.
138 'He who comes to you when you are united and wants to divide you, kill him' in *Ṣāḥīḥ Muslim: kitāb al-imāra, bāb ḥukm man farraqa amra al-muslimīn wa-huwa mujtamiʿ*.
139 Warren, 'Cleansing the Nation of the 'Dogs of Hell': ʿAli Jumʿa's Nationalist Legal Reasoning in Support of the 2013 Egyptian Coup and Its Bloody Aftermath.'
140 Brown, 'The Rise and Fall of the Salafi Al-Nour Party.'
141 Ismail, *Rethinking Salafism*, 55.
142 Lacroix, 'Egypt's Pragmatic Salafis,' 13–14.
143 Lacroix, 15.
144 Lacroix, 13.
145 Lacroix, 14–15.
146 Lacroix, 2.

147 Nadine Dahan, 'Popular Egyptian Preacher Silenced Following Spat with Tv Personality,' *Middle East Eye*, September 25, 2018, https://www.middleeasteye.net/news/popular-egyptian-preacher-silenced-following-spat-tv-personality.
148 Frederic Wehrey and Anouar Boukhars, *Salafism in the Maghreb: Politics, Piety, and Militancy* (New York, NY: Oxford University Press, 2019), 55.
149 Hani Mohamad, 'Egypt: Salafist TV Sheikh Renounces Salafism in Court,' *Daraj*, June 17, 2021, https://daraj.media/en/egypt-salafist-tv-sheikh-renounces-salafism-in-court/. Hassan's testimony in August 2021 was reported in a rather innocuous manner and concentrated on his unsurprising disavowal of the Muslim Brotherhood; see 'An Egyptian Preacher Disavowed the Brotherhood,' *Arab Observer*, August 8, 2021, https://www.arabobserver.com/an-egyptian-preacher-disavowed-the-brotherhood/.
150 Lacroix, 'Egypt's Pragmatic Salafis,' 18.
151 See 'Egypt's Salafist Nour Party Endorses Sisi for Another Term,' *The New Arab*, October 5, 2023, https://www.newarab.com/news/egypts-salafist-nour-party-endorses-sisi-another-term; and Reuters, 'Egypt's Sisi Wins Third Term as President After Amending Constitution,' *The Guardian*, December 19, 2023, https://www.theguardian.com/world/2023/dec/19/egypt-2023-presidential-election-results-abdel-fattah-al-sisi-wins-no-challengers.
152 Besnik Sinani, 'Post-Salafism: Religious Revisionism in Contemporary Saudi Arabia,' *Religions* 13, no. 4 (April 2022): 340, https://doi.org/10.3390/rel13040340.
153 Mohamed Mokhtar Qandil, 'The Muslim Brotherhood and Saudi Arabia: From Then to Now,' *The Washington Institute*, May 18, 2018, https://www.washingtoninstitute.org/policy-analysis/muslim-brotherhood-and-saudi-arabia-then-now.
154 'Saudi Arabia Takes Aim at Muslim Brotherhood before Democrats Take over in Washington,' *The Economic Times*, November 18, 2020, https://economictimes.indiatimes.com/news/international/saudi-arabia/saudi-arabia-takes-aim-at-muslim-brotherhood-before-democrats-take-over-in-washington/articleshow/79286964.cms?from=mdr.
155 Sermon delivered Nov 11, 2020, from the Grand Mosque. See *Al-Shaykh ʿAbd al-Raḥmān al-Sudays Jamāʿat al-Ikhwān al-Muslimīn Jamāʿa Irhābiyya* (YouTube, 2020), https://www.youtube.com/watch?v=koCa9nJ0pQg.
156 The story of the Muslim Brotherhood in modern Palestine is dominated by their creation of Hamas, and so it is not of direct relevance to our discussion of the Brotherhood and Salafism – as Hamas has become its own political entity, and not merely a Muslim Brotherhood organization.
157 Wagemakers, *Salafism in Jordan*, 102.
158 Cited in Weismann, 'The Politics of Popular Religion,' 52.
159 Raphael Lefevre, *Ashes of Hama: The Muslim Brotherhood in Syria*, 1st ed. (Oxford University Press, 2013), 86–90.
160 Wagemakers, *Salafism in Jordan*, 103; Hamdeh, *Salafism and Traditionalism*, 52–55.
161 Pierret, *Religion and State in Syria*, 107 and 169.
162 Thomas Hegghammer, *The Caravan: Abdallah Azzam and the Rise of Global Jihad*, 1st ed. (Cambridge: Cambridge University Press, 2020), 92.
163 'IUMS Mourns the Death of Sheikh Zuhair Al-Shawish.'
164 Umar F. Abd-Allah and Hamid Algar, *Islamic Struggle in Syria*, 1st ed. (Berkeley: Mizan Pr, 1983); Lefevre, *Ashes of Hama*.
165 Hegghammer, *The Caravan*, 198–99.
166 Conduit, *The Muslim Brotherhood in Syria*, 21–26.
167 Wickham, *The Muslim Brotherhood*, 195.
168 Wagemakers, *Salafism in Jordan*, 230; Pierret, *Religion and State in Syria*, 107; Hamdeh, *Salafism and Traditionalism*, 49.
169 Wagemakers, *Salafism in Jordan*, 59 and 90.
170 Wagemakers, 106.

171 Hamdeh, *Salafism and Traditionalism*, 49–52.
172 Wagemakers, *Salafism in Jordan*, 106 and 111–12.
173 Wagemakers, 219.
174 Wagemakers, 157–58.
175 Wagemakers, 220–23.
176 This section is largely indebted to the research of Courtney Freer, 'The Rise of Pragmatic Islamism in Kuwait's Post-Arab Spring Opposition Movement,' *The Brookings Institution*, Rethinking Political Islam, August 2015.
177 Wagemakers, *Salafism in Jordan*, 109–10 and 113–14.
178 Bjørn Olav Utvik, 'The Ikhwanization of the Salafis: Piety in the Politics of Egypt and Kuwait,' *Middle East Critique* 23, no. 1 (January 2, 2014): 5–27, https://doi.org/10.1080/19436149.2014.896597.

## 5 THE PHENOMENON OF JIHADI-SALAFISM

1 Hegghammer, *The Caravan*, 40.
2 ʿAbd al-Hakim, ʿUmar, *The Global Resistance Call*, 1060.
3 For a discussion of essentially Qur'anic notions of peace and war, see Ramon Harvey, *The Qur'an and the Just Society*, 1st ed. (Edinburgh: Edinburgh University Press, 2019), chaps 6 and 7.
4 For a discussion of jihad as a state policy aimed at establishing God's religion in the world, spanning from the Prophetic era in 623 CE for over a century until the decline of the Umayyads, prior to the onset of military weakness, defeats, and diminishing support for persisting in unsuccessful missions, see Khalid Yahya Blankinship, *The End of the Jihad State: The Reign of Hisham Ibn 'abd Al-Malik and the Collapse of the Umayyads* (Albany: State University of New York Press, 1994). For a more general discussion of the history of jihad, including its application by various Islamic dynasties such as the Abbasids and the Ottomans, both of whom notably reinvigorated the state-led obligation to partake in jihad – with the Ottomans achieving remarkable feats like the conquest of Constantinople in 1453, see Michael Bonner, *Jihad in Islamic History: Doctrines and Practice*, 1st ed. (Princeton: Princeton University Press, 2006).ng
5 Alexander Thurston, 'Jihadists of North Africa and the Sahel: Local Politics and Rebel Groups,' *Journal of Islamic Studies*, June 11, 2024, 1, https://doi.org/10.1093/jis/etae019.
6 Alexander Thurston, 'Algeria's GIA: The First Major Armed Group to Fully Subordinate Jihadism to Salafism,' *Islamic Law and Society* 24, no. 4 (2017): 412–36; Jerome Drevon, *Institutionalizing Violence: Strategies of Jihad in Egypt* (Oxford; New York: Oxford University Press, 2022), chap. 3.
7 ʿAbd al-Hakim, ʿUmar, *The Global Resistance Call*, 1060.
8 On the complexity surrounding this popular categorization, see Joas Wagemakers, 'A Purist Jihadi-Salafi: The Ideology of Abu Muhammad al-Maqdisi,' *British Journal of Middle Eastern Studies* 36, no. 2 (2009): 281–97; Wagemakers, 'Revisiting Wiktorowicz: Categorising and Defining the Branches of Salafism'; Reuven Paz, 'Debates Within the Family: Jihadi-Salafi Debates on Strategy, Takfir, Extremism, Suicide Bombings, and the Sense of the Apocalypse,' in *Global Salafism: Islam's New Religious Movement*, ed. Roel Meijer (Oxford University Press, 2014), 0, https://doi.org/10.1093/acprof:oso/9780199333431.003.0012; for a discussion on how the three groups of Salafis identified by Wiktorowicz differ on even theological issues, see Meijer, 'Yūsuf Al-ʿUwayrī.'
9 Alexander Thurston, *Salafism in Nigeria: Islam, Preaching, and Politics*, Reprint ed. (London: Cambridge University Press, 2018), 195 and 209–10.

10 Darryl Li, 'Will the Real Jihadi Please Stand Up?: On "Jihadism" as a Conceptual Weapon,' in *Disentangling Jihad, Political Violence and Media*, ed. Simone Pfeifer, Christoph Günther, and Robert Dörre (Edinburgh: Edinburgh University Press, 2023), 125, 127 and 135.
11 Jonathan A. C. Brown, *Slavery and Islam* (London: Oneworld Academic, 2019), 234.
12 See Marc Weitzmann, 'France's Great Debate Over the Sources and Meaning of Muslim Terror.' *Tablet*, May 24, 2021, https://www.tabletmag.com/sections/news/articles/roy-kepel-marc-weitzmann.
13 François Burgat, *Understanding Political Islam*, 1st ed. (Manchester: Manchester University Press, 2019), 205.
14 For an analysis that prioritizes the political rather than the religious side of jihadists movements, in particular Al-Qaeda, see Michael Scheuer, *Imperial Hubris: Why the West Is Losing the War on Terror* (Potomac Books, 2007).
15 Jaan S. Islam, 'The Portrayal of Jihadi-Salafism: The Role of Knowledge Production in Fabricating a Global Enemy,' in *Disentangling Jihad, Political Violence and Media*, ed. Simone Pfeifer, Christoph Günther, and Robert Dörre (Edinburgh University Press, 2023), 32–33, https://www.jstor.org.queens.ezproxy.cuny.edu/stable/10.3366/jj.9941193.8.
16 Thomas Hegghammer, 'Jihadi-Salafis Or Revolutionaries? On Religion and Politics in the Study of Militant Islamism,' in *Global Salafism: Islam's New Religious Movement*, ed. Roel Meijer (Oxford University Press, 2014), 246, https://doi.org/10.1093/acprof:oso/9780199333431.003.0011.
17 Hegghammer, 251; Islam, 'The Portrayal of Jihadi-Salafism,' 43 and 48.
18 See Hegghammer, 'Jihadi-Salafis Or Revolutionaries?' 245.
19 In addition to Paz, 'Debates Within the Family'; see Eli Alshech, 'The Doctrinal Crisis within the Salafi-Jihadi Ranks and the Emergence of Neo-Takfirism,' *Islamic Law and Society* 21 (September 22, 2014): 419–52, https://doi.org/10.1163/15685195-00214p04; Darryl Li, 'Taking the Place of Martyrs: Afghans and Arabs Under the Banner of Islam,' *Arab Studies Journal* 20, no. 1 (Spring 2012): 137.
20 See Paz, 'Debates Within the Family.'
21 On the point of the Taliban as Sufis, albeit with its complex relationship with popular Sufism, see Brannon D. Ingram, *Revival from Below: The Deoband Movement and Global Islam*, 1st ed. (Oakland: University of California Press, 2018), 208–10.
22 The first three chapters of this work provide detailed insights into the history and key concepts of Salafism.
23 See Thomas Hegghammer, '"Classical" and "Global" Jihadism in Saudi Arabia,' in *Saudi Arabia in Transition: Insights on Social, Political, Economic and Religious Change*, ed. Bernard Haykel, Stéphane Lacroix, and Thomas Hegghammer (Cambridge: Cambridge University Press, 2015), 221–23, https://doi.org/10.1017/CBO9781139047586.014.
24 Paz, 'Debates Within the Family.'
25 Hegghammer, 'Jihadi-Salafis Or Revolutionaries?' 251–52.
26 On the complexity surrounding this popular categorization, see Wagemakers, 'A Purist Jihadi-Salafi,' 281–97; Wagemakers, 'Revisiting Wiktorowicz: Categorising and Defining the Branches of Salafism'; for a discussion on how the three groups of Salafis identified by Wiktorowicz differ on even theological issues, see Meijer, *Global Salafism*, 221–43.
27 Wiktorowicz, 'Anatomy of the Salafi Movement,' 213.
28 Hassan Abu Haniyeh co-founded the *Jamʿiyyat al-Kitāb wa-l-Sunna*, which was officially recognized under Jordanian law in 1993. Although Wiktorowicz (see the next footnote) and Wagemakers identify Abu Haniyeh and the group with JS, Abu Haniyeh classified the organization as being between quietist and Jihadi-Salafi trends, namely 'reform-salafism' (*al-salafiyya al-iṣlāḥiyya*). The notion of their

non-jihadist positioning is supported by the fact that they operate under Jordanian law and work with mainstream organizations, like the Muslim World League. Abu Haniyeh later left Salafism and became a researcher, with a specialty in Salafism. See Wagemakers, *Salafism in Jordan*, 204–6; Sturla Godø Sæther, 'Humanitarian Salafism – a Contradiction in Terms?: A Study of the Salafi Organisation "the Book and the Sunna Society" and Their Efforts in Relief Work in Jordan' (MA Thesis, Oslo, Norway, University of Oslo, 2013), 32–33 and 41, http://urn.nb.no/URN:NBN:no-42263.

29 Wiktorowicz, 'Anatomy of the Salafi Movement,' 213–14 and 225–28.

30 See Thurston, 'Algeria's GIA,' 413.

31 See Brynjar Lia, '"Destructive Doctrinarians": Abu Mus'ab al-Suri's Critique of the Salafis in the Jihadi Current,' in *Global Salafism: Islam's New Religious Movement*, ed. Roel Meijer (Oxford University Press, 2014), 281–300, https://doi.org/10.1093/acprof:oso/9780199333431.003.0013.

32 Shiraz Maher, *Salafi-Jihadism: The History of an Idea* (London: C Hurst & Co, 2016), 200–202.

33 Bunzel, 'Manifest Enmity,' 17–18.

34 Maher, *Salafi-Jihadism*, 177–81.

35 Maher, 181–206.

36 See Alkhateeb, *Lost Islamic History*, 45; Muhammad Al-Yaqoubi, *Refuting ISIS: A Rebuttal Of Its Religious And Ideological Foundations* (Middletown: Sacred Knowledge, 2015), 11–14.

37 Bunzel, 'Manifest Enmity,' 17.

38 Maher, *Salafi-Jihadism*, 89–93.

39 Maher, 95.

40 Maher, 31–35.

41 Cited in Brynjar Lia, *Architect of Global Jihad: The Life of Al-Qaeda Strategist Abu Mus'ab Al-Suri*, 1st ed. (Oxford: Oxford University Press, 2009), 428, 978-0199326457.

42 Tafsīr al-Ṭabarī, vol. 2, 190.

43 Maher, *Salafi-Jihadism*, 49.

44 Maher, 49–54.

45 Wagemakers, 'The Transformation of a Radical Concept,' 85–91.

46 Wagemakers, 90.

47 Wagemakers, 91.

48 al-Maqdisi, *Millat Ibrāhīm*, 39–45, and other sections.

49 Maher, *Salafi-Jihadism*, 134–38.

50 Muhammad Al-Yaqoubi, *Refuting ISIS: A Rebuttal Of Its Religious And Ideological Foundations* (Middletown: Sacred Knowledge, 2015), 18–19.

51 Fawaz A. Gerges, *The Far Enemy: Why Jihad Went Global*, 2nd ed. (Cambridge; New York: Cambridge University Press, 2009), 5.

52 Sajjan M. Gohel, *Doctor, Teacher, Terrorist: The Life and Legacy of Al-Qaeda Leader Ayman Al-Zawahiri* (New York, NY: Oxford University Press, 2024), 36.

53 Maher, *Salafi-Jihadism*, 178–83; for a discussion of the premodern roots of the concept of ḥākimiyya expounded by Qutb and Mawdudi, the latter being the pivotal founding father of Islamism in the Indian subcontinent and influencing the thought of Qutb on this matter, see Usaama Al-Azami, 'Locating Ḥākimiyya in Global History: The Concept of Sovereignty in Premodern Islam and Its Reception after Mawdūdī and Quṭb,' *Journal of the Royal Asiatic Society* 32, no. 2 (April 2022): 355–76, https://doi.org/10.1017/S1356186321000675.

54 Alex Strick van Linschoten and Felix Kuehn, *An Enemy We Created: The Myth of the Taliban-Al Qaeda Merger in Afghanistan* (Oxford; New York: Oxford University Press, 2012), 28–29.

55 Maher, *Salafi-Jihadism*, 88–90.

56 Stephane Lacroix, 'Ayman Al-Zawahiri, Veteran of Jihād,' in *Al Qaeda in Its Own Words*, ed. Gilles Kepel (Cambridge, Mass.: Belknap Press, 2010), 163–64.
57 Meir Hatina, 'Remembering Our Heroes: Global Jihad's Militancy in a Comparative Perspective,' *Middle East Law and Governance* 13, no. 1 (March 4, 2021): 98–124, https://doi.org/10.1163/18763375-13010002.
58 Gilles Kepel, *Jihad: The Trail of Political Islam*, trans. Anthony F. Roberts, Unstated ed. (Cambridge, Mass.: Belknap Press: An Imprint of Harvard University Press, 2003), 136.
59 Al-Rasheed, *A History of Saudi Arabia*, 130 and 138.
60 Strick van Linschoten and Kuehn, *An Enemy We Created*, 51.
61 Hegghammer, *The Caravan*, 179.
62 Hegghammer, 322–25.
63 Li, 'Taking the Place of Martyrs,' 137.
64 Strick van Linschoten and Kuehn, *An Enemy We Created*, 51.
65 Hegghammer, *The Caravan*, 365.
66 Strick van Linschoten and Kuehn, *An Enemy We Created*, 42 and 51.
67 Trofimov, *The Siege of Mecca*, 245.
68 Hegghammer, *The Caravan*, 333–34.
69 Gilles Kepel, ed., *Al Qaeda in Its Own Words* (Cambridge, Mass.: Belknap Press, 2010), 154–55.
70 Hegghammer, *The Caravan*, 246.
71 Strick van Linschoten and Kuehn, *An Enemy We Created*, 63.
72 Strick van Linschoten and Kuehn, 93.
73 Al-Suri is a complex case and is often seen as a Jihadi-Salafi because of his involvement with their ranks and his leading role within Al-Qaeda; however, his approach was more ecumenical than those who are Salafi-inclined. He argued that the Salafis were 'the most conflict-prone of all groups,' and he was somewhat ambivalent on the theological differences between Salafis and Ashʿarīs, and other groups like Sufis and Tablighis. Indeed, al-Suri criticized Salafis for weakening the jihad ranks through their insistence on Salafi doctrine throughout the movement, which led to arguments, divisions and diversions; and his criticism of the leading Jihadi-Salafi theorist Abu Qatadah al-Filastini, his former collaborator, demonstrates his disdain. Moreover, he was one of the Taliban's biggest supporters in the face of Salafi-Arab fighters exhibiting dismissive stances towards the Taliban on account of their non-Salafi religious methodology. He opposed and fell out with Osama bin Laden over the Al-Qaeda bombings in Africa in 1998. Yet, al-Suri did indicate, in 2005, his endorsement of public terrorist acts in the West, although he was not seemingly supportive of the 9/11 attacks. See Lia, '"Destructive Doctrinarians,"' 313–16 and 340–42; Strick van Linschoten and Kuehn, *An Enemy We Created*, 175–76; Thurston, 'Algeria's GIA,' 428–31; Although al-Suri emerged with the Syrian Muslim Brotherhood's military wing, the Fighting Vanguard (al-Tali'a al-Muqatila), he was critical of the Brotherhood; see Lefevre, *Ashes of Hama*, 102–7, 116–17 and 121–22.
74 See the words of Ayman al-Zawahiri, in his Knights Under the Prophet's Banner, as cited in Strick van Linschoten and Kuehn, *An Enemy We Created*, 63.
75 Lacroix, *Awakening Islam*, 115.
76 Hegghammer, *Jihad in Saudi Arabia*, 38.
77 Upon being imprisoned in Egypt many years later, he would recant from his Jihadism, after which al-Zawahiri would release a scathing critique and refutation against him.
78 Strick van Linschoten and Kuehn, *An Enemy We Created*, 92–94.
79 Strick van Linschoten and Kuehn, 72.
80 Hegghammer, *The Caravan*, 419.
81 Strick van Linschoten and Kuehn, *An Enemy We Created*, 82.
82 Hegghammer, *The Caravan*, 638.
83 Strick van Linschoten and Kuehn, *An Enemy We Created*, 101.

84 Strick van Linschoten and Kuehn, 109.
85 Strick van Linschoten and Kuehn, 52; Azzam has been expertly discussed in numerous publications, of which the most significant are: Hegghammer, *The Caravan* which is the most extensive treatment of Azzam in English; which is an incredibly succinct summary of Azzam's importance and thought; Darryl Li, *The Universal Enemy: Jihad, Empire, and the Challenge of Solidarity* (Stanford: Stanford University Press, 2019), 84–87; and Kepel, *Al Qaeda in Its Own Words* which has a good sample of translations of Azzam's writings.
86 Hegghammer, *The Caravan*, 88 and 463.
87 Kepel, *Al Qaeda in Its Own Words*, 82–85; Hegghammer, *The Caravan*, 18 and 30.
88 Kepel, *Al Qaeda in Its Own Words*, 85–88.
89 Hegghammer, *The Caravan*, 75 and 79.
90 Hegghammer, 121.
91 Strick van Linschoten and Kuehn, *An Enemy We Created*, 30 and 50.
92 Hegghammer, *The Caravan*, 122.
93 See Hegghammer, 206–43.
94 Martijn de Koning, 'Changing World Views and Friendship: An Exploration of the Life Stories of Two Female Salafis in the Netherlands,' in *Global Salafism: Islam's New Religious Movement*, ed. Roel Meijer (Oxford University Press, 2014), 443–44, https://doi.org/10.1093/acprof:oso/9780199333431.003.0019.
95 See Li, *The Universal Enemy*, 86; Li, 'Taking the Place of Martyrs,' 21–26 and 37.
96 Cited in Hegghammer, *The Caravan*, 298.
97 Cited in Darryl Li, 'Taking the Place of Martyrs: Afghans and Arabs Under the Banner of Islam,' *Arab Studies Journal* 20, no. 1 (Spring 2012): 23–24. For a discussion of Azzam's clear use of Sufi terminology, as well as referring to Sufi masters, see Thomas Hegghammer, *The Caravan: Abdallah Azzam and the Rise of Global Jihad*, 1st ed. (Cambridge: Cambridge University Press, 2020), 299.
98 An argument advanced by Li in Li, *The Universal Enemy*, 85.
99 See extracts in Kepel, *Al Qaeda in Its Own Words*, 102.
100 Cited in Hegghammer, *The Caravan*, 305.
101 See Hegghammer, 304–5.
102 Cited in Kepel, *Al Qaeda in Its Own Words*, 117.
103 See extracts in Kepel, 110–12, 117–18 and 124; see also Hegghammer, *The Caravan*, 391.
104 Al-Maqdisi has spoken of departing from 'Azzam's camp in Afghanistan because he could not tolerate that 'Azzam 'considered the tomb worshippers and amulet-wearers mujahidin,' see Thurston, 'Jihadists of North Africa and the Sahel,' 36.
105 For the theories that Hegghammer proposes regarding the assassination, see Hegghammer, *The Caravan*, chap. 15.
106 Cited in Hegghammer, 80.
107 Hegghammer, 309.
108 Hegghammer, 312.
109 See Hegghammer, 310–11.
110 Hegghammer, 289–90 and chap. 16.
111 Hegghammer, 307–8.
112 Cited in Hegghammer, 28.
113 Cited in Hegghammer, 40.
114 Hegghammer, 92–94 and 130–33.
115 Hegghammer, 290.
116 Strick van Linschoten and Kuehn, *An Enemy We Created*, 52; Thurston, 'Algeria's GIA,' 8.
117 Dilip Hiro, *War Without End: The Rise of Islamist Terrorism and Global Response*, rev. ed. (London; New York: Routledge, 2002), 78; Hegghammer, *The Caravan*, 418.

118 Cited in Hegghammer, *The Caravan*, 182.
119 Cited in Hegghammer, 425.
120 Hegghammer, 422.
121 Cited in Hegghammer, 464; for Azzam's legacy in comprehensive detail, see Hegghammer, chap. 16.
122 For studies of Jihadi-Salafism in such African countries, see Wehrey and Boukhars, *Salafism in the Maghreb*; Thurston, 'Jihadists of North Africa and the Sahel.'
123 For a study of Jihadi-Salafism in Sweden and Denmark, see Magnus Ranstorp, Linda Ahlerup, and Filip Ahlin, eds, *Salafi-Jihadism and Digital Media: The Nordic and International Context*, Political Violence (London; New York: Routledge, Taylor & Francis Group, 2022).
124 Maher, *Salafi-Jihadism*, 86–87.
125 Maher, 87.
126 Maher, 87.
127 See Gilles Kepel, *Muslim Extremism in Egypt: The Prophet and Pharaoh, With a New Preface for 2003*, First Edition, With a New Preface for 2003 (University of California Press, 2003), 70–102.
128 See Jeffrey B. Cozzens, 'Al-Takfir Wa'l Hijra: Unpacking an Enigma,' *Studies in Conflict & Terrorism* 32, no. 6 (May 28, 2009): 489–510, https://doi.org/10.1080/10576100902886044; Drevon, *Institutionalizing Violence*, chap. 3.
129 See Jerome Drevon, 'The Emergence and Construction of the Radical Salafi Milieu in Egypt,' in *Political Violence in Context: Time, Space and Milieu*, ed. Lorenzo Bosi, Niall Ó Dochartaigh, and Daniela Pisoiu, 2015, 215–35.
130 See Kepel, *Al Qaeda in Its Own Words*, 136.
131 See Cozzens, 'Al-Takfir Wa'l Hijra'; Abu Hamza al-Misri, *Khawaarij & Jihad* (Birmingham: Maktabah Al-Ansar, 2000).
132 See Hamied N. Ansari, 'The Islamic Militants in Egyptian Politics,' *International Journal of Middle East Studies* 16, no. 1 (1984): 123–44.
133 Drevon, *Institutionalizing Violence*, chap. 3.
134 See Moneep, *Islamic Movements in Egypt: A Map and Guidance*, 42–45.
135 See Drevon, 'The Emergence,' 215–35.
136 Moneep, *Islamic Movements in Egypt: A Map and Guidance*, 44.
137 Jeffrey T. Kenney, *Muslim Rebels: Kharijites and the Politics of Extremism in Egypt* (Oxford; New York: Oxford University Press, 2006), 125–26.
138 See Ansari, 'The Islamic Militants in Egyptian Politics,' 125–26.
139 Kenney, *Muslim Rebels*, 125–26.
140 See Moneep, *Islamic Movements in Egypt: A Map and Guidance*, 48–49; Drevon, *Institutionalizing Violence*, chap. 3.
141 See Hiro, *War Without End*, 78–80; Kenney, *Muslim Rebels*, 136–37; Gerges, *The Far Enemy*, 5.
142 al-Gama'ah al-Islamiyah, *Initiative to Stop the Violence: Sadat's Assassins and the Renunciation of Political Violence*, ed. Sherman A. Jackson, World Thought in Translation (New Haven: Yale University Press, 2015), 128n17.
143 Analyses of this work can be found in Kepel, *Muslim Extremism in Egypt*, 192–204; Kenney, *Muslim Rebels*, 135–36; J. J. G. Jansen, 'The Creed of Sadat's Assassins. The Contents of "The Forgotten Duty" Analysed,' *Die Welt Des Islams* 25, no. 1/4 (1985): 1–30, https://doi.org/10.2307/1571075.
144 Gerges, *The Far Enemy*, 44.
145 See Kenney, *Muslim Rebels*, 135–36; Kenney, 194–99; for a discussion of Ibn Taymiyya's various fatwas on the Mongols, and how his views hardened in relation to the Mongols until he called them disbelievers in the third and final fatwa, see Hoover, *Ibn Taymiyya*, 2020, 12–18 and 30–31.
146 See Kepel, *Muslim Extremism in Egypt*, 205; Hiro, *War Without End*, 87 and 81.

147 See Kepel, *Al Qaeda in Its Own Words*, 153.
148 See Kepel, 153.
149 Hiro, *War Without End*, 80.
150 See the note by Jackson in al-Gama'ah al-Islamiyah, *Initiative to Stop the Violence*, 128–129n27.
151 See Jackson's introduction in al-Gama'ah al-Islamiyah, 7–10.
152 al-Gama'ah al-Islamiyah, 9.
153 Cited in al-Gama'ah al-Islamiyah, 13.
154 Kenney, *Muslim Rebels*, 176.
155 al-Gama'ah al-Islamiyah, *Initiative to Stop the Violence*, 124–125n4.
156 See Jackson's introduction in al-Gama'ah al-Islamiyah, 46.
157 Rifa'i Taha would eventually leave the EIG on account of such differences, and in 1998 he joined Osama bin Laden's World Islamic Front for Jihad against Jews and Crusaders, and signed Bin Laden's infamous edict calling for the indiscriminate killing of Americans.
158 See Jackson's introduction in al-Gama'ah al-Islamiyah, *Initiative to Stop the Violence*, 15–19.
159 Gerges, *The Far Enemy*, 214.
160 Gerges, 214–17.
161 See Jackson's notes in al-Gama'ah al-Islamiyah, *Initiative to Stop the Violence*, 142.
162 See Jackon's introduction in al-Gama'ah al-Islamiyah, *Initiative to Stop the Violence*.
163 See Gerges, *The Far Enemy*, 301.
164 Wagemakers, 'The Transformation of a Radical Concept,' 91.
165 Hegghammer and Lacroix, 'Rejectionist Islamism in Saudi Arabia,' 122n79.
166 See Wagemakers, 'A Purist Jihadi-Salafi,' 285; Strick van Linschoten and Kuehn, *An Enemy We Created*, 40; Juhaymān had written in his Risalat al-Imarah wa'l-Bay'ah wa'l-Ta'ah (*The Message of Governance, Pledge of Allegiance and Obedience*) that 'these [Muslim] rulers have no pledge of allegiance from Muslims and they should not be obeyed. Yet, they should not be excommunicated… We believe that by staying in power, these rulers will destroy the religion of God glorious and exalted, even if they professed Islam; we ask God to relieve us from all of them.' See Rabil, *Salafism in Lebanon*, 38.
167 Nasir al-Huzaimi, *The Mecca Uprising: An Insider's Account of Salafism and Insurrection in Saudi Arabia*, trans. David Commins (London; New York; Oxford; New Delhi; Sydney: I.B. Tauris, 2021), 85–86.
168 See Trofimov, *The Siege of Mecca*.
169 Thomas Hegghammer and Stéphane Lacroix, 'Rejectionist Islamism in Saudi Arabia: The Story of Juhayman al-ʿUtaybi Revisited,' *International Journal of Middle East Studies* 39, no. 1 (2007): 109–110.
170 Hegghammer and Lacroix, 111.
171 Hegghammer and Lacroix, 116.
172 Kepel, *Jihad*, 137.
173 Al-Rasheed, *A History of Saudi Arabia*, 154–55.
174 Hegghammer and Lacroix, 'Rejectionist Islamism in Saudi Arabia,' 118.
175 For more on 'Uyayri, see Hegghammer, *Jihad in Saudi Arabia*, 118–28.
176 See Hegghammer, 71–76.
177 Hegghammer, 117.
178 Hegghammer and Lacroix, 'Rejectionist Islamism in Saudi Arabia,' 118.
179 On the Shu'aybi school, see Hegghammer, *Jihad in Saudi Arabia*, 83–87; Al-Sarhan, 'The Struggle for Authority,' 181–206.
180 Hegghammer, *Jihad in Saudi Arabia*, 128, 143, 147–55, 185 and 199.
181 Hegghammer, 199 and 223–25.
182 Stéphane Lacroix, 'To Rebel or Not to Rebel: Dilemmas Among Saudi Salafis in a Revolutionary Age,' in *Salafism After the Arab Awakening: Contending with People's*

*Power*, ed. Francesco Cavatorta and Fabio Merone (Oxford University Press, 2017), 63, https://doi.org/10.1093/acprof:oso/9780190274993.003.0005.

183 Paz, 'Debates Within the Family,' 274.

184 For a discussion on e-jihad and online jihad chat forums, as well as the indigenousness of Saudi Jihadi-Salafis, even while engaging in a global discourse, see Madawi Al-Rasheed, 'The Local and the Global In Saudi Salafi-Jihadi Discourse,' in *Global Salafism: Islam's New Religious Movement*, ed. Roel Meijer (Oxford University Press, 2014), 302–20, https://doi.org/10.1093/acprof:oso/9780199333431.003.0014.

185 Gerges, *The Far Enemy*, 311.

186 Kepel, *Jihad*, 84.

187 Shahin, *Through Muslim Eyes*, 181.

188 Marvine Howe, *Morocco: The Islamist Awakening and Other Challenges* (New York: Oxford University Press, 2005), 127.

189 This movement has been analyzed in David Cook, 'Paradigmatic Jihadi Movements' (West Point, NY: The Combating Terrorism Center United States Military Academy, 2006), 6–11; Shahin, *Through Muslim Eyes*, 181–88; Emilie Siobhan François, 'The Movement for Unicity and Reform' (PhD thesis, Oxford, University of Oxford, 2016), 24–106.

190 Cook, 'Paradigmatic Jihadi Movements,' 4 and 6; François, 'The Movement for Unicity and Reform,' 50–51 and 60–69.

191 Cook, 'Paradigmatic Jihadi Movements,' 9–10.

192 It is not possible to definitively establish Mouti's movements upon leaving Morocco. See Henry Munson, *Religion and Power in Morocco* (Yale University Press, 1993), 160–61, https://doi.org/10.2307/j.ctt1xp3srm.

193 See François Burgat and William Dowell, *The Islamic Movement in North Africa*, Middle East Monograph Series (Austin: Univ. of Texas, 1993), 150.

194 Mohamed Darif, 'The Moroccan Combat Group,' *Real Instituto Elcano*, March 30, 2004.

195 Wehrey and Boukhars, *Salafism in the Maghreb*, 47.

196 Howe, *Morocco*, 323–42 and 352–57.

197 Abdelkader Filali, *Salafi Jihadism, Disengagement, and the Monarchy: Exploring the Case of Morocco* (Université d'Ottawa / University of Ottawa, 2019), 122.

198 Filali, 362.

199 See Mohammed Masbah, 'Salafi Movements and the Political Process in Morocco,' in *Salafism After the Arab Awakening: Contending with People's Power*, ed. Francesco Cavatorta and Fabio Merone (Oxford University Press, 2017), 83–98, https://doi.org/10.1093/acprof:oso/9780190274993.003.0006.

200 Filali, *Salafi Jihadism, Disengagement, and the Monarchy*, 48 and 119.

201 Masbah, 'Moroccan Foreign Fighters: Evolution of the Phenomenon, Promotive Factors, and the Limits of Hardline Policies,' German Institute for International and Security Affairs, October, 2015, https://www.swp-berlin.org/publications/products/comments/2015C46_msb.pdf.

202 See these words from Abu Mus'ab al-Suri cited in Strick van Linschoten and Kuehn, *An Enemy We Created*, 126.

203 See Hugh Roberts, *The Battlefield: Algeria, 1988–2002: Studies in a Broken Polity* (London; New York: Verso, 2003).

204 For a study of this period, see Michael Willis, *The Islamist Challenge in Algeria: A Political History*, 1st ed. (New York: New York Univ. Press, 1997).

205 Willis, chap. 3.

206 Cook, 'Paradigmatic Jihadi Movements,' 14.

207 Wehrey and Boukhars, *Salafism in the Maghreb*, 66.

208 Cook, 'Paradigmatic Jihadi Movements,' 14; Thurston, 'Jihadists of North Africa and the Sahel,' 37; Thurston, 'Algeria's GIA.'

209 Willis, *The Islamist Challenge in Algeria*, chap. 4.
210 Kepel, *Jihad*, 152–54.
211 Thurston, 'Algeria's GIA,' 420.
212 Kepel, *Jihad*, 145–61.
213 Kepel, 233–37.
214 Kepel, 158–59 and chap. 11.
215 Thurston, 'Algeria's GIA,' 241.
216 Gilles Kepel, *Jihad: The Trail of Political Islam*, trans. Anthony F. Roberts, Unstated ed. (Cambridge, Mass.: Belknap Press: An Imprint of Harvard University Press, 2003), 338–39.
217 Kepel, 241–42.
218 Kepel, 242–44.
219 Thurston, 'Jihadists of North Africa and the Sahel,' 42.
220 Kepel, *Jihad*, 244–45.
221 See Thurston, 'Algeria's GIA,' 427.
222 Kepel, *Jihad*, 246–47.
223 Cited in Kepel, 248; in 2004, al-Suri published a memoir, under a pseudonym ʿUmar ʿAbd al-Ḥakīm, entitled *Mukhtaṣar Shahādatī ʿalā al-Jihad fī al-Jazāʾir 1988–1996* (*A Summary of My Testimony on the Jihad in Algeria 1988–1996*), and he proceeded to attack Zitouni for turning the GIA into murderers of civilians and engaging in liberal excommunication, and blamed the failure of the Algerian jihad on the overly-zealous Salafis and their doctrinal extremism, for which he included Abu Qatadah. See Thurston, 'Algeria's GIA,' 428–31.
224 Lawrence Wright, *The Looming Tower: Al-Qaeda and the Road to 9/11*, 1. Vintage Books ed, National Bestseller (New York: Vintage Books, 2007), 190.
225 Lia, *Architect of Global Jihad*, 155–58.
226 See Kepel, *Jihad*, 249–251 and 382 (notes 31 and 32).
227 Thurston, 'Algeria's GIA,' 426.
228 Amel Boubekeur, 'Salafism and Radical Politics in Postconflict Algeria,' *Carnegie Endowment for International Peace*, 2008, 16–17; Wehrey and Boukhars, *Salafism in the Maghreb*, 70.
229 Thurston, 'Algeria's GIA,' 432–35.
230 Thurston, 'Jihadists of North Africa and the Sahel,' 54; Boubekeur, 'Salafism and Radical Politics in Postconflict Algeria,' 10.
231 Wehrey and Boukhars, Salafism in the Maghreb, 69.
232 Thurston, 'Jihadists of North Africa and the Sahel,' 43.
233 Thurston, 48–66.
234 Thurston, 53–54.
235 Thurston, 68–69.
236 Paz, 273–74.
237 Boubekeur, 'Salafism and Radical Politics in Postconflict Algeria,' 11.
238 Thurston, 'Jihadists of North Africa and the Sahel,' 85 and 97.
239 Wehrey and Boukhars, *Salafism in the Maghreb*, 79.
240 For a discussion on the divide between the Taliban and Al-Qaeda, see Strick van Linschoten and Kuehn, *An Enemy We Created.*
241 Important foundational histories of Al-Qaeda in Afghanistan can be read in Strick van Linschoten and Kuehn; Anne Stenersen, *Al-Qaida in Afghanistan* (Cambridge: Cambridge University Press, 2017), 287–95.
242 Lia, *Architect of Global Jihad*, 265.
243 Strick van Linschoten and Kuehn, *An Enemy We Created*, 99.
244 Hegghammer, *The Caravan*, 351.
245 Strick van Linschoten and Kuehn, *An Enemy We Created*, 96.
246 Thurston, 'Algeria's GIA,' 418.

247 Strick van Linschoten and Kuehn, *An Enemy We Created*, 99.
248 Strick van Linschoten and Kuehn, 93, 103 and 126.
249 For a discussion on the jihad in Bosnia, Tajikistan and other smaller battles of a like nature, see Hegghammer, *Jihad in Saudi Arabia*, 48–58.
250 Strick van Linschoten and Kuehn, *An Enemy We Created*, 129.
251 Hegghammer, *Jihad in Saudi Arabia*, 100.
252 Strick van Linschoten and Kuehn, *An Enemy We Created*, 136.
253 For excerpts and analysis of this Declaration, see Kepel, *Jihad*, 291–92; Kepel, *Al Qaeda in Its Own Words*, 47–50.
254 Strick van Linschoten and Kuehn, *An Enemy We Created*, 147 and 477.
255 See Kepel, *Jihad*, 293; Kepel, *Al Qaeda in Its Own Words*, 53–56.
256 Strick van Linschoten and Kuehn, *An Enemy We Created*, 152–53 and 176.
257 Strick van Linschoten and Kuehn, 162–68 and 174.
258 Stenersen, *Al-Qaida in Afghanistan*, 170–72.
259 Stenersen, 229–30.
260 See, in particular, the discussion on the document produced by Abu al-Walid al-Masri in criticism of Bin Laden in Gerges, *The Far Enemy*, 192–99.
261 Strick van Linschoten and Kuehn, *An Enemy We Created*, 242–43 and 256.
262 Strick van Linschoten and Kuehn, 231 and 264–65.
263 Gerges, *The Far Enemy*, 217.
264 Gerges, 200–210.
265 Strick van Linschoten and Kuehn, *An Enemy We Created*, 272–80.
266 For a study of Jihadi-Salafism in such areas, see Thurston, 'Jihadists of North Africa and the Sahel.'
267 Gerges, *The Far Enemy*, 96.
268 Joas Wagemakers, 'Al-Qā ʿida's Post-Arab Spring Jihad: Confirmation or Re-Evaluation?' accessed June 12, 2024, https://doi.org/10.1515/9781474485531-011.
269 See Farhad Khosrokhavar, 'The Arab Revolutions and Jihadism,' in *Violence in Islamic Thought from European Imperialism to the Post-Colonial Era*, ed. Mustafa Baig and Robert Gleave (Edinburgh: Edinburgh University Press, 2021), https://doi.org/10.1515/9781474485531-012.
270 For a study of IS-K, see Antonio Giustozzi, *The Islamic State in Khorasan: Afghanistan, Pakistan and the New Central Asian Jihad* (London: Hurst & Company, 2018). The following information has been largely drawn from this work.
271 Peter Baker, Helene Cooper, and Mark Mazzetti, 'Bin Laden Is Dead, Obama Says.' *The New York Times*, May 1, 2011, https://www.nytimes.com/2011/05/02/world/asia/osama-bin-laden-is-killed.html.
272 See David Smith, Joanna Walters, and Jason Burke, 'Ayman Al-Zawahiri: Al-Qaida Leader Killed in US Drone Strike in Afghanistan, Joe Biden Says,' *The Guardian*, August 2, 2022, https://www.theguardian.com/world/2022/aug/01/us-strike-afghanistan-kills-al-qaida-leader-ayman-al-zawahiri.
273 For a study of Jihadi-Salafism in Indonesia, and its impact on the Malay Archipelago, see Solahudin et al., *The Roots of Terrorism in Indonesia: From Darul Islam to Jema'ah Islamiyah* (Ithaca: Cornell University Press, 2013); see also Julie Chernov Hwang and Kirsten E. Schulze, 'Why They Join: Pathways into Indonesian Jihadist Organizations,' *Terrorism and Political Violence* 30, no. 6 (November 2, 2018): 911–32, https://doi.org/10.1080/09546553.2018.1481309. This section has been derived from these works.
274 For an overview of his life, see Gilles Kepel and Omar Saghi, eds, 'Osama Bin Laden, the Iconic Orator,' in *Al Qaeda in Its Own Words* (Cambridge, Mass.: Belknap Press, 2010), 11–40.
275 Strick van Linschoten and Kuehn, *An Enemy We Created*, 34.
276 Yaroslav Trofimov, *The Siege of Mecca: The 1979 Uprising at Islam's Holiest Shrine*, 1st Anchor Books ed. (New York: Anchor Books, 2007), 246–47.

277 Khashoggi was a dissident Saudi journalist who was slain in the Saudi Embassy in Istanbul in 2018, and made the subject of a documentary in 2020. See *The Dissident*.
278 Hegghammer, *The Caravan*, 210.
279 Mustafa Hamid and Leah Farrall, *The Arabs at War in Afghanistan* (Oxford University Press, 2015), 30.
280 Lacroix, *Awakening Islam*, 115.
281 Hegghammer, *The Caravan*, 361.
282 Hegghammer, 360–61.
283 Strick van Linschoten and Kuehn, *An Enemy We Created*, 103.
284 Baker, Cooper, and Mazzetti, 'Bin Laden Is Dead, Obama Says.' *The New York Times*.
285 Lia, *Architect of Global Jihad*, 293–99.
286 For an overview of his life, see Stéphane Lacroix, 'Ayman Al-Zawahiri,' in *Al Qaeda in Its Own Words*, ed. Gilles Kepel (Cambridge, Mass.: Belknap Press, 2010), 147–70; for a detailed study, see Gohel, *Doctor, Teacher, Terrorist*. Most of the material in this section is taken from this work.
287 Gohel, *Doctor, Teacher, Terrorist*, xxv–xxvi.
288 Montasser al-Zayyāt, *The Road to Al-Qaeda: The Story of Bin Laden's Right-Hand Man*, ed. Sara Nimis, trans. Ahmed Fekry (Pluto Books, 2015), 16, https://doi.org/10.2307/j.ctt18fs95x.
289 Scott Baldauf, 'The "cave man" and Al Qaeda,' *Christian Science Monitor*, 31 October 2001, published at https://www.csmonitor.com/2001/1031/p6s1-wosc.html. Retrieved 8 October 2019.
290 Maher, *Salafi-Jihadism*, 16.
291 Gerges, *The Far Enemy*, 39.
292 See Meir Hatina, 'Contesting Violence in Radical Islam: Sayyid Imām al-Shaīf's Ethical Perception,' *Islamic Law and Society* 23, no. 1/2 (2016): 120–40.
293 Gerges, *The Far Enemy*, 301–3.
294 Wagemakers, 'A Purist Jihadi-Salafi,' 281–97.
295 Hegghammer, *The Caravan*, 420–21.
296 Hegghammer and Lacroix, 'Rejectionist Islamism in Saudi Arabia,' 115.
297 Joas Wagemakers, in *Global Salafism*, 438.
298 al-Maqdisi, *Millat Ibrāhīm*, 39–216.
299 Wagemakers, 'A Purist Jihadi-Salafi,' 292–94.
300 Johnsen, 'The Rise of ISIS,' 14.
301 Hegghammer, *The Caravan*, 475.
302 Hegghammer, 475.
303 Areej Abuqudairi, 'Jordan Releases Anti-ISIL Salafi Leader | ISIL/ISIS News |,' *Al Jazeera*, June 17, 2014, https://www.aljazeera.com/news/2014/6/17/jordan-releases-anti-isil-salafi-leader.
304 Hegghammer, *The Caravan*, 470; for an overview of al-Zarqawi's life, see Jean-Pierre Milelli, 'Abu Musʿab Al-Zarqawi, Jihad in "Mesopotamia,"' in *Al Qaeda in Its Own Words*, ed. Gilles Kepel (Cambridge, Mass.: Belknap Press, 2010), 237–50; Fawaz A. Gerges, *ISIS: A History* (Princeton; Oxford, UK: Princeton University Press, 2016), 56–64 and 67–93.
305 Gerges, *ISIS*, 57.
306 Gerges, 57.
307 Johnsen, 'The Rise of ISIS,' 14.
308 Lia, *Architect of Global Jihad*, 265–71.
309 Gerges, *The Far Enemy*, 254.
310 Gerges, 259.
311 Gerges, 261–63.
312 Cited in Hatina, 'Contesting Violence in Radical Islam,' 136.
313 Paz, 'Debates Within the Family,' 270–71.

314 Paz, 270–71; Gerges, *The Far Enemy*, 257.
315 Johnsen, 'The Rise of ISIS,' 15.
316 See Jason Burke, *The New Threat: The Past, Present, and Future of Islamic Militancy* (New York City, NY: New Press, 2017).
317 For a comprehensive study of this movement, see Gerges, *ISIS*.
318 This fell to US$1 billion in 2015 and lowered in later years.
319 Gerges, *ISIS*, xii and 1–2.
320 Gerges, 97–98.
321 Gerges, 136.
322 Gerges, 136–43.
323 See Steven Strasser, ed., *The Abu Ghraib Investigations: The Official Reports of the Independent Panel and Pentagon on the Shocking Prisoner Abuse in Iraq*, 1st ed. (New York: Public Affairs, 2004).
324 Gerges, *ISIS*, 135–38.
325 Johnsen, 'The Rise of ISIS,' 16–20.
326 Gerges, *ISIS*, 147.
327 Paz, 'Debates Within the Family,' 270–71.
328 Gerges, *ISIS*, 97–99.
329 Cited in Gerges, 13.
330 Gerges, 145–47 and chap. 5.
331 Lizzie Dearden, 'Al-Qaeda Leader Denounces Isis "Madness and Lies" as Two Terrorist Groups Compete for Dominance,' *The Independent*, January 13, 2017, https://www.independent.co.uk/news/world/middle-east/al-qaeda-leader-ayman-al-zawahiri-isis-madness-lies-extremism-islamic-state-terrorist-groups-compete-middle-east-islamic-jhadis-a7526271.html.
332 Dearden, 19.
333 See Mathias Ghyoot, '"Nay, We Obeyed God When We Burned Him": Debating Immolation (Taḥrīq) Between the Islamic State and Al-Qāʿida,' in *Violence in Islamic Thought from European Imperialism to the Post-Colonial Era*, ed. Mustafa Baig and Robert Gleave (Edinburgh: Edinburgh University Press, 2021), 249–88, http://www.jstor.org/stable/10.3366/j.ctv1ns7mwk.16; Edinburgh University Press, 2021. For the criticism of ISIS by Salman al-Oudah and Muhammad Hassan on this point, see Ismail, *Rethinking Salafism*, 137–38.
334 Johnsen, 'The Rise of ISIS,' 21–22; see also Omar Anchassi, 'The Logic of the Conquest Society: Isis, Apocalyptic Violence and the "Reinstatement" of Slave Concubinage,' in *Legitimate and Illegitimate Violence in Islamic Thought*, ed. Mustafa Baig and Robert Gleave (Edinburgh: Edinburgh University Press, 2021), 225–48, https://doi.org/10.1515/9781474485531-013.
335 Laurie Goodstein, 'Muslim Leaders Wage Theological Battle, Stoking ISIS' Anger,' *The New York Times*, May 8, 2016, https://www.nytimes.com/2016/05/09/us/isis-threatens-muslim-preachers-who-are-waging-theological-battle-online.html.
336 Johnsen, 'The Rise of ISIS,' 19.
337 Gerges, *ISIS*, 99.
338 *Ṣāḥīḥ ḥMuslim: kitāb al-fitan wa-asharāṭ al-sāʿa, bāb fatḥ qusṭunṭīnīyyat wa-khurūj al-dajjāl wa-nuzūl Īsā ibn Maryam*. This is part of a much larger hadith predicting a great war that would trigger the end of times. ISIS was, in fact, trying to hasten the end of times with this move.
339 On the accusation of apartheid on the part of Israel, see Ilan Pappé, *The Ethnic Cleansing of Palestine*, Reprint ed. (Oxford: Oneworld Publications, 2007); Ilan Pappé, ed., *Israel and South Africa: The Many Faces of Apartheid* (London: Zed Books, 2015); Uri Davis, *Apartheid Israel: Possibilities for the Struggle Within* (London: Zed Books, 2003); Norman G. Finkelstein, *Gaza: An Inquest into Its Martyrdom* (Oakland, California: University of California Press, 2018).

340 Gerges, *ISIS*, 273–74.
341 Fawaz A. Gerges, 'Qurayshi Death: The Islamic State Has Become a Resilient Insurgency,' *Foreign Policy*, February 7, 2022, https://foreignpolicy.com/2022/02/07/qurayshi-death-leader-islamic-state-current-strength/.
342 For a comprehensive study of the movement, see Alexander Thurston, *Boko Haram: The History of an African Jihadist Movement* (Princeton University Press, 2017), https://doi.org/10.2307/j.ctvc779gc; the latter builds on the study in Thurston, *Salafism in Nigeria*, pt. III.
343 Thurston, *Boko Haram*, 2–3 and 17–18.
344 Emmanuel Akinwotu, Emmanuel Akinwotu West Africa correspondent, and Isaac Abrak, 'Suspected Islamist Attack Frees Hundreds of Prisoners in Nigeria,' *The Guardian*, July 6, 2022, https://www.theguardian.com/world/2022/jul/06/suspected-boko-haram-attack-frees-hundreds-of-prisoners-in-nigeria-abuja.
345 Thurston, *Salafism in Nigeria*, 194.
346 See Thurston, 66.
347 Cited in Abdulbasit Kassim, 'Defining and Understanding the Religious Philosophy of Jihādī-Salafism and the Ideology of Boko Haram,' *Politics, Religion & Ideology* 16 (September 1, 2015): 1–28, https://doi.org/10.1080/21567689.2015.1074896.
348 See Thurston, *Boko Haram*, 98–104; Thurston, *Salafism in Nigeria*, 208–214; 'The Popular Discourses of Salafi Radicalism and Salafi Counter-Radicalism in Nigeria: A Case Study of Boko Haram,' January 1, 2012, 123–39, https://doi.org/10.1163/15700666-12341224.
349 Cited from a 2015 edition of ISIS' publication Dabiq, cited in Thurston, *Boko Haram*, 18.
350 Cited in Kassim, 'Defining and Understanding the Religious Philosophy of Jihādī-Salafism and the Ideology of Boko Haram,' 193.
351 Kassim, 193.
352 Cited in Thurston, *Boko Haram*, 173–74.
353 Thurston, 272–76.
354 For a succinct introduction to Dan Fodio's life and spiritual teaching, see Rudolph T. Ware, Zachary Valentine Wright, and Amir Syed, eds., 'Part 1: Shaykh 'Uthman Bin Fudi,' in *Jihad of the Pen: The Sufi Literature of West Africa* (Cairo; New York: The American University in Cairo Press, 2018); for a more elaborate study of Dan Fodio's life and thought, see Ibraheem Sulaiman, *The African Caliphate: The Life, Works and Teaching of Shaykh Usman Dan Fodio (1754–1817)* (Diwan Press, 2019); Abdullah Hakim Quick, 'Aspects of Islamic Social Intellectual History in Hausaland, 'Uthman Ibn Fudi, 1774–1804 C.E' (PhD thesis, Toronto, University of Tornoto, 1995), https://hdl.handle.net/1807/10830.
355 Thurston, *Boko Haram*, 3–4.
356 There are a number of insightful studies of Al-Shabaab, including Stig Jarle Hansen, *Al-Shabaab in Somalia: The History and Ideology of a Militant Islamist Group, 2005–2012* (Oxford University Press, 2013); Harun Maruf and Dan Joseph, *Inside Al-Shabaab: The Secret History of Al-Qaeda's Most Powerful Ally* (Indiana University Press, 2018), https://doi.org/10.2307/j.ctv6mtfn2; Mary Harper, *Everything You Have Told Me Is True: The Many Faces of Al Shabaab* (Oxford University Press, 2019); see also a number of relevant articles in Michael Keating and Matt Waldman, eds, *War and Peace in Somalia: National Grievances, Local Conflict and Al-Shabaab*, 1st ed. (Oxford University Press, 2019), https://doi.org/10.1093/oso/9780190947910.001.0001; However, a concise overview of the movement can be found in Christopher Anzalone, *Continuity and Change: The Evolution and Resilience of Al-Shabab's Media Insurgency, 2006–2016* (Oslo, Norway: Hate Speech International, 2016). The following overview of the group's history has been largely derived from this latter work.
357 See Anzalone, *Continuity and Change*.

358 Christopher Anzalone, *Localizing 'Global' Jihad: The Organization and Narration of Violence and Community in Islamist Insurgencies* (McGill University Libraries, 2019), 461–63 and 466.
359 Thurston, *Boko Haram*, 304–5.
360 Godane's support of Al-Qaeda must be attributed, in some way, to his historic ties to the Egyptian Islamic Jihad (EIJ). Between 1989 and 1996, while he was a student at the International Islamic University of Islamabad (IIUI), where he spent six years in gaining a degree in economics and a master's in finance and Islamic banking, after spending one initial year at a madrasa in Karachi, Godane developed ties with the EIJ, who took him to Peshawar and Afghanistan. Godane's worldview would be forever shaped by that time and its enduring impact and the network it provided him. See Maruf and Joseph, *Inside Al-Shabaab*, 63–66.
361 Maruf and Joseph, 265.
362 'US Offers $10m for Information on Al-Shabab Leaders, Finances,' *Al Jazeera*, November 14, 2022, https://www.aljazeera.com/news/2022/11/14/us-offers-10m-for-information-on-al-shabab-leaders-finances.
363 This focus on those who communicated widely in English excludes a number of prominent Jihadi-Salafi exiles who found asylum in the West, most notably in London, and whose Arabic writings, even from the location of their refuge, have had a significant impact on Arabic-speaking and Arab-based Jihadi-Salafis. Significant examples include Abu Qatadah al-Filastini, who has been discussed on numerous occasions in this chapter, and Abu Basir al-Tartusi. For introductory studies on these latter two figures, see Petter Nesser, 'Abū Qatāda and Palestine,' January 1, 2013, https://doi.org/10.1163/15685152-5334P0005; Joas Wagemakers, 'Between Purity and Pragmatism? Abu Basir al-Tartusi's Nuanced Radicalism,' in *Jihadi Thought and Ideology*, ed. Rüdiger Lohlker and Tamara Abu-Hamdeh (Logos Verlag, 2014), 16–36; for a study of Jihadism in Europe in general, see Farhad Khosrokhavar, *Jihadism in Europe: European Youth and the New Caliphate*, 1st ed. (Oxford University PressNew York, 2021), https://doi.org/10.1093/oso/9780197564967.001.0001.
364 Alexander Meleagrou-Hitchens, *Incitement: Anwar Al-Awlaki's Western Jihad* (Cambridge, Mass.: Harvard University Press, 2020), 2.
365 In the context of European-based Jihadis, Farhad Khosrokhavar found common biographical details to be 'stigmatization, delinquency, repeat offense, radicalization, and travel in countries at war in the name of jihad.' Moreover, he provides examples of middle-class Jihadis which mitigate against stereotyping Jihadis, whether in Muslim or non-Muslim countries, as always coming from socially deprived backgrounds. Khosrokhavar, *Jihadism in Europe*, 344 and 348–50; On other Jihadis from privileged, middle-class backgrounds, like Omar Saeed Sheikh, the 'Crawley group' and the '7/7' cell from England, see Petter Nesser, *Islamist Terrorism in Europe: A History* (New York: Oxford University Press, 2015), 168–90. This is similar to the trend explored earlier in relation to the Jihadis in Egypt who came from prosperous backgrounds, most notably Ayman al-Zawahiri.
366 Meleagrou-Hitchens, *Incitement*, 19–21.
367 Scott Shane, *Objective Troy: A Terrorist, a President, and the Rise of the Drone*, 1st ed. (New York: Tim Duggan Books, 2015), 56–65.
368 Shane, 82–102. This view has come to be challenged, with the argument that an analysis of his output over fifteen years shows 'no radical or sudden transformation,' but his view on Muslims in the West did alter: 'Patient and long-term Islamic activism was discarded in favor of the instant gratification and apparent results of violence.' See Meleagrou-Hitchens, *Incitement*, 264–66. However, the turn to advocating violence against Western civilians is a radical transformation.
369 Shane, *Objective Troy*, 303.

370 Shane, 102–5.
371 Shane, 109–15.
372 Shane, 106–9.
373 Scott Shane, 'Born in U.S., a Radical Cleric Inspires Terror,' *Herald-Tribune*, November 19, 2009, https://www.heraldtribune.com/story/news/2009/11/19/born-in-u-s-radical/28905016007/.
374 Meleagrou-Hitchens, *Incitement*, 29.
375 Shane, *Objective Troy*, 119–21 and 124–25.
376 The Mad Mamluks, 'The First American Jihadi | Ismail Royer,' accessed October 12, 2019, https://themadmamluks.com/the-first-american-jihadi-ismail-royer/. For the record, I will share my own analysis of this incident, based on my own sources who were close to Awlaki and al-Timimi in the late 1990s. There seems to have been an inexplicable and sudden change of heart in Awlaki in the early part of 2002. Awlaki most certainly was a Salafi, but he was not sympathetic to Salafi-Jihadist thought throughout the '90s and immediately following the 9/11 attacks. The morning after this alleged incident to entrap al-Timimi, al-Timimi confided in a close friend that he felt Awlaki was an informant, based on the types of questions and the demeanor Awlaki displayed during his private interaction with al-Timimi. Awlaki's roommates at the time also claimed that Awlaki spontaneously decided to leave America one night, after appearing extremely agitated, and hastily packed his bags, purchased a ticket for the next day, and left many personal items behind. Everyone who knew him from the '90s expressed surprise at the sudden turn of events. One surmises that Awlaki felt trapped by the FBI (which was clearly trying to recruit him to spy on others), and worried about the potential exposure of his personal file. It appears that he felt his best recourse was to flee the country while he was able to and viewed embracing a more radical stance as his only option. One hopes the public release of the FBI files will tell us more about the details of this incident.
377 Meleagrou-Hitchens, *Incitement*, 60–64.
378 Meleagrou-Hitchens, 155–59.
379 Meleagrou-Hitchens, 159–61.
380 Shane, *Objective Troy*, 145–49.
381 For a study of Nidal Hasan in the context of al-Awlaki, see Meleagrou-Hitchens, *Incitement*, 189–208.
382 Shane, *Objective Troy*, 190–95.
383 For a study of Umar Farouk Abdulmutallab in the context of al-Awlaki, see Meleagrou-Hitchens, *Incitement*, 165–88; I also met and taught Umar, before he decided that mainstream Salafism was not satisfactory for him and traveled to Yemen to meet Awlaki. My thoughts on that encounter are published in an online blog. See Yasir Qadhi, 'The Lure of Radicalism and Extremism Amongst Muslim Youth,' Muslimmatters, October 2010, https://muslimmatters.org/2010/10/18/yasir-qadhi-the-lure-of-radicalism-amongst-muslim-youth/.
384 Shane, *Objective Troy*, 301–2.
385 For a study of Zachary Adam Chesser in the context of al-Awlaki, see Meleagrou-Hitchens, *Incitement*, 209–35.
386 Meleagrou-Hitchens, 291.
387 Meleagrou-Hitchens, 294.
388 Yasir Qadhi, 'Opinion | Assassinating Al-Awlaki Was Counterproductive,' *The New York Times*, October 1, 2011, https://www.nytimes.com/2011/10/02/opinion/sunday/assassinating-al-awlaki-was-counterproductive.html.
389 Meleagrou-Hitchens, *Incitement*, 2.
390 The opinion of Donald Holbrook, cited in Hegghammer, *The Caravan*, 475.
391 Meleagrou-Hitchens, *Incitement*, 2 and 252.
392 Jytte Klausen, *Western Jihadism: A Thirty Year History* (Oxford; New York: Oxford University Press, 2021), 157; see also Sean O'Neill and Daniel McGrory, *The Suicide*

*Factory: Abu Hamza and the Finsbury Park Mosque* (London: Harper Perennial, 2006), for an account of an undercover agent who spent time in the Finsbury Park mosque, see Omar Nasiri, *Inside the Jihad: My Life with Al Qaeda: A Spy's Story* (New York: Basic Books, 2006).

393 Jarret M. Brachman, *Global Jihadism: Theory and Practice*, Transferred to digital print, Political Violence (London: Routledge, 2010), 168.

394 Nesser, *Islamist Terrorism in Europe*, 41.

395 Hegghammer, *The Caravan*, 255.

396 Klausen, *Western Jihadism*, 240.

397 *Sahih Muslim, Kitāb al-fitan wa ashāṭ al-sāʿah, bāb fī al-ayāt allathī takūn qabl al-sāʿah.*

398 Klausen, *Western Jihadism*, 240–45.

399 See O'Neill and McGrory, *The Suicide Factory*, 47–48 and 66–75.

400 Nesser, *Islamist Terrorism in Europe*, 41–42.

401 Abdullah Faisal, *100 Fabricated Hadith*, 7, accessed June 12, 2024, http://archive.org/details/100FabricatedHadithShaikhAbdullahFaisal_201707; for a case study of al-Faisal, see Abdul Haqq Baker, *Extremists in Our Midst: Confronting Terror* (Houndmills, Hampshire: Palgrave Macmillan, 2011), 146–59.

402 The Brixton mosque became synonymous with Salafism by the mid-1990s, but it had a short-lived, hard-line Sufi period, under the direction of the Murabitun, a politico-Sufi group headed by a Scottish convert Ian Dallas (aka 'Abdalqadir as-Sufi), shortly before the committee was overthrown for its seemingly excessive measures to monopolize the direction of the community; the Sufi-inclined committee was replaced with an overt Salafi committee, which ushered in the dominance of a Salafi ethos into the previously diverse community, to such an extent that it is now simply seen as a Salafi mosque. See Baker, *Extremists in Our Midst: Confronting Terror*, 22–28.

403 For a case study of Moussaoui, including his links to Al-Qaeda, in addition to al-Faisal, see Baker, 106–29.

404 For a case study of Reid, see Baker, 129–46.

405 Cited in Khosrokhavar, *Jihadism in Europe*, 216.

406 Cited in Baker, *Extremists in Our Midst: Confronting Terror*, 151.

407 Cited in Baker, 152–53.

408 'Hate Preaching Cleric Jailed,' *BBC*, March 7, 2003, http://news.bbc.co.uk/2/hi/uk_news/england/2829059.stm.

409 Nicola Harley, 'Radical July 7 Preacher Arrested in Undercover Sting Trying to Recruit Jihadis,' August 26, 2017, https://www.telegraph.co.uk/news/2017/08/25/radical-july-7-preacher-arrested-undercover-sting-trying-recruit/; and 'Abdullah Al-Faisal,' Counter Extremism Project, March 23, 2023, https://www.counterextremism.com/extremists/abdullah-al-faisal.

410 Kenney, *Muslim Rebels*, 121–34.

411 See ʿAbd al-Raḥmān ibn Muʿallā Luwayḥiq and Jamaal Al-Din M. Zarabozo, *Religious Extremism in the Lives of Contemporary Muslims* (Denver, Colo: Al-Basheer Company for Publications and Translations, 2001).

412 Cited in Nader Hashemi, 'The ISIS Crisis and the Broken Politics of the Arab World,' in *Routledge Handbook on Human Rights and the Middle East and North Africa*, ed. Anthony Tirado Chase, Routledge Handbooks Online (Abingdon, Oxon: Routledge, 2016).

413 Cited in Ismail, *Rethinking Salafism*, 136.

414 See Razavian, 'Post-Salafism: Salman al-Ouda and Hatim al-Awni,' 181–85.

415 See Cole Bunzel, *The Kingdom and the Caliphate: Duel of the Islamic States* (Carnegie Endowment for International Peace, 2016).

416 ʿAbd al-Hakim, ʿUmar, *The Global Resistance Call*, 842.

417 ʿAbd al-Hakim, ʿUmar, *The Global Resistance Call*, 1060.

418 Steffen Hertog and Diego Gambetta, 'Why Are There so Many Engineers among Islamic Radicals?' *European Journal of Sociology* 50 (August 1, 2009): 7, https://doi.org/10.1017/S0003975609990129; see also Diego Gambetta and Steffen Hertog, *Engineers of Jihad: The Curious Connection between Violent Extremism and Education* (Princeton: Princeton University Press, 2016).

## 6 GLOBAL SALAFISM IN THE CONTEMPORARY WORLD

1 From a live radio broadcast, *Nūr ʿala al-darb, fatwa* no. 1452, in which a Syrian caller asked Ibn Bāz to describe Salafism and Wahhabism. The transcription is available from his official website 'Al-Mawqiʿ al-Rasmī Li-Shaykh ʿAbd al-ʿAzīz Bin Bāz.'

2 Taken from '"The Salafi Da'wah Is Now in Disarray": Al-Albani,' *Darul Tahqiq* (blog), accessed June 10, 2024, https://www.darultahqiq.com/the-salafi-dawah-is-now-in-disarray-al-albani/.

3 See, for example, Borhan Osman, 'Bourgeois Jihad: Why Young, Middle-Class Afghans Join the Islamic State,' *United States Institute of Peace* (blog), June 1, 2020, https://www.usip.org/publications/2020/06/bourgeois-jihad-why-young-middle-class-afghans-join-islamic-state. This overview highlights that Salafism developed in Afghanistan during the war with the Soviet Union, primarily around the group of Jamil al-Rahman in Kunar in eastern Afghanistan, as well as other groups in Nuristan and in Badakhshan; but these quickly dissipated. There was widespread opposition to such Salafi groups, which were based mainly in northern and eastern Afghanistan, and this hostility continued under the first Taliban rule, despite them tolerating, with some internal conflict, Jihadi-Salafis like Al-Qaeda. Then after the American invasion of Afghanistan after 9/11, there was greater freedom for Salafi groups to operate. However, over time the most apparent Salafi trend became the Jihadi-Salafi Islamic State in Khorasan (IS-K), which came into conflict with the resurgent Taliban. This was discussed in Chapter 5 of this book.

4 See Terje Østebø, *Localising Salafism: Religious Change among Oromo Muslims in Bale, Ethiopia* (Leiden: Brill, 2011), https://brill.com/display/title/19533.

5 See Terje Østebø, 'African Salafism: Religious Purity and the Politicization of Purity,' *Islamic Africa* 6, no. 1–2 (2015): 1–29.

6 See Mohamed-Ali Adraoui, 'Salafism in France: Ideology, Practices and Contradictions,' in *Global Salafism: Islam's New Religious Movement*, ed. Roel Meijer (Oxford University Press, 2014), 365–83, https://doi.org/10.1093/acprof:oso/9780199333431.003.0017.

7 See Koning, 'Changing World Views and Friendship.'

8 See Susanne Olsson, *Contemporary Puritan Salafism: A Swedish Case Study*, Comparative Islamic Studies (Sheffield, UK Bristol, CT: Equinox, 2016); Susanne Olsson, Simon Sorgenfrei, and Jonas Svensson, 'Puritan Salafis in a Liberal Democratic Context,' in *Salafi-Jihadism and Digital Media: The Nordic and International Context*, ed. Magnus Ranstorp, Linda Ahlerup, and Filip Ahlin, Political Violence (London; New York: Routledge, Taylor & Francis Group, 2022), 92–112.

9 See Nina Wiedl, *The Making of a German Salafiyya: The Emergence, Development and Missionary Work of Salafi Movements in Germany* (Centre for Studies in Islamism and Radicalisation (CIR), Department of Political Science, Aarhus University, 2012); Sabine Damir-Geilsdorf and Mira Menzfeld, '"Looking at the Life of the Prophet and How He Dealt with All These Issues." Self-Positioning, Demarcations and Belongingness of German Salafis from an Emic Perspective,' *Contemporary Islam* 10 (September 1, 2016), https://doi.org/10.1007/s11562-016-0361-7.

10 Chanfi Ahmed, 'West African ʿulamāʾ and Salafism in Mecca and Medina' (Leiden: Brill, 2015), https://brill.com/display/title/24534.

11 In speaking about me, Christopher Pooya Razavian wrote, 'Qadhi is arguably the most famous foreign graduate of the Islamic University of Medinah (IUM), and one of America's most influential Muslims.' Razavian, 'Post-Salafism: Salman al-Ouda and Hatim al-Awni,' 172–73. I would say that I was heavily involved with the movement as an insider from 1991 to around 2010. Then, in 2013, I publicly dissociated from the movement with my online article 'On Salafi Islam.'

12 For studies of Salafi thought and practice in Egypt in the twentieth century, see Aaron Rock-Singer, *Practicing Islam in Egypt: Print Media and Islamic Revival* (Cambridge: Cambridge University Press, 2019), https://doi.org/10.1017/9781108590877; Rock-Singer, *In the Shade of the Sunna.*

13 For a discussion on this modernist-Salafi phenomenon in Morocco, see Lauzière, *The Making of Salafism*, 2016, 23 and 148–54.

14 Wehrey and Boukhars, *Salafism in the Maghreb*, chap. 3.

15 Henri Lauzière, 'The Evolution of the Salafiyya in the Twentieth Century Through the Life and Thought of Taqi Al-Din al-Hilali,' *Georgetown University-Graduate School of Arts & Sciences* (thesis, Georgetown University, 2008), 211–13, https://repository.library.georgetown.edu/handle/10822/558204.

16 Lauzière, *The Making of Salafism*, 2016, 64–66.

17 Lauzière, 156–57.

18 Lauzière, 157–60.

19 Lauzière, 173–75.

20 Lauzière, 179–80.

21 Lauzière, 180–81.

22 Lauzière, 185–98.

23 François, 'The Movement for Unicity and Reform,' 70.

24 Lauzière, *The Making of Salafism*, 2016, 199–200 and 210.

25 Mohammed Masbah, 'Between Preaching and Activism: How Politics Divided Morocco's Salafis,' *MIPA Institute*, October 6, 2024, https://mipa.institute/en/5615.

26 Wehrey and Boukhars, *Salafism in the Maghreb*, 44–48.

27 The preceding paragraphs have been derived from Masbah, 'Salafi Movements and the Political Process in Morocco.'

28 Wehrey and Boukhars, *Salafism in the Maghreb*, 55–57.

29 On the use of 'Salafi' the adjective to *salafiyya* the abstract noun, see Lauzière, *The Making of Salafism*, 2016, 16–23; Henri Lauzière, 'Salafism Against Hadith Literature: The Curious Beginnings of a New Category in 1920s Algeria,' *Journal of the American Oriental Society* 141, no. 2 (August 27, 2021): 407–10, https://doi.org/10.7817/jameroriesoci.141.2.0403.

30 Wehrey and Boukhars, *Salafism in the Maghreb*, 67.

31 Boubekeur, 'Salafism and Radical Politics in Postconflict Algeria,' 8.

32 Boubekeur, 27.

33 Ferkous used the story of the conversion of the King of Ethiopia, al-Najashi, during the time of the Prophet to back his stance, saying that he 'neither applied Shariʿa in his realm nor engaged in legitimate jihad, but God forgave him nonetheless, as his people were not Muslims and would not have supported its application.' This spinning contrasts with how Islamists and political Salafis have used this story. For example, Hamad Kabbaj, the Moroccan Salafi who turned politico from a quietist Salafism over the Arab Spring, and was discussed earlier, utilizes the story of al-Najashi to justify a political pragmatism whereby he was permitted by the Prophet to not abdicate his throne but to do as much good as possible, even if not ideal, as abdication would cause greater harm to the Muslim community in Arabia. See Wehrey and Boukhars, *Salafism in the Maghreb*, 57 and 76.

34 Wehrey and Boukhars, 73–77.

35 Wehrey and Boukhars, 59–60.

36 Wehrey and Boukhars, 110.

37 Mohamed A. El-Khuwas, 'Qaddafi and Islam in Libya,' *American Journal of Islam and Society* 1, no. 1 (April 1, 1984): 61–81, https://doi.org/10.35632/ajis.v1i1.2821.

38 Alison Pargeter, 'Qadhafi and Political Islam in Libya,' in *Libya since 1969*, ed. Dirk Vandewalle (New York: Palgrave Macmillan US, 2008), 83–104, https://doi.org/10.1007/978-0-230-61386-7_4.

39 Wehrey and Boukhars, *Salafism in the Maghreb*, 108.

40 'Madkhalī' as a reference to Libyan factions began in Libya around late 2013, in an attempt to demonize the growing Salafi tendencies from eastern Libya as foreign agents, under the direction of Saudi Arabia. See Wehrey and Boukhars, 131.

41 Frederic Wehrey and Anouar Boukhars, *Salafism in the Maghreb: Politics, Piety, and Militancy* (New York, NY: Oxford University Press, 2019), 114–15.

42 For a discussion of these actors, see Bonnefoy, *Salafism in Yemen*.

43 The following Libyan Salafis sided with al-Ma'ribi: Sha'ban Madud Khalifah Hadiyah (aka Abu Ubaydah al-Zway), Ahmad Gumatah (aka Abu Harun), Nadir Umrani, Mahmud bin Musa and 'Abd al-Qadir al-Na'rut; and those who sided with al-Madkhalī include, in addition to Hafalah, Muhammad al-Anqar and Muhammad Mika'ili Nazal (aka Abu Abdillah al-Abyari). See Wehrey and Boukhars, *Salafism in the Maghreb*, 172n42.

44 Wehrey and Boukhars, 112–13.

45 Hafalah was born in Tripoli, with roots in western Libya. Ethnically, he is Amazigh. He studied in Saudi Arabia and then in Yemen with Muqbil; and he was originally aligned with al-Ma'ribi, before switching to the loyalist Rabi' al-Madkhalī. See Wehrey and Boukhars, 173n55.

46 Wehrey and Boukhars, 117–18.

47 Wehrey and Boukhars, 120–21 and 173n86.

48 For a detailed analysis of the period from 2011 until 2019, see Wolfram Lacher, *Libya's Fragmentation: Structure and Process in Violent Conflict* (London: I.B. Tauris, 2020).

49 Wehrey and Boukhars, *Salafism in the Maghreb*, 174n75.

50 Lacher, *Libya's Fragmentation*, 30–31.

51 Wehrey and Boukhars, *Salafism in the Maghreb*, 30–31.

52 Lacher, *Libya's Fragmentation*, 33–36.

53 Haftar had been a general under Gaddafi, but defected in the 1980s and had become a CIA asset, before returning to Libya in 2011, after being exiled in the United States. See Frederic Wehrey and Anouar Boukhars, *Salafism in the Maghreb: Politics, Piety, and Militancy* (New York, NY: Oxford University Press, 2019), 122.

54 Wehrey and Boukhars, 122–23.

55 Wehrey and Boukhars, 123–24.

56 Wehrey and Boukhars, 125–27.

57 Wehrey and Boukhars, 127–28.

58 Wehrey and Boukhars, 129.

59 Wehrey and Boukhars, 178n139.

60 Wehrey and Boukhars, 129–30 and 178n142.

61 Wehrey and Boukhars, 133–34.

62 Wehrey and Boukhars, 134.

63 Nadir al-Umrani was my close personal friend during my days at IUM. He was a gentle, caring soul who was well-loved and admired by professors and students alike, and his brutal and senseless death shocked people around the world.

64 Wehrey and Boukhars, *Salafism in the Maghreb*, 130–32.

65 Thurston, *Salafism in Nigeria*, 15 and 34.

66 The pivotal study on this country is Alexander Thurston, *Salafism in Nigeria: Islam, Preaching, and Politics*, Reprint ed. (London: Cambridge University Press, 2018).

67 For discussions on Gumi's life and thought, see Thurston, *Salafism in Nigeria*, 81–86; Roman Loimeier, *Islamic Reform and Political Change in Northern Nigeria* (Evanston, Illinois: Northwestern University Press, 2011).
68 Thurston, *Salafism in Nigeria*, 77–81.
69 Thurston, 86–87.
70 Thurston, 90.
71 Thurston, 89–06, 153, 162–94.
72 Abu Hajar would come to be expelled by the British from Sudan, and thereafter he was appointed by King Ibn Sa'ud as the president of the Organization of Enjoining the Good and Forbidding the Evil (*al-amr bi-l-ma'ruf wa-l-nahy 'an al-munkar)* in Jeddah.
73 Noah Salomon, 'The Salafi Critique of Islamism: Doctrine, Difference and the Problem of Islamic Political Action in Contemporary Sudan,' in *Global Salafism: Islam's New Religious Movement*, ed. Roel Meijer (Oxford University Press, 2014), 144–68, https://doi.org/10.1093/acprof:oso/9780199333431.003.0007.
74 Einas Ahmed, 'Militant Salafism in Sudan,' *Islamic Africa* 6, no. 1–2 (2015): 177–78.
75 Ahmed, 'Militant Salafism in Sudan'; Liv Tønnessen, 'Ansar Al-Sunna and Women's Agency in Sudan: A Salafi Approach to Empowerment through Gender Segregation,' *Frontiers: A Journal of Women Studies* 37, no. 3 (2016): 92–124, https://doi.org/10.5250/fronjwomestud.37.3.0092. These two articles provide the substance of the majority of the information in this section.
76 Ahmed, 'Militant Salafism in Sudan,' 170–71.
77 See Noah Salomon, *For Love of the Prophet: An Ethnography of Sudan's Islamic State* (Princeton: Princeton University Press, 2016), 91–93.
78 Omar al-Bashir was himself deposed by a coup in 2019, marking the beginning of a relatively unsettled period in Sudan.
79 Salomon, *For Love of the Prophet*, 181–82.
80 Alexander Thurston, 'Islam and Politics in Postcolonial Mauritania,' in *Oxford Research Encyclopedia of African History*, by Alexander Thurston (Oxford University Press, 2022).
81 See Wehrey and Boukhars, *Salafism in the Maghreb*, chap. 2.
82 Alexander Thurston, 'Shaykh Muhammad Al-Hasan al-Dedew (b. 1963), a Salafi Scholar in Contemporary Mauritania,' 2012, 64–67, https://www.semanticscholar.org/paper/Shaykh-Muhammad-al-Hasan-al-Dedew-(b.-1963)%2C-a-in-Thurston/1bf5df0a8020e10c84b6cd191ea7c326435a8f6d#citing-papers.
83 Thurston, 'Islam and Politics in Postcolonial Mauritania.'
84 Thurston.
85 Pierret, *Religion and State in Syria*, 105–6.
86 Pierret, 108.
87 Pierret, 108–9.
88 Pierret, 108–12.
89 This organization was first formed in 1980 as the Royal Academy for Islamic Civilization Research; and in 2000 its name was changed to the Royal Aal al-Bayt Institute for Islamic Thought. It has been a crucial element in trying to create an 'official Islam' for the Jordanian kingdom. See Wagemakers, *Salafism in Jordan*, 147–48.
90 For a discussion on how Salafism both influenced the adherents of the Syrian 'old orthodoxy' and how Syrians have joined the 'anti-Salafi international,' but not without some traditionalist Syrian discontent with the direction of this movement, see Pierret, *Religion and State in Syria*, 113–29.
91 These include *Aḥrar al-Sham* (mainly in the north-west of Syria), who have support from activist Salafis in Kuwait, the *Army of Islam* (formerly called the Islam Brigade, led by Zahran 'Allush, whose father was connected to the Saudi religious establishment) and *Suqur al-Sham* (which had been active in Idlib, and formed at

the end of 2011). These three were co-founders of the Islamic Front (al-Jabhat al-Islamiyya, IF), along with non-Salafi factions. The IF received support from Ṣaḥwa Salafis in Saudi Arabia like Salman al-Oudah and Nasir al-ʻUmar; the Army of Islam had support from al-ʻArʻur and activist Kuwaiti Salafis, as well as Saudi Arabia, who perhaps saw it as a useful force against ISIS, or even as a way of appeasing their own nationals who were angered at Saudi's backing of the 2013 coup in Egypt against the democratically-elected Mohamed Morsi of the Muslim Brotherhood. However, Saudi did not endorse *Aḥrar al-Sham*. Yet the IF had its most important support from Turkey and Qatar. We shall return to *Aḥrar al-Sham* in the final section of this chapter.

92 The main forms of this thought are Jabhat al-Nusra and ISIS.

93 It is noteworthy that the few large Islamist groups linked to the urban middle class (Fastaqim Kama Umirt in Aleppo and Shabab al-Huda in Damascus) are not Salafi. See Thomas Pierret, 'Salafis at War in Syria: Logics of Fragmentation and Realignment,' in *Salafism After the Arab Awakening: Contending with People's Power*, ed. Francesco Cavatorta and Fabio Merone (Oxford University Press, 2017), 137–154, https://doi.org/10.1093/acprof:oso/9780190274993.003.0009.

94 Eido, 'The Rise of Syrian Salafism,' 262–67.

95 For a comprehensive study of Salafism in Jordan, see Wagemakers, *Salafism in Jordan*. Much of this section has been derived from the latter work.

96 Wagemakers, 96–97.

97 Wagemakers, 38.

98 Wagemakers, 99–100.

99 Wagemakers, 219.

100 See Khaled Hroub, 'Salafi Formations in Palestine: The Limits of a De-Palestinised Milieu,' in *Global Salafism: Islam's New Religious Movement*, ed. Roel Meijer (Oxford University Press, 2014), 221–43, https://doi.org/10.1093/acprof:oso/9780199333431.003.0010.

101 Wagemakers, *Salafism in Jordan*, 116.

102 It should be noted that, unsurprisingly, al-Madkhalī and al-Halabi were no longer on good terms until the latter's death in 2020.

103 Wagemakers, *Salafism in Jordan*, 75–77 and 110–11.

104 Wagemakers, 140; Pall, *Salafism in Lebanon*, 65–76.

105 Wagemakers, *Salafism in Jordan*, chap. 7.

106 See Wagemakers, 204–12; Lacroix, 'Between Revolution and Apoliticism,' 69.

107 Wagemakers, *Salafism in Jordan*, 119; the following account of the discord is extracted from Wagemakers, chap. 4.

108 Mūrad Shukrī, *Iḥkām Al-Taqrīr Li-Aḥkām Masʾalat al-Takfīr* (Riyadh: Dār al-Ṣamīʿī, 1994); for a short overview on the work, see Wagemakers, *Salafism in Jordan*, 123–26.

109 The center opened with Salim al-Hilali as director, Muhammad Musa Nasr as deputy and al-Halabi, Mashhur ibn Hasan and Husayn al-ʿAwayisha as key members. See Wagemakers, *Salafism in Jordan*, 139.

110 Wagemakers, 196.

111 See Wagemakers, 150–51.

112 Wagemakers, 217–26.

113 See Adham Saouli, 'Lebanon's Salafis,' in *Salafism After the Arab Awakening*, ed. Francesco Cavatorta and Fabio Merone (Oxford University Press, 2017), 43–60, https://doi.org/10.1093/acprof:oso/9780190274993.003.0004.

114 Pall, *Lebanese Salafis between the Gulf and Europe*, 39.

115 Pall, 40; Rabil, *Salafism in Lebanon*, 4.

116 Pall, *Lebanese Salafis between the Gulf and Europe*, 51.

117 Robert G. Rabil, *Salafism in Lebanon: From Apoliticism to Transnational Jihadism* (Washington, DC: Georgetown University Press, 2014), 4–5 and 82.

118 Pall, *Lebanese Salafis between the Gulf and Europe*, 62; Rabil, *Salafism in Lebanon*, 82–83.
119 Rabil, *Salafism in Lebanon*, 82–83.
120 Pall, *Lebanese Salafis between the Gulf and Europe*, 51.
121 Pall, 66.
122 Pall, 77.
123 See Saouli, 'Lebanon's Salafis,' 69–73.
124 Pall, *Lebanese Salafis between the Gulf and Europe*, 83–87.
125 Pall, 82–83.
126 Pall, 9.
127 Hegghammer and Lacroix, 'Rejectionist Islamism in Saudi Arabia,' 111.
128 Pall, *Lebanese Salafis between the Gulf and Europe*, 87–89.
129 Zoltan Pall, 'Kuwaiti Salafism and Its Growing Influence in the Levant,' *Carnegie Endowment for International Peace*, May 7, 2014, 7.
130 Other Kuwaiti Madkhalīs who emerged around this time include Hamad 'Uthman, Salim al-Tawil, Falah Mundakar, Ahmad al-Siba'i and Muhammad al-'Anjari. See Zoltán Pall, 'Salafi Dynamics in Kuwait: Politics, Fragmentation and Change,' in *Salafism After the Arab Awakening: Contending with People's Power*, ed. Francesco Cavatorta and Fabio Merone (Oxford University Press, 2017), 178, https://doi.org/10.1093/acprof:oso/9780190274993.003.0011.
131 Pall, *Lebanese Salafis between the Gulf and Europe*, 90–94.
132 Pall, 'Kuwaiti Salafism,' 8–11.
133 Pall, 10; Pall, 'Salafi Dynamics in Kuwait,' 181–86.
134 Pall, 'Kuwaiti Salafism,' 10–12.
135 Ismail, *Rethinking Salafism*, 52.
136 See Pall, 'Salafi Dynamics in Kuwait.'
137 See Bonnefoy, *Salafism in Yemen*; Judit Kuschnitzki, 'The Establishment and Positioning of Al-Rashad: A Case Study of Political Salafism in Yemen,' in *Salafism After the Arab Awakening: Contending with People's Power*, ed. Francesco Cavatorta and Fabio Merone (Oxford University Press, 2017), 0, https://doi.org/10.1093/acprof:oso/9780190274993.003.0007; Maysaa Shujaa Aldeen, 'Yemen's War-Torn Rivalries for Religious Education,' in *Islamic Institutions in Arab States: Mapping the Dynamics of Control, Co-Option, and Contention*, ed. Frederic Wehrey (Washington, DC: Carnegie Endowment for International Peace, 2021), 33–52.
138 Bonnefoy, *Salafism in Yemen*, 54–59.
139 Hegghammer and Lacroix, 'Rejectionist Islamism in Saudi Arabia,' 108 and 120n24.
140 al-Huzaimi, *The Mecca Uprising*, 76.
141 Hegghammer and Lacroix, 'Rejectionist Islamism in Saudi Arabia,' 111.
142 al-Huzaimi, *The Mecca Uprising*, 93.
143 Lacroix, *Awakening Islam*, 101.
144 See Bonnefoy, *Salafism in Yemen*, 158.
145 Laurent Bonnefoy, 'How Transnational Is Salafism In Yemen?' in *Global Salafism: Islam's New Religious Movement*, ed. Roel Meijer (Oxford University Press, 2014), 333–35, https://doi.org/10.1093/acprof:oso/9780199333431.003.0015.
146 Aldeen, 'Yemen's War-Torn Rivalries,' 42.
147 Bonnefoy, 'How Transnational Is Salafism In Yemen?' 325.
148 Bonnefoy, *Salafism in Yemen*, 142–43.
149 Bonnefoy, 206–7.
150 Bonnefoy, 259.
151 Bonnefoy, 264–65.
152 Bonnefoy, 'How Transnational Is Salafism In Yemen?' 338.
153 Laurent Bonnefoy, 'Quietist Salafis, the Arab Spring and the Politicisation Process,' in *Salafism After the Arab Awakening: Contending with People's Power*, ed. Francesco

Cavatorta and Fabio Merone (Oxford University Press, 2017), 212, https://doi.org/10.1093/acprof:oso/9780190274993.003.0013.

154 Kuschnitzki, 'The Establishment and Positioning of Al-Rashad,' 101–2.

155 Kuschnitzki, 102–3.

156 Bonnefoy, *Salafism in Yemen*, 76.

157 Kuschnitzki, 'The Establishment and Positioning of Al-Rashad,' 104–15.

158 Bonnefoy, 'Quietist Salafis, the Arab Spring and the Politicisation Process,' 216–17.

159 Aldeen, 'Yemen's War-Torn Rivalries,' 33 and 45.

160 Lauzière, 'The Construction of Salafiyya,' 383.

161 Olidort, 'In Defense of Tradition,' 219n650.

162 Thurston, *Salafism in Nigeria*, 90.

163 See Dietrich Reetz, *Islam in the Public Sphere: Religious Groups in India 1900–1947.* (Oxford: Oxford University Press, 2006), 74; Zahab, 'Salafism in Pakistan: The Ahl-e Ḥadīth Movement,' 126–42.

164 Lauzière, *The Making of Salafism*, 2016, 74, 90–91 and 105–13.

165 On the complex aspects of the relationship, see Walī Riḍā Naṣr, *Mawdudi and the Making of Islamic Revivalism* (New York: Oxford University Press, 1996), 17, 110–11, 174n11 and 177n66.

166 See Maszlee Malik, 'Salafism in Malaysia: Historical Account on Its Emergence and Motivations,' *Sociology of Islam* 5, no. 4 (December 5, 2017): 303–33, https://doi.org/10.1163/22131418-00504003.

167 Thurston, *Salafism in Nigeria*, 90.

168 See Noorhaidi Hasan, 'The Salafi Madrasas of Indonesia,' in *The Madrasa in Asia*, ed. Farish A Noor, Yoginder Sikand, and Martin Van Bruinessen (Amsterdam University Press, 2009), 247–274, https://doi.org/10.1515/9789048501380-011; Din Wahid, 'Nurturing Salafi Manhaj A Study of Salafi Pesantrens in Contemporary Indonesia,' *Wacana* 15, no. 2 (July 1, 2015): 367, https://doi.org/10.17510/wacana.v15i2.413; the distinction between madrasa and pesantren is sometimes difficult to maintain; Hasan, 'The Salafi Madrasas of Indonesia,' 271n1.

169 See Noorhaidi Hasan, 'Salafism, Education, and Youth: Saudi Arabia's Campaign for Wahhabism in Indonesia,' in *Wahhābism and the World: Understanding Saudi Arabia's Global Influence on Islam*, ed. Peter Mandaville (Oxford University Press, 2022), 135–157, https://doi.org/10.1093/oso/9780197532560.003.0007. This important article has been used for much of the contents of this section.

170 See Noorhaidi Hasan, 'Between Transnational Interest and Domestic Politics: Understanding Middle Eastern Fatwās on Jihad in the Moluccas,' January 1, 2005, 73–92, https://doi.org/10.1163/1568519053123885; Noorhaidi Hasan, 'Ambivalent Doctrines and Conflicts In the Salafi Movement In Indonesia,' in *Global Salafism: Islam's New Religious Movement*, ed. Roel Meijer (Oxford University Press, 2014), 169–88., https://doi.org/10.1093/acprof:oso/9780199333431.003.0008.

171 Hasan, 'Salafism, Education, and Youth,' 136.

172 Hasan, 'The Salafi Madrasas of Indonesia,' 270.

173 See Chris Chaplin, 'Salafi Islamic Piety as Civic Activism: Wahdah Islamiyah and Differentiated Citizenship in Indonesia,' *Citizenship Studies* 22, no. 2 (February 17, 2018): 208–23, https://doi.org/10.1080/13621025.2018.1445488; Chris Chaplin, *Salafism and the State: Islamic Activism and National Identity in Contemporary Indonesia, Chaplin* (Copenhagen: NIAS Press, 2021), https://press.uchicago.edu/ucp/books/book/distributed/S/bo239343105.html.

174 See the points relating to Salafis adapting their method in Hasan, 'Salafism, Education, and Youth,' 148–49.

175 A broad outline of Salafism in the UK, albeit with a lack of emphasis on the role of the *Ahl-e-Hadith* movement (discussed here), can be found in Sadek Hamid, *Sufis, Salafis and Islamists: The Contested Ground of British Islamic Activism*, Library of Modern

Religion 46 (London; New York: I.B. Tauris, 2016), 55–67; Innes Bowen, *Medina in Birmingham, Najaf in Brent: Inside British Islam* (London: Hurst, 2014), 59–81; Anabel Inge, *The Making of a Salafi Muslim Woman: Paths to Conversion* (New York: Oxford University Press, 2017), 26–32.

176 For an overview of the formation of the MJAH in the UK and its relationship to Salafism, see R. Ahmad Azami, *Ahl-e-Hadith in Britain: History, Establishment, Activites and Objectives* (London: The Muslim College and Ta-Ha Publishers, 1995); Hira Amin, 'Salafism and Islamism in Britain, 1965–2015' (PhD thesis, Cambridge, University of Cambridge, 2017), https://www.repository.cam.ac.uk/handle/1810/269730; Amin and Majothi, 'The Ahl-e-Hadith,' 1–31.

177 Amin, 'Salafism and Islamism in Britain, 1965–2015,' 53 and 68; Majothi, 'Translating Salafism into English,' 70–71.

178 Majothi, 'Translating Salafism into English,' 71.

179 Azhar Majothi, 'Translating Salafism into English: Anglo–Salafi Print Culture in Britain' (PhD thesis, Nottingham, England, University of Nottingham, 2023), 72–73, http://eprints.nottingham.ac.uk/74265/.

180 Majothi, 71–72.

181 See Hira Amin, 'The Shifting Contours of Saudi Influence in Britain,' in *Wahhabism and the World: Understanding Saudi Arabia's Global Influence on Islam*, ed. Peter Mandaville (Oxford University Press, 2022), 294 and 302, https://doi.org/10.1093/oso/9780197532560.003.0015.

182 Iman Dawood, 'Reworking the Common Sense of British Muslims: Salafism, Culture, and Politics within London's Muslim Community' (PhD thesis, London, The London School of Economics and Political Science, 2021), 80 and 84, and also chaps 3 and 8.

183 See Dawood, 'Reworking the Common Sense of British Muslims'; Majothi, 'Translating Salafism into English.'

184 Suhaib Hasan received his PhD from the University of Birmingham in 1991, which was eventually published as a monograph, as Hasan, *The Concept of the Mahdi Among Ahl Al-Sunna*.

185 Majothi, 'Translating Salafism into English,' 189.

186 Amin, 'Salafism and Islamism in Britain, 1965–2015,' 72.

187 Amin, 75–76; Majothi, 'Translating Salafism into English,' 73 and 79.

188 Amin, 'Salafism and Islamism in Britain, 1965–2015,' 77.

189 For instance, see Majothi, 'Translating Salafism into English,' 144–46.

190 For a good overview of the history of JIMAS, see Dawood, 'Reworking the Common Sense of British Muslims,' 77–81, and also 105 on on comments regarding Abu Muntasir's leadership style that was interpreted as dictatorial.

191 The relationship and nature of these organizations have been examined in Majothi, 'Translating Salafism into English.'

192 Dawood, 'Reworking the Common Sense of British Muslims,' 85; 'Abdurraheem Green: "Returning Jihadis Aren't so Bad, I Used to Be One,"' *5 Pillars* (blog), October 30, 2014, https://5pillarsuk.com/2014/10/30/abdur-raheem-green-returning-jihadis-arent-so-bad-i-used-to-be-one/.

193 Abu Aaliyah (aka Surkheel Sharif), a key member of the emerging Salafi trend that would develop into JIMAS, speaks of the nature of Salafism at this formative time: 'There was no invitation to Salafiya [in JIMAS] because Salafiya as a concept did not exist. As far as we were concerned, Abu Muntasir [the leader of the organization] was on "Qur'an and Sunna" … Salafism came, by name, at a slightly more developed stage; but we were Salafi before we were Salafi, unbeknown to us.' Furthermore, Abu Aaliyah/Sharif is also quoted on how the developing Salafi movement started to make the opinions of al-Albānī the sole criteria for establishing Islamic validity in areas that were legitimately differed upon in 'classical' scholarship. See Iman Dawood, 'Who Is a "Salafi"? Salafism and the Politics of Labelling in the UK,' March 3, 2020, 243–44,

https://doi.org/10.1163/22117954-12341416; Abu Aaliyah/Sharif has been described as Abu Muntasir's 'right hand man' in JIMAS, after taking Abu Muntasir as a mentor from the early 1980s; see Dawood, 'Reworking the Common Sense of British Muslims,' 76–79; Abu Aaliyah/Sharif has undertaken an intellectual journey which has led him to call for the refinement of many facets of Salafism; Surkheel Sharif, *Salafism Reconsidered* (forthcoming), n.d., 84.

194 Dawood, 'Reworking the Common Sense of British Muslims,' 84.

195 Bowen, *Medina in Birmingham, Najaf in Brent*, 78.

196 Al-Haddad remained with al-Muntada for five years, before he left and formed the Muslim Research and Development Forum (MRDF), and then influenced the creation of the Islam21C website. These initiatives have a trace of Salafism, but they also display an ecumenical approach, as well as, unsurprisingly, showing a high level of political engagement, and distance themselves from being called Salafi. See Dawood, 'Reworking the Common Sense of British Muslims,' 119–22 and 207–10.

197 Lacroix, *Awakening Islam*, 192.

198 Bowen, *Medina in Birmingham, Najaf in Brent*, 78; Majothi, 'Translating Salafism into English,' 144–45.

199 For a study of Madkhali's thought, see Meijer, 'Politicising Al-Jarḥ Wa-l-Taʿdīl.'

200 The Jamiyya were described in Chapter 3, as the followers of the Ethiopian scholar Muhammad Bin Amān al-Jāmī (1930–1995), who led the pro-Saudi regime charge against the Ṣaḥwa, while he was a teacher at IUM. For a study of Jami, together with Muhammad Surur, see Ahmed Khalid Ayong, 'The Nature of the 'Jāmī/Surūrī' Dispute and Its Impact on the Islamic University in Medina' (draft paper prepared for the CSIA, University of Oxford).

201 In 2009, MJAH produced a defense of their Salafism with a passionately worded document entitled *In Defense of MJAH: A Response to the Unjust, Deceptive and Slanderous Allegations Made Against Markazi Jamiat Ahle Hadith UK* (Birmingham: MJAH, 2008, and then edited in 2009).

202 Dawood, 'Reworking the Common Sense of British Muslims,' 110.

203 See section 6.5 on Salafism in North America for a more detailed discussion of the AlMaghrib Institute.

204 I was briefly a lecturer with the AlKauthar Institute when it first launched in 2006.

205 Dawood, 'Reworking the Common Sense of British Muslims,' 198.

206 See Baker, *Extremists in Our Midst: Confronting Terror*, 25–26.

207 For a study of the importance of Salafism in the lives of Salafi women in the UK, see Inge, *The Making of a Salafi Muslim Woman*, chap. 6.

208 Farquhar, *Circuits of Faith*, 162.

209 The authorship of this book, as noted earlier in Chapter 2, has now been convincingly attributed to Ghulām Khalīl and not al-Barbahārī. See section 2.2.4, note 68.

210 Dawood, 'Reworking the Common Sense of British Muslims,' 84.

211 See Alexander Meleagrou-Hitchens, *Salafism in America: History, Evolution, Radicalization* (George Washington University, Program on Extremism, 2018), 21–22.

212 Lewys Bruce, a government advisor on extremism, with a special focus on 'incel' ideology, has criticized Shawcross's focus on Muslim extremists over right-wing extremists as indicative of his attitude being incorrectly stuck in the period between 2004 and 2007, around the time of the London bombings in 2005. See Mark Townsend, 'Anti-Terrorism Programme Must Keep Focus on Far Right, Say Experts,' *The Observer*, May 22, 2022, https://www.theguardian.com/uk-news/2022/may/22/anti-terrorism-programme-must-keep-focus-on-far-right-say-experts.

213 See Matt Dathan, 'Cabinet Row Holds Up Prevent Counterterrorism Review,' *The Times*, May 22, 2022, https://www.theguardian.com/uk-news/2022/may/22/anti-terrorism-program-must-keep-focus-on-far-right-say-experts.

214 See the press release of Bindmans solicitors in the aftermath of their client's legal victory, 'Dr Salman Butt Secures Apology, Substantial Libel Damages and Costs against the Secretary of State for the Home Department,' *Bindmans*, November 15, 2021, https://www.bindmans.com/knowledge-hub/news/dr-salman-butt-secures-apology-substantial-libel-damages-and-costs-against-the-secretary-of-state-for-the-home-department/.
215 See William Shawcross, 'Independent Review of Prevent,' Government Report (London: House of Commons, February 2023), https://assets.publishing.service.gov.uk/government/uploads/system/uploads/attachment_data/file/1134987/Independent_Review_of_Prevent__print_.pdf.
216 A study of the backlash against Salafism in the UK by other Sunni groups can be seen in Iman Dawood, 'Reworking the Common Sense of British Muslims: Salafism, Culture, and Politics within London's Muslim Community' (PhD thesis, London, The London School of Economics and Political Science, 2021), chap. 4, http://etheses.lse.ac.uk/id/eprint/4347. Dawood, 153–56 tackles the spiritual crisis felt by UK Salafis, and their varying responses to it. And Dawood, 160 quotes Abu Aaliyah and Green.
217 For the contents of this section, see Andrew Hammond, 'Salafi Thought in Turkish Public Discourse Since 1980,' *International Journal of Middle East Studies* 49, no. 3 (2017): 417–35.
218 His official website contains many of his articles and lectures in Turkish, see 'Nureddin Yıldız,' n.d., https://www.nureddinyildiz.com/.
219 See Harun Karčić, 'Arab Brothers, Arms, and Food Rations: How Salafism Made Its Way to Bosnia and Herzegovina,' in *Wahhabism and the World: Understanding Saudi Arabia's Global Influence on Islam*, ed. Peter Mandaville (Oxford University Press, 2022), 272–89, https://doi.org/10.1093/oso/9780197532560.003.0014.
220 Karčić, 276 and 278.
221 See Li, *The Universal Enemy*, 53–54 and 68.
222 Darryl Li, 'Expert Report on the Bosnian Jihad: Prepared for US. v. Bahar Ahmad and US. v. Syed Talha Ahsan' (New Haven, CT: United States District Court for the District of Connecticut, 2014), https://www.academia.edu/28287134/Expert_Opinion_on_Foreign_Fighters_in_the_Bosnian_Jihad.
223 Karčić, 'Arab Brothers, Arms, and Food Rations,' 281.
224 See the introductory portions of Mohamed-Ali Adraoui, *Salafism Goes Global: From the Gulf to the French Banlieues*, Religion and Global Politics (Oxford; New York: Oxford University Press, 2020).
225 Adraoui, 'Salafism in France,' 365; Adraoui, *Salafism Goes Global*.
226 Adraoui, *Salafism Goes Global*, chaps 1 and 2.
227 Adraoui, 'Salafism in France,' 370–76; Adraoui, *Salafism Goes Global*, chap. 2.
228 Mohamed-Ali Adraoui, 'Radical Milieus and Salafis Movements in France: Ideologies, Practices, Relationships with Society and Political Visions,' *European University Institute*, 2014, 7, https://cadmus.eui.eu/handle/1814/31911.
229 'Salafism Seeks to Impose Itself in the Muslim World,' *La Croix International*, April 7, 2016, https://international.la-croix.com/news/religion/salafism-seeks-to-impose-itself-in-the-muslim-world/2942.
230 'Charlie Hebdo: Magazine Republishes Controversial Mohammed Cartoons,' September 1, 2020, https://www.bbc.com/news/world-europe-53985407.
231 'France "Expels" Controversial Salafist Preacher to Algeria,' *France 24*, April 20, 2018, https://www.france24.com/en/20180420-france-expels-controversial-salafist-preacher-algeria.
232 'France Deports Salafist Preacher to Algeria,' *The New Arab*, June 15, 2023, https://www.newarab.com/news/france-deports-salafist-preacher-algeria.

233 Matthew A. MacDonald, 'What Is a Salafi Reformist?: Tariq Ramadan and Sayyid Qutb in Conversation,' *Political Theology* 15, no. 5 (September 2014): 385–405, https://doi.org/10.1179/1462317X14Z.00000000083.

234 Angelique Chrisafis, 'Tariq Ramadan Acquitted of Charges of Rape and Sexual Coercion by Swiss Court,' *The Guardian*, May 24, 2023, https://www.theguardian.com/world/2023/may/24/tariq-ramadan-cleared-rape-sexual-coercion-swiss-court.

235 Ellen van de Bovenkamp, 'Tariq Ramadan: A Voice for Decoloniality in France and in Morocco,' February 18, 2022, https://doi.org/10.1163/22117954-bja10045.

236 For an overview of Salafism in North America, with a particular emphasis on the United States, see Meleagrou-Hitchens, *Salafism in America*; Razavian, 'Yasir Qadhi and the Development of Reasonable Salafism'; Shadee Elmasry, 'The Salafis in America: The Rise, Decline and Prospects for a Sunni Muslim Movement among African-Americans,' *Journal of Muslim Minority Affairs* 30 (June 1, 2010): 217–36, https://doi.org/10.1080/13602004.2010.494072.

237 Farquhar, *Circuits of Faith*, 162. I am the eighteenth American graduate in 2000 and the first non-covert from America.

238 Sherman A. Jackson, *Islam and the Blackamerican* (Oxford University Press, 2005), 49, https://doi.org/10.1093/acprof:oso/9780195180817.001.0001.

239 Dr Bilal Philips helped in the publication of my first book in English. See Yasir Qadhi, *Riyaa: Hidden Shirk* (Sharjah, UAE: Dar Al Fatah, 1996). I met him in London in the early 2000s on a number of occasions.

240 See *Meet Dr Bilal Philips – Communist to Islam | Young Smirks Podcast Ep14*, Meet Dr Bilal Philips, 2019, https://www.youtube.com/watch?v=kAGtgEvag1Q. Abdullah Hakim Quick cannot be defined as a Salafi, although he is an instructor with the post-Salafi AlMaghrib Institute, discussed below.

241 For a study of this movement, see Muhammad Khalid Masud, *Travellers in Faith: Studies of the Tablīghī Jamā'at as a Transnational Islamic Movement for Faith Renewal*, Social, Economic, and Political Studies of the Middle East and Asia (Boston: Brill, 2000), http://bvbr.bib-bvb.de:8991/F?func=service&doc_library=BVB01&local_base=BVB01&doc_number=008979001&line_number=0001&func_code=DB_RECORDS&service_type=MEDIA.

242 See *Interview with Dr. Bilal on Islam and Education [Arabic with Subtitles]*, 2019, https://www.youtube.com/watch?v=AQugDiStEIw.

243 His PhD was reworked into a monograph, and published as Abu Ameenah Bilal Philips, *The Exorcist Tradition in Islam* (Al-Hidaayah Publishing, 2008).

244 See 'Founder IOU,' International Open University, accessed December 25, 2022, https://iou.edu.gm/founder/.

245 See Dawood, 'Who Is a "Salafi"?' 249–50, 253 and 255.

246 See *Sh. Al-Jibaly Interview*, 2008, https://www.youtube.com/watch?v=QdLO-qqVuk8M.

247 Cited in Meleagrou-Hitchens, *Salafism in America*, 56.

248 Meleagrou-Hitchens, 50–51.

249 Milton Viorst, 'The Education of Ali Al-Timimi,' *The Atlantic*, June 1, 2006, https://www.theatlantic.com/magazine/archive/2006/06/the-education-of-ali-al-timimi/304884/.

250 In this regard, al-Timimi translated the work of 'Abd al-Rahman 'Abd al-Khaliq from Arabic in English and distributed it. See Abdur-Rahman Abdul-Khaliq, *The Wisdom behind the Islamic Laws Regarding Women*, trans. Ali al-Timimi (IslamKotob, n.d.).

251 'Ali Al-Timimi: A Life of Learning,' *SunnahOnline.Com* (blog), accessed June 11, 2024, https://sunnahonline.com/library/biographies/651-ali-al-timimi-a-life-of-learning.

252 Meleagrou-Hitchens, *Salafism in America*, 67–78; 'Ali Al-Timimi: A Life of Learning.'

253 In relation to students based in London who attended AlMaghrib sessions, see Dawood, 'Reworking the Common Sense of British Muslims,' 229.
254 Zareena Grewal, *Islam Is a Foreign Country: American Muslims and the Global Crisis of Authority*, Nation of Newcomers: Immigrant History as American History (New York: New York University Press, 2014), 330.
255 Dawood, 'Reworking the Common Sense of British Muslims,' 123.
256 See Razavian, 'Post-Salafism: Salman al-Ouda and Hatim al-Awni,' 172–73.
257 See Shabbir Akhtar, 'Finding and Following Jesus: The Muslim Claim to the Messiah,' *Yaqeen Insitutue for Islamic Research*, December 24, 2018, https://yaqeeninstitute.org/read/paper/finding-and-following-jesus-the-muslim-claim-to-the-messiah.
258 See Surkheel Sharif, 'Is Islam a Conquest Ideology? On Jihad, War, & Peace,' *Yaqeen Insitutue for Islamic Research*, April 16, 2018.
259 Materials form this section are culled from these sources: Sinani, 'Post-Salafism'; Razavian, 'Post-Salafism: Salman al-Ouda and Hatim al-Awni'; Alexander Thurston, 'An Emerging Post-Salafi Current in West Africa and Beyond,' *Maydan* (blog), October 15, 2018, https://themaydan.com/2018/10/emerging-post-salafi-current-west-africa-beyond/.
260 Thurston, 'An Emerging Post-Salafi Current in West Africa and Beyond.'
261 The Islamic Seminary of America, based in Dallas, TX – an institute of which I am the Dean – is one such Seminary. Our curriculum integrates a study of the tradition from classical sources along with a contemporary analysis of Islam.
262 Thurston, 'Islam and Politics in Postcolonial Mauritania.'
263 Al-Rasheed, *Contesting the Saudi State*, 33 and 65; Madawi Al-Rasheed, 'Divine Politics Reconsidered: Saudi Islamists on Peaceful Revolution,' PDF, 2015, 10, https://doi.org/10.21953/LSE.RO.62240.
264 Al-Rasheed, 'Divine Politics Reconsidered,' 16.
265 Mark C. Thompson, *Saudi Arabia and the Path to Political Change: National Dialogue and Civil Society*, Library of Modern Middle East Studies 159 (London, England; New York: I.B. Tauris, 2014), 116.
266 Al-Rasheed, 'Divine Politics Reconsidered,' 11.
267 Salmān al-ʿOuda, *As'ilat Al-Thawra* (Riyadh: Markaz Namāʾ, 2012).
268 Al-Rasheed, 'Divine Politics Reconsidered,' 16.
269 Al-Rasheed, 'Divine Politics Reconsidered'; Razavian, 'Post-Salafism: Salman al-Ouda and Hatim al-Awni,' 175–80.
270 For studies on Outdah, see Razavian, 'Post-Salafism: Salman al-Ouda and Hatim al-Awni'; Usaama al-Azami, 'Legitimising Political Dissent: Islamist Salafi Discourses on Obedience and Rebellion After the Arab Revolutions,' in *Salafi Social and Political Movements*, ed. Masooda Bano (Edinburgh University Press, 2021), 61–86, https://doi.org/10.1515/9781474479158-008.
271 See Yasir Qadhi, 'Reformation or Reconstruction: Dr. Hatem al-Awni's Critiques of Wahhabism (Unpublished)' (Future of Salafism, Oxford, UK, 2018).
272 Cited in Ismail, *Rethinking Salafism*, 137.
273 See Razavian, 'Post-Salafism: Salman al-Ouda and Hatim al-Awni,' 180–88.
274 Sinani, 'Post-Salafism,' 340.
275 Of the various interactions with al-Awni on these matters by Salafis, the *Taḥqīq al-ifādah bi-taḥrīr mafhūm al ʿibāda* of the Salafi Sụltan al-ʿUmayri, a lecturer at Umm al-Qura University in Mecca, is highly illustrative of the issues at stake between such parties. As this work is not a mere parody or simple polemic, it attracted some serious attention in the English-speaking world. In response, students of al-Awni wrote a number of articles clarifying the matters between the works of al-Awni and al-ʿUmayri. See 'Tawhid Essays – Medium,' *Medium* (blog), accessed June 11, 2024, https://medium.com/@tawhidessays.
276 Ismail, *Rethinking Salafism*, 136.

277 See Robert F. Worth, 'A Black Imam Breaks Ground in Mecca,' *The New York Times*, April 10, 2009, https://www.nytimes.com/2009/04/11/world/middleeast/11saudi.html; 'Leading Saudi Cleric Says IS and Saudi Arabia "Follow the Same Thought,"' *Middle East Eye*, January 28, 2016, https://www.middleeasteye.net/news/leading-saudi-cleric-says-and-saudi-arabia-follow-same-thought; Eman Alhussein, 'The Enlightened Sheikhs of the New Saudi Arabia,' *AGSIW*, June 27, 2018, https://agsiw.org/the-enlightened-sheikhs-of-the-new-saudi-arabia/.

278 See Ahmad Al-Raysuni, *Imam Al-Shatibi's Theory of the Higher Objectives and Intents of Islamic Law*, trans. Nancy Roberts (London: International Institute of Islamic Thought, 2013).

279 See Jasser Auda, *Maqasid Al-Shariah as Philosophy of Islamic Law: A Systems Approach* (London: International Institute of Islamic Thought, 2008); Jasser Auda, 'A Maqāṣidī Approach to Contemporary Application of the Sharī'ah,' *Intellectual Discourse* 19 (December 1, 2011).

280 Tariq Ramadan, *Western Muslims and the Future of Islam*, 1, issued as an Oxford University Press paperback (Oxford; New York, NY: Oxford Univ. Press, 2005), 26–27. It should be noted that Tariq Ramadan has been accused of various predatory crimes – charges that he has strenuously denied – and therefore has been largely absent from the public sphere for the last few years.

281 Tariq Ramadan, *What I Believe* (Oxford; New York: Oxford University Press, 2009), 47–48 and 136n9.

282 Andrew F. March, 'Reading Tariq Ramadan: Political Liberalism, Islam, and "Overlapping Consensus,"' *Ethics & International Affairs* 21, no. 4 (2007): 405–6, https://doi.org/10.1111/j.1747-7093.2007.00114.x.

283 See Tracy McVeigh, '"Recruiter" of UK Jihadis: I Regret Opening the Way to Isis,' *The Observer*, June 13, 2015, https://www.theguardian.com/world/2015/jun/13/godfather-of-british-jihadists-admits-we-opened-to-way-to-join-isis.

284 See Yasir Qadhi, 'On Salafī Islam,' *Muslimmatters.Org*, April 22, 2014, https://muslimmatters.org/wp-content/uploads/On-Salafi-Islam_Dr.-Yasir-Qadhi.pdf.

285 'Pledge of Mutual Respect and Cooperation Between Sunni Muslim Scholars, Organizations, and Students of Sacred Knowledge' (Muslimmatters.org, 2017), https://muslimmatters.org/wp-content/uploads/2007/09/pledge-of-mutual-respect-and-cooperation-between-sunni-muslim-scholars-and-organizations-2.pdf.

286 Surkheel Abu Aaliyah, 'On True Salafism, False Salafism & Ijma' Theology (2/2) – The Humble I,' *The Humble I* (blog), June 3, 2021, https://thehumblei.com/2021/06/03/on-false-salafism-true-salafism-ijma-theology-2-2/.

287 For this movement, see Sam Heller, 'Ahrar Al-Sham's Revisionist Jihadism,' *War on the Rocks* (blog), September 30, 2015, https://warontherocks.com/2015/09/ahrar-al-shams-revisionist-jihadism/; Tore Hamming, *Jihadi Politics: The Global Jihadi Civil War, 2014–2019* (Oxford University Press, 2023); Mokhtar Awad, 'Revolutionary Salafism: The Case of Ahrar Movement | Hudson,' *Hudson Institute* (blog), April 29, 2016, https://www.hudson.org/national-security-defense/revolutionary-salafism-the-case-of-ahrar-movement.

## EPILOGUE

1 https://www.nytimes.com/2011/03/20/magazine/mag-20Salafis-t.html (last accessed Mar 2024).

# BIBLIOGRAPHY


5 Pillars. 'Abdurraheem Green: "Returning Jihadis Aren't so Bad, I Used to Be One,"' October 30, 2014. https://5pillarsuk.com/2014/10/30/abdur-raheem-green-returning-jihadis-arent-so-bad-i-used-to-be-one/.

Abd-Allah, Umar F., and Hamid Algar. *Islamic Struggle in Syria*. 1st ed. Berkeley: Mizan Pr, 1983.

Abdel Haleem, M. 'Early Kalām.' In *History of Islamic Philosophy*, edited by Oliver Leaman and Seyyed Hossein Nasr, 1st ed., 71–88. London: Routledge, 2001.

ʿAbduh, Muḥammad. *Risālat al-tawḥīd*. Beirut: Dār Ibn Ḥazm, 2001.

Abdul-Khaliq, Abdur-Rahman. *The Wisdom behind the Islamic Laws Regarding Women*. Translated by Ali al-Timimi. IslamKotob, n.d.

Abou El Fadl, Khaled. *The Great Theft: Wrestling Islam from the Extremists*. Paperback ed. New York, NY: HarperOne, 2007.

'About – Fiqh Council of North America.' Accessed June 9, 2024. https://fiqhcouncil.org/about/.

Abrahamov, Binyamin. *Islamic Theology: Traditionalism and Rationalism*. 1st ed. Edinburgh: Edinburgh University Press, 1998.

——. 'Scripturalist and Traditionalist Theology.' In *The Oxford Handbook of Islamic Theology*, edited by Sabine Schmidtke, Reprint ed., 263–80. Oxford, United Kingdom: Oxford University Press, 2018.

Abu Aaliyah, Surkheel. 'On True Salafism, False Salafism & Ijmaʿ Theology (2/2) – The Humble I.' *The Humble I* (blog), June 3, 2021. https://thehumblei.com/2021/06/03/on-false-salafism-true-salafism-ijma-theology-2-2/.

Abū Dāwūd al-Sijistānī, Sulaymān b. al-Ashʿath. *Sunan Abī Dāwūd*. 2 vols. Beirut: Dār Iḥyāʾ al-Turāth al-ʿArabī, n.d.

Abu Iyaad. 'Al-Fawzan, Al-Luhaydan, Aal Al-Shaykh: The Ikhwan (Muslim Brotherhood) Are From the 72 Sects, Use Secrecy and Aim Only to Seek Power.' *Ikhwanis.Com* (blog). Accessed August 10, 2019. http://www.ikhwanis.com/articles/lwakzes-the-ikhwan-muslim-brotherhood-are-from-the-72-sects.cfm.

Abū Yaʿlā b. al-Farrāʾ. *Ibṭāl al-taʾwīlat li-akhbār al-ṣifāt*. Edited by Abū ʿAbd Allāh Muḥammad b. Ḥamad al-Ḥamūd al-Najdī. Kuwait: Ghirās li-l-Nashr wa-l-Tawzīʿ, 2013.

ʿAbūd, Ṣāliḥ b. ʿAbd Allāh al-. *Aqīdat Al-Shaykh Muḥammad Ibn ʿAbd al-Wahhāb al-Salafiyya Wa-Atharuhā Fī al-ʿĀlam al-Islāmī*. 2 vols. Medina: Maktabat al-Ghurabāʾ, 1996.

Abuqudairi, Areej. 'Jordan Releases Anti-ISIL Salafi Leader | ISIL/ISIS News |.' *Al Jazeera*, June 17, 2014. https://www.aljazeera.com/news/2014/6/17/jordan-releases-anti-isil-salafi-leader.

Adamson, Peter, and Fedor Benevich. 'Fakhr Al-Din al-Razi.' In *The Stanford Encyclopedia of Philosophy*, edited by Edward N. Zalta and Uri Nodelman, Spring 2023. Metaphysics Research Lab, Stanford University, 2023. https://plato.stanford.edu/archives/spr2023/entries/al-din-al-razi/.

Adang, Camilla. 'The Beginnings of the Zahiri Madhhab in Al-Andalus.' In *The Islamic School of Law: Evolution, Devolution, and Progress*, edited by Peri Bearman, Rudolph Peters, and Frank E. Vogel, 117–25. Harvard Series in Islamic Law 2. Cambridge, Mass.: Harvard Univ. Press, 2005.

Adang, Camilla, Hassan Ansari, Maribel Fierro, and Sabine Schmidtke, eds. *Accusations of Unbelief in Islam: A Diachronic Perspective on Takfīr*. Leiden, The Netherlands: Brill, 2015. https://brill.com/edcollbook/title/32385.

Adem, Rodrigo. 'The Intellectual Genealogy of Ibn Taymīya.' PhD, The University of Chicago. Accessed August 14, 2023. https://www.proquest.com/docview/1707671365/abstract/6A56EF0EF62D487DPQ/1.

Adraoui, Mohamed-Ali. 'Radical Milieus and Salafis Movements in France: Ideologies, Practices, Relationships with Society and Political Visions.' *European University Institute*, 2014. https://cadmus.eui.eu/handle/1814/31911.

——. *Salafism Goes Global: From the Gulf to the French Banlieues*. Religion and Global Politics. Oxford; New York: Oxford University Press, 2020.

——. 'Salafism In France: Ideology, Practices and Contradictions.' In *Global Salafism: Islam's New Religious Movement*, edited by Roel Meijer, 365–83. Oxford University Press, 2014. https://doi.org/10.1093/acprof:oso/9780199333431.003.0017.

Afsaruddin, Asma. *The First Muslims: History and Memory*. Oxford: Oneworld, 2008.

Ahmad, Mohiuddin. *Saiyid Ahmad Shahid: His Life and Mission*. Academy of Islamic Research and Publications Series ; No. 93. Lucknow: Academy of Islamic Research and Publications, 1975. https://catalog.lib.uchicago.edu/vufind/Record/114529.

Ahmad, Muzzammil, and Ian Greer. 'Shāh Walī Allāh in Defence of Ibn Taymiyyah.' *Islamic Studies* 61, no. 1 (March 31, 2022): 25–44. https://doi.org/10.52541/isiri.v61i1.2243.

Ahmad, Qeyamuddin. *The Wahhabi Movement in India*. 2nd rev. ed. New Delhi: Manohar, 1994. https://catalog.lib.uchicago.edu/vufind/Record/2428820.

Ahmed, Chanfi. 'West African ʿulamāʾ and Salafism in Mecca and Medina.' Leiden: Brill, 2015. https://brill.com/display/title/24534.

Ahmed, Einas. 'Militant Salafism in Sudan.' *Islamic Africa* 6, no. 1–2 (2015): 164–84.

Ahmed Khalid Ayong. 'The Nature of the 'Jāmī/Surūrī' Dispute and Its Impact on the Islamic University in Medina (Fourthcoming),' n.d.

Akhtar, Shabbir. 'Finding and Following Jesus: The Muslim Claim to the Messiah.' *Yaqeen Insitutue for Islamic Research*, December 24, 2018. https://yaqeeninstitute.org/read/paper/finding-and-following-jesus-the-muslim-claim-to-the-messiah.

Akinwotu, Emmanuel, Emmanuel Akinwotu West Africa correspondent, and Isaac Abrak. 'Suspected Islamist Attack Frees Hundreds of Prisoners in Nigeria.'

*The Guardian*, July 6, 2022. https://www.theguardian.com/world/2022/jul/06/suspected-boko-haram-attack-frees-hundreds-of-prisoners-in-nigeria-abuja.

Āl al-Shaykh, Muḥammad b. Ibrāhīm. *Fatāwā wa-rasāʾil samāḥat al-shaykh Muḥammad ibn Ibrāhīm ibn ʿAbd al-Laṭīf Āl al-Shaykh*. Edited by Muḥammad b. ʿAbd al-Raḥmān Ibn Qāsim. 13 vols. Mecca: Maṭbaʿat al-Ḥukūma, 1978.

——. *Risālat taḥkīm al-qawānīn*, n.d.

Āl al-Shaykh, ʿAbd al-Raḥmān b. Ḥasan. *Fatḥ al-majīd li-sharḥ kitāb al-tawḥīd*. Edited by al-Walīd b. ʿAbd al-Raḥmān Āl Furayyān. Riyadh: Dār al-Ṣumayʿī, n.d.

Āl Ḥamza, Khālid b. Fawzī b. ʿAbd al-Ḥamīd. *Muḥammad Rashīd Riḍā: Ṭūd wa-iṣlāḥ daʿwa wa-dāʿiya*. 2nd ed. 1 vols. Dār ʿUlamāʾ al-Salaf, 1994.

*Al Jazeera*. 'US Offers $10m for Information on Al-Shabab Leaders, Finances.' November 14, 2022. https://www.aljazeera.com/news/2022/11/14/us-offers-10m-for-information-on-al-shabab-leaders-finances.

Āl ʿAbd al-Laṭīf, ʿAbd al-ʿAzīz b. Muḥammad. *Daʿāwā al-munāwiʾīn li-daʿwat al-shaykh Muḥammad ibn ʿAbd al-Wahhāb*. Riyadh: Dār Ṭayba, 1989.

Al-Arian, Abdullah A. *Answering the Call: Popular Islamic Activism in Sadat's Egypt*. Religion and Global Politics. Oxford; New York: Oxford University Press, 2014.

Al-Atawneh, Muhammad K. *Wahhabi Islam Facing the Challenges of Modernity: Dar Al-Ifta in the Modern Saudi State*. Studies in Islamic Law and Society 32. Leiden; Boston: Brill, 2010.

Alavi, Seema. *Muslim Cosmopolitanism in the Age of Empire*. Cambridge, Mass.; London: Harvard University Press, 2015. https://doi.org/10.4159/9780674286894.

——. 'Siddiq Hasan Khan (1832–90) and the Creation of a Muslim Cosmopolitanism in the 19th Century.' *Journal of the Economic and Social History of the Orient* 54, no. 1 (January 1, 2011): 1–38. https://doi.org/10.1163/156852011X567373.

Al-Azami, Usaama. *Islam and the Arab Revolutions: The Ulama Between Democracy and Autocracy*. Oxford: Oxford University Press, 2022.

——. 'Legitimising Political Dissent: Islamist Salafi Discourses on Obedience and Rebellion After the Arab Revolutions.' In *Salafi Social and Political Movements*, edited by Masooda Bano, 61–86. Edinburgh University Press, 2021. https://doi.org/10.1515/9781474479158-008.

——. 'Locating Ḥākimiyya in Global History: The Concept of Sovereignty in Premodern Islam and Its Reception after Mawdūdī and Quṭb.' *Journal of the Royal Asiatic Society* 32, no. 2 (April 2022): 355–76. https://doi.org/10.1017/S1356186321000675.

——. 'Neo-Traditionalist Sufis and Arab Politics: A Preliminary Mapping of the Transnational Networks of Counter-Revolutionary Scholars after the Arab Revolutions.' In *Global Sufism: Boundaries, Structures, and Politics*, edited by Mark Sedgwick and Francesco Piraino. London: Hurst, 2019.

Albānī, Muḥammad Nāṣir al-Dīn al-. *al-Fatāwā Kuwaytiyya wa-l-fatāwā al-Ustrāliyya*. Cairo: Dār al-Ḍiyāʾ, 2007.

——. *al-Tawassul: Anwāʿuhu wa-aḥkāmuhu*. Riyadh: Maktabat al-Maʿārif, 2001.

——. *Durūs li-shaykh Muḥammad Nāṣir al-Dīn al-Albānī*. Audio lessons transcribed by the Islamic Network website http://www.islamweb.net, made available on Shāmila at https://shamela.ws/book/7682, n.d. Accessed May 8, 2024.

——. 'Hadhihī hiya al-Salafiyya [This Is Salafism].' *Majalla Al-Āṣāla* 54 (1993): 54–55.

——. *Ḥukm tārik al-ṣalāt*. Edited by ʿAlī al-Ḥalabī. Jordan: al-Maktab al-Islāmyya, 1992.

——. *Ṣifat ṣalāt al-nabī ṣalallahu ʿalaihi wa wallam min al-takbīr ilā-l-taslīm kaʾannaka tarāhā*. 10th ed. Riyadh: Maktabat al-Maʿārif, 1990.

——. *Silsilat al-aḥādīth al-ṣaḥīḥah wa-shayʾ min fiqhihā wa-fawā idihā*. 7 vols. Riyadh: Maktabat al-Maʿārif, 1995.

——. *Silsilat al-hudā wa-l-nūr*, n.d.

Aldeen, Maysaa Shujaa. 'Yemen's War-Torn Rivalries for Religious Education.' In *Islamic Institutions in Arab States: Mapping the Dynamics of Control, Co-Option, and Contention*, edited by Frederic Wehrey, 33–52. Washington, DC: Carnegie Endowment for International Peace, 2021.

Al-Fahad, Abdulaziz H. 'From Exclusivism to Accommodation: Doctrinal and Legal Evolution of Wahhabism.' *New York University Law Review* 79, no. 2 (519 485AD).

Al-Gama'ah al-Islamiyah. *Initiative to Stop the Violence: Sadat's Assassins and the Renunciation of Political Violence*. Edited by Sherman A. Jackson. World Thought in Translation. New Haven: Yale University Press, 2015.

Algar, Hamid. *Wahhabism: A Critical Essay*. 1st ed. Oneonta, NY: Islamic Publications International, 2002.

Alhussein, Eman. 'The Enlightened Sheikhs of the New Saudi Arabia.' *AGSIW*, June 27, 2018. https://agsiw.org/the-enlightened-sheikhs-of-the-new-saudi-arabia/.

ʿAlī al-Qarī, Mullā. *Sharḥ Kitāb al-Fiqh al-akbar*. Beirut: Dār al-Kutūb al-ʿIlmiyya, n.d.

Ali, Mohamed Bin. *The Roots of Religious Extremism: Understanding the Salafi Doctrine of Al-Wala' Wal Bara'*. Insurgency and Terrorism Series. Imperial College Press, 2015. https://doi.org/10.1142/p924.

Al-Jamil, Tariq. 'Ibn Taymiyya and Ibn Al-Muṭahhar al-Ḥillī: Shiʿī Polemics and the Struggle for Religious Authority in Medieval Islam.' In *Ibn Taymiyya and His Times*, edited by Youssef Rapoport and Shahab Ahmed, 229–46. Karachi: Oxford University Press, 2010.

——. *Power and Knowledge in Medieval Islam: Shi'i and Sunni Encounters in Baghdad*. I.B. Tauris, 2025.

'Al-Jāmiʿa al-Islāmiyya Bi-l-Madīna al-Munawwara.' Accessed June 9, 2024. https://www.iu.edu.sa/.

Alkhateeb, Firas. *Lost Islamic History: Reclaiming Muslim Civilisation from the Past*. Revised and Updated ed. London: Hurst & Company, 2017.

'Al-Masjid al-Kabīr.' Accessed June 9, 2024. https://thegrandmosque.awqaf.gov.kw/ar.

Al-Matroudi, Abdul Hakim I. *The Hanbali School of Law and Ibn Taymiyyah: Conflict or Conciliation*. 1st ed. Routledge, 2006.

'Al-Mawqiʿ al-Rasmī Li-Shaykh ʿAbd al-ʿAzīz Bin Bāz.' Accessed May 15, 2024. https://binbaz.org.sa/.

Al-Rasheed, Madawi. *A History of Saudi Arabia*. 2nd ed. New York: Cambridge University Press, 2010.

——. *Contesting the Saudi State: Islamic Voices from a New Generation*. Cambridge Middle East Studies. Cambridge: Cambridge University Press, 2006. https://doi.org/10.1017/CBO9780511492181.

——. 'Divine Politics Reconsidered: Saudi Islamists on Peaceful Revolution.' PDF, 2015, 507 KB. https://doi.org/10.21953/LSE.RO.62240.

——. 'Introduction: The Dilemas of a New Era.' In *Salman's Legacy: The Dilemmas of a New Era in Saudi Arabia*, edited by Madawi Al-Rasheed, 1–28. Oxford; New York, NY: Oxford University Press, 2018.

——. 'King Salman and His Son: Winning the United States, Losing the Rest.' In *Salman's Legacy: The Dilemmas of a New Era in Saudi Arabia*, edited by Madawi Al-Rasheed, 235–50. Oxford; New York, NY: Oxford University Press, 2018.

——, ed. *Kingdom Without Borders: Saudi Arabia's Political, Religious, and Media Frontiers*. New York: Columbia University Press, 2008.

——, ed. *Salman's Legacy: The Dilemmas of a New Era in Saudi Arabia*. Oxford; New York, NY: Oxford University Press, 2018.

——. 'The Local and the Global In Saudi Salafi-Jihadi Discourse.' In *Global Salafism: Islam's New Religious Movement*, edited by Roel Meijer, 302–20. Oxford University Press, 2014. https://doi.org/10.1093/acprof:oso/9780199333431.003.0014.

Al-Raysuni, Ahmad. *Imam Al-Shatibi's Theory of the Higher Objectives and Intents of Islamic Law*. Translated by Nancy Roberts. London: International Institute of Islamic Thought, 2013.

Al-Sarhan, Saud. 'Early Muslim Traditionalism: A Critical Study of the Works and Political Theology of Aḥmad Ibn Ḥanbal.' PhD thesis, University of Exeter, 2011. http://hdl.handle.net/10036/3374.

——. 'The Struggle for Authority: The Shaykhs of Jihadi-Salafism in Saudi Arabia, 1997–2003.' In *Saudi Arabia in Transition: Insights on Social, Political, Economic and Religious Change*, edited by Bernard Haykel, Stéphane Lacroix, and Thomas Hegghammer, 181–206. Cambridge: Cambridge University Press, 2015. https://doi.org/10.1017/CBO9781139047586.013.

*Al-Shaykh ʿAbd al-Raḥmān al-Sudays Jamāʿat al-Ikhwān al-Muslimīn Jamāʿa Irhābiyya*. YouTube, 2020. https://www.youtube.com/watch?v=koCa9nJ0pQg.

Alshech, Eli. 'The Doctrinal Crisis within the Salafi-Jihadi Ranks and the Emergence of Neo-Takfirism.' *Islamic Law and Society* 21 (September 22, 2014): 419–52. https://doi.org/10.1163/15685195-00214p04.

Ālūsī, Maḥmūd al-. *Rūh al-maʿānī fī tafsīr al-Qurʾān al-ʿaẓīm wa sabʿ al-mathānī*. Edited by ʿAlī ʿAbd al-Bārī ʿAṭiyya. 1st ed. 15 vols. Beirut: Dār al-Kutub al-ʿIlmiyya, 1994.

Ālūsī, Nuʿmān al-. *Jalāʾ Al-ʿaynayn fī muḥākamat al-Aḥmadayn*. Cairo: Maṭbaʿat Būlāq, 1880.

Al-Yaqoubi, Muhammad. *Refuting ISIS: A Rebuttal Of Its Religious And Ideological Foundations*. Middletown: Sacred Knowledge, 2015.

'Ambassador – Embassy of Sierra Leone, Saudi Arabia.' Accessed June 9, 2024. https://sa.slembassy.gov.sl/ambassador-2/.

Ambrosio, Alberto Fabio. 'Isma'il Rusuhi Ankaravi: An Early Mevlevi Intervention into the Kadizadeli-Sufi Conflict.' In *Sufism and Society: Arrangements of the Mystical in the Muslim World, 1200-1800*, edited by John Curry and Erik Ohlander. Milton Park, Abingdon, Oxon; New York: Routledge, 2012.

Amin, Hira. 'Salafism and Islamism in Britain, 1965–2015.' PhD thesis, University of Cambridge, 2017. https://www.repository.cam.ac.uk/handle/1810/269730.

——. 'The Shifting Contours of Saudi Influence in Britain.' In *Wahhabism and the World: Understanding Saudi Arabia's Global Influence on Islam*, edited by Peter Mandaville, 290–314. Oxford University Press, 2022. https://doi.org/10.1093/oso/9780197532560.003.0015.

Amin, Hira, and Azhar Majothi. 'The Ahl-e-Hadith: From British India to Britain.' *Modern Asian Studies* 56, no. 1 (January 2022): 176–206. https://doi.org/10.1017/S0026749X21000093.

Amin, Kamaruddin. 'Nāṣiruddīn Al-Albānī on Muslim's Ṣaḥīḥ: A Critical Study of His Method.' *Islamic Law and Society* 11, no. 2 (2004): 149–76.

Aminrazavi, Mehdi. 'Mysticism in Arabic and Islamic Philosophy.' In *The Stanford Encyclopedia of Philosophy*, edited by Edward N. Zalta, Spring 2021. Metaphysics Research Lab, Stanford University, 2021. https://plato.stanford.edu/archives/spr2021/entries/arabic-islamic-mysticism/.

Amir-Moezzi, Mohammad Ali. 'Early Shīʿī Theology.' In *The Oxford Handbook of Islamic Theology*, edited by Sabine Schmidtke, Reprinted ed., 81–90. Oxford, United Kingdom: Oxford University Press, 2018.

'AMJA Members | AMJA Online.' Accessed June 9, 2024. https://www.amjaonline.org/about/amja-members/.

Anani, Khalil al-. 'Unpacking the Sacred Canopy: Egypt's Salafis between Religion and Politics.' In *Salafism After the Arab Awakening: Contending with People's Power*, edited by Francesco Cavatorta and Fabio Merone. London: Oxford University Press, 2017. https://doi.org/10.1093/acprof:oso/9780190274993.003.0003.

Anastasopoulos, Antonis. *Political Initiatives 'from the Bottom Up' in the Ottoman Empire*. Crete University Press, 2012.

Anchassi, Omar. 'The Logic of the Conquest Society: Isis, Apocalyptic Violence and the 'Reinstatement' of Slave Concubinage.' In *Legitimate and Illegitimate Violence in Islamic Thought*, edited by Mustafa Baig and Robert Gleave. Edinburgh: Edinburgh University Press, 2021. https://doi.org/10.1515/9781474485531-013.

Anjum, Ovamir. *Politics, Law and Community in Islamic Thought: The Taymiyyan Moment*. Cambridge Studies in Islamic Civilization. Cambridge; New York: Cambridge University Press, 2012.

Ansari, Hamied N. 'The Islamic Militants in Egyptian Politics.' *International Journal of Middle East Studies* 16, no. 1 (1984): 123–44.

Ansari, M. Abdul Haq. 'Ibn 'Arabī: The Doctrine of Waḥdat Al-Wujūd.' *Islamic Studies* 38, no. 2 (1999): 149–92.
——. 'Ibn Taymiyyah and Sufism.' *Islamic Studies* 24, no. 1 (1985): 1–12.
Anthony, Sean W. *The Caliph and the Heretic: Ibn Saba' and the Origins of Shī'ism*. Leiden; Boston: Brill, 2011.
Anzalone, Christopher. *Continuity and Change: The Evolution and Resilience of Al-Shabab's Media Insurgency, 2006–2016*. Oslo, Norway: Hate Speech International, 2016.
——. *Localizing 'Global' Jihad: The Organization and Narration of Violence and Community in Islamist Insurgencies*. McGill University Libraries, 2019.
Anzalone, Christopher, and Yasir Qadhi. 'From Dir'iyya to Riyadh: The History and Global Impact of Saudi Religious Propagation and Education.' In *Wahhabism and the World: Understanding Saudi Arabia's Global Influence on Islam*, edited by Peter Mandaville, 53–75. Religion and Global Politics. Oxford; New York: Oxford University Press, 2022.
Āqḥiṣārī, Aḥmad b. Muḥammad al-Rūmī al-Ḥanafī al-. *Against Smoking: An Ottoman Manifesto*. Translated by Yahya Michot. Markfield: Kube Publishing Ltd, 2011.
——. *Majālis al-abrār wa masālik al-akhbār*. Edited by Irshād al-Ḥaqq al-Atharī. Alexandria: Dār al-Kutub al-'Arabiyya, 2009.
*Arab News*. 'Naif Says Muslim Brotherhood Cause of Most Arab Problems.' November 28, 2002. https://www.arabnews.com/node/226291.
*Arab Observer*. 'An Egyptian Preacher Disavowed the Brotherhood.' August 8, 2021. https://www.arabobserver.com/an-egyptian-preacher-disavowed-the-brotherhood/.
Arafat, Alaa Al-Din. *Egypt in Crisis: The Fall of Islamism and Prospects of Democratization*. 1st ed. Cham: Palgrave Macmillan, 2017.
Ash'arī, Abū al-Ḥasan al-. *Al-Ibāna 'an Uṣūl al-Diyāna*. Edited by Fawqiyya Ḥusayn Maḥmūd. Cairo: Dār al-Anṣār, 1977.
——. *Maqālāt Al-Islāmiyyīn*. Edited by Helmut Ritter. Beirut: Dār al-Nashr, 1980.
Auda, Jasser. 'A Maqāṣidī Approach to Contemporary Application of the Sharī'ah.' *Intellectual Discourse* 19 (December 1, 2011).
——. *Maqasid Al-Shariah as Philosophy of Islamic Law: A Systems Approach*. London: International Institute of Islamic Thought, 2008.
Awad, Mokhtar. 'Revolutionary Salafism: The Case of Ahrar Movement | Hudson.' *Hudson Institute* (blog), April 29, 2016. https://www.hudson.org/national-security-defense/revolutionary-salafism-the-case-of-ahrar-movement.
'Awnī, al-Sharīf Ḥātim b. 'Ārif al-. *al-'Ibāda: bawābat al-tawḥīd wa-bawābat al-takfīr*. Riyadh: Markaz Namā', 2012.
——. *Takfīr ahl al-shahādatayn mawāni'ūhu wa manāṭatuhu*. 1st ed. Riyadh: Markaz Namā', 2015.
Azami, R. Ahmad. *Ahl-e-Hadith in Britain: History, Establishment, Activites and Objectives*. London: The Muslim College and Ta-Ha Publishers, 1995.
Azzam, A. R. *Saladin: The Triumph of the Sunni Revival*. 2nd ed. Cambridge, UK: Islamic Texts Society, 2014.

Baker, Abdul Haqq. *Extremists in Our Midst: Confronting Terror*. Houndmills, Hampshire: Palgrave Macmillan, 2011.

Baker, Peter, Helene Cooper, and Mark Mazzetti. 'Bin Laden Is Dead, Obama Says.' *The New York Times*, May 1, 2011. https://www.nytimes.com/2011/05/02/world/asia/osama-bin-laden-is-killed.html.

Baljon, J. M. S. *Religion and Thought of Shāh Walī Allāh Dihlawī, 1703–1762*. Leiden: Brill, 1986.

Banani, Amin, Richard G. Hovannisian, and Georges Sabagh, eds. *Poetry and Mysticism in Islam: The Heritage of Rūmī*. Giorgio Levi Della Vida Conferences, 11th conference. New York: Cambridge University Press, 1994.

Bannā, Ḥasan al-. *A Treatise on the Islamic Faith*. Edited by Uwais Namazi Nadwi. Translated by Mustafa Umar, n.d.

——. *Five Tracts of Ḥasan Al-Bannā (1906–1949): A Selection from the Majmū'at Rasā'il Al-Imām Al-Shahīd Ḥasan Al-Bannā*. Translated by Charles Wendell. University of California Publications : Near Eastern Studies ; v. 20. Berkeley: University of California Press, 1978.

Bano, Masooda. 'In Today's Saudi Arabia: The State, the Society and the Scholars.' In *Salafi Social and Political Movements: National and Transnational Contexts*, edited by Masooda Bano, 51–55. Edinburgh: Edinburgh University Press, 2021.

——. *Modern Islamic Authority and Social Change, Volume 1: Evolving Debates in Muslim Majority Countries*. Edinburgh University Press, 2018. https://doi.org/10.1515/9781474433242.

——, ed. *Salafi Social and Political Movements: National and Transnational Contexts*. S.l.: Edinburgh University Press, 2023.

Barbahārī [or Ghulām Khalīl], al-Ḥasan b. ʿAlī al-. *Explanation of the Creed [Sharḥ al-Sunna]*. Translated by Dawood Burbank. 1st ed. Al-Hidaayah, 1995.

——. *Sharḥ al-sunna*. Edited by Muḥammad b. Saʿīd al-Qaḥṭānī. Cairo: Maktabat al-Sunna, 1996.

Barnstone, Willis, and Marvin W. Meyer, eds. 'Islamic Mystical Literature.' In *The Gnostic Bible*, Revised ed., 667–759. Boulder: Shambhala, 2009.

——, eds. *The Gnostic Bible*. Revised ed. Boulder: Shambhala, 2009.

Barzegar, Abbas. 'The Persistence of Heresy: Paul of Tarsus, Ibn Saba, and Historical Narrative in Sunni Identity Formation.' *Numen* 58, no. 2–3 (January 1, 2011): 207–31. https://doi.org/10.1163/156852711X562290.

Bayhaqī, Abū Bakr al-. *al-Asmāʾ wa-l-ṣifāt*. Edited by ʿAbd Allāh al-Ḥāshīdī. 1st ed. 2 vols. Jeddah: Maktab al-Sawādī, 1993.

*BBC*. 'Hate Preaching Cleric Jailed.' March 7, 2003. http://news.bbc.co.uk/2/hi/uk_news/england/2829059.stm.

Bdaiwi, Ahab. 'Jamāl Al-Dīn al-Afghānī.' In *Christian Muslim Relations Online II*. Leiden: Brill, March 1, 2018. https://referenceworks.brill.com/doi/10.1163/2451-9537_cmrii_COM_31239.

Bearman, Peri, Rudolph Peters, and Frank E. Vogel, eds. *The Islamic School of Law: Evolution, Devolution, and Progress*. Harvard Series in Islamic Law 2. Cambridge, Mass.: Harvard Univ. Press, 2005.

Beránek, Ondřej, and Pavel Ťupek. *The Temptation of Graves in Salafi Islam: Iconoclasm, Destruction and Idolatry*. Paperback ed. Edinburgh: Edinburgh University Press, 2019.

*Bindmans*. 'Dr Salman Butt Secures Apology, Substantial Libel Damages and Costs against the Secretary of State for the Home Department.' November 15, 2021. https://www.bindmans.com/knowledge-hub/news/dr-salman-butt-secures-apology-substantial-libel-damages-and-costs-against-the-secretary-of-state-for-the-home-department/.

Birkawī [also: al-Birkalī], Muḥammad b. ʿAlī al-. *al-Ṭarīqa al-Muḥammadiyya wa-l-sīra al-Aḥmadiyya*. Edited by Muḥammad Raḥmat Allāh Ḥāfiẓ Muḥammad Nāẓim al-Nadawī. 1st ed. Damascus: Dār al-Qalam, 2011.

Blankinship, Khalid Yahya. *The End of the Jihad State: The Reign of Hisham Ibn 'abd Al-Malik and the Collapse of the Umayyads*. Albany: State University of New York Press, 1994.

'Board of Directors | Union of African Muslim Schollars.' Accessed May 9, 2024. http://africanulama.org/en/membre-admin/.

Bonacina, Giovanni. *The Wahhabis Seen Through European Eyes 1772–1830: Deists and Puritans of Islam*. Leiden; Boston: Brill Academic Pub, 2015.

Bonnefoy, Laurent. 'How Transnational Is Salafism In Yemen?' In *Global Salafism: Islam's New Religious Movement*, edited by Roel Meijer, 321–41. Oxford University Press, 2014. https://doi.org/10.1093/acprof:oso/9780199333431.003.0015.

——. 'Quietist Salafis, the Arab Spring and the Politicisation Process.' In *Salafism After the Arab Awakening: Contending with People's Power*, edited by Francesco Cavatorta and Fabio Merone, 205–18. Oxford University Press, 2017. https://doi.org/10.1093/acprof:oso/9780190274993.003.0013.

——. *Salafism in Yemen: Transnationalism and Religious Identity*. Place of publication not identified: Oxford University Press, 2012.

Bonner, Michael. *Jihad in Islamic History: Doctrines and Practice*. 1st ed. Princeton: Princeton University Press, 2006.

Bori, Caterina. 'A New Source for the Biography of Ibn Taymiyya.' *Bulletin of the School of Oriental and African Studies, University of London* 67, no. 3 (2004): 321–48.

——. 'Ibn Taymiyya (14th to 17th Century): Transregional Spaces of Reading and Reception.' *The Muslim World* 108, no. 1 (2018): 87–123. https://doi.org/10.1111/muwo.12230.

——. 'Ibn Taymiyya Wa-Jama'Atuhu: Authority, Conflict and Consensus in Ibn Taymiyya's Circle.' In *Ibn Taymiyya and His Times*, edited by Youssef Rapoport and Shahab Ahmed, 23–52. Karachi: Oxford University Press, 2010.

Bori, Caterina, and Livnat Holtzman, eds. *A Scholar in the Shadow: Essays in the Legal and Theological Thought of Ibn Qayyim Aal-Jawziyya*. Oriente Moderno, nuova serie, anno 90, 1, 2010. Roma: Istituto per l'Oriente C.A. Nallino, 2010. https://catalog.lib.uchicago.edu/vufind/Record/9348472.

Boubekeur, Amel. 'Salafism and Radical Politics in Postconflict Algeria.' *Carnegie Endowment for International Peace*, 2008, 1–20.

Bovenkamp, Ellen van de. 'Tariq Ramadan: A Voice for Decoloniality in France and in Morocco,' February 18, 2022. https://doi.org/10.1163/22117954-bja10045.

Bowen, Innes. *Medina in Birmingham, Najaf in Brent: Inside British Islam.* London: Hurst, 2014.
Böwering, Gerhard, ed. 'Fundamentalism.' In *The Princeton Encyclopedia of Islamic Political Thought*, 184–88. Princeton, NJ: Princeton University Press, 2013.
Brachman, Jarret M. *Global Jihadism: Theory and Practice*. Transferred to digital print. Political Violence. London: Routledge, 2010.
Brown, Daniel W. *Rethinking Tradition in Modern Islamic Thought*. 1st paperback ed. Cambridge: Cambridge University Press, 1999.
Brown, Jonathan A. C. *Hadith: Muhammad's Legacy in the Medieval and Modern World*. 2nd reprint ed. Foundations of Islam. London: Oneworld Academic, 2020.
——. 'Is Islam Easy to Understand or Not?: Salafis, the Democratization of Interpretation and the Need for the Ulema.' *Journal of Islamic Studies* 26, no. 2 (2015): 117–44.
——. *Misquoting Muhammad: The Challenge and Choices of Interpreting the Prophet's Legacy*. Paperback ed. London: Oneworld Publications, 2015.
——. 'Salafis and Sufis in Egypt.' *Carnegie Endowment for International Peace*, December 20, 2011, 1–16.
——. *Slavery and Islam*. London: Oneworld Academic, 2019.
——. *The Canonization of Al-Bukhārī and Muslim: The Formation and Function of the Sunnī Ḥadīth Canon*. Leiden; Boston: Brill, 2011.
——. 'The Rise and Fall of the Salafi Al-Nour Party in Egypt.' *Jadaliyya* (blog), November 14, 2013. https://www.jadaliyya.com/Details/29813.
Bukhārī, Muḥammad b. Ismāʿīl al-. *Khalq afʿāl al-ʿibād wa-l-radd ʿalā al-jahmiyya wa-aṣḥāb al-taʿṭīl*. Cairo: Maktab al-Turāth al-Islāmī, n.d.
Bulliet, Richard W. *The Patricians of Nishapur; a Study in Medieval Islamic Social History*. Cambridge, Mass.: Harvard University Press, 1972.
Bunzel, Cole M. 'Manifest Enmity: The Origins, Development, and Persistence of Classical Wahhābism (1153-1351/1741-1932).' Princeton University, 2018. http://arks.princeton.edu/ark:/88435/dsp01ms35tc409.
——. *The Kingdom and the Caliphate: Duel of the Islamic States*. Carnegie Endowment for International Peace, 2016.
——. *Wahhābism: The History of a Militant Islamic Movement*. Princeton: Princeton University Press, 2023.
Burckhardt, John Lewis. *Notes on the Bedouins and Wahabys*. London: Henry Colburn Press, 1831.
Burgat, François. *Understanding Political Islam*. 1st ed. Manchester: Manchester University Press, 2019.
Burgat, François, and William Dowell. *The Islamic Movement in North Africa*. Middle East Monograph Series. Austin: Univ. of Texas, 1993.
Burke, Jason. *The New Threat: The Past, Present, and Future of Islamic Militancy*. New York City, NY: New Press, 2017.
Busool, Assad Nimer. 'Shaykh Muhammad Rashid Rida's Relations with Jamal Al-Din Al-Afghani and Muhammad 'Abduh.' *The Muslim World (Hartford)* 66, no. 4 (1976): 272.

Būṭī, Muḥammad Saʿīd Ramaḍān al-. *al-Salafiyya: Marḥala zamanīyya mubārakah lā mudhhab islāmī*. Damascus: Dār al-Fikr, 1988.

Calvert, John. *Sayyid Qutb and the Origins of Radical Islamism*. 1st ed. New York, NY: Oxford University Press, 2018.

Cavatorta, Francesco, and Fabio Merone, eds. *Salafism After the Arab Awakening*. London: Hurst, 2017.

Çavuşoğlu, Semiramis. 'The Ḳāḍīzādeli Movement: An Attempt of Seri'at-Minded Reform in the Ottoman Empire.' Princeton University, 1990.

Chalcraft, John. 'Egypt's 25 January Uprising, Hegemonic Contestation, and the Explosion of the Poor.' In *The New Middle East: Protest and Revolution in the Arab World*, edited by Fawaz A. Gerges, 155–79. Cambridge: Cambridge University Press, 2013. https://doi.org/10.1017/CBO9781139236737.009.

Chaplin, Chris. 'Salafi Islamic Piety as Civic Activism: Wahdah Islamiyah and Differentiated Citizenship in Indonesia.' *Citizenship Studies* 22, no. 2 (February 17, 2018): 208–23. https://doi.org/10.1080/13621025.2018.1445488.

——. *Salafism and the State: Islamic Activism and National Identity in Contemporary Indonesia, Chaplin*. Copenhagen: NIAS Press, 2021. https://press.uchicago.edu/ucp/books/book/distributed/S/bo239343105.html.

'Charlie Hebdo: Magazine Republishes Controversial Mohammed Cartoons.' September 1, 2020. https://www.bbc.com/news/world-europe-53985407.

Chaudri, Zeeshan. 'Demarcating the Contours of the Deobandi Tradition via a Study of the "Akābirīn."' PhD, SOAS University of London, 2022. https://doi.org/10.25501/SOAS.00037291.

Chittick, William C. 'Ibn 'Arabî.' In *The Stanford Encyclopedia of Philosophy*, edited by Edward N. Zalta, Spring 2020. Metaphysics Research Lab, Stanford University, 2020. https://plato.stanford.edu/archives/spr2020/entries/ibn-arabi/.

——. 'Rûmî and Wahdat Al-Wujûd.' In *Poetry and Mysticism in Islam: The Heritage of Rūmī*, edited by Amin Banani, Richard G. Hovannisian, and Georges Sabagh, 70–111. Giorgio Levi Della Vida Conferences, 11th conference. New York: Cambridge University Press, 1994.

——. *Sufism: A Beginner's Guide*. London: Oneworld Publications, 2007.

——. *The Sufi Path of Knowledge: Ibn al-ʿArabi's Metaphysics of Imagination*. Albany, NY: State University of New York Press, 1989.

Chrisafis, Angelique. 'Tariq Ramadan Acquitted of Charges of Rape and Sexual Coercion by Swiss Court.' *The Guardian*, May 24, 2023. https://www.theguardian.com/world/2023/may/24/tariq-ramadan-cleared-rape-sexual-coercion-swiss-court.

Christmann, Andreas. 'Islamic Scholar and Religious Leader: A Portrait of Shaykh Muhammad Sa Id Ramadan Al-Buti.' *Islam & Christian Muslim Relations* 9, no. 2 (July 1998): 149.

*CNN*. 'al-Iftāʾ al-Suʿūdiyya: Jamāʿat al-Ikhwān Ḍālla wa-lā Tamut li-al-Islām bi-Ṣilah.' November 15, 2020. https://arabic.cnn.com/middle-east/article/2020/11/16/saudi-ifta-muslim-brotherhood.

*CNN*. 'Ṣūra 'Miṣr 3 Yūliyū 2013': Taʿarraf ʿalā Man Taraqā.. Wa-Man Ẓalla Fī Manṣibih.. Wa-Man Yugharrid Khārij al-Kādir.' July 3, 2015. https://arabic.cnn.com/middleeast/2015/07/03/egypt-memory-picture.

Commins, David. 'From Wahhabi to Salafi.' In *Saudi Arabia in Transition: Insights on Social, Political, Economic and Religious Change*, edited by Bernard Haykel, Stéphane Lacroix, and Thomas Hegghammer, 151–66. Cambridge: Cambridge University Press, 2015. https://doi.org/10.1017/CBO9781139047586.011.

——. *Islamic Reform: Politics and Social Change in Late Ottoman Syria*. Studies in Middle Eastern History. Oxford; New York: Oxford University Press, 1990.

——. *The Wahhabi Mission and Saudi Arabia*. London; New York: I.B. Tauris, 2006.

——. 'Wahhabis, Sufis and Salafis in Early Twentieth Century Damascus.' In *Guardians of Faith in Modern Times: ʿUlamaʾ in the Middle East*, edited by Meir Hatina, 231–46. Brill, 2009. https://doi.org/10.1163/9789047442936_012.

Conduit, Dara. *The Muslim Brotherhood in Syria*. Cambridge Middle East Studies. New York, NY: Cambridge University Press, 2019.

Cook, David. 'Paradigmatic Jihadi Movements.' West Point, NY: The Combating Terrorism Center United States Military Academy, 2006.

Cook, Michael. *Commanding Right and Forbidding Wrong in Islamic Thought*. Cambridge, UK ; New York: Cambridge University Press, 2000.

——. 'On the Origins of Wahhābism.' *Journal of the Royal Asiatic Society* 2, no. 2 (July 1992): 191–202. https://doi.org/10.1017/S1356186300002376.

Coppens, Pieter. 'Jamāl Al-Dīn al-Qāsimī's Treatise on Wiping over Socks and the Rise of a Distinct Salafi Method.' *Die Welt Des Islams* 62, no. 2 (October 28, 2021): 154–87. https://doi.org/10.1163/15700607-61040014.

Counter Extremism Project. 'Abdullah Al-Faisal,' March 23, 2023. https://www.counterextremism.com/extremists/abdullah-al-faisal.

Cozzens, Jeffrey B. 'Al-Takfir Wa'l Hijra: Unpacking an Enigma.' *Studies in Conflict & Terrorism* 32, no. 6 (May 28, 2009): 489–510. https://doi.org/10.1080/10576100902886044.

Currie, James Muhammad Dawud. 'Kadizadeli Ottoman Scholarship, Muḥammad Ibn ʿabd Al-Wahhāb, and the Rise of the Saudi State.' *Journal of Islamic Studies* 26, no. 3 (2015): 265–88.

Curry, John, and Erik Ohlander, eds. *Sufism and Society: Arrangements of the Mystical in the Muslim World, 1200–1800*. Milton Park, Abingdon, Oxon; New York: Routledge, 2012.

Curtis, Mark. *Secret Affairs: Britain's Collusion with Radical Islam*. New updated version. London: Serpent's Tail, 2012.

Dahan, Nadine. 'Popular Egyptian Preacher Silenced Following Spat with Tv Personality.' *Middle East Eye*, September 25, 2018. https://www.middleeasteye.net/news/popular-egyptian-preacher-silenced-following-spat-tv-personality.

Daḥlān, Aḥmad b. Zaynī. *Fitnat al-Wahhābiyya*. Istanbul: Işık Kitabevi, 1974.

Dakake, Maria Massi. *The Charismatic Community: Shiʿite Identity in Early Islam*. Albany: State University of New York Press, 2007.

Damir-Geilsdorf, Sabine, and Mira Menzfeld. '"Looking at the Life of the Prophet and How He Dealt with All These Issues." Self-Positioning, Demarcations and Belongingness of German Salafis from an Emic Perspective.' *Contemporary Islam* 10 (September 1, 2016). https://doi.org/10.1007/s11562-016-0361-7.

Darif, Mohamed. 'The Moroccan Combat Group.' *Real Instituto Elcano*, March 30, 2004.

Dārimī, ʿUthmān b. Saʿīd al-. *al-Radd ʿalā al-jahmiyya*. Edited by Badr b. ʿAbd Allāh al-Badr. Kuwait: Dār ibn al-Athīr, 1995.

——. *Naqḍ ʿUthmān ibn Saʿīd ʿalā al-Marīsī al-jahmī al-ʿanīd fī mā aftara ʿalā Allāh al-tawḥīd*. Edited by Manṣūr b. ʿAbd al-ʿAzīz al-Simārī. Riyadh: Maktabat Aḍwāʾ al-Salaf, 1999.

——. *Radd al-imām al-Dārimī ʿUthman ibn Saʿīd ʿalā Bishr al-Marīsī al-ʿanīd*. Edited by Muḥammad Ḥamīd al-Faqqī. Beirut: Dār al-Kutūb al-ʿIlmiyya, 2004.

Darul Tahqiq. '"The Salafi Da'wah Is Now in Disarray": Al-Albani.' Accessed June 10, 2024. https://www.darultahqiq.com/the-salafi-dawah-is-now-in-disarray-al-albani/.

Dathan, Matt. 'Cabinet Row Holds Up Prevent Counterterrorism Review.' *The Times*, May 22, 2022. https://www.theguardian.com/uk-news/2022/may/22/anti-terrorism-program-must-keep-focus-on-far-right-say-experts.

Davis, Uri. *Apartheid Israel: Possibilities for the Struggle Within*. London: Zed Books, 2003.

Dawood, Iman. 'Reworking the Common Sense of British Muslims: Salafism, Culture, and Politics within London's Muslim Community.' PhD thesis, The London School of Economics and Political Science, 2021. http://etheses.lse.ac.uk/id/eprint/4347.

——. 'Who Is a "Salafi"? Salafism and the Politics of Labelling in the UK,' March 3, 2020. https://doi.org/10.1163/22117954-12341416.

Dawsirī, Muhammmad b. Sālim al-. *Rafʿ Al-Lāʾima ʿan Fatwā al-Lajna al-Dāʾima*. 2nd ed. Riyadh: Dār ʿĀlam al-Fawāʾid, 2001.

Dearden, Lizzie. 'Al-Qaeda Leader Denounces Isis "Madness and Lies" as Two Terrorist Groups Compete for Dominance.' *The Independent*, January 13, 2017. https://www.independent.co.uk/news/world/middle-east/al-qaeda-leader-ayman-al-zawahiri-isis-madness-lies-extremism-islamic-state-terrorist-groups-compete-middle-east-islamic-jhadis-a7526271.html.

DeLorenzo, Yusuf Talal. *Imam Bukhari's Book of Muslim Morals and Manners*. Alexandria, VA: Al-Saadawi, 1997.

Demiri, Lejla, Philip Dorroll, and Dale J. Correa, eds. *Maturidi Theology: A Bilingual Reader*. Bilingual ed. Tübingen: Mohr Siebrek Ek, 2022.

Dhahabī, Shams al-Dīn al-. 'Dhayl tārīkh al-Islām.' In *al-Jāmiʿ li-sīrat shaykh al-Islām Ibn Taymiyya khilāla sabʿat qurūn*, edited by Muḥammad ʿUzayr Shams and ʿAlī b. Muḥammad al-ʿImrān, 2nd ed., 267–72. Riyadh: Dār ʿĀlam al-Fawāʾid, 2001.

——. *Mukhtaṣar al-ʿulūw li-l-ʿAlī al-Ghaffār*. Edited by Muhammad Nāṣir al-Dīn al-Albānī. 1st ed. Damascus: al-Maktab al-Islāmī, 1981.

——. *Siyar aʿlām al-nubalāʾ*. Edited by Bashshār ʿAwwād Maʿrūf. 3rd ed. 25 vols. Beirut: Muʾassasat al-Risāla, 1985.

Dihlawī, Shāh Walī Allāh al-. 'Risāla fī nanāqib Ibn Taymiyya wa-l-difāʿ ʿanhu.' In *al-Jāmiʿ li-sīrat shaykh al-Islām Ibn Taymiyya khilāla sabʿat qurūn*, edited by Muḥammad ʿUzayr Shams and ʿAlī b. Muḥammad al-ʿImrān, 2nd ed., 641–46. Riyadh: Dār ʿĀlam al-Fawāʾid, 2001.

Drevon, Jerome. *Institutionalizing Violence: Strategies of Jihad in Egypt*. Oxford; New York: Oxford University Press, 2022.

——. 'The Emergence and Construction of the Radical Salafi Milieu in Egypt.' In *Political Violence in Context: Time, Space and Milieu*, edited by Lorenzo Bosi, Niall Ó Dochartaigh, and Daniela Pisoiu, 215–35, 2015.

Dumairieh, Naser. *Intellectual Life in the Ḥijāz before Wahhabism: Ibrāhīm al-Kūrānī's (d. 1101/1690) Theology of Sufism*. Islamicate Intellectual History, volume 9. Leiden; Boston, Mass.: Brill, 2022.

Duwaysh, Aḥmad b. ʿAbd al-Razzāq al-. *Fatāwā Al-Lajna al-Dāʾima Li-l-Buḥūth al-ʿIlmiyya Wa-l-Iftā*. 23 vols. Riyahd: Dār al-Muʾayyad, 2003.

Eddy, William A. 'King Ibn Sa'ūd: "Our Faith and Your Iron."' *Middle East Journal* 17, no. 3 (1963): 257–63.

Eido, Issam. 'The Rise of Syrian Salafism: From Denial to Recognition.' In *The Syrian Uprising*, edited by Raymond Hinnebusch and Omar Imady, 1st ed. London: Routledge, 2018.

El-Bizri, Nader. 'God: Essence and Attribute.' In *The Cambridge Companion to Classical Islamic Theology*, edited by T. J. Winter, 121–40. Cambridge Companions to Religion. Cambridge; New York: Cambridge University Press, 2008.

El-Khuwas, Mohamed A. 'Qaddafi and Islam in Libya.' *American Journal of Islam and Society* 1, no. 1 (April 1, 1984): 61–81. https://doi.org/10.35632/ajis.v1i1.2821.

Elliott, Andrea. 'Why Yasir Qadhi Wants to Talk About Jihad.' *The New York Times*, March 17, 2011, sec. Magazine. https://www.nytimes.com/2011/03/20/magazine/mag-20Salafis-t.html.

Elmasry, Shadee. 'The Salafis in America: The Rise, Decline and Prospects for a Sunni Muslim Movement among African-Americans.' *Journal of Muslim Minority Affairs* 30 (June 1, 2010): 217–36. https://doi.org/10.1080/13602004.2010.494072.

El-Omari, Racha. 'The Muʿtazilite Movement (I): The Origins of the Muʿtazila.' In *The Oxford Handbook of Islamic Theology*, edited by Sabine Schmidtke, Reprint ed., 131–41. Oxford, UK: Oxford University Press, 2018.

——. *The Theology of Abū L-Qāsim al-Balkhī/al-Kaʿbī (d. 319/931)*. Islamic Philosophy, Theology and Science 99. Boston; Leiden: Brill, 2016.

El-Rouayheb, Khaled. 'From Ibn Hajar Al-Haytami (d. 1566) to Khayr al-Din al-Alusi (d. 1899): Changing Views of Ibn Taymiyya amongst Sunni Islamic Scholars.' In *Ibn Taymiyya and His Times*, edited by Youssef Rapoport and Shahab Ahmed, 269–318. Karachi: Oxford University Press, 2010.

——. *Islamic Intellectual History in the Seventeenth Century: Scholarly Currents in the Ottoman Empire and the Maghreb*. Cambridge University Press, 2015. https://doi.org/10.1017/CBO9781107337657.

El-Sherif, Ashraf. 'Egypt's Salafists at a Crossroads.' *Carnegie Endowment for International Peace*, 2015, 1–28.

El-Tobgui, Carl Sharif. *Ibn Taymiyya on Reason and Revelation: A Study of Darʾ Taʿāruḍ al-ʿaql Wa-l-Naql*. Leiden; Boston: Brill, 2019.

'EPIC's Team – EPIC Masjid.' Accessed June 9, 2024. https://epicmasjid.org/epics-team/.

Eppel, Michael. 'Note about the Term Effendiyya in the History of the Middle East.' *International Journal of Middle East Studies* 41, no. 3 (2009): 535–39.

Ess, Josef van. *Theology and Society in the Second and Third Centuries of the Hijra*. Translated by Gwendolin Goldbloom. Vol. 3. 5 vols. Leiden: Brill, 2017. https://brill.com/display/title/34588.

——. *Theology and Society in the Second and Third Centuries of the Hijra*. Translated by Gwendolin Goldbloom. Vol. 4. 5 vols. Leiden: Brill, 2018. https://brill.com/display/title/34744.

'European Council For Fatwa And Research.' Accessed June 9, 2024. https://www.e-cfr.org/en/.

Evered, Emine Ö. 'Rereading Ottoman Accounts of Wahhabism as Alternative Narratives: Ahmed Cevdet Paşa's Historical Survey of the Movement.' *Comparative Studies of South Asia, Africa and the Middle East* 32, no. 3 (December 1, 2012): 622–32. https://doi.org/10.1215/1089201X-1891615.

'Executive Member – All India Muslim Personal Law Board.' Accessed June 9, 2024. https://aimplb.org/executive-members/.

Fadel, Mohammad. 'Islamic Law and Constitution-Making: The Authoritarian Temptation and the Arab Spring.' *Osgoode Hall Law Journal* 53, no. 2 (January 1, 2016): 472–507. https://doi.org/10.60082/2817-5069.2994.

Faisal, Abdullah. *100 Fabricated Hadith*. Accessed June 12, 2024. http://archive.org/details/100FabricatedHadithShaikhAbdullahFaisal_201707.

Fandy, Mamoun. *Saudi Arabia and the Politics of Dissent*. 1st ed. Basingstoke: Palgrave, 2001.

Farquhar, Michael [also: Mike]. *Circuits of Faith: Migration, Education, and the Wahhabi Mission*. Stanford: Stanford University Press, 2016.

Farquhar, Michale [also: Mike]. 'The Islamic University of Medina since 1961: The Politics of Religious Mission and the Making of a Modern Salafi Pedagogy.' In *Shaping Global Islamic Discourses: The Role of al-Azhar, al-Medina and al-Mustafa*, edited by Masooda Bano and Keiko Sakurai, 0. Edinburgh University Press, 2015. https://doi.org/10.3366/edinburgh/9780748696857.003.0002.

Field, Nathan, and Ahmed Hamam. 'Salafi Satellite TV in Egypt.' *Arab Media & Society* Spring (January 1, 2009).

Filali, Abdelkader. *Salafi Jihadism, Disengagement, and the Monarchy: Exploring the Case of Morocco*. Université d'Ottawa / University of Ottawa, 2019.

Filoramo, Giovanni. *A History of Gnosticism*. Reprint ed. Cambridge, MA: Blackwell, 1994.

Finkel, Caroline. *Osman's Dream: The Story of the Ottoman Empire, 1300–1923*. New York: Basic Books, 2007.

Finkelstein, Norman G. *Gaza: An Inquest into Its Martyrdom*. Oakland, California: University of California Press, 2018.

*France 24*. 'France "Expels" Controversial Salafist Preacher to Algeria.' April 20, 2018. https://www.france24.com/en/20180420-france-expels-controversial-salafist-preacher-algeria.

François, Emilie Siobhan. 'The Movement for Unicity and Reform.' PhD thesis, University of Oxford, 2016.

Frank, Richard M. *Beings and Their Attributes: The Teaching of the Basrian School of the Mu'tazila in the Classical Period*. Studies in Islamic Philosophy and Science. Albany: State University of New York Press, 1978.

Freer, Courtney. 'The Rise of Pragmatic Islamism in Kuwait's Post-Arab Spring Opposition Movement.' *The Brookings Institution*, Rethinking Political Islam, August 2015.

Friedman, Yaron. 'Ibn Taymiyya's Fatāwā against the Nuṣayrī-ʿAlawī Sect' 82, no. 2 (December 12, 2005): 349–63. https://doi.org/10.1515/islm.2005.82.2.349.

——. *The Nuṣayrī-ʿalawīs: An Introduction to the Religion, History, and Identity of the Leading Minority in Syria*. Leiden; Boston: Brill, 2010.

Gambetta, Diego, and Steffen Hertog. *Engineers of Jihad: The Curious Connection between Violent Extremism and Education*. Princeton: Princeton University Press, 2016.

Gauvain, Richard. *Salafi Ritual Purity: In the Presence of God*. 1st ed. Routledge Islamic Studies Series. New York, NY: Routledge, 2017.

——. 'Salafism in Modern Egypt: Panacea or Pest?' *Political Theology* 11, no. 6 (December 15, 2010): 802–25. https://doi.org/10.1558/poth.v11i6.802.

Gerges, Fawaz A. *ISIS: A History*. Princeton; Oxford, UK: Princeton University Press, 2016.

——. 'Qurayshi Death: The Islamic State Has Become a Resilient Insurgency.' *Foreign Policy*, February 7, 2022. https://foreignpolicy.com/2022/02/07/qurayshi-death-leader-islamic-state-current-strength/.

——. *The Far Enemy: Why Jihad Went Global*. 2nd ed. Cambridge; New York: Cambridge University Press, 2009.

Gershoni, Israel, and James P. Jankowski. *Redefining the Egyptian Nation, 1930–1945*. Cambridge Middle East Studies. Cambridge: Cambridge University Press, 1995. https://doi.org/10.1017/CBO9780511523991.

Ghanem, Tarek. 'Muslim Media in the Post-Arab Spring: The Curious Case of Egypt.' March 18, 2020. *Maydan* (blog). Accessed January 14, 2023. https://themaydan.com/2020/03/muslim-media-in-the-post-arab-spring-the-curious-case-of-egypt/.

Ghazali, Zainab al-. *Return of the Pharaoh: Memoir in Nasir's Prison*. Leicester: The Islamic Foundation, 1994.

Ghitani, Gamal al-. *The Mahfouz Dialogs*. Translated by Humphrey Davies. 1st ed. Cairo: The American University in Cairo Press, 2008.

Ghyoot, Mathias. '"Nay, We Obeyed God When We Burned Him": Debating Immolation (Taḥrīq) Between the Islamic State and Al-Qāʿida.' In *Violence in Islamic Thought from European Imperialism to the Post-Colonial Era*, edited by Mustafa Baig and Robert Gleave, 249–88. Edinburgh: Edinburgh University Press, 2021. http://www.jstor.org/stable/10.3366/j.ctv1ns7mwk.16.

Giustozzi, Antonio. *The Islamic State in Khorasan: Afghanistan, Pakistan and the New Central Asian Jihad*. London: Hurst & Company, 2018.

Godelek, Kamuran. 'The Neoplatonist Roots of Sufi Philosophy.' *The Paideia Archive: Twentieth World Congress of Philosophy* 5 (1998): 57–60. https://doi.org/10.5840/wcp20-paideia19985114.

Gohel, Sajjan M. *Doctor, Teacher, Terrorist: The Life and Legacy of Al-Qaeda Leader Ayman Al-Zawahiri*. New York, NY: Oxford University Press, 2024.

Goldziher, Ignaz [also: Ignác]. *Le Dogme et La Loi de l'Islam; Histoire Du Développement Dogmatique et Juridique de La Religion Musulmane*. Paris: Geuthner, 1920.

——. 'The Ẓāhirīs: Their Doctrine and Their History. A Contribution to the History of Islamic Theology.' In *The Ẓāhirīs*. Brill, 2007. https://brill.com/display/title/14350.

Goodstein, Laurie. 'Muslim Leaders Wage Theological Battle, Stoking ISIS' Anger.' *The New York Times*, May 8, 2016. https://www.nytimes.com/2016/05/09/us/isis-threatens-muslim-preachers-who-are-waging-theological-battle-online.html.

Gräf, Bettina, and Jakob Skovgaard-Petersen, eds. *Global Mufti: The Phenomenon of Yūsuf al-Qaraḍāwī*. London: C. Hurst & Company, 2009.

Grewal, Zareena. *Islam Is a Foreign Country: American Muslims and the Global Crisis of Authority*. Nation of Newcomers: Immigrant History as American History. New York: New York University Press, 2014.

Griffel, Frank. 'Ibn Taymiyya and His Ash'arite Opponents on Reason and Revelation: Similarities, Differences, and a Vicious Circle.' *Muslim World* 108, no. 1 (January 1, 2018): 11–39.

Haddad, Mahmoud. 'Arab Religious Nationalism in the Colonial Era: Rereading Rashid Rida's Ideas on the Caliphate.' *Journal of the American Oriental Society* 117, no. 2 (June 1997): 253–77.

Ḥāfī, ʿAbd Allāh b. Yūsuf al-. *al-Ikhtiyārāt wa-l-tarjīḥāt li-shaykh Ibn ʿUthaymīn fī kitābihī al-sharḥ al-mumtiʿ*. Kuwait: Dār al-Ilāf, 1999.

Haider, Najam. 'Zaydism.' In *Handbook of Islamic Sects and Movements*, edited by Muhammad Afzal Upal and Carole M. Cusack, 203–34. Brill Handbooks on Contemporary Religion, volume 21. Leiden; Boston: Brill, 2021. https://catalog.lib.uchicago.edu/vufind/Record/12616489.

Ḥalabī, ʿAlī al-. *Maʿa shaykhinā Nāṣir al-sunna wa-l-dīn Muḥammad Nāṣir al-Dīn al-Albānī mujaddid al-qarn wa-muḥaddith al-ʿaṣr fī shuhūr ḥayātihi al-akhīra*. Ras al-Khaimah, UAE: Maktabat Dār al-Ḥadīth, 1999.

Halevi, Leor. *Modern Things on Trial: Islam's Global and Material Reformation in the Age of Rida, 1865–1935*. New York: Columbia University Press, 2019.

Hallaq, Wael B. *Authority, Continuity, and Change in Islamic Law*. Cambridge, UK; New York: Cambridge University Press, 2001.

——. *Sharīʿa: Theory, Practice, Transformations*. Cambridge, UK; New York: Cambridge University Press, 2009.

——. 'Takhrij and the Construction of Juristic Authority.' In *Studies in Islamic Legal Theory*, edited by Bernard G. Weiss, 317–35. Leiden: Brill, 2002.

——. *The Origins and Evolution of Islamic Law*. Themes in Islamic Law 1. Cambridge, UK; New York: Cambridge University Press, 2005.

Halm, Heinz. *Shi'ism*. Translated by Janet Watson and Marian Hill. 2nd ed. New York: Columbia University Press, 2004.

Halverson, Jeffry R. *Theology and Creed in Sunni Islam: The Muslim Brotherhood, Ash'arism, and Political Sunnism*. New York, NY: Palgrave Macmillan, 2010.

Hamdeh, Emad. *Salafism and Traditionalism: Scholarly Authority in Modern Islam*. New York: Cambridge University Press, 2020.
——. 'Shaykh Google as Ḥāfiẓ Al-ʿAṣr: The Internet, Traditional ʿUlamā', and Self Learning.' *American Journal of Islam and Society* 37, no. 1–2 (May 15, 2020): 67–102. https://doi.org/10.35632/ajis.v37i1-2.851.
——. 'The Formative Years of an Iconoclastic Salafi Scholar.' *The Muslim World* 106, no. 3 (July 2016): 411–32. https://doi.org/10.1111/muwo.12157.
Hamdi, Mohamed Elhachmi. *The Politicisation of Islam: A Case Study of Tunisia*. State, Culture & Society in Arab North Africa. Boulder, Colo.: Westview Press, 1998.
Hamid, Mustafa, and Leah Farrall. *The Arabs at War in Afghanistan*. Oxford University Press, 2015.
Hamid, Sadek. *Sufis, Salafis and Islamists: The Contested Ground of British Islamic Activism*. Library of Modern Religion 46. London; New York: I.B. Tauris, 2016.
Hamming, Tore. *Jihadi Politics: The Global Jihadi Civil War, 2014–2019*. Oxford University Press, 2023.
Hammond, Andrew. 'Salafi Publishing and Contestation over Orthodoxy and Leadership in Sunni Islam.' In *Wahhabism and the World: Understanding Saudi Arabia's Global Influence on Islam*, edited by Peter Mandaville, 80–84. Religion and Global Politics. Oxford; New York: Oxford University Press, 2022.
——. 'Salafi Thought in Turkish Public Discourse Since 1980.' *International Journal of Middle East Studies* 49, no. 3 (2017): 417–35.
Hansen, Stig Jarle. *Al-Shabaab in Somalia: The History and Ideology of a Militant Islamist Group, 2005–2012*. Oxford University Press, 2013.
Harley, Nicola. 'Radical July 7 Preacher Arrested in Undercover Sting Trying to Recruit Jihadis,' August 26, 2017. https://www.telegraph.co.uk/news/2017/08/25/radical-july-7-preacher-arrested-undercover-sting-trying-recruit/.
Harper, Mary. *Everything You Have Told Me Is True: The Many Faces of Al Shabaab*. Oxford University Press, 2019.
Hartung, Jan-Peter. 'Making Sense of "Political Quietism": An Analytical Intervention.' In *Political Quietism in Islam: Sunni and Shi'i Practice and Thought*, edited by Saud al-Sarhan, 15–32. King Faisal Center for Research and Islamic Studies Series. London; New York, NY: I.B. Tauris, 2020.
Harvey, Ramon. *The Qur'an and the Just Society*. 1st ed. Edinburgh: Edinburgh University Press, 2019.
——. *Transcendent God, Rational World: A Maturidi Theology*. 1st ed. Edinburgh University Press, 2023.
Hasan, Masudul. *History of Islam*. Vol. 2. 2 vols. Adam Publishers, 1998.
Hasan, Noorhaidi. 'Ambivalent Doctrines and Conflicts in the Salafi Movement in Indonesia.' In *Global Salafism: Islam's New Religious Movement*, edited by Roel Meijer, 0. Oxford University Press, 2014. https://doi.org/10.1093/acprof:oso/9780199333431.003.0008.
——. 'Between Transnational Interest and Domestic Politics: Understanding Middle Eastern Fatwās on Jihad in the Moluccas,' January 1, 2005. https://doi.org/10.1163/1568519053123885.

——. 'Salafism, Education, and Youth: Saudi Arabia's Campaign for Wahhabism in Indonesia.' In *Wahhābism and the World. Understanding Saudi Arabia's Global Influence on Islam*, edited by Peter Mandaville, 135–57. Oxford University Press, 2022. https://doi.org/10.1093/oso/9780197532560.003.0007.

——. 'The Salafi Madrasas of Indonesia.' In *The Madrasa in Asia*, edited by Farish A Noor, Yoginder Sikand, and Martin Van Bruinessen, 247–74. Amsterdam University Press, 2009. https://doi.org/10.1515/9789048501380-011.

Hasan, Suhaib. *The Concept of the Mahdi Among Ahl Al-Sunna*. London: Al-Qur'an Society, 2019.

Hashemi, Nader. 'The ISIS Crisis and the Broken Politics of the Arab World.' In *Routledge Handbook on Human Rights and the Middle East and North Africa*, edited by Anthony Tirado Chase, Routledge Handbooks Online. Abingdon, Oxon: Routledge, 2016.

Hassan, Hassan. 'The "Conscious Uncoupling" of Wahhabism and Saudi Arabia.' *New Lines Magazine*, February 22, 2022. https://newlinesmag.com/argument/the-conscious-uncoupling-of-wahhabism-and-saudi-arabia/.

Hatina, Meir. 'Contesting Violence in Radical Islam: Sayyid Imām al-Shaīf's Ethical Perception.' *Islamic Law and Society* 23, no. 1/2 (2016): 120–40.

——. 'Remembering Our Heroes: Global Jihad's Militancy in a Comparative Perspective.' *Middle East Law and Governance* 13, no. 1 (March 4, 2021): 98–124. https://doi.org/10.1163/18763375-13010002.

Hawwa, Saʿid. *al-Ijābāt*. Cairo: Daral-Salam, 1984.

——. *Hadhihi tajribatī wa-hadhihi shahādatī*. Cairo: Maktabat Wahba, 1987.

Haykel, Bernard. 'Anti-Wahhabism: A Footnote.' *Middle East Strategy at Harvard* (blog), March 27, 2008. https://archive.blogs.harvard.edu/mesh/2008/03/anti_wahhabism_a_footnote/.

——. 'On the Nature of Salafi Thought and Action.' In *Global Salafism*, edited by Roel Meijer, 34–57. Oxford University Press, 2014. https://doi.org/10.1093/acprof:oso/9780199333431.003.0002.

——. *Revival and Reform in Islam: The Legacy of Muhammad al-Shawkani*. Illustrated ed. Cambridge, UK; New York: Cambridge University Press, 2003.

Hegghammer, Thomas. '"Classical" and "Global" Jihadism in Saudi Arabia.' In *Saudi Arabia in Transition: Insights on Social, Political, Economic and Religious Change*, edited by Bernard Haykel, Stéphane Lacroix, and Thomas Hegghammer, 207–28. Cambridge: Cambridge University Press, 2015. https://doi.org/10.1017/CBO9781139047586.014.

——. *Jihad in Saudi Arabia: Violence and Pan-Islamism Since 1979*. Cambridge Middle East Studies 33. Cambridge, UK; New York: Cambridge University Press, 2010.

——. 'Jihadi-Salafis Or Revolutionaries? On Religion and Politics in the Study of Militant Islamism.' In *Global Salafism: Islam's New Religious Movement*, edited by Roel Meijer, 0. Oxford University Press, 2014. https://doi.org/10.1093/acprof:oso/9780199333431.003.0011.

——. *The Caravan: Abdallah Azzam and the Rise of Global Jihad*. 1st ed. Cambridge: Cambridge University Press, 2020.

Hegghammer, Thomas, and Stéphane Lacroix. 'Rejectionist Islamism in Saudi Arabia: The Story of Juhayman al-ʿUtaybi Revisited.' *International Journal of Middle East Studies* 39, no. 1 (2007): 103–22.

Heller, Sam. 'Ahrar Al-Sham's Revisionist Jihadism.' *War on the Rocks* (blog), September 30, 2015. https://warontherocks.com/2015/09/ahrar-al-shams-revisionist-jihadism/.

Henderson, John B. *The Construction of Orthodoxy and Heresy: Neo-Confucian, Islamic, Jewish, and Early Christian Patterns*. Albany, NY: State University of New York Press, 1998.

Hermansen, Marcia. 'Eschatology.' In *The Cambridge Companion to Classical Islamic Theology*, edited by T. J. Winter, 308–24. Cambridge Companions to Religion. Cambridge; New York: Cambridge University Press, 2008.

Hertog, Steffen, and Diego Gambetta. 'Why Are There so Many Engineers among Islamic Radicals?' *European Journal of Sociology* 50 (August 1, 2009). https://doi.org/10.1017/S0003975609990129.

Ḥillī, Ibn Muṭahhar al-. *Minhāj al-karāma fī ithbāt al-imāma*. Lithographic reprint of a manuscript. [Iran], 1877.

Hiro, Dilip. *War Without End: The Rise of Islamist Terrorism and Global Response*. Rev. ed. London; New York: Routledge, 2002.

Hodgson, Marshall G. S. *The Venture of Islam: Conscience and History in a World Civilization*. 3 vols. Chicago: University of Chicago Press, 1974.

Høigilt, Jacob, and Frida Nome. 'Egyptian Salafism in Revolution.' *Journal of Islamic Studies* 25 (January 8, 2014): 33–54. https://doi.org/10.1093/jis/ett056.

Holtzman, Livnat. 'Al-Lālakāʾī, Abū l-Qāsim.' In *Encyclopaedia of Islam Three Online*, edited by Kate Fleet, Gudrun Krämer, Denis Matringe, John Nawas, and Devin J. Stewart. Brill, 2020. https://doi.org/10.1163/1573-3912_ei3_COM_35783.

——. *Anthropomorphism in Islam: The Challenge of Traditionalism*. 1st ed. Edinburgh: Edinburgh University Press, 2019.

——. 'The Caliph Al-Qādir Bi-Llāh and the Qādirī Creed.' In *Rulers as Authors in the Islamic World*, edited by Maribel Fierro, Sonja Brentjes, and Tilman Seidensticker, 143–209. Leiden: Brill, 2024. https://doi.org/10.1163/9789004690615_008.

Hoover, Jon. 'Hanbali Theology.' In *The Oxford Handbook of Islamic Theology*, edited by Sabine Schmidtke, 626–46. Oxford Handbooks. Oxford, UK: Oxford University Press, 2016.

——. 'Ḥanbali Theology.' In *The Oxford Handbook of Islamic Theology*, edited by Sabine Schmidtke, 625–46. Oxford, UK: Oxford University Press, 2018.

——. 'Ḥashwiyya.' In *Encyclopaedia of Islam Three Online*. Brill, 2016. https://doi.org/10.1163/1573-3912_ei3_COM_30377.

——. *Ibn Taymiyya*. London: Oneworld Academic, 2020.

——. 'Ibn Taymiyya.' In *The Stanford Encyclopedia of Philosophy*, edited by Edward N. Zalta and Uri Nodelman, Summer 2024. Metaphysics Research Lab, Stanford University, 2024. https://plato.stanford.edu/archives/sum2024/entries/ibn-taymiyya/.

——. 'Ibn Taymiyya.' Accessed August 14, 2023. https://sites.google.com/site/jhoover363/taymiyyan-studies/ibn-taymiyya

——. 'Ibn Taymiyya Between Moderation and Radicalism.' In *Reclaiming Islamic Tradition: Modern Interpretations of the Classical Heritage*, edited by Elisabeth Kendall and Ahmad Khan, 177–203. Edinburgh: Edinburgh University Press, 2016.

——. 'Withholding Judgment on Islamic Universalism: Ibn al-Wazīr (d. 840/1436) on the Duration and Purpose of Hell-Fire.' In *Locating Hell in Islamic Traditions*, edited by Christian Lange, 208–37. Brill, 2016. https://doi.org/10.1163/9789004301368_011.

Hourani, Albert. *Arabic Thought in the Liberal Age 1798–1939*. Cambridge: Cambridge University Press, 1983. https://doi.org/10.1017/CBO9780511801990.

——. 'Rashid Rida and the Sufi Orders: A Footnote to Laoust.' *Bulletin d'études Orientales* 29 (1977): 231–41.

Howe, Marvine. *Morocco: The Islamist Awakening and Other Challenges*. New York: Oxford University Press, 2005.

Hroub, Khaled. 'Salafi Formations in Palestine: The Limits of a De-Palestinised Milieu.' In *Global Salafism: Islam's New Religious Movement*, edited by Roel Meijer, 221–43. Oxford University Press, 2014. https://doi.org/10.1093/acprof:oso/9780199333431.003.0010.

Hurvitz, Nimrod. *The Formation of Hanbalism: Piety into Power*. 1st ed. New York: Routledge, 2011.

——. 'The Mihna (Inquisition) and the Public Sphere.' In *The Public Sphere in Muslim Societies*, edited by Miriam Hoexter, S. N. Eisenstadt, and Nehemia Levtzion, 17–29. Albany: State University of New York Press, 2002.

Ḥusayn, Aḥmad b. ʿAbd al-ʿAzīz al-. *Daʿwat al-Imām Muḥammad Ibn ʿAbd al-Wahhāb Salafiyya lā Wahhābiyya*. 1st ed. Riyadh: Dār ʿĀlam al-Kutub, 1999.

Huzaimi, Nasir al-. *The Mecca Uprising: An Insider's Account of Salafism and Insurrection in Saudi Arabia*. Translated by David Commins. London; New York; Oxford; New Delhi; Sydney: I.B. Tauris, 2021.

Hwang, Julie Chernov, and Kirsten E. Schulze. 'Why They Join: Pathways into Indonesian Jihadist Organizations.' *Terrorism and Political Violence* 30, no. 6 (November 2, 2018): 911–32. https://doi.org/10.1080/09546553.2018.1481309.

Ibn ʿAbd al-Wahhāb, Muḥammad. *Kashf al-shubuhāt*. Maktabat al-Himma, 2016.

——. *Kitāb al-tawḥīd alladhī huwa ḥaqq Allāh ʿalā al-ʿabīd*. Edited by Daghash b. Shabīb al-ʿAjmī. Kuwait: Maktabat Ahl al-Athar, 2014.

——. *Majmūʿat rasāʾil fī Al-tawḥīd wa-l-īmān*. Edited by Ismāʿīl b. Muḥammad al-Anṣārī. Riyadh: Jāmiʿat al-Imām Muḥammad ibn Suʿūd al-Islāmiyya, n.d.

——. *Muʾallafāt al-shaykh al-imām Muḥammad ibn ʿAbd al-Wahhāb*. Edited by ʿAbd al-ʿAzīz b. Zayd al-Rūmī, Muḥammad Baltājī, and Sayyid Ḥijāb. Riyadh: Jāmiʿat al-Imām Muḥammad ibn Suʿūd al-Islāmiyya, 1976.

——. *Uṣūl al-īmān*. Edited by Bāsam Fayṣal al-Jawābira. 5th ed. Medina: Wizārat al-Shuʾūn al-Islāmiyya wa-l-Awqāf wa-l-Daʿwa wa-l-Irshād, 1999.

Ibn ʿAbd al-Wahhāb, Sulaymān. *al-Ṣawāʿiq al-ilāhiyya fī al-radd ʿalā al-Wahhābiyya*. Edited by al-Sarrājī. 1st ed. Beirut: Dār Dhū al-Qarnayn, 1998.

——. *The Divine Lightning*. London: Lulu Press, 2003.

Ibn Abī Yaʿlā al-Farrāʾ, Abū al-Ḥusayn Muḥammad. *Ṭabaqāt al-Ḥanābila*. Edited by ʿAbd al-Raḥmān b. Sulaymān al-ʿUthaymīn. 3 vols. Riyadh: al-Amāna al-ʿĀmma li-l-Iḥtifāl bi-Murūr Miʾat ʿĀmʿalā Taʾsīs al-Mamlaka, 1999.

Ibn ʿAfāliq, Muḥammad b. ʿAbd al-Raḥmān. *Tahakkum al-muqallidīn fī muddaʿī tajdīd al-dīn*, n.d. https://dn790009.ca.archive.org/0/items/lionsunna_TAHAKKOMU_ALMUKALLEDIN/lmlkmltkmrl.pdf.

Ibn Aḥmad, ʿAbd Allāh. *Kitāb al-sunna*. Edited by Muḥammad b. Saʿīd b. Sālim al-Qaḥṭānī. 2 vols. Dammam: Dār Ibn al-Qayyim, 1986.

Ibn ʿAlawī al-Mālikī al-Ḥasanī, Muḥammad. *Notions That Must Be Corrected [Mafāhim Yajib ʿan Tuṣāhhah]*. Translated by Suraqah Abdul Aziz. The Netherlands: Sunni Publications, n.d.

Ibn ʿAsākir, ʿAlī b. al-Ḥasan. *Tabyīn kadhib al-muftarī fī-mā nusiba ilā al-imām Abī al-Ḥasan al-Ashʿarī*. 2nd ed. Damascus: Dār al-Fikr, 1979.

Ibn-al-Aṯīr, ʿIzz-ad-Dīn Abu-'l-Ḥasan ʿAlī. *The Annals of the Saljuq Turks: Selections from al-Kāmil Fī 'l-Taʾrīkh of ʿIzz al-Dīn Ibn al-Athīr*. Translated by Donald S. Richards. Studies in the History of Iran and Turkey. London: RoutledgeCurzon, 2002.

Ibn al-Jawzī, Abū al-Faraj ʿAbd al-Raḥmān. *A Medieval Critique of Anthropomorphism: Ibn Al-Jawzī's Kitāb Akhbār Aṣ-Ṣifāt*. Translated by Merlin L. Swartz. Leiden: Brill, 2002.

——. *al-Muntaẓam fī taʾrīkh al-mulūk wa-l-umam*. Edited by Muḥammad ʿAbd al-Qādir ʿAṭā and Muṣṭafā ʿAbd al-Qādir ʿAṭā. 19 vols. Beirut: Dār al-Kutūb al-ʿIlmiyya, 1992.

——. *Dafʿ shubah al-tashbīh bi-akuff al-tanzīh fī al-radd ʿalā al-mujassima wa-l-mushabbiha*. Edited by Muḥammad Zāhid al-Kawtharī. Cairo: al-Maktaba al-Tawfīqiyya, 1977.

——. *Naqd al-ʿilm wa-l-ʿulamāʾ aw talbīs Iblīs*. Cairo: Maṭbaʿat al-Saʿāda, 1921.

——. *The Attributes of God: Ibn al-Jawzi's Daf' Shubah al-Tashbih Bi-Akaff al-Tanzih*. Translated by Abdullah bin Hamid 'Ali. 1st ed. Amal Press, 2006.

——. *The Life of Ibn Ḥanbal*. Translated by Michael Cooperson. Abridged ed. New York: NYU Press, 2016.

Ibn al-Jawzī, Sibṭ. *Mirʾāt al-zamān fī tawārīkh al-aʿyān*. Edited by Muḥammad Barakāt, Kamāl Muḥammad al-Kharāṭ, Ammār Rīḥāwī, and Muḥammad Riḍwān ʿArqasūsī. Vol. 23. Damascus: Dār al-Risālāt al-ʿĀlamiyya, 2013.

Ibn al-ʿUthaymīn, Muḥammad b. Ṣāliḥ. *al-Sharḥ al-mumtiʿ ʿalā zād al-mustaqniʿ*. Edited by Abū Ayyūb al-Sulaymān. 15 vols. Dammam, Saudi Arabia: Dār Ibn al-Jawzī, 2008.

——. *Liqāʾ al-bāb al-maftūḥ*. Transcribed by the Islamic Network website http://www.islamweb.net, made Available on Shāmila at https://shamela.ws/book/7687,. Liqāʾ al-bāb, 1992. https://shamela.ws/book/7687.

——. *Sharḥ Kitāb Kashf Al-Shubuhāt Wa-Yalīhi Sharḥ al-Uṣūl al-Sittah*. Edited by Fahd b. Nāṣir b. Ibrāhīm al-Sulaymān. 1st ed. Riyadh: Dār al-Thurayyā li-l-Nashr, 1996.

——. *ʿAqīdat Ahl Al-Sunna Wa-l-Jamāʿa*. 4th ed. Riyadh: al-Maktab al-Taʿawunī, 2001.

Ibn al-Wazīr, Muḥammad b. Ibrāhīm. *al-ʿAwāṣim wa al-qawāṣim fī al-dhabb ʿan sunna Abī al-Qāsim*. Edited by Shuʿayb al-Arnaʾūṭ. 3rd ed. 9 vols. Beirut: Muʾassasat al-Risāla li-al-Ṭibāʿa wa-l-Nashr wa-l-Tawzīʿ, 1994.

Ibn al-Zāghūnī, Abū al-Ḥasan. *al-Īḍāḥ fī uṣūl al-dīn*. Edited by ʿIṣām Sayyid Maḥmūd. Riyadh: Markaz al-Malik Fayṣal li-l-Buḥūth wa-l-Dirāsāt al-Islāmiyya, 2003.

Ibn Baṭṭa al-ʿUkbarī, Abū ʿAbd Allāh. *al-Ibāna ʿan sharīʿat al-firaq al-nājiya wa-l-mujānabat al-firaq al-madhmūma [also: al-Ibāna al-kubrā]*. Edited by Riḍā b. Naʿsān Muʿṭī. 2nd ed. 7 vols. Riyadh: Dār al-Rāya, 1994.

——. *al-Sharḥ wa-l-ibāna ʿalā uṣūl al-sunna wa-l-diyāna [also: al-Ibāna al-ṣughrā]*. Edited by Riḍā b. Naʿsān Muʿṭī. 1st ed. Maktabat al-ʿUlūm wa-l-Ḥikam, 2002.

Ibn Bāz, ʿAbd al-ʿAzīz. 'Ḥukm Duʿāʾ Ghayr Allāh ʿan Jahl bi-al-Tawḥīd (Fatwa No. 1210).' *al-Mawqiʿ al-Rasmī li-Shaykh ʿAbd al-ʿAzīz bin Bāz*. Accessed May 15, 2024. https://binbaz.org.sa/fatwas/1210/%D8%AD%D9%83%D9%85-%D8%AF%D8%B9%D8%A7%D8%A1-%D8%BA%D9%8A%D8%B1-%D8%A7%D9%84%D9%84%D9%87-%D8%B9%D9%86-%D8%AC%D9%87%D9%84-%D8%A8%D8%A7%D9%84%D8%AA%D9%88%D8%AD%D9%8A%D8%AF.

——. *Majmūʿ fatāwā wa-maqālāt mutanawwiʿa*. Edited by Muḥammad b. Saʿd al-Shuwayʿir. 30 vols. Saudi Arabia: Riʾāsat Idārat al-Buḥūth al-ʿIlmiyya wa-l-Iftāʾ, n.d.

——. *Naqd al-qawmiyya al-ʿArabiyya ʿalā ḍawʾ al-Islām wa-l-wāqiʿ*. 6th ed. Riyadh: al-Riʾāsa al-ʿĀmma li-Idārāt al-Buḥūth al-ʿIlmiyya wa-l-Iftā, 1991.

Ibn Ghannām, Ḥusayn b. Abī Bakr. *Tārīkh Ibn Ghannām al-musammā rawḍat al-afkār wa-l-afhām li-murtād ḥāl al-imām wa-taʿdād ghazawāt dhawī-l-Islām*. Edited by Sulaymān b. Ṣāliḥ al-Kharāshī. 2 vols. Riyadh: Dār al-Thulūthiyya, 2010.

Ibn Ḥajar ʿAsqalānī, Aḥmad b. ʿAlī. *Bulūgh al-marām min adillat al-aḥkām*. Edited by Samīr b. Amīn al-Zuhrī. 7th ed. Riyadh: Dār al-Falaq, 2003.

——. *Inabāʾ al-ghumr bi-abānaʾ al-ʿumr fī al-tārīkh*. 9 vols. Hyderabad: Maṭbaʿat Majlis Dāʾirat al-Maʿārif al-ʿUthmāniyya, 1967.

Ibn Ḥanbal, Aḥmad. *Musnad al-imām Aḥmad ibn Ḥanbal*. Edited by Shuʿayb al-Arnaʾūṭ and ʿĀdil Murshid. 52 vols. Beirut: Muʾassasat al-Risāla, 1993.

[pseudo-]Ibn Ḥanbal, Aḥmad. *Uṣūl al-sunna*. 1st ed. Al-Kharj, Saudi Arabia: Dār al-Manār, 1990.

Ibn Kathīr, Abū al-Fidāʾ Ismāʿīl. *al-Bidāya wa-l-nihāya*. Edited by ʿAbd al-Rahmān al-Lādqī and Muḥammad Ghāzī Bayḍūn. 8 vols. Beirut: Dār al-Maʿarifa, 2010.

Ibn Khuzayma, Abū Bakr. *Kitāb al-tawḥīd wa-ithbāt ṣifāt al-rabb ʿazza wa-jalla*. Edited by ʿAbd al-ʿAzīz al-Shahwān. 2 vols. Riyadh: Dār al-Rushd, 1994.

——. *Ṣaḥīḥ Ibn Khuzayma*. Edited by Muṣṭafā al-Aʿẓamī. Beirut: al-Maktab al-Islāmī, 1970.

Ibn Nāsir al-Dīn al-Dimashqī, Muḥammad b. ʿAbd Allāh. *al-Radd al-wāfir ʿalā man zaʿam bi-anna man sammā Ibn Taymiyya Shaykh al-Islām kāfir*. Edited by Zuhayr al-Shāwīsh. 3rd ed. Beirut: al-Maktab al-Islāmī, 1991.

Ibn Qāḍī Shuhba, Taqī al-Dīn Abū Bakr b. Aḥmad. *Tārīkh Ibn Qāḍī Shuhba*. Edited by Adnān Darwīsh. 4 vols. Damascus: Institut Français de Damas, 1977.

Ibn Qāsim, ʿAbd al-Raḥmān b. Muḥammad. *al-Durar al-saniyya fī al-ajwiba al-najdiyya*. 6th ed. 16 vols., 1996.

Ibn Qayyim al-Jawziyya, Shams al-Dīn. *Ijtimāʿ al-juyūsh al-islāmiyya*. Edited by ʿAwwād b. ʿAbd Allāh al-Muʿtiq. Riyadh: Maktabat al-Rushd, 1995.

——. *Matn al-Qaṣīda al-nūniyya*. 2nd ed. Cairo: Maktabat Ibn Taymiyya, 1996.

——. *Ranks of the Divine Seekers: A Parallel English-Arabic Text*. Translated by Ovamir Anjum. 2 vols. Islamic Translation Series, volume 14. Leiden; Boston, Mass.: Brill, 2020.

Ibn Qayyim al-Jawziyya, Shams al-Dīn, and Shams al-Dīn Muḥammad ibn al-Mawṣilī. *Mukhtaṣar al-ṣawāʿiq al-mursala ʿalā al-jahmiyya wa-l-muʿaṭṭila*. Edited by Muḥammad Ḥamīd al-Fiqī and Muḥammad ʿAbd al-Razzāq Ḥamza. al-Maṭbaʿa al-Salafiyya wa-Maktabatuhā, 1929.

——. *Mukhtaṣar al-ṣawāʿiq al-mursala ʿalā al-jahmiyya wa-l-muʿaṭṭila*. Edited by al-Ḥasan b. ʿAbd al-Raḥman al-ʿAlawī. 1st ed. 4 vols. Riyadh: Aḍwāʾ al-Salaf, 2004.

Ibn Qudāma, Muwaffaq al-Dīn. *al-Mughnī sharḥ mukhtaṣar al-Khiraqī*. Edited by ʿAbd Allāh b. ʿAbd al-Muḥsin al-Turkī and ʿAbd al-Fattāḥ Muḥammad al-Ḥilū. 3rd ed. 15 vols. Riyadh: Dār ʿĀlam al-Kutub, 1997.

Ibn Qutayba, Abū Muḥammad. *al-Ikhtilāf fī al-lafẓ wa-l-radd ʿalā al-jahmiyya wa-l-mushabbiha*. Edited by ʿUmar b. Maḥmūd Abū ʿUmar. Riyadh: Dār al-Rāya, 1991.

——. *Taʾwīl mukhtalif al-ḥadīth*. Edited by Salīm b. ʿĪd al-Hilālī. Annotated by ʿUmar b. Maḥmūd Abū ʿUmar. Riyadh: Dār Ibn al-Qayyim, 2009.

Ibn Taymiyya, Taqī al-Dīn. *Against Extremisms*. Translated by Yahya Michot. Beirut: Albouraq Editions, 2012.

——. *al-Fatwā al-Ḥamawiyya al-kubrā*. Edited by Ḥamad b. ʿAbd al-Muḥsin al-Tuwayjirī. Riyadh: Dār al-Ṣumayʿī, 2004.

——. *al-Fatwā al-kubrā*. Edited by Ismāʿīl al-Khaṭīb. 5 vols. Beirut: Dār al-Qalam, 1987.

——. *al-Īmān*. Edited by Muḥammad Nāṣir al-Dīn al-Albānī. 5th ed. Amman, Jordan: al-Maktab al-Islāmī, 1996.

——. *al-Istighātha fi al-radd ʿalā al-Bakrī*. Edited by ʿAbdallāh b. Dujayn al-Sahlī. 4th ed. Riyadh: Maktabat Dār al-Minhāj, 2014.

——. *al-Jawāb al-Ṣaḥīḥ li-man baddala dīn al-Masīḥ*. Edited by ʿAlī b. Ḥasan, ʿAbd al-ʿAzīz b. Ibrāhīm al-ʿAskar, and Ḥamdān b. Muḥammad al-Ḥamdān. 7 vols. Riyadh: Dār al-ʿĀṣima, 1999.

——. *al-Tadmuriyya: Taḥqīq al-ithbāt fī al-asmāʾ wa-l-ṣifāt wa-l-ḥaqīqat al-jamʿ bayna al-qadar wa-l-sharʿ*. Edited by Muḥammad b. ʿAwda al-Saʿawī. 6th ed. Riyadh: Maktabat al-ʿUbaykān, 2000.

——. *Bayān talbīs al-jahmiyya fī taʾsīs bidaʿihim al-kalāmiyya*. Edited by Yaḥyā b. Muḥammad al-Hunaydī, et al., et al., and et al. 10 vols. Medina: Mujammaʿ al-Malik Fahd li-Ṭibāʿat al-Muṣḥaf al-Sharīf, 2005.

——. *Darʾ taʿāruḍ al-ʿaql wa-l-naql*. Edited by Muḥammad Rashād Sālim. 2nd ed. 10 vols. Riyadh: Jāmiʿat al-Imām Muḥammad ibn Suʿūd al-Islāmiyya, 1991.

——. *Ibn Taimiya's Struggle Against Popular Religion*. Translated by Muhammad Umar Memon. Reprint 2012 ed. The Hague: De Gruyter Mouton, 1976.

——. *Ibn Taymiyya Against the Greek Logicians*. Translated by Wael B. Hallaq. 1st ed. Oxford : New York: Clarendon Press, 1993.

——. *Iqtiḍāʾ al-ṣirāṭ al-mustaqīm li-mukhālafat aṣḥāb al-Jaḥīm*. Edited by Nāṣir b. ʿAbd al-Karīm al-ʿAql. 2 vols. Riyadh: Dār al-ʿĀṣima, 1998.

——. *Majmūʿ fatāwā shaykh al-Islām Aḥmad ibn Taymiyya*. Edited by ʿAbd al-Raḥmān b. Muḥammad b. Qāsim and Muḥammad b. ʿAbd al-Raḥmān ibn Qāsim. 37 vols. Riyadh: Maṭābiʿ al-Riyāḍ, 1962.

——. *Minhāj al-sunna al-nabawiyya fī naqḍ kalām al-Shīʿa al-qadariyya*. Edited by Muḥammad Rashād Sālim. 9 vols. Riyadh: Jāmiʿat al-Imām Muḥammad ibn Suʿūd al-Islāmiyya, 1986.

——. *Minhāj al-sunna al-nabawiyya fī naqḍ kalām al-Shīʿa al-qadariyya*. Edited by Rashād Sālim. 8 vols. Riyadh: Muʾassasat al-Rayyān, 2003.

——. *Naqḍ asās al-taqdīs*. Edited by Mūsā b. Sulaymān al-Duwaysh. Medina: Maktabat al-ʿUlūm wa-l-Ḥikam, 2004.

——. *Qāʿida jalīla fī al-tawassul wa-l-wasīla*. Edited by Shuʿayb al-Arnaʾūṭ. Beirut: Riʾāsah ʿIlmiyya, 1999.

Inge, Anabel. *The Making of a Salafi Muslim Woman: Paths to Conversion*. New York: Oxford University Press, 2017.

Ingram, Brannon D. *Revival from Below: The Deoband Movement and Global Islam*. 1st ed. Oakland: University of California Press, 2018.

International Open University. 'Founder IOU.' Accessed December 25, 2022. https://iou.edu.gm/founder/.

International Union of Muslim Scholars. 'IUMS Mourns the Death of Sheikh Zuhair Al-Shawish,' 2013. https://www.iumsonline.org/en/ContentDetails.aspx?ID=2251.

*Interview with Dr. Bilal on Islam and Education [Arabic with Subtitles]*, 2019. https://www.youtube.com/watch?v=AQugDiStEIw.

ʿĪsā, Yusuf al-. 'Kayfa munḥa al-shaykh Ibn ʿUthaymīn jāʾizat al-malik fayṣal al-ʿālamiyya.' *Al-Jazirah*, January 13, 2001. https://www.al-jazirah.com/2001/20010113/ln6.htm.

Islam, Jaan S. 'The Portrayal of Jihadi-Salafism: The Role of Knowledge Production in Fabricating a Global Enemy.' In *Disentangling Jihad, Political Violence and Media*, edited by Simone Pfeifer, Christoph Günther, and Robert Dörre, 31–52. Edinburgh University Press, 2023. https://www.jstor.org.queens.ezproxy.cuny.edu/stable/10.3366/jj.9941193.8.

'Islamic University of Madinah Joins Guinness World Records.' Accessed June 9, 2024. https://www.spa.gov.sa/2364981.

'Islamic University of Medinah.' Accessed May 9, 2024. https://iu.edu.sa/Postgraduates.

Ismail, Raihan. *Rethinking Salafism: The Transnational Networks of Salafi 'Ulama in Egypt, Kuwait, and Saudi Arabia*. Oxford; New York: Oxford University Press, 2021.

Ismāʿīl, Shāh Muḥammad. *Radd al-ishrāk*. Edited by Ismāʿīl b. ʿAbd al-Ghanī and Muḥammad ʿUzair Shams. Lahore: al-Maktaba al-Salafiyya, 1988.

Ivanyi, Katharina A. *Virtue, Piety and the Law: A Study of Birgivī Meḥmed Efendī's al-Ṭarīqa al-Muḥammadīyya*. The Ottoman Empire and Its Heritage 72. Leiden, The Netherlands: Koninklijke Brill NV, 2021.

Jackson, Sherman A. 'Ijtihād and Taqlīd: Between the Islamic Legal Tradition and Autonomous Western Reason.' In *Routledge Handbook of Islamic Law*, edited by Khaled Abou El Fadl, Ahmad Atif Ahmad, and Said Fares Hassan, 1st ed. Routledge Handbooks. London; New York: Routledge, Taylor & Francis Group, 2019.

———. *Islam and the Blackamerican*. Oxford University Press, 2005. https://doi.org/10.1093/acprof:oso/9780195180817.001.0001.

———. *Islam and the Problem of Black Suffering*. Oxford: Oxford University Press, 2014.

Jansen, J. J. G. 'The Creed of Sadat's Assassins. The Contents of "The Forgotten Duty" Analysed.' *Die Welt Des Islams* 25, no. 1/4 (1985): 1–30. https://doi.org/10.2307/1571075.

Jarrar, Maher, and Sebastian Günther, eds. 'Doctrinal Instruction in Early Islam: The Book of the Explanation of the Sunna by Ghulām Khalīl (d. 275/888).' In *Doctrinal Instruction in Early Islam*. Brill, 2020. https://brill.com/edcollbook/title/57361.

Jayyusi, Salma Khadra, Renata Holod, Antillio Petruccioli, and André Raymond, eds. 'The City in the Islamic World.' In *The City in the Islamic World (2 Vols.)*. Brill, 2008. https://brill.com/edcollbook/title/17776.

Johnsen, Gregory D. 'The Rise of ISIS.' *Great Decisions*, 2016, 13–24.

Judaiʿ, ʿAbd Allāh b. Yūsuf al-. *Aḍwāʾ ʿalā ḥadīth al-iftirāq*. Beirut: Muʾassasat al-Rayyān, 2007.

Karamustafa, Ahmet T. *Sufism: The Formative Period*. Berkeley: University of California Press, 2007.

Karčić, Harun. 'Arab Brothers, Arms, and Food Rations: How Salafism Made Its Way to Bosnia and Herzegovina.' In *Wahhabism and the World: Understanding Saudi Arabia's Global Influence on Islam*, edited by Peter Mandaville, 272–89. Oxford University Press, 2022. https://doi.org/10.1093/oso/9780197532560.003.0014.

Kassim, Abdulbasit. 'Defining and Understanding the Religious Philosophy of Jihādī-Salafism and the Ideology of Boko Haram.' *Politics, Religion & Ideology* 16 (September 1, 2015): 1–28. https://doi.org/10.1080/21567689.2015.1074896.

Katz, Marion Holmes. *The Birth of the Prophet Muhammad: Devotional Piety in Sunni Islam*. Culture and Civilization in the Middle East 11. London: Routledge, 2009.

Keating, Michael, and Matt Waldman, eds. *War and Peace in Somalia: National Grievances, Local Conflict and Al-Shabaab*. 1st ed. Oxford University Press, 2019. https://doi.org/10.1093/oso/9780190947910.001.0001.

Kendall, Elisabeth, and Ahmad Khan, eds. *Reclaiming Islamic Tradition: Modern Interpretations of the Classical Heritage*. Edinburgh: Edinburgh University Press, 2016.

Kenney, Jeffrey T. *Muslim Rebels: Kharijites and the Politics of Extremism in Egypt*. Oxford; New York: Oxford University Press, 2006.

Kepel, Gilles, ed. *Al Qaeda in Its Own Words*. Cambridge, Mass.: Belknap Press, 2010.

———. *Jihad: The Trail of Political Islam*. Translated by Anthony F. Roberts. Unstated ed. Cambridge, Mass.: Belknap Press: An Imprint of Harvard University Press, 2003.

——. *Muslim Extremism in Egypt: The Prophet and Pharaoh, With a New Preface for 2003*. 1st ed. University of California Press, 2003.

Kepel, Gilles, and Omar Saghi, eds. 'Osama Bin Laden, the Iconic Orator.' In *Al Qaeda in Its Own Words*, 11–40. Cambridge, Mass.: Belknap Press, 2010.

Khan, Adil Hussain. *From Sufism to Ahmadiyya: A Muslim Minority Movement in South Asia*. Bloomington: Indiana University Press, 2015.

Khan, Ahmad. *Heresy and the Formation of Medieval Islamic Orthodoxy: The Making of Sunnism, from the Eighth to the Eleventh Century*. Cambridge: Cambridge University Press, 2023. https://doi.org/10.1017/9781009093033.

——. 'Islamic Tradition in an Age of Print: Editing, Printing and Publishing the Classical Heritage.' In *Reclaiming Islamic Tradition: Modern Interpretations of the Classical Heritage*, edited by Elisabeth Kendall and Ahmad Khan, 52–99. Edinburgh: Edinburgh University Press, 2016.

Khan, Muin-ud-din Ahmad. 'A Diplomat's Report on Wahhabism of Arabia.' *Islamic Studies* 7, no. 1 (1968): 33–46.

——. *Selections from Bengal Government Records on Wahhabi Trials (1863–1870)*. Asiatic Society of Pakistan, 1961.

Khān, Ṣiddīq Ḥasan. *An Interpreter of Wahabiism*. Calcutta, 1884. http://archive.org/details/interpreterofwah00muhauoft.

——. *Qitf Al-Thamar Fī Bayān ʿAqīdat Ahl al-Athar*. Edited by ʿĀṣim al-Qaryūtī. Riyadh: Jāmiʿat al-Imām Muḥammad ibn Suʿūd al-Islāmiyya, 2011.

——. *Tarjumān-e-Wahhābīyya*. Agra: Mufīd-e-ʿĀm Press, 1884.

Khatab, Sayed. *The Political Thought of Sayyid Qutb: The Theory of Jahiliyyah*. London: Routledge, 2006. https://doi.org/10.4324/9780203086438.

——. *The Power of Sovereignty: The Political and Ideological Philosophy of Sayyid Qutb*. 1st ed. London: Routledge, 2006.

Khaṭīb al-Baghdādī, Abū Bakr Aḥmad b. ʿAlī b. Thābit al-. *Tārīkh madīnat al-salām wa-dhayluh wa-l-mustafād (Tārīkh Baghdād)*. Edited by Bashār ʿAwwād Maʿrūf. 1st ed. 21 vols. Beirut: Dār al-Gharb al-Islāmī, 2001.

Khosrokhavar, Farhad. *Jihadism in Europe: European Youth and the New Caliphate*. 1st ed. Oxford University Press New York, 2021. https://doi.org/10.1093/oso/9780197564967.001.0001.

——. 'The Arab Revolutions and Jihadism.' In *Violence in Islamic Thought from European Imperialism to the Post-Colonial Era*, edited by Mustafa Baig and Robert Gleave. Edinburgh: Edinburgh University Press, 2021. https://doi.org/10.1515/9781474485531-012.

Kindawi, Ahmad. 'A New Synthesis: Saudi Salafism and the Contested Ideologies of Muhammad Surur.' MA Thesis, Rowan University, 2020. https://rdw.rowan.edu/etd/2784.

Kingsley, Patrick. 'Egypt Massacre Was Premeditated, Says Human Rights Watch.' *The Guardian*, August 12, 2014. https://www.theguardian.com/world/2014/aug/12/egypt-massacre-rabaa-intentional-human-rights-watch.

Klausen, Jytte. *Western Jihadism: A Thirty Year History*. Oxford; New York: Oxford University Press, 2021.

Knysh, Alexander. 'Ibrāhīm Al-Kūrānī (d. 1101/1690), an Apologist for "Waḥdat al-Wujūd."' *Journal of the Royal Asiatic Society* 5, no. 1 (1995): 39–47.

——. *Islamic Mysticism: A Short History*. Leiden, The Netherlands; Boston: Brill, 2000.

Koning, Martijn de. 'Changing World Views and Friendship: An Exploration of the Life Stories of Two Female Salafis in the Netherlands.' In *Global Salafism: Islam's New Religious Movement*, edited by Roel Meijer, 404–23. Oxford University Press, 2014. https://doi.org/10.1093/acprof:oso/9780199333431.003.0019.

Krämer, Gudrun. *Hasan Al-Banna*. Oxford: Oneworld Academic, 2009.

Kramer, Martin, ed. *Shi'ism, Resistance and Revolution*. 1st ed. Routledge, 2019.

——. 'Syria's Alawis and Shi'ism.' In *Shi'ism, Resistance and Revolution*, edited by Martin Kramer, 1st ed., 237–54. Routledge, 2019.

Krawietz, Birgit, and Georges Tamer, eds. *Islamic Theology, Philosophy and Law: Debating Ibn Taymiyya and Ibn Qayyim Al-Jawziyya*. Berlin ; Boston: De Gruyter, 2013.

Kūrī, Muḥammad Dāwūd. *Daʿwa jamāʿa qāḍīzādah al-iṣlāḥiyya fī al-dawla al-ʿUthmāniyya*. Cairo: Dār al-Luʾluʾa li-l-Nashr wa-l-Tawzīʿ, 2018.

Kuschnitzki, Judit. 'The Establishment and Positioning of Al-Rashad: A Case Study of Political Salafism in Yemen.' In *Salafism After the Arab Awakening: Contending with People's Power*, edited by Francesco Cavatorta and Fabio Merone, 0. Oxford University Press, 2017. https://doi.org/10.1093/acprof:oso/9780190274993.003.0007.

*La Croix International*. 'Salafism Seeks to Impose Itself in the Muslim World.' April 7, 2016. https://international.la-croix.com/news/religion/salafism-seeks-to-impose-itself-in-the-muslim-world/2942.

Lacher, Wolfram. *Libya's Fragmentation: Structure and Process in Violent Conflict*. London: I.B. Tauris, 2020.

Lacroix, Stéphane. *Awakening Islam: The Politics of Religious Dissent in Contemporary Saudi Arabia*. Translated by George Holoch. Cambridge, Mass.: Harvard University Press, 2011.

——. 'Ayman Al-Zawahiri.' In *Al Qaeda in Its Own Words*, edited by Gilles Kepel, 147–70. Cambridge, Mass.: Belknap Press, 2010.

——. 'Between Revolution and Apoliticism: Nasir al-Din al-Albani and His Impact on the Shaping of Contemporary Salafism.' In *Global Salafism: Islam's New Religious Movement*, edited by Roel Meijer, 0. Oxford University Press, 2014. https://doi.org/10.1093/acprof:oso/9780199333431.003.0003.

——. 'Egypt's Pragmatic Salafis: The Politics of Hizb Al-Nour.' *Carnegie Endowment for International Peace.*, November 1, 2016. https://carnegieendowment.org/research/2016/11/egypts-pragmatic-salafis-the-politics-of-hizb-al-nour?lang=en.

——. 'Egypt's Salafi Awakening in the 1970s: Revisiting the History of a Crucial Decade for Egyptian Islamic Activism.' *Religions* 13, no. 4 (April 2, 2022): 316. https://doi.org/10.3390/rel13040316.

——. 'To Rebel or Not to Rebel: Dilemmas Among Saudi Salafis in a Revolutionary Age.' In *Salafism After the Arab Awakening: Contending with People's Power*, edited by Francesco Cavatorta and Fabio Merone, 61–82. Oxford University Press, 2017. https://doi.org/10.1093/acprof:oso/9780190274993.003.0005.

——. 'Unpacking the Saudi-Salafi Connection in Egypt.' In *Wahhabism and the World: Understanding Saudi Arabia's Global Influence on Islam*, edited by Peter Mandaville, 255–71. Religion and Global Politics. Oxford; New York: Oxford University Press, 2022.

Laher, Suheil Ismail. 'Re-Forming the Knot: ʿAbdullāh al-Ghumārī's Iconoclastic Sunnī Neo-Traditionalism.' *Journal of College of Sharia and Islamic Studies*, 2018. https://doi.org/10.29117/jcsis.2018.0207.

Lālakāʾī, Abū al-Qāsim Ḥibat Allāh al-. *Sharḥ uṣūl iʿtiqād ahl al-Sunna wa-l-jamāʿa*. Edited by Aḥmad ibn Saʿd Ibn Ḥamdān. 8th ed. 4 vols. Riyadh: Dār Ṭayba, 2003.

Lambert-Hurley, Siobhan. *Muslim Women, Reform and Princely Patronage: Nawab Sultan Jahan Begam of Bhopal*. Royal Asiatic Society Books. London; New York: Routledge, 2007. https://catalog.lib.uchicago.edu/vufind/Record/6276410.

Lange, Christian, ed. 'Locating Hell in Islamic Traditions.' In *Locating Hell in Islamic Traditions*. Brill, 2015. https://brill.com/edcollbook-oa/title/31679.

Lauzière, Henri. 'Rejoinder: What We Mean Versus What They Meant by "Salafi": A Reply to Frank Griffel.' *Die Welt Des Islams* 56, no. 1 (April 19, 2016): 89–96. https://doi.org/10.1163/15700607-00561p06.

——. 'Salafism Against Hadith Literature: The Curious Beginnings of a New Category in 1920s Algeria.' *Journal of the American Oriental Society* 141, no. 2 (August 27, 2021). https://doi.org/10.7817/jameroriesoci.141.2.0403.

——. 'The Construction of Salafiyya: Reconsidering Salafism from the Perspective of Conceptual History.' *International Journal of Middle East Studies* 42, no. 3 (August 2010): 369–89. https://doi.org/10.1017/S0020743810000401.

——. 'The Evolution of the Salafiyya in the Twentieth Century Through the Life and Thought of Taqi Al-Din al-Hilali.' *Georgetown University-Graduate School of Arts & Sciences*. Thesis, Georgetown University, 2008. https://repository.library.georgetown.edu/handle/10822/558204.

——. *The Making of Salafism: Islamic Reform in the Twentieth Century*. Religion, Culture, and Public Life. New York: Columbia University Press, 2016.

Lefevre, Raphael. *Ashes of Hama: The Muslim Brotherhood in Syria*. 1st ed. Oxford University Press, 2013.

Li, Darryl. 'Expert Report on the Bosnian Jihad: Prepared for US. v. Bahar Ahmad and US. v. Syed Talha Ahsan.' New Haven, CT: United States District Court for the District of Connecticut, 2014. https://www.academia.edu/28287134/Expert_Opinion_on_Foreign_Fighters_in_the_Bosnian_Jihad.

——. 'Taking the Place of Martyrs: Afghans and Arabs Under the Banner of Islam.' *Arab Studies Journal* 20, no. 1 (Spring 2012): 12–39.

——. *The Universal Enemy: Jihad, Empire, and the Challenge of Solidarity*. Stanford: Stanford University Press, 2019.

——. 'Will the Real Jihadi Please Stand Up?: On "Jihadism" as a Conceptual Weapon.' In *Disentangling Jihad, Political Violence and Media*, edited by Simone Pfeifer, Christoph Günther, and Robert Dörre, 119–37. Edinburgh: Edinburgh University Press, 2023.

Lia, Brynjar. *Architect of Global Jihad: The Life of Al-Qaeda Strategist Abu Mus'ab Al-Suri*. 1st ed. Oxford: Oxford University Press, 2009. 978-0199326457.

——. '"Destructive Doctrinarians": Abu Mus'ab al-Suri's Critique of the Salafis in the Jihadi Current.' In *Global Salafism: Islam's New Religious Movement*, edited by Roel Meijer, 281–300. Oxford University Press, 2014. https://doi.org/10.1093/acprof:oso/9780199333431.003.0013.

——. *The Society of the Muslim Brothers in Egypt: The Rise of an Islamic Mass Movement 1928–1942*. 1st ed. Reading, England: Ithaca Press, 1999.

Little, Donald P. 'Did Ibn Taymiyya Have a Screw Loose?' *Studia Islamica*, no. 41 (1975): 93–111. https://doi.org/10.2307/1595400.

——. 'The Historical and Historiographical Significance of the Detention of Ibn Taymiyya.' *International Journal of Middle East Studies* 4, no. 3 (1973): 311–27.

Loimeier, Roman. *Islamic Reform and Political Change in Northern Nigeria*. Evanston, Illinois: Northwestern University Press, 2011.

Lucas, Scott C. *Constructive Critics, Hadith Literature, and the Articulation of Sunni Islam: The Legacy of the Generation of Ibn Sa'd, Ibn Ma'īn, and Ibn Ḥanbal*. Leiden; Boston: Brill, 2004.

Luwayḥiq, ʿAbd al-Raḥmān ibn Muʿallā, and Jamaal Al-Din M. Zarabozo. *Religious Extremism in the Lives of Contemporary Muslims*. Denver, Colo: Al-Basheer Company for Publications and Translations, 2001.

MacDonald, Matthew A. 'What Is a Salafi Reformist?: Tariq Ramadan and Sayyid Qutb in Conversation.' *Political Theology* 15, no. 5 (September 2014): 385–405. https://doi.org/10.1179/1462317X14Z.00000000083.

Madelung, Wilfred. 'Early Ibāḍī Theology.' In *The Oxford Handbook of Islamic Theology*, edited by Sabine Schmidtke, Reprinted ed., 242–51. Oxford, UK: Oxford University Press, 2018.

Maher, Shiraz. *Salafi-Jihadism: The History of an Idea*. London: C Hurst & Co, 2016.

'Majlisul Ulama Zimbabwe.' Accessed June 9, 2024. https://majlis.org.zw/index.html.

Majothi, Azhar. 'Indian Wahhabism: The Case of the Ahl-i-Ḥadīth in Colonial India.' University of Wales Trinity Saint David, 2017.

——. 'Translating Salafism into English: Anglo–Salafi Print Culture in Britain.' PhD thesis, University of Nottingham, 2023. http://eprints.nottingham.ac.uk/74265/.

Makdisi, George. *Ibn ʿAqil: Religion and Culture in Classical Islam*. 1st ed. Edinburgh: Edinburgh University Press, 1997.

——. 'Muslim Institutions of Learning in Eleventh-Century Baghdad.' *Bulletin of the School of Oriental and African Studies, University of London* 24, no. 1 (1961): 1–56.

Malik, Maszlee. 'Salafism in Malaysia: Historical Account on Its Emergence and Motivations.' *Sociology of Islam* 5, no. 4 (December 5, 2017): 303–33. https://doi.org/10.1163/22131418-00504003.

Mandaville, Peter, ed. *Wahhabism and the World: Understanding Saudi Arabia's Global Influence on Islam*. Religion and Global Politics. Oxford; New York: Oxford University Press, 2022.

Maqdisī, Abū Muḥammad al-. *Millat Ibrāhīm*. Minbar al-Tawḥīd wa-l-Jihād, n.d.

Maqsood, Abdul. 'Shaykh Abdul Maqsood's Ruling on the Events in Egypt.' *Virtual Mosque* (blog), February 5, 2011. https://www.virtualmosque.com/society/international/shaykh-abdul-maqsoods-ruling-on-the-events-in-egypt/.

March, Andrew F. 'Reading Tariq Ramadan: Political Liberalism, Islam, and "Overlapping Consensus."' *Ethics & International Affairs* 21, no. 4 (2007): 399–413. https://doi.org/10.1111/j.1747-7093.2007.00114.x.

Markaz al-Imām al-Albānī lil-Dirāsāt wa-al-Abḥāth. 'Majallat Al-Aṣāla – ʿAwdat Ilā al-Kitāb Wa-al-Sunna Bi-Fahm Salaf al-Umma.' Al-Albany.org. Accessed June 5, 2024. https://www.alalbany.org/asala/.

Maruf, Harun, and Dan Joseph. *Inside Al-Shabaab: The Secret History of Al-Qaeda's Most Powerful Ally*. Indiana University Press, 2018. https://doi.org/10.2307/j.ctv6mtfn2.

Masbah, Mohammed. 'Between Preaching and Activism: How Politics Divided Morocco's Salafis.' *MIPA Institute*, October 6, 2024. https://mipa.institute/en/5615.

——. 'Moroccan Foreign Fighters: Evolution of the Phenomenon, Promotive Factors, and the Limits of Hardline Policies.' German Institute for International and Security Affairs, October 2015. https://www.swp-berlin.org/publications/products/comments/2015C46_msb.pdf

——. 'Salafi Movements and the Political Process in Morocco.' In *Salafism After the Arab Awakening: Contending with People's Power*, edited by Francesco Cavatorta and Fabio Merone, 83–98. Oxford University Press, 2017. https://doi.org/10.1093/acprof:oso/9780190274993.003.0006.

Masud, Muhammad Khalid. *Travellers in Faith: Studies of the Tablīghī Jamāʿat as a Transnational Islamic Movement for Faith Renewal*. Social, Economic, and Political Studies of the Middle East and Asia. Boston: Brill, 2000. http://bvbr.bib-bvb.de:8991/F?func=service&doc_library=BVB01&local_base=BVB01&doc_number=008979001&line_number=0001&func_code=DB_RECORDS&service_type=MEDIA.

Matthiesen, Toby. 'Migration, Minorities, and Radical Networks: Labour Movements and Opposition Groups in Saudi Arabia, 1950–1975.' *International Review of Social History* 59, no. 3 (2014): 473–504.

Mawdūdī, Sayyid Abū al-Aʿlā al-. *A Short History of the Revivalist Movement in Islam*. Translated by Al-Ashʿari. Lahore: Islamic Publications, 1963.

McCarthy, Richard J. *The Theology of Al-Ashʿarī: The Arabic Texts of Al-Ashʿarī's Kitāb Al-Lumaʿ and Risālat Istiḥsān Al-Khawḍ Fī ʿilm Al-Kalām, with Briefly Annotated Translations, and Appendices Containing Material Pertinent to the Study of Al-Ashʿarī*. Beyrouth: Impr. catholique, 1953.

McVeigh, Tracy. '"Recruiter" of UK Jihadis: I Regret Opening the Way to Isis.' *The Observer*, June 13, 2015. https://www.theguardian.com/world/2015/jun/13/godfather-of-british-jihadists-admits-we-opened-to-way-to-join-isis.

Medium. 'Tawhid Essays – Medium.' Accessed June 11, 2024. https://medium.com/@tawhidessays.

*Meet Dr Bilal Philips – Communist to Islam | Young Smirks Podcast Ep14*. Meet Dr Bilal Philips, 2019. https://www.youtube.com/watch?v=kAGtgEvag1Q.

Meijer, Roel, ed. *Global Salafism: Islam's New Religious Movement*. Oxford University Press, 2014. https://doi.org/10.1093/acprof:oso/9780199333431.001.0001.

——. 'Politicising Al-Jarḥ Wa-l-Taʿdīl: Rabīʿ b. Hādī al-Madkhalī and the Transnational Battle for Religious Authority.' In *The Transmission and Dynamics of the Textual Sources of Islam*, edited by Nicolet Boekhoff-van Der Voort, Kees Versteegh, and Joas Wagemakers, 375–99. Brill, 2011. https://doi.org/10.1163/9789004206786_019.

——. 'Yūsuf Al-ʿUwayrī and the Making of a Salafi Praxis.' In *Kingdom Without Borders: Saudi Arabia's Political, Religious, and Media Frontiers*, edited by Madawi Al-Rasheed, 422–59. New York: Columbia University Press, 2008.

Melchert, Christopher. *Ahmad Ibn Hanbal*. Oxford: Oneworld Academic, 2006.

——. 'Aḥmad Ibn Ḥanbal and the Qur'an.' *Journal of Qur'anic Studies* 6, no. 2 (October 2004): 22–34. https://doi.org/10.3366/jqs.2004.6.2.22.

——. *Before Sufism: Early Islamic Renunciant Piety*. Islam – Thought, Culture, and Society, volume 4. Berlin ; Boston: De Gruyter, 2020.

——. 'Muḥammad Nāṣīr Al-Dīn Al-Albānī and Traditional Hadith Criticism.' In *Reclaiming Islamic Tradition: Modern Interpretations of the Classical Heritage*, edited by Elisabeth Kendall and Ahmad Khan, 33–51. Edinburgh: Edinburgh University Press, 2016.

——. 'The Adversaries of Aḥmad Ibn Ḥanbal.' *Arabica* 44, no. 2 (1997): 234–53.

——. *The Formation of the Sunni Schools of Law, 9th–10th Centuries CE*. Leiden; New York: Brill, 1997.

Meleagrou-Hitchens, Alexander. *Incitement: Anwar Al-Awlaki's Western Jihad*. Cambridge, Massachusetts ; London, Massachusetts: Harvard University Press, 2020.

——. *Salafism in America: History, Evolution, Radicalization*. George Washington University, Program on Extremism, 2018.

Memon, Muhammad Umar. *Ibn Taimiya's Struggle Against Popular Religion: With an Annotated Translation of His Kitab Iqtida as-Sirat al-Mustaqim Mukhalafat Ashab al-Jahim*. De Gruyter, 2013. https://doi.org/10.1515/9783111662381.

Metcalf, Barbara Daly, ed. *Islam in South Asia in Practice*. Princeton Readings in Religions. Princeton: Princeton University Press, 2009.

——. *Islamic Revival in British India: Deoband, 1860–1900*. Princeton: Princeton University Press, 1982.

——. 'The Taqwiyyat Al-Iman (Support of the Faith) by Shah Ismaʿil Shahid.' In *Islam in South Asia in Practice*, edited by Barbara Daly Metcalf, 201–11. Princeton Readings in Religions. Princeton: Princeton University Press, 2009.

Metcalf, Barbara Daly, and Thomas R. Metcalf. *A Concise History of Modern India*. 3rd ed. Cambridge: Cambridge University Press, 2012.

Mez, Adam. *Die Renaissance Des Islams*. Heidelberg: Carl Winters, 1922.

——. *The Renaissance of Islam: History, Culture and Society in the 10th Century Muslim World*. Edited by Julia Bray. Translated by Salahuddin Khuda Bukhsh and D. S. Margolliouth. New ed. London: Bloomsbury Publishing, 2024.

Micheau, Françoise. 'Baghdad In The Abbasid Era: A Cosmopolitan and Multi-Confessional Capital.' In *The City in the Islamic World (2 Vols.)*, edited by Salma Khadra Jayyusi, Renata Holod, Antillio Petruccioli, and André Raymond,

219–45. Brill, 2008. https://brill.com/display/book/edcoll/9789047442653/Doj.9789004116202.i 1500_011.xml

Michel, Thomas F., ed. *A Muslim Theologian's Response to Christianity: Ibn Taymiyya's Al-Jawab Al-Sahih*. Delmar, NY: Caravan Books, 1656.

Michot, Yahya. 'Ibn Taymiyya's "New Mardin Fatwa". Is Genetically Modified Islam (GMI) Carcinogenic?' *The Muslim World* 101, no. 2 (2011): 130–81. https://doi.org/10.1111/j.1478-1913.2011.01351.x.

——. *Muslims Under Non-Muslim Rule: Ibn Taymiyya*. Oxford: Interface Publications, 2006.

*Middle East Eye*. 'Leading Saudi Cleric Says IS and Saudi Arabia "Follow the Same Thought."' January 28, 2016. https://www.middleeasteye.net/news/leading-saudi-cleric-says-and-saudi-arabia-follow-same-thought.

Milani, Milad. 'Mysticism in the Islamicate World: The Question of Neoplatonic Influence in Sufi Thought.' In *Later Platonists and Their Heirs among Christians, Jews, and Muslims*, edited by Eva Anagnostou and Ken Parry, 513–44. Brill, 2022. https://doi.org/10.1163/9789004527850_023.

Milelli, Jean-Pierre. 'Abu Musʿab Al-Zarqawi, Jihad in "Mesopotamia."' In *Al Qaeda in Its Own Words*, edited by Gilles Kepel, 237–50. Cambridge, Mass.: Belknap Press, 2010.

Minault, Gail. *The Khilafat Movement Religious Symbolism and Political Mobilization in India*. 1st ed. New York: Columbia University Press, 1982.

Misri, Abu Hamza al-. *Khawaarij & Jihad*. Birmingham: Maktabah Al-Ansar, 2000.

Mitchell, Richard P. *The Society of the Muslim Brothers*. New York: Oxford University Press, 1993.

'Mogadishu University.' Accessed June 9, 2024. https://mu.edu.so/.

Mohamad, Hani. 'Egypt: Salafist TV Sheikh Renounces Salafism in Court.' *Daraj*, June 17, 2021. https://daraj.media/en/egypt-salafist-tv-sheikh-renounces-salafism-in-court/.

Moneep, Abdelmonem. *Islamic Movements in Egypt: A Map and Guidance*. 2nd ed., 2018.

Mottahedeh, Roy. *Loyalty and Leadership in an Early Islamic Society*. 2nd ed. London; New York: New York: I.B. Tauris, 2001.

Mouline, Nabil. *The Clerics of Islam: Religious Authority and Political Power in Saudi Arabia*. Translated by Ethan S. Rundell. New Haven/Conn: Yale University Press, 2014.

Mudayhish, Ibrāhīm b. ʿAbd Allāh. *Al-Najdiyyūn Fī al-Hind: ʿUlamāʾ Najd al-Ladhīn Raḥalū Ilā al-Hind Li-l-Istiẓādat Min al-Ḥadīth al-Nabawī,*. 1st ed. Riyadh: Dār al-Thulūthiyya, 2019.

'Mufti Ismail Musa Menk | The Muslim 500.' Accessed June 9, 2024. https://themuslim500.com/profiles/mufti-ismail-musa-menk/.

Munson, Henry. *Religion and Power in Morocco*. Yale University Press, 1993. https://doi.org/10.2307/j.ctt1xp3srm.

Muslim ibn al-Ḥajjāj, Abū al-Ḥusayn. *Ṣaḥīḥ Muslim*, n.d.

Muzaffarpūrī, Faḍl Ḥusain. *Al-Ḥayāt Baʿd al-Mamāt*. Agra: Akbari Press, 1908.

Nadwi, Abul Hasan Alī. *Saviours of Islamic Spirit*. Translated by S. Mohiuddin Ahmad. Vol. 4. 5 vols. Lucknow: Academy of Islamic Research and Publications, 1993.

Nadwi, Mohammad Akram. *Shaykh 'Abū al-Ḥasan 'Alī Nadwī*. Translated by Mahomed Mahomedy, n.d.

Nafi, Basheer M. 'A Teacher of Ibn 'Abd Al-Wahhāb: Muḥammad Ḥayāt al-Sindī and the Revival of Aṣḥāb al-Ḥadīth's Methodology.' *Islamic Law and Society* 13, no. 2 (2006): 208–41.

——. 'Abu Al-Thana' al-Alusi: An Alim, Ottoman Mufti, and Exegete of the Qur'an.' *International Journal of Middle East Studies* 34, no. 3 (2002): 465–94.

——. 'Salafism Revived: Nu'mān al-Alūsī and the Trial of Two Ahmads.' *Die Welt Des Islams* 49, no. 1 (January 1, 2009): 49–97. https://doi.org/10.1163/157006008X424959.

——. 'Taṣawwuf and Reform in Pre-Modern Islamic Culture: In Search of Ibrāhīm al-Kūrānī.' *Die Welt Des Islams* 42, no. 3 (2002): 307–55.

Nasiri, Omar. *Inside the Jihad: My Life with Al Qaeda: A Spy's Story*. New York: Basic Books, 2006.

Naṣr, Walī Riḍā. *Mawdudi and the Making of Islamic Revivalism*. New York: Oxford University Press, 1996.

National Commission on Terrorist Attacks upon the United States, ed. *The 9/11 Commission Report: Final Report of the National Commission on Terrorist Attacks Upon the United States*. Authorized ed., 1st ed. New York: Norton, 2004.

Nawawī, Yaḥyā b. Sharaf al-. *Ṣāḥīḥ Muslim Bi-Sharḥ al-Nawawī*. 2nd ed. 18 vols. Cairo: Mu'assasat Qurṭuba, 1994.

Nesser, Petter. 'Abū Qatāda and Palestine,' January 1, 2013. https://doi.org/10.1163/15685152-5334P0005.

——. *Islamist Terrorism in Europe: A History*. New York: Oxford University Press, 2015.

Nguyen, Martin. 'Sufi Theological Thought.' In *The Oxford Handbook of Islamic Theology*, edited by Sabine Schmidtke, Reprinted ed., 325–43. Oxford, UK: Oxford University Press, 2018.

'Nureddin Yıldız,' n.d. https://www.nureddinyildiz.com/.

O'Bagy, Elizabeth. 'Jihad in Syria.' *Institute for the Study of War*, 2012. https://www.understandingwar.org/sites/default/files/Jihad-In-Syria-17SEPT.pdf.

Olidort, Jacob. 'In Defense of Tradition: Muḥammad Nāṣir Al-Dīn al-Albānī and the Salafī Method.' PhD, Princeton University, 2015. http://arks.princeton.edu/ark:/88435/dsp01nz8062003.

Olsson, Susanne. *Contemporary Puritan Salafism: A Swedish Case Study*. Comparative Islamic Studies. Sheffield, UK Bristol, CT: Equinox, 2016.

Olsson, Susanne, Simon Sorgenfrei, and Jonas Svensson. 'Puritan Salafis in a Liberal Democratic Context.' In *Salafi-Jihadism and Digital Media: The Nordic and International Context*, edited by Magnus Ranstorp, Linda Ahlerup, and Filip Ahlin, 92–112. Political Violence. London; New York: Routledge, Taylor & Francis Group, 2022.

O'Neill, Sean, and Daniel McGrory. *The Suicide Factory: Abu Hamza and the Finsbury Park Mosque*. London: Harper Perennial, 2006.

Osman, Amr. *The Ẓāhirī Madhhab (3rd/9th–10th/16th Century): A Textualist Theory of Islamic Law*. Brill, 2014. https://brill.com/display/title/26592.

Osman, Borhan. 'Bourgeois Jihad: Why Young, Middle-Class Afghans Join the Islamic State.' *United States Institute of Peace* (blog), June 1, 2020. https://www.usip.org/publications/2020/06/bourgeois-jihad-why-young-middle-class-afghans-join-islamic-state.

Østebø, Terje. 'African Salafism: Religious Purity and the Politicization of Purity.' *Islamic Africa* 6, no. 1–2 (2015): 1–29.

——. 'Growth and Fragmentation: The Salafi Movement in Bale, Ethiopia.' In *Global Salafism: Islam's New Religious Movement*, edited by Roel Meijer, 342–63. Oxford University Press, 2014. https://doi.org/10.1093/acprof:oso/9780199333431.003.0016.

——. *Localising Salafism: Religious Change among Oromo Muslims in Bale, Ethiopia*. Leiden: Brill, 2011. https://brill.com/display/title/19533.

ʿOuda, Salmān al-. *As ʾilat al-thawra*. Riyadh: Markaz Namāʾ, 2012.

Pall, Zoltan. 'Kuwaiti Salafism and Its Growing Influence in the Levant.' *Carnegie Endowment for International Peace.*, May 7, 2014, 1–26.

——. *Lebanese Salafis Between the Gulf and Europe: Development, Fractionalization and Transnational Networks of Salafism in Lebanon*. Forum Publications. Amsterdam: Amsterdam University Press, 2013.

——. 'Salafi Dynamics in Kuwait: Politics, Fragmentation and Change.' In *Salafism After the Arab Awakening: Contending with People's Power*, edited by Francesco Cavatorta and Fabio Merone, 169–86. Oxford University Press, 2017. https://doi.org/10.1093/acprof:oso/9780190274993.003.0011.

——. *Salafism in Lebanon: Local and Transnational Movements*. 1st ed. New York: Cambridge University Press, 2018.

Pappé, Ilan, ed. *Israel and South Africa: The Many Faces of Apartheid*. London: Zed Books, 2015.

——. *The Ethnic Cleansing of Palestine*. Repr. Oxford: Oneworld Publ, 2007.

Pargeter, Alison. 'Qadhafi and Political Islam in Libya.' In *Libya since 1969*, edited by Dirk Vandewalle, 83–104. New York: Palgrave Macmillan US, 2008. https://doi.org/10.1007/978-0-230-61386-7_4.

——. *The Muslim Brotherhood: From Opposition to Power*. New ed. London: Saqi, 2013.

Paz, Reuven. 'Debates Within the Family: Jihadi-Salafi Debates on Strategy, Takfir, Extremism, Suicide Bombings, and the Sense of the Apocalypse.' In *Global Salafism: Islam's New Religious Movement*, edited by Roel Meijer, 0. Oxford University Press, 2014. https://doi.org/10.1093/acprof:oso/9780199333431.003.0012.

Peacock, A. C. S. *The Great Seljuk Empire*. 1st ed. Edinburgh: Edinburgh University Press, 2015.

Pelham, Nicolas. 'MBS: Despot in the Desert.' *The Economist*. Accessed May 10, 2024. https://www.economist.com/1843/2022/07/28/mbs-despot-in-the-desert.

Pfeifer, Simone, Christoph Günther, and Robert Dörre, eds. *Disentangling Jihad, Political Violence and Media*. Edinburgh: Edinburgh University Press, 2023.

Philips, Abu Ameenah Bilal. *The Exorcist Tradition in Islam*. Al-Hidaayah Publishing, 2008.

——. *The Fundamentals of Tawḥeed: Islamic Monotheism*. 2nd ed. Riyadh: International Islamic Publ. House, 2006.

Picken, Gavin. 'Ibn Ḥanbal and Al-Muḥāsibī: A Study of Early Conflicting Scholarly Methodologies.' *Arabica* 55, no. 3/4 (2008): 337–61.

Pierret, Thomas. *Religion and State in Syria: The Sunni Ulama from Coup to Revolution*. Cambridge Middle East Studies. Cambridge: Cambridge University Press, 2013. https://doi.org/10.1017/CBO9781139207720.

——. 'Salafis at War in Syria: Logics of Fragmentation and Realignment.' In *Salafism After the Arab Awakening: Contending with People's Power*, edited by Francesco Cavatorta and Fabio Merone, 137–54. Oxford University Press, 2017. https://doi.org/10.1093/acprof:oso/9780190274993.003.0009.

Pirbhai, M. Reza. 'Intention and Implication: The Disputed Legacy of Shah Wall Allah.' *Journal of Islamic and Muslim Studies* 5, no. 2 (November 1, 2020): 24–48. https://doi.org/10.2979/jims.5.2.02.

'Pledge of Mutual Respect and Cooperation Between Sunni Muslim Scholars, Organizations, and Students of Sacred Knowledge.' Muslimmatters.org, 2017. https://muslimmatters.org/wp-content/uploads/2007/09/pledge-of-mutual-respect-and-cooperation-between-sunni-muslim-scholars-and-organizations-2.pdf.

Preckel, Claudia. 'Screening Ṣiddīq Ḥasan Khān's Library: The Use of Ḥanbalī Literature in 19th-Century Bhopal.' In *Islamic Theology, Philosophy and Law*, edited by Birgit Krawietz and Georges Tamer, 162–219. De Gruyter, 2013. https://doi.org/10.1515/9783110285406.162.

'Professor Choi Young Kil-Hamed – King Faisal Foundation.' Accessed June 9, 2024. https://www.kff.com/king-faisal-prize/professor-choi-young-kil-hamed/.

Qadhi [also: Kazi], Yasir. *An Explanation of Muhammad Ibn 'Abd al-Wahhab's Kashf al-Shubuhat: A Critical Study of Shirk*. Birmingham, UK: Al-Hidaayah Publishing, 2003.

——. 'On Salafī Islam.' *Muslimmatters.Org*, April 22, 2014. https://muslimmatters.org/wp-content/uploads/On-Salafi-Islam_Dr.-Yasir-Qadhi.pdf.

——. 'Opinion | Assassinating Al-Awlaki Was Counterproductive.' *The New York Times*, October 1, 2011. https://www.nytimes.com/2011/10/02/opinion/sunday/assassinating-al-awlaki-was-counterproductive.html.

——. 'Reconciling Reason and Revelation in the Writings of Ibn Taymiyya (d. 728/1328): An Analytical Study of Ibn Taymiyya's "Dar' al-Ta'arud."' PhD, Yale University. Accessed August 14, 2023. https://www.proquest.com/pqdtglobal/docview/1432424222/abstract/4EF6277D3A51420BPQ/1.

——. 'Reformation or Reconstruction: Dr. Hatem al-Awni's Critiques of Wahhabism (Unpublished).' Oxford, UK, 2018.

——. *Riyaa: Hidden Shirk*. Sharjah, UAE: Dar Al Fatah, 1996.

——. 'The Lure of Radicalism and Extremism Amongst Muslim Youth.' Muslimmatters, October 2010. https://muslimmatters.org/2010/10/18/yasir-qadhi-the-lure-of-radicalism-amongst-muslim-youth/.

——. '"The Unleashed Thunderbolts" of Ibn Qayyim al-Ǧawziyyah: An Introductory Essay,' August 12, 2010. https://doi.org/10.1163/22138617-09001007.

Qandil, Mohamed Mokhtar. 'The Muslim Brotherhood and Saudi Arabia: From Then to Now.' *The Washington Institute*, May 18, 2018. https://www.washingtoninstitute.org/policy-analysis/muslim-brotherhood-and-saudi-arabia-then-now.

Qāsimī, Jamāl al-Dīn al-. *al-Jahmiyya wa-l-Muʿtazila.* 1 vols. Beirut: Muʾassasat al-Risāla, 1979.

——. *Irshād al-khalq ilā al-ʿamal bi-khabar al-barq, wa-yalīhi ʿudda min fatāwā al-ishrāf fī al-ʿamal bi-al-tilighrāf.* Damascus: Maṭbaʿat al-Muqtabis, 1911.

Qasmi, Ali Usman. *Questioning the Authority of the Past: The Ahl al-Qur'an Movements in the Punjab*. 1st ed. Karachi: Oxford University Press, 2012.

Quick, Abdullah Hakim. 'Aspects of Islamic Social Intellectual History in Hausaland, 'Uthman Ibn Fudi, 1774–1804 C.E.' PhD thesis, University of Tornoto, 1995. https://hdl.handle.net/1807/10830.

Qureshi, Jawad. 'Zuhayr Al-Shāwīsh (1925–2013) and al-Maktab al-Islāmī: Print, Hadith Verification, and Authenticated Islam,' 2016.

Qureshi, M. Naeem. *Pan-Islam in British Indian Politics: A Study of the Khilafat Movement, 1918–1924*. Leiden; Boston: Brill, 1999.

Quṭb, Sayyid. *A Child from the Village*. Translated by John Calvert and William E. Shepard. 1st ed. Middle East Literature in Translation. Syracuse: Syracuse University Press, 2016. https://catalog.lib.uchicago.edu/vufind/Record/12353393.

——. *al-Taṣwīr al-fannī fi al-Qurʾān*. 9th printing. Cairo: Daral-Shuruq, 1987.

——. *Ṭifl min al-qarya*. 4th ed. Beirut, 1967. https://catalog.lib.uchicago.edu/vufind/Record/2121622.

Rabil, Robert G. *Salafism in Lebanon: From Apoliticism to Transnational Jihadism*. Washington, DC: Georgetown University Press, 2014.

Ramadan, Tariq. *Western Muslims and the Future of Islam*. 1. Issued as an Oxford University Press paperback. Oxford; New York, NY: Oxford Univ. Press, 2005.

——. *What I Believe*. Oxford; New York: Oxford University Press, 2009.

Ramli, Harith Bin. 'The Sālimiyya and Abū Ṭālib Al-Makkī: The Transmission of Theological Teachings in a Basran Circle of Mystics.' In *Les Maîtres Soufis et Leurs Disciples Des IIIe-Ve Siècles de l'hégire (IXe-XIe): Enseignement, Formation et Transmission*, edited by Geneviève Gobillot and Jean-Jacques Thibon, 101–29. Études Arabes, Médiévales et Modernes. Beyrouth: Presses de l'Ifpo, 2012. https://doi.org/10.4000/books.ifpo.3073.

Ranstorp, Magnus, Linda Ahlerup, and Filip Ahlin, eds. *Salafi-Jihadism and Digital Media: The Nordic and International Context*. Political Violence. London; New York: Routledge, Taylor & Francis Group, 2022.

Rapoport, Youssef, and Shahab Ahmed, eds. *Ibn Taymiyya and His Times*. Karachi: Oxford University Press, 2010.

Razavian, Christopher Pooya. 'Post-Salafism: Salman al-Ouda and Hatim al-Awni.' In *Modern Islamic Authority and Social Change, Volume 1*, edited by Masooda Bano, 172–92. Evolving Debates in Muslim Majority Countries. Edinburgh:

Edinburgh University Press, 2018. http://www.jstor.org.queens.ezproxy.cuny.edu/stable/10.3366/j.ctv7n0978.12.

——. 'Yasir Qadhi and the Development of Reasonable Salafism.' In *Modern Islamic Authority and Social Change, Volume 2: Evolving Debates in the West*, edited by Masooda Bano, 155–79. Edinburgh: Edinburgh University Press, 2018. https://www.cambridge.org/core/books/modern-islamic-authority-and-social-change-volume-2/yasir-qadhi-and-the-development-of-reasonable-salafism/2F67387111A8965C3814FD1999ADE283.

Rāzī, Abū Ḥātim al-. *Kitāb aṣl al-sunna wa iʿtiqād al-dīn*. Edited by Ibrāhīm al-Ḥāzimī. Riyadh: Dār al-Sharīf, 1992.

Reetz, Dietrich. *Islam in the Public Sphere: Religious Groups in India 1900–1947*. Oxford: Oxford University Press, 2006.

Reuters. 'Egypt's Sisi Wins Third Term as President After Amending Constitution.' *The Guardian*, December 19, 2023. https://www.theguardian.com/world/2023/dec/19/egypt-2023-presidential-election-results-abdel-fattah-al-sisi-wins-no-challengers.

Riexinger, Martin. 'Ibn Taymiyya's Worldview and the Challenge of Modernity: A Conflict Among the Ahl-i Ḥadīth in British India.' In *Islamic Theology, Philosophy and Law: Debating Ibn Taymiyya and Ibn Qayyim Al-Jawziyya*, edited by Birgit Krawietz and Georges Tamer. Berlin ; Boston: De Gruyter, 2013.

Rizvi, Saiyid Athar Abbas. *Shāh 'Abd Al-'Azīz: Puritanism, Sectarian Polemics and Jihād*. Canberra, Australia: Ma'rifat Pub. House, 1982. https://catalog.lib.uchicago.edu/vufind/Record/510526.

——. *Shāh Walī-Allāh and His Times: A Study of Eighteenth Century Islām, Politics, and Society in India*. Ma'rifat Publishing, 1980.

Rizvi, Sayyid Muhammad. 'Muhibb Al-Din al-Khatib: A Portrait of a Salafi-Arabist.' Simon Fraser University, 1991. https://summit.sfu.ca/item/3579.

Roberts, Hugh. *The Battlefield: Algeria, 1988–2002: Studies in a Broken Polity*. London; New York: Verso, 2003.

Rock-Singer, Aaron. *In the Shade of the Sunna: Salafi Piety in the Twentieth-Century Middle East*. Oakland (Calif.): University of California press, 2022.

——. *Practicing Islam in Egypt: Print Media and Islamic Revival*. Cambridge: Cambridge University Press, 2019. https://doi.org/10.1017/9781108590877.

Roy, Oliver. *Islam and Resistance in Afghanistan*. 1st ed. Cambridge, UK; New York: Cambridge University Press, 1986.

Rudolph, Ulrich. *Al-Maturidi and the Development of Sunni Theology in Samarqand*. Translated by Rodrigo Adem. Translated ed. Leiden; Boston: Brill, 2014.

Ryad. *Islamic Reformism and Christianity*. Illustrated ed. Leiden; Boston: Brill, 2009.

Ryad, Umar. 'A Printed Muslim 'Lighthouse' in Cairo al-Manār's Early Years, Religious Aspiration and Reception (1898–1903),' January 1, 2009, 27–60. https://doi.org/10.1163/157005809X398636.

Ryzova, Lucie. 'Egyptianizing Modernity through the 'New Effendiya': Social and Cultural Constructions of the Middle Class in Egypt under the Monarchy.' In

*Re-Envisioning Egypt 1919–1952*, edited by Arthur Goldschmidt and Amy J. Johnson, 0. American University in Cairo Press, 2005. https://doi.org/10.5743/cairo/9789774249006.003.0006.

Ṣābūnī, Abū ʿUthmān Ismāʿīl b. ʿAbd al-Raḥmān al-. *ʿAqīdat al-Salaf wa aṣḥāb al-ḥadīth [also: al-Risāla fī iʿtiqād ahl al-Sunna wa aṣḥāb al-ḥadīth wa-l-aʾimma]*. Edited by Nāṣir b. ʿAbd al-Raḥmān al-Judaiʿ. Riyadh: Dār al-ʿĀṣima, 1998.

Sæther, Sturla Godø. 'Humanitarian Salafism – a Contradiction in Terms?: A Study of the Salafi Organisation "The Book and the Sunna Society" and Their Efforts in Relief Work in Jordan.' MA Thesis, University of Oslo, 2013. http://urn.nb.no/URN:NBN:no-42263.

Saffārīnī, Muḥammad b. Aḥmad al-. *al-Ḍurra al-muḍiyya fī ʿaqd al-firqa al-marḍiyya*. Edited by Abū Muḥammad Ashraf b. ʿAbd al-Maqṣūd. 1st ed. Riyadh: Maktabat Aḍwāʾ al-Salaf, 1998.

——. *Lawāmiʿ al-anwār al-bahiyya wa-l-sawāṭiʿ al-asrār al-athariyya*. Edited by ʿAbd al-Raḥmān Abā Buṭayn and Sulaymān Ibn Suḥmān [also: Siḥmān]. 3rd ed. Beirut; Riyadh: al-Maktab al-Islāmī; Dār al-Khānī, 1991.

Said, Edward W. *Orientalism*. 25th anniversary ed. with a new preface by the author. New York: Vintage Books Edition, 2014.

Salahi, Adil, trans. *Ṣaḥīḥ Muslim: With the Full Commentary by Imam Al-Nawawi*. Vol. 2. London: Islamic Foundation, 2019.

Salahi, Adil. 'Scholar of Renown Sheikh Ali Al-Tantawi.' *Arab News*, June 19, 2001. https://www.arabnews.com/node/212775.

——. 'Scholar of Renown: Sheikh Ali Al-Tantawi: II.' *Arab News*, June 25, 2001. https://www.arabnews.com/node/213339.

Sālim, Aḥmad, and ʿAmr Basyūnī. *Mā baʿd al-salafiyya*. Riyadh: Markaz Namāʾ, 2015.

Salīm, ʿAmr ʿAbd al-Munʿim. *al-Manhaj al-Salafī ʿinda al-shaykh Nāṣir al-Dīn al-Albānī*. Tanta, Egypt: Dār al-Ḍiyāʾ, n.d.

Salomon, Noah. *For Love of the Prophet: An Ethnography of Sudan's Islamic State*. Princeton: Princeton University press, 2016.

——. 'The Salafi Critique of Islamism: Doctrine, Difference and the Problem of Islamic Political Action in Contemporary Sudan.' In *Global Salafism: Islam's New Religious Movement*, edited by Roel Meijer, 144–68. Oxford University Press, 2014. https://doi.org/10.1093/acprof:oso/9780199333431.003.0007.

Sanyal, Usha. *Ahmad Riza Khan Barelwi: In the Path of the Prophet*. Oxford: Oneworld Academic, 2005.

Ṣanʿānī, Muḥammad b. Ismāʿīl al-Amīr al-. *Irshād Dhawī Al-Albāb Ilā Ḥaqīqat Aqwāl Ibn ʿAbd al-Wahhāb*. Edited by ʿAbd al-Karīm Aḥmad Jadbān. Majālis Āl Muḥammad, 2008. https://shamela.org/pdf/9586c8f2aee7169e2ce8cb2fb94ea413.

——. *Subul Al-Salām Sharḥ Bulūgh al-Marām*. Edited by ʿIṣām al-Ṣabbābīṭī and ʿImād al-Sayyid. 5th ed. 4 vols. Cairo: Dār al-Ḥadīth, 1997.

Saouli, Adham. 'Lebanon's Salafis.' In *Salafism After the Arab Awakening*, edited by Francesco Cavatorta and Fabio Merone, 43–60. Oxford University Press, 2017. https://doi.org/10.1093/acprof:oso/9780190274993.003.0004.

Ṣarāf, Aḥmad al-. 'Hal maqūlat ʿAbduhu kādhība?' *Al-Qabas*, 2018. https://www.alqabas.com/article/558966-%D9%87%D9%84-%D9%85%D9%82%D9%88%D9%84%D8%A9-%D8%B9%D8%A8%D8%AF%D9%87-%D9%83%D8%A7%D8%B0%D8%A8%D8%A9%D8%9F.

Sarḥān, Sa'ūd ibn Ṣāliḥ, ed. *Political Quietism in Islam: Sunni and Shi'i Practice and Thought*. King Faisal Center for Research and Islamic Studies Series. London; New York, NY: I.B. Tauris, 2020.

Sariyannis, Marinos. 'The Kadizeli Movement as a Social and Political Phenomenon: The Rise of a "Mercantile Ethic"?' In *Political Initiatives 'from the Bottom up' in the Ottoman Empire*, edited by Antonis Anastasopoulos, 263–89. Rethymno: Crete University Press, 2012.

Scharbrodt, Oliver. *Muhammad 'Abduh: Modern Islam and the Culture of Ambiguity*. London; New York; Oxford: I.B. Tauris, 2022.

Scheuer, Michael. *Imperial Hubris: Why the West Is Losing the War on Terror*. Potomac Books, 2007.

Schlegell, B. R. von. *Sufism in the Ottoman Arab World: Shaykh 'Abd Al-Ghanī Al-Nābulusī (d.1143/1731)*. University of California, Berkeley, 1997.

Schmidtke, Sabine. 'Neuere Forschungen Zur Muʿtazila Unter Besonderer Berücksichtigung Der Späteren Muʿtazila Ab Dem 4./10. Jahrhundert.' *Arabica* 45, no. 4 (1998): 379–408. https://doi.org/10.1163/1570058987742304l9.

——, ed. *The Oxford Handbook of Islamic Theology*. Reprint ed. Oxford, UK: Oxford University Press, 2018.

Schöck, Cornelia. 'Jahm b. Ṣafwān (d. 128/745–6) and the 'Jahmiyya' and Ḍirār b.ʿAmr (d. 200/815).' In *The Oxford Handbook of Islamic Theology*, edited by Sabine Schmidtke, Reprint ed., 55–80. Oxford, UK: Oxford University Press, 2018.

Scholars of MJAH UK. *C: A Response to the Unjust, Deceptive and Slanderous Allegations Made against Markazi Jamiat Ahle Hadith UK*. Birmingham: MJAH, 2018.

Schönig, Hanne (Halle/Saale). 'Kalam.' In *Brill's New Pauly*. Brill, October 1, 2006. https://referenceworks.brillonline.com/entries/brill-s-new-pauly/*-e605450.

Schwartz, Stephen. *The Two Faces of Islam: The House of Saʿud from Tradition to Terror*. 1 ed. New York: Doubleday, 2003.

Selim, Hebatullah Nazy Sayed. 'Religionizing Politics: Salafis and Social Change in Egypt.' PhD, University of Birmingham, 2017. https://etheses.bham.ac.uk/id/eprint/7636/.

*Sh. Al-Jibaly Interview*, 2008. https://www.youtube.com/watch?v=QdLOqqVuk8M.

Shāgif, Aḥmad. *Qurrat al-ʿayn fī tarjama al-Sayyid Nadhīr Ḥusayn*. Lahore: al-Maktaba al-Salafiyya, 2002.

Shah, Mustafa. 'Ibn Qudāma, al-Maqdisi.' In *Encyclopaedia of Islam Three Online*, edited by Kate Fleet, Gudrun Krämer, Denis Matringe, John Nawas, and Devin J. Stewart. Brill, 2018. https://doi.org/10.1163/1573-3912_ei3_COM_32175.

Shahin, Emad Eldin. *Through Muslim Eyes: M. Rashid Rida and the West*. Herndon, Va., USA, 1993.

Shāhīn, Imād al-Dīn. *Political Ascent: Contemporary Islamic Movements in North Africa*. Boulder, Colo. Oxford: Westview, 1998.

Shalata, Ahmed Zaghloul. 'The Salafist Call in Alexandria: The Trajectory of the Organization and Outcomes of Its Politics.' *Contemporary Arab Affairs* 9, no. 3 (2016): 351–64.

Shams, Muḥammad ʿUzayr, and ʿAlī b. Muḥammad al-ʿImrān, eds. *Al-Jāmiʿ Li-Sīrat Shaykh al-Islām Ibn Taymiyya Khilāla Sabʿat Qurūn*. 2nd ed. Riyadh: Dār ʿĀlam al-Fawāʾid, 2001.

Shamsy, Ahmed El. *Rediscovering the Islamic Classics: How Editors and Print Culture Transformed an Intellectual Tradition*. Princeton University Press, 2022.

Shane, Scott. 'Born in U.S., a Radical Cleric Inspires Terror.' *Herald-Tribune*, November 19, 2009. https://www.heraldtribune.com/story/news/2009/11/19/born-in-u-s-radical/28905016007/.

——. *Objective Troy: A Terrorist, a President, and the Rise of the Drone*. First edition. New York: Tim Duggan Books, 2015.

Sharif, Surkheel. 'Is Islam a Conquest Ideology? On Jihad, War, & Peace.' *Yaqeen Insitutue for Islamic Research*, April 16, 2018.

——. *Salafism Reconsidered (Forthcoming)*, n.d.

Shawcross, William. 'Independent Review of Prevent.' Government Report. London: House of Commons, February 2023. https://assets.publishing.service.gov.uk/government/uploads/system/uploads/attachment_data/file/1134987/Independent_Review_of_Prevent__print_.pdf.

Shawkānī, Muḥammad b. ʿAlī al-. *A Critique of the Ruling of Al-Taqlid*. Translated by Adnan Karim. Dar al-Arqam, 2020.

——. *Al-Qawl al-Mufīd Fī Adillat al-Ijtihād Wa-l-Taqlīd*. Edited by ʿAbd al-Raḥmān ʿAbd al-Khāliq. 1st ed. Kuwait: Dār al-Qalam, 1976.

'Sheikh Abdullah Awad Al Juhany Biography – Inside the Haramain.' Accessed June 9, 2024. https://www.haramainsharifain.com/sheikh-abdullah-awad-al-juhany-biography/.

Sheikh, Mustapha. *Ottoman Puritanism and Its Discontents: Ahmad al-Rumi al-Aqhisari and the Qadizadelis*. 1st ed. Oxford: Oxford University Press, 2017.

Shukrī, Mūrad. *Iḥkām Al-Taqrīr Li-Aḥkām Masʾalat al-Takfīr*. Riyadh: Dār al-Ṣamīʿī, 1994.

Sieny, Mahmoud Esma'il. *Heroes of Islam*. Dar-us-Salam Publications, 2000.

Sinani, Besnik. 'Normative Spirituality in Wahhābī Prophetology: Saʿīd b. Wahf al-Qaḥṭānī's (d. 2018) Raḥmatan Li-l-ʿĀlamīn as Reparatory Theology.' *Religions* 15, no. 5 (April 28, 2024): 543. https://doi.org/10.3390/rel15050543.

——. 'Post-Salafism: Religious Revisionism in Contemporary Saudi Arabia.' *Religions* 13, no. 4 (April 2022): 340. https://doi.org/10.3390/rel13040340.

Sindī, Muḥammad Ḥayāt al-. *al-Īqāf ʿalā asbāb al-ikhtilāf*. Edited by Aḥmad ʿAbd al-Mālik ʿAbd al-Raḥman al-Saʿadī. Damascus: Dār Saʿad al-Dīn, 2012.

——. *Tuḥfat al-anām fī al-ʿamal bi-ḥadīth al-nabī ʿalayhi al-ṣalā wa-l-salām*. 1st ed. Beirut: Dār Ibn Ḥazm li-l-Nashr wa-l-Tawzīʿ, 1993.

Sirriyeh, Elizabeth. 'Rashid Rida's Autobiography of the Syrian Years, 1865–1897.' *Arabic & Middle Eastern Literature* 3, no. 2 (July 1, 2000): 179–94. https://doi.org/10.1080/13666160008718238.

Sirry, Mun'im. 'Jamāl Al-Dīn al-Qāsimī and the Salafi Approach to Sufism.' *Die Welt Des Islams* 51, no. 1 (2011): 75–108.

Smith, David, Joanna Walters, and Jason Burke. 'Ayman Al-Zawahiri: Al-Qaida Leader Killed in US Drone Strike in Afghanistan, Joe Biden Says.' *The Guardian*, August 2, 2022. https://www.theguardian.com/world/2022/aug/01/us-strike-afghanistan-kills-al-qaida-leader-ayman-al-zawahiri.

Sobhani, Ayatollah Jafar. *Doctrines of Shi'i Islam: A Compendium of Imami Beliefs and Practices*. Translated by Reza Shah Kazemi. London: I.B.Tauris, 2001.

Solahudin, Dave McRae, Greg Fealy, and Solahudin. *The Roots of Terrorism in Indonesia: From Darul Islam to Jema'ah Islamiyah*. Ithaca: Cornell University Press, 2013.

Stenersen, Anne. *Al-Qaida in Afghanistan*. First published. Cambridge, UK; New York, NY; Port Melbourne, VIC; Delhi; Singapore: Cambridge University Press, 2017.

Stephane Lacroix. 'Ayman Al-Zawahiri, Veteran of Jihād.' In *Al Qaeda in Its Own Words*, edited by Gilles Kepel, 147–70. Cambridge, Mass.: Belknap Press, 2010.

Strasser, Steven, ed. *The Abu Ghraib Investigations: The Official Reports of the Independent Panel and Pentagon on the Shocking Prisoner Abuse in Iraq*. 1st ed. New York: Public Affairs, 2004.

Strick van Linschoten, Alex, and Felix Kuehn. *An Enemy We Created: The Myth of the Taliban-Al Qaeda Merger in Afghanistan*. Oxford; New York: Oxford University Press, 2012.

Subkī, Tāj al-Dīn al-. *Ṭabaqāt al-Shāfiʿiyya al-kubrā*. Edited by Maḥmūd al-Ṭanāḥī and ʿAbd al-Fattāḥ al-Ḥulw. 2nd ed. 10 vols. Cairo: Dār Hajr, 1992.

Sulaiman, Ibraheem. *The African Caliphate: The Life, Works and Teaching of Shaykh Usman Dan Fodio (1754–1817)*. Diwan Press, 2019.

Suleiman, Farid. *Ibn Taymiyya and the Attributes of God*. Translated by Carl Sharif El-Tobgui. Islamic Philosophy, Theology and Science, volume 125. Leiden; Boston: Brill, 2023.

Sunarwoto, A. 'Negotiating Salafī Islam and the State: The Madkhaliyya in Indonesia,' May 27, 2020. https://doi.org/10.1163/15700607-06023P03.

SunnahOnline.com. 'Ali Al-Timimi: A Life of Learning.' Accessed June 11, 2024. https://sunnahonline.com/library/biographies/651-ali-al-timimi-a-life-of-learning.

Suyūṭī, Jalāl al-Dīn ʿAbd al-Raḥmān al-. *Al-Ashbāh Wa-l-Naẓāʾir Fī Qawāʿid Wa-Furūʿ Fiqh al-Shāfiʿiyya*. 1st ed. Beirut: Dār al-Kutub al-ʿIlmiyya, 1983.

Talmon-Heller, Daniella. 'ʿAbd Al-Ghanī al-Maqdisi.' In *Encyclopaedia of Islam Three Online*, edited by Kate Fleet, Gudrun Krämer, Denis Matringe, John Nawas, and Devin J. Stewart. Brill, 2022. https://doi.org/10.1163/1573-3912_ei3_COM_46424.

Tammam, Husam. 'Yūsuf Qaraḍāwī and the Muslim Brothers: The Nature of a Special Relationship.' In *Global Mufti: The Phenomenon of Yūsuf al-Qaraḍāwī*, edited by Bettina Gräf and Jakob Skovgaard-Petersen, 55–83. London: C. Hurst & Company, 2009.

Tareen, SherAli K. *Defending Muḥammad in Modernity*. Notre Dame, Indiana: University of Notre Dame Press, 2020.

*Tawḍīḥ min al-Shaykh Ṣāliḥ al-Mughāmisī ḥawla tashbīhih qiṣṣat Jamāl Khāshuqjī bi-qiṣṣat Khālid ibn al-Walīd*, 2018. https://www.youtube.com/watch?v=R6LeKnAvO-Y.

*The Dissident*. Documentary, Crime, Thriller. Orwell Productions, Diamond Docs, Human Rights Foundation, 2021.

*The Economic Times*. 'Saudi Arabia Takes Aim at Muslim Brotherhood before Democrats Take over in Washington.' November 18, 2020. https://economictimes.indiatimes.com/news/international/saudi-arabia/saudi-arabia-takes-aim-at-muslim-brotherhood-before-democrats-take-over-in-washington/articleshow/79286964.cms?from=mdr.

The Embassy of the Kingdom of Saudi Arabia. 'King Fahd's Speech on the Issuance of the Basic Law of Governance.' Accessed March 10, 2024. https://www.saudiembassy.net/king-fahds-speech-issuance-basic-law-governance.

'The Islamic Seminary of America.' Accessed June 9, 2024. https://islamicseminary.us/about-us/.

'The Islamic Sharia Council.' Accessed June 9, 2024. https://www.islamic-sharia.org/.

The Mad Mamluks. 'The First American Jihadi | Ismail Royer.' Accessed October 12, 2019. https://themadmamluks.com/the-first-american-jihadi-ismail-royer/.

*The New Arab*. 'Egypt's Salafist Nour Party Endorses Sisi for Another Term.' October 5, 2023. https://www.newarab.com/news/egypts-salafist-nour-party-endorses-sisi-another-term.

*The New Arab*. 'France Deports Salafist Preacher to Algeria.' June 15, 2023. https://www.newarab.com/news/france-deports-salafist-preacher-algeria.

*The New York Times*. 'Sad and Qaddafi Fly to Saudi Arabia.' February 21, 1974, sec. Archives. https://www.nytimes.com/1974/02/21/archives/sadat-and-qaddafi-fly-to-saudi-arabia-special-to-the-new-york-times.html.

'The Popular Discourses of Salafi Radicalism and Salafi Counter-Radicalism in Nigeria: A Case Study of Boko Haram,' January 1, 2012. https://doi.org/10.1163/15700666-12341224.

*The Salafi Fallacy*, 2012. https://www.youtube.com/watch?v=1MRXs5fqlXQ.

Thiele, Jan. 'Abū Hāshim Al-Jubbāʾī's (d. 321/933) Theory of "States" (Aḥwāl) and Its Adaption by Ashʿarite Theologians.' In *The Oxford Handbook of Islamic Theology*, edited by Sabine Schmidtke, Reprint ed., 364–85. Oxford, UK: Oxford University Press, 2018.

Tholib, Udjang. 'The Reign of the Caliph Al-Qādir Billāh (381/991–422/1031).' McGill University, 2002. https://escholarship.mcgill.ca/concern/theses/ng451k215.

Thompson, Mark C. *Saudi Arabia and the Path to Political Change: National Dialogue and Civil Society*. Library of Modern Middle East Studies 159. London, England; New York: I.B. Tauris, 2014.

Thurston, Alexander. 'Algeria's GIA: The First Major Armed Group to Fully Subordinate Jihadism to Salafism.' *Islamic Law and Society* 24, no. 4 (2017): 412–36.

——. 'An Emerging Post-Salafi Current in West Africa and Beyond.' *Maydan* (blog), October 15, 2018. https://themaydan.com/2018/10/emerging-post-salafi-current-west-africa-beyond/.

——. *Boko Haram: The History of an African Jihadist Movement*. Princeton University Press, 2017. https://doi.org/10.2307/j.ctvc779gc.

——. 'Islam and Politics in Postcolonial Mauritania.' In *Oxford Research Encyclopedia of African History*, by Alexander Thurston. Oxford University Press, 2022. https://doi.org/10.1093/acrefore/9780190277734.013.1292.

——. 'Jihadists of North Africa and the Sahel: Local Politics and Rebel Groups.' *Journal of Islamic Studies*, June 11, 2024, etae019. https://doi.org/10.1093/jis/etae019.

——. *Salafism in Nigeria: Islam, Preaching, and Politics*. Reprint ed. London: Cambridge University Press, 2018.

——. 'Shaykh Muhammad Al-Hasan al-Dedew (b. 1963), a Salafi Scholar in Contemporary Mauritania,' 2012. https://www.semanticscholar.org/paper/Shaykh-Muhammad-al-Hasan-al-Dedew-(b.-1963)%2C-a-in-Thurston/1bf5df0a8020e10c84b6cd191ea7c326435a8f6d#citing-papers.

Tirmidhī, Abū ʿĪsā al-. *al-Jāmiʿ al-ṣaḥīḥ wa-huwa Sunan al-Tirmidhī*. Edited by Aḥmad Muḥammad Shākir, Muḥammad Fuʾād ʿAbd al-Bāqī, and Ibrāhīm ʿAṭwa ʿAwaḍ. 5 vols. Cairo: Maṭbaʿat Muṣṭafā al-Bābī al-Ḥalabī, 1978.

'Tomasz Miśkiewicz.' Accessed June 9, 2024. https://mzr.pl/zyciorys/.

Tønnessen, Liv. 'Ansar Al-Sunna and Women's Agency in Sudan: A Salafi Approach to Empowerment through Gender Segregation.' *Frontiers: A Journal of Women Studies* 37, no. 3 (2016): 92–124. https://doi.org/10.5250/fronjwomestud.37.3.0092.

Townsend, Mark. 'Anti-Terrorism Programme Must Keep Focus on Far Right, Say Experts.' *The Observer*, May 22, 2022. https://www.theguardian.com/uk-news/2022/may/22/anti-terrorism-programme-must-keep-focus-on-far-right-say-experts.

Traboulsi, Samer. 'An Early Refutation of Muḥammad Ibn ʿAbd Al-Wahhāb's Reformist Views.' *Die Welt Des Islams* 42, no. 3 (2002): 373–415.

Treiger, Alexander. 'Origins of Kalām.' In *The Oxford Handbook of Islamic Theology*, edited by Sabine Schmidtke, 28–44. Oxford Handbooks. Oxford, UK: Oxford University Press, 2016.

Trimingham, J. Spencer. *The Sufi Orders in Islam*. New York; Oxford: Oxford University Press, 1998.

Trofimov, Yaroslav. *The Siege of Mecca: The 1979 Uprising at Islam's Holiest Shrine*. 1st Anchor Books ed. New York: Anchor Books, 2007.

Turner, John P. *Inquisition in Early Islam: The Competition for Political and Religious Authority in the Abbasid Empire*. Library of Middle East History, v. 35. London: I.B. Tauris, 2013.

Ukeles, Raquel Margalit. 'Innovation or Deviation: Exploring the Boundaries of Islamic Devotional Law.' PhD, Harvard University, 2006.

Ulumiddin, Ahya. 'Socio-Political Turbulence of the Ottoman Empire: Reconsidering Sufi and Kadizadeli Hostility in 17th Century.' *Ulumuna* 20, no. 2 (December 1, 2016): 319–52. https://doi.org/10.20414/ujis.v20i2.807.

Umar Lee. *The Rise and Fall of the Salafi Dawah in America*. Kindle ed., n.d.

Upal, Muhammad Afzal. 'The Cultural Genetics of the Aḥmadiyya Muslim Jamāʿat.' In *Handbook of Islamic Sects and Movements*, edited by Muhammad Afzal Upal and Carole M. Cusack. Brill Handbooks on Contemporary Religion, volume 21. Leiden; Boston: Brill, 2021. https://catalog.lib.uchicago.edu/vufind/Record/12616489.

Upal, Muhammad Afzal, and Carole M. Cusack, eds. *Handbook of Islamic Sects and Movements*. Brill Handbooks on Contemporary Religion, volume 21. Leiden; Boston: Brill, 2021. https://catalog.lib.uchicago.edu/vufind/Record/12616489.

Usmani, Muhammad Taqi. *Islam and Politics: A Translation of Islam Awr Siyasi Nazariyat*. Translated by Z. Baintner. Turath Publishing, 2017.

——. *The Legal Status of Following a Madhab*. Translated by Mohammed Amin Kholwadia. Karachi: Zam Zam Publishing, 2009.

Utvik, Bjørn Olav. 'The Ikhwanization of the Salafis: Piety in the Politics of Egypt and Kuwait.' *Middle East Critique* 23, no. 1 (January 2, 2014): 5–27. https://doi.org/10.1080/19436149.2014.896597.

Vinklát, Marek. 'Sufism and Gnosticism: A Comparison.' Accessed March 17, 2024. https://www.academia.edu/428804/Sufism_and_Gnosticism_A_Comparison.

Viorst, Milton. 'The Education of Ali Al-Timimi.' *The Atlantic*, June 1, 2006. https://www.theatlantic.com/magazine/archive/2006/06/the-education-of-ali-al-timimi/304884/.

Voll, John. 'Muḥammad Ḥayyā Al-Sindī and Muḥammad Ibn 'Abd al-Wahhāb: An Analysis of an Intellectual Group in Eighteenth-Century Madīna.' *Bulletin of the School of Oriental and African Studies* 38, no. 1 (February 1975): 32–39. https://doi.org/10.1017/S0041977X00047017.

Wagemakers, Joas. 'A Purist Jihadi-Salafi: The Ideology of Abu Muhammad al-Maqdisi.' *British Journal of Middle Eastern Studies* 36, no. 2 (2009): 281–97.

——. 'Al-Qā ʿida's Post-Arab Spring Jihad: Confirmation or Re-Evaluation?' Accessed June 12, 2024. https://doi.org/10.1515/9781474485531-011.

——. 'Between Purity and Pragmatism? Abu Basir al-Tartusi's Nuanced Radicalism.' In *Jihadi Thought and Ideology*, edited by Rüdiger Lohlker and Tamara Abu-Hamdeh, 16–36. Logos Verlag, 2014.

——. 'Revisiting Wiktorowicz: Categorising and Defining the Branches of Salafism.' In *Salafism After the Arab Awakening*, edited by Francesco Cavatorta and Fabio Merone, 7–24. Oxford University Press, 2017. https://doi.org/10.1093/acprof:oso/9780190274993.003.0002.

——. 'Salafism: Generalisation, Conceptualisation and Categorisation.' Edited by Magnus Ranstorp. *Contextualising Salafism and Salafi Jihadism*, March 2020.

——. *Salafism in Jordan: Political Islam in a Quietist Community*. Cambridge: Cambridge University Press, 2016. https://doi.org/10.1017/CBO9781316681534.

——. 'The Citadel of Salafism.' In *Handbook of Islamic Sects and Movements*, 333–47. Brill, 2021. https://doi.org/10.1163/9789004435544_019.

——. 'The Enduring Legacy of the Second Saudi State: Quietist and Radical Wahhabi Contestations of Al-Walāʾ Wa-l-Barāʾ.' *International Journal of Middle East Studies* 44, no. 1 (2012): 93–110.

——. 'The Transformation of a Radical Concept: Al-Wala' Wa-l-Bara' in the Ideology of Abu Muhammad Al-Maqdisi.' In *Global Salafism: Islam's New*

*Religious Movement*, edited by Roel Meijer, 81–106. Oxford University Press, 2014. https://doi.org/10.1093/acprof:oso/9780199333431.003.0004.

Wahhabis.com. 'Muhammad Bin Abd Al-Wahhab and the Excuse of Ignorance for Muslims Who Fall Into Affairs of Shirk.' Accessed June 7, 2024. http://www.wahhabis.com/articles/lxygyii-muhammad-bin-abd-al-wahhab-and-the-excuse-of-ignorance-for-muslims-who-fall-into-affairs-of-shirk.cfm.

Wahid, Din. 'Nurturing Salafi Manhaj A Study of Salafi Pesantrens in Contemporary Indonesia.' *Wacana* 15, no. 2 (July 1, 2015): 367. https://doi.org/10.17510/wacana.v15i2.413.

Ware, Rudolph T., Zachary Valentine Wright, and Amir Syed, eds. *Jihad of the Pen: The Sufi Literature of West Africa*. Cairo; New York: The American University in Cairo Press, 2018.

——, eds. 'Part 1: Shaykh 'Uthman Bin Fudi.' In *Jihad of the Pen: The Sufi Literature of West Africa*. Cairo; New York: The American University in Cairo Press, 2018.

Warren, David H. 'Cleansing the Nation of the "Dogs of Hell": ʿAli Jumʿa's Nationalist Legal Reasoning in Support of the 2013 Egyptian Coup and Its Bloody Aftermath.' *International Journal of Middle East Studies* 49, no. 3 (2017): 457–77.

——. *Rivals in the Gulf: Yusuf al-Qaradawi, Abdullah Bin Bayyah, and the Qatar-Uae Contest Over the Arab Spring and the Gulf Crisis*. Islam in the World. London; New York: Routledge, Taylor & Francis Group, 2021.

Watt, W. Montgomery. *Islamic Philosophy and Theology: An Extended Survey*. 2nd ed. Edinburgh: Edinburgh University Press, 1995.

——. *The Formative Period of Islamic Thought*. New ed. Oxford: Oneworld Publications, 1998.

Wehrey, Frederic, and Anouar Boukhars. *Salafism in the Maghreb: Politics, Piety, and Militancy*. New York, NY: Oxford University Press, 2019.

Weismann, Itzchak. 'Between Ṣūfī Reformism and Modernist Rationalism: A Reappraisal of the Origins of the Salafiyya from the Damascene Angle.' *Die Welt Des Islams* 41, no. 2 (2001): 206–37.

——. 'Dāwūd b. Jirjīs.' In *Encyclopaedia of Islam Three Online*. Leiden: Brill, 2012. https://referenceworks.brill.com/doi/10.1163/1573-3912_ei3_COM_25935.

——. *Taste of Modernity: Sufism, Salafiyya and Arabism in Late Ottoman Damascus*. 2nd unrevised ed. Islamic History and Civilization 34. Leiden: Brill, 2004.

——. 'The Politics of Popular Religion: Sufis, Salafis, and Muslim Brothers in 20th-Century Hamah.' *International Journal of Middle East Studies* 37, no. 1 (February 2005): 39–58. https://doi.org/10.1017/S002074380505004X.

Weiss, Bernard. 'Interpretation in Islamic Law: The Theory of Ijtihad.' *The American Journal of Comparative Law* 26, no. 2 (1978): 199. https://doi.org/10.2307/839668.

Weitzmann, Marc. 'France's Great Debate Over the Sources and Meaning of Muslim Terror.' *Tablet*, May 24, 2021. https://www.tabletmag.com/sections/news/articles/roy-kepel-marc-weitzmann.

Wickham, Carrie Rosefsky. *The Muslim Brotherhood: Evolution of an Islamist Movement*. 1st ed. Princeton: Princeton University Press, 2013.

Wiedl, Nina. *The Making of a German Salafiyya: The Emergence, Development and Missionary Work of Salafi Movements in Germany*. Centre for Studies in Islamism and Radicalisation (CIR), Department of Political Science, Aarhus University, 2012.

'Wifaq Ul Madaris Al Arabia Pakistan.' Accessed June 9, 2024. https://www.wifaqulmadaris.org/.

Wiktorowicz, Quintan. 'Anatomy of the Salafi Movement.' *Studies in Conflict & Terrorism* 29, no. 3 (May 2006): 207–39. https://doi.org/10.1080/10576100500497004.

Wildberg, Christian. 'Neoplatonism.' In *The Stanford Encyclopedia of Philosophy*, edited by Edward N. Zalta, Winter 2021. Metaphysics Research Lab, Stanford University, 2021. https://plato.stanford.edu/archives/win2021/entries/neoplatonism/.

Willi, Victor J. *The Fourth Ordeal: A History of the Muslim Brotherhood in Egypt, 1968–2018*. Cambridge, UK; New York, NY: Cambridge University Press, 2021.

Willis, Michael. *The Islamist Challenge in Algeria: A Political History*. 1st ed. New York: New York Univ. Press, 1997.

Winter, T. J., ed. *The Cambridge Companion to Classical Islamic Theology*. Cambridge Companions to Religion. Cambridge; New York: Cambridge University Press, 2008.

Worth, Robert F. 'A Black Imam Breaks Ground in Mecca.' *The New York Times*, April 10, 2009. https://www.nytimes.com/2009/04/11/world/middleeast/11saudi.html.

Wright, Lawrence. *The Looming Tower: Al-Qaeda and the Road to 9/11*. 1st Vintage Books ed. National Bestseller. New York: Vintage Books, 2007.

Yazigi, Maya. 'Ḥadīth Al-'Ashara or the Political Uses of a Tradition.' *Studia Islamica*, no. 86 (1997): 159–67. https://doi.org/10.2307/1595809.

Zahab, Mariam Abou. 'Salafism in Pakistan: The Ahl-e Ḥadīth Movement.' In *Global Salafism: Islam's New Religious Movement*, edited by Roel Meijer, 1st ed., 128–29. New York: Oxford University Press, 2014.

Zarabozo, Jamaal al-Din M. *Purification of the Soul: Concept, Process and Means*. Denver, CO: Al-Basheer Publications & Translations, 2002.

——. *The Life, Teachings And Influence Of Muhammad Ibn Abdul Wahhaab*. Ministry of Islamic Affairs, 2003.

Zayyāt, Montasser al-. *The Road to Al-Qaeda: The Story of Bin Laden's Right-Hand Man*. Edited by Sara Nimis. Translated by Ahmed Fekry. Pluto Books, 2015. https://doi.org/10.2307/j.ctt18fs95x.

Zilfi, Madeline C. 'The Kadizadelis: Discordant Revivalism in Seventeenth-Century Istanbul.' *Journal of Near Eastern Studies* 45, no. 4 (1986): 251–69.

Zollner, Barbara. *The Muslim Brotherhood: Hasan Al-Hudaybi and Ideology*. 1st ed. London; New York: Routledge, 2008.

Zysow, Aron. 'Karrāmiyya.' In *The Oxford Handbook of Islamic Theology*, edited by Sabine Schmidtke, Reprint ed., 252–62. Oxford, UK: Oxford University Press, 2018.

——. *The Economy of Certainty: An Introduction to the Typology of Islamic Legal Theory*. Resources in Arabic and Islamic Studies 2. Atlanta, GA: Lockwood Press, 2013.

——. 'Two Unrecognized Karrāmī Texts.' *Journal of the American Oriental Society* 108, no. 4 (1988): 577–87. https://doi.org/10.2307/603146.

# INDEX

*Note:* Page numbers in italics are figures.

in Egypt 235, 236
in Indonesia 392
in Jordan 377, 378
in Kuwait 382, 383
in Libya 363
in Sudan 370, 371
in Yemen 384, 386–7, 388
Ādam, Ja'far 368, 369
Adib, Dawud 408
Adly, Muhammad Syed 408
Adraoui, Mohamed-Ali 405
al-Afghānī, Djafar (Mourad Si Ahmed) 297
al-Afghānī, Jamāl al-Dīn 96–7
Afghanistan, and Jihadi-Salafism 266–9, 301–9
Afghan–Soviet War 194, 224, 266–7
Africa
Algeria 293–301, 358–61
Libya 361–7
Mauritania 371–2
Morocco 290–3, 352–8
Nigeria 367–9
Sudan 369–71
*see also* Egypt
*ahl al-ḥadīth* 4, 46, 50, 118
*ahl al-ra'y* 46
'*ahl al-Sunna wa-l-jamā'a*' 13
*Ahl-e Ḥadīth* movement 87–95, 158, 200, 388–90, 394–6
*Aḥrar al-Sham* (The Freedom Fighters of Syria) 422
Aided Group 13
Akef, Mohammed Mahdī 220
al-Albānī, Muhammad Nasir al-Din 17, 19–20, 27, 38–9, 109–17, 118, 171, 350
and Azzam 274
and IUM 201
and Jihadi-Salafism 258, 300
and JIMAS 397
and the JMB 247
and Kuwait 249
and al-Madkhalī 192
*The Prophet's Prayer* 400
and al-Qāsimī 106
on Sayyid Qutb 213
and Shaqrah and al-Salik 375–6
and the SMB 246
Algeria 293–301, 358–61
al-'Ali, Hamid 382
Ali, Manwar (Abu Muntasir) 397, 398
Ali Benhadj 359
AlKauthar Institute 399
AlMaghrib Institute 399, 411–12
aloofists 33, *34*, *38*, *39*, *40*
Alp Arsalan 61–2
Alsawy, Dr Salah 412
Alshareef, Muhammad 411
al-Ālūsī, Abū al-Thanā Maḥmūd 107–8
al-Ālūsī, Maḥmūd Shukrī 108–9
al-Ālūsī, Nu'mān Khayr al-Dīn 108
America, North 406–14
*see also* United States (US)
Amritsārī 94–5
'Anatomy of the Salafi Movement' (Wiktorowicz) 29
Andirja, Firanda 393
*Angkatan Belia Islam Malaysia* (Muslim Youth Movement or ABIM) 391
Anjum, Ovamir 74
*Ansar al-Sunna* (Helpers of the Sunnah) (Sudan) 369, 370–1
Anṣār al-Sunna al-Muḥammadiyya (Helpers of the Prophetic Sunna) (Egypt) 200, 214, 222, 226, 228
and al-Azhar 229
founded by Al-Fiqī 102, 212
and *al-Jama'a al-Salafiyya al-Muḥtasiba* 171
and Madkhalis 231
and the Muslim Brotherhood 215
al-Anṣārī, Ismā'īl 113
anti-madhhabists 17, 18–19
Aouissat, Abdelghani 359, 360
apolitical Salafism
in Algeria 358, 359, 360
in Egypt 231, 232, 233, 242, 243
in Jordan 247
in Libya 361

in Morocco 354, 355–6, 357, 358
in Syria 373–4
apostates 12, 135
and al-Baghdadi 325
and First-Wave Wahhabism 169
and Ibn ʿAbd al-Wahhāb 130, 137, 138, 141, 175
and Ibn Ibrahim 168
and Ibn ʿUthaymīn 182
and the *Ikhwān* 161
and ISIS 263, 326
and Jihadism 259, 260–1, 280
and the Ottomans 155, 159
and Sulaymān b. ʿAbd Allāh Āl al-Shaykh 144
and Third-Wave Wahhabism 176
al-Āqḥiṣārī, Aḥmad al-Rūmī 77–8
*al-ʿAqīda al-Wāsiṭiyya* (*The Wāṣit Creed*) (Ibn Taymiyya) 70
*ʿAqīdat ahl al-Sunna wa-l-jamāʿa* (*The Creed of the People of the Sunna and the Community*) 11
*ʿAqīdat al-salaf wa aṣḥāb al-ḥadīth* (*The Creed of the Predecessors and the Partisans of Hadith*) (al-Sābūnī) 58
Arab Spring 232, 233, 246
how viewed in Jordan 248, 378, 379
and Kuwait 383–4
in Saudi Arabia 243
Aramco (Arabian American Oil Company) 163
Armed Islamic Group (*Groupe Islamique Armé* or GIA) 262–3, 295, 297–9
Armed Islamic Movement (*Mouvement islamique armé* or MIA) 294–5, 297
al-ʿA'rur, ʿAdnan 374
*al-Aṣāla* (*The Foundations*) 115
al-Ashʿarī, Abū al-Ḥasan 57
Ashʿarī/Māturīdī schools 10
Ashʿarīs 52, 59, 61, 70
Ashʿarī scholars 61, 94, 200
Ashʿarīsm 51, 64, 118
al-Ashqar, Umar 381
Asia 87–95, 157, 388–94
*see also* Egypt; Saudi Arabia
*As'ilat al-Thawra* (*Questions on the Arab Spring*) (al-Oudah) 418
Asim, Fazal Karim 394, 395
Assembly of Muslim Jurists of America (AMJA) 412, 413
association and dissociation 11–12
*Atharī* 6
al-Attar, Issam 245
al-Awlaki, Anwar 333–4, 336–42
al-Awni, Dr al-Sharif Hatim 347, 419–20
Ayro, Aden Hashi Farah 333
al-Azhar, Shaykh (Mahmu Shaltut) 229
al-Azhar University 65, 282–3
Azzam, Abdullah 268, 269–76, 310, 314, 342

b. ʿAbd al-Azīz, Saʿūd 154, 164
b. ʿAbd Allāh Āl al-Shaykh, Sulaymān 144, 158
b. ʿAbd al-Laṭīf Āl al-Shaykh, ʿAbdullāh 159
b. ʿAbd al-Wahhāb, Sulaymān 126, 128
b. ʿAfāliq, Muḥammad 139
Baghdad 107–9
al-Baghdadi, Abu Bakr 324, 325, 327
Baker, Abdul Haqq 400–1
al-Bakrī, Nūr al-Dīn 73–4
b. ʿAlawī al-Mālikī al-Ḥasanī, Muḥammad 25
b. ʿAlī al-Shawkānī, Muḥammad 19
Bali bombings 312
*balkafa* 48, 52, 54, 70
b. Anas, Mālik 48–9
al-Bannā, Ḥasan 209–12, 214, 216
al-Barbahārī, al-Ḥasan b. ʿAlī 56–8
Barelwī movement 87
al-Barqawi, Yusuf 375
Basyouni, Waleed 413
b. ʿAṭāʾ, Wāṣil 46
b. ʿAtīq, Hamad 93, 158

Battle of Sibilla 162
*Bayān talbīs al-jahmiyya* (*The Elucidation of the Deception of the Jahmiyya*) (Ibn Taymiyya) 71
Benghazi Defense Brigades 364
Benhadj, Ali 295–6
Ben Jelloun, Omar 292
b. Faisal, ʿAbd Allāh 158
b. Faisal, Saʿūd 158
b. Fawzan al-Fawzan, Salih 183
b. Fayrūz, Muḥammad 152
b. Hādī al-Madkhalī, Rabīʿ 28
b. Ḥamad, Saʿd 93–4
b. Ḥanbal, Aḥmad 41, 51–2
b. Ibrahīm, Muḥammad 176–7
*bidʿa* 21, 24, 42
  *see also* innovation
bin Laden, Osama 230, 257, 267, 268, 271, 303, 313–15
  on Azzam 275
  co-founded Al-Qaeda 194
  and the Darul Islam movement 311
  and Dr Faḍl 318
  on Al-Shabaab 333
  and al-Zarqawi 321, 323
  executed in Pakistan 309
al-Birgawī, Muḥammad b. ʿAlī (Birgili Meḥmed Efendi) 77
b. Ismāʿīl al-Bukhārī, Muḥammad 49
b. Ismāʿīl al-Sanʿānī, Muḥammad 19
al-Bīṭār, Muḥammad Bahjat 105
blind-following 42, 171
  *see also taqlīd*
Boko Haram 328–31, 369
*The Book of Jihad* (Ibn Nuhās) 338, 339
Bosnia and Herzegovina 403–4
Bouslimani, Mohamed 298
Bouyali, Mustafa 294, 295
b. Rāhawayh, Isḥāq 49
Brixton Mosque 399
b. Salman (popularly known as 'MBS'), Crown Prince Muhammad 195–9
b. Salman, Mashhur 247
b. Saʿūd, Muhammad 154
al-Bukhārī, ʿAlā al-Dīn 80
Bukhari Institute (*Ma'had al-Bukhari*) 380
Burbank, Daawood 397, 400
Burckhardt, Johann 155
Burhami, Yasir 227, 234, 235, 238
al-Buṣayrī, Buddah 372
al-Buti, Muhammad Sa'id Ramadan 373
Butt, Salman 401
b. Zaynī Daḥlān, Aḥmad 150–1, 152

Caillet, Romain 320
Cairene Salafis 236
caliphate jihadis 34, 36, 37
*The Call for Global Islamic Resistance* (Abu Mus'ab al-Suri) 291
Camp Bucca 324, 325
Çelebi, Kātib (Ḥajjī Khalīfah) 78
Center for Islamic Information and Education (CIIE) (also known as *Dar al-Arqam*) 410
Chesser, Zachary Adam 340
Commercial Courts 168–9
Companions of the Prophet 44–5
comparative law 200–1
Council of Senior Religious Scholars (*Hay'at Kibār al-ʿUlamā)* 170, 243–4
Council on American Islamic Relations (CAIR) 409
critical-madhhabists 17, 18

Dadullah, Mullah 307, 308
*al-Dalāʾil fī ḥukm muwālāt Ahl al-ishrāk* (*Manifest Evidence Regarding Showing Loyalty to the People of Polytheism*) (al-Shaykh) 144
*al-Dalāʾil fī ḥukm muwālāt Ahl al-Ishrāk* (*The Evidences for the Ruling Regarding Alliance with the Infidels*) (Sulaymān b. ʿAbd Allāh Āl al-Shaykh) 158
*dalīl* 17, 18, 20, 427
Damascus 103–7, 112

dan Fodio, 'Uthman 331
*Dar al Arqam* (also known as Center for Islamic Information and Education) 410
*Dar al-Hadith* (Yemen) 385, 386
*Dar al-Hadith al-Hassaniyyah* (Morocco) 354
al-Dārimī, ʿUthmān b. Saʿīd 53–4
Darul Islam movement 310–11
*al-Daʿwah ila al-Qurʾan waʾl-Sunna* (The Call to the Qurʾan and the Sunna) 355
*Daʿwat al-Haqq* (*The Call to Truth*) 353
al-Dawla, Fakhr 64
*Declaration of Jihad against the Americans Occupying the Land of the Two Holy Places* (bin Laden) 303
al-Dedew, Muhammad al-Hasan 372
*In Defense of Muslim Lands* (Azzam) 271–2
defensive jihad 254, 256
Deobandī movement 87
Derbala, Mohammed Essam 306, 307
*Dewan Dakwah Islamiyah Indonesia* (Indonesian Council for Islamic Propagation or DDII) 391
al-Dhahabī, Sham al-Dīn 69, 70
Dialogue Forums 417–18
*Difficult Questions Regarding Extremism in the Religion* (Al-Rahman Luwayhiq) 347
al-Dihlawī, Shāh Walī Allāh 81, 87
divine attributes 46–9
and Ibn Ḥanbal 52
and Ibn Khuzayma 55–6
and Ibn Qutayba 50–1
and Ibn Taymiyya 71
*al-Diyaʾ* (*The Light*) 390
Doudi, El Hadi 405
driving for women 197–8
Durman, Tariq 365–6
*al-Ḍurra al-muḍiyya fī ʿaqd al-firqa al-marḍiyya* (*The Radiant Pearl on the Doctrine of the Delighted Party*) (al-Saffārīnī) 82
al-Duwaysh, Faisal 162

El Hadi Doudi 405
*The Economy of Certainty* (Zysow) 16
Efendi, Birgili Meḥmed (Muḥammad b. ʿAlī al-Birgawī) 77
Efendi, Ebusuûd (Abū al-Saʿud al-Afandī ) 77
Efendi, Qāḍīzāde Meḥmed 78
Effendi, Ahmad 154
Egypt 96–103, 209, 233–9, 242, 243
and Jihadi-Salafism 276–86
and the Muslim Brotherhood 215, 216, 225–9, 231–2, 251
Egyptian Islamic Group (EIG) 267, 282, 285–6, 306–7, 404
and ʿAbd al-Raḥmān 280, 281
Egyptian Islamic Jihad (EIJ) 267, 268, 316–17
Egyptian-Jihadi-Salafism (EJS) 193, 194
El-Affendi, Abdelwahab 370
El-Helbawy, Kamal 220
'Enlightenment' project 96, 209
Europe 394–406
European Islam 420–1
*The Evolution of Fiqh* (Philips) 400, 407
excommunication, *see takfir*
expansionist jihad 254
*Explanation of the Creed* 400
*Extremism in the Religion* (Al-Rahman Luwayhiq) 347

Fadel, Mohammad 233
Faḍl, Dr (Sayyid Imām al-Sharif) 264, 268, 275, 278, 285, 317
on bin Laden and al-Zawahiri 318
and the Egyptian Islamic Jihad 316
on ISIS 327
Fahd, King 185–6, 187, 230
al-Fahd, Nasir b. Ḥamad 195
al-Faisal, Abdullah (born Trevor William Forrest) 343–5

Faisal, King 164–5, 166, 169–70, 219, 221
faith, conception of 11–14
Faraj 280
Farid, Ahmad 227
*al-Farīḍah al-Ghā'ibah* (*The Neglected Obligation*) (Faraj) 280
*Fatāwā al-'Ulamā' al-Akābir fī-mā Uhdira min Dimā' fī al-Jazā'ir* (*The Opinions of Major Scholars on the Blood Spilled in Algeria*) ('Abd al-Malik al-Ramdani) 299–300
*Fatḥ al-Majīd* (*The Victory of the Exalted*) '(Abd al-Raḥmān) 157
*al-Fatwā al-Ḥamawiyya al-kubrā* (*The Large Verdict from Hama*) (Ibn Taymiyya) 70
fatwas
 and al-Albānī 115
 and Azzam 271–2
 and bin Laden 311
 and First-Wave Wahhabi thought 159
 and Ibn Bāz 178–9, 246
 and Ibn Taymiyya 24, 72, 75, 149, 280
 on the Muslim Brotherhood 225–6, 239
al-Fawzan, Salih 225
FBI 337, 338
Ferkous, Mohamed Ali 359, 360
Finsbury Park Mosque 342–3
*fiqh* 15, 16, 17, 19
al-Fiqī, Muḥammad Ḥāmid 102–3, 215, 216
al-Firqa al-Nājiyya 12–14
First Saudi State 153, 154–6
First-Wave Wahhabism 153–63, 168, 169, 183, 207
 and Juhaymān 174
 and al-Maqdisi 319
FIS (Islamic Salvation Front) 295–6, 359, 396
*al-Fitnat al-Wahhābiyya* (*The Wahhabi Tribulation*) (Daḥlān) 150–1
Fizazi, Mohammed 293
*Fī Ẓilāl al-Qur'ān* (*In the Shade of the Qur'an*) (Qutb) 264–5
FJP ( Freedom and Justice Party) 237, 238
*Foresight and Persistence* (Kabbaj) 356
*Forum Komunikasi Ahlus Sunna wal Jama'ah* (Forum for Followers of the Sunna and the Community of the Prophet or FKASWJ) 393
Fotouh, Abdel Moneim Aboul 237
Founding Day (*yawm al-ta'sīs*) 197
France 405–6
Front for Islamic Constitution (FIC) 370
*The Fundamentals of Tawheed* (Philips) 400, 407

Gabriel, hadith 7–8
Gaddafi, Colonel Muammar 361, 362
Gaddafi, Saadi 361, 362
Gaddafi, Saif al-Islam 361–2
Gambetta, Diego 348
General National Congress (GNC)/Libya 363
Gerges, Fawaz A. 321, 324, 325
Ghaffour, Emad Abdel 234, 237, 238
al-Ghariani, Sadiq 367
al-Ghazālī, Abū Ḥāmid 64
Ghaznavids 61
Ghoneim, Wagdy 239
GIA (Armed Islamic Group of Algeria (*Groupe Islamique Armé*) 262–3, 295, 297–9
global jihadis 34, 36, 256, 290, 343
*The Global Resistance Call* (Abu Mus'ab al-Suri) 253, 291
Godane, Ahmed 333, 334
God's attributes 9–11
God's perfect unicity 47
Goldziher, Ignaz 64
Gomaa, Ali 233, 241
Gondalavi, Muhammad 389
Gousmi, Cherif 298
Government of National Accord (GNA)/Libya 364

graves 73, 164, 334
and excommunication 85
of saints 24, 67, 134
visitation of 77, 83, 124, 353
Green, Abdur Raheem 402
Green Lane Masjid 398
GSPC (Salafist Group for Preaching and Combat) 300–1
Gumi, Abubakar 367–8

al-Hādī al-Sindī, Abū al-Ḥasan Muḥammad b. ʿAbd 81–2
hadith of Gabriel 7–8
Hadiyah, Sha'ban Madud Khalifah 363, 364
Hafalah, Majdi 362
Haftar, General Khalifah 364, 365, 366
*Hajar al-Zawiya* (*Corner Stone*) 418
al-Hajuri, Yahya 385, 386, 387, 388
*al-ḥākimiyya* 259–60
*al-Hakimiyya wa'l-siyasa al-shar'iyya* (*God's Rule and Political Rule*) ('Adl Sayyid) 231–2
al-Halabi, 'Ali 106, 375, 376, 377–8, 379
Hamadache, Abdelfattah 360
al-Hamid, Muhammad 245, 246
Ḥanafī school 16, 18
*Ḥanbalī,* definition 6
Ḥanbalīs 56, 59, 61
Ḥanbalī school 16, 18, 19, 47, 200
Ḥanbalism 57–8, 60
Al-Haneef Publications (later Al-Hidaayah Publishing & Distribution) 399, 400
*al-Harakah al-Salafiyyah* (The Salafi Movement) 383
*Harakat al-Shabibah al-Islamiyyah* 291–2
harakis 31, 32
Haramayn Charity Foundation (*Mu'assasat al-Haramayn al-Khayriyyah*) 385
al-Harīrī, Muḥammad b. Khalīl 75
al-Ḥārith al-Muḥāsibī 52
al-Ḥasan b. ʿAlī b. Ishāq (Niẓām al-Mulk) 62
Hasan, Nidal 339–40
Hasan, Suhaib 395–6
Hassan, Muhammad 227, 232, 235, 241
Hattab, Hassan 300
al-Ḥawālī, Safar 187, 188, 376
Hawwa, Saʿid 245, 246
Hayden, Michael V. 290
Haykel, Bernard 192
al-Hayy, Hayy 382
Hegghammer, Thomas 274, 290
Hell 24, 73, 86, 183
heresy 4, 10, 49, 116, 169
and Ibn ʿAbd al-Wahhāb 125
and Ibn Bāz 179
and *Sharḥ al-Sunna* 57
Hertog, Steffen 348
Hezbollah 380–1
Al-Hidaayah Publishing & Distribution (Al-Haneef Publications) 399
*al-Hikmah* 386–7
al-Hilali, Muhammad Taqi al-Din 215, 352–5, 390
al-Hilali, Salim 378
*al-Ḥiṣād al-Murr: al-Ikhwān al-Muslimūn fī Sittīn ʿāmā* (*Bitter Harvest: Sixty Years of the Muslim Brotherhood*) (al-Zawahiri) 265
*Hizb al-Umma* (Umma Party) 383
al-Hudaybi, Hasan 218, 277, 291, 346
*Ḥukm tārik al-ṣalāt* (*The Ruling on the One Who Abandons the Prayer*) (al-Albānī) 116
Hussein, Saddam 187

*al-Ibāna al-kubrā* (*The Large Elucidations*) (Ibn Baṭṭa) 58
*al-Ibā-ṣughrā* (*The Small Elucidations*) (Ibn Baṭṭa) 58
Ibn ʿAbd al-Wahhāb 9, 19, 41, 120, 154, 259
and apostates 175
and excommunication 139–45
his life from two paradigms 121–31

and Ibn Taymiyya 83–4
and innovation 124
and theology 131–9
thought original or based on scholarly precedent? 147–9
writings 145–7
Ibn Abī al-ʿIzz 75
Ibn Abī Ḥātim 49
Ibn ʿAfāliq 151, 152
Ibn al-Amīr al-Ṣanʿānī (Muḥammad b. Ismaʿīl) 82, 151–2
Ibn al-Jawzī 66
Ibn al-Khattab 257
Ibn al-Saʿdī 180
Ibn al-Uthaymin 11
Ibn al-Wazīr 86
Ibn al-Zāghūnī 65, 66
Ibn ʿAqīl 66
Ibn ʻAtiq 158–9
Ibn Baṭṭa 58–9
Ibn Bāz 17, 18, 27, 170–1, 176–80, 187, 208, 350
and al-Albānī 113
and Asim 395
and Azzam 272
and al-Hilali 354–5
on Jihadi-Salafis 300
and Juhaymān's followers 172
and 'The Letter of Demands' 188
and Masjid al-Tawhid 396
and Sayyid Qutb 219, 225
and the SMB 246
and al-Timimi 409
Ibn Dawwās 126, 127
Ibn Ḥāmid 65
Ibn Ḥanbal 41, 51–2
Ibn Ibrahim 166–70
Ibn Khuzayma (Abū Bakr Muḥammad b. Isḥāq) 54–6
Ibn Muʿammar 124, 125, 129, 139, 141
Ibn Nāsir al-Dīn al-Dimashqī 80
Ibn Qayyim 26, 53, 70
Ibn Qudāma 67
Ibn Qutayba (ʿAbd Allāh b. Muslim) 50–1
Ibn Sallām 48
Ibn Saʿūd 125, 127, 129, 130, 159–62, 163–4
Ibn Taymiyya 8, 11, 19, 24, 25, 41, 43, 67–76, 118
and al-Ālūsī 108
and Faraj 280
and Ibn ʿAbd al-Wahhāb 83–4, 147–9
and Ibn al-Wazīr 86
influence of during the Interlude 79–80
and Muḥammad ʿAbduh 98
and the Qāḍīzādelī movement 77
Ibn Tumart 353
Ibn ʿUthaymīn, Shaykh 180–3
Ibrahim, Nageh Abdullah 306, 307
idolatry 9, 25
Idrees, Jafar Shaikh 410
Idris, Ismail 368
*Ighāthat al-lahfān* (*Aid for the Afflicted*) (al-Birgawī ) 77
*Ihya al-Sunna* (The Revival of the Sunna) 392
*ijtihād* 104, 415
*Ikhwān* (*The Brotherhood*) 160–2
ʿImād al-Dīn al-Kundurī 61, 62
Imam al-Albānī Centre 378
*Imām al-Ḥaramayn* 61
Imam Muhammad ibn Saud Islamic University 199
*īmān* 11–14
India 87–95, 157, 388–90
Indonesia 309–12, 391–4
Initiative to Stop the Violence 282–3
innovation 2, 21–2, 24, 41, 42
and al-Albānī 116
and Ibn ʿAbd al-Wahhāb 124, 134
and Ibn Taymiyya 25, 72, 148
and the *Ikhwān* 161
'The Inquisition (*Miḥna*) of the Ashʿarīs' 61, 62
International Institute for Islamic Thought (IIIT) 406
*iqamat al-ḥujja* 176

*Iqtiḍā᾽ al-ṣirāṭ al-mustaqīm li-mukhālafat aṣḥāb al-jaḥīm* (*Following the Straight Path by Opposing the People of Hellfire*) (Ibn Taymiyya) 72
Iranian Revolution 223–4, 381
Iran–Iraq War 224
IS-Central 308
ISI (Islamic State in Iraq) 324, 325
ISIS (Islamic State in Iraq and Syria) 263, 264, 312, 323–8, 331, 334–5
'ISIS Imbala cell' case 242–3
ISIS Jihadi-Salafis 36
ISIS-Salafism 40
IS-K (Islamic State in Khorasan) 308–9
*Islam and the Challenges of the Twenty-First Century* (Ibrahim) 306
al-Islambouli, Khalid 280–1
Islamic Assembly of North America (IANA) 409, 410
Islamic Constitutional Movement (ICM) 248–50
Islamic Courts Union (ICU) 332
Islamic Group (*Gama'a Islamiyya*) 223
Islamic Representative Group (IRC) 391
*Islamic Revolution is the Destiny of Present-day Morocco* (Mouti) 291
Islamic Salvation Front (FIS) 295–6, 359, 396
Islamic Society of North America (ISNA) 406
Islamic University of Medina (IUM) 84, 199–206, 368, 389, 391–2
  and American students 406, 407
  and Bosnian students 404
  delegation visited the UK 394–5
  and UK students 399
Islamism (political Islam) 208
Islamist Party of Justice and Development (PJD)/Morocco 356, 357
*isnād* system 45
al-Issawi, Abu Abdullah Mohamed al-Mansour 324
*istighātha* 25, 133–4, 148
*al-Ittihad al-Islami* 331–2
*Ittihad al-Rashad* (*Rashad Union*) 387
IUM, *see* Islamic University of Medina (IUM)

*Jabhat al-Nusrah* (Front for the Conquest of the Levant) 325–6
Jackson, Sherman A. 282–4
*Jahabersa* 391
Jahmī school 46
Jahmiyya 53–4
*Jalā᾽ al-ʿaynayn fī muḥākamat al-Aḥmadayn* (*Revealing to the Eyes the Trial of the Two Aḥmads*) (al-Ālūsī) 108
*al-Jamaʿa al-Salafiyya al-Muḥtasiba* (The Salafi Group That Commands Right and Forbids Wrong or JSM) 171–4, 222, 384
*al-Jamaʿah al-Islamiyyah* 280
*Jamaah Ansharus Syariah* (Community of the Helpers of Shariah or JAS) 312
*Jamaah Anshorut Tauhid* (Helpers of Tawḥīd Congregation or JAT) 312
Jamaal al-Din Zarabozo 26
*Jamāʿat al-Muslimīin* (The Group of the Muslims) 277, 278
*Jamaʿat Ansar al-Sunna al-Muhammadiyya* 215
  *see also* Anṣār al-Sunna al-Muḥammadiyya
*Jamaat-e-Islami* 389, 390
*Jamāʿat Izālat al-Bidʿa wa-Iqāmat al-Sunna* (The Society for Removing Heretical Innovation and Establishing the Sunna) 368
Jamālīs 104
*Jamiah Salafiyyah* seminary 389
*Jamʾiat Ihyaa' Minhaaj-al-Sunna* (The Society for the Revival of the Prophetic Way or JIMAS) 396–7, 398

Jāmīs 33, 189
*Jam'iyyat al-Hidayah wa'l-Ihsan al-Islamiyyah* (Islamic Association of Guidance and Charity) 379, 380
*Jam'iyyat al-Khayriyyah al-Hikmah al-Yamaniyyah* (Yemeni Wisdom Charity Association, known simply as *al-Hikmah*) 386–7
*Jam'iyyat Ihya' al-Turath al-Islami* (The Revival of Islamic Heritage Society, or RIHS) 380, 382, 383, 392
*jarḥ* 52
*al-Jawāb al-ṣaḥīḥ li-man baddala dīn al-Masīḥ* (*The Correct Response to Those who Altered the Message of Christ*) (Ibn Taymiyya) 72
*Jemaah Islamiyah* (JI) 311–12
al-Jibaly, Muhammad 408
jihad 28, 261–2
  definition 252
  concept of in Islam 253–5
  and Wahhabism 138–9
jihadi movements 255–8
  *see also* Al-Qaeda; Al-Shabaab; Boko Haram; ISIS (Islamic State in Iraq and Syria)
jihadis 30, 31–2, 33–4
Jihadi-Salafis 12, 275, 300
  definition 256
  key doctrines 258–63
Jihadi-Salafism (ISIS) *40*
Jihadi-Salafism (JS) 193–5, 253, 256, 264–5, 421–2
  definition 257–8
  in Algeria 293–301
  and Egypt 276–86
  in Morocco 290–3
  Muslim Brotherhood blamed for by Saudi government 264–5
  in Saudi Arabia 286–90
jihadism, definition 256
Jihadi-Sufis 257
*Join the Caravan* (Azzam) 272
Jordan 38–9, 113–14, 375–9
Jordanian Muslim Brotherhood (JMB) 247–8, 376
Juraysha, Ali 221
al-Juwaynī, Abū al-Ma'ālī 61, 62

Kabbaj, Hamad 356, 357–8
*kalām* 10, 71, 118
al-Kalbani, Adil 347, 420
Karrāmīs 53, 61
Kartosuwirjo, Sekarmadji Maridjan 310
*Kashf al-Shubuhāt* (*The Removal of Doubts*) (Ibn 'Abd al-Wahhāb) 146
*Kaum Muda* (Young People) 390
al-Kawtharī 107
Kepel, Gilles 254–5
Khaksar, Mullah Muhammad 303–4
Khalid Sheikh Mohammed 271, 288, 304
Khalīfah, Ḥajjī (Kātib Çelebi) 78
Khān, Ṣiddīq Ḥasan 91, 92–4, 95
Kharijites 260
Khashoggi, Jamal 197
al-Khaṭṭāb, Zayd b. 129
al-Khuḍayr, 'Ali b. Khuḍayr 195
King 'Abd al-'Aziz University 220
Kingdom of Saudi Arabia
  declared by Ibn Sa'ūd 163–6
  and Salafi attitude to politics 26–8
  *see also* Saudi Arabia
King Fahd Mosque 404
*Kitāb al-Tawhīd* (*The Book of Monotheism*) (Ibn 'Abd al-Wahhāb) 124, 129, 145–6
*Kitāb al-tawḥīd wa-l-ithbāt ṣifāt al-rabb* (*The Book of Monotheism and Affirmation of the Attributes of the Lord*) (Ibn Khuzayma) 54, 55
*Knights under the Prophet's Banner* (al-Zawahiri) 316
*kufr* 4, 74, 76, 135, 179, 428
  and Commercial Courts 169
  and Hell 73
  and the Madkhalis 192
  and monism 24
  and the Shubra Salafi School 236

al-Kūrānī, Ibrāhīm b. Ḥasan 80–1
Kuwait 248–50, 381–4

al-Lālakāʾī, Hibat Allāh 58
*Lashkar-e-Taiba* (*Army of the Good*) 389
*Laskar Jihad Ahlus Sunna Wal Jamaʻah* (Warriors of Jihad of the People of the Sunnah) 393
law
  shariʿa and fiqh 15–20
  Sunna and bidʿa 21–2
*Lawāmiʿ al-anwār al-bahiyya* (*The Shining of the Magnificent Lights*) (al-Saffārīnī) 82
Layada, Abdelhaq 297
Lebanon 379–81
*Lembaga Ilmu Pengetahuan Islam dan Bahasa Arab* (Institute of Islamic and Arabic Studies or LIPIA) 391–2
'The Letter of Demands' (*khitab al-matalib*) 188, 189
Li, Darryl 253
Libya 361–7
Libya Dawn 364
Libyan National Army (LNA) 364
Libyan Revolutionaries Operations Rooms (LROR) 363
*Lisan al-Din* (*The Language of Religion*) 353
loyalists 33, *34*
al-Luhaydan, Salih 225

*Maʿālim fī al-Tarīq* (*Milestones on the Path*) (Qutb) 264–5
Madani, Abbassi 295, 296
*Madārij al-Sālikīn* (*The Ranks of the Divine Seekers*) (Ibn Qayyim) 26
*madhhabs* 17, 18, 19, 20
Madhkhalīs 12, 33, 190, 231, 383
  in Libya 362, 363, 364, 365, 366–7
  in the UK 398–9
*Madkhalī 28*
al-Madkhalī, Muhammad ibn Hadi 360
al-Madkhalī, Rabīʿ b. Hādi 190, 192, 360, 362, 364, 382, 385, 398
  and Azzam 272–3
  and Ibn Bāz and al-Albānī 191
Madkhalism 189–93
al-Maghamisi, Saleh 198
al-Maghrawi, Muhammad ibn 'Abd al-Rahman 355–7
Mahdī 172–3, 174
*Majālis al-Abrār* (*The Councils of the Pious*) (al-Āqḥiṣārī) 77
al-Majdhub, Muhammad 220–1
al-Majlisi, Muhammad Salim 372
*Majmūʿa Muʾallafat al-Shaykh Muḥammad ibn ʿAbd al-Wahhāb* (*The Collected Works of Shaykh Muḥammad ibn ʿAbd al-Wahhāb*) 147
Makdisi, George 60
Makhioun, Younes 239
*al-Maktab al-Islāmī* (*The Islamic Bookshop*) 112–13
Malay Archipelago 309–12
Malaysia 390–1
Mālikī school 16
*al-Manār* (*The Lighthouse*) 99
*Manhaj al-Anbiyā fi-l-daʿwah ilā Allah fihī al-Ḥikmah wa-l-ʿaql* (*The Method Followed by the Prophets in Religious Preaching Contains Wisdom and Reason*) (Al-Madkhalī) 190
*manhaj*-wars 192
*maqāsid al-sharīʿa* 415, 420
al-Maqdisi, Abū Muḥammad 287, 312, 318–20, 326
  on ISIS 327
  and *Millat Ibrāhīm* 138, 263
al-Ma'ribi (Abu al-Hasan al-Misri) 362, 385, 387
*Markaz Dirasat al-Sunna al-Nabawwiyah* (Centre for the Teaching of the Sunnah of the Prophet) 397–8
*Markaz Jamiat Ahl-e-Hadith* UK (MJAH) 394–6, 398

al-Masjid al-Ḥarām siege 224
Masjid al-Tawhid 395–6
al-Masri, Abu al-Walid 305
*al-Maṭbaʿa al-Salafiyya* 102–3, 106–7
Mauritania 371–2
al-A'la Mawdudi, Sayyid Abu 90, 259, 390
MBS (Crown Prince Muhammad b. Salman) 195–9
Mecca, Sharif 127
Mecca, Siege 162, 173–4, 194, 286, 287
Mehmed IV, Sultan 78
Meijer, R. 193
'The Memorandum of Advice' (*Mudhakkirat al-nasiha*) 188–9
MIA (Armed Islamic Movement) (*Mouvement islamique armé*) 294–5, 297
Middle East
  Jordan 38–9, 113–14, 375–9
  Kuwait 248–50, 381–4
  Lebanon 379–81
  Syria 373–4
  Yemen 85–7, 384–8
  *see also* Egypt; Saudi Arabia
*Milestones on the Path* (Qutb) 276
*Millat Ibrāhīm* (*The Creed of Abraham*) (al-Maqdisi) 138, 263, 319
*Minhāj al-sunna al-nabawiyya* (*The Prophetic Way of the Sunna*) (Ibn Taymiyya) 71–2
al-Misri, Abu Hamza 299, 342–3
al-Misri, Imad 404
MJAH (*Markaz Jamiat Ahl-e-Hadith*) 394–6, 398
monism 24
monotheism 8–11, 25, 132
  *see also tawḥīd*
Moroccan Islamic Combatant Group (GICM) 293
Morocco 290–3, 352–8
Morsi, Mohamed 237, 238, 239, 240
Mouline, Nabil 164, 185
Mourad Si Ahmed (also known as Djafar al-Afghānī) 297
Mouti, Abdelkrim 291, 292
*Mu'assassat al-Haramayn al-Khayriyyah* (Haramayn Charity Foundation) 380
*Mu'assassat Shaykh Eid al-Thani al-Khayriyah* (Shaykh Eid al-Thani Charitable Organization) 380
al-Mubarak, Muhammad 220
Mubarak, President Hosni 231, 233, 234, 281
al-Muhajjer, Abu Hamza 327
Muhammad Ali 425
Muhammad b. Salman, Crown Prince 243
Muḥammad Ismāʿīl, Shāh 88, 90
Muḥibb al-Dīn al-Khaṭīb 106–7
*muḥsin* 8
*mujāhidīn* 266, 269, 310, 403–4
al-Mujāhīdīn Abdullah Yusuf Azzam, Shaykh 252
al-Mulk, Niẓām 62, 63, 64
*muʾmin* 8
*al-Muntada al-Islami* (Islamic Forum) 368, 398
al-Muqaddam, Muhammad Isma'il 227, 241
al-Muqtadī, Caliph 63–4
Muslim Brotherhood 186–7, 208–9, 251
  and 9/11 attacks 230–1
  and Arab Spring 232
  in Egypt 214–16
  and Jihadi-Salafism 264–5
  in Jordan 247–8
  in Kuwait 248–50, 381
  leaders 209–13
  and al-Madkhalī 190
  in Malaysia 391
  and migration and exile to Saudi Arabia 216–18
  and Nasser 276
  and political Salafism 223–9
  and the Salafi Call 234–44
  and Saudi Arabia 213–16, 219–23
  in Syria 244–6
Muslim Brotherhood of Egypt 165

Muslim Students Association (MSA) 106
Muslim World League (*Rabitat al-'Alam al-Islami*) 218
*Musnad* 51, 210, 214
Mustafa, Shukri 273, 277
al-Mutairi, Hakim 382, 383
Muʿtazilī school 46, 50
Muʿtazilism 47
*Muttahidat Majliṣ-e-Amal* (United Assembly of Action or MMA) 389
mysticism 22–3

al-Nabhānī, Yūsuf 109
al-Nadwi, Masʿud ʿAlam 390
al-Nadwi, Sulayman 390
*Nahdlatul Ulama* (Revival of the Umma) 394
*Naqd al-qawmiyya al-ʿArabiyyh ʿala daw' al-Islam wa'l-waqiʿ* (*Critique of Arab Nationalism in the Light of Islam and Reality*) (Ibn Bāz) 177
Naqshbandī, Maulānā Khālid 107
*Al-Nas* (The People) 232
Nasser, Gamal Abdel 186, 276
National Islamic Front (NIF)/Sudan 370
National Salvation Front (NSF)/Egypt 239
Nayef ibn ʿAbd al-ʿAziz, Prince 230
*Negara Islam Indonesia* (Indonesian Islamic State or NII) 392
Nigeria 367–9
non-Salafi jihadists 256–7
North America 406–14
*Notions That Must Be Corrected* (al-Misri) 404
Nour Party (*Ḥizb al-Nūr*) 234, 235, 236, 237
  endorsed Sisi's candidacy for the 2023 presidential election 243
  and National Salvation Front 238–9
  poor performance in the 2015 elections 241–2
  was the sole Islamic party to endorse the military coup 240
Nuṣayrīs 72

oil 163–4
Organization of Islamic Conference (OIC) 165
*The Origins and Evolution of Islamic Law* (Hallaq) 15
'the other' 7
the Ottomans 154, 155–6, 159
Ottoman-Wahhabi War 156
al-Oudah, Salman 187, 347, 362, 409, 417–19
Ould Addoud, Muhammad Salim 372
Ould Lembrabott, Ahmad 372

Pakistan 389, 390
Pall, Zoltan 30–2
Pasha, Ibrāhīm 156
Pasha, Muḥammad ʿAlī 155–6
peace treaties 254
Philips, Bilal 400, 407–8, 409
Pious Predecessors 5, 6, 14, 44
PJD (Islamist Party of Justice and Development)/Morocco 356, 357
political Islam 208
Political Isolation Law (Libya) 363
political Salafis 221, 240, 241, 242, 357
  in Algeria 359
  in Kuwait 248–9, 383
  in Libya 362
political Salafism 223–9, 251, 377, 378
  in Egypt 209
  in Kuwait 249, 250
politicians (Salafi classification) 33, *34*
politico-purists 31, 32
politicos 30, 31, 33
politics, Salafi attitude to 26–8
polytheism 124, 125–6, 130, 133, 146
  *see also shirk*
post-Salafi Jihadism 421–2
post-Salafism 413–14, 418–21
  definitions and trajectory 414–16
  history and origins 416–17
predestination 46, 55, 80, 118
Prevent counter-terrorism policy 400, 401

propagandists 33, *34*
*The Prophet's Prayer* (al-Albānī) 400
proto-Ash'arism 49
proto-Ḥanbalism 47
proto-Salafism 43, 46, 49
proto-Salafi theology 51–60
proto-Sunnism 47, 49
purification 19, 22, 23, 27, 115
purists 29–30, 31, 32
purists-rejectionists 31, 32
puritan Salafis 258, 299, 344, 352, 355, 386
puritan Salafism 2, 99, 106, 355

*qadar* 46, 55, 118
al-Qādī, Abū Ya'lā 65, 66
al-Qādir bi-llāh, Caliph 59, 60
Qādirī Creed 51, 59–60
Qāḍīzādelī movement 77–9
Al-Qaeda 194, 230, 262, 263, 264, 268
  in Afghanistan 302–9
  and Salafist Group for Preaching and Combat (GSPC) 300, 301
  and Shekau 330
  and al-Zarqawi 322–3
  and al-Zawahiri 317
Al-Qaeda Central (AQC) 324, 325
Al-Qaeda in Iraq (AQI) 324, 325
Al-Qaeda in the Islamic Maghreb (AQIM) 300–1, 306
Al-Qaeda on the Arabian Peninsula (AQAP) 195, 288, 289–90, 306, 387, 388
*Al Qaeda Strategy: Mistakes and Dangers* (Derbala) 306
al-Qaḥṭānī, Muḥammad b. 'Abd Allāh 172, 173
al-Qalqili, Abdallah 375
al-Qaradawi, Yusuf 233, 247
al-Qari Haji Salleh, Abdullah 390
al-Qarni, Aid 198
*Qasīdat al-Burda* (*Ode of the Mantle*) 24–5
al-Qāsim b. Sallām, Abū 'Ubayd 47–8
al-Qāsimī, Jamāl al-Dīn 104–5, 106, 108
al-Qattan, Ibrahim 375
al-Qattan, Manna 218
*Al-Qawā'id al-Arba'* (*The Four Fundamentals*) (Ibn 'Abd al-Wahhāb) 146
*al-Qawl al-mufīd fī adillat al-ijtihād wa-l-taqlīd* (*The Useful Speech Regarding The Evidences For Juristic Reasoning and Blind Following*) (al-Shawkānī) 86
quietist Salafis
  classification 32–3
  in Algeria 359, 360–1
  in Jordan 377, 379
  in Kuwait 383
  in Saudi Arabia 244
  in Syria 374
  in Yemen 386, 387
quietist Salafism 209, 247, 248, 251
  in North America 408, 412
  *see also* apolitical Salafism
*al-Qur'an was-Sun-*(QSS) 408–9, 410
al-Qushayrī, Abū al-Qāsim 61
Qutb, Muhammad 221
Qutb, Sayyid 212–13, 219, 225, 247–8, 276–7, 278
  and al-Albānī 376–7
  and Jihadi-Salafism 264–5
  and al-Zawahiri 316

*al-Rabitah al-Nahdhah wa'l-Taghiy-ir* (The League of Revival and Change or LRC) 387
*al-Rabitah al-shar'iah li'l-'ulama' wa'l-du'at* (The Legitimate League for Religious Scholars) 369–70
*Rabitat al-Du'at al-Kuwaitiyyah* (League of Islamic Preachers of Kuwait or LDK) 383
*al-Radd 'alā al-Jahmiyya* (*Refutation of the Jahmiyya*) (Al-Dārimī ) 53–4
*Radd 'alā al-Marīsī al-'anīd* (*Refutation of al-Marīsī, the Arrogant*) (Al-Dārimī) 54
*Radd al-ishrāk* (*The Refutation of Idolatry*) (Shāh Muḥammad Ismā'īl) 90

*al-Radd al-wāfir* (*The Ample Response*) (Ibn Nāṣir al-Dīn al-Dimashqī) 80
al-Rafush, Adil 357
*Al-Rahma* (Mercy) 232
al-Rahman, 'Umar 'Abd 275, 280, 281, 283
Ramadan, Tariq 405–6, 420–1
Al-Rasheed, Madawi 187, 418
Razavian, Christopher Pooya 411
al-Rāzī, Fakhr al-Dīn 71
Reign of Islamic Daʿwah (TROID) 408
'Revisiting Wiktorowicz' (Wagemakers) 32
revolutionaries 34
Riḍā, Rashīd 94–5, 96, 98–102, 105, 108, 110
  on expansionist wars 254
al-Rifaʿi, Muhammad Nasib 375
RIHS (*Jamʿiyyat Ihya' al-Turath al-Islami*) (The Revival of Islamic Heritage Society) 249, 382, 383
*al-Risāla al-Tadmuriyya* (*Epistle to Palmyra*) (Ibn Taymiyya) 70
*The Road to Al-Qaeda* (al-Zayyat) 348
Robow, Mukhtar 334
Roosevelt, Franklin 163
Roy, Olivier 254
Royer, Ismail 337–8
*rubūbiyya* 132, 147, 148, 149
*Rūh al-maʿānī fī tafsīr al-Qurʾān al-ʿaẓīm wa sabʿ al-mathānī* (*The Soul of Meaning in the Exegesis of the Great Qurʾan and the Repeated Seven Verses*) (al-Ālūsī) 107, 108
Rushdi, Osama 284

al-Sāʾātī, Aḥmad Fawzī 105–6
*Sabil al-najat wa'l-fikak min muwalat al-murtaddin wa-l-atrak* (*The Path of Success and Fleeing from Loyalty to the Apostates and Turks*) (Ibn 'Atiq) 158–9
al-Sabt, 'Abdullah 381, 382
al-Sābūnī, Ismāʿīl 58
Sadat, President 280–1
al-Saffārīnī, Muḥammad b. Aḥmad b. Sālim 82, 151
Sageman, Marc 348
*Ṣaḥwa* movement 28, 39–40, 185–9, 191, 376–7
*Ṣaḥwa* scholars
  condemned the 9/11 attacks 289
  dispute with the so-called 'Shuʿaybi school' 195, 289
  and al-Timimi 410
*Ṣaḥwis* 224–5
Said, Edward 7
saints 24, 25, 67, 132–3, 134
Saladin (Ṣalāḥ ad-Dīn Ayyūbī) 65
Salafi brothers 110–11
Salafi Call (*al-Daʿwah al-Salafiyya*) 223, 233–5, 236, 239, 241
  and the Muslim Brotherhood 228, 238, 240
  suffered for its political opportunism 242
Salafi Publications (UK) 399
Salafism, definition 3, 5
'Salafism: Generalisation, Conceptualisation and Categorisation' (Wagemakers) 34
Salafist Group for Preaching and Combat (GSPC) 300–1
Ṣalāḥ ad-Dīn Ayyūbī (Saladin) 65
Ṣalāḥ al-Dīn 105
Salih, Ali Abdullah 386
al-Salik, Ahmad 375–6
Salman, King 195
Salman, Mashhur Hasan 376
al-Ṣanʿānī, ibn al-Amīr 86
al-Sananirī, Kamāl 270
Saqib, Abdul Karim 395
Saʿūd, King 217, 218, 389
Saudi Arabia 26–8, 168–9, 170, 187–8
  and 9/11 attacks 229–31
  and Afghanistan 266
  and Jihadi-Salafism 286–90
  kingdom declared by Ibn Saʿūd 163–6

and Muslim Brotherhood 214–15, 216–18, 219–23, 243–4
and political Salafism 223–6
Saudiazation 202
Saudi-establishment Salafism 39
Saudi-Jihadi-Salafism (SJS) 193, 194, 195, 288–9
Saudi States 153, 154–60
Saudi Wahhabis 99
Saved Sect 12–14
Sayah, Abderrahim 405
Sayyid Aḥmad Shahīd 88–90, 92
Sayyid Awlād Ḥasan 91–2
Sayyid Nadhīr Ḥusayn 90–1, 94
schisms 12, 13
scholarly Salafism, in North America 412–13
Second Saudi State 153, 157–9
Second-Wave Wahhabism 163–74, 183, 207
Services Bureau (*Maktab al-Khadamāt*) 270–1
Al-Shabaab 331–5
Shāfiʿī school 18
Shahadah, Usamah 377, 378
al-Shahal, Salim 379
Shakir, Abdullah 235
Shaltut, Mahmud (Shaykh al-Azhar) 229
al-Shami, Abu Anas 322–3
Shaqra, Muhammad Ibrahim 375–6, 378
*al-Sharḥ al-Mumtiʿ ʿalā Zād al-Mustaqniʿ* (*The Pleasing Commentary of Zād al-Mustaqniʿ*) (Ibn ʿUthaymīn) 181–2
*Sharḥ al-Sunna* (*The Explanation of the Sunna*) ( al-Barbahārī) 56–7
*Sharḥ uṣūl iʿtiqād ahl al-Sunna wa-l-jamāʿa min al-kitāb wa-l-sunna wa ijmāʿ al-ṣaḥāba* (*The Explanation of the Creed of the Partisans of the Sunna and the Community Based on the Book, the Sunna, and the Consensus of the Companions*) ( al-Lālakāʾī) 58
Shariʿa 15, 16, 17
Sharif, Abu Aliyah Surkheel 421
al-Sharif, Sayyid Imām, *see* Faḍl, Dr (Sayyid Imām al-Sharif)
*The Sharp Sword* 299
al-Shathri, Saad 348
al-Shawish 112, 113, 246
al-Shawkānī, Muḥammad b. ʿAlī 86–7, 152
al-Shayiji, ʻAbd al-Razzaq 382
al-Shaykh, Salih Āl 225–6
Shekau, Abubakar 330
Shiʿism 72, 123, 129
al-Shinqīṭī, Muḥammad al-Amīn 201
al-Shinqiti, Muhammad al-Khadir 375
*shirk* 9, 25, 133, 135, 149
*see also* polytheism
al-Shuʿaybi, Ḥamūd b. ʿAbd Allah al-ʿUqla 195
Shuʿaybi school 195, 289
Shubra Salafi School 236
al-Siba'i, Hani 284
al-Sibaʿi, Mustafa 245
Siege of Mecca 162, 173–4, 194
*Ṣifat ṣalāt al-Nabī* (*The Prophet's Prayer Described*) 116
*Signs of the Merciful in the Afghan Jihad* (Azzam) 271
*Silsilat al-aḥādīth al-ḍaʿīfah wa-l-mawḍūʿa wa-atharuhā al-sayyʾ fī al-umma* (*The Series of Weak and Forged Hadith Reports and Their Bad Influence on the Community*) (al-Albānī) 111–12
*Silsilat al-aḥādīth al-ṣaḥīḥah* (*The Series of Sound Hadith Reports*) (al-Albānī) 112
al-Sindī, Muḥammad Hayāt 82, 128
Sirriyyah, Sāliḥ 279
al-Sisi, General Abdel Fattah 240, 243
Society for the Revival of Islamic Heritage (*Jamʿiyyat Ihyaʾ al-Turath al-Islami* or RIHS) 249, 382, 383
soft-madhhabists 17, 18
Somalia 331–2

Soviet–Afghan War 194, 224, 266–7
Special Deterrence Force 363, 364–5
speculative theology 10, 41
spirituality 22–6
*The Straight Path* 399
Strategy to Reach, Empower, and Educate Teenagers (STREET) 400–1
*Subul al-Salām* (*The Pathways of Peace*) (al-Ṣanʿānī) 86
Sudan 369–71
Sufism 22–3, 25–6, 73, 211
Suleiman II 78–9
Sungkar, Abdullah 310, 311
Sunna 4, 21, 27
  and al-Albānī 113, 114
  and Ḥanbalī thought 57
  and Ibn Baṭṭa 58
  and Wiktorowicz 29
Sunni Revival 65
Sunnism 47, 60, 72
al-Suri, Abū Musʿab 252, 259, 262, 267, 304, 348
  and *The Global Resistance Call* 253, 291
al-Surur, Muhammad 187, 370, 397–8
Sururis 187, 370, 392, 398
al-Suwaydī, Shaykh ʿAlī 107
al-Suyūṭī 176
Syria, and Jihadi-Salafism 422
Syrian Muslim Brotherhood (SMB) 111, 244–6, 374

*tabdī*ʿ 178, 428
*tafwīḍ* 10, 49
*Tahakkum al-muqallidīn* (*The Destruction of Those who Blindly Follow*) (Ibn ʿAfāliq) 151
*Taḥkīm al-Qawānīn* (*A Treatise Regarding the Canonization of Laws*) (Ibn Ibrahim) 168
*al-Tajammu*ʿ *al-Salafi al-Islami* (Salafi Islamic Gathering) 382
*takfīr* 134–6, 139–45, 176, 260–1, 287, 428
  and graves 85
  and al-Maqdisi 319
*takfīrīs* 275
*al-Takfīr wa'l-Hijrah* (The Party of Excommunication and Emigration) 277, 278
Taliban 256–7, 301, 305, 309
al-Tantawi, ʿAli 113, 220
Tantawi, Isma'il 278, 279
*Tanzim al-Jihad* (The Organization of Jihad) 280, 281
*taqlīd* 16, 17, 18, 19, 20, 171
  and Ibn al-Wazīr 86
  and Rashīd Riḍā 100
*tarawīh* 113, 116
Tareen, SherAli 81
*al-Ṭarīqa al-Muḥammadiyya* (*The Muhammadan Path*) (al-Birgawī) 77
*Tariqa-e-Muḥammadiya* (*The Muhammadan Spiritual Order*) 89, 90
*Tarjumān-e-Wahhābīyya* (*A History of Wahhabism*) (Ṣiddīq Ḥasan Khān) 92
al-Tartusi, Abu Basir 260–1
*Tashih ul-Afkar al-Mutatarrifah* (Rectifying Extremist Ideologies or TAM) 412
*ṭawāghīt*, definition 260
*tawassul* 25, 75, 105
*tawḥīd* 8–11, 25, 132, 259–60, 426
  and Ibn Taymiyya 69
  and Wahhabism 84–5
*Tehrik-e-Mujahidin* (*Movement of Mujahidin*) 389
Thalib, Ja'far 'Umar 392, 393
theology 7–14
Third Saudi State 153, 159–60
Third-Wave Wahhabism 175–85, 207
Thurston, Alexander 258, 328
al-Timimi, Ali 338, 409–11
traditionalist Salafism 358, 370
Transitional Federal Government (TFG) 332

*Treatise Exonerating the Nation of the Pen and the Sword from the Blemish of the Accusation of Weakness and Fatigue* (al-Zawahiri) 317–18
*The Treatise on Faith* (Sirriyyah) 279
'Trial (*fitna*) of al-Qushayrī' 62–3
Trofimov, Yaroslav 287
TROID (Reign of Islamic Daʿwah) 408
al-Turabi, Hasan 370
al-Turki, Homaidan 336
Turkish-Islamic Synthesis (*Türk İslam Sentezi*) 402
Türkiye 402–3

*al-ʿudhr bi-l-jahl* 176
al-ʿUkbarī, ʿUbayd Allāh b. Muḥammad (Ibn Baṭṭa) 58–9
*ulūhiyya* 148, 149
ʿUmar, Mullah Muhammad 303, 304–5
al-Umrani, Nadir 367
unicity, God's perfect 47
United Kingdom (UK) 394–402
United States (US)
and 9/11 attacks 229–30
and Afghanistan 266
and Saudi Arabia 163, 187–8
unity of being 23, 24
*Uṣūl al-Īmān* (*Principles of Faith*) (Ibn ʿAbd al-Wahhāb) 146
*al-Uṣūl al-Thalātha* (*The Three Principles*) (Ibn ʿAbd al-Wahhāb) 146
usury 100
al-ʿUtaybi, Ihsan 377
al-ʿUtaybī, Juhaymān 172–3, 174, 194, 263, 286–7
'Uthman dan Fodio 329–30
al-Uyayri, Yusuf 195

Virginia Jihad Network 410

al-Wadi'ī, Muqbil ibn Hadi 384–5
*Waʿd Kissinjar* (*The Promise of Kissinger*) (al-Ḥawālī) 188
Wagemakers, Joas 32–4, 36
al-Wahhāb, Muḥammad b. ʿAbd 82–3
Wahhabi-Jihadi-Salafis (WJS) 193, 194, 195
Wahhabi-Jihadi-Salafism (WJS) 253, 289
Wahhabism 84–5, 101, 105, 138–9, 206–7
First-Wave 153–63, 168, 169, 174, 183, 319
and Jihadi-Salafism 263–4
reactions to 149–52
Second-Wave 163–74, 183
Third-Wave 175–85
*al-walāʾ wa-l-barāʾ* 11–12, 52, 136–8, 263, 287, 289
*Waqafāt maʿa Thamarāt al-Jihad* (*An Assessment of the Fruits of Jihadist Efforts*) (al-Maqdisi) 312, 320
Warren, David H. 233
*Wathīqat tarshīd al-ʿamal al-jihādī fī Miṣr wa'l-ʿālam* (*The Document of Right Guidance for Jihad Activity in Egypt and the World*) (Faḍl) 317
Wiktorowicz, Quintan 29–30, 258
women's driving 197–8
World Assembly of Muslim Youth (*al-Nadwa al-ʿAlamiyya li'l-Shabab al-Islami*)/WAMY 165, 219–20

Yaqeen Institute 413–14
Yassine, Abdessalam 355
Yemen 85–7, 384–8
Yildiz, Nureddin 402
Yolcu, Abdullah 402
Yusuf, Muhammad 328, 329, 369

al-Zahhawi, Amjad 218
Zaid, Kareem Abu 414
al-Zāki, 'Ala al-Din 370
al-Zarqawi, Abu Mus'ab 308, 320–3
al-Zawahiri, Ayman 264, 267, 268, 281–2, 308, 310, 315–18
and Dr Fadl 275, 286
and *al-Ḥiṣād al-Murr: al-Ikhwān al-Muslimūn fī Sittīn ʿāmā 265*

and ISI 325
on ISIS 326
took over leadership from bin Laden 309
Zaydī Shiʿism 85
al-Zayyat, Montasser 348
Zitouni, Djamel 298, 299
Zouabri, Antar 299
Zuhdi, Karam 282, 306
Zysow, Aron 16